P9-ECS-832

a Wolters Kluwer business

GAAS Guide

by Mark S. Beasley and Joseph V. Carcello

Highlights

CCH's *GAAS Guide* highlights professional standards, including recent pronouncements, for CPAs involved in audit, attestation, compilation, and review engagements. The 2011 *GAAS Guide* includes detailed analyses of critical components of the complete listing of Statements on Auditing Standards (SASs), Statements on Standards for Attestation Engagements, and Statements on Standards for Accounting and Review Services, along with numerous practitioner aids that can easily be incorporated into any CPA firm's practice. The book's sensible organization tracks the arrangement of the AICPA's Professional Standards (Volumes I and II), making it easy to move from the AICPA's original language to an analysis of these standards.

2011 Edition

The 2011 Edition of CCH's *GAAS Guide* has been updated to reflect the latest available professional standards. This edition includes coverage of SAS-117 (AU 801) (Compliance Audits), issued in December 2009, SAS-118 (AU 550 and AU 551) (Other Information in Documents Containing Audited Financial Statements), issued in February 2010, SAS-119 (AU 551) (Supplementary Information in Relation to the Financial Statements as a Whole), issued in February 2010, SAS-120 (AU 558) (Required Supplementary Information), issued in February 2010, SSAE-16 (AT 801) (Reporting on Controls at a Service Organization) issued in April 2010, SSARS-19 (AR 60, AR 80, and AR 90) (Compilation and Review Engagements), issued in December 2009, several interpretations of SASs, PCAOB standards, and exposure drafts. The 2011 Edition of the *GAAS Guide* incorporates these new requirements throughout the affected auditing standards and includes coverage of the following:

- Statements on Auditing Standards Nos. 1 through 120

- Auditing Interpretations

- Statements on Standards for Attestation Engagements Nos. 1 through 16, including all issued interpretations

- Statements on Standards for Accounting and Review Services Nos. 1 through 19, including all issued interpretations

The extensive coverage of these AICPA standards is particularly relevant to CPAs who serve nonpublic entity clients. The above standards represent those applicable to nonpublic company engagements. The guidance contained in this edition is also relevant to CPAs who serve public company clients. Although the Public Company Accounting Oversight Board (PCAOB) is now responsible for establishing professional standards applicable to audits of public companies, the guidance contained in this edition is also directly relevant to CPAs serving public companies because the PCAOB's Interim Auditing Standards continue to embrace most of the provisions in the AICPA's professional standards.

The 2011 *GAAS Guide* contains an appendix to help CPAs understand the key provisions of recent changes affecting the auditing profession resulting from the passage of the Sarbanes-Oxley Act of 2002 (SOX):

- *Appendix A: The Sarbanes-Oxley Act of 2002*   This appendix provides an excellent one-source overview of the key provisions of SOX. CPAs wanting a quick, reader-friendly summary of SOX's provisions will find this appendix helpful.

To help CPAs recognize important unique considerations for audits of public companies, this edition includes summaries of issues having implications for audits of public companies. These summaries, labeled "Public Company Implication," are incorporated throughout the coverage of AICPA Statements on Auditing Standards. CPAs who audit public companies will find that these summaries help them identify key differences between audits of public and nonpublic companies.

Owing to the focus on recent corporate scandals involving allegations of fraudulent financial reporting, the need for auditors to detect material misstatements due to fraud is critical. To help sensitize CPAs to issues affecting auditor responsibility for fraud, this edition contains "Fraud Pointers," which integrate fraud issues related to a particular professional standard's requirement. This should aid CPAs in considering fraud risks throughout the entire audit engagement.

To keep CPAs abreast of potential changes affecting the AICPA Professional Standards and other developments affecting auditing practice, this edition contains overviews of outstanding exposure drafts. In particular, several exposure drafts of Statements on Auditing Standards have been issued by the Auditing Standards Board to redraft existing standards to converge them to International Statements on Auditing (ISAs) issued by the International Auditing and Assurance Standards Board (IAASB) and make them more readable and understandable. Throughout the book, highlights labeled "Important Notice for 2011" explain key elements of potential changes, including proposed redrafts of existing professional standards and other regulatory changes, alerting CPAs to issues that may affect their engagements.

Sample letters, reports, and checklists on the free companion CD-ROM can be printed and customized to meet your auditing needs.

Automate your CCH Engagement Guides with ProSystem *fx* Engagement

By integrating your CCH *Engagement Guides* with ProSystem *fx* Engagement, you can achieve a fully paperless audit workflow. ProSystem *fx* Engagement, a member of the CCH ProSystem *fx* Office suite, enables firms to increase convenience and efficiency by automating workpaper preparation, management, and workflow within a state-of-the-art paperless engagement system. ProSystem *fx* and CCH are pleased to offer this high-quality combination of software and content to the accounting community. To sample ProSystem *fx* Engagement, please call 1-800-PFX-9998, or visit the ProSystem *fx* web site at CCHGroup.com/ProSystem.

CCH Learning Center

CCH's goal is to provide you with the clearest, most concise, and up-to-date accounting and auditing information to help further your professional development, as well as a convenient method to help you satisfy your continuing professional education requirements. The CCH Learning Center* offers a complete line of self-study courses covering complex and constantly evolving accounting and auditing issues. We are continually adding new courses to the library to help you stay current on all the latest

---

*CCH is registered with the National Association of State Boards of Accountancy (NASBA) as a sponsor of continuing professional education on the National Registry of CPE Sponsors. Participating State boards of accountancy have final authority on the acceptance of individual courses for CPE credit. Complaints regarding registered sponsors may be addressed to NASBA, 150 Fourth Avenue North, Suite 700, Nashville, TN 37219-2417. Telephone: 615-880-4200.

*CCH is registered with the National Association of State Boards of Accountancy (NASBA) as a Quality Assurance Service (QAS) sponsor of continuing professional education. Participating state boards of accountancy have final authority on the acceptance of individual courses for CPE credit. Complaints regarding QAS program sponsors may be addressed to National Registry of CPE Sponsors, 150 Fourth Avenue North, Suite 700, Nashville, TN 37219-2417. Telephone: 615-880-4200.

developments. The CCH Learning Center courses are available 24 hours a day, seven days a week. You'll get immediate exam results and certification. To view our complete accounting and auditing course catalog, go to: **http://cch.learningcenter.com.**

Accounting Research Manager™

Accounting Research Manager is the most comprehensive, up-to-date, and objective online database of financial reporting literature. It includes all authoritative and proposed accounting, auditing, and SEC literature, plus independent, expert-written interpretive guidance. And, in addition to our standard accounting and SEC libraries, you can enjoy the full spectrum of financial reporting with our Audit library.

The Audit library covers auditing standards, attestation engagement standards, accounting and review services standards, audit risk alerts, and other vital auditing-related guidance. You'll also have online access to our best-selling *GAAS Practice Manual, Audit Procedures, Compilations & Reviews, CPA's Guide to Effective Engagement Letters, CPA's Guide to Management Letter Comments,* and be kept up-to-date on the latest authoritative literature via the *GAAS Update Service.*

With **Accounting Research Manager**, you maximize the efficiency of your research time, while enhancing your results. Learn more about our content and our experts by visiting us at **http://www.accountingresearch-manager.com**.

10/10

2011

GAAS

G U I D E

A Comprehensive Restatement of
Standards for Auditing, Attestation,
Compilation, and Review

MARK S. BEASLEY, Pʜ.D., CPA
JOSEPH V. CARCELLO, Pʜ.D., CPA

CCH
a Wolters Kluwer business

ISBN: 978-0-8080-2407-1
ISSN: 1088-9159

No claim is made to original government works; however, within this Product or Publication, the following are subject to CCH's copyright: (1) the gathering, compilation, and arrangement of such government materials; (2) the magnetic translation and digital conversion of data, if applicable; (3) the historical, statutory and other notes and reference; and (4) the commentary and other materials.

Portions of this work were published in a previous edition.

Printed in the United States of America

SUSTAINABLE FORESTRY INITIATIVE — Certified Fiber Sourcing — www.sfiprogram.org

Our Peer Review Policy

Thank you for purchasing the 2011 *GAAS Guide*. Each year we bring you the best engagement guides available, with accompanying electronic audit documents and practice aids. To confirm the technical accuracy and quality control of our materials, CCH, a Wolters Kluwer business, voluntarily submitted to a peer review of our publishing system and our publications (see the Peer Review Statement on the following page).

In addition to peer review, our publications undergo strict technical and content reviews by qualified practitioners. This ensures that our books, audit documents, and practice aids meet "real world" standards and applicability.

Our publications are reviewed every step of the way — from conception to production — to ensure that we bring you the finest guides on the market.

Updated annually, peer reviewed, technically accurate, convenient, and practical — the 2011 *GAAS Guide* shows our commitment to creating books and audit documentation you can trust.

Peer Review Statement

 *Caldwell, Becker, Dervin, Petrick & Co., L.L.P.*
CERTIFIED PUBLIC ACCOUNTANTS

Quality Control Materials Review Report

November 12, 2009

Executive Board
CCH, a Wolters Kluwer business
and the National Peer Review Committee

We have reviewed the system of quality control for the development and maintenance of GAAS Guide (2010 Edition) (hereafter referred to as *materials*) of CCH, a Wolters Kluwer business (the organization) and the resultant materials in effect at October 31, 2009. Our quality control materials peer review was conducted in accordance with the Standards for Performing and Reporting on Peer Reviews established by the Peer Review Board of the American Institute of Certified Public Accountants. The organization is responsible for designing a system of quality control and complying with it to provide users of the materials with reasonable assurance that the materials are reliable aids to assist them in conforming with those professional standards that the materials purport to encompass. Our responsibility is to express an opinion on the design of the system and the organization's compliance with that system based on our review. The nature, objectives, scope, limitations of, and the procedures performed in a Quality Control Materials Review are described in the standards at www.aicpa.org/prsummary.

In our opinion, the system of quality control for the development and maintenance of the quality control materials of CCH, a Wolters Kluwer business was suitably designed and was being complied with during the year ended October 31, 2009, to provide users of the materials with reasonable assurance that the materials are reliable aids to assist them in conforming with those professional standards the materials purport to encompass. Also, in our opinion, the quality control materials referred to above are reliable aids at October 31, 2009. Organizations can receive a rating of *pass*, *pass with deficiency(ies)*, or *fail*. CCH, a Wolters Kluwer business has received a peer review rating of *pass*.

CALDWELL, BECKER, DERVIN, PETRICK & CO., LLP.
CALDWELL, BECKER, DERVIN, PETRICK & CO., L.L.P.

20750 Ventura Boulevard, Suite 140 • Woodland Hills, CA 91364
(818) 704-1040 • FAX (818) 704-5536

Contents

Our Peer Review Policy iii
Peer Review Statement iv
Preface ix
About the Authors xiii

AU 100: Introduction

Section 110: Responsibilities and Functions
of the Independent Auditor 3
Section 120: Defining Professional Requirements in
Statements on Auditing Standards 5
Section 150: Generally Accepted Auditing Standards 8
Section 161: The Relationship of Generally Accepted
Auditing Standards to Quality Control Standards 14

AU 200: The General Standards

Section 201: Nature of the General Standards 23
Section 210: Training and Proficiency of the
Independent Auditor 24
Section 220: Independence 27
Section 230: Due Care in the Performance of Work 33

AU 300: The Standards of Field Work

Section 311: Planning and Supervision 43
Section 312: Audit Risk and Materiality in Conducting
an Audit 68
Section 314: Understanding the Entity and Its Environment and
Assessing the Risks of Material Misstatement 96
Section 315: Communications between Predecessor and
Successor Auditors 144
Section 316: Consideration of Fraud in a Financial
Statement Audit 155
Section 317: Illegal Acts by Clients 187
Section 318: Performing Audit Procedures in Response to
Assessed Risks and Evaluating the Audit Evidence
Obtained 194
Section 322: The Auditor's Consideration of the Internal
Audit Function in an Audit of Financial Statements 218
Section 324: Service Organizations 225
Section 325: Communication of Internal Control Related
Matters Noted in an Audit 245
Section 326: Audit Evidence 257

Section 328: Auditing Fair Value Measurements and
    Disclosures 269
Section 329: Analytical Procedures 281
Section 330: The Confirmation Process 306
Section 331: Inventories 324
Section 332: Auditing Derivative Instruments, Hedging
    Activities, and Investments in Securities 332
Section 333: Management Representations 342
Section 334: Related Parties........................... 353
Section 336: Using the Work of a Specialist 361
Section 337: Inquiry of a Client's Lawyer Concerning
    Litigation, Claims, and Assessments 369
Section 339: Audit Documentation 379
Section 341: The Auditor's Consideration of an Entity's
    Ability to Continue as a Going Concern 395
Section 342: Auditing Accounting Estimates 407
Section 350: Audit Sampling 430
Section 380: The Auditor's Communication with
    Those Charged with Governance 472
Section 390: Consideration of Omitted Procedures after
    the Report Date 483

AU 400: The First, Second, and Third Standards of Reporting

Section 410: Adherence to Generally Accepted Accounting
    Principles 489
Section 411: The Meaning of "Present Fairly in
    Conformity with Generally Accepted Accounting
    Principles" 491
Section 420: Consistency of Application of Generally
    Accepted Accounting Principles 499
Section 431: Adequacy of Disclosures in Financial
    Statements 508
Section 435: Segment Information 512

AU 500: The Fourth Standard of Reporting

Section 504: Association with Financial Statements 515
Section 508: Reports on Audited Financial Statements 522
Section 530: Dating of the Independent Auditor's Report 561
Section 532: Restricting the Use of an Auditor's Report 565
Section 534: Reporting on Financial Statements Prepared
    for Use in Other Countries 571
Section 543: Part of Audit Performed by Other
    Independent Auditors 578

Section 544: Lack of Conformity with Generally Accepted
Accounting Principles. 586
Section 550: Other Information in Documents Containing
Audited Financial Statements 588
Section 551: Reporting on Information Accompanying the Basic
Financial Statements in Auditor-Submitted Documents . . . 594
Section 552: Reporting on Condensed Financial Statements
and Selected Financial Data 602
Section 558: Required Supplementary Information 606
Section 560: Subsequent Events 612
Section 561: Subsequent Discovery of Facts Existing at the
Date of the Auditor's Report 618

AU 600: Other Types of Reports

Section 623: Special Reports 629
Section 625: Reports on the Application of Accounting
Principles 655
Section 634: Letters for Underwriters and Certain Other
Requesting Parties 663

AU 700: Special Topics

Section 711: Filings under Federal Securities Statutes 691
Section 722: Interim Financial Information 697

AU 800: Compliance Auditing

Section 801: Compliance Audits 727

AU 900: Special Reports of the Committee on Auditing Procedure

Section 901: Public Warehouses — Controls and Auditing
Procedures for Goods Held 745

AT Section: Statements on Standards for Attestation Engagements

AT Section 20: Defining Professional Requirements in
Statements on Standards for Attestation Engagements . . . 749
AT Section 50: SSAE Hierarchy 751
AT Section 101: Attest Engagements 753
AT Section 201: Agreed-Upon Procedures Engagements 779
AT Section 301: Financial Forecasts and Projections 787

AT Section 401: Reporting on Pro Forma Financial
   Information   812
AT Section 501: Reporting on an Entity's Internal Control
   over Financial Reporting   822
AT Section 601: Compliance Attestation   850
AT Section 701: Management's Discussion and Analysis   866
AT Section 801: Reporting on Controls at a Service
   Organization   897

AR Section: Statements on Standards for Accounting and Review Services

AR Section 60: Framework for Performing and Reporting on
   Compilation and Review Engagements   925
AR Section 80: Compilation of Financial Statements   932
AR Section 90: Review of Financial Statements   953
AR Section 110: Compilation of Specified Elements,
   Accounts, or Items of a Financial Statement 1017
AR Section 120: Compilation of Pro Forma Financial
   Information 1019
AR Section 200: Reporting on Comparative Financial
   Statements 1021
AR Section 300: Compilation Reports on Financial
   Statements in Certain Prescribed Forms 1037
AR Section 400: Communications between Predecessor
   and Successor Accountants 1040
AR Section 600: Reporting on Personal Financial Statements
   Included in Written Personal Financial Plans 1046

Appendix A: The Sarbanes-Oxley Act of 2002   **1049**

Accounting Resources on the Web   **1069**

Cross-Reference   **1077**

Index   **1097**

About the CD-ROM   **1153**

CD-ROM Contents   **1155**

Preface

CCH's 2011 *GAAS Guide* describes the engagement standards, practices, and procedures in use today, including Statements on Auditing Standards (SASs) and their Interpretations, Statements on Standards for Attestation Engagements (SSAEs) and their Interpretations, and Statements on Standards on Accounting and Review Services (SSARS) and their Interpretations.

The 2011 Edition of the *GAAS Guide* has been updated to reflect the latest available professional standards. This edition includes coverage of SAS-117 (AU 801) (Compliance Audits), issued in December 2009; SAS-118 (AU 550 and AU 551) (Other Information in Documents Containing Audited Financial Statements), issued in February 2010; SAS-119 (AU 551) (Supplementary Information in Relation to the Financial Statements as a Whole), issued in February 2010; SAS-120 (AU 558) (Required Supplementary Information), issued in February 2010; SSAE-16 (AT 801) (Reporting on Controls at a Service Organization) issued in April 2010, SSARS-19 (AR 60, AR 80, and AR 90) (Compilation and Review Engagements), issued in December 2009, several interpretations of SASs, PCAOB standards, and exposure drafts. The *GAAS Guide* incorporates these new requirements throughout the affected auditing standards and includes coverage of AICPA pronouncements up through the following standards:

- SAS-120 (AU 558) (Required Supplementary Information)

- SSAE-16 (AT 801) (Reporting on Controls at a Service Organization)

- SSARS-19 (Compilation and Review Engagements)

The edition's organization follows the arrangement of the AICPA's Professional Standards (Volumes I and II) so that you can easily go from the AICPA's original language to our analyses of the standards. All the exhibit materials in the book appear on the accompanying CD-ROM. All the sample letters, reports, and checklists found in the text can be printed and customized to meet all your auditing, attestation, compilation, and review engagement needs.

Each section is organized using a consistent structure that is simple and insightful. The opening of each section begins with a list of "Authoritative Pronouncements" that identifies the specific professional standards pertinent to that section. That list is followed by an "Overview" that highlights key provisions of the relevant section followed by a "Promulgated Procedures Checklist" that identifies the essential professional responsibilities that must be satisfied in each part of your engagement. Next, under the label "Analysis and Application of Procedures," you'll find a concise discussion of how each specific promulgated procedure should be applied. Finally, many of the sections contain "Practitioner Aids" to help you apply the promulgated standards to your specific engagements.

A continuing feature of the 2011 Edition is the inclusion throughout most sections of additional insights to help you identify unique issues related to your implementation of the professional standards requirements, including suggestions to help you better plan and execute your engagements. This highlighted guidance is summarized as one of the following:

- Engagement Strategy

- Fraud Pointer

- Important Notice for 2011

- Observation

- Planning Aid Reminder

- Public Company Implication

These highlights are easy to find and can help you understand many of the important subtleties contained in the professional standards guidance.

The AICPA's Auditing Standards Board issues auditing standards applicable to the audits of nonpublic companies. The 2011 *GAAS Guide* contains up-to-date AICPA professional standard guidance applicable to those engagements.

The Public Company Accounting Oversight Board (PCAOB), which was created by the Sarbanes-Oxley Act of 2002 (SOX), announced that the PCAOB "will establish auditing and other professional standards for registered public accounting firms." The PCAOB adopted all existing Statements on Auditing Standards (SASs) in effect as of April 16, 2003 (up through SAS-101) as its Interim Auditing Standards. As a result, much of the guidance contained in this 2011 Edition is relevant to auditors of public companies. The 2011 Edition contains Public Company Implications, which highlight issues that are unique for audits of public companies.

To help CPAs understand the impact of the Sarbanes-Oxley Act of 2002, we have included an appendix that highlights key provisions of the act:

- *Appendix A: The Sarbanes Oxley Act of 2002*   This appendix provides an excellent one-source overview of the key provisions of SOX. CPAs wanting a quick and reader-friendly summary of SOX's provisions will find this appendix helpful.

The PCAOB has issued its own auditing standards that apply to audits of financial statements of public companies. As the 2011 Edition of the *GAAS Guide* went to press the PCAOB had issued 15 PCAOB Auditing

Standards (one of which has been superseded). Although the PCAOB Auditing Standards continue to embrace SAS-1 through SAS-101 as the PCAOB's "Interim Auditing Standards," auditors of public companies should continue to monitor the standards-setting activities of the PCAOB.

This 2011 Edition continues to provide what has always been the most important feature of the *GAAS Guide* — readability. The utmost care has been exercised to avoid the difficult language and organization of many of the original pronouncements. Essential material is placed at your fingertips for quick integration into your practice. There is no more need to wonder exactly what a standard means or how it is to be used in a real engagement.

Acknowledgments

Thanks are due Vincent J. Love, CPA, of New York, NY, for his thoughtful, thorough review of the 2011 edition.

Mark S. Beasley
Raleigh, North Carolina

Joseph V. Carcello
Knoxville, Tennessee

About the Authors

Mark S. Beasley is the Deloitte Professor of Enterprise Risk Management and Professor of Accounting in the Department of Accounting at North Carolina State University, in Raleigh, N.C., where he teaches auditing courses in the undergraduate and masters programs. He currently serves as a member of the COSO Board. Dr. Beasley received a BS in accounting from Auburn University and a Ph.D. from Michigan State University. He is a Certified Public Accountant (CPA) in North Carolina and has worked in public accounting, where he was an Audit Manager with Ernst & Young. Dr. Beasley also worked as a Technical Manager with the AICPA's Auditing Standards Division, in New York City. He is a member of the American Institute of Certified Public Accountants, the American Accounting Association, the Institute of Internal Auditors, and the Association of Certified Fraud Examiners. Dr. Beasley also serves as Director of North Carolina State University's Enterprise Risk Management Initiative, which provides thought leadership on enterprise risk management and its integration with strategy planning and governance.

Dr. Beasley actively conducts research related to financial statement fraud, corporate governance, and auditor quality. His work has been published in journals such as the *Journal of Accounting Research, Contemporary Accounting Research, Auditing: A Journal of Practice & Theory, Accounting Horizons, Journal of the American Taxation Association, Journal of Accountancy*, and *The CPA Journal*, among numerous others. He recently served on COSO's Enterprise Risk Management project Advisory Council and the AICPA's Antifraud Programs and Controls Task Force. He has previously served on Auditing Standards Board task forces, including the SAS No. 99 Fraud Task Force. Dr. Beasley is the co-author of several continuing education courses, an auditing textbook, and an auditing casebook.

Joseph V. Carcello is a Professor in the Department of Accounting and Information Management and the Director of Research of the Corporate Governance Center at the University of Tennessee, in Knoxville, Tenn., where he teaches auditing and financial accounting courses in the undergraduate and MAcc. programs. Dr. Carcello received a BS in accounting from SUNY at Plattsburgh, a MAcc from the University of Georgia, and a Ph.D. from Georgia State University. He is a Certified Public Accountant (CPA), a Certified Internal Auditor (CIA), and a Certified Management Accountant (CMA). Dr. Carcello worked in public accounting, where he was an Audit Senior with Ernst & Young. He is a member of the American Institute of Certified Public Accountants, the American Accounting Association, the American Bar Association (associate), the Association of Certified Fraud Examiners, the Financial Executives

International, the Institute of Internal Auditors, the Institute of Management Accountants, and the National Association of Corporate Directors.

Dr. Carcello has taught continuing professional education courses for two of the Big 4 accounting firms, AICPA, Institute of Internal Auditors, The Institute of Management Accountants, the Tennessee and Florida Societies of CPAs, local and regional accounting firms, and he has provided consulting services on revenue recognition to the software industry. He has also served as an expert witness for the Securities and Exchange Commission and testified before the U.S. Treasury Advisory Committee on the Auditing Profession. Dr. Carcello is a member of the PCAOB's Investor Advisory Group, and he previously served as a member of the PCAOB's Standing Advisory Group and of COSO's Small Business Control Guidance Advisory Group Task Force.

Dr. Carcello actively conducts research related to corporate governance (particularly audit committee performance), fraudulent financial reporting, and going-concern reporting. His work has been published in journals such as *The Accounting Review, Journal of Accounting Research, Contemporary Accounting Research, Auditing: A Journal of Practice & Theory, Accounting Horizons, Journal of Accounting and Public Policy*, and *Journal of Accountancy*, among numerous others. Dr. Carcello is the co-author of CCH's *GAAP Guide, Volume I* and a financial accounting textbook.

AU 100

Introduction

Section 110: Responsibilities and Functions of the
    Independent Auditor 3

Section 120: Defining Professional Requirements in Statements
    on Auditing Standards 5

Section 150: Generally Accepted Auditing Standards 8

Section 161: The Relationship of Generally Accepted Auditing
    Standards to Quality Control Standards 14

SECTION 110

RESPONSIBILITIES AND FUNCTIONS OF THE INDEPENDENT AUDITOR

Authoritative Pronouncements

SAS-1 — Codification of Auditing Standards and Procedures (Section 110, Responsibilities and Functions of the Independent Auditor)

> **IMPORTANT NOTICE FOR 2011:** The Auditing Standards Board (ASB) is in the process of redrafting all of the auditing sections in *Codification of Statements on Auditing Standards* to converge U.S. GAAS with the International Standards on Auditing issued by the International Auditing and Assurance Standards Board. As part of this process, the newly redrafted standards will follow certain clarity drafting conventions adopted by the ASB. These clarity drafting conventions include: (1) establishing objectives for each standard; (2) including a definitions section, if appropriate; and (3) separating requirements from application guidance and other material. The ASB is planning to have all redrafted standards become effective on the same date, which is for audits of financial statements for periods ending on or after December 15, 2012. It is possible that the effective date might be delayed beyond that date. The ASB's clarity and convergence project will have a significant effect on the auditing standards applicable to audits of nonpublic companies, and the 2012 *GAAS Guide* will be appropriately modified to reflect these changes once the effective date of the standards is certain.

Overview

The purpose of an audit engagement is to express an opinion in an auditor's report about a client's financial statements. The opinion may be unqualified, qualified, or adverse; in some circumstances the auditor may disclaim an opinion on the financial statements. Although the auditor expresses an opinion on the client's financial statements, the responsibility for the financial statements rests with management. Nonetheless, the auditor can make suggestions to the client about the form and content of the financial statements or may draft the financial statements based on information the client provides.

> **PUBLIC COMPANY IMPLICATIONS:** Section 302 of the Sar-
> banes-Oxley Act of 2002 (SOX) requires the CEO and CFO of
> public companies to prepare a written statement that certifies
> the appropriateness of the annual and quarterly financial
> statements and disclosures, including certification that based
> on their knowledge those financial statements and disclosures
> fairly present, in all material respects, the operations and fi-
> nancial condition of the issuer. Thus, in an audit of a public
> company's financial statements, the auditor would not be
> responsible for drafting the financial statements based on in-
> formation provided by the client. Rather, management is re-
> sponsible for preparing the financial statements.

In order to perform the services of an auditor of financial statements, an individual must possess an appropriate educational background and have adequate experience. An auditor is not expected to have the background necessary to accept the responsibilities of another profession. For example, an auditor is not expected to fulfill the role of an attorney or asset appraiser.

In order to express an opinion on a client's financial statements, an auditor is expected to exercise professional judgment in a number of areas, ranging from selecting auditing procedures to determining the appropriateness of an accounting principle or method. The judgments made by an auditor are that of a qualified professional, but that judgment is not infallible.

Finally, an auditor has a responsibility to his or her profession to observe professional standards, including the AICPA's Code of Professional Conduct.

> **PUBLIC COMPANY IMPLICATIONS:** SOX authorizes the Pub-
> lic Company Accounting Oversight Board (PCAOB) to issue
> auditing standards for audits of public company financial state-
> ments. In April 2003, the PCAOB adopted existing auditing
> standards previously issued by the Auditing Standards Board
> as the PCAOB's "Interim Auditing Standards." Thus, GAAS
> promulgated by the Auditing Standards Board as of April 16,
> 2003 constitute the "Interim Auditing Standards." Since then,
> the PCAOB has begun to issue PCAOB Auditing Standards
> that amend or supersede portions of the "Interim Auditing
> Standards."

SECTION 120

DEFINING PROFESSIONAL REQUIREMENTS IN STATEMENTS ON AUDITING STANDARDS

Authoritative Pronouncements

SAS-102 — Defining Professional Requirements in Statements on Auditing Standards

> **IMPORTANT NOTICE FOR 2011:** The Auditing Standards Board (ASB) is in the process of redrafting all of the auditing sections in *Codification of Statements on Auditing Standards* to converge U.S. GAAS with the International Standards on Auditing issued by the International Auditing and Assurance Standards Board. As part of this process, the newly redrafted standards will follow certain clarity drafting conventions adopted by the ASB. These clarity drafting conventions include: (1) establishing objectives for each standard; (2) including a definitions section, if appropriate; and (3) separating requirements from application guidance and other material. The ASB is planning to have all redrafted standards become effective on the same date, which is for audits of financial statements for periods ending on or after December 15, 2012. It is possible that the effective date might be delayed beyond that date. The ASB's clarity and convergence project will have a significant effect on the auditing standards applicable to audits of nonpublic companies, and the 2012 *GAAS Guide* will be appropriately modified to reflect these changes once the effective date of the standards is certain.

Overview

SAS-102 specifies the auditor's performance responsibility under the Statements on Auditing Standards and provides guidance on when an auditor *must* perform an auditing procedure, when the auditor *should* perform an auditing procedure, and when an auditor *may* perform an auditing procedure.

> **OBSERVATION:** SAS-102 defines an auditor's performance responsibilities with more specificity than has previously existed in the auditing literature. Therefore, the authors expect that auditors will be held to these performance standards by

regulators and the judicial system. For these reasons auditors are well advised to pay particularly close attention to the inclusion of the words "must," "is required," "should," and "may" in existing and future professional standards.

PUBLIC COMPANY IMPLICATION: PCAOB standards are very similar to SAS-102 as it relates to the auditor's performance responsibility. The PCAOB's Rule 3101 states that its standards create unconditional responsibilities, presumptively mandatory responsibilities, and responsibilities to consider. Unconditional responsibilities are denoted by the words "must," "shall," and "is required." Presumptively mandatory responsibilities are denoted by the word "should." Responsibilities to consider are denoted by the words "may," "might," "could," and similar language.

A SAS contains both professional requirements and related guidance in applying it. In fulfilling professional responsibilities, the auditor has a responsibility to consider the entire text of a SAS. There are two types of professional requirements imposed by a SAS: (1) unconditional requirements and (2) presumptively mandatory requirements.

An auditor must comply with unconditional requirements, assuming the circumstances that a requirement applies to exist. The existence of an unconditional requirement is indicated by the words "must" or "is required" in a SAS.

In most cases, auditors are also required to comply with presumptively mandatory requirements. In rare cases, an auditor can depart from a presumptively mandatory requirement. But, in these rare cases, the auditor must document (1) the reasons why the presumptively mandatory requirement was not followed and (2) how alternative procedures achieved the objectives that the presumptively mandatory requirement was designed to meet. The existence of a presumptively mandatory requirement is indicated by the word "should."

ENGAGEMENT STRATEGY: The auditor must achieve the objectives that a presumptively mandatory requirement is designed to achieve, either by performing the procedures specified in the SAS or by employing alternative procedures that accomplish the same objective.

A SAS may specify that an auditor "should consider" a procedure. In this instance, there is a presumptive requirement that the auditor will consider the procedure. However, although an auditor essentially has to consider the procedure, he or she does not necessarily have to perform the procedure.

A SAS also contains related guidance in applying the standard. This related guidance is also referred to as "explanatory material." Explanatory material in a SAS is intended to be descriptive rather than imperative (i.e., it does not impose a performance obligation upon the auditor). For example, explanatory material may (1) explain the objective of the professional requirements, (2) explain why particular audit procedures are recommended or required, and (3) provide additional information that the auditor may find helpful in applying his or her professional judgment. Explanatory material may discuss other procedures or actions that the auditor might perform. These other procedures or actions are suggestive and do not impose a professional requirement on the auditor. These suggested procedures and actions in a SAS are denoted by the words "may," "might," or "could."

> **OBSERVATION:** SAS-102 reiterates SAS-95's guidance that interpretive publications are not professional standards but, rather, provide guidance on the application of a SAS to a particular circumstance. Interpretive guidance includes auditing interpretations of the SASs, appendixes to SASs, auditing guidance in AICPA Audit and Accounting Guides, and AICPA auditing Statements of Position. The words "must" or "should" in an interpretive document do *not* represent unconditional requirements or presumptively mandatory requirements, respectively. Although interpretive publications do not create a professional requirement, SAS-95 indicates that the auditor should be aware of and should consider interpretive publications. Moreover, if the auditor does not apply the interpretive guidance, the auditor should be *prepared to explain* how he or she complied with the specific SAS provision that the interpretive guidance pertained to.

> **PUBLIC COMPANY IMPLICATION:** An auditor's professional requirements as specified in SAS-102 are quite similar to an auditor's professional requirements in the audit of a public company, as specified by the PCAOB in Rule 3101 (Certain Terms Used in Auditing and Related Professional Practice Standards).

SECTION 150

GENERALLY ACCEPTED AUDITING STANDARDS

Authoritative Pronouncements

SAS-95 — Generally Accepted Auditing Standards
SAS-98 — Omnibus Statement on Auditing Standards — 2002
SAS-105 — Amendment to Statement on Auditing Standards No. 95, Generally Accepted Auditing Standards
SAS-113 — Omnibus Statement on Auditing Standards — 2006

> **IMPORTANT NOTICE FOR 2011:** The Auditing Standards Board (ASB) is in the process of redrafting all of the auditing sections in *Codification of Statements on Auditing Standards* to converge U.S. GAAS with the International Standards on Auditing issued by the International Auditing and Assurance Standards Board. As part of this process, the newly redrafted standards will follow certain clarity drafting conventions adopted by the ASB. These clarity drafting conventions include: (1) establishing objectives for each standard; (2) including a definitions section, if appropriate; and (3) separating requirements from application guidance and other material. The ASB is planning to have all redrafted standards become effective on the same date, which is for audits of financial statements for periods ending on or after December 15, 2012. It is possible that the effective date might be delayed beyond that date. The ASB's clarity and convergence project will have a significant effect on the auditing standards applicable to audits of nonpublic companies, and the 2012 *GAAS Guide* will be appropriately modified to reflect these changes once the effective date of the standards is certain.

Overview

Auditing standards deal with the quality of an audit performed by an independent auditor. The members of the American Institute of Certified Public Accountants (AICPA) have approved and adopted ten generally accepted auditing standards (GAAS) that apply to the audits of nonpublic entities. These standards are divided into three groups: (1) general standards, (2) standards of fieldwork, and (3) standards of reporting. Under Rule 202 of the Code of Professional Conduct, every member of the AICPA who audits a nonpublic company must comply with GAAS.

> **OBSERVATION:** Many state boards of accountancy require CPAs licensed in their state to comply with the AICPA Code of Professional Conduct and other AICPA authoritative standards even if those CPAs are not members of the AICPA.

General standards

The most important factor in any profession is the people who make up the profession. The personal characteristics of an auditor are described below in a discussion of the three general standards. Desirable traits are difficult to describe in any individual, much less a profession. Therefore, these general standards are quite broad and are open to a considerable degree of reasonable interpretation.

- *General Standard No. 1* The auditor must have adequate technical training and proficiency to perform the audit.

- *General Standard No. 2* The auditor must maintain independence in mental attitude in all matters related to the audit.

- *General Standard No. 3* The auditor must exercise due professional care in the performance of the audit and the preparation of the report.

Standards of fieldwork

- *Standard of Fieldwork No. 1* The auditor must adequately plan the work and must properly supervise any assistants.

- *Standard of Fieldwork No. 2* The auditor must obtain a sufficient understanding of the entity and its environment, including its internal control, to assess the risk of material misstatement of the financial statements whether due to error or fraud, and to design the nature, timing, and extent of further audit procedures.

- *Standard of Fieldwork No. 3* The auditor must obtain sufficient appropriate audit evidence by performing audit procedures to afford a reasonable basis for an opinion regarding the financial statements under audit.

Standards of reporting

- *Reporting Standard No. 1* The auditor must state in the auditor's report whether the financial statements are presented in accordance with generally accepted accounting principles (GAAP).

- *Reporting Standard No. 2* The auditor must identify in the auditor's report those circumstances in which such principles have not been consistently observed in the current period in relation to the preceding period.

- *Reporting Standard No. 3* When the auditor determines that informative disclosures are not reasonably adequate, the auditor must so state in the auditor's report.

- *Reporting Standard No. 4* The auditor must either express in his or her report an opinion regarding the financial statements taken as a whole or state that an opinion cannot be expressed. When the auditor cannot express an overall opinion, the auditor should state the reasons therefore in the auditor's report. In all cases where an auditor's name is associated with financial statements, the auditor should clearly indicate the character of the auditor's work, if any, and the degree of responsibility the auditor is taking, in the auditor's report.

Statements on Auditing Standards

The AICPA's Auditing Standards Boards issues Statements on Auditing Standards (SASs) that apply to the audits of nonpublic entity financial statements. An auditor must be familiar with all SASs to determine which are appropriate for a particular engagement. In applying the SASs, the auditor is expected to use professional judgment, including considering materiality and audit risk. In addition, SAS-102 defines an auditor's professional requirements in applying the SASs (see AU Section 120). An auditor may, in rare circumstances, depart from a presumptively mandatory requirement. In these situations, the auditor must document why he or she departed from the presumptively mandatory requirement and how he or she accomplished the objective of the presumptively mandatory requirement through other procedures.

> **ENGAGEMENT STRATEGY:** An engagement planning strategy is to start with the assumption that all SASs apply, given that most are relevant in every audit. As planning proceeds, the auditor might identify exceptions that exist for unique situations. For example, the use of specialists, audits of service organizations, or the audit of derivative instruments might not be applicable. Auditors may wish to identify a list of the most frequent exceptions, which could be used when planning all audit engagements, and assume that all other SASs are applicable.

Interpretative publications

Interpretative publications are issued under the authority of the Auditing Standards Board and include the following:

- Appendixes to SASs (does not include previously issued appendixes to original pronouncements that when adopted modified other SASs)
- Auditing Interpretations of the SASs
- AICPA Audit and Accounting Guides
- AICPA Auditing Statements of Position

Guidelines established in interpretative publications are not auditing standards but, rather, provide specific direction on how auditing standards are to be observed in particular situations, especially for clients who operate in specialized industries. An auditor is expected to be aware of interpretative publications and, if they are relevant, follow their guidance in a particular engagement.

Auditing Interpretations are discussed throughout this text. AICPA Audit and Accounting Guides are listed below and may be purchased from the AICPA:

- Analytical Procedures
- Audit Sampling
- Auditing Derivative Instruments, Hedging Activities, and Investments in Securities
- Auditing Revenue in Certain Industries
- Audits of Agricultural Producers and Agricultural Cooperatives
- Audits of Airlines
- Audits of Casinos
- Audits of Employee Benefit Plans
- Audits of Entities with Oil and Gas Producing Activities
- Audits of Federal Government Contractors
- Audits of Investment Companies
- Audits of Property and Liability Insurance Companies
- Audits of State and Local Governmental Units
- Brokers and Dealers in Securities

- Common Interest Realty Associations

- Consideration of Internal Control in a Financial Statement Audit

- Construction Contractors

- Depository and Lending Institutions: Banks and Savings Institutions, Credit Unions, Finance Companies, and Mortgage Companies

- Government Auditing Standards and Circular A-133 Audits

- Guide for Prospective Financial Information

- Guide for the Use of Real Estate Appraisal Information

- Health Care Organizations

- Life and Health Insurance Entities

- Not-for-Profit Organizations

- Service Organizations: Applying SAS No. 70, as Amended

- Personal Financial Statements Guide

AICPA Statements of Position (Auditing and Attestation), which address specific auditing and accounting issues, may be purchased from the AICPA.

Other auditing publications

Auditing guidance is also provided in a variety of other publications including textbooks, articles, and various instructional materials. An auditor is not "expected to be aware of the full body of other auditing publications"; however, if such guidance is followed, the auditor is responsible for determining whether the guidance is relevant to a particular engagement.

> **PUBLIC COMPANY IMPLICATIONS:** SOX authorizes the Public Company Accounting Oversight Board (PCAOB) to issue auditing standards for audits of public company financial statements. In April 2003, the PCAOB adopted existing auditing standards previously issued by the Auditing Standards Board as the PCAOB's "Interim Auditing Standards." Thus, GAAS promulgated by the Auditing Standards Board as of April 16, 2003 constitute the "Interim Auditing Standards." Since then, the PCAOB has begun to issue PCAOB Auditing Standards that amend or supersede portions of the "Interim Auditing Standards."

PLANNING AID REMINDER: In December 2005, the Auditing Standards Board issued SAS-102 (Defining Professional Requirements in Statements on Auditing Standards), which defines the degree of responsibility imposed on a practitioner when the words "must," "is required," or "should" appear in a SAS. The words "must" or "is required" indicate mandatory obligations of a practitioner, assuming the circumstances that the requirement applies to exist. The word "should" indicates a presumptive requirement. In rare circumstances, a practitioner may justify departure from a presumptive requirement if (1) he or she documents the reasons for the departure and (2) documents how alternative procedures he or she performed accomplished the objectives of the presumptive requirement. SAS-102 does not apply to Auditing Interpretations issued by the Auditing Standards Board or to any other interpretive guidance.

SECTION 161

THE RELATIONSHIP OF GENERALLY ACCEPTED AUDITING STANDARDS TO QUALITY CONTROL STANDARDS

Authoritative Pronouncements

SAS-25 — The Relationship of Generally Accepted Auditing Standards to Quality Control Standards

SAS-98 — Omnibus Statement on Auditing Standards — 2002

SQCS-7 — A Firm's System of Quality Control

> **IMPORTANT NOTICE FOR 2011:** The Auditing Standards Board (ASB) is in the process of redrafting all of the auditing sections in *Codification of Statements on Auditing Standards* to converge U.S. GAAS with the International Standards on Auditing issued by the International Auditing and Assurance Standards Board. As part of this process, the newly redrafted standards will follow certain clarity drafting conventions adopted by the ASB. These clarity drafting conventions include: (1) establishing objectives for each standard; (2) including a definitions section, if appropriate; and (3) separating requirements from application guidance and other material. The ASB is planning to have all redrafted standards become effective on the same date, which is for audits of financial statements for periods ending on or after December 15, 2012. It is possible that the effective date might be delayed beyond that date. The ASB's clarity and convergence project will have a significant effect on the auditing standards applicable to audits of nonpublic companies, and the 2012 *GAAS Guide* will be appropriately modified to reflect these changes once the effective date of the standards is certain.

Overview

An accounting firm should adopt a system of quality controls to provide reasonable assurance that generally accepted auditing standards (GAAS) are followed by the professional staff of the firm (SAS-25). Quality control standards relate to the conduct of a firm's audit practice. GAAS relates to the conduct of an individual audit engagement. In this way, quality control standards and GAAS are related.

The AICPA's Auditing Standards Board has the authority to issue pronouncements on quality control standards for CPA firms that are members of the American Institute of Certified Public Accountants (AICPA).

> **OBSERVATION:** SAS-98 points out that if a firm is found to have deficiencies in its system of quality control or violates specific policies or controls, it does not mean that a particular audit engagement was not performed in accordance with generally accepted auditing standards.

The actual design of the system of quality controls will vary from firm to firm, depending on such factors as the size of the professional staff, the number of offices, and the geographical location of the offices.

Quality control standards are based on Statements on Quality Control Standards No. 7 (SQCS-7) (A Firm's System of Quality Control). SQCS-7 requires that a firm establish a system of quality control designed to provide it with reasonable assurance that the firm and its personnel comply with professional standards and applicable regulatory and legal requirements, and that the firm or engagement partners issue reports that are appropriate in the circumstances. SQCS-7 defines a system of quality control as consisting of policies designed to achieve these objectives and the procedures necessary to implement the policies and monitor compliance with them.

SQCS-7 notes that the firm's system of quality control should include policies and procedures addressing each of the following elements:

- Leadership responsibilities for quality within the firm (the "tone at the top")
- Relevant ethical requirements
- Acceptance and continuance of client relationships and specific engagements
- Human resources
- Engagement performance
- Monitoring

The standards established by SQCS apply to a firm's "accounting and auditing practice," which is defined as follows by SQCS-7:

> Accounting and auditing practice refers to all audit, attest, compilation, review, and other services for which standards have been established by the AICPA Auditing Standards Board

or the AICPA Accounting and Review Services Committee under Rules 201 or 202 of the AICPA Code of Professional Conduct.

> **OBSERVATION:** Other AICPA senior technical committees may establish standards. Engagements subject to those standards do not fall under the scope of an accounting and auditing practice.

The AICPA Professional Issues Task Force published Practice Alert No. 01-1, titled "Common Peer Review Recommendations," which identifies common peer review findings that are helpful to professionals as they consider critical and significant issues in planning and performing audits. The issues are grouped in the following categories: (1) implementation of new professional standards or pronouncements, (2) application of GAAP pertaining to equity transactions, (3) application of GAAP pertaining to revenue recognition considerations, (4) documentation of audit procedures and audit findings, and (5) miscellaneous findings. Practice Alerts can be downloaded from the AICPA Web site (http://www.aicpa.org).

Promulgated Quality Control Component Checklist

A public accounting firm should consider the following components in the design of an effective quality control system:

- Leadership responsibilities for quality within the firm (the "tone at the top")
- Relevant ethical requirements
- Acceptance and continuance of client relationships and specific engagements
- Human resources
- Engagement performance
- Monitoring

Although these components are discussed separately in the following analysis, an effective system of quality control recognizes that all of the components are interrelated.

Analysis and Application of Quality Control Components

A firm's system of quality control should include policies and procedures that address each of the following elements.

Leadership responsibilities for quality within the firm (the "tone at the top")

The firm should promote an internal culture based on the recognition that quality is essential in performing engagements, and it should establish policies and procedures to support that culture. The policies and procedures should require the firm's leadership (managing partner or board of managing partners, chief executive officer, or equivalent) to assume ultimate responsibility for the firm's system of quality control.

Relevant ethical requirements

The firm should establish policies and procedures designed to provide it with reasonable assurance that the firm and its personnel comply with relevant ethical requirements. The AICPA's *Code of Professional Conduct* establishes the fundamental principles of professional ethics.

Acceptance and continuance of client relationships and specific engagements

The firm should establish policies and procedures for the acceptance and continuance of client relationships and specific engagements. The policies should be designed to provide the firm with reasonable assurance that it will undertake or continue relationships and engagements only where the firm

- Has considered the integrity of the client, including the identity and business reputation of the client's principal owners, key management, related parties, and those charged with its governance, and the risks associated with providing professional services in the particular circumstances.

- Is competent to perform the engagement and has the capabilities and resources to do so; and

- Can comply with legal and ethical requirements.

Human resources

The firm should establish policies and procedures designed to provide it with reasonable assurance that it has sufficient personnel with the capabilities, competence, and commitment to ethical principles necessary to perform the engagements in accordance with professional standards and regulatory and legal requirements and enable it to issue reports that are appropriate in the circumstances. Such policies and procedures should address recruiting and hiring; determining capabilities and competencies; assigning personnel to engagements, if applicable; professional development; and performance evaluation, compensation, and advancement.

Engagement performance

The firm should establish policies and procedures designed to provide it with reasonable assurance that engagements are consistently performed in accordance with professional standards and regulatory and legal requirements, and that the firm or the engagement partner issues reports that are appropriate in the circumstances. These policies should address engagement performance, supervision responsibilities, and review responsibilities.

Monitoring

The firm should establish policies and procedures designed to provide it and its engagement partners with reasonable assurance that the policies and procedures relating to the system of quality control are relevant, adequate, operating effectively, and are complied with in practice.

Documentation of Operation of Quality Control

SQCS-7 requires the firm to establish policies and procedures requiring appropriate documentation to provide evidence of the operation of each element of its system of quality control. The form and content of the documentation evidencing the operation of each of the elements of the system of quality control is a matter of judgment. Such documentation depends on a number of factors, including the size of the firm, the number of offices, and the nature and complexity of the firm's practice and organization.

Firms should establish policies and procedures that require retention of documentation for a period of time sufficient to permit those performing monitoring procedures and peer review to evaluate the firm's compliance with its system of quality control or for a longer period of time, if required by law or regulation.

> **PUBLIC COMPANY IMPLICATION:** The PCAOB's AS-7 (Engagement Quality Review) establishes standards for the performance of an engagement quality review. AS-7 applies to all firms registered with the PCAOB (prior to AS-7, only firms that were members of the AICPA's SECPS were required to perform a concurring review).

In addition to applying to audits performed under PCAOB standards, AS-7 also applies to reviews. However, the procedures required to be performed by the engagement quality reviewer for a review of interim financial information would be more limited. For all such engagements, an engagement review would be required to be conducted before the report is issued. The engagement reviewer would be required to be a partner of the firm performing the engagement, another person in an equivalent position in the firm, or an individual outside the firm who is associated with a registered public accounting firm. The engagement reviewer would be required to have competence, independence, integrity, and objectivity. He or she would be required to have the level of competence needed to have an overall responsibility for the engagement under review (although the quality reviewer is not actually serving as the engagement partner). To maintain objectivity, the engagement reviewer would not be permitted to make decisions for the engagement team or assume responsibilities of the team. In addition, a partner cannot serve as the engagement quality reviewer for a client if the partner had served as the engagement partner for either of the clients two previous audits; however, this prohibition does not apply to certain small auditing firms that are exempt from the audit partner rotation rules under SEC regulation. Certain review procedures are required on every audit engagement, and review procedures generally involve discussions with engagement personnel and review of documents. Review procedures must be performed with due professional care and professional skepticism. Required engagement quality review procedures are more limited when the service being reviewed is an interim review. In addition, the engagement quality reviewer would be required to review documentation in the areas that he or she reviewed. The engagement quality reviewer would be required to assess whether this documentation indicates that the engagement team responded appropriately to significant risks (audit engagements only) and whether the documentation supports conclusions reached by the engagement team (both for audit and review engagements). The engagement quality reviewer must adequately document his or her review procedures. The firm would not be permitted to issue its report (or communicate its conclusion to the client if no report was to be issued) until the engagement quality reviewer granted his or her concurring approval. The PCAOB has stated that compliance with ASB standards (e.g., SQCS-7) is not sufficient to comply with AS-7.

AU 200

The General Standards

Section 201: Nature of the General Standards 23

Section 210: Training and Proficiency of the Independent
    Auditor 24

Section 220: Independence 27

Section 230: Due Care in the Performance of Work 33

SECTION 201

NATURE OF THE GENERAL STANDARDS

Authoritative Pronouncements

SAS-1 — Codification of Auditing Standards and Procedures (Section 201, Nature of the General Standards)

> **IMPORTANT NOTICE FOR 2011:** The Auditing Standards Board (ASB) is in the process of redrafting all of the auditing sections in *Codification of Statements on Auditing Standards* to converge U.S. GAAS with the International Standards on Auditing issued by the International Auditing and Assurance Standards Board. As part of this process, the newly redrafted standards will follow certain clarity drafting conventions adopted by the ASB. These clarity drafting conventions include: (1) establishing objectives for each standard; (2) including a definitions section, if appropriate; and (3) separating requirements from application guidance and other material. The ASB is planning to have all redrafted standards become effective on the same date, which is for audits of financial statements for periods ending on or after December 15, 2012. It is possible that the effective date might be delayed beyond that date. The ASB's clarity and convergence project will have a significant effect on the auditing standards applicable to audits of nonpublic companies, and the 2012 *GAAS Guide* will be appropriately modified to reflect these changes once the effective date of the standards is certain.

Overview

The general standards of generally accepted auditing standards (GAAS) are personal and relate to the qualifications of the auditor and to the professional care exercised in a particular engagement. The standards address who is qualified to perform an audit engagement and the need for adequate technical training and proficiency, independence, and the exercise of due professional care. However, the general standards, standards of fieldwork, and reporting standards are all interrelated and must be applied accordingly.

SECTION 210

TRAINING AND PROFICIENCY OF THE INDEPENDENT AUDITOR

Authoritative Pronouncements

SAS-1 — Codification of Auditing Standards and Procedures (Section 210, Training and Proficiency of the Independent Auditor)

> **IMPORTANT NOTICE FOR 2011:** The Auditing Standards Board (ASB) is in the process of redrafting all of the auditing sections in *Codification of Statements on Auditing Standards* to converge U.S. GAAS with the International Standards on Auditing issued by the International Auditing and Assurance Standards Board. As part of this process, the newly redrafted standards will follow certain clarity drafting conventions adopted by the ASB. These clarity drafting conventions include: (1) establishing objectives for each standard; (2) including a definitions section, if appropriate; and (3) separating requirements from application guidance and other material. The ASB is planning to have all redrafted standards become effective on the same date, which is for audits of financial statements for periods ending on or after December 15, 2012. It is possible that the effective date might be delayed beyond that date. The ASB's clarity and convergence project will have a significant effect on the auditing standards applicable to audits of nonpublic companies, and the 2012 *GAAS Guide* will be appropriately modified to reflect these changes once the effective date of the standards is certain.

Overview

General Standard No. 1 states that "the auditor must have adequate technical training and proficiency to perform the audit." This first standard addresses two characteristics that an auditor must possess: adequate technical training and proficiency as an auditor.

A technical body of accounting and auditing knowledge must be mastered as a prerequisite for the successful practice of auditing. This body of knowledge encompasses an understanding of generally accepted accounting principles (GAAP) and generally accepted auditing standards (GAAS). The foundations of this knowledge can initially be acquired by the completion of an accounting degree at a college or university.

However, adequate technical training goes beyond the completion of certain accounting and auditing courses. Accounting educators and practitioners do not agree on what specific courses a prospective auditor should complete. In one respect, the practitioner's problem of technical training has been solved by the state boards of accountancy, in that these boards establish the minimum number of credits a candidate must complete before taking the certified public accounting (CPA) examination.

For a number of reasons, the practitioner should not take a passive role in accepting the state boards' prescribed course requirements. Not all newly hired auditors will take the uniform CPA examination; some might never meet the state-mandated requirements. In addition, the needs of a particular firm might require that an employee have specialized accounting or auditing training. Most importantly, adequate technical training is a dynamic concept and the need for it should not apply only to newly hired employees. Technical training includes a continual awareness of business and professional developments. Knowledge of new pronouncements on accounting principles and audit procedures as they are developed by authoritative bodies is critical to possessing technical training. Having passed the CPA examination ten years ago does not necessarily mean that a CPA is adequately trained today. Thus, a CPA firm must view technical training of its employees in the context of its clientele and (1) establish minimum courses that an employee should complete and (2) design a training program that reflects changes in the accounting profession.

Many firms use a combination of continuing professional education (CPE) courses and staff training to make certain that members of the firm have adequate technical training. The AICPA and state boards of accountancy have requirements for licensees to complete a certain amount of CPE as a prerequisite for renewing their licenses. CPE courses offer CPAs and their firm members the opportunity to update their knowledge and obtain new knowledge.

Adequate technical training for an auditor does not go beyond the bounds of accounting and auditing knowledge. A firm may encounter a situation in which the practitioner needs technical training in other disciplines in order to successfully complete an audit engagement. For example, the fairness of the financial statements may be dependent on geological conclusions or actuarial computations. SAS-73 (AU 336) (Using the Work of a Specialist) recognizes the technical limitations of an auditor and establishes guidelines for the use of members of other disciplines. In much the same way, SAS-12 (AU 337) (Inquiry of a Client's Lawyer Concerning Litigation, Claims, and Assessments) provides guidelines for the use of a lawyer in applying ASC 450 (FAS-5, *Accounting for Contingencies*).

The second part of the first general standard refers to an auditor's need for proficiency. Success in auditing goes beyond receiving an education and training. Proficiency as an auditor is also obtained through ongoing professional experience. With proper supervision and review by a more experienced auditor, a less-experienced auditor can develop proficiency as he or she applies knowledge in an actual engagement. Thus, proficiency is gained through on-the-job experience. It should be noted that the basis for proficiency is adequate training and education. Therefore, the practitioner must apply the first general standard on an integrated basis, recognizing the interrelationship of training and proficiency.

> **PLANNING AID REMINDER:** If the first general standard were applied literally to an engagement, only experienced auditors could be used, because of the proficiency requirement. However, General Standard No. 1 must be evaluated in conjunction with the first standard of fieldwork, which notes that assistants must be properly supervised. Thus, compliance with professional standards can be achieved if a firm matches the background of its staff with the complexities of a particular engagement and designs a plan of supervision that reflects both the background and the complexities.

SECTION 220

INDEPENDENCE

Authoritative Pronouncements

SAS-1, Codification of Auditing Standards and Procedures (Section 220, Independence)

> **IMPORTANT NOTICE FOR 2011:** The Auditing Standards Board (ASB) is in the process of redrafting all of the auditing sections in *Codification of Statements on Auditing Standards* to converge U.S. GAAS with the International Standards on Auditing issued by the International Auditing and Assurance Standards Board. As part of this process, the newly redrafted standards will follow certain clarity drafting conventions adopted by the ASB. These clarity drafting conventions include: (1) establishing objectives for each standard; (2) including a definitions section, if appropriate; and (3) separating requirements from application guidance and other material. The ASB is planning to have all redrafted standards become effective on the same date, which is for audits of financial statements for periods ending on or after December 15, 2012. It is possible that the effective date might be delayed beyond that date. The ASB's clarity and convergence project will have a significant effect on the auditing standards applicable to audits of nonpublic companies, and the 2012 *GAAS Guide* will be appropriately modified to reflect these changes once the effective date of the standards is certain.

Overview

General Standard No. 2 states that "The auditor must maintain independence in mental attitude in all matters relating to the audit." Although every profession should demand that its members be trained and proficient, the second general standard is unique to the auditing profession. The need for independence is a result of the auditor's responsibility to users of the financial statements. Because the users of financial statements have no way of verifying the fairness of the financial statements, they must rely on the work of an independent auditor. If it is suspected that the auditor is not independent, then the integrity and fairness of the financial statements are questionable and the auditor's assurance is of little value to the reader.

- The Code of Professional Conduct provides guidelines for accounting practitioners in the conduct of their professional affairs. A member of the American Institute of Certified Public Accountants (AICPA) must observe the Rules of Conduct. The applicability of the Code of Professional Conduct is based on the guidance provided by the AICPA, paraphrased as follows:

- The Rules of Conduct that follow apply to all professional services performed except (1) where the wording of the rule indicates otherwise and (2) that a member who is practicing outside the United States will not be subject to discipline for departing from any of the rules stated herein as long as the member's conduct is in accord with the rule of the organized accounting profession in the country in which he or she is practicing. Where a member's name is associated with financial statements under circumstances that entitle the reader to assume that United States practices were followed, however, the member must comply with the requirements of Rules 202 and 203.

- All persons associated with a member in the practice of public accounting and who are either under the member's supervision or are the member's partners or shareholders may hold the member responsible for compliance with the rules.

- A member shall not permit others to carry out on his or her behalf, either with or without compensation, acts which, if carried out by the member, would place the member in violation of the rules.

> **OBSERVATION:** Each licensing jurisdiction either has its own code of conduct or references the AICPA's code. All CPAs should consider adhering to the AICPA's code of conduct, regardless of whether or not they are AICPA members.

> **PUBLIC COMPANY IMPLICATIONS:** SOX authorizes the PCAOB to issue independence and ethics standards applicable to audits of public company financial statements. Additionally, SOX also explicitly includes provisions related to the performance of nonaudit services, audit partner rotation, and auditor acceptance of employment at the client. In April 2003, the PCAOB adopted the provisions of the AICPA's Code of Professional Conduct on integrity and objectivity (Rule 102) as its "Interim Ethics Standards." The PCAOB also designated Rule 101 of the Code of Professional Conduct and the related interpretations and ethical rulings plus Standards Nos. 1, 2, and 3, and Interpretations 99-1, 00-1, and 00-2 of the Independence Standards Board (ISB) as its "Interim Independence Standards." ISB Standard No. 1 and Interpretations 00-1 and 00-2 have been superseded by PCAOB Rule 3526.

> **PUBLIC COMPANY IMPLICATION:** PCAOB Rule 3526 requires the registered public accounting firm to make certain disclosures to the client's audit committee regarding independence both before it accepts an initial engagement and no less frequently than yearly thereafter. Before accepting an initial engagement, the registered firm must (1) communicate in writing to the audit committee all relationships between the firm and the potential client and individuals in financial reporting oversight roles at the potential client that may potentially affect the firm's independence and (2) discuss with the audit committee the potential independence effects of these relationships. These communications must be updated at least annually. And, at least annually, the registered firm must communicate to the audit committee in writing that the firm is independent. The registered firm must document these communications.

A member of the AICPA must also be aware of Interpretations of the AICPA Rules of Conduct. After having been exposed to state societies and state boards of accountancy, Interpretations of the AICPA Rules of Conduct are published, modified, or deleted by the Executive Committee of the Professional Ethics Division. Interpretations are not intended to limit the scope or application of the Rules of Conduct. A member of the AICPA who departs from the guidelines provided in the Interpretations has the burden of justifying such departure in the event that there are AICPA disciplinary hearings.

> **OBSERVATION:** Most state societies and boards of accountancy have similar rules or adopt the AICPA model; however, there are subtle differences between states that are important to consider.

Rule 101 — Independence

A member in public practice shall be independent in the performance of professional services as required by standards promulgated by bodies designated by AICPA Council.

"Independence" is a highly subjective term, because it concerns an individual's ability to act with integrity and objectivity. Integrity relates to an auditor's honesty, while objectivity is the ability to be neutral during the conduct of the engagement and the preparation of the auditor's report. Two facets of independence are independence in fact and independence in appearance. The second general standard of generally accepted auditing standards (GAAS) requires that an auditor be independent in mental attitude in all matters relating to an engagement. In essence, the second standard embraces the concept of independence in fact. However, independence in appearance is also critical. Public confidence would be impaired if the auditor actually lacked independence. That confidence would also be impaired if the public believed circumstances existed that might influence the auditor's independence. Thus, auditors should avoid situations that could cast doubt on their independence.

Independence, in fact, is impossible to measure, since it is a mental attitude; the Code of Professional Conduct takes a more pragmatic approach to the concept of independence.

- Rule 101 is applicable to professional services provided by a CPA that require independence. Engagements that require that a CPA be independent include the following: Professional services subject to Statements on Auditing Standards (SASs)

  — Audits of financial statements prepared in accordance with generally accepted accounting principles (GAAP)

  — Audits of financial statements prepared in accordance with a comprehensive basis of accounting other than GAAP [SAS-62 (AU 623) (Special Reports)]

  — Reports expressing an opinion on one or more specified elements, accounts, or items of a financial statement [SAS-62 (AU 623)]

  — Reports on compliance with aspects of contractual agreements or regulatory requirements related to audited financial statements [SAS-62 (AU 623)]

  — Reports on information accompanying the basic financial statements in auditor-submitted documents [SAS-29 (AU 551) (Reporting on Information Accompanying the Basic Financial Statements in Auditor-Submitted Documents)]

  — Reports on reviews of interim financial information [SAS-100 (AU 722) (Interim Financial Information)]

  — Reports on condensed financial statements and selected financial data [SAS-42 (AU 552) (Reporting on Condensed Financial Statements and Selected Financial Data)]

  — Special-purpose reports on internal accounting control at service organizations [SAS-70 (AU 324) (Service Organizations)]

  — Reports on financial statements prepared for use in other countries [SAS-51 (AU 534) (Reporting on Financial Statements Prepared for Use in Other Countries)]

- Professional services subject to Statements on Standards for Attestation Engagements (SSAE)

— Agreed-upon procedures (AUP) engagements

— Financial forecasts and projections engagements

— Reporting on pro forma financial information engagements

— Reporting on an entity's internal control over financial reporting engagements

— Compliance attestation engagements

— Reporting on management's discussion and analysis engagements

— Trust Services Engagements, including WebTrust and SysTrust

• Professional services subject to Statements on Standards for Accounting and Review Services (SSARS)

— Reviews of financial statements prepared by nonpublic entities

— Compilations of financial statements prepared by nonpublic entities

OBSERVATION: Practitioners should determine whether state societies, state boards of accountancy, and state regulatory agencies impose additional requirements for assessing whether independence has been compromised. Also, if the client is a public entity, regulations established by the Securities and Exchange Commission and the PCAOB must be considered.

PUBLIC COMPANY IMPLICATION: PCAOB Rule 3520 requires registered public accounting firms to be independent of their clients. Under Rule 3521 a registered public accounting firm is not independent if it performs any service for a client during the audit or professional engagement period for a contingent fee or commission. Under Rule 3522 a registered public accounting firm is not independent if it performs tax services during the audit or professional engagement period that involve the marketing, planning, or opining in favor of the tax treatment of a transaction if the transaction is confidential (i.e., the taxpayer cannot disclose the transaction) or involves an aggressive tax position as defined by the PCAOB. The audit period is the period covered by the financial statements being audited or reviewed. The professional engagement period begins on the earlier of when the initial engagement letter is signed or the audit, review, or attest procedures begin, and it ends when the registered firm or the client notifies the SEC that there is no longer a client relationship. In addition, under Rule 3523 a registered public accounting firm is generally not independent if it provides tax services to a client person in a financial reporting oversight role or a family member of such a person during the professional engagement period. A person in a financial reporting oversight role has the ability to influence the contents of the financial statements or those who prepare the financial statements (e.g., board members, CEO, president, CFO, COO, general counsel, chief accounting officer, controller, director of internal audit, director of financial reporting, treasurer). However, if a board member is in a financial reporting oversight role solely because he or she is a member of the board, the registered firm is not prohibited from providing tax services to the board member. Finally, if a registered public accounting firm seeks to perform allowable tax services or allowable nonaudit services related to internal control over financial reporting for a client, the registered firm, as required by the Sarbanes-Oxley Act, must obtain pre-approval from the audit committee to perform the service. In either instance, the registered firm must (1) describe in writing to the audit committee the scope of the service and the potential effect of the service on the firm's independence and (2) document the substance of its discussion with the audit committee (Rules 3524 and 3525). Additionally, in the case of allowable tax services, the registered firm must disclose (1) the fee structure for the arrangement, (2) the existence of any side letter or other amendment or agreement related to the service, and (3) whether the registered firm has any referral agreement, referral fee, or fee-sharing arrangement with a third party related to the service (Rule 3524).

SECTION 230

DUE CARE IN THE PERFORMANCE OF WORK

Authoritative Pronouncements

SAS-1 — Codification of Auditing Standards and Procedures (Section 230, Due Professional Care in the Performance of Work)

SAS-99 — Consideration of Fraud in a Financial Statement Audit

SAS-104 — Amendment to Statement on Auditing Standards No. 1, Codification of Auditing Standards and Procedures (Section 230, Due Professional Care in the Performance of Work)

> **IMPORTANT NOTICE FOR 2011:** The Auditing Standards Board (ASB) is in the process of redrafting all of the auditing sections in *Codification of Statements on Auditing Standards* to converge U.S. GAAS with the International Standards on Auditing issued by the International Auditing and Assurance Standards Board. As part of this process, the newly redrafted standards will follow certain clarity drafting conventions adopted by the ASB. These clarity drafting conventions include: (1) establishing objectives for each standard; (2) including a definitions section, if appropriate; and (3) separating requirements from application guidance and other material. The ASB is planning to have all redrafted standards become effective on the same date, which is for audits of financial statements for periods ending on or after December 15, 2012. It is possible that the effective date might be delayed beyond that date. The ASB's clarity and convergence project will have a significant effect on the auditing standards applicable to audits of nonpublic companies, and the 2012 *GAAS Guide* will be appropriately modified to reflect these changes once the effective date of the standards is certain.

Overview

General Standard No. 3 states that "The auditor must exercise due professional care in the performance of the audit and the preparation of the report." This general standard recognizes that even if an auditor is competent and independent, these qualities alone will not necessarily result in a successful audit. Besides possessing these qualities, an auditor must be conscientious in conducting the engagement.

In some respects, the standard of due professional care encompasses the other nine generally accepted auditing standards (GAAS). The auditor must observe the standards of fieldwork and reporting in order to comply with the concept of due professional care. The fieldwork and reporting standards can be achieved only if the auditor is adequately trained and experienced and has an independent mental attitude.

On the other hand, the standard of due professional care is more than just the observance of the other nine standards. This standard is the synthesizer for the entire audit process. The auditor is expected to pull together all the facts gathered during the engagement and to use his or her experience and professional judgment to reach a conclusion about the fairness of the financial statements or some other specific facet of the engagement. Two fundamental aspects of this audit process are (1) professional skepticism and (2) reasonable assurance.

> **PUBLIC COMPANY IMPLICATION:** PCAOB Rule 3502 prohibits an individual at a registered public accounting firm from knowingly or recklessly taking an action, or failing to take a required action, where the individual's behavior is likely to lead to the registered firm's violation of the Sarbanes-Oxley Act, PCAOB rules and standards, SEC rules, or provisions of the securities laws.

Professional skepticism

Every task performed by a professional person is approached with a mental attitude. In an audit engagement, that mental attitude is described as professional skepticism. Professional skepticism does not suggest that the auditor assumes the client's management is dishonest or that everything management says is incorrect. According to SAS-1, the appropriate mental state the auditor assumes is "an attitude that includes a questioning mind and a critical assessment of audit evidence." For example, as a gesture of courtesy, a client's employee might offer to mail confirmations that the auditor has just prepared. Although the auditor might be certain that the offer is genuine, professional skepticism requires that the auditor exercise due care in performing the audit and deliver the confirmations directly to the U.S. Postal Service.

> **FRAUD POINTER:** SAS-99 emphasizes the importance of exercising professional skepticism when assessing the risk of material misstatements in the financial statements due to fraud. First, the auditor should approach the engagement with a questioning mind-set that recognizes that fraud is possible in any entity, regardless of the auditor's prior experience

with the entity and the auditor's views about management integrity. Second, the auditor should critically evaluate evidence obtained throughout the performance of audit procedures by always questioning whether the evidence obtained suggests that fraud might be present. The auditor should not let his or her beliefs about management's integrity allow him or her to accept less than persuasive evidence.

Reasonable assurance

The performance of an audit is a complex process, and no matter how professionally it may be performed the auditor cannot offer a guarantee or insurance (absolute assurance) that the financial statements are not materially misstated. Fundamentally, the audit process is based on professional judgment in planning the engagement and determining the nature, timing, and extent of audit procedures to obtain reasonable assurance.

The concept of reasonable assurance is defined as a "high, but not absolute, level of assurance." When performing the audit, the auditor must plan and perform the audit to obtain sufficient and appropriate audit evidence so that audit risk will be limited to a low level that is, in the auditor's professional judgment, appropriate for expressing an opinion on the financial statements. The high, but not absolute, level of assurance is expressed in the auditor's report as obtaining reasonable assurance about whether the financial statements are free of material misstatement. Absolute assurance is not attainable because of the nature of audit evidence and the characteristics of fraud.

- For example, an audit generally involves the selective testing of data, rather than a 100% examination. There is no guarantee that material misstatements due to errors or fraud are absent in the items not tested. Even for those items tested, the auditor must use judgment in assessing the implications for the audit and, as in all professional services, the assessment might not always be correct. Besides, the accounting process is based on numerous estimates and judgments, which may or may not be confirmed by future events. In the audit environment, the best an auditor can do is to collect appropriate and sufficient evidence that is persuasive rather than convincing. For this reason, the auditor's opinion on the financial statements is based on reasonable assurance but not absolute assurance. In addition to these limitations, fraud is another factor that restricts the level of assurance that the auditor can obtain. SAS-99 notes that characteristics of fraud include the following:

- Concealment is based on collusion among management, employees, or other parties

- Documents are withheld, misrepresented, or falsified

- Management has overridden or instructed others to override otherwise effective controls

There is always a chance, even when an engagement has been properly planned and executed, that the auditor might fail to detect a material misstatement of the financial statements caused by error or fraud. Auditing standards rarely require the authentication of documentation by auditors, and auditors are not experts in such authentication. Furthermore, auditing standards note that collusion can lead an auditor to conclude that the evidence obtained is persuasive when it is in fact false.

SAS-1 states that "the subsequent discovery that a material misstatement, whether from error or from fraud, exists in the financial statements does not, in and of itself, evidence (a) failure to obtain reasonable assurance; (b) inadequate planning, performance, or judgment; (c) the absence of due professional care; or (d) a failure to comply with generally accepted auditing standards."

> **FRAUD POINTER:** Enforcement actions against auditors often mention a lack of due professional care and a lack of appropriate professional skepticism.

Practitioner's Aids

Professional skepticism is a key element of observing the General Standard No. 3 of GAAS. The practitioner's aid presented in Exhibit AU 230-1 is based on the guidance provided in the AICPA's Practice Alert 98-2 (Professional Skepticism and Related Topics). Practice Alerts are based on existing auditing standards and are issued by the AICPA to help practitioners improve the efficiency and effectiveness of their audits.

EXHIBIT AU 230-1 — PROFESSIONAL SKEPTICISM

Key Questions on Skepticism	Suggested Guidance Provided by Practice Alert 98-2
• What is professional skepticism?	Professional skepticism is an attitude that includes a questioning mind and working practices that encompass a

Key Questions on Skepticism	*Suggested Guidance Provided by Practice Alert 98-2*
	critical assessment of audit evidence.
• Should professional skepticism be exercised throughout the audit?	Because audit evidence is gathered and evaluated throughout an engagement, professional skepticism must be exercised throughout the entire engagement.
• Does professional skepticism mean that statements made by management should never be accepted?	The auditor should strike a balance between disbelief and unquestioning acceptance. Generally there is a need to corroborate management's responses.
• What level of evidence should the auditor obtain in exercising professional skepticism?	Evidence should be persuasive rather than convincing.
• Do representations by management provide persuasive evidence?	Representations by management, without further corroboration, rarely provide persuasive evidence.
• What are some audit areas that may demand particular scrutiny?	Management responses to questions resulting from the application of analytical procedures.

Representations regarding recoverability of assets or deferred charges

Accruals (or lack thereof), particularly for unusual events or transactions

Substance of large and unusual (particularly period-end) transactions

Vague contract terms or conditions

Key Questions on Skepticism	Suggested Guidance Provided by Practice Alert 98-2
Existence of nonstandard journal entries	
Lack of copies of original documents	
Presence of fraud or illegal acts	

- Which conditions related to nonstandard journal entries may suggest heightened skepticism with respect to a particular account balance?

  Transactions that are complex or unusual in nature

  Estimates and period-end adjustments.

  Journal entries indicative of potential problems with the accounting systems

  Item has been prone to client error in the past

  Item has not been reconciled on a timely basis or contains old reconciling items

  Represents a particular risk specific to the client's industry

  Represents account balances affecting the company's book value and liquidity (e.g., account balances that are used in determining loan covenant ratios).

  Journal entries processed outside the normal course of business

- Does the use of photocopies or draft copies (rather than originals) have an effect on audit skepticism?

  Yes; it may be more difficult to identify alterations on photocopied material, and draft copies might not include all relevant information. With the use of scanners, original

Key Questions on Skepticism	Suggested Guidance Provided by Practice Alert 98-2
	documents can be altered in a way that makes detection especially difficult.
• When originals are not available, what alternative procedures are available to the auditor?	The auditor should consider whether the originals should be obtained and inspected.
• Should the auditor accept fax or e-mail confirmation responses?	The auditor should consider whether (1) to confirm the information over the telephone and/or (2) to request that the original confirmation be returned directly to the auditor.

AU 300

The Standards of Field Work

Section 311: Planning and Supervision 43

Section 312: Audit Risk and Materiality in Conducting
    an Audit 68

Section 314: Understanding the Entity and Its
    Environment and Assessing The Risks of Material
    Misstatement 96

Section 315: Communications between Predecessor and
    Successor Auditors 144

Section 316: Consideration of Fraud in a Financial
    Statement Audit 155

Section 317: Illegal Acts by Clients 187

Section 318: Performing Audit Procedures in Response to
    Assessed Risks and Evaluating the Audit Evidence
    Obtained... 194

Section 322: The Auditor's Consideration of the Internal
    Audit Function in an Audit of Financial Statements . 218

Section 324: Service Organizations 225

Section 325: Communication of Internal Control Related
    Matters Noted in an Audit 245

Section 326: Audit Evidence 257

Section 328: Auditing Fair Value Measurements
    and Disclosures 269

Section 329: Analytical Procedures 281

Section 330: The Confirmation Process 306

Section 331: Inventories   324

Section 332: Auditing Derivative Instruments, Hedging
     Activities, and Investments in Securities   332

Section 333: Management Representations   342

Section 334: Related Parties   353

Section 336: Using the Work of a Specialist   361

Section 337: Inquiry of a Client's Lawyer Concerning
     Litigation, Claims, and Assessments   369

Section 339: Audit Documentation.   379

Section 341: The Auditor's Consideration of an Entity's
     Ability to Continue as a Going Concern   395

Section 342: Auditing Accounting Estimates   407

Section 350: Audit Sampling   430

Section 380: The Auditor's Communication with
     Those Charged with Governance   472

Section 390: Consideration of Omitted Procedures after
     the Report Date   483

SECTION 311

PLANNING AND SUPERVISION

Authoritative Pronouncements

SAS-108 — Planning and Supervision

Auditing Interpretation No. 1 of AU 311 (February 1980) — Communications Between the Auditor and Firm Personnel Responsible for Non-Audit Services

> **IMPORTANT NOTICE FOR 2011:** The Auditing Standards Board (ASB) is in the process of redrafting all of the auditing sections in *Codification of Statements on Auditing Standards* to converge U.S. GAAS with the International Standards on Auditing issued by the International Auditing and Assurance Standards Board. As part of this process, the newly redrafted standards will follow certain clarity drafting conventions adopted by the ASB. These clarity drafting conventions include: (1) establishing objectives for each standard; (2) including a definitions section, if appropriate; and (3) separating requirements from application guidance and other material. The ASB is planning to have all redrafted standards become effective on the same date, which is for audits of financial statements for periods ending on or after December 15, 2012. It is possible that the effective date might be delayed beyond that date. The ASB's clarity and convergence project will have a significant effect on the auditing standards applicable to audits of nonpublic companies, and the 2012 *GAAS Guide* will be appropriately modified to reflect these changes once the effective date of the standards is certain.

Overview

The first standard of fieldwork requires that an engagement be adequately planned and that assistants be properly supervised. This standard recognizes that the successful completion of an audit engagement is a difficult task and, like most difficult tasks, requires proper planning. Adequate planning of an audit encompasses features such as understanding the basic characteristics of the client, determining personnel requirements, and determining how to use a firm's resources in an effective manner.

Before the auditor can plan the audit the auditor must be appointed. It is best if the independent auditor is appointed well before year-end. This enables him or her to have ample time to plan and perform the audit. However, the auditor is not precluded from accepting an engagement near the end of the fiscal year or even after year-end. Before accepting an engagement with a late appointment date, the auditor should evaluate whether he or she will be able to conduct an adequate audit and express an unqualified opinion. If not, the auditor should communicate with those charged with governance that a qualified opinion or a disclaimer of opinion may have to be issued. In some cases the problems associated with a late appointment of the auditor can be addressed (e.g., the physical inventory observation can be delayed or reperformed so that the auditor can be present).

The auditor should also communicate (1) the objectives and limitations of an audit engagement, (2) the responsibilities of the auditor, and (3) the responsibilities of the client. This is all part of establishing an understanding with the client.

The nature, timing, and extent of planning depend on (1) the size and complexity of the entity, (2) the auditor's previous experience serving the entity, and (3) the auditor's knowledge of the entity and its environment, including its internal control. Obtaining an understanding of the entity and its environment, including its internal control, is essential in effectively planning an audit.

The audit plan must be responsive to the auditor's identification of the risk of material misstatement. Although planning is performed before the auditor begins fieldwork, planning is not a discrete process but, rather, is an iterative process. As the auditor performs planned audit procedures, he or she considers the need to revise the nature, timing, and extent of audit procedures that were selected during the initial phase of planning the audit.

The first standard of fieldwork also requires that staff assistants be properly supervised. In most audit engagements, several auditors with varying degrees of experience are used. Supervision includes (1) instructing assistants, (2) keeping assistants informed of developments on the engagement, (3) reviewing the work of assistants, and (4) dealing with differences of opinion between engagement personnel. The degree of supervision over an assistant depends on a variety of factors, such as the background of the assistant and the nature of the work he or she is performing.

An important aspect of supervision is informing assistants of where the entity's financial statements may be susceptible to material misstatement, whether due to error or fraud. The auditor with final responsibility should particularly emphasize the susceptibility of the entity's financial statements to material misstatement due to fraud, and emphasize to assistants the importance of professional skepticism in gathering and evaluating audit evidence.

PUBLIC COMPANY IMPLICATION: In 2010 the PCAOB issued eight auditing standards (AS-8 through AS-5) related to the auditor's assessment of and response to risk. The proposed standards bear many similarities to the eight risk-assessment standards adopted by the Auditing Standards Board in 2006. AS-9 (Audit Planning) and AS-10 (Supervision of the Audit Engagement) are the new PCAOB standards that affect audit planning and supervision. AS-9 establishes requirements related to planning the audit, including requirements related to developing an appropriate audit strategy and audit plan. AS-10 describes the auditor's responsibilities for supervising the engagement, and it applies to the engagement partner and other audit team members who assist the partner in supervising others. Although there are a number of differences between the PCAOB's and ASB's risk standards, the risk-assessment concepts contained in the PCAOB standards should be familiar to most auditors. As is currently the case, audit risk is the risk that the auditor will issue an inappropriate opinion on financial statements that are materially misstated. The auditor is to reduce audit risk to a low level through the application of audit procedures. As a result, the amount of audit effort devoted to particular accounts, classes of transactions, and disclosures should vary based on their respective risk.

Promulgated Procedures Checklist

The auditor should perform the following procedures related to his or her appointment and in determining whether an appropriate understanding has been established with the client:

- Communicate with the predecessor auditor (if applicable)

- Identify the basic understandings related to the engagement

- Consider other matters that should be part of the understanding

- Document the understanding in the audit files

In order to properly plan the audit the auditor should

- Evaluate whether to accept a new client engagement or continue to serve an existing client, including evaluating whether the auditor is independent

- Develop an overall strategy for the audit engagement

- Develop an audit plan

- Consider whether special information technology or other specialized skills are needed to perform the audit engagement

- Communicate with management and with those charged with governance

In order to properly supervise assistants, if there are any, the auditor should

- Inform assistants of their responsibilities and the purpose of audit procedures they perform

- Request assistants to identify significant accounting and auditing questions raised during their performance of audit procedures

- Inform assistants of procedures that should be used when there are disagreements concerning accounting and auditing matters among audit personnel who work on the engagement

- Review assistants' work to determine its effects on the audit report

Analysis and Application of Procedures

Communicate with the predecessor auditor (if applicable)

AU 315 (SAS-84) requires the auditor to communicate with the predecessor auditor before accepting an engagement. Inquiry of the predecessor auditor might provide useful information relevant to the successor auditor's decision about whether to accept the engagement.

> **ENGAGEMENT STRATEGY:** As part of any new client engagement strategy, the auditor might want to add an item in the engagement letter checklist that reminds him or her of the requirement to communicate first with the predecessor auditor before obtaining an engagement letter signed by the client.

Identify the basic understandings related to an engagement

The auditor should prepare written documentation of the understanding between the auditor and the client of the services to be performed. In most cases, the auditor and management reach an understanding of the services to be performed, although in some cases the auditor reaches this understanding with those charged with governance of the entity. Individuals charged with governance of the entity are responsible for overseeing the entity's strategic direction and the financial reporting and disclosure process. These individuals are often members of the entity's board of directors or of its audit committee. The understanding between the auditor and the client usually includes the following:

- That the purpose of an audit is to express an opinion on the financial statements

- That management is responsible for its financial statements and the selection and application of accounting principles

- That management is responsible for establishing and maintaining effective internal control over financial reporting

- That management is responsible for designing and implementing anti-fraud programs and controls

- That management is responsible for identifying the laws and regulations applicable to its activities and ensuring that the entity complies with these laws and regulations

- That management is responsible for making all financial records and related information available to the auditor

- That at the conclusion of the engagement management will provide the auditor with a letter that confirms certain representations made during the audit

- That management is responsible for adjusting the financial statements to remove any material misstatements

- That management is responsible for stating in the representation letter that any misstatements identified by the auditor and not corrected are immaterial, "both individually and in the aggregate," with respect to the financial statements taken as a whole

- That the auditor is responsible for conducting the audit in accordance with generally accepted auditing standards (GAAS). GAAS standards require that the auditor obtain reasonable, rather than absolute, assurance about whether the financial statements are free of material misstatement, whether caused by error or by fraud. Accordingly, a material misstatement might remain undetected. Also, an audit is not designed to detect error or fraud that is immaterial to the financial statements. If for any reason the auditor is unable to complete the audit or is unable to form or has not formed an opinion, he or she may decline to express an opinion or to issue a report as a result of the engagement.

- That an audit includes obtaining an understanding of the entity and its environment, including its internal control, sufficient to understand the risks of material misstatement and to determine the nature, timing, and extent of audit procedures to be performed. An audit of financial statements is not designed to provide assurance on internal control or to identify significant deficiencies. However, the auditor is responsible for ensuring that those charged with governance are aware of any significant deficiencies or material weakness that come to his or her attention.

> **OBSERVATION:** In December 2008, the ASB issued SAS-115 (Communication of Internal Control Related Matters Identified in an Audit), which requires the auditor of financial statements to communicate in writing to management and those charged with governance significant deficiencies and material weaknesses that were identified. Although an audit of financial statements is not designed to perform procedures to detect control deficiencies, SAS-115 requires the communications when the auditor identifies significant deficiencies and material weaknesses in internal control over financial reporting. The ASB adopted the PCAOB definitions of "control deficiency," "significant deficiency," and "material weakness."

> **PUBLIC COMPANY IMPLICATION:** SOX requires all public companies to issue an internal control report that includes management's assessment of the effectiveness of internal controls. Furthermore, the auditor must attest to and issue a report on management's assessment of internal control. Thus, in the audit of public companies, the auditor must issue an opinion on the financial statements and an opinion on internal controls. The audit of financial statements and the audit of internal controls are meant to be integrated. For this reason, when obtaining an understanding with the client in the audit of a public company, the auditor must modify the discussion to reflect the unique responsibility for internal controls that is applicable to public companies.

Consider other matters that should be part of the understanding

SAS-108 also notes that an auditor may include other matters, such as the following, as part of the understanding with the client:

- Arrangements regarding the conduct of the engagement (timing, client assistance regarding the preparation of schedules, and the availability of documents and electronic evidence)

- Arrangements concerning involvement of specialists or internal auditors, if applicable

- Arrangements involving a predecessor auditor

- Arrangements regarding fees and billing

- Any limitation or other arrangements regarding the liability of the auditor or the client, such as indemnification to the auditor for liability arising from known misrepresentations to the auditor by management (regulators may restrict or prohibit such liability limitation arrangements)

- Conditions under which access to the auditor's documentation may be granted to others

- Additional services to be provided relating to regulatory requirements

- Arrangements regarding other services to be provided in connection with the engagement

Document the understanding in the audit files

The auditor should document in an engagement letter the understanding of the objectives and limitations of an audit and the responsibilities of the auditor and the client. Because the auditor should document this understanding in an engagement letter, it is a presumptively mandatory requirement. The auditor should neither accept nor perform an audit if he or she has not reached an understanding with the client regarding the services to be performed.

> **PLANNING AID REMINDER:** The presumptively mandatory requirement to prepare an engagement letter differs from current practice. Auditors should be certain to make sure that an engagement letter is prepared for every audit engagement.
>
> **ENGAGEMENT STRATEGY:** Given that the use of engagement letters is essentially required, the auditor may want to develop preformatted engagement letter templates that include matters that must be understood by the client. Such preformatted letters can be an effective starting point for auditors as they seek to obtain this required understanding in every audit engagement.
>
> **OBSERVATION:** The engagement letter is an important part of the documentation of an auditor's understanding with the client of the scope of, and limitations on, his or her services. It should not be used as a marketing tool. It memorializes the responsibilities of all of the parties and acts as a contract

between the auditor and client. The engagement letter should include the cautionary language concerning the purpose of the engagement and the limitations on the expectations of a GAAS audit. If the scope of the engagement goes beyond the auditor's responsibility to perform a GAAS audit and report on the financial statements taken as a whole, he or she should adequately describe the services or commitments and any related expectation limitations. The auditor should list any other services or commitments contained in the letter in a checklist. The services and commitments listed should be initialed and dated when the additional service is delivered or the commitment is satisfied.

PLANNING AID REMINDER: The guidance established by SAS-108 is written in the context of an audit engagement; however, the understanding should be modified to reflect the type of service provided by the auditor. For example, modifications would be required by an engagement subject to SAS-100 AU 722 (Interim Financial Information) and SAS-74 (AU 801) (Compliance Auditing Considerations in Audits of Governmental Entities and Recipients of Governmental Financial Assistance).

PUBLIC COMPANY IMPLICATION: SOX specifically mandates that the audit committee of a public company be directly responsible for the appointment, compensation, and oversight of the work of the auditor. In effect, the audit committee, and not management, of a public company is to be viewed as "the client." Treating the audit committee as the client has implications for the auditor when establishing the understanding with the client. Auditors of public companies need to direct their efforts related to obtaining an understanding of the engagement with the client to the audit committee.

Evaluate whether to accept a new client engagement or continue to serve an existing client, including evaluating whether the auditor is independent

Before deciding whether to accept a new client engagement, the auditor should perform his or her normal client acceptance procedures and communicate with the predecessor auditor (assuming a change in auditors). An important aspect of client acceptance (and continuance) procedures is an evaluation of management integrity. The auditor also needs to ascertain that he or she is independent before commencing the audit engagement.

In a first-year audit, the auditor should also consider the following factors in developing the audit plan:

- The need to make arrangements with the previous auditor to review their documentation

- Any major issues discussed with management before being retained, the need to communicate these issues to those charged with governance, and the effect of these issues on the audit plan

- The need to obtain appropriate audit evidence for account balances as of the beginning of the year

- The assignment of appropriate staff to the engagement

- Other steps required by the firm's system of quality control (e.g., the involvement of a second partner to review the audit plan before work begins)

> **PLANNING AID REMINDER:** The process of planning the audit is typically more extensive in the first year of an engagement than in later years.

For a continuing engagement, the auditor should apply his or her normal client continuance procedures. The auditor also needs to make certain that he or she is independent. These procedures often occur shortly after the completion of the previous audit engagement.

> **PLANNING AID REMINDER:** Although the auditor evaluates whether he or she is independent before commencing the engagement, he or she needs to monitor his or her continuing independence throughout the period of the professional engagement.

Develop an overall strategy for the audit engagement

The specific audit strategy for an engagement is based on the characteristics of the client. Specific factors that the auditor should consider include the following:

- Characteristics of the client's business and the related industry (e.g., the client's basis of reporting, locations, etc.)

- The nature of reports expected to be rendered, including deadlines and key dates for expected communications

- Preliminary judgment of materiality levels, and material locations and account balances (including setting materiality levels for auditors of other locations)

- Conditions where there may be a higher risk of material misstatement

- Whether to test the operating effectiveness of internal control

- Identification of recent events affecting the entity or its industry, including recent financial reporting developments

> **PLANNING AID REMINDER:** The auditor should also consider his or her knowledge gained from performing other engagements for the entity.

In developing an overall audit strategy, the auditor should consider (1) the scope of the audit engagement and (2) the engagement's reporting objectives, timing, and required communications. In determining the scope of the audit engagement, the auditor normally considers the following:

- Industry-specific reporting requirements

- Expected audit coverage (e.g., number of client locations where audit procedures are going to be performed)

- Nature of control relationships between a parent and a subsidiary

- Use of other auditors

- The entity's reporting currency

- Any statutory or regulatory audit requirements

- The use of client personnel (e.g., internal audit) in performing the audit engagement

- The client's use of service organizations, and how the auditor will test the design and operating effectiveness of controls at the service organization

- The auditor's planned use of audit evidence obtained in prior periods

- The effect of information technology on audit procedures, including the availability of electronic data and the use of computer-assisted audit techniques

- The availability of client personnel and data

- Engagement budgeting, including allocating sufficient time to audit areas with greater risk

- Audit areas with a higher risk of material misstatement

- The entity's volume of transactions (which may affect whether the auditor decides to test the operating effectiveness of internal control)

- Management's commitment to internal control and the results of previous evaluations of the operating effectiveness of internal control, including management's efforts to remedy significant deficiencies or material weaknesses

- Significant recent developments affecting the entity (e.g., business, industry, legal, regulatory)

In determining the engagement's reporting objectives, timing, and required communications, the auditor may consider

- Due dates of financial reports, including interim reports

- Planned meeting dates with management and those charged with governance

- The expected type and timing of reports to be issued (e.g., audit report, management letter, etc.)

- Periodic updates to management on the progress of the audit throughout the engagement

- The type and timing of reports from other auditors involved in performing the engagement

- The schedule of audit team meetings during the audit and the planned schedule for reviewing audit work

- Whether there are any required communications with third parties

> **ENGAGEMENT STRATEGY:** Auditing Interpretation No. 1 of AU 311 notes that the auditor should consider whether the nature of nonaudit services performed had an effect on the client's financial statements or the performance of audit procedures. If the auditor concludes that the nonaudit services may have had these effects, he or she should (1) discuss the matter with firm personnel who performed the nonaudit service and consider how the services may affect the conduct and scope of the audit and (2) consider reviewing the accountant's documentation that supports the nonaudit service. The auditor should also consult ET Section 100 (Independence, Integrity, and Objectivity) in the AICPA's Code of Conduct.

> **PUBLIC COMPANY IMPLICATION:** SOX and revised SEC rules prohibit the auditor of a public company from performing certain nonaudit services for that company. Many of these services were prohibited under existing SEC rules on independence adopted in November 2000. The new rules clarify many of the existing prohibitions and expand the circumstances in which the services are prohibited. Furthermore, SOX requires that any allowed nonaudit service be pre-approved by the audit committee of the public company. There are a number of differences between SEC/PCAOB independence rules and the independence rules that apply to auditors of private (non-SEC registrants) companies.

An outcome of preparing the audit strategy is that it helps the auditor to determine the allocation of audit resources; for example:

- The nature of audit staff to assign to specific audit areas (e.g., assign experienced staff to high-risk areas)

- The number of staff to assign to specific audit areas

- The timing of when audit staff are to be assigned

- The supervision, management, and direction of audit staff

Changes in circumstances may require the auditor to revise his or her overall audit strategy. Any such change should be documented.

Because the nature, timing, and extent of audit planning depends in part on the size and complexity of the client, the planning for a small entity does not have to be complex or time-consuming. A brief memorandum that outlines issues from the previous audit, updated based on conversations with the owner-manager, can serve as the basis for planning the current audit.

Develop an audit plan

The auditor should prepare a detailed audit plan that reflects the overall strategy for performing the audit engagement. The nature, timing, and extent of audit procedures to be performed in carrying out the audit strategy must be documented (i.e., the audit plan is captured in a written audit program). The audit procedures to be performed must be expected to reduce audit risk to an acceptably low level.

The audit plan should include (1) the nature, timing, and extent of audit procedures to identify the risks of material misstatement, (2) the nature, timing, and extent of further audit procedures at the assertion level for each material class of transactions, account balances, and disclosures, and (3) any other audit procedures to be performed to comply with GAAS (e.g., obtaining a management representation letter). The nature, timing, and extent of further audit procedures depends on whether the auditor has decided to test the operating effectiveness of controls, and specifies the nature, timing, and extent of substantive procedures to be performed.

> **ENGAGEMENT STRATEGY:** The auditor should document any changes to the original audit plan as a result of a change in circumstances and the results of additional audit procedures that were performed.

Consider whether special information technology or other specialized skills are needed to perform the audit engagement

Specialized skills are often needed in performing an audit (e.g., information technology, valuation, forensic, etc.). In planning the audit, the auditor should consider whether individuals with specialized skills are likely to be needed. An individual with specialized skills may be on the auditor's own staff or an outside professional. The auditor should determine whether the individual with specialized skills will function as a member of the audit team. If the specialist is to function as a member of the audit team, the auditor's responsibilities for supervising that individual are the same as his or her responsibilities for supervising any other assistant. If the auditor is responsible for supervising the specialist, he or she needs sufficient knowledge to specify the audit objectives that the specialist needs to meet and to evaluate the specialist's procedures and findings.

The audit engagement team often needs an individual possessing information technology (IT) skills to (1) determine the effect of IT on the audit, (2) understand IT controls, and (3) design and perform tests of IT controls and substantive procedures. An IT professional is more likely to be needed on the engagement if

- The entity's systems and IT controls are complex

- The entity has made significant changes to existing systems or has implemented new systems

- The entity has significant involvement with electronic commerce

- The entity uses emerging technologies

- Significant audit evidence is available only in electronic form

- Significant data sharing exists between systems

An IT specialist may perform the following audit procedures: (1) analyze how the entity initiates, authorizes, records, processes, and reports transactions; (2) analyze the design of the entity's internal controls; (3) inspect the entity's system documentation; (4) observe the operation of IT controls; and (5) plan and perform tests of IT controls.

> **PLANNING AID REMINDER:** When outside computer professionals are used, the auditor must have sufficient computer-related knowledge to be able to describe the objective of the work that the outside professional is to perform and evaluate the results of the procedures performed in order to determine whether they satisfy the requirements of the engagement.

Communicate with management and with those charged with governance

The auditor may discuss the results of his or her planning efforts with those charged with governance of the entity. These discussions typically include the overall audit strategy, including the timing of audit work and are often intended to facilitate the effective administration of the engagement. Although these discussions are acceptable, and are often helpful, the auditor should be careful that he or she doesn't communicate something that will reduce the effectiveness of the audit. For example, the auditor should be cautious in describing the nature and timing of detailed audit procedures. Such communication may make the audit procedures too predictable, thereby reducing their effectiveness.

Inform assistants of their responsibilities and the purpose of audit procedures they perform

Assistants used in an engagement should know their role in relationship to specific audit objectives and the reason they are performing audit procedures outlined in the audit program. Assistants should be informed of possible accounting and auditing issues affecting the client, particularly in those areas where assistants are performing audit procedures. The degree of direction will vary depending on the experience of assistants and the complexity of the procedures to be performed.

> **PLANNING AID REMINDER:** Often there is an inverse relationship between the time spent with an assistant in the planning stage and the time needed to review the assistant's workpapers. A little extra time spent up front with an assistant may eliminate the need to redo work later.

Request assistants to identify significant accounting and auditing questions raised during their performance of audit procedures

Assistants should be instructed to bring accounting and auditing issues that may be of significance to the financial statements or to the auditor's report to the attention of the auditor with final responsibility for the engagement. Assistants should also be instructed to report difficulties that they encounter in performing the engagement (e.g., missing documents, client unwillingness to respond to inquiries or to provide information).

Inform assistants of procedures that should be used when there are disagreements concerning accounting and auditing matters among audit personnel who work on the engagement

Assistants have a professional responsibility to inform the appropriate individuals within the firm of disagreements or concerns regarding accounting or auditing issues that are significant to the financial statements or to the auditor's report. All members of the audit engagement team should be aware of the procedures to be followed when differences of opinion arise between members of the engagement team. An assistant should have the right and responsibility to document any dissenting position taken if he or she chooses not to be associated with the final resolution of an accounting or auditing matter. The basis for final resolution should also be documented.

> **FRAUD POINTER:** SAS-99 (Consideration of Fraud in a Financial Statement Audit) requires that communication among the audit team members about the risks of material misstatements due to fraud continue throughout the audit. For example, at or near the completion of fieldwork, the auditor with final responsibility for the audit is required to determine that there has been appropriate communication with other team members throughout the audit about information or circumstances that might indicate there are risks of material misstatements due to fraud.

Review the work of assistants to determine the effects on the audit report

The supervising auditor should allow adequate time to review the results of the assistants' audit documentation to make sure that those results are consistent with the audit conclusion that is being expressed in the report.

Practitioner's Aids

AU 311-1 is an example of an engagement letter that establishes an appropriate understanding with a nonpublic company client.

Use a planning checklist

The auditor may use an engagement planning checklist to control the planning phase of the audit engagement. AU 311-2 is an example of such a checklist.

Practitioner's Aids

EXHIBIT AU 311-1 — ENGAGEMENT LETTER

Mr. Robert J. Bray, President
Averroes Company
1800 Carolina Avenue
Cherry Hill, NJ 08003

Dear Mr. Bray:

In accordance with the agreement reached in our conference on October 14, 20X5, we are to perform an audit of the balance sheet of Averroes Company as of December 31, 20X5, and of the related statements of income, stockholder's equity, and cash flows for the fiscal year then ended. The audit report will be mailed to you and to the Board of Directors. During our conference we discussed a number of factors, and we have reached the following understanding with you and your management:

- The purpose of our audit is to express an opinion on the financial statements of Averroes Company based on the performance of generally accepted auditing standards. Those standards require that we obtain reasonable rather than absolute assurance about whether the financial statements are free of material misstatement, whether caused by error or by fraud. Accordingly, a material misstatement may remain undetected. Also, our audit is not designed to detect error or fraud that is immaterial to the financial statements. If, for any reason, we are unable to complete the audit or we are unable to form an opinion on the financial statements, we may decline to express an opinion or decline to issue a report as a result of the engagement.

- Management is responsible for preparing the financial statements, including the selection and application of accounting principles. Management is also responsible for designing and implementing an effective system of internal control over financial reporting, including antifraud programs and controls.

- Management is responsible for providing us with all financial records and related information that we need to conduct the audit.

- Management is responsible for adjusting the financial statements to correct material misstatements and for affirming to us in a representation letter that the effects of any uncorrected misstatements aggregated by us during the current engagement and pertaining to the latest period presented are immaterial, both individually and in the aggregate, to the financial statements taken as a whole.

- At the conclusion of the engagement, we will request that your management provide us with a letter that confirms certain representations made during the audit.

- Our audit will include obtaining an understanding of the entity and its environment, including internal control, sufficient to understand the risks of material misstatement and to determine the nature, timing, and extent of audit procedures to be performed. An audit is not designed to provide assurance on internal control or to identify significant deficiencies or material weaknesses. However, we are responsible for ensuring that those charged with governance are aware of any significant deficiencies or material weaknesses that come to our attention.

In addition to the performance of an audit of your financial statements, we will prepare the federal and state income tax returns for the fiscal year ending December 31, 20X5.

Based on our discussion with your personnel and the predecessor auditor and after a preliminary review of your accounting records, we estimate that the cost of the audit engagement, including the preparation of the related tax returns, will be between $75,000 and $80,000. It should be recognized that the estimated fee could be affected by unusual circumstances we cannot foresee at this time. However, if we should encounter such problems, we will contact you to discuss the implications of the new developments.

Whenever possible, we will attempt to use your company's personnel in the preparation of company information necessary for the audit. This effort should substantially reduce our time requirements and help us perform an efficient audit.

We appreciate the opportunity to serve your company. Do not hesitate to contact us if you have questions about the engagement or desire other professional services.

If the terms designated in this letter are satisfactory, please sign in the space provided below and return the copy of the letter to us.

Sincerely,
Penny J. Nichols, CPA

Accepted by:
Title:
Date:

EXHIBIT AU 311-2 — AUDIT ENGAGEMENT PLANNING CHECKLIST

Use the following checklist as a guide for planning audit procedures in a continuing engagement. The checklist is only a guide, and professional judgment should be exercised to determine how the checklist should be modified by revising questions listed or adding questions to the checklist where appropriate.

Check the appropriate response. If the question is not relevant to this particular audit engagement, place "N/A" (not applicable) in the space provided for the audit documentation reference. If additional explanation is needed with respect to a question, provide a proper cross-reference to another audit schedule.

Client Name: _____

Date of Financial Statements: _____

	Yes	No	Audit Documentation Reference

1. Is the scope of the audit engagement limited to a single financial statement? ⎯ ⎯ ⎯⎯⎯

   • If yes, have we identified the notes and other disclosures that are appropriate for a single financial statement presentation? ⎯ ⎯ ⎯⎯⎯

   • If yes, are the other financial statements going to be available for our perusal in order to identify events, transactions, and balances that may have implications for the audited financial statements? ⎯ ⎯ ⎯⎯⎯

2. Are comparative financial statements presented? ⎯ ⎯ ⎯⎯⎯

   • If yes, are we responsible for reporting on the previous year's financial statements? ⎯ ⎯ ⎯⎯⎯

3. If a predecessor CPA is reporting on the previous year's financial statements, have we:

   • Discussed relevant matters with the predecessor CPA before accepting the engagement? ⎯ ⎯ ⎯⎯⎯

   • Considered what matters to discuss with the predecessor CPA? ⎯ ⎯ ⎯⎯⎯

   • Arranged to communicate matters discovered in the current engagement to the predecessor CPA? ⎯ ⎯ ⎯⎯⎯

   • Arranged to provide the predecessor with a preliminary draft of the current and previous year's financial statements and our audit report? ⎯ ⎯ ⎯⎯⎯

   • Considered the format and content of the representation letter to be issued to the predecessor CPA? ⎯ ⎯ ⎯⎯⎯

4. Have we considered the effect on audit procedures if the client has decided not to present a statement of cash flows? ⎯ ⎯ ⎯⎯⎯

	Yes	*No*	*Audit Documentation Reference*
5. If the client has decided to present supplementary information, which is not part of the basic financial statements, are we engaged to review the supplementary information?	___	___	_____
6. If a portion of the financial statements is audited by another CPA, have we determined whether we can serve as the principal CPA?	___	___	_____
7. If we can serve as the principal CPA, have we considered whether to refer in our audit report to the work done by the other CPA?	___	___	_____
8. Have we identified the bases (operating income, total assets, etc.) and percentages of those amounts that should be used by subordinates to identify material misstatement?	___	___	_____

9. In designing the specific inquiries to be made, have we considered:

	Yes	*No*	Reference
• The nature and materiality of items?	___	___	_____
• The likelihood of misstatement?	___	___	_____
• Knowledge obtained during current and previous engagements?	___	___	_____
• The stated qualifications of the entity's accounting personnel?	___	___	_____
• The extent to which a particular item is affected by management's judgment?	___	___	_____
• The inadequacies in the entity's underlying financial data?	___	___	_____
• The potential for related-party transactions	___	___	_____

10. Have we acquired an adequate understanding of specialized accounting principles and practices of the client's industry by:

	Yes	*No*	Reference
• Reviewing relevant AICPA Accounting/Audit Guides?	___	___	_____

	Yes	*No*	*Audit Documentation Reference*

- Reviewing financial statements of other entities in the same industry? ____ ____ _____

- Consulting with other individuals familiar with accounting practices in the specialized industry? ____ ____ _____

- Reading periodicals, textbooks, and other publications? ____ ____ _____

- Performing other procedures? (Describe.) ____ ____ _____

11. Have we developed an understanding of the client's organization, including:

- The form of business organization? ____ ____ _____

- The history of the client? ____ ____ _____

- The principals involved in the organization by review of the organizational chart or similar analysis? ____ ____ _____

- Changes in capital structure ____ ____ _____

- Other relevant matters? (Describe.) ____ ____ _____

12. Have we developed an understanding of the client's operating characteristics, including:

- An understanding of the client's products and services? ____ ____ _____

- Identification of operating locations? ____ ____ _____

- An understanding of production methods? ____ ____ _____

- Degree of reliance on information technology, including the use of outside service centers? ____ ____ _____

- Other operating characteristics? (Describe.) ____ ____ _____

13. Have we developed an understanding of the nature of the client's assets, liabilities, revenues, and expenses by:

- Reviewing the client's chart of accounts? ____ ____ _____

- Reviewing the previous year's financial statements? ____ ____ _____

	Yes	No	Audit Documentation Reference
• Considering the relationships between specific accounts and the nature of the client's business?	___	___	_____
• Performing other procedures? (Describe.)	___	___	_____
14. Have we made inquiries concerning accounting principles, practices, and methods?	___	___	_____
15. Have we made inquiries concerning the accounting procedures and processes used by the client, including:			
• Recording transactions?	___	___	_____
• Classifying transactions?	___	___	_____
• Summarizing transactions?	___	___	_____
• Accumulating information for making disclosures in the financial statements?	___	___	_____
• Other accounting procedures? (Describe.)	___	___	_____
16. Have we obtained an adequate understanding of internal control over financial reporting, including whether to test the operating effectiveness of controls?	___	___	_____
17. Have we made inquiries concerning the effect on the financial statements due to actions taken at meetings of:			
• Stockholders?	___	___	_____
• The board of directors?	___	___	_____
• Other committees? (Describe.)	___	___	_____
18. If there were changes in the application of accounting principles:			
• Did the change in accounting principle include the adoption of another acceptable accounting principle?	___	___	_____
• Was the change properly justified?	___	___	_____

	Yes	No	*Audit Documentation Reference*

- Were the effects of the change presented in the financial statements, including adequate disclosure, in a manner consistent with GAAP? ____ ____ _____

- Were there other matters that we took into consideration? ____ ____ _____

19. Have we made inquiries concerning changes in the client's business activities or industry that may require the adoption of different accounting principles, and have we considered the implication of this change for the financial statements? ____ ____ _____

20. Have we made inquiries concerning the occurrence of events subsequent to the date of the financial statements that may require:

  - Adjustments to the financial statements? ____ ____ _____

  - Disclosures in the financial statements? ____ ____ _____

21. Have we considered whether other professional services are needed in order to complete the audit engagement, including:

  - Preparing a working trial balance? ____ ____ _____

  - Preparing adjusting journal entries? ____ ____ _____

  - Consulting matters fundamental to the preparation of acceptable financial statements? ____ ____ _____

  - Preparing tax returns? ____ ____ _____

  - Providing bookkeeping or data processing services that do not include the generation of financial statements? ____ ____ _____

  - Other services considered necessary before an audit can be performed? (Describe.) ____ ____ _____

	Yes	No	Audit Documentation Reference
22. Have we performed preliminary analytical review procedures as required by SAS-56?	____	____	_____
23. Have we obtained reports from other CPA(s) who reported on the financial statements of components of the client-reporting entity if we have decided to rely on their reports?	____	____	_____

Prepared By: _____

Date: _____

Supervision checklist

The auditor may use a supervision checklist, such as the one illustrated in Exhibit AU 311-3, in an engagement.

EXHIBIT AU 311-3 — AUDIT ENGAGEMENT SUPERVISION CHECKLIST

Use the following checklist as a guide for supervising an audit engagement. The checklist is only a guide, and professional judgment should be exercised to determine how the checklist should be modified by revising questions listed or adding questions to the checklist where appropriate.

Check the appropriate response. If the question is not relevant to this particular audit engagement, place "N/A" (not applicable) in the space provided for the workpaper reference. If additional explanation is needed with respect to a question, provide a proper cross-reference to another workpaper.

Client Name: _____

Date of Financial Statements: _____

In-Charge Accountant: _____

Assistants: _____

		Yes	No	Audit Documentation Reference
1.	Have assistants adequately prepared for the engagement, including:	____	____	_____
	• Reviewing the previous year's audit documentation?	____	____	_____
	• Reviewing the previous year's financial statements?	____	____	_____
	• Informing them of developments that affect the current engagement?	____	____	_____
	• Discussing the engagement budget?	____	____	_____
	• Other matters? (Describe.)	____	____	_____
2.	Have assistants been instructed to communicate significant problems to the in-charge accountant (and, if necessary, to the auditor with final responsibility for the engagement) on a timely and ongoing basis?	____	____	_____
3.	Have we made arrangements to review audit documentation on a timely basis?	____	____	_____
4.	Have assistants been instructed to discuss their disagreements concerning professional matters with the in-charge accountant (and, if necessary, to the auditor with final responsibility for the engagement)?	____	____	_____
5.	Have assistants been informed about procedures available to document their disagreements concerning professional matters?	____	____	_____
6.	Have other matters relative to supervising the engagement been identified? (Describe.)	____	____	_____

Prepared By: _____

Date: _____

SECTION 312

AUDIT RISK AND MATERIALITY IN CONDUCTING AN AUDIT

Authoritative Pronouncements

SAS-96 — Audit Documentation

SAS-98 — Omnibus Statement on Auditing Standards — 2002

SAS-99 — Consideration of Fraud in a Financial Statement Audit

SAS-107 — Audit Risk and Materiality in Conducting an Audit

> **IMPORTANT NOTICE FOR 2011:** The Auditing Standards Board (ASB) is in the process of redrafting all of the auditing sections in *Codification of Statements on Auditing Standards* to converge U.S. GAAS with the International Standards on Auditing issued by the International Auditing and Assurance Standards Board. As part of this process, the newly redrafted standards will follow certain clarity drafting conventions adopted by the ASB. These clarity drafting conventions include: (1) establishing objectives for each standard; (2) including a definitions section, if appropriate; and (3) separating requirements from application guidance and other material. The ASB is planning to have all redrafted standards become effective on the same date, which is for audits of financial statements for periods ending on or after December 15, 2012. It is possible that the effective date might be delayed beyond that date. The ASB's clarity and convergence project will have a significant effect on the auditing standards applicable to audits of nonpublic companies, and the 2012 *GAAS Guide* will be appropriately modified to reflect these changes once the effective date of the standards is certain.

Overview

In determining the nature, timing, and extent of audit procedures, the auditor must consider, among other factors, materiality and audit risk.

"Materiality" is defined in the FASB's Statement of Financial Accounting Concepts No. 2 (CON-2) (Qualitative Characteristics of Accounting Information) as "the magnitude of an omission or misstatement of accounting information that, in the light of surrounding circumstances, makes it probable that the judgment of a reasonable person relying on the information would have been changed or influenced by the omission or misstatement.''

''Audit risk'' is ''the risk that the auditor may unknowingly fail to appropriately modify his or her opinion on financial statements that are materially misstated.'' The concept of audit risk is based on the reality that the audit process can result in only reasonable assurance (not absolute assurance) that the auditor will detect material misstatements in financial statements, whether caused by error or fraud. SAS-107 explains how the auditor should integrate the concepts of materiality and audit risk into the planning and execution of an audit engagement.

A misstatement in the financial statements includes (1) a difference between the amount, classification, or presentation of a reported financial statement element, account, or item and the amount, classification, or presentation that would have been reported under GAAP; (2) the omission of a financial statement element, account, or item; (3) a financial statement disclosure that is not presented in accordance with GAAP; or (4) the omission of information required to be disclosed in accordance with GAAP.

> **OBSERVATION:** Audit risk and materiality in an audit engagement relate to the assertions that are explicitly stated or implied in the financial statements. SAS-106 outlines three classes of assertions: assertions related to classes of transactions, assertions related to account balances, and assertions related to presentation and disclosure.

An auditor's opinion refers to materiality of the financial statements in the context of the financial statements taken as a whole. SAS-107 notes that in performing the audit ''the auditor is concerned with matters that, either individually or in the aggregate, could be material to the financial statements. The auditor's responsibility is to plan and perform the audit to obtain reasonable assurance that material misstatements, whether caused by error or fraud, are detected.'' An auditor has no responsibility to plan and perform an engagement in order to obtain reasonable assurance that immaterial misstatements (from error or from fraud) will be detected.

Errors refer to unintentional misstatements or omissions of amounts or disclosures from financial statements, whereas fraud is intentional and based on the perpetrator's deceit; however, the auditor's responsibility with respect to material misstatement in the financial statements is the same for errors as for fraud. Despite similarities in detection responsibilities, the auditor's response to the discovery of an error during an engagement is different from the auditor's response to the discovery of fraud during an engagement. That difference is illustrated as follows: Generally, an isolated, immaterial error in processing accounting data or applying accounting principles is not significant to the audit. In contrast, when fraud is detected, the auditor should consider the implications for the integrity of management or employees and the possible effect on other aspects of the audit even if the detected misstatement due to fraud is immaterial.

> **ENGAGEMENT STRATEGY:** The auditor is concerned with audit risk and materiality levels during both the planning phase and the evaluation phase of an engagement. Although conceptually possible, generally, the assessment of materiality levels will not be the same at the planning stage as at the evaluation stage. Because the auditor will have more complete information to better assess materiality for a particular engagement, the materiality level at the end of the audit can differ from the materiality used in the planning stage. In fact, if the level of materiality is significantly less at the evaluation stage than at the planning stage, the auditor will generally need to "reevaluate the sufficiency of the audit procedures he or she has performed."

SAS-107 emphasizes that there are two types of misstatements:

1. *Known misstatements.* Misstatements identified during the audit arising from the incorrect selection or misapplication of accounting principles or misstatements of facts identified.

2. *Likely misstatements.* Misstatements arising from (1) differences between management's and the auditor's judgments concerning accounting estimates that the auditor considers unreasonable or inappropriate or (2) the extrapolation from audit evidence obtained (e.g., projecting sample results to the population).

> **PUBLIC COMPANY IMPLICATION:** In 2010 the PCAOB issued eight auditing standards (AS-8 through AS-5) related to the auditor's assessment of and response to risk. The proposed standards bear many similarities to the eight risk-assessment standards adopted by the Auditing Standards Board in 2006. AS-9 (Audit Planning) and AS-10 (Supervision of the Audit Engagement) are the new PCAOB standards that affect audit planning and supervision. AS-9 establishes requirements related to planning the audit, including requirements related to developing an appropriate audit strategy and audit plan. AS-10 describes the auditor's responsibilities for

supervising the engagement, and it applies to the engagement partner and other audit team members who assist the partner in supervising others. Although there are a number of differences between the PCAOB's and ASB's risk standards, the risk-assessment concepts contained in the PCAOB standards should be familiar to most auditors. As is currently the case, audit risk is the risk that the auditor will issue an inappropriate opinion on financial statements that are materially misstated. The auditor is to reduce audit risk to a low level through the application of audit procedures. As a result, the amount of audit effort devoted to particular accounts, classes of transactions, and disclosures should vary based on their respective risk.

Promulgated Procedures Checklist

The auditor should design the audit approach so that materiality and audit risk is integrated into the audit engagement at the following points:

- Determine audit risk and materiality during the planning phase of the engagement.
- Assess audit risk based on the results of substantive procedures.
- Communicate misstatements to management.
- Document audit results.

Analysis and Application of Procedures

Determine audit risk and materiality during the planning phase of the engagement

During the planning phase of the engagement, the auditor must consider audit risk and materiality (1) at the financial statement level and (2) at the individual account-balance or class-of-transactions level.

Financial statement level

The auditor considers audit risk and materiality for the financial statement as a whole to accomplish the following objectives:

- Determine the extent and nature of risk assessment procedures
- Identify and assess the risks of material misstatements

- Determine the nature, timing, and extent of further audit procedures

- Evaluate whether the financial statements taken as a whole are presented fairly, in all material respects, in conformity with generally accepted accounting principles.

Audit risk is a function of two conditions: (1) the financial statements contain a material misstatement and (2) the auditor fails to detect the misstatement. The acceptable level of audit risk is defined by SAS-107 as being "limited to a low level that is, in [the auditor's] professional judgment, appropriate for expressing an opinion on the financial statements." Because audit risk deals with the chance that material misstatements in the financial statements go undetected by the auditor, it is appropriate for the professional standards to require that all engagements be planned and executed with a low level of audit risk.

The level of audit risk may be expressed in quantitative terms or nonquantitative terms. For example, the auditor may conclude that audit risk should be established at 5% and use this threshold as a basis for the planning and the performance of audit procedures — a quantitative measure. On the other hand, an auditor can plan and perform audit procedures based on a non-quantitative measure (such as high, medium, or low) and not attempt to be specific concerning audit risk.

> **ENGAGEMENT STRATEGY:** In practice, auditors often express audit risk in both quantitative terms and nonquantitative terms. For example, when statistical sampling is used for one or more parts of the engagement, audit risk must be quantified. Many areas of the engagements will not be susceptible to statistical sampling, however, and the auditor will use the nonquantitative guideline of low audit risk in order to guide the planning and execution of audit procedures. Also, due to the complexity of an audit engagement and the numerous variables that must be considered in determining audit risk, it is likely that an auditor would not be comfortable with a conclusion about audit risk expressed entirely in quantitative terms. For example, to conclude at the end of an audit engagement that the audit opinion is based on, say, 5% audit risk is to misunderstand the nature of the audit process and the environment in which it is applied.

SAS-107 requires the auditor to perform "risk assessment procedures" to assess the risks of material misstatements at both the financial statement level and the relevant assertions level. When considering risks at the financial statement level, the auditor considers risks of material misstatements that relate pervasively to the financial statements as a whole and potentially affect many relevant assertions. Risks of this nature often relate to the entity's control environment and include risks arising from fraud, such as the risk of management's override of internal control. SAS-107 notes that the auditor's consideration of audit risk and materiality are affected by the following factors:

- The size and complexity of the entity

- The auditor's experience with the entity

- The auditor's knowledge of the entity's business and its environment, including its internal control.

Auditors are required to perform risk assessment procedures in every audit. The second standard of fieldwork requires auditors to obtain an understanding of the entity and its environment, including its internal control, to assess the risks of material misstatements at the financial statement and relevant assertion levels. Risk assessment procedures do not by themselves provide sufficient appropriate audit evidence to base the audit opinion on and must be supplemented by further audit procedures, which consist of tests of controls and substantive tests. The auditor's prior experience with and knowledge of an entity and its environment may affect his or her assessment of audit risk and materiality. If the auditor concludes that there is significant risk of material misstatement, the nature, timing, and extent of further audit procedures should take this assessment into consideration.

When developing a response to the risks of material misstatement at the overall financial statement level, the auditor should consider the need to alter the mix of personnel assigned to the engagement to include individuals with the appropriate knowledge, skill, and ability to respond to the assessed risks. In certain situations, the auditor may request the assistance of specialists or modify the level of supervision of assistants involved in the engagement to respond to the overall financial statement risk.

> **FRAUD POINTER:** SAS-99 explicitly requires the auditor to gather information necessary to identify risks of material misstatements due to fraud. Auditors are required to obtain this information to assess fraud risk by (1) making inquiries of management and others within the entity about fraud risks, (2) evaluating the results of analytical procedures performed during the planning stage of the audit, (3) considering fraud risk factors, and (4) considering certain other information, such as information obtained during client acceptance and continuance, reviews of interim financial statements, and consideration of inherent risks.

The assessment of risk of material misstatement should also be related to an audit of a client with operations in multiple components or locations. SAS-107 requires that, in determining whether the activities at a location or at a component should be considered in the planning of the engagement, the auditor should consider factors such as the following:

- The nature and amount of assets and transactions executed at the location or component

- The degree of centralization of records or information processing

- The effectiveness of the control environment, particularly with respect to management's direct control over the exercise of authority delegated to others and its ability to effectively supervise activities at the location or component

- The frequency, timing, and scope of monitoring activities by the entity or others at the location or component

- Judgments about materiality of the location or component

- Risks associated with the location, such as political or economic stability

During the planning phase of the audit, the auditor must determine a materiality level for the financial statements taken as a whole when establishing the overall audit strategy. This materiality level for the financial statements as a whole is to be used by the auditor as guide when performing risk assessment procedures and when planning the nature, timing, and extent of further audit procedures.

The auditor must use professional judgment to establish materiality levels for an engagement based on the characteristics unique to that engagement. There are no specific standards for determining materiality levels; however, in general terms the auditor must consider both quantitative and qualitative factors.

Quantitative materiality considerations

From a quantitative perspective, an auditor generally focuses on various amounts that appear in the financial statements as a basis for determining materiality levels. These amounts may include such financial statement elements as revenue, gross profit, net income, total assets, current assets, and total liabilities. Using the FASB's broad definition of "materiality," the auditor must determine, in his or her opinion, what amount of misstatement in the various numbers contained in the financial statements may result in a material misstatement. Often the auditor applies a percentage to a chosen benchmark as a step in determining materiality. Auditors often consider common financial statement elements (e.g., assets, liabilities, pre-tax income, etc.) and specific financial statement accounts or elements that will be the focus of financial statement users' attention. For example, assume that the auditor has established the following analysis as a preliminary step in establishing materiality levels in an engagement:

Financial Statement Element	Financial Statements Amount (unaudited)	Percentage Misstatement Considered Material	Amount Misstatement Considered Material
Gross profit	$4,000,000	6%	$240,000
Income before taxes from continuing items	3,000,000	7%	210,000
Total assets	4,000,000	10%	400,000
Current assets	3,000,000	8%	240,000

PLANNING AID REMINDER: In some instances income or loss from continuing operations includes significant, unusual, or infrequently occurring items. Under these circumstances, it may be appropriate to exclude the unusual or infrequent items in developing a base for measuring materiality.

ENGAGEMENT STRATEGY: In the above example, materiality levels are based on unaudited financial statement amounts. In some situations, the auditor may have to make preliminary estimates of current financial statement amounts based on annualized interim financial statements or financial statements from previous periods given the timing of audit planning for most engagements. SAS-107 recognizes that materiality judgments may have to be based on preliminary or unadjusted amounts, and it states that such an approach is acceptable as long as the auditor considers the effects of major changes in the entity's circumstances (for example, a significant merger) and relevant changes in the economy as a whole or the industry in which the entity operates.

Although the auditor may be concerned with the misstatement of several financial statement elements, generally the smallest materiality level is used in the planning phase of the engagement. This approach is justified because of the interrelationship of the financial statements and the need for audit efficiency. In the current example, the overall materiality level for the financial statements would be $210,000.

ENGAGEMENT STRATEGY: When the auditor uses a single materiality threshold for all of the financial statements, the planned audit risk is lower for those items that have a materiality threshold level higher than the single materiality level selected for planning purposes. In the current example, the planned audit risk is lower for the balance sheet (total assets) because the materiality level is $210,000 rather than $400,000. However, SAS-107 does allow the auditor to use two different levels of materiality for the income statement and balance sheet as part of the engagement strategy. In this example, the auditor may conclude that misstatements aggregating $210,000 are material to the income statement but that misstatements to the balance sheet would have to aggregate to $400,000, as long as balance sheet misstatements have no impact on the income statement.

Qualitative considerations

Besides establishing a quantitative materiality level during the planning phase of the engagement, the auditor should also be sensitive to possible misstatements that could be qualitatively material. Qualitative factors include such items as the discovery of a fraudulent transaction in the previous engagement, or the existence of a loan covenant that, if violated, provides a creditor with the right to demand immediate payment of an obligation. SAS-107 requires the auditor to consider whether there are circumstances where misstatements of lesser amounts than the materiality level determined for the financial statements as a whole might affect economic decisions of users of the financial statements. For example, accounting standards, regulations, or laws may affect user expectations regarding the measurement or disclosure of certain items. Additionally, the industry or environment the entity operates in may place importance on key disclosures.

OBSERVATION: In assessing the significance of a misstatement, the auditor should consider the pervasiveness of the misstatement (such as whether the amounts and presentation of numerous financial statement items are affected), and the effect of the misstatement on the financial statements taken as a whole. We list qualitative factors that the auditor might consider in assessing materiality in the "Practitioner's Aids" at the end of this section.

PUBLIC COMPANY IMPLICATION: The SEC Staff has issued guidance about materiality considerations relevant to financial statements for public companies. That guidance, published as SEC Staff Accounting Bulletin No. 99 (SAB-99)

(Materiality) contains the SEC staff's views that the auditor's exclusive reliance on certain quantitative benchmarks to assess materiality in preparing financial statements and performing audits of those financial statements is inappropriate; misstatements are not immaterial simply because they fall beneath a numerical threshold. SAB-99 emphasizes the importance of evaluating qualitative aspects of materiality and provides guidance to auditors of useful qualitative characteristics to consider. Auditors of public companies should examine SAB-99 guidance.

PLANNING AID REMINDER: There is an inverse relationship between audit risk and materiality, which can be expressed in the following generalizations: (1) the risk that an item could be misstated by an extremely large amount is generally low and (2) the risk that an item could be misstated by an extremely small amount is generally high. Thus, as the planned level of materiality is reduced, the scope of the audit approach must be increased.

Individual account-balance or class-of-transactions level

SAS-107 notes that when determining the nature, timing, and extent of audit procedures at the specific account level, the auditor

> should design procedures to obtain reasonable assurance of detecting misstatements that the auditor believes, based on the judgment about materiality, could be material, when aggregated with misstatements in other balances, classes, or disclosures, to the financial statements taken as a whole.

The auditor considers audit risk at the account balance, class of transaction, and disclosure level in such a way that ultimately enables him or her at the completion of the audit to express an opinion on the financial statements taken as a whole at an appropriately low level of audit risk. The auditor must use professional judgment to determine how preliminary judgments concerning materiality should affect the audit of a specific account balance or class of transactions. The auditor must perform the audit to obtain reasonable assurance of detecting misstatements that he or she believes could be large enough, individually or in the aggregate, to be quantitatively material to the financial statements. The auditor should consider the possibility that misstatements at amounts less than the overall financial statement level materiality could in the aggregate result in material misstatements in the financial statements. To do this, the auditor should determine one or more levels of tolerable misstatement that reflect the maximum error in a class of transactions or account balance that he or she is willing to accept. Tolerable misstatement amounts are normally lower than the materiality levels. To illustrate one approach, assume that, based on the previous example (where materiality was set at $210,000), the auditor is considering the effect of materiality on the selection of audit procedures for the following balance sheet accounts:

Account Title	Balance	Materiality Level for Each Account (5.25%)
Cash	$ 500,000	$ 26,250
Accounts receivable	1,400,000	73,500
Inventories	1,100,000	57,750
Property, plant, and equipment (net)	1,000,000	52,500
	$4,000,000	$210,000

In the above example, the overall preliminary materiality level is 5.25% ($210,000/$4,000,000). The auditor could decide that a misstatement of 5.25% for each account or financial statement element individually is to be considered material for that account or financial statement element.

In contrast to allocating a set percentage to determine tolerable misstatement for each account balance or financial statement element, the auditor may allocate the total materiality amount among the items based on professional judgment. For example, the auditor may decide to allocate the $210,000 in the following manner:

Account Title	Balance	Materiality Level for Each Account
Cash	$ 500,000	$ 10,000
Accounts receivable	1,400,000	50,000
Inventories	1,100,000	50,000
Property, plant, and equipment (net)	1,000,000	100,000
Total	$4,000,000	$210,000 (5.25%)

In this instance, the auditor has used his or her judgment to allocate materiality to individual accounts. The individual materiality amounts (e.g., tolerable misstatements) relative to the related accounts differ in percentage amounts. For example, tolerable misstatement for cash represents 2% ($10,000 divided by $500,000) of the cash balance, whereas tolerable misstatement for property, plant, and equipment (net) represents 10% ($100,000 divided by $1,000,000) of the account balance. However, the aggregate of all tolerable misstatements sums to $210,000, which is 5.25% of the aggregate account balances.

> **PLANNING AID REMINDER:** Factors that may be relevant in determining how to allocate the overall materiality amount to specific accounts include the extent of errors in a particular account discovered during previous audit engagements or the sensitivity of an account balance to external factors (such as the relationship of the business cycle to the estimate of doubtful accounts).

Selecting a materiality level at the individual account-balance level or class-of-transactions level (e.g., tolerable misstatements) affects the scope of the audit approach for each individual item. For example, SAS-107 notes that as the level of materiality is reduced for a particular account (holding other planning considerations equal), the auditor must do one or more of the following:

- Select a more effective auditing procedure (nature of procedures)

- Perform auditing procedures closer to year-end (timing of procedures)

- Increase the extent of a particular auditing procedure (extent of procedures)

The determination of the audit scope during the planning stage is important because it provides a basis for the auditor to restrict audit risk at the individual balance or class level in such a way that will enable him or her, "at the completion of the audit, to express an opinion on the financial statements taken as a whole at an appropriately low level of audit risk." Audit risk at the account balance, class of transaction, relevant assertion, or disclosure level consists of three types of risk:

1. Inherent risk

2. Control risk

3. Detection risk

Inherent risk and control risk relate to material misstatements caused by either error or fraud. SAS-107 describes the risk of material misstatement as the auditor's combined assessment of inherent risk and control risk. The auditor may make separate assessments of inherent risk and control risk or a combined assessment of inherent and control risk to represent the risk of material misstatement.

Inherent risk

The nature of the account balance or class of transactions and the fundamental characteristics of the entity being audited determine the level of inherent risk. SAS-107 defines "inherent risk" as "the susceptibility of a relevant assertion to a misstatement that could be material, either individually or when aggregated with other misstatements, assuming that there are no related controls."

There are many factors that can affect inherent risk but, in general, these factors relate to broad characteristics of the entity as well as factors unique to the individual account balance or class of transactions. Factors to be considered include the need for estimates, sensitivity to external economic forces, complexity of the underlying accounting, technological developments affecting product obsolescence, and characteristics of the industry in which the company operates.

As a general rule, there is less inherent risk associated with an account that is based on actual transactions than with an account based on estimates. For example, there is less risk associated with rent expense than with warranty expense based on this single factor (estimate-based), and there is more inherent risk associated with the inventory of a company that is part of an industry experiencing rapid technological changes than there is for a company in a stable industry.

Control risk

The client's design of internal control will have an impact on the level of audit risk. "Control risk" is defined by SAS-107 as "the risk that a misstatement that could occur in a relevant assertion and that could be material, either individually or when aggregated with other misstatements, will not be prevented or detected on a timely basis by the entity's internal control." Control risk and inherent risk are the entity's risks and exist independent of the audit of the financial statements. As a result, they are risks that cannot be changed by the auditor.

In general, the stronger (in both design and operation) the internal control, the greater the likelihood that the system will prevent or detect material misstatements (whether caused by error or fraud). Some control risk will always exist because of the inherent limitations of internal control.

The level of control risk will be based on the auditor's consideration of the client internal control. SAS-107 notes that "if the auditor believes controls are unlikely to pertain to an assertion or are unlikely to be effective, he or she would assess control risk for that assertion at the maximum."

> **PLANNING AID REMINDER:** Often, inherent risk and control risk are evaluated as a single risk factor because it is sometimes difficult to classify risk conditions. For example, the risk of inventory loss through theft may be a combination of poor internal controls as well as the physical nature of the inventory. The evaluation of the risks as a single factor is acceptable because the inherent risk and control risk are both unique to the client and cannot be changed by the auditor.

SAS-107 requires the auditor to make an assessment of the risk of material misstatement at the relevant assertion level to provide a basis for further audit procedures. Whether the auditor makes a combined or separate assessment of inherent and control risks, he or she must have an appropriate basis for the assessment. The basis for that assessment may be obtained through the auditor's performance of risk assessment procedures and tests of controls.

> **PLANNING AID REMINDER:** Even if inherent risk is assessed as low, the auditor cannot ignore the assessment of control risk in his or her assessment of the combined risks of material misstatements. The auditor is required to assess the combined risk of material misstatement. Thus, the auditor cannot ignore control risk regardless of the auditor's assessment of inherent risk. Although auditing standards do not require separate assessments to be performed, they do require an assessment of the risk of material misstatement that includes control risk.

The auditor must be careful that his or her judgment about inherent risk is not influenced by the effect of certain controls. The AICPA issued Technical Practice Aid (TIS) 8200.09 to emphasize that an auditor's separate assessment of inherent risk should exclude the effect of related controls. TIS 8200.09 provides the following example to illustrate this point. Assume an auditor is auditing a balance sheet account that he or she expects to have only one adjustment per month posted to it. The auditor believes that the monthly adjustment is relatively easy to calculate and assesses inherent risk as low because the amount is easy to calculate. In addition, the auditor has not identified a misstatement in this account in prior years, and the bookkeeper is capable of recording the correct monthly amount. In this case, the auditor's assessment of inherent risk was influenced by his or her belief that the bookkeeper is competent and has never made an error in prior years. In that case, the auditor's assessment of inherent risk did not assume there are no controls in place, because there are controls in place that the bookkeeper uses each month to post the adjustments.

SAS-107 no longer allows auditors to assess control risk "at the maximum" without having a basis for that assessment. Thus, there no longer is a "default" to maximum control risk. Although the risk of material misstatement is based on judgment rather than a precise measurement of risk, the auditor is required to have a basis for his or her assessment.

> **ENGAGEMENT STRATEGY:** Many audit firm methodologies allow a "default to maximum" assessment for control risk despite the presence of internal controls at a client. SAS-107 no longer allows this automatic "default to maximum." Now, auditors must have a basis for their risk assessments, including a basis for assessing control risk at maximum. Auditors are required to obtain a sufficient understanding of internal controls in every audit in order to assess the risk of material misstatement. After identifying and assessing the risk of material misstatement at the assertion level, the auditor may adopt a substantive audit strategy because the costs of testing the operating effectiveness of controls exceed their benefits. In this circumstance, the auditor may assess control risk at the maximum.

Detection risk

Even though the auditor performs a variety of audit procedures, it is possible that a material misstatement will not be detected. SAS-107 defines "detection risk" as "the risk that the auditor will not detect a misstatement that exists in a relevant assertion that could be material, either individually or when aggregated with other misstatements." In part, detection risk arises because not all items that make up an account balance are examined (sampling risk) and audit procedures are not properly applied or interpreted (nonsampling risk).

During the planning phase of the engagement, the auditor must consider inherent risk, control risk, and detection risk and must select an audit strategy that will result in a low level of audit risk once the engagement is complete. There is an inverse relationship between the auditor's assessment of inherent and control risks and the level of detection risk. If inherent risk and control risks are high, the auditor should establish a low level of detection risk.

At the individual account-balance or class-of-transactions level, the auditor can express the interrelationship of the various risk factors as follows:

$$\text{Audit Risk} = \text{Risk of Material Misstatement} \times \text{Detection Risk}$$

As noted previously, the risk of material misstatement consists of the product of inherent risk and control risk. Thus, the above expression can also be stated as follows:

Audit Risk = Inherent Risk × Control Risk × Detection Risk

Control risk and inherent risk exist based on the client's characteristics. It is the auditor's responsibility to assess inherent risk and control risk at the appropriate levels based on those characteristics. Furthermore, as required by professional standards, audit risk must be set at an appropriately low level. Thus, the auditor's ability to change risk factors is limited to detection risk. For these reasons and for analytical purposes, the formula presented above can be manipulated with the following results:

$$\text{Detection Risk} = \frac{\text{Audit Risk}}{\text{Inherent Risk} \times \text{Control Risk}}$$

For example, if the auditor establishes audit risk at 5%, and inherent risk and control risk are both assessed at 40%, the detection risk would be established at about 31%, as follows:

$$31\% = \frac{.05}{.4 \times .4}$$

PLANNING AID REMINDER: The formula to compute detection risk is more conceptual than mathematical. That is, the formula shows the interrelationship of the various risk factors, but in practice it is useful as a broad guide as well as a technique for quantifying detection risk. Although numbers are used here to illustrate the audit risk model, many practitioners apply the formula by assessing inherent, control, and detection risk on a qualitative basis (e.g., high, medium, and low).

If inherent risk and control risk are assessed at higher levels—say, 60%—the auditor would decrease the detection risk to about 14%, as shown below:

$$14\% = \frac{.05}{.6 \times .6}$$

The level of detection risk has an impact on the design of the auditor's substantive procedures. In general, if a low level of detection risk is appropriate, based on the assessment of inherent risk and control risk, the auditor would (1) expand the sample of substantive procedures (extent of procedures), (2) be less likely to perform substantive procedures at interim dates (timing of procedures), and/or (3) perform audit procedures that result in more appropriate audit evidence. Thus, as detection risk is lowered, the nature, timing, and/or extent of substantive procedures are adjusted to intensify the search for possible misstatements. Detection risk can be disaggregated into additional components of tests of details risk and substantive analytical procedures risk.

SAS-107 states that "it is not appropriate, however, for an auditor to rely completely on assessments of inherent risk and control risk to the exclusion of performing substantive procedures of account balances and classes of transactions where misstatements could exist that might be material when aggregated with misstatements in other balances or classes." As a result, the auditor will plan to perform further audit procedures that include tests of details or substantive analytical procedures.

The identification of audit risk and materiality at the individual account-balance and class-of-transactions level is preliminary and necessary in order for the auditor to plan the scope of the engagement; however, the professional judgments made are tentative. The audit process is cumulative in that as the engagement progresses the auditor should consider additional information obtained. For this reason, the auditor may need to reassess risk factors and adjust the scope of the engagement accordingly. For example, the auditor may discover excessive misstatements that were not anticipated in the preliminary planning stage of the engagement and that require a reduction in the level of materiality initially considered appropriate. In that situation, the auditor should reconsider the appropriateness of the nature, timing, and extent of further audit procedures.

> **FRAUD POINTER:** When assessing the risk of material misstatement due to fraud at the account level related to revenue recognition, SAS-99 notes that the auditor should ordinarily presume that fraud risk is high. Material misstatements due to fraud often result from overstatements of revenues (e.g., through fictitious sales or through premature recording of sales transactions) or understatements of revenues (e.g., through delays in recording sales transactions). Accordingly, the auditor should develop appropriate audit responses in light of this risk assessment.

Assess the audit risk based on the results of substantive procedures

Based on the performance of audit procedures, the auditor may identify known and likely misstatements in the financial statements. The auditor must accumulate all known and likely misstatements identified during the audit, unless he or she believes the misstatements are trivial.

Initially the auditor should consider the effects of uncorrected misstatements both individually and in the aggregate. For example, one misstatement could have the effect of increasing income while another misstatement could have the opposite effect and when considered in the aggregate the two misstatements could more or less have little effect on income. Although the two misstatements offset one another, the evaluation of whether the financial statements are materially misstated is incomplete.

Specifically, the auditor must consider the materiality of each misstatement on the financial statements. For example if one misstatement materially overstates gross profit while the other misstatement materially understates administrative expenses but the two combined do not have a material effect on net income, the two misstatements would still be considered individually material and should be corrected by the client or the auditor's report should be modified.

On the other hand, a number of relatively small misstatements might have been discovered that individually are not material but when aggregated cause the financial statements to be misstated. Looking at the uncorrected misstatements individually is not enough; they must also be aggregated and evaluated.

The auditor's evaluation of possible material misstatements in the financial statements should include the auditor's best estimate of the total misstatements (the likely misstatements), which is in part based on the specifically identified misstatements (the known misstatements). In a simple illustration of this approach, an auditor who identifies a known misstatement of $20,000 based on testing might project a likely misstatement of $80,000 if the sample tested represented 25% of the total account balance. Additionally, the auditor would combine the quantitative results of his or her misstatement analysis with relevant qualitative factors (such as an estimate of the risk that the sample is not representative of the population) to determine the risk that material misstatements exist.

> **OBSERVATION:** Auditing Interpretation No. 2 of AU 312 provides guidance for determining the amount of the likely misstatement to be aggregated. If the auditor has concluded, based on audit procedures employed, that a particular balance likely falls within a range, then the likely misstatement is the difference between the balance recorded in the financial statement and the upper or lower boundary of the range. For example, if the range is likely to be between $200,000 and $300,000 and the recorded balance is $315,000, the misstatement to be aggregated is $15,000 ($315,000-$300,000). However, if the auditor's assessment of the balance is based on a point estimate (say, $290,000) rather than a range, the misstatement to be aggregated is the difference between the point estimate and the financial statement balance [in this case $25,000 ($315,000-$290,000)].

An auditor may apply substantive analytical procedures to an account balance or a class of transactions; however, due to the nature of substantive analytical procedures, it is ordinarily unlikely that the auditor would identify specific known misstatements and draw a conclusion concerning whether a material misstatement exists. Thus, the auditor's application of substantive analytical procedures can provide only an indication that an account balance or class of transactions might be misstated. When a substantive analytical procedure indicates a likelihood of a material misstatement, the auditor generally first requests management to investigate the unusual expectation and then, if necessary, expands his or her audit procedures to determine whether a misstatement actually exists in the account balance or class of transactions.

As noted earlier, there is more audit risk for an account balance or a class of transactions that is based on estimates than there is for an account or class of transactions based on objective, factual data. Because accounts based on estimation require subjective judgments to be made about future events, they are inherently risky. Additionally, estimates may increase the risk of misstatement due to inadequate or inappropriate data that may be misapplied. A projected amount for an account balance or a class of transactions based on audit sampling will seldom be equal to the actual estimated amount in the financial statements. Generally, this difference should not be treated as a misstatement as long as the auditor believes the difference is reasonable. If the auditor believes the difference is not reasonable, the difference between the amount on the financial statements and the closest reasonable estimate should be treated as a misstatement. Next, the difference should be evaluated individually and in the aggregate with other likely misstatements in determining whether a material misstatement exists in the financial statements taken as a whole.

Although each account balance or class of transactions is audited individually, the auditor should take a broader perspective to determine whether the client has a bias to misstate all or most of its estimated amounts. SAS-107 states that "if each accounting estimate included in the financial statements was individually reasonable, but the effect of the difference between each estimate and the estimate best supported by the audit evidence was to increase income, the auditor should reconsider the estimates taken as a whole."

After estimating the total misstated projected amount (likely misstatement) individually and in the aggregate, the auditor should compare that amount to materiality. If the likely misstatement is greater than the amount designated as material, the auditor should request the client to investigate the financial statement balance that appears to be misstated. If additional procedures are not performed or if the client refuses to modify the financial statements in order to eliminate the material misstatement, the auditor would express either a qualified opinion or an adverse opinion on the financial statements. If the likely misstatement is less than the materiality amount, the auditor must use professional judgment to assess audit risk; for example, as the likely misstatement approaches the materiality amount, the level of audit risk rises. As noted earlier, SAS-107 states that the audit risk should be established at a relatively low level. Thus, the comparison and the analysis of the relationship of the likely misstatement and the level of materiality are critical. For example, if the auditor has estimated the aggregate likely misstatement (either focusing on the misstatement as an individual misstatement or focusing on all aggregated misstatements) to be $200,000 and the level of materiality is $210,000, it is likely that audit risk is too great to conclude that the financial statements are fairly stated. On the other hand, if the estimated likely misstatement (either individually or in the aggregate) had been $50,000 rather than $200,000, it is more likely that the auditor would conclude that a low level of audit risk had been achieved.

> **OBSERVATION:** The current year's financial statements may be affected by misstatements from the prior year's engagement financial statements because such misstatements were not considered material and therefore no adjustment was made in the prior year. If the auditor believes that "there is an unacceptably high risk" that the current year's financial statements are materially misstated when the prior year's misstatements are taken into consideration, the auditor should include the likely misstatement amount due to the prior year's misstatement with the current year's likely misstatement amount to determine whether the current year's financial statements appear to be materially misstated.

> **ENGAGEMENT STRATEGY:** During the engagement, the auditor may identify a minimum level of misstatement to be used to determine known misstatements and the likely misstatements. The amount must be set low enough, however, so that "any such misstatements, either individually or when aggregated with other such misstatements, would not be material to the financial statements, after the possibility of further undetected misstatements is considered."

When evaluating the results of substantive procedures, the auditor should consider both qualitative and quantitative aspects of the noted misstatement. In some instances, a relatively small misstatement may be deemed material. For example, misstatements that involve an illegal act, change a loss to net income, or increase the entity's compliance with contracts and regulatory provisions may have a material effect on the financial statements.

The auditor's response to intentional misstatements

Securities laws and auditing standards [SAS-54 (AU 317) and SAS-99 (AU 316)] both require that an auditor report fraudulent acts to the appropriate level of management. If the auditor believes that a misstatement is, or may be, the result of fraud, he or she should consider the implications of the misstatement in relation to other aspects of the audit, even if the misstatement is not material to the financial statements.

> **ENGAGEMENT STRATEGY:** In addition to reporting fraudulent acts to the appropriate level of management, the auditor must also consider how the discovery of such facts affects the nature, timing, and extent of audit procedures. In some instances it may be appropriate, after seeking competent legal advice, for the auditor to resign from an engagement.

GAAP precedent over industry practice

When there is a conflict between GAAP and industry accounting practice, clearly GAAP must be observed. Thus, if a client prepares a portion of its financial statements to conform to industry accounting practices that are inconsistent with GAAP, these departures must be evaluated to determine whether the financial statements are materially misstated.

General comments

The SEC recognizes that determining when financial statements are materially misstated can be a complex process. This is especially true when the application of GAAP to a particular transaction or balance is not clear. Under these conditions, a client may account for an item "based on analogies to similar situations or other factors." When these conditions arise, an auditor is encouraged to discuss ambiguous accounting and reporting issues with the SEC staff on a timely basis.

> **ENGAGEMENT STRATEGY:** When the client is not a public company, the auditor should have in place procedures that encourage staff accountants to discuss difficult reporting issues with appropriate personnel within the firm.

Communicate misstatements to management

The auditor should communicate all known and likely misstatements to an appropriate level of management. This communication should be made timely to allow management an opportunity to evaluate whether the items are misstatements and to take any necessary action. The appropriate level of management to receive the communication from the auditor may be based on factors such as the nature, size, and frequency of the misstatement and which level of management can take the appropriate action.

When making these communications, the auditor should distinguish between known and likely misstatements. The auditor should request management to record adjustments needed to correct all known misstatements, unless they are considered to be trivial, including the effect of prior-period misstatements. For likely misstatements based on a sample, the auditor should request management to examine the class of transactions, account balance, or disclosure in order to identify and correct misstatements. For likely misstatements based on differences in estimates, the auditor should request management to review the assumptions and methods used in developing management's estimate. Once management has made these evaluations, the auditor should then re-evaluate the amount of likely misstatement.

If management decides not to correct some or all of the known and likely misstatements communicated to management by the auditor, he or she should obtain an understanding about management's reasons for not making the corrections. The auditor should take that understanding into account when considering the qualitative aspects of the entity's accounting practices and implications related to his or her report.

Document audit results

SAS-107 requires the auditor to document the following:

- The levels of materiality and tolerable misstatement used in the audit and the basis on which those levels were determined

- A summary of uncorrected misstatements related to known and likely misstatements (unless they are trivial)

- The auditor's conclusion as to whether uncorrected misstatements, individually or in the aggregate, do or do not cause the financial statements to be materially misstated, and the basis for that conclusion.

- All known and likely misstatements (except those that are trivial) identified by the auditor during the audit that have been corrected by management.

SAS-107 further requires that the auditor document all uncorrected misstatements in a manner that allows the auditor to

- Separately consider the effects of known and likely misstatements, including uncorrected misstatements identified in prior periods

- Consider the aggregate effect of misstatements on the financial statements

- Consider the qualitative factors that are relevant to the auditor's consideration of whether the misstatements are material

Practitioner's Aids

Checklist of qualitative factors in determining materiality

The following qualitative factors may be relevant in determining the materiality of an item:

- Items that have an effect on trends (particularly profitability trends)

- Items that change losses to income or vice versa

- Items that have an impact on segment information

- Items that are relevant in determining whether loan covenants and similar items have been violated

- Items that have an effect on materiality thresholds that are established by statute or regulation

- Items that mask a change in earnings or other trends

- Items that increase management's compensation

- Items that affect the vulnerability of the financial statements to possible fraud, illegal acts, or other similar situations

- Particular nature of the item misstated (such as recurring items versus nonrecurring items)

- Items that are misclassified (such as misclassification of an item that should be considered operating but is classified as nonoperating)

- The significance of the item in relationship to known user needs

- The character of the misstatement (for example, the degree to which an account balance is based on an estimate)

- The possible motivation of management for the misstatement

- The existence of offsetting effects of individually significant items

- The possibility that a currently immaterial item could have a material impact on subsequent financial statements

- The cost of making a correction

- The risk that other undetected misstatements would affect the auditor's opinion

- Items that reflect unfavorably on management's integrity

SEC Staff Accounting Bulletin: "Materiality"

The Financial Accounting Standards Board (FASB) and the American Institute of Certified Public Accountants (AICPA) have provided little guidance for determining what constitutes a material item in financial statements. The Securities and Exchange Commission (SEC) has addressed this issue in a Staff Accounting Bulletin (SAB) titled "Materiality" (SAB-99). Although the SEC addresses only publicly traded companies, this Bulletin, discussed below, provides valuable guidance in the performance of audits in general. This Practitioner's Aid summarizes the guidance in the SAB.

SAB-99 discusses how the auditor of a public company should do the following:

- Assess materiality

- Aggregate and net misstatements

- Consider immaterial misstatements that are intentional

Assessing materiality

FASB Concepts Statement No. 2 (CON-2) (Qualitative Characteristics of Accounting Information) characterizes "materiality" as follows:

> The omission or misstatement of an item in a financial report is material if, in the light of surrounding circumstances, the magnitude of the item is such that it is probable that the judgment of a reasonable person relying upon the report would have been changed or influenced by the inclusion or correction of the item.

While everyone agrees with this description of materiality, applying the concept in practice requires a considerable amount of professional judgment. In many engagements, an auditor establishes a material threshold or a rule of thumb, such as 5% or 10%, and a misstatement(s) that is less than the specific threshold is not considered material. SEC SAB-99 points out that the creation of a specific materiality percentage or dollar value for determining whether a particular item is material "has no basis in the accounting literature or the law."

An auditor deals with two broad types of materiality during an engagement. First, in order to help plan an engagement, the auditor must identify a materiality factor. That is, the auditor must make some determination of what may be material in determining the nature, timing, and extent of audit procedures. Generally, as the materiality threshold falls from, say, 10% to 5%, the extent of audit procedures that are necessary to achieve the auditor's objective is increased. The SEC has no problem with an auditor using preliminary definitions of "materiality" in determining the audit approach in a particular engagement.

The second type of materiality the auditor must address in an engagement involves determining whether specific misstatements are in the aggregate large enough for the auditor to conclude that the financial statements may be materially misstated. The SEC points out that in this phase of the audit engagement, using hard and fast materiality thresholds is not appropriate. That is, concluding whether or not an item is material is not a procedural process (asking whether an item exceeds a specific threshold) but rather an analytical process (asking whether it could affect one's assessment of a particular company). To support the argument that acceptance of the analytical process is the appropriate approach, the SEC refers to the following legal conclusion: "Magnitude by itself, without regard to the nature of the item and the circumstances in which the judgment has to be made, will not generally be a sufficient basis for a materiality judgment." That is, the SEC reminds auditors that both quantitative and qualitative factors must be considered in determining whether an item is material to the financial statements taken as a whole.

SEC SAB-99 points out that the qualitative factors used to evaluate a matter that is below the quantitative threshold should include the following:

- Whether the misstatement arises from an item capable of precise measurement or from an estimate and, if from an estimate, the degree of imprecision inherent in the estimate

- Whether the misstatement masks a change in earnings or other trends

- Whether the misstatement hides a failure to meet analysts' consensus expectations for the enterprise

- Whether the misstatement changes a loss into income or vice versa

- Whether the misstatement concerns a segment or other portion of the registrant's business that has been identified as playing a significant role in the registrant's operations or profitability

- Whether the misstatement affects the registrant's compliance with regulatory requirements

- Whether the misstatement affects the registration's compliance with loan covenants or other contractual requirements

- Whether the misstatement has the effect of increasing management's compensation — for example, by satisfying requirements for the award of bonuses or other forms of incentive compensation

- Whether the misstatement involves concealment of an unlawful transaction

The SEC also notes that an auditor must be particularly careful when audit results suggest that management has intentionally made misstatements in the preparation of its financial statements that appear to have the objective of "managing earnings." In this regard, the SAB-99 makes the following Observation:

> The staff believes that investors generally would regard as significant a management practice to over- or under-state earnings up to an amount just short of a percentage threshold in order to "manage" earnings. Investors presumably also would regard as significant an accounting practice that, in essence, rendered all earnings figures subject to a management-directed margin of misstatement.

Based on the SEC's reasoning and plain common sense, an auditor should not establish a materiality threshold and then blindly apply it in an engagement. That is not exercising judgment; it is reducing the audit process to a mechanical process that can be more efficiently performed by a computer.

Aggregating and netting misstatements

In determining whether financial statements are materially misstated, the misstatement should be evaluated both individually and in the aggregate. This determination should be made on the basis of both quantitative thresholds and qualitative factors (such as those discussed in the previous section), and the analysis should be directed to "individual line item amounts, subtotals, or totals in the financial statements."

When an individual item by itself is material, it is incorrect to offset its significance with another item that has the opposite impact on the financial statements. For example, if sales are materially overstated and cost of goods sold is materially overstated by more or less the same amount, it would not be proper to suggest that the income statement is not materially misstated because net income is not materially affected by the offsetting misstatements.

SAB-99 warns auditors that they must be careful when aggregating the effects of two or more misstatements that net to a smaller effect on a particular total or subtotal. This is especially true when two misstatements are offset and one is based on an estimate and the other on a precise measurement.

> **ENGAGEMENT STRATEGY:** The auditor must take into consideration in the current engagement misstatements that were made in previous years but were considered immaterial. Those previous years' misstatements could have a material impact on the current year's financial statements, since the quantitative and qualitative factors that are relevant to identifying material items in the current engagement may have changed.

Consider immaterial misstatements that are intentional

SAB-99 raises the question of whether a client can make deliberate adjustments to its financial statements that are inconsistent with generally accepted accounting principles (GAAP) even though the effect is immaterial. The SEC takes the position that such action by a client is inappropriate and may in fact be in violation of securities laws that require that the books and records be accurate in "reasonable detail." The "reasonable detail" is more stringent than the materiality threshold. In determining what is reasonable detail, the auditor should consider the materiality factors (quantitative and qualitative factors discussed earlier) as well as additional factors such as the following:

- *The significance of the misstatement* Though the staff does not believe that registrants need to make finely calibrated determinations of significance with respect to immaterial items, plainly it is "reasonable" to treat misstatements whose effects are clearly inconsequential differently than more significant ones.

- *How the misstatement arose* It is unlikely that it is ever "reasonable" for registrants to record misstatements or not to correct known misstatements — even immaterial ones — as part of an ongoing effort directed by or known to senior management for the purposes of "managing" earnings. On the other hand, insignificant misstatements that arise from the operation of systems or recurring processes in the normal course of business generally will not cause a registrant's books to be inaccurate "in reasonable detail."

- *The cost of correcting the misstatement* The books and records provisions of the Exchange Act do not require registrants to make major expenditures to correct small misstatements. Conversely, where there is little cost or delay involved in correcting a misstatement, failing to do so is unlikely to be "reasonable."

- *The clarity of authoritative accounting guidance with respect to the misstatement* Where reasonable minds may differ about the appropriate accounting treatment of a financial statement item, a failure to correct it may not render the registrant's financial statements inaccurate "in reasonable detail." Where, however, there is little ground for reasonable disagreement, the case for leaving a misstatement uncorrected is correspondingly weaker.

SECTION 314

UNDERSTANDING THE ENTITY AND ITS ENVIRONMENT AND ASSESSING THE RISKS OF MATERIAL MISSTATEMENT

Authoritative Pronouncements

SAS-109 — Understanding the Entity and Its Environment and Assessing the Risks of Material Misstatement

> **IMPORTANT NOTICE FOR 2011:** The Auditing Standards Board (ASB) is in the process of redrafting all of the auditing sections in *Codification of Statements on Auditing Standards* to converge U.S. GAAS with the International Standards on Auditing issued by the International Auditing and Assurance Standards Board. As part of this process, the newly redrafted standards will follow certain clarity drafting conventions adopted by the ASB. These clarity drafting conventions include: (1) establishing objectives for each standard; (2) including a definitions section, if appropriate; and (3) separating requirements from application guidance and other material. The ASB is planning to have all redrafted standards become effective on the same date, which is for audits of financial statements for periods ending on or after December 15, 2012. It is possible that the effective date might be delayed beyond that date. The ASB's clarity and convergence project will have a significant effect on the auditing standards applicable to audits of nonpublic companies, and the 2012 *GAAS Guide* will be appropriately modified to reflect these changes once the effective date of the standards is certain.

Overview

The second standard of fieldwork requires the auditor to obtain a sufficient understanding of the entity and its environment, including its internal control, to understand the risk of material misstatement of the financial statements whether caused by error or fraud. This understanding is also used by the auditor to plan the nature, timing, and extent of further audit procedures (i.e., tests of operating effectiveness of controls and substantive procedures).

In performing procedures to understand the risk of material misstatement in the financial statements, the audit team should discuss where and how the entity's financial statements are susceptible to material misstatement, whether caused by error or fraud.

PLANNING AID REMINDER: SAS-99 requires the audit team to brainstorm on where and how an entity's financial statements might be susceptible to material misstatement due to fraud. SAS-109 extends this requirement — requiring a discussion of where and how the entity's financial statements are susceptible to material misstatement, whether caused by fraud or by error.

A major part of planning an audit is obtaining an understanding of an entity's internal control. SAS-109, relying on the work of the Committee of Sponsoring Organizations (COSO) of the Treadway Commission in its *Internal Control—Integrated Framework* document, defines internal control as

> Internal control is a process — effected by those charged with governance, management, and other personnel — designed to provide reasonable assurance about the achievement of the entity's objectives with regard to: (1) reliability of financial reporting, (2) effectiveness and efficiency of operations, and (3) compliance with applicable laws and regulations.

Internal control also relates to the safeguarding of assets — to prevent the unauthorized acquisition, use, or disposition of assets. This objective pertains to both the reliability of financial reporting and the efficiency and effectiveness of operations.

The auditor should obtain an understanding of the following five components of internal control:

1. *Control environment* The control environment sets the tone of an organization, which influences the control consciousness of its employees. The control environment is the foundation for all other components of internal control, because it provides discipline and structure.

2. *Risk assessment by the entity* Risk assessment is the process that an entity must conduct in order to identify and assess any relevant risks to its objectives. Once this assessment is performed, management must determine how the risks should be managed.

3. *Information and communication systems* Information and communication systems are used to identify, capture, and exchange the information needed for employees to carry out their responsibilities.

4. *Control activities* Control activities are the policies and procedures that help ensure that management directives are carried out.

5. *Monitoring* Monitoring is a process that an entity uses to assess the quality of its internal control performance over time.

> **PUBLIC COMPANY IMPLICATION:** SOX requires all public companies to issue an "internal control report" that includes the following: (1) a statement that management is responsible for establishing and maintaining adequate internal control over financial reporting and (2) an assessment of the effectiveness of internal control over financial reporting as of the end of the company's fiscal year. Auditors are also required to perform a separate evaluation of the effectiveness of internal control. Related SEC rules require management to explicitly state their responsibility for internal control and to identify material weaknesses in internal control. The framework that management uses as a basis for its evaluation of internal control must be one that has been established by a body or group that followed a due-process procedure that allowed for public comment. Most public companies use COSO's Internal Control — Integrated Framework. The concepts in SAS-109 are based on that framework.

> **FRAUD POINTER:** Gaining an understanding of internal control provides useful information about the presence of one of the three fraud conditions: opportunity. Nonexistent or weak internal controls can provide management or employees with opportunities or circumstances that allow them to carry out material misstatements in the financial statements. For this reason, auditors should consider the information they obtain through understanding internal control as they evaluate the presence of other risk factors related to conditions of fraud. The more fraud risk factors the auditor observes, the greater the likelihood of a material misstatement due to the occurrence of fraud.

> **PUBLIC COMPANY IMPLICATION:** In 2010 the PCAOB issued eight auditing standards (AS-8 through AS-5) related to the auditor's assessment of and response to risk. The proposed standards bear many similarities to the eight risk-assessment standards adopted by the Auditing Standards Board in 2006. AS-9 (Audit Planning) and AS-10 (Supervision of the Audit Engagement) are the new PCAOB standards that affect audit planning and supervision. AS-9 establishes requirements related to planning the audit, including requirements related to developing an appropriate audit strategy and audit plan. AS-10 describes the auditor's responsibilities for supervising the engagement, and it applies to the engagement partner and other audit team members who assist the partner

in supervising others. Although there are a number of differences between the PCAOB's and ASB's risk standards, the risk-assessment concepts contained in the PCAOB standards should be familiar to most auditors. As is currently the case, audit risk is the risk that the auditor will issue an inappropriate opinion on financial statements that are materially misstated. The auditor is to reduce audit risk to a low level through the application of audit procedures. As a result, the amount of audit effort devoted to particular accounts, classes of transactions, and disclosures should vary based on their respective risk.

Control Environment

The success or failure of internal control depends on the environment in which the internal control process takes place (i.e., the control environment). The control environment is also referred to as "the tone at the top," and it is the foundation for all the other elements of internal control. SAS-109 identifies the following as elements that affect an entity's control environment:

- Integrity and ethical values

- Commitment to competence

- Participation of those charged with governance

- Management's philosophy and operating style

- Organizational structure

- Assignment of authority and responsibility

- Human resource policies and practices

Exhibit AU 314-1 provides examples of elements of the control environment.

The effectiveness of an entity's controls cannot exceed the integrity and ethical values of those who design, administer, and monitor controls. Given this fact, an entity's control consciousness is heavily influenced by those charged with governance.

> **FRAUD POINTER:** In January 2005, the AICPA's Antifraud Programs and Controls Task Force issued a document entitled "Management Override of Internal Controls: The Achilles' Heel of Fraud Prevention," which provides guidance to audit committees to help them address the ever-present risk of fraud

resulting from management override of internal control. The document notes that the audit committee (or the board where there is no audit committee) plays a vital role in overseeing the actions of management. For many organizations, the audit committee is in the best position to prevent, deter, and detect fraud resulting from management override of controls. The document identifies specific actions an audit committee can take to address the risk of management override of internal controls. Auditors may find the document helpful as they assess the "participation of those charged with governance" element of the control environment.

Risk assessment by the entity

The design of internal control related to financial reporting should include management's identification, analysis, and management of risk factors that may prevent financial statements from being prepared in accordance with GAAP. When designing internal controls, management should consider "external and internal events and circumstances that may occur and adversely affect an entity's ability to initiate, authorize, record, process, and report financial data consistent with the assertions of management in the financial statements." Risk assessment is an ongoing process, and Exhibit AU 314-2 provides examples of factors affecting entity risks.

> **OBSERVATION:** In 2004, the Committee of Sponsoring Organizations of the Treadway Commission (COSO) issued a new enterprise risk management framework to assist boards of directors, management, and others within entities to effectively manage risks across the enterprise. The framework builds on the five elements of internal control to create eight elements of effective enterprise risk management. Auditors might benefit from understanding the key elements of enterprise risk management as they evaluate a client's risk assessment process.

> **PUBLIC COMPANY IMPLICATION:** COSO's Enterprise Risk Management — Integrated Framework is likely to be particularly useful to auditors of public companies who are assessing an entity's risk assessment process as part of auditing the effectiveness of internal control over financial reporting.

Information and communication systems

The auditor needs to obtain an understanding of the entity's financial reporting system. A financial reporting system generally consists of computer hardware, software, people, automated and manual procedures, and data used by the entity to initiate, authorize, record, process, and report its transactions and events and maintain accountability for assets, liabilities, and equity. Exhibit AU 314-3 provides a description of information systems' objectives.

The auditor also needs to understand how the entity communicates to individuals their roles and responsibilities related to the financial reporting process. Communication occurs in written form (e.g., manuals), orally, electronically, and through management actions.

Control activities

Control activities are those policies and procedures that help ensure that management's objectives and strategies are carried out. Within the domain of financial reporting controls, control activities should be designed to address risks of material misstatement to the financial statements. Examples of control activities are authorizations, segregation of duties, safeguarding of assets and records, and asset accountability (e.g., reconciliations). Control activities may be either automated or manual. Exhibit AU 314-4 provides other examples of control activities germane to internal control over financial reporting. The auditor typically does not obtain an understanding of the control activities related to every relevant assertion or each transaction class, account balance, and disclosure in the financial statements.

> **ENGAGEMENT STRATEGY:** The requirement that the auditor obtain an understanding of all five components of internal control does not suggest that this gathering of information is accomplished as five distinct tasks. The auditor might, for example, develop an understanding of some control activities as part of his or her consideration of the information and communication component of internal control.

Monitoring

Once internal controls are implemented, management must assess the controls (both from a design perspective and an operational perspective) on a timely basis and make modifications when appropriate. Monitoring of controls involves assessing the quality of internal control performance over time, and is accomplished through ongoing activities, separate evaluations, or both.

Ongoing monitoring should be part of the routine activities of effective internal control, and include supervisory and management activities. Separate evaluations are often performed by an internal audit function, which does not have to represent a formal internal audit department. In such instances, strengths and weaknesses of controls are identified and communicated to appropriate managerial personnel. In addition, external parties can have an important role in monitoring internal controls. For example, as part of its role, a regulatory agency might evaluate internal control or the client's customers might complain about billing errors or incorrect shipment of materials. All of these factors make up the monitoring component of internal control.

Auditor objectives related to internal control

The auditor's primary objective in understanding internal control is to understand whether and how a control prevents, or detects and corrects, material misstatements in relevant assertions related to classes of transactions, account balances, or disclosures. The primary objective is not necessarily to evaluate each of the five internal control components. Therefore, an auditor may define internal control using different terminology or a different framework as long as the internal control objectives underlying the five internal control components are met.

The auditor should obtain an understanding of internal control over financial reporting sufficient to understand the design of controls and whether the controls have been implemented. The auditor uses this knowledge to (1) identify the types of possible misstatements, (2) identify the factors that affect the risk of material misstatement, and (3) design further audit procedures (tests of the operating effectiveness of controls and substantive procedures).

> **PLANNING AID REMINDER:** AICPA Technical Practice Aid TIS 8200.05 clarifies that when the auditor believes an entity may not have effective internal control, he or she is required to obtain an understanding of internal control in every audit. This requirement applies even if the auditor intends to design a substantive audit approach and not rely on controls. Additionally, AICPA Technical Practice Aid TIS 8200.11 notes that the auditor cannot skip the evaluation and documentation of controls when he or she believes the controls over financial reporting are nonexistent or ineffective. The auditor is required to obtain a sufficient understanding of internal controls to assess their design and implementation. The purpose of obtaining such an understanding in every audit is to evaluate the design of controls to provide the auditor with information to assess the risk of material misstatements. When the auditor believes, based on his or her understanding of internal controls, that controls do

not exist to prevent or detect material misstatements in financial statements, he or she would plan and perform substantive procedures to respond to the assessed risks. The auditor needs to be satisfied that only performing substantive procedures provides sufficient appropriate evidence to support his or her opinion. Additionally, the auditor must evaluate identified control deficiencies to determine whether any are deemed to be significant deficiencies or material weaknesses for communication in writing to management and those charged with governance.

Limitations of internal control

The basic characteristics of internal control can provide reasonable, but not absolute, assurance that the entity's objectives will be achieved. No matter how well internal controls are designed, they do have inherent limitations. For example, one of the design principles of internal control is that duties and responsibilities of departments and individuals need to be properly segregated. If collusion exists, the effectiveness of this principle may be completely invalidated. Additionally, internal controls can be circumvented by management. Other factors, such as employee carelessness, misunderstanding of instructions, mistakes, and errors in judgment, have a similar impact on the effectiveness of internal control. Finally, a basic concept in the design of internal control is the expectation that controls must be cost-effective. That is, the benefits derived from an internal control procedure should exceed the cost of adopting the procedure. When designing internal control, an entity cannot measure the cost-benefit relation precisely, but a reasonable analysis combined with appropriate judgment and estimates is useful.

> **FRAUD POINTER:** One of the limitations of internal control is that management is in a unique position to commit fraud because it can override established controls. The risk of management override when the entity is run by an owner-manager depends heavily on the entity's control environment and on the owner-manager's attitude toward internal control. Since the risk of management override of internal control is present in virtually all audits, SAS-99 mandates that certain audit procedures be performed in every audit to respond to the ever-present risk of management override. Auditors must (1) examine journal entries and other adjustments, (2) review accounting estimates for bias, and (3) evaluate the business reason for significant unusual transactions.

Effect of Information Technology

In considering an entity's internal control, an auditor recognizes that information technology (IT) may affect any of the five components of internal control. IT processing can affect the fundamental manner by which transactions are initiated, authorized, recorded, processed, and reported. An entity's transactions can be initiated either manually or electronically through programmed procedures. Authorization involves transaction approval by the appropriate level of management. Certain authorizations can be pre-approved and integrated into automated procedures (e.g., the extension of trade credit). Recording involves identifying and capturing relevant information about transactions and events (e.g., amount, account, and period). Examples of processing procedures include edit and validation, calculation, valuation, summarization, and reconciliation. IT is particularly efficient in performing processing tasks. Reporting involves preparing both financial and other reports. Clients whose accounting systems use IT employ both automated controls and manual controls. Manual controls (1) may be independent of IT, (2) may use information generated by the IT system, (3) may be used to monitor IT functioning and automated controls, and (4) may be used to handle exceptions from normal transaction processing.

Although an auditor may be well versed in controls related to a manual system, such as written authorization for a transaction and appropriate segregation of duties and responsibilities, special attention must be paid to the advantages and disadvantages of a client's use of IT-based controls. The use of IT-based controls can benefit internal control because of the following IT system characteristics:

- Predefined business rules and complicated calculations can be consistently applied by IT to a large number of similar transactions

- Information can be processed accurately by IT and be available to internal users in a timely fashion

- A variety of analytical tools can be applied by IT to the processed information

- An entity's IT-based activities and its policies and procedures can be better monitored

- The risk that IT controls can be circumvented can be reduced

- Security controls for applications, databases, and operating systems can be implemented to enhance the effective segregation of duties

On the other hand, the use of IT controls introduces a variety of specific risks related to the internal control environment. Risks that are related to IT-based controls can arise through the following situations:

- A reliance on automated procedures that are incorrectly processing data or that are processing incorrect data

- Changing, destroying, or introducing new data into the system without proper authorization

- An unauthorized change of data in a master file

- An unauthorized change to a system or a program

- The failure to make necessary changes to a system or a program

- Inappropriate manual intervention (i.e., override of IT-based processing)

- The potential loss of data

The risks associated with IT-based transaction processing and IT-based controls vary depending on the nature and characteristics of the entity's information system. For example, effective segregation of duties is threatened when IT personnel or other users are given access privileges that exceed the needs of their job.

Although IT controls offer many advantages and are increasingly common in today's business environment, manual controls may be more appropriate where judgment and discretion are needed. For example, manual controls are particularly germane in the case of (1) transactions that are large, unusual, or nonrecurring, (2) transactions or events where defining or predicting misstatements is difficult, (3) rapidly changing circumstances where a unique or custom control response may be needed, and (4) monitoring the performance of automated controls. However, manual controls have a number of limitations, and therefore their use should generally be limited to the four circumstances just listed. Relative to IT controls, it is easier to bypass, override, or ignore manual controls. Also, manual controls are more prone to error or mistake because they are performed by people. The auditor cannot assume that manual controls have been applied on a consistent basis. As a result, the auditor should test a sample of transactions where the manual control is expected to operate to evaluate the operating effectiveness of any manual control that the auditor plans to rely on.

> **PLANNING AID REMINDER:** If the auditor decides to use an outside professional with specialized IT skills to evaluate and test IT systems and controls, the guidance in SAS-73 (AU 336) (Using the Work of a Specialist) should be followed.

Promulgated Procedures Checklist

In developing an understanding of the entity and its environment, including internal control, the auditor should perform the following types of procedures:

- Risk assessment procedures
- Understanding the entity and its environment
- Understanding internal control
- Assessing the risks of material misstatement
- Completing the required documentation

Analysis and Application of Procedures

Risk assessment procedures

Although much of the auditor's effort in identifying and assessing risks occurs in planning the audit, the auditor should continue to assess risk throughout the audit and, if necessary, modify his or her overall risk evaluation and the nature, timing, and extent of audit procedures to reflect any modification to the auditor's initial risk assessments.

> **PLANNING AID REMINDER:** In assessing the entity's risks, the auditor should also be mindful of the specific fraud-risk-assessment requirements contained in SAS-99. For example, SAS-99 requires the auditor to assess the risk of material misstatement due to fraud and to modify audit procedures in response to this risk. A heightened risk of material misstatement due to fraud might call for an overall response (e.g., more supervision, more experienced staff, greater skepticism); a response tailored to classes of transactions, account balances, or disclosures (e.g., modify the nature, timing, and extent of audit procedures to be performed); or both.

The auditor should (1) perform analytical procedures, (2) make inquiries of management and others within the entity, and (3) observe activities and inspect documents and records in performing risk assessment procedures. Although the auditor should perform all three of these risk assessment procedures, he or she is not required to perform all three of these procedures for every area of risk being assessed.

The auditor may perform other risk assessment procedures in addition to the three types of procedures that are required. For example, the auditor may make inquiries of individuals outside the entity (e.g., the entity's outside counsel, bankers, and valuation experts). The auditor also may examine information developed by outside sources (e.g., analyst reports, reports by credit rating agencies, trade journals, etc.).

> **ENGAGEMENT STRATEGY:** In performing risk assessment procedures the auditor may also gather evidence about the operating effectiveness of controls even though the risk assessment procedures were not specifically designed to accomplish this purpose. Also, due to efficiency concerns, the auditor may choose to perform tests of controls or substantive procedures at the same time that he or she performs risk assessment procedures.

Perform analytical procedures

SAS-56 (AU 329) requires the auditor to perform analytical procedures in planning the audit. These procedures are useful in obtaining an understanding of the entity and its environment and in identifying financial statement risk areas. Analytical procedures may also help the auditor identify unusual transactions and events. In performing analytical procedures, the auditor should develop his or her own independent expectation as to the recorded account balance or ratio. A difference between the auditor's expectation and the entity's recorded account balance (or a ratio computed using recorded account balances) may indicate a higher risk of material misstatement.

> **FRAUD POINTER:** Auditors sometimes perform analytical procedures at a highly aggregated level. For example, an auditor might compare the entity's recorded total revenue amount to his or her expectation of total revenue. Analytical procedures performed at such an aggregated level may not be effective in identifying risks of material misstatement. The auditor should consider performing analytical procedures on a more disaggregated basis (e.g., analyze revenue amounts by quarter or month, by operating unit, by product line, etc.).

Inquiries of management and others

Auditors direct many of their inquiries to management and to those responsible for the entity's financial reporting process. In addition, an auditor may want to extend his or her inquiries to other parties within the entity. These other parties can often provide a valuable (different) perspective that may be useful in identifying risks of material misstatement. In deciding on other parties to talk with and on what to ask, an auditor should focus on obtaining information that will help him or her identify risks of material misstatement. Other parties that may be uniquely helpful to the auditor, and the types of information they might provide, are as follows:

Internal Party	Type of Risk Information Provided
Those charged with governance	An understanding of the entity's control environment
Internal audit	Results of audits performed during the year, including control deficiencies that were identified and management's responses to these findings
Those involved with initiating, authorizing, processing, or recording complex or unusual transactions	An understanding of the business purpose of the transaction and an understanding of the accounting policy that was selected and how it was applied
In-house legal counsel	Pending or threatened litigation, compliance with laws or regulations, any known or suspected fraud, and an understanding of contract terms and provisions with financial reporting implications
Marketing, sales, or production personnel	Changes in marketing strategies, sales trends, production methods, or agreements with customers

Observation and inspection

Auditors typically observe procedures and inspect documents and records in assessing client risks. Examples of these activities include the following:

- Tour some of the entity's locations and plants
- Observe the operations of the entity, including selected control procedures
- Inspect documents, records, and control manuals
- Trace the processing of transactions from initiation through its inclusion in the financial statements
- Read reports prepared by management, internal audit, and those charged with governance

Other sources of information in assessing client risks

The auditor should consider information gathered (1) during the client acceptance and continuance process, (2) in performing other engagements for the client, and (3) during prior-year audits. The auditor performs a number of procedures to identify client risk before accepting or agreeing to continue to serve an existing client. These procedures can be useful to the auditor in identifying the risks of material financial statement misstatements. The auditor may have become aware of financial statement risks by performing other engagements for the client (e.g., tax services, review of interim financials, etc.).

Based on prior-year audits, the auditor has knowledge of the entity's business, organizational structure, controls, past misstatements, and management's efforts to correct past misstatements. This knowledge is useful in assessing risks in the current year's audit. Before relying on this information, the auditor should assess its continued relevance given any changes to the entity or its environment that may have occurred.

Required discussion among the audit team

The audit team should discuss the risks of material misstatement in the client's financial statements, whether caused by error or fraud. Key members of the audit team and the auditor with final responsibility for the engagement should participate in this discussion, and this discussion should occur at the same time as the audit team brainstorming session required by SAS-99. The auditor should use his or her judgment in determining when and where this meeting is to occur, and the nature and extent of the items to be discussed. Although at a minimum key members of the audit team are to participate in this discussion, it is not expected that all members of the team will have the same level of knowledge of audit-related matters. The auditor with final responsibility for the engagement should inform members of the audit team who were not present about the content of the discussion based on his or her judgment.

> **ENGAGEMENT STRATEGY:** A sole practitioner may be performing the audit. In this case, he or she meets the audit team discussion requirement by preparing a memo outlining the risks of material misstatement in the client's financial statements.

The objective of the required audit team discussion is to identify those aspects of the entity's financial statements that are susceptible to material misstatement that are being assigned to each audit team member. Each audit team member should obtain an understanding of how the procedures that he or she is to perform may affect other aspects of the audit, giving particular attention to the following:

- The susceptibility of the entity's financial statements to misstatement due to fraud

- Financial statement areas susceptible to management override of controls

- Client accounting procedures that are unusual

- Materiality at both the financial statement and account level

- Important control systems

> **FRAUD POINTER:** The importance of exercising professional skepticism should be emphasized during the audit team discussion. Audit team members should be reminded of the importance of being alert to information that may indicate the existence of a material misstatement whether due to error or fraud, and to rigorously follow up on any such information to determine whether the financial statements are in fact materially misstated.

Understanding the entity and its environment

The auditor obtains an understanding of the entity and its environment to help him or her in identifying risks of material misstatement in the financial statements and to plan the nature, timing, and extent of further audit procedures. The extent of the understanding to be obtained is a function of the auditor's professional judgment. A thorough understanding of the entity and its environment helps the auditor to

- Determine planning materiality

- Evaluate the accounting policies selected and financial statement disclosures

- Identify audit areas requiring greater effort (e.g., related-party transactions, complex or unusual transactions, etc.)

- Develop independent expectations for performing analytical procedures

- Design further audit procedures (i.e., tests of operating effectiveness of controls and substantive procedures)

- Evaluate the audit evidence gathered

OBSERVATION: The auditor's understanding of the entity and its environment, including its internal control, is not expected to equal the level of understanding possessed by management.

PUBLIC COMPANY IMPLICATION: The PCAOB has issued Staff Audit Practice Alert No. 3 (Audit Considerations in the Current Economic Environment), which states that the events in the financial markets and the economy may have implications for the valuation, impairment, or recoverability of assets and for the completeness and valuation of liabilities. The Staff Audit Practice Alert is designed to help auditors identify matters that may affect audit risk and require additional audit effort. The alert provides guidance on (1) overall audit considerations, (2) auditing fair value measurements, (3) auditing accounting estimates, (4) auditing the adequacy of disclosures, (5) the auditor's consideration of an entity's ability to continue as a going concern, and (6) additional audit considerations in other areas.

As it relates to overall audit considerations, the Staff Audit Practice Alert provides guidance on planning, fraud, internal controls, substantive procedures, and audit committee communications. For example, internal controls over the identification and review of assets for recoverability and impairment and the use of specialists may require additional audit attention. Staff Audit Practice Alert No. 3 emphasizes that Practice Alert No. 2 (Matters Related to Auditing Fair Value Measurements of Financial Instruments and the Use of Specialists) remains applicable in the current environment. Staff Audit Practice Alert No. 3 reminds auditors of the sensitivity of various accounting estimates and the approaches that auditors should consider in auditing estimates. The alert also reminds auditors that they should perform a retrospective review of significant accounting estimates from the prior year. Such a retrospective review may identify deficiencies in the client's estimation process, including possible management bias. With respect to disclosures, the alert reminds auditors of the client's disclosure obligations related to significant risks and uncertainties under SOP 94-6 (Disclosure of Certain Significant Risks and Uncertainties). The alert reminds auditors that the omission of a required disclosure should result in their issuing a qualified or adverse report. The alert emphasizes the requirements in SAS-59. In addition to the factors listed in SAS-59 that relate to management's plans to mitigate the conditions or events that give rise to a going-concern doubt, the auditor may also consider the client's participation in a program of federal assistance. Staff Audit Practice Alert No. 3 suggests that audit risk may be elevated in the following areas as a result of the current economic environment: (1) consolidation; (2) contingencies and guarantees;

(3) derivatives, especially credit derivatives; (4) debt obligations; (5) deferred tax assets; (6) goodwill, intangibles, and other long-lived assets; (7) inventory; (8) other-than-temporary impairment of investment securities; (9) pension and other postretirement benefits; (10) receivables; (11) restructuring; (12) revenue recognition; and (13) share-based payments.

In obtaining an understanding of the entity and its environment, the auditor typically considers

- Industry, regulatory, and other external factors
- Nature of the entity
- Objectives and strategies of the entity and the resulting business risks
- Financial performance of the entity

It is particularly important for the auditor to identify significant changes in any of the above factors from prior periods, which are often indicative of a heightened risk of material misstatement. The extent of the audit procedures needed to understand the entity and its environment are related to the particular circumstances of the engagement — for example, the size and complexity of the engagement and the auditor's previous experience serving the client.

Industry, regulatory, and other external factors

The auditor should understand the industry and regulatory factors that affect the client. These factors include industry conditions, regulations affecting the client, the legal and political environment, environmental requirements affecting the client, and other factors. Some industries pose unique risks of material misstatements (e.g., financial institutions, high technology companies), and the auditor should consider whether the engagement is staffed with individuals with an appropriate degree of industry expertise. Exhibit AU 314-5 provides examples of industry, regulatory, and other external factors.

Nature of the entity

The auditor should understand the nature of the entity, including an understanding of its operations, structure, ownership, governance, sources of funds (i.e., how the entity has been financed), uses of funds (i.e., how the entity has deployed the funds it has received). This understanding informs the auditor about the classes of transactions, account balances, and disclosures that are likely to appear in the entity's financial statements. For example, an entity with a complex structure (e.g., numerous subsidiaries, a number of which are located in foreign locations) may present issues related to preparing consolidated financial statements, the allocation of goodwill across different operating units, asset impairment testing, and foreign currency translation. Also, understanding the relationships between management, owners, and those charged with governance is useful in identifying related-party transactions. Exhibit AU 314-6 provides examples of entity-specific factors to consider and their link to relevant standards of financial reporting (GAAP).

Objectives and strategies of the entity and the resulting business risks

The auditor should obtain an understanding of the entity's objectives and strategies and the business risks that result from them. Objectives are management's overall plans for the entity. Strategies are management's detailed approach for accomplishing its objectives. Business risks are those factors that might prevent the entity from achieving its objectives or implementing its strategies, as well as the risk that the entity has designed flawed objectives or strategies. Entity objectives and strategies are dynamic, changing, and evolving over time.

> **OBSERVATION:** The entity's business risk includes the risk of material misstatement in the financial statements but is much broader.

The successful identification of client business risks helps the auditor assess the risks of material misstatement in the financial statements; however, the auditor is not expected to identify all business risks. Rather, the auditor focuses on business risks that have financial statement implications. Examples of client strategies and factors affecting the client's business and the related business risks include the following:

Client Strategy or Factor Affecting the Client's Business	Business Risk
Expansion into new markets	The client lacks the expertise and personnel needed to effectively compete in the new markets; failure to accurately forecast demand
Introduction of new products	Lack of customer acceptance; cost overruns in producing the product; lack of historical data on customer returns and warranty claims; increased liability exposure

Client Strategy or Factor Affecting the Client's Business	Business Risk
Issuance of new accounting pronouncements	The client implements the new pronouncement incorrectly or fails to apply it
Changes in industry-specific regulations	Loss of key licenses; increased compliance costs; increased liability exposure
Issuance of new equity or debt securities	Failure to complete the offering in the amount expected; additional restrictions imposed on the entity's operations
Introduction of a new information processing system	Existing systems and processes are not compatible; failure to effectively manage the conversion from the old system to the new system

Financial performance of the entity

The auditor should obtain an understanding of the entity's financial performance, including how management measures and reviews the entity's performance. The measurement of the entity's financial performance — whether via internal or external measures — creates performance pressure on management. This performance pressure can appropriately cause management to take steps to improve the entity's operating performance but, in some instances, performance pressure can lead to inappropriate managerial actions that result in material misstatements in the financial statements.

Management may use the following internally generated performance measures in evaluating the entity's financial performance:

• Key performance indicators and operating ratios

• Measures of employee performance

• Actual-to-budget comparisons

• Comparative financial statements

• Department, division, or subsidiary performance reports

• Comparison of the entity's performance with that of competitors

The information used by management in evaluating an entity's performance is typically generated by its internal information system. In some cases the auditor wants to rely on this same information in performing audit procedures. The auditor needs to either test the design and operating effectiveness of the controls associated with this information or test the accuracy of the internally generated information directly. Otherwise the auditor has no basis for relying on the accuracy of the internally generated information. Also, for the auditor to be able to detect material misstatements, he or she needs to consider whether financial performance measures used by management are precise enough.

The auditor's use of performance measures may help him or her identify risks of material misstatement. For example, client growth that significantly outpaces that of the rest of the industry may be a risk factor. Unexplained client growth may be of particular concern when coupled with very aggressive employee compensation plans (a high ratio of variable-based compensation to fixed compensation).

> **OBSERVATION:** Management's measurement, review, and investigation of (unexpected) financial performance are not part of the monitoring element of internal control; rather, such activity is a type of manual, detective control activity.

Understanding internal control

The auditor is required to obtain an understanding of internal control in every engagement. In obtaining the understanding of internal control necessary to assess the risks of material misstatement and to have an adequate basis to plan the nature, timing, and extent of audit procedures that are responsive to these risks, the auditor should

- Understand the entity's accounting policies

- Evaluate those elements of internal control over financial reporting

- Determine the extent of internal control understanding that is needed

- Perform required audit procedures related to the control environment, risk assessment by the entity, information and communication systems, control activities, and monitoring

> **PLANNING AID REMINDER:** AU Section 314 requires the auditor to obtain an understanding of internal control. Auditors may perform walk-throughs of transactions to confirm the auditor's understanding of internal control relevant to transaction processing. Walk-throughs are considered to be a good practice, and an auditor might (although is not required to) perform a walk-through of significant accounting cycles every year. AICPA Technical Practice Aid (TIS) 8200.12 notes that a walk-through performed every year might be an effective technique that the auditor performs to update his or her understanding of the control in order to allow him or her to rely on certain audit evidence obtained in prior years that is based on the continued performance of that control in the current fiscal period. In that instance, the walk-through may be an efficient and effective technique to obtain an understanding of the

> continued relevance of the audit evidence obtained in prior years. Furthermore, when performing a walk-through of controls, the auditor might identify improvements to the controls that the client should consider implementing. A by-product of obtaining an understanding of controls is that suggestions for improvements can be made to the client, which adds value to the audit process.

While the auditor is developing an understanding of internal control, he or she may encounter circumstances indicating that the financial statements cannot be audited. These circumstances include the following: (1) a lack of management integrity raises doubts about the overall reliability of internal control and (2) the accounting records are inadequate and do not provide sufficient appropriate audit evidence to base an opinion on. The auditor might be able to issue a qualified opinion or a disclaimer of opinion in these cases, but in many instances the more prudent course of action is to withdraw from the engagement.

> **PUBLIC COMPANY IMPLICATION:** SOX requires all public companies to issue an "internal control report" by management. Furthermore, SOX requires that auditors issue a separate opinion based on their evaluation of the effectiveness of internal control over financial reporting. Auditors of all entities, including auditors of public companies, must obtain an understanding of internal control over financial reporting. Auditors of public companies must also perform tests of controls in every audit that are sufficient to provide separate assurance about the design and operating effectiveness of internal control over financial reporting.

Understand the entity's accounting policies

The auditor should understand how the entity selects and applies accounting policies. Furthermore he or she should evaluate whether the accounting policies used are appropriate for the entity's business and are consistent with both GAAP and the accounting policies typically used in the entity's industry. The auditor should understand (1) the methods the entity uses to account for significant and unusual transactions, (2) the effect of significant accounting policies in controversial or emerging areas where authoritative guidance is lacking, and (3) the nature of any change in accounting policies. If the entity has changed an accounting policy, or its method of applying an existing policy the auditor should consider the reasons for the change and evaluate whether the reasons and the application of the new accounting policy are consistent with GAAP. The auditor also needs to consider new financial reporting standards and regulations that apply to the entity and when and how the entity will apply these new standards or regulations. The auditor needs to remember that the presentation of financial statements in accordance with GAAP requires adequate disclosure of material matters.

Evaluate elements of internal control over financial reporting

SAS-109 notes that management develops internal control related to a broad spectrum of objectives ranging from financial reporting matters to the efficient execution of operational activities. However, the auditor's consideration of internal controls in an audit of financial statements is specific. The auditor is concerned with internal control and its components as they relate to the reliability of financial reporting. More specifically, the auditor is concerned with relevant assertions over classes of transactions, account balances, and presentation and disclosure.

The auditor is not required to assess all controls that are designed to reduce the risk of a material misstatement in the financial statements. The determination of which controls to be assessed is a function of the auditor's professional judgment. However, in exercising his or her professional judgment, the auditor should consider the following:

- Materiality of the assertion related to the class of transaction, account balance, or disclosure that the control pertained to

- The entity's size (see Exhibit AU 314-7 for examples of the application of internal control concepts to small and midsize entities)

- The nature of the entity's business (e.g., organizational and ownership characteristics) and information systems

- The diversity and complexity of the entity's operations

- Legal and regulatory requirements

> **PLANNING AID REMINDER:** During the planning stage of the audit engagement, the auditor's responsibility to gain an understanding of internal control is limited to understanding the design of the system of controls and determining whether internal controls are in place; it does not include determining whether those controls are operating effectively. (Determining whether controls are operating effectively is part of further audit procedures, which are discussed later.)

The auditor is not primarily concerned with controls related to the efficiency and effectiveness of operations or that relate to compliance with laws and regulations; however, these controls may be relevant if they relate to the generation of information or data that the auditor will use in performing other audit procedures. For example, quality control data may be useful for testing the assertion in the financial statements that the allowance for returned goods is properly valued. Likewise, controls related to compliance with laws and regulations are likely to be relevant if noncompliance could have a material and direct effect on financial statement amounts and disclosures (e.g., compliance with income tax laws and regulations).

Determine the extent of internal control understanding needed

The auditor needs to test whether controls have been designed and implemented (i.e., the control exists and is being used). The focus is on determining whether the control is likely to prevent (or detect and correct) material misstatements in the financial statements. A control that is improperly designed may represent a material weakness, and the auditor will have to make this evaluation.

An auditor evaluates the design and implementation of controls by performing a combination of procedures — inquiry, observation, inspection of documents and reports, and tracing transactions through the accounting system. Reliance on inquiry alone is not sufficient. In most cases, obtaining an understanding of the design of a control is not sufficient to conclude that the control is operating effectively. However, if the control is automated, and the entity has strong general computer controls (particularly over computer security and program changes), the auditor's testing of the design and implementation of an automated control may provide evidence of the operating effectiveness of the control.

> **FRAUD POINTER:** SAS-99 reminds the auditor that as part of gaining an understanding of an entity's internal control, he or she should evaluate whether the internal controls that address identified risks of material misstatement due to fraud have been suitably designed and placed in operation. These controls may be specific controls designed to mitigate specific fraud risks, or they may be broad programs and controls designed to prevent, deter, and detect fraud.

Required audit procedures related to the control environment

The auditor should perform the following procedures related to the control environment:

- Evaluate the entity's antifraud programs and controls

- Understand the attitudes of those charged with governance toward internal control and financial reporting

- Evaluate the independence of those charged with governance

- Evaluate the financial expertise of those charged with governance

- Evaluate whether control environment elements have been implemented

- Determine the effect of the auditor's evaluation of the control environment on further audit procedures

> **PLANNING AID REMINDER:** The control environment may be less formal in smaller entities than larger entities. AICPA Technical Practice Aid TIS 8200.08 reminds auditors that auditing standards require the auditor to understand all components of internal control, including the control environment, sufficiently to evaluate the design of the controls and to determine whether they have been placed in operation. Even in smaller entities, auditors may rely on the control environment to determine the nature, timing, and extent of further audit procedures. Thus, auditors are required to understand the control environment even when it is less formal. When auditors rely on aspects of the control environment, they are required to test those controls. Because of the potential impact on audit strategy, auditors are encouraged to evaluate the control environment early in the audit process.

Evaluate the entity's antifraud programs and controls

Management and those charged with governance are responsible for preventing and detecting fraud and error. One means of preventing and detecting fraud is to have programs and controls that are designed to reduce the risk of fraud (e.g., a hotline process by which employees can anonymously raise concerns regarding the entity's accounting and financial reporting process). The auditor should evaluate these programs and controls. An entity with inadequate or nonexistent antifraud programs and controls may have a significant deficiency in internal control or a material weakness.

> **FRAUD POINTER:** The risk of fraud can be reduced through a combination of fraud prevention, deterrence and detection programs, and controls. The exhibit in the AICPA's SAS-99 provides guidance for boards of directors and management about specific antifraud programs and controls that can be designed and implemented to prevent, deter, and detect fraud. Many of these antifraud programs and controls relate

to the control environment component. Auditors might find the information contained in the SAS-99 exhibit useful in evaluating a client's control environment.

Understand the attitudes of those charged with governance toward internal control and financial reporting

The auditor should obtain an understanding of the attitudes, awareness, and actions of those charged with governance toward internal control and the reliability of financial reporting. In other words the auditor attempts to assess the entity's "tone at the top" — that is, how important are strong internal controls and reliable financial reporting to those ultimately responsible for the entity's operations and performance? The auditor should examine those controls that have been implemented because in some cases established controls are largely ignored in the day-to-day activities of the entity.

Evaluate the independence of those charged with governance

The auditor should consider the independence from management of those charged with governance (e.g., the board of directors, audit committee). For example, if management's compensation is highly variable and that variability is tied (directly or indirectly) to reported financial results (e.g., bonuses, stock options, grants, and other awards) there is a tension between management's desire to increase their compensation and the requirement to produce accurate financial statements. Those charged with governance are one of the few checks on management's behavior in this situation; however, the effectiveness of these individuals in acting as a check on management is often dependent on their independence from management.

Evaluate the financial expertise of those charged with governance

The auditor should evaluate whether individuals among those charged with governance have financial expertise (i.e., an understanding of the entity's business transactions, including how the transactions should be recorded under GAAP). Although nonpublic companies are not required to have financial experts among those charged with governance, the entity's control environment is likely to be stronger if individuals with financial expertise are involved in overseeing the affairs of the entity.

Evaluate whether control environment elements have been implemented

The auditor should evaluate whether control environment elements have been implemented. For example, an entity may claim to have a hotline process, but the auditor should determine whether the hotline has been established, whether employees know about it, and whether it is being used. Also, an entity may state that employees must sign an acknowledgement on a yearly basis that they are in compliance with the entity's code of conduct, but is there any evidence that these employee certifications are taking place and does the entity follow up with employees who fail to provide the certification? The auditor should obtain sufficient, appropriate audit evidence through inquiries, supplemented with observation and inspection, to determine whether control environment elements have been implemented.

Determine the effect of the auditor's evaluation of the control environment on further audit procedures

In making an overall evaluation of the control environment component, the auditor should consider the strengths and weaknesses in the various control environment elements. A strong control environment reduces the risk of material misstatement, particularly the risk of material misstatement due to fraud. Because the control environment is the foundation for all the other elements of internal control, this component has a pervasive effect on the risks of material misstatement and therefore the auditor's evaluation of the nature, timing, and extent of further audit procedures. However, the operation of the control environment is not specific enough to provide substantial audit comfort that material misstatements in individual classes of transactions, account balances, or disclosures will be prevented or detected.

Required audit procedures related to risk assessment by the entity

The auditor should perform the following procedures related to the entity's risk assessment process:

- Understand how the entity identifies, analyzes, and manages risks
- Understand the business risks identified by management

Understand how the entity identifies, analyzes, and manages risks

The auditor should acquire an understanding of how the entity identifies risks related to the possible occurrence of errors for particular transactions, accounts, and disclosures. The auditor should understand how management (1) identifies business risks that could result in a material misstatement to the financial statements, (2) assesses the likelihood of a misstatement and the potential amount of any misstatement, (3) designs controls responsive to an identified risk. For example, if the entity receives a significant amount of returned goods, the auditor should understand how management identifies returned goods and similar financial reporting risks and how risks of this nature are managed so that the financial statements are not materially misstated.

Understand the business risks identified by management

The auditor should inquire about business risks identified by management and consider whether they increase the likelihood of a material misstatement in the financial statements. Not all of the business risks identified by management necessarily have financial statement implications (i.e., not all business risks represent audit risks of a material misstatement).

> **ENGAGEMENT STRATEGY:** The auditor may identify business risks or risks of a material misstatement in the financial statements that the entity's risk assessment process failed to identify. Such a finding may necessitate the auditor's reevaluation of his or her initial evaluation of the entity's risk assessment process.

Required audit procedures related to the information and communication system

The auditor should perform the following procedures related to the entity's information and communication system:

- Obtain an overall understanding of the entity's information system

- Understand the automated and manual procedures used in preparing the financial statements

- Understand how the entity communicates financial reporting roles and responsibilities

Obtain an overall understanding of the entity's information system

The auditor should

- Understand the classes of transactions in the entity's operations that are significant to its financial statements, and how transactions originate within the entity's business processes

- Understand how those transactions are initiated, authorized, recorded, processed, and reported, whether through manual or automated procedures. The auditor should also understand how errors in processing transactions are resolved.

- Understand the accounting records, whether electronic or manual, other supporting information, and specific accounts in the financial statements involved in the processing and reporting of transactions

- Understand how the accounting system identifies and records events and conditions other than transactions that require recording in the financial statements

- Understand the financial reporting process for preparing financial statements, including significant accounting estimates and disclosures

Understand the automated and manual procedures used in preparing the financial statements

The auditor should understand how the entity's financial statements are prepared, including the required disclosures, sufficiently to identify where misstatements might occur. The auditor needs to understand how (1) transaction totals are entered into the general ledger; (2) journal entries in the general ledger are initiated, authorized, recorded, and processed; (3) recurring and nonrecurring adjustments are initiated and recorded (i.e., adjustments that are not captured in formal journal entries); (4) general ledger accounts are combined; (5) the trial balance is prepared; (6) consolidation processes are executed; and (7) the financial statements and related disclosures are prepared.

> **ENGAGEMENT STRATEGY:** When transaction totals are entered into the general ledger automatically and when financial statements are prepared using IT, there may be little in the way of an audit trail. In these situations, it is important that the auditor be able to rely on the client's IT-controls. Also, the auditor may want to consider having a computer audit specialist on the engagement and/or using computer-assisted audit techniques.

> **FRAUD POINTER:** To address the risk of management override of internal controls, SAS-99 requires the auditor in every audit to examine journal entries and other adjustments for evidence of possible misstatements. The required understanding of both automated and manual procedures related to the process for recording journal entries and adjustments helps the auditor in examining journal entries and other adjustments for evidence of possible misstatements. The auditor's understanding of the entity's financial reporting process can help in identifying the type, number, and monetary value of journal entries and other adjustments that are typically made in preparing the financial statements.

*Understand how the entity communicates financial reporting roles
and responsibilities*

The auditor should understand how the entity communicates financial reporting roles and responsibilities to affected employees and how it communicates matters related to financial reporting to affected parties. Communication often occurs through policy manuals and financial reporting manuals, which the auditor should consider examining.

Employees should understand how their roles and responsibilities relate to the work of others, and they should understand the entity's processes for reporting financial reporting exceptions to their supervisors and other levels of management within the entity. Finally, the auditor should understand communication channels and the nature of communications between management and those charged with governance (especially the audit committee, if one exists), and between the entity and relevant outside parties (e.g., regulators).

Required audit procedures related to control activities

The auditor should perform the following procedures related to the entity's control activities:

- Understand the entity's process for reconciling subsidiary ledger accounts to the general ledger for significant accounts

- Understand how a control activity reduces the risk of material misstatement

- Understand how the entity's use of IT affects control activities, including whether the entity has responded appropriately to IT-related risks

*Understand the entity's process for reconciling subsidiary ledger accounts
to the general ledger for significant accounts*

For significant accounts, the auditor should examine whether the entity reconciles subsidiary ledger accounts to the general ledger. The auditor will want to consider (1) how often the reconciliation is performed, (2) who performs and reviews the reconciliation, (3) who investigates and resolves reconciling items, including the timeliness and completion of this process, and (4) whether the reconciliations are current.

*Understand how a control activity reduces the risk of a
material misstatement*

In reviewing control activities, the auditor's primary consideration is understanding how a control activity alone or in combination with other control activities either prevents or detects and corrects material misstatements in the financial statements. The focus is on identifying and understanding control activities in those financial statement areas where a material misstatement is most likely to occur.

Understand how the entity's use of IT affects control activities,
including whether the entity has responded appropriately to IT-related risks

To understand how IT affects control activities, the auditor should obtain an understanding of both application controls and general computer controls. Some application controls are referred to as "user controls" because they involve the interaction between the IT system and an individual. The auditor should understand that the effectiveness of user controls; for example, the review and follow-up of items on a system-generated exception report depends on the accuracy of the underlying system-generated information.

The entity's control activities should be designed to respond to IT-related risks. For example, effective general computer controls reduce the risks associated with relying on application controls. The auditor's focus is on those controls that maintain the integrity and security of system-generated information (i.e., that prevent or detect unauthorized additions, modifications, or deletions) to this information.

Required audit procedures related to monitoring

The auditor should perform the following procedures related to the monitoring component of internal control:

- Understand the activities that the entity performs to monitor internal control

- Understand the sources of information used by management in performing monitoring activities

Understand the activities that the entity performs to monitor
internal control

The auditor should understand the specific ongoing activities and separate evaluations that the entity uses in monitoring controls. The auditor also should understand how the monitoring function leads to corrective actions when controls are not operating as intended, and to changes in controls when needed due to changes in conditions.

Understand the sources of information used by management in performing monitoring activities

Management often relies on internally generated information in performing monitoring activities. Management may assume that the information is accurate, but this assumption should not be made unless the controls over the generation of the information are designed and operating effectively or the accuracy of the information has been directly tested. The auditor should understand the information sources used by management in performing monitoring activities, and management's basis for relying on this information.

Assessing the risks of material misstatement

After identifying the risk of material misstatement by considering the entity and its environment, including its internal control, the auditor should assess the risk of material misstatement at the financial statement level and at the assertion level for classes of transactions, account balances, and disclosures. In addition, for each identified risk, the auditor should consider both the *significance* and the *likelihood* of the risk. Significance relates to the potential magnitude of any misstatement that might occur in the financial statements as a result of the risk. Likelihood refers to the probability that a misstatement might occur as a result of the risk. Risks that are more likely to result in a financial statement misstatement, or risk areas where any such misstatement are expected to be larger than other areas, should receive greater attention by the auditor. That is, the auditor should modify the nature, timing, and extent of further audit procedures in response to the risks identified.

The risk of material misstatement may relate directly to a particular assertion for classes of transactions, account balances, or disclosures or it may pertain to the financial statements taken as a whole. If the risk of material misstatement pertains to the overall financial statements, many assertions will be affected. Risks related to the financial statements taken as a whole often relate to a weak control environment. Weaknesses in the control environment often have a pervasive effect on the audit and may call for an overall response by the auditor (e.g., assign more experienced personnel to the engagement, devote more partner and manager time to supervising the engagement, increase the overall skepticism that the engagement is performed with).

The auditor's assessment of the risk of material misstatement may be based on the assumption that controls are operating effectively. The auditor must test the operating effectiveness of controls to support this assumption.

Auditor's evaluation of controls

In evaluating controls, the auditor primarily focuses on those controls that are likely to prevent or detect and correct material misstatements in relevant assertions. In some cases multiple controls must operate effectively to reduce the risk of material misstatement for a particular assertion to an appropriately low level. In other cases a single control activity may be sufficient to achieve a control objective for a relevant assertion. For example, the entity's controls related to completing the count of physical inventory are designed to address the existence and completeness assertions for the inventory account balance.

Some controls are directly related to an assertion, other controls are indirectly related to an assertion. For example, preventive controls, especially those that are control activities, tend to be directly related to an assertion. Detective controls (e.g., management reviews of business performance) are more likely to be indirectly related to an assertion. In general, more direct controls are more effective in reducing the risk of material misstatement.

> **OBSERVATION:** The auditor may identify deficiencies in internal control as part of the risk assessment process. If these deficiencies rise to the level of significant deficiencies or material weaknesses, they must be communicated in writing to those charged with governance.

Significant risks requiring special audit attention

As the auditor assesses risks, he or she should identify those risks requiring special audit consideration (i.e., significant risks). The identification of significant risks is a matter of the auditor's professional judgment, although at least some significant risks are likely to exist on all audit engagements. The auditor should evaluate the design and implementation of controls (including control activities) that are responsive to the significant risks identified.

In evaluating significant risks, the auditor should consider the inherent risk that a class of transactions, account balance, or disclosure would be materially misstated before considering the operation of the entity's internal control. In assessing inherent risk, the auditor should consider the nature of the risk, the likely magnitude of any misstatement as a result of the risk, and the likelihood of the risk occurring. Exhibit AU 314-8 presents factors that may indicate a heightened risk of material misstatement.

Issues requiring the auditor's attention are (1) the nature of the risk, (2) risks related to nonroutine transactions, (3) risks related to judgmental matters, and (4) management controls over nonroutine transactions and judgmental matters.

Nature of risk

A risk factor is more likely to represent a significant risk if the risk

- Relates to fraud
- Relates to recent changes in accounting, economic, or industry conditions
- Relates to significant transactions with related parties
- Relates to subjective accounting judgments and measurements
- Relates to highly complex transactions
- Relates to significant nonroutine transactions, especially if these transactions occur outside the normal course of business. A nonroutine transaction is unusual — because of either its size or its nature — and therefore occurs infrequently.

Risks related to nonroutine transactions

Nonroutine transactions are more likely to represent a significant risk when (1) management is involved in specifying the accounting treatment, especially operating management, (2) the transaction involves complex accounting principles or computations, (3) the transaction is with related parties, (4) the transaction is not subject to the entity's normal internal control processes, and (5) there is extensive manual involvement in collecting and processing the data underlying the transaction.

Risks related to judgmental matters

Financial statement amounts and disclosures whose determination involves significant judgment, especially accounting estimates, are more likely to represent a significant risk. In particular, estimates that are dependent on the occurrence or nonoccurrence of future events are more prone to misstatement. Additionally, judgments involving revenue recognition for certain types of transactions can be subject to differing interpretations, increasing the likelihood of a misstatement.

Management controls over nonroutine transactions and judgmental matters

Although nonroutine transactions and judgmental matters are less likely to be subject to routine controls, management still needs to develop controls over these issues. The auditor should consider *whether* and *how* management responds to nonroutine transactions and judgmental matters. For example, when assumptions are involved in determining recorded amounts, the assumptions should be reviewed by senior management or experts. In addition, management should have implemented formal processes for developing significant accounting estimates, including review by senior management and, in some instances, those charged with governance.

> **OBSERVATION:** If the entity does not have effective controls over significant risks and the auditor evaluates this deficiency as either a significant deficiency or a material weakness, he or she should communicate this matter to those charged with governance.

Risks where substantive procedures alone are not sufficient

The auditor may not be able to reduce detection risk to an acceptably low level using only substantive procedures when an entity processes significant classes of business transactions (e.g., revenues, purchases, cash receipts, and cash disbursements) entirely using automated processing. In these instances, audit evidence might exist only in electronic form and the reliability of such electronic evidence depends on the design and operating effectiveness of the controls over the generation of the evidence. There is also a heightened risk that information can be improperly initiated or altered if the initiation, authorization, recording, processing, or reporting of transactions occurs only in electronic form. Therefore, in certain situations where the entity relies exclusively on IT-based processing, the auditor will have to rely on the effectiveness of internal controls, at least to some extent, to reduce detection risk to an appropriately low level.

Assessment of risk throughout the engagement

The auditor assesses the risk of material misstatement in the planning stage of the audit based on his or her understanding of the entity and its environment, including internal control. As the auditor performs further audit procedures, his or her initial assessment may change. For example, the auditor might find that controls that he or she planned to rely on are not operating effectively. The auditor might also find errors in performing substantive tests that are larger and more frequent than he or she expected based on his or her initial risk assessment. In these situations, the auditor should revise his or her risk assessments and modify the nature, timing, and extent of audit procedures as appropriate.

Required documentation related to the auditor's understanding

The auditor should document his or her understanding of the entity and its environment, including its internal control. The documentation should include the following:

- The audit team's discussion of the susceptibility of the entity's financial statements to material misstatement, whether caused by error or fraud, including (1) when and how the discussion occurred, (2) who participated, (3) what was discussed, (4) changes to the audit plan as a result of the discussion.

- Key elements of the auditor's understanding of the entity and its environment, including (1) industry, regulatory, and other external factors; (2) nature of the entity; (3) entity objectives and strategies and the resulting business risks; and (4) entity financial performance. The auditor's documentation should also include his or her sources of information and the risk assessment procedures followed.

- Key elements of the auditor's understanding of the entity's internal control, including (1) control environment, (2) risk assessment by the entity, (3) information and communication systems, (4) control activities, and (5) monitoring. The auditor's documentation should also include his or her sources of information and the risk assessment procedures followed.

- The auditor's assessment of risk of material misstatement at the financial statement and assertion levels and the basis for the auditor's assessment.

- The identification of any significant risks requiring special audit consideration, and the specific controls that management has established in response to these risks.

The auditor uses his or her professional judgment in determining the nature and extent of documentation. The nature and extent of the auditor's documentation depends on (1) the nature, size, and complexity of the entity and its environment, including its internal control; (2) how much information is available from the entity; (3) the extent of the auditor's procedures; and (4) the auditor's specific audit methodology. Generally, the larger and more complex the entity and the greater the extent of the auditor's procedures, the more extensive the auditor's documentation. Methods of documentation include the preparation of flowcharts, internal control questionnaires, narrative descriptions, checklists, decision tables, and memoranda.

> **PLANNING AID REMINDER:** Although it is recommended that an entity document its controls so that the auditor can

efficiently understand them, assess the risk of material misstatement, and test them for operating effectiveness, controls do not have to be documented by the client for them to be tested, as emphasized in AICPA Technical Practice Aid (TIS) 8200.13. If the entity does not document a control and it is an important control, AU Section 314 requires the auditor to document the control as part of his or her risk assessment procedures to identify and assess the risks of material misstatements. TIS 8200.13 notes that it may not be practical to test the operating effectiveness of controls throughout the audit period without some level of documentation of the control by the client.

Practitioner's Aids

The exhibits on the following pages may be used as practitioner's aids.

EXHIBIT AU 314-1 — EXAMPLES OF ELEMENTS OF THE CONTROL ENVIRONMENT

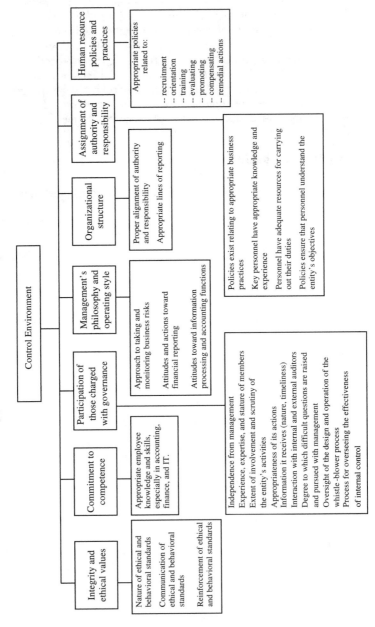

EXHIBIT AU 314-2—EXAMPLES OF FACTORS AFFECTING ENTITY RISKS

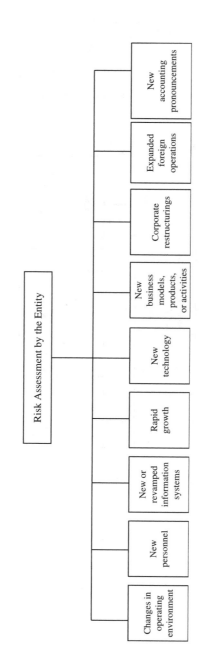

EXHIBIT AU 314-3—OBJECTIVES OF INFORMATION SYSTEMS

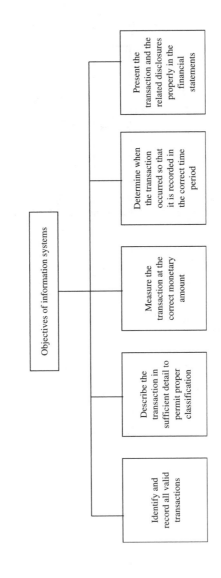

EXHIBIT AU 314-4—EXAMPLES OF CONTROL ACTIVITIES GERMANE TO INTERNAL CONTROL OVER FINANCIAL REPORTING

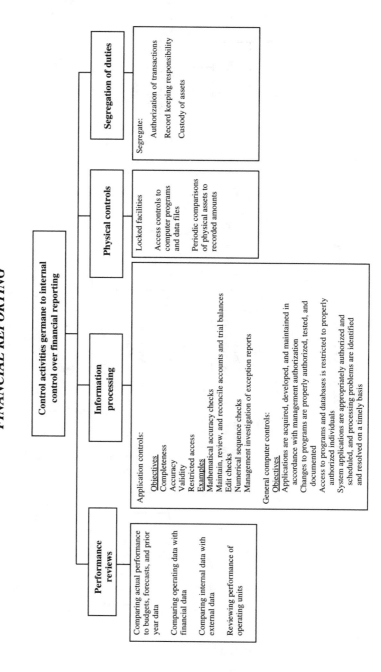

*EXHIBIT AU-314-5—EXAMPLES OF INDUSTRY, REGULATORY,
AND OTHER EXTERNAL FACTORS*

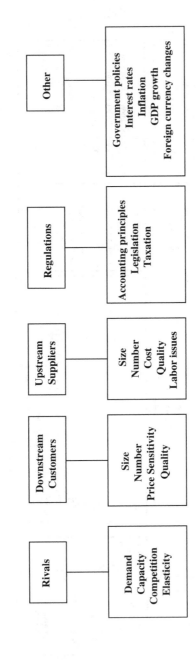

EXHIBIT AU 314-6—NATURE OF THE ENTITY AND RELEVANT STANDARDS OF FINANCIAL REPORTING

Nature of the Entity	Examples	Relevant Standards of Financial Reporting[a]
Business operations	Geographic segments	ASC 280 (FAS-131)
	Joint ventures	ASC 323 (APB-18)
	Key customers	ASC 280 (FAS-131)
	Long-term supply contracts	ASC 440, ASC 470 (FAS-47)
	Major customers	ASC 280 (FAS-131)
	Pension, other postretirement benefits, and other postemployment benefits	ASC 715 (FAS-87, FAS-88, FAS-106, FAS-132, FAS-158), ASC 712 (FAS-112), ASC 958 (FAS-158)
	Related-party transactions	ASC 850 (FAS-57)
	Research and development activities	ASC 730 (FAS-2), ASC 985 (FAS-86)
	Sources of revenue	ASC 605 (SAB-104)
	Stock option plans	ASC 718, ASC 505 (FAS-123R)
	Subsidiaries or divisions	ASC 810 (ARB-51, FAS-94), ASC 840 (FAS-94)
	Warranties	ASC 450 (FAS-5)
Investments	Acquisitions, mergers, and disposals	ASC 350 (FAS-142), ASC 805 (FAS-141)
	Investments in securities	ASC 320 (FAS-115), ASC 323 (APB-18)
	Derivatives	ASC 815 (FAS-133, FAS-138, FAS-155)
	Capital expenditures	ASC 835 (FAS-34)
Financing	Off-balance-sheet financing	ASC 460 (FIN-45)
	Leasing	ASC 840 (FAS-13, FAS-22, FAS-23, FAS-28, FAS-29, FAS-91, FAS-98)
Financial reporting	Revenue recognition	ASC 605 (FAS-48)
	Fair-value accounting	

Nature of the Entity	Examples	Relevant Standards of Financial Reporting[a]
		ASC 820 (FAS-157), ASC 825 (FAS-107, FAS-159)
	Foreign currency transactions and translation	ASC 830 (FAS-52)

[a]Not a complete list. Readers desiring a more complete list or a detailed discussion of these pronouncements might refer to CCH's *GAAP Guide, Volume I*, by Williams, Carcello, and Neal.

EXHIBIT AU 314-7 — APPLICATION OF INTERNAL CONTROL CONCEPTS TO SMALL AND MIDSIZED ENTITIES

Internal control is a critical element in helping the client to prepare financial statements that reflect generally accepted accounting principles (GAAP). However, SAS-109 recognizes that internal control will often be designed and implemented differently for a large company than for a small or even a midsized company. For example, the five components of internal control may not be clearly distinguishable in a smaller entity; rather, the owner-manager in a smaller entity may perform functions that cut across the five components of internal control. Although the internal control objectives underlying the internal control components should be met in every entity regardless of size, how the control objectives are achieved can vary from client to client. For example, the following features of a small or midsized entity's internal control may be as effective as the features adopted by a larger entity:

- *Control environment* Controls related to the control environment might not be as extensively documented in a formal manner but, rather, may be communicated orally and by management example to affected personnel. For example, although a formal code of conduct might not be reduced to written form, the essence of such a code might be part of the culture of the entity. In addition, smaller companies might not have independent or outside members among the group charged with governance of the entity. In fact, in some very small entities, it is often the owner-manager him- or herself who is charged with governance.

- *Risk assessment by entity* Risk assessment related to the preparation of financial statements might be less formal in a small company. However, all entities regardless of size, should have established financial reporting objectives. They may just be implicit rather than explicit in smaller entities. It is often the case that because of their involvement in the day-to-day operations of the entity, key managerial personnel (including owner-managers), are fully aware of the relationship between various operational activities and financial reporting objectives. The auditor should discuss with management how risks are identified and how they are managed.

- *Information and communication systems* Documentation of the information and communication system and related controls might not be as extensive or formal in a small company. The active involvement by a relatively small number of managerial personnel might not require formal accounting manuals or sophisticated accounting records. Also, communication in a smaller entity is often easier to achieve.

- *Control activities* Management involvement might substitute for certain types of control activities in smaller entities (e.g., management may specifically authorize the entity to enter into transactions through its direct involvement). Segregation of duties can often be a challenge in a smaller entity. However, reasonable segregation of duties can often be achieved even in an entity with only a few employees through (1) appropriate assignment of responsibilities to these few individuals, (2) management oversight of incompatible activities, or (3) utilization of embedded controls in packaged software programs.

- *Monitoring* Ongoing monitoring activities in smaller entities are likely to be informal. However, management's day-to-day involvement in operational activities may provide an adequate separate evaluation of the effectiveness of the design and operation of internal control.

The auditor's process of obtaining an understanding of the entity and its environment is also typically different for a small entity than for a midsize or large entity. For example, smaller entities often don't reduce their objectives and strategies to written form. These entities also may not have formal processes for managing business risks. The auditor obtains an understanding of the entity and its environment through discussions with management, and through his or her observation of how the business is run (i.e., what the implicit objectives and strategies are) and risks are managed.

Smaller entities may not have a formal process for measuring and reviewing their financial performance. Management of these entities may nonetheless rely on key indicators that they know from experience are accurate barometers of business performance. The auditor should discuss how management measures and reviews the entity's financial performance and document this discussion in the workpapers.

EXHIBIT AU 314-8 — FACTORS THAT MIGHT INDICATE A HEIGHTENED RISK OF MATERIAL MISSTATEMENT

Operating Factors

- The entity operates in a region that is economically unstable (e.g., highly inflationary economies, countries with political and economic instability).

- The entity has operations in volatile markets (e.g., derivatives trading).

- The entity is struggling to meet objectives it has set, especially if the entity has publicly committed to meeting the objectives.

- The entity has begun offering new products or services.

- The entity has changed its sales, distribution, and production methods.

- There has been turnover among key personnel, especially among senior executives and individuals with financial reporting oversight responsibilities.

- The entity is subject to complex regulations.

- The entity's industry is subject to rapid changes.

Financing Factors

- The entity's ability to access capital and credit is constrained.

- The entity has completed a large acquisition or divestiture during the period under audit.

- The entity enters into complex alliances, joint venture agreements, special-purpose entities, and other types of off-balance-sheet financing.

Financial Reporting Factors

- There are questions about the ability of the entity to continue as a going concern.

- The entity lacks an adequate number of personnel with accounting and financial reporting skills.

- The entity has implemented a new information system, or made significant modification to existing information systems.

- New accounting pronouncements apply to the entity.

- The entity has changed the accounting policies it uses or the methods used to apply an existing accounting policy.

- The entity's financial reports depend on complex measurements and/or highly subjective judgments (e.g., fair-value accounting).

- The entity enters into material related-party transactions.

- There are weaknesses in the entity's internal control over financial reporting.

- The entity has a history of past misstatements and/or significant material audit adjustments.

- Regulators or others are investigating or have alleged financial reporting improprieties.

- The entity faces pending litigation and other types of contingent liabilities.

- The entity has entered into large revenue transactions at the end of the period.

- The entity has entered into nonroutine and nonsystematic transactions that are material.

- The accounting for material transactions depends on management intent.

EXHIBIT 314-9 — RELATIONSHIP OF ASSESSED RISKS OF MATERIAL MISSTATEMENT AND AUDITOR'S RESPONSES

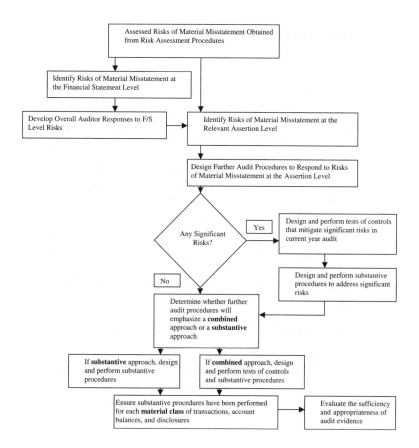

SECTION 315

COMMUNICATIONS BETWEEN PREDECESSOR AND SUCCESSOR AUDITORS

Authoritative Pronouncements

SAS-84—Communications Between Predecessor and Successor Auditors

SAS-93—Omnibus Statement on Auditing Standards—2000

> **IMPORTANT NOTICE FOR 2011:** The Auditing Standards Board (ASB) is in the process of redrafting all of the auditing sections in *Codification of Statements on Auditing Standards* to converge U.S. GAAS with the International Standards on Auditing issued by the International Auditing and Assurance Standards Board. As part of this process, the newly redrafted standards will follow certain clarity drafting conventions adopted by the ASB. These clarity drafting conventions include: (1) establishing objectives for each standard; (2) including a definitions section, if appropriate; and (3) separating requirements from application guidance and other material. The ASB is planning to have all redrafted standards become effective on the same date, which is for audits of financial statements for periods ending on or after December 15, 2012. It is possible that the effective date might be delayed beyond that date. The ASB's clarity and convergence project will have a significant effect on the auditing standards applicable to audits of nonpublic companies, and the 2012 *GAAS Guide* will be appropriately modified to reflect these changes once the effective date of the standards is certain.

Overview

A variety of auditing problems can arise when a client changes from one auditor to another auditor. SAS-84 defines a "predecessor auditor" as an auditor with either of the following characteristics.

* An auditor who has reported on the most recent audited financial statements or was engaged to perform but did not complete the engagement of any subsequent financial statements.

* An auditor who has resigned, has declined to stand for reappointment, or has been notified that his or her services have been or may be terminated.

When an auditor is replaced before an engagement is completed, the replaced auditor is considered a predecessor auditor. In this circumstance there are two predecessor auditors: the auditor who performed the audit and the auditor who was replaced during the engagement. A successor auditor is the auditor who is considering accepting an audit engagement but has not communicated with the predecessor auditor or who has not accepted the audit engagement.

> **PLANNING AID REMINDER:** The standards established by SAS-84 do not apply to an engagement if the most recently audited financial statements are dated more than two years prior to the earliest period being audited by the successor auditor.

Promulgated Procedures Checklist

The auditor should perform the following procedures when a predecessor/successor auditor relationship arises or when issues related to a new client arise:

- The successor auditor should communicate with the predecessor auditor.

- The predecessor auditor should cooperate with reasonable requests made by a successor auditor.

In addition, the change of auditors may create the need to perform the following audit procedures:

- Obtain audit evidence to support beginning account balances.

- Perform audit procedures related to a reaudit engagement.

- Perform audit procedures related to the discovery of misstatements in previously issued financial statements.

Analysis and Application of Procedures

The successor auditor should communicate with the predecessor auditor

A successor auditor is required to communicate with the predecessor auditor before accepting an engagement; however, an auditor may make a proposal on an engagement before the communication has been made. The responsibility to initiate the communication, which can be either oral or written, rests with the successor auditor.

Communications before an engagement is accepted

SAS-84 requires that an auditor attempt to communicate with the predecessor auditor before accepting an engagement. This communication is necessary to determine whether there are prior client-auditor problems that might cause the successor auditor to refuse the engagement.

> **ENGAGEMENT STRATEGY:** Rule 301 of the Code of Professional Conduct prohibits an auditor from disclosing confidential information except when the client agrees to the disclosure. To reconcile the requirements of SAS-84 with Rule 301, the successor auditor should ask the prospective client to grant permission to discuss the impending engagement with the predecessor auditor. The client should not place any restrictions on the exchange of information between the successor and predecessor auditors. If the successor auditor cannot obtain required information from the predecessor auditor because of client restrictions, the successor auditor should consider the reasons for the restrictions and take the circumstances into consideration when deciding whether to accept the client.

SAS-84 notes that inquiries directed by the successor auditor to the predecessor auditor should be "specific and reasonable" and should include matters such as the following:

- Information related to the integrity of management

- Disagreements between the predecessor auditor and the client concerning accounting principles, audit procedures, or other "similarly significant matters"

- Predecessor auditor's communications with the client audit committee (or others with equivalent authority and responsibility, such as the members of the board of directors or the trustees or an owner-manager) concerning fraud, illegal acts by the client, and matters related to the client's internal control

- The predecessor auditor's understanding of the reason for the change in auditors

> **FRAUD POINTER:** SAS-99 (Consideration of Fraud in a Financial Statement Audit) notes that the auditor should consider other information obtained in an audit, such as procedures related to the acceptance and continuance of clients, when assessing the risks of material misstatements due to fraud. Information obtained from the predecessor auditor about management's integrity, disagreements between management and the predecessor auditor, and the reasons for the change in auditors can provide relevant insights to the successor auditor, particularly when combined with other information gathered by the successor auditor to assess fraud risks.

Other communications

Communications between the predecessor auditor and the successor auditor, other than the type listed above, may be helpful in planning the audit engagement, but they do not have to be made before the successor auditor accepts the client. For example, the successor auditor should request access to the predecessor's audit documentation, and in turn the predecessor auditor should make him- or herself available to the successor auditor.

Although the predecessor auditor must use professional judgment in determining which audit documentation should be made available to the successor auditor, SAS-84 points out that generally the predecessor auditor should grant the successor access to audit files, such as those documenting (1) planning the engagement; (2) internal control; (3) audit results; and (4) matters related to continuing accounting and auditing significance, such as analyses of balances and contingencies.

The predecessor auditor should cooperate with reasonable requests made by a successor auditor

During the change of auditors, more than one auditor may make a proposal on the same engagement. Under this circumstance, the predecessor auditor is not expected to respond to inquiries made by the auditor until (1) the client has selected a successor auditor and (2) the successor auditor has accepted the engagement subject to the consideration of the responses received from the predecessor auditor. Once these conditions are satisfied, the predecessor auditor should respond promptly to inquiries made by the successor auditor. However, the predecessor auditor may decide not to respond to the inquiries or to respond in a limited way under unusual circumstances such as pending litigation or disciplinary proceedings.

> **OBSERVATION:** If the predecessor auditor is owed fees for prior work, the auditor does not need to comply with a request until those fees are paid.

> **PLANNING AID REMINDER:** When the most recent financial statements have been compiled or reviewed, a successor-predecessor auditor relationship does not exist; however, the auditor is not prohibited from following the guidance established by SAS-84.

Before allowing access to audit documentation, the predecessor auditor should reach an understanding with the successor auditor regarding the use of the audit documentation. This understanding may be documented in a letter prepared by the predecessor auditor and acknowledged by the successor. Exhibit AU 315-1 is an example of such a letter. In order to further document the process related to the review of the predecessor's audit documentation, the predecessor auditor may request a consent and acknowledgment letter from the client. Exhibit AU 315-2 is an example of such a letter.

Obtain audit evidence to support beginning account balances

Beginning balances and the consistency standard

In order to express an opinion on the financial statements for an initial engagement, the successor auditor must obtain sufficient appropriate audit evidence (1) relating to the opening balances of balance sheet accounts and (2) satisfying the consistency standard. Auditing standards state that audit evidence to support these audit objectives may be obtained from the following:

- Reading of the previous year's financial statements and the related predecessor auditor's report

- Inquiries made of the predecessor auditor

- Review of the predecessor's audit documentation

- Audit procedures applied to the current year's transactions that substantiate opening balances (for example, the review of subsequent cash collections that apply to the opening balance of accounts receivable)

- Audit procedures applied by the successor auditor to opening balances and transactions from the previous year

With respect to the client's opening balances and the investigation of the application of the consistency standard, the successor auditor's approach may be influenced by the review of the predecessor's audit documentation. However, ultimately the nature, timing, and extent of audit procedures used during the initial engagement will be based solely on the successor auditor's professional judgment.

> **OBSERVATION:** Although he or she is not required to do so by the standards established by SAS-84, an auditor may decide to make inquiries concerning the reputation of the predecessor auditor based on guidance established by SAS-1, AU 543 (Part of Audit Performed by Other Independent Auditors). However, even though the successor auditor may be influenced by the work performed by the predecessor auditor, the successor auditor's report on the current year's financial

statements should not refer to the work performed by the predecessor auditor.

Perform audit procedures related to a reaudit engagement

In some instances the successor auditor is requested to reaudit the financial statements that were previously audited by the predecessor auditor. A re-audit engagement creates a successor auditor – predecessor auditor relationship, and the communications described above must be followed — except that the successor auditor must explain to the predecessor auditor that the purpose of the request for information is the performance of a reaudit. The audit schedules that the successor auditor requests to review should include the predecessor auditor's documentation for the year under reaudit and for the previous year. However, information the successor auditor obtains through inquiries made of the predecessor auditor or through review of the predecessor auditor's documentation is not sufficient to enable the successor auditor to express an opinion on the previous year's financial statements.

The successor auditor must plan the reaudit in a manner that, based on the successor auditor's professional judgment, will satisfy generally accepted auditing standards (GAAS). If GAAS cannot be satisfied, the successor auditor should express a qualified opinion or disclaim an opinion on the previous year's financial statements based on the circumstances of the reaudit engagement. Evidence obtained by the successor auditor during the audit of the current year's financial statements, if appropriate, "may be considered in planning and performing the reaudit of the preceding period or periods and may provide audit evidence that is useful in performing the reaudit."

Of course, the successor auditor will be unable to observe inventory or perform other related procedures as described in SAS-1, AU 331, paragraphs 9 – 11. In determining the nature, timing, and extent of audit procedures related to inventory balances (beginning and ending) in the financial statements subject to reaudit, the successor auditor may take into consideration knowledge obtained from the review of the predecessor auditor's documentation and inquiries of the predecessor. However, SAS-84 requires that the successor auditor "observe or perform some physical counts of inventory at a date subsequent to the period of the reaudit, in connection with a current audit or otherwise, and apply appropriate tests of intervening transactions." The appropriate tests may include tests of transactions, review of records showing prior physical counts, and the use of analytical procedures.

SAS-84 draws the following conclusions with respect to the reaudit engagement:

- The successor cannot assume responsibility for the predecessor auditor's work or assume divided responsibility with the predecessor auditor in a manner described in SAS-1, AU 543 (Part of Audit Performed by Other Independent Auditors).

- The work of the predecessor auditor should not be considered the work by a specialist as described in SAS-73 (AU 336) (Using the Work of a Specialist).

- The work of the predecessor auditor should not be considered work by an internal auditor as described in SAS-65 (AU 322) (The Auditor's Consideration of the Internal Audit Function in an Audit of Financial Statements).

Perform audit procedures related to the discovery of misstatements in previously issued financial statements

During the audit or reaudit of the new client's financial statements, the successor auditor may discover information that suggests that the financial statements reported on by the predecessor auditor were misstated. Under this circumstance, the successor auditor should inform the client of the situation and request the client to inform the predecessor auditor of the matter. In addition, the successor auditor should communicate information to the predecessor auditor that will enable the predecessor auditor to evaluate the situation based on the guidance established by SAS-1, AU 561 (Subsequent Discovery of Facts Existing at the Date of the Auditor's Report). Also, report guidance established by AU 561 should be observed.

When the successor auditor discovers a possible misstatement, ideally the three parties meet and resolve the issue. However, if the client refuses to inform the predecessor auditor of the matter or if the successor is not satisfied with resolution of the matter, SAS-84 states that the successor auditor should consider, perhaps after consultation with legal counsel, whether it is appropriate to resign from the engagement.

Practitioner's Aids

Exhibit AU 315-1 is an example of a letter of understanding between the predecessor and successor auditors. This letter is reproduced, with minor modifications, from Appendix B of SAS-84.

EXHIBIT AU 315-1 — LETTER OF UNDERSTANDING FROM PREDECESSOR TO SUCCESSOR AUDITOR

We have previously audited, in accordance with generally accepted auditing standards, the December 31, 20X7, financial statements of Averroes Company. We rendered a report on those financial statements and have not performed any audit procedures subsequent to the audit report date. In connection with your audit of Averroes Company's 20X8 financial statements, you have requested access to our audit documentation prepared in connection with that audit. Averroes Company has authorized our firm to allow you to review the audit documentation.

Our audit, and the audit documentation prepared in connection therewith, of Averroes Company's financial statements was not planned or conducted in contemplation of your review. Therefore, items of possible interest to you may not have been specifically addressed. Our use of professional judgment and the assessment of audit risk and materiality for the purpose of our audit mean that matters may have existed that would have been assessed differently by you. We make no representation as to the sufficiency or appropriateness of the information in our audit documentation for your purposes.

We understand that the purpose of your review is to obtain information about Averroes Company and that our 20X7 audit results will assist you in planning your 20X8 audit of Averroes Company. For that purpose only, we will provide you access to our audit documentation that relate to that objective.

Upon request, we will provide copies of those audit schedules that provide factual information about Averroes Company. You agree to subject any such copies or information otherwise derived from our audit documentation to your normal policy for retention of audit documentation and protection of confidential client information. Furthermore, in the event of a third-party request for access to your audit documentation prepared in connection with your audits of Averroes Company, you agree to obtain our permission before voluntarily allowing any such access to our audit documentation or information otherwise derived from our audit documentation, and to obtain on our behalf any releases that you obtain from such third party. You agree to notify us promptly of any such third-party request and provide us with a copy of any subpoena, summons, or other court order for access to your audit documentation that include copies of our audit documentation or information otherwise derived therefrom.

Please confirm your agreement with the foregoing by signing and dating a copy of this letter and returning it to us.

Very truly yours,

[Predecessor Auditor]

By:

Accepted:
[*Successor Auditor*]
By:

Date:

SAS-84 notes that in order to further document the process related to the review of the predecessor's audit documentation, the predecessor auditor may request a consent and acknowledgment letter from the client. Exhibit AU 315-2 is an example of such a letter (reproduced from Appendix A of SAS-84).

EXHIBIT AU 315-2 — CLIENT CONSENT AND ACKNOWLEDGMENT LETTER

You have given your consent to allow [*name of successor CPA firm*], as successor independent auditors for Averroes Company, access to our audit documentation for our audit of the December 31, 20X7, financial statement of Averroes Company. You also have given your consent to us to respond fully to [*name of successor CPA firm*] inquiries. You understand and agree that the review of our audit documentation is undertaken solely for the purpose of obtaining an understanding of Averroes and certain information about our audit of the December 31, 20X8, financial statement of Averroes Company.

Please confirm your agreement with the foregoing by signing and dating a copy of this letter and returning it to us.

Attached is the form of the letter we will furnish [*name of successor CPA firm*] regarding the use of the workpapers.

Very truly yours,
[*Predecessor Auditor*]
By:

Accepted:
[*Averroes Company*]
By:

Date:

Prospective client The degree of planning of an audit engagement is greatly affected by whether an engagement is new or recurring. Exhibit AU 315-3 is a prospective client evaluation form that can be helpful in determining whether a client should be accepted. Once a client is accepted, the form can be used as an integral part of the planning of the accepted engagement.

EXHIBIT AU 315-3 — PROSPECTIVE CLIENT EVALUATION FORM

Use this form to document the evaluation of a prospective client who has requested audited financial statements. The memo format is only a guide. The auditor should exercise professional judgment to determine how the form should by modified by adding, deleting, or revising captions to the memo format.

The evaluation process does not imply that our firm is vouching for the integrity or reliability of the prospective client.

Name of Prospective Client: _____

Date of Financial Statements: _____

1. Describe how contact was established with the prospective client.

   _____
   _____
   _____

2. Provide a background of the principals that represent the client.

   _____
   _____
   _____

3. Describe the nature of the products and/or services provided by the prospective client.

   _____
   _____
   _____

4. Describe the services and dates of services provided by the predecessor CPA.

   _____
   _____
   _____

5. Explain the reason(s) why the prospective client has decided to seek the services of another CPA.

   _____
   _____
   _____

6. Summarize the explanation for the change of accountants as understood by the predecessor CPA. (If the predecessor CPA firm has not been contacted, provide the reason that contact was not made.)

   _____
   _____
   _____

7. Summarize the history of the prospective client and other CPA firms (other than the predecessor CPA firm) that have provided service for the past 10 years.

    _____

    _____

    _____

8. Explain why the client desires audited financial statements, and identify external parties who may rely on the statements.

    _____

    _____

    _____

9. Describe any litigation that the client and its principals have been involved in during the past 5 years.

    _____

    _____

    _____

10. Summarize information obtained from credit bureaus, etc., concerning the credit rating of the client and its principals.

    _____

    _____

    _____

11. Other information: _____

    _____

    _____

Prepared By: _____

Date: _____

Client Accepted (Yes or No): _____

Acceptance Date: _____

Signature of CPA: _____

_____

SECTION 316

CONSIDERATION OF FRAUD IN A FINANCIAL STATEMENT AUDIT

Authoritative Pronouncements

SAS-99 — Consideration of Fraud in a Financial Statement Audit
SAS-113 — Omnibus Statement on Auditing Standards — 2006

> **IMPORTANT NOTICE FOR 2011:** The Auditing Standards Board (ASB) is in the process of redrafting all of the auditing sections in *Codification of Statements on Auditing Standards* to converge U.S. GAAS with the International Standards on Auditing issued by the International Auditing and Assurance Standards Board. As part of this process, the newly redrafted standards will follow certain clarity drafting conventions adopted by the ASB. These clarity drafting conventions include: (1) establishing objectives for each standard; (2) including a definitions section, if appropriate; and (3) separating requirements from application guidance and other material. The ASB is planning to have all redrafted standards become effective on the same date, which is for audits of financial statements for periods ending on or after December 15, 2012. It is possible that the effective date might be delayed beyond that date. The ASB's clarity and convergence project will have a significant effect on the auditing standards applicable to audits of nonpublic companies, and the 2012 *GAAS Guide* will be appropriately modified to reflect these changes once the effective date of the standards is certain.

Overview

SAS-99 states that an auditor "has a responsibility to plan and perform the audit to obtain reasonable assurance about whether the financial statements are free of material misstatement, whether caused by fraud or error." SAS-99 defines fraud as "an intentional act that results in a material misstatement in financial statements that are the subject of an audit" and identifies two types of intentional misstatements, namely (1) misstatements arising from fraudulent financial reporting and (2) misstatements arising from misappropriations of assets.

> **PUBLIC COMPANY IMPLICATION:** In 2010 the PCAOB issued eight auditing standards (AS-8 through AS-15) related

to the auditor's assessment of and response to risk. The proposed standards bear many similarities to the eight risk-assessment standards adopted by the Auditing Standards Board in 2006. The PCAOB's standards emphasize the importance of considering fraud risk in a financial statement audit, and they require the auditor to integrate his or her assessment of fraud risk into his or her general risk-assessment procedures. In particular, a discussion of fraud risk is contained in AS-8, AS-9, AS-12, AS-13, and AS-14. AS-12 and AS-13 provide the most detailed discussion of the auditor's responsibility in assessing and responding to fraud risk. Although there are a number of differences between the PCAOB's and ASB's risk standards, the risk-assessment concepts contained in the PCAOB standards should be familiar to most auditors. As is currently the case, audit risk is the risk that the auditor will issue an inappropriate opinion on financial statements that are materially misstated. The auditor is to reduce audit risk to a low level through the application of audit procedures. As a result, the amount of audit effort devoted to particular accounts, classes of transactions, and disclosures should vary based on their respective risk.

Fraudulent financial reporting

The intentional misstatement of information (through either commission or omission) in financial statements is referred to as "fraudulent financial reporting." SAS-99 lists the following as examples of fraudulent financial reporting:

- Intentional misapplications of accounting principles relating to amounts, classification, manner of presentation, or disclosure [e.g., disclosing a loss contingency based on the standards established by FAS-5 (ASC 450) (Accounting for Contingencies) when, in fact, the contingency should be accrued].

- Manipulation, falsification, or alteration of the accounting records or supporting documents that financial statements are prepared from (e.g., the inclusion of false amounts in the accounts receivable subsidiary ledger).

- Misrepresentation in, or intentional omission from, the financial statements of events, transactions, or other significant information [e.g., not capitalizing leases that are in-substance purchases as defined by FAS-13 (ASC 840)].

IMPORTANT NOTICE FOR 2011: In 2007 the U.S. Department of the Treasury, at the behest of Treasury Secretary Henry Paulson, created the Advisory Committee on the Auditing Profession. The Advisory Committee, co-chaired by Arthur Levitt, a former SEC chairman, and Donald Nicolaisen, a former SEC chief accountant was created to examine the sustainability of a strong and viable auditing profession, and its recommendations have the potential to affect auditing practice. The Advisory Committee has made three recommendations that involve fraudulent financial reporting: (1) that the SEC and PCAOB clarify in the auditor's report the auditor's responsibility for detecting fraud, (2) that parties with an interest in fraud (e.g., academics, auditors, investors, public companies, regulators, and users) develop best practices with respect to fraud prevention and detection, (3) that a center (under the auspices of the PCAOB) be created for auditing firms and others to share experiences, practices, data, and commission research regarding fraud prevention and detection. The PCAOB has decided to establish a National Fraud Resource Center in accordance with the recommendations of the Treasury Advisory Committee.

Misappropriation of assets

The theft of assets that results in the misstatement of financial statements is referred to as "misappropriation of assets" (theft or defalcation). Misappropriation can result from a variety of deliberate actions, such as the unauthorized removal of inventory and the payment for assets that have never been received by the client. The auditor is required to plan and perform the audit to detect material misstatements due to misappropriation of assets.

OBSERVATION: In 2010 the Committee of Sponsoring Organizations of the Treadway Commission (COSO) issued a study titled "Fraudulent Financial Reporting 1998 – 2007: An Analysis of U.S. Public Companies" that examined about 350 cases of SEC enforcement actions against public companies alleging financial statement fraud. Of those cases, the majority involved fraudulent financial reporting. Only 14% of the cases involved misappropriations of assets. However, auditors of nonpublic entities might conclude that the risk of material misstatements due to misappropriations of assets is likely to be higher in nonpublic companies than in public companies.

Exercise Professional Skepticism During the Engagement

An important element in identifying fraudulent financial statements is the mind-set the auditor brings to an engagement. That mind-set should include an appropriate level of professional skepticism, which SAS-99 defines as "an attitude that includes a questioning mind and a critical assessment of audit evidence." An auditor should guard against becoming complacent in the collection and evaluation of audit evidence even when past experience with the client has provided no hint of dishonesty or deception on the part of management. SAS-99 states that "the auditor should not be satisfied with less-than-persuasive evidence because of a belief that management is honest." Although fraud is not a purely random event, the auditor should always consider that fraud could occur in any audit engagement no matter what the circumstances.

> **PLANNING AID REMINDER:** Common characteristics of litigation related to fraudulent financial statements include (1) accepting management's representations without obtaining corroborative evidence, (2) allowing management to influence the scope of audit procedures, and (3) ignoring conditions that suggest that there is an unreasonable degree of risk related to the engagement.

Promulgated Procedures Checklist

The auditor should perform the following procedures in considering the possibility that fraud related to financial statements exists in an audit engagement:

1. Discuss the potential for material misstatement of the financial statements due to fraud.

2. Obtain information needed to identify the risks of material misstatement due to fraud.

3. Identify risks that may result in a material misstatement due to fraud.

4. Perform risk assessment in the context of related programs and controls.

5. Respond to the results of the assessment.

6. Evaluate audit evidence.

7. Communicate possible fraud to management, the audit committee, and others.

8. Document the consideration of fraud.

Analysis and Application of Procedures

Discuss the potential for material misstatement of the financial statements due to fraud

SAS-99 requires the audit team to discuss the potential for material misstatement of the financial statements because of fraud. That does not necessarily mean that every member of the audit team should be part of the discussion. The size, structure, and complexity of the client are factors that should be considered in determining which members should actively participate in the discussion.

The scope of the discussion among audit members should include the following:

- Brainstorming session(s) among audit members

- Maintenance of professional skepticism throughout the engagement

> **ENGAGEMENT STRATEGY:** The discussion or process may be performed prior to the execution of the other procedures listed in SAS-99 (and discussed in the remainder of this Section) or as part of those procedures. In practice, the discussion for the potential for material misstatement of the financial statements due to fraud will generally be fluid and take a course dictated to some degree by the developments during the engagement. It is not particularly important when this procedure is performed but rather it is the professional attitude maintained by the auditor with respect to the procedure that is important. If the procedure is merely part of a checklist along with other audit procedures, it is unlikely that an effective audit will be performed. On the other hand, if the auditor believes that fraud could arise in any engagement and he or she remains sensitive to this possibility throughout the engagement, the chance of identifying material fraudulent financial statements will be enhanced.

Brainstorming sessions among audit team members

SAS-99 recognizes that the discovery of fraud in an engagement is more of an art than a science and therefore members of the audit team need to exchange ideas about the possibility of client fraud as an unstructured and free-flowing exchange of ideas. SAS-99 attempts to provide context for this discussion, noting that the discussion should take into consideration known external and internal factors, which might include the following:

- Circumstances that might increase either the incentive or pressure for management or others to commit fraud

- Circumstances that might provide the opportunity to commit fraud (including the risk of management overriding controls)

- Existence of a client culture that might encourage management to rationalize the commission of fraud

> **FRAUD POINTER:** If conducted with the appropriate mind-set, the brainstorming among audit team members about how and where they believe material misstatements due to fraud might occur and how management could perpetrate and conceal fraud can provide important insights to all audit team members about the presence of fraud risks. By setting aside prior beliefs about management's integrity, the brainstorming session can be an effective tool in reminding audit team members about the importance of maintaining an appropriate questioning mind-set that recognizes that fraud is possible in any engagement. Ordinarily the brainstorming discussion should involve all key members of the audit team. The brainstorming session is meant to be a dialogue of information exchanged between all audit team members. It is not intended to be a one-way communication from the audit partner or manager to all other audit team members. Even though a sole practitioner has no team members, he or she should document his or her thoughts on these matters.

Maintenance of professional skepticism throughout the engagement

During the exchange among audit members, there should be an emphasis on the need to maintain a questioning mind-set and to critically evaluate audit evidence gathered throughout the engagement. That is, the audit approach should be driven by the need to be analytically critical of audit evidence obtained rather than the need to satisfy the audit budget, which can encourage even the best auditors to rationalize away inconsistencies, inaccuracies, and incomplete evidence.

Obtain information needed to identify the risks of material misstatement due to fraud

The second standard of fieldwork requires the auditor to obtain an understanding of the entity and its environment, including internal controls, to assess the risk of material misstatements in the financial statements, whether due to error or fraud, and to design the nature, timing, and extent of further audit procedures. SAS-109 requires the auditor to identify and assess the risk of material misstatement at the financial statement level and at the relevant assertion level related to classes of transactions, account balances, and disclosures. To assess the risk of material misstatement due to fraud, SAS-99 requires, as part of an auditor's development of an understanding of the client's business and industry, that the following procedures be performed as the basis for identifying risks of material misstatement due to fraud:

- Make inquiries of appropriate personnel in order to identify their views on the risks of fraud and how those risks have been addressed.

- Consider unusual or unexpected relationships that have been identified during the performance of analytical procedures as part of the planning of the engagement.

- Consider whether fraud risk factors exist.

- Consider whether other information provides insight into the possible existence of fraud risk factors.

> **FRAUD POINTER:** SAS-99 expands the set of information to be gathered by the auditor to assess fraud risks beyond that previously required by SAS-82. Prior to SAS-99, auditors frequently completed fraud risk factor checklists as their sole source of information to assess fraud risks. Although auditors continue to assess fraud risk factors under SAS-99, they combine that information with information obtained through inquiries of others within the entity, from the performance of planning phase analytical procedures, and through the performance of other procedures. More complete sets of information from multiple sources are expected to increase the auditor's ability to identify circumstances where fraud risk is heightened.

Information gathered through inquiries

Make inquiries of appropriate personnel in order to identify their views on the risks of fraud and how those risks have been addressed. The auditor's quizzing of management and other appropriate personnel should encompass the following:

- Awareness of the existence of any fraud or suspected fraud including allegations of fraud from parties such as former employees, suppliers, or regulators

- Understanding of possible risk of fraud within the client, including any identification of the risk with respect to specific accounts or transactions

- Existence of programs and controls related to the control environment, risk assessment, control activities, information and communication, and monitoring that are designed to mitigate specific fraud risks

- Existence of controls related to operating units in multiple locations

- Identification of operating units in multiple locations that exhibit a higher degree of possible fraud risk

- How, if at all, management's view on business practices and ethical behavior are communicated to employees

- Whether management has communicated to the audit committee (or others with equivalent responsibility) how its internal control has been structured to prevent, deter, or detect material misstatements due to fraud

> **ENGAGEMENT STRATEGY:** SAS-85 requires that the client make certain written representations concerning fraud that relate to management's knowledge of fraud or suspected fraud affecting the entity that involve management, employees who have significant roles in internal control, or others where fraud could materially misstate financial statements. The representations also relate to management's knowledge of fraud or suspected fraud received from communications by others, such as employees, former employees, analysts, regulators, and short sellers, among others. As auditors make the required SAS-99 inquiries, an effective engagement strategy is to consider making specific inquiries of the items to be explicitly addressed in the management representation letter. The auditor might find it helpful to state at the time of inquiry that he or she will be requesting written representations of management's responses at the end of fieldwork. That might lead to less confusion at the end of fieldwork, because the representation letter is signed by management.

In addition to making the inquires listed above, the auditor should also make inquiries of the audit committee (or at least its chair) that include (1) the committee's views concerning the occurrence of fraud, (2) whether the committee is aware of fraud or suspected fraud, and (3) the committee's oversight role in the assessment of fraud risk and prevention (if the committee performs such an oversight activity).

> **FRAUD POINTER:** In January 2005, the AICPA's Antifraud Programs and Controls Task Force issued a document entitled "Management Override of Internal Controls: The Achilles' Heel of Fraud Prevention," which provides guidance to audit committees to help them address the ever-present fraud risk resulting from management override of internal control. The document notes that the audit committee, or the board when there is no audit committee, plays a vital role in overseeing the actions of management. For many organizations,

> the audit committee is in the best position to most likely prevent, deter, and detect fraud resulting from management override of controls. The document identifies specific actions an audit committee can take to address the risk of management override of internal controls. Auditors may find the document helpful in their discussions with audit committees about how the audit committee is addressing this ever-present risk of fraud.

For clients that have an internal audit function, the auditor should make inquiries about (1) views concerning the occurrence of fraud, (2) whether internal audits have been conducted during the year to identify fraud and whether management has appropriately responded to audit findings, and (3) whether internal audit is aware of fraud or suspected fraud.

Often fraud is revealed by others outside the financial reporting process. For this reason, "the auditor should use professional judgment to determine those others within the entity to whom inquiries should be directed and the extent of such inquiries." For example, those others may include the following:

- Nonmanagerial personnel that the auditor has spoken with in conducting other phases of the engagement

- Operating personnel not involved in the financial reporting process

- Nonmanagerial personnel responsible for initiating, recording, or processing complex or unusual transactions

- In-house legal counsel

> **FRAUD POINTER:** Forensic experts note that the use of inquiry can be an effective tool in fraud investigation. People who might be reluctant to voluntarily share information about actual or possible fraud are often more likely to reveal that information if directly asked. As a result, auditors should take seriously the inquiries they make of those within an entity — the information obtained could be invaluable.

Information gathered through analytical procedures

Professional standards (AU 329) require the auditor to perform analytical procedures as part of the planning of the engagement in order to identify unusual circumstances that have engagement implications. Auditors should consider unusual or unexpected relationships that have been identified during the performance of planning analytical procedures to determine whether that information, when combined with other information obtained by the auditor, indicates a higher risk of material misstatements due to fraud. SAS-99 specifically requires that the auditor perform analytical procedures related to revenue accounts in order to identify circumstances that might indicate fraudulent financial reporting. Although the performance of analytical procedures can help to identify risks related to fraudulent financial reporting, the auditor should be aware that those procedures are generally performed on an aggregate basis and therefore provide only a broad insight into the risk of fraud. As a result, the information obtained should be evaluated in light of other information gathered by the auditor.

Information gathered through considering fraud risk factors

Consider whether fraud risk factors exist — which are often present when fraud exists. SAS-99 refers to these as "fraud risk factors" and describes them as "events or conditions that indicate incentives/pressures to perpetrate fraud, opportunities to carry out the fraud, or attitudes/rationalizations to justify a fraudulent action." For example, a fraud risk factor exists if key management personnel's compensation is significantly dependent on operating results. The circumstance does not mean that fraud exits but rather that the likelihood of fraud is influenced by the circumstance and as the number of fraud risk factors increase the audit approach must reflect that environment.

> **FRAUD POINTER:** Three conditions are present when fraud exists: (1) an incentive or pressure that motivates management or others to engage in fraud; (2) an opportunity for the individual to carry out the fraud; (3) the perpetrator has an attitude or set of ethical beliefs that allow him or her to justify committing an unethical or dishonest act. SAS-99 organizes the examples of fraud risk factors along these three conditions of fraud. When auditors identify fraud risk factors across the three conditions, fraud risk is likely to be high.

Information gathered through other procedures

Other information obtained through the performance of other procedures might provide insight into the possible existence of fraud risk factors. Specific information about risks of material misstatement due to fraud should be combined with other information, such as the following, that has come to the auditor's attention:

• Discussions among engagement personnel (as discussed earlier)

• Information considered when the engagement was accepted (if a new engagement) or continued

- Results from the review of interim financial statements
- Consideration of inherent risk

Identify risks that might result in a material misstatement due to fraud

Based on the information gathered, the auditor should consider that information in the context of the three conditions of fraud to identify risks that a material misstatement due to fraud might exist. This evaluation should be made in the context of three conditions, namely (1) management or other employees have incentives or are under pressures that provide reasons to commit fraud, (2) opportunities exist to commit fraud (for example, management can override controls), and (3) individuals are able to rationalize fraudulent acts or they possess attitudes of dishonesty. The number of conditions that are present and the degree to which each condition exists increases the likelihood that fraud might be committed.

> **FRAUD POINTER:** SAS-99 points out that the absence of one or all three of the conditions listed above does not suggest that the auditor should conclude that the possibility of fraudulent acts is nonexistent or very low. In fact, it is often difficult for an auditor to observe management's attitude or ability to rationalize a fraudulent act, because it involves management's state of mind.

In addition to establishing a broad assessment of risk, the auditor should consider the risk factors as they relate to the financial statements taken as a whole and to specific account balances and classes of transactions. If the risk factors are more specific than broad, the auditor can design the nature, timing, and extent of audit procedures to test for possible fraud occurrence. For example, if the three conditions listed above exist and can be related to investments in derivatives, the auditor would design his or her audit procedures to corroborate the assertions related to those investments.

> **ENGAGEMENT STRATEGY:** The Committee of Sponsoring Organizations of the Treadway Commission (COSO) issued a study in 2010 ("Fraudulent Financial Reporting: 1998–2007, An Analysis of U.S. Public Companies") that found that 61% of the fraudulent financial reporting enforcement actions by the SEC involved revenue recognition. SAS-99 states that "the auditor should ordinarily presume that there is a risk of material misstatement due to fraud relating to revenue recognition."

> **PLANNING AID REMINDER:** Even when the auditor has not identified specific risks related to fraud, SAS-99 notes that there is always the possibility of management's override of controls. For

this reason, this broad risk should be addressed by the auditor separate and apart from risks that are more specific.

Perform risk assessment in the context of related programs and controls

Once risks of material misstatement due to fraud have been identified, the auditor should assess the risk of fraud after taking into consideration the client's strategies for addressing such risks. Thus, as part of the development of an understanding of the client's business and environment, including its internal control, as described in SAS-109 (AU 314), the auditor should determine whether the client's controls and programs related to identification of risks of fraud have been appropriately designed and placed in operation. These programs and controls may be designed for broad objectives (for example, to encourage ethical behavior) or more narrow objectives (for example, those related to specific account balances or classes of transactions).

Respond to the results of the assessment

After the completion of the procedures described so far, the auditor is in a position to determine how to respond to identified risks of material misstatements due to fraud through the performance of audit procedures. SAS-99 states that the auditor may respond by modifying the

1. Overall approach to the audit

2. Nature, timing, and extent of procedures that are affected by specific risks

3. Procedures related to possible management override of controls

> **ENGAGEMENT STRATEGY:** In some instances, the risks related to fraudulent financial statements are so great that the prudent course of action is withdrawal from the engagement.

Overall audit approach is affected by identified risks

SAS-99 states that the auditor's assessment of identified risks of material misstatement due to fraud can have a broad effect on the audit approach in the following three ways:

1. *Assignment of personnel and supervision:* The level of assessment of the risks of material misstatement due to fraud should be matched with the capabilities of those who participate in the engagement. For example, in some instances it is appropriate for the auditor to assign personnel with special skills, such as information technology or even forensic

experience, and in other instances it is appropriate that in general more experienced auditors participate in the engagement. The intensity of the supervision of the engagement should reflect the assessed level of risk.

2. *Accounting principles:* The auditor's concern with the appropriateness and quality of accounting principles selected and applied (especially for subjective and complex applications) should increase as the level of assessed risks increases. For example, if accounting principles appear to be selected and applied in a manner that consistently has the same overall effect on the financial statements (e.g., an increase in earnings per share) the auditor should be more critical in its evaluation of the client's selection of its accounting principles and policies that might result in a material misstatement of the financial statements. SAS-99 notes that the guidance established by SAS-114 (AU 380) (The Auditor's Communication with Those Charged with Governance) provides insights into developing judgments about the quality of accounting principles and that "the auditor should consider whether their collective application indicates a bias that may create such a material misstatement of the financial statements."

3. *Predictability of audit procedures:* As the assessment of the risks of material misstatement due to fraud increases, the auditor should likewise increase the unpredictability of the audit approach. This strategy may range from changing the timing of audit procedures to varying the locations the procedures are employed at.

The nature, timing, and extent of procedures are affected by identified risks

The specific nature (i.e., use procedures that generate more reliable evidence), timing (i.e., perform procedures at or near year-end), and extent (i.e., the size of the audit sample) of audit procedures (generally for both substantive tests and tests of operating effectiveness of programs and controls) are affected by the level of risks of material misstatement due to fraud.

> **ENGAGEMENT STRATEGY:** SAS-99 points out that because management can override controls, it is unlikely that audit risk can be reduced to an appropriately low level by performing only tests of controls. As a result, substantive testing is a required part of the engagement strategy. The possibility of management override of controls is discussed in the next section.

Procedures related to possible management override of controls are affected

SAS-99 recognizes that management is in a unique position to engage in fraud by bypassing existing controls. Therefore, an auditor must always consider the risk of management override of controls. In this regard, the auditor should perform the following procedures to address the risk of management override of controls:

1. Review journal entries and other adjustments

2. Consider accounting estimates for biases

3. Analyze the business basis for significant unusual transactions

Review journal entries and other adjustments: A client prepares a number of journal entries and adjustments during an accounting period. Often, fraud is perpetrated by management who records inappropriate or unauthorized journal entries or adjustments. To assess the appropriateness of those entries and adjustments, the auditor should do the following:

*   Develop an understanding of the financial reporting process.

*   Develop relevant criteria for the selection of entries to be tested.

*   Determine the timing of the testing of entries.

*   Make inquiries of appropriate individuals.

In developing an understanding of the financial reporting process the auditor should determine such characteristics as (1) the source of data that is the foundation for the entry, (2) the required approval for an entry, (3) the monetary value of routine entries, and (4) control procedures used to identify inappropriate entries or unsuccessfully proposed entries. An understanding of the journal entry process will enable the auditor to identify entries that are atypical and prime suspects for further investigation.

Once the auditor has an understanding of the financial reporting process for entries, the selection of specific entries for testing (as well as the nature and timing of how those entries will be tested) should be based on factors such as the following:

*   Risk factors or other conditions that relate to specific classes of entries

*   The quality of controls that relate to entries

*   The financial reporting process and the client's evidential support (including electronic support) for entries

*   Entries with unusual characteristics such as unique authorization sources, posting dates, dollar amounts, and accounts involved

*   Entries that affect accounts that are characterized by their complexity, high degree of subjectivity because of estimates, past history of errors, or

identification with risk factors suggesting possible material misstatement due to fraud

- Entries that are not considered part of the routine (sales, purchases, payroll, etc.) journal entries made during the period

> **PLANNING AID REMINDER:** SAS-99 points out that in planning which entries should be tested, the auditor should take into consideration that fraudulent entries are often made at the end of an accounting period.

Consider biases in accounting estimates

Because of the uncertainty associated with estimates, accounting information based on estimates is sometimes subject to fraudulent manipulation by management. The auditor should compare estimates reflected in the financial statements with the best estimates that are supported by the audit process. Individually, management's estimates might appear reasonable, but if every estimate has the same bias (for example, increased earnings per share), the auditor should reconsider the effect of the estimates taken as a whole and whether that reconsideration is a risk factor that affects the possibility of material misstatement due to fraud.

> **ENGAGEMENT STRATEGY:** Challenging estimates made by a client and supporting those challenges can be difficult; however, SAS-99 requires that the auditor perform a retrospective review of estimates made in previous years by the client. If the client has exhibited consistent bias in the past, that history should be considered in assessing material misstatement due to fraud. As part of the engagement strategy, the auditor should have access to information obtained in prior years about significant estimates in order to evaluate the consistency of management's assumptions and judgments in the current year relative to prior years.

Analyze the business basis for significant unusual transactions

Business transactions should make sense given the fundamental characteristics of a client. Transactions that appear unusual to the auditor should be investigated in order to determine their rationale. This process should include the following procedures:

- Consider whether the transaction is overly complex.

- Analyze the economic substance of the transaction, not just the accounting and legal form.

- Determine whether the transaction has been discussed with the audit committee or board of directors.

- Consider whether the transaction is driven by its accounting implication rather than sound business strategy.

- Determine whether a transaction that involves unconsolidated related parties has been properly reviewed and approved by the audit committee or board of directors.

- Determine whether a transaction that involves a (1) previously unidentified related party or (2) party that cannot fulfill its obligation without support from the client.

Evaluate audit evidence

SAS-99 emphasizes the critical evaluation of audit evidence related to the occurrence of possible fraud across four key areas of the audit:

1. Assessing fraud risks throughout the engagement

2. Evaluating the results of analytical procedures performed as part of substantive procedures or in the overall review stage of the engagement

3. Evaluating risks at or near the completion of fieldwork

4. Responding to misstatements that might relate to fraud

Assessing fraud risks throughout the engagement

The auditor's concern with the possible occurrence of material misstatement due to fraud should not be compartmentalized but rather should continue through the entire engagement. For example, the initial assessment by the auditor might result in a minimum level of risk of material misstatement due to fraud; however, during the performance of substantive procedures the auditor might discover documents that appear to have been altered. The auditor must be alert to evidence gathered at any point in the engagement that might have implications in assessing risks of material misstatement due to fraud.

Evaluating the results of analytical procedures performed as part of substantive tests or in the overall review stage of the engagement

As required by SAS-56 (AU 329) (Analytical Procedures) analytical procedures should be performed as part of the overall review of financial information and considered for possible performance as part of substantive procedures. The performance of these latter (nonplanning stage) analytical procedures might identify fraud risks that had not previously come to the auditor's attention.

> **PLANNING AID REMINDER:** SAS-99 requires (as part of the overall review stage of the engagement) the auditor to apply substantive analytical procedures to revenue through the end of the period.

Professional judgment must be exercised to identify trends and relationships that appear to be unusual and therefore subject to further investigation; however, SAS-99 points out that unusual relationships might come to the auditor's attention "because management or employees generally are unable to manipulate certain information to create seemingly normal or expected relationships." For example, the following unexpected relationships might be based on fraudulent activities:

- There are material differences between sales according to the accounting records and sales according to production reports because fictitious sales have been recorded by the management personnel who had access to the accounting records but not to production statistics.

- There are unusual relationships between the current year's inventory, accounts payable, sales, or costs of goods sold and those of the previous year because of inventory theft and the perpetrator was unable to adjust the affected accounts.

- There is an unusual relationship between net income and cash flows from operations because fictitious revenue was recorded through receivables and not cash.

> **FRAUD POINTER:** SAS-99 states that unusual and unexpected relationships involving year-end revenue and income should be particularly relevant to the auditor's concern with the possible existence of fraudulent financial statements. For example, the recognition of unusually large amounts of revenue from unusual transactions needs to be considered by the auditor.

Evaluating risks at or near the completion of fieldwork

Once the engagement's fieldwork has been or nearly been completed, the auditor should make a final assessment of the risks of material misstatement due to fraud based on all audit evidence gathered to that point. As part of that assessment, "the auditor with final responsibility for the audit should ascertain that there has been appropriate communication with the other audit team members throughout the audit regarding information or conditions indicative of risks of material misstatement due to fraud."

> **FRAUD POINTER:** The auditor should evaluate management's responses to inquiries (particularly inquiries related to substantive analytical procedures and analytical procedures performed as part of the overall review stage of the audit) to determine whether the responses are vague, implausible, or inconsistent with other evidence obtained. Management representations on significant issues should be supported by corroborating audit evidence.

Responding to misstatements that might relate to fraud

During the engagement, the auditor might identify a number of misstatements in the financial statements and those misstatements must be evaluated to determine whether their occurrence arose from fraudulent activities. The difference between an error and a fraudulent act is intent and the auditor must use professional judgment to make that differentiation.

> **PLANNING AID REMINDER:** The identification of fraudulent acts has an effect on the auditor's determination of materiality because the level of materiality is a function of both quantitative and qualitative factors. That is, if fraudulent misstatements are identified during the engagement, the level of materiality for the engagement decreases.

When a fraudulent act or possible fraudulent act is discovered and that act does not appear to have a material impact on the financial statements, the auditor should nonetheless consider the implications of the fraud, especially the person(s) involved in the act. For example, if the fraudulent act that has financial statement implications was conducted by a high-level management individual, the auditor should consider whether the circumstance calls into question the integrity of management. Under this circumstance the auditor should reconsider the assessment of risk of material misstatement due to fraud, which could lead to a change in the nature, timing, and extent of audit procedures and to a reassessment of the effectiveness of controls if control risk has been established below the maximum. On the other hand, when the fraudulent act is conducted by nonmanagerial personnel and the amount of the fraud that could be executed at that level is petty, the assessment of risk of material misstatement due to fraud would generally not change.

When a fraudulent act or possible fraudulent act is discovered and (1) that act could have a material impact on the financial statements or (2) the possible impact on the financial statements has not been determined, the auditor should do the following:

- Attempt to gather additional evidence to determine whether fraud has occurred and its impact on the financial statements.

- Consider reassessing the risk of material misstatement due to fraud (including changes in the nature, timing, and extent of audit procedures and the reassessment of the effectiveness of controls if control risk has been established below the maximum).

- Discuss the event with an appropriate level of management (at least one level above the level of occurrence), senior level management, and the audit committee.

- Recommend that the client consider discussing the event with legal counsel.

> **ENGAGEMENT STRATEGY:** The risk of the possible existence of materially misstated financial statements due to fraud might be so great that the auditor decides (perhaps after consultation with legal counsel) to withdraw from the engagement. If the auditor withdraws from the engagement, the reason for the withdrawal should be communicated to the audit committee or others with equivalent authority and responsibility.

Communicate possible fraud to management, the audit committee, and others

When the auditor believes fraud might have occurred (whether consequential or inconsequential), the matter should be communicated to the appropriate level of management. If the fraudulent act involves senior management or has a material effect on the financial statements, the matter should be communicated directly to the audit committee.

> **ENGAGEMENT STRATEGY:** The auditor and the audit committee should come to an understanding about the need for communication with the audit committee when lower-level employees are involved in fraudulent acts.

> **FRAUD POINTER:** When the auditor has identified risks of material misstatement due to fraud that have implications for the client's internal control, the guidance related to communicating significant deficiencies and material weaknesses as described in SAS-115 (Communication of Internal Control Related Matters Identified in an Audit) should be considered.

Generally, the auditor is not required to communicate the possible or actual existence of fraud to other parties due to the confidential relationship with the client; however, SAS-99 points out that it might be necessary to communicate such information under the following circumstances:

- Communication might be required by law or regulation or to satisfy a subpoena.

- Communication might be appropriate because of a successor-predecessor relationship as described in SAS-84 (AU 315) (Communications between Predecessor and Successor Auditors).

- Communication might be required by a governmental agency that provides funding to the client.

> **RISK ASSESSMENT STRATEGY:** The auditor should consider seeking legal counsel when determining whether a third party should be informed of possible fraud related to a client's financial statements.

Document the consideration of fraud

SAS-99 requires that the auditor document the following in his or her audit documentation with respect to the consideration of fraud in a financial statement audit:

- The discussion among audit team members concerning planning the engagement as it relates to the financial statements' susceptibility to material misstatement due to fraud, including:

  — When and how the discussion took place

  — Team members that participated in the discussion

  — Subject matter discussed

- The audit procedures performed in relationship to the identification and assessment of risks of material misstatement due to fraud

- Descriptions of specific risk factors identified and the auditor's response to their discovery

- If the auditor has not identified revenue recognition as a particular risk of material misstatement due to fraud, the reason this was not done

- Procedures performed related to the risk of management override of controls

- The basis for employing additional audit procedures or other responses

- The nature of communications with management, the audit committee, or others regarding acts of fraud

Practitioner's Aid

Exhibit AU 316-1 discusses authoritative guidance that is helpful in the audit of revenue reported in a client's financial statements. Exhibit AU 316-1 summarizes an approach described in the AICPA's Audit Guide titled "Auditing Revenue in Certain Industries." The Audit Guide (which is available for purchase from the AICPA) notes that based on SEC Accounting and Auditing Enforcement Releases from between January 1987 and 1997 "more than half of the frauds involved overstating revenues by recording them either fictitiously or prematurely."

EXHIBIT AU 316-1 — GUIDANCE FOR AUDITING REVENUE IN CERTAIN INDUSTRIES

Revenue should be recognized when it has been earned or substantially earned. Generally this means that revenue is recorded when goods are delivered or services are performed. Management has the primary responsibility for the fair presentation of revenue and related accounts such as allowances for uncollectible accounts, sales returns, and provisions for customer rebates and refunds. The Audit Guide points out that factors such as the (1) tone at the top, (2) role of the audit committee, (3) effectiveness of the internal audit function, and (4) adoption of effective internal control that has an impact on the proper reporting of revenue in the financial statements based on GAAP.

The recognition of revenue consistent with GAAP can involve the application of a variety of pronouncements, including the following:

- ASC 360 (FAS-66, Accounting for Sales of Real Estate)

- ASC 470 (FAS-49, Accounting for Product Financing Arrangements)

- ASC 605 (Accounting Research Bulletin No. 45, "Long-Term Construction-Type Contracts")

- ASC 605 (AICPA Statement of Position 81-1, "Accounting for Performance of Construction-Type and Certain Production-Type Contracts")

- ASC 605 (EITF 2000-21, "Accounting for Revenue Arrangements with Multiple Deliverables," and numerous other consensus positions of the FASB's Emerging Issue Task Force (EITF))

- ASC 605 (FAS-48, Revenue Recognition When Right of Return Exists)

- ASC 605 (SEC Staff Accounting Bulletin 104, "Revenue Recognition")

- ASC 605 (SEC Staff Accounting Bulletin No. 101, "Revenue Recognition in Financial Statements")

- ASC 952 (FAS-45, Accounting for Franchise Fee Revenue)

- ASC 985 (AICPA Statement of Position 97-2, "Software Revenue Recognition")

The Audit Guide identifies the following specific factors that might indicate that a client is not reporting revenues in accordance with GAAP:

- Side agreements

- Channel stuffing

- Related-party transactions and significant unusual transactions

- Nature of business and accounting for revenue

- Integrity of evidence

Side agreements

Arrangements whereby the normal terms of a sale are modified in order to encourage a particular customer to accept shipment of goods that it would generally not accept (or record as a purchase) constitute a side agreement. These arrangements are generally characterized as relieving "the customer of some of the risk and rewards of ownership." Side agreements often result in revenue being recorded when the recognition is not in accordance with GAAP. Since side agreements are an exception to the normal sales conditions and are known only to a few key management personnel, this circumstance presents a challenge to the auditor; however, the Audit Guide points out that being aware that such an agreement could exist is a starting point for discovering their actual existence.

Channel stuffing

The Audit Guide defines the channel stuffing strategy as a "marketing practice that suppliers sometimes use to boost sales by inducing distributors to buy substantially more inventory than they can promptly resell.'' The client's objective is to record more sales in the current period than typically would be recorded if sales were simply driven by market conditions. The auditor should be alert to identifying irregular sales patterns and consider their effect on the current financial statements. For example, there may be a need to create or increase provisions for returned goods or special discounts related to side agreements.

Related-party transactions and significant unusual transactions

Related-party transactions can be the basis for the recording of fraudulent transactions. For example, a client might sell inventory or capital assets to a related-party at an inflated price. The Audit Guide points out that individual related-party transactions that are kept relatively small but executed frequently could nonetheless have a material impact on the financial statements.

Another transaction type that can result in the reporting of fraudulent information in the financial statements involves highly complex transactions whether or not they involve related parties.

Nature of business and accounting for revenue

Revenue is generally recognized when earned; however, the nature of the client's industry can increase the risk that fraudulent revenue recognition schemes are present. The Audit Guide reminds auditors to consider factors such as the following as they relate to the probability that a client could inappropriately recognize revenue:

- The manner by which the client recognizes revenue based on the nature of its industry

- A recent change in the manner by which a client recognizes revenue

- The existence of client sales and payment terms that differ from industry norms or the client's normal internal policies

- Shipment policies that provide a basis for the inappropriate recognition of revenue

> **PUBLIC COMPANY IMPLICATION:** The SEC staff has issued guidance specific to revenue recognition that is relevant to auditors of public companies. SAB-101 and SAB-104 summarize the SEC staff's views of the appropriate accounting for revenue recognition in financial statements. The guidance

includes an analysis of the criteria that must be satisfied in order to recognize revenue. Auditors of public companies should consider the guidance in SAB-101 and SAB-104.

Integrity of evidence

The integrity of the evidence that supports the recognition of revenue is another risk factor that should be considered by the auditor. The Audit Guide lists the following as some of the conditions related to evidence that can suggest the improper recording of revenue:

- Responses from management with respect to revenue recognition are "inconsistent, vague, or implausible."

- Audit evidence to support revenue transactions is missing.

- Company personnel have signed bills of lading (rather than the common carrier).

- Shipping documents have been altered.

Indicators of improper revenue recognition

There is no comprehensive checklist to determine when conditions suggest that a client might be inappropriately recording revenue; however, the Audit Guide presents the following (categorized as [1] absence of an agreement, [2] lack of delivery, and [3] incomplete earnings process) as indicators that should raise the auditor's suspicions about fraudulent revenue transactions.

Absence of an agreement

- Sales are based on letters of intent rather than signed contracts or agreements.

- Goods are shipped before they are authorized by a customer.

- Sales are recorded at date of shipment to a new customer even though the customer can return the goods with no obligation.

- Sales are recorded even though the customer has the right to cancel the sale.

- Sales are recorded even though certain terms of the agreement, such as a consignment sales arrangement, have not been satisfied.

Lack of delivery

- Sales are recorded before delivery occurs.

- Sales are based on transactions that were executed after the end of the accounting period.

- Sales are based on shipments to warehouses or other locations that have not been authorized by the customer.

- Sales are recorded but a critical component of the order has not been shipped.

- Sales are recorded based on the receipt of purchase orders.

Incomplete earnings process

- Sales are recorded but receipt of payment from the customer is based on other material conditions that must be satisfied by the client.

- Sales are recorded but goods are unassembled.

- Sales are recorded based on shipments to freight forwarders but the goods will be returned to the client for modifications as dictated by the customer.

- Sales are recorded even though the client is obliged to perform additional work (such as debugging a client application).

Audit Procedures

The Audit Guide lists the following as authoritative and nonauthoritative procedures that the auditor should consider in obtaining "reasonable as-surance about whether the financial statements are free of material mis-statement, whether caused by error or fraud":

- Determine an appropriate audit risk level.

- Develop a knowledge of the business.

- Consider internal control over revenue recognition.

- Consider fraud in the financial statements.

- Consider related-party transactions.

- Perform analytical procedures.

- Perform cutoff tests, vouch transactions, and perform other tests.

- Send appropriate confirmations.

- Evaluate accounting estimates related to revenue transactions.

- Observe inventory.

- Obtain appropriate management representations.

- Consider the adequacy of financial statement disclosures.

- Evaluate audit evidence.

Determine an appropriate audit risk level

The auditor's awareness of fraud risk factors, related-party transactions, and other questionable revenue recognition characteristics of a client can occur as part of accepting or continuing an engagement, as part of planning the engagement, as part of developing an understanding of a client's business and environment, including its internal control, or during the performance of tests of controls and substantive procedures. For this reason, during the entire engagement the auditor may need to reevaluate the levels of inherent risk and control risk related to revenue recognition to determine the nature, timing, and extent of audit procedures appropriate for the audit of revenue and related accounts.

Develop knowledge of the business

The Audit Guide notes that an auditor should be aware of a variety of characteristics of a client's revenue recognition process, including the following:

- Products and services sold

- The effect of seasonal or cyclical trends on revenue

- Marketing and sales policies, both internal and industry-wide

- Policies with respect to pricing, returns, discount credit granting, and payment terms

- Personnel (particularly in the marketing and sales activities) who record sales, extend credit, and authorize shipments

- Compensation benefits that are related to sales volume

- Classes and categories of customers

- The client's role in "placing products with end users, and how the company manages, tracks and controls its inventory that is held by distributors"

- Accounting principles that are appropriate for the client's sales activities

The Audit Guide points out that making inquiries of appropriate management personnel can help to better understand high-audit-risk conditions such as unusual or complex revenue transactions and sales contracts with unusual or complex terms.

> **FRAUD POINTER:** Making appropriate inquiries is only a starting point in determining whether the client has recognized revenue inappropriately. The auditor should attempt to corroborate representations obtained through inquiry using other audit procedures, such as obtaining written confirmation from an independent source.

The auditor should read sales contracts in order to understand the responsibilities accepted by the client and their implications for revenue recognition. The Audit Guide notes that reading sales contracts and sales correspondence might alert the auditor to the existence of side agreements.

When a client executes complex sales agreements or is involved in related-party transactions, care must be taken in the assignment of personnel to ensure that the training and experience of an auditor is sufficient for the demands of this phase of the engagement. In some instances it is appropriate to seek expert assistance from members of the firm that are not part of the engagement, and in some instances it is necessary to use the work of an outside specialist.

Consider internal control over revenue recognition

As with other significant components of a client's internal control, the auditor should develop an understanding of internal control over revenue transactions that satisfies the requirements established by SAS-109 (AU 314) (Understanding the Entity and Its Environment and Assessing the Risks of Material Misstatement). Internal control related to revenue recognition should, among other things, include an understanding of (1) how nonstandard revenue contracts are approved, (2) the accounting implications for changing standard contracts, (3) the development of estimates related to revenue transactions, and (4) related-party transactions. Based on the auditor's understanding of internal control related to revenue recognition, an appropriate level of control risk should be assessed and in turn tests of controls should be performed. If the results from performing tests of controls suggest that internal control over revenue recognition is ineffective, the nature, timing, or extent of substantive procedures must be modified in order to provide more persuasive audit evidence.

Consider fraud in the financial statements

As discussed in the main body of this Section, SAS-99 requires that an auditor specifically assess the risk of material misstatement of the financial statements due to fraud and consider that assessment in designing the audit procedures to be performed. The Audit Guide points out that the auditor's assessment relative to financial statement fraud is dependent upon factors such as (1) professional skepticism and its affect on the nature, timing, and extent of audit procedures, (2) management's selection and application of accounting principles for revenue recognition, and (3) management's ability to circumvent internal control related to revenue recognition.

Consider related-party transactions

SAS-45 (AU 334) (Related Parties) provides guidance for the planning and application of procedures for related-party transactions. The Audit Guide identifies the following as procedures that may be appropriate for substantive procedures for revenue recognition that involves a related party:

- Understand the purpose of the transaction.

- Examine documentation that supports the transaction.

- Determine whether the board of directors (or other appropriate personnel) has approved the transaction.

- Confirm the details of the transaction with external parties.

- When the transaction raises questions about its substance, refer to various sources of information to determine whether the transaction appears to be reasonable.

- When the transaction creates material uncollected balances or obligations, obtain information about the financial viability of the related party.

Perform analytical procedures

SAS-56 (AU 329) (Analytical Procedures) provides guidance for the performance of analytical procedures in an audit engagement. The Audit Guide notes that the following analytical procedures "are particularly useful in identifying unusual fluctuations in the revenue cycle that warrant additional consideration":

- Compare monthly and quarterly sales to comparable periods for the current year and previous years and evaluate the amounts in the context of current industry conditions and current client strategies.

- Review sales recorded a few days before and a few days after the end of the year.

- Compare gross profit ratios to those for previous years and to budgeted amounts, and evaluate the amounts in the context of current industry conditions and current client strategies.

- Compare the amount of inventory in the distribution channel with the amounts for prior periods to consider whether there may be channel stuffing.

- Compare the trends of sales in the distributor channel and evaluate the amounts in the context of current industry conditions and current client strategies.

- Compare revenue deductions, such as discounts, to those of the previous year and budgeted amounts, and evaluate the amounts in the context of current industry conditions and current client strategies.

- Evaluate sales credits and returns after the end of the year with regard to the figures for similar periods of the previous year to determine whether there may have been contingent sales or other unusual sales arrangements.

- Evaluate the ratio of returns and allowances to sales.

- Compare the aged trial balance of receivables with those of previous years.

- Evaluate the amount of cash receipts collected after the end of the year to cash receipts activities during the year to determine whether receipts are unusually slow to materialize.

Perform cutoff tests, vouch transactions, and perform other tests

The auditor should perform appropriate cutoff tests, vouch transactions, and perform other audit procedures to determine whether sales and related transactions are recorded in the appropriate accounting period.

Send appropriate confirmations

SAS-67 (AU 330) (The Confirmation Process) provides guidance for the use of confirmations in an audit engagement. The Audit Guide notes that the auditor should consider confirming the details of complicated or unusual sales transactions, including possible unfilled obligations on the part of the client.

PLANNING AID REMINDER: SAS-99 states that there is generally a heightened risk of fraud involving revenue recognition. Therefore, the auditor should consider confirming the terms of material revenue transactions, including inquiring about the existence of side agreements. The auditor should be more likely to confirm the terms of revenue transactions if they are unusual or complex. In addition, AICPA Practice Alert 03-1 (Audit Confirmations) states that the auditor should be more likely to confirm transaction terms and the existence of side agreements if any of the following conditions exist: (1) significant sales or sales volume at or near the end of the reporting period, (2) use of nonstandard contracts or contract clauses, (3) use of letters of authorization instead of signed contracts or agreements, (4) altered dates on contracts or shipping documents, (5) contracts or agreements that are linked with each other or that happen concurrently (e.g., sales to and purchases from the same party), (6) lack of evidence that the customer has accepted the product, (7) presence of bill-and-hold transactions, (8) sales with extended payment terms or nonstandard installment receivables, (9) sales without involvement from the accounting/finance department or where the accounting/finance department does not monitor relationships with distributors/retailers, (10) unusual sales volume to distributors/retailers, (11) sales involving a commitment for future upgrades, especially if not involving software, (12) sales involving significant uncertainties or obligations for the seller, (13) sales to value-added resellers or distributors whose financial viability is questionable, (14) an abnormally large increase in a receivable from a customer, and (15) aggressive accounting policies and practices by the client.

Evaluate accounting estimates related to revenue transactions

SAS-57 (AU 342) (Auditing Accounting Estimates) describes the auditor's responsibilities and the audit procedures with respect to estimates that are part of the client's financial statements. The Audit Guide notes that this general guidance should be applied to material accounts such as sales, sales returns, the allowance for doubtful accounts, and revenue recognized under the percentage-of-completion method used to account for long-term construction contracts.

Observe inventory

The Audit Guide reminds auditors that appropriate cutoff procedures for the observation of inventories at the end of the year have implications for the recognition of revenues in the proper accounting period. In addition, the Guide notes that if a client has numerous shipping facilities the auditor should (1) observe inventory counts at all locations on the same date or (2) observe only some of the locations on an unannounced basis. Also, if the client is in an industry where inventory obsolescence is an issue, the auditor should determine whether client personnel used to count the inventory have the expertise to identify obsolete inventory.

Obtain appropriate management representations

SAS-89 (AU 333) (Management Representations) provides guidance in obtaining written representations from a client. The Audit Guide states that some of the items that should be considered for representation by the client are

- There has been no fraud that could have a material effect on the financial statements.

- Related-party transactions, including sales and amounts receivable from related parties, have been properly recorded and disclosed.

- All financial records and related data have been made available.

- Significant estimates and material concentrations that are required to be disclosed in accordance with SOP 94-6 (Disclosure of Certain Significant Risks and Uncertainties) have been disclosed.

- The effects of any uncorrected financial statement misstatements aggregated by the auditor during the current engagement and pertaining to the latest period presented are immaterial, both individually and in the aggregate, to the financial statements taken as a whole. (A summary of such items should be included in or attached to the letter.)

If the client has been involved in unusual revenue transactions, the auditor should consider whether it is appropriate to ask for representation concerning the details of these transactions.

Consider the adequacy of financial statement disclosures

The financial statements should reflect disclosures "with regard to revenue recognition policies, information about major customers or significant concentrations of credit risk, related-party transactions, and the effect of significant revisions to estimates in percentage-of-completion contracts."

Evaluate audit evidence

The Audit Guide points out that "to the extent the auditor remains in substantial doubt about any assertion of material significance, he or she must refrain from forming an opinion until he or she has obtained sufficient appropriate audit evidence to remove such substantial doubt, or the auditor must express a qualified or disclaimer of opinion."

> **OBSERVATION:** In addition to providing general guidance for the audit of revenue and related accounts, the Audit Guide provides specific guidance for the high-technology manufacturing industry.

SECTION 317

ILLEGAL ACTS BY CLIENTS

Authoritative Pronouncements

SAS-54 — Illegal Acts by Clients

Auditing Interpretation No. 1 of AU 317 (October 1978) — Consideration of the Internal Control Structure in a Financial Statement Audit and the Foreign Corrupt Practices Act

Auditing Interpretation No. 2 of AU 317 (October 1978) — Material Weakness in Internal Control and the Foreign Corrupt Practices Act

> **IMPORTANT NOTICE FOR 2011:** The Auditing Standards Board (ASB) is in the process of redrafting all of the auditing sections in *Codification of Statements on Auditing Standards* to converge U.S. GAAS with the International Standards on Auditing issued by the International Auditing and Assurance Standards Board. As part of this process, the newly redrafted standards will follow certain clarity drafting conventions adopted by the ASB. These clarity drafting conventions include: (1) establishing objectives for each standard; (2) including a definitions section, if appropriate; and (3) separating requirements from application guidance and other material. The ASB is planning to have all redrafted standards become effective on the same date, which is for audits of financial statements for periods ending on or after December 15, 2012. It is possible that the effective date might be delayed beyond that date. The ASB's clarity and convergence project will have a significant effect on the auditing standards applicable to audits of nonpublic companies, and the 2012 *GAAS Guide* will be appropriately modified to reflect these changes once the effective date of the standards is certain.

Overview

Although the purpose of an audit is not to determine whether an act is illegal, an auditor should be aware that such acts could occur and materially misstate financial statements. SAS-54 defines "illegal acts" as "violations of laws or governmental regulations," including acts committed by management and the entity's employees acting on behalf of the entity. An illegal act, for purposes of SAS-54, does not include acts arising from the personal conduct of an employee of the entity unrelated to business activities.

An entity must observe many laws and regulations. In general, the auditor lacks the expertise to identify and evaluate all illegal acts. For purposes of determining the auditor's responsibilities for detecting illegal acts, illegal acts are classified as either those having a direct effect on the financial statements or those having only an indirect effect on the financial statements.

Illegal acts with direct effects on financial statements

Some laws and regulations directly apply to the determination of financial statement amounts or disclosures and are, therefore, taken into consideration when the auditor plans his or her audit procedures. For example, the auditor would likely evaluate compliance with Internal Revenue Code (IRC) and related regulations when determining whether the provision for income taxes is fairly presented in the financial statements. The auditor's responsibility for detecting illegal acts relating to laws and regulations having a direct and material effect on the financial statements is the same as the responsibility relating to the detection of errors and fraud [see previous discussion of SAS-99 (AU 316)]. The auditor must design the audit to provide reasonable assurance of detecting such acts.

> **OBSERVATION:** Auditing Interpretation No. 1 of AU 317 (October 1978) titled "Consideration of the Internal Control in a Financial Statement Audit and the Foreign Corrupt Practices Act" notes that the auditor is not required to expand the scope of the audit engagement because of the Foreign Corrupt Practices Act of 1977, beyond the normal scope required by the second standard of fieldwork.

Illegal acts with indirect effects on financial statements

Most laws and regulations have only an indirect effect on financial statements; that is, when an illegal act related to this type of law or regulation has occurred, the effects are often indirect in that they only require disclosure in the financial statements based on their classification as a contingent liability. Illegal acts of this type are generally related to the operations of the organization rather than to the financial and accounting aspects of the entity. Furthermore, under many circumstances, the auditor has no basis for determining whether this type of law or regulation has been violated.

SAS-54 addresses illegal acts relating to laws and regulations that have an indirect effect on financial statements. Although the auditor is not responsible for the detection of illegal acts, during various phases of the engagement specific information might be discovered that raises questions about whether indirect effect illegal acts have occurred. SAS-54 lists the following as examples of specific information that raises questions about the existence of illegal acts:

- Unauthorized transactions, improperly recorded transactions, or transactions not recorded in a complete or timely manner in order to maintain accountability for assets

- Investigation by a governmental agency, an enforcement proceeding, or payment of unusual fines or penalties

- Violations of laws or regulations cited in reports of examinations by regulatory agencies made available to the auditor

- Large payments for unspecified services to consultants, affiliates, or employees

- Sales commissions or agents' fees that appear excessive in relation to those normally paid by the client or to the services actually received

- Unusually large payments in cash, purchases of bank cashiers' checks in large amounts payable to bearer, transfers to numbered bank accounts, or similar transactions

- Unexplained payments made to government officials or employees

- Failure to file tax returns or pay government duties or similar fees common to the entity's industry or the nature of its business

> **PLANNING AID REMINDER:** SAS-54 establishes professional standards relating to the auditor's responsibility for detecting illegal acts in the course of the audit of the entity's financial statements. An auditor might accept other engagements that impose a different responsibility for detecting illegal acts. Such engagements include professional services subject to governmental auditing standards or special engagements designed to determine compliance with specific laws or regulations.

> **PLANNING AID REMINDER:** Auditing Interpretation No. 2 of AU 317 notes that when a material weakness comes to the auditor's attention in an engagement covered by the Foreign Corrupt Practices Act, the auditor should discuss with management and the auditor's legal counsel whether the material weakness is a violation of the Act.

Promulgated Procedures Checklist

The auditor should perform the following procedures with respect to indirect effect illegal acts in an audit engagement:

- Perform audit procedures that are appropriate when there is no suspicion of indirect effect illegal acts.

- Perform audit procedures that are appropriate when there is suspicion of indirect effect illegal acts.

- Evaluate the results of performing procedures related to indirect effect illegal acts.

- Communicate illegal acts to the client's audit committee.

- Determine the effects of an illegal act on the audit report.

Analysis and Application of Procedures

Perform audit procedures that are appropriate when there is no suspicion of indirect effect illegal acts

Typically, the engagement does not include audit procedures specifically directed to identifying indirect effect illegal acts when no specific information has come to the attention of the auditor that would suggest that any such illegal acts occurred. Nonetheless, the auditor should make the following inquiries of management:

- Entity's compliance with laws and regulations

- Entity's policies that may prevent illegal acts

- Entity's directives and periodic representations obtained by the entity concerning compliance with laws and regulations

> **PLANNING AID REMINDER:** Also, the auditor should request a written representation from the entity stating that no violations or possible violations of laws or regulations have occurred that may require accrual or disclosure in the financial statements. Management should also represent that it has informed the auditor of all possible illegal acts that it is aware of.

Perform audit procedures that are appropriate when there is suspicion of indirect effect illegal acts

If an auditor is aware of information concerning a possible illegal act, the auditor should (1) understand the nature of the act, (2) understand the circumstances surrounding the act, and (3) obtain sufficient information to evaluate the effects of the act on the financial statements. If possible, the auditor should deal with management at least one level above those involved in the act.

When management cannot provide sufficient information to demonstrate that an illegal act did not take place, the auditor should:

• Consult with the entity's legal counsel or other specialists (the entity should make the arrangements for meeting with its legal counsel).

• If necessary to obtain a further understanding of the act, perform additional procedures such as the following:

— Inspect supporting documentation and compare it with the accounting records

— Confirm information with other parties and intermediaries

— Determine if the transaction has been properly authorized

— Consider whether other similar transactions have occurred, and attempt to identify them

> **FRAUD POINTER:** In November 2004, the AICPA issued a Practice Alert on illegal acts, which states that the client is normally expected to perform an investigation if an illegal act might have occurred. (These investigations are typically performed by an outside law firm, with the assistance of forensic accountants, under the supervision of the audit committee.) The auditor should request that he or she be allowed to attend the presentation of the investigation team's report at the completion of the engagement and discuss the results of the investigation with senior management and the audit committee.

Evaluate the results of performing procedures related to indirect effect illegal acts

When an illegal act has occurred or probably occurred, the auditor should evaluate the effects of the act on the financial statements.

> **OBSERVATION:** The possible loss arising from the illegal act should be evaluated to determine whether the amount is material. All costs related to the loss, such as penalties and fines, should be considered. The need for accrual and/or disclosure in the financial statements should be evaluated in the context of guidelines established by by ASC 450 (FAS-5, Accounting for Contingencies). The auditor must consider both quantitative and qualitative factors in evaluating the materiality of the illegal act. Qualitative factors are often more important than the immediate quantitative effect in evaluating the materiality of an illegal act. For example, penalties and fines can sometimes exceed the amount of the illegal act itself.

The illegal act should also be evaluated to determine whether other aspects of the engagement are affected. This is particularly applicable to the evaluation of the reliability of management representations. Such facts as the perpetrators involved, the methods of concealment, and the nature of internal control procedures overridden should be considered in the evaluation.

FRAUD POINTER: The AICPA's Practice Alert on illegal acts states that the auditor is to evaluate management's conclusions after receiving the investigation report. After the auditor considers the results of the special investigation and discusses the investigation report with senior management and the audit committee, he or she must determine (1) whether additional audit procedures need to be performed, (2) the nature of any needed disclosures in the financial statements and notes, (3) whether internal control deficiencies exist and need to be communicated, and (4) whether the audit report needs to be modified. The auditor should also consider whether it is appropriate to withdraw from the engagement.

Communicate illegal acts to the client's audit committee

An auditor should ensure that an illegal act has been communicated to the client's audit committee (or to "individuals with a level of authority and responsibility equivalent to an audit committee in organizations that do not have one, such as the board of directors, the board of trustees, an owner in an owner-managed enterprise, or others who may have engaged the auditor"). The communication should include the following:

- Description of the illegal act
- Circumstances surrounding the illegal act
- Auditor's evaluation of the effects of the illegal act on the financial statements

FRAUD POINTER: If members of senior management are involved in the illegal act, the auditor should communicate directly with the audit committee (or equivalent individuals). The communication can be written or oral, and in either case it should be adequately documented in the audit files.

OBSERVATION: The auditor's communication to the audit committee can be either oral or written. If it is oral, the auditor should document the discussion.

Notifying parties other than management and the audit committee (or equivalent individuals) about the occurrence of an illegal act is not required; however, SAS-54 notes that under the following circumstances the auditor may be called on to inform another party of an illegal act:

- SEC disclosure requirements based on a change of auditors

- Inquiries received from a successor auditor

- Subpoena issued by a court

- Governmental audit requirements applicable to entities that have received financial aid

> **ENGAGEMENT STRATEGY:** Because of the confidential relationship between the entity and the auditor, the auditor may find it advisable to contact legal counsel before illegal acts are disclosed to outside parties.

Determine the effects of an illegal act on the audit report

If the effects of an illegal act are not properly accrued or are not properly disclosed in the financial statements, either an adverse opinion or a qualified opinion should be expressed. If the entity does not allow the auditor to collect sufficient appropriate audit evidence to determine whether an illegal act has taken place or whether an illegal act has a material effect on the financial statements, usually a disclaimer of opinion should be expressed. If the entity refuses to accept the modified auditor's report, the auditor should withdraw from the engagement and notify the board of directors and the audit committee (or equivalent individuals) of the reason for the withdrawal.

In some circumstances it is not possible to determine whether an illegal act has occurred, because audit evidence does not exist to resolve the issue or because there is disagreement about the interpretation of the law or regulation. In this case, the auditor is faced with an uncertainty and must determine whether the auditor's report should be modified (see the discussion in AU 508, titled "Auditor's Reports").

SECTION 318

PERFORMING AUDIT PROCEDURES IN RESPONSE TO ASSESSED RISKS AND EVALUATING THE AUDIT EVIDENCE OBTAINED

Authoritative Pronouncements

SAS-110—Performing Audit Procedures in Response to Assessed Risks and Evaluating the Audit Evidence Obtained

> **IMPORTANT NOTICE FOR 2011:** The Auditing Standards Board (ASB) is in the process of redrafting all of the auditing sections in *Codification of Statements on Auditing Standards* to converge U.S. GAAS with the International Standards on Auditing issued by the International Auditing and Assurance Standards Board. As part of this process, the newly redrafted standards will follow certain clarity drafting conventions adopted by the ASB. These clarity drafting conventions include: (1) establishing objectives for each standard; (2) including a definitions section, if appropriate; and (3) separating requirements from application guidance and other material. The ASB is planning to have all redrafted standards become effective on the same date, which is for audits of financial statements for periods ending on or after December 15, 2012. It is possible that the effective date might be delayed beyond that date. The ASB's clarity and convergence project will have a significant effect on the auditing standards applicable to audits of nonpublic companies, and the 2012 *GAAS Guide* will be appropriately modified to reflect these changes once the effective date of the standards is certain.

Overview

The third standard of fieldwork requires the auditor to obtain sufficient appropriate audit evidence by performing audit procedures to afford a reasonable basis for an opinion regarding the financial statements as a whole. SAS-110 establishes the standards and procedures to assist the auditor in fulfilling the requirements of this third standard of fieldwork. SAS-110 provides guidance to assist the auditor with the following:

- Determining the overall response to the risk of material misstatement at the financial statement level.

- Designing and performing further audit procedures in response to risks of material misstatement at the relevant financial statement assertion level.

- Evaluating the sufficiency and appropriateness of audit evidence obtained.

- Satisfying the related documentation requirements.

The auditor's performance of risk assessment procedures should lead to the identification of those account balances, classes of transactions, or disclosures where material misstatements are most likely to occur. The risk assessment procedures should provide the basis for designing and performing further audit procedures. To reduce audit risk to an acceptably low level, the auditor performs further audit procedures, whose nature, timing, and extent are responsive to the assessed risks of material misstatement. SAS-110 provides guidance to assist auditors in the design and performance of these further audit procedures to address the risks of material misstatement identified. Exhibit 314-9 provides an overview of the linkage between the assessed level of risk of material misstatements and the auditor's responses to the risks that are identified (described elsewhere in this section).

> **PUBLIC COMPANY IMPLICATION:** In 2010 the PCAOB issued eight auditing standards (AS-8 through AS-15) related to the auditor's assessment of and response to risk. The proposed standards bear many similarities to the eight risk-assessment standards adopted by the Auditing Standards Board in 2006. AS-13 (The Auditor's Responses to the Risks of Material Misstatement) and AS-14 (Evaluating Audit Results) are the new PCAOB standards that provide guidance to the auditor in performing audit procedures. AS-13 establishes requirements for responding to audit risk, both at the overall level and at the level of significant accounts and disclosures. AS-14 describes the auditor's responsibilities for evaluating audit results. The auditor must evaluate whether he or she has obtained sufficient appropriate audit evidence, and the auditor is required to consider (1) uncorrected misstatements and control deficiencies, (2) overall financial statement presentation, including disclosures, and (3) potential management bias in preparing the financial statements. Although there are a number of differences between the PCAOB's and ASB's risk standards,

the risk-assessment concepts contained in the PCAOB standards should be familiar to most auditors. As is currently the case, audit risk is the risk that the auditor will issue an inappropriate opinion on financial statements that are materially misstated. The auditor is to reduce audit risk to a low level through the application of audit procedures. As a result, the amount of audit effort devoted to particular accounts, classes of transactions, and disclosures should vary based on their respective risk.

Overall Responses at the Financial Statement Level

The auditor's risk assessment procedures may identify risks pervasive to the financial statements. In particular, the auditor's understanding of the control environment obtained as part of the auditor's risk assessment procedures may affect the assessment of the risk of material misstatement at the overall financial statement level. When weaknesses in the control environment exist, the auditor's confidence in internal control and the reliability of evidence generated internally by the client's internal control system may lead the auditor to perform audit procedures closer to period end than at interim and seek more audit evidence from the performance of substantive procedures. Thus, consideration of matters affecting the control environment or other factors that affect the overall risks of material misstatements at the financial statement level has a significant effect on the general approach to the audit.

To respond to assessed risks of material misstatement at the financial statement level, the auditor's response may include the following:

- Emphasizing to the audit engagement team the importance of maintaining professional skepticism in gathering and evaluating audit evidence

- Assigning more experienced staff or those with specialized skills or using specialists

- Providing more supervision

- Incorporating additional elements of unpredictability in the selection of further audit procedures to be performed

- Shifting further audit testing from interim periods to periods closer to year-end

Audit responses to risks of material misstatement at the relevant assertion level

Based on his or her performance of risk assessment procedures, the auditor may identify risks of material misstatements at the relevant assertion level for account balances, classes of transactions, or disclosures. SAS-110 requires the auditor to design and perform further audit procedures to respond to the assessed risks of material misstatements at the relevant assertion level. This ensures a direct linkage between the risk assessment and the nature, timing, and extent of further audit procedures. Further audit procedures may emphasize the performance of substantive procedures (a substantive approach) or use both tests of controls and substantive procedures (a combined approach).

To determine the appropriateness of further audit procedures, the auditor considers several factors:

• The significance of the risk

• The likelihood that a material misstatement will occur

• The characteristics of the class of transactions, account balance, or disclosure involved

• The nature of the specific controls used by the entity, in particular, whether they are manual or automated

• Whether the auditor expects to obtain audit evidence from tests of controls (to determine whether the controls are operating effectively to prevent or detect material misstatement)

In some cases, the auditor may respond by only performing substantive procedures and exclude the effect of controls. However, in doing so, he or she must be satisfied that only performing substantive procedures for the relevant assertions is appropriate for effectively reducing detection risk to an acceptable level. Often, however, auditors determine that a combined approach of performing both tests of controls and substantive procedures is most effective.

> **PLANNING AID REMINDER:** Because there are limitations in any system of internal control in preventing or detecting material misstatements, tests of controls do not eliminate the need for the performance of substantive procedures. SAS-110 requires the auditor to design and perform substantive procedures for all relevant assertions related to each material class of transactions, account balance, and disclosure. Furthermore,

performance of substantive analytical procedures as the sole substantive procedures may not be sufficient. Thus, in many cases, tests of detail of account balances are required.

Considering the nature of further audit procedures

The nature of the audit procedures is of most importance when designing and performing further audit procedures to respond to risks of material misstatement. The nature of further audit procedures refers to the purpose and type of further audit procedures. The purpose relates to whether the procedures are designed to be tests of controls or to provide substantive evidence about an account balance, class of transaction, or disclosure. The type of further audit procedure relates to whether the procedures involve inspection, observation, inquiry, confirmation, recalculation, reperformance, or analytical procedure.

As the risks of material misstatement for a relevant assertion increase, the auditor may modify the nature of the further audit procedure by changing the purpose from a test of control to a substantive procedure, because evidence from substantive procedures is often more reliable and relevant. The auditor may also modify the type of procedure in order to obtain evidence that is more reliable.

The reasons for the assessment of risk of material misstatement for the relevant assertion should affect the nature of the further audit procedures. Information affecting the auditor's assessment of inherent risk and his or her understanding of internal control will directly affect his or her determination of the appropriate nature of further audit procedures. For example, if the auditor believes internal controls are effectively designed and in operation, he or she may plan to perform tests of controls and modify the nature of substantive procedures accordingly. In other situations when the auditor's assessment of risk of material misstatement is low, the auditor may conclude that the performance of substantive analytical procedures provides sufficient appropriate audit evidence.

Considering the timing of further audit procedures

Timing refers to when the auditor performs further audit procedures or the period or date that the audit evidence applies to. The auditor's decision about the timing of further audit procedures is affected by the auditor's assessment of the risks of material misstatement at the relevant assertion level. As the risks of material misstatement increase, the auditor may decide to perform substantive procedures closer to the period end or that are unannounced or conducted at unpredictable times.

When the auditor performs procedures before period end, he or she should consider the additional evidence that might be necessary for the remaining untested period. In some cases, audit procedures performed at interim periods help the auditor identify important matters at an early stage of the audit. Having determined that further audit tests are to be performed at earlier interim periods, the auditor should consider whether additional testing is required between the interim and period-end time frame.

The timing of the performance of audit procedures may be affected by when the relevant information is available. In some cases, electronic evidence may be overwritten and thus must be examined on a timely basis before that occurs. In other cases, the nature of risks may affect the timing of procedures. For example, if there is a risk of material misstatement related to the cutoff of revenue transactions, the auditor may wait to inspect transactions near period end. Certain audit procedures can only be performed at or after period end, such as reconciling accounting records to the financial statements.

Considering the extent of further audit procedures

The extent of further audit procedures encompasses the sufficiency or quantity of a specific audit procedure to be performed. Several factors affect the auditor's considerations of the extent of further audit
procedures:

- The auditor's consideration of tolerable misstatement: The extent increases as tolerable misstatement decreases.

- The assessed risk of material misstatement: As the risk increases, the extent of further audit testing may need to increase, assuming the procedure is relevant to the specific risk and is reliable.

- The degree of assurance the auditor plans to obtain from the further audit procedures: The greater the assurance needs, the greater the extent of testing needed.

The increase in the extent of further audit procedures is effective as long as the nature of the test is relevant to the risks identified.

PLANNING AID REMINDER: SAS-110 emphasizes that the auditor must provide a clear linkage between the assessment of the risk of material misstatement and the nature, timing, and extent of further audit procedures and document it. Although audit procedures performed in prior audits and example audit procedures in illustrative audit programs may be useful to the auditor, the assessment of the risk of material misstatement in the current period forms the primary basis for designing further audit procedures.

Tests of controls

Further audit procedures consist of tests of controls and substantive procedures. The auditor performs tests of controls when the auditor expects the operating effectiveness of controls to reduce his or her assessment of the risks of material misstatement or when substantive procedures alone will not provide sufficient appropriate evidence relevant to an assertion. Generally, an audit is more efficient when the auditor can rely to some degree on the client's internal control.

Tests of controls are only performed on controls that the auditor has determined to be suitably designed to prevent or detect a material misstatement in a relevant assertion. In those circumstances, the linkage of the control to be tested and the specific assertions affected must be identified. Some controls are directly related to specific assertions, and other controls are related only indirectly to specific assertions. The more direct the relationship between controls and an assertion, the more likely the control can provide a basis for reducing the overall risk of material misstatement.

> **PLANNING AID REMINDER:** The auditor performs tests of controls when he or she expects the operating effectiveness of controls to reduce his or her assessment of the risks of material misstatements or when substantive procedures alone will not provide sufficient appropriate evidence. According to AICPA Technical Practice Aid TIS 8200.06, the phrase "expectation of the operating effectiveness of controls" means that the auditor's understanding of all five components of internal control enable him or her to initially assess control risk at less than the maximum. In that case, the auditor's strategy is to perform a combination of tests of controls and substantive procedures. The auditor's initial assessment of control risk is preliminary and subject to satisfactory results from the tests of the operating effectiveness of those controls.

Tests of controls differ from the auditor's risk assessment procedures that he or she performs to determine whether relevant controls exist and are in use. Tests of controls seek to determine whether the controls operate effectively, including how they were applied during the period under audit, the consistency with which they were applied, and by whom they were applied.

Although the objective of tests of controls differs from the auditor's risk assessment procedures, he or she may determine that testing the operating effectiveness of controls can be efficiently and effectively performed as part of procedures performed to assess their design and implementation. For example, risk assessment procedures performed to determine whether an automated control has been designed and placed in operation may serve as the test of that control's operating effectiveness, because of the inherent consistency of IT processing as long as IT general controls are operating effectively. In that case, the auditor may test the automated control once to determine that it is in use. Because IT processing should work consistently as long as there are strong controls over IT security and program changes, that one test may also serve as the auditor's test of the automated control. The auditor would then need to test the operating effectiveness of IT security and program change controls.

Nature of tests of controls

The nature of tests of controls ordinarily includes the following procedures:

• Inquiries of appropriate entity personnel

• Inspection of documents, reports, or electronic files for indication of the performance of the control

• Observation of the application of the control

• Reperformance by the auditor of the application of the control

The nature of the test of controls is affected by the desired assurance to be obtained about the operating effectiveness of the controls. As the planned level of assurance increases, the auditor should design and perform tests of controls that are more reliable and relevant. Evidence obtained from inspection or reperformance generally provides more assurance than evidence obtained from inquiry or observation. Furthermore, inquiry alone is not sufficient to obtain evidence about the operating effectiveness of controls. As the desired level of assurance from controls increases, auditors usually change the nature of tests of controls from a combination of inquiry and observation to inspection and reperformance. For example, an auditor may combine inquiry with reperformance procedures to test the operating effectiveness of controls.

The nature of tests of controls is directly affected by the nature of the underlying control. For some controls, operating effectiveness is best evidenced by documentation. In those situations, the auditor's tests of controls most likely involve inspection of documentation. For other controls, such as those related to the control environment, the most reliable and relevant evidence may be obtained through inquiry and observation.

The impact of technology on the performance of a control may affect the nature of the auditor's tests of controls. When a control is based on a combination of user review of IT-generated information, the nature of the auditor's test of the control not only relates to considering the effectiveness of the user's review but also the effectiveness of controls related to the accuracy of information generated by the IT system.

Because of the inherent consistency of IT processing, the nature of the auditor's tests of an automated control may be affected by his or her testing of the operating effectiveness of IT general controls, particularly those related to security and program change controls. That is, the automated control might require limited testing because once the control is implemented it functions the same way each time unless the program or underlying data is changed. The auditor may test the automated control once it is implemented and then test the overall effectiveness of general IT controls, particularly those related to security and program changes, to ensure that the automated control has not changed since it was implemented. This evaluation may require the skills of an IT specialist.

> **PLANNING AID REMINDER:** The auditor may design a test of a control that is to be performed at the same time as a test of detail on the same transaction. The objective of the test of the control is to determine whether it is operating effectively. The objective of the test of detail is to support relevant assertions or detect material misstatements at the relevant assertion level. Procedures performed simultaneously through tests of controls and a test of details on the same transaction are referred to as "dual-purpose tests." When performing dual-purpose tests, the auditor must evaluate the outcome of each test to determine its impact on substantive procedures. For example, if the tests of controls determine that the controls are not operating effectively, the auditor should evaluate the adequacy of the sample size for the related substantive procedure.

Timing of tests of controls

The timing of the auditor's tests of controls depends on the period of time he or she intends to rely on those controls. If the auditor only intends to rely on the performance of controls as of a point in time (for example, relying on controls related to the physical inventory taken as of the balance sheet date), tests of the controls may be conducted as of that particular time. If the auditor intends to rely on the performance of controls throughout the period under audit, the tests of controls should be performed to determine that they operated effectively during that period.

For many controls, the auditor's tests may be performed during an interim period. In those circumstances, the auditor must determine what additional evidence should be obtained for the remaining period between interim and period end. Several factors affect the need for additional evidence about the remaining untested period:

- The significance of the assessed risks of material misstatements

- The specific controls that were tested during the interim period

- The degree to which audit evidence about the operating effectiveness of those controls was obtained

- The length of the remaining period

- The extent to which the auditor intends to reduce further substantive procedures based on the reliance of controls

- The control environment

- The extent of changes in internal control occurring subsequent to the interim period

The auditor may be able to rely on tests of controls performed in prior-year audits. To rely on tests of controls performed in prior audits, the auditor must obtain evidence about whether changes in those specific controls have occurred subsequent to the prior-year audit. For example, the auditor may have determined that an automated control operated effectively in a prior-year audit. The auditor should consider whether changes have been made to that automated control by making inquiries of management and by inspecting program change control logs. If changes have been made since the prior-year testing, the auditor should test the operating effectiveness of those controls in the current-year audit.

> **PLANNING AID REMINDER:** If the auditor plans to rely on controls that have not changed since they were last tested, he or she should test the operating effectiveness of the controls at least once in every third year of an annual audit.

The extent of time that has elapsed since the last testing of a control is directly impacted by the extent of risk of material misstatement or the extent of reliance on controls. More recent retesting of a control occurs when the control environment is weak, there are weak monitoring controls, there is a significant manual element to the control, personnel changes have occurred that affect the application of the control, there are weak general IT controls, and there are other circumstances that indicate a need for changes in the control.

There may be circumstances where there are several controls affecting the auditor's planned audit evidence that were tested in prior audits. SAS-110 requires the auditor to test the operating effectiveness of some of those controls each year (thus, the auditor cannot rely solely on tests of all those controls conducted in prior audits). This requirement ensures that there is some rotation of testing of those controls throughout each audit period within the last three years.

As the risk of material misstatement increases, the need for more audit evidence about the operating effectiveness of controls relevant to that risk should increase. The auditor must perform tests of controls in the current audit period for all controls intended to mitigate a significant risk. As a result, the auditor should not rely on tests of controls performed in a prior audit when those controls are designed to mitigate a significant risk. Exhibit 318-1 provides a summary of decisions auditors make about the timing of the testing of controls for current-year audits.

Extent of tests of controls

The extent of tests of controls relates to the sufficiency of the tests. Several factors affect the extent of tests of controls:

• The frequency of the performance of the control by the entity during the period

• The length of time during the audit period that the auditor is relying on the control

• The relevance and reliability of the audit evidence to be obtained in supporting that the control prevents or detects and corrects material misstatements at the relevant financial statement level

• The extent to which audit evidence is obtained from tests of other controls related to the relevant assertion

- The extent to which the auditor plans to rely on the operating effectiveness of the control in the assessment of risk

- The expected deviation from the control

As the auditor's reliance on the operating effectiveness of the control increases, the extent of his or her testing of the control should increase. Similarly, when the expected control deviation rate increases, the auditor's extent of testing of the related control should increase.

> **PLANNING AID REMINDER:** Because an automated IT control should function consistently until the underlying program or data is changed, the auditor may be able to limit the testing of IT processing controls to a few instances of the control's operation. Once the testing of the automated control occurs, the auditor should perform tests to determine that the control continues to function effectively, such as determining whether program changes have occurred, that the authorized version of the program is used for processing, and that other general controls are operating effectively.

Substantive procedures

The objective of a substantive procedure is to detect material misstatements at the relevant assertion level for an account balance, class of transaction, or disclosure. Substantive procedures consist of two types: (1) substantive analytical procedures and (2) tests of details of classes of transactions, account balances, and disclosures.

Generally, the nature, timing, and extent of substantive procedures are affected by the assessed level of risk of material misstatement. However, SAS-110 notes that the auditor should design and perform substantive procedures for all relevant assertions pertaining to each account balance, disclosure, and material class of transactions. As a result, substantive procedures are required in every audit because (1) the auditor's assessment of risks of material misstatements is judgmental and may not be sufficiently precise to identify all risks of material misstatements and (2) there are inherent limitations in any system of internal control.

SAS-110 requires the auditor's substantive procedures related to the financial reporting process to include the following audit procedures:

- Agreeing the financial statements, including their accompanying notes, to the underlying accounting records

- Examining material journal entries and other adjustments made during the course of preparing the financial statements

PLANNING AID REMINDER: An AICPA Technical Practice Aid (TIS) clarifies that adjustments made during the course of preparing the financial statements noted in the bulleted point above refer to journal entries and adjustments prepared by the entity during the process of preparing its financial statements, such as consolidating entries or elimination entries between subsidiaries. It does not refer to journal entries recorded by the entity in the general ledger during the year. However, AU Section 316 reminds auditors that they are required to design audit procedures to test the appropriateness of journal entries recorded by the entity in the general ledger during the year as part of their considerations of the risk of material misstatement due to fraud.

FRAUD POINTER: SAS-99 requires the auditor to respond to the risk of management override of internal controls in every audit by examining journal entries. Thus, the auditor's examination of journal entries and other adjustments as part of his or her substantive procedures should be coordinated with the examination of journal entries required by SAS-99 to address the ever-present risk of management override of internal control.

In addition to the foregoing required substantive procedures at the financial statement reporting level, SAS-110 requires the auditor to perform substantive procedures for all significant risks. For example, if the auditor determines that the risk of material misstatement in accounts receivable is high related to the existence assertion, the auditor may not only confirm outstanding account balances of related customer balances, but also other details related to transactions affecting customers' account balances.

PLANNING AID REMINDER: In certain instances, the auditor may plan an all substantive approach even if his or her understanding of internal control causes him or her to believe that controls are designed effectively. AICPA Technical Practice Aid (TIS) 8200.07 clarifies that after the auditor obtains an understanding of the entity and its environment, including internal controls, and assesses the risk of material misstatement, he or she may consider the cost-benefit to determine the most effective set of further audit procedures. If the auditor believes that the benefit of testing the operating effectiveness of internal controls is less than the costs of testing them, he or she may adopt an audit strategy that consists solely of substantive procedures to respond to the risk of material misstatement.

Nature of substantive procedures

The nature of substantive procedures is directly affected by whether the procedure is a substantive analytical procedure or a test of details. Substantive analytical procedures are generally more applicable to larger volumes of transactions that tend to be predictable over time, such as income statement accounts. Tests of details are generally more appropriate for obtaining audit evidence about account balances, particularly existence and valuation.

The nature of substantive procedures should be responsive to the level of planned detection risk. In many instances the auditor's planned level of detection risk is affected by his or her tests of controls. Thus, the nature of substantive testing is affected by the audit evidence obtained through tests of controls. For example, substantive analytical procedures may be sufficiently responsive to the planned level of detection risk for some accounts, particularly when the tests of operating effectiveness have reduced the auditor's assessed level of the risk of material misstatements. In other situations, only a test of details or a combination of tests of details and substantive analytical procedures is appropriate to respond to the planned level of detection risk.

The nature of substantive procedures is directly affected by the nature of the relevant assertion. For example, to test the existence assertion, the nature of the auditor's substantive procedures should include the selection of items for testing from those recorded in the accounting records. To test the completeness assertion, the nature of the auditor's substantive procedures should include the selection of items for testing from audit evidence that indicates that an item has occurred and should be recorded in the accounting records. Exhibit 318-2 provides an example of illustrative substantive procedures linked to the inventory account balance assertions and the inventory presentation and disclosure assertions.

Several factors should affect the nature of the design of substantive analytical procedures. First, the auditor should consider the suitability of using substantive analytical procedures given the assertions. Second, the auditor should evaluate the reliability of the data used to develop the analytical procedure. Third, the level of precision that will be required from the analytical procedure to achieve the desired level of assurance must be considered. Fourth, the amount of any difference in recorded amounts from expected values that is acceptable will affect the design of the substantive analytical procedure.

When relying on substantive analytical procedures to achieve the planned level of detection risk, the auditor should consider performing tests of controls over the preparation of information that is to be used to perform the substantive analytical procedure. As the operating effectiveness of controls over the information generation increases, the auditor's confidence in the reliability of the underlying information used to develop the substantive analytical procedure increases.

> **FRAUD POINTER:** Auditors should consider the risk of management override of controls that relate to the generation of information used in developing a substantive analytical procedure. Management's override of such controls may allow them to make adjustments outside the normal period-end financial reporting process that artificially change the financial statement relationships being analyzed. As a result, substantive analytical procedures alone are not effective at detecting some types of fraud.

Timing of substantive procedures

Similar to tests of controls, the auditor may decide to perform substantive procedures at an interim date or at periods close to or as of period end. When substantive procedures are performed at interim dates, there is a risk that material misstatement that exists at the period end will not be detected by the auditor. As the length of the period between interim testing and period end increases, this risk increases. As a result, when the auditor decides to perform substantive tests at an interim date, he or she should perform further substantive procedures, sometimes in combination with tests of controls, to cover the remaining period to provide a basis for extending the audit conclusions from interim substantive procedures to period end. Exhibit 318-3 provides an illustrative example of how interim substantive procedures can be rolled forward to period end.

Several factors affect the auditor's decision to perform substantive procedures at an interim date:

- The strength of the control environment and other relevant controls
- The availability of information at a later date that is necessary for the auditor's procedures
- The objective of the substantive procedure
- The assessed level of material misstatement

- The nature of the account balance or class of transactions and relevant assertions

- The ability of the auditor to reduce the risk that misstatements that exist at the period end are not detected by performing appropriate substantive procedures, including those combined with tests of controls.

> **FRAUD POINTER:** When the auditor identifies risks of material misstatements due to fraud, one of his or her responses might include a change in the timing of substantive procedures to perform tests at or closer to the end of the reporting period.

Unlike the auditor's tests of controls, he or she is unable to rely on substantive procedures performed in prior audits to reduce detection risk in the current audit. In most cases, audit evidence obtained from prior audits provides little or no evidence to reduce detection risk in the current audit. As a result, substantive procedures should generally be performed during the current audit.

Extent of Substantive Procedures

As the risk of material misstatement increases, the extent of substantive testing must increase to achieve a reduced level of planned detection risk. Because the risk of material misstatement may be affected by the operating effectiveness of relevant internal controls, the auditor's tests of controls may reduce the extent of substantive procedures.

The extent of substantive procedures is often addressed through the sample size examined in the substantive procedure. Sample size is impacted by the planned level of detection risk, tolerable misstatement, expected misstatement, and the nature of the population (see AU 350 for further discussion about determining sample sizes). Other matters may also affect the extent of substantive procedures, including whether the population of items for testing can be stratified into homogeneous subpopulations or identified for testing due to their size or unusual nature, which requires a greater extent of testing.

The extent of substantive analytical procedures is directly affected by the amount of difference between expected and actual values that can be accepted by the auditor without further testing. As the acceptable level of difference decreases, the desired level of assurance to be obtained from the substantive analytical procedure increases.

Procedures to evaluate the adequacy of presentation and disclosure

SAS-110 requires the auditor to perform audit procedures to evaluate whether the overall presentation in the financial statements, including the related disclosures, are in accordance with generally accepted accounting principles. This includes the auditor's consideration of whether the individual financial statements reflect the appropriate classification and description of financial information and include adequate disclosure of material matters.

One of the main auditor considerations is the completeness and accuracy of disclosure information. The auditor should consider whether management should have disclosed a particular matter in light of a specific situation. The auditor's assessment of the risk of material misstatement should affect the auditor's evaluation of disclosure.

Evaluating the Sufficiency and Appropriateness of Audit Evidence Obtained

The third standard of fieldwork requires the auditor to obtain sufficient appropriate audit evidence in order to obtain a reasonable basis for his or her opinion about the financial statements. The sufficiency and appropriateness of audit evidence to support the auditor's conclusions made throughout the audit are a matter of professional judgment. Several factors affect the sufficiency and appropriateness of audit evidence:

- Significance of the potential misstatement in the relevant assertion and the likelihood of it having a material effect on the financial statements

- Effectiveness of management's responses and controls to address the risks

- Experience gained during previous audits with respect to similar potential misstatements

- Results of audit procedures performed, including whether such audit procedures identified specific instances of fraud or error

- Source and reliability of audit evidence

- Persuasiveness of audit evidence

- Understanding of the entity and its environment, including its internal control

The auditor's accumulation of audit evidence in an audit is cumulative and iterative. As the auditor performs the audit procedures and obtains related audit evidence, he or she should evaluate whether assessments of the risks of material misstatement at the relevant assertion level remain appropriate.

Evidence obtained from risk assessment procedures or further audit procedures, including tests of controls and substantive procedures, may have an impact on the nature, timing, and extent of audit procedures. For example, information may come to the auditor's attention that differs from the information he or she used to assess the risk of material misstatement or information obtained from tests of controls may identify deviations in those controls. That information may require the auditor to modify the assessed level of risk of material misstatement, in turn requiring changes in the nature, timing, or extent of other planned audit procedures that should be performed.

When the auditor's tests of controls identify deficiencies in the operating effectiveness of those controls, SAS-110 requires the auditor to make specific inquiries to understand whether the deviations were caused by factors such as changes in key personnel, significant seasonal fluctuations in the volume of transactions, or human error and their potential consequences. Furthermore, the auditor should determine whether any misstatements identified by substantive procedures alter his or her assessment of the effectiveness of related controls. In light of these findings, the auditor then assesses whether additional tests of controls are necessary or the risks of material misstatements should be addressed using substantive procedures.

FRAUD POINTER: A deficiency commonly cited in enforcement actions against auditors is their overreliance on internal controls, particularly their failure to expand testing in light of known control weaknesses.

Before the conclusion of the audit, the auditor should evaluate whether audit risk has been reduced to an appropriately low level and whether the nature, timing, and extent of the audit procedures should be reconsidered. In some instances, the auditor may need to reconsider the nature, timing, and extent of substantive procedures or the audit evidence obtained through tests of controls.

The auditor should attempt to obtain further audit evidence if he or she has not obtained sufficient appropriate audit evidence. If the auditor is unable to obtain sufficient appropriate audit evidence, he or she should express a qualified or disclaimer of opinion.

FRAUD POINTER: When the auditor identifies a material misstatement due to fraud, he or she should not assume that the fraud instance is an isolated occurrence. The auditor should consider the implications for the overall financial statement audit and may need to modify his or her overall response to the risk of material misstatements or his or her response at the relevant assertion level.

Documentation of the auditor's responses to the assessed risks

SAS-110 includes specific responsibilities related to the auditor's documentation of matters related to the responses to the assessed risks of material misstatements. Specifically, the auditor must document the following:

- The overall responses to address the assessed risks of misstatement at the financial statement level.

- The nature, timing, and extent of the further audit procedures (tests of controls and substantive procedures).

- The linkage of those procedures with the assessed risks at the relevant assertion level.

- The results of the audit procedures.

- The conclusions reached about the audit evidence used in the current audit that pertains to the operating effectiveness of controls that was obtained in a prior audit.

Practitioner's Aids

The exhibits on the following pages may be used as practitioner's aids.

EXHIBIT 318-1 — DECISION TREE FOR DESIGNING AND PERFORMING CURRENT YEAR TESTS OF CONTROLS

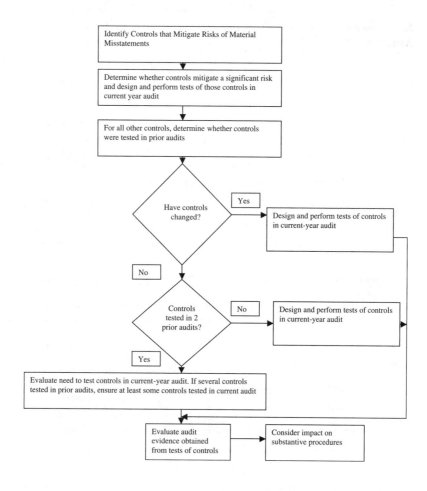

EXHIBIT 318-2—EXAMPLES OF SUBSTANTIVE PROCEDURES RELEVANT TO INVENTORY ASSERTIONS

Inventory Account Balance Assertions	Examples of Substantive Procedures
Existence Inventories included in the balance sheet physically exist	Conduct a physical examination of inventory items
	Obtain confirmation of inventory items held at outside locations
	Inspect documentation related to the purchase and sale of inventory between the physical inventory date and the balance sheet date
Completeness Inventory items on hand at the balance sheet date are included in the balance sheet.	Conduct a physical examination of inventory items and determine that the items are recorded in the inventory listing
	Inspect shipping and receiving transactions near year-end for recording in the proper period
Valuation Inventories are stated at cost (except when market is lower).	Examine invoices paid to vendors for inventory purchases and compare product unit prices to those appropriate given the underlying selected accounting policy (e.g. LIFO versus FIFO)
	Inspect inventory publications and other market data for current market prices and determine whether unit prices used to value inventory are at lower of cost or market
	Recalculate unit price times quantity for selected items included in the inventory listing
	Watch for evidence of slow-moving items while present for the physical examination of inventory

Inventory Account Balance Assertions	Examples of Substantive Procedures
Rights and obligations The entity has legal title or similar rights of ownership to the inventories.	Obtain confirmation of inventory held at other locations to confirm title of goods held
	Examine vendor invoices for evidence of consignment arrangements
	Examine sales invoices and related shipping documents to ensure inventories exclude items billed to customers or owned by others

Inventory Presentation and Disclosure Assertions	Examples of Substantive Procedures
Rights and obligations Any pledge or assignment of inventories is appropriately disclosed	Obtain confirmation of inventories pledged under loan agreements
Completeness The financial statements include all disclosures related to inventories specified by GAAP	Use a disclosure checklist to determine whether required GAAP disclosures are included in the footnotes
Understandability Inventories are properly classified in the balance sheet as current assets and all related disclosures are understandable	Examine drafts of the financial statements for appropriate balance sheet classification
	Read the inventory footnote disclosures for clarity
Accuracy and valuation The major categories of inventories and their bases of valuation are accurately disclosed in the financial statements.	Examine the drafts of the financial statements for appropriate disclosure

EXHIBIT AU 318-3 — EXAMPLES OF ROLL FORWARD OF SUBSTANTIVE PROCEDURES FROM INTERIM TO PERIOD END

Professional judgment must be used to determine which balance sheet accounts can be subjected to substantive tests prior to the balance sheet date. To illustrate how this approach may be applied, assume that an auditor has decided to confirm accounts receivable at an interim date. The confirmation procedures normally applied at year-end would be applied to the trial balance of accounts receivable as of the interim date. Returned confirmations would be evaluated, and the auditor would develop various confirmation statistics. For transactions occurring after the interim date, the auditor would rely upon the client's internal control to process data in an acceptable manner. Summary data in the sales journal and cash receipts journal would be reviewed for unusual items. In addition, the client could be requested to prepare an aged trial balance at the end of the year, and the auditor could perform the analysis. During the review, the auditor would look for significant amounts from customers that were not listed on the interim trial balance. Other items that are unusual or that otherwise come to the attention of the auditor could be subject to confirmation as of the year-end date.

The following illustrates an audit schedule format that an auditor could use to document the approach of performing substantive tests on data processed by the client after the interim date:

Averroes Company

Analysis of Accounts Receivable from Interim to Year-End Date	12/31/X6	
Accounts Receivable Balance @ 9/30/X6		$450,000
		See audit schedule
		@ AR110
Sales — October (a)	80,000	
November (a)	85,000	
December (a)	82,000	
		247,000

Cash receipts — October (b)	78,000		
November (b)	81,000		
December (b)	79,000		
		238,000	
Write-offs — October (c)	450		
November (c)	230		
December (c)	1,850		
		−2,530	
Accounts Receivable Balance @12/31/X6		$456,470	

See audit schedule

@ AR100

(a) Traced to Sales Journal — Footed November and December journals

(b) Traced to Cash Receipts Journal — Footed October

(c) Traced to approvals and reviewed with credit manager

Prepared By: _____JB_____

Date: _____1/29/X7_____   AR101

SECTION 322

THE AUDITOR'S CONSIDERATION OF THE INTERNAL AUDIT FUNCTION IN AN AUDIT OF FINANCIAL STATEMENTS

Authoritative Pronouncements

SAS-65 — The Auditor's Consideration of the Internal Audit Function in an Audit of Financial Statements

> **IMPORTANT NOTICE FOR 2011:** The Auditing Standards Board (ASB) is in the process of redrafting all of the auditing sections in *Codification of Statements on Auditing Standards* to converge U.S. GAAS with the International Standards on Auditing issued by the International Auditing and Assurance Standards Board. As part of this process, the newly redrafted standards will follow certain clarity drafting conventions adopted by the ASB. These clarity drafting conventions include: (1) establishing objectives for each standard; (2) including a definitions section, if appropriate; and (3) separating requirements from application guidance and other material. The ASB is planning to have all redrafted standards become effective on the same date, which is for audits of financial statements for periods ending on or after December 15, 2012. It is possible that the effective date might be delayed beyond that date. The ASB's clarity and convergence project will have a significant effect on the auditing standards applicable to audits of nonpublic companies, and the 2012 *GAAS Guide* will be appropriately modified to reflect these changes once the effective date of the standards is certain.

Overview

An internal audit function, if it exists, is part of the client's internal control. SAS-65 describes how the auditor should evaluate the internal audit function in order to plan the audit engagement (designing the nature, timing, and extent of subsequent audit procedures).

An internal audit function may consist of a variety of activities, some or all of which might not be related to the recording, processing, and reporting of financial information. The auditor should obtain an understanding of the internal audit function as part of obtaining an understanding of the entity and its environment, including its internal controls. Although the special circumstances of each engagement will dictate the specific audit approach, the auditor should make inquiries to gain an understanding of the following issues:

- Internal audit's status within the organizational hierarchy of the entity

- Internal audit's application of professional standards, such as professional internal auditing standards

- Internal audit's audit plan, including the nature, timing, and extent of its work

- Internal audit's ability to assess records and any restrictions on the scope of their activities

Certain internal audit activities might not be relevant to the audit of financial statements, such as operational audits performed by internal audit. If after gaining an understanding of the internal audit function the auditor determines that internal audit's activities are not relevant to the audit of financial statements, he or she does not have to further consider the internal audit function.

> **PUBLIC COMPANY IMPLICATION:** In 2003, the New York Stock Exchange (NYSE) changed its listing requirements to mandate that all NYSE registrants have an internal audit function.

Promulgated Procedures Checklist

If the auditor concludes that relevant activities are being performed by internal auditors, and it appears that it would be efficient to rely on those activities in lowering the assessment of control risk, the auditor should perform the following:

- Assess the objectivity and competence of the internal audit function

- Determine the effect of the internal audit function on understanding the internal control

- Determine the effect of the internal audit function on the assessment of the risk of material misstatement

- Determine the degree of reliance on the internal audit function

- Evaluate internal audit's work

> **PLANNING AID REMINDER:** SAS-65 requires that, in all engagements, the auditor develop some understanding of

the internal audit function and determine whether that function is relevant to the assessment of control risk. Thus, if there is an internal audit function, it must be evaluated. The evaluation is not optional.

Analysis and Application of Procedures

Assess the objectivity and competence of the internal audit function

The auditor should evaluate the objectivity of internal auditors by determining the organizational status of the internal audit function and by examining the policies that may enhance the likelihood that the internal auditors are objective.

> **OBSERVATION:** The standard of objectivity is different from the standard of independence. Although it could be argued that it is simply a matter of semantics, the differentiation is based on the reasonable assumption that an internal auditor cannot achieve independence, because he or she is an employee of the client.

SAS-65 states that factors relevant to determining organizational status of the internal audit function include the following:

- Direct reporting to an officer, which implies broad audit coverage and adequate consideration of audit findings

- Direct access and reporting to the board of directors, the audit committee, or the owner/manager

- For internal audit employment decisions, oversight responsibility that rests with the board of directors, the audit committee, or the owner/manager

In addition, policies that minimize the placement of internal auditors in situations where they have an existing relationship (for example, auditing a department where a spouse works) or may have a future relationship (possible assignment to a department once the internal audit stint is completed) can contribute to the objectivity of the internal audit function and should be considered by the auditor.

In assessing the competence of the internal auditors, the auditor should review background information on the internal auditors, such as their educational achievements (degrees, certifications, continuing education) and professional experience. In addition, the auditor should consider operational practices such as the assignment of internal auditors, supervision and review of personnel within the department, quality of audit documentation, and specific performance evaluations. Audit policies, programs, and procedures are also relevant, when evaluating the internal audit functions.

SAS-65 states that in some instances it is necessary to test the effectiveness of the client's controls on objectivity and competency. For example, rather than simply accepting an assertion that the audit committee is involved in the hiring of internal auditors, the auditor may decide to interview members of the committee and ask them specifically about their roles in hiring and overseeing internal audit staff.

> **ENGAGEMENT STRATEGY:** The degree to which the effectiveness of controls will be tested should be based on the anticipated degree to which the internal audit function will be a factor in the planning of subsequent audit procedures: The greater the reliance on the internal audit function, the greater the degree to which the controls should be tested.

If the auditor concludes that the internal audit function possesses an acceptable level of objectivity and competence, the auditor should determine the effect of the function on (1) the understanding of the internal control, (2) the assessment of risk, and (3) the design of substantive procedures.

Determine the effect of the internal audit function on understanding the internal control

The auditor's responsibility with regard to the client's internal control generally consists of obtaining an understanding of the design and determining whether controls have been placed in operation. Work performed by internal auditors may affect one or both of these phases of the engagement. For example, internal auditors may have documented the cash disbursements system by preparing a flowchart and supportive narrative descriptions. In addition, the internal auditors may have inspected canceled voucher packages to determine whether certain specific control procedures depicted on the flowchart were followed. The auditor could rely on this documentation to gain an initial understanding of the cash disbursement system (understanding design phase) and could review the number and types of control deviations discovered by the internal auditors (placed in operation phase).

Determine the effect of the internal audit function on the assessment of risk of material misstatement

The auditor assesses risk at the financial statement level and at the account balance or class-of-transaction level. Risk at the financial statement level is broad in nature in that it applies to assessing the risk of material misstatement in many financial statement assertions. Generally, factors related to the control environment have a broad effect on numerous accounts. Thus, an evaluation of the internal audit function as an element of the client's internal control can have an effect on the auditor's assessment of risk at the financial statement level because internal audit can affect many account assertions.

Risk at the account balance or class-of-transaction level is directed to specific control activities and the related assertions that appear in the financial statements. Having internal auditors perform tests of controls may influence the level of risk assessed at the account balance level or class-of-transaction level. For example, if internal auditors have tested specific assertions in the cash disbursement system, the auditor reviewing internal audit's tests may decide that control risk as it relates to assertions concerning certain operating expenses (such as advertising expense and utilities expense) can be assessed at a level less than maximum.

> **FRAUD POINTER:** SAS-99 requires auditors to inquire of internal audit personnel, if there is an internal audit function, about internal audit's views related to the risks of fraud. Auditors must also inquire about whether internal audit has performed any procedures to identify or detect fraud during the year and whether management has responded satisfactorily to internal audit's findings regarding fraud risks. Auditors must also ask internal audit whether they have knowledge of any fraud or suspected fraud.

Determine the degree of reliance on the internal audit function

Although the role of the internal audit function should be considered as part of understanding internal control, assessing risk, and designing substantive procedures, the independent auditor is solely responsible for the opinion expressed on the financial statements. For this reason, the auditor should carefully consider the extent to which the internal audit function should influence the audit approach. The fundamental guidance for determining the role the internal audit function should play in the audit is simple: Audit evidence obtained indirectly from an internal auditor is less reliable than the same audit evidence developed directly by the independent auditor.

> **OBSERVATION:** SAS-65 states that the auditor should consider three factors: (1) the materiality of balances or classes of transactions, (2) the degree of inherent risk and control risk that affects assertions, and (3) the degree of subjectivity needed to evaluate evidence to support assertions in the financial statements — in

determining the degree of reliance on the internal audit function. As each one of these factors increases, the degree of reliance on work performed by internal auditors should decrease (and vice versa).

SAS-65 reiterates that when assertions related to material amounts are characterized by a high risk of material misstatement or a high degree of subjectivity (or both), the auditor must be in a position to accept sole responsibility for satisfying the standards of fieldwork with respect to these assertions and the related internal control. Furthermore, the work of the internal auditors cannot solely be used as a basis for eliminating the auditor's performance of substantive procedures on those assertions. SAS-65 suggests that the following assertions have either a high degree of risk or a high degree of subjectivity in the evaluation of audit evidence:

- Significant accounting estimates that are the basis for valuing assets or liabilities

- Existence and disclosure of related-party transactions

- Existence and disclosure of contingencies and other uncertainties

- Existence and disclosure of subsequent events

Although the work of internal auditors may be used in a variety of circumstances, SAS-65 states that the following judgments should be made by the auditor and not by internal auditors:

- Assessments of inherent risk and control risk

- Sufficiency of audit tests performed

- Evaluation of significant accounting estimates

Other similar judgments also should be made exclusively by the auditor. SAS-65 states that if the internal auditors are requested to directly assist in the audit, the auditor should follow the guidelines listed below:

- Assess the competence and objectivity of the internal auditors

- Supervise, review, evaluate, and test the work performed by the internal auditors

- Describe to the internal auditors their responsibilities

- Describe the objective of the work that is being performed by internal audit

- Describe circumstances that could affect the nature, timing, and extent of audit procedures

- Direct internal auditors to inform the auditor of all significant accounting and auditing issues that arise during the performance of their work

Evaluate internal audit's work

When the auditor concludes that the work of internal auditors may be used to determine an understanding of internal control, to assess risk, or as substantive procedures, the auditor should evaluate the quality of that work. Factors that might be considered in assessing the work of internal auditors are the following:

- Whether the scope of the work is consistent with audit objectives

- Adequacy of internal audit programs

- Adequacy of audit documentation, including evidence of supervision and review

- Appropriateness of conclusions drawn

- Whether the internal audit reports are consistent with the nature of the work performed

The auditor's evaluation of the effectiveness of the procedures conducted by internal auditors should include the testing of the internal auditors' work related to significant financial statement assertions. The auditor can satisfy the need for such evaluation either by (1) examining controls, transactions, or balances examined by the internal auditors or by (2) examining similar controls, transactions, or balances not actually examined by the internal auditors. The auditor should then compare his or her own results to those of the internal auditors. The degree to which the auditor performs such tests is a matter of professional judgment.

SECTION 324

SERVICE ORGANIZATIONS

Authoritative Pronouncements

SAS-70 — Service Organizations

SAS-78 — Consideration of Internal Control in a Financial Statement Audit: An Amendment to SAS-55

SAS-88 — Service Organizations and Reporting on Consistency

SAS-98 — Omnibus Statement on Auditing Standards — 2002

Auditing Interpretation No. 1 of AU 324 (April 1995) — Describing Tests of Operating Effectiveness and the Results of Such Tests

Auditing Interpretation No. 2 of AU 324 (April 1995) — Service Organizations That Use the Services of Other Service Organizations (Subservice Organizations)

Auditing Interpretation No. 4 of AU 324 (February 2002) — Responsibilities of Service Organizations and Service Auditors with Respect to Forward-Looking Information in a Service Organization's Description of Controls

Auditing Interpretation No. 5 of AU 324 (February 2002) — Statements about the Risk of Projecting Evaluations of the Effectiveness of Controls to Future Periods

> **IMPORTANT NOTICE FOR 2011:** The Auditing Standards Board (ASB) issued Statement on Standards for Attestation Engagements (SSAE) No. 16 (Reporting at a Service Organization) in April 2010. The purpose of SSAE-16 is to move the guidance for service auditors contained in AU 324 from auditing standards to the attest standards. The guidance for user auditors will continue to reside in the audit standards. As of April 2010, the ASB had completed a revision to AU 324 that is part of the ASB's process of redrafting all of the auditing sections in *Codification of Statements on Auditing Standards* to converge U.S. GAAS with the International Standards on Auditing issued by the International Auditing and Assurance Standards Board. The redrafted AU 324 conforms the guidance for user auditors contained here to the clarity drafting conventions adopted by the ASB. Although the guidance in

SSAE-16 is effective for service auditors' reports for periods ending on or after June 15, 2011 (with early application permitted), the redrafted AU 324 guidance for user auditors will become effective with all other redrafted standards. The ASB is planning to have all redrafted standards become effective on the same date, which is for audits of financial statements for periods ending on or after December 15, 2012. It is possible that the effective date will be delayed beyond that date. The ASB's clarity and convergence project will have a significant effect on the auditing standards applicable to audits of non-public companies, and the 2012 *GAAS Guide* will be appropriately modified to reflect these changes once the effective date of the standards is certain.

Overview

The guidance established by SAS-70 (as amended by SAS-88) applies to the audit of a client that uses the services of another entity (service organization), whereby those services are considered to be part of the client's information system used to process transactions because they affect one or more of the following:

- Classes of transactions significant to the entity's financial statements

- Procedures used to initiate, record, process, and report transactions in the financial statements

- The client's accounting records, supporting information, and specific accounts in the financial statements

- The procedures, both manual and automated, used to process accounting transactions (from the initiation of a transaction to the impact of the transaction on the financial statements)

- The process used to prepare the client's financial statements (including significant accounting estimates and disclosures)

For example, a mortgage company may use the services of another entity to receive and process monthly mortgage payments from its customers, or a company may engage a computer processing service to record and process routine transactions related to payroll, trade receivables, and trade payables.

The activities performed by the service organization may be considered part of the client's internal control and therefore may require that the auditor develop a sufficient understanding of the controls in place at the service organization's facilities. However, it may be costly to have the client's auditor visit the other organization to obtain such an understanding. Also, it could be disruptive to the other organization to have several of its customers' auditors review and test its internal control.

To provide a reasonable solution to this problem, the American Institute of Certified Public Accountants (AICPA) issued SAS-70, which identifies and defines the following four parties relative to reporting on processing of transactions by service organizations:

1. *User organization* The entity that has engaged a service organization and whose financial statements are being audited

2. *User auditor* The auditor who reports on the financial statements of the user organization

3. *Service organization* The entity (or segment of an entity) that provides services to the user organization

4. *Service auditor* The auditor who reports on the processing of transactions by a service organization

> **PLANNING AID REMINDER:** The standards established by SAS-70 are also applicable to service organizations that develop, provide, and maintain software used by user organizations. However, the standards are not applicable to the audit of a client's transactions that arise from financial interests in partnerships, corporations, and joint ventures, when the entity's proprietary interest is accounted for and reported. In addition, SAS-70 would not apply when the service organization executes transactions based on specific authorization granted by the user organization. For example, the user auditor would not consider the control procedures of a broker that simply executes security transactions for the user organization.

ROLE OF THE USER AUDITOR

When a user organization employs a service organization, the user organization's ability to institute effective internal controls over the activities performed by the service organization can vary.

In many instances, internal controls of the service organization are an extension of the user organization's accounting system. Generally, transactions authorized by the user organization are transferred to the service organization for additional processing, and internal controls are maintained by both the user and the service organization. In other instances, the service organization may execute transactions and maintain related accountability, and the user organization might not have effective internal controls over such transactions.

Promulgated Procedures Checklist: User Auditor

The user auditor should perform the following procedures in determining the degree to which the work of the service auditor should be utilized:

- Determine the degree of understanding that should be obtained about the service organization's internal controls.

- Consider the internal controls at the service organization in assessing control risk.

- Consider obtaining a service auditor's report.

- Make inquiries concerning the service auditor's professional reputation.

- Determine whether the work of the service auditor can be used.

Analysis and Application of Procedures: User Auditor

Determine the degree of understanding that should be obtained about the service organization's internal controls

When a service organization's activities are considered to be part of the client's information system (as described earlier), the requirements established in SAS-109 (AU 314) (Understanding the Entity and Its Environment and Assessing the Risks of Material Misstatement) and SAS-110 (AU 318) (Performing Audit Procedures in Response to Assessed Risks and Evaluating the Audit Evidence Obtained) apply to the tasks performed by the service organization. That is, the auditor must obtain an understanding of the entity and its environment, including related controls instituted by both the client and the service organization in order to

- Identify the nature of potential misstatements that might occur

- Consider relevant factors that affect the risk of a material misstatement in the financial statements

- Design test of controls

- Design substantive procedures

Information about relevant controls instituted by a service organization can be identified from a number of sources, including the following:

- User manuals

- System overviews

- Technical manuals

- The contract between the two parties

- Reports by other parties including the service auditor, internal auditors, and regulatory authorities

One of the ways user auditors can obtain information useful to gaining an understanding of internal controls at the service organization is through a report provided by the service auditor to the user auditor. A service auditor can provide a report on controls placed in operation at the service center. That report should be helpful in providing information to an auditor obtaining an understanding of internal controls at the service center in order to plan his or her audit of the user organization. However, it is important to note that such a report provides no evidence about the operating effectiveness of relevant controls. It merely provides information about the design of controls at the service center and whether they have been placed in operation.

SAS-88 notes that when the activities performed by the service organization are routine and highly standardized, a review of information obtained by the user auditor in previous experience with the service center might be useful in planning the current engagement.

On the basis of these factors, and others that the user auditor may consider relevant, the user auditor should decide whether the service organization should be contacted to obtain specific information needed to understand internal controls relevant to the audit. If the user auditor concludes that there is sufficient information about the service organization's internal control to plan the audit, there is no need to contact the service organization.

> **ENGAGEMENT STRATEGY:** If it is concluded that the information is insufficient for adequate planning of the audit, the user auditor should consider contacting the service organization (through the client). The user auditor could (1) request additional information from the service organization, (2) request that a service auditor be engaged by the service organization (see later discussion titled "Role of the Service Auditor"), or (3) visit the service organization and obtain the desired information.

*Consider the internal controls at the service organization in
assessing control risk*

When assessing control risk, the user auditor should consider controls that
are employed by the service organization, as well as those established by
the user organization. SAS-109 (AU 314) states that control risk can be
assessed at a level below the maximum level only when (1) specific controls
relate to specific assertions and (2) those procedures are subject to tests of
controls. When certain service center controls permit the user auditor to
assess control risk below the maximum, evidence about the operating
effectiveness of those controls can be obtained in the following ways:

- By performing tests of controls at the user organization's location

- By performing tests of controls at the service organization

- By obtaining a service auditor's report on controls placed in operation, as
  well as tests of operating effectiveness

- By obtaining a service auditor's report on the application of agreed-upon
  procedures that describes appropriate tests of controls

> **PLANNING AID REMINDER:** Although the user auditor can
> obtain information about tests of controls in a variety of ways,
> the information should be carefully evaluated to determine
> whether it is relevant to and sufficient for the assessment of
> control risk at a level that is less than the maximum level.

Consider obtaining a service auditor's report

Professional standards describe two reports that user auditors may obtain
from service auditors. Discussions between the user auditor, user organization, service auditor, and service organization will help the auditor
determine the most suitable report to obtain. These two reports address
the following elements.

Report on controls placed in operation

The report on controls placed in operation can be useful to user auditors,
particularly in meeting their responsibility to obtain an understanding of
internal controls when planning the audit. In this report, the service auditor
reports on the service organization's description of internal controls that
might be relevant to the user organization's internal control and whether
the design of controls is suitable for achieving specific control objectives.
In addition, the service auditor reports on whether the controls have been

placed in operation as of a specific date. This report does not, however, report on tests of controls. Thus, it does not provide the user auditor with a basis for assessing control risk below maximum.

Report on controls placed in operation and tests of operating effectiveness

The report on controls placed in operation and tests of operating effectiveness is useful to user auditors. In addition to providing the information described above for the report on controls placed in operation, the service auditor reports on the operating effectiveness of controls that were tested to provide reasonable assurance that the control objectives were achieved during the period tested. This report can provide a basis for the user auditor to lower the assessment of control risk below maximum.

The service auditor may also perform agreed-upon audit procedures that substantiate transactions and balances that appear in the user organization's financial statements. Such procedures should be agreed to by the user organization, user auditor, service organization, and service auditor. Similarly, governmental auditing regulations or other arrangements might require the service auditor to perform specific substantive procedures. The user auditor might take into consideration the results of performing such procedures.

> **PUBLIC COMPANY IMPLICATION:** SOX requires all public companies to issue an "internal control report" by management. Furthermore, SOX requires the auditor to issue a separate opinion based on his or her evaluation of the effectiveness of internal control over financial reporting. That responsibility includes a requirement for the auditor to arrive at his or her own assessment of the operating effectiveness of the internal controls. When auditing a public company that uses a service organization to process transactions relevant to financial statements, the auditor should consider the guidance contained in AU 324. In many cases the auditor is required to obtain a service auditor's report on controls placed in operation and tests of operating effectiveness.

Make inquiries concerning the service auditor's professional reputation

As suggested earlier, the user auditor might obtain a service auditor's report on (1) controls placed in operations (used to obtain an understanding of internal control in order to plan the engagement) or (2) controls placed in operation and tests of operating effectiveness (used to obtain an understanding of internal control in order to plan the engagement and assess control risk). Before either of these reports is relied on, the user auditor should make inquiries concerning the service auditor's professional reputation. Guidance for making such inquiries can be found in SAS-1, AU 543 (Part of Audit Performed by Other Independent Auditors).

> **ENGAGEMENT STRATEGY:** Although the user auditor may rely on the work of the service auditor, there should be no reference to such work in the user auditor's report on the financial statements of the user organization. This is not a "division of responsibility" reporting circumstance as described in SAS-1, AU 543.

Determine whether the work of the service auditor can be used

If it is concluded that the service auditor's professional reputation is acceptable, there should be a determination of whether the work performed by the service auditor is sufficient to achieve the user auditor's objectives. To make this determination, the user auditor should consider performing one or more of the following procedures:

• Communicating with the service auditor and discussing the application and results of audit procedures performed

• Reviewing the audit programs used by the service auditor

• Reviewing the audit documentation of the service auditor

> **ENGAGEMENT STRATEGY:** If it is concluded that the work of the service auditor does not fully meet the needs of the user auditor, (1) the user auditor might request (with the permission of the user organization and the service organization) that the service auditor perform agreed-upon procedures or (2) the user auditor might perform appropriate procedures at the service organization's location.

ROLE OF THE SERVICE AUDITOR

When a service auditor reports on the processing of transactions by a service organization, the general standards — and the relevant standards of fieldwork and reporting — should be observed. Although the service auditor must be independent with respect to the service organization, it is not necessary to be independent from every user organization.

If the service auditor becomes aware of illegal acts, fraud, or uncorrected errors (that are other than inconsequential) that affect a user organization, the service auditor should determine whether the user organization has been informed of the matter. If such matters have not been communicated by management of the service organization to the user organization, the service auditor should inform the service organization's audit committee (or equivalent party) of the matter. If, after being informed of the matter, the audit committee does not take appropriate action, the service auditor should consider withdrawing from the engagement.

The service organization should determine what type of engagement the service auditor should perform; however, in an ideal situation, the user organization would discuss the matter with the service organization and its auditors to ensure that all parties will be satisfied with the service auditor's report.

The service auditor should observe the following guidance:

- Prepare an appropriate service audit report.

- Make inquiry concerning subsequent events that might affect the user organization's information systems

- Obtain written representations from the service organization.

Analysis and Application of Procedures: Service Auditor

Prepare an appropriate service audit report

SAS-70 defines a "report on controls placed in operation" (PPPO report) as follows:

> A service auditor's report on a service organization's description of the controls that may be relevant to a user organization's internal control as it relates to an audit of financial statements, on whether such controls were suitably designed to achieve specified control objectives, and on whether they had been placed in operation as of a specific date.

A "report on controls placed in operation and tests of operating effectiveness" (PPPO/TOE report) is defined as follows:

> A service auditor's report on a service organization's description of its controls that may be relevant to a user organization's internal control as it relates to an audit of financial statements, on whether such controls were suitably designed to achieve specified control objectives, on whether they had been placed in operation as of a specific date, and on whether the controls that

were tested were operating with sufficient effectiveness to provide reasonable, but not absolute, assurance that the related control objectives were achieved during the period specified.

The user auditor may use the PPPO report to obtain an understanding of the user organization's internal control as it relates to the activities performed by the service organization. The report may be used to plan tests of controls and substantive procedures in the audit of the user organization's financial statements, but it cannot be the basis for reducing the user auditor's assessment of control risk below the maximum level. A PPPO/TOE report, however, can be used by the user auditor to reduce the assessment of control risk below the maximum level, as well as to obtain an understanding and plan tests.

The service auditor issuing a PPPO report or a PPPO/TOE report should obtain a description of the relevant controls of the service organization's internal control that satisfies the needs of the user auditor. To determine whether the service organization has placed the controls in operation, the service auditor should consider the following audit procedures:

- Refer to results from previous experience with the service organization (may include results from the audit of the service organization's financial statements)

- Make inquiries of appropriate service organization personnel

- Inspect relevant documents and records of the service organization

- Observe activities conducted by the service organization

> **OBSERVATION:** When issuing a PPPO/TOE report, the service auditor should complete the above procedures and also perform tests of controls based on guidance established in SAS-109 (AU 314) and SAS-39 (AU 350) to determine the effectiveness of the relevant controls identified.

> **PUBLIC COMPANY IMPLICATION:** A PPPO report is also referred to as a "Type 1 SAS-70 report" and a PPPO/TOE report is also referred to as a "Type 2 SAS-70 report." Under PCAOB AS-5, only a PPPO/TOE report is acceptable because the auditor must be comfortable that internal controls at the service organization are properly designed and operating effectively.

The service auditor should make inquiries about changes in controls that may have occurred before fieldwork was begun. If there have been significant changes in controls (limited to changes within the last 12 months), those controls should be included in the description of the service organization's controls. If such changes are not included in the description of the service organization's controls, the service auditor should include them in his or her report.

For PPPO reports and PPPO/TOE reports, the description of relevant controls placed in operation at the service organization may be prepared by the service organization or by the service auditor. In either case, the representations made in the description are those of the management of the service organization. In order for the service auditor to express an opinion on the description, the following conditions must exist:

- There must be an appropriate identification and description of control objectives and the relevant controls at the service organization covered by the report.

- The service auditor must evaluate the relationships between the control objective and the relevant controls.

- The service auditor must obtain sufficient evidence to provide a basis for expressing an opinion on the description.

During the engagement, the service auditor should consider whether there are significant deficiencies in the service organization's controls that suggest that control objectives could not be satisfied. In addition, the service auditor should consider any additional information, whether or not it is related to specific control objectives, that (1) questions the ability of the service organization to initiate, record, process, or report financial data to user organizations without error and (2) indicates that the user organizations generally would not have controls in place to discover such deficiencies.

> **PLANNING AID REMINDER:** The service auditor should evaluate the control objectives (unless they are established by an outside party) to determine whether they are reasonable and consistent with the service organization's contractual obligations.

In both PPPO and PPPO/TOE reports, the service auditor should obtain evidence of whether controls have been placed in operation at the service center. Such evidence is generally obtained through previous experience with the service organization, through procedures involving inquiry of service organization's management, inspection of documentation at the service organization, and by observing service organization's activities and procedures.

In addition to including a description of relevant controls, a service auditor's PPPO/TOE report on the processing of transactions by the service organization should be accompanied by a separate description of tests of specified service organization controls designed to obtain evidence about the operating effectiveness of the relevant controls. That description should include the following:

- Controls that were tested

- Control objectives that the controls were intended to achieve

- Tests applied to the controls

- Results of the tests applied

- Description of the nature, timing, and extent of tests (presented in sufficient detail to enable user auditors to determine the effect on the assessment of control risk for the user organizations)

- Relevant information about exceptions discovered by the service auditor, including causative factors and corrective actions taken

The service organization determines which control objectives are to be subjected to tests of controls. The service auditor determines which controls are relevant to achieving specific control objectives and then establishes the nature, timing, and extent of audit procedures to test their effectiveness. The test period for relevant controls should generally cover a period of not less than six months, and sample items should be selected over the entire period.

SAS-70 establishes the following procedures for preparing PPPO and PPPO/TOE reports:

- Refer to the applications, services, products, or other aspects of the service organization covered by the report.

- Describe the scope and nature of the procedures performed.

- Identify the party that specified the control objectives.

- Indicate the purpose of the engagement.

- State an opinion on whether the description presents fairly, in all material respects, the relevant aspects of the service organization's controls that had been placed in operation as of a specific date.

- State the inherent limitations of the potential effectiveness of controls and the risk of projecting to future periods any evaluation of the description.

- Identify the parties for which the report is intended.

A PPPO report should also state an opinion on whether the controls were suitably designed to provide reasonable assurance that the specified control objectives would be achieved if those controls were satisfactorily complied with, and it should disclaim an opinion on the operating effectiveness of the controls.

A PPPO/TOE report, on the other hand, should also state an opinion on whether the controls tested were operating with sufficient effectiveness to provide a reasonable assurance that the related control objectives were achieved during the period. Therefore, in this type of report, the service auditor must also

- Refer to the description of tests of specified service organization controls.

- Disclose the period covered by tests of specified controls.

- State an opinion on whether controls tested were operating with sufficient effectiveness to provide a reasonable assurance that the related control objectives were achieved during the period.

- State that the effectiveness of specific service organization controls depends on their interaction with individual user organizations' controls, and other factors.

- If all control objectives listed in the description of controls were not covered by tests of operating effectiveness, state that the opinion is not applicable to those control objectives not listed in the description of tests performed.

- State that the service auditor has not performed procedures to determine the effectiveness of controls for user organizations.

According to SAS-70, PPPO reports and PPPO/TOE reports should be addressed to the service organization. An example of a PPPO report (Exhibit AU 324-1) and an example of a PPPO/TOE report (Exhibit AU 324-2) are presented at the end of this section.

If the service auditor concludes that the description that accompanies the PPPO or PPPO/TOE report is inaccurate or incomplete, the report should state this, and it should contain additional details to provide the user auditor with an appropriate understanding of the controls.

An effective design of internal controls at the service organization may be based on the assumption that complementary controls are in place at the user organization. Under this circumstance, the user organization's complementary controls should be part of the description of the service organization's relevant internal controls. Also, when the user organization's controls are considered necessary to achieve the stated control objectives, the report should be modified by adding an additional statement to the phrase "complied with satisfactorily" in the scope paragraph (first paragraph) and the opinion paragraph (third paragraph in the PPPO report, second paragraph in the PPPO/TOE report). The additional phrase is

> . . . and user organizations applied the internal controls contemplated in the design of the Service Organization's controls.

When the service auditor concludes that the description of controls is inaccurate or incomplete, the report should be changed by adding an explanatory paragraph (placed immediately before the opinion paragraph) that describes the deficiency and by qualifying the opinion paragraph. SAS-70 presents the following as an example of a qualified PPPO or PPPO/TOE report on a service organization's controls.

[Explanatory paragraph:]

The accompanying description states that X Service Organization uses operator identification numbers and passwords to prevent unauthorized access to the system. Based on inquiries of staff personnel and inspections of activities, we determined that such procedures are employed in Applications A and B but are not required to access the system in Applications C and D.

[Opinion paragraph:]

In our opinion, except for the matter referred to in the preceding paragraph, the accompanying description of the aforementioned application presents fairly, in all material respects, the relevant aspects of X Service Organization's controls that had been placed in operation as of [*identify date*]. Also, in our opinion, the controls, as described, are suitably designed to provide reasonable assurance that the specified control objectives would be achieved if the described controls were complied with satisfactorily.

When the service auditor concludes that there are significant deficiencies in the design or operation of relevant controls, the report should be changed by adding an explanatory paragraph (placed immediately before the opinion paragraph) that describes the deficiency and by qualifying the opinion paragraph. SAS-70 presents the following as an example of a qualified PPPO or PPPO/TOE report on a service organization's controls:

[Explanatory paragraph:]

As discussed in the accompanying description, from time to time the Service Organization makes changes in application programs to correct deficiencies or to enhance capabilities. The procedures followed in determining whether to make changes, designing the changes, and implementing them do not include review and approval by authorized individuals who are independent from those involved in making the changes. There are also no specified requirements to test such changes or to provide test results to an authorized reviewer prior to implementing the changes.

[Opinion paragraph:]

In our opinion, the accompanying description of the aforementioned application presents fairly, in all material respects, the relevant aspects of X Service Organization's controls that had been placed in operation as of [*identify date*]. Also, in our opinion, except for the deficiency referred to in the preceding paragraph, the controls, as described, are suitably designed to provide reasonable assurance that the specified control objectives would be achieved if the described controls were complied with satisfactorily.

Make inquiry concerning subsequent events

The service auditor has no responsibility to discover subsequent events; however, SAS-98 requires that the auditor inquire as to whether subsequent events have occurred after the period covered by the report but on or before the report date that might have an effect on user organizations. The service auditor should consider the following two types of subsequent events:

1. *Related to conditions that existed during the period covered by the report:* These subsequent events should be evaluated by the service auditor to determine whether they have implications for the auditor's assessment of controls that could affect user organizations' systems covered by the period reported on by the service auditor.

2. *Related to conditions that arose after the period covered by the report:* These subsequent events generally do not have an effect on the service auditor's assessment of controls applicable to the current engagement, but they must be disclosed by management in a section of the report containing "Other Information Provided by the Service Organization." If the service organization does not make the disclosure, the service auditor should disclose the subsequent event in the section of the report containing "Other Information Provided by the Service Auditor" and/or in the service auditor's report.

Obtain written representations from the service organization

The service auditor should obtain a written representation from the service organization's management that includes the following matters:

- Acknowledgment that management is responsible for establishing and maintaining appropriate controls related to the processing of transactions for user organizations

- Acknowledgment of the appropriateness of the control objectives specified

- Statement that the description of controls presents fairly, in all material respects, the aspects of the service organization's controls that may be relevant to a user organization's internal control

- Statement that controls, as described, had been placed in operation as of a specified date

- Statement that management has disclosed any significant changes in controls that have occurred since the service organization's last examination

- Statement that management has disclosed any illegal acts, fraud, or uncorrected errors that may affect one or more user organizations

- Statement that management has disclosed all design deficiencies in controls of which it is aware, including those for which the costs may exceed the benefits

- Statement that management has disclosed all instances, of which it is aware, when controls have not operated with sufficient effectiveness to achieve the specified control objectives (required only for PPPO/TOE reports)

- Statement that management has disclosed any subsequent events that would have a significant effect on user organizations

> **PLANNING AID REMINDER:** Auditing Interpretation No. 1 of AU 324 states that the report on the controls placed in operation and tests of operating effectiveness should provide a sufficient description of the tests performed and their results to enable the user auditor to adequately assess control risk for assertions related to the tasks performed by the service organization.

> **PLANNING AID REMINDER:** Interpretation No. 2 of AU 324 states that the user auditor must consider evaluating controls of a subservice organization that performs work for the service organization.

> **PLANNING AID REMINDER:** Auditing Interpretation No. 4 of AU 324 states that the service auditor does not have to identify in his or her report "design deficiencies that do not

affect processing during the period covered by the service auditor's examination but may represent potential problems in future periods."

Practitioner's Aids

Exhibit AU 324-1 is an example of a controls-placed-in-operation report (PPPO) and Exhibit AU 324-2 is an example of a controls-placed-in-operation and tests of operating effectiveness report (PPPO/TOE).

EXHIBIT AU 324-1 — REPORT ON CONTROLS PLACED IN OPERATION AT A SERVICE ORGANIZATION (PPPO)

We have examined the accompanying description of controls related to the [*identify service applications*] of X Service Organization. Our examination included procedures to obtain reasonable assurance about whether (1) the accompanying description presents fairly, in all material respects, the aspects of X Service Organization's controls that may be relevant to a user organization's internal control as it relates to an audit of financial statements; (2) the controls included in the description were suitably designed to achieve the control objectives specified in the description, if those controls were complied with satisfactorily; and (3) such controls had been placed in operation as of [*identify specific date*]. The control objectives were specified by [*identify party who specified control objectives*]. Our examination was performed in accordance with standards established by the American Institute of Certified Public Accountants and included those procedures we considered necessary in the circumstances to obtain a reasonable basis for rendering our opinion.

We did not perform procedures to determine the operating effectiveness of controls for any period. Accordingly, we express no opinion on the operating effectiveness of any aspects of X Service Organization's controls, individually or in the aggregate.

In our opinion, the accompanying description of the aforementioned application presents fairly, in all material respects, the relevant aspects of X Service Organization's controls that had been placed in operation as of [*identify date*]. Also, in our opinion, the controls, as described, are suitably designed to provide reasonable assurance that the specified control objectives would be achieved if the described controls were complied with satisfactorily.

The description of controls at X Service Organization is as of [*identify date*], and any projection of such information to the future is subject to the risk that, because of change, the description may no longer portray the controls in existence. The potential effectiveness of specific controls at the Service Organization is subject to inherent limitations and, accordingly, errors or fraud may occur and not be detected. Furthermore, the projection of any conclusions, based on our findings, to future periods is subject to the risk that changes may alter the validity of such conclusions.

This report is intended solely for use by the management of X Service Organization, its customers, and the independent auditors of its customers.

EXHIBIT AU 324-2 — REPORT ON CONTROLS PLACED IN OPERATION AT A SERVICE ORGANIZATION AND TESTS OF OPERATING EFFECTIVENESS (PPPO/TOE)

We have examined the accompanying description of controls related to the [*identify service applications*] of X Service Organization. Our examination included procedures to obtain reasonable assurance about whether (1) the accompanying description presents fairly, in all material respects, the aspects of X Service Organization's controls that may be relevant to a user organization's internal control as it relates to an audit of financial statements, (2) the controls included in the description were suitably designed to achieve the control objectives specified in the description, if those controls were complied with satisfactorily, and (3) such controls had been placed in operation as of [*identify specific date*]. The control objectives were specified by [*identify party who specified control objectives*]. Our examination was performed in accordance with standards established by the American Institute of Certified Public Accountants and included those procedures we considered necessary in the circumstances to obtain a reasonable basis for rendering our opinion.

In our opinion, the accompanying description of the aforementioned application presents fairly, in all material respects, the relevant aspects of X Service Organization's controls that had been placed in operation as of [*identify date*]. Also, in our opinion, the controls, as described, are suitably designed to provide reasonable assurance that the specified control objectives would be achieved if the described controls were complied with satisfactorily.

In addition to the procedures we considered necessary to render our opinion as expressed in the previous paragraph, we applied tests to specific controls, listed in Schedule A, to obtain evidence about their effectiveness in meeting the control objectives, described in Schedule A, during the period from [*identify period covered*]. The specific controls and the nature, timing, extent, and results of the tests are listed in Schedule A. This information has been provided to user organizations of X Service Organization and to their auditors to be taken into consideration, along with information about the internal control at user organizations, when making assessments of control risk for user organizations. In our opinion the controls that were tested, as described in Schedule A, were operating with sufficient effectiveness to provide reasonable, but not absolute, assurance that the control objectives specified in Schedule A were achieved during the period [*identify period covered*].

The relative effectiveness and significance of specific controls at X Service Organization and their effect on assessments of control risk at user organizations are dependent on their interaction with the controls, and other factors present at individual user organizations. We have performed no procedures to evaluate the effectiveness of controls at individual user organizations.

The description of controls at X Service Organization is as of [*identify date*], and information about tests of the operating effectiveness of specified controls covers the period from [*identify period covered*]. Any projection of such information to the future is subject to the risk that, because of change, the description may no longer portray the controls in existence. The potential effectiveness of specific controls at the Service Organization is subject to inherent limitations and, accordingly, errors or fraud may occur and not be detected. Furthermore, the projection of any conclusions, based on our findings, to future periods is subject to the risk that changes may alter the validity of such conclusions.

This report is intended solely for use by the management of X Service Organization, its customers, and the independent auditors of its customers.

> **OBSERVATION:** If all of the control objectives identified in the description of controls were not subject to tests of controls, the following should be added as the last sentence to the third paragraph in the preceding example: "However, the scope of our engagement did not include tests to determine whether control objectives not listed in Schedule A were achieved; accordingly, we express no opinion on the achievement of control objectives not included in Schedule A."

Auditing Interpretation No. 5 (February 2002) titled "Statements about the Risk of Projecting Evaluations of the Effectiveness of Controls to Future Periods" points out that the report illustrated above could be expanded by referring to the risk of projecting to the future conclusions drawn in the current engagement. Language that could be included in the report, as suggested by the Interpretation, is reproduced below (the following would be placed just before the restricted-use paragraph):

> The description of controls at X Service Organization is as of [*identify specific date*], and information about tests of the operating effectiveness of specific controls covers the period from [*identify period covered*]. Any projection of such information to the future is subject to the risk that, because of change, the description may no longer portray the controls in existence. The potential effectiveness of specific controls at the Service Organization is subject to inherent limitations and, accordingly, errors or fraud may occur and not be detected. Furthermore, the projection of any conclusions, based on our findings, to future periods is subject to the risk that changes made to the system or controls, or the failure to make needed changes to the system or controls, may alter the validity of such conclusions.

SECTION 325

COMMUNICATION OF INTERNAL CONTROL RELATED MATTERS NOTED IN AN AUDIT

Authoritative Pronouncements

SAS-115 — Communication of Internal Control Related Matters Identified in an Audit

Auditing Interpretation No. 1 of AU 325 (June 2007, revised March 2010) — Communicating Deficiencies in Internal Control over Compliance in an Office of Management and Budget Circular A-133 Audit

Auditing Interpretation No. 2 of AU 325 (November 2009) — Communication of Significant Deficiencies and Material Weaknesses Prior to Completion of the Compliance Audit for Participants in Office of Management and Budget Single Audit Pilot Project

Auditing Interpretation No. 3 of AU 325 (November 2009) — Communication of Significant Deficiencies and Material Weaknesses Prior to Completion of the Compliance Audit for Auditors That are Not Participants in Office of Management and Budget Single Audit Pilot Project

Auditing Interpretation No. 4 of AU 325 (November 2009) — Appropriateness of Identifying No Significant Deficiencies or No Material Weaknesses in an Interim Communication

> **IMPORTANT NOTICE FOR 2011:** The Auditing Standards Board (ASB) is in the process of redrafting all of the auditing sections in *Codification of Statements on Auditing Standards* to converge U.S. GAAS with the International Standards on Auditing issued by the International Auditing and Assurance Standards Board. As part of this process, the newly redrafted standards will follow certain clarity drafting conventions adopted by the ASB. These clarity drafting conventions include: (1) establishing objectives for each standard; (2) including a definitions section, if appropriate; and (3) separating requirements from application guidance and other material. The ASB is planning to have all redrafted standards become effective on the same date, which is for audits of financial statements for periods ending on or after December 15, 2012. It is possible that the effective date might be delayed beyond that date. The ASB's clarity and convergence project will have a significant effect on the auditing standards applicable to audits of nonpublic companies, and the 2012 *GAAS Guide* will be

appropriately modified to reflect these changes once the effective date of the standards is certain.

Overview

During an audit engagement, the auditor may discover deficiencies related to the entity's internal controls over financial reporting that should be reported to management and those charged with governance. SAS-115 requires auditors to communicate in writing to management and those charged with governance any noted significant deficiencies or material weaknesses in internal control related to financial reporting. SAS-115 notes that internal control related to financial reporting pertains to internal controls related to the preparation of reliable financial statements that are fairly presented in conformity with generally accepted accounting principles (GAAP).

A control deficiency exists, as defined by SAS-115, when "the design or operation of a control does not allow management or employees, in the normal course of performing their assigned functions, to prevent, or detect and correct misstatements on a timely basis." SAS-115 notes that a deficiency in design exists when (1) a control necessary to meet the control objective is missing or (2) an existing control is not properly designed, so that even if the control operates as designed, the control objective would not be met. A deficiency in operation exists when (1) a properly designed control does not operate as designed or (2) the person performing the control does not possess the necessary authority or competence to perform the control effectively.

Auditors are required to communicate deficiencies that are deemed to be significant deficiencies or material weaknesses. SAS-115 defines "material weaknesses" and "significant deficiencies" as follows:

> A *material weakness* is a deficiency, or combination of deficiencies, in internal control, such that there is a reasonable possibility that a material misstatement of the entity's financial statements will not be prevented or detected and corrected on a timely basis.
>
> A *significant deficiency* is a deficiency, or combination of deficiencies, in internal control that is less severe than a material weakness, yet important enough to merit the attention by those charged with governance.

The auditor's communication is directed to management and those charged with governance, which often includes the board of directors, committees of the board, partners, management committees, or other similar governance parties. For certain small entities, management and those charged with governance may be the same person(s).

> **PUBLIC COMPANY IMPLICATION:** SAS-115 aligns the defi-
> nitions of various kinds of deficiencies in internal control with
> the definitions of internal control deficiencies in the PCAOB's
> AS-5 (An Audit of Internal Control that is Integrated with an
> Audit of Financial Statements).

Promulgated Procedures Checklist

The auditor should perform the following procedures with respect to the communication of internal control related matters to management and those charged with governance:

- Identify deficiencies in internal control that are deemed to be significant deficiencies or material weaknesses

- Consider the communication of other internal control matters to management or those charged with governance

- Prepare a written report that communicates all significant deficiencies and material weaknesses in internal control over financial reporting

Analysis and Application of Procedures

Identify deficiencies in internal control over financial reporting that are deemed to be significant deficiencies or material weaknesses

The scope of an audit of financial statements does not include the performance of procedures to identify all control deficiencies. However, in performing the audit of financial statements, the auditor is required to obtain an understanding of internal control as part of the auditor's risk assessment procedures. Additionally, the auditor performs tests of controls to support a control risk assessment that is below the maximum. The auditor may also identify control deficiencies when performing other procedures to assess the risk of material misstatement or support an account balance, transaction, or disclosure. The extent that the auditor becomes aware of control deficiencies will vary within each audit depending on the nature, timing, and extent of audit procedures that are performed.

> **PLANNING AID REMINDER:** An auditor may decide not to
> test controls and instead perform all substantive audit proce-
> dures. AICPA Technical Practice Aid 8200.15 notes that the
> decision to not test controls does not automatically mean there

is a control deficiency that must be evaluated. If the auditor decides not to test a control because it is nonexistent or is not properly designed, then that would represent a control deficiency that needs to be assessed in order to determine whether it is a significant deficiency or material weakness. If the design of the control is appropriate but the auditor decides not to test it for other reasons, then he or she has not identified a control deficiency.

SAS-115 requires the auditor to identify those deficiencies, individually or in combination, that are significant deficiencies or material weaknesses. The determination of whether a control deficiency constitutes a significant deficiency or material weakness is a matter of professional judgment. When making this determination, the auditor considers the likelihood and magnitude of misstatement.

Several factors can affect the likelihood that a deficiency might fail to prevent or detect a misstatement. For example, the nature of the account or transaction, the susceptibility of assets or liabilities to loss, the subjectivity and complexity of the amount involved, and the judgment required to determine the value of an account or transaction might increase the likelihood of a deficiency leading to a misstatement. In addition, the interaction or relationship of the control with other controls and the interaction of the control among other deficiencies also affect the auditor's judgment about whether there is a reasonable possibility that a deficiency or combination of deficiencies will result in a misstatement of an account balance or disclosure.

The magnitude of the misstatement caused by a control deficiency may be affected by size of the financial statement amounts or disclosures impacted by the deficiency and by the volume of activity in an account balance or class of transactions. In evaluating the magnitude of the potential misstatement, the maximum amount by which an account balance or total of transactions can be overstated is generally the recorded amount, whereas understatements could be larger. In some instances, a deficiency may be individually insignificant; however, when combined with other deficiencies that affect the same account balance or disclosure, the combination of deficiencies can lead to a higher likelihood of a material misstatement.

> **PLANNING AID REMINDER:** Internal control deficiencies might be discovered during various phases of the engagement. Deficiencies can be related to any of the five components of internal control. In addition, deficiencies can arise because of poor design or poor operation of the control. For example, a deficiency could be related to lack of proper segregation of

duties and responsibilities (design within internal control) or lack of timely preparation of bank reconciliations (execution within internal control).

Certain deficiencies in internal control may be mitigated by other effective compensating controls. SAS-115 defines a "compensating control" as a "control that may limit the severity of the deficiency and prevent it from being a significant deficiency or material weakness." Although compensating controls offset the effects of a control deficiency, they do not eliminate the control deficiency. The auditor is not required to consider the effects of compensating controls related to a deficiency in operation. However, the auditor may consider the effects of compensating controls related to a deficiency in operation provided he or she has tested the compensating controls for operating effectiveness as part of the financial statement audit.

> **PUBLIC COMPANY IMPLICATION:** SOX requires the auditor of a public company to issue a report on the operating effectiveness of its internal control over financial reporting. The audit of internal controls and the audit of the financial statements of a public company are to be integrated. In order to provide reasonable assurance about the operating effectiveness of internal controls, the auditor is to perform tests of controls over financial reporting. Information about significant deficiencies and material weaknesses obtained through work performed as part of the financial statement audit should be considered when reporting on internal controls (and vice versa).

SAS-115 identifies the following areas of controls in which existing deficiencies are indicators of material weaknesses:

- Identification of fraud, whether or not material, on the part of management

- Restatement of previously issued financial statements to reflect the correction of a material misstatement due to error or fraud

- Identification by the auditor of a material misstatement in the financial statements under audit in circumstances that indicate that the misstatements would not have been detected by the entity's internal control

- Ineffective oversight of the entity's financial reporting and internal control by those charged with governance

Exhibit AU 325-1 provides guidance regarding what items may be considered deficiencies in internal control over financial reporting.

Consider the communication of other internal control matters to management or those charged with governance

SAS-115 requires the auditor to communicate in writing all identified significant deficiencies and material weaknesses to management and those charged with governance. A client may request that an auditor communicate other matters related to internal control that are not necessarily significant deficiencies or material weaknesses. Additionally, the auditor may choose to communicate recommendations for operational or administrative efficiency that might benefit the entity. The auditor may choose to communicate these other matters orally or in writing. If communicating orally, the auditor should document the communication.

Prepare a written report that communicates all significant deficiencies and material weaknesses in internal control over financial reporting

SAS-115 requires the auditor's communication of significant deficiencies and material weaknesses to be in writing. This communication requirement applies to all significant deficiencies or material weaknesses identified during the current audit, in addition to significant deficiencies and material weaknesses communicated in previous audits that have not yet been remediated.

The written communication must include the following components:

- Statement that the purpose of the audit is to express an opinion on the financial statements and not to express an opinion on the effectiveness of internal control over financial reporting

- Statement that the auditor is not expressing an opinion on the effectiveness of internal control

- Definition of the terms "significant deficiency" and "material weakness" (when relevant)

- Identification of those matters deemed to be significant deficiencies and those deemed to be material weaknesses

- Statement that the communication is intended solely for the information of management and those charged with governance

If governmental regulations require submission of the report, the report should include a reference to the regulatory agency.

> **OBSERVATION:** When no significant deficiencies or material weaknesses are identified in the audit, the auditor is prohibited from issuing a written communication stating that no significant deficiencies or material weaknesses were identified. This

> prohibition exists because of the potential for misinterpretation of the limited assurance that would be provided by such communication.
>
> **ENGAGEMENT STRATEGY:** The auditor may include additional statements describing general inherent limitations of internal control, including the possibility of management override of controls or descriptive information about the auditor's consideration of internal control in the financial statement audit.

The timing of the written communication is best if made by the report release date, which is the date the auditor grants the entity permission to use the auditor's report in connection with the financial statements. SAS-115 does require that the written communication be made no later than 60 days after the report release date. Some matters may be communicated to management or those charged with governance at an earlier date to allow management the opportunity to remediate the deficiency on a timely basis. The early communication does not have to be in writing; however, the auditor must ultimately communicate all significant deficiencies and material weaknesses in writing.

> **OBSERVATION:** For some significant deficiencies or material weaknesses, management or those charged with governance may make a conscious decision to accept the risk of the deficiency leading to a material misstatement due to the cost or other considerations associated with remediating the deficiency. Despite management's decision, the auditor is still required to communicate all significant deficiencies and material weaknesses in writing. When significant deficiencies or material weaknesses that were previously communicated have not been remediated, the auditor may communicate such matters by referring to the previously issued written communication and the date of the communication.
>
> **PUBLIC COMPANY IMPLICATION:** In the audit of internal control over financial reporting required by SOX for public companies, the presence of one or more material weaknesses prohibits the auditor from concluding that internal control over financial reporting is operating effectively.
>
> **IMPORTANT NOTICE FOR 2011:** In October 2009 the Office of Management and Budget (OMB) began a pilot project that is a collaborative effort between volunteer nonfederal entities expending American Recovery and Reinvestment Act of 2009 (ARRA) awards (referred to as the auditees here), the auditors performing compliance audits of auditees with ARRA expenditures under OMB Circular A-133, Audits of States, Local

Governments, and Non-Profit Organizations, and the federal government. For auditees that volunteer, the pilot project requires their auditors to issue to management an early written communication of significant deficiencies and material weaknesses in internal control over compliance at an interim date prior to the completion of the compliance audit. This communication is to be based on internal control work performed on specified compliance requirements for two major programs with ARRA expenditures chosen from a list of approved ARRA pilot project programs. This communication would also be required to be submitted by management to the cognizant agency for audit. Interpretation 2 of AU 325 clarifies that an auditor may issue such an interim communication in accordance with AU 325 (Communicating Internal Control Related Matters Identified in an Audit). The interpretation notes that AU 325A permits an auditor to communicate to management identified significant deficiencies and material weaknesses before the completion of a financial statement audit. It would be appropriate for a compliance audit as well. Regardless of how early the communication is delivered, the auditor must communicate all significant deficiencies and material weaknesses in writing to management and those charged with governance in accordance with AU 325.

Practitioner's Aids

Exhibit 325-1 includes SAS-115 examples of possible control deficiencies, significant deficiencies, and material weaknesses. Exhibit 325-2 is an example of a written communication required by SAS-115. Exhibit 325-3 includes examples of possible material weaknesses for a small business enterprise.

EXHIBIT AU 325-1 — EXAMPLES OF POSSIBLE DEFICIENCIES

- Deficiencies in internal control design

  — Inadequate overall internal control design over financial statement preparation

  — Inadequate design over a significant account or process

  — Inadequate documentation of internal control

  — Insufficient control consciousness across the organization

— Inadequate segregation of duties

— Absent or inadequate controls over safeguarding of assets

— Inadequate design of information technology general and application controls

— Unqualified or inadequately trained employees or management

— Inadequate design of monitoring controls

— Absence of an internal process to report deficiencies in internal control to management on a timely basis

- Failures in the operation of internal control

— Evidence of failure in the operation of an effectively designed control over a significant account or process

— Evidence of failure of the information and communication component of internal control to provide complete and accurate output because of deficiencies in timeliness, completeness, or accuracy

— Evidence of failure of controls designed to safeguard assets from loss, damage, or misappropriation

— Lack of performance of reconciliations of significant accounts

— Presence of undue bias or lack of objectivity by those responsible for accounting decisions

— Misrepresentation by client personnel to the auditor

— Management override of controls

— Failure of an application control caused by a deficiency in the design or operation of an IT general control

EXHIBIT AU 325-2 — EXAMPLE OF A WRITTEN COMMUNICATION ABOUT SIGNIFICANT DEFICIENCIES AND MATERIAL WEAKNESSES

In planning and performing our audit of the financial statements of X Corporation as of and for the year ended December 31, 20X5, in accordance with auditing standards generally accepted in the United States of America, we considered X Corporation's internal control over financial reporting (internal control) as a basis for designing our audit procedures for the purpose of expressing our opinion on the financial statements, but not for the purpose of expressing an opinion on the effectiveness of X Corporation's internal control. Accordingly, we do not express an opinion on the effectiveness of the company's internal control.

Our consideration of internal control was for the limited purpose described in the preceding paragraph and was not designed to identify all deficiencies in internal control that might be significant deficiencies or material weaknesses and, therefore, there can be no assurance that all deficiencies, significant deficiencies, or material weaknesses have been identified. However, as discussed below, we identified certain deficiencies in internal control that we consider to be material weaknesses [*and other deficiencies that we consider to be significant deficiencies*].

A deficiency in internal control exists when the design or operation of a control does not allow management or employees, in the normal course of performing their assigned functions, to prevent, or detect and correct misstatements on a timely basis. A material weakness is a deficiency, or a combination of deficiencies, in internal control such that there is a reasonable possibility that a material misstatement of the entity's financial statements will not be prevented, or detected and corrected on a timely basis. We consider the following deficiencies in X Corporation's internal control to be material weaknesses:

[*Describe the material weaknesses that were identified.*]

A significant deficiency is a deficiency, or a combination of deficiencies, in internal control that is less severe than a material weakness, yet important enough to merit attention by those charged with governance. We consider the following deficiencies to be significant deficiencies:

[*Describe the significant deficiencies that were identified.*]

This communication is intended solely for the information and use of management, [*identify those charged with governance*], others within the organization, and [*identify any specified governmental authorities*] and is not intended to be and should not be used by anyone other than these specified parties.

EXHIBIT AU 325-3 — EXAMPLES OF POSSIBLE MATERIAL WEAKNESSES: SMALL BUSINESS ENTERPRISE

Note: A "material weakness is a deficiency, or combination of deficiencies, in internal control, such that there is a reasonable possibility that a material misstatement of the entity's financial statements will not be prevented, or detected and corrected on a timely basis."

Determining whether a specific condition is a material weakness is based on exercising professional judgment in the context of the existing characteristics of a particular client. The following list includes examples of conditions that the auditor may identify as a material weakness for a small business enterprise. The list is illustrative only and is not intended to be comprehensive. Also, because the assumption is that the client is a small business enterprise, there is an emphasis on cash and related cash transactions, inventory, and property, plant, and equipment.

- *Cash and credit sales*

  — Credit sales are approved by the bookkeeper, who is responsible for the write-off of bad debts.

  — A bookkeeper maintains cash receipts records, opens the mail, and prepares the bank deposit.

  — Cash payments for expenditures using cash receipts for the day.

  — Cash receipts are deposited at the end of the week, net of expenditures paid during the week.

  — Several sales clerks have access to the single cash drawer used during the day to record cash sales.

  — Cash registers used during the day are not read and reconciled after the end of each shift.

  — A bookkeeper is responsible for the purchase of goods and services.

  — There is no formal documentation that shows that goods purchased were received.

  — Documentation to support cash disbursements is maintained on a haphazard basis.

  — The office manager authorizes the payment of invoices, prepares checks, and reconciles the bank statements.

- *Cash and purchases of goods and services*

  — Purchase orders are not used to authorize the acquisition of goods and services.

  — Invoices and other supporting documentation are not marked as "canceled" or "paid."

  — The hiring and firing of employees is not centralized.

— Paychecks are given to an immediate supervisor for distribution.

— The number of hours or days worked is not controlled through the use of time clocks or otherwise approved by supervisory personnel.

— An unusually large amount of petty cash is maintained, and support for expenditures is lacking.

— Numerous checking accounts are used, and prenumbered checks are not accounted for.

— Numerous employees are authorized to sign checks.

— Checks are often written to "cash."

— Bank reconciliations are seldom prepared.

• *Inventory controls*

— The periodic inventory count is not under the control of the owner or manager.

— The inventory is not subject to reasonable limited access (for both employees and customers) based on the characteristics of the business.

— Inventory shipments to customers are not based on appropriate shipping authorization.

— Inventory receipts are not properly counted and inspected.

— The year-end inventory summarization is not analyzed and evaluated by the owner or manager for unusual variations in gross profit percentages, obsolete inventory lines, unreasonable inventory counts, missing items, inappropriate cost data, etc.

• *Property, plant, and equipment*

— A plant ledger is not maintained.

— The owner or manager does not periodically verify the existence and condition of property items.

— The sale of used property items is not approved by the owner or manager.

SECTION 326

AUDIT EVIDENCE

Authoritative Pronouncements

SAS-106 — Audit Evidence

Auditing Interpretation No. 1 of AU 326 (October 1980) — Audit Evidence for an Audit of Interim Financial Statements

Auditing Interpretation No. 2 of AU 326 (June 2003) — The Effect of an Inability to Obtain Evidential Matter Relating to Income Tax Accruals

Auditing Interpretation No. 3 of AU 326 (April 1986) — The Auditor's Consideration of the Completeness Assertion

> **IMPORTANT NOTICE FOR 2011:** The Auditing Standards Board (ASB) is in the process of redrafting all of the auditing sections in *Codification of Statements on Auditing Standards* to converge U.S. GAAS with the International Standards on Auditing issued by the International Auditing and Assurance Standards Board. As part of this process, the newly redrafted standards will follow certain clarity drafting conventions adopted by the ASB. These clarity drafting conventions include: (1) establishing objectives for each standard; (2) including a definitions section, if appropriate; and (3) separating requirements from application guidance and other material. The ASB is planning to have all redrafted standards become effective on the same date, which is for audits of financial statements for periods ending on or after December 15, 2012. It is possible that the effective date might be delayed beyond that date. The ASB's clarity and convergence project will have a significant effect on the auditing standards applicable to audits of nonpublic companies, and the 2012 *GAAS Guide* will be appropriately modified to reflect these changes once the effective date of the standards is certain.

Overview

The third standard of fieldwork states the following:

> The auditor must obtain sufficient appropriate audit evidence by performing audit procedures to afford a reasonable basis for an opinion regarding the financial statements under audit.

Audit evidence includes all the information considered by the auditor in supporting his or her opinion. Audit evidence is cumulative in nature, and includes evidence from (1) procedures performed during the audit, (2) results from prior-year audits, and (3) the firm's quality control process for client acceptance and continuance.

Management is responsible for the financial statements, and they are prepared using the entity's accounting records. Accounting records consist of general and specialized journals, ledgers, manuals, and supporting worksheets and spreadsheets and other analyses. The auditor should test the accounting records — for example, that the accounting records are internally consistent and agree to the financial statements. Other tests of the accounting records include retracing transactions through the accounting system, recomputing allocations, and performing other mathematical calculations. However, solely testing the accounting records is not sufficient to support an opinion on the financial statements. Therefore, the auditor should gather corroborating audit evidence. Other types of audit evidence includes minutes of meetings, confirmations, controls manuals, and information obtained by the auditor from audit procedures such as inquiry, observation, inspection, and reperformance.

> **PUBLIC COMPANY IMPLICATION:** In 2010 the PCAOB issued eight auditing standards (AS-8 through AS-15) related to the auditor's assessment of and response to risk. The proposed standards bear many similarities to the eight risk-assessment standards adopted by the Auditing Standards Board in 2006. AS-15 (Audit Evidence) defines what constitutes audit evidence, and it provides guidance to the auditor in evaluating the sufficiency and appropriateness of audit evidence. Although there are a number of differences between the PCAOB's and ASB's risk standards, the risk-assessment concepts contained in the PCAOB standards should be familiar to most auditors. As is currently the case, audit risk is the risk that the auditor will issue an inappropriate opinion on financial statements that are materially misstated. The auditor is to reduce audit risk to a low level through the application of audit procedures. As a result, the amount of audit effort devoted to particular accounts, classes of transactions, and disclosures should vary based on their respective risk.

Promulgated Procedures Checklist

The auditor should consider the following factors in collecting and evaluating audit evidence to support his or her opinion on the client's financial statements:

- Significant assertions contained in the client's financial statements
- Sufficient appropriate audit evidence

- Risk assessment procedures, tests of controls, and substantive procedures
- Types of and performance of audit procedures
- Effect of the client's information technology on the audit process
- Audit evidence evaluation

Analysis and Application of Procedures

Significant assertions contained in the client's financial statements

The collection and evaluation of sufficient appropriate audit evidence can be described, and it should be applied as a logical process. SAS-106 attempts to provide the logical framework for the audit process. Conceptually, the auditor should design his or her tests by relating assertions made by management in the financial statements to specific audit procedures designed to test the validity of the assertions. The three general classes of assertions relate to (1) transactions or events for the audit period, (2) account balances at period end, and (3) presentation and disclosure.

There are five assertions that relate to classes of transactions or events for the period under audit:

1. *Occurrence* The entity has entered into the transactions and events that are recorded.

2. *Completeness* All transactions and events that affected the entity during the period have been recorded.

3. *Accuracy* Transactions and events are recorded at the right amount.

4. *Cutoff* Transactions and events are recorded in the right period.

5. *Classification* Transactions and events are recorded in the right account.

There are four assertions that relate to account balances at the end of the period under audit:

1. *Existence* Assets, liabilities, and owners' interests exist.

2. *Rights and obligations* The entity holds or controls the rights to recorded assets, and recorded liabilities are obligations of the entity.

3. *Completeness* All of the entity's assets, liabilities, and owners' interests have been recorded.

4. *Valuation and allocation* Assets, liabilities, and owners' interests are correctly valued in accordance with GAAP.

There are four assertions that relate to presentation and disclosure:

1. *Occurrence and rights and obligations* Events and transactions that are disclosed have occurred and pertain to the entity.

2. *Completeness* All required disclosures are included in the financial statements.

3. *Classification and understandability* Financial information is appropriately presented and described, and disclosures are understandable.

4. *Accuracy and valuation* Financial and other information is properly disclosed and at appropriate amounts.

> **OBSERVATION:** The auditor may use the foregoing list of assertions or develop his or her own list of assertions (as long as the objectives underlying the foregoing assertions are met).

The auditor should focus on those assertions that have a meaningful bearing on whether an account is fairly stated (defined as relevant assertions). The auditor is to consider the different types of potential misstatements that may occur, and then design his or her audit procedures accordingly. This approach is to be followed for each significant class of transaction, account balance, and presentation and disclosure. In determining whether a particular assertion is relevant the auditor considers

- The nature of the assertion

- The volume of transactions or data related to the assertion

- The nature and complexity of the systems that generate the data underlying the assertion

Often a single assertion will lead to more than one audit objective. For example, a balance sheet may represent that inventories are valued at a particular amount. In turn, this single financial statement assertion may lead to the following audit objectives: (1) inventories are stated at first in, first out (FIFO) cost and (2) defective inventories are stated at net realizable value. Having identified an audit objective, the auditor selects audit procedures to achieve the particular audit objective. Of course, an audit objective may require that more than one audit procedure be employed. Likewise, a single audit procedure may contribute information to the evaluation of several audit objectives.

> **RISK ASSESSMENT POINT:** Auditing Interpretation No. 3 of AU 326 states that an auditor's reliance on the internal control and the written representations of management does not provide sufficient audit evidence to support the assertion that all

account balances and transactions have been properly included in the financial statements (completeness assertion). An auditor must evaluate the audit risk of omission and whether any accounts and/or transactions have been improperly omitted from the financial statements. Substantive procedures that are designed to obtain evidence about the completeness assertion are used to reduce the audit risk of omission. These substantive tests should include analytical procedures and tests of details of related account balances. The type and quantity of substantive tests may vary depending on the auditor's assessment of control risk.

Sufficient appropriate audit evidence

The third standard of fieldwork requires the auditor to gather "sufficient appropriate" audit evidence. Evidence is "sufficient" if there is enough of it to support the auditor's opinion on the financial statements (i.e., sufficiency refers to the quantity of evidence gathered). Evidence is "appropriate" if it is relevant and reliable in providing support for or detecting misstatements in the classes of transactions, account balances, and disclosures (i.e., appropriateness refers to the quality of audit evidence).

Audit judgment is used to determine when sufficiency is achieved, just as judgment is used to determine the appropriateness of audit evidence. The concept of sufficiency recognizes that the auditor can never reduce audit risk to zero, and a fundamental concept in auditing is that the accumulation of evidence should be persuasive rather than conclusive. However, the auditor has not obtained reasonable assurance unless the evidence accumulated is at least persuasive. The requirement to obtain persuasive rather than conclusive audit evidence is consistent with the idea that the auditor is not free to collect unlimited amounts of evidence, because he or she must work within economic limits. However, the cost or difficulty of an audit procedure cannot be the justification for not performing the procedure if there is no appropriate alternative.

> **FRAUD POINTER:** The auditor should exercise professional skepticism in evaluating whether the quantity and quality of audit evidence is sufficient.

Relevant audit evidence relates to the specific assertion being tested by the auditor. For example, observation of the client's physical inventory count provides relevant audit evidence related to the existence assertion for the inventory account balance.

The reliability of audit evidence is determined by referring to its source and its nature. Although there are exceptions to these general principles, audit evidence is more reliable when it

- Is obtained from a knowledgeable, independent source external to the entity

- Is produced by a system with effective internal control

- Is obtained directly by the auditor (e.g., observation, reperformance) rather than indirectly (e.g., inquiry)

- Exists in documentary form

- Exists in original form (rather than as a copy or a fax)

- Is consistent with audit evidence obtained from other sources or audit evidence of a different nature (the auditor needs to perform additional audit procedures to resolve inconsistencies between two different sources of audit evidence)

> **ENGAGEMENT PLANNING STRATEGY:** Auditing Interpretation No. 1 of AU 326 notes that the third standard of fieldwork (sufficient appropriate audit evidence) must be satisfied when an auditor expresses an opinion on financial statements, including interim financial statements.

The auditor needs to gather more audit evidence when audit risk (the risk of a material misstatement) is greater, and the quality of that evidence should also be higher when the auditor is facing greater risk. In addition, the auditor can obtain less audit evidence if the quality of the evidence gathered is higher. Conversely, the auditor cannot make up for evidence of a lower quality by merely gathering more of the same type of evidence.

The auditor often uses information produced by the entity as the source for other audit procedures. When the auditor uses client-generated information, he or she needs to test whether the information is accurate and complete. The auditor may test the completeness and accuracy of client-generated information at the same time that the auditor is performing another audit procedure using that data. Rather than directly testing the accuracy and completeness of client-generated information, the auditor, may, alternatively test the controls over the production and maintenance of the information.

> **FRAUD POINTER:** Although the auditor is expected to evaluate the reliability of audit evidence, he or she is not expected to authenticate the validity of written documents. The auditor is not trained in authenticating documents and GAAS does not expect auditors to have this expertise. Nonetheless, many frauds are perpetrated through the creation of bogus documentation or the alteration of legitimate documentation. The auditor should be cognizant of this risk, and may want to involve forensic specialists in high risk engagements, particularly where questions about the authenticity of documentation arise.

Risk assessment procedures, tests of controls, and substantive procedures

In performing the audit, the auditor should perform three types of procedures: (1) risk assessment procedures, (2) tests of controls, and (3) substantive procedures. The auditor must perform risk assessment procedures for the purpose of understanding the entity and its environment, including obtaining an understanding of the design of the entity's internal control. The objective of these procedures is to assess the risk of material misstatement, at both the financial statement and assertion levels. Risk assessment procedures alone do not provide an adequate basis for issuing an opinion on the financial statements and must be supplemented by tests of controls and/ or substantive procedures.

The auditor performs tests of the *operating effectiveness* of controls when required or when the auditor concludes that relying on internal controls would improve the efficiency or effectiveness of the audit. These tests of controls should be designed to test operating effectiveness at the assertion level. Tests of controls are required (1) if the auditor's risk assessment assumes that controls are operating effectively or (2) if relying solely on substantive procedures does not provide sufficient appropriate audit evidence to support an opinion on the financial statements.

The auditor performs substantive tests to detect material misstatements in classes of transactions, account balances, and in presentations and disclosures. Substantive procedures include tests of details and substantive analytical procedures. Substantive procedures should be designed to detect material misstatements at the assertion level. The extent of substantive tests is a function of the auditor's assessed level of detection risk, and detection risk reflects the results of testing controls. Although auditors reduce the extent of substantive testing if internal control is designed and operating effectively, they should perform at least some substantive procedures for all relevant assertions related to all material classes of transactions, account balances, and disclosures. This requirement reflects the fact that no system of internal control, no matter how well designed and operated, is foolproof. For example, management can override internal control, individuals with control responsibilities can make mistakes, and changes to systems can render a previously effective system ineffective.

Types and performance of audit procedures

Audit evidence gathering procedures include (1) inspection of records or documents, (2) inspection of tangible assets, (3) observation, (4) inquiry, (5) confirmation, (6) recalculation, (7) reperformance, and (8) analytical procedures. The auditor should perform one or more of these types of procedures. The auditor may need to perform multiple types of procedures to obtain sufficient appropriate audit evidence related to tests of controls and substantive procedures. In some cases, audit evidence gathered in previous years' audits may have continuing relevance, but the auditor should perform audit procedures to ascertain the continuing relevance of this evidence from prior years.

> **PLANNING AID REMINDER:** Often the accounting data and corroborating evidence only exist in electronic form, and that evidence may only exist at a certain point in time. As a result, some of that evidence may not be visible in written form and it might not be retrievable after certain points in time. As part of planning the audit, the auditor should identify the time that evidence might exist or is available and consider that timing when planning the audit. In some cases, the auditor might determine that the use of IT specialists and/or CAATs (computer-assisted audit techniques) is appropriate in performing the audit.

Inspection of records or documents

Inspection involves examining documents or records. The reliability of the audit evidence obtained from inspecting documents or records varies depending on the nature and source of the documents and records, and on the strength of internal control for internally generated documents and records.

Inspection of tangible assets

Inspection of tangible assets involves physically examining the asset. Inspection of tangible assets can provide useful audit evidence regarding the existence of the asset. It is a less effective procedure for providing evidence related to valuation of an asset and the entity's right to use it. Inspection is sometimes paired with observation as an evidence-gathering technique — for example auditors often inspect individual assets during a physical inventory observation.

Observation

Observation involves looking at a client-performed process or procedure (e.g., observation of the entity's process for counting inventory, observation of the performance of a control procedure). Observation is limited to providing evidence about the state of a process or procedure at the time its performance is observed. Also, the very act of observing a process or procedure may change its performance — that is, client personnel may perform a process or procedure differently than normal when they know the auditor is watching.

Inquiry

Inquiry involves asking questions to obtain information from knowledgeable sources. The auditor should consider making inquiries of both financial and nonfinancial personnel and of personnel both inside and external to the entity. Inquiry involves both formal written inquiries and informal oral questions. Inquiry is typically a complementary procedure to another audit evidence-gathering technique, and its effectiveness depends on the auditor's ability to evaluate the responses received.

Inquiry typically involves the following steps:

- Deciding on the specific individuals both inside and outside the entity to talk with. In making this determination, the auditor should consider an individual's knowledge, objectivity, experience, responsibilities, and qualifications.

- Asking clear, concise, and relevant questions

- Knowing how and when to use open- and closed-end questions, and using each as appropriate

- Employing effective listening approaches (e.g., maintaining eye contact, paraphrasing the interviewees' response to confirm understanding)

- Asking follow-up questions as needed

- Evaluating the response. This includes assessing whether the response (1) makes sense (is the response consistent with what the auditor knows about the entity, its industry, and the overall economy, and is the response consistent with GAAP), (2) is sufficient (if the inquiry relates to explaining a difference between the auditor's expectation and the recorded account balance, does the response (if true) explain most or all of the difference), and (3) can be corroborated with other evidence.

Inquiry alone is neither sufficient to test the operating effectiveness of controls nor serve as the sole substantive procedure. Inquiry alone is not likely to be effective in detecting a material misstatement at the assertion level. Inquiry may be used in assessing management intent where such intent is determinative of the accounting under GAAP (e.g., the classification of securities held as investments). Management may state that it has the positive intent and ability to hold a debt security to maturity, but finding evidence to corroborate this management representation may be difficult.

In such cases, management's past history of doing what it says may provide evidence either to support or refute its representations.

> **FRAUD POINTER:** Inquiry of senior management is likely to be particularly ineffective in cases of fraud where top management is involved.

> **ENGAGEMENT STRATEGY:** Some responses to inquires are of sufficient importance that they should be included in the management letter of representations.

Confirmation

A confirmation is a specific type of inquiry. It involves asking a third party to make a representation about certain information or of an existing condition (e.g., confirmation of an accounts receivable balance). Often confirmations are used to provide audit evidence related to account balances, but they can also be used to confirm the existence of any agreements that may affect an account balance (e.g., a side agreement allowing a customer to return goods if the customer is not able to resell them).

Recalculation

Recalculation is a procedure that involves checking the mathematical accuracy of documents or records.

Reperformance

The auditor may reperform a procedure or control that is part of the entity's internal control. For example, an entity may have a control that involves the assistant controller reviewing the account coding for cash disbursements. The auditor could reperform this procedure.

Analytical procedures

Analytical procedures involve analyzing the reasonableness of financial information by comparing it with other financial and nonfinancial data. For example, the auditor might evaluate the reasonableness of the allowance for doubtful accounts by relating the allowance to the ratio of days' sales in receivables. In performing analytical procedures, the auditor should develop his or her own independent expectation of the account balance (or ratio etc.) *before* performing the analytical procedure. The effectiveness of an analytical procedure largely depends on the auditor's subsequent investigation of fluctuations or relationships that are inconsistent with other data or that deviate significantly from the auditor's expectations.

> **FRAUD POINTER:** In some cases the auditor uses the prior year's audited balance as the implicit expectation and then focuses on differences between the recorded amount and the prior year's balance in performing the analytical procedure. In some cases the lack of a difference between the recorded amount and the prior year's balance is just as problematic as the existence of a difference.

Scanning is a type of an analytical procedure. Scanning involves reviewing accounting records (e.g., transaction listings, subsidiary ledgers, general ledger control accounts, adjusting entries, suspense accounts, reconciliations) for large or unusual items and then testing them. The effectiveness of scanning depends on the auditor's ability to define unusual items. Scanning is implemented most effectively through the use of CAATs.

Effect of the client's information technology on the audit process

The client's use of digital technology to process financial data does not change the auditor's fundamental responsibility, which is to collect sufficient appropriate evidence upon which to base an opinion on the financial statements. The client's use of technology, however, can have an effect on the design of the audit strategy and specific audit procedures that may be employed in an engagement.

In general, reducing detection risk to an acceptable level may be impossible without performing tests of controls. This generalization applies to all types of systems, including those that rely heavily on electronic data processing procedures. For example, for a client where significant information is transmitted, processed, maintained, or accessed electronically, it may be impractical or impossible to reduce detection risk for some assertions to an acceptable level by performing only substantive procedures. In this circumstance, it would be necessary to perform tests of controls and to consider the results of these tests in the assessment of control risk.

> **ENGAGEMENT STRATEGY:** Auditing Interpretation No. 2 of AU 326 points out that (1) a client is responsible for the tax accrual, related disclosures, and the support for the accrual and disclosures, (2) when a client does not provide the auditor with appropriate information to support the tax accrual and related disclosures or limits the auditor's access to such infor-

mation, that circumstance creates a scope limitation that may lead to a modification of the auditor's report on the financial statements, (3) the auditor should adequately document audit procedures and conclusions reached as part of the audit of the tax accrual and related disclosures and the documentation may include copies of the client's documents, schedules, and analyses, and (4) the auditor cannot adequately substantiate the tax accrual and related disclosures simply by accepting the conclusions of a third-party tax adviser (functioning as a third-party expert) that has been hired by the client for such a purpose.

Evaluation of audit evidence

Before issuing an audit report on the financial statements, the auditor should evaluate whether sufficient, appropriate evidence has been obtained for specified audit objectives. Throughout the audit, the auditor should maintain an attitude of professional skepticism, including a questioning mind-set and a critical evaluation of audit evidence. The auditor should be satisfied that the evidence obtained is persuasive, regardless of the auditor's belief about management's integrity. That is, the auditor should not accept less-than-persuasive evidence based on his or her belief that management is honest.

> **FRAUD POINTER:** A very common deficiency in enforcement actions against auditors is the auditors' failure to gather adequate audit evidence. In some cases, the auditors' failure to gather adequate evidence may have prevented them from detecting material misstatement due to fraud.

SECTION 328

AUDITING FAIR VALUE MEASUREMENTS AND DISCLOSURES

Authoritative Pronouncements

SAS-101 — Auditing Fair Value Measurements and Disclosures

SAS-113 — Omnibus Statement on Auditing Standards — 2006

Auditing Interpretation No. 1 (July 2005) — Auditing Interests in Trusts Held by a Third-Party Trustee and Reported at Fair Value

> **IMPORTANT NOTICE FOR 2011:** The Auditing Standards Board (ASB) is in the process of redrafting all of the auditing sections in Codification of Statements on Auditing Standards to converge U.S. GAAS with the International Standards on Auditing issued by the International Auditing and Assurance Standards Board. As part of this process, the newly redrafted standards will follow certain clarity drafting conventions adopted by the ASB. These clarity drafting conventions include (1) establishing objectives for each standard; (2) including a definitions section, if appropriate; and (3) separating requirements from application guidance and other material. The ASB is planning to have all redrafted standards become effective on the same date, which is for audits of financial statements for periods ending on or after December 15, 2012. It is possible that the effective date might be delayed beyond that date. The ASB's clarity and convergence project will have a significant effect on the auditing standards applicable to audits of non-public companies, and the 2012 GAAS Guide will be appropriately modified to reflect these changes once the effective date of the standards is certain.

Overview

Accounting standards are slowly changing to reflect, either on the face of the financial statements or in notes to those statements, items reported at fair value rather than historical cost. FASB's Statement of Financial Accounting Concepts No. 7 (CON-7) (Using Cash Flow Information and Present Value in Accounting Measurements) defines the fair value of an asset (liability) as "the amount at which that asset (or liability) could be bought (or incurred) or sold (or settled) in a current transaction between willing parties, that is, other than in a forced or liquidation sale."

Determining the fair value of an asset that is held or a liability that exists is relatively easy if there is an established public market. For example, the fair value of an investment in the equity securities of a public company is generally readily determinable based on prices reflected in public markets. However, the more an item is unique and less like a commodity, the less likely it is that there is an established market with a large number of buyers and sellers to provide reliable information about the item's fair value at a particular point in time. For this reason, the fair value of an asset or liability might have to be estimated based on a variety of methods including discounted cash flows, estimates of reconstruction costs, professional appraisals, and various pricing models.

As is the case for all other information in its financial statements, the client is responsible for designing procedures to determine fair values that must be presented in financial statements in order for those statements to conform to generally accepted accounting principles. When market quotations are not available, the client's estimate of fair value is often based on "assumptions about future conditions, transactions, or events whose outcome is uncertain and will therefore be subject to change over time." SAS-101 provides general guidance for the audit of fair value measurements and disclosures.

> **PLANNING AID REMINDER:** SAS-101 does not identify audit procedures for specific types of assets and liabilities that must be measured or disclosed at their estimated fair values. The auditor must be aware of other standards (for example, SAS-92 [Auditing Derivative Instruments, Hedging Activities, and Investments in Securities]) that provide guidance that is more specific.

> **PUBLIC COMPANY IMPLICATION:** The PCAOB has issued Staff Audit Practice Alert No. 2 (Matters Related to Auditing Fair Value Measurements of Financial Instruments and the Use of Specialists). The Practice Alert is designed to provide guidance related to auditing fair values, particularly in light of the FASB's issuance of FAS-157 (ASC 820) (Fair Value Measurements). The auditor needs to understand the company's process for determining fair value measurements and disclosures, including related internal controls. The auditor should also evaluate whether (1) management's assumptions in determining fair value are reasonable and not inconsistent with market information, (2) management reliance on historical financial information continues to be justified (e.g., use of historical default rates may not be appropriate when credit markets are deteriorating), and (3) the company's determination of fair value is applied consistently and whether this is appropriate. For example, a company may apply a model consistently

in determining fair value but because of changes in the environment it may be more appropriate for the company to change the relative weights of model inputs. In addition, the auditor should recognize that model inputs based on the company's own data are generally more susceptible to bias and take appropriate audit steps to respond to this increased risk. Finally, GAAP provides for many required disclosures relating to fair value measurements. The auditor needs to recognize that material disclosures that depart from GAAP represent a misstatement of the financial statements.

PUBLIC COMPANY IMPLICATION: The PCAOB has issued Staff Audit Practice Alert No. 4 (Auditor Considerations Regarding Fair Value Measurements, Disclosures, and Other-than-Temporary Impairments), which is designed to inform auditors about the potential implications on annual audits and interim reviews of three FASB Staff Positions (FSPs): (1) FSP FAS 157-4 (ASC 820) (Determining Fair Value When the Volume and Level of Activity for the Asset or Liability Have Significantly Decreased and Identifying Transactions That Are Not Orderly), (2) FSP FAS 115-2 (ASC 320) and FAS 124-2 (ASC 320) (Recognition and Presentation of Other-than-Temporary-Impairment), and (3) FSP FAS 107-1 (ASC 825) and APB 28-1 (ASC 825) (Interim Disclosures about Fair Value of Financial Instruments). Staff Audit Practice Alert No. 4 states that the auditor should include inquiries about the application of these FSPs in a review of interim financial information. For audits of financial statements, the Practice Alert emphasizes the need for auditors to obtain sufficient appropriate evidence to support accounting estimates, including their measurement and disclosure. For example, in certain cases FSP FAS 115-2 (ASC 320) requires losses from other-than-temporary impairments to be separated between credit losses and other factors. Such a determination involves significant judgment. Staff Audit Practice Alert No. 4 also reminds auditors of their responsibility to read other information in documents containing interim and annual financial statements. If this other information is inconsistent with the financial statements, either the audit report, the financial statements, or the other information needs to be changed. The application of these FSPs may require communication to the audit committee because their application might involve a change in (1) accounting policy, (2) accounting estimates, (3) the process by which management develops sensitive estimates, and (4) the auditor's judgment about the quality, not just the acceptability, of the client's accounting policies. These required disclosures to the audit committee pertain to both annual audits and interim reviews.

Promulgated Procedures Checklist

The auditor should perform the following procedures to obtain sufficient appropriate audit evidence to substantiate fair value measurements and disclosures made in the financial statements:

- Understand the client's process for fair value determinations and risk assessments.

- Evaluate conformity of fair value measurements and disclosures with GAAP.

- Consider the use of a specialist.

- Test the fair value measurements and disclosures.

- Evaluate fair value disclosures.

- Evaluate the results of audit procedures.

- Obtain management representations about fair values.

- Consider communicating with the audit committee.

> **PLANNING AID REMINDER:** Interpretation No. 1 of AU 328 (Auditing Fair Value Measurements and Disclosures) addresses the situation where an entity holds an interest in a trust that is managed by a third-party trustee. GAAP may require the assets in the trust to be reported at fair value (see ASC 958 (FAS-136, (Transfers of Assets to a Not-for-Profit Organization or Charitable Trust that Raises or Holds Contributions for Others)). The receipt of a confirmation from the trustee, where the investments held are confirmed on an aggregate basis, is not sufficient. However, the existence assertion is supported if the auditor receives confirmation from the trustee as to the individual investments held by the trustee. The valuation assertion is not supported even if the trustee confirms the investments held by the trust on an individual basis. Management, not the third-party trustee, is responsible for determining the fair values of investments held in the trust. Management needs to develop a process for determining the fair value of investments held in a trust. The auditor needs to (1) understand management's process, (2) evaluate whether the fair value measurements are in conformity with GAAP, and (3) test management's fair value determinations. If the auditor is unable to gather sufficient appropriate audit evidence related to either the existence or valuation assertions, a scope limitation may exist, requiring either a qualified audit opinion or a disclaimer of opinion.

Analysis and Application of Procedures

Understand the client's process for fair value determinations and risk assessments

The client's internal control should incorporate appropriate procedures for the processing and reporting in the financial statements fair value information and the auditor should obtain an understanding of the process based on the responsibilities described in SAS-109 (AU 314) (Consideration of Internal Control in a Financial Statement Audit). Specifically SAS-101 states that the auditor's understanding should consider the following:

- Specific controls over procedures to determine fair value measurements

- Level of expertise and experience of personnel involved in the process

- Extent of the role that information technology plays in the process

- Types of accounts or transactions affected by fair value measurements and disclosures

- Extent, if any, to which a service organization is used to provide fair value information (if a service organization is used, the auditor should consider the guidance established by SAS-70 [AU 324] [Service Organizations])

- Extent, if any, that the client uses the services of specialists in determining fair value measurements and disclosures

- Significant management assumptions (including how they were developed) used to develop fair value information, documentation created to support those assumptions, and procedures in place to monitor changes in assumptions

- Security controls in place relative to changes made in valuation models and relevant information systems

- Controls relative to the consistency, timeliness, and reliability of data used in valuation models

- Complexity of the process used to develop fair value information

These and other factors are used by the auditor to assess the risk of material misstatement, and they form the basis for determining the nature, timing, and extent of audit procedures.

> **FRAUD POINTER:** The auditor should consider the guidance established in SAS-99 (Consideration of Fraud in a Financial Statement Audit) for the possibility of management override of

controls related to fair value information presented in financial statements.

Evaluate conformity of fair value measurements and disclosures with GAAP

The auditor should evaluate whether the fair value measurements and disclosures are in accordance with GAAP, and SAS-101 emphasizes that this determination presupposes the auditor's understanding of GAAP as well as the nature of the client's business operations.

> **ENGAGEMENT STRATEGY:** Although this may be obvious, the Auditing Standards Board recognizes that accounting standards, especially those related to fair value, are becoming sophisticated and that auditors must stay current with financial accounting theory. For example, the valuation and disclosures related to derivatives as established by ASC 815 (FAS-133, Accounting for Derivative Instruments and Hedging Activities) and the application of the standards related to goodwill as established by ASC 350 (FAS-142, Goodwill and Other Intangible Assets) can be challenging even to the most seasoned auditor. It is more important than ever that the auditor devote a part of his or her professional life to professional development in order to deliver an audit product that satisfies professional standards. In some instances an effective engagement strategy includes the use of a specialist who is knowledgeable about fair value instruments, measurements, and disclosures.

The intent of management is fundamental to the correct implementation of GAAP. For example, the application of GAAP to the specific measurement of the impairment of a long-lived asset depends on whether the client plans to keep the asset in production or hold it for resale. SAS-101 points out that the auditor must use professional judgment to evaluate management intent; however, the auditor would make appropriate inquiries of management and also corroborate those responses through procedures such as the following:

- Analyze management's past history of executing stated intentions with respect to assets and liabilities

- Review written documentation that supports management's intentions

- Consider management's reason for a particular intention

- Consider whether management is financially or otherwise capable of executing a particular strategy

In some instances, the corroboration of fair value information is simple in that there is an established market with timely quotations; however, when no such market exists, SAS-101 states that the auditor should determine the rationale for the client's use of a particular valuation approach and consider the following issues:

- Has the client sufficiently evaluated and appropriately applied the criteria, if any, provided by GAAP to support the valuation method?

- Is the valuation method appropriate based on the circumstances under which it is applied and the nature of the asset or liability?

- Is the valuation method appropriate based on the business, industry, and environment in which the client operates?

Once selected, the client should apply the valuation method consistently unless circumstances or GAAP change. The auditor should be satisfied that a change in the use of a valuation method is appropriate.

> **PLANNING AID REMINDER:** The client may have more than one valuation method and identified a range of significantly different estimates of fair value. SAS-101 requires that the auditor evaluate how the client has investigated these differences in establishing a particular valuation.

Consider the use of a specialist

In some instances, the auditor does not have the expertise to plan and perform audit procedures that corroborate the client's presentation of fair value information in the financial statements. Under this circumstance the auditor should follow the guidance established in SAS-73 (AU 336) (Using the Work of a Specialist).

Test the fair value measurements and disclosures

Because of the variety of fair value information that is required by GAAP, the specific testing (nature, timing, and extent of audit procedures) of this information will vary depending upon the complexity of the information being tested and/or the complexity of the method used to determine the fair value of the information. Although professional judgment must be used to establish a strategy for testing fair value information, SAS-101 suggests that the approach could include the following:

- Test significant assumptions, the valuation model, and the underlying data.

- Review subsequent events and transactions.

- Consider developing independent fair value estimates.

Test significant assumptions, the valuation model, and the underlying data: SAS-101 states that the testing of fair value measurements and disclosures should include the following:

- Evaluate management's assumptions to determine whether they are reasonable and consistent with market information.

- Evaluate management's valuation models to determine whether they are appropriate.

- Evaluate relevant information that was used by management to determine whether it was reasonably available at the time.

The three items listed above are broad and should provide the auditor with a general approach in testing management's significant assumptions, valuation models, and underlying data; however, professional judgment must be exercised to determine how specific fair value information is to be tested for reasonableness in the context of the financial statements taken as a whole. The auditor does not offer an opinion on the assumptions, valuation models, or the underlying data themselves. Rather, the auditor's tests are performed in the context of auditing the client's financial statements.

> **ENGAGEMENT STRATEGY:** Fair value information may be based on sensitive assumptions. That is, a change in an assumption can have a significant impact on the dollar value of fair value information. SAS-101 states, "where applicable, the auditor encourages management to use techniques such as sensitivity analysis to help identify particularly sensitive assumptions." Furthermore, if management has not used sensitivity analysis in this manner, the auditor should consider whether to use the approach as part of the engagement strategy to identify such assumptions.

When evaluating the reasonableness of management's assumptions, each assumption should be considered individually as well as its relationship to the entire set of assumptions. That is, an assumption may appear reasonable in isolation but in the context of the overall valuation approach it may be inconsistent with other assumptions. SAS-101 points out that the following should be taken into consideration in determining whether assumptions are realistic and consistent with:

- Assumptions made in prior periods, if applicable?

- Available market information?

- Economic conditions in general, those of the industry, and those specifically related to the client's circumstances?

- Other assumptions used by management to prepare the financial statements?

- Past experience, if applicable?

- The client's plans?

- The risk related to cash flows including variability, timing, and the effect of the discount rate?

> **OBSERVATION:** When the client uses a valuation model to quantify measurements and disclosures, the auditor neither serves as an appraiser nor substitutes his or her judgment for that of the client. The auditor's role is to review the model and determine whether the client has used reasonable assumptions based on the relevant circumstances.

Finally, the auditor should perform appropriate procedures to test data used to determine (1) whether data are accurate, complete, and relevant and (2) whether the fair value information represents such data and management's assumptions. These procedures could include recomputation, verification of source data, and determination of data consistency with management's intentions and ability to carry out certain actions.

Consider developing independent fair value estimates

The auditor may decide to independently develop estimates of fair value information. For example, an auditor-developed model may be used. SAS-101 points out that if this procedure is employed as part of the testing of the entity's fair value measurements and disclosures, the following guidelines should be observed:

- Use the general guidance established by SAS-56 (AU 329) (Analytical Procedures).

- When the independent estimate is based on management's assumptions, use the guidance discussed above.

- When the independent estimate is based on the auditor's assumptions, (1) develop an understanding of management's assumptions, (2) use management's assumptions to ensure that all significant variables are also used by the auditor, and (3) evaluate significant differences between estimates made by management and those derived from the auditor-developed approach.

Irrespective of whether the auditor uses management's assumptions or develops his or her own assumptions, the auditor should perform appropriate procedures to test data used to determine (1) whether data are accurate, complete, and relevant, and (2) whether the fair value information represents such data and management's (or the auditor's) assumptions. These procedures could include recomputation, verification of source data, and determination of data consistency.

Review subsequent events and transactions

In some instances, insight into the fair value of information reported in the year-end financial statements can be obtained by events and transactions that occur after the balance-sheet date but before the date of the auditor's report. Only events or transactions that reflect conditions that existed as of the balance-sheet date should be considered. For example, the sales price of an investment in a publicly traded security that occurs after the balance-sheet date would generally not be useful in measuring the fair value of the investment at the date of the balance sheet because economic conditions have changed between the balance sheet date and the date of the transaction. On the other hand, the sale after the balance-sheet date of an asset that does not have an established market can be helpful in substantiating or questioning the fair value information presented in the balance sheet. In such a case the audit procedures described in the section titled "Test significant assumptions, the valuation model, and the underlying data" may be omitted or minimized.

> **PLANNING AID REMINDER:** The audit procedure described in the previous paragraph is a substantive procedure and is not part of the review of subsequent events described in SAS-1 (AU 560) (Codification of Auditing Standards and Procedures-Subsequent Events).

Evaluate fair value disclosures

A client may present in its notes to the financial statements both fair value information required by GAAP and voluntary disclosures. Generally the same audit procedures that are applied to fair value measurements that are reflected directly on the financial statements are also applied to fair value information (both required and voluntary) presented in the notes. That is, "the auditor obtains sufficient appropriate audit evidence that valuation principles are appropriate under GAAP and are being consistently applied, and that the method of estimation and significant assumptions used are adequately disclosed in accordance with GAAP."

> **PLANNING AID REMINDER:** When there is a high degree of uncertainty with respect to fair value measurements, the auditor should determine whether the degree of uncertainty is adequately disclosed. In making this determination, the general guidance established by AICPA SOP 94-6 (Disclosure of Certain Significant Risks and Uncertainties) should be followed.

Evaluate the results of audit procedures

Once the procedures described above and other procedures deemed appropriate are applied, the auditor must determine whether fair value information is presented in accordance with GAAP and applied on a consistent basis. Making this determination should be consistent with the guidance established by SAS-107 (AU 312) (Audit Risk and Materiality in Conducting an Audit).

> **FRAUD POINTER:** In 2010 the Committee of Sponsoring Organizations of the Treadway Commission (COSO) issued a study entitled "Fraudulent Financial Reporting: 1998–2007, An Analysis of U.S. Public Companies" that found that 51% of the fraudulent financial reporting enforcement actions by the SEC involved asset overstatements. Assets related to fair value measurement and disclosure might involve heightened fraud risk because of the significant opportunities for management to perpetrate fraud related to those accounts. The significant dependence on management assumptions and the related complexities associated with measuring and disclosing fair value instruments can create significant opportunities for management to engage in fraud.

Obtain management representations about fair values

Generally the written representations covering the following should be obtained from management concerning fair value information:

- The reasonableness of significant assumptions used to determine fair value information

- The significant assumptions reflect management's intentions

- The ability of management to carry out specific strategies related to the measurement of fair value information

SAS-101 also notes that, depending on the nature, materiality, and complexity of fair value measurements and disclosures, the following additional written representations should be provided by management:

- The appropriateness of measurement methods used

- The completeness and adequacy of disclosures

- Whether subsequent events affect the fair value information

Consider communicating with the audit committee

Appendix B of SAS-114 (AU 380) describes the nature of auditor communications to those charged with governance about certain matters regarding accounting estimates. Specifically that communication should include the process used to make accounting estimates and the auditor's basis for determining the reasonableness of accounting estimates. Estimates related to fair value information are included in the scope of this communication requirements, and SAS-101 states that the auditor should consider communicating the following:

- The nature of significant assumptions that are the basis of fair value estimates

- The degree of subjectivity related to the significant assumptions

- The relative materiality of the fair value measurements to the financial statements taken as a whole

SECTION 329

ANALYTICAL PROCEDURES

Authoritative Pronouncements

SAS-56 — Analytical Procedures

Audit Guide — Analytical Procedures

> **IMPORTANT NOTICE FOR 2011:** The Auditing Standards Board (ASB) is in the process of redrafting all of the auditing sections in *Codification of Statements on Auditing Standards* to converge U.S. GAAS with the International Standards on Auditing issued by the International Auditing and Assurance Standards Board. As part of this process, the newly redrafted standards will follow certain clarity drafting conventions adopted by the ASB. These clarity drafting conventions include: (1) establishing objectives for each standard; (2) including a definitions section, if appropriate; and (3) separating requirements from application guidance and other material. The ASB is planning to have all redrafted standards become effective on the same date, which is for audits of financial statements for periods ending on or after December 15, 2012. It is possible that the effective date might be delayed beyond that date. The ASB's clarity and convergence project will have a significant effect on the auditing standards applicable to audits of nonpublic companies, and the 2012 *GAAS Guide* will be appropriately modified to reflect these changes once the effective date of the standards is certain.

Overview

Analytical procedures are used to determine whether relationships between information presented in financial statements is consistent with the auditor's expectations. For example, if an auditor is aware that a client has invested heavily in new machinery, depreciation expense would be expected to be significantly greater in the current period than in the prior period. To successfully employ analytical procedures, an auditor must have a thorough knowledge of the client and the industry in which the entity operates. Because analytical procedures are applied in a broad manner in the collection of evidence and because such an approach has limitations in achieving audit objectives, analytical procedures should only be employed by (or supervised closely by) experienced staff.

Expectations concerning financial information and assumptions that affect financial information may be developed by the auditor from sources such as the following:

- Prior-period financial information (if appropriate, modified for new conditions and events)

- Budgeted, forecasted, and projected financial information

- Interrelationships of financial information

- Industry characteristics and developments

- Nonfinancial information that may affect financial information

> **PUBLIC COMPANY IMPLICATION:** In 2010 the PCAOB issued eight auditing standards (AS-8 through AS-15) related to the auditor's assessment of and response to risk. The proposed standards bear many similarities to the eight risk-assessment standards adopted by the Auditing Standards Board in 2006. The discussion of analytical procedures is integrated across these eight new risk-assessment standards. In particular, analytical procedures are discussed in AS-12, AS-13, AS-14, and AS-15. Although there are a number of differences between the PCAOB's and ASB's risk standards, the risk-assessment concepts contained in the PCAOB standards should be familiar to most auditors. As is currently the case, audit risk is the risk that the auditor will issue an inappropriate opinion on financial statements that are materially misstated. The auditor is to reduce audit risk to a low level through the application of audit procedures. As a result, the amount of audit effort devoted to particular accounts, classes of transactions, and disclosures should vary based on their respective risk.

Analytical Procedures Process

The AICPA Audit Guide titled "Analytical Procedures" states that the process of using analytical procedures consists of the following four phases:

1. Formation of auditor expectations

2. Identification of differences between account balances and auditor expectations

3. Investigation of differences

4. Evaluation of results

Formation of auditor expectations

The auditor incorporates all of his or her experiences, both general and client-specific, to develop expectations of relationships between financial and nonfinancial data. Thus, at this stage the auditor must formulate an expectation about a relationship involving an amount that appears in the client's accounting system. Because of the varying nature of information processed and otherwise developed by a client, the Audit Guide notes that the effectiveness of developing an expectation depends on the following factors:

• Nature of account or assertion

• Reliability and other characteristics of data

• Inherent precision of an analytical procedure

Nature of account or assertion

Auditor expectations must be based on plausible relationships between financial and nonfinancial data. The more predictable a relationship, the more plausible the auditor's expectation. For example, there is a relationship between the amount of interest-bearing debt on the balance sheet (as reported throughout the year) and the interest expense reported on the operating statement. Developing an expected relationship between two amounts such as these is relatively easy to do; however, expectations about other relationships can be more difficult to identify with an acceptable degree of precision. For example, the relationship between accounts receivable and the allowance for uncollectible accounts can be difficult to predict if the client has changed its credit policies or the economics of the client's industry have significantly changed. The Audit Guide lists the following as examples of factors that an auditor may consider in establishing a relationship between accounts (assertions) on the financial statements:

• The degree of subjectivity exercised to develop the account balance (for example, an account may simply be an aggregation of transactions (low degree of subjectivity) or be based on estimates (high degree of subjectivity).

• The product mix

- The client's profile (for example, the manner in which it distributes its products)

- Management's discretion

- Various measurements of the client's environment (for example, changes in economic, technological, or regulatory conditions)

- The type of account (balance sheet or operating account)

Reliability and other characteristics of data

The precision of the auditor's expectation (how close the expectation is to the correct amount, not the reported amount) depends on the quality of the data used to form the expectation. If the reliability of the data is poor, the quality of the audit evidence created by performing an analytical procedure will be poor and perhaps irrelevant. The Audit Guide identifies the following as factors that are useful in determining the usefulness of data used to develop auditor expectations:

- The client's internal control (the stronger the internal control, the more reliable the data)

- The source of data (data based on outside parties are more reliable than internally generated data)

- Audited data (data that have been subjected to audit procedures [generally financial data] are more reliable than data that have not been audited [generally nonfinancial data])

- The degree of aggregation (the more aggregated data, the more difficult it is to develop a precise expectation)

Inherent precision of an analytical procedure

The Audit Guide broadly classifies analytical procedures as (1) trend analysis, (2) ratio analysis, (3) reasonableness test, and (4) regression analysis. These broad analytical procedures are not substitutes for one another. The auditor, using professional judgment, selects the appropriate analytical procedure based on the desired level of assurance that the account (assertion) is not materially misstated.

Trend analysis is based on the analysis of changes in a balance over a period of time that can vary from two years (the current year compared with the previous year) to several years. Generally trend analysis is most effective when the client is in a stable environment. For example, the reasonableness of current-year sales may be appropriately tested by comparing that amount to sales in the previous year if there is an absence of increased competition in the area serviced by the client, changing local economic conditions, changing consumer preferences, and an absence of change in a host of other environmental conditions.

The advantage of using trend analysis is its simplicity; however, its effectiveness is limited by the fact that it does not take into consideration changes in the client's environment. In addition, the use of this approach is based on an implicit rather than an explicit expectation. That is, in trend analysis the auditor does not explicitly establish an expected dollar amount but, rather, compares two numbers that because of changed conditions might not be comparable. Trend analysis is also limited to a single predictor and cannot take into consideration operating data or external data.

Ratio analysis can be used to compare the relationship between (1) accounts over time (inventory turnover), (2) an account and nonfinancial information (for example, sales per square foot of space), (3) accounts of the client and data from the client's industry (for example, the percentage of uncollectible accounts), and (4) a combination of the foregoing three items.

Like trend analysis, ratio analysis is most effective when the environmental characteristics of the client are stable; however, the Audit Guide points out that ratio analysis can be more effective than trend analysis "because comparisons between the balance sheet and operating statement can often reveal unusual fluctuations that an analysis of the individual accounts would not." Furthermore using ratio analysis that is based in part on industry data can only be effective if the client's operating and financing activities do not deviate significantly from industry norms.

Reasonableness tests utilize financial and nonfinancial data to determine the acceptability of an account balance or a change in an account balance. For example, the current year's payroll expense expectation may take into consideration last year's account balance and other factors such as the average pay rate change, the timing of pay rate adjustments, and the expansion or contraction of the labor force. The advantage of a reasonableness test over trend analysis and ratio analysis is that in a reasonableness test the auditor takes into consideration a client's changed environment and, using professional judgment, assesses whether the current-year balance appears to be appropriate. In applying a reasonableness test the auditor must be careful to identify all the significant factors that could have an impact on the account balance being investigated.

Regression analysis is the most sophisticated analytical procedure in that it is based on a statistical model to predict the relationship between the account balance and various other factors. Generally the difference between a reasonableness test and regression analysis is that regression analysis produces a quantitative prediction (expressed as a range) of what the current year's balance should be.

The most difficult analytical procedure to employ is regression analysis, but it has all of the advantages of reasonableness tests and, additionally, it provides a measure of statistical precision. That is, the auditor does not attempt to predict a single amount but, rather, estimates a projected amount plus or minus a dollar value.

> **PLANNING AID REMINDER:** The effectiveness of analytical procedures is increased if the data sets are disaggregated. For example, applying a trend analysis approach to divisional information rather than consolidated financial information will generally result in more precise expectations. Be aware that when conducting regression analyses, one needs a sufficient number of data points to obtain a statistically valid result. Usually 18 to 20 data points are sufficient. Quarterly results can be used if the data is accurate. Microsoft Excel and other spreadsheet programs contain easy-to-use statistical analysis programs.

Identification of differences between account balance and auditor expectations

The second phase of the analytical procedure process is the identification of differences, which simply means that the auditor computes the difference between the expectation and the recorded account balance. The computed difference is then compared with the auditor's measure of materiality. When the analytical procedure is part of substantive testing, the auditor will accept the recorded amount balance when the difference is less than the materiality threshold for the account (e.g., the tolerable misstatement). If the difference is greater than the materiality threshold, the difference must be investigated.

Investigation of differences

The Audit Guide points out that differences between the expected amount and the recorded account balance can arise for one or more of the following reasons:

- The recorded account balance is misstated.

- The recorded account balance is affected by inherent factors related to the nature of the account to a degree not anticipated by the auditor.

- The expected amount is affected by the reliability of databases used to establish the expected amount to a degree not anticipated by the auditor.

Initially the auditor should evaluate the expectation results by determining whether there is an apparent problem with the precision of the estimate (the second and third items listed above). If it is concluded that the analytical procedure created a too imprecise expectation, then the auditor must decide whether the cost related to employing a more precise analytical procedure can be justified. For example, the auditor might have used trend analysis to develop an implicit expectation about a client's current sales figure, but if the difference between the expected amount and the recorded sales amount is too great, it may be concluded that regression analysis should be used to test the acceptability of the sales figure.

If the auditor concludes that the level of precision does not appear to be the reason for the unacceptable difference between the expected amount and the recorded amount, the investigation should consider whether there is a plausible explanation for the difference. Generally a plausible explanation is related to unexpected events, changes in the business environment, or accounting changes. The Audit Guide states that a plausible explanation should be evaluated in the context of such factors as the following:

- The development of audit evidence in other parts of the engagement, especially evidence obtained that relates to the database used to formulate the original expectation.

- Reports by management or the board of directors that identify and explain significant variances between budgeted and actual results.

- Relevant information identified in the minutes of the board of directors.

- Information about unusual events that occurred in previous years that may have reoccurred in the current period.

When an analytical procedure is performed as part of substantive testing, reasons that support a plausible explanation must be investigated and corroborated. The specific form of corroboration will depend on the nature of the account and the plausible explanation, but the Audit Guide notes that one or more of the following procedures may be useful to an auditor:

- Confirm related factors with outside parties.

- Make inquiries of internal personnel who did not provide the plausible explanation to the auditor.

- Perform other auditing procedures (perhaps on the data that were used to establish the expectation).

- Inspect documents that support the plausible explanation.

If the auditor cannot corroborate the plausible explanation, the difference must be evaluated as unexplained.

Evaluation of results

The final step in the analytical procedures process is the evaluation of results arising from the application of the procedure. Professional judgment must be exercised to determine how the results of applying an analytical procedure affect the audit engagement. The Audit Guide points out that "the auditor should attempt to quantify that portion of the difference for which plausible explanations can be obtained and, where appropriate, corroborate and determine that the amount that cannot be explained is sufficiently small to enable him or her to conclude on the absence of material misstatement." More specifically when a plausible explanation cannot be supported, the auditor should aggregate misstatements that the entity has not corrected in a way that enables him or her to consider whether, in relation to individual amounts, subtotals, or totals in the financial statements, they materially misstate the financial statements taken as a whole. Qualitative considerations also influence the auditor in reaching a conclusion as to whether misstatements are material.

> **FRAUD POINTER:** SAS-99 (Consideration of Fraud in a Financial Statement Audit) requires the auditor to consider the results of analytical procedures performed when planning the audit when obtaining information necessary to identify fraud risks. When the auditor identifies through the use of planning analytical procedures unusual or unexpected relationships between recorded amounts and the auditor's expectations, he or she should consider the results of those procedures in identifying the risks of material misstatements due to fraud.

Promulgated Procedures Checklist

The auditor should do the following as part of implementing analytical procedures as part of the audit engagement:

- Perform analytical procedures as part of the planning of the engagement.

- Perform analytical procedures as part of the overall review of financial information.

- Consider performing analytical procedures as part of substantive procedures.

- Document results of performing analytical procedure related to substantive procedures.

> **PLANNING AID REMINDER:** Analytical procedures must be used in planning the nature, timing, and extent of audit procedures and in conducting an overall review of the financial information. The auditor must use professional judgment to determine whether analytical procedures should be used as a substantive procedure to collect audit evidence related to account balances or classes of transactions.

> **ENGAGEMENT STRATEGY:** Although SAS-56 does not require that analytical procedures be used as part of substantive testing, it does imply that it may be difficult to achieve certain audit objectives efficiently without applying them as a substantive procedure.

Analysis and Application of Procedures

Perform analytical procedures as part of the planning of the engagement

An auditor must perform analytical procedures to provide a basis for determining the nature, timing, and extent of subsequent audit procedures. Analytical procedures are employed to reduce to an acceptable level the possibility that a material misstatement or omission in the financial statements may occur (detection risk). When establishing an acceptable level of detection risk, the auditor must consider the susceptibility of an account to be misstated (inherent risk), the control structure related to the account (control risk), and materiality.

> **ENGAGEMENT STRATEGY:** Analytical procedures applied early in the engagement can help the auditor understand factors that must be used to establish a satisfactory level of detection risk.

The planning phase of an engagement should include review of financial information that is generally aggregated to identify unexpected relationships or trends. This may be accomplished through comparisons of general ledger balances with similar balances from prior periods and with budgeted or forecasted balances. Various ratios or trends may be computed to facilitate the analysis; however, the evaluation should be sensitive to changing conditions that may explain unexpected variations or may raise expectations that variations should in fact be present in the financial information. For example, the balance in the current legal expense account might be consistent with both last year's amount and the budgeted amount, but such expense stability might be unwarranted, because the client experienced unanticipated legal problems. In planning subsequent audit procedures, the auditor should select procedures to determine whether the client's legal counsel is billing its services on a timely basis.

Formulating Expectation

An auditor should be careful to use analytical procedures in this stage of the engagement as an effective audit planning tool. That is, in some engagements, auditors may see analytical procedures as a nuisance and not as an integral part of the engagement. Under this circumstance, it may be easy to gather corroborative evidence and then, based on the audit results, let the evidence drive the documentation of the "expectations" that should have been driven by the original performance of analytical procedures. For example, an auditor may conclude, as a result of performing procedures related to the substantiation of bad debts expense, that bad debts expense as a percentage of credit sales has fallen significantly compared with the previous year's engagement because more rigorous credit review policies have been implemented during the year. This is a backward approach to the use of analytical procedures and is a violation of professional standards.

To encourage staff personnel to use analytical procedures correctly, it may be useful to document the preliminary expectations prior to the performance of planning analytical procedures. That documentation should include the expected impact of the results of the analytical procedures on the design of the timing, extent, and nature of audit procedures to be used as part of substantive procedures. A Practitioner's Aid at the end of this section illustrates how preliminary expectations may be documented in an engagement.

> **PLANNING AID REMINDER:** In addition to financial information, nonfinancial data may be taken into consideration as part of the performance of analytical procedures. For example, quality control reports prepared near year-end may identify production problems, which may suggest that significant amounts of inventory sold during the latter part of the year may be returned or may significantly increase future warranty claims.

Perform analytical procedures as part of the overall review of financial information

An auditor must perform analytical procedures as part of the final review of the audited financial information in order to determine whether the anticipated opinion on the financial statements appears to be warranted. Analytical procedures performed in the overall review stage of the audit generally involve reading the financial statements and notes to consider the adequacy of evidence gathered in response to unusual or unexpected relationships and to identify unusual or unexpected relationships not previously noted and investigated. Based on this analysis, the auditor might determine that additional audit evidence should be collected.

Consider performing analytical procedures as part of substantive procedures

Analytical procedures may be used as part of substantive procedures (tests of financial statement assertions) to achieve desired audit objectives or to achieve those objectives in an efficient manner. In general, the auditor uses analytical procedures as part of the substantive procedures by evaluating aggregated information to form conclusions about specific assertions contained in the financial statements. For example, an aged trial balance may be prepared and analyzed to test the assertion that accounts receivable are presented at net realizable value. In many instances the auditor will use both analytical procedures and tests of details to examine financial statement balances and classes of transactions.

In determining whether and to what extent analytical procedures should be used, an auditor should consider the following factors:

• Nature of the assertion being tested

• Plausibility and predictability of the relationship

• Reliability and availability of the data used to develop the expectation

• Precision of the expectation

These four factors should be considered in assessing the relative efficiency and effectiveness of analytical procedures as compared to tests of details.

The nature of the assertion being tested should be evaluated to determine whether analytical procedures may satisfy the related audit objective in a more efficient and effective way than tests of details. In general, it may be more appropriate to test assertions related to the completeness assertion (all transactions and accounts are reflected in the financial statements) by using analytical procedures. For example, the validity of an allowance for returned merchandise may be more effectively tested by using analytical procedures (review of sales volume, history of returned goods, maintenance of production standards, etc.) than by using tests of details (vouching actual sales returned).

The applicability of analytical procedures depends on the plausibility and predictability of the relationship between data. There is seldom a one-to-one relationship between data; however, the stronger the relationship, the more likely it is that analytical procedures can satisfy some audit objectives. The following generalizations may be useful in identifying plausible relationships:

- Relationships in a relatively stable environment tend to be more predictable than those in an unstable environment. (For example, bad debts expense and credit sales tend to be closely related to a stable economic environment.)

- Relationships among data on the income statement tend to be more predictable than relationships among data on the balance sheet. (For example, sales and sales commission expense tend to be more closely related than trade accounts payable and inventories.)

- Relationships that are subject to management discretion are more difficult to evaluate. (For example, loss contingency accruals associated with the number of pending lawsuits tend not to be predictable.)

For the auditor to be able to draw an inference about an account balance or a class of transactions based on applying analytical procedures, the data from which the inference is made must be reliable and available. In evaluating the reliability of data, the following generalizations are useful:

- Audited data (current or prior years) are more reliable than unaudited data.

- Internal data tend to be more reliable when developed from records maintained by personnel who are not responsible for the audited amount.

- Internal data tend to be more reliable when developed under an adequate control structure.

- Data from an external source tend to be more reliable than data from an internal source.

- Reliability of expectations increases as sources of data increase.

Because analytical procedures generally lead to fairly broad conclusions about assertions in the financial statements, an auditor should consider the precision of the established expectation. In some instances, an auditor may be satisfied with a fairly imprecise expectation. For example, expectations concerning the relationship between warranty expense and sales subject to warranty may be imprecise (say, from 1% to 8% of sales) if significant changes in warranty expenses are unlikely to have a material effect on the financial statements. On the other hand, a more precise expectation may be demanded for sales returns when the client is in an industry that experiences significant returns and a change of a percentage point or two could have a material effect on the financial statements. Factors that affect the precision of an expectation include

- The number of relevant variables that affect a relationship (the more variables, the more precise the expectation)

- The number of relevant variables that are evaluated by the auditor (the more variables evaluated, the more precise the expectation)

- The level of detail in the data used to construct the expectation (the more detailed the data, the more precise the expectation)

> **ENGAGEMENT STRATEGY:** When planning analytical procedures, the auditor should set the materiality thresholds for acceptable deviations from expected amounts. The amount of an acceptable deviation from the expected amount should be less than what is considered material when those deviations are combined with other errors in other account balances and classes of transactions.

When a significant deviation from an expected amount is encountered, the auditor should attempt to identify and corroborate reasons to explain the deviation. The corroborative process may include the following:

- Use of information obtained in other parts of the audit

- Explanation provided by the client

- Use of extended audit procedures

> **ENGAGEMENT STRATEGY:** The corroborative process is employed to reasonably ensure that the significant deviation is not caused by an error or fraud. The more precise and reliable an expectation, the greater the likelihood that a significant deficiency is the result of error or fraud. And the more precise and reliable an expectation, the more an auditor must be skeptical about explanations that seek to justify a significant deviation.

Document results of performing analytical procedure related to
substantive procedures

The auditor should document the following in the audit files when an analytical procedure has been used as a principal substantive test of a significant financial statement assertion:

- The expected result (when that expectation is not obvious) and factors considered in developing the expectation

- The results arising from the comparison of the expected results with the recorded amounts or ratios developed from the recorded amounts

- Any additional procedures that resulted from the comparison of the expected results with recorded amounts or ratios developed from the recorded amounts

- The results arising from the performance of the additional procedures listed above

Practitioner's Aids

Exhibits AU 329-1 and AU 329-2 are examples of audit documentation that could be used to document the performance and results of analytical procedures. Exhibit AU 329-3 illustrates an approach to the performance of preliminary analytical review. Exhibit AU 329-4 illustrates an approach to the performance of final analytical review.

EXHIBIT AU 329-1 — DOCUMENTATION OF THE EFFECT OF ANALYTICAL PROCEDURES ON THE PLANNING OF SUBSTANTIVE AUDIT PROCEDURES

Use this audit schedule to document the effect of analytical procedures on planned substantive audit procedures. The evaluation of the preliminary condition's effect on planned substantive audit procedures is preliminary, and the nature, extent, and timing of audit procedures may be revised based on additional information obtained during the engagement.

Client Name: _____

Date of Financial Statements: _____

Preliminary Condition	Implication of Preliminary Condition on Planning Substantive Audit Procedures	Substantive Audit Documentation Reference
• **Account Balance/Transaction:** Description of preliminary condition:	Nature of Procedure: Timing of Procedure: Extent of Procedure:	
• **Account Balance/Transaction:** Description of preliminary condition:	Nature of Procedure: Timing of Procedure: Extent of Procedure:	
• **Account Balance/Transaction:** Description of preliminary condition:	Nature of Procedure: Timing of Procedure: Extent of Procedure:	
• **Account Balance/Transaction:** Description of preliminary condition:	Nature of Procedure: Timing of Procedure: Extent of Procedure:	
• **Account Balance/Transaction:** Description of preliminary condition:	Nature of Procedure: Timing of Procedure: Extent of Procedure:	
• **Account Balance/Transaction:** Description of preliminary condition:	Nature of Procedure: Timing of Procedure: Extent of Procedure:	
• **Account Balance/Transaction:** Description of preliminary condition:	Nature of Procedure: Timing of Procedure: Extent of Procedure:	

Preliminary Condition	Implication of Preliminary Condition on Planning Substantive Audit Procedures	Substantive Audit Documentation Reference
• **Account Balance/Transaction:** Description of preliminary condition:	Nature of Procedure:	
	Timing of Procedure:	
	Extent of Procedure:	
• **Account Balance/Transaction:** Description of preliminary condition:	Nature of Procedure:	
	Timing of Procedure:	
	Extent of Procedure:	
• **Account Balance/Transaction:** Description of preliminary condition:	Nature of Procedure:	
	Timing of Procedure:	
	Extent of Procedure:	
• **Account Balance/Transaction:** Description of preliminary condition:	Nature of Procedure:	
	Timing of Procedure:	
	Extent of Procedure:	

Analysis Performed by: _____

Date: _____

Reviewed by: _____

Date: _____

_____

EXHIBIT AU 329-2 — PERFORMANCE OF ANALYTICAL PROCEDURES

Use this form to document the performance of analytical procedures. The form is only a guide, and professional judgment should be exercised to determine how the form should be modified by omitting or adding analytical procedures.

Client Name: _____

Date of Financial Statements: _____

COMPARISON OF CURRENT FINANCIAL STATEMENTS WITH COMPARABLE PRIOR-PERIOD FINANCIAL STATEMENTS

The following ratios were computed:

_____ Using financial data that reflects adjustments proposed to date.

_____ Using financial data that does not reflect adjustments.

	Formula
LIQUIDITY RATIOS	
1. Current ratio	$\dfrac{\text{Current Assets}}{\text{Current Liabilities}}$
2. Acid-test ratio	$\dfrac{\text{Quick Assets}}{\text{Current Liabilities}}$
3. Days' sales in accounts receivable	$\dfrac{\text{Average Accounts Receivable} \times 365 \text{ Days}}{\text{Net Credit Sales}}$
4. Current liabilities to total assets	$\dfrac{\text{Current Liabilities}}{\text{Total Assets}}$
ACTIVITY RATIOS	
1. Inventory turnover	$\dfrac{\text{Cost of Goods Sold}}{\text{Average Inventory}}$
2. Receivable turnover	$\dfrac{\text{Net Credit Sales}}{\text{Average Accounts Receivable}}$
OTHER RATIOS	
3. Asset turnover	$\dfrac{\text{Net Sales}}{\text{Average Total Assets}}$
4. Gross profit percentage	$\dfrac{\text{Gross Profit}}{\text{Net Sales}}$
PROFITABILITY RATIOS	
1. Bad debt to sales	$\dfrac{\text{Bad Debt Expense}}{\text{Net Sales}}$
2. Return on assets	$\dfrac{\text{Net Income}}{\text{Total Assets}}$
3. Return on equity	$\dfrac{\text{Net Income}}{\text{Total Equity}}$
4. Net margin	$\dfrac{\text{Net Income}}{\text{Net Sales}}$

	Formula

COVERAGE RATIOS

1. Debt to total assets

$$\frac{\text{Total Debt}}{\text{Total Assets}}$$

2. Interest expense to sales

$$\frac{\text{Interest Expense}}{\text{Net Sales}}$$

3. Number of times interest earned

$$\frac{\text{Income before Interest and Taxes}}{\text{Interest Expenses}}$$

1. Effective tax rate

$$\frac{\text{Income Taxes}}{\text{Income before Taxes}}$$

2. Bad debt rate

$$\frac{\text{Allowance for Bad Debts}}{\text{Accounts Receivable}}$$

3. Depreciation rate

$$\frac{\text{Depreciation Expense}}{\text{Depreciable Property}}$$

4. Accounts payable to purchases

$$\frac{\text{Accounts Payable}}{\text{Purchases}}$$

5. Dividend rate

$$\frac{\text{Dividends}}{\text{Common Stock (Par)}}$$

6. Interest rate

$$\frac{\text{Interest Expense}}{\text{Average Interest-Bearing Debt}}$$

7. Payroll rate

$$\frac{\text{Payroll Expense}}{\text{Net Sales}}$$

8. Dividend return

$$\frac{\text{Dividend Income}}{\text{Average Equity Investments}}$$

9. Interest income return

$$\frac{\text{Interest Income}}{\text{Average Debt Investments}}$$

OTHER

COMPARISON OF CURRENT FINANCIAL STATEMENTS WITH ANTICIPATED RESULTS

	20XX		
Acct # Account Name	*Actual*	*Budgeted*	*Difference*
Cash in bank — name			
Petty cash			
Cash in bank — payroll			

		20XX		
Acct #	Account Name	Actual	Budgeted	Difference
	Investment marketable — equity securities (current)			
	Allowance for decline in market value — marketable equity securities (current)			
	Accounts receivable			
	Allowance for doubtful accounts			
	Other receivables (current)			
	Accrued interest receivable			
	Notes receivable (current)			
	Discount on notes receivable			
	Dividends receivable			
	Inventory (year-end balance)			
	Prepaid insurance			
	Prepaid rent			
	Prepaid advertising			
	Land			
	Buildings			
	Accumulated depreciation — buildings			
	Delivery equipment			
	Accumulated depreciation — delivery equipment			
	Fixtures			
	Accumulated depreciation — fixtures			
	Office equipment			
	Accumulated depreciation — Office equipment			
	Property — capital leases			
	Investment — marketable equity securities (noncurrent)			
	Allowance for decline in market value — marketable equity securities (noncurrent)			
	Deferred bond issuance costs			
	Other receivables (noncurrent)			
	Investment — convertible bonds			
	Land held for investment			
	Accounts payable			
	Accrued liabilities			
	Payroll taxes and other withholdings			
	Interest payable			

		20XX		
Acct #	*Account Name*	*Actual*	*Budgeted*	*Difference*
	Notes payable			
	Discounts/premiums — notes payable			
	Obligations — capital leases (current)			
	Dividends payable			
	Income taxes payable			
	Notes payable (noncurrent)			
	Bonds payable			
	Discounts/premiums — bonds payable			
	Obligations — capital leases (noncurrent)			
	Common stock			
	Paid-in capital in excess of par			
	Unappropriated retained earnings			
	Appropriated retained earnings			
	Unrealized loss — marketable equity securities (noncurrent)			
	Sales			
	Sales returns and allowances			
	Sales discounts			
	Cost of goods sold			
	Purchases			
	Freight-in			
	Bad debt expense			
	Utilities expense			
	Travel expense			
	Advertising expense			
	Delivery expense			
	Miscellaneous expense			
	Insurance expense			
	Rent expense			
	Professional fees expense			
	Salaries and wages expense			
	Payroll taxes expense			
	Depreciation expense — buildings			
	Depreciation expense — delivery equipment			
	Depreciation expense — fixtures			
	Depreciation expense — office equipment			
	Depreciation expense — capital leases			

Acct #	Account Name	20XX		
		Actual	*Budgeted*	*Difference*
	Repairs and maintenance expense			
	Miscellaneous income			
	Extraordinary items			
	Dividend income			
	Interest income			
	Interest expense			
	Loss/gain on sale of assets			
	Unrealized loss — marketable equity securities			
	Recovery of market reduction of marketable equity securities (current) recorded in prior years			
	Loss on exchange of assets			
	Loss due to permanent decline in value of security investments			
	Loss/gain on sale of investments			
	Income tax expense			
	Totals			

Prepared By: _____

Reviewed By: _____

STUDY OF FINANCIAL STATEMENT ELEMENTS AND UNEXPECTED RELATIONSHIPS

Unexpected Relationships	*Summary of Analysis*
_____	_____
_____	_____
_____	_____
_____	_____
_____	_____
_____	_____
_____	_____
_____	_____
_____	_____
_____	_____
_____	_____

OTHER ANALYTICAL PROCEDURES

Summary of findings: _____

_____

_____

_____

_____

_____

_____

_____

_____

_____

_____

Prepared By: _____

Date: _____

Reviewed By: _____

Date: _____

EXHIBIT AU 329-3 — EXAMPLE OF PRELIMINARY ANALYTICAL REVIEW

CLIENT:

DATE: 6/30/XX

Preliminary analytical review is to be performed for all audit engagements. The purpose of preliminary analytical review procedures is to spot areas that warrant more intensive auditing procedures, and to identify areas that are either not material or appear to be of low risk and warrant consideration of less-intensive procedures. Preliminary analytical review should be performed early in the audit work to enable us to most efficiently plan the nature and scope of our test work and substantive procedures.

Consider the following the procedures:

	WP	REF
1. Compare current-year balances with those of prior years, noting unusual fluctuations.	_____	_____

	WP	REF

2. Identify amounts that because of their size represent significant elements of the financial statements, regardless of consistency or lack of consistency with prior years.   _____   _____

3. If the entity prepares a budget, consider comparing actual current year to budget and investigate significant variances.   _____   _____

4. Identify elements within the statements that would be expected to have predictable relationships (e.g., current ratio, quick ratio, inventory turnover, days of sales in A/R, gross profit percentage, percent of payroll taxes, workers' comp, etc.) to salary expenses and percentages of variable costs to gross revenue.   _____   _____

5. Identify elements that show heightened risk of fraud.   _____   _____

The results of the foregoing procedures may be documented on comparative T/Bs or material variance reports or in narrative form in memoranda or on specific account workpapers.

EXHIBIT AU 329-4— EXAMPLE OF FINAL ANALYTICAL REVIEW

Client: _____

Name: _____

At this stage of the engagement it is important to consider the financial statements as a whole in light of the audit evidence that has been accumulated and in light of known and likely user expectations. The objective of this phase of the audit is to answer one very important question about the statement as they are presented:

Do these financial statements make sense? Yes___   No___

Consider the following broad significant financial statement categories (please check):

Cash   _____

Accounts receivable   _____

Inventory	_____
Fixed assets	_____
Investments	_____
Accounts payable & accrued expenses	_____
Notes payable	_____
Equity	_____
Revenues	_____
Cost of goods sold	_____
Payroll	_____
Other expenses	_____

	Yes	No	N/A
1. Do they appear reasonable compared to			
a. Prior years?	____	____	____
b. Industry norms?	____	____	____
c. Current budget?	____	____	____
2. Does related data within the statement appear to be congruent? For example	____	____	____
a. Cost of sales compared to sales?	____	____	____
c. Cost of sales compared to inventory?	____	____	____
d. Payroll taxes, benefits, workers' compensation, compared to payroll?	____	____	____
d. Current assets compared to current liabilities?	____	____	____
e. Percent relations of income statement amounts to gross income?	____	____	____
f. Percent relations of significant expenses to total expenses?	____	____	____
g. Percent relation of significant assets/liabilities to total assets?	____	____	____

	Yes	No	N/A
3. Is there known nonfinancial information that corroborates financial data in the statements?			

Explain:

_____

_____

_____

4. Attach a draft copy of statements to this workpaper and make notations on them as appropriate.

SECTION 330

THE CONFIRMATION PROCESS

Authoritative Pronouncements

SAS-67 — The Confirmation Process

Auditing Interpretation No. 1 (November 2008)—Use of Electronic Confirmations

> **IMPORTANT NOTICE FOR 2011:** The Auditing Standards Board (ASB) is in the process of redrafting all of the auditing sections in *Codification of Statements on Auditing Standards* to converge U.S. GAAS with the International Standards on Auditing issued by the International Auditing and Assurance Standards Board. As part of this process, the newly redrafted standards will follow certain clarity drafting conventions adopted by the ASB. These clarity drafting conventions include: (1) establishing objectives for each standard; (2) including a definitions section, if appropriate; and (3) separating requirements from application guidance and other material. The ASB is planning to have all redrafted standards become effective on the same date, which is for audits of financial statements for periods ending on or after December 15, 2012. It is possible that the effective date might be delayed beyond that date. The ASB's clarity and convergence project will have a significant effect on the auditing standards applicable to audits of nonpublic companies, and the 2012 *GAAS Guide* will be appropriately modified to reflect these changes once the effective date of the standards is certain.

Overview

The auditor can obtain audit evidence by confirming with, or acquiring information from, third parties. The confirmation process can be used as part of the audit of a number of account balances, transactions, and other information. For example, accounts receivable and payable may be confirmed with customers and vendors, respectively; a complex transaction may be confirmed with the counterparty; and the relationship between two (related) parties may be explained by the other party.

In general, audit evidence obtained through the confirmation process is often considered to be appropriate evidence because it is obtained from sources outside the entity. SAS-106 (AU 326) (Audit Evidence) reinforces this position by stating that "audit evidence is more reliable when it is obtained from knowledgeable independent sources outside the entity."

> **PLANNING AID REMINDER:** The confirmation of accounts receivable is a generally accepted auditing procedure, but confirmations can be effective in auditing many other areas: cash, notes receivable, inventory, consigned merchandise, construction and production contracts, investment securities, market values, accounts payable, notes payable, lines of credit, and actual and contingent liabilities. Confirmations can also be used to confirm the terms of unusual transactions and transactions with related parties (in accordance with AICPA Practice Alert 03-1 (Audit Confirmations)).

Promulgated Procedures Checklist

The auditor should perform the following procedures for the confirmation process to provide reliable evidence:

- Design the confirmation request to satisfy audit objectives.
- Perform confirmation procedures to satisfy audit objectives.
- Evaluate confirmation response received from the third party.

Analysis and Application of Procedures

Design the confirmation request to satisfy audit objectives

When designing a confirmation request, the auditor should identify related audit objectives and then format the confirmation request so that information requested will achieve those objectives. Audit objectives are established to test the numerous assertions (both explicit and implicit) that are included in a client's financial statements. Account balance assertions can be grouped into the following four categories:

1. Existence
2. Completeness
3. Rights and obligations
4. Valuation or allocation

Although confirmation requests may be designed to enable the auditor to obtain evidence to support all four assertions, evidence acquired through confirmation generally is either not relevant to all four assertions or more persuasive in testing one assertion than the others. For example, when an account receivable is confirmed, the audit evidence created through confirmation is often persuasive with respect to the existence assertion, but is almost irrelevant to the completeness assertion. Thus, when evaluating the evidence from confirmation requests, the auditor should recognize the limitations of the confirmation process.

If an important assertion will not be tested as part of the confirmation process, the auditor must select other audit procedures that satisfactorily test the remaining assertions.

In designing the confirmation request, factors such as the following should be considered.

- Confirmation request form

- Prior auditor experience

- Information being confirmed

- Characteristics of respondents

> **OBSERVATION:** Clients sometimes ask the auditor not to send a confirmation request to a particular party. Often the stated reason is that there is a dispute between the client and the party as to the account balance. Audit Practice Alert 03-1 (Audit Confirmations) states that a dispute is not by itself a sufficient reason not to send a confirmation. Although there may be valid reasons for honoring a management request not to send a confirmation request to a particular party, the auditor should corroborate the reasons management is making this request. Simple reliance on management representations as corroboration is not sufficient. If the auditor concludes that management's request not to send a confirmation is not reasonable, and the restriction significantly limits the audit scope, he or she should normally either disclaim an opinion or withdraw from the engagement.

Confirmation request form

An auditor may use either a positive confirmation form or a negative confirmation form.

A positive confirmation form may be designed in two ways. The information to be confirmed may be indicated in the confirmation request or the request may be blank, requiring the respondent to fill in the missing information. In either circumstance, audit evidence is dependent on the receipt of responses from the recipients of confirmation requests.

ENGAGEMENT STRATEGY: There is a trade-off between selecting the complete format and selecting the incomplete format as part of the engagement strategy. When a respondent completes and returns an incomplete form, more appropriate evidence is created than when the respondent is simply asked to sign a complete confirmation form. However, when the incomplete form is used, the response rate generally will be lower and less accurate (sufficiency of evidence matter), and it may be necessary to perform alternative audit procedures to supplement the confirmation process. When a positive confirmation is used and the request is not returned, no evidence is created.

PLANNING AID REMINDER: AICPA Practice Alert 03-1 (Audit Confirmations) states that the auditor can increase confirmation response rates by (1) using clear wording, (2) sending the confirmation to a specific person, (3) naming the company being audited, (4) have the client manually sign the confirmation request, (5) provide deadlines for receiving a response, (6) sending second and third requests, and (7) calling the respondent for an oral confirmation and request that the written request be subsequently mailed. In addition, accounts receivable confirmation requests may receive greater attention if they are included with the monthly statement sent to the customer.

A negative confirmation form requires the respondent to return the confirmation only if there is disagreement. When negative confirmations are not returned, the evidence generated is different from that generated when positive confirmations are used. That is, the lack of returned negative confirmations provides only implicit evidence that the information is correct.

ENGAGEMENT STRATEGY: Unreturned negative confirmations do not provide explicit evidence that the intended third parties received the confirmation requests and verified that the information contained on them is correct. Auditors should factor this limitation into their engagement strategy.

Because of the limitation described above, the negative confirmation form should be used only when all of the following conditions are met:

- The combined assessed level of inherent risk and control risk is low.

- The audit population contains a large number of relatively small individual balances.

- There is no reason to believe that respondents will not give adequate attention to confirmation requests.

> **ENGAGEMENT STRATEGY:** Even under the conditions described above, there is a concern that the use of negative confirmations will not generate sufficient appropriate audit evidence and that the auditor should consider performing other substantive procedures to supplement the use of negative confirmations. For example, if the auditor uses negative confirmations to test the existence of accounts receivable, it may also be advisable to use additional tests (such as reviewing subsequent cash collections and vouching) to determine with reasonable assurance that accounts receivable do exist. Also, if negative confirmations are used, the auditor should generally send more confirmation requests than if positive confirmation requests had been used.

When a response is received from a negative confirmation, the auditor should investigate the reason for the disagreement. If there are a number of disagreements or if the disagreements appear to be significant, the auditor should reconsider the original assessment of the level of inherent and control risk. This reassessment may lead to the conclusion that the combined assessed level of inherent risk and control risk is not low, in which case the auditor should appropriately modify the originally planned audit approach.

Prior auditor experience

In designing confirmation requests, the auditor should consider prior experience with the client and with similar clients. Prior experience may suggest, for example, that a confirmation form was improperly designed or that previous response rates were so low that audit procedures other than confirmations should be considered.

Information being confirmed

The auditor should consider the capabilities of the respondent in determining what should be included in the response to the confirmation request. Respondents can confirm only what they are capable of confirming, and there is a tendency to confirm only what is relatively easy to confirm. For example, in designing an accounts receivable confirmation, the auditor should consider whether respondents are more capable of verifying an individual account balance or transactions that make up a single receivable balance. The auditor's understanding of the nature of transactions as they relate to respondents is fundamental to determining what information should be included in a confirmation request.

Information to be confirmed with respondents does not have to be limited to dollar or other amounts. For example, in complex transactions it may be appropriate to confirm terms of contracts or other documentation that support such transactions. In addition, it may be appropriate to confirm information that is based on oral modifications and therefore not part of the formal documentation. The following guidance from SAS-67 may be useful with respect to oral modifications:

> When the auditor believes there is a moderate or high degree of risk that there may be significant oral modifications, he or she should inquire about the existence and details of any such modifications to written agreements.

If the client's response to the auditor's inquiry about the presence of oral modifications is that there are no oral modifications to an agreement, the auditor should consider confirming with the *other* party to the agreement that no oral modifications exist.

Characteristics of respondents

Confirmation requests should be addressed to respondents who, when they respond to the requests, will generate meaningful and appropriate audit evidence. Factors to be considered include the following:

- Competence of respondent

- Knowledge of respondent

- Objectivity of respondent

If information concerning the above factors (as well as other relevant factors) comes to the auditor's attention and that information suggests that meaningful and appropriate audit evidence will not result from the confirmation process, the auditor should consider using other audit procedures to test assertions.

> **FRAUD POINTER:** The auditor should be aware that under some circumstances the level of professional skepticism should be increased, resulting in a closer scrutiny of the respondent's competence, knowledge, and objectivity. For example, increased skepticism is appropriate when there has been an unusual transaction or a significant balance or transaction. For these as well as other circumstances, SAS-67 does not state specifically what the auditor's actions should be. Presumably,

the auditor could decide to investigate the characteristics of the respondents more closely or to employ other audit procedures to reduce the risk of material misstatements in the financial statements.

Perform confirmation procedures to satisfy audit objectives

The confirmation process should be executed so that the client does not have an opportunity to intercept requests when they are mailed or when they are returned from respondents. However, the work of internal auditors may be used in the confirmation process if the guidance established by SAS-65 (AU 322) (The Auditor's Consideration of the Internal Audit Function in an Audit of Financial Statements) is observed.

The confirmation process ideally involves the auditor mailing a confirmation request directly to a respondent and receiving the returned confirmation directly from the respondent. When positive confirmations are used, and there is no response, the auditor should consider sending second and possibly third requests.

> **ENGAGEMENT STRATEGY:** Confirmation requests (either positive or negative) may be returned as undeliverable. In this case, it is important for the auditor to corroborate that the intended recipient actually exists. AICPA Practice Alert 03-1 (Audit Confirmations) states that the auditor may want to discuss confirmations returned as undeliverable with a client official not related to the area being audited.

SAS-67 does recognize that other means of confirmation may be used, but it notes that the auditor must consider using additional audit procedures to reasonably ensure that a response is authentic and relevant. Specifically, SAS-67 discusses the use of fax and oral responses.

When the auditor receives a fax from a respondent as part of the confirmation process, the same degree of uncertainty concerning the source of the information arises. To reduce that risk, the auditor may employ procedures such as the following:

- Verify the source and content of the fax through a telephone call to the respondent.

- Request the respondent to mail the original confirmation directly to the auditor.

The procedures performed and the conclusions reached when a confirmation is received either electronically or via fax should be documented in the working papers.

ENGAGEMENT STRATEGY: When information is confirmed orally, the content of and circumstances surrounding the confirmation should be documented in the audit files. If the information confirmed orally is significant, the information should be confirmed in writing.

OBSERVATION: AU 330 states that a confirmation normally involves a written confirmation mailed to the auditor. Given technological advances, it is possible for the auditor to both send and receive confirmations electronically. Interpretation No. 1 of AU 330 (Use of Electronic Confirmations) states that properly controlled electronic confirmations can provide reliable audit evidence. The risks that the auditor faces are that (1) the confirmation is received from a source that is not authentic, (2) the respondent is not authorized to respond or is not knowledgeable about the information to be confirmed, and (3) the integrity of the information may have been compromised. Encryption, electronic digital signatures, and authentication of Web sites are tools the auditor can use to verify that the confirmation response is received from an authorized, appropriate source. Also, if a system or process is used to facilitate electronic confirmation between the auditor and the respondent, an assurance trust services report or another auditor's report can provide evidence of the design and operating effectiveness of electronic and manual controls used in the process.

Evaluate confirmation information received from the third party

The auditor often is unable to obtain a 100% response rate when positive confirmations are used. When information has not been confirmed, alternative audit procedures must be used. The specific nature of alternative procedures depends on the account balance or transaction and the adequacy of the client's internal control. For example, when a customer will not confirm an account receivable, the existence of the account could be substantiated through the review of a subsequent cash collection(s) or the inspection of documentation for the transaction(s) that created the year-end balance.

It may be acceptable to omit the use of alternative procedures if both of the following two circumstances exist:

1. Unconfirmed balances do not appear to be unique.

2. Unconfirmed balances are immaterial when projected as 100% misstatements.

Unconfirmed balances do not appear to be unique

The auditor should review those accounts that respondents will not confirm to determine whether they are unusual. Although it is difficult to define "unusual," transactions that are complex and not routine, and balances that do not follow a dollar-value pattern, would increase the level of audit risk and generally preclude the auditor from omitting alternative procedures. For example, most auditors would be skeptical if most of the unconfirmed accounts receivable were from customers who also had other relationships with the client.

Unconfirmed balances are immaterial

The auditor may treat all accounts that respondents do not confirm as misstatements if collectively those misstatements could not have a material effect on the financial statements. In determining the misstatements, the auditor must project the assumed misstatements from the unconfirmed balances to the total population.

Based on the evidence obtained through the confirmation process and the use of alternative audit procedures, the auditor should determine whether related assertions have been sufficiently tested. The auditor should consider the following factors when making this determination:

- The reliability of evidence obtained through the confirmation process and alternative procedures

- The nature and implications of exceptions discovered

- Evidence that may have been obtained through the use of procedures other than confirmation and alternative audit procedures

> **PLANNING AID REMINDER:** If the auditor anticipates that audit evidence obtained through the confirmation process, alternative audit procedures, and other audit procedures may not be sufficient to substantiate relevant assertions in the financial statements, additional evidence must be obtained. The additional evidence may be acquired by employing whatever procedures the auditor may deem appropriate, including additional confirmations, tests of details, and analytical procedures.

> **PLANNING AID REMINDER:** Auditors must be cautious when confirming the fair value of assets with parties that were originally involved in the acquisition of the assets being investigated. Because the respondent party might not provide objective evidence, the auditor should consider

whether it is necessary to communicate with a party that is not involved in the transaction in order to collect appropriate audit evidence concerning the fair value of an asset.

Procedures for the confirmation of accounts receivable

In addition to providing standards for employing the confirmation process, SAS-67 specifically addresses the confirmation of accounts receivable. The term "accounts receivable" is defined as follows:

* The entity's claims against customers that have arisen from the sale of goods or services in the normal course of business

* A financial institution's loans

> **OBSERVATION:** Although SAS-67 defines the term "accounts receivable," that definition also encompasses notes receivable and other receivables that use descriptive terms, assuming the account balance arose from the sale of goods or services in the normal course of business.

The confirmation of accounts receivable is a generally accepted auditing procedure and should be employed in all audit engagements except under one or more the following circumstances:

* The accounts receivable balance is immaterial.

* It is expected that the use of confirmations would be ineffective (for example, prior experience may suggest that the response rate is too low or responses are expected to be unreliable).

* Confirmation is not necessary to reduce audit risk to an acceptably low level.

The last circumstance arises when the combined assessed level of inherent and control risk is low, and the expected evidence created from analytical procedures and tests of details results in the achievement of an acceptable level of audit risk.

> **PLANNING AID REMINDER:** Although the confirmation of accounts receivable is not necessary when audit risk can otherwise be reduced to an "acceptably low level," SAS-67 appears to warn auditors that such a situation is unusual by stating that "in many situations, both confirmation of accounts

receivable and tests of details are necessary to reduce audit risk to an acceptably low level for the applicable financial statement assertions."

When the auditor concludes that it is not necessary to confirm accounts receivable, that position must be documented in the audit files. Thus, the audit documentation must include a full explanation based on one or more of the three circumstances listed above.

> **FRAUD POINTER:** Enforcement actions against auditors often result from deficiencies in the accounts receivable confirmation process. In some cases auditors failed to confirm accounts receivable; other cases involved auditors' failure to control the confirmation process (e.g., allowed the client to handle mailing and receipt of confirmations and the related responses). Finally, auditors sometimes failed to perform alternative procedures when confirmations were not returned or were returned with material exceptions.

> **ENGAGEMENT STRATEGY:** Although confirming accounts payable is not a generally accepted auditing procedure, accounts payable confirmations can be useful in providing audit evidence related to the existence and completeness assertions. In particular, it may be appropriate to send accounts payable confirmations to major suppliers, including those with small or zero balances. In addition, confirming accounts payable can be useful in detecting round-trip or linked transactions (an entity simultaneously sells to and buys from another party). AICPA Practice Alert 03-1 (Audit Confirmations) states that the following circumstances suggest that confirming accounts payable is appropriate: (1) the client has weak controls over payables and cash disbursements, (2) the client's industry poses a higher risk of unrecorded liabilities or inappropriate accounting, and (3) the complexity of the client's environment increases the risk of unrecorded liabilities. In confirming accounts payable, a blank confirmation request form is generally used. An important aspect of confirming accounts payable is the generation of a reliable and complete vendor list. The auditor should (1) review the accounts payable subsidiary ledger, (2) review invoice files by supplier, (3) review disbursement records by supplier, and (4) ask client personnel for the names of major suppliers. If an accounts payable confirmation is not returned, the auditor should perform alternative procedures, including examining subsequent cash disbursements. Subsequent cash disbursements might indicate amounts that should have been recorded as a liability at the balance sheet date.

Practitioner's Aids

In the confirmation of accounts receivable the auditor may use a positive confirmation or a negative confirmation or a combination of both. An example of a positive confirmation is presented in Exhibit AU 330-1. An example of a negative confirmation is presented in Exhibit AU 330-2. Positive and negative confirmations may take a variety of forms. For example, the negative confirmation may be a stamp or a sticker placed directly on the monthly statements sent to the client's customers; for a positive confirmation it may be a letter in a format similar to the one used in Exhibit AU 330-1.

The standards related to the confirmation process apply to all confirmations, not just those that involve the confirmation of receivables. Exhibits AU 330-3 and AU 330-4 illustrate other types of confirmations, namely, the confirmation of a lease obligation and a mortgage obligation.

Exhibit AU 330-5 illustrates an audit program for the confirmation of accounts receivable.

Exhibit AU 330-6 provides an example of an audit schedule that summarizes the results of the accounts receivable confirmation process.

EXHIBIT AU 330-1 — POSITIVE CONFIRMATION

[*Client's Letterhead*]

[*Customer's Name and Address*]

Dear _____:

In accordance with the request of our auditors, please confirm the correctness of your account as listed below.

Account # _____
Date of Account Balance _____
                       (Confirmation Date)
Account Balance $ _____

If the amount is correct, sign in the space provided and return this letter to our auditor in the enclosed self-addressed envelope.

If the amount is incorrect, sign in the space provided, explain the difference on the back of this letter, and return this letter to our auditor in the enclosed self-addressed envelope.

This is not a request for payment.

Thank you for your prompt attention to this matter.

Very truly yours.

[*Client's Signature*]

The above balance at the confirmation date is correct, except as noted on the back of this letter.

[*Customer's Signature*]

[*Title*]

EXHIBIT AU 330-2 — NEGATIVE CONFIRMATION

CONFIRMATION REQUEST

Please examine this statement carefully. If it is not correct, please notify our auditors of any differences. For your convenience a stamped, self-addressed envelope is enclosed.

If you do not reply to this request, it will be assumed that the balance is correct.

This is not a request for payment.

EXHIBIT AU 330-3—OBLIGATION UNDER LONG-TERM LEASES

[*Client's Letterhead*]

[*Lessor's Name and Address*]

Dear _____:

In accordance with the request of our auditors, please confirm the correctness of terms of our lease (and related matters) with your company.

    Initial date of lease:_____

    Monthly payments: $_____

    Number of months covered by the lease:_____

    Renewal date (if applicable):_____

      Monthly renewal payments $_____

      Period covered by renewal options: From:_____To:_____

    Purchase option (if applicable)

      Purchase option price: $_____

      Dates covered by purchase option: From:_____To:_____

    Date of last lease payment received:_____

    Other information:

_____

_____

_____

_____

If the above information is correct, sign in the space provided and return this letter to our auditor in the enclosed self-addressed envelope.

If the above information is incorrect, sign in the space provided, explain the difference on the back of this letter, and return this letter to our auditor in the enclosed self-addressed envelope.

Thank you for your prompt attention to this matter.

Very truly yours,

_____

[*Client's Signature*]

The above information is correct, except as noted on the back of this letter.

_____

[*Lessor's Signature*]   [*Title*]

EXHIBIT AU 330-4 — MORTGAGE OBLIGATION

[*Client's Letterhead*]

[*Mortgagor's Name and Address*]

Dear _____:

In accordance with the request of our auditors, please confirm the correctness of terms of our mortgage (and related matters) with your company.

Initial date of mortgage: _____

Monthly payments: $_____

Number of months covered by the mortgage: _____

Interest rate: _____%

Unpaid balance as of (Date): $_____

Date of last mortgage payment received: _____

Purpose of mortgage:

_____

_____

Description of mortgaged property:

_____

_____

Escrow amount held by you: $_____

Amount of property taxes paid during (Date): $_____

Amount of insurance paid during (Date): $_____

Other information:

_____

_____

If the above information is correct, sign in the space provided and return this letter to our auditor in the enclosed self-addressed envelope.

If the above information is incorrect, sign in the space provided, explain the difference on the back of this letter, and return this letter to our auditor in the enclosed self-addressed envelope.

Thank you for your prompt attention to this matter.

Very truly yours,

_____

[*Client's Signature*]

The above information is correct, except as noted on the back of this letter.

_____

[*Mortgagor's Signature*]   [*Title*]

EXHIBIT AU 330-5 — AUDIT PROGRAM — CONFIRMATION OF ACCOUNTS RECEIVABLE

Use the following procedures as a guide for confirming accounts receivable. The audit program is only a guide, and professional judgment should be exercised to determine how the procedures should be modified by revising procedures listed or adding procedures to the audit program.

Initial and date each procedure as it is completed. If the procedure is not relevant to this particular audit engagement, place "N/A" (not applicable) in the space provided for an initial.

Client Name:_____

Date of Financial Statements:_____

Audit Report Date:_____

	Yes	No	Audit Documentation Reference
1. Obtain or prepare an aged trial balance of accounts receivable.	_____	_____	_____
2. Foot and crossfoot the aged trial balance and trace the total to the general ledger.	_____	_____	_____
3. Trace a sample of accounts listed on the aged trial balance to the account in the accounts receivable subsidiary ledger.	_____	_____	_____
4. Trace a sample of accounts in the accounts receivable subsidiary ledger to the aged trial balance.	_____	_____	_____
5. From the aged trial balance select a sample of account balances for confirmation.	_____	_____	_____
6. If confirmations are prepared by the client, substantiate the information on the confirmation with information contained in the subsidiary ledger.	_____	_____	_____

	Yes	No	*Audit Documentation Reference*
7. Mail confirmations directly with the U.S. Postal Service and include in the mailings a self-addressed return envelope.	_____	_____	_____
8. Trace returned confirmation to information contained in the list of confirmations mailed.	_____	_____	_____
9. Investigate exceptions noted in returned confirmation.	_____	_____	_____
10. Send second requests for confirmations not returned.	_____	_____	_____
11. Apply alternative procedures (such as review of subsequent cash collection and inspection of documentation that substantiate the original balance) to confirmations not returned.	_____	_____	_____
12. Prepare summary statistics based on confirmations mailed and results of confirmation process.	_____	_____	_____

Reviewed by:_____

Date:_____

_____

EXHIBIT AU 330-6 — SUMMARY OF ACCOUNTS RECEIVABLE CONFIRMATION STATISTICS

Averroes Company
Accounts Receivable Confirmation Statistics
12/31/X5

	Dollar Value	*Number of Accounts*	Relative to Total Accounts Receivable		Relative to Total Confirmations Sent	
			Dollar Value	*Number of Accounts*	*Dollar Value*	*Number of Accounts*
Total Accounts Receivable	$351,574.31	426				
Total Confirmations Mailed	223,876.12	235	63.70%	55.20%		
Accounts Confirmed (including exceptions cleared)	184,392.13	177	52.50%	41.60%	82.40%	75.30%
Unconfirmed Accounts Verified through Alternative Procedures	36,726.75	43	10.40%	10.10%	16.40%	18.30%
Exceptions not cleared(a)	2,757.24	15	0.80%	3.50%	1.20%	6.40%
Totals	$223,876.12	235	63.70%	55.20%	100.00%	100.00%

(a) — See analysis of exceptions not cleared at AR201.

Prepared By: ___JB___

Date: ___2/18/X6___   AR200

SECTION 331

INVENTORIES

Authoritative Pronouncements

SAS-1 — Codification of Auditing Standards and Procedures (Section 331, Inventories)

SAS-43 — Omnibus Statement on Auditing Standards

SAS-67 — The Confirmation Process

> **IMPORTANT NOTICE FOR 2011:** The Auditing Standards Board (ASB) is in the process of redrafting all of the auditing sections in *Codification of Statements on Auditing Standards* to converge U.S. GAAS with the International Standards on Auditing issued by the International Auditing and Assurance Standards Board. As part of this process, the newly redrafted standards will follow certain clarity drafting conventions adopted by the ASB. These clarity drafting conventions include: (1) establishing objectives for each standard; (2) including a definitions section, if appropriate; and (3) separating requirements from application guidance and other material. The ASB is planning to have all redrafted standards become effective on the same date, which is for audits of financial statements for periods ending on or after December 15, 2012. It is possible that the effective date might be delayed beyond that date. The ASB's clarity and convergence project will have a significant effect on the auditing standards applicable to audits of nonpublic companies, and the 2012 *GAAS Guide* will be appropriately modified to reflect these changes once the effective date of the standards is certain.

Overview

The observation of inventories is a generally accepted auditing procedure. That is, the auditor has the burden of justifying his or her audit opinion when observations of inventory have not occurred. The observation requirement may be satisfied in a number of ways.

Promulgated Procedures Checklist

The auditor should observe the following broad guidelines in order to substantiate the existence of inventories owned by the client:

- Observe inventories when inventory quantities are determined solely by a physical count.

- Observe inventories when well-kept perpetual inventory records are maintained and periodically checked by the client's physical counts.

- Observe inventories when statistical sampling is used to estimate the inventory count.

- Substantiate the inventory count made in a previous year.

- Substantiate inventory held in a public warehouse or by another outside custodian.

> **ENGAGEMENT STRATEGY:** AU 311 addresses only issues related to the substantiation of the inventory count. AU 311 does not contain guidance pertaining to other aspects that affect the fair presentation of the inventory account, such as the proper valuation of the inventory balance.

Analysis and Application of Procedures

Observe inventories when inventory quantities are determined solely by a physical count

When a client determines the inventory quantity solely by a physical count as of the balance sheet date (or within a reasonable time period before or after the date of the balance sheet), the auditor should observe the physical inventory count. The objective of the observation is to determine the physical existence of the inventory and its condition.

> **FRAUD POINTER:** SAS-99 (Consideration of Fraud in a Financial Statement Audit) notes that when the auditor believes there is a risk of material misstatement due to fraud, he or she may consider observing inventory on unexpected dates or at unexpected locations on a surprise basis. For situations in which the risk of material misstatement in inventory due to fraud is perceived to be high, SAS-99 notes that the auditor's examination of the entity's inventory records might help identify locations or items that require specific attention during or after the physical count. For example, the auditor may decide to count inventory at multiple locations on the same date.

Observe inventories when well-kept perpetual inventory records are maintained

When the client effectively maintains perpetual inventory records and substantiates the balances in these records by appropriate physical counts throughout the year, the auditor's observation tests can generally be performed either during the year or after year-end.

> **FRAUD POINTER:** SAS-99 notes that the auditor may request that the client count inventory at year-end or on a date closer to year-end to minimize the risk of inventory balances being manipulated between the count date and the balance sheet date.

Observe inventories when statistical sampling is used to estimate the inventory count

A client may determine its inventory by using a statistical sampling method, which makes unnecessary an annual physical count of each item of inventory. When statistical sampling is used, the auditor must determine the validity and application of the statistical plan to determine whether its results are sufficiently reliable, i.e., substantially the same as a physical count. The auditor must also observe such counts as he or she deems necessary.

> **ENGAGEMENT STRATEGY:** If an auditor has not substantiated the existence of inventory based on one of the approaches described above, testing solely the client's inventory records will not be sufficient to satisfy professional standards. SAS-1 states that under this circumstance the auditor should observe the client's count or should actually make inventory counts of the inventory and test intervening transactions between the count date and the balance sheet date. These procedures should be performed in concert with documentation created and procedures performed by the client.

Substantiate the inventory count made in a previous year

In some instances an auditor will be requested to audit the financial statements of a previous year as part of the current-year engagement. The auditor may substantiate inventory quantities for the previous year by using procedures such as tests of prior transactions, reviews of the client's inventory count, and gross profit tests. This can be successful only if the auditor is satisfied with the client's current inventory count.

Substantiate inventory held in a public warehouse or by another outside custodian

Generally, the direct confirmation of the inventory held by outside custodians provides sufficient evidence to validate the existence and ownership of the inventory. However, if the inventory held by an external party is significant in relation to current assets and total assets, confirmation must be supplemented with the performance of the following procedures:

- Discuss with the client (owner of the goods) the client's control procedures in investigating the warehouseman, including tests of related audit evidence.

- Observe the warehouseman's or client's count of goods whenever practical and reasonable.

- If warehouse receipts have been pledged as collateral, confirm details with the lenders to the extent the auditor deems necessary.

- Obtain an independent auditor's report on the warehouseman's control procedures relevant to custody of goods and, if applicable, pledge receipts; or apply alternative procedures at the warehouse to gain reasonable assurance that information received from the warehouseman is reliable.

> **PLANNING AID REMINDER:** Some companies are in the business of counting, recording, and pricing inventories. The auditor's responsibility for the count and other tasks performed by an inventory-taking company is similar to the responsibility for tasks normally performed directly by the client. Therefore, the auditor should (1) review the client's inventory-counting program, (2) make or observe a test of physical counts, (3) make appropriate mathematical checks, and (4) test the valuation of the inventory.

Practitioner's Aids

EXHIBIT AU 331-1 — AUDIT PROGRAM: INVENTORY OBSERVATION PROCEDURES

Use the following procedures as a guide for the observation of inventories. The audit program is only a guide, and professional judgment should be exercised to determine how the procedures should be modified by revising procedures listed or adding procedures to the audit program.

Initial and date each procedure as it is completed. If the procedure is not relevant to this particular audit engagement, place "N/A" (not applicable) in the space provided for an initial.

Client Name: _____

Date of Financial Statements: _____

Audit Report Date: _____

	Yes	*No*	*Audit Documentation Reference*

Planning Phase

1. Review with appropriate personnel the inventory count procedures to be used by the client. ___ ___ _____

2. Attend meetings in which the client instructs personnel concerning the inventory count. ___ ___ _____

3. Identify inventory count issues that need special attention (such as the use of a specialist, inventory held by consignees, inventory held for other parties). ___ ___ _____

4. Determine the number of staff personnel and level of experience needed to cover the client's inventory count. ___ ___ _____

Inventory Count Phase

5. Meet with client personnel to identify any new issues that need to be addressed before the count begins. ___ ___ _____

6. Determine whether inventory that should not be counted (such as consigned goods, inventory to be shipped during the day) has been appropriately segregated or otherwise identified. ___ ___ _____

7. Obtain inventory control count information (such as range of ticket numbers or count sheet numbers to be used during the count). ___ ___ _____

8. Obtain inventory cutoff information from the shipping department (such as bill of lading numbers) and the receiving department (such as receiving report numbers). ___ ___ _____

9. Test inventory counts on a sample basis, and determine whether items are being counted and described correctly and identified as obsolete or damaged if appropriate. ___ ___ _____

	Yes	*No*	*Audit Documentation Reference*

10. Record some test counts that can be used later to test the client's summarization of inventory counts. ___ ___ _____

11. Determine whether all inventory items are counted and clearly marked as "counted." ___ ___ _____

12. Determine whether inventory that is moved from one location to another is appropriately identified to avoid double counting or omission from the count. ___ ___ _____

13. Once the inventory count is completed, obtain inventory control information (such as last ticket or counting sheet number used). ___ ___ _____

Inventory Count Summary Phase

14. Trace inventory test counts made during the inventory count to client inventory summarization sheets. ___ ___ _____

15. Determine whether inventory numbers used in the client's summarization sheets are consistent with inventory control information obtained at the conclusion of the physical inventory count. ___ ___ _____

16. Select inventory amount in the inventory summarization, and trace to either (1) inventory test count information or (2) consistency of ticket control information. ___ ___ _____

17. Determine whether inventory items identified as damaged or obsolete during the inventory count were appropriately identified in the client's inventory summarization. ___ ___ _____

18. Determine whether inventory cutoff information obtained during the inventory count is consistent with sales information and purchases information shortly before and after the year-end date. ___ ___ _____

Reviewed by: _____

Date: _____

EXHIBIT AU 331-2 — CONFIRMATION REQUEST FOR INVENTORY HELD BY ANOTHER PARTY

[Client's Letterhead]

[Custodian's Name and Address]

Dear _____:

In accordance with the request of our auditors, please confirm the correctness of the inventory items owned by us but held by your company as of December 31, 20X5. For your convenience we have included with this correspondence a list of these items based on our records.

Also, please answer the following questions:

1. How did you determine the number of inventory items held by you as of December 31, 20X5?

_____
_____
_____

2. Are any of the items held by you for us damaged?

_____
_____
_____

3. Are there any negotiable or nonnegotiable warehouse receipts issued, and if so, to your knowledge have any of the receipts been assigned or pledged?

_____
_____
_____

4. Are there any liens against the inventory?

_____
_____
_____

5. Do we owe you any amount of money as of December 31, 20X5?

_____
_____
_____

If the amounts and descriptions included in the attachment are correct, please sign the space provided and return this letter to our auditor in the enclosed self-addressed envelope.

If the amounts are incorrect or there is other relevant information that you want to communicate to our auditors, sign in the space provided, explain the difference in a separate letter, and return this letter and any other relevant information to our auditor in the enclosed self-addressed envelope.

Thank you for your prompt attention to this matter.

Very truly yours,

[*Client's Signature*]

The above balance at the confirmation date is correct, except as noted on the back of this letter.

[*Custodian's Signature*]   [*Title*]

SECTION 332

AUDITING DERIVATIVE INSTRUMENTS, HEDGING ACTIVITIES, AND INVESTMENTS IN SECURITIES

Authoritative Pronouncements

SAS-92 — Auditing Derivative Instruments, Hedging Activities, and Investments in Securities

Auditing Interpretation No. 1 (July 2005) — Auditing Investments in Securities Where a Readily Determinable Fair Value Does Not Exist

> **IMPORTANT NOTICE FOR 2011:** The Auditing Standards Board (ASB) is in the process of redrafting all of the auditing sections in *Codification of Statements on Auditing Standards* to converge U.S. GAAS with the International Standards on Auditing issued by the International Auditing and Assurance Standards Board. As part of this process, the newly redrafted standards will follow certain clarity drafting conventions adopted by the ASB. These clarity drafting conventions include: (1) establishing objectives for each standard; (2) including a definitions section, if appropriate; and (3) separating requirements from application guidance and other material. The ASB is planning to have all redrafted standards become effective on the same date, which is for audits of financial statements for periods ending on or after December 15, 2012. It is possible that the effective date might be delayed beyond that date. The ASB's clarity and convergence project will have a significant effect on the auditing standards applicable to audits of nonpublic companies, and the 2012 *GAAS Guide* will be appropriately modified to reflect these changes once the effective date of the standards is certain.

Overview

SAS-92 provides guidance for the audit of derivative instruments and hedging activities and securities included in financial statements.

For derivative instruments and hedging activities SAS-92 provides guidance for the accounting and reporting standards established in ASC 815 (FAS-133, Accounting for Derivative Instruments and Hedging Activities). ASC 815 defines a derivative instrument as a financial instrument or other contract with all three of the following characteristics:

1. It has (1) one or more underlyings and (2) one or more notional amounts or payment provisions or both. Those terms determine the

amount of the settlement or settlements, and, in some cases, whether or not a settlement is required.

2. It requires no initial net investment or an initial net investment that is smaller than would be required for other types of contracts that would be expected to have a similar response to changes in market factors.

3. Its terms require or permit net settlement, it can readily be settled net by a means outside the contract, or it provides for delivery of an asset that puts the recipient in a position not substantially different from net settlement.

For purposes of financial reporting, all derivative instruments must be classified as follows:

- No hedge designation

- Fair value hedge

- Cash flow hedge

- Foreign currency hedge

SAS-92 provides guidance for "hedging activities in which the entity designates a derivative or a nonderivative financial instrument as a hedge of exposure for which FASB Statement No. 133 [ASC 815] permits hedge accounting."

> **PUBLIC COMPANY IMPLICATION:** The PCAOB has issued Staff Audit Practice Alert No. 2 (Matters Related to Auditing Fair Value Measurements of Financial Instruments and the Use of Specialists). The Practice Alert is designed to provide guidance related to auditing fair values, particularly in light of the FASB's issuance of FAS-157 (ASC 820) (Fair Value Measurements). The auditor needs to understand the company's process for determining fair value measurements and disclosures, including related internal controls. The auditor should also evaluate whether (1) management's assumptions in determining fair value are reasonable and are not inconsistent with market information, (2) management's reliance on historical financial information continues to be justified (e.g., use of historical default rates may not be appropriate when credit markets are deteriorating), and (3) the company's determination of fair value is applied consistently and whether this is appropriate. For example, a company may apply a model consistently in determining fair value, but because of changes in the environment it may be more appropriate for the company to change the relative weights of model inputs. In addition, the auditor should recognize that model inputs based on the

company's own data are generally more susceptible to bias and take appropriate audit steps to respond to this increased risk. Finally, GAAP provides many required disclosures relating to fair value measurements. The auditor needs to recognize that material disclosures that depart from GAAP represent a misstatement of the financial statements.

Securities

The standards established by SAS-92 apply to all securities (both debt securities and equity securities) held by an entity. The financial accounting and reporting standards that a client should follow depend on the client's characteristics. For example, commercial enterprises must observe the standards established by ASC 320 (FAS-115, Accounting for Certain Investments in Debt and Equity Securities); not-for-profit entities must follow the guidance established by ASC 958 (FAS-124, Accounting for Certain Investments Held by Not-for-Profit Organizations), and governmental entities must refer to the standards identified in GASB-31 (I 50) (Accounting and Financial Reporting for Certain Investments and for External Investment Pools).

> **OBSERVATION:** SAS-92 applies to both marketable and non-marketable debt and equity securities. The standards also apply to securities accounted for using the equity method as described in APB-18 (The Equity Method of Accounting for Investments in Common Stock).

Promulgated Procedures Checklist

The auditor should perform the following procedures to obtain sufficient appropriate audit evidence to substantiate the presentation of derivative instruments and securities:

- Develop an understanding of the derivative/security

- Consider audit risk and materiality

- Design appropriate substantive procedures

- Consider management's intent

> **PLANNING AID REMINDER:** Interpretation No. 1 of AU 332 addresses the situation of an entity that has investments in securities where, although GAAP requires the investments to be recorded at fair value, a readily determinable fair value may not exist. For example, investments in a hedge fund may be reported at fair value even though fair value is not readily

determinable. The hedge fund management might not provide details on how the fair value of its investments is determined, and it might only confirm the aggregate amount of a company's investment in the hedge fund. The receipt by an auditor of a confirmation where investments are confirmed on an aggregate basis is not sufficient. However, the existence assertion is supported if the auditor receives confirmation from the hedge fund as to the individual investments held by the fund. The valuation assertion is not supported even if the fund manager confirms the investments held by the hedge fund on an individual basis. Management, not the hedge fund manager, is responsible for determining the fair values of investments held by the fund. Management needs to develop a process for determining the fair value of investments held in the hedge fund. The auditor needs to (1) understand management's process, (2) evaluate whether the fair value measurements are in conformity with GAAP, and (3) test management's fair value determinations. If the auditor is unable to gather sufficient appropriate audit evidence related to either the existence or valuation assertions, a scope limitation may exist, requiring either a qualified audit opinion or a disclaimer of opinion.

Analysis and Application of Procedures

Develop an understanding of the derivative/security

Some derivatives and securities have complicated characteristics, and in order to properly audit these items an auditor must have an adequate understanding of them. SAS-92 presents the following audit procedures that may be needed in this area:

- Understand the nature of a derivative/security and related generally accepted accounted principles (GAAP)

- Understand the information system used to process and account for the derivative or security (including the use of an outside service organization)

- Obtain skills necessary to understand how computer applications are used to transmit, process, maintain, and access derivative or security transactions and balances

- Understand various models that may be used to determine the fair value of a derivative or security

- Assess inherent risk and control risk related to the assertions related to derivatives that are used in hedge transactions

Consider audit risk and materiality

AU 312 (Audit Risk and Materiality in Conducting an Audit) provides general guidance for planning and executing audit procedures in an engagement. Two important elements in the planning of audit procedures are the assessments of inherent risk and control risk.

> **PLANNING AID REMINDER:** If an auditor decides to use the work of a client's internal auditor in this part of the engagement, the guidance established by AU 322 should be followed.

Assessment of Inherent Risk

SAS-107 (AU 312) (Audit Risk and Materiality in Conducting an Audit) defines inherent risk as "the susceptibility of a relevant assertion to a misstatement that could be material, either individually or when aggregated with other misstatements, assuming there are no related controls." SAS-92 lists the following as examples of factors that can affect an auditor's assessment of inherent risk for a derivative or security:

- Management's objective for acquiring a derivative or security

- The complex nature of the derivative or security

- Whether the origination of the derivative or security did not involve the exchange of cash

- Entity's past experience with the derivative or security

- Whether the derivative is freestanding or an embedded feature of an agreement

- Whether external factors, such as credit, market, basis, or legal risk, affect the related assertions in the financial statements

- The changing nature of derivatives and whether accounting standards address the related measurement and reporting issues

- The degree to which the client understands how a derivative is valued and client reliance on external expertise

- Whether GAAP requires the development of assumptions about future conditions

Assessment of Control Risk

SAS-107 (AU 312) defines control risk as "the risk that a misstatement that could occur in a relevant assertion and that could be material, either individually or when aggregated with other misstatements, will not be prevented or detected on a timely basis by an entity's internal control." SAS-92 points out that control features that may be adopted by a client who uses derivative transactions extensively include the following:

- Separate monitoring by client personnel who are fully independent of derivative activities

- Required approval by senior management of derivative transactions that exceed previously approved transaction limits

- Senior management's determination of the appropriateness of actions that deviated from previously approved derivative strategies, including limit excesses

- Controls that determine whether the communication of derivative positions in the risk measurement system have been accurate

- Controls that determine whether there have been appropriate reconciliations "to ensure data integrity across the full range of derivatives"

- Controls to ensure that derivative strategies have been properly evaluated and complied with by derivative traders, risk managers, and senior management

- Identification of an appropriate group to review controls and financial results of derivative activities and strategies

- Established reviews when limits that relate to strategies, risk tolerance, and market conditions are changed

The auditor's assessment of controls related to derivatives and securities transactions is performed based on the guidance established by professional standards including SAS-109 (AU 314) and SAS-70 (AU 324).

Design Appropriate Substantive Procedures

The nature, timing, and extent of substantive procedures for financial statement assertions related to derivatives and securities are based on the auditor's assessment of inherent risk and control risk. Although this approach is conceptually the same for all assertions included in financial statements, SAS-92 identifies several illustrative procedures (enumerated in a "Practitioner's Aid" at the end of this section) that may be appropriate substantive procedures for derivatives and securities.

Consider Management's Intent

The auditor should obtain written representations from management "confirming aspects of management's intent and ability that affect assertions about derivatives and securities, such as its intent and ability to hold a debt security until its maturity or to enter into a forecasted transaction for which hedge accounting is applied.''

Implications of Using a Service Organization

In those instances where a service organization performs duties that are an important part of a client's information system, the auditor must incorporate this circumstance into the design of the nature, timing, and extent of audit procedures. Professional judgment must be used to determine how the role of the service organization might affect the design of the audit plan; however, SAS-92 provides the examples in Exhibit AU 332-1 of services that would affect substantive procedures.

EXHIBIT AU 332-1 — SERVICES THAT AFFECT SUBSTANTIVE PROCEDURES

Activity Performed By The Service Organization	Effect on Substantive Procedures
Documentation that supports derivative/security transactions is maintained at the service organization	Relevant documentation should be inspected by either (a) the principal auditor, (b) an auditor employed by the principal auditor, or (c) an auditor employed by the service auditor
Significant information about the client's securities may be accessed by external parties, including data processors and investor advisers	Principal auditor may have to identify and test the operating effectiveness of related controls at the client and/or service organization in order to reduce audit risk to an acceptable level
Security transactions may be initiated by the service organization and securities may be held and serviced by the organization	Principal auditor may have to evaluate the controls at the service organization (such as segregation of duties) in order to determine the level of detection risk for substantive procedures

Practitioner's Aid

Exhibit AU 332-2 illustrates substantive procedures that may be appropriate for the audit of financial statement assertions related to derivatives and securities accounts and transactions.

EXHIBIT AU 332-2 — ILLUSTRATIVE SUBSTANTIVE PROCEDURES FOR DERIVATIVES AND SECURITIES

Existence or occurrence assertion Management asserts that derivatives and securities reported in the balance sheet exist and that related transactions recorded in the income statement or cash flows statement occurred. To obtain evidence about this assertion, the auditor should consider performing one or more of the following substantive procedures:

- Confirm balances or transactions with the issuer

- Confirm securities with holder or confirm derivatives with counterparty

- Confirm settled transactions with broker-dealer or counterparty

- Physically inspect security or derivative contract

- Read executed partnership or similar agreement

- Inspect underlying agreements and related documentation for (1) amount reported, (2) evidence that would preclude the sales treatment of a transfer, or (3) unrecorded repurchase agreement

- Inspect underlying documentation for settlements made after year-end

- Perform analytical procedures

Completeness assertion Management asserts that all derivatives and securities that exist or occurred are recorded in the financial statements. To obtain evidence for this assertion, the auditor should consider performing one or more of the following substantive procedures:

- Request a counterparty or holder to provide a complete description of the transaction

- Query previously active counterparties or holders that current accounting records indicate presently have no involvement in derivative/security transactions about whether they are a party to a current transaction

- Inspect current documentation to determine whether agreements include embedded derivatives

- Review documentation for activities that occurred subsequent to the year-end date

- Perform analytical procedures

- Identify transactions that have been settled to determine whether treating them as sales was appropriate

- Read other information such as minutes of meetings of the board of directors or relevant committees

Rights and obligations assertion Management makes an assertion about the entity's rights and obligations associated with derivatives and securities reported in the financial statements, including pledging arrangements. To obtain evidence for this assertion, the auditor should consider performing one or more of the following substantive procedures:

- Confirm significant terms of an agreement with the counterparty or holder

- Inspect documentation that supports derivative or security transactions

- Consider evidence obtained in other areas of the engagement

Valuation and allocation assertion Management asserts that derivatives and securities reported in the financial statements were determined in accordance with GAAP. To obtain evidence about this assertion, the auditor should consider performing one or more of the following substantive procedures:

- For items reported at historical cost, inspect appropriate documentation

- For items reported based on the valuation of an investee's financial results, review the financial statements and consider obtaining additional evidence related to other matters such as (1) significant differences in fiscal year-ends, (2) changes in ownership, (3) material transactions between the investor and investee companies, and (4) the issuance of unaudited financial statements

- For items reported at fair value, determine whether the method of valuation is specified by GAAP, fully understand how the method is employed (such as pricing models), determine whether it is necessary to obtain information from more than one source, and where appropriate follow the guidance established by SAS-70 (AU 324) and SAS-73 (AU 336)

- For items that are required to be evaluated for possible impairment losses that are other than temporary, obtain relevant information concerning the loss of value of a particular item

- For derivatives that are hedges, obtain evidence that demonstrates that management has complied with the hedge accounting requirements of GAAP

- For securities, obtain evidence that demonstrates that management has complied with the investment accounting requirements of GAAP

Presentation and disclosure assertions Management asserts that the classification, description, and disclosure of derivatives and securities in the financial statements conform with GAAP, that all disclosed events occurred and are complete, and that the disclosures are understandable and disclosed at fair and accurate amounts. To obtain evidence for these assertions, the auditor should consider performing one or more of the following procedures:

- Determine that the accounting method used is acceptable and appropriate under the circumstances

- Determine that the financial statements are "informative of matters that may affect their use, understanding, and interpretation"

- Determine that the financial statements are classified and summarized in a reasonable, understandable manner

- Determine that the financial statements reflect the underlying transactions and events within a range of acceptable limits

SECTION 333

MANAGEMENT REPRESENTATIONS

Authoritative Pronouncements

SAS-85 — Management Representations

SAS-89 — Audit Adjustments

SAS-99 — Consideration of Fraud in a Financial Statement Audit

SAS-113 — Omnibus Statement on Auditing Standards — 2006

Auditing Interpretation No. 1 of AU 333 (March 1979) — Management Representations on Violations and Possible Violations of Laws and Regulations

> **IMPORTANT NOTICE FOR 2011:** The Auditing Standards Board (ASB) is in the process of redrafting all of the auditing sections in *Codification of Statements on Auditing Standards* to converge U.S. GAAS with the International Standards on Auditing issued by the International Auditing and Assurance Standards Board. As part of this process, the newly redrafted standards will follow certain clarity drafting conventions adopted by the ASB. These clarity drafting conventions include: (1) establishing objectives for each standard; (2) including a definitions section, if appropriate; and (3) separating requirements from application guidance and other material. The ASB is planning to have all redrafted standards become effective on the same date, which is for audits of financial statements for periods ending on or after December 15, 2012. It is possible that the effective date might be delayed beyond that date. The ASB's clarity and convergence project will have a significant effect on the auditing standards applicable to audits of nonpublic companies, and the 2012 *GAAS Guide* will be appropriately modified to reflect these changes once the effective date of the standards is certain.

Overview

During the course of an engagement, the client's personnel make a variety of representations in response to questions raised by the auditor. Generally accepted auditing standards require that in order to reduce the likelihood of misunderstandings between the client and the auditor, written representations be obtained from the client to confirm explicit and implicit representations made by management during the engagement.

Written representations received from management are audit evidence, and they often support other audit evidence the auditor obtains. For example, the auditor may inspect client documentation to determine whether there are liens against certain capital assets; however, the auditor should obtain a written representation from management stating that no liens exist. In other instances, written representations by management may be a source of audit evidence to support an assertion stated or implied in the financial statements. For example, certain current liabilities may be classified as noncurrent based on the guidance established by ASC 470 (FAS-6, Classification of Short-Term Obligations Expected to Be Refinanced). Part of that guidance requires that management must intend to refinance the obligation on a long-term basis. Under this circumstance, the auditor's support for management's intent may be management's written representation in addition to other sources of audit evidence. In general, written representations are not a substitute for other auditing procedures necessary to form the basis for the auditor's opinion.

Written representations should be addressed to the auditor and should apply to all periods covered in the auditor's report. Even though current management may not have been present during all of the periods covered by the report, written representations must cover all periods. The representations should be made by management as of the date of the auditor's report and should be signed by the chief executive officer and chief financial officer or others "with overall responsibility for financial and operating matters whom the auditor believes are responsible for and knowledgeable about, directly or through others in the organization, the matters covered by the written representations."

> **FRAUD POINTER:** In enforcement actions against auditors an overreliance on inquiry as a form of evidence was often mentioned. Auditors were often cited for a failure to corroborate management's explanations with other evidence. Instead, auditors relied on only management's representations or failed to challenge inconsistent explanations or explanations that were refuted by other evidence.

Promulgated Procedures Checklist

The auditor should perform the following procedures with respect to management representations in an audit engagement:

- Obtain certain minimum written representations from management.

- Consider whether written management representations beyond the minimum required should be obtained.

- Evaluate inconsistencies between representations made by management and evidence otherwise obtained.

- Consider whether written representations should be obtained from parties other than management.

- Consider whether an "updating representation letter" should be obtained.

- If applicable, consider the circumstances under which management has refused to provide written representations.

Analysis and Application of Procedures

Obtain certain minimum written representations from management

SAS-85 requires that in all audit engagements, the auditor must obtain from management written representations that relate to the following matters, and they must include management's acknowledgment of the following:

- Financial statements

  - Responsibility for the fair presentation in the financial statements of financial position, results of operations, and cash flows in conformity with generally accepted accounting principles

  - The belief that the financial statements are fairly presented in conformity with generally accepted accounting principles

  - The belief that any misstatements identified by the auditor and not corrected are immaterial, "both individually and in the aggregate" with respect to the financial statements taken as a whole. (The representation letter or an attachment should summarize the uncorrected errors.)

- Completeness of information

  — The availability of all financial records and related data

  — The completeness and availability of all minutes of meetings of stockholders, directors, and committees of directors

  — The completeness of communications from regulatory agencies concerning noncompliance with or deficiencies in financial reporting practices

— The absence of unrecorded transactions

- Recognition, measurement, and disclosure

  — Responsibility for the design and implementation of programs and controls to prevent and detect fraud

  — Knowledge of fraud or suspected fraud involving (1) management, (2) employees who have significant roles in internal control, or (3) others where the fraud could have a material effect on the financial statements

  — Knowledge of any allegations of fraud or suspected fraud based on information from other parties

  — The existence of plans or intentions that may affect the carrying value or classification of assets or liabilities

  — The existence of information concerning related-party transactions and amounts receivable from or payable to related parties

  — The existence of guarantees, whether written or oral, under which the entity is contingently liable

  — Significant estimates and material concentrations known to management exist that are required to be disclosed in accordance with the AICPA's Statement of Position 94-6 (ASC 275) (Disclosure of Certain Significant Risks and Uncertainties)

  — The existence of violations or possible violations of laws or regulations whose effects should be considered for disclosure in the financial statements or as a basis for recording a loss contingency

  — The existence of unasserted claims or assessments that the entity's lawyer has advised are probable of assertion and must be disclosed in accordance with Financial Accounting Standards Board Statement No. 5 (FAS-5) (ASC 450) (Accounting for Contingencies)

  — The existence of other liabilities and gain or loss contingencies that are required by FAS-5 (ASC 450) to be accrued or disclosed

  — The existence of satisfactory title to assets, liens, or encumbrances on assets, and assets pledged as collateral

  — Compliance with aspects of contractual agreements that may affect the financial statements

- Subsequent events

  — The existence of information concerning subsequent events

PLANNING AID REMINDER: The minimum representations also apply to financial statements that use a comprehensive basis of accounting other than accrual accounting as described in SAS-62 (AU 623) (Special Reports).

FRAUD POINTER: SAS-99 requires the auditor to make specific inquiries of management related to the risk of material misstatements due to fraud (see AU 316.20 – .21). Related to these inquiries, AU 333 (Management Representations) requires the auditor to obtain selected written representations from management regarding fraud.

SAS-85 notes that representations made by management may be limited to items that are material to the client's financial statements, if "management and the auditor have reached an understanding on materiality for this purpose." That understanding, expressed either in quantitative or qualitative terms, may be part of the management representation letter. However, some items that are the basis for management representations do not relate to dollar values and therefore are not affected by materiality considerations. For example, the management representation that all financial records and related data have been made available to the auditor is not subject to a materiality threshold.

As noted above, management must represent to the auditor that any uncorrected misstatements discovered during the audit are immaterial and that there should be a summary of these items in or attached to the representation letter. SAS-89 notes that if management does not agree with the auditor about a particular misstatement, the following may be added to the representation letter:

We do not agree that items [*identify the items*] constitute misstatements, because [*give reasons for the disagreement*].

In addition, SAS-107 (AU 312) (Audit Risk and Materiality in Conducting an Audit) points out that an auditor may establish a minimum amount that a misstatement must reach before it is accumulated by the auditor. The representation letter need not list these misstatements.

FRAUD POINTER: SAS-85 specifically notes that materiality does not apply to representations related to fraud involving management and employees who have significant roles in internal control.

Consider whether written management representations beyond the minimum required should be obtained

In addition to the specific representations listed above, the auditor must use professional judgment to determine whether additional representations are appropriate based on the characteristics of the engagement, including the industry in which the client operates. For example, SAS-85 points out that certain AICPA Audit Guides identify a variety of written representations that the auditor should consider. These additional representations could relate to such matters as the client's use of the cost method when the client owns less than 20% of an investee company's voting stock, the recognition of losses arising from purchase commitments, and the provision for losses related to environmental issues.

> **PUBLIC COMPANY IMPLICATION:** SOX requires the auditor of a public company to issue an audit report on the financial statements and a report on the effectiveness of internal control over financial reporting. The audit of financial statements and the audit of internal controls are to be integrated and the report dates should be the same. As a result, auditors may consider combining representations from management related to the audit of financial statements with representations made by management about internal control matters. Management representations required by AS-5 should be included in the combined representation letter.

Evaluate inconsistencies between representations made by management and evidence otherwise obtained

When a management representation contradicts evidence the auditor has obtained, "the auditor should investigate the circumstances and consider the reliability of the representation made." Depending on the results of the investigation, the auditor should consider whether the inconsistency of the management representation has implications for other areas of the audit engagement.

> **FRAUD POINTER:** SAS-85 provides practical insight into the auditor's reliance on statements made by management. It states, "The auditor neither assumes that management is dishonest nor assumes unquestioned honesty. In exercising professional skepticism, the auditor should not be satisfied with less than persuasive evidence because of a belief that management is honest."

Consider whether written representations should be obtained from parties other than management

SAS-85 notes that under some circumstances, such as the following, the auditor may obtain written representations from other individuals:

- Written representations concerning completeness may be obtained from the individual responsible for keeping the minutes of meetings of stockholders, board of directors, and committees of the board of directors.

- Written representations concerning matters such as related party transactions may be obtained from a parent company when the auditor's engagement is limited to expressing an opinion on a subsidiary's financial statements.

Consider whether an "updating representation letter" should be obtained

Under some circumstances, such as the following, an auditor should obtain an "updating representation letter" from management:

- A predecessor auditor has been requested to reissue previously issued reports covering financial statements that will be presented on a comparative basis with financial statements audited by a successor auditor.

- The auditor is performing subsequent audit procedures related to a filing under the Securities Act of 1933.

The updating written representations should state (1) whether subsequent information has come to the attention of management that would affect written representations previously expressed and (2) whether any subsequent events have occurred that would require adjustment or disclosure in the latest financial statement reported on by the auditor.

> **PLANNING AID REMINDER:** SAS-1 (AU 530) (Dating of the Independent Auditor's Report), provides guidance for situations in which the auditor's report should be "dual-dated." SAS-85 points out that the auditor should consider whether it is appropriate to obtain a written representation about the subsequent event that created the dual-dating situation.

If applicable, consider the circumstances under which management has refused to provide written representations

If management is unwilling to provide appropriate written representations, the auditor should consider whether that refusal has an effect on the auditor's reliance on other representations made by management during the engagement. Based on professional judgment, the auditor must determine whether it is necessary to withdraw from the engagement or disclaim an opinion on the financial statements because of the scope limitation.

SAS-85 does note that "based on the nature of the representations not obtained or the circumstances of the refusal, the auditor may conclude that a qualified opinion is appropriate." However, the expression of an unqualified opinion on the financial statements is precluded.

> **OBSERVATION:** The audit report date must not be earlier than the date on which the auditor has obtained sufficient appropriate audit evidence to support the opinion. A management representation letter is required for the auditor to issue an unqualified report because management must assert its responsibility for the financial statements. According to an AICPA Technical Practice Aid, the auditor need not have physical possession of the management representation letter before the date of the audit report; however, before the auditor can date the report management must have reviewed the representation letter and orally confirmed that it will sign the representation letter as written. In addition, the auditor must be in physical possession of the management representation letter before he or she releases the audit report.

Auditing Interpretation No. 6 (June 1983) of SAS-12 (AU 337) titled "Client Has Not Consulted Lawyer" states that when a client has not consulted outside legal counsel concerning litigation, claims, and assessments, the auditor will usually rely on internal documentation and representations made by management. In this event, the client's representation may read as follows:

> We are not aware of any impending or threatened litigation, claims, or assessments, or unasserted claims or assessments, that are required to be accrued or disclosed in the financial statements in accordance with ASC 450 (FAS-5). We have not consulted a lawyer concerning litigation, claims, or assessments.

> **ENGAGEMENT STRATEGY:** Auditing Interpretation No. 1 of AU 333 states that the auditor's request for written representations from management on significant violations or possible violations of laws and regulations need not include matters beyond those described in ASC 450 (FAS-5).

Practitioner's Aids

Exhibit AU 333-1 illustrates a management representation letter similar to the one included in the appendix of SAS-85.

EXHIBIT AU 333-1 — MANAGEMENT REPRESENTATION LETTER

We are providing this letter in connection with your audit(s) of the [*identify financial statements*] of [*name of entity*] as of [*dates*] and the [*periods*] for the purpose of expressing an opinion as to whether the (consolidated) financial statements present fairly, in all material respects, the financial position, results of operations, and cash flows of [*name of entity*] in conformity with generally accepted accounting principles. We confirm that we are responsible for the fair presentation of the (consolidated) financial statements of financial position, results of operations, and cash flows in conformity with generally accepted accounting principles.

Certain representations in this letter are described as being limited to matters that are material. Items are considered material, regardless of size, if they involve an omission or misstatement of accounting information that, in the light of surrounding circumstances, makes it probable that the judgment of a reasonable person relying on the information would be changed or influenced by the omission or misstatement.

We confirm, to the best of our knowledge and belief [*as of (date of auditor's report)*], the following representations made to you during your audit(s).

1. The financial statements referred to above are fairly presented in conformity with accounting principles generally accepted in the United States of America.

2. We have made available to you all
    a. Financial records and related data.
    b. Minutes of the meetings of stockholders, directors, and committees of directors, or summaries of actions of recent meetings for which minutes have not yet been prepared.

3. There have been no communications from regulatory agencies concerning noncompliance with or deficiencies in financial reporting practices.

4. All material transactions have been properly recorded in the accounting records underlying the financial statements.

5. The company is responsible for the design and implementation of programs and controls to prevent and detect fraud.

6. The company has no knowledge of any fraud or suspected fraud affecting the entity involving (a) management, (b) employees

who have significant roles in internal control, or (c) others where the fraud could have a material effect on the financial statements.

7. The company has no knowledge of any allegations of fraud or suspected fraud affecting the entity received in communications from employees, former employees, analysts, regulators, short sellers, or others.

8. The company has no plans or intentions that may materially affect the carrying value or classification of assets and liabilities.

9. We believe that the uncorrected misstatements in the financial statements that are summarized in the accompanying schedule are immaterial, both individually and in the aggregate, to the financial statements taken as a whole.

10. The following have been properly recorded or disclosed in the financial statements:
    a. Related-party transactions, including sales, purchases, loans, transfers, leasing arrangements, and guarantees, and amounts receivable from or payable to related parties.
    b. Guarantees, whether written or oral, under which the company is contingently liable.
    c. Significant estimates and material concentrations known to management that are required to be disclosed in accordance with ASC 275 (AICPA Statement of Position 94-6, "Disclosure of Certain Significant Risks and Uncertainties"). (Significant estimates are estimates at the balance sheet date that could change materially within the next year; concentrations refer to volumes of business, revenues, available sources of supply, or markets or geographic areas for which events could occur that would significantly disrupt normal finances within the next year.)

11. There are no
    a. Violations or possible violations of laws or regulations whose effects should be considered for disclosure in the financial statements or as a basis for recording a loss contingency.
    b. Unasserted claims or assessments that our lawyer has advised us are probable of assertion and must be disclosed in accordance with ASC 450 (FAS 5, Accounting for Contingencies).
    c. Other liabilities or gain or loss contingencies that are required to be accrued or disclosed by ASC 450 (FAS-5).

12. The company has satisfactory title to all owned assets, and there are no liens or encumbrances on such assets nor has any asset been pledged as collateral.

13. The company has complied with all aspects of contractual agreements that would have a material effect on the financial statements in the event of noncompliance.

To the best of our knowledge and belief, no events have occurred subsequent to the balance sheet date and through the date of this letter that would require adjustment to our disclosure in the aforementioned financial statements.

SECTION 334

RELATED PARTIES

Authoritative Pronouncements

SAS-45 — Omnibus Statement on Auditing Standards 1983

Auditing Interpretation No. 4 of AU 334 (April 1979) — Exchange of Information Between the Principal and Other Auditor on Related Parties

Auditing Interpretation No. 5 of AU 334 (April 1979) — Examination of Identified Related Party Transactions with a Component

Auditing Interpretation No. 6 of AU 334 (May 1986) — The Nature and Extent of Auditing Procedures for Examining Related Party Transactions

Auditing Interpretation No. 7 of AU 334 (May 2000) — Management's and Auditor's Responsibilities with Regard to Related Party Disclosures Prefaced by Terminology Such As "Management Believes That"

> **IMPORTANT NOTICE FOR 2011:** The Auditing Standards Board (ASB) is in the process of redrafting all of the auditing sections in *Codification of Statements on Auditing Standards* to converge U.S. GAAS with the International Standards on Auditing issued by the International Auditing and Assurance Standards Board. As part of this process, the newly redrafted standards will follow certain clarity drafting conventions adopted by the ASB. These clarity drafting conventions include: (1) establishing objectives for each standard; (2) including a definitions section, if appropriate; and (3) separating requirements from application guidance and other material. The ASB is planning to have all redrafted standards become effective on the same date, which is for audits of financial statements for periods ending on or after December 15, 2012. It is possible that the effective date might be delayed beyond that date. The ASB's clarity and convergence project will have a significant effect on the auditing standards applicable to audits of nonpublic companies, and the 2012 *GAAS Guide* will be appropriately modified to reflect these changes once the effective date of the standards is certain.

Overview

An audit of financial statements cannot be expected to provide assurance that all related-party transactions were identified. However, an auditor must be alert for the possible occurrence of related party transactions and should evaluate them with a higher degree of skepticism than transactions that are executed by parties that are not related. SAS-45 establishes guidelines for evaluating related party transactions that are discovered during an audit engagement.

An accounting transaction generally reflects the resources exchanged and obligations incurred when parties to a transaction are unrelated. The auditor may verify the values assigned to the accounts by examining the supporting documentation. For example, if a client purchases machinery for $10,000 cash, inspection of the vendor invoice will usually satisfy the auditor that the fair value of the asset acquired at the transaction date was in fact $10,000. However, if the parties to the transaction are related, it cannot always be assumed that the recorded amounts properly reflect the true economic substance of the transaction. Moreover, the inspection of supporting documentation might not provide the auditor with appropriate audit evidence. Professional guidelines for related party transactions are contained in SAS-45 and ASC 850 (FAS-57, Related Party Disclosures).

> **PLANNING AID REMINDER:** Auditing Interpretation No. 4 of AU 334 states that the principal auditor and other auditors of related entities should exchange information on the names of known related parties in the early stages of their examinations.

Promulgated Procedures Checklist

The auditor should perform the following procedures with respect to related party transactions:

- Determine whether conditions exist for related party transactions.

- Perform audit procedures that are likely to identify related party transactions.

- Determine whether the client has made appropriate disclosures for related party transactions that have been identified.

Analysis and Application of Procedures

Determine whether conditions exist for related party transactions

A related party transaction occurs when one party to a transaction has the ability to impose contract terms that would not have occurred if the parties had been unrelated. ASC 850 (FAS-57) states that related parties consist of all affiliates of an enterprise, including (1) its management and their immediate families; (2) its principal owners and their immediate families;

(3) investments accounted for by the equity method; (4) beneficial employee trusts that are managed by the management of the enterprise; and (5) any party that may, or does, deal with the enterprise and has ownership, control, or significant influence over the management or operating policies of another party to the extent that an arm's-length transaction might not be achieved.

> **PLANNING AID REMINDER:** Auditing Interpretation No. 5 of AU 334 states that principal auditors ordinarily should allow access to the relevant portions of their audit documentation to other auditors who are auditing a component or subsidiary of the entity (and vice versa). This enables other auditors to understand the related party transactions.

In addition to relationships that may lead to the auditor's identification of a related party transaction, certain transactions suggest that the parties may be related. SAS-45 lists the following as examples:

- Contracts that carry no interest rate or that carry an unrealistic interest rate

- Real estate transactions that are made at a price significantly different from appraised values

- Nonmonetary transactions that involve the exchange of similar assets

- Loan agreements that contain no repayment schedule

Finally, certain conditions may increase the possibility that a related party transaction may occur. These conditions include the following:

- Inadequate working capital or lines of credit

- Management's desire for strong earnings to support the market price of the company's stock

- Earnings forecast that was too optimistic

- A declining industry

- Excess capacity

- Significant legal problems

- Exposure to technological changes

> **OBSERVATION:** Although these conditions do not usually result in related party transactions, they indicate that the auditor must be more alert to the increased possibility.

> **FRAUD POINTER:** SAS-99 notes that the presence of significant related-party transactions not in the ordinary course of business or with related parties who are not audited or who are audited by another firm can create opportunities for management or others to engage in fraudulent financial reporting. When evaluating business transactions involving previously unidentified related parties, auditors should exercise appropriate professional skepticism.

Perform audit procedures that are likely to identify related party transactions

ASC 850 (FAS-57), which is reviewed at the end of this section, covers related party transactions and how they should be identified and disclosed in the financial statements. SAS-45 states that until special accounting rules are promulgated, the auditor should evaluate related party transactions in the context of existing generally accepted accounting principles and should consider whether material transactions are adequately disclosed in the financial statements in accordance with GAAP.

Auditing Interpretation No. 6 of AU 334 states that the auditor should apply sufficient audit procedures to provide reasonable assurance that related party transactions are adequately disclosed in the financial statements and that material misstatements associated with identified related party transactions do not exist.

> **ENGAGEMENT STRATEGY:** Since the audit risk associated with management's assertions concerning related party transactions is generally higher than the audit risk associated with other transactions, the audit procedures that are applied to related party transactions should be more extensive or effective. For example, to obtain additional evidence or a better understanding of a related party transaction, the auditor may apply selected audit procedures to, or may actually audit, the financial statements of the related party as part of the engagement strategy.

Initially the auditor should select audit procedures that are likely to identify transactions with related parties. These procedures are as follows:

- Supply audit team members the names of known related parties of the client and its divisions, segments, etc., to all audit personnel.

- Read the minutes of the board of directors meetings and executive or operating committee meetings.

- Review proxy and other material filed with the SEC and comparable data filed with other regulatory agencies for information on material related party transactions.

- Read conflict-of-interest statements prepared by the client's key personnel.

- Review major transactions for indications of previously undisclosed relationships.

- Consider whether any transactions are occurring but at little or no cost or are not being recorded.

- Review significant or nonroutine transactions, especially those occurring near the end of the accounting period.

- Review confirmations of compensating-balance agreements for suggestions that balances are or were maintained for or by related parties.

- Review invoices from law firms to see whether a related party is involved.

- Review loan confirmations to determine if guarantees exist.

> **PLANNING AID REMINDER:** The auditor should consider obtaining written representations from senior management of an entity and its board of directors regarding whether they or other related parties were involved in transactions with the entity.

> **PUBLIC COMPANY IMPLICATION:** Because related-party transactions are not conducted at arm's length, there is often a lack of independence and objectivity between management and the related party. In light of this, SOX prohibits related-party transactions that involve personal loans to executives of public companies. It is now illegal for any public company to extend or maintain credit, to arrange for the extension of credit, or to renew the extension of credit in the form of a personal loan to any director or executive officer of the public company. These restrictions do not apply to any loan, such as a home loan or credit card agreement, made by a bank or other insured financial institution under normal banking operations using market terms. Auditors of public companies should be alert for prohibited loans to executives and deal with them as illegal acts.

When a related party transaction is identified, the auditor should consider performing the following procedures:

- Understand the business purpose of the transaction.

- Examine documentation that supports the transaction.

- Determine whether the board of directors or other senior officials approved the transaction.

- Test the reasonableness of amounts compiled for possible disclosure in the financial statements.

- If appropriate, arrange for the audit of intercompany account balances. Use the same audit date cutoff for all balances.

- If appropriate, arrange for the examination of transactions by the auditors for each of the parties.

- Determine the transferability and value of collateral, if any.

> **ENGAGEMENT STRATEGY:** If the auditor is not satisfied with the results of the above procedures, he or she may select additional procedures to obtain a complete understanding of the nature of the transaction. These procedures may include confirming data with the other party, discussing transactions with banks or other parties, inspecting documents held by others, or verifying the existence of the other party by referring to trade journals or other sources.

> **PLANNING AID REMINDER:** The auditor is required to understand the business rationale for significant related-party transactions. AICPA Practice Alert 03-1 (Audit Confirmations) states that confirmation of the terms of related-party transactions can help auditors obtain this understanding. Specifically, the auditor might confirm the transaction amount and terms, including any guarantees, with the other party to the transaction. Because client management may be on both sides of a related-party transaction, the auditor should consider confirming the terms of the transaction with intermediaries (e.g., agents, attorneys, banks, guarantors).

Auditing Interpretation No. 7 of AU 334 points out that management may use phraseology such as "management believes that" or "it is the Company's belief that" in describing a related party transaction. The use of this or similar terminology does not change management's responsibility to substantiate its representations concerning a related party transaction that it believes was executed on terms equivalent to those similar to an arm's-length transaction.

> **ENGAGEMENT STRATEGY:** If management does not adequately substantiate its representation with respect to the related party transaction, the auditor should express a qualified or adverse opinion on the financial statements if the matter is considered material.

Determine whether the client has made appropriate disclosures for related party transactions that have been identified

The Financial Accounting Standards Board (FASB) requires disclosure of related party transactions that (1) are not eliminated in consolidated or combined financial statements and (2) are necessary to understand the entity's financial statements.

If separate financial statements of an entity that has been consolidated are presented in a financial report that includes the consolidated financial statements, duplicate disclosure of the related party transactions is not necessary. Thus, disclosure of the related party transactions in the consolidated statements is all that is required. However, disclosure of related party transactions is required in separate financial statements of (1) a parent company, (2) a subsidiary, (3) a corporate joint venture, or (4) an investee that is less than 50% owned. The minimum financial statement disclosures required by ASC 850 (FAS-57) for related party transactions that (1) are not eliminated in consolidation or combination and (2) are necessary to the understanding of the financial statements are as follows:

1. The nature of the related party relationship. The name of the related party should also be disclosed if it is essential to the understanding of the relationship.

2. A description of the related party transactions, including amounts and other pertinent information for each period in which an income statement is presented.

3. Related party transactions of no amount, or of nominal amounts, must also be disclosed. In other words, all information that is necessary for an understanding of the effects of the related party transactions on the financial statements must be disclosed, assuming this information is material.

4. The effects of any change in terms between the related parties from terms used in prior periods. In addition, the dollar amount of transactions for each period in which an income statement is presented must be disclosed.

5. If not apparent in the financial statements, (1) the terms of related party transactions; (2) the manner of settlement to related party transactions; and (3) the amount due to, or due from, related parties must all be disclosed.

6. The nature of any control relationship, even if there were no transactions between the related parties, must be disclosed in all circumstances.

The amount of information disclosed for related party transactions must be sufficient for the user of the financial statements to be able to understand the related party transaction. Thus, the disclosure of the total amount of a specific type of related party transaction, or the effects of the relationship between the related parties, may be all that is necessary. The auditor must determine whether the related party transaction affects the financial statements to such a degree that they are materially misstated and must modify the report accordingly.

> **OBSERVATION:** One cannot assume that a related party transaction is consummated in the same manner as an arm's-length transaction. Disclosures or other representations of related party transactions in financial statements should not, under any circumstances, indicate that the transaction was made on the same basis as an arm's-length transaction.

SECTION 336

USING THE WORK OF A SPECIALIST

Authoritative Pronouncements

SAS-73 — Using the Work of a Specialist

Auditing Interpretation No. 1 of AU 336 (December 2001) — The Use of Legal Interpretations as Evidential Matter to Support Management's Assertion That a Transfer of Financial Assets Has Met the Isolation Criterion in Paragraph 9(a) of Financial Accounting Standards Board Statement No. 140

> **IMPORTANT NOTICE FOR 2011:** The Auditing Standards Board (ASB) is in the process of redrafting all of the auditing sections in *Codification of Statements on Auditing Standards* to converge U.S. GAAS with the International Standards on Auditing issued by the International Auditing and Assurance Standards Board. As part of this process, the newly redrafted standards will follow certain clarity drafting conventions adopted by the ASB. These clarity drafting conventions include: (1) establishing objectives for each standard; (2) including a definitions section, if appropriate; and (3) separating requirements from application guidance and other material. The ASB is planning to have all redrafted standards become effective on the same date, which is for audits of financial statements for periods ending on or after December 15, 2012. It is possible that the effective date might be delayed beyond that date. The ASB's clarity and convergence project will have a significant effect on the auditing standards applicable to audits of nonpublic companies, and the 2012 *GAAS Guide* will be appropriately modified to reflect these changes once the effective date of the standards is certain.

Overview

In some instances the dollar amounts reflected in the financial statements are based on audit evidence that an auditor is not capable of evaluating. For example, pension costs depend on an actuarial analysis that is usually beyond the expertise of an auditor. SAS-73 provides guidance in engagements that require the services of a specialist. A specialist is a person or firm that possesses specialized knowledge or skill in a nonaccounting or nonauditing field. Although there is no complete list of circumstances that require the use of a specialist, SAS-73 provides the following examples:

- Valuation of inventories, property, plant, and equipment, financial instruments, and works of art for which the question of a write-down due to the application of the lower of cost or market rule or the cost recoverability rule is relevant

- Valuation of an environmental contingency

- Physical measurements and conditions (tons, barrels, etc.) of raw materials

- Dollar valuations based on specialized measurement techniques such as actuarial computations

- Interpretation of technical material such as legal documents and regulatory standards and guidance

> **PLANNING AID REMINDER:** SAS-73 did not change the requirement established by SOP 92-4 (Auditing Insurance Entities' Loss Reserves) that a "loss reserve specialist," not an employee or officer of the client, must be used to audit the loss reserve for property and liability insurance companies.

> **ENGAGEMENT STRATEGY:** SAS-73 states that the auditor has the expertise necessary to consider the financial statement implications (accrual, disclosure, and presentation) of income tax matters. This presupposes an understanding of income tax laws and regulations that apply to a particular client and the standards established by ASC 740 (FAS-109, Accounting for Income Taxes) and other related pronouncements.

SAS-73 does not provide guidelines for the use of a lawyer who is requested to make representations concerning litigation, claims, or assessments (see SAS-12 [AU 337] [Inquiry of a Client's Lawyer Concerning Litigation, Claims, and Assessments]); however, SAS-73 does apply to using the expertise of a lawyer in other circumstances.

The standards established by SAS-73 apply to the audit of financial statements prepared in accordance with generally accepted accounting principles (GAAP) as well as to engagements discussed in SAS-62 (AU 623) (Special Reports); however, they do not apply to specialists employed by the auditor when those specialists are part of the audit team. When a auditor employs a specialist as a member of the audit team in an engagement, the standards established by SAS-108 (AU 311) (Planning and Supervision) must be observed.

An auditing firm must apply the standards established by SAS-73 in the following circumstances:

- When management engages a specialist and the auditor is considering using the work of that specialist as part of substantive testing

- When management engages a specialist to perform advisory services and the auditor employs that specialist to perform services related to substantive testing (Under this circumstance, the auditor should consider the effect on independence.)

- When the auditor engages a specialist as part of substantive testing

> **ENGAGEMENT STRATEGY:** An entity's use of information technology is likely to have a significant impact on internal control. AU 314 notes that the auditor should consider whether specialized IT skills are needed for the auditor to understand the effect of IT on the audit. In some instances, an outside IT specialist is needed to inquire of client IT personnel about IT-based transaction processing and related automated controls, including examination of system documentation and planning and performance of tests of IT controls. An auditor who engages an IT specialist should have sufficient IT-related knowledge to communicate the audit objectives to the specialist, to evaluate whether the specialist's procedures satisfy audit objectives, and to evaluate the results of the specialist's work.

> **FRAUD POINTER:** As part of the auditor's mandated responses to address the risk of management override of internal controls, SAS-99 (Consideration of Fraud in a Financial Statement Audit) requires the auditor to examine journal entries and other adjustments for evidence of possible material misstatements due to fraud. SAS-99 notes that journal entries and other adjustments might only exist in electronic form for entities that use IT in the financial reporting process. In some circumstances, an IT specialist might be needed to extract electronic evidence needed by the auditor to test journal entries and other adjustments.

Promulgated Procedures Checklist

Once an auditor determines that a specialist is appropriate in an engagement, the following procedures should be performed:

- Determine the qualifications of the specialists.

- Evaluate the effects of using a specialist on audit evidence.

- Determine the extent to which the work of the specialist should be used.

- Consider the effect of using the work of a specialist on the audit report.

- If applicable, consider using the work of a specialist to determine whether there has been a transfer of financial assets as defined by ASC 860 (FAS-140).

Analysis and Application of Procedures

Determine the qualifications of the specialists

Initially, the auditor must determine the nature of the work to be performed by a specialist as it relates to gathering appropriate audit evidence. That is, the auditor should identify the *assertions* (as defined by SAS-106 [AU 326] [Audit Evidence]) in the financial statements (either explicitly or implicitly) that can be substantiated only through evidence obtained or developed by a specialist. For example, presentation and disclosure assertions related to the projected benefit obligation that appear in a note to the financial statements (as required by ASC 715 (FAS-87, Employers' Accounting for Pensions) require the expertise of an actuary. Specifically, SAS-73 requires that the auditor obtain an understanding of the following with respect to nature of the services to be provided by a specialist:

- The objectives and scope of the specialist's services

- The relationship between the specialist and the client

- The methods and assumptions to be used in the work

- A comparison of the methods and assumptions proposed for the current engagement with those used in the previous engagement

- The appropriateness of the work of the specialist in relationship to the assertions to be substantiated

- The form and content of the results of work of the specialist and how they relate to the auditor's need to evaluate that work

> **ENGAGEMENT STRATEGY:** SAS-73 notes that the auditor may need to inform the specialist that his or her work will be used to substantiate certain assertions in the financial statements. Although SAS-73 does not provide any guidance on when this contact may be appropriate, it generally would be necessary to ensure that the specialist understands the need to provide a "usable link" between the specialist's work and the assertions to be substantiated. Essentially, the prudent auditor must make sure that the technical nature of the specialist's work makes sense in the context of the audit engagement. This should be determined early in the strategy planning for the engagement.

Before the auditor places reliance on the work of a specialist, the qualifications and experience of the specialist should be established, for example, by identifying the professional designations (certification, license, etc.) and the professional reputation and standing of the specialist. In addition, the specialist's professional work experience provides insight into whether the qualifications of the specialist are acceptable.

Evaluate the effects of using a specialist on audit evidence

Perhaps the most sensitive aspect of using the work of a specialist is to determine the relationship between the specialist and the client, and the effect of that relationship on an auditor's collection of appropriate audit evidence. If the specialist is biased in favor of the client, the work performed by the specialist and used as evidence by the auditor will be tainted.

Ideally, the specialist would not have a relationship with the client that could provide an opportunity for the client to "directly or indirectly control or significantly influence the specialist." The concept of a "relationship" is broad and encompasses such circumstances as that of an employer/employee or a member of the same family. If there is no relationship between the client and the specialist (that is, the auditor hires the specialist and there are no other direct or indirect relationships between the client and the specialist), there is a greater chance that the work the specialist performs will be reliable.

> **ENGAGEMENT STRATEGY:** SAS-73 notes that the term "relationship" includes (but is not limited to) those relationships included in Note 1 of SAS-45 (AU 334). The SAS-45 (AU 334) note is based on the definition of "related parties" contained in SAS-57 (AU 342).

If a relationship does exist between the client and the specialist, the auditor is required to obtain an understanding of the relationship, as the existence of a relationship does not in itself preclude the auditor from relying on the specialist's work. In this circumstance, SAS-73 requires that the auditor "assess the risk that the specialist's objectivity might be impaired." If the auditor concludes that the specialist's objectivity might be impaired, the auditor must perform additional procedures. These procedures should focus on "some or all of the specialist's assumptions, methods, or findings." When the results of performing the additional procedures do not dispel the auditor's concern with the specialist's objectivity, the auditor should engage another specialist.

Determine the extent to which the work of the specialist should be used

The auditor's role in the evaluation of the evidence created by a specialist is to determine whether the specialist's findings are reasonable. SAS-73 states that the auditor should use the following approach to assess the reasonableness of the findings:

- Obtain an understanding of the specialist's methods and assumptions.

- Test the data provided to the specialist by the client. (The nature, timing, and extent of the testing should be based on the auditor's assessment of the client's control risk.)

- Evaluate whether the relevant assertions in the financial statements are substantiated by the specialist's findings.

> **PLANNING AID REMINDER:** If, on the basis of the above and other procedures deemed appropriate by the auditor, the auditor concludes that the findings are reasonable, the evidence can be relied on as the basis for forming an opinion on the financial statements. On the other hand, if the auditor's evaluation does not suggest that the findings are reasonable, SAS-73 requires that the auditor perform additional procedures. If the matter still is unresolved after the performance of additional procedures, the auditor should obtain the opinion of another specialist.

> **PUBLIC COMPANY IMPLICATION:** The PCAOB has issued Staff Audit Practice Alert No. 2 (Matters Related to Auditing Fair Value Measurements of Financial Instruments and the Use of Specialists), which includes a discussion of the auditor's use of a specialist in auditing fair values. The auditor should consider using a specialist when he or she lacks the necessary skill and knowledge to plan and perform audit procedures relating to fair value measurements in the financial statements. The auditor should be more likely to use a specialist given a greater client use of unobservable inputs, greater complexity in valuation techniques, and fair value amounts that are large. If the auditor chooses to rely on the work of a specialist, he or she must obtain an understanding of the specialist's methods and evaluate whether they will result in a measurement that is in accordance with GAAP. In addition, the auditor needs to evaluate the specialist's assumptions. Finally, the auditor should evaluate the specialist's qualifications, including his or her experience in performing the type of work that the auditor is considering relying upon.

Consider the effect of using the work of a specialist on the audit report

When the auditor concludes that the specialist's findings support the particular assertions in the financial statements, the third standard of fieldwork has been satisfied. An unqualified opinion, without reference to the work of the specialist, can be expressed.

On the other hand, when the findings of the specialist do not support the relevant assertions in the financial statements, the auditor should perform additional procedures to resolve the problem. If the auditor cannot resolve the issue by performing additional procedures or obtaining the services of another specialist, the auditor must determine whether the circumstance is (1) a deviation from GAAP or (2) a scope limitation.

A deviation from GAAP arises when the auditor concludes that the relevant assertions in the financial statements are not supported by findings of the specialist and by other procedures (perhaps including the work of another specialist) that the auditor may perform. Under this circumstance, the auditor should express either a qualified opinion or an adverse opinion on the financial statements.

A scope limitation arises when the auditor concludes that the performance of additional audit procedures would not provide a reasonable basis for either substantiating or refuting the relevant assertions in the financial statements. Under this circumstance, the auditor should either express a qualified opinion or disclaim an opinion on the financial statements.

SAS-73 states that, generally, the auditor's report, whether unqualified or modified, should not make reference to the findings of a specialist, because the reference may be interpreted as (1) a qualification or (2) an attempt to divide the responsibility for the report between the auditor and the specialist. However, SAS-73 allows the auditor to add explanatory language to an unqualified report or a modified report if "the auditor believes such reference will facilitate an understanding of the reason for the explanatory paragraph or the departure from the unqualified opinion." Thus, the auditor may decide to express an unqualified opinion and add an explanatory paragraph (after the opinion paragraph but with no reference in the opinion paragraph to the explanatory paragraph) that refers to the findings of a specialist. In addition, the auditor may decide to express an opinion that is other than unqualified, and the paragraph that describes the basis for the report modification could then refer to the findings of a specialist. In each circumstance, the explanatory paragraph may refer to and identify the specialist.

If applicable, consider using the work of a specialist to determine whether there has been a transfer of financial assets as defined by ASC 860 (FAS-140)

ASC 860 (paragraph 9(a) of FAS-140, Accounting for Transfers and Servicing of Financial Assets and Extinguishments of Liabilities) provides the following guidance for determining when the transfer of financial assets may be treated as a sale:

> The transferred assets have been isolated from the transferor — put presumptively beyond the reach of the transferor and its creditors, even in bankruptcy or other receivership.

Auditing Interpretation No. 1 of AU 336 states that determining whether the above condition (the isolation criterion) has been satisfied is "largely a matter of law." The Interpretation notes that the need for the work of a specialist (lawyer) generally depends on the complexity of the transfer. When the transfer is routine and there is no continuing involvement in the assets by the transferor, the use of a lawyer may not be necessary. On the other hand, if the transfer involves complex legal structures, the opinion of a legal specialist may be required.

When it is concluded that the opinion of a legal specialist is needed, the following factors should be considered in assessing the adequacy of the legal opinion:

- The legal experience of the specialist in the area (including exposure to the U.S. Bankruptcy Code and other relevant statutes)

- An understanding by the auditor of the assumptions that are used by the legal specialist

- The performance by the auditor of appropriate tests on relevant information that has been provided to the specialist by management

> **OBSERVATION:** The Interpretation notes that the specialist's work is usually expressed "in the form of a reasoned legal opinion that is restricted to particular facts and circumstances relevant to the specific transaction." If the auditor concludes that the legal opinion provided by the specialist is inadequate or inappropriate, the auditor must determine how the audit report should be modified.

SECTION 337

INQUIRY OF A CLIENT'S LAWYER CONCERNING LITIGATION, CLAIMS, AND ASSESSMENTS

Authoritative Pronouncements

SAS-12 — Inquiry of a Client's Lawyer Concerning Litigation, Claims and Assessments

Auditing Interpretation No. 1 of AU 337 (March 1977) — Specifying Relevant Date in an Audit Inquiry Letter

Auditing Interpretation No. 2 of AU 337 (March 1977) — Relationship Between Date of Lawyer's Response and Auditor's Report

Auditing Interpretation No. 3 of AU 337 (March 1977) — Form of Audit Inquiry Letter When Client Represents That No Unasserted Claims and Assessments Exist

Auditing Interpretation No. 4 of AU 337 (March 1977) — Documents Subject to Lawyer-Client Privilege

Auditing Interpretation No. 5 of AU 337 (June 1983) — Alternative Wording of the Illustrative Audit Inquiry Letter to a Client Lawyer

Auditing Interpretation No. 6 of AU 337 (June 1983) — Client Has Not Consulted a Lawyer

Auditing Interpretation No. 7 of AU 337 (February 1997) — Assessment of a Lawyer's Evaluation of the Outcome of Litigation

Auditing Interpretation No. 8 of AU 337 (June 1983) — Use of the Client's Inside Counsel in the Evaluation of Litigation, Claims, and Assessments

Auditing Interpretation No. 9 of AU 337 (February 1990) — Use of Explanatory Language About the Attorney-Client Privilege or the Attorney Work-Product Privilege

Auditing Interpretation No. 10 of AU 337 (January 1997) — Use of Explanatory Language Concerning Unasserted Possible Claims or Assessments in Lawyer's Response to Audit Inquiry Letters

IMPORTANT NOTICE FOR 2011: The Auditing Standards Board (ASB) is in the process of redrafting all of the auditing sections in *Codification of Statements on Auditing Standards* to converge U.S. GAAS with the International Standards on

Auditing issued by the International Auditing and Assurance Standards Board. As part of this process, the newly redrafted standards will follow certain clarity drafting conventions adopted by the ASB. These clarity drafting conventions include: (1) establishing objectives for each standard; (2) including a definitions section, if appropriate; and (3) separating requirements from application guidance and other material. The ASB is planning to have all redrafted standards become effective on the same date, which is for audits of financial statements for periods ending on or after December 15, 2012. It is possible that the effective date might be delayed beyond that date. The ASB's clarity and convergence project will have a significant effect on the auditing standards applicable to audits of nonpublic companies, and the 2012 *GAAS Guide* will be appropriately modified to reflect these changes once the effective date of the standards is certain.

Overview

SAS-12 provides guidance for the collection of audit evidence to determine whether litigation, claims, and assessments have been properly reflected in the financial statements in accordance with generally accepted accounting principles (GAAP). Financial reporting standards with respect to litigation, claims, and assessments were established by FAS-5 (ASC 450) (Accounting for Contingencies). ASC 450 requires that a loss contingency be accrued if (1) information available before the issuance of the financial statements indicates that it is probable that an asset had been impaired or a liability incurred at the date of the financial statements and (2) the amount of loss can be reasonably estimated. If these two conditions are not both met but there is a reasonable possibility that a loss or an additional loss may be incurred, the loss contingency must be disclosed in the financial statements, usually in a note.

Promulgated Procedures Checklist

The auditor should perform the following procedures with respect to the identification of litigation, claims, and assessments:

- Identify litigation, claims, and assessments that may have to be accrued or disclosed in the financial statements.

- Obtain a letter of audit inquiry from the client's lawyer.

- Consider whether it is appropriate to accept oral representations made by the client's lawyer.

- Determine the effect on the audit report when the client's lawyer does not respond to the letter of audit inquiry.

Analysis and Application of Procedures

Identify litigation, claims, and assessments that may have to be accrued or disclosed in the financial statements

SAS-12 recognizes that the auditor ordinarily lacks the expertise to evaluate litigation, claims, and assessments in the context of the financial reporting requirements established by ASC 450 (FAS-5). For this reason, the auditor must rely a great deal on the client's lawyer regarding litigation, claims, and assessments. It is the auditor's responsibility to collect audit evidence (1) to identify circumstances that may result in a loss contingency, (2) to identify the period in which the event occurred that may lead to the loss contingency, (3) to support the probability of the loss, and (4) to support the estimated amount of the loss or the estimated range of the loss. To achieve these audit objectives, the auditor should employ the following procedures:

- Discuss with management its processes for identifying, evaluating, and accounting for litigation, claims, and assessments.

- Obtain a description and evaluation of litigation, claims, and assessments from the client that existed as of the balance sheet date.

- Obtain a representation from the client, preferably in writing, that they have complied with ASC 450 (FAS-5) requirements with respect to litigation, claims, and assessments.

- Examine documents relative to legal liability matters, including correspondence and invoices from lawyers.

- Obtain from the client a statement in writing that the client has disclosed unasserted claims that the lawyer believes will probably be asserted and must be disclosed in the financial statements.

- After obtaining permission from the client, notify the client's lawyer that the client has made the assurances described above. Notification may be in the form of a separate letter or as part of the letter of audit inquiry.

- Send letters of inquiry to lawyers who have been consulted concerning legal matters.

- Read contracts, loan agreements, leases, and correspondence from taxing authorities.

- Read minutes of stockholders, directors, and other committee meetings during the year and through the end of fieldwork.

- Obtain information from banks concerning loan agreements.

- Review other documents for possible guarantees the client has made.

> **PLANNING AID REMINDER:** Auditing Interpretation No. 6 of AU 337 states that SAS-12 is expressly limited to inquiries of lawyers with whom management has consulted. If the client has not consulted a lawyer during the period, the auditor should rely on (1) the review of internal information available and (2) written representations from management stating it had not consulted a lawyer about litigation, claims, and assessments.
>
> **ENGAGEMENT STRATEGY:** The Auditing Interpretation No. 4 of AU 337 states that it is not necessary for the auditor to examine documents held by the client that are subject to the lawyer-client privilege.
>
> **FRAUD POINTER:** SAS-99 requires the auditor to consider making inquiries of others separate from management about the risks of fraud. As part of these inquiries, auditors may make inquiries of in-house legal counsel about the risks of fraud.

Obtain a letter of audit inquiry from the client's lawyer

Representations that the client makes with respect to litigation, claims, and assessments must be substantiated by letters of audit inquiry to the client's lawyers. Letters of audit inquiry should be sent to those lawyers who have the primary responsibility for and knowledge about particular litigation, claims, and assessments. In some circumstances the client's in-house counsel will be the recipient of the letter and may provide the auditor with the necessary corroboration concerning litigation, claims, and assessments. A letter of audit inquiry typically would include, but is not limited to, the following matters:

1. Identification of the client and the date of the audit

2. A list prepared by management or legal counsel that describes and evaluates pending and threatened litigation, claims, and assessments

3. A list prepared by management that describes and evaluates unasserted claims and assessments

4. A request that the lawyer reply directly to the independent auditor if his or her views differ from management's regarding item 2, above

5. A statement that the client understands that whenever its lawyer has formed a professional conclusion concerning a possible claim or assessment, the lawyer has so advised the client and has consulted with the client concerning the question of disclosure provided for by GAAP

6. A request that the lawyer confirm whether the understanding in item 5 (above) is correct

7. A request that the lawyer identify the nature of and reasons for any limitation in his or her response

Exhibit AU 337-1, which is taken from Appendix A of SAS-12, illustrates an audit inquiry letter to legal counsel.

Exhibit AU 337-2, which is based on Auditing Interpretation No. 5 of AU 337, illustrates an audit inquiry letter whereby management has requested that the lawyer prepare the list of pending or threatened litigation, claims, and assessments.

Auditing Interpretation No. 10 of AU 337 notes that some lawyers include the following or similar language in their response to the auditor's letter of inquiry:

> Please be advised that, pursuant to clauses (b) and (c) of Paragraph 5 of the ABA Statement of Policy (American Bar Association's Statement of Policy Regarding Lawyers' Responses to Auditors' Requests for Information) and the related Commentary referred to in the last paragraph of this letter, it would be inappropriate for this firm to respond to a general inquiry relating to the existence of unasserted possible claims or assessments involving the Company. We can only furnish information concerning those unasserted possible claims or assessments upon which the Company has specifically requested in writing that we comment. We also cannot comment upon the adequacy of the Company's listing, if any, of unasserted possible claims or assessments or its assertions concerning the advice, if any, about the need to disclose same.

The Interpretation notes that inclusion of this type of language does not limit the scope of the audit engagement.

ENGAGEMENT STRATEGY: Auditing Interpretation No. 8 of AU 337 notes that audit inquiry letters "should be sent to those lawyers, which may be either inside counsel or outside lawyers, who have the primary responsibility for, and knowledge about, particular litigation, claims and assessments."

Consider whether it is appropriate to accept oral representations made by the client's lawyer

Under special circumstances, the lawyer may make representations orally. For example, the details and accounting implications of complex litigation may best be evaluated in a conference attended by the client, the lawyer, and the auditor.

> **ENGAGEMENT STRATEGY:** Auditing Interpretation No. 1 of AU 337 states that the audit inquiry letter to a client's attorney should specify (1) the earliest acceptable effective date of the attorney's response and (2) the latest date for return to the auditor. A two-week period between the dates is recommended. If the attorney does not specify an effective date of the response, the effective date is assumed to be the date of the response. Auditing Interpretation No. 2 of AU 337 recommends that the effective date requested in a letter to the client's attorney be as close as possible to the date of the auditor's report.

> **PLANNING AID REMINDER:** Auditing Interpretation No. 9 of AU 337 notes that some clients state in their letter of audit inquiry that the letter is not intended to infringe on the attorney-client privilege or the attorney work-product privilege. Likewise, legal counsel's response to the letter may state that counsel has been advised by the client that the request for information is not intended to waive the privileged relationship with the client. Such comments in the client letter of audit inquiry or counsel's response to the letter do not result in a limitation of the scope of an audit.

Determine the effect on the audit report when the client's lawyer does not respond to the letter of audit inquiry

Under some circumstances a lawyer might not respond to the auditor's letter of audit inquiry. If the lawyer decides not to respond, there is a scope limitation, and the auditor should issue a qualified opinion or a disclaimer opinion. When the lawyer cannot reasonably respond to the letter because of significant uncertainties surrounding the possible outcome of a certain legal matter, there is an uncertainty, and the auditor's report should be modified.

> **ENGAGEMENT STRATEGY:** Auditing Interpretation No. 7 of AU 337 states that when the auditor is uncertain about the meaning of the lawyer's evaluation of litigation, claims, or assessments, he or she should request clarification either in a follow-up letter or in a conference with the client and lawyer. The clarification should be adequately documented in the auditor's files.

> **ENGAGEMENT STRATEGY:** The lawyer's response to the auditor's letter of audit inquiry should be addressed to the auditor, should apply to circumstances that existed from the date of the balance sheet through the auditor's report date, and should have an effective date within two or three weeks of the report date.

Practitioner's Aids

EXHIBIT AU 337-1 — ILLUSTRATIVE AUDIT INQUIRY LETTER TO LEGAL COUNSEL

In connection with an audit of our financial statements at [*balance sheet date*] and for the [*period*] then ended, management of the Company has prepared, and furnished to our auditors [*name and address of auditors*], a description and evaluation of certain contingencies, including those set forth below involving matters with respect to which you have been engaged and to which you have devoted substantive attention on behalf of the Company in the form of legal consultation or representation. These contingencies are regarded by management of the Company as material for this purpose [*management may indicate a materiality limit if an understanding has been reached with the auditor*]. Your response should include matters that existed at [*balance sheet date*] and during the period from that date to the date of your response.

Pending or Threatened Litigation [excluding unasserted claims]

[Ordinarily the information would include the following: (1) the nature of the litigation, (2) the progress of the case to date, (3) how management is responding or intends to respond to the litigation (for example, to contest the case vigorously or to seek an out-of-court settlement), and (4) an evaluation of the likelihood of an unfavorable outcome and an estimate, if one can be made, of the amount or range of potential loss.]

Please furnish to our auditors such explanation, if any, that you consider necessary to supplement the foregoing information, including an explanation of those matters as to which your views may differ from those stated and an identification of the omission of any pending or threatened litigation, claims, and assessments or a statement that the list of such matters is complete.

Unasserted Claims and Assessments [considered by management to be probable of assertion and that, if asserted, would have at least a reasonable possibility of an unfavorable outcome]

[Ordinarily, management's information would include the following: (1) the nature of the matter, (2) how management intends to respond if the claim is asserted, and (3) an evaluation of the likelihood of an unfavorable outcome and an estimate, if one can be made, of the amount or range of potential loss.]

Please furnish to our auditors such explanation, if any, that you consider necessary to supplement the foregoing information, including an explanation of those matters as to which your views may differ from those stated.

We understand that whenever, in the course of performing legal services for us with respect to a matter recognized to involve an unasserted possible claim or assessment that may call for financial statement disclosure, if you have formed a professional conclusion that we should disclose or consider disclosure concerning such possible claim or assessment, as a matter of professional responsibility to us, you will so advise us and will consult with us concerning the question of such disclosure and the applicable requirements of Statement of Financial Accounting Standards No. 5. Please specifically confirm to our auditors that our understanding is correct.

Please specifically identify the nature of and reasons for any limitation on your response.

[*The auditor may request the client to inquire about additional matters — for example, unpaid or unbilled charges — or specified information on certain contractually assumed obligations of the company, such as guarantees or indebtedness of others.*]

PLANNING AID REMINDER: Auditing Interpretation No. 3 of AU 337 notes that when the client believes there are no unasserted claims or assessments to be identified that are probable of assertion and that, if asserted, would have a reasonable possibility of an unfavorable outcome, that section of the letter may be replaced with the following:

Unasserted claims and assessments — We have represented to our auditors that there are no unasserted possible claims that you have advised us are probable of assertion and must be disclosed, in accordance with Statement of Financial Accounting Standards No. 5. The second paragraph in the letter illustrated above would not be changed.

EXHIBIT AU 337-2 — ILLUSTRATIVE AUDIT INQUIRY LETTER TO LEGAL COUNSEL WHEREBY MANAGEMENT HAS REQUESTED THAT THE LAWYER PREPARE THE LIST OF PENDING OR THREATENED LITIGATION, CLAIMS, AND ASSESSMENTS

In connection with an audit of our financial statements as of [*balance sheet date*] and for the [*period*] then ended, please furnish our auditors, [*name and address of auditors*], with the information requested below concerning certain contingencies involving matters with respect to which you have devoted substantive attention on behalf of the Company in the form of legal consultation or representation. [*When a materiality limit has been established based on an understanding between management and the auditor, the following sentence should be added:* This request is limited to contingencies that amount to [*amount*] individually or items involving lesser amounts that exceed [*amount*] in the aggregate.]

Pending or Threatened Litigation, Claims, and Assessments

Regarding pending or threatened litigation, claims, and assessments, please include in your response (1) the nature of each matter; (2) the progress of each matter to date; (3) how the Company is responding or intends to respond (for example, to contest the case vigorously or seek an out-of-court settlement); and (4) an evaluation of the likelihood of an unfavorable outcome and an estimate, if one can be made, of the amount or range or potential loss.

Unasserted Claims and Assessments

We have represented to our auditors that there are no unasserted possible claims or assessments that you have advised us are probable of assertion and must be disclosed in accordance with FASB Statement

No. 5 (ASC 450). We understand that whenever, in the course of performing legal services for us with respect to a matter recognized to involve an unasserted possible claim or assessment that may call for financial statement disclosure, you have formed a professional conclusion that we should disclose or consider disclosure concerning such possible claim or assessment, as a matter of professional responsibility to us, you will so advise us and will consult with us concerning the question of such disclosure and the applicable requirements of FASB Statement No. 5 (ASC 450). Please specifically confirm to our auditors that our understanding is correct.

Other Matters

Your response should include matters that existed as of [*balance-sheet date*] and during the period from that date to the effective date of your response.

Please specifically identify the nature of and reasons for any limitations on your response.

Our auditors expect to have the audit completed about [*expected completion date*]. They would appreciate receiving your reply by that date with a specified effective date no earlier than [*ordinarily two weeks before expected completion date*].

SECTION 339

AUDIT DOCUMENTATION

Authoritative Pronouncements

SAS-103 — Audit Documentation (redrafted)

Auditing Interpretation No. 1 of AU 339 (June 1996) — Providing Access to, or Copies of, Audit Documentation to a Regulator

> **IMPORTANT NOTICE FOR 2011:** The Auditing Standards Board (ASB) is in the process of redrafting all of the auditing sections in *Codification of Statements on Auditing Standards* to converge U.S. GAAS with the International Standards on Auditing issued by the International Auditing and Assurance Standards Board. As part of this process, the newly redrafted standards will follow certain clarity drafting conventions adopted by the ASB. These clarity drafting conventions include: (1) establishing objectives for each standard; (2) including a definitions section, if appropriate; and (3) separating requirements from application guidance and other material. The ASB is planning to have all redrafted standards become effective on the same date, which is for audits of financial statements for periods ending on or after December 15, 2012. It is possible that the effective date might be delayed beyond that date. The ASB's clarity and convergence project will have a significant effect on the auditing standards applicable to audits of nonpublic companies, and the 2012 *GAAS Guide* will be appropriately modified to reflect these changes once the effective date of the standards is certain.

Overview

Audit documentation (working papers) should (1) support the auditor's representation that the engagement has been performed in accordance with GAAS and (2) substantiate the type of audit report (such as an unqualified or qualified opinion) issued; however, the specific type, content, and extent of documentation is to some degree dependent upon the characteristics of the particular engagement and the audit methodology employed. The specific nature of the audit documentation is a matter of the auditor's professional judgment.

The auditor must prepare audit documentation for each engagement in sufficient detail for an experienced auditor with no previous involvement with the engagement to understand the following:

- The nature, timing, and extent of audit procedures performed

- The results of the audit tests performed and the evidence collected

- Conclusions drawn on significant matters

- That the accounting records agree or reconcile to the audited financial statements (or other audited information)

An experienced auditor is an individual who has the competencies and skills that would have enabled him or her to have performed the engagement. This hypothetical experienced auditor may be either inside or outside the auditor's firm. The individual should have practical audit experience and a reasonable understanding of the audit process, generally accepted auditing standards and related regulatory requirements, the business environment in which the entity operates, and the auditing and financial reporting issues relevant to the entity's industry.

> **PUBLIC COMPANY IMPLICATION:** The standard for audit documentation for an audit of a public company is the PCAOB's AS-3 (Audit Documentation). Audit documentation represents the written record of the auditor's work, and it serves as the primary support for the auditor's conclusions. Audit planning, procedures performed, evidence gathered, and conclusions reached are all to be documented. The PCAOB states that a failure to prepare adequate audit documentation is serious, and inadequate audit documentation in a high-risk area is a very serious (authors' emphasis) violation of PCAOB standards. The PCAOB also states that an oral explanation of audit procedures without written documentary evidence is insufficient. In addition, audit documentation should be prepared at the time the audit procedure is performed.
>
> Audit documentation must be sufficient to permit an experienced auditor who has no previous connection to the audit engagement to (1) understand the nature, timing, extent, and results of the procedures performed, evidence obtained, and conclusions reached; (2) who did the work and when; and (3) who reviewed the work and when the review was done. Failure to maintain sufficient documentation leads to the presumption that the procedures were not applied, the evidence was not obtained, and the conclusions reached lacked adequate support.
>
> Significant findings and issues must be documented in an engagement completion document, which must document the auditor's response to all significant findings and issues and the basis for his or her conclusions with respect to each matter. The auditor also must document (and include as part of the audit documentation) any information that he or she acquires that is inconsistent with or that contradicts his or her final conclusions. The auditor

must document how he or she responded to the inconsistent information, including details on how differences in professional judgment between members of the engagement team were resolved.

AS-3 provides two important dates with respect to the preparation and retention of audit documentation: (1) the report release date and (2) the documentation completion date. The report release date is the date when the auditor gives the client permission to use his or her audit report. Prior to the report release date, the auditor must have completed all audit procedures (including clearing review notes) and accumulated sufficient evidence to support his or her conclusions and representations in his or her report. If the auditor performs additional audit procedures after the report release date, he or she should follow the guidance in interim auditing standards AU 390 (Consideration of Omitted Procedures after the Report Date) and AU 561 (Subsequent Discovery of Facts Existing at the Date of the Auditor's Report). Any addition to the audit documentation after the report release date must document the nature of the change, the date of the change, who prepared the change, and the reason for the change. If audit documentation is amended after the report release date, no previously existing documentation should be discarded.

The auditor has 45 days after the report release date to assemble and complete a final set of audit documentation (i.e., the documentation completion date). Additions to audit documentation can be made after the documentation completion date, but existing documentation must not be deleted or discarded. Any documentation added must include the date of the addition, who prepared it, and the reason for the addition.

IMPORTANT NOTICE FOR 2011: The Auditing Standards Board (ASB) issued a redraft of SAS-103 (Audit Documentation) to apply the ASB's drafting clarity conventions and converge audit documentation guidance with the International Standards on Auditing. The redrafted SAS-103 is similar to existing guidance. The major difference is that sections of the prior version of SAS-103 that were redundant with other auditing and quality control standards have been removed.

Standards of Fieldwork

Audit documentation (which may be in hard-copy form, electronic form, or other medium) developed for an engagement should demonstrate that the three standards of fieldwork were satisfied. The documentation generally includes the following:

- Audit programs

- Analyses

- Memoranda

- Confirmation letters

- A representation letter

- Checklists

- Correspondence concerning and summaries of significant findings or issues

- Abstracts/copies of entity documents (including significant contracts or agreements that support the accounting for specific transactions)

- Schedules or commentaries prepared by the auditor

- Schedules or commentaries prepared by the client and substantiated by the auditor

Audit documentation should identify the member of the audit team who performed a particular task (such as drawing a conclusion concerning the audit evidence obtained) and the date that the procedure was performed on. In addition, the documentation should identify who reviewed the audit work and the date on which the review took place. Although who reviewed the working papers must be documented, each individual working paper is not required to contain evidence of its review.

Nature and extent of documentation for specific audit objectives and procedures

While the nature and extent of audit documentation for (1) a particular audit area or (2) the employment of a specific audit procedure will vary, the following factors should be considered:

- The risk of material misstatement related to an account or class of transaction

- The degree of professional judgment required to perform the procedures and evaluate the results

- The nature of audit procedures used

- The significance of the audit evidence obtained to satisfy an audit objective being tested

- The nature and extent of exceptions identified during the engagement

- The need to document a conclusion (or the basis for a conclusion) that is not evident from reviewing the documentation of the work performed.

The auditor is not required to document every matter considered during the audit. The auditor also cannot rely on oral explanations to support the work performed or the conclusions reached, although oral explanations can supplement the audit documentation.

> **ENGAGEMENT STRATEGY:** The auditor is required to document auditor independence and staff training. The most efficient means of documenting these items may be centrally within the firm, although the firm can choose to include the documentation at the engagement level.

Identification of items tested

Specific items tested as part of the tests of operating effectiveness of controls and tests of details that are based on the inspection of documents or written confirmations should be identified in the audit documentation. For example, if 50 payroll transactions are tested as part of the tests of controls, the audit documentation must specifically identify which 50 items were tested. For example, the payroll check numbers could be listed in the audit documentation. Likewise, if accounts are confirmed as part of the audit of receivables, the specific accounts confirmed must be documented.

> **PLANNING AID REMINDER:** In some instances it is not necessary to specifically list each item tested. For example, if systematic sampling is used it is sufficient to identify the starting point and the selection interval. However, the method of documentation must enable an experienced auditor to reconstruct which specific sample items were tested as part of the engagement.

Significant audit findings or issues

Significant audit findings or issues encountered during an engagement should be documented. The documentation should include (1) a description of the audit finding or issue, (2) the audit procedures adopted to address the matter, and (3) the basis for drawing a particular conclusion about the matter. The Auditing Standards Board does not define a significant audit finding or issue; however, it does identify the following as examples:

- Significant matters related to the selection, application, and consistency of accounting principles, particularly related to the accounting for complex or unusual transactions and the accounting for items dependent on estimates, uncertainties, and management assumptions

- The results of employing audit procedures suggest that the financial statements (including the related notes) could be materially misstated

- The results of employing audit procedures cause the auditor to modify his or her assessment of the risk of material misstatement and his or her response to this reassessment

- The application of required audit procedures was difficult (e.g., problems receiving confirmations, missing documents, etc.)

- Findings that could lead to a modification of the standard auditor's report

- Audit adjustments

The auditor should document discussions that he or she has with management regarding significant findings or issues, including management's responses. The documentation should include a description of the significant findings or issues, the member of management who the issue was discussed with, and when the discussion took place. The auditor may also discuss significant findings and issues with other parties, including those charged with governance (e.g., the board of directors or audit committee), individuals in a financial reporting oversight role, others within the entity (e.g., internal audit), and outside parties (e.g., outside counsel).

The auditor should document the resolution of significant findings or issues. In some cases, the auditor may be aware of other information that is inconsistent with or contradicts the auditor's final conclusion. The auditor should document how he or she reconciled the final conclusion with any seemingly inconsistent other information.

> **ENGAGEMENT STRATEGY:** Documentation as discussed in this section is essential in supporting an auditor against claims of malpractice. Auditors should ensure that their audit procedures, results, and conclusions are well documented and carefully reviewed. Such steps are an important part of minimizing liability risk.

Documentation of departure from GAAS

SAS-102 defines an auditor's professional responsibilities in applying the SASs. Certain audit procedures are presumptively mandatory (denoted by the word "should" in the SAS). In those rare instances where an auditor departs from a presumptively mandatory requirement, he or she must document (1) why he or she departed from the presumptively mandatory requirement, and (2) how alternative procedures that were performed accomplished the objective of the presumptively mandatory requirement.

Dating of the auditor's report

The auditor should not date the audit report earlier than when he or she has obtained sufficient appropriate audit evidence to support the audit opinion (i.e., the audit report date). Sufficient appropriate audit evidence means that the (1) audit documentation has been reviewed, (2) financial statements, including the notes, have been prepared, and (3) management has taken responsibility for the financial statements. Normally the audit report date is near the report release date, the date that the auditor allows the client to use the audit report.

Assembly, retention, and protection of audit documentation

The audit documentation for an entire engagement is referred to as an audit file. The auditor should finish assembling the final audit file within 60 days of the report release date (documentation completion date), and the report release date is to be documented. Prior to the documentation completion date, the auditor may change the audit documentation to

- Complete the documentation and assembly of the audit evidence that was gathered prior to the date of the auditor's report

- Assemble the audit file (e.g., delete or discard superseded documentation)

- Sign off on file completion checklists

- Add information to the file received after the date of the auditor's report (e.g., a hard-copy confirmation that was previously faxed)

The auditor must not delete or discard any audit documentation between the documentation completion date and end of the document retention period. Audit documentation should be retained for a period of time that is sufficient to meet the objectives of the CPA firm, and to meet any applicable legal or regulatory requirements. In no instance can the document retention period be less than five years from the report release date. In some circumstances, the auditor may need to make an addition to the audit file after the documentation completion date. In such circumstances, the auditor should document (1) who made (reviewed) the change and when, (2) why the change was made, and (3) any effect of the change on the auditor's conclusions.

The auditor is responsible for developing appropriate controls over the generation, maintenance, and protection of audit documentation. These controls should

- Capture when and by whom audit documentation is created, changed, or reviewed

- Protect the integrity of the audit documentation throughout the audit

- Prevent unauthorized changes to the audit documentation

- Limit access to the audit documentation to the audit team and other authorized parties

> **PUBLIC COMPANY IMPLICATIONS:** SOX required the PCAOB to adopt an auditing standard that requires auditors to prepare and maintain audit documentation for a period of at least seven years. The nature and extent of documentation retained must be in sufficient detail to support the auditor's conclusions. SOX makes the knowing and willful destruction of audit documentation within the seven-year period a criminal offense. The PCAOB issued AS-3 (Audit Documentation), which contains the audit documentation requirements applicable to audits of public companies. SAS-103 bears many similarities to AS-3.

Confidentiality of audit documentation

A CPA firm should adopt reasonable administrative procedures to maintain the confidentiality (including preventing unauthorized access) of audit documentation in order to satisfy the AICPA Code of Professional Conduct (Rule 301) and related legal or regulatory requirements.

> **PLANNING AID REMINDER:** When audit documentation is maintained electronically, a CPA firm should be careful to retain the computer applications (that may be periodically upgraded or otherwise modified) that enable access to the documentation during the entire retention period.

Other required documentation

SAS-103 provides both general guidance and some limited, specific requirements for audit documentation. However, more specific documentation requirements are identified in other SASs. These requirements, along with those required by SAS-103, are listed in Exhibit AU 339-1.

Access to audit documentation

Audit documentation is the property of the auditor. The auditor may at his or her option make available to the client copies of the audit documentation as long as the independence and validity of the audit process is not compromised. In addition, governmental regulators may have a right to the audit documentation based on law, regulation, or the audit contract. Auditing Interpretation No. 1 of AU 339 states that when regulators have requested access to audit documentation, the auditor should observe the following guidance:

- Consider notifying the client that regulators have requested access to the audit documentation, and state that the auditor intends to comply with the request.

- Make arrangements (time, date, place, etc.) with the regulators concerning access to the audit documentation.

- Establish procedures that allow the auditor to maintain control over the audit documentation.

In addition to the above procedures, the auditor should consider sending a letter to the regulatory agency (probably requesting a signed acknowledgment of receipt of the letter) that explains the role of the auditor and the nature of the audit documentation. (Exhibit AU 339-2 is an example of such a letter.) The auditor should not agree to transfer the ownership of the audit documentation to the regulatory agency.

When a regulatory agency requests the auditor's audit documentation but there is no legal basis for the request (no applicable law, regulation, or audit contract requirement), the auditor should evaluate the purpose for the request. That evaluation may include consultation with legal counsel. If the auditor agrees with the request, the auditor should obtain permission for access to the audit documentation from the client (preferably in writing). In some instances the client may request an inspection of the audit documentation before granting the regulatory agency access to it. If the auditor agrees to the client's request, the auditor should maintain control over the audit documentation.

Some regulatory agencies may hire a third party to inspect audit documentation. Under this circumstance, the auditor should follow the same procedures that would apply if the regulatory agency itself were inspecting the audit documentation. In addition, the auditor should obtain from the regulatory agency a statement (preferably in writing) that the third party is "acting on behalf of the regulator and agreement from the third party that he or she is subject to the same restriction on disclosure and use of audit documentation and the information contained therein as the regulator."

> **OBSERVATION:** The guidance established by the Interpretation does not apply to requests from (1) the Internal Revenue Service, (2) peer review programs (and similar programs) established by the AICPA or state societies of CPAs, (3) proceedings arising from alleged violations of ethical standards, or (4) subpoenas. In addition, audit documentation can be shown to another firm during the due diligence process to sell or merge an accounting practice, but the firm must take appropriate precautions to protect client data (e.g., require a signed confidentiality agreement).

Practitioner's Aids

Exhibit AU 339-1 is a checklist for audit documentation required by various SASs, including SAS-103.

EXHIBIT AU 339-1 — SASs THAT IDENTIFY SPECIFIC AUDIT DOCUMENTATION

Pronouncement	Nature of Documentation	Reference
SAS-1 (Codification of Auditing Standards and Procedures [AU 561])	When and by whom additional auditing procedures were performed as a result of subsequent discovery of facts that existed at the date of the report but that were not known to the auditor at that time	Paragraph 25 (AU 339.25)
	When and by whom the additional procedures were reviewed	
	The results obtained from performing additional audit procedures	
	The effect on the auditor's conclusions (including the continuing appropriateness of the original audit opinion issued) as a result of the subsequent discovery of facts that existed at the date of the audit report	
SAS-12 (Inquiry of a Client's Lawyer Concerning Litigation, Claims, and Assessments [AU 337])	Obtain assurances from management concerning unasserted claims.	Paragraph 5d (AU 337.5d)
	Obtain a response concerning matters covered by the audit inquiry letter in a conference.	Paragraph 10 (AU 337.10)
SAS-46 (Consideration of Omitted Procedures after the Report Date [AU 390])	When and by whom the omitted procedure was performed and reviewed	Paragraph 24 (AU 339.24)
	The reasons why the omitted procedure needs to be performed and the results obtained from performing the procedure	
	Any effect of performing the procedure on the auditor's conclusions	
SAS-47 (Audit Risk and Materiality in Conducting an Audit [AU 312])	Document the nature and effect of aggregated misstatements and audit conclusions.	Paragraph 40 (AU 312.40), as amended by SAS-96
SAS-51 (Reporting on Financial Statements Prepared for Use in Other Countries [AU 534])	Obtain written representations from management concerning the purpose and use of the financial statements prepared using the accounting principles of another country.	Paragraph 2 (AU 534.02)

Pronouncement	Nature of Documentation	Reference
SAS-54 (Illegal Acts by Clients [AU 317])	Document certain oral communications to the audit committee or its equivalent regarding illegal acts.	Paragraph 17 (AU 317.17)
SAS-56 (Analytical Procedures [AU 329])	Document (1) expectations where not evident from work performed, (2) results of comparing expectations to recorded amounts or ratios computed and (3) additional procedures (and their results) arising from identifying unexpected results.	Paragraph 22 (AU 329.22), as amended by SAS-96
SAS-58 (Reports on Audited Financial Statements [AU 508])	Obtain representations from the successor auditor and management before reissuing report.	Paragraph 71 (AU 508.71)
SAS-59 (The Auditor's Consideration of an Entity's Ability to Continue as a Going Concern [AU 341])	Document (1) circumstances that raised substantial doubt about the entity's ability to continue as a going concern, (2) procedures performed to evaluate management's plans, (3) audit conclusions, and (4) the effect of the matter on the financial statements and the audit report.	Paragraph 17 (AU 341.17), as amended by SAS-96
SAS-67 (The Confirmation Process [AU 330])	Document oral confirmations.	Paragraph 29 (AU 330.29)
	Document the reason for not confirming accounts receivables, if applicable.	Paragraph 35 (AU 330.35)
SAS-74 (Compliance Auditing Considerations in Audits of Governmental Entities and Recipients of Governmental Financial Assistance [AU 801])	Document certain oral communications to management and the audit committee or its equivalent.	Paragraph 23 (AU 801.23)
SAS-85 (Management Representations [AU 333])	Obtain written representations from management.	Paragraphs 1-14 (AU 333.01-333.14)
SAS-95 (Generally Accepted Auditing Standards [AU 150])	Document justification for a departure from a presumptively mandatory requirement in a SAS	Paragraph 4 (AU 150.04), as amended by SAS-103
SAS-99 (Consideration of Fraud in a Financial Statement Audit [AU 316])	Document the audit team brainstorming discussion on fraud (when it occurred, who participated, and what was discussed)	Paragraph 83 (AU 316.83)
	Procedures performed to identify and assess the risks of material misstatement due to fraud	

Pronouncement	Nature of Documentation	Reference
	Risks identified and the auditor's response	
	If revenue recognition is not identified as a risk factor, the reasons why	
	Results of procedures related to management override of controls	
	Other conditions or analytical procedures that led the auditor to perform additional auditing procedures	
	Fraud-related communications to management, the audit committee, and others	
SAS-107 (Audit Risk and Materiality in Conducting an Audit [AU 312])	Materiality and tolerable misstatement, including how determined	Paragraph 69 (AU 312.69)
	Summary of nontrivial uncorrected misstatements	
	Audit conclusion as to whether the uncorrected misstatements cause a material misstatement	
	Misstatements identified during the audit that were corrected by management	
	Uncorrected misstatements should be documented so that the auditor can	
	• Separately consider the effects of known and likely misstatements, including uncorrected misstatements from prior periods	Paragraph 70 (AU 312.70)
	• Consider the aggregate effect of misstatements	
	• Consider the qualitative factors that affect an evaluation of materiality	
SAS-108 (Planning and Supervision [AU 311])	Prepare written audit programs	Paragraph 20 (AU 311.20)
SAS-109 (Understanding the Entity and Its Environment and Assessing the Risks of Material Misstatement [AU 314])	Audit team discussion of the susceptibility of the client's financial statements to error or fraud (when the discussion occurred, who participated, subjects discussed, and planned audit responses)	Paragraph 122 (AU 314.122)

Pronouncement	Nature of Documentation	Reference
	The auditor's understanding of the entity's environment and its internal control (including sources of information and risk assessment procedures)	
	The auditor's assessment of the risk of material misstatement at the financial statement level and the assertion level and the auditor's basis for these assessments	
	Risks identified and evaluation of related controls	
SAS-110 (Performing Audit Procedures in Response to Assessed Risks and Evaluating the Audit Evidence Obtained [AU 318])	Overall audit response to the assessed risk of misstatement at the financial statement level	Paragraph 77 (AU 318.77)
	Nature, timing, and extent of audit procedures	
	Linkage of procedures to risks at the assertion level	
	Results of audit procedures	
	Decision regarding the operating effectiveness of controls obtained in a prior audit and their use in the current audit	
SAS-114 (The Auditor's Communication with Those Charged with Governance) [AU 380]	Required communications to those charged with governance about matters involving the auditor's responsibilities, the planned scope and timing of the audit, and significant audit findings	Paragraph 64 (AU 380.64)
SAS-115 (Communication of Internal Control Related Matters Identified in an Audit [AU 325])	Communication of significant deficiencies and material weaknesses in internal control made to management and those charged with governance	Paragraph 17 (AU 325.17)
SAS-116 (Interim Financial Information [AU 722])	Documentation in support of the review of interim financial information, including	Paragraph 52 (AU 722.52)
	• Findings or issues that may indicate that the interim financial information is materially misstated and the auditor's actions to address these findings	

Pronouncement	Nature of Documentation	Reference
	• Basis for the auditor's final conclusions	
	• Nature, timing, and extent of procedures performed and results	
	• Who performed and reviewed the work	
	• Evidence that the interim financial statements reconciled to the underlying accounting records	

Exhibit AU 339-2 is an example of a letter that may be sent to a regulatory agency in response to its request for access to the auditor's documentation.

EXHIBIT AU 339-2 — LETTER FOR REGULATORY AGENCY THAT REQUESTS ACCESS TO AUDIT DOCUMENTATION

Your representatives have requested access to our audit documentation in connection with our audit of the December 31, 20X8 financial statements of [*name of client*]. It is our understanding that the purpose of your request is [*state purpose: for example*, "to facilitate your regulatory examination"].

Our audit of [*name of client*]'s December 31, 20X8 financial statements was conducted in accordance with auditing standards generally accepted in the United States of America, the objective of which is to form an opinion as to whether the financial statements, which are the responsibility and representations of management, present fairly, in all material respects, the financial position, results of operations, and cash flows in conformity with generally accepted accounting principles. Under generally accepted auditing standards, we have the responsibility, within the inherent limitations of the auditing process, to design our audit to provide reasonable assurance that errors and fraud that have a material effect on the financial statements will be detected, and to exercise due care in the conduct of our audit. The concept of selective testing of the data being audited, which involved judgment both as to the number of transactions to be audited and as to the areas to be tested, has been generally accepted as a valid and sufficient basis for an audit to express an opinion on financial statements. Thus, our audit, based on the concept of selective testing, is subject to the inherent risk that material errors or fraud, if they exist, would not be detected. In addition, an audit does not address the possibility that material errors or fraud may occur in the future. Also, our use of professional judgment and the assessment of materiality for the purpose of our audit means that matters may have existed that would have been assessed differently by you.

The audit documentation was prepared for the purpose of providing the principal support for our report on [*name of client*]'s December 31, 20X8, financial statements and to aid in the conduct and supervision of our audit. The audit documentation is the principal record of auditing procedures performed, evidence obtained, and conclusions reached in the engagement. The auditing procedures that were performed were limited to those we considered necessary under generally accepted auditing standards to enable us to formulate and express an opinion on the financial statements taken as a whole. Accordingly, we make no representation as to the sufficiency or appropriateness, for your purposes, of either the information contained in our audit documentation or our auditing procedures. In addition, any notations, comments, and individual conclusions appearing on any of the audit documents do not stand alone, and should not be read as an opinion on any individual amounts, accounts, balances, or transactions.

Our audit of [*name of client*]'s December 31, 20X8, financial statement was performed for the purpose stated above and has not been planned or conducted in contemplation of your [*state purpose: for example*, "regulatory examination"] or for the purpose of assessing [*name of client*]'s compliance with laws and regulations. Therefore, items of possible interest to you may not have been specifically addressed. Accordingly, our audit and the audit documentation prepared in connection therewith, should not supplant other inquiries and procedures that should be undertaken by the [*name of regulatory agency*] for the purpose of monitoring and regulating the financial affairs of the [*name of client*]. In addition, we have not audited any financial statements of [*name of client*] since [*date of audited balance sheet referred to in the first paragraph above*] nor have we performed any auditing procedures since [*date*], the date of our auditor's report, and significant events or circumstances may have occurred since that date.

The audit documentation constitutes and reflects work performed or evidence obtained by [*name of auditor*] in its capacity as independent auditor for [*name of client*]. The documents contain trade secrets and confidential commercial and financial information of our firm and [*name of client*] that is privileged and confidential, and we expressly reserve all rights with respect to disclosures to third parties.

Accordingly, we request confidential treatment under the Freedom of Information Act or similar laws and regulations when requests are made for the audit documentation or information contained therein or any derived there from. We further request that written notice be given to our firm before distribution of the information in the audit documentation [*or copies thereof*] to others, including other governmental agencies, except when such distribution is required by law or regulations. [*If it is expected that copies will be requested, add the following:* Any copies of our audit documentation that we agree to provide you will be identified as "Confidential Treatment Requested by [*name of auditor, address, and telephone number*]."]

The above illustrative letter should be appropriately modified to reflect the circumstances of the engagement. Some of the modifications that may be needed include the following:

- When the audit has been conducted in accordance with GAAS and other established auditing procedures (such as generally accepted governmental auditing standards), the letter should be appropriately modified.

- When the audit was conducted in accordance with the Single Audit Act of 1984, and other federal audit requirements, the letter should be modified to explain the object of the audit.

- When the letter is sent to the regulatory agency at the request of management (rather than by law, regulation, or audit contract), the letter should state that "the management of X Company has authorized us to provide you access to our audit documentation in order to facilitate your regulatory examination."

- When the financial statements are based on regulatory accounting principles, the letter should be appropriately modified.

- When the regulatory agency has asked for photocopies of the audit documentation, the letter should state that "any photocopies of our audit documentation we agree to provide you will be identified as 'Confidential Treatment Request by [*name of auditor, address, telephone number*].'"

- When the audit engagement has not been completed, the letter should be modified to describe that fact and to put the regulatory agency on guard that the workpapers may change based on the performance of additional audit procedures (generally, the auditor should not agree to supply the regulatory agency with incomplete audit documentation).

SECTION 341

THE AUDITOR'S CONSIDERATION OF AN ENTITY'S ABILITY TO CONTINUE AS A GOING CONCERN

Authoritative Pronouncements

SAS-59 — The Auditor's Consideration of an Entity's Ability to Continue as a Going Concern

SAS-64 — Omnibus Statement on Auditing Standards — 1990

SAS-77 — Amendments to Statements on Auditing Standards No. 22, "Planning and Supervision," No. 59 "The Auditor's Consideration of an Entity's Ability to Continue as a Going Concern," and SAS-62, "Special Reports"

SAS-103 — Audit Documentation

SAS-113 — Omnibus Statement on Auditing Standards — 2006

SAS-114 — The Auditor's Communication with Those Charged with Governance

Auditing Interpretation No. 1 of AU 341 (August 1995) — Eliminating a Going Concern Explanatory Paragraph from a Reissued Report

> **IMPORTANT NOTICE FOR 2011:** The Auditing Standards Board (ASB) is in the process of redrafting all of the auditing sections in *Codification of Statements on Auditing Standards* to converge U.S. GAAS with the International Standards on Auditing issued by the International Auditing and Assurance Standards Board. As part of this process, the newly redrafted standards will follow certain clarity drafting conventions adopted by the ASB. These clarity drafting conventions include: (1) establishing objectives for each standard; (2) including a definitions section, if appropriate; and (3) separating requirements from application guidance and other material. The ASB is planning to have all redrafted standards become effective on the same date, which is for audits of financial statements for periods ending on or after December 15, 2012. It is possible that the effective date might be delayed beyond that date. The ASB's clarity and convergence project will have a significant effect on the auditing standards applicable to audits of nonpublic companies, and the 2012 *GAAS Guide* will be appropriately modified to reflect these changes once the effective date of the standards is certain.

Overview

Financial statements are usually prepared on the assumption that the entity will continue as a going concern. When a company decides or is forced to liquidate, the going-concern concept is not appropriate, and assets should be presented at their estimated net realizable values and legally enforceable liabilities should be classified according to priorities established by law.

SAS-59 (The Auditor's Consideration of an Entity's Ability to Continue as a Going Concern) states that as part of an audit, the auditor should evaluate conditions or events discovered during the engagement that raise questions about the appropriateness of the going-concern assumption. The auditor may identify such conditions or events at various points during the engagement, including during the performance of analytical procedures, when reading of responses received from the entity's legal counsel, and when evaluating the entity's compliance with restrictions imposed by loan agreements.

> **PLANNING AID REMINDER:** Information that raises questions about going concern generally relates to the entity's ability to meet its maturing obligations without selling operating assets, restructuring debt, or revising operations based on outside pressures or similar strategies. SAS-59 states that the projection of the going-concern concept is limited to a "reasonable period of time," which is defined by SAS-59 as not exceeding one year beyond the date of the financial statements being audited.

Promulgated Procedures Checklist

The auditor should perform the following procedures when considering an entity's ability to continue as a going concern:

- Evaluate relevant information obtained during the course of the engagement.

- Identify and evaluate management's plans related to going concern.

- Consider the effect of the evidence on disclosures and the audit report.

- Document audit results.

Analysis and Application of Procedures

Evaluate relevant information obtained during the course of the engagement

Although the auditor is not specifically required to employ procedures to identify conditions or events that might raise substantial doubt, he or she should be sensitive to implications pertaining to going concern in the audit evidence collected during the audit.

SAS-59 provides the examples in Exhibit AU 341-1 as conditions and events that may raise substantial doubt about an entity's ability to continue as a going concern.

EXHIBIT AU 341-1 — CONDITIONS AND EVENTS THAT MAY RAISE A SUBSTANTIAL-DOUBT QUESTION

Condition or Event	Specific Example
Negative trends	• Recurring operating losses • Working capital deficiencies • Negative cash flows from operations • Adverse key financial ratios
Other indications of possible agreements	• Default on loan or similar financial difficulties • Arrearages in dividends
Other indications of possible financial difficulties	• Denial of usual trade credit from vendors • Restructuring of debt • Noncompliance with statutory capital requirements • Need to seek new sources of financing • Need to sell substantial assets
Internal matters	• Labor difficulties, such as work stoppages • Substantial dependence on the success of a particular project • Uneconomic long-term commitments • Need to significantly revise operations
External matters or similar matters that might affect the entity's ability to continue operations	• Legal proceedings, legislation • Loss of key franchise, license, or patent • Loss of principal customer or vendor • Occurrence of uninsured catastrophe

When the audit evidence raises substantial doubt, the auditor might consider obtaining additional evidence that could remove the auditor's substantial doubt.

FRAUD POINTER: The Committee of Sponsoring Organizations of the Treadway Commission (COSO) issued a study in 2010 entitled "Fraudulent Financial Reporting: 1998 – 2007, An Analysis of U.S. Public Companies" that analyzed SEC enforcement actions alleging violations of the antifraud provisions of the securities acts. The study found that many of the companies involved in fraud were financially distressed in periods preceding the fraud. Over a quarter of the companies faced net losses, and several experienced downward trends in net income preceding the first year of the fraud. As auditors observe conditions affecting an entity's ability to continue as a going concern, they should consider whether those conditions create significant incentives or pressures that might lead management to perpetrate fraudulent financial reporting.

Identify and evaluate management's plans related to going concern

If the auditor concludes that there is substantial doubt about the continued existence of the entity as a going concern for a reasonable period of time, he or she should identify and evaluate management's plans to mitigate the effects of the adverse conditions or events. SAS-59 identifies the examples in Exhibit AU 341-2 as plans and factors that are relevant to the evaluation of those plans.

EXHIBIT AU 341-2 — PLANS AND FACTORS RELEVANT TO THE EVALUATION OF MANAGEMENT'S PLANS

Planned Action	*Factors Relevant to Evaluation of Planned Action*
Sale of assets	• Restrictions on the sale of assets
	• Likely marketability of assets
	• Effects from sale of assets
Borrow or restructure debt	• Likelihood of raising funds based on existing or committed debt arrangements
	• Existing or committed arrangements for restructuring debt or obtaining guarantees for loans
	• Restrictions on ability to borrow or use assets as collateral
Reduce or delay expenditures	• Feasibility of reducing or postponing expenditures
	• Effects of reducing or postponing expenditures

Planned Action	Factors Relevant to Evaluation of Planned Action
Increase ownership equity	• Feasibility of increasing equity based on existing or committed arrangements
	• Flexibility of dividend policy
	• Ability to raise funds from affiliates or other investors

The auditor should consider obtaining audit evidence to support planned actions that are significant to the substantial-doubt question.

Some management strategies may in part be evaluated through the auditor's investigation of management's prospective financial statements. Specific audit procedures that the auditor may employ include the following:

- Read the prospective financial statements.

- Identify fundamental assumptions used to prepare the prospective financial statements.

- Evaluate the prospective financial statements on the basis of the auditor's familiarity with the client's operations.

- Compare the prospective financial statements for prior periods with actual results.

- Compare the prospective financial statements for the current period with actual results to date.

During the evaluation of fundamental assumptions used to prepare the prospective financial statements, the auditor should direct special emphasis to the following assumptions:

- Assumptions that have a material effect on the prospective financial statements

- Assumptions that have a high degree of uncertainty

- Assumptions that are inconsistent with past patterns

> **OBSERVATION:** If the auditor discovers material factors that are not reflected in the preparation of the prospective financial statements, such discoveries should be discussed with management with the understanding that the statements may have to be revised.

Consider the effect of the evidence on disclosures and the audit report

Once the auditor has evaluated management's strategies designed to mitigate the adverse effects of conditions or events that raise substantial doubt about continued existence, the auditor must determine whether substantial doubt exists about the going-concern concept.

When events or conditions exist that, when considered in the aggregate, indicate there could be substantial doubt about the entity's ability to continue as a going concern for a reasonable period of time, the auditor is required to communicate certain matters to those charged with governance. These required communications include the nature of the events or conditions identified, the possible effect on the financial statements and the adequacy of related disclosures in the financial statements, and the effects on the auditor's report.

If substantial doubt does not exist, there is no need to modify the auditor's report. However, the auditor should consider whether the conditions or events that originally created the question about going concern should be disclosed in the financial statements. The disclosure might include the possible effect of the conditions or events and mitigating factors (including management's plans).

If the auditor concludes that substantial doubt exists, the effects of conditions or events should be considered as they relate to (1) adequate disclosures in the financial statements and (2) modification to the auditor's report.

Adequate disclosures

If the auditor concludes that substantial doubt exists about the client's ability to continue in existence, care must be taken to ensure that presentations and related disclosures in the financial statements properly reflect the (1) recoverability and classification of assets and (2) amount and classification of liabilities. In addition, the auditor should consider whether disclosures related to the possible discontinuation of operations are adequate in the financial statements. SAS-59 notes that the disclosure might include the following:

- Conditions or events that gave rise to the substantial doubt concerning continued existence

- Possible effects of the conditions or events

- Management's assessments concerning the significance of the conditions or events

- Other factors that may aggravate or mitigate the conditions or events

- Management's strategies that will attempt to deal with the adverse conditions or events

- Possible discontinuance of operations

Report modifications

If an auditor concludes that substantial doubt exists about the continued existence of the client, the audit report should be modified by adding an explanatory paragraph. When the auditor believes that the financial statements can still be relied on, the report modification is limited to a reference to the going-concern matter in the report, but the opinion expressed is unqualified.

The substantial-doubt question is discussed in an explanatory paragraph following the opinion paragraph. SAS-64 (AU 341, AU 508, AU 543) (Omnibus Statement on Auditing Standards — 1990) requires that the explanatory paragraph include the phrase "substantial doubt about its [the entity's] ability to continue as a going concern," or similar wording. If similar wording is used, the terms "substantial doubt" and "going concern" must be used in the phrase.

When an auditor concludes that there is substantial doubt about an entity's ability to continue as a going concern, the audit report should not use language that suggests that the conclusion is conditional on future events. Specifically, SAS-77 (AU 311, AU 341, AU 623) notes that the use of conditional terminology — such as "if the company is unable to obtain re-financing, there may be substantial doubt about the company's ability to continue as a going concern" — is precluded.

The introductory, scope, and opinion paragraphs make no reference to the explanatory paragraph. An example of an explanatory paragraph based on a substantial-doubt question is presented below:

> The accompanying financial statements have been prepared assuming that the Company will continue as a going concern. As discussed in Note X to the financial statements, the Company is involved in litigation concerning alleged patent infringement. Because operations of the Company could be substantially impeded if the charges are upheld, the pending litigation raises substantial doubt about its ability to continue as a going concern. Management's plans in regard to the litigation are also described in Note X. The financial statements do not include any adjustments that might result from the outcome of this uncertainty.

When the auditor concludes that the uncertainty related to the substantial-doubt question is so significant that an opinion cannot be expressed on the financial statements, a disclaimer of opinion may be expressed.

The modification of the auditor's report because of a substantial-doubt question in the current year does not imply that the auditor's report on a prior year's financial statements (presented on a comparative basis) should also be modified.

During the current year, a question of substantial doubt contained in an auditor's report on a prior year's financial statements may no longer be applicable. Under this circumstance, the explanatory paragraph should not be repeated in the auditor's report on the comparative financial statements.

> **ENGAGEMENT STRATEGY:** To not include the explanatory paragraph is not a change in the opinion expressed by the auditor; therefore, not including the paragraph does not require that the auditor observe the report guidelines established in SAS-58 (AU 508) concerning changes of opinions.

Although the auditor is responsible for including an explanatory paragraph in the auditor's report when a substantial-doubt question arises, the auditor is not responsible for predicting the outcome of future events. Thus, the liquidation of an entity (even within one year of the date of the financial statements) does not imply that the audit was substandard when an explanatory paragraph has not been included in the auditor's report. Similarly, the lack of including an explanatory paragraph in the auditor's report should not be taken as an assurance that the entity will continue as a going concern within a reasonable period of time. The auditor's evaluation is based on his or her knowledge of relevant conditions and events that exist at or have occurred prior to the date of the auditor's report.

SAS-77 (AU 311, AU 341, AU 623) prohibits the use of conditional language when a substantial-doubt explanatory paragraph is presented. Two examples of unacceptable language that are provided by SAS-77 (AU 311, AU 341, AU 623) are as follows:

> If the company continues to suffer recurring losses from operations and continues to have a net capital deficiency, there may be substantial doubt about its ability to continue as a going concern.
>
> The company has been unable to renegotiate its expiring credit agreements. Unless the company is able to obtain financial support, there is substantial doubt about its ability to continue as a going concern.

The going-concern paragraph should be included in subsequent auditor's reports as long as substantial doubt about the entity's existence continues. If the substantial-doubt condition ceases in a future period, there is no need to include the substantial-doubt explanatory paragraph for reports that cover previous periods in which the substantial-doubt condition was originally applicable.

After the auditor has issued a report that refers to a going-concern issue, the client may request the auditor to reissue the report and remove the going-concern reference because the client believes the circumstances that led to the uncertainty have been changed. Because the request by the client constitutes a new engagement, the auditor is not obligated to accept it. If the auditor accepts the engagement, the circumstances related to the going-concern issue should be examined to determine whether it is appropriate to revise the report.

Auditing Interpretation No. 1 of AU 341 (August 1995) titled "Eliminating a Going-Concern Explanatory Paragraph from a Reissued Report" notes that the auditor is not obligated to reissue a report; however, if the auditor decides to do so, he or she should perform the following procedures:

- Audit the event or transaction that prompted the request to delete the going-concern paragraph.

- Perform procedures related to subsequent events as described in AU 560.11 – AU 560.12.

- Consider the factors related to the going-concern concept as described in AU 341.06 – AU341.11.

> **ENGAGEMENT STRATEGY:** In addition to the listed procedures, the auditor should conduct other procedures he or she deems appropriate. Based on the results of applying those procedures, the auditor should reassess the going-concern status of the client.

Document audit results

The auditor should document the following in the audit files when a going-concern issue has been raised and investigated based on the standards discussed in AU 341:

- Conditions or events that are the basis for the going-concern substantial doubt

- Elements of management's plans that have a significant effect on overcoming the adverse effects of the conditions or events identified above

- Audit procedures performed and evidence gathered related to the significant elements of management's plans

- The auditor's conclusion about the ability of the client to continue as a going concern for a reasonable period of time

- If the auditor concludes that there is substantial doubt about the client continuing as a going concern, document the possible effects on the financial statements (including disclosures)

- If the auditor concludes that the substantial doubt issue has been alleviated, document the conclusion regarding the need for disclosure of the conditions or events

- The conclusion regarding whether an explanatory paragraph should be included in the audit report

- If disclosures in the financial statements concerning the going-concern issue are inadequate, document the conclusion regarding whether the audit report should be qualified or an adverse opinion should be expressed

> **FRAUD POINTER:** The Committee of Sponsoring Organizations of the Treadway Commission (COSO) issued a study in 2010 entitled "Fraudulent Financial Reporting: 1998–2007, An Analysis of U.S. Public Companies" that analyzed SEC enforcement actions alleging fraud. The study found that a large portion of the companies engaging in fraud filed for Chapter 11 bankruptcy, were defunct, taken over by a regulator, delisted from a stock exchange, or sold within two years of the SEC investigation. Auditors of companies where fraud has allegedly occurred should be sensitive to conditions affecting going concern in periods after the alleged fraud has been revealed.

Practitioner's Aids

EXHIBIT AU 341-3 — EVALUATING AN ENTITY'S ABILITY TO CONTINUE AS A GOING CONCERN

Use the following procedures, which are adapted from guidance found in SAS-59 (The Auditor's Consideration of an Entity's Ability to Continue as a Going Concern), as a guide for evaluating an entity's ability to continue as a going concern. The program is only a guide, and professional judgment should be exercised to determine how the guidance established should be adapted to a particular engagement.

Initial and date each procedure as it is completed. If the procedure is not relevant to this engagement, place "N/A" (not applicable) in the space provided for an initial.

Client Name: _____

Date of Financial Statements: _____

	Initials	Date	Audit Documentation Reference
1. Evaluate relevant information obtained during the course of the engagement.	___	___	_____
2. Identify and evaluate management's plans related to going concern.	___	___	_____
3. Consider the effect of the evidence on disclosures and the engagement report.	___	___	_____
4. Consider whether the following disclosures in the financial statements are appropriate:	___	___	_____
• Factors that are the basis for raising the question of going concern	___	___	_____
• Possible effects on the financial statements of the factors that raised the question of going concern	___	___	_____
• Management's assessment of the significance of the factors and any mitigating circumstances	___	___	_____
• Possible discontinuance of operations	___	___	_____

	Initials	Date	*Audit Documentation Reference*

- Management's plans to deal with the current circumstances (including relevant prospective information) ___ ___ _____

- Information related to asset re-coverability and classification and the amount and classification of liabilities ___ ___ _____

Other engagement procedures: _____

_____
_____
_____
_____

Reviewed by: _____
Date: _____

_____

OBSERVATION: If through performing other audit procedures the auditor identifies conditions and events that may raise questions about the entity's ability to continue as a going concern and management has not developed plans to address the issue, he or she would ordinarily conclude that doubts about the going-concern issue are valid and would consider modifying his or her report in a manner required by SAS-59.

SECTION 342
AUDITING ACCOUNTING ESTIMATES

Authoritative Pronouncements

SAS-57 — Auditing Accounting Estimates

SAS-113 — Omnibus Statement on Auditing Standards — 2006

Auditing Interpretation No. 1 of AU 342 (October 2000) — Performance and Reporting Guidance Related to Fair Value Disclosures

> **IMPORTANT NOTICE FOR 2011:** The Auditing Standards Board (ASB) is in the process of redrafting all of the auditing sections in *Codification of Statements on Auditing Standards* to converge U.S. GAAS with the International Standards on Auditing issued by the International Auditing and Assurance Standards Board. As part of this process, the newly redrafted standards will follow certain clarity drafting conventions adopted by the ASB. These clarity drafting conventions include: (1) establishing objectives for each standard; (2) including a definitions section, if appropriate; and (3) separating requirements from application guidance and other material. The ASB is planning to have all redrafted standards become effective on the same date, which is for audits of financial statements for periods ending on or after December 15, 2012. It is possible that the effective date might be delayed beyond that date. The ASB's clarity and convergence project will have a significant effect on the auditing standards applicable to audits of nonpublic companies, and the 2012 *GAAS Guide* will be appropriately modified to reflect these changes once the effective date of the standards is certain.

Overview

SAS-57 (Auditing Accounting Estimates) defines "accounting estimate" as "an approximation of a financial statement element, item, or account." Accounting estimates are made to measure past transactions or events (loss contingency arising from pending lawsuits) or to measure assets (net realizable value of accounts receivable) or liabilities (accrual related to warranty contracts).

It is management's responsibility to establish reasonable accounting estimates — by reviewing past experiences and evaluating these experiences in the context of current and expected future conditions. Thus, accounting estimates are based on both objective factors (past transactions and events) and subjective factors (projecting the likely outcome of future transactions and events). Although management is responsible for accounting estimates, the auditor must collect sufficient audit evidence to determine that accounting estimates are reasonable. Because of the uncertainty related to accounting estimates and the higher possibility of misstatement, an auditor must have a greater degree of skepticism when planning and performing procedures related to the audit of accounting estimates.

Auditing estimates that are part of financial statements can often prove to be a significant engagement challenge because they often require a considerable amount of professional judgment. The AICPA has published an Audit Practice Guide titled "Auditing Estimates and Other Soft Accounting Information," which is summarized in a Practitioner's Aid at the end of this Section.

> **FRAUD POINTER:** As described in SAS-99, one of the three conditions of fraud is the presence of "opportunities," or circumstances that allow fraud to be perpetrated. The presence of accounting estimates in financial statements can create significant opportunities for management to materially misstate financial statements. The complexity involved in the estimation process and the need for assumptions to be made by management when developing an estimate can provide a significant opportunity for the estimate to be materially misstated. As they identify and evaluate factors related to fraud risks, auditors should consider the extent that estimates are required in client financial statements.

Management's internal control

As for all classes of transactions and events that affect the financial statements, management should adopt, either formally or informally, a process for developing accounting estimates. The process should include identifying circumstances that require accounting estimates, and collecting and evaluating information that leads to the development of reasonable accounting estimates.

Many factors, such as the availability of reliable data, the required complexity of the evaluation process, and the extent that assumptions must be made by management, can increase the likelihood of accounting estimates leading to material misstatement in the financial statements. In addition, when assessing the risk of misstatement the auditor should consider the entity's internal control relating to the development of accounting estimates. The entity's internal control should include the following elements:

- Use of controls that allow the entity to identify circumstances requiring the development of accounting estimates

- Development of sufficient and reliable data

- Use of competent personnel

- Review and approval of accounting estimates by appropriate personnel (including the review of relevant factors and assumptions and the determination of whether there is a need for a specialist)

- Comparison of previous accounting estimates with actual results

- Determination that accounting estimates are consistent with management's plans

Promulgated Procedures Checklist

The auditor should perform the following procedures with respect to accounting estimates in an audit of a client's financial statements:

- Determine whether all circumstances that give rise to accounting estimates have been identified by the entity.

- Determine whether accounting estimates are reasonable.

- Obtain sufficient audit evidence to support fair value disclosures.

Analysis and Application of Procedures

Determine whether all circumstances that give rise to accounting estimates have been identified by the entity

To determine whether the entity has identified all circumstances that require accounting estimates, the auditor should consider the entity's operating characteristics and the industry in general — including any new pronouncements that affect the industry. On the basis of a review of these factors, the auditor should consider performing the following procedures:

- Read the financial statements, and identify those assertions implied in the financial statements that may require an accounting estimate.

- Refer to evidence gathered in other parts of the engagement, including the following:

  — Changes made or contemplated by the entity or the industry that would affect the operations of the business

  — Changes made in the manner in which information is accumulated

— Identified litigation and other contingencies

— Relevant information contained in minutes of the board of directors, stockholders, and other significant committees

— Relevant information contained in regulatory reports, supervisory correspondence, and similar information from relevant regulatory agencies

- Discuss with management situations that may require an accounting estimate.

Exhibit AU 342-2 lists common financial statement estimates that require evaluation by an auditor.

Determine whether accounting estimates are reasonable

To determine which specific accounting estimates are reasonable, an auditor should concentrate on fundamental factors and assumptions that are material to an estimate and for which changes in the factor or assumption would have a significant effect on the accounting estimate. In addition, attention should be directed to factors and assumptions that are different from past patterns or that are highly subjective.

The audit approach should encompass an understanding of the entity's process for developing accounting estimates. Having gained such an understanding, the auditor should adopt one or a combination of the following approaches:

- Review and test the accounting estimation process.

- Develop an independent estimate.

- Review subsequent events or transactions.

Procedures that the auditor should consider when deciding to review and test the accounting estimation process include the following:

- Identify management controls and supporting data.

- Identify sources of data and factors used by management.

- Consider whether data and factors are relevant, reliable, and sufficient to support the estimate.

- Determine whether other factors or assumptions are appropriate.

- Determine if assumptions are internally consistent with other assumptions and supporting data.

- Determine that historical data used are comparable and consistent with data of the period under audit and that such data are reliable.

- Determine whether changes during the current period require that other factors be considered in developing assumptions.

- Review documentation supporting assumptions used to make accounting estimates.

- Inquire about other plans management may have adopted that could have an effect on assumptions related to accounting estimates.

- Determine whether a specialist is needed to evaluate assumptions.

- Recompute calculations made to convert assumptions and key factors into the accounting estimate.

> **FRAUD POINTER:** To address the ever-present risk of management override of internal control, SAS-99 requires the auditor in every audit to review accounting estimates for biases that could result in material misstatements due to fraud. As part of that review, SAS-99 requires the auditor to perform a retrospective review of significant accounting estimates reflected in the financial statements of the prior year. The purpose of this retrospective review is to determine whether management judgments and assumptions related to the estimates indicate possible management bias. The management judgments and assumptions examined by the auditor should include those estimates that are based on highly sensitive assumptions or are otherwise significantly impacted by management's judgment. In performing this retrospective review, the auditor is able to take advantage of the benefit of hindsight to determine the extent of bias on the part of management in developing the prior-year estimate. When bias is detected, the auditor should evaluate whether it indicates a risk of material misstatement due to fraud.

The auditor may test the reasonableness of accounting estimates by making an independent calculation. In making the calculation, the auditor should use other factors or alternative assumptions that he or she considers relevant.

Finally, the auditor may decide to test the reasonableness of an accounting estimate by reviewing subsequent events or transactions that occur after the date of the balance sheet but before the audit report date. Such information may make it unnecessary to evaluate factors and assumptions related to the accounting estimate. In other circumstances, the uncertainty related to the evaluation of factors and assumptions may be significantly reduced.

> **OBSERVATION:** The purpose of the audit of accounting estimates is to determine whether estimates are reasonable. Thus, an auditor might conclude that an estimate is reasonable even though it is not the best estimate. The difference between the reasonable estimate and the best estimate should not necessarily be treated as a misstatement; however, if most estimates appear to reflect a particular bias, such as the tendency to understate expenses, the auditor should consider whether all misstatements combined could result in a material misstatement.

Once the auditor has determined that an accounting estimate has been identified and properly valued, the auditor must determine whether the accounting estimate is properly presented and disclosed in the financial statements. In making that assessment, the auditor must consider the nature of the accounting estimate, relevant accounting and reporting standards, and the general rule of disclosure when making this determination.

> **ENGAGEMENT STRATEGY:** Auditing Interpretation No. 1 of AU 342 states that when auditing estimates related to FAS-107 (CT F25) (Disclosures about Fair Value of Financial Instruments) the auditor should collect appropriate audit evidence to reasonably assure (1) that valuation methods are acceptable, are applied consistently, and are adequately documented; and (2) that estimation methods and significant assumptions are disclosed.

Obtain sufficient audit evidence to support fair value disclosures

ASC 825 (FAS-107, Disclosures about Fair Value of Financial Instruments) requires that "an entity shall disclose, either in the body of the financial statements or in the accompanying notes, the fair value of financial instruments for which it is practicable to estimate that value." Some companies disclose only the information required by ASC 825 (FAS-107); others voluntarily disclose the fair value of assets and liabilities not required by ASC 825 (FAS-107). Auditing Interpretation No. 1 of AU 342 provides guidance for auditing and reporting on fair value disclosures:

The auditor must collect sufficient audit evidence to satisfy the following:

- Valuation principles are acceptable.

- Valuation principles are consistently applied and their application is adequately documented.

- Estimation methods used and significant assumptions made are properly disclosed.

> **PUBLIC COMPANY IMPLICATION:** The PCAOB has issued Staff Audit Practice Alert No. 2 (Matters Related to Auditing Fair Value Measurements of Financial Instruments and the Use of Specialists). The Practice Alert is designed to provide guidance related to auditing fair values, particularly in light of the FASB's issuance of ASC 820 (FAS-157, Fair Value Measurements). The auditor needs to understand the company's process for determining fair value measurements and disclosures, including related internal controls. The auditor should also evaluate whether (1) management's assumptions in determining fair value are reasonable and not inconsistent with market information, (2) management reliance on historical financial information continues to be justified (e.g., use of historical default rates may not be appropriate when credit markets are deteriorating), and (3) the company's determination of fair value is applied consistently and whether this is appropriate. For example, a company may apply a model consistently in determining fair value but because of changes in the environment it may be more appropriate for the company to change the relative weights of model inputs. In addition, the auditor should recognize that model inputs based on the company's own data are generally more susceptible to bias and take appropriate audit steps to respond to this increased risk. Finally, GAAP provides for many required disclosures relating to fair value measurements. The auditor needs to recognize that material disclosures that depart from GAAP represent a misstatement of the financial statements.

Reporting on required information

When a client reports only the disclosures required by ASC 825 (FAS-107) and the auditor has satisfied the three conditions listed above, a standard auditor's report is issued with no reference to the fair value disclosures. If the required disclosures are not made, the auditor must decide, depending on his or her assessment of the materiality of the disclosures omitted from the financial statements, whether to modify the standard report (qualified opinion or adverse opinion).

> **ENGAGEMENT STRATEGY:** The Interpretation notes that it may be appropriate to expand the standard report by adding an emphasis-of-a-matter paragraph when fair value is based on management's best estimate rather than on quoted market prices.

Reporting on required and voluntary information

When voluntary information on fair values is presented, that information may be audited only when the following conditions are met:

- Criteria used to measure and disclose the information are reasonable.

- Application of the disclosure and measurement criteria by competent persons would result in similar information.

The Interpretation states that voluntary disclosures may result in the presentation of essentially a complete balance sheet or an incomplete balance sheet based on fair values.

Complete balance sheet

The Interpretation states that if the fair value disclosures (both required and voluntary) encompass all material items in the balance sheet, the auditor should expand the report by adding the following paragraph:

> We have also audited in accordance with auditing standards generally accepted in the United States of America the supplemental fair value balance sheet of X Company as of December 31, 20X5. As described in Note X, the supplemental fair value balance sheet has been prepared by management to present relevant financial information that is not provided by the historical-cost balance sheets and is not intended to be a presentation in conformity with generally accepted accounting principles. In addition, the supplemental fair value balance sheet does not purport to present the net realizable, liquidation, or market value of X Company as a whole. Furthermore, amounts ultimately realized by X Company from the disposal of assets may vary significantly from the fair values presented. In our opinion, the supplemental fair value balance sheet referred to above presents fairly, in all material respects, the information set forth therein as described in Note X.

Incomplete balance sheet

If the fair value disclosures do not include all of the material items in the balance sheet and the disclosures are made either on the face of the financial statements or in notes, the Interpretation states that there is no need to make reference to the disclosures in the auditor's report. However, if the disclosures are presented in a supplemental schedule or exhibit, the auditor should add the following paragraph to the report:

> Our audit was conducted for the purpose of forming an opinion on the basic financial statements taken as a whole. The fair value disclosures contained in Schedule X are presented for purposes

of additional analysis and are not a required part of the basic financial statements. Such information has been subjected to the auditing procedures applied in the audit of the basic financial statements and, in our opinion, is fairly stated in all material respects in relation to the basic financial statements taken as a whole.

Reporting when disclosures are not audited

The auditor may not be requested to audit voluntary fair value disclosures or may be unable to audit the information because the conditions listed earlier may not be satisfied. When voluntary fair value disclosures are not audited but are presented in an auditor-submitted document, and they appear on the face of the financial statements, in the notes, or in a supplemental schedule to the basic financial statements, the disclosures should be labeled "unaudited" and the paragraph below should be added to the auditor's report:

> Our audit was conducted for the purpose of forming an opinion on the basic financial statements taken as a whole. The fair value disclosures contained in Schedule X are presented for purposes of additional analysis and are not a required part of the basic financial statements. Such information has not been subjected to the auditing procedures applied in the audit of the basic financial statements, and, accordingly, we express no opinion on them.

> **PLANNING AID REMINDER:** When the unaudited voluntary disclosures are presented in a client-prepared document and the information is included on the face of the financial statements, in the notes, or in a supplemental schedule, the disclosures should be labeled "unaudited." There is no need to disclaim an opinion on the information. If the unaudited voluntary disclosures are not presented on the face of the financial statements, in the notes, or in a supplemental schedule, the auditor should read the information in a manner consistent with the guidance established by SAS-118 (AU 550) (Other Information in Documents Containing Audited Financial Statements).

Practitioner's Aid

Exhibit AU 342-1 discusses nonauthoritative guidance that is helpful in the audit of so-called soft accounting information (estimates). This appendix summarizes an approach explained in the AICPA's Audit Practice Guide titled "Auditing Estimates and Other Soft Accounting Information." The Audit Practice Guide is available for purchase from the AICPA.

EXHIBIT AU 342-1 — NONAUTHORITATIVE GUIDANCE FOR AUDITING SOFT ACCOUNTING INFORMATION

The AICPA's Audit Practice Guide provides the following broad guidelines for the audit of accounting estimates:

• Auditing soft accounting information and engagement planning

• Evaluating the persuasiveness of audit evidence related to soft accounting information

• Communicating the nature of soft accounting information

Auditing soft accounting information and engagement planning

Financial statements are based on a variety of accounting estimates ranging from the percentage of accounts receivable expected to be uncollectible to actuarial assumptions required by ASC 715 (FAS-87, Employers' Accounting for Pension Plans) in order to recognize pension expense. The client needs to understand and appreciate the role of estimates in the financial reporting process and that the determination of those estimates is the responsibility of the client, not the auditor.

For the planning phase of the engagement the Audit Practice Guide addresses the following issues:

• Identify estimates with high risk.

• Determine the client's involvement in accounting estimates.

• Advise and support the client in making accounting estimates.

Identify estimates with high risk

Financial statements incorporate a variety of estimates. During the planning stage of an engagement the auditor should identify areas where there is a high degree of risk for specific estimates. One factor that can help mitigate the risk related to a particular estimate is the client's established procedures. For example, internal reports that are timely, reviewed, and are the basis of managerial action can help ensure that an estimate is well understood and to some degree controlled. On the other hand, poorly designed procedures increase the likelihood that an estimate that has not received an appropriate amount of attention harbors a relatively high degree of risk. The Audit Practice Guide identifies the following as conditions that can increase the audit risk related to estimates:

- The client might be new and its previous years' financial statements might have been compiled or audited and the client might not have given adequate attention to the role of estimates in financial reporting.

- The client might have switched from another comprehensive basis of accounting to GAAP-based reporting. For example, many estimates are based on the accrual accounting concept and if a cash or a modified accrual basis has been used by the client, procedures related to the development of estimates might be nonexistent.

- There has been an issuance of new accounting standards that contain accounting and reporting requirements that rely on client estimates. For example, ASC 360 (FAS-144, Accounting for the Impairment or Disposal of Long-Lived Assets) requires under certain conditions the estimate of future net cash flows to determine whether a long-lived asset has a cost recoverability problem.

- The operations of the client have changed in a manner whereby previous years' experience with estimating account balances is no longer relevant or is less relevant to current estimates. For example, the client has added a line of electronic components that is characterized by rapid technological change compared to previously manufactured components. Previously employed procedures for identifying inventory that needs to be written down might not be appropriate for the new components.

- The customer base of the client has been modified. For example, the client might have decided to sell its products in foreign markets and has limited experience with collection issues related to accounts receivable.

Determine the client's involvement in accounting estimates

The Audit Practice Guide notes that once the estimates that have a higher degree of audit risk are identified the next step is to determine the extent to which the client has developed an information base to address the estimation issue. This approach should include asking the following questions:

- What are the specific procedures used by the client to develop the data?

- Are the data collected by the client relevant to the account estimate and sufficient to make a reliable estimate?

- What are the procedures (model) used by the client to convert the data into the account estimate?

- Are the procedures used logical and does the process represent a reasonable approximation of the existing conditions?

In the audit of some clients, especially small or newly organized companies, it is possible that the client's procedures do not address many, if any, accounting estimates. This could be especially true of companies dominated by a manager-owner. The Audit Practice Guide points out that under this condition the auditor must determine whether the lack of procedures requires the auditor to withdraw from the engagement or remain in the engagement and help the client develop reasonable estimates for the preparation of the financial statements.

The Audit Practice Guide states that "when the estimates or soft accounting information are vital to the management of the business and are pervasive throughout the financial statements, the client's lack of a process for making these estimates should lead you to consider whether the entity is even auditable." For example, assume that a client manufactures a component for a large computer manufacturer and the controls in the supply chain are so deficient that the client often has fairly large quantities of inventory that become obsolete and of nominal value. If the client has maintained no records from previous years' inventory obsolescence experience, it is possible that the engagement is not auditable if current levels of inventory are material.

> **OBSERVATION:** If the client has essentially no procedures related to the development of an estimate fundamental to the financial statements but still believes that the financial statements are auditable, the auditor should consider whether the condition gives rise to a significant deficiency or material weakness in internal control.

Advise and support the client in making accounting estimates

On the other hand, the client's lack of procedures related to estimating account balances does not always imply that a prudent auditor should withdraw from an engagement. In many small engagements the client lacks the in-house expertise to fully understand the role of estimations in financial reporting or develop appropriate data to make those estimations. Obviously the auditor cannot simply walk away from these engagements (assuming they are auditable) but, rather, must develop a commonsense approach to the situation. The Audit Practice Guide describes the following as an approach that could be useful under this circumstance:

- Explain the role of estimates to the client.

- Assist the client in developing an estimation model.

- Assist the client in developing relevant key assumptions.

- Assist the client in obtaining relevant information about key assumptions.

- Let the client make the final assumptions.

- Assist the client in making the final estimate.

Explain the role of estimates to the client

Many individuals with a limited financial background (including businesspeople) see accounting as black and white with no room for estimates; it can be a challenge to explain to such individuals the accrual basis of accounting. The way an auditor conveys the explanation is personal and dependent upon his or her imagination. It is often best to leave out all of the jargon and technical references and find an everyday, close-to-home context to explain the need for estimates. In the final analysis an auditor must take time to educate the client and make sure they are committed to "getting the numbers right."

Assist the client in developing an estimation model

All estimates are based on a model (mathematical equation), some of which are simple and some of which are elaborate. For example, the aging of accounts receivable in order to estimate the amount of uncollectible accounts is based on a model with two or more variables (the bad-account percentage increases with the age of the account).

The key to developing a successful model (one that represents more or less the real world) is inquisitiveness in the context of the client's operations. The client brings to this project a thorough understanding of its operations and should be able to rely on in-house expertise to be reasonably certain that all of the relevant factors are considered. An auditor brings to this project a more limited knowledge of the client but a great deal of experience with various other clients and industries. Furthermore, the auditor brings a degree of rigor that might not always be the domain of the client. For example, the auditor can analyze factors raised by the client and determine which are relevant, how they interrelate with one another, and the possible financial outcome of their interplay.

Finally an auditor should be careful not to restrict the scope of the information that may be gathered to deal with the estimation issue. The Auditor Practice Guide notes that "many practitioners make the mistake of building a model based only on the information they know exists." With the explosion of information and data-retrieval tools, the client and auditor need to be willing to spend an adequate amount of time considering relevant data sources.

Assist the client in developing relevant key assumptions

The auditor should discuss with the client the key assumptions that are likely to be the basis for developing an acceptable account estimate. The assumptions may include a variety of factors such as management's desire to maintain strong customer relations (the liberal application of a warranty clause), reliable costs estimates (for pending lawsuits), and business strategies that relate to future cash flow assumptions (in applying the cost recoverability test to various assets).

Assist the client in obtaining relevant information about key assumptions

Often a client needs help in the collection of information that relates to the key assumptions identified by the client. This is a research task that can include searching databases and other sources of information maintained by industry trade associations, business libraries, and reference sources maintained by the client. As sources of information are identified the auditor must determine whether the information is relevant to the estimate that needs to be made by the client. Like all accounting information, the information must be relevant to the estimation that needs to be made, reliable, and sufficient to support the assertions that will be made in the financial statements.

Let the client make the final assumptions

Even though the auditor is involved in developing the procedures used to make an account estimate, professional standards require that the client, not the auditor, make the assumptions related to the estimation. This is often a very difficult phase of the process. Up to this point the auditor has worked with the client to develop the approach and suddenly the auditor must tell the client that the client has the responsibility for developing an estimate that is included in the financial statements. The client knows that the estimates he or she develops must be acceptable to the auditor and often asks "What is the correct number?" The auditor should point out that it is not so much the specific number that an auditor is concerned with but, rather, the client's approach in developing the number. After all, the estimate is just that, an estimate. The Audit Practice Guide notes that it may be helpful to explain to the client the thought process that the auditor goes through in determining whether the process and assumptions used by the client are acceptable. For example, the auditor would raise the following questions as part of the audit process:

- Are the assumptions internally consistent with one another and consistent with other information developed?

- Do the assumptions reflect current changes and trends that are likely to have an effect on the eventual payments or write-downs related to the estimate?

- Are the assumptions consistent with the client's future plans?

Assist the client in making the final estimate

The final estimate made by the client must satisfy the client as well as the auditor and is fundamentally a trade-off between the cost of developing a highly precise estimate and the materiality of the estimate to the financial statements. If the estimate is clearly not material to the financial statements, a minimum amount of time should be devoted to the process. As the materiality of the estimate increases the auditor must be prepared to expend more audit effort in order to reduce the audit risk to an acceptable level.

Only a seasoned auditor who is familiar with the client and the client's industry should make the decision on how important an estimate is and how much audit time should be allocated to the process. The Audit Practice Guide points out that the auditor should also realize that becoming familiar with a particular estimation process should not be limited to the context of the client. For example, building expertise in a particular area can (1) benefit other audit engagements who have a similar issue or (2) build "valuable skills that later clients will pay for."

PLANNING AID REMINDER: The auditor might not have the expertise to develop an estimation process or evaluate the process used by the client, in which case the guidance established by SAS-73 (AU 336) (Using the Work of a Specialist) should be observed.

Evaluating the persuasiveness of audit evidence related to soft accounting information

Audit evidence related to estimates is different from that which supports historical cost transactions reflected in the financial statements. Past transactions can be corroborated by inspecting documentation, confirming specifics related to the transactions or performing other similar audit procedures that generally created high quality audit evidence. Estimates are future related because they are based on subsequent decisions, events, or transactions and the quality of audit evidence to corroborate estimates will be somewhat limited. The Audit Practice Guide states that in order to be comfortable with an estimate the following two factors are important to the audit process:

1. The reliability of the estimation process

2. The quality of the assumptions used in the estimation process

The reliability of the estimation process

There is an inverse relationship between the time and effort expended by management to develop an estimate and the audit risk related to the estimate. That is, if management has little interest in a particular estimate, the level of audit risk is greater than when management's approach to the estimate is both thoughtful and rigorous. The Audit Practice Guide points out that the following are factors of a reliable estimation process:

• Management's good faith effort

• The appropriateness of the estimation model

• The quality of information used to make the estimate

Management's good faith effort

In determining whether the estimation process is reliable, management's attitude toward the process should be considered. The Audit Practice Guide notes that good faith effort includes (1) being diligent in developing appropriate assumptions, (2) being cautious so as not to include misleading information in the financial statements, and (3) incorporating information that is consistent with management's plans and strategies.

The appropriateness of the estimation model

An appropriate balance can only be created when the model used is a reasonable representation of the real-world conditions that affect the estimate. Key elements of the model should be investigated to determine whether they are consistent with the existing conditions. For example, if a warranty liability is being estimated and one of the key elements of the estimation model is that only parts and not repair service are covered by the warranty, the auditor should determine whether in practice service costs are also covered depending on the nature of the relationship between the client and its customers.

The quality of information used to make the estimate

Obviously the auditor must be reasonable in determining the quality of information that is acceptable in developing an estimate. Professional judgment must be exercised based on the costs to the client and the benefits of producing financial statements that are not materially misstated.

The quality of the assumptions used in the estimation process

The Audit Practice Guide identifies the following as techniques that can be used to evaluate the appropriateness of estimates made by the client:

- Use of hindsight
- Identify ranges of estimates
- Use alternative approaches

Use of hindsight In limited situations an auditor may be able to review transactions and events that occur during the stub period (after the date of the financial statements but before the financial statements are released). For example, if a client made an estimate for returned goods that were shipped before the end of the year, a review of returned goods during the stub period might provide important insight into whether the estimate was reasonable.

Identify ranges of estimates One thing that is almost always certain about a point estimate is that it will be wrong. In most situations the auditor develops an acceptable range for the estimate, and if the client's estimate falls within that range, the auditor might be satisfied with the account balance.

> **OBSERVATION:** The Audit Practice Guide warns that "the process used to develop a range should be as rigorous" as the process used to develop a point estimate.

Use alternative approaches Often the auditor can use alternative ways to determine whether an estimation process used by the client is acceptable. For example, an estimate for warranty costs for a new product could have been made by the client using assessments made by its engineering staff. As an alternative approach, the auditor could select a previously introduced product and review the warranty cost pattern for that product to see if it is reasonably consistent with the one developed by the client. The Audit Practice Guide notes that "wide differences in the results obtained from two or more valid models should be a red flag that causes you to investigate further."

> **OBSERVATION:** The Audit Practice Guide points out that there are three types of estimates that are required by financial accounting standards, namely (1) management's ability and intent, (2) estimates of future cash flows, and (3) fair value estimates. For example, (1) ASC 320 (FAS-115, Accounting for Certain Investments in Debt and Equity Securities) requires that management classify investments into three possible portfolios that are accounted for in three different ways, (2) ASC 360 (FAS-144, Accounting for the Impairment or Disposal of Long-Lived Assets) requires a client to estimate future cash flows for certain long-lived assets, and (3) ASC 718 (FAS-123R, Share-Based Payment) requires that the fair value of compensatory stock option plans be determined. All of these estimation approaches present challenges for the auditor in determining whether the soft accounting information is not misleading as reported in the financial statements.

Communicating the nature of soft accounting information

The inherent nature of estimates constrains the precision and effectiveness of financial reporting. No matter how sophisticated the client's procedure for constructing estimates or how rigorous the auditor's evaluation of those estimates, the information in the current financial statements that is based on estimates is tentative to some degree. The uncertainty related to estimates needs to be communicated to users in a way that allows them to build that uncertainty into their decision making process. The Audit Practice Guide lists the following two broad techniques that can help users better understand this uncertainty:

1. Required disclosures

2. Optional disclosures

Required disclosures

Financial reporting mandates a variety of required disclosures that specifically focus on uncertainties related to financial reporting. ASC 275 (SOP 94-6, Disclosure of Certain Significant Risks and Uncertainties) provides the "primary guidance on disclosures related to estimates and soft accounting information." ASC 275 (SOP 94-6) requires certain disclosures when the following conditions are present:

- It is at least reasonably possible that the estimate of the effect on the financial statements of a condition, situation, or set of circumstances that existed at the date of the financial statements will change in the near term due to one or more future confirming events.

- The effect of the change would have a material effect on the financial statements.

If the above conditions are present, the following disclosures should be made:

- If an estimate requires disclosure under ASC 450 (FAS-5) or another pronouncement, an indication also shall be made that it is at least reasonably possible that a change in the estimate will occur in the near term.

- An estimate that does not require disclosure under ASC 450 (FAS-5) (such as estimates associated with long-term operating assets and amounts reported under profitable long-term contracts) may meet the standards described above and, if so, require the following: (1) disclosure of its nature and (2) an indication that it is reasonably possible that a change in the estimate will occur in the near term.

The scope of ASC 275 (SOP 94-6) is general and can apply to a variety of financial reporting issues as indicated by the following examples that are included in the pronouncement:

- Inventory subject to rapid technological obsolescence

- Specialized equipment subject to technological obsolescence

- Valuation allowances for deferred tax assets based on future taxable income

- Capitalized motion picture film product costs

- Capitalized computer software costs

- Deferred policy acquisition costs of insurance enterprises

- Valuation allowances for commercial and real estate loans

- Environmental remediation-related obligations

- Litigation-related obligations

- Contingent liabilities for obligations of other entities

- Amounts reported for long-term obligations (e.g., pensions and other postretirement benefits)

- Estimated net proceeds recoverable, the provisions for expected loss to be incurred, etc., on disposition of a business or assets

- Amounts reported for long-term contracts

Optional disclosures

Disclosures are not limited to those required by specific accounting pronouncements. The general disclosure principle requires that financial statements include information that could reasonably make a difference in assessments made by financial statement users. This general disclosure principle provides both management and the auditor with an opportunity to step back from the promulgated standards and ask whether the financial statements convey a reasonable description of the financial position and results of operations of the client. The Audit Practice Guide points out that the following optional disclosures may be helpful in portraying the risks and uncertainties related to soft accounting information:

- Disclose significant estimates.

- Describe limitations of estimates.

- Describe models used to make estimates.

- Describe the basis used to make assumptions.

- Describe recognition criteria.

- Explain why an estimate cannot be made.

- Disclose the time period related to future cash flow estimates.

Disclose significant estimates

The listing of estimates used by a client in the preparing of financial statements has become boilerplate and for that reason not very informative. As a supplement, the auditor may encourage the client to disclose and explain significant estimates that are fundamental to presentation of the financial statements.

Describe limitations of estimates

One of the misconceptions of financial reporting is the implication that a number presented is correct with no room for imprecision. This impression can be remedied to some extent by the client's describing the uncertainty related to specific significant estimates used to prepare the financial statements. Management should supplement boilerplate language with a succinct description of the risks that management is aware of and planned strategies to address these issues.

Describe models used to make estimates

The Audit Practice Guide points out that in some instances, such as one-time events, it is helpful to describe in a note to the financial statements "significant features of the process, the key assumptions made, and the rationale for such assumptions." These disclosures could remind the readers of the financial statements of the uncertainty associated with a particular account balance and the practical difficulties with making a reasonable estimate based on existing conditions.

Describe the basis used to make assumptions

Along with describing the elements related to the model used to make an estimate it may be equally insightful to the financial statement reader to be informed of "the rationale, the sources of information, and the thought process" used to construct assumptions that were fundamental to making the estimate.

Describe recognition criteria

In some instances it is not apparent or obvious to a financial statement user the criteria that were used to make an estimate. For example, ASC 450 (FAS-5) uses terms such as "probable," "reasonably possible," and "remote" in determining whether a loss contingency is to be recorded, disclosed in a note, or omitted from the financial statements. Descriptions of these terms in the context of the specific estimates may assist the user in understanding the degree of uncertainty related to certain account balances.

Explain why an estimate cannot be made

In some instances management is unable to make a reasonable estimate because of the lack of relevant information even after an appropriate estimation process has been constructed and executed. Rather than simply state in a note to the financial statements that an estimate cannot be made, the disclosure may "explain why a particular estimate cannot be made and give some indication of when an estimate will be possible."

Disclose the time period related to future cash flow estimates

Accounting estimates may be in part based on estimates of future cash flows. Disclosing the period of time used for the estimate and why a particular length of time was used can better convey to the financial statement user the degree of uncertainty surrounding an estimate.

EXHIBIT AU 342-2 — COMMON FINANCIAL STATEMENT ESTIMATES REQUIRING AUDITOR EVALUATION

Assets

- Allowance for doubtful accounts

- Allowance for sales returns and allowances

- Evaluation of when a software vendor has established technological feasibility for the purpose of capitalizing computer software development costs

- Estimates of fair-market value of available-for-sale and trading securities (not traded in an active market)

- Impairment of long-lived assets and intangible assets

- Inventory obsolescence reserve

- Recoverability of deferred tax assets (more likely than not)

- Useful lives and salvage values of fixed assets

- Useful lives of intangible assets (those without an indefinite useful life)

Liabilities

- Discount rate, assumed return on plan assets, among other assumptions, for defined benefit pension plans

- Discount rate, health-care-cost trend rate, among other estimates, for retiree health-care-benefit plans

- Salvage value for leased assets, implicit rate of return in a lease contract, among other estimates, for lease contracts

- Warranty obligations

Revenues

- Percentage-of-completion for long-term construction contracts

- Sales discounts

- Sales returns

Expenses

- Amortization expense

- Bad debts expense

- Cost of goods sold

- Depreciation expense

- Income tax expense

- Pension expense (income)

- Postretirement benefit expense other than pension

- Warranty expense

Gains and Losses

- Loss on asset impairment

- Unrealized gains and losses on nonpublic or thinly traded securities

SECTION 350

AUDIT SAMPLING

Authoritative Pronouncements

SAS-39 — Audit Sampling

SAS-43 — Omnibus Statement on Auditing Standards

SAS-45 — Omnibus Statement on Auditing Standards — 1993

SAS-111 — Amendment to Statement on Auditing Standards No. 39, Audit Sampling

Auditing Interpretation No. 1 of AU 350 (January 1985) — Applicability

> **IMPORTANT NOTICE FOR 2011:** The Auditing Standards Board (ASB) is in the process of redrafting all of the auditing sections in *Codification of Statements on Auditing Standards* to converge U.S. GAAS with the International Standards on Auditing issued by the International Auditing and Assurance Standards Board. As part of this process, the newly redrafted standards will follow certain clarity drafting conventions adopted by the ASB. These clarity drafting conventions include: (1) establishing objectives for each standard; (2) including a definitions section, if appropriate; and (3) separating requirements from application guidance and other material. The ASB is planning to have all redrafted standards become effective on the same date, which is for audits of financial statements for periods ending on or after December 15, 2012. It is possible that the effective date might be delayed beyond that date. The ASB's clarity and convergence project will have a significant effect on the auditing standards applicable to audits of nonpublic companies, and the 2012 *GAAS Guide* will be appropriately modified to reflect these changes once the effective date of the standards is certain.

Overview

The third standard of fieldwork requires the auditor to obtain sufficient appropriate audit evidence by performing audit procedures sufficient to afford a reasonable basis for an opinion on the financial statements. "Audit evidence" represents all the information used by an auditor in arriving at the conclusions that his or her audit opinion is based on.

Examining the documentation for every transaction of a business is costly and time-consuming. Because most audit objectives do not require that amount of evidence, auditors frequently use sampling techniques and procedures. SAS-39 (Audit Sampling), as amended, notes that there may be other reasons (other than performing sampling) why an auditor would examine fewer than all of the items in a given population, such as when performing risk-assessment procedures to obtain an understanding of the entity and its environment, including its internal controls. Under these circumstances, guidelines established in SAS-39 are not applicable.

Nonsampling plans

Although sampling is an important audit strategy in many engagements, a sampling approach is not appropriate for many situations. Auditing Interpretation No. 1 of AU 350 (January 1985) (Applicability) states that when less than 100% of the items in a given population are not examined, the following circumstances would not be considered sampling:

- The auditor does not intend to extend the sample results to the remainder of the items in the population.

- Although he or she might not be examining all of the items in the population, the auditor might be examining 100% of the items that make up a subgroup of the entire population.

- The auditor is performing tests of controls on an undocumented procedure (e.g., observing the client counting his or her inventory).

- The auditor is not performing a test of details (e.g., applying substantive analytical procedures).

For example, an auditor examining a client's trial balance of accounts receivable may discover that the balance is composed of only four accounts, and each amount due is individually significant. In this circumstance it would be appropriate, for example, to confirm each of the four receivables and evaluate each for likelihood of collection. Also, when testing automated controls, sampling concepts might not apply. Automated controls may be tested only once if there are effective general controls over information technology.

Nonstatistical sampling plans

The strategy of sampling is to examine less than 100% of the items in a given population and to draw from this examination a conclusion about certain characteristics of the total population. The conclusion can be expressed in quantitative terms (statistical sampling) or nonquantitative terms (nonstatistical sampling). For example, a sample of customer credit orders might be examined to determine whether appropriate credit approval has been made on each order. If the auditor used nonstatistical sampling, he or she may say in the conclusion, "Based on the number of errors and the nature of those errors, I believe that the credit approval process is working effectively." On the other hand, if the auditor used statistical sampling, he or she may conclude, "Based on the number of errors and the nature of those errors, I am 95% certain that the maximum error rate for nonapproval of credit is 1.2%."

SAS-39 was issued to provide guidance for the auditor's design and implementation of audit sampling plans. SAS-39 endorses both a nonstatistical approach and a statistical approach to sampling by concluding that either approach can provide sufficient audit evidence, as required by the third standard of fieldwork. Both nonstatistical sampling and statistical sampling are based on judgment, and the same factors are used in both approaches in order to determine the appropriate sample size and to evaluate the sample results.

The difference between the two approaches is that in statistical sampling the sample approach and the sample results are quantified, whereas in nonstatistical sampling qualitative terms are used to express the sampling results. Because of the similarities of the professional judgments in the two approaches, the following discussion applies to both nonstatistical and statistical sampling. It should be emphasized that although the concepts used in SAS-39 appear to be directed to statistical sampling, they (and the terminology) apply equally to nonstatistical sampling.

When an auditor designs a nonstatistical sampling plan or a statistical sampling plan, the purpose of the plan is to draw a conclusion about either an attribute or a dollar value. Attribute sampling measures the frequency of a specific occurrence in a particular population. This sampling technique is used to discover how often exceptions occur in the population under examination. Thus, attribute sampling is concerned with the qualitative characteristics of a sample. Generally, attribute sampling is associated with tests of controls, the results of which are the basis for assessing control risk at a level less than the maximum level.

Variable sampling is used to estimate the dollar value of a population and to determine the reasonableness of specific balances on the financial statements. Thus, variable sampling is concerned with the quantitative characteristics of a population. Generally, variable sampling is associated with substantive procedures, which are performed to gather audit evidence concerning the validity and the propriety of specific transactions and balances.

Audit risk

Even when every transaction and balance is examined 100%, there is always a degree of audit risk present in an engagement. This degree of audit risk is referred to in SAS-39 as a combination of nonsampling risk and sampling risk. Examples of nonsampling risk are (1) the selection of inappropriate auditing procedures and (2) the failure to identify an error on a document that the auditor is examining. Nonsampling risk cannot be measured, but it can be reduced to an acceptable level if the auditor implements an effective quality control system.

> **FRAUD POINTER:** SAS-99 notes that one of the auditor's overall responses to the risk of material misstatement due to fraud is to change the extent of audit procedures applied. When the risk of material misstatement due to fraud is considered high, auditors may decide to increase sample sizes or test the entire population instead of using a sample.

Sampling risk occurs because fewer than 100% of the sample units in a population are reviewed. For this reason, the auditor can reduce sampling risk by increasing the size of the sample. Sampling risks are classified as follows:

- *Risk of assessing control risk too low (tests of controls)* The risk that the assessed level of control risk based on the sample is less than the true operating effectiveness of the internal control policy or procedure. In other words, the internal control is not as effective as the auditor believes it to be.

- *Risk of assessing control risk too high (tests of controls)* The risk that the assessed level of control risk based on the sample is greater than the true operating effectiveness of the internal control policy or procedure. In other words, the internal control is more effective than the auditor believes it to be.

- *Risk of incorrect acceptance (substantive procedures)* The risk that the selected sample supports the auditor's conclusion that the recorded account balance is not materially misstated, when in fact the recorded account balance is materially misstated. In other words, on the basis of the selected sample, the auditor concludes that the recorded account balance is not materially misstated, when in fact, based on the total population, the recorded account balance is materially misstated.

- *Risk of incorrect rejection (substantive procedures)* The risk that the selected sample supports the auditor's conclusion that the recorded account balance is materially misstated, when in fact the recorded account balance is not materially misstated. In other words, on the basis of the selected sample, the auditor concludes that the recorded account balance is materially misstated, when in fact, based on the total population, the recorded account balance is not materially misstated.

Both the risk of incorrectly assessing control risk too high and the risk of incorrect rejection of a recorded account balance are associated with the efficiency of the audit. For example, by assessing control risk at a high level (when in fact the control risk is lower), the auditor may increase the extent of substantive procedures unnecessarily. Thus, the audit was not performed efficiently, because the auditor could have selected, for example, a smaller sample for substantive procedures.

Both the risk of incorrectly assessing control risk too low on internal control and the risk of incorrect acceptance of a recorded account balance are associated with the effectiveness of the audit. For example, when an auditor concludes that a recorded account balance is correct when in fact the balance is not correct, the effectiveness of the audit is impaired.

Thus, the risk of assessing control risk too high and the risk of incorrect rejection may affect the efficiency of an audit, whereas the risk of assessing control risk too low and the risk of incorrect acceptance may affect the effectiveness of an audit. An auditor is more concerned with the risk of assessing control risk too low and the risk of incorrect acceptance than with the risk of assessing control risk too high and the risk of incorrect rejection, because the effectiveness of the audit is more important than the efficiency of the audit. For this reason, the risk of assessing control risk too low and the risk of incorrect acceptance of an incorrectly recorded account balance are emphasized in SAS-39.

The implications of testing less than 100% of a population

Sampling is concerned with selecting less than 100% of the items that make up a population to project the results of testing the sample to the total population. For example, an auditor may select a sample of accounts to be confirmed and, based on the results of the confirmed items, make a statement about a characteristic of the total accounts receivable balance. This approach is sampling and is subject to the guidance established by SAS-39.

However, the fact that an auditor tests less than 100% of a population does not mean that the approach is always sampling and, therefore, subject to the guidance established by SAS-39. For example, an auditor might decide to confirm all receivables that have a balance of $1,000 or more. Previous AICPA Audit Risk Alerts point out that in this case an auditor cannot project the results of the confirmed items to the total balance of accounts receivable, because the auditor has not drawn a sample from all of the receivables. The auditor cannot project the results of sampling to the population as a whole unless all of the items in the total population have had some chance for selection.

SAMPLING TESTS OF CONTROLS (NONSTATISTICAL AND STATISTICAL SAMPLING APPROACHES)

As stated earlier, attribute sampling measures the frequency of a specific occurrence in a particular population. This sampling technique is used to discover how often exceptions occur in the population under examination. Thus, attribute sampling is concerned with the qualitative characteristics of a sample — with tests of controls, which the auditor must perform in order to assess control risk at less than the maximum level.

Promulgated Procedures Checklist

The auditor may use the following steps to apply attribute sampling to tests of controls:

1. Determine the objectives of the test.
2. Define the deviation conditions.
3. Define the population:

    a. Define the period covered by the test.

    b. Define the sampling unit.

    c. Consider the completeness of the population.

4. Determine the method of selecting the sample:

    a. Random-number sampling

    b. Systematic sampling

    c. Other sampling

5. Determine the sample size:

    a. Consider the allowable risk of assessing control risk too low.

    b. Consider the maximum rate of deviations from prescribed internal controls that would support the auditor's planned assessed level of control risk (tolerable rate).

    c. Consider the expected population deviation rate.

    d. Consider the effect of the population size.

    e. Consider statistical or nonstatistical sampling methods.

6. Perform the sampling plan.
7. Evaluate the sample results:

    a. Calculate the deviation rate.

    b. Consider the sampling risk.

    c. Consider the qualitative aspects of the deviations.

    d. Reach an overall conclusion.

8. Document the sampling procedures.

Analysis and Application of Procedures

Step 1 — Determine the objectives of the test

Generally, the use of sampling techniques in tests of controls applies only to those internal controls that generate documentary evidence. Thus, sampling techniques generally cannot be used in tests of controls for segregation of duties or the competency of personnel.

Tests of controls are concerned with determining whether a client's internal control operates in accordance with prescribed policies. Each internal control procedure has an objective and prescribed rules to obtain that objective. For example, in the credit department of a business, a control might state that orders must be appropriately approved for acceptance of credit risk before being processed. The objective of this control is to ensure that credit is approved before an order is accepted. This control must also include the prescribed rules for attaining the objective. One of the rules for attaining this particular objective for the credit department might be that no additional credit may be extended to any customer who has an outstanding balance more than sixty days old. The head of the credit department is responsible for ensuring that this control and its prescribed rules are consistently followed.

Every control objective must have one or more stated control techniques, which are designed to achieve the control objective.

Controls may be classified as preventive or detective. Preventive controls are established to prevent errors from occurring. Detective controls are established to detect errors that have occurred.

When performing tests of controls, the auditor must determine whether a specific internal control operates as designed and whether the control objective is being achieved. In this respect the auditor might be concerned with (1) who performed the control, (2) where the control was performed, and (3) whether the control was performed in accordance with prescribed policy.

The audit objective must be defined in terms of specific compliance characteristics that can be tested.

> **FRAUD POINTER:** To address the ever-present risk of management override of internal control, SAS-99 requires the auditor to examine journal entries and other adjustments for evidence of possible material misstatement due to fraud. One objective of the auditor's examination of journal entries is to determine the effectiveness of internal controls over journal entries and other adjustments. In light of the volume of journal entries to be examined as part of testing controls related to the journal entry process, auditors are likely to base their testing on samples of journal entries. Thus, the auditor's objective in this sample application is to obtain evidence that the internal controls over the journal entry process operate effectively.

> **PUBLIC COMPANY IMPLICATIONS:** SOX requires all public companies to issue a report by the auditor on the effectiveness of the entity's internal control over financial reporting. To provide the basis for the auditor's report on internal control, he or she performs tests of controls over financial reporting. In many circumstances, the auditor performs tests of controls of samples selected from the population of transactions subject to the internal controls being examined. Thus, the guidance in this section is especially relevant to public company auditors.

Step 2 — Define the deviation conditions

A *deviation* is a departure from the prescribed internal control. The auditor must identify any significant deviation conditions that exist in a control. A significant deviation condition exists when a necessary step to achieve a particular internal control objective is not performed as prescribed. The auditor might consider that some internal controls, such as multiple approvals, are unimportant and need not be tested.

Step 3 — Define the population

The population selected for examination must be complete and must provide the auditor with the opportunity to satisfy the established audit objective. A sample should be selected in a manner that is representative of the population from which it is selected. If the population is not complete in all respects, the selected sample will not be representative of the complete population. For example, the audit objective may be to determine whether all goods that are shipped are properly billed. For this audit objective, the auditor should define the population as bills of lading or other shipping records prepared during the audit period — rather than sales invoices, which may or may not represent goods that have been shipped.

Step 3a — Define the period covered by the test

A conclusion can be drawn about a population only if all items in the population have a chance of being selected for examination. The population from which the sample is selected should include all transactions for the accounting period under examination. However, professional standards recognize that it may be appropriate to perform tests of controls at interim dates and review subsequent transactions when the auditor performs year-end audit procedures.

Step 3b — Define the sampling unit

A population consists of a number of sampling units, such as canceled checks or sales invoices. For example, if the audit objective is to determine whether vouchers have been properly approved, the sampling items may be the line items in the voucher register rather than the checks used to pay the vouchers. Once the auditor adequately defines the population, the sample unit should not be difficult to define.

Step 3c — Consider the completeness of the population

The physical representation of the population must be consistent with the definition of the population. For example, the auditor might be concerned with all cash disbursements made during the period and define the population as all canceled checks during the period. The auditor must determine that the defined population is complete; otherwise, a representative sample cannot be drawn from the population.

Step 4 — Determine the method of selecting the sample

Sampling units must be selected from the defined population so that each sampling unit has a chance of being selected. SAS-39 requires that a representative sample be selected for both nonstatistical sampling and statistical sampling. When statistical sampling is used, the sample must be selected on an unbiased basis (usually a random selection).

> **ENGAGEMENT STRATEGY:** SAS-39 notes that auditors should select sample items so that the sample is representative of the population. A representative sample is one in which all items in a population have an equal opportunity of being included in the sample. A randomly selected sample meets that definition, and random selection is often the technique used to select samples for statistical sampling applications. However, auditors also often use random selection techniques for non-statistical sampling plans to increase the likelihood that those samples are representative of the population. The use of a representative sample reduces sampling risk.

Step 4a — Random-number sampling

A sample may be selected from the population on a random basis using random numbers generated by a computer or numbers chosen from a random-number table.

Step 4b — Systematic sampling

The auditor may select a random sample using the systematic-selection method, whereby every nth item is selected. Systematic selection is also referred to as sequential sampling. The following steps should be followed when systematic selection is used:

1. Determine the population (N).

2. Determine the sample size (n).

3. Compute the interval size by dividing N by n.

4. Select a random start (a random-number table can be used to determine the starting point).

5. Determine the sample items selected by successively adding the interval to the random starting point.

To illustrate the systematic-selection method, assume that the auditor has defined the population as 3,000 sales invoices listed in the sales journal (N) and would like to select 100 sales invoices for testing (n). Thus, the interval is every thirtieth sales invoice (3,000/100). If it is assumed that the auditor selects the number 12 as a random starting point, the first sales invoice selected would be the twelfth invoice, the second would be the forty-second invoice $(12 + 30)$, and so on, until the sample of 100 items is selected.

A client might summarize or group a population in a specific order, and thus such a population would not be random. A sample selected from a nonrandom population using the systematic-selection method might not be appropriate for drawing statistical conclusions about a population, unless the auditor takes steps to solve the randomness problem. The auditor should examine the population to determine whether it has been grouped or summarized in a particular order. Inquiries of client personnel may also be made to ascertain how individual transactions are accumulated or individual balances listed. If the population is in a specific order, it should be stratified and proportional samples should be drawn from each stratum. In this event, the auditor might want to test one or more of the strata more extensively.

Even if the population is not in a specific order, it usually is advisable for the auditor to have two or more random starts.

Step 4c — Other sampling

Block sampling refers to selecting contiguous sampling units, such as all checks numbered from 420 to 440. Block sampling cannot be used when the auditor uses a statistical sampling approach. When the auditor uses only a few blocks to select the sample, block sampling also would be inappropriate for a nonstatistical sampling approach.

Haphazard sampling consists of selecting sampling units without any conscious bias. For example, the selection would be biased if the auditor had a tendency to select vendor folders that had the most vendor invoices in them. If properly applied, haphazard sampling can be used for nonstatistical sampling but not for a statistical sampling approach.

Step 5 — Determine the sample size

A considerable amount of professional judgment is necessary to determine the proper sample size. The method for reaching a decision for determining the sample size is the same for nonstatistical sampling as it is for statistical sampling. In statistical sampling, the auditor will quantify the factors that are used to determine the sample size; in nonstatistical sampling, the factors will be described in subjective terms. For example, in statistical sampling, the auditor may conclude that a 10% factor should be assigned to the risk of assessing control risk too low. In nonstatistical sampling, the auditor may conclude that the client's internal controls appear to be well-designed. Both conclusions are highly subjective and are based on the same fundamental analysis, although the conclusion associated with statistical sampling is more precise.

EXHIBIT AU 350-1—AUDIT JUDGMENT FACTORS USED IN NONSTATISTICAL AND STATISTICAL SAMPLING TO DETERMINE SAMPLE SIZE FOR TESTS OF CONTROLS

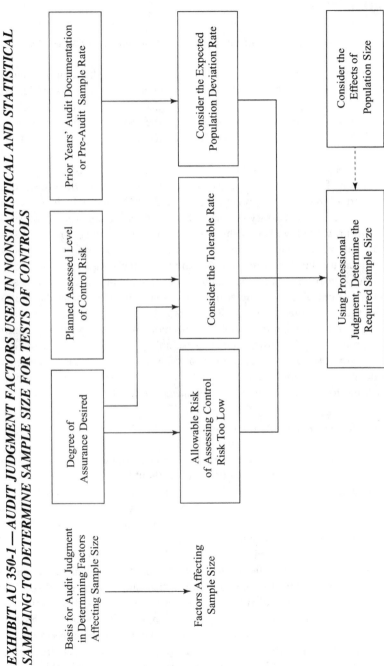

The audit decision process as described in SAS-39 is summarized in Exhibit AU 350-1.

Step 5a — Consider the allowable risk of assessing control risk too low

The level of sampling risk is influenced by the size of the sample. There is always a risk that the auditor will not draw a representative sample. The larger the sample, the more audit hours it takes to test the sample. Achieving an acceptable level of sampling risk is the result of a trade-off between trying to avoid overauditing on the one hand and underauditing on the other.

Establishing an allowable risk of assessing control risk too low is a function of the degree of assurance indicated by the audit evidence selected as part of the sample process. If the auditor desires a high degree of assurance, it is necessary to establish a relatively small risk of assessing control risk too low. Establishing a small risk of assessing control risk too low will require that (assuming all other factors remain constant) the auditor increase the size of the sample. The larger the sample size, the higher the degree of assurance the auditor can offer about the effectiveness of internal control. For example, if using a nonstatistical sample, the auditor must select a larger sample in order to establish a low risk of underestimating control risk rather than establishing a moderate risk of assessing control risk too low. When using statistical sampling, the auditor must select a larger sample size in order to make a statement about the maximum error rate at a 99% confidence level (or a 1% allowable risk of assessing control risk too low) rather than at a 90% confidence level.

Step 5b — Consider the tolerable rate

The "tolerable rate" is the maximum percentage of deviations (errors) in a population that an auditor will tolerate without changing the planned assessed level of control risk. SAS-39 states that the establishment of a tolerable rate in an engagement is based on (1) the planned assessed level of control risk and (2) the degree of assurance indicated by the audit evidence in the sample.

The planned assessed level of control risk results from obtaining an understanding of the client's internal control. Having gained an understanding of the client's internal control, the auditor then establishes the planned level of control risk, which in turn is a factor in determining the sample size for tests of control. For example, if an internal control is considered highly relevant to a critical financial statement assertion, the auditor would initially plan to rely relatively heavily on the control procedure and there would be a tendency to establish a small tolerable rate.

Step 5c — Consider the expected population deviation rate

The purpose of attribute sampling for nonstatistical as well as statistical sampling is to provide some insight into the deviation rate of a particular characteristic in a population. For example, the auditor may be interested in the rate of pricing errors the client made in preparing customer invoices. However, before sampling can begin, the auditor must make a preliminary estimate of the deviation rate. The expected population deviation rate is the anticipated deviation rate in the entire population. Ideally, the estimate should be based on the results of audits of prior years, taking into consideration any subsequent modifications of the client's internal control. The auditor may review audit documentation for the last few years to obtain an idea of the expected population deviation rate. In a new engagement, the auditor can estimate the expected population deviation rate by selecting and auditing a preliminary sample of about 25 items. The results of the test should be properly documented, because the preliminary sample becomes part of the final sample.

As the expected population deviation rate approaches the tolerable rate that the auditor established, the required sample size increases because the auditor must make an allowance for sampling risk. That is, if the auditor establishes a tolerable rate of 5% but the preliminary estimate of the deviation rate is 4%, in most situations the risk is too great that the actual deviation rate is more than 5%. In nonstatistical and statistical sampling it is misleading to think of estimating a single error rate. It is more useful to think of estimating an error range. In the current example, if the auditor is using nonstatistical sampling, it is better to think of the preliminary estimate of the deviation rate of being somewhere around 4%. If statistical sampling is used, the auditor may state that the estimated deviation rate is 4% plus or minus 2% (a range between 2% and 6%). Clearly, when the expected population deviation rate for a particular internal control is equal to or greater than the tolerable rate, the auditor should establish the control risk at its maximum level and generally not complete the test of controls, at least for the particular control(s) under investigation.

Step 5d — Consider the effect of the population size

In most circumstances, the size of the population has little and sometimes no effect on the determination of the required sample size in attribute sampling.

Step 5e — Consider a statistical or nonstatistical sampling method

The auditor may use either a nonstatistical sampling method or a statistical sampling method.

Sample size and nonstatistical sampling   When using nonstatistical sampling, the auditor takes into consideration the risk of assessing control risk too low, the tolerable rate, and the expected population deviation rate, and determines the sample size by professional judgment. The auditor should observe the following generalizations in determining the sample size when nonstatistical sampling is employed:

- As the risk of assessing control risk too low increases, the required sample size decreases.

- As the risk of assessing control risk too low decreases, the required sample size increases.

- As the tolerable rate increases, the required sample size decreases.

- As the tolerable rate decreases, the required sample size increases.

- As the expected population deviation rate increases, the required sample size increases.

- As the expected population deviation rate decreases, the required sample size decreases.

Sample size and statistical sampling For statistical sampling, the auditor can use tables or computer applications to determine the appropriate sample size. To use either tables or computer applications, the following must be established by the auditor:

- The risk of assessing control risk too low

- The tolerable error rate

- The expected population deviation rate

For example, if an auditor established (1) the risk of assessing control risk too low at 5%, (2) a tolerable error rate of 9%, and (3) an expected population deviation rate of 4%, the required sample size would be about 100.

Step 6 — Perform the sampling plan

After the sample has been selected, the auditor should apply audit procedures to each sampling unit to determine whether there has been a deviation from the established internal control procedure. Usually, a deviation occurs if the auditor is unable to perform an audit procedure or apply alternative audit procedures to a sampling unit. As a general rule, sampling units that are selected but not examined, such as voided transactions or unused documents, should be replaced with new sampling units. Voided transactions or unused documents are not considered deviations if the established procedure of accounting for these items has been properly followed.

Step 7 — Evaluate the sample results

After the audit procedures have been applied to each sampling unit, and the deviations, if any, from the prescribed internal controls have been summarized, the auditor must evaluate the results of the sampling.

Step 7a — Calculate the deviation rate

The deviation rate is computed by dividing the number of deviations by the number of units in the sample. The sample deviation rate is the auditor's best estimate of the population deviation rate.

Step 7b — Consider the sampling risk

The auditor must consider the degree of sampling risk involved in the sample results. Sampling risk arises because the auditor does not examine all of the sampling units in a population. An auditor can reach an entirely different conclusion on the basis of sample results than if the entire population is examined. When the auditor's estimate of the population deviation is less than the tolerable rate for the population, there is still a possibility that the true deviation rate in the population (maximum population deviation) is greater than the tolerable rate. The auditor can determine the degree of sampling risk in the sample results by computing the maximum population deviation rate.

Sampling risk and nonstatistical sampling When the auditor employs nonstatistical sampling, the sampling risk cannot be quantified; the auditor should nonetheless take that risk into consideration in determining whether the potential error rate in the population is unacceptable. The auditor should observe the following generalizations when evaluating the results of non-statistical sampling:

• The auditor may rely on the planned assessed level of control risk when the auditor's best estimate of the population deviation rate (based on the sample results) is equal to or less than the expected population deviation rate.

- The auditor cannot rely on the planned assessed level of control risk when the auditor's best estimate of the population deviation rate is greater than the expected population deviation rate.

When the deviation rate is greater than the tolerable rate, the planned assessed level of control risk is not justified. Thus, the auditor may, for example, decide not to rely on the client's internal control (assess control risk at the maximum) in the performance of substantive procedures.

Sampling risk and statistical sampling   When using statistical sampling, the auditor can use tables or computer applications to measure the allowance for sampling risk. To use either tables or computer applications, the following must be established by the auditor:

- The risk of assessing control risk too low

- The number of actual deviations found in the sample

- The sample size

- The expected deviation rate

To illustrate the above procedures, assume that the risk the auditor has established for assessing control risk too low is 5%, the sample size established by the auditor is 100, the tolerable rate established by the auditor is 9%, and the expected population deviation rate established by the auditor is 4%. If the auditor examines the 100 sample units and discovers two errors, the maximum population deviation rate (obtained from tables in Appendix A of the AICPA Audit Sampling Guide) is 6.2%. The maximum population deviation rate is also referred to as the upper limits or the upper precision limits.

In the above illustration, the auditor can be 95% certain that the maximum population deviation rate is 6.2%. The 95% certainty percentage is the complement of the 5% risk factor (100% minus 5%). Since the maximum deviation rate of 6.2% is less than the tolerable rate of 9% established by the auditor, the planned assessed level of control risk is not changed. However, when the maximum population deviation rate is greater than the tolerable rate established by the auditor, the planned assessed level of control risk is not justified.

Step 7c — Consider the qualitative aspects of the deviations

The auditor should consider the qualitative aspects of each deviation. The nature and cause of each deviation should be analyzed and deviations should be classified into unintentional deviations (errors) or intentional deviations (acts of fraud). The auditor should make a determination about whether the deviation resulted from a misunderstanding of instructions or from carelessness. The discovery of an act of fraud would require more attention from the auditor than the discovery of an error.

Step 7d — Reach an overall conclusion

The auditor must determine whether the overall audit approach supports the planned assessed level of control risk. To make this overall evaluation, the auditor should consider the following factors:

- Sample results of tests of controls

- Results of inquiries about controls that do not leave an audit trail

- Results of observations concerning control procedures that are based on the segregation of responsibilities

Professional judgment is required in reaching a conclusion on how the results of the tests of controls will affect the nature, timing, and extent of the subsequent substantive procedures.

Step 8 — Document the sampling procedures

To satisfy the requirements of SAS-103 (AU 312, AU 329, AU 339, AU 341) (Audit Documentation), the auditor should consider the following matters for documentation in the audit files:

- Description of internal controls tested

- Objective of the tests of controls

- Definition of population and sampling unit

- Definition of deviation conditions

- Method of determining sample size

- Method of sample selection

- Description of audit procedures employed and list of deviations discovered by the auditor [deviations should be classified as unintentional and (suspected) intentional acts]

- Evaluation of sample results and overall conclusions

SAMPLING IN TESTS OF DETAILS
(NONSTATISTICAL AND STATISTICAL SAMPLING APPROACHES)

Variable sampling (which is used in the performance of substantive tests of transactions and balances) is used to estimate the dollar value of a population and determine the reasonableness of financial statement balances. The purpose of substantive procedures is to obtain evidence of the validity and propriety of accounting balances and classes of transactions.

Promulgated Procedures Checklist

The auditor may use the following steps to apply variable sampling to substantive procedures:

1. Determine the audit objective of the test.
2. Define the population:

    a. Define the sampling unit.

    b. Consider the completeness of the population.

    c. Identify individually significant items.

3. Choose an audit sampling technique.
4. Determine the sample size:

    a. Consider variations within the population.

    b. Consider the acceptable level of risk.

    c. Consider the tolerable misstatement.

    d. Consider the expected amount of error.

    e. Consider the population size.

5. Determine the method of selecting the sample.
6. Perform the sampling plan.
7. Evaluate the sample results:

    a. Project the misstatement to the population and consider sampling risk.

    b. Consider the qualitative aspects of misstatements and reach an overall conclusion.

8. Document the sampling procedures.

Analysis and Application of Procedures

Step 1 — Determine the audit objective of the test

The audit objective of performing substantive procedures is to determine whether the dollar value assigned by management to an account balance or group of transactions is reasonable.

Step 2 — Define the population

The population the auditor defines must include all items that are related to the audit objective of the procedures. If items relevant to the audit objective are omitted from the population, the audit objective of the procedure will not be achieved. For example, the audit objective may be to determine whether the repairs and maintenance expense account is reasonably stated. The definition of the population could be all line items that make up the detail of the account, but such a definition would probably be deficient because other accounts — especially property, plant, and equipment — could contain expenditures that were capitalized when they should have been expensed. A better definition of the population would be all repairs and maintenance work orders authorized during the period.

Step 2a — Define the sampling unit

The population is made up of individual sampling units that may be individual transactions, documents, customer or vendor balances, or an individual entry. The auditor must consider the efficiency of the audit when selecting the sampling unit. For example, it may be more efficient to define the sampling unit as the individual sales invoice — rather than as the individual accounts receivable, which may be made up of several invoices.

Step 2b — Consider the completeness of the population

The physical representation of the population must be consistent with the definition of the population. For example, the auditor may be concerned with all cash disbursements made during the period and define the population as all canceled checks during the period. The auditor must determine that the defined population is complete; otherwise, a representative sample cannot be drawn from the population.

Step 2c — Identify individually significant items

The population should be reviewed for items that should be individually examined because of the audit exposure related to these items. Items that should be examined individually include large dollar items, related party transactions, and accounts with a history of errors. When items are examined individually, they are not part of the sampling results; however, these items must be considered in determining the possible misstatement in the population. There is, therefore, no sampling risk associated with these items.

Step 3 — Choose an audit sampling technique

Initially, the auditor must determine whether a nonstatistical or a statistical sampling approach should be employed. As stated earlier, SAS-39 indicates no preference of one over the other. Whether a nonstatistical or a statistical sampling approach is used, many different types of sampling techniques are used in practice. Irrespective of the sampling approach or specific sampling technique the auditor uses, he or she must observe the following steps as established by SAS-39 in the performance of substantive procedures based on sampling.

Step 4 — Determine the sample size

The auditor must use professional judgment to determine the sample size. The decision process for determining the sample size is the same for nonstatistical sampling as it is for statistical sampling. In statistical sampling the auditor will quantify the relevant factors, whereas in nonstatistical sampling the factors will be described in a less structured manner.

The audit decision process for determining the sample size as described in SAS-39 is summarized in Exhibit AU 350-2.

Step 4a — Consider variations within the population

A basic concept in sampling is the need to obtain a representative sample from the population. If the population is composed of various items, the auditor must examine a sufficiently large sample to be reasonably assured that a representative sample has been selected.

For accounting populations, the variation within a population may be expressed in dollar amounts. It is not unusual for an accounting population to be composed of a few large balances, several medium balances, and

EXHIBIT AU 350-2—AUDIT JUDGMENT FACTORS USED TO DETERMINE SAMPLE SIZE FOR SUBSTANTIVE PROCEDURES

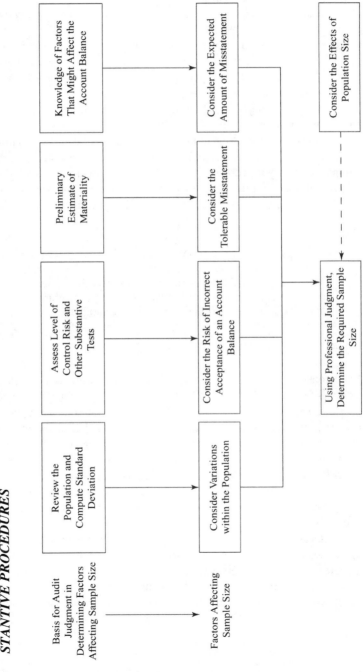

numerous smaller balances. The required sample size increases as the variability in the population increases.

When nonstatistical sampling is employed, the auditor may review the population or the prior years' audit documentation to acquire an understanding of the variation within the population. When a classical variable statistical sampling technique is employed, the auditor measures the variation in the population by computing the estimate of the standard deviation of the sample mean.

It may be efficient to stratify a population with a high degree of variation. "Stratification" simply means that the population is divided into groups (strata) of sampling units that have the same or approximately the same dollar values, and samples are selected from each group. Stratification is necessary to reduce the effect of the variation in the population on the size of the sample. (In both nonstatistical sampling and statistical sampling, as the variation increases, the auditor needs to select a larger sample size.)

> **ENGAGEMENT STRATEGY:** When probability proportional to size (PPS) sampling is used, there is no need to consider the variation within the population, because this technique automatically considers that factor since it is a combination of both attribute sampling and variable estimation.

Step 4b — Consider the acceptable level of risk

When considering whether to accept or reject the results of a sample, the auditor is faced with the risks of (1) incorrect rejection of a balance and (2) incorrect acceptance of a balance. The risk of incorrect rejection of a balance is the risk that the results of a sample will lead the auditor to conclude that the recorded account balance is materially misstated when, in fact, the recorded account balance is not materially misstated. The risk of incorrect acceptance of a balance is the risk that the results of a sample will lead the auditor to conclude that the recorded account balance is not materially misstated when, in fact, the recorded account balance is materially misstated.

In determining an acceptable level of risk of incorrect acceptance for tests of details, the auditor should consider (1) the assessed risk of material misstatement (inherent risk and control risk) and (2) the risk that other relevant substantive procedures (including substantive analytical procedures) would not detect a material misstatement. These risk factors and interrelationships must be considered in nonstatistical sampling plans as well as in statistical sampling plans. These relationships are illustrated in an appendix to SAS-39 in the following manner:

$$TD = AR/(IR \times CR \times AP)$$

where:

- AR = the allowable audit risk that monetary misstatements equal to tolerable misstatement might remain undetected for the account balance or class of transactions and related assertions after the auditor has completed all audit procedures deemed necessary.

- IR = the susceptibility of an assertion to a material misstatement assuming there are no related internal controls.

- CR = the risk that a material misstatement that could occur in an assertion will not be prevented or detected on a timely basis by the entity's internal controls. (The auditor assesses control risk on the basis of the sufficiency of audit evidence obtained to support the effectiveness of internal controls.)

- AP = the risk that analytical procedures and other relevant substantive procedures would fail to detect misstatements that could occur in an assertion equal to tolerable misstatement, given that such misstatements occur and are not detected by the internal control.

- TD = the allowable risk of incorrect acceptance for the test of details, given that misstatements equal to tolerable misstatement occur in an assertion and are not detected by internal control or analytical procedures and other relevant substantive procedures.

The above equation emphasizes relationships among the various factors that the auditor must consider when determining the allowable risk of incorrect acceptance. For example, as control risk rises, the allowable risk of incorrect acceptance must decrease to achieve a stated level of audit risk. That relationship is based on the simple logic that as the perceived effectiveness of internal control decreases, the auditor is less willing to establish a high allowable risk of incorrect acceptance of an account balance. Stated in terms of its effect on sample size, it is necessary to increase the size of the sample as control risk increases to reduce the level of risk of incorrect acceptance. Thus, from the perspective of sample size and all other factors remaining constant, there is an inverse relationship between control risk and the allowable risk of incorrect acceptance.

Although the relationships established in the above equation are intuitive, it is unlikely that an auditor would assign an absolute value to audit risk; rather he or she would evaluate the risk in an abstract manner. Even when statistical sampling is employed, most auditors would use the relationships established by the equation as a guide, avoiding a strict and comprehensive quantitative approach arrived at by simply plugging in risk factors. Even if an auditor insists on a strictly quantitative approach, that does not imply that judgment has been removed from the process. In a strictly quantitative approach, the process may appear to be unbiased, but as discussed in this section, the risk factors are based on a number of decisions that depend heavily on professional judgments. Those judgments are the same for nonstatistical sampling and statistical sampling.

Step 4c — Consider the tolerable misstatement

The tolerable misstatement is an estimate of the maximum monetary misstatement that may exist in an account balance or group of transactions when combined with misstatement in other accounts, without causing the financial statements to be materially misstated. The tolerable misstatement is based on the auditor's definition of "materiality," or the maximum amount by which the financial statements could be misstated and still be in accordance with generally accepted accounting principles. There is an inverse relationship between the tolerable misstatement and the required sample size. Thus, the sample size must be increased when the tolerable misstatement is decreased.

Tolerable misstatement is related to the auditor's planned level of materiality for the financial statements as a whole such that tolerable misstatement when combined for all planned audit procedures does not exceed materiality for the financial statements. Thus, auditors should set tolerable misstatement for a specific audit procedure at an amount less than the financial statements so that when the results are aggregated, the required level of overall assurance is obtained.

Step 4d — Consider the expected amount of misstatement

An estimate of the expected amount of misstatement in a particular account balance or group of transactions is based on the following factors:

- Understanding of the entity's business
- Prior years' tests of the population
- Results of a pre-audit sample
- Results of tests of controls

The required sample size increases as the auditor's estimate of the expected amount of misstatement in the population increases.

> **PLANNING AID REMINDER:** In practice it is often difficult to determine the expected amount of misstatement, but this can be overcome by combining the effects of the tolerable misstatement and the expected amount of misstatement. This can be accomplished by establishing a materiality threshold and then dividing that amount by "about 2" in order to establish the tolerable misstatement. For example, if materiality is established at $100,000, then the tolerable misstatement would be about $50,000 ($100,000/2). Then only the (adjusted) tolerable misstatement would be used to determine the required sample size.

Step 4e — Consider the population size

The population size generally has an effect on the sample size, depending on which sampling technique the auditor employs.

Step 5 — Determine the method of selecting the sample

The auditor must select sampling units from the defined population in such a way that each sampling unit has a chance of being selected. The auditor's objective is to select a representative sample of all items from the population. If statistical sampling is used, the sample selection must be random.

Step 6 — Perform the sampling plan

Once the sample has been selected, the auditor should apply appropriate audit procedures. If the auditor is unable to perform an audit procedure on a sampling unit selected for examination, alternative audit procedures should be considered. If the sampling unit does not have an effect on the conclusion the auditor reaches concerning the acceptability of the population, alternative audit procedures do not have to be applied, and the sampling unit may be treated as a misstatement for evaluation purposes. In addition, the auditor should determine whether the inability to apply an audit procedure has an effect on the assessed level of control risk or the assessment of risk on representations made by the client.

Step 7 — Evaluate the sample results

After testing the sample units, the auditor should evaluate the sample results to determine whether the account balance or group of transactions is correct and in accordance with generally accepted accounting principles.

Step 7a — Project the misstatement to the population and consider sampling risk

The misstatements discovered in the sampling units should be projected to the total population. In its simplest form, a $2,000 misstatement in a sample that represents 20% of the population would be projected as a total misstatement of $10,000 ($2,000/20%). The method of projecting the misstatement to the total population will depend on the type of sampling technique the auditor uses.

If the projected misstatement is greater than the tolerable misstatement, the account balance cannot be accepted as correct. If the projected misstatement is significantly less than the tolerable misstatement, the auditor may conclude that the account balance is not materially misstated. For example, if the projected misstatement is $10,000 and the tolerable misstatement is $50,000, in most instances the risk of accepting an incorrect balance would be acceptable. As the projected misstatement approaches the tolerable misstatement, the risk of accepting an incorrect balance increases, and the auditor must use professional judgment in deciding whether to accept a balance as correct. For example, if the projected misstatement is $40,000 and the tolerable misstatement is $50,000, in most instances the risk of accepting an incorrect balance would not be acceptable.

Step 7b — Consider the qualitative aspects of misstatements and reach an overall conclusion

Each misstatement the auditor discovers by testing the sample should be evaluated to determine why the misstatement was made and whether the misstatement has an effect on other phases of the engagement. For example, the discovery of a fraudulent act would have broader implication to the auditor than the discovery of a routine error.

The results of the substantive procedures may suggest that the assessed level of control risk was too low. Such a condition would require the auditor to consider whether substantive procedures should be expanded.

Step 8 — Document the sampling procedures

To satisfy the requirements of SAS-103 (AU 312, AU 329, AU 339, AU 341), the auditor should consider the following matters for documentation in the audit files:

- Description of audit procedures and objectives tested

- Definition of population and sampling unit

- Definition of a misstatement

- Basis for establishment of risk of incorrect acceptance, incorrect rejection, tolerable misstatement, and expected misstatement

- Audit sampling technique used

- Method of sampling selection

- Description of sampling procedures performed and list of misstatements discovered [deviations should be classified as unintentional and (suspected) intentional acts]

- Evaluation of sample and summary of overall conclusions

NONSTATISTICAL SAMPLING FOR TESTS OF DETAIL

This section is based on the discussion in the previous section, but it focuses exclusively on nonstatistical sampling for tests of detail. The guidance provided here is based on material in Chapter 5 of the AICPA's Audit Guide titled "Audit Sampling" (the AICPA released a new edition of the guide on May 1, 2008).

Promulgated Procedures Checklist

The auditor may use the following steps to apply nonstatistical sampling concepts to tests of details.

- Identify individually significant items

- Determine the sample size

- Select the sample

- Evaluate the sample results

Analysis and Application of Procedures

Identify individually significant items

Initially the auditor should review the items that make up the population to determine whether certain items should be tested 100% rather than sampled. The items selected for 100% testing might be based on the dollar value of the item or unusual characteristics of the item. For example, an auditor may review the trial balance of accounts receivable and decide that all receivables that exceed $1,000 should be selected for confirmation. Generally, larger dollar amounts within a population are selected for 100% testing based on the auditor's judgment.

Determine the sample size

The size of the sample in nonstatistical sampling is based on professional judgment. The auditor cannot simply decide to use a rule of thumb in all engagements and expect to satisfy professional standards or to perform an effective engagement. For example, if the auditor has a rule of thumb that he or she always confirms 10% of the dollar value of accounts receivable, that approach is a violation of generally accepted auditing standards.

The Audit Guide "Audit Sampling" points out that when an auditor uses nonstatistical sampling to perform test of details, the following factors (discussed in the previous section) must be taken into consideration:

- Population variation

- Risk of incorrect acceptance

- Tolerable misstatement and expected misstatement

- Population size

Although these four factors sound like concepts that are found in a statistics course, they are actually based on common sense.

> **PLANNING AID REMINDER:** Although the auditor must take the four factors listed above into consideration in determining the size of the sample, the auditor does not have to quantify these factors. Also, some auditors believe that there is some simple solution to determining sample size that does not have to take into consideration the four factors listed above. There is no simple rule-of-thumb solution. An auditor must take these factors into consideration and use professional judgment

to determine the size of a sample, even when nonstatistical sampling is used.

Population variation

In general, the more homogenous the population, the smaller the sample size can be. That is, for example, if the trial balance of accounts receivable is made up of balances that range from $150 to $220, there is little variation in the population. For this reason, an auditor can test relatively few items in order to get a representative sample of the accounts receivable. On the other hand, if the range of balances in accounts receivable is from $5 to $25,000, this population exhibits more variability and it would be necessary to test a larger number of accounts receivable.

> **ENGAGEMENT STRATEGY:** In practice it is unlikely that an accounting population will have as small degree of variation as suggested in the above paragraph; however, it is possible to divide the population into groupings (population stratification) and thus significantly reduce the degree of variation in each grouping. Also, it should be remembered that a group of the population may be tested 100% (as discussed earlier) and evaluated separately. Stratification and testing some of the items 100% will almost always reduce the overall size of the sample.

The auditor can get a feel for the variation within a population by reviewing the items that make up the population. For example, a simple review of the trial balance of accounts receivable should give the auditor a reasonable impression of the variability of the population. A more precise measurement of variability can be determined quickly if the trial balance is digitized and can be subjected to analysis by various file analyzers. For example, if the trial balance of accounts receivable is maintained in a spreadsheet file, such as an Excel spreadsheet, it might be possible to create statistics such as the variance or standard deviation of the population.

Risk of incorrect acceptance

As discussed earlier in this section, an interplay exists among audit risk, inherent risk, and control risk. These relationships can be summarized as follows:

- When the combined inherent and control risks are assessed at a lower level, a greater risk of incorrect acceptance for planned substantive procedures can be established. Under this circumstance, the required sample size is decreased.

• When the combined inherent and control risks are assessed at a higher level, a lower risk of incorrect acceptance for planned substantive procedures can be established. Under this circumstance, the required sample size is increased.

• When the auditor relies more heavily on other substantive procedures (including analytical procedures) to achieve the same audit objective, a greater risk of incorrect acceptance for planned substantive procedures can be established. Under this circumstance, the required sample size is decreased.

• When the auditor relies less heavily on other substantive procedures (including analytical procedures) to achieve the same audit objective, a lesser risk of incorrect acceptance for planned substantive procedures can be established. Under this circumstance, the required sample size is increased.

Tolerable misstatement and expected misstatement

The establishment of a sample size in nonstatistical sampling must take into consideration the tolerable misstatement (the size of the error that the auditor considers to be tolerable) and the expected misstatement. In general, as the size of the tolerable misstatement increases, the required sample size decreases. For example, if the auditor believes that a tolerable misstatement in the accounts receivable balance is $30,000 rather than $10,000, the number of items that must be in the sample is decreased.

In determining the size of a sample, the auditor should also take into consideration the expected misstatement in the population. As the expected misstatement in the population increases, the required sample size must be increased. That is, if an auditor does not have much faith in the balances under investigation, common sense would require an auditor to test more items from the population.

Population size

The size of the population has little effect on the size of the sample. Thus, if one trial balance of accounts receivable has 2,000 line items and another trial balance has 4,000 line items, assuming all other factors are equal, both populations would require essentially the same sample size.

> **ENGAGEMENT STRATEGY:** It is easy for auditors to over-emphasize the size of the population in determining the required sample size for a particular balance. For example, if the auditor has a rule of thumb that he or she samples 10% of the items of the population, the result is a misapplication of auditing standards. In the previous example, the auditor would select 200 items from the first population and 400 items from the second, but that doubling of the sample size in the second population is not supported by sampling concepts. It is far more important for the auditor to thoughtfully look at the other three factors discussed above, rather than population size, in determining the required sample size for a population.

Consider the interplay of the four factors   The auditor uses professional judgment to evaluate the four factors described above and, based on this evaluation, determines the required sample size. There is no single approach that an auditor should use to make this determination; however, for illustrative purpose the AICPA Audit Sampling Guide describes the following as an approach that an auditor may consider:

- Consider the level of inherent risk

- Consider the effectiveness of controls related to the financial statement assertions

- Establish the risk of incorrect acceptance

- Establish a tolerable misstatement level

- Evaluate the effect of other related tests of details

- Determine the population reported amount

- Compute the preliminary sample size

- Adjust the preliminary sample size

> **ENGAGEMENT STRATEGY:** The AICPA Audit Guide "Audit Sampling" is careful not to endorse any particular method for determining sample size but describes the usefulness of the approach described above as follows: The model is provided only to illustrate the relative effect of different planning considerations on sample size; it is not intended as a substitute for professional judgment. The auditor can find this approach useful to get a feel for how various assessments of the four factors described earlier can have on the required sample size.

Consider the level of inherent risk   Initially the auditor assesses the level of inherent risk related to the particular assertions in the financial statements that will be tested once the sample is selected. SAS-107 (AU 312) (Audit Risk and Materiality in Conducting an Audit) defines inherent risk as "the susceptibility of an assertion to a material misstatement, assuming that there are no related controls." SAS-106 (AU 326) (Audit Evidence) attempts to provide the logical framework for the audit process by identifying the following broad assertions that must be tested:

• Assertions for classes of transactions

• Assertions for account balances

• Assertions for presentation and disclosure

> **OBSERVATION:** For a discussion of inherent risk see AU 312, and for a discussion of financial statements assertions see AU 326.

Consider the effectiveness of controls related to the financial statement assertions   Once the specific financial statement assertions are identified, the auditor should consider the effectiveness of the controls related to the prevention and detection of material misstatements related to the assertions. SAS-107 (AU 312) defines control risk as "the risk that a material misstatement that could occur in an assertion will not be prevented or detected on a timely basis by the entity's internal control."

Establish the risk of incorrect acceptance   The judgments made in the first two steps should be combined and the auditor should determine the risk of incorrect acceptance (which was described earlier in this section). That is, inherent risk and control risk related to specific assertions included in the financial statements provide insight into how much risk the auditor is willing to accept for those particular assertions. Although there are innumerable levels that could be identified in practice, some auditors think about the risk of incorrect acceptance using quantitative measures such as 5%, 10%, 15%, and so forth, whereas other auditors qualitatively express the risk of incorrect acceptance using the following categories:

• Maximum

• Slightly below maximum

• Moderate

• Low

If the auditor believes that particular assertions have a high inherent risk and that the controls related to the assertions are weak, the auditor would be less willing to bear the risk of incorrect acceptance. On the other hand, if there is relatively low inherent risk related to assertions and the related controls are effective, the auditor would be willing to bear a higher risk of incorrect acceptance.

Establish a tolerable misstatement level   The tolerable misstatement is an estimate of the maximum monetary misstatement that may exist in an account balance or group of transactions when combined with misstatement in other accounts, without causing the financial statements to be materially misstated.

Evaluate the effect of other related tests of details   When a single audit procedure is performed, the results of that procedure often test the validity of more than one assertion that appears in the financial statements. For this reason, the auditor should assess the risk that other audit procedures may have an impact on the assertions that are the focus of the current sample determination using the following framework.

- *Maximum risk*   No other substantive procedures are performed to test the same assertions

- *Moderate risk*   Other substantive procedures that are performed to test the same assertions are expected to be moderately effective in detecting material misstatements in those assertions

- *Low risk*   Other substantive procedures that are performed to test the same assertions are expected to be highly effective in detecting material misstatements in those assertions

Determine the population reported amount   The dollar value of the population is simply the amount reported in the financial statements less items that make up this value that are to be tested 100%.

Compute the preliminary sample size   The preliminary sample size is a function of the auditor's determination of the risk of incorrect acceptance, expected rate of misstatement in the population, tolerable misstatement, and the reported population amount. The expected rate of misstatement is the expected monetary misstatement that may exist in an account balance or group of transactions. The illustrative sample sizes in Exhibit AU 350-3 are based on Table 4.5 from the *Audit Guide*.

EXHIBIT AU 350-3 — ILLUSTRATIVE SAMPLE SIZES

Risk of Incorrect Acceptance	Ratio of Expected Misstatement to Tolerable Misstatement	Tolerable Misstatement as % of Population	Sample Size
5%	0	5%	60
5%	0.2	5%	93
5%	0.2	2%	232
10%	0	5%	47
10%	0.2	5%	69
10%	0.2	3%	114
15%	0	5%	38
15%	0.2	5%	55
15%	0	2%	95

As Exhibit AU 350-3 illustrates, holding other factors constant, the sample size increases given (1) a lower risk of incorrect acceptance, (2) a larger ratio of expected misstatement to tolerable misstatement, and (3) a smaller ratio of tolerable misstatement as a percentage of the reported population amount.

Adjust the preliminary sample size   The preliminary sample size must be adjusted upward because nonstatistical rather than statistical sampling is used. The AICPA Audit Guide "Audit Sampling" notes that "auditors typically adjust the sample size from 10% to 50% if the sample is not selected in a statically efficient manner." For example, if a population that has a great deal of variation has not been stratified, the auditor should increase the preliminary sample size.

To illustrate this approach, assume an auditor is trying to decide the sample size for the confirmation of accounts receivable under the following conditions:

- *Consider the level of inherent risk*   This particular audit procedure is concerned with the existence of accounts receivable, and the level of inherent risk is considered to be moderate based on the nature of accounts receivable and other factors related to the client.

- *Consider the effectiveness of controls related to the financial statement assertions*   Based on the evaluation of the client's internal control related to the processing of accounts receivable and cash receipts, the auditor has concluded that internal controls are weak and control risk is assessed at the maximum level.

- *Evaluate the effect of other related tests of details*   The auditor has identified another audit procedure that will help to determine the existence of accounts receivable (for example, the review of subsequent cash receipts) and assessed as moderate the risk that other substantive procedures will fail to detect a material misstatement.

- *Establish the risk of incorrect acceptance*   The auditor considers the assessed level of inherent risk (moderate), control risk (maximum), and the effect of other related tests of details (moderate) in determining the risk of incorrect acceptance. The auditor decides to assess the risk of incorrect acceptance at 10% (or, qualitatively, at a level slightly below maximum).

- *Establish a tolerable misstatement level*   Based on the assessment of materiality, the auditor decides to establish a tolerable misstatement level of $11,500.

- *Estimate the expected misstatement level*   Based on the auditor's previous experience auditing accounts receivable for this client, expected misstatement is $2,000.

- *Determine the population reported amount*   The general ledger balance of accounts receivable is reported at $250,000 but accounts receivable that exceed $4,000 will be tested 100%. The accounts that will be tested 100% are reported at $20,000. Thus, the population subject to sampling has a reported amount of $230,000.

- *Compute the preliminary sample size*   The auditor has established the risk of incorrect acceptance at 10%. Expected misstatement, $2,000, is approximately 20% of tolerable misstatement, $11,500. And tolerable misstatement is 5% of the population balance subject to sampling ($11,500/$230,000). Using the table in Exhibit AU 350-3, the preliminary sample size is 69 sample items (i.e., customer accounts receivable balances to be confirmed).

- *Adjust the preliminary sample size*   The auditor, based on the review of the trial balance of accounts receivable, decided not to stratify the sample (except for the items that are tested 100%), even though there was a moderate amount of variation in the account balances. For this reason, the auditor decided to increase the size of the sample by 30%. Thus, the required sample size is 90 (69 × 1.3).

Select the sample

Once the sample size has been determined, the sample itself should be selected so that each item in the population has a chance of selection (representative sample). One way to select the sample is to divide the population into categories based on dollar values, selecting more items from the category with the greatest dollar value. The allocation in Exhibit AU 350-4 illustrates this approach based on the example presented earlier in this section.

EXHIBIT AU 350-4 — SELECTING THE SAMPLE

Category	Reported Amount	Allocation Fraction	Total Required Sample Size	Sample Size for Category
$1 to $500	100,000	100/230	90	39
$501 to $2,000	80,000	80/230	90	31
$2,001 to $4,000	50,000	50/230	90	20
Totals	$230,000			90

Thus, 39 receivables will be selected from those receivables that have a balance of $500 or less, and so on. Within each category, the specific items selected for confirmation could be selected on a random basis or an interval basis.

> **OBSERVATION:** In this example, the population has been stratified for sample selection purposes but not for sample evaluation purposes.

Evaluate the sample results

In order to evaluate the sample results when a nonstatistical sampling approach is used, the auditor must do the following:

- Project the misstatement in the population
- Consider the sampling risk
- Consider qualitative characteristics

Project the misstatement in the population

Once the specific items are selected for testing, the appropriate audit procedures are performed. Based on the performance of the audit procedures, the auditor would determine the amount of the misstatements found in the sample items. This misstatement must then be projected to the total population. To continue with the current illustration, assume the 90 accounts selected for confirmation have a total account balance of $23,000 and assume that the auditor discovered misstatements equal to $600. The projected total misstatement for the sampled population would be $6,000 ($600/[$23,000/$230,000]).

When the auditor has tested a segment of the population 100%, the misstatement found for these items must be added to the projected total misstatement for the sampled item in order to determine the projected total misstatement for the total population. For example, in the current illustration all receivables with a balance greater than $4,000 were tested. If the misstatement discovered in this group of receivables was $1,000, the projected total misstatement for the population would be $7,000 ($6,000 + $1,000).

Consider sampling risk

Once the auditor has determined the projected total misstatement for the population, he or she must be careful not to draw a conclusion about the population based on this single estimate. That is, the auditor cannot say that the best estimate of the misstatement is a specific amount ($7,000 in the current example), but rather he or she must recognize that sampling risk must be considered. Sampling risk arises because not all the items in the population were tested; therefore, the best estimate of the misstatement is not a single amount but a range around that single amount.

Determining, based on the sampling results, whether a population's dollar value is probably not misstated involves a considerable amount of professional judgment. The focus of the judgment is the relationship between the tolerable misstatement and the projected misstatement. The broad generalizations in Exhibit AU 350-5 are helpful in making that judgment.

EXHIBIT AU 350-5 — MISSTATEMENTS AND
PROFESSIONAL JUDGMENT

Relationship of Projected Misstatement and Tolerable Misstatement for the Sample	*Examples*	*Analysis and Judgment*
The projected misstatement is significantly less than the tolerable misstatement.	Assume the projected misstatement is $1,000 and the tolerable misstatement is $9,000.	The projected misstatement is so much less than the tolerable misstatement, it is probably unlikely that the actual misstatement (if the entire population were sampled) would be greater than the tolerable misstatement. *Conclusion:* The auditor is reasonably assured that the population balance is not misstated.
The projected misstatement is equal to or greater than the tolerable misstatement.	Assume the projected misstatement is $10,000 and the tolerable misstatement is $9,000.	The projected misstatement implies that the balance is materially misstated. *Conclusion:* The auditor may request that the client review the population for possible adjustment. Once adjustments are made, the auditor should reevaluate the balance to determine whether it is acceptable.
The projected misstatement is neither close to nor far from the tolerable misstatement.	Assume the projected misstatement is $7,500 and the tolerable misstatement is $9,000.	When the projected misstatement is neither close to nor far from the tolerable misstatement, the decision process becomes more difficult because the conclusion that can be drawn is not as obvious as it is in the two situations described above.

Relationship of Projected Misstatement and Tolerable Misstatement for the Sample	Examples	Analysis and Judgment
		Conclusion: Under this circumstance, the auditor might want to (1) increase the sample size (concluding that the original sample might not have been representative) or (2) perform alternative audit procedures in order to obtain additional evidence concerning the possible misstatement of the population.

Consider qualitative characteristics

When a misstatement is discovered, an auditor should not mechanically respond to the misstatement as simply part of the projection of the total misstated amount in the population. Each misstatement should be analyzed to determine whether it arose from an error (an unintentional action) or from possible fraud (an intentional action). If fraud is suspected, the auditor should follow the guidance established in AU 316 (Consideration of Fraud in a Financial Statement Audit).

Practitioner's Aids

EXHIBIT AU 350-6 — REQUIRED SAMPLE SIZE FOR NONSTATISTICAL TESTS OF DETAILS

Use the following procedures as a guide for determining the required sample size for the performance of tests of details based on a non-statistical sampling approach. The checklist is only a guide, and professional judgment should be exercised to determine how it should be modified by revising or adding procedures. Initial and date each procedure as it is completed. Each procedure should be cross-referenced to an audit schedule that is the basis for the judgment or factor that is used to determine the required sample size.

Client Name: _____

Account Balance or Transactions Tested: _____

Date of Financial Statements: _____

	Initials	Date	Audit Documentation Reference
1. Establish the level of inherent risk.	____	____	_____
— — Maximum			
— — Slightly below maximum			
— — Moderate			
— — Low			
2. Consider the effectiveness of controls related to the financial statement assertions (control risk).	____	____	_____
— — Maximum			
— — Slightly below maximum			
— — Moderate			
— — Low			
3. Establish the risk of incorrect acceptance.	____	____	_____
— — Maximum			
— — Slightly below maximum			
— — Moderate			
— — Low			
4. Establish a tolerable misstatement level, both as a dollar amount and as a percentage of the population amount subject to sampling procedures.	____	____	_____
5. Estimate the expected misstatement amount, both as a dollar amount and as a percentage of tolerable misstatement.	____	____	_____

	Initials	*Date*	*Audit Documentation Reference*

6. Evaluate the effect of other related tests of details.   ____   ____   _____

— — Maximum

— — Slightly below maximum

— — Moderate

— — Low

7. Determine the population reported amount subject to sampling procedures.   ____   ____   _____

$_____

8. Compute the preliminary sample size using the table in Exhibit AU 350-3 or using Table 4.5 in the AICPA's *Audit Sampling* guide.

9. Adjust the preliminary sample size.   ____   ____   _____

Required sample size:————

Reviewed by: _____

Date: _____

SECTION 380

THE AUDITOR'S COMMUNICATION WITH THOSE CHARGED WITH GOVERNANCE

Authoritative Pronouncements

SAS-114 — The Auditor's Communication with Those Charged with Governance

> **IMPORTANT NOTICE FOR 2011:** The Auditing Standards Board (ASB) has already issued a redrafted SAS-114 to apply the ASB's drafting clarity conventions and converge audit documentation guidance with the International Standards on Auditing. The redrafted SAS is similar to previously existing guidance. The major difference is that certain sections of previously existing SAS-114 were removed because they are redundant with other auditing standards. In addition, the requirement for the auditor to communicate his or her responsibility related to other information in documents containing audited financial statements, including any audit procedures performed and their results, has been moved to AU Section 550. The effective date of all redrafted SASs is audits of financial statements for periods beginning no earlier than on or after December 15, 2012. This date is far enough into the future to provide sufficient time for firms to update their methodologies and to provide needed training.

Overview

Effective governance over the entity's processes, including those related to financial reporting, is a critical element of an entity's internal controls. Persons should be in place who have responsibility for overseeing the strategic direction of the entity and obligations related to the accountability of the entity to its key stakeholders, including oversight of the financial reporting process. Governance structures vary by entity, often depending on the entity's size and organizational structure.

SAS-114 establishes standards and provides guidance on the auditor's communication with those charged with governance in relation to the audit of financial statements. The intent of SAS-114 is to provide a framework for an effective two-way communication between the auditor and those charged with governance, and it identifies specific matters to be communicated. Auditors are required to communicate matters that in their judgment are significant and relevant to the responsibilities of those charged with governance over the financial reporting responsibilities.

The principal purposes of the auditor's communications with those charged with governance include the following:

- Communicate clearly the responsibilities of the auditor in relation to the financial statement audit, including an overview of the scope and timing of the audit.

- Obtain information relevant to the audit from those charged with governance.

- Provide those charged with governance with timely information about observations arising from the audit that are relevant to their governance responsibilities in the oversight of the financial reporting processes.

The intended recipient of the auditor's communication is *those charged with governance*, which may vary across entities. For many, those charged with governance include the board of directors or its audit committee. For others, those charged with governance may reside outside the entity, such as a government agency, or those charged with governance may include those who have management responsibilities. Determination of who those charged with governance are is based on the auditor's judgment.

Promulgated Procedures Checklist

The auditor should perform the following procedures related to communications with those charged with governance:

- Determine the appropriate recipients of the auditor's communication

- Determine the specific matters to be communicated to those charged with governance

- Determine the form and timing of the communication process and assess the adequacy of communications

Analysis and Application of Procedures

Determine the appropriate recipients of the auditor's communication

The intended recipients of the auditor's communication are those charged with governance, which varies from one entity to another. The auditor's understanding of the entity's governance structure and processes obtained in connection with the requirements in SAS-109 provide relevant input to his or her determination of the appropriate recipients of his or her communication.

Those charged with governance might include one or more of the following:

- Board of directors or supervisory board

- Subgroup of the board, such as the audit committee

- Partners or proprietors

- Committee of management or trustees

- Owner-manager or sole trustee

SAS-114 does not establish communication requirements with an entity's management or owners unless they also are charged with a governance role.

In many instances, communication with the audit committee (or another equivalent subgroup of those charged with governance) adequately fulfills the auditor's responsibility to communicate with those charged with governance. Audit committees exist in many entities and are often responsible for oversight of the financial reporting process.

> **PUBLIC COMPANY IMPLICATION:** Both the New York Stock Exchange and the NASDAQ require registrants to have audit committees. SOX specifically mandates that the audit committee of a public company be directly responsible for the appointment, compensation, and oversight of the work of the auditor. In effect, the audit committee, and not the management, of a public company is to be viewed as "the client."

The auditor's determination of whether the audit committee (or equivalent subgroup) constitutes those charged with governance should include consideration of the following:

- The respective responsibilities of the governing body and the subgroup

- The nature of the matter to be communicated

- Relevant legal or regulatory requirements

- The authority of the subgroup to be able to take action in relation to the information communicated

- The ability of the subgroup to provide further information and explanations needed by the auditor

- Whether there are potential conflicts of interest between the subgroup and the other members of the governing body

- Whether the auditor will also have to communicate information in full or summary form to the governing body

For many entities, the auditor will determine that the audit committee constitutes the appropriate communication recipients.

> **OBSERVATION:** In evaluating whether the audit committee represents those charged with governance, the auditor should assess whether the audit committee exercises good governance principles. Effective audit committee processes include facilitating access between the auditor and the audit committee, including regular meetings with the auditor and the audit committee chair and others on the audit committee, with at least one of those meetings each year occurring without management present.

> **ENGAGEMENT STRATEGY:** The auditor is likely to discuss many matters with management in the course of conducting the audit that include matters to be communicated with those charged with governance. In most instances, communication of those matters to management in addition to the communications with those charged with governance is appropriate. Often discussions with management help clarify facts and issues. However, it may not be appropriate to discuss with management questions of management's competence or integrity.

Determine the specific matters to be communicated to those charged with governance

SAS-114 requires the auditor to communicate with those charged with governance about the following matters:

- The auditor's responsibilities under generally accepted auditing standards

- Overview of the planned audit scope and timing

- Significant findings from the audit

SAS-114 does not preclude the auditor from communicating other matters in addition to those required.

> **PUBLIC COMPANY IMPLICATION:** PCAOB Rule 3526 requires the registered public accounting firm to make certain

disclosures to the client's audit committee regarding independence both before it accepts an initial engagement and no less
frequently than yearly thereafter. Before accepting an initial
engagement, the registered firm must (1) communicate in
writing to the audit committee all relationships between
the firm and the potential client and individuals in financial
reporting oversight roles at the potential client that may potentially affect the firm's independence and (2) discuss with the
audit committee the potential independence effects of these
relationships. These communications must be updated at
least annually. And, at least annually, the registered firm
must communicate to the audit committee in writing that the
firm is independent. The registered firm must document these
communications.

Auditor's responsibilities under GAAS

The auditor should communicate to those charged with governance the
auditor's responsibilities under generally accepted auditing standards.
When making these communications, the auditor describes that his or
her responsibility is to form and express an opinion about whether the
financial statements are presented fairly in all material respects in conformity with generally accepted accounting principles.

The auditor emphasizes to those charged with governance that the financial
statements have been prepared by management, with the oversight of those
charged with governance. To emphasize the responsibilities of management
and those charged with governance, SAS-114 requires that the auditor communicate that the audit of the financial statements does not relieve management or those charged with governance of their responsibilities.

Although it is not required, the auditor may also emphasize to those
charged with governance that the audit is designed to provide reasonable,
but not absolute, assurance about whether the financial statements contain
material misstatements. The auditor may also consider communicating that
although the auditor considers internal control for purposes of designing
audit procedures, his or her consideration of internal control does not
provide a basis for expressing an opinion on the effectiveness of internal
control. Finally, the auditor may choose to communicate that generally
accepted auditing standards do not require him or her to design procedures
for the purpose of identifying other matters to be communicated to those
charged with governance.

ENGAGEMENT STRATEGY: The auditor may communicate
these required matters regarding the auditor's GAAS responsibilities through an engagement letter or other form of contract, as long as that letter or contract is provided to those
charged with governance.

Overview of the planned scope and timing of the audit

The auditor should communicate with those charged with governance an overview of the planned scope and timing of the audit. Communication of these matters may assist the auditor in better understanding the entity and its environment, which is required by the second standard of fieldwork. These communications also assist those charged with governance in understanding better the consequences of the auditor's work for their oversight activities and help those charged with governance better understand the auditor's consideration of risks and materiality.

The auditor should exercise caution when communicating matters related to the planned scope and timing of the audit. It is important that the auditor's communication of these matters not compromise the effectiveness of the audit. This caution is especially relevant when those charged with governance are involved in managing the entity, such as an owner-manager. The auditor should avoid disclosing information that makes his or her procedures predictable.

Typical matters related to the planned scope and timing that the auditor may communicate include the following:

- How the auditor plans to address significant risks of material misstatements

- The auditor's approach to internal control

- The concept of materiality that the auditor uses during planning and execution of the audit

- The extent the auditor will use internal audit, if applicable

Discussions with those charged with governance about the planned scope and timing of the audit may provide the auditor with useful insights about their attitude and actions. For example, the communications may reveal information about the attitudes, awareness, and actions of those charged with governance regarding their responsibilities for the oversight of the financial reporting process, including responsibility for internal control and assessing fraud risk.

Significant finding from the audit

A primary component of the required auditor communications is to inform those charged with governance about significant findings from the audit. Communications about significant findings from the audit include matters that directly relate to the financial reporting oversight of those charged with governance. SAS-114 requires communication of the following matters related to significant findings from the audit:

- Auditor views about qualitative aspects of the entity's significant accounting practices

- Significant difficulties encountered during the audit

- Uncorrected misstatements, other than those deemed trivial

- Disagreements with management, if any

- Other findings or issues, if any, arising from the audit that are significant and relevant to those charged with governance

Exhibit AU 380-1 summarizes the topics that SAS-114 states should be communicated with those charged with governance.

Determine the form and timing of the communication process and assess the adequacy of communications

To help establish an effective two-way communication, a mutual understanding should be established between the auditor and those charged with governance regarding the form, timing, and expected general content of the communications. Clear communications about the auditor's GAAS responsibilities, the planned audit scope and timing, and the nature of expected communications strengthen the communications between the auditor and those charged with governance. Thus, SAS-114 requires the auditor to establish a mutual understanding of these matters with those charged with governance.

Clarification of the purpose of the required communications with those charged with governance and the form and timing of those communications in advance of making the required communications with those charged with governance contributes to an effective two-way communication. Explicit understanding about the auditor's expectation that the communication is designed to be a two-way communication reinforces to those charged with governance the importance of their providing relevant information to the auditor that might affect the audit of financial statements.

Form of communication

The auditor is required to communicate in writing to those charged with governance significant findings from the audit (see matters identified in Exhibit 380-1) when in his or her judgment oral communication would not be adequate. The auditor does not have to include in the written communications to those charged with governance those matters that have been satisfactorily resolved that he or she communicated during the course of the audit.

Whether to communicate orally or in writing is determined by the auditor's judgment. In making those determinations, the auditor should consider the following matters:

- Significance of the particular matter

- Whether the matter has been satisfactorily resolved

- Whether management previously communicated the matter to those charged with governance

- The size, operating structure, control environment, and legal structure of the entity

- Legal or regulatory requirements to communicate certain audit findings in writing

- Amount of ongoing contact and dialogue the auditor has with those charged with governance

- Whether there have been significant changes in the composition and membership of the governing body

When the communications are made orally, SAS-114 requires the auditor to document the matters that were communicated. For example, minutes of meetings of those charged with governance that contain an appropriate record of the communication may provide adequate documentation for inclusion in the auditor's files. When the communications are made in writing, the auditor should retain a copy of the communication as part of his or her documentation.

Timing of the communication

For the required communications to be useful to those charged with governance, timely communication of matters identified by the auditor is important. The auditor should communicate on a sufficiently timely basis to enable those charged with governance to take appropriate action.

The appropriate timing will vary with the circumstances, depending on the significance and nature of the matter and the action expected to be taken by those charged with governance. Matters related to audit planning, such as the overview of the auditor's responsibilities and the planned scope and timing of the audit, are likely to be discussed early in the engagement as part of clarifying the terms of the engagement. Significant findings from the audit may be communicated as they are encountered (for example, significant difficulties) so that they can be overcome in a timely fashion.

Adequacy of the communication

The objective of the required communications is to create a two-way dialogue between the auditor and those charged with governance. The auditor should evaluate whether the two-way communication between the auditor and those charged with governance has been adequate. Inadequate communication may signal an ineffective control environment, which should impact the auditor's assessment of risk of material misstatements, and it may signal an increased risk that the auditor may not have obtained all the audit evidence required to form an opinion on the financial statements.

To address concerns about the adequacy of the communications, the auditor may discuss concerns with those charged with governance. If the situation remains unresolved, the auditor may consider modifying the opinion on the financial statements due to a scope limitation, obtaining legal advice, communicating with those outside the entity, or withdrawing from the engagement.

SAS-114 does not change requirements in other standards to communicate certain matters to those charged with governance. The following communications required by other standards remain in effect:

- Communications with the audit committee or others with equivalent authority and responsibility pertaining to illegal acts that come to the auditor's attention (see AU 317)

- Communications to management and the audit committee or others with equivalent authority and responsibility when the auditor becomes aware during the audit that the entity is subject to an audit requirement that may not be encompassed in the terms of the engagement, and that an audit in accordance with generally accepted auditing standards may not satisfy the relevant legal, regulatory, or contractual requirements (see AU 801)

- Required direct inquiry of the audit committee (or at least its chair) regarding the audit committee's views about the risk of fraud and whether the audit committee has knowledge of any fraud or suspected fraud affecting the entity (see AU 316)

- Communications to those charged with governance about fraud caused by senior management and fraud (whether caused by senior management or others) that causes a material misstatement in the financial statements (see AU 316)

- Communications in writing to management and those charged with governance regarding control deficiencies identified during an audit that upon evaluation are considered to be significant deficiencies or material weaknesses (see AU 325)

Practitioner's Aids

Exhibit AU 380-1 presents examples of significant findings from the audit that should be communicated by the auditor to those charged with governance.

EXHIBIT AU 380-1 TOPIC AND NATURE
OF COMMUNICATIONS ABOUT SIGNIFICANT
FINDINGS

Topic of Communication	*Nature of Communication*
Qualitative aspects of entity's significant accounting practices	• Appropriateness and acceptability of accounting policies to the circumstances
	• Initial selection of and changes to accounting policies, including application of new pronouncements
	• Effect of significant accounting policies in controversial or emerging areas
	• Effect of the timing of transactions in relation to the period they are recorded
	• Process used to make accounting estimates
	• Auditor's basis for assessing the reasonableness of accounting estimates
	• Overall neutrality, consistency, and clarity of disclosures in financial statements
Significant difficulties encountered during the audit	• Significant delays in management providing required information
	• Unnecessary short time frame to complete the audit
	• Extensive unexpected effort required to obtain sufficient, appropriate evidence
	• Restrictions imposed by management on the auditors
	• Unavailability of expected information

Topic of Communication	Nature of Communication
Uncorrected misstatements	• Information about misstatements communicated by the auditor to management that remain uncorrected
	• Impact of uncorrected misstatements on the auditor's report and request for correction
	• Discussion of the implications of failure to correct known and likely misstatements
Disagreements with management	• Disagreements with management (whether or not satisfactorily resolved) about matters that individually or in the aggregate could be significant to the financial statements
	• Significant disagreements with management concerning applicability of accounting principles, scope of the engagement, or wording of the audit report
Management's consultation with other accountants	• Auditor's view of management's consultation with other accountants concerning the applicability of accounting principles, scope of engagement, or wording of the auditor's report
Significant issues discussed with or subject to correspondence with management	• Significant issues that were discussed or were the subject of correspondence with management such as business conditions affecting the entity that increase the risk of material misstatement and discussions in connection with the retention of the auditor or discussions about the application of accounting principles and auditing standards

SECTION 390

CONSIDERATION OF OMITTED PROCEDURES AFTER THE REPORT DATE

Authoritative Pronouncements

SAS-46—Consideration of Omitted Procedures after the Report Date

> **IMPORTANT NOTICE FOR 2011:** The Auditing Standards Board (ASB) is in the process of redrafting all of the auditing sections in *Codification of Statements on Auditing Standards* to converge U.S. GAAS with the International Standards on Auditing issued by the International Auditing and Assurance Standards Board. As part of this process, the newly redrafted standards will follow certain clarity drafting conventions adopted by the ASB. These clarity drafting conventions include: (1) establishing objectives for each standard; (2) including a definitions section, if appropriate; and (3) separating requirements from application guidance and other material. The ASB is planning to have all redrafted standards become effective on the same date, which is for audits of financial statements for periods ending on or after December 15, 2012. It is possible that the effective date might be delayed beyond that date. The ASB's clarity and convergence project will have a significant effect on the auditing standards applicable to audits of nonpublic companies, and the 2012 *GAAS Guide* will be appropriately modified to reflect these changes once the effective date of the standards is certain.

Overview

SAS-46 provides guidance when the auditor concludes, subsequent to the date of the auditor's report, that one or more procedures were omitted from an engagement. This situation is different from the circumstance where the auditor, subsequent to the date of the report, discovers facts existing at the date of the auditor's report.

> **OBSERVATION:** Disclosure that procedures were omitted often comes as a result of a quality review or peer review of the auditor's engagement.

Promulgated Procedures Checklist

The auditor should perform the following procedures when it is suspected that audit procedures were omitted:

- Assess the significance of omitted procedures and consider whether to apply audit procedures.

- Determine the proper course of action if significant procedures or alternative procedures cannot be performed.

Analysis and Application of Procedures

Assess the significance of omitted procedures and consider whether to apply audit procedures

Initially, the auditor should assess the importance of the omitted audit procedure within the context of the engagement. This assessment may include a review of the audit documentation and discussions with other personnel within the firm. The auditor must determine whether the third standard of fieldwork (audit evidence) was observed. If it is concluded that a significant audit procedure was omitted, and it is likely that the financial statements are being relied on or will be relied on by others, the auditor must take corrective action. If possible, the auditor should apply the omitted audit procedure or an alternative audit procedure.

> **ENGAGEMENT STRATEGY:** Applying the omitted audit procedure or an alternative audit procedure may lead the auditor to conclude that facts did exist at the date of the report that could have had an effect on the audit approach or the auditor's report.

The auditor should document the performance of the omitted audit procedure, including the following:

- When and by whom the omitted audit procedure was performed and reviewed

- The reasons why the omitted audit procedure needs to be performed and the results obtained from performing the procedure

- Any effect of performing the procedure on the auditor's conclusions

Determine the proper course of action if significant procedures or alternative procedures cannot be performed

If the auditor is unable to apply the omitted or the alternative audit procedure, he or she should consult an attorney and discuss the appropriateness of the following actions:

• Notification of regulatory authorities (SEC etc.)

• Notification of persons relying, or likely to rely, on the financial statements

Practitioner's Aids

EXHIBIT AU 390-1 — OMISSION OF ENGAGEMENT PROCEDURES DISCOVERED AFTER THE REPORT DATE

Use the following procedures, which are adapted from guidance found in SAS-46 (Consideration of Omitted Procedures after the Report Date), as a guide for evaluating the omission of engagement procedures discovered after the report date. The program is only a guide, and professional judgment should be exercised to determine how the guidance established in the auditing standards should be adapted to a particular engagement.

Initial and date each procedure as it is completed. If the procedure is not relevant to this engagement, place "N/A" (not applicable) in the space provided for an initial.

Client Name: _____

Date of Financial Statements: _____

	Initials	*Date*	*Audit Documentation Reference*
1. Establish the level of inherent risk.	____	____	_____
2. Assess the significance of omitted procedures and consider whether to apply audit procedures.	____	____	_____

	Initials	*Date*	*Audit Documentation Reference*
3. If doing so is appropriate, apply the omitted procedures and consider the effect that the evidence gathered has on the auditor's conclusions.	____	____	_____
4. Determine the proper course of action if significant procedures or alternative procedures cannot be performed.	____	____	_____

Other engagement procedures: _____

Reviewed by: _____

Date: _____

AU 400

The First, Second, and Third Standards of Reporting

Section 410: Adherence to Generally Accepted Accounting
    Principles 489

Section 411: The Meaning of "Present Fairly in Conformity
    with Generally Accepted Accounting Principles" 491

Section 420: Consistency of Application of Generally
    Accepted Accounting Principles 499

Section 431: Adequacy of Disclosures in Financial
    Statements 508

Section 435: Segment Information 512

SECTION 410

ADHERENCE TO GENERALLY ACCEPTED ACCOUNTING PRINCIPLES

Authoritative Pronouncements

SAS-1 — Codification of Auditing Standards and Procedures (Section 410, Adherence to Generally Accepted Accounting Principles)

SAS-62 — Special Reports

Auditing Interpretation No. 3 of AU 410 (February 1997) — The Impact of the Auditor's Report of a FASB Statement Prior to the Statement's Effective Date

> **IMPORTANT NOTICE FOR 2011:** The Auditing Standards Board (ASB) is in the process of redrafting all of the auditing sections in *Codification of Statements on Auditing Standards* to converge U.S. GAAS with the International Standards on Auditing issued by the International Auditing and Assurance Standards Board. As part of this process, the newly redrafted standards will follow certain clarity drafting conventions adopted by the ASB. These clarity drafting conventions include: (1) establishing objectives for each standard; (2) including a definitions section, if appropriate; and (3) separating requirements from application guidance and other material. The ASB is planning to have all redrafted standards become effective on the same date, which is for audits of financial statements for periods ending on or after December 15, 2012. It is possible that the effective date might be delayed beyond that date. The ASB's clarity and convergence project will have a significant effect on the auditing standards applicable to audits of nonpublic companies, and the 2012 *GAAS Guide* will be appropriately modified to reflect these changes once the effective date of the standards is certain.

Overview

The first standard of reporting requires that "the auditor must state in the auditor's report whether the financial statements are presented in accordance with generally accepted accounting principles." At the conclusion of an engagement, the auditor offers an opinion as to whether the financial statements are prepared in accordance with generally accepted accounting principles. Note that the auditor offers an opinion on the financial statements rather than a statement of fact. An opinion is based on various judgments that must be made during the audit engagement and by its very nature is not a statement of fact that can be verified in a manner that results in a guarantee that the financial statements conform to generally accepted accounting principles. If the auditor is unable to perform the audit procedures that are considered appropriate for a particular engagement, a qualified opinion or disclaimer of opinion must be expressed on the financial statements

> **OBSERVATION:** If a client's financial statements are based on a comprehensive basis of accounting other than generally accepted accounting principles, the auditor satisfies the first standard of reporting by stating in the audit report that "the statements have been prepared in conformity with another comprehensive basis of accounting other than generally accepted accounting principles" and by expressing an opinion on a basis of accounting identified in AU 623 (Special Reports).

> **PLANNING AID REMINDER:** Auditing Interpretation No. 3 of AU 410 states that the auditor must evaluate the adequacy of the client's disclosure of the use of an accounting principle that currently is acceptable but (1) will not be acceptable in the future because of the effective date of a new FASB Statement and (2) the new FASB Statement requires the restatement of prior years' financial statements when it is adopted.

SECTION 411

THE MEANING OF "PRESENT FAIRLY IN CONFORMITY WITH GENERALLY ACCEPTED ACCOUNTING PRINCIPLES"

Authoritative Pronouncements

SAS-69 — The Meaning of "Present Fairly in Conformity with Generally Accepted Accounting Principles"

SAS-91 — Federal GAAP Hierarchy

SAS-93 — Omnibus Statement on Auditing Standards — 2000

Auditing Interpretation No. 3 of AU 411 (October 2000) — The Auditor's Consideration of Management's Adoption of Accounting Principles for New Transactions or Events

[*Note:* The Auditing Standards Board's Exposure Draft titled "Amendment to Statement on Auditing Standards No. 69, The Meaning of Present Fairly in Conformity with Generally Accepted Accounting Principles, for Nongovernmental Entities" if adopted, will amend AU Section 411.]

> **IMPORTANT NOTICE FOR 2011:** The Auditing Standards Board (ASB) is in the process of redrafting all of the auditing sections in *Codification of Statements on Auditing Standards* to converge U.S. GAAS with the International Standards on Auditing issued by the International Auditing and Assurance Standards Board. As part of this process, the newly redrafted standards will follow certain clarity drafting conventions adopted by the ASB. These clarity drafting conventions include: (1) establishing objectives for each standard; (2) including a definitions section, if appropriate; and (3) separating requirements from application guidance and other material. The ASB is planning to have all redrafted standards become effective on the same date, which is for audits of financial statements for periods ending on or after December 15, 2012. It is possible that the effective date might be delayed beyond that date. The ASB's clarity and convergence project will have a significant effect on the auditing standards applicable to audits of nonpublic companies, and the 2012 *GAAS Guide* will be appropriately modified to reflect these changes once the effective date of the standards is certain.

Overview

SAS-1 describes "generally accepted accounting principles" as a "technical accounting term that encompasses the conventions, rules, and procedures necessary to define accepted accounting practice at a particular time." Thus, generally accepted accounting principles include broad guidelines of general application (for example, the concept of depreciation) as well as detailed practices and procedures (straight-line deprecation). SAS-1 requires that in determining whether a client's financial statements are presented fairly in conformity with generally accepted accounting principles, the auditor must make the following judgments:

- The accounting principles selected and applied have generally acceptance.

- The accounting principles are appropriate in the circumstances.

- The financial statements, including the related notes, are informative of matters that may affect their use, understanding, and interpretation (see AU 431 — Adequacy of Disclosure in Financial Statements).

- The information presented in the financial statements is classified and summarized in a reasonable manner; that is, it is neither too detailed nor too condensed (see AU 431).

- The financial statements reflect the underlying transactions and events in a manner that presents the financial position, results of operations, and cash flows stated within a range of acceptable limits, that is, within limits that are reasonable and practicable to attain in financial statements.

To determine how a particular transaction or event should be accounted for and reported in the financial statements, the auditor must refer to the applicable authoritative literature. FAS-168 (ASC 105) (The FASB Accounting Standards Codification and the Hierarchy of Generally Accepted Accounting Principles), issued by the FASB, establishes the hierarchy of accounting principles for nongovernmental entities. All accounting literature included within the FASB's Accounting Standards Codification (ASC) is considered authoritative; accounting literature not included within the Codification is non-authoritative. In addition, because the FASB no longer clears pronouncements of AICPA member bodies, no authoritative Statements of Position, Industry Accounting and Auditing Guides, or Practice Bulletins will be issued in the future. SAS-69 establishes the hierarchy of accounting principles for state, local, and federal governmental entities.

IMPORTANT NOTICE FOR 2011: At the time that CCH's 2011 *GAAS Guide* went to press, the Auditing Standards Board

(ASB) had outstanding a proposed Statement on Auditing Standards titled "Amendment to Statement on Auditing Standards No. 69, The Meaning of "Present Fairly in Conformity with Generally Accepted Accounting Principles" for Nongovernmental Entities." Given the issuance of FAS-168 (ASC 105), the proposed SAS moves the delineation of the GAAP hierarchy for nongovernmental entities from the auditing literature to the accounting literature.

PUBLIC COMPANY IMPLICATION: The PCAOB's AS-6 (Evaluating Consistency of Financial Statements and Conforming Amendments) removes the GAAP hierarchy from the auditing literature for public companies. GAAP for public companies will be defined by reference to the requirements of the Securities and Exchange Commission.

ENGAGEMENT STRATEGY: SAS-69 notes that state and local governmental entities include public benefit corporations and authorities, public employee retirement systems, governmental utilities, governmental hospitals and other governmental health care providers, and public colleges and universities.

The nongovernmental, state and local government, and federal accounting hierarchies are presented in Exhibits AU 411-1, AU 411-2, and AU 411-3, respectively.

The absence of official pronouncements or unofficial writings forces an enterprise to review other actual accounting and reporting practices. Practitioners can identify specific practices by reviewing surveys and reports published by professional organizations. For example, the AICPA annually publishes *Accounting Trends and Techniques*, which summarizes the accounting practices followed by 600 large business enterprises. Periodically the AICPA publishes its *Financial Report Survey*, which discusses the actual reporting practices of many companies for a specific accounting topic. Many accounting firms maintain departments that answer questions raised by professional staff members or clients about accounting methods or practices. As specific problems are solved, they are documented by the firm. This serves as a basis for the selection of accounting methods in similar situations. Some accounting firms have an informal arrangement whereby they share experiences and technical opinions with other accounting firms.

New transactions or events

Auditing Interpretation No. 3 (October 2000) titled "The Auditor's Consideration of Management's Adoption of Accounting Principles for New Transactions or Events" makes the following points for when a client adopts accounting principles for new transactions or events that are not specifically addressed by the Accounting Standards Codification.

- The auditor should understand the basis by which the client determined how to account for the item.

- In determining the appropriateness of the basis used by the client, the auditor may consider analogous transactions or events for which accounting principles have been established.

- In determining the appropriateness of the basis the client used, the auditor may consider other accounting literature (as discussed in the non-authoritative accounting literature category of the Accounting Standards Codification) depending on (1) its relevance to the new transaction or event, (2) the specificity of the guidance, and (3) the "general recognition of the issuer or author as an authority."

The Interpretation also notes that in engagements that are covered by the standards established by AU 380 (The Auditor's Communication with Those Charged with Governance), the auditor should determine that the audit committee (or its equivalent) has been informed of the newly adopted accounting principle. The audit committee should also be informed of accounting methods used "to account for significant unusual transactions and the effect of significant accounting policies in controversial or emerging areas for which there is a lack of authoritative guidance or consensus."

> **FRAUD POINTER:** SAS-99 notes that nonfinancial management's participation in or preoccupation with the selection of accounting principles can represent a risk factor reflective of the attitudes or rationalization condition of fraud. Reliance on nonfinancial management to select accounting principles might provide an indication about management's lack of emphasis on quality financial reporting.

Practitioner's Aids

EXHIBIT AU 411-1 — SOURCES OF GAAP FOR NONGOVERNMENTAL ENTITIES

Authoritative GAAP

Presented here is authoritative GAAP in accordance with FAS-168 (ASC 105). FAS-168 states that the source of all GAAP for nongovernmental entities is contained in the Accounting Standards Codification (as a result of the Codification, there is no longer a GAAP hierarchy and literature not included within the Codification is non-authoritative). The types of pronouncements subsumed by the Codification include the following:

- FASB Statements
- FASB Interpretations
- SEC Staff Accounting Bulletins (authoritative for public companies)
- Accounting Principles Board (APB) Opinions
- AICPA Accounting Research Bulletins
- FASB Staff Positions
- FAS-133 Implementation Issues
- FASB Technical Bulletins
- AICPA Industry Audit and Accounting Guides (if cleared by the FASB)
- AICPA Statements of Position (if cleared by the FASB)
- FASB Emerging Issues Task Force consensus positions, including Appendix D topics
- AICPA Accounting Standards Executive Committee (AcSEC) Practice Bulletins (if cleared by the FASB)
- AICPA Accounting Interpretations
- Implementation Guides (Qs and As) published by the FASB staff

If guidance is not found in the Codification, a practitioner may consider non-authoritative sources.

Non-authoritative Sources of GAAP

Examples of non-authoritative sources of GAAP are as follows:

- Practices widely recognized and prevalent generally or in an industry
- FASB Statements of Financial Accounting Concepts
- AICPA Issues Papers
- International Financial Reporting Standards of the International Accounting Standards Board

- Pronouncements of other professional associations or regulatory agencies

- AICPA Technical Practice Aids

- Accounting textbooks, handbooks, and articles

EXHIBIT AU 411-2 — STATE AND LOCAL GOVERNMENT ACCOUNTING HIERARCHY

Authoritative GAAP

Level A

- GASB Statements

- GASB Interpretations

- FASB pronouncements made applicable by a GASB Statement or GASB Interpretation

- AICPA pronouncements made applicable by a GASB Statement or GASB Interpretation

Level B

- GASB Technical Bulletins

- AICPA Industry Audit and Accounting Guides made applicable by the AICPA

- AICPA Statements of Position made applicable by the AICPA

Level C

- AICPA AcSEC Practice Bulletins made applicable by the AICPA

- GASB Emerging Issues Task Force consensus positions (if created)

Level D

- GASB Implementation Guides (Qs and As)

- Practices widely recognized and prevalent in state and local governments

Other Non-authoritative Accounting Literature

- GASB Concepts Statements

- Sources identified in Levels A through D in the nongovernmental entity accounting hierarchy that have not been made applicable by the action of the GASB

- FASB Statements of Financial Accounting Concepts, FASB Statements, Interpretations, Technical Bulletins, and Concept Statements

- AICPA Issues Papers

- International Financial Reporting Standards of the International Accounting Standards Board

- Pronouncements of other professional associations or regulatory agencies

- AICPA Technical Practice Aids

- Accounting textbooks

- Handbooks

- Articles

EXHIBIT AU 411-3 — FEDERAL GAAP HIERARCHY

Authoritative GAAP

Level A

- FASAB (Federal Accounting Standards Advisory Board) Statements

- FASAB Interpretations

- AICPA and FASB pronouncements made applicable by a FASAB Statement or Interpretation

Level B

- FASAB Technical Bulletins

- AICPA Industry Audit and Accounting Guides made applicable by the AICPA and cleared by the FASAB

- AICPA Statements of Position made applicable by the AICPA and cleared by the FASAB

Level C

- AICPA AcSEC Practice Bulletins if made applicable and cleared by the FASAB
- Technical releases of the Accounting and Auditing Policy Committee of the FASAB

Level D

- FASAB Implementation Guides
- Practices widely recognized and prevalent in the federal government

Other Non-authoritative Accounting Literature

- FASAB Concepts Statements
- Sources identified in Levels A through D in the private-sector accounting hierarchy that have not been made applicable by the action of the FASAB
- FASB Concepts Statements
- GASB Statements, Interpretations, Technical Bulletins, and Concepts Statements
- AICPA Issues Papers
- International Financial Reporting Standards of the Internal Accounting Standards Board
- Pronouncements of other professional associations or regulatory agencies
- AICPA Technical Practice Aids
- Accounting textbooks
- Handbooks
- Articles

SECTION 420

CONSISTENCY OF APPLICATION OF GENERALLY ACCEPTED ACCOUNTING PRINCIPLES

Authoritative Pronouncements

SAS-1 — Codification of Auditing Standards and Procedures (AU 420, Consistency of Application of Generally Accepted Accounting Principles)

SAS-43 — Omnibus Statement on Auditing Standards

SAS-88 — Service Organizations and Reporting on Consistency

Auditing Interpretation No. 2 of AU 420 (February 1974) — The Effect of APB Opinion 28 on Consistency

Auditing Interpretation No. 3 of AU 420 (April 1989) — Impact of the Auditor's Report of FIFO to LIFO Change in Comparative Financial Statements

Auditing Interpretation No. 8 of AU 420 (June 1993) — The Effect of Accounting Changes by an Investee on Consistency

Auditing Interpretation No. 10 of AU 420 (December 1980) — Change in Presentation of Accumulated Benefit Information in the Financial Statements of a Defined Benefit Pension Plan

Auditing Interpretation No. 12 of AU 420 (April 2002) — The Effect on the Auditor's Report of an Entity's Adoption of a New Accounting Standard That Does Not Require the Entity to Disclose the Effect of the Change in the Year of Adoption

IMPORTANT NOTICE FOR 2011: The Auditing Standards Board (ASB) is in the process of redrafting all of the auditing sections in *Codification of Statements on Auditing Standards* to converge U.S. GAAS with the International Standards on Auditing issued by the International Auditing and Assurance Standards Board. As part of this process, the newly redrafted standards will follow certain clarity drafting conventions adopted by the ASB. These clarity drafting conventions include: (1) establishing objectives for each standard; (2) including a definitions section, if appropriate; and (3) separating requirements from application guidance and other material. The ASB is planning to have all redrafted standards become effective on the same date, which is for audits of financial statements for periods ending on or after December 15, 2012. It is possible that the effective date might be delayed beyond that date. The ASB's clarity and convergence project will have a significant effect on the auditing standards applicable to audits of nonpublic companies, and the 2012 *GAAS Guide* will be appropriately modified to reflect these changes once the effective date of the standards is certain.

Overview

The second standard of reporting states that "the auditor must identify in the auditor's report those circumstances in which such principles have not been consistently observed in the current period in relation to the preceding period."

FAS-154 (ASC 250) (Accounting Changes and Error Corrections — a Replacement of APB Opinion No. 20 and FASB Statement No. 3) classifies "accounting changes" as (1) changes in an accounting principle, (2) changes in a reporting entity, and (3) changes in an accounting estimate. For each accounting change, FAS-154 (ASC 250) establishes appropriate accounting and reporting standards. In general, changes in accounting principles are accounted for by retrospectively applying the new accounting principle unless explicit transition requirements are provided in a newly issued accounting standard.

Under the following conditions, the auditor does not refer to the consistent application of accounting principles in the standard three-paragraph report:

• There have been no changes in the application of accounting principles in the preparation of the current year's financial statements.

• There have been changes in the application of accounting principles in the preparation of the current year's financial statements, but the effects of the changes are considered immaterial.

When there has been a change in the application of an accounting principle and the effects of the change are considered material, an explanatory paragraph should be added to the standard auditor's report. The explanatory paragraph should immediately follow the opinion paragraph and should include the following:

• Reference to the note to the financial statements that discusses the change in accounting principle

• Discussion of the nature of the change in accounting principle

The following is an example of an explanatory paragraph resulting from a change in an accounting principle:

As discussed in Note X to the financial statements, the Company changed its method of valuing inventories in 20X5.

Even though there has been a violation of the consistency standard, the auditor's report is not qualified, and there is no reference to the explanatory paragraph in the opinion paragraph.

> **PLANNING AID REMINDER:** Auditing Interpretation No. 8 of AU 420 states that the auditor's report on an investor company that uses the equity method to account for its interest in an investee company must include an explanatory paragraph when the investee company changes an accounting principle.

> **PLANNING AID REMINDER:** Auditing Interpretation No. 10 of AU 420 states that changes in the formatting of information related to the presentation of accumulated benefits are reclassifications and not changes in an accounting principles and therefore do not require the addition of an explanatory paragraph.

> **PLANNING AID REMINDER:** Auditing Interpretation No. 12 of AU 420 provides guidance for when a new standard is issued that does not require the client to disclose the effects of the change in a note to the financial statements. Under this circumstance the CPA is not required to determine the effect of the change, and the determination of whether the change has a material impact on the financial statements should be based on (1) the relative size of the cumulative-effects adjustment, if any, that is made (either on the income statement or to the beginning balance of retained earnings) and (2) if applicable, voluntary disclosures made by the client, including related supporting analysis. The Interpretation states that an explanatory paragraph concerning consistency should be added to the audit report only if "the cumulative effect of the change is material or if management discloses that it believes that the effect is or may be material in the year of adoption."

> **PUBLIC COMPANY IMPLICATION:** The PCAOB's AS-6 (Evaluating Consistency of Financial Statements and Conforming Amendments) requires the auditor to evaluate whether financial statements between periods are comparable. Financial statements might not be comparable, because of a change in accounting principle or an adjustment to correct a misstatement in previously issued financial statements. If there is a change in accounting principle, the auditor should evaluate whether (1) the new accounting principle is generally accepted, (2) the accounting for the change in accounting principle is

in accordance with GAAP, (3) the disclosures surrounding the change are adequate, and (4) the change in accounting principle is preferable. Assuming these four criteria are met, the auditor should add an explanatory paragraph to the audit report describing the lack of consistency in the financial statements. If the four criteria are not met, the financial statements are not in accordance with GAAP and the auditor should issue either an adverse opinion or a qualified opinion. In addition, if the financial statements are adjusted to correct a material misstatement in previously issued financial statements, the auditor's report should include an explanatory paragraph describing the lack of consistency due to the correction of the previously issued financial statements (i.e., the financial statements for earlier years included for comparative purposes in the current year's filing will differ from previously filed statements). Finally, a change in how items are classified in the financial statements does not need to be recognized in the auditor's report unless it represents a change in accounting principle or the correction of a material misstatement.

PUBLIC COMPANY IMPLICATION: The PCAOB's AS-6 (Evaluating Consistency of Financial Statements and Conforming Amendments) requires the auditor to evaluate whether financial statements between periods are comparable. When the financial statements are not comparable, the auditor is to add an explanatory paragraph to the audit report. If the financial statements are not comparable because of a change in accounting principle due to the adoption of a new FASB standard, the explanatory paragraph should state that the company has changed its method of accounting due to the adoption of the specific FASB standard and refer the reader to the particular note describing the change. If the financial statements are not comparable because of a voluntary change in accounting principle, the explanatory paragraph should refer to the elective nature of the change and refer the reader to the particular note describing the elective change. If the financial statements are not comparable because of the correction of a previous period's misstatement, the explanatory paragraph should refer to the correction of a misstatement and refer the reader to the particular note describing the misstatement.

Promulgated Reporting Checklist

The auditor should consider the effect on the consistency standard under the following circumstances:

- Report covers only a single (current) year

- Reporting subsequent to the year of change

- Change in the format of the statement of cash flows
- Changing to an acceptable accounting principle
- Correction of an error
- Change in an accounting estimate
- Change in an accounting principle inseparable from a change in estimate
- Change in the reporting entity
- Substantially different transactions or events
- Change that may have a material effect in the future

Analysis and Application of Reporting Standards

Report covers only a single (current) year

When the auditor's report covers only a single (current) year, the auditor must determine whether generally accepted accounting principles have been consistently applied in the current year and in the previous year. When the auditor's report covers two or more years, the auditor must determine whether generally accepted accounting principles have been applied on a consistent basis (1) between or among the financial statements reported on and (2) between the earliest set of financial statements reported on and the immediately previous year's set of financial statements (not reported on) if the previous year's statements are presented.

Reporting subsequent to the year of change

Reporting a change in an accounting principle in a period after the change has occurred is dependent on whether (1) the change was accounted for through the retroactive restatement of prior years' financial statements and (2) the change was from FIFO (first in, first out) to LIFO (last in, first out).

Retroactive restatement

When a change in an accounting principle is accounted for by the retroactive restatement of prior years' financial statements, there is comparability among the financial statements since all financial statements are prepared (after restatement) using the same accounting principles. For this reason, an explanatory paragraph (as illustrated earlier) describing a change in accounting principle needs to be added to the standard auditor's report only in the year of the change.

No retroactive restatement

When a change in an accounting principle is accounted for in a manner that does not result in the retroactive restatement of prior years' financial statements, there is a lack of complete comparability among financial statements due to the cumulative-effect adjustment reflected in the financial statements for the year of the change. For this reason, an explanatory paragraph describing the change in accounting principle must be added to the standard auditor's report for as long as the financial statements for the year of the change are presented with subsequent statements.

FIFO to LIFO change

FAS-154 (ASC 250) provides specific guidance for when an entity changes from the FIFO inventory method to the LIFO inventory method. A change from FIFO to LIFO requires that the LIFO inventory method be applied prospectively as of the earliest date practicable. Auditing Interpretation No. 3 of AU 420 on consistency (April 1989) titled "Impact on the Auditor's Report of FIFO to LIFO Change in Comparative Financial Statements" states that a FIFO-to-LIFO accounting change requires an explanatory paragraph in the auditor's report for (1) the year of the change and (2) all subsequent years until the year of change is the earliest year reported on by the auditor.

> **PLANNING AID REMINDER:** Audit Interpretation No. 2 of AU 420 states that the auditor should not add an explanatory paragraph in those circumstances in which accounting principles and practices used in preparing the annual financial information have been modified in accordance with APB-28 (ASC 270) (Interim Financial Reporting).

Change in the format of the statement of cash flows

FAS-95 (ASC 230) (Statement of Cash Flows) allows some flexibility in the preparation of the statement of cash flows. For example, either the direct method or the indirect method can be used to compute cash flows from operations. SAS-43 (Omnibus Statement on Auditing Standards) states that changes of this nature are not a violation of the consistency standard, and if prior years' financial statements are reclassified to conform to another format, the auditor's report need not refer to the change. SAS-43 considers these changes to be reclassifications.

PLANNING AID REMINDER: FAS-154 (ASC 250) is not applicable to reclassifications. When a reclassification occurs, prior years' financial statements should be reclassified so that all statements are comparable. However, the reclassifications, if significant, should be disclosed in the financial statements or footnotes thereto.

Changing to an acceptable accounting principle

A change from an unacceptable accounting principle to a generally accepted accounting principle is considered to be a correction of an error in financial statements of a prior period. Prior-period errors in financial statements are corrected by restatement of the prior years' financial statements that are presented on a comparative basis with the current year's statements. The nature of the error and the effect of its correction on income before extraordinary items, net income, and the related per-share data must be fully disclosed in the period the error is discovered and corrected.

When there has been a change from an unacceptable accounting principle to an acceptable accounting principle, a paragraph, similar to the one illustrated below, would be added to the standard auditor's report after the opinion paragraph.

As discussed in Note X to the financial statements, in 20X5 the Company changed from an unacceptable method of accounting for depreciation to an acceptable method. The change in accounting principles has been accounted for as a correction of an error and prior years' financial statements have been restated.

Correction of an error

A correction of an error that arises from circumstances other than a change from an unacceptable accounting principle to an acceptable principle is not an accounting change. For this reason, the auditor's report does not refer to a consistency violation in the year the error is discovered and corrected.

PLANNING AID REMINDER: If the auditor has previously reported on the prior years' financial statements that are being corrected, standards established by SAS-1, AU 561 (Subsequent Discovery of Facts Existing at the Date of the Auditor's Report) should be observed.

Change in an accounting estimate

FAS-154 (ASC 250) states that a change in an accounting estimate must be accounted for prospectively. Thus, the effect of a change in an accounting estimate is accounted for (1) in the period of change, if the change affects only that period (for example, a change that affects the allowance for doubtful accounts), or (2) in the period of change and in future periods, if the change affects both periods (for example, a change in the remaining life of a depreciable asset). If the auditor is satisfied that the change in an accounting estimate is reasonable, the auditor's report is not qualified or otherwise modified.

Change in an accounting principle inseparable from a change in estimate

A change in an accounting estimate that is inseparable from the effect of a related change in accounting principle must be reported as a change in an accounting estimate. Although such a change is reported as a change in accounting estimate, it also involves a change in accounting principle for which the auditor's report must be expanded. In this case, an explanatory paragraph must be added to the auditor's report in which the accounting change is described; however, the opinion paragraph is unqualified, with no reference to the explanatory paragraph.

Change in the reporting entity

SAS-88 notes that a change in a reporting entity generally results from a "transaction or event, such as the creation, cessation, or complete or partial purchase or disposition of a subsidiary or other business unit" and includes the following examples:

- Consolidated or combined financial statements are presented in the current year, but individual financial statements were presented in the previous year.

- Consolidated financial statements for the current year do not include the same subsidiaries that were used to prepare the previous year's consolidated financial statements.

- Combined financial statements for the current year do not include the same companies that were used to prepare the previous year's combined financial statements.

A change in a reporting entity, such as the ones described above, does not require the inclusion of an explanatory paragraph about a consistency violation in the auditor's report.

> **PLANNING AID REMINDER:** A change in a reporting entity that does not result from a transaction or event must be included in an explanatory paragraph.

Substantially different transactions or events

An accounting principle may be changed when transactions or events have a material effect on the financial statements. An accounting change of this nature is not a violation of the consistency standard, and therefore the auditor's report is not modified. For example, a company may account for transactions on a cash basis because the affect on the financial statements is considered immaterial; however, in a subsequent year, the volume of transactions may increase, resulting in the need to adopt an accrual method. The adoption of the accrual method is not considered a change in an accounting principle.

In addition, when an accounting principle is changed to account for transactions or events that are clearly different from previous transactions or events, the accounting change is not a violation of the consistency standard.

Change that may have a material effect in the future

As noted earlier, the auditor's report is not modified when the effect of a change in an accounting principle is immaterial. If it is expected that the change may have a material effect on future financial statements, that expectation should be disclosed in a note to the financial statements; however, there is no need to refer to the change in accounting principle in the auditor's report in the current or future years.

SECTION 431

ADEQUACY OF DISCLOSURES IN FINANCIAL STATEMENTS

Authoritative Pronouncements

SAS-32 — Adequacy of Disclosures in Financial Statements

> **IMPORTANT NOTICE FOR 2011:** The Auditing Standards Board (ASB) is in the process of redrafting all of the auditing sections in *Codification of Statements on Auditing Standards* to converge U.S. GAAS with the International Standards on Auditing issued by the International Auditing and Assurance Standards Board. As part of this process, the newly redrafted standards will follow certain clarity drafting conventions adopted by the ASB. These clarity drafting conventions include: (1) establishing objectives for each standard; (2) including a definitions section, if appropriate; and (3) separating requirements from application guidance and other material. The ASB is planning to have all redrafted standards become effective on the same date, which is for audits of financial statements for periods ending on or after December 15, 2012. It is possible that the effective date might be delayed beyond that date. The ASB's clarity and convergence project will have a significant effect on the auditing standards applicable to audits of nonpublic companies, and the 2012 *GAAS Guide* will be appropriately modified to reflect these changes once the effective date of the standards is certain.

Overview

Adequate disclosure in financial statements is a broad concept and encompasses many factors including the following items:

- The format of the financial statements

- The arrangement of items in the financial statements

- The specific content of items in the financial statements

- Notes to the financial statements

- Terminology used in the financial statements

- Classification of items in the financial statements

The auditor must use professional judgment to determine whether the disclosure in the financial statements is adequate. If the auditor concludes that adequate disclosure has not been achieved, the auditor's report should be qualified or an adverse opinion should be expressed. If practicable, the omitted disclosure should be included in the auditor's report. "Practicable" means that "the information is reasonably obtainable from management's accounts and records and providing the information in his or her report does not require the auditor to assume the position of a preparer of financial information."

> **ENGAGEMENT STRATEGY:** An auditor of a nonpublic entity may assist management in the preparation of its financial statements, including the preparation of notes. Despite this involvement, under this circumstance the financial statements and the accompanying notes are the representations of management and there is no need for the auditor to modify the audit report. By contrast, the auditor of a public company is prohibited from assisting management in the preparation of financial statements.

> **OBSERVATION:** The auditor should not make information obtained during the engagement available to other parties without the consent of management, unless the information is required to be disclosed or presented in order for the financial statements to be prepared in accordance with generally accepted accounting principles.

EXHIBIT AU 431-1 — ENGAGEMENT PROGRAM FOR SOP 94-6

Use the following procedures as a guide for implementing the guidance established by SOP 94-6 (Disclosure of Certain Significant Risks and Uncertainties). The program is only a guide, and professional judgment should be exercised to determine how the standards established in SOP 94-6 should be observed.

Initial and date each procedure as it is completed. If the procedure is not relevant to this engagement, place "N/A" (not applicable) in the space provided for an initial.

Client Name: _____

Date of Financial Statements: _____

	Initials	Date	Audit Documentation Reference
1. Has the client made appropriate disclosures for estimates that have the following characteristics?	____	____	_____
• It is at least reasonably possible that the estimate of the effect on the financial statements of a condition, situation, or set of circumstances that existed at the balance sheet date will change in the near term due to one or more future confirming events.	____	____	_____
• The effect of the change would have a material effect on the financial statements.	____	____	_____
2. Have estimates that require disclosure based on the standards established by FAS-5 (ASC 230) or another pronouncement been described by the client as being at least reasonably possible that a change in the estimate will occur in the near term?	____	____	_____
3. If an estimate does not require disclosure under FAS-5 (ASC 230) but the estimate meets the standards described in question 1 above, has the client made the following disclosures related to the estimate?	____	____	_____
• Disclosure concerning the nature of the estimate	____	____	_____
• Disclosure indicating that it is reasonably possible that a change in the estimate will occur in the near term	____	____	_____

4. Other comments: ————————————————————

————————————————————————————————

————————————————————————————————

Reviewed by: ————————————————————————

Date: ————————————————————————————

————————————————————————————————

SECTION 435

SEGMENT INFORMATION

FAS-14 (Financial Reporting for Segments of a Business Enterprise) provided guidance for the reporting of segment information for certain companies, and SAS-21 (Segment Information) provided guidance for the audit of segment information. In June 1997, FAS-131 (ASC 280) (Disclosures about Segments of an Enterprise and Related Information) superseded FAS-14, and because the audit guidance provided by SAS-21 was inappropriate for the standards established by FAS-131 (ASC 280), SAS-21 was rescinded. Audit guidance for segment information is now covered by Auditing Interpretation No. 4 of AU 326 (June 2003) titled "Applying Auditing Procedures to Segment Disclosures in Financial Statements," which is discussed in AU 326 (Audit Evidence).

AU 500

The Fourth Standard

of Reporting

Section 504: Association with Financial Statements 515

Section 508: Reports on Audited Financial Statements 522

Section 530: Dating of the Independent Auditor's Report ... 561

Section 532: Restricting the Use of an Auditor's Report ... 565

Section 534: Reporting on Financial Statements Prepared
for Use in Other Countries 571

Section 543: Part of Audit Performed by Other Independent
Auditors 578

Section 544: Lack of Conformity with Generally Accepted
Accounting Principles 586

Section 550: Other Information in Documents Containing
Audited Financial Statements 588

Section 551: Reporting on Information Accompanying the
Basic Financial Statements in Auditor-Submitted
Documents 594

Section 552: Reporting on Condensed Financial
Statements and Selected Financial Data 602

Section 558: Required Supplementary Information 606

Section 560: Subsequent Events 612

Section 561: Subsequent Discovery of Facts Existing at the
Date of the Auditor's Report 618

SECTION 504

ASSOCIATION WITH FINANCIAL STATEMENTS

Authoritative Pronouncements

SAS-26 — Association with Financial Statements

Auditing Interpretation No. 1 of AU 504 (November 2002) — Annual Report Disclosure of Unaudited Fourth Quarter Interim Data

Auditing Interpretation No. 4 of AU 504 (November 1979) — Auditor's Identification with Condensed Financial Data

Auditing Interpretation No. 5 of AU 504 (November 1979) — Applicability of Guidance on Reporting When Not Independent

> **IMPORTANT NOTICE FOR 2011:** The Auditing Standards Board (ASB) is in the process of redrafting all of the auditing sections in *Codification of Statements on Auditing Standards* to converge U.S. GAAS with the International Standards on Auditing issued by the International Auditing and Assurance Standards Board. As part of this process, the newly redrafted standards will follow certain clarity drafting conventions adopted by the ASB. These clarity drafting conventions include (1) establishing objectives for each standard; (2) including a definitions section, if appropriate; and (3) separating requirements from application guidance and other material. The ASB is planning to have all redrafted standards become effective on the same date, which is for audits of financial statements for periods ending on or after December 15, 2012. It is possible that the effective date might be delayed beyond that date. The ASB's clarity and convergence project will have a significant effect on the auditing standards applicable to audits of nonpublic companies, and the 2012 *GAAS Guide* will be appropriately modified to reflect these changes once the effective date of the standards is certain.

Overview

The fourth reporting standard establishes very definite reporting obligations when an auditor is associated with financial statements. SAS-26 (Association with Financial Statements) describes the meaning of "association" when the client is a public entity or a nonpublic entity whose financial statements are audited. Reporting requirements for a nonpublic entity whose financial statements are unaudited are established by Statements on Standards for Accounting and Review Services (SSARS). An auditor is associated with financial statements under the following circumstances:

- The accountant agrees to the use of his or her name in a report or similar document that contains the financial statements.

- The accountant submits to the client or third parties financial statements that the accountant has prepared or has assisted in preparing. (Whether the accountant's name appears on the financial statements is irrelevant.)

Interpretation No. 4 of AU 504 (November 1979) (Auditor's Identification with Condensed Financial Data) states that an accountant is not associated with *condensed* financial data published by a financial reporting service even when the accountant is identified by the service as being the entity's auditor.

> **OBSERVATION:** SAS-26 refers specifically to financial statements and is not applicable to data presented in an alternative format. Although SAS-26 does not define the meaning of "financial statement," SAS-62 (AU 623) states that financial statements would include information that purports to describe the assets and obligations of an organization or the changes of the assets and obligations over a period of time. In addition, SAS-62 (AU 623) recognizes that financial statements encompass those prepared in accordance with GAAP as well as those that reflect a comprehensive basis of accounting other than GAAP. Finally, SAS-26 states that a tax return prepared solely for a tax authority is beyond the scope of SAS-26.

> **PLANNING AID REMINDER:** Interpretation No. 1 of AU 504 notes that the auditor is not required to audit interim information unless specifically engaged to do so.

Promulgated Reporting Checklist

The auditor may be associated with certain financial statements that have not been audited or reviewed, as follows:

- Unaudited financial statements of a public entity

- Unaudited financial statements prepared on a comprehensive basis of accounting other than GAAP

- Unaudited financial statements arising because the auditor is not independent

- Unaudited financial statements presented on a comparative basis with audited financial statements

- Unaudited financial statements that require a modified disclaimer

Analysis and Application of Reporting Standards

Unaudited financial statements of a public entity

An accountant who is associated with the financial statements of a public entity whose financial statements have not been audited or reviewed should issue a disclaimer of opinion on the unaudited financial statements. The disclaimer may be placed directly on the unaudited financial statements, or it may be expressed in the accountant's report that accompanies the financial statements. Exhibit AU 504-1 is an example of a disclaimer that accompanies the unaudited financial statements.

> **PLANNING AID REMINDER:** When the accountant issues a disclaimer of opinion under this circumstance, the accountant is not required to perform any procedures except to read the financial statements for obvious material misstatements. If the accountant has performed other procedures, those procedures should not be referred to in the disclaimer of opinion.

If the accountant becomes aware that a public company is going to use his or her name in a client-prepared document that contains financial statements that have not been audited or reviewed, the accountant should request that his or her name not be used in the document or that the financial statements be marked as "unaudited" and that the document contain a notation that the accountant does not express an opinion on the financial statements.

> **OBSERVATION:** If the client refuses the accountant's request, the client should be informed that it does not have permission to use the accountant's name in the document and the accountant should consider what other steps may be appropriate, including seeking the advice of legal counsel.

> **OBSERVATION:** A disclaimer of opinion should not include negative assurances unless specifically allowed by standards established by the American Institute of Certified Public Accountants. (For example, see AU 634 [Letters for Underwriters and Certain Other Requesting Parties].)

Unaudited financial statements prepared on a comprehensive basis of accounting other than GAAP

An accountant may be associated with financial statements of a public entity whose financial statements are prepared on a comprehensive basis of accounting other than generally accepted accounting principles. Under this circumstance, the accountant should follow the guidance provided in the previous Section, except the disclaimer should be appropriately modified to reflect the guidance established by SAS-62 (AU 623) (Special Reports).

Exhibit AU 504-2 is an example of a disclaimer that accompanies unaudited financial statements prepared on a comprehensive basis of accounting other than generally accepted accounting principles.

> **PLANNING AID REMINDER:** Financial statements that are prepared on a comprehensive basis of accounting other than generally accepted accounting principles must include a note that describes the basis of presentation and how it differs from generally accepted accounting principles. The monetary effects of the differences between the two bases of accounting need not be included in the note.

Unaudited financial statements arising because the auditor is not independent

When an accountant is not independent but is associated with a client's financial statements, the accountant should disclaim an opinion on the financial statements. The reason for the lack of independence should not be disclosed. If the accountant has performed any procedures with respect to the financial statements, those procedures should not be disclosed in the accountant's report.

Exhibit AU 504-3 is an example of a disclaimer that arises from the accountant's lack of independence.

> **PLANNING AID REMINDER:** If the client is a nonpublic company, the financial statements must be compiled or reviewed based on the standards established by Statements on Standards for Accounting and Review Services.

Interpretation No. 5 of AU 504 (Applicability of Guidance on Reporting When Not Independent) notes that the accountant must use professional judgment to determine when independence has been impaired with respect to unaudited financial statements. The Interpretation notes further that the same factors should be used to make that determination that are used to make the judgment when the financial statements have been audited.

*Unaudited financial statements are presented on a comparative basis
with audited financial statements*

Unaudited financial statements may be presented on a comparative basis
with audited financial statements that are included in a document filed with
the Securities and Exchange Commission (SEC). Under this circumstance,
the unaudited financial statements must clearly be marked as "unaudited."

When unaudited financial statements are presented on a comparative
basis with audited financial statements in other circumstances (not part of
a filing with the SEC), the unaudited financial statements must again be
clearly marked as "unaudited" and either of the following must be observed:

- The report on the prior period should be reissued.

- The report on the current period should be expanded to include a separate
  paragraph that describes the responsibility assumed for the financial
  statements of the prior period.

When the current-period financial statements are unaudited and the prior-
period financial statements are audited and a separate paragraph is included
in the current report, the separate paragraph should include the following:

- A statement that the prior-period financial statements were previously
  audited

- The date of the previous report

- The type of opinion previously expressed on the prior-period financial
  statements (if the opinion is other than unqualified, the reason for modifying the previous report must be described)

- A statement that no auditing procedures were performed after the date of
  the prior-year financial statements

When the current-period financial statements are audited and the prior-
period financial statements are unaudited and a separate paragraph is included in the current report, the separate paragraph should include the following:

- A statement of the type of service performed in the previous year

- The report date of the previous service

- A description of any modifications to the previous year's report

- A statement that the service performed was less than an audit and did not
  provide a basis for expressing an opinion on the financial statements

- If the client is a public entity, a disclaimer of opinion on the prior-year
  financial statements

When the client is a nonpublic entity, the separate paragraph should include a description of either a compilation (see Exhibit AU 504-4) or a review (see Exhibit AU 504-5).

Unaudited financial statements that require a modified disclaimer

When an accountant issues a disclaimer of opinion on unaudited financial statements, the accountant may be aware that the financial statements are not consistent with generally accepted accounting principles. Under this circumstance, the accountant should modify the disclaimer of opinion by doing the following:

* Describing the departure from generally accepted accounting principles

* If practicable, describing the effect of the departure on the financial statements or including the required disclosure in his or her report

* If the effects on the financial statements are not reasonably determinable or it is unreasonable to make the appropriate disclosures, stating so in the report

> **OBSERVATION:** If the client will not agree to the modification of the disclaimer of opinion, the accountant should refuse to be associated with the financial statements and, if appropriate, withdraw from the engagement.

Practitioner's Aids

EXHIBIT AU 504-1 — DISCLAIMER OF OPINION ON UNAUDITED FINANCIAL STATEMENTS

The accompanying balance sheet of Bluefield Company as of December 31, 20X5, and the related statements of income, retained earnings, and cash flows for the year then ended were not audited by us and, accordingly, we do not express an opinion on them.

EXHIBIT AU 504-2 — DISCLAIMER OF OPINION ON UNAUDITED FINANCIAL STATEMENTS THAT ARE PREPARED ON A COMPREHENSIVE BASIS OF ACCOUNTING OTHER THAN GENERALLY ACCEPTED ACCOUNTING PRINCIPLES

The accompanying statement of assets and liabilities, resulting from cash transactions of Bluefield Company as of December 31, 20X5, and the related statement of revenues collected and expenses paid during the year then ended were not audited by us and, accordingly, we do not express an opinion on them.

EXHIBIT AU 504-3 — DISCLAIMER OF OPINION ON UNAUDITED FINANCIAL STATEMENTS BECAUSE THE ACCOUNTANT IS NOT INDEPENDENT

We are not independent with respect to Bluefield Company, and the accompanying balance sheet as of December 31, 20X5, and the related statements of income, retained earnings, and cash flows for the year then ended were not audited by us and, accordingly, we do not express an opinion on them.

EXHIBIT AU 504-4 — DESCRIPTION OF A COMPILATION IN A SEPARATE PARAGRAPH WHEN REPORTING ON AUDITED AND UNAUDITED FINANCIAL STATEMENTS IN COMPARATIVE FORM

The 20X5 financial statements were compiled by us, and our report thereon, dated February 14, 20X6, stated that we did not audit or review those financial statements and, accordingly, express no opinion or other form of assurance on them.

EXHIBIT AU 504-5 — DESCRIPTION OF A REVIEW IN A SEPARATE PARAGRAPH WHEN REPORTING ON AUDITED AND UNAUDITED FINANCIAL STATEMENTS IN COMPARATIVE FORM

The 20X5 financial statements were reviewed by us, and our report thereon, dated February 14, 20X6, stated that we were not aware of any material modifications that should be made to those statements for them to be in conformity with accounting principles generally accepted in the United States. However, a review is substantially less in scope than an audit and does not provide a basis for the expression of an opinion on the financial statements taken as a whole.

SECTION 508

REPORTS ON AUDITED FINANCIAL STATEMENTS

Authoritative Pronouncements

SAS-58 — Reports on Audited Financial Statements

SAS-64 — Omnibus Statement on Auditing Standards — 1990

SAS-79 — Amendments to Statement on Auditing Standards No. 58, "Reports on Audited Financial Statements"

SAS-85 — Management Representations

SAS-93 — Omnibus Statement on Auditing Standards — 2000

SAS-98 — Omnibus Statement on Auditing Standards — 2002

Auditing Interpretation No. 1 (October 2000) — Report of an Outside Inventory-Taking Firm as an Alternative Procedure for Observing Inventories

Auditing Interpretation No. 8 (October 2000) — Reporting on Financial Statements Prepared on a Liquidation Basis of Accounting

Auditing Interpretation No. 12 (January 1989) — Reference in Auditor's Standard Report to Management's Report

Auditing Interpretation No. 14 (May 2008) — Reporting on Audits Conducted in Accordance with Auditing Standards Generally Accepted in the United States of America and in Accordance with International Standards on Auditing

Auditing Interpretation No. 15 (November 2002) — Reporting as Successor Auditor When Prior-Period Audited Financial Statements Were Audited by a Predecessor Auditor Who Has Ceased Operations

Auditing Interpretation No. 16 (June 2003) — Effect on Auditor's Report of Omission of Schedule of Investments by Investment Partnerships That Are Exempt from Securities and Exchange Commission Registration under the Investment Company Act of 1940

Auditing Interpretation No. 17 (June 2004) — Clarification in the Audit Report of the Extent of Testing of Internal Control over Financial Reporting in Accordance with Generally Accepted Auditing Standards

Auditing Interpretation No. 18 (June 2004) — Reference to PCAOB Standards in an Audit Report on a Nonissuer

Auditing Interpretation No. 19 (May 2008) — Financial Statements Prepared in Conformity with International Financial Reporting Standards as Issued by the International Accounting Standards Board

> IMPORTANT NOTICE FOR 2011: The Auditing Standards Board (ASB) is in the process of redrafting all of the auditing sections in *Codification of Statements on Auditing Standards* to converge U.S. GAAS with the International Standards on Auditing issued by the International Auditing and Assurance Standards Board. As part of this process, the newly redrafted standards will follow certain clarity drafting conventions adopted by the ASB. These clarity drafting conventions include (1) establishing objectives for each standard; (2) including a definitions section, if appropriate; and (3) separating requirements from application guidance and other material. The ASB is planning to have all redrafted standards become effective on the same date, which is for audits of financial statements for periods ending on or after December 15, 2012. It is possible that the effective date might be delayed beyond that date. The ASB's clarity and convergence project will have a significant effect on the auditing standards applicable to audits of non-public companies, and the 2012 *GAAS Guide* will be appropriately modified to reflect these changes once the effective date of the standards is certain.

Overview

The format of the standard auditor's report is mandated by the following four standards:

1. The report shall state whether the financial statements are presented in accordance with generally accepted accounting principles.

2. The report shall identify those circumstances in which such principles have not been consistently observed in the current period in relation to the preceding period.

3. Informative disclosures in the financial statements are to be regarded as adequate unless otherwise stated in the report.

4. The report shall contain either an expression of opinion regarding the financial statements, taken as a whole, or an assertion to the effect that an opinion cannot be expressed. When an overall opinion cannot be expressed, the reasons there for must be stated. In all cases where an auditor's name is associated with financial statements, the report must contain a clear-cut indication of the character of the auditor's examination, if any, and the degree of responsibility the auditor is taking.

SAS-58 states that the standard auditor's report should include the following:

- A title that includes the word "independent"

- A statement that the financial statements identified in the report were audited

- A statement that the financial statements are the responsibility of the entity's management and that the auditor's responsibility is to express an opinion on the financial statements based on the audit

- A statement that the audit was conducted in accordance with generally accepted auditing standards and an identification of the country of origin of those standards (for example, auditing standards generally accepted in the United States of America or U.S. generally accepted auditing standards [GAAS])

- A statement that generally accepted auditing standards require that the auditor plan and perform the audit to obtain reasonable assurance about whether the financial statements are free of material misstatement

- A statement that the audit included:

  — An examination of evidence supporting the amounts and disclosures in the financial statements on a test basis

  — An assessment of the accounting principles used and significant estimates made by management

  — An evaluation of the overall financial statement presentation

- A statement that the auditor believes that the audit provides a reasonable basis for his or her opinion

- An opinion of whether the financial statements present fairly, in all material respects, the financial position of the entity as of the balance sheet date and the results of its operations and its cash flows for the period then ended in conformity with generally accepted accounting principles (GAAP), and the opinion should include an identification of the country of origin of those accounting principles (for example, accounting principles generally accepted in the United States of American or U.S. generally accepted accounting principles [GAAP])

- A manual or printed signature of the auditor's firm

- The date of the audit report

PUBLIC COMPANY IMPLICATION: For public companies, PCAOB Auditing and Related Professional Practice Standard

No. 1 (AS-1) (References in Auditors' Reports to the Standards of the Public Company Accounting Oversight Board) requires that the scope paragraph of the audit report state that the audit was conducted "in accordance with the standards of the Public Company Accounting Oversight Board (United States)."

PUBLIC COMPANY IMPLICATION: The auditor's opinion relates to whether the financial statements are fairly presented. Auditors have historically assumed that if the financial statements are in accordance with GAAP, then the financial statements are fairly stated. This assumption might no longer be valid for public company audits. For example, Section 302 of SOX requires management to certify whether the financial statements fairly present in all material respects the financial condition and results of operations of the entity. There is no reference to compliance with GAAP in evaluating whether the financial statements are fairly stated. All auditors, but particularly public company auditors, should only issue an unqualified report if the client's financial statements accurately represent the economics of the client's financial position and results of operations, regardless of compliance with GAAP.

PUBLIC COMPANY IMPLICATION: In 2007 the U.S. Department of the Treasury, at the behest of Treasury Secretary Henry Paulson, created the Advisory Committee on the Auditing Profession. The Advisory Committee, co-chaired by Arthur Levitt, a former SEC chairman, and Donald Nicolaisen, a former SEC chief accountant was created to examine the sustainability of a strong and viable auditing profession, and its recommendations have the potential to affect auditing practice. The Advisory Committee has made one recommendation that will affect the auditor's report, if adopted; namely, it recommends that the SEC and PCAOB clarify in the auditor's report the auditor's responsibility for detecting fraud.

The body of the standard auditor's report should include an introductory paragraph, a scope paragraph, and an opinion paragraph. In the introductory paragraph, the auditor (1) states that an audit has been performed and (2) describes the responsibility assumed by the entity's management and the auditor with respect to the financial statements.

In the scope paragraph, the auditor states that generally accepted auditing standards were observed in the performance of the audit and briefly describes the audit. In the concluding sentence of the scope paragraph, the auditor states that the audit has provided a reasonable basis for expressing an opinion on the financial statements.

PLANNING AID REMINDER: Interpretation No. 18 of AU 508 states that although an audit for a nonpublic entity should be conducted in accordance with generally accepted auditing standards, an auditor is not precluded from performing the audit in accordance with both generally accepted auditing standards and the standards of the PCAOB. If the auditor chooses to perform an audit in accordance with both sets of standards, the scope paragraph of the auditor's standard report needs to be modified appropriately. Exhibit AU 508-12 presents an example of an audit report in which the standards of both the ASB and the PCAOB were followed in the performance of the audit. The additional language in Exhibit 508-12 related to internal control should not be used when a nonpublic company engages its auditor to audit and report on the entity's effectiveness of internal control over financial reporting.

In the opinion paragraph, the auditor states that the financial statements present fairly, in all material respects, the entity's financial position, results of operations, and cash flows. The auditor also states that the financial statements are presented in accordance with generally accepted accounting principles; however, the auditor does not refer to the consistent application of accounting principles.

Financial statements are presented fairly in accordance with generally accepted accounting principles if those accounting principles represent U.S. GAAP (see AU 411). In addition, in accordance with Interpretation 19 of AU 508, the financial statements are fairly presented in accordance with generally accepted accounting principles if the statements are in accordance with International Financial Reporting Standards (IFRS) as issued by the International Accounting Standards Board (IASB). This reflects the fact that AICPA Council has designated the IASB as the body to promulgate international financial reporting standards under Rules 202 and 203 of the AICPA's Code of Professional Conduct. The auditor would state in his or her report that the financial statements were prepared in accordance with IFRS as issued by the IASB rather than U.S. GAAP. An auditor *cannot* report under AU 508 if the financial statements are prepared using IFRS as modified by a particular foreign country (e.g., IFRS as issued by the IASB have been modified for use in the European Union).

Exhibit AU 508-1 is an example of the standard auditor's report.

EXHIBIT AU 508-1 — STANDARD AUDITOR'S REPORT

Independent Auditor's Report

Penney and Nichols, CPAs
45789 Beachwood Drive
Centerville, New Jersey 08000

Board of Directors and Stockholders
X Company

We have audited the accompanying balance sheet of X Company as of December 31, 20X5, and the related statements of income, retained earnings, and cash flows for the year then ended. These financial statements are the responsibility of the Company's management. Our responsibility is to express an opinion on these financial statements based on our audit.

We conducted our audit in accordance with auditing standards generally accepted in the United States of America. Those standards require that we plan and perform the audit to obtain reasonable assurance about whether the financial statements are free of material misstatement. An audit includes examining, on a test basis, evidence supporting the amounts and disclosures in the financial statements. An audit also includes assessing the accounting principles used and significant estimates made by management, as well as evaluating the overall financial statement presentation. We believe that our audit provides a reasonable basis for our opinion.

In our opinion, the financial statements referred to above present fairly, in all material respects, the financial position of X Company as of December 31, 20X5, and the results of its operations and its cash flows for the year then ended in conformity with accounting principles generally accepted in the United States of America.

[Report Date]

[Signature]

PLANNING AID REMINDER: Interpretation No. 17 of AU 508 states that the auditor can modify the scope paragraph of his or her report to indicate the purpose and extent of internal control testing in an audit performed for a nonpublic entity in accordance with generally accepted auditing standards. The following sentences would be added to the scope paragraph: "An audit includes consideration of internal control over financial reporting as a basis for designing audit procedures that are appropriate in the circumstances, but not for the purpose of expressing an opinion on the effectiveness of the Company's internal control over financial reporting. Accordingly, we express no such opinion." This language is not appropriate when a nonpublic entity engages its auditor to audit and report on the entity's effectiveness of internal control over financial reporting.

> **OBSERVATION:** The audit reports presented in this chapter assume that the entity does not have other "comprehensive income" components as defined by ASC 220 (FAS-130, Reporting Comprehensive Income). If the entity has such components and presents a statement of comprehensive income, the first line in each report should refer to "the accompanying balance sheet of X Company as of December 31, 20X5, and the related statements of income, comprehensive income, retained earnings, and cash flows for the year then ended."

Interpretation No. 14 of AU 508 states that an auditor may (but is not required to) indicate that the audit was conducted in accordance with another set of auditing standards (in addition to U.S. GAAS) if the other standards have been followed. Under this reporting circumstance the first sentence of the standard audit report is modified to read as follows (for illustrative purposes it is assumed that the other set of auditing standards satisfied were those established by the International Auditing and Assurance Standards Board):

> We conducted our audit in accordance with auditing standards generally accepted in the United States of America and in accordance with International Standards on Auditing.

> **PLANNING AID REMINDER:** When the audit report refers to another set of auditing standards, all the other auditing standards and related interpretations must be observed. For example, if the report refers to International Standards of Auditing, the Interpretation notes that "it is necessary to consider the text of the International Standards on Auditing in their entirety, including the basic principles and essential procedures together with the related guidance included in the International Standards on Auditing."

The report is dated to coincide with the date that the auditor has gathered sufficient evidence to support the audit opinion. Generally, the auditor is not required to perform audit procedures after the report date. The report is signed by a firm's partner (or sole proprietor), which legally binds the CPA firm to the assertions made in the report.

The auditor's report may be addressed to the client, its board of directors, or its stockholders. For an unincorporated client, the report may be addressed to the partners or the sole proprietor. When an audit is performed at the request of a party other than the management or owners of the audited entity, the report should be addressed to the party that requested the audit.

> **PUBLIC COMPANY IMPLICATION:** Under SOX, the audit committee of the client's board of directors is directly responsible

for the appointment, compensation, and oversight of the auditor. As such, the client in a public company audit is now the audit committee. Therefore, public company audit reports should no longer be addressed to the company or to the company's management.

The standard report illustrated above is referred to as an unqualified report. When an unqualified report is issued, the auditor makes the following assurances:

- That accounting principles selected by the client have general acceptance

- That accounting principles are appropriate for the client

- That disclosures, such as financial statement notes, are adequate to enable the user to use, understand, and interpret the financial statements

- That data presented in the financial statements are classified and summarized in a reasonable manner

- That underlying events and transactions, within a range of acceptable limits, are reflected in the financial statements

> **PLANNING AID REMINDER:** Interpretation No. 12 of AU 508 states that when an annual shareholders' report or other client-prepared document that includes audited financial statements contains a statement that management is responsible for the financial statements, the auditor's report should not modify the standard audit report by referring to management's report. Such a modification could imply that the auditor is making assurances about various statements contained in the management report.

Reporting on comprehensive income

ASC 220 (FAS-130) describes "comprehensive income" as net income plus other comprehensive income components. The components of other comprehensive income include "revenues, expenses, gains, and losses that under generally accepted accounting principles are included in comprehensive income but excluded from net income." The components of other comprehensive income include items that have the appearance of nominal accounts (income statement accounts) but are currently reported as part of owners' equity (either as an increase or decrease). Specifically, other comprehensive income components include the provision for the "minimum pension liability" identified in ASC 715 (FAS-87, Employers' Accounting for Pension Plans), unrealized gains and losses on investments classified as part of the available-for-sale portfolio identified in ASC 320 (FAS-115,

Accounting for Certain Investments in Debt and Equity Securities), the valuation of certain hedge contracts reported at fair value as required by ASC 320 (FAS-115), and foreign currency translation adjustments as described by ASC 830 (FAS-52, Foreign Currency Translation).

The language of the standard auditor's report must be changed slightly when comprehensive income is presented depending upon how comprehensive income is presented in the client's financial statements. Although ASC 220 (FAS-130) does not require a specific presentation format, the following presentations would be acceptable:

- A separate statement of comprehensive income

- A combined statement of income and comprehensive income

- A statement of change in equity (that includes comprehensive income)

Separate statement of comprehensive income

A separate statement of comprehensive income would include net income and other comprehensive income components. Under this circumstance, the report must be modified to include reference to the separate statement. Presented below is the language of a standard auditor's report for financial statements that include a separate statement of comprehensive income:

> We have audited the accompanying balance sheet of X Company as of December 31, 20X5, and the related statements of income, comprehensive income, retained earnings, and cash flows for the year then ended. These financial statements are the responsibility of the Company's management. Our responsibility is to express an opinion on these financial statements based on our audit.
>
> We conducted our audit in accordance with auditing standards generally accepted in the United States of America. Those standards require that we plan and perform the audit to obtain reasonable assurance about whether the financial statements are free of material misstatement. An audit includes examining, on a test basis, evidence supporting the amounts and disclosures in the financial statements. An audit also includes assessing the accounting principles used and significant estimates made by management, as well as evaluating the overall financial statement presentation. We believe that our audit provides a reasonable basis for our opinion.
>
> In our opinion, the financial statements referred to above present fairly, in all material respects, the financial position of X Company as of December 31, 20X5, and the results of its operations and its cash flows for the year then ended in

conformity with accounting principles generally accepted in the United States of America.

Combined statement of income and comprehensive income

A combined statement of income and comprehensive income would include net income and other comprehensive income components, all included in a single financial statement. Under this circumstance, the audit report must be changed so that the reference is to the combined financial statement. The following illustrates an audit report on financial statements that include a combined statement of income and comprehensive income.

> We have audited the accompanying balance sheet of X Company as of December 31, 20X5, and the related statements of combined income and comprehensive income, retained earnings, and cash flows for the year then ended. These financial statements are the responsibility of the Company's management. Our responsibility is to express an opinion on these financial statements based on our audit.
>
> We conducted our audit in accordance with auditing standards generally accepted in the United States of America. Those standards require that we plan and perform the audit to obtain reasonable assurance about whether the financial statements are free of material misstatement. An audit includes examining, on a test basis, evidence supporting the amounts and disclosures in the financial statements. An audit also includes assessing the accounting principles used and significant estimates made by management, as well as evaluating the overall financial statement presentation. We believe that our audit provides a reasonable basis for our opinion.
>
> In our opinion, the financial statements referred to above present fairly, in all material respects, the financial position of X Company as of December 31, 20X5, and the results of its operations and its cash flows for the year then ended in conformity with accounting principles generally accepted in the United States of America.

Statement of change in equity (that includes comprehensive income)

In some instances the components of other comprehensive income may be included in the statement of change in equity, which includes a separate column that reconciles the beginning and ending balances of the equity (permanent) account that tracks the changes in other components of comprehensive income. Under this circumstance, the audit report must be changed so that there is a reference to the statement of change in equity.

The following report illustrates a standard audit report on financial statements that include a statement of change in equity.

> We have audited the accompanying balance sheet of X Company as of December 31, 20X5, and the related statements of income, retained earnings, change in equity, and cash flows for the year then ended. These financial statements are the responsibility of the Company's management. Our responsibility is to express an opinion on these financial statements based on our audit.
>
> We conducted our audit in accordance with auditing standards generally accepted in the United States of America. Those standards require that we plan and perform the audit to obtain reasonable assurance about whether the financial statements are free of material misstatement. An audit includes examining, on a test basis, evidence supporting the amounts and disclosures in the financial statements. An audit also includes assessing the accounting principles used and significant estimates made by management, as well as evaluating the overall financial statement presentation. We believe that our audit provides a reasonable basis for our opinion.
>
> In our opinion, the financial statements referred to above present fairly, in all material respects, the financial position of X Company as of December 31, 20X5, and the results of its operations and its cash flows for the year then ended in conformity with accounting principles generally accepted in the United States of America.

Promulgated Reporting Standards Checklist

The auditor's report may be modified due to one of the following circumstances:

- There is a departure from generally accepted accounting principles (GAAP).

- There is a departure from an accounting principle promulgated by an authoritative body designated by the AICPA to promulgate such principles, and the auditor agrees with the departure.

- Informative disclosures in the financial statements are not reasonably adequate.

- There is a change from an acceptable accounting principle to an unacceptable accounting principle.

- The treatment of a change in an accounting principle is inappropriate.

- Management has not provided reasonable justification for a change in accounting principles.

- Sufficient appropriate audit evidence has not been collected.

- There are other scope limitations.

- The reporting engagement is limited (e.g., a report on the balance sheet only).

- There are uncertainties related to going concern.

- There are uncertainties related to loss contingencies.

- An event, condition, or transaction affecting the financial statements is emphasized.

- The auditor is not independent with respect to the financial statements.

- There is a piecemeal opinion (prohibited).

- There are negative assurances (prohibited).

- The auditor reports on comparative financial statements.

Analysis and Application of Reporting Standards

There is a departure from GAAP

Generally accepted accounting principles include promulgated rules, as well as unwritten rules that have gained acceptance through general usage. When a client has not observed generally accepted accounting principles, the auditor must decide whether to issue an unqualified, a qualified, or an adverse opinion. The selection of the appropriate opinion depends on the materiality of the departure, the effects of the departure, and the number of accounts affected by the departure. An unqualified opinion can be issued if the departure is not significant to the fair presentation of the financial statements. If the departure affects the fairness of the financial statements but overall the statements can be relied on, a qualified opinion can be issued. On the other hand, when the departure is so significant that the financial statements should not be relied on, an adverse opinion must be issued.

When a qualified or adverse opinion is issued, an explanatory paragraph must describe the departure and its effects, if determinable, on the financial statements. If a qualified opinion is issued, the opinion paragraph should specifically refer to the explanatory paragraph as illustrated in Exhibit AU 508-2.

If the auditor concludes that an adverse opinion is to be issued, language similar to that in Exhibit AU 508-3 is used in the opinion paragraph. The opinion paragraph should specifically refer to the paragraph that discloses the basis for the adverse opinion.

> **OBSERVATION:** If practicable, an auditor should provide information required by GAAP that has not been disclosed in the financial statements, unless the omission of the information from the auditor's report is recognized as appropriate by another SAS. "Practicable" means that the required information is reasonably obtainable from management's accounts and records and that by providing the information, the auditor is not required to assume the position of preparer of the financial information.

The above guidance also applies to those situations in which the auditor expresses a qualified or an adverse opinion because of a departure from GAAP that is not related to disclosure.

When generally accepted accounting principles have not been used to prepare the financial statements, a note to the financial statements may describe the nature and effects of the departure. Rather than repeat this information in an explanatory paragraph, the auditor's report may incorporate the information in the note by reference. For example, the explanatory paragraph could read as follows:

> As described more fully in Note 12 to the financial statements, the Company reports all of its sales on the installment method for financial accounting purposes and on its tax return. In our opinion, generally accepted accounting principles require that sales be reported on the accrual basis with an appropriate provision for deferred taxes.

The opinion paragraph (either a qualified or an adverse opinion) would refer to the deviation described in the explanation.

> **OBSERVATION:** An auditor may incorporate the information in a note to the financial statements into the auditor's report by reference; however, the auditor must be careful that matters in the note that are inconsistent with the auditor's opinion are not also incorporated. For example, the note may attempt to justify the departure from generally accepted accounting principles in a manner that is inappropriate or misleading. Under this circumstance, it would be advisable to not make reference to the note and to simply repeat the relevant information in the explanatory paragraph.

*There is a departure from an accounting principle promulgated
by an authoritative body designated by the AICPA to promulgate
such principles, and the auditor agrees with the departure*

Generally accepted accounting principles include written as well as unwritten accounting principles, methods, and procedures. Rule 203 of the AICPA Code of Professional Conduct states:

> A member shall not (1) express an opinion or state affirmatively that the financial statements or other financial data of any entity are presented in conformity with generally accepted accounting principles or (2) state that he or she is not aware of any material modifications that should be made to such statements or data in order for them to be in conformity with generally accepted accounting principles, if such statements or data contain any departure from an accounting principle promulgated by bodies designated by Council to establish such principles that has a material effect on the statements or data taken as a whole. If, however, the statements or data contain such a departure and the member can demonstrate that due to unusual circumstances the financial statements or data would otherwise have been misleading, the member can comply with the rule by describing the departure, its approximate effects, if practicable, and the reasons why compliance with the principle would result in a misleading statement.

The AICPA Council has adopted resolutions designating the Financial Accounting Standards Board (FASB) and the Governmental Accounting Standards Board (GASB) as having the authority to promulgate accounting standards for commercial enterprises and governmental entities, respectively.

When an accounting principle is promulgated, strict interpretation and application of the rule may in some cases result in misleading financial statements. To prevent this situation, Rule 203 permits a client to use an alternative method. If the auditor agrees with the client's conclusion that the use of a promulgated rule would result in misleading financial statements, he or she may issue an unqualified opinion. However, an explanatory paragraph must be included in the standard report in which the nature, effect, and reason for the departure from the promulgated rule are described. The introductory, scope, and opinion paragraphs are not modified, and no reference is made to the explanatory paragraph in the opinion paragraph.

> **OBSERVATION:** Although Rule 203 may be needed to provide flexibility in the application of accounting principles, the rule

must be used with a great deal of caution. When the rule is used, the auditor is, in effect, promulgating an accounting rule for a specific client, which is a heavy responsibility to undertake. Not surprisingly, there are very few examples where Rule 203 has been employed concerning the adaptation of different accounting methods.

Informative disclosures in the financial statements are not reasonably adequate

The third standard of reporting states that informative disclosures in the financial statements are assumed sufficient unless specifically noted otherwise in the auditor's report. Informative disclosure includes the format and content of the financial statements, all related notes, terminology, account classification, parenthetical comments, and the degree of detail in the statements and related notes. In general, the financial information should not be abbreviated to the extent that informative disclosures are not communicated. On the other hand, the informative disclosures should not be so detailed that they might be misunderstood.

Information not adequately disclosed in the financial statements should be disclosed in an explanatory paragraph, if practical, when (1) informative disclosures are not considered adequate, (2) the report must be qualified, or (3) an adverse opinion is issued. SAS-32 (AU 431) (Adequacy of Disclosure of Financial Statements) defines "practical" to mean that (1) the information can be obtained from management's records and (2) the auditor's efforts in gathering the information do not constitute the actual preparation of the financial information. Thus, the auditor is not expected to actually prepare basic financial statements or any other financial information in an effort to include such data in the report. SAS-58 specifically states that when a client does not include a statement of cash flows, the auditor is not required to prepare and present such a statement in the report. However, an explanatory paragraph in the auditor's report must clearly state that the client has declined to include a statement of cash flows and that such a statement is required by GAAP. When such a statement is not presented in the financial statements, the auditor's report must be qualified. In all cases, when the auditor issues a qualified or adverse opinion, the explanatory paragraph in the report must be referred to in the opinion paragraph of the report. Exhibit AU 508-4 illustrates an auditor's report that is qualified because the client did not present a statement of cash flows.

Interpretation No. 16 of AU 508 provides clarification for paragraphs 7.10 through 7.14 of the AICPA Audit and Accounting Guide titled "Audits of Investment Companies." Paragraphs 7.10–7.14 of the Guide identify information that must be disclosed in an entity's Schedule of

Investments. The Interpretation states that when an entity omits disclosures required by the Schedule of Investments, it is not sufficient simply to "describe the nature of the omitted disclosures" and then express either a qualified or adverse opinion on the financial statements. For some disclosures, it is practical to present in the auditor's report some of the disclosures required by the Guide because the auditor can obtain the information from management's records and doing so does not constitute the actual preparation of the financial information. Thus, the auditor's report may contain two broad types of information concerning the omitted disclosures; namely, (1) those that are more or less what the entity should have disclosed and (2) those that are described in general (that is, the nature of the information that is not practicable to present in the auditor's report).

> **OBSERVATION:** The modification of an audit report because of a violation of the consistency standard is discussed in AU 420.

There is a change from an acceptable accounting principle to an unacceptable accounting principle

A newly adopted accounting principle must be evaluated to determine if it has general acceptance. If the auditor concludes that the accounting principle is not generally accepted, a decision must be made about whether a qualified opinion or an adverse opinion must be issued based on the deviation from generally accepted accounting principles. An explanatory paragraph(s), similar to the one presented below, should immediately precede the opinion (qualified or adverse) paragraph.

> During 20X5, the Company changed its method of valuing land held for investment from the cost method to the appraisal method. The increase resulting from the reevaluation amounted to $500,000 and is presented as an increase to stockholders' equity (appraisal capital). In our opinion, the newly adopted accounting principle (appraisal method) is not in conformity with generally accepted accounting principles.

There is no need to add an explanatory paragraph on consistency, because the change in accounting principle has been described adequately in the explanatory paragraph that discusses the selection of an unacceptable accounting principle.

For the years following the adoption of the unacceptable accounting principle, the auditor should continue to express the qualified or adverse opinion on the financial statements for the year in which the change was made. In addition, the auditor must determine whether the effects of applying an unacceptable accounting principle also require the modification of opinion(s) on subsequent financial statements.

The treatment of a change in an accounting principle is inappropriate

FAS-154 (ASC 250) (Accounting Changes and Error Corrections — a Replacement of APB Opinion No. 20 and FASB Statement No. 3) provides standards for accounting for changes in accounting principles. A change in an accounting principle usually results in retrospective application of the new accounting principle to prior periods. If the standards established by ASC 250 (FAS-154) are not observed, the auditor must decide whether the auditor's report should be modified because of a deviation from generally accepted accounting principles. If it is concluded that the report should be modified, a paragraph similar to the one illustrated below should immediately precede the opinion (qualified or adverse) paragraph:

> During 20X5, the Company changed its method of accounting for depreciation, as described in Note X to the financial statements. The effects of the change to the new method were accounted for on a prospective basis. In our opinion, the change was not accounted for in accordance with generally accepted accounting principles in that the change should have been applied retrospectively. If the change had been accounted for retrospectively, net income would be decreased $70,000 and earnings per share would be decreased $.50 in the prior year. Additionally, net property, plant, and equipment would be decreased $100,000, and deferred income tax liabilities would be decreased $30,000 in the prior year. (Only two years of financial statements are assumed.)

For the years following the incorrect treatment in accounting for the accounting change, the auditor should continue to express the qualified or adverse opinion on the financial statements for the year in which the change was made. If the accounting for the change in an accounting principle was accounted for prospectively when a cumulative-effect adjustment or a restatement of prior years' financial statements was appropriate, subsequent financial statements should be evaluated to determine whether a qualified or adverse opinion is appropriate.

Management has not provided reasonable justification for a change in accounting principles

Once an accounting principle is adopted, the principle should not be changed unless it can be demonstrated that another accounting principle is preferable as well as acceptable. If management does not adequately justify the change in accounting principles, the auditor should determine whether the report should be modified. If the auditor concludes that the report should be modified, a paragraph similar to the one presented below should immediately precede the opinion paragraph:

> During 20X5, the Company changed its method of accounting for amortization, as described in Note X to the financial statements. In previous years, the Company used an accelerated amortization method but has now changed to the straight-line method. Although the straight-line method of amortization is in conformity with generally accepted accounting principles, in our opinion the Company has not provided reasonable justification for making this change as required by generally accepted accounting principles.

There is no need to add an explanatory paragraph on consistency, because the change in accounting principle has been described adequately in the explanatory paragraph that discusses the lack of reasonable justification for making the change in accounting principles.

> **OBSERVATION:** SAS-58 does not discuss whether a lack of reasonable justification for an accounting change could lead to an adverse opinion. Under most, if not all, circumstances, it would be difficult to argue that an adverse opinion should be expressed.

For the years following the adoption of the new accounting principle, the auditor should continue to express the qualified opinion on the financial statements for the year in which the change was adopted. However, it is not appropriate to express a qualified opinion on subsequent financial statements, since the newly adopted accounting principle is a generally accepted accounting principle.

Sufficient appropriate audit evidence has not been collected

The third standard of fieldwork requires that the auditor's opinion be based on sufficient appropriate audit evidence. If adequate evidence is not collected, a scope limitation occurs. In this case, the auditor should express a qualified opinion or issue a disclaimer of opinion on the financial statements. A scope limitation may result from circumstances of the engagement or restrictions imposed by the client. The significance of the restriction depends on the number of accounts affected by the scope limitation and their potential impact on the financial statements.

> **PLANNING AID REMINDER:** SAS-58 notes that when significant scope limitations are imposed by the client, the auditor generally should express a disclaimer of opinion on the financial statements.

When an auditor concludes that a qualified opinion should be expressed, there is no change in the introductory paragraph; however, the auditor modifies the scope paragraph by referring to the scope limitation that is described in an explanatory paragraph. The explanatory paragraph should contain a description of the nature of the scope limitation and the accounts involved. The description of the scope limitation should not be incorporated in the auditor's report by reference to a note to the financial statements, because the auditor, not the client, is responsible for the description of the scope limitation. Finally, the opinion paragraph should refer to the explanatory paragraph as the basis for the qualification, and it should contain the phrase "except for" in describing the qualification. This type of report is illustrated in Exhibit AU 508-5.

If the scope limitation requires the expression of a disclaimer of opinion, the format illustrated in Exhibit AU 508-6 should be used.

In addition, the second paragraph of the standard report is omitted and an explanatory paragraph is added to describe the scope limitation. If the auditor is aware of any departures from generally accepted accounting principles, these deficiencies should also be described in another separate explanatory paragraph. The opinion paragraph should refer to the explanatory paragraph that describes the scope limitation and also should state that an opinion is not expressed on the financial statements.

Typical scope limitations include an inability to (1) observe the physical inventory, (2) confirm receivables, or (3) obtain financial statements related to an investment in another (investee) company. If the auditor is able to obtain sufficient appropriate audit evidence through alternative audit procedures (such as the review of subsequent cash receipts when a receivable is not confirmed), there is no scope limitation and the three-paragraph (unqualified) report should be issued.

> **PLANNING AID REMINDER:** SAS-58 reiterates the point that although alternative procedures may be used when the auditor cannot observe the physical inventory count, "it will always be necessary for the auditor to make, or observe, some

physical counts of the inventory and apply appropriate tests of intervening transactions."

PLANNING AID REMINDER: Interpretation No. 2 of AU 326 (The Effect of an Inability to Obtain Evidential Matter Relating to Income Tax Accruals) requires the auditor to disclaim an opinion on the financial statements if the client limits the auditor's access to tax accrual documentation and to the appropriate client personnel responsible for the tax calculation.

There are other scope limitations

When notes to the financial statements include unaudited information, the audit approach used depends on whether the information is essential to the fair presentation of the financial statements. If the information is considered essential to fair presentation, the auditor must perform procedures to determine whether the information is fairly presented. When the auditor is unable to apply the procedures considered necessary, a qualified opinion or a disclaimer of opinion should be expressed.

If the information is not considered essential for fair presentation of the financial statements, the disclosures may be "identified as unaudited or as not covered by the auditor's report." However, if the information is based on a subsequent event that occurs after the audit report date but before the financial statements are issued, the auditor must do one of the following:

- Dual-date the report

- Date the report as of the subsequent event

- Extend procedures to enable the auditor to review all subsequent events to the extended date of the report

> **OBSERVATION:** In the above circumstances, the auditor cannot accept the labeling of the subsequent event as "unaudited."

> **PLANNING AID REMINDER:** Some companies are in the business of counting, recording, and pricing inventories. Interpretation No. 1 of AU 508 states that the auditor's responsibility for the count and other tasks performed by an inventory-taking company is similar to the responsibility for tasks normally performed directly by the client. Therefore, the auditor should (1) review the client's inventory-counting program, (2) make or observe a test of physical counts, (3) make appropriate mathematical checks, and (4) test the valuation of the inventory.

*The reporting engagement is limited (e.g., a report on
the balance sheet only)*

An auditor may be engaged to audit one or more, but not all, of the
financial statements. This type of engagement is not considered a limitation of the scope of an engagement. It is instead described as a limited
reporting engagement. Of course, no scope limitation exists if the auditor is
unrestricted in the performance of audit procedures considered necessary
under the circumstances.

In a limited reporting engagement, the auditor's report is modified so
that only the financial statement(s) audited is identified. An example of a
limited report on a balance sheet is presented in Exhibit AU 508-7.

> **PLANNING AID REMINDER:** In a limited reporting engage-
> ment, the auditor must employ procedures to determine whe-
> ther accounting principles have been applied consistently with
> those used in the previous year. If the consistency standard has
> been violated, an explanatory paragraph should be added to
> the auditor's report (after the opinion paragraph). An unquali-
> fied opinion, however, is expressed on the financial statement(s).

There are uncertainties related to going concern

The auditor is required to assess the ability of the client to continue as a
going concern for one year from the financial statement date. Although a
number of factors can suggest that there is substantial doubt about an
entity's ability to continue as a going concern, the following factors can
be particularly important:

- Losses from operations for a period of years, particularly when those
  losses are growing over time

- Negative cash flow from operations, particularly when this amount is
  growing over time

- An inability to make interest and principal payments on debt

- Loss of a major customer, significant labor strikes, uninsured catastrophes

- Loss of key legal rights (e.g., franchise, patent), or other adverse legal or
  regulatory developments

If the auditor has substantial doubt about the ability of an entity to continue
as a going concern, he or she should consider management's plans for
addressing the entity's going-concern difficulties. These plans might
involve the disposition of assets, borrowing money or restructuring debt,

reducing or delaying expenditures, or increasing ownership equity. If, after considering management's plans, the auditor still has substantial doubt about the ability of the entity to continue as a going concern for one year from the financial statement date, he or she should modify the audit report by adding a fourth paragraph following the opinion paragraph where the going concern uncertainty is discussed. See AU Section 341 for a more detailed discussion of the auditor's consideration of an entity's ability to continue as a going concern, including an example of the applicable report wording when the auditor issues a modified report due to substantial doubt about the ability of the entity to continue as a going concern.

There are uncertainties related to loss contingencies

During the preparation of financial statements, a client must make a variety of accounting estimates, such as the estimated useful life of depreciable assets, a provision for doubtful accounts receivable, and an accrual for a loss contingency. In most instances, the auditor is able to collect sufficient appropriate evidence to support the reasonableness of accounting estimates. In this case, the auditor's standard report is not modified.

ASC 450 (FAS-5, Accounting for Contingencies) provides accounting and reporting standards applicable to one type of uncertainty, namely, loss contingencies. A loss contingency is defined as "an existing condition, situation, or set of circumstances involving uncertainty as to possible loss to an enterprise that will ultimately be resolved when one or more future events occur or fail to occur." Furthermore, the following classifications are used to categorize loss contingencies:

- *Probable*   The future event or events are likely to occur.

- *Reasonably possible*   The chance of the future event or events occurring is more than remote but less than likely.

- *Remote*   The chance of the future event or events occurring is slight.

> **OBSERVATION:** ASC 450 (FAS-5) is not applicable to all uncertainties; however, the Statement provides the only broad guidance in this area and may be used as a general frame of reference when evaluating other uncertainties. Additional guidance is established by ASC 275 (SOP 94-6, Disclosure of Certain Significant Risks and Uncertainties).

The accounting and reporting standards for loss contingencies are summarized in Exhibit AU 508-8.

EXHIBIT AU 508-8—ACCOUNTING AND REPORTING STANDARDS FOR LOSS CONTINGENCIES

Characteristics of Loss Contingency	*Presentation in the Financial Statements*
Probable and a reasonable estimate (or range) of the loss can be made	Accrual of loss contingency
Probable but no reasonable estimate of the loss can be made	Disclosure of loss contingency
Reasonable estimate of the loss can be made, but the loss is less than probable but more than remote	Disclosure of loss contingency
Remote likelihood of occurrence	No accrual or disclosure

> **OBSERVATION:** With the issuance of SAS-79, the Auditing Standards Board no longer requires that an audit report be modified when uncertainties exist, assuming the accounting and reporting standards established by ASC 450 (FAS-5) have been observed. However, although it is no longer required, the auditor may still choose to add a paragraph to the standard audit report to emphasize certain loss contingencies, specifically those loss contingencies that are particularly material. The next section discusses the use of a modified report to emphasize an event, condition, or transaction affecting the financial statements.

> **PLANNING AID REMINDER:** Matters of uncertainty should not be confused with scope limitations and deviations from generally accepted accounting principles. A scope limitation arises when audit evidence exists with respect to the uncertainty but has not been made available to the auditor. A deviation from generally accepted accounting principles occurs when (1) the uncertainty is not adequately disclosed, (2) an inappropriate accounting principle is used, or (3) an unreasonable accounting estimate is made. Scope limitations may lead to the expression of a qualified opinion or a disclaimer of opinion. Deviations from generally accepted accounting principles may lead to a qualified opinion or an adverse opinion.

An event, condition, or transaction affecting the financial statements is emphasized

Although reporting standards and rules are very detailed, it would be difficult to promulgate rules to provide guidance in every reporting situation.

To provide some reporting flexibility, the auditor's report may emphasize a matter without qualifying the opinion. SAS-58 presents the following as matters that could be emphasized:

- The entity reported on is a component of a larger entity.

- There have been significant transactions with a related party.

- A significant subsequent event has taken place.

- Comparability of financial statements has been affected by the accounting treatment of an event or transaction.

When the auditor decides to emphasize a matter, the auditing standards do not specify the placement of the emphasis paragraph, but they do state that the introductory, scope, and opinion paragraphs should not refer to the explanatory paragraph. An unqualified opinion should be expressed. An example of an explanatory paragraph that emphasizes a matter is as follows:

> Company X, a wholly owned subsidiary of Z Company, sells 15% of its output to Z Company. As described more fully in Note Y to the financial statements, these intercompany sales are based on negotiated prices between the Company and Z Company, at approximate market prices that exist within the industry.

> **PLANNING AID REMINDER:** When an explanatory paragraph contains more information than the related financial statement disclosure, the auditor should consider whether the financial statements have been prepared in accordance with GAAP (inadequate disclosure).

The auditor is not independent with respect to the financial statements

The second general standard requires that the auditor be independent. Many of the relationships that should be avoided in order not to impair independence or not to suggest the loss of independence in the eyes of others are established by the Code of Professional Conduct. When the independent auditor concludes that he or she is no longer independent, a disclaimer of opinion must be expressed. Under these circumstances, no introductory, scope, or explanatory paragraphs are included in the auditor's report. The disclaimer of opinion should simply state that the auditor is not independent and that no opinion is expressed on the financial statements. The reason for the lack of independence must not be described in the auditor's report.

An example of a disclaimer of an opinion because the auditor is not independent is as follows:

> We are not independent with respect to X Company, and the accompanying balance sheet as of December 31, 20X5, and the related statements of income, retained earnings, and cash flows for the year then ended were not audited by us and, accordingly, we do not express an opinion on them.

When the auditor is not independent, and the client is a nonpublic entity, a review report cannot be issued. A compilation report may be issued if the standards established by Statements on Standards for Accounting and Review Services (SSARS) are observed.

> **PUBLIC COMPANY IMPLICATION:** As a result of SOX, auditors of public companies are prohibited from performing a number of nonaudit services for a public company audit client. The auditor is not deemed to be independent if he or she performs any of the following nonaudit services for a public company audit client: (1) bookkeeping and other related services; (2) financial information systems design and implementation; (3) appraisal or valuation services, fairness opinions, or contribution-in-kind reports; (4) actuarial services; (5) internal audit outsourcing services; (6) management functions or human resources; (7) broker/dealer, investment adviser, investment banking; or (8) legal services and expert services. On a more conceptual level, the auditor cannot (1) function in the role of management, (2) audit his or her own work, and (3) serve in an advocacy role for the client.

There is a piecemeal opinion (prohibited)

When an adverse opinion or a disclaimer of opinion is expressed, the auditor is prohibited from issuing a piecemeal opinion on some items that appear in the financial statements.

There are negative assurances (prohibited)

When an auditor expresses a disclaimer of opinion on the financial statements, the disclaimer should not be contradicted by a negative assurance. A negative assurance implies that the financial statements, or other financial information, may be in accordance with generally accepted accounting principles, since nothing to the contrary was discovered during the engagement.

The auditor reports on comparative financial statements

Most financial statements are presented on a comparative basis. SAS-58 requires that prior-year financial statements presented with the current year be reported on by the continuing auditor or, when appropriate, by the predecessor auditor. When all financial statements presented have been audited by the same accounting firm, the introductory, scope, and opinion paragraphs refer to and report on all the financial statements. This simply means that plural terms are substituted for singular terms, so that reference will be made to balance sheets, income statements, and so forth. SAS-58, as amended by SAS-98, requires that the auditor's report on comparative financial statements be as of the audit report date for the most recent engagement. An example of an auditor's report that covers comparative statements for two years is illustrated in Exhibit AU 508-9.

If one or more of the financial statements presented on a comparative basis require that the auditor's report be modified, the normal report modification should be applied. For example, the prior year's financial statements may be presented in accordance with GAAP and the current year's financial statements may not be presented in accordance with GAAP. In this event, (1) the introductory paragraph refers to both the current and the prior years' financial statements, (2) an explanatory paragraph is added that contains an explanation of the deviation from GAAP in the current year's financial statements, and (3) the opinion paragraph contains an unqualified opinion on the prior year's financial statements and a qualified opinion (with reference to the explanatory paragraph) on the current year's financial statements.

Exhibit AU 508-10 is an example of an auditor's report with different opinions on the comparative financial statements. In this example, the auditor's opinion on the prior year's income statement is qualified because of a departure from generally accepted accounting principles, but an unqualified opinion is expressed on the current year's financial statements.

Updated opinion different from previous opinion

When a continuing auditor repeats a previous opinion on a prior year's financial statements, it is referred to as updating the report. Updating means that the auditor has considered the appropriateness of the prior opinion in the context of the results of the current engagement. Thus, it must be determined whether the prior opinion is still applicable to the prior financial statements. If it is concluded that the prior opinion is still appropriate, the reporting guidelines applicable to comparative financial statements discussed above are followed.

If the auditor believes the prior opinion is not appropriate, the current report (which covers both years) must include an explanatory paragraph stating why a different opinion on the prior financial statements is being expressed. The explanatory paragraph must disclose (1) that the updated opinion is different from the prior original opinion, (2) the reason the opinion is being revised, (3) the type of opinion previously issued, and (4) the date of the prior audit report. If the revised prior-year opinion is not unqualified, the current report must include an additional explanatory paragraph describing the deficiency.

When an explanatory paragraph is added because of a change in the opinion expressed on a previous year's financial statements, the introductory, scope, and opinion paragraphs would not refer to the explanatory paragraph and an unqualified opinion would be expressed on both years' financial statements (assuming that unqualified opinions are appropriate under the circumstances). An example of the explanatory paragraph is as follows:

> In our report dated February 18, 20X8, we expressed an opinion that the 20X7 statement of income did not fairly present the results of operations in conformity with accounting principles generally accepted in the United States of America because a net provision for loss on abandonment of equipment had been presented as an extraordinary charge against earnings for 20X7. As described in Note X, the Company has changed its presentation of the net provision by revising the 20X7 statement of income so that the statement is now presented in accordance with generally accepted accounting principles. Accordingly, our present opinion on the 20X7 financial statements, as presented herein, is different from that expressed in our previous report.

Reporting by predecessor auditor

In most circumstances, a predecessor auditor will be in a position to "reissue" the report. Reissuance is different from updating a report, in that the predecessor auditor is not in a position to evaluate his or her opinion in the context of the current year's examination. However, before reissuing the report, the predecessor auditor is required to (1) read and compare the current year's financial statements with the prior year's financial statements and (2) obtain a representation letter from management of the former client and from the successor auditor. The representation letter from management of the former client should state whether its previous representations can still be relied upon and whether any events have occurred after the date of the previous year's financial statements that would require disclosure in or adjustment to those previous year's statements. The successor auditor should represent to the predecessor auditor whether its current-year audit indicates a need for any adjustments to or disclosures modified in the prior year's financial statements. If the predecessor auditor concludes, on the basis of these limited procedures, that the prior year's opinion is still appropriate, the prior year's report is reissued as it was originally, including the same original report date. If the predecessor auditor concludes that the prior year's opinion is no longer appropriate, he or she may issue a revised report. In an explanatory paragraph, the predecessor auditor must fully describe the type of original opinion issued and the reason for changing the opinion. The reissued report should be dual-dated, showing the original report date and the revised report date. Language such as the following should be used: "March 3, 20X5, except for Note 12 as to which the date is February 26, 20X6." (It is important to remember that an auditor is responsible for material subsequent events up to the date appearing on the report.)

If the predecessor auditor's report is omitted from the current year's comparative financial statements, the successor auditor must modify the introductory paragraph of the current report. The introductory paragraph should state that the prior-year financial statements were audited by another CPA, also noting the type of opinion expressed and the date of the report. If the predecessor's report was not unqualified, the reason for the modification must also be explained. The successor auditor's opinion paragraph refers only to the current year's financial statements.

Exhibit AU 508-11 is an example of a successor auditor's report in which the predecessor auditor's report is not presented.

> **PLANNING AID REMINDER:** Reference to the predecessor auditor's name is prohibited in the successor auditor's report except when the predecessor auditor's practice has been acquired by or merged into the practice of the successor auditor.

'If the prior year's financial statements have been restated, the introductory paragraph of the successor auditor's report should state that the predecessor auditor reported on the previous year's financial statements before they were restated. When the successor auditor has been engaged to audit the restatement adjustments, and has applied sufficient procedures to determine that the adjustments are appropriate, the following paragraph may be added to the successor auditor's report.

> We also audited the adjustments described in Note X that were applied to restate the 20X4 financial statements. In our opinion, such adjustments are appropriate and have been properly applied.

> **PUBLIC COMPANY IMPLICATION:** The PCAOB staff has issued a series of questions and answers surrounding auditor reporting responsibilities when prior-period financial statements are adjusted. Adjustments to prior-period financial statements can relate to reporting a discontinued operation,

restatements to correct errors, and retrospective applications of changes in accounting principles. Either the predecessor or successor auditor may audit the adjustments to the prior-period financial statements, as long as the auditor is independent and registered with the PCAOB. If the predecessor auditor audits the adjustments, the predecessor auditor should dual date his or her report and the successor auditor should obtain an understanding of the adjustments and their effects on the current-period financial statements. In deciding whether the successor auditor can audit the adjustments or has to re-audit the prior-period financial statements, the successor auditor should consider (1) the extent of the adjustments, (2) the reason for the adjustments, and (3) the cooperation of the predecessor auditor. In addition, the successor auditor must have completed the audit of the current-period financial statements to audit adjustments to prior-period financial statements.

Reporting as successor auditor when prior-period audited financial statements were audited by a predecessor auditor who has ceased operations

Interpretation No. 15 of AU 508 addresses complications that arise when financial statements of a prior period have been reported on a by a predecessor auditor that has ceased operations. The Interpretation notes that operations are considered ceased when a firm no longer issues audit opinions on financial statements either in its own name or in the name of a successor firm in the case of a merger.

When prior-period financial statements have not been restated, the successor auditor should add the following to the introductory paragraph of the current year's audit report (based on the general reporting guidance established by AU 508.74):

- State that the prior-period financial statements were audited by another auditor that has ceased operations

- Disclose the date of the predecessor auditor's report

- Disclose the type of report issued by the predecessor auditor

- If the predecessor auditor's report was other than a standard report, explain the basis for modification

The name of the predecessor auditor should not be referred to in the successor auditor's report.

It should be noted that the information described above should be included in the successor auditor's introductory paragraph even when the predecessor auditor's report is reprinted and presented with the current auditor's report. Reprinting a previous audit report is not the same as reissuing a report.

> **PLANNING AID REMINDER:** The above guidance should also be followed when the financial statements have been restated and the client does not file annual financial statements with the SEC. In addition, the introductory paragraph should point out that the predecessor auditor reported on the prior-year's financial statements before they were restated.

When prior-year financial statements have been restated, management may request that the successor auditor re-audit the prior-period financial statements or audit only the restatement adjustments. If only the restatement adjustments are audited the successor auditor may report on the results by (1) following the general reporting guidance established by AU 508.74 (as discussed above) or (2) by adding the following paragraph to the report:

> As discussed above, the financial statements of X Company as of December 31, 20X4, and for the year then ended were audited by other auditors who have ceased operations. As described in Note X, these financial statements have been restated [revised]. We audited the adjustments described in Note X that were applied to restate [revise] the 20X4 financial statements. In our opinion, such adjustments are appropriate and have been properly applied. However, we were not engaged to audit, review, or apply any procedures to the 20X4 financial statements of the Company other than with respect to such adjustments and, accordingly, we do not express an opinion or any other form of assurance on the 20X4 financial statements taken as a whole.

> **OBSERVATION:** The term "restated" refers to changing amounts that appear directly in the financial statements, whereas the term "revised" refers to modification or expansion of disclosures found in the financial statements. For purposes of the Interpretation, the guidance applies equally to restatements and revisions.

> **PLANNING AID REMINDER:** In determining the nature, timing, and extent of audit procedures related to the restatement adjustments the successor auditor should consider the guidance established by AU 561 (Subsequent Discovery of Facts Existing at the Date of the Auditor's Report).

If the successor auditor is not requested to re-audit the prior-year's financial statements or audit the restatement adjustments, the note to the financial statements that describes the restatement adjustments should be identified as "Unaudited."

> **ENGAGEMENT STRATEGY:** Alternatively, it may be appropriate to identify the prior-year's financial statements as "Unaudited" depending on the nature and extent of the restatement adjustments.

When the client is a public company, the predecessor auditors previous year's audit report should be reproduced in the current filing (both the SEC filing and the annual report) with the following legends on the previous report:

- The report is a copy of the previously issued report

- The predecessor auditor has not reissued the report

In addition, the successor auditor's current report should, in the introductory paragraph, refer to the predecessor auditor's report in a manner similar to the guidance established by AU 508.74 (described earlier). If the prior year's financial statements have been restated, the introductory paragraph should state that the predecessor auditor reported on the financial statements before they were restated.

> **PLANNING AID REMINDER:** A successor auditor that is engaged to audit only the restatement adjustments is not required to perform procedures to identify other adjustments that may be appropriate; however, if the successor auditor, as part of the current year's audit, discovers information that suggest that amounts in the previous year's financial statements need revision, the guidance established by AU 315 should be followed.

> **OBSERVATION:** In some instances, the prior year's financial statements are modified in ways that amount to editorial changes. Such changes are not considered restatements or revisions for purposes of the Interpretation.

> **PLANNING AID REMINDER:** A successor auditor can report on restated financial statements previously audited by a predecessor auditor in the manner described above only when reporting on comparative financial statements. Thus, a successor auditor cannot report only on the restatement adjustments.

Practitioner's Aids

The following exhibits are presented in this section:

- Exhibit AU 508-2 — Qualified Auditor's Report

- Exhibit AU 508-3 — Adverse Auditor's Report

- Exhibit AU 508-4 — Qualified Auditor's Report Because Statement of Cash Flow Is Omitted

- Exhibit AU 508-5 — Qualified Auditor's Report Because of a Scope Limitation

- Exhibit AU 508-6 — Disclaimer Report

- Exhibit AU 508-7 — Auditor's Report Only on the Balance Sheet

- Exhibit AU 508-9 — Auditor's Report on Comparative Financial Statements

- Exhibit AU 508-10 — Auditor's Report on Comparative Financial Statements with Different Opinions

- Exhibit AU 508-11 — Auditor's Report When a Predecessor Auditor's Report Is Not Presented

- Exhibit AU 508-12 — Auditor's Report When the Standards of Both the Auditing Standards Board and the Public Company Accounting Oversight Board Are Followed in Performing the Audit

EXHIBIT AU 508-2 — QUALIFIED AUDITOR'S REPORT

We have audited the accompanying balance sheet of X Company as of December 31, 20X5, and the related statements of income, retained earnings, and cash flows for the year then ended. These financial statements are the responsibility of the Company's management. Our responsibility is to express an opinion on these financial statements based on our audit.

We conducted our audit in accordance with auditing standards generally accepted in the United States of America. Those standards require that we plan and perform the audit to obtain reasonable assurance about whether the financial statements are free of material misstatement. An audit includes examining, on a test basis, evidence supporting the amounts and disclosures in the financial statements. An audit also includes assessing the accounting principles used and significant estimates made by management, as well as evaluating the overall financial statement presentation. We believe that our audit provides a reasonable basis for our opinion.

As more fully described in Note 12 to the financial statements, a net provision for loss on abandonment of certain property of $800,000 after related income taxes has been presented as an extraordinary charge against earnings for 20X5. In our opinion, generally accepted accounting principles require that the gross amount of such provision be included in the determination of income before income taxes and that the per-share amount of the provisions ($.75) not be separately presented in the statement of income.

In our opinion, except for the effect of the matter described in the preceding paragraph on the statement of income, the financial statements referred to above present fairly, in all material respects, the financial position of X Company as of December 31, 20X5, and the results of its operations and its cash flows for the year then ended in conformity with accounting principles generally accepted in the United States of America.

EXHIBIT AU 508-3 — ADVERSE AUDITOR'S REPORT

We have audited the accompanying balance sheet of X Company as of December 31, 20X5, and the related statements of income, retained earnings, and cash flows for the year then ended. These financial statements are the responsibility of the Company's management. Our responsibility is to express an opinion on these financial statements based on our audit.

We conducted our audit in accordance with auditing standards generally accepted in the United States of America. Those standards require that we plan and perform the audit to obtain reasonable assurance about whether the financial statements are free of material misstatement. An audit includes examining, on a test basis, evidence supporting the amounts and disclosures in the financial statements. An audit also includes assessing the accounting principles used and significant estimates made by management, as well as evaluating the overall financial statement presentation. We believe that our audit provides a reasonable basis for our opinion.

As disclosed in Note 12 to the financial statements, the Company reports all of its sales on the installment method for financial accounting purposes and on its tax return. In our opinion, generally accepted accounting principles require that sales be reported on the accrual basis with an appropriate provision for deferred taxes. As a result of these departures from generally accepted accounting principles, gross profit on sales is understated by $123,456 and income tax expense is understated by $14,222. The total effect of these departures on retained earnings is $109,234, which results in an increase in earnings per share of $1.42.

In our opinion, because of the effects of the matters discussed in the preceding paragraphs, the financial statements referred to above do not present fairly, in conformity with accounting principles generally accepted in the United States of America, the financial position of X Company as of December 31, 20X5, or the result of its operations or its cash flows for the year then ended.

EXHIBIT AU 508-4 — QUALIFIED AUDITOR'S REPORT BECAUSE STATEMENT OF CASH FLOW IS OMITTED

We have audited the accompanying balance sheet of X Company as of December 31, 20X5, and the related statements of income and retained earnings for the year then ended. These financial statements are the responsibility of the Company's management. Our responsibility is to express an opinion on these financial statements based on our audit.

We conducted our audit in accordance with auditing standards generally accepted in the United States of America. Those standards require that we plan and perform the audit to obtain reasonable assurance about whether the financial statements are free of material misstatement. An audit includes examining, on a test basis, evidence supporting the amounts and disclosures in the financial statements. An audit also includes assessing the accounting principles used and significant estimates made by management, as well as evaluating the overall financial statement presentation. We believe that our audit provides a reasonable basis for our opinion.

The Company did not present a statement of cash flows for the year ended December 31, 20X5. Presentation of such statement summarizing the Company's operating, investing, and financing activities is required by generally accepted accounting principles.

In our opinion, except that the omission of a statement of cash flows results in an incomplete presentation as explained in the preceding paragraph, the financial statements referred to above present fairly, in all material respects, the financial position of X Company as of December 31, 20X5, and the results of its operations for the year then ended in conformity with accounting principles generally accepted in the United States of America.

EXHIBIT AU 508-5 — QUALIFIED AUDITOR'S REPORT BECAUSE OF A SCOPE LIMITATION

We have audited the accompanying balance sheet of X Company as of December 31, 20X5, and the related statements of income, retained earnings, and cash flows for the year then ended. These financial statements are the responsibility of the Company's management. Our responsibility is to express an opinion on these financial statements based on our audit.

Except as discussed in the following paragraph, we conducted our audit in accordance with auditing standards generally accepted in the United States of America. Those standards require that we plan and perform the audit to obtain reasonable assurance about whether the financial statements are free of material misstatement. An audit includes examining, on a test basis, evidence supporting the amounts and disclosures in the financial statements. An audit also includes assessing the accounting principles used and significant estimates made by management, as well as evaluating the overall financial statement presentation. We believe that our audit provides a reasonable basis for our opinion.

We were not able to confirm accounts receivable as of December 31, 20X5, stated at $500,000. The receivables were principally due from agencies of the U.S. government. In addition, we were unable to determine the validity of the accounts through the use of alternative procedures.

In our opinion, except for the effects of such adjustment, if any, as might have been determined to be necessary had we been able to determine the validity of accounts receivable, the financial statements referred to in the first paragraph above present fairly, in all material respects, the financial position of X Company as of December 31, 20X5, and the results of its operations and its cash flows for the year then ended in conformity with accounting principles generally accepted in the United States of America.

EXHIBIT AU 508-6 — DISCLAIMER REPORT

We were engaged to audit the accompanying balance sheet of X Company as of December 31, 20X5, and the related statements of income, retained earnings, and cash flows for the year then ended. These financial statements are the responsibility of the Company's management.

No physical inventory was taken for merchandise held for sale by the Company as of December 31, 20X4, or December 31, 20X5, and inventory quantities are stated in the accompanying financial statements at $150,000 and $400,000, respectively.

Since the Company did not take physical inventories and we were not able to apply alternative auditing procedures to satisfy ourselves as to inventory quantities, the scope of our work was not sufficient to enable us to express, and we do not express, an opinion on the financial statements referred to above.

EXHIBIT AU 508-7 — AUDITOR'S REPORT ONLY ON THE BALANCE SHEET

We have audited the accompanying balance sheet of X Company as of December 31, 20X5. This financial statement is the responsibility of the Company's management. Our responsibility is to express an opinion on this financial statement based on our audit.

We conducted our audit in accordance with auditing standards generally accepted in the United States of America. Those standards require that we plan and perform the audit to obtain reasonable assurance about whether the balance sheet is free of material mis-statement. An audit includes examining, on a test basis, evidence supporting the amounts and disclosures in the balance sheet. An audit also includes assessing the accounting principles used and significant estimates made by management, as well as evaluating the overall balance sheet presentation. We believe that our audit provides a reasonable basis for our opinion.

In our opinion, the balance sheet referred to above presents fairly, in all material respects, the financial position of X Company as of December 31, 20X5, in conformity with accounting principles generally accepted in the United States of America.

EXHIBIT AU 508-9 — AUDITOR'S REPORT ON COMPARATIVE FINANCIAL STATEMENTS

We have audited the accompanying balance sheets of X Company as of December 31, 20X5 and 20X4, and the related statements of income, retained earnings, and cash flows for the years then ended. These financial statements are the responsibility of the Company's management. Our responsibility is to express an opinion on these financial statements based on our audits.

We conducted our audits in accordance with auditing standards generally accepted in the United States of America. Those standards require that we plan and perform the audit to obtain reasonable assurance about whether the financial statements are free of material misstatement. An audit includes examining, on a test basis, evidence supporting the amounts and disclosures in the financial statements.

An audit also includes assessing the accounting principles used and significant estimates made by management, as well as evaluating the overall financial statement presentation. We believe that our audits provide a reasonable basis for our opinion.

In our opinion, the financial statements referred to above present fairly, in all material respects, the financial position of X Company as of December 31, 20X5 and 20X4, and the results of its operations and its cash flows for the years then ended in conformity with accounting principles generally accepted in the United States of America.

EXHIBIT AU 508-10 — AUDITOR'S REPORT ON COMPARATIVE FINANCIAL STATEMENTS WITH DIFFERENT OPINIONS

We have audited the accompanying balance sheets of X Company as of December 31, 20X5 and 20X4, and the related statements of income, retained earnings, and cash flows for the years then ended. These financial statements are the responsibility of the Company's management. Our responsibility is to express an opinion on these financial statements based on our audits.

We conducted our audits in accordance with auditing standards generally accepted in the United States of America. Those standards require that we plan and perform the audit to obtain reasonable assurance about whether the financial statements are free of material misstatement. An audit includes examining, on a test basis, evidence supporting the amounts and disclosures in the financial statements. An audit also includes assessing the accounting principles used and significant estimates made by management, as well as evaluating the overall financial statement presentation. We believe that our audits provide a reasonable basis for our opinion.

As more fully described in Note 7 to the financial statements, a net provision for loss on abandonment of equipment of $14,000,000 after related income taxes has been presented as an extraordinary charge against earnings for 20X4. In our opinion, generally accepted accounting principles require that the gross amount of such provision be part of the determination of income from operations before taxes and that the per-share amount of the provision not be separately presented in the statement of income.

In our opinion, except for the effects of the matter described in the previous paragraph on the 20X4 statement of income, the financial statements referred to above present fairly, in all material respects, the financial position of X Company as of December 31, 20X5 and 20X4, and the results of its operations and its cash flows for the years then ended in conformity with accounting principles generally accepted in the United States of America.

EXHIBIT AU 508-11 — AUDITOR'S REPORT WHEN A PREDECESSOR AUDITOR'S REPORT IS NOT PRESENTED

We have audited the balance sheet of X Company as of December 31, 20X5, and the related statements of income, retained earnings, and cash flows for the year then ended. These financial statements are the responsibility of the Company's management. Our responsibility is to express an opinion on these financial statements based on our audit. The financial statements of X Company as of December 31, 20X4, were audited by other auditors whose report, dated February 18, 20X5, expressed an unqualified opinion on those statements.

We conducted our audit in accordance with auditing standards generally accepted in the United States of America. Those standards require that we plan and perform the audit to obtain reasonable assurance about whether the financial statements are free of material misstatement. An audit includes examining, on a test basis, evidence supporting the amounts and disclosures in the financial statements. An audit also includes assessing the accounting principles used and significant estimates made by management, as well as evaluating the overall financial statement presentation. We believe that our audit provides a reasonable basis for our opinion.

In our opinion, the 20X5 financial statements referred to above present fairly, in all material respects, the financial position of X Company as of December 31, 20X5, and the results of its operations and its cash flows for the year then ended in conformity with accounting principles generally accepted in the United States of America.

EXHIBIT AU 508-12 — AUDITOR'S REPORT WHEN THE STANDARDS OF BOTH THE AUDITING STANDARDS BOARD AND THE PUBLIC COMPANY ACCOUNTING OVERSIGHT BOARD ARE FOLLOWED IN PERFORMING THE AUDIT

We have audited the accompanying balance sheet of X Company as of December 31, 20X5, and the related statements of income, stockholders' equity, and cash flows for the year then ended. These financial statements are the responsibility of the Company's management. Our responsibility is to express an opinion on these financial statements based on our audits.

We conducted our audit in accordance with generally accepted auditing standards as established by the Auditing Standards Board (United States) and in accordance with the auditing standards of the Public Company Accounting Oversight Board (United States). Those standards require that we plan and perform the audit to obtain reasonable assurance about whether the financial statements are free of material misstatement. The Company is not required to have, nor were we engaged to perform, an audit of its internal control over financial reporting. Our audit included consideration of internal control over financial reporting as a basis for designing audit procedures that are appropriate in the circumstances, but not for the purpose of expressing an opinion on the effectiveness of the Company's internal control over financial reporting. Accordingly we express no such opinion. An audit also includes examining, on a test basis, evidence supporting the amounts and disclosures in the financial statements, assessing the accounting principles used and significant estimates made by management, as well as evaluating the overall financial statement presentation. We believe that our audit provides a reasonable basis for our opinion.

In our opinion, the financial statements referred to above present fairly, in all material respects, the financial position of X Company as of December 31, 20X5, and the results of its operations and its cash flows for the year then ended in conformity with accounting principles generally accepted in the United States of America.

SECTION 530

DATING OF THE INDEPENDENT AUDITOR'S REPORT

Authoritative Pronouncements

SAS-1 — Codification of Auditing Standards and Procedures (Section 530, Dating of the Independent Auditor's Report)

SAS-29 — Reporting on Information Accompanying the Basic Financial Statements in Auditor-Submitted Documents

SAS-98 — Omnibus Statement on Auditing Standards — 2002

SAS-103 — Audit Documentation

> **IMPORTANT NOTICE FOR 2011:** The Auditing Standards Board (ASB) is in the process of redrafting all of the auditing sections in *Codification of Statements on Auditing Standards* to converge U.S. GAAS with the International Standards on Auditing issued by the International Auditing and Assurance Standards Board. As part of this process, the newly redrafted standards will follow certain clarity drafting conventions adopted by the ASB. These clarity drafting conventions include (1) establishing objectives for each standard; (2) including a definitions section, if appropriate; and (3) separating requirements from application guidance and other material. The ASB is planning to have all redrafted standards become effective on the same date, which is for audits of financial statements for periods ending on or after December 15, 2012. It is possible that the effective date might be delayed beyond that date. The ASB's clarity and convergence project will have a significant effect on the auditing standards applicable to audits of non-public companies, and the 2012 *GAAS Guide* will be appropriately modified to reflect these changes once the effective date of the standards is certain.

Overview

The audit report should be dated no earlier than the date on which the auditor has gathered sufficient audit evidence to support the opinion. The auditor has not obtained sufficient audit evidence to support the opinion until (1) the audit documentation has been reviewed, (2) the financial statements, including required disclosures have been prepared, and (3) management has accepted responsibility for the financial statements.

auditor has no responsibility to perform audit procedures subsequent to the audit report date except under the following circumstances:

- A subsequent event of the type requiring adjustment of the financial statements occurs after the audit report date but before the issuance of the financial statements

- Reissuance of the audit report

> **OBSERVATION:** Auditors have typically dated the audit report as of the last day of fieldwork. SAS-103 appears to eliminate the phrase "completion of fieldwork," replacing it with the phrase "date on which the auditor has obtained sufficient appropriate audit evidence to support the opinion." The audit will now be dated (i.e., the audit report date) based on the date when the auditor has obtained sufficient audit evidence to support the opinion.

A subsequent event of the type requiring adjustment of the financial statements occurs after the audit report date but before the issuance of the financial statements

AU 560 identifies subsequent events that occur after the client's balance sheet date but require that (1) the financial statements be adjusted or (2) the event be disclosed in the financial statements.

> **PLANNING AID REMINDER:** SAS-98 makes it clear that subsequent events discussed in this section are those that occur up to the date of the issuance of the financial statements.

Events that require adjustment

When a subsequent event that requires adjustment occurs after the date of the audit report but before the financial statements have been issued (and the auditor becomes aware of the event), the financial statements should be appropriately adjusted or the auditor should not issue an unqualified opinion on the financial statements. When an adjustment is made and the event is not otherwise disclosed in the financial statements, the date of the audit report should be based on the original audit report date. If the client refuses to make the appropriate adjustment or if the adjustment is made and the event is disclosed in the financial statements, the auditor should date the report in either one of the two following methods.

Dual-dating method Under this approach, the report is dated based on the original audit report date and an exception similar to the following is noted in the report date:

> March 3, 20X5, except for Note X, for which the date is March 15, 20X5.

If the auditor dual-dates the report, his or her responsibility is limited to the specific subsequent event and not to other subsequent events that may occur between the two dates (March 3 and March 15).

Single-dating method Under this approach, a single report date (the date that refers to the subsequent event) is used; however, using a single report date means that the auditor's responsibility for all subsequent events extends to the date identified with the specific subsequent event (March 15 in this example).

> **PLANNING AID REMINDER:** When the single-dating method is used, the auditor should follow the guidance established by AU 560 with respect to subsequent events.

Events that require disclosure

When a subsequent event that requires disclosure occurs after the date of the audit report but before the financial statements have been issued (and the auditor becomes aware of the event), the financial statements should include the appropriate disclosure or the auditor should not issue an unqualified opinion on the financial statements. When the appropriate disclosure is made, the audit report should be dated using the dual-dating method or the single-dating method, as described above.

Reissuance of the audit report

An auditor may be requested to reissue the original audit report under a number of circumstances, such as the following:

- Subsequent annual reports are filed with the Securities and Exchange Commission or other regulatory agency.

- Subsequent documents are submitted to the client or other parties.

- The client requests that the auditor submit additional copies of the original audit report.

Generally, the auditor has no responsibility to perform audit procedures subsequent to the original engagement and should use the original audit report date except under certain circumstances. For example, the auditor may have become aware of a subsequent event that requires that the original financial statements be adjusted or that the event be disclosed in the financial statements as required by AU 560. In this instance, the reissued financial statement should not be adjusted unless the circumstances satisfy the conditions for a prior-period adjustment. Furthermore, the auditor should follow the guidance described above (single-dating or dual-dating) to determine how the reissued audit report should be dated.

If the subsequent event occurred between the original report date and the date of the reissued financial statements and the event requires only financial statement disclosure, the event may be disclosed in separate note to the financial statements with the following caption:

Event (Unaudited) Subsequent to the Date of the Independent Auditor's Report

Under this circumstance, the original audit report date should be used in the reissued audit report.

> **PLANNING AID REMINDER:** Additional guidance for dating the auditor's report can be found in AU 711 (Filings Under Federal Securities Statutes), which addresses the audit report included in a registration statement filed under the Securities Act of 1933, and in AU 508 (Reports on Audited Financial Statements), which provides guidance for a predecessor auditor.

SECTION 532

RESTRICTING THE USE OF AN AUDITOR'S REPORT

Authoritative Pronouncements

SAS-87—Restricting the Use of an Auditor's Report

> **IMPORTANT NOTICE FOR 2011:** The Auditing Standards Board (ASB) is in the process of redrafting all of the auditing sections in *Codification of Statements on Auditing Standards* to converge U.S. GAAS with the International Standards on Auditing issued by the International Auditing and Assurance Standards Board. As part of this process, the newly redrafted standards will follow certain clarity drafting conventions adopted by the ASB. These clarity drafting conventions include (1) establishing objectives for each standard; (2) including a definitions section, if appropriate; and (3) separating requirements from application guidance and other material. The ASB is planning to have all redrafted standards become effective on the same date, which is for audits of financial statements for periods ending on or after December 15, 2012. It is possible that the effective date might be delayed beyond that date. The ASB's clarity and convergence project will have a significant effect on the auditing standards applicable to audits of non-public companies, and the 2012 *GAAS Guide* will be appropriately modified to reflect these changes once the effective date of the standards is certain.

Overview

Generally, when an auditor reports on financial statements that are prepared in conformity with generally accepted accounting principles (GAAP) or an other comprehensive basis of accounting (OCBOA) other than GAAP, the distribution of the audit report is not limited (general-use reports). However, under certain conditions the auditor's report may be intended for specified parties (restricted-use reports), in which case the last paragraph of the report should describe the restriction using language such as the following:

> This report is intended solely for the information and use of [*the specified parties*] and is not intended to be and should not be used by anyone other than these specified parties.

ENGAGEMENT STRATEGY: The client, rather than the auditor, controls the actual distribution of an auditor's report. However, it is advised that the auditor inform the client that nonspecified parties should not receive a restricted-use report, even when the restricted-use report is included in a document that contains a separate general-use report. The auditor may want to formalize this understanding as part of the terms of the engagement. When restricted-use reports are filed with a regulatory agency, they may become public based on statute or regulatory requirements.

PLANNING AID REMINDER: The specified parties may be listed in the report or may be referred to in a list of specified parties included elsewhere in the document that includes the auditor's report. When the engagement is covered by guidance established by U.S. Office of Management and Budget (OMB) Circular A-123 and "Audits of States, Local Governments and Non-Profit Organizations," the specified parties can simply be described as "federal awarding agencies and pass-through entities."

PLANNING AID REMINDER: When the auditor issues a single report that covers both general-use and restricted-use situations, the single report must be restricted. However, when a document includes both a separate restricted-use report and a general-use report, there is no need to restrict the use of the general-use report.

The reporting guidance provided by AU 532 does not apply to the following situations:

- SAS-70 — Service Organizations (AU 324)
- SAS-72 — Letters for Underwriters and Certain Other Requesting Parties (AU 634)

Promulgated Reporting Standards Checklist

The auditor's report should be restricted for distribution in the following circumstances:

- The basis-of-reporting criteria are contained in contractual agreements, or regulatory provisions are not GAAP or OCBOA.

- The report is a by-product of an audit of a client's financial statements.

    OBSERVATION: When the above situations are encountered, the auditor must issue a restricted-use report. The auditor is not prohibited from restricting the distribution of reports that are not listed above.

Analysis and Application of Reporting Standards

The basis of reporting criteria are contained in contractual agreements, or regulatory provisions are not GAAP or OCBOA.

A CPA may accept an engagement whereby the subject matter or presentation is based on measurement or disclosure criteria contained in a contractual agreement or regulatory provisions that do not conform to GAAP or OCBOA. For example, SAS-62 (AU 623) (Special Reports) notes that an auditor may be requested to report on special-purpose financial statements that have been prepared to satisfy a contractual agreement or governmental regulatory requirements. SAS-62 (AU 623) identifies the following as types of special-purpose financial statement presentations:

- A special-purpose financial presentation prepared in compliance with a contractual agreement or regulatory provision that does not constitute a complete presentation of the entity's assets, liabilities, revenues, and expenses but is otherwise prepared in conformity with GAAP or OCBOA

- A special-purpose financial presentation (may be a complete set of financial statements or a single financial statement) prepared on a basis of accounting prescribed in an agreement that does not result in a presentation in conformity with GAAP or an other comprehensive basis of accounting

Because of the nature of these engagements, the auditor should prepare a restricted-use report.

Exhibit AU 532-1 illustrates a report on a statement of assets sold and liabilities transferred to comply with a contractual agreement. Exhibit AU 532-2 illustrates a report on financial statements prepared pursuant to a loan agreement that results in a presentation not in conformity with GAAP or OCBOA.

> **PLANNING AID REMINDER:** For a discussion of the guidance established by SAS-62, see AU 623.

During or subsequent to an engagement directed to reporting on subject matter or presentations based on measurement or disclosure criteria contained in contractual agreements or regulatory provisions, the auditor may be asked to add other specified parties that may use the report. The auditor may agree to this request, but should consider why the parties are being added. If the auditor agrees to add the other parties, an acknowledgment (usually in writing) should be obtained from these parties affirming that they understand the nature of the engagement, the measurement or disclosure criteria used, and the nature of the report. If the parties are added after the report has been issued, the auditor may reissue a revised report (using the original report date) or may acknowledge in a separate communication that the other parties have been added as specified parties (the communication should note that no additional procedures were performed after the date of the original report).

The report is a by-product of an audit of a client's financial statements

In some instances the auditor may audit a client's financial statements and as a by-product report separately on matters that came to his or her attention during the audit engagement. Examples of this reporting circumstance are discussed in the following promulgations:

- SAS-62 — Special Reports (paragraphs 19 – 21) (AU 623)

- SAS-112 (AU 325) (Communication of Internal Control Related Matters Identified in an Audit)

- SAS-114 (AU 380) (The Auditor's Communication with Those Charged with Governance)

> **OBSERVATION:** A by-product report may be issued in other engagements conducted in accordance with generally accepted auditing standards, such as an engagement to express an opinion on a specified element, account, or item in a financial statement.

Because the report on the above-listed Statements on Auditing Standards is a by-product of the audit of the client's financial statements, the auditor should issue a restricted-use report on these matters. AU 532 of the AICPA standards specifically notes that the restricted-use report for these matters should be distributed to the following parties only:

- The entity's audit committee

- The entity's board of directors

- The entity's management and others within the organization

- Specified regulatory agencies

- Parties to the contract or agreement for reports on compliance with aspects of the contractual agreement

Practitioner's Aids

EXHIBIT AU 532-1 — RESTRICTED AUDIT REPORT ON SPECIAL-PURPOSE FINANCIAL STATEMENT PRESENTATION

We have audited the accompanying statement of net assets sold of X Company as of July 15, 20X7. This statement of net assets sold is the responsibility of X Company's management. Our responsibility is to express an opinion on the statement of net assets sold based on our audit.

We conducted our audit in accordance with auditing standards generally accepted in the United States of America. Those standards require that we plan and perform the audit to obtain reasonable assurance about whether the statement of net assets sold is free of material misstatement. An audit includes examining, on a test basis, evidence supporting the amounts and disclosures in the statement. An audit also includes assessing the accounting principles used and significant estimates made by management, as well as evaluating the overall presentation of the statement of net assets sold. We believe that our audit provides a reasonable basis for our opinion.

The accompanying statement was prepared to present the net assets of X Company sold to Z Company pursuant to the purchase agreement described in Note 1, and is not intended to be a complete presentation of X Company's assets and liabilities.

In our opinion, the accompanying statement of net assets sold presents fairly, in all material respects, the net assets of X Company as of July 15, 20X7, sold pursuant to the purchase agreement referred to in Note 1, in conformity with accounting principles generally accepted in the United States of America.

This report is intended solely for the information and use of the boards of directors and managements of X Company and Z Company and is not intended to be and should not be used by anyone other than these specified parties.

EXHIBIT AU 532-2 — RESTRICTED AUDIT REPORT ON FINANCIAL STATEMENTS PREPARED PURSUANT TO A LOAN AGREEMENT

We have audited the special-purpose statement of assets and liabilities of X Company as of December 31, 20X7 and 20X8, and the related special-purpose statements of revenues and expenses and cash flows for the years then ended. These financial statements are the responsibility of the Company's management. Our responsibility is to express an opinion on these financial statements based on our audits.

We conducted our audits in accordance with auditing standards generally accepted in the United States of America. Those standards require that we plan and perform the audit to obtain reasonable assurance about whether the financial statements are free of material misstatement. An audit includes examining, on a test basis, evidence supporting the amounts and disclosures in the financial statements. An audit also includes assessing the accounting principles used and significant estimates made by management, as well as evaluating the overall financial statement presentation. We believe that our audits provide a reasonable basis for our opinion.

The accompanying special-purpose financial statements were prepared for the purpose of complying with Section A of a loan agreement between the Company and the First State Bank as discussed in Note 1, and are not intended to be a presentation in conformity with accounting principles generally accepted in the United States of America.

In our opinion, the special-purpose financial statements referred to above present fairly, in all material respects, the assets and liabilities of X Company as of December 31, 20X7 and 20X8, and the revenues, expenses, and cash flows for the years then ended, on the basis of accounting described in Note 1.

This report is intended solely for the information and use of the boards of directors and managements of X Company and the First State Bank and is not intended to be and should not be used by anyone other than these specified parties.

SECTION 534

REPORTING ON FINANCIAL STATEMENTS PREPARED FOR USE IN OTHER COUNTRIES

Authoritative Pronouncements

SAS-51 — Reporting on Financial Statements Prepared for Use in Other Countries

Auditing Interpretation No. 1 (May 1996) — Financial Statement for General Use Only Outside of the U.S. in Accordance with International Accounting Standards and International Standards on Auditing

Auditing Interpretation No. 2 (May 2008) — Financial Statements Prepared in Conformity with International Financial Reporting Standards as Issued by the International Accounting Standards Board

Auditing Interpretation No. 3 (May 2008) — Financial Statements Audited in Accordance with International Standards on Auditing

> **IMPORTANT NOTICE FOR 2011:** The Auditing Standards Board (ASB) is in the process of redrafting all of the auditing sections in *Codification of Statements on Auditing Standards* to converge U.S. GAAS with the International Standards on Auditing issued by the International Auditing and Assurance Standards Board. As part of this process, the newly redrafted standards will follow certain clarity drafting conventions adopted by the ASB. These clarity drafting conventions include (1) establishing objectives for each standard; (2) including a definitions section, if appropriate; and (3) separating requirements from application guidance and other material. The ASB is planning to have all redrafted standards become effective on the same date, which is for audits of financial statements for periods ending on or after December 15, 2012. (i.e., for calendar-year companies, financial statements dated December 31, 2011). It is possible that the effective date might be delayed beyond that date. The ASB's clarity and convergence project will have a significant effect on the auditing standards applicable to audits of nonpublic companies, and the 2012 *GAAS Guide* will be appropriately modified to reflect these changes once the effective date of the standards is certain.

Overview

A U.S. practicing auditor may be engaged by a U.S. entity to report on financial statements that are intended to be used outside the United States and that are to be prepared in conformity with accounting principles generally accepted in another country. Guidance for reporting on such financial statements is provided by SAS-51. For the purposes of SAS-51, a "U.S. entity" is one that is either organized or domiciled in the United States.

An auditor should have a clear understanding of the purpose and uses of financial statements that are prepared in conformity with accounting principles of another country. The auditor should obtain management's written representations before reporting on such statements. When using the standard report of another country instead of the U.S.-style auditor's standard report, an auditor must determine whether he or she is exposed to any additional legal responsibilities.

> **OBSERVATION:** Auditing Interpretation 2 of AU 534 states that the guidance in AU 508, rather than in AU 534, applies when the auditor is engaged to opine on financial statements prepared in accordance with International Financial Reporting Standards (IFRS) as issued by the International Accounting Standards Board (IASB). If, however, the financial statements use IFRS as modified by a foreign country (i.e., they deviate from IFRS as originally issued by the IASB) then AU 534 applies.
>
> Auditing Interpretation No. 3 of AU 534 states that a U.S. auditor can perform an audit using the International Standards on Auditing, regardless of whether the financial statements are prepared using U.S. GAAP, IFRS, or accounting principles generally accepted in another country. If the financial statements are for use outside the United States, the guidance in AU 534 applies. The auditor must comply with the general and fieldwork standards of U.S. GAAS, as well as any additional requirements of the International Standards on Auditing. The auditor's report can be in either the U.S. format or the format of the International Standards on Auditing. If the financial statements are intended for use in the United States, the guidance in AU 508 is applicable (including Interpretation 14).

Promulgated Procedures Checklist

The auditor should perform the following procedures when reporting on financial statements prepared for use in another country:

- Observe the general standards and the standards of fieldwork established by the United States Auditing Standards Board.

- Consider whether foreign auditing standards must be observed.

- Prepare an appropriate audit report.

Analysis and Application of Procedures

Observe the general standards and the standards of fieldwork established by the United States Auditing Standards Board

Before reporting on financial statements prepared in accordance with accounting principles of another country, the auditor must consider which auditing standards are applicable in the engagement. In some engagements, an auditor may be required to follow both U.S. generally accepted auditing standards (GAAS) and auditing standards established by a foreign country.

In reporting on financial statements prepared in accordance with accounting principles of another country, the auditor must observe the three general standards and the three fieldwork standards that are part of U.S. generally accepted auditing standards. In this event, the auditor is also required to comply with all related SASs and SAS Interpretations.

Consider whether foreign auditing standards must be observed

When the auditor is required to comply with auditing standards of another country, both those standards and U.S. generally accepted auditing standards must be observed during the engagement. Thus, some audit procedures will be employed to comply with U.S. GAAS, whereas other audit procedures will be performed to satisfy auditing standards of the foreign country.

Prepare an appropriate audit report

The reporting standards that must be observed in the preparation of the auditor's report on financial statements prepared in accordance with accounting principles of another country are dependent on the purpose of the financial statements. These purposes may be classified as (1) foreign GAAP/foreign use, (2) dual statements (foreign GAAP/U.S. GAAP), and (3) foreign GAAP/general United States distribution. Each of these purposes is discussed below.

Foreign GAAP/foreign use

When financial statements of a U.S. entity that are prepared in accordance with accounting principles of another country are to be used exclusively outside the United States, the auditor may use either the U.S.-style standard auditor's report or the standard auditor's report of the foreign country.

The auditor should observe the following reporting standards when deciding to use a U.S.-style standard auditor's report for financial statements prepared in accordance with accounting principles of a foreign country:

- The report must use the word "independent" in the title.

- The report must state that the financial statements were audited.

- The report must refer to the note to the financial statements that discloses the basis of presentation, including the nationality of the accounting principles.

- The report must state that the financial statements are the responsibility of management and that the auditor's responsibility is to express an opinion on them.

- The report must state that the audit was conducted in accordance with U.S. generally accepted auditing standards (and if applicable, the auditing standards of the foreign country).

- The report must state that U.S. standards require the auditor to plan and perform the audit to obtain a reasonable assurance on whether the financial statements are free of material misstatement.

- The report must state that an audit includes (1) examining, on a test basis, evidence supporting the amounts and disclosures in the financial statements; (2) assessing the accounting principles used and significant estimates made by management; and (3) evaluating the overall financial statement presentation.

- The report must state that the auditor believes that the audit provides a reasonable basis for his or her opinion.

- The report must state an opinion on the financial statements with respect to the basis of accounting described. (If the financial statements are not fairly presented, the opinion should be modified appropriately and should refer to a separate paragraph that describes the deficiency.)

- If there is an inconsistent application of the basis of accounting described, the report must contain a separate paragraph that explains the deficiency and the opinion must refer to the note that describes the inconsistency.

An example of a U.S.-style standard auditor's report is presented in Exhibit AU 534-1.

The standard report should be modified when the auditor concludes that the financial statements are not fairly presented in accordance with the basis of accounting described in the note. When the report is modified, a separate paragraph should contain a description of the accounting deficiency. The opinion paragraph should refer to the additional paragraph as the basis of the modification and should contain the appropriate opinion on the financial statements (qualified or adverse).

Rather than use the U.S.-style standard auditor's report, the auditor may use the standard auditor's report of the foreign country, provided two conditions are met. First, the standard report of the foreign country must be the same report that would have been issued by auditors of the foreign country under the same circumstances. Second, the auditor must understand the assertions made in the standard auditor's report of the foreign country and it must be appropriate for the auditor to take the responsibility for those assertions. With respect to the second condition, it must be recognized that the assertions in the standard auditor's report of another country may be different from those in the U.S.-style standard auditor's report.

The fundamental assertion in the U.S.-style standard auditor's report is that the financial statements are prepared in accordance with generally accepted accounting principles. On the other hand, a foreign country's standard auditor's report may imply or state that the financial statements are prepared in compliance with existing statutory regulations. Thus, before issuing a foreign country's standard auditor's report, the U.S. auditor must fully understand the auditing standards, accounting principles, and laws that are applicable in the foreign country. To gain the appropriate understanding, the U.S. auditor might need to consult with auditors who are familiar with the auditing standards, accounting principles, and laws of the particular foreign country.

When the U.S. practicing auditor concludes that it is appropriate to issue the foreign country's standard auditor's report, the reporting standards of the foreign country should be observed.

Dual statements (foreign GAAP/U.S. GAAP)

One set of financial statements may be prepared in accordance with U.S. generally accepted accounting principles (GAAP) and a second set in accordance with accounting principles acceptable in a foreign country, to provide relevant information to users in both countries. For the financial statements presented in accordance with U.S. generally accepted accounting principles, the auditor should observe the Statements on Auditing Standards issued by the American Institute of Certified Public Accountants (AICPA) Auditing Standards Board in preparing the auditor's report. For the financial statements prepared in accordance with accounting principles acceptable in a foreign country and to be used outside of the United States, the auditor may prepare the U.S.-style standard auditor's report, which was described earlier, or may use the standard report of another country.

Some confusion may arise when the same financial statements of a U.S. entity are prepared on two different accounting bases. SAS-51 suggests that to reduce the possibility of a misunderstanding, one or both of the audit reports should contain a statement advising the reader of the other audit report, which has been issued on the same financial statements but is based on the accepted accounting principles of another country. The auditor's report also may refer to the note to the financial statements, if presented, that describes the significant differences between the two bases of accounting. An example of the auditor's reference to such a note is as follows:

We also have reported separately on the financial statements of Company X for the same period presented in accordance with accounting principles generally accepted in [*insert name of foreign country*]. The significant differences between the accounting principles accepted in [*insert name of foreign country*] and those generally accepted in the United States are summarized in Note 1.

Foreign GAAP/general United States distribution

Financial statements prepared in accordance with the accepted accounting principles of a foreign country might be intended for more than a limited distribution in the United States. When the auditor is asked to report on this type of financial statement, there are two acceptable reporting formats.

First, reporting guidance established by SAS-58 (AU 508) (Reports on Audited Financial Statements) should be followed for the U.S.-distributed financial statements. Thus, significant departures from United States generally accepted accounting principles, if any, would result in an expression of a qualified opinion or an adverse opinion. The auditor may include an additional paragraph in the standard report to express an opinion on whether the financial statements also are presented in conformity with the accepted accounting principles of another country.

Second, the auditor may present two reports: (1) either the U.S.-style auditor's report or the foreign country's standard report for foreign distribution (see earlier discussion for a description of these reports) and (2) an audit report based on SAS-58 (AU 508), as described in the previous paragraph for U.S. distribution.

OBSERVATION: SAS-51 does not preclude the limited distribution of financial statements to users within the United States who deal directly with the U.S. entity, as long as the users can discuss with the U.S. entity the significance of the differences between U.S. accounting principles and the foreign accounting principles that were used to prepare the financial statements.

PLANNING AID REMINDER: Interpretation No. 1 of AU 534 states that an auditor may audit financial statements of a U.S.

entity that presents its financial statements in accordance with International Accounting Standards for general use only outside of the United States. Under this circumstance, the U.S. auditor must observe the guidance established by SAS-51.

Practitioner's Aids

Exhibit AU 534-1 is an example of a U.S.-style standard auditor's report.

EXHIBIT AU 534-1 — U.S.-STYLE STANDARD AUDITOR'S REPORT

We have audited the accompanying balance sheet of X Company as of December 31, 20X5, and the related statements of income, retained earnings, and cash flows for the year then ended, which, as described in Note X, have been prepared on the basis of accounting principles generally accepted in [*insert name of foreign country*]. These financial statements are the responsibility of the Company's management. Our responsibility is to express an opinion on these financial statements based on our audit.

We conducted our audit in accordance with auditing standards generally accepted in the United States of America. U.S. standards require that we plan and perform the audit to obtain reasonable assurance about whether the financial statements are free of material misstatement. An audit includes examining, on a test basis, evidence supporting the amounts and disclosures in the financial statements. An audit also includes assessing the accounting principles used and significant estimates made by management, as well as evaluating the overall financial statement presentation. We believe that our audit provides a reasonable basis for our opinion.

In our opinion, the financial statements referred to above present fairly, in all material respects, the financial position of X Company as of December 31, 20X5, and the results of its operations and its cash flows for the year then ended in conformity with accounting principles generally accepted in [*insert name of foreign country*].

Note: If the audit satisfies the auditing standards of another country (in addition to U.S. auditing standards), the first sentence of the second paragraph in Exhibit AU 534-1 is modified to read "We conducted our audit in accordance with auditing standards generally accepted in the United States of America and in [*name of other country*]."

SECTION 543

PART OF AUDIT PERFORMED BY OTHER INDEPENDENT AUDITORS

Authoritative Pronouncements

SAS-1 — Codification of Auditing Standards and Procedures (Section 543, Part of Audit Performed by Other Independent Auditors)

SAS-64 — Omnibus Statement on Auditing Standards — 1990

Auditing Interpretation No. 1 (November 1996) — Specific Procedures Performed by the Other Auditor at the Principal Auditor's Request

Auditing Interpretation No. 2 (April 1979) — Inquiries of the Principal Auditor by the Other Auditor

Auditing Interpretation No. 3 (April 1979) — Form of Inquiries of the Principal Auditor Made by the Other Auditor

Auditing Interpretation No. 4 (April 1979) — Form of Principal Auditor's Response to Inquiries from Other Auditors

Auditing Interpretation No. 5 (April 1979) — Procedures of the Principal Auditor

Auditing Interpretation No. 6 (December 1981) — Application of Additional Procedures Concerning the Audit Performed by the Other Auditor

> **IMPORTANT NOTICE FOR 2011:** The Auditing Standards Board (ASB) is in the process of redrafting all of the auditing sections in *Codification of Statements on Auditing Standards* to converge U.S. GAAS with the International Standards on Auditing issued by the International Auditing and Assurance Standards Board. As part of this process, the newly redrafted standards will follow certain clarity drafting conventions adopted by the ASB. These clarity drafting conventions include (1) establishing objectives for each standard; (2) including a definitions section, if appropriate; and (3) separating requirements from application guidance and other material. The ASB is planning to have all redrafted standards become effective on the same date, which is for audits of financial statements for periods ending on or after December 15, 2012. It is possible that the effective date might be delayed beyond that date. The ASB's clarity and convergence project will have a significant effect on the auditing standards applicable to audits of nonpublic companies, and the 2012 *GAAS Guide* will be

appropriately modified to reflect these changes once the effective date of the standards is certain.

Overview

An auditor must decide whether to make reference to the report of another auditor when part of the examination is made by another auditor. When part of an examination, such as the audit of a subsidiary, has been performed by another auditor, the principal auditor must decide whether that participation permits him or her to act as the principal auditor. If it does, the auditor must decide whether or not reference should be made to the other auditor. This decision is a matter of professional judgment and should be based on the materiality of the portions examined by each auditor. After a decision is reached about who is the principal auditor, the principal auditor must decide whether to refer to the other auditor in the report or to assume sole responsibility for the report. However, regardless of the decision of the principal auditor, the other auditor remains responsible for his or her own work and report.

Promulgated Procedures Checklist

The auditor should perform the following procedures when part of the work in an audit engagement is performed by another independent auditor:

- Perform basic audit procedures irrespective of whether the work of the other auditor is to be referred to in the report.

- Consider performing additional procedures when the work of the other auditor is not referred to in the report.

- Prepare an appropriate audit report.

Analysis and Application of Procedures

Perform basic audit procedures irrespective of whether the work of the other auditor is to be referred to in the report

Whether the principal auditor decides to make reference to another auditor or not, the following basic audit procedures must be performed:

- Determine the professional reputation and standing of the other auditor.

- Obtain a representation from the other auditor that he or she is independent of the client.

- Notify the other auditor that his or her audited financial statements may be included in the consolidated or combined financial statements reported on by the principal auditor.

- Notify the other auditor that his or her report may be relied on and, if appropriate, referred to by the principal auditor.

- Determine whether the other auditor is familiar with generally accepted accounting principles (GAAP) and generally accepted auditing standards (GAAS) and whether he or she uses these standards in engagements and the resulting reports.

- If the client is a public company, determine whether the other auditor is familiar with SEC and PCAOB reporting practices and standards and is registered with the PCAOB.

- Notify the other auditor that there may be a review of adjusting and eliminating intercompany transactions.

> **PLANNING AID REMINDER:** Interpretation No. 2 of AU 543 states that it may be necessary for the other auditor to make inquiries of the principal auditor. For example, inquiry may be appropriate when the other auditor is making inquiries concerning related parties. In addition, the other auditor may make inquiries of the principal auditor about any matter considered significant to his or her examination. Usually the inquiry should be made in writing and should note that the response should be made in writing. Also, the inquiry should specify the date by which the principal auditor should respond. The principal auditor should identify what stage of completion the examination is in as of the date of the reply. Also, the principal auditor should state that all the information requested by the other auditor would not necessarily be revealed by procedures used by the principal auditor. The principal auditor is not required to perform any procedures directed toward identifying matters that would not affect his or her own audit.

If the principal auditor concludes that the report of the other auditor cannot be relied on, a scope limitation exists and a qualified opinion or a disclaimer of opinion should be expressed.

Consider performing additional procedures when the work of the other auditor is not referred to in the report

When the principal auditor decides not to refer to the report of another auditor, it might be appropriate for the principal auditor to perform one or more of the following procedures:

- Visit the other auditor and discuss the audit procedures the other auditor employed and the results that auditor obtained during the engagement.

- Review the other auditor's audit program.

- Review the other auditor's workpapers.

- Consider whether instructions should be given to the other auditor as to the scope of work.

- Consider whether the principal auditor should discuss relevant matters directly with personnel of the consolidating or combining entity and/or should perform additional tests.

> **ENGAGEMENT STRATEGY:** Interpretation No. 6 of AU 543 states that a principal auditor who decides not to make reference to the audit of another auditor may consider various factors when determining whether to apply procedures to obtain information about the adequacy of the other auditor's examination. One factor that may be taken into consideration involves knowledge of the other auditor's quality control policies and procedures that provide the other auditor with reasonable assurance of conformity with GAAS. Other factors that may be considered are (1) past experience with the other auditor, (2) the materiality of the financial statements examined by the other auditor in relationship to the combined or consolidated financial statements, (3) the degree of control exercised by the principal auditor over the work performed by the other auditor, and (4) the results of audit procedures performed by the principal auditor that suggest that the other auditor may have to perform additional procedures.

> **PUBLIC COMPANY IMPLICATION:** The PCAOB has issued Auditing Standard No. 3 (AS-3) (Audit Documentation and Amendment to Interim Auditing Standards), which amends paragraph .12 of AU 543. AS-3 specifies appropriate audit documentation when the principal auditor does not refer to the work of the other auditors. The principal auditor must obtain and review the following prior to issuing his or her audit report: (1) an engagement completion document; (2) a list of significant fraud risk factors, the other auditor's response, and the results from these procedures; (3) information on any matters that are inconsistent with or contradict the auditor's final conclusions; (4) any findings that affect the consolidating or combining of accounts in the consolidated financial statements; (5) the information necessary for the principal auditor to reconcile the amounts audited by the other auditor to the consolidated financial statements; (6) a schedule of audit adjustments, including the nature and cause of each adjustment; (7) a listing

of all significant deficiencies and material weaknesses in internal control, with each group listed separately; (8) management representation letters; (9) any matters to be communicated to the audit committee. In addition to these documentation requirements, the principal auditor should consider discussing the other auditors' audit procedures and related results, and consider reviewing the audit programs used by other auditors.

Generally, an auditor decides not to refer to another auditor when (1) the other auditor is an associate or correspondent, (2) the principal auditor actually engages the other auditor, or (3) the financial statements examined by the other auditor are immaterial in relation to the consolidated or combined group.

Prepare an appropriate audit report

Reporting when reference is made

If the principal auditor decides to refer to the other auditor's examination, the report should, in both the scope and opinion paragraphs, clearly indicate the degree of responsibility and the portions of the financial statements examined by each. (This may be expressed in percentages, total assets, total revenue, or other appropriate criteria.) In addition, the principal auditor may name the other auditor only with his or her express permission.

Reference to another auditor by the principal auditor does not constitute a qualification of opinion but, rather, a description of responsibility between the two auditors.

If the other auditor's opinion is qualified, the principal auditor must decide whether the subject of the qualification is material in relation to the consolidated statements. If the principal auditor decides that it is not, the principal auditor does not need to refer to the qualification in the report.

> **PLANNING AID REMINDER:** Interpretation No. 1 of AU 543 states that when a principal auditor requests that the other auditor perform specific procedures, the principal auditor is responsible for determining the extent of the procedures to be performed.

When the principal auditor decides to refer to the report of another auditor, the basic audit procedures described previously must be performed.

> **OBSERVATION:** An auditor is placed in the role of principal auditor when a long-term investment is accounted for by the

equity method. Furthermore, an auditor may be placed in the role of principal auditor even if the cost method is used to account for a long-term investment. This circumstance can arise when the work of the other auditor constitutes a major element of evidence with respect to the investment account. Presumably, this occurs when there is some question about whether there has been a permanent impairment in the carrying value of the investment.

Practitioner's Aids

Exhibit AU 543-1 illustrates an auditor's report in which reference is made to the work of another auditor. Exhibit AU 543-2 is an example of the other auditor's inquiry of the principal auditor. Exhibit AU 543-3 is an example of the principal auditor's response to inquiries from the other auditor.

EXHIBIT AU 543-1 — REFERENCE TO THE WORK OF ANOTHER AUDITOR IN THE AUDIT REPORT

We have audited the consolidated balance sheet of X Company as of December 31, 20X5, and the related consolidated statements of income, retained earnings, and cash flows for the year then ended. These financial statements are the responsibility of the Company's management. Our responsibility is to express an opinion on these financial statements based on our audit. We did not examine the financial statements of Z Company, a consolidated subsidiary whose statements reflect total assets and revenues constituting 15% and 12%, respectively, of the related consolidated totals. Those statements were audited by other auditors whose report has been furnished to us, and our opinion, insofar as it relates to the amounts included for Z Company, is based solely on the report of the other auditors.

We conducted our audit in accordance with auditing standards generally accepted in the United States of America. Those standards require that we plan and perform the audit to obtain reasonable assurance about whether the financial statements are free of material misstatement. An audit includes examining, on a test basis, evidence supporting the amounts and disclosures in the financial statements. An audit also includes assessing the accounting principles used and significant estimates made by management, as well as evaluating the overall financial statement presentation. We believe that our audit and the report of other auditors provide a reasonable basis for our opinion.

In our opinion, based on our audit and the report of other auditors, the consolidated financial statements referred to above present fairly, in all material respects, the financial position of X Company as of December 31, 20X5, and the results of its operations and its cash flows for the year then ended in conformity with accounting principles generally accepted in the United States of America.

EXHIBIT AU 543-2 — EXAMPLE OF INQUIRY BY THE OTHER AUDITOR DIRECTED TO THE PRINCIPAL AUDITOR

We are auditing the financial statements of [name of client] as of [date] and for the [period of audit] for the purpose of expressing an opinion as to whether the financial statements present fairly, in all material respects, the financial position, results of operations, and cash flows of [name of client] in conformity with generally accepted accounting principles.

A draft of the financial statements referred to above and a draft of our report are enclosed solely to aid you in responding to this inquiry. Please provide us [in writing/orally] with the following information in connection with your current examination of the consolidated financial statement of [name of parent company]:

1. Transactions or other matters (including adjustment made during consolidation or contemplated at the date of your reply) that have come to your attention that you believe require adjustment to or disclosure in the financial statements of [name of client] being audited by us.

2. Any limitation on the scope of your audit that is related to the financial statements of [name of client] being audited by us, or that limits your ability to provide us with the information requested in this inquiry.

Please make your response as of a date near [expected date of the other auditor's report].

EXHIBIT AU 543-3 — EXAMPLE OF PRINCIPAL AUDITOR'S RESPONSE TO INQUIRY MADE BY OTHER AUDITOR

This letter is furnished to you in response to your request that we provide you with certain information in connection with your audit of the financial statements of [*name of component*], a [*subsidiary, division, branch or investment*] of Parent Company for the year ended [*date*].

We are in the process of performing an audit of the consolidated financial statements of Parent Company for the year ended [*date*] [*but have not completed our work as of this date*]. The objective of our audit is to enable us to express an opinion on the consolidated financial statements of Parent Company, and, accordingly, we have performed no procedures directed toward identifying matters that would not affect our audit or our report. However, solely for the purpose of responding to your inquiry, we have read the draft of the financial statement of [*name of component*] as of [*date*] and for the [*period of audit*] and the draft of your report on them, included with your inquiry dated [*date of inquiry*].

Based solely on the work we have performed [*to date*] in connection with our audit of the consolidated financial statements, which would not necessarily reveal all or any of the matters covered in your inquiry, we advise you that:

1. No transactions or other matters (including adjustments made during consolidation or contemplated at this date) have come to our attention that we believe require adjustment to or disclosure in the financial statements of [*name of component*] being audited by you.

2. No limitation has been placed by Parent Company on the scope of our audit that, to our knowledge, is related to the financial statements of [*name of component*] being audited by you, that has limited our ability to provide you with the information requested in your inquiry.

OBSERVATION: Interpretation No. 5 of AU 543 states that the above response should be made by the auditor "with final responsibility for the engagement," and that auditor should perform steps considered reasonable under the circumstances to respond in an appropriate manner to the request made by the other auditor. If relevant information is discovered after the principal auditor has responded to the request but before the completion of the audit, the other auditor should be informed of the new information. If the principal auditor discovers information relevant to the other auditor's request after a response has been sent, the guidance established by AU 561 (Subsequent Discovery of Facts Existing at the Date of the Auditor's Report) should be followed.

SECTION 544

LACK OF CONFORMITY WITH GENERALLY ACCEPTED ACCOUNTING PRINCIPLES

Authoritative Pronouncements

SAS-1 — Codification of Auditing Standards and Procedures (Section 544, Lack of Conformity with Generally Accepted Accounting Principles)

SAS-62 — Special Reports

SAS-77 — Amendments to Statements on Auditing Standards No. 22, "Planning and Supervision," No. 59, "the Auditor's Consideration of an Entity's Ability to Continue as a going Concern," and SAS-62, "Special Reports"

[*Note:* The Auditing Standards Board's Exposure Draft titled "Amendment to Statement on Auditing Standards No. 69, The Meaning of Present Fairly in Conformity with Generally Accepted Accounting Principles, for Nongovernmental Entities," if adopted, will amend AU Section 411.]

> **IMPORTANT NOTICE FOR 2011:** The Auditing Standards Board (ASB) is in the process of redrafting all of the auditing sections in *Codification of Statements on Auditing Standards* to converge U.S. GAAS with the International Standards on Auditing issued by the International Auditing and Assurance Standards Board. As part of this process, the newly redrafted standards will follow certain clarity drafting conventions adopted by the ASB. These clarity drafting conventions include (1) establishing objectives for each standard; (2) including a definitions section, if appropriate; and (3) separating requirements from application guidance and other material. The ASB is planning to have all redrafted standards become effective on the same date, which is for audits of financial statements for periods ending on or after December 15, 2012. It is possible that the effective date might be delayed beyond that date. The ASB's clarity and convergence project will have a significant effect on the auditing standards applicable to audits of non-public companies, and the 2012 *GAAS Guide* will be appropriately modified to reflect these changes once the effective date of the standards is certain.

Overview

Generally accepted accounting principles apply to all commercial enterprises, including those enterprises whose accounting practices are established by a governmental agency. For example, insurance companies must file financial statements with the appropriate state insurance commissioner and must observe the accounting and reporting standards established by that state's commissioner. When financial statements of these enterprises are prepared for purposes other than for filing with the regulatory agency that establishes the accounting and reporting principles, those statements must follow generally accepted accounting principles as defined in the authoritative literature (see AU 411). If the regulated enterprise does not revise its general-purpose financial statements to conform to authoritative accounting standards, the auditor must determine whether a qualified opinion or an adverse opinion must be expressed on the financial statements. SAS-1 notes that when an adverse opinion is expressed, the auditor's report may be accompanied by an opinion on a supplementary presentation that is consistent with generally accepted accounting principles.

> **PLANNING AID REMINDER:** The auditor may follow the reporting standards established by SAS-62 (AU 544, AU 623) (Special Reports) in order to report on financial statements that are prepared in accordance with regulatory accounting standards and that are to be used only to satisfy the filing requirement established by the governmental regulatory authority.

In some instances the enterprise's financial statements, prepared using regulatory accounting standards, may have to be filed "in presentations for distribution in other than filings with the entity's regulatory agency." If the auditor is requested to express an opinion on the financial statements under this circumstance, the guidance established by SAS-58 (AU 508) (Reports on Audited Financial Statements) must be observed, and any material differences with generally accepted accounting principles would require that a qualified opinion or an adverse opinion be expressed. The auditor's report should include an additional paragraph stating whether the financial statements are prepared in accordance with the regulatory accounting standards.

SECTION 550

OTHER INFORMATION IN DOCUMENTS CONTAINING AUDITED FINANCIAL STATEMENTS

Authoritative Pronouncements

SAS-118—Other Information in Documents Containing Audited Financial Statements

> **IMPORTANT NOTICE FOR 2011:** The Auditing Standards Board (ASB) is in the process of redrafting all of the auditing sections in *Codification of Statements on Auditing Standards* to converge U.S. GAAS with the International Standards on Auditing issued by the International Auditing and Assurance Standards Board. As part of this process, the newly redrafted standards will follow certain clarity drafting conventions adopted by the ASB. SAS-118 (which superseded SAS-8) represents the redrafted and clarified guidance for AU 550. Although the ASB expects that the redrafted standards will become effective on the same date, the effective date for the guidance in AU 550 has been accelerated to address certain practice issues. SAS-118 is effective for audits of financial statements for periods beginning on or after December 15, 2010. Early application is permitted.

Overview

The auditor's report may be included in a document that contains other information. For example, a company's annual report may include a message from the chief executive officer and descriptions of operations and future plans, as well as a variety of charts and graphs accompanied by explanations.

AU 550 establishes the responsibilities of the independent auditor with respect to other information in (1) annual reports sent to holders of securities, (2) annual reports of government and charitable or philanthropic organizations available to the public, and (3) other documents reviewed by the auditor at the client's request.

> **PLANNING AID REMINDER:** A designated accounting standard setter such as the Financial Accounting Standards Board may have issued guidance or standards regarding the form and content of other information. This AU Section addresses this other information when it is voluntarily presented in a

document containing the audited financial statements and auditor's report, but if the other information is required to be included by a designated accounting standard setter, the auditor should follow the guidance in AU 558.

Although he or she is not required to audit the other information, the auditor must read it to determine whether, compared with the information presented in the financial statements, there is (1) a material inconsistency or (2) a material misstatement of fact. By reading the other information, the auditor can respond appropriately if other information is presented that could undermine the credibility of the audited financial statements and the auditor's report.

Definitions

Term	Definition
Other information	Financial and nonfinancial information (other than the financial statements, auditor's report, and required supplementary information) that is included in a document containing audited financial statements and the auditor's report.
Inconsistency	Other information that conflicts with information in the audited financial statements. A material inconsistency may raise doubt about the audit conclusions drawn and the basis for the auditor's opinion on the financial statements.
Misstatement of fact	Other information unrelated to matters appearing in the audited financial statements that is incorrectly stated or presented. A material misstatement of fact may undermine the credibility of the document containing audited financial statements.

Requirements

The auditor is presumptively required to perform the following procedures on other information in documents containing audited financial statements.

Reading other information

1. Read any other information the auditor is aware of to identify any material inconsistencies with the audited financial statements.

2. Arrange with management or those charged with governance to obtain other information prior to the report release date, or, if that is not possible, read other information as soon as practicable.

3. Communicate with those charged with governance regarding the auditor's responsibility for other information as well as any procedures performed related to other information and their results.

Material inconsistencies

4. If a material inconsistency is identified when reading the other information, determine whether revision of the audited financial statements or other information is needed.

5. If the auditor discovers information prior to the report release date requiring revision of the audited financial statements and management refuses to make the revision, modify the auditor's report in accordance with AU 508.

6. If revision of the other information is necessary and management refuses to make the revision, communicate the matter to those charged with governance and include an explanatory paragraph in the auditor's report describing the material inconsistency in accordance with AU 508, withhold the auditor's report, or withdraw from the engagement where withdrawal is legally permitted.

7. If the auditor becomes aware of other information subsequent to the report release date and revision of the audited financial statements is necessary, refer to the guidance in AU 561.

8. If revision of the other information obtained subsequent to the report release date is necessary and management agrees to make the revision, carry out the necessary procedures under the circumstances (see AU 561). If management refuses to make the revision, the auditor should notify those charged with governance of his or her concerns and take further appropriate action.

Material misstatements of fact

9. If the auditor becomes aware of an apparent material misstatement of fact when reading the other information, discuss the matter with management.

10. If the auditor still considers there to be an apparent material misstatement of fact after such discussions, request that management consult with a qualified third party such as legal counsel and the auditor should consider the advice the entity receives.

11. If the auditor concludes there is a material misstatement of fact in the other information that management refuses to correct, the auditor should notify those charged with governance of his or her concerns and take appropriate further action.

Analysis and Application of Procedures

Other Information

Items that may comprise other information include the following:

- A report on operations by management or those charged with governance

- Financial summaries or highlights

- Employment data

- Planned capital expenditures

- Financial ratios

- Names of officers and directors

- Selected quarterly data

Other information does not include information on a company's Web site, information contained in analyst briefings, or a press release or cover letter accompanying the document containing audited financial statements and the auditor's report.

Reading Other Information

The other information is not required to be referenced in the auditor's report on the financial statements. However, an explanatory paragraph disclaiming an opinion on the other information may be included to prevent users from inferring an unintended level of assurance on the other information. An example of such an explanatory paragraph is as follows:

> Our audit was conducted for the purpose of forming an opinion on the basic financial statements as a whole. The [*identify the other information*] is presented for purposes of additional analysis and is

not a required part of the basic financial statements. Such information has not been subjected to the auditing procedures applied in the audit of the financial statements, and, accordingly, we do not express an opinion or provide any assurance on it.

The auditor may find an agreement with management to be helpful in obtaining the other information on a timely basis. The auditor may also consider delaying release of his of her report until the client provides him or her with the other information.

Material Inconsistencies

When material inconsistencies are identified in other information obtained prior to the report release date and management refuses to make revisions, the auditor may use legal counsel's advice to decide on further appropriate action. In instances where withdrawal from the engagement is not legally permitted, the auditor may issue a report to those charged with governance and the appropriate statutory body detailing the identified inconsistency.

When material inconsistencies are identified in other information obtained subsequent to the report release date and management agrees to make revisions, the auditor's procedures may include reviewing steps taken by management to inform recipients of the issued financial statements, auditor's report, and other information of the revision. If management refuses to make revisions that the auditor deems necessary, the auditor may take further action, including obtaining advice from legal counsel.

Material Misstatements of Fact

It is more difficult to identify a material misstatement of fact in an annual report, because the nature of much of the other information is nonaccounting and beyond the expertise of the auditor. The auditor may conclude that valid differences of judgment or opinion exist if he or she is unable to evaluate the validity of some disclosures in the other information or of management's responses to inquiries.

> **FRAUD POINTER:** AU 550 is vague in this area of material misstatement of fact, because it relies on the auditor's limited expertise in relation to the other information. In other words, the auditor must proceed with caution. However, if he or she discovers a material misstatement of fact and the client refuses to change the other information but the auditor still issues a report, it might be wise for the auditor to follow the reporting format prescribed when a material misstate-

ment is encountered in the financial statements or accompanying notes.

If the auditor concludes there is a material misstatement of fact that management refuses to correct, the auditor may take further actions, including obtaining advice from legal counsel, withholding the auditor's report if not already issued, or withdrawing from the engagement.

SECTION 551

REPORTING ON INFORMATION ACCOMPANYING THE BASIC FINANCIAL STATEMENTS IN AUDITOR-SUBMITTED DOCUMENTS

Authoritative Pronouncements

SAS-118—Other Information in Documents Containing Audited Financial Statements

SAS-119—Supplementary Information in Relation to the Financial Statements as a Whole

> **IMPORTANT NOTICE FOR 2011:** The Auditing Standards Board (ASB) is in the process of redrafting all of the auditing sections in *Codification of Statements on Auditing Standards* to converge U.S. GAAS with the International Standards on Auditing issued by the International Auditing and Assurance Standards Board. As part of this process, the newly redrafted standards will follow certain clarity drafting conventions adopted by the ASB. SAS-119 (which superseded the guidance in AU 551) represents the redrafted and clarified guidance for AU 551. Although the ASB expects that the redrafted standards will become effective on the same date, the effective date for the guidance in AU 551 has been accelerated to address certain practice issues. SAS-119 is effective for audits of financial statements for periods beginning on or after December 15, 2010. Early application is permitted.

Overview

AU 551 applies to engagements in which the auditor expresses an opinion on whether supplementary information is fairly stated, in all material respects, in relation to the financial statements as a whole. The supplementary information that this AU Section applies to is not required in order for the financial statements to be fairly presented in accordance with the applicable financial reporting framework.

This guidance may also be applied if the auditor is engaged to express an opinion on whether required supplementary information is fairly stated in all material respects in relation to the financial statements as a whole. However, AU 550 addresses the auditor's responsibilities for other information outside the financial statements, and AU 558 addresses the auditor's responsibilities for information required by a designated accounting standard setter to accompany an entity's basic financial statements. Furthermore, if the auditor is engaged to express an opinion on specified elements, accounts, or items of financial statements for the purpose of a separate presentation, the guidance in AU 623 applies. An engagement to examine supplementary information or an assertion related to the supplementary information may also be performed in accordance with AT 101.

Definitions

Term	Meaning
Supplementary information	Information other than the financial statements, auditor's report, and required supplementary information that is not considered necessary for the financial statements to be fairly presented in accordance with the applicable financial reporting framework. This information includes details, explanations, or historical summaries of financial statement items, consolidating information, statistical data, and other information which may come from sources outside the accounting system or the entity. This information may be presented with or separate from the audited financial statements. Supplementary information may be prepared in accordance with an applicable financial reporting framework, management's criteria, or by regulatory, contractual, or other requirements.

Requirements

The auditor is presumptively required to apply the following procedures for opining on supplementary information in relation to the financial statements as a whole.

Procedures

1. Determine the following in order to express an opinion on whether supplementary information is fairly stated in all material respects in relation to the financial statements as a whole:

    a. Supplementary information relates to the same period as the financial statements and was derived from and directly relates to the underlying accounting and other records used to prepare those statements

b.   The financial statements were audited, an adverse opinion or disclaimer of opinion was not issued, and the auditor served as the principal auditor in the engagement

c.   The supplementary information will accompany the audited financial statements or the entity will make those statements readily available

2.   Obtain management's agreement that it acknowledges and understands its responsibility:

a.   To prepare the supplementary information in accordance with the applicable criteria

b.   To provide the auditor with the written representations described in requirement 3f (below)

c.   To include the auditor's report on the supplementary information in any document containing the supplementary information and indicate the auditor has reported on that information

d.   To present the supplementary information with the audited financial statements or make the audited financial statements readily available to the supplementary information's intended users no later than the date the supplementary information and auditor's report on that information are issued

3.   Perform the following procedures in addition to procedures performed during the financial statement audit, using the same materiality level used in the financial statement audit, in order to express an opinion on whether supplementary information is fairly stated in all material respects in relation to the financial statements as a whole:

a.   Inquire of management about the purpose of supplementary information and the criteria used to prepare that information

b.   Obtain an understanding about the methods of preparing the information including whether those methods have changed from prior periods and the reasons why as well as whether the form and content of the information complies with established criteria

c.   Compare and reconcile the information to the financial statements or to the underlying accounting and other records used in preparing the financial statements

     d. Inquire of management about any significant assumptions or interpretations underlying the information's measurement or presentation

     e. Evaluate the appropriateness and completeness of the information, considering procedures and other knowledge obtained during the financial statement audit

     f. Obtain written representations from management: acknowledging responsibility for the supplementary information; stating that the information's form and content is in accordance with prescribed guidelines; stating that measurement and presentation methods have not changed from the prior period or the reasons for any such changes; about any significant assumptions or interpretations underlying information measurement or presentation; and that when supplementary information is not presented with the audited financial statements those statements will be made readily available to the supplementary information's intended users no later than the date the supplementary information and auditor's report are issued.

4. The auditor has no responsibility for considering subsequent events with respect to the supplementary information. However, if information comes to the auditor's attention before or after the auditor's report on the financial statements is released regarding events that affect the financial statements, he or she should follow the guidance in AU 560 or AU 561, respectively.

Reporting

5. If the auditor expresses an opinion on the supplementary information in relation to the financial statements as a whole that is presented with the financial statements, include an explanatory paragraph in the auditor's report on the financial statements or issue a separate report on the supplementary information with the following statements:

     a. The audit was conducted for the purpose of forming an opinion on the financial statements as a whole

     b. Supplementary information is presented for additional analysis purposes and is not a required part of the financial statements

     c. Supplementary information is management's responsibility and was derived from and directly relates to the underlying accounting and other records used to prepare the financial statements

     d. Supplementary information has been subjected to the auditing procedures applied in the financial statement audit and certain additional procedures, including comparing and reconciling such information directly to the underlying accounting and other records used to prepare the financial statements and other additional procedures as prescribed by auditing standards generally accepted in the United States of America

e.   If the financial statement opinion is unqualified and the supplementary information is fairly stated, include a statement that, in the auditor's opinion, the other supplementary information is fairly stated in all material respects, in relation to the financial statements as a whole.

f.   If the financial statement opinion is qualified and the qualification has an effect on the supplementary information, include a statement that, in the auditor's opinion, except for the effects on the supplementary information of (refer to the paragraph in the auditor's report explaining the qualification), such information is fairly stated in all material respects in relation to the financial statements as whole.

6.   If the auditor expresses an opinion on supplementary information and the audited financial statements are not presented with the supplementary information, the report on the supplementary information should include all of the above elements and a reference to the financial statement report, the date of that report, the opinion expressed on the financial statements, and any report modifications.

7.   If an adverse opinion or disclaimer of opinion is issued on the financial statements, the auditor may not express an opinion on the supplementary information and may withdraw from the engagement to report on such information where permitted by law or regulation. If the auditor does not withdraw from the engagement, the report on the supplementary information should state that because of the significance of the matter disclosed in the auditor's report, it is inappropriate for the auditor to express an opinion on the supplementary information.

8.   The date of the auditor's opinion on the supplementary information should not be earlier than the date on which the auditor completed the required procedures.

9.   If the auditor concludes the supplementary information is materially misstated in relation to the financial statements as a whole, he or she should discuss the matter with management and propose appropriate revision of the information. If management does not revise the supplementary information, the auditor should modify his or her opinion on the information and describe the misstatement in his or her report, or, if

a separate report is being issued on the supplementary information, withhold his or her report on the supplementary information.

Analysis and Application of Procedures

Reporting on Supplementary Information

Although the auditor is not obligated to report on supplementary information presented outside the basic financial statements, he or she may choose to apply auditing procedures to the information in order to express an opinion on it. Management information not directly related to the basic financial statements is not ordinarily subjected to auditing procedures. However, when that information has been obtained or derived from accounting records the auditor has tested, the auditor may be in a position to express an opinion on it in relation to the financial statements as a whole.

Procedures

To express an opinion on other supplementary information in relation to the financial statements as a whole, the auditor is not required to obtain a separate understanding of internal control or assess fraud risk. The auditor may consider testing accounting or other records through observation or examination of source documents or other procedures ordinarily performed in a financial statement audit to evaluate the appropriateness and completeness of the supplementary information.

> **PLANNING AID REMINDER:** The materiality level used for the supplementary information is the overall audit materiality used in the financial statement audit or for the entire governmental entity in a government audit. Therefore, the procedures required to express an opinion on the supplementary information in relation to the financial statements as a whole do not need to be as extensive as if the auditor was expressing an opinion on the supplementary information by itself.

Other guidance the auditor may follow in determining whether supplementary information is fairly stated in relation to the financial statements as a whole includes the following:

- Obtaining an updating representation letter in accordance with AU 333

- Performing subsequent events procedures in accordance with AU 560

- Sending the client's lawyer a letter of inquiry regarding supplementary information in accordance with AU 337

Audited financial statements are considered readily available if a third-party user can obtain them without any further action by the entity. For example, financial statements available on an entity's Web site are readily available, but if the statements are only available upon request, they are not readily available.

> **ENGAGEMENT STRATEGY:** The auditor may consider restricting the use of a separate report on supplementary information to avoid potential misinterpretation or misunderstanding of supplementary information that is not presented with the financial statements.

Practitioner's Aids

Exhibit AU 551-1 provides an example of an explanatory paragraph that may be used in the auditor's report on the financial statements when the auditor is engaged to report on supplementary information in relation to the financial statements as a whole, an unqualified opinion is being issued on the financial statements, and the auditor has concluded that the supplementary information is fairly stated, in all material respects, in relation to the financial statements as a whole.

EXHIBIT AU 551-1 — EXPLANATORY PARAGRAPH USED WHEN REPORTING ON SUPPLEMENTARY INFORMATION

Our audit was conducted for the purpose of forming an opinion on the financial statements as a whole. The [*identify accompanying supplementary information*] is presented for purposes of additional analysis and is not a required part of the financial statements. Such information is the responsibility of management and was derived from and relates directly to the underlying accounting and other records used to prepare the financial statements. The information has been subjected to the auditing procedures applied in the audit of the financial statements and certain additional procedures, including comparing and reconciling such information directly to the underlying accounting and other records used to prepare the financial statements or to the financial statements themselves, and other additional procedures in accordance with auditing standards generally accepted in the United States of America. In our opinion, the information is fairly stated in all material respects in relation to the financial statements as a whole.

Exhibit AU 551-2 provides a reporting example the auditor may use when reporting separately on supplementary information in relation to the financial statements as a whole, an unqualified opinion has been issued on the financial statements, and an unqualified opinion is being issued on the supplementary information.

EXHIBIT AU 551-2 — REPORTING ON SUPPLEMENTARY INFORMATION SEPARATELY FROM THE FINANCIAL STATEMENTS AS A WHOLE

We have audited the financial statements of ABC Entity as of and for the year ended December 31, 20X5, and have issued our report thereon dated [*date of the auditor's report on the financial statements*], which contained an unqualified opinion on those financial statements. Our audit was performed for the purpose of forming an opinion on the financial statements as a whole. The [*identify accompanying supplementary information*] is presented for purposes of additional analysis and is not a required part of the financial statements. Such information is the responsibility of management and was derived from and relates directly to the underlying accounting and other records used to prepare the financial statements. The information has been subjected to the auditing procedures applied in the audit of the financial statements and certain additional procedures, including comparing and reconciling such information directly to the underlying accounting and other records used to prepare the financial statements or to the financial statements themselves, and other additional procedures in accordance with auditing standards generally accepted in the United States of America. In our opinion, the information is fairly stated in all material respects in relation to the financial statements as a whole.

SECTION 552

REPORTING ON CONDENSED FINANCIAL STATEMENTS AND SELECTED FINANCIAL DATA

Authoritative Pronouncements

SAS-42 — Reporting on Condensed Financial Statements and Selected Financial Data

> **IMPORTANT NOTICE FOR 2011:** The Auditing Standards Board (ASB) is in the process of redrafting all of the auditing sections in *Codification of Statements on Auditing Standards* to converge U.S. GAAS with the International Standards on Auditing issued by the International Auditing and Assurance Standards Board. As part of this process, the newly redrafted standards will follow certain clarity drafting conventions adopted by the ASB. These clarity drafting conventions include (1) establishing objectives for each standard; (2) including a definitions section, if appropriate; and (3) separating requirements from application guidance and other material. The ASB is planning to have all redrafted standards become effective on the same date, which is for audits of financial statements for periods ending on or after December 15, 2012. It is possible that the effective date might be delayed beyond that date. The ASB's clarity and convergence project will have a significant effect on the auditing standards applicable to audits of non-public companies, and the 2012 *GAAS Guide* will be appropriately modified to reflect these changes once the effective date of the standards is certain.

Overview

SAS-42 (Reporting on Condensed Financial Statements and Selected Financial Data) is applicable to reports on condensed financial statements or selected financial data that are derived from audited financial statements and that appear in a client-prepared document. Specifically, the reporting guidelines established by SAS-42 relate to the following:

- Condensed financial statements that are derived from audited financial statements of a public entity that is required to file, at least annually, complete financial statements with a regulatory agency

- Selected financial data that are derived from audited financial statements of a public or nonpublic entity and presented in a document containing audited financial statements or incorporated by reference to information filed with a regulatory agency

    OBSERVATION: If the condensed financial information or selected financial data are presented in an auditor-submitted document, SAS-119 (AU 551) (Supplementary Information in Relation to the Financial Statements as a Whole) should be followed.

Promulgated Procedures Checklist

The auditor should report on condensed financial statements and selected financial data by observing the following guidelines:

- Express an opinion on condensed financial statements.

- Express an opinion on selected financial data.

Analysis and Application of Procedures

Express an opinion on condensed financial statements

The very nature of condensed financial statements is that they are presented in less detail than conventional financial statements. For this reason, they do not fairly present the financial position or results of operation of an entity. When an auditor is engaged to report on condensed financial statements derived from audited financial statements of a public entity, the auditor should observe the following reporting guidelines in preparing the auditor's report:

- State that the complete financial statements have been audited.

- Disclose the date of the auditor's report on the complete financial statements.

- Describe the type of opinion expressed. If the opinion was other than unqualified, explain the nature of and reason for the modification.

- State whether the condensed information is fairly stated in relation to the audited financial statements from which the information was extracted.

The following paragraph illustrates an auditor's report on condensed financial statements that reflects the reporting guidelines described previously:

> We have audited, in accordance with auditing standards generally accepted in the United States of America, the consolidated balance sheet of B Company and its subsidiaries as of December 31, 20X5, and the related consolidated statements of income, retained earnings, and cash flows for the year then ended (not presented herein), and in our report dated February 12, 20X6, we expressed an unqualified opinion on those consolidated financial statements.
>
> In our opinion, the information set forth in the accompanying condensed consolidated financial statements is fairly stated in all material respects in relation to the consolidated financial statements from which it has been derived.

> **PLANNING AID REMINDER:** When the condensed financial statements are presented with financial statements of a subsequent interim period and the auditor's review report on the interim financial statements, the auditor is considered to be associated with the condensed financial statements. Under this circumstance, the auditor would add an additional paragraph, similar to the one described above, to the review report to cover the condensed financial statements.

Express an opinion on selected financial data

Selected financial data for a public or nonpublic company may be presented, along with audited financial statements, in a client-prepared document. For example, some reports filed with the SEC must contain selected financial data for a five-year period. The auditor is not required to audit this data, but, as required by SAS-8 (AU 550) (Other Information in Documents Containing Audited Financial Statements), the auditor must read the data for possible material inconsistencies between it and the audited financial statements.

> **OBSERVATION:** SAS-118 (AU 550) is not applicable to filings under the Securities Act of 1933. SAS-37 (AU 711) (Filings under Federal Securities Statutes) provides guidance for filings under the Securities Act of 1933.

Selected financial data are not an integral part of the basic financial statements of a public or nonpublic company and, as noted above, may not be audited. Under certain circumstances, the auditor may be asked or required to examine the supplementary information. In this case, the report should observe the following guidelines:

- State that the complete financial statements have been audited.

- Describe the type of opinion expressed. If the opinion was other than unqualified, explain the nature of and reason for the modification.

- State whether the selected financial data are fairly stated in relation to the audited financial statements from which the data were derived.

- If appropriate, identify the statements that were audited by another CPA firm, but express no opinion on the selected data derived from those financial statements.

The auditor may meet these reporting requirements by adding an additional paragraph to the standard auditor's report. For example, the following explanatory paragraph is applicable to the audited (comparative) financial statements for 20X4 and 20X5 and the selected financial data from 20X1 through 20X5.

> We previously audited, in accordance with generally accepted auditing standards, the consolidated balance sheets as of December 31, 20X3, 20X2, and 20X1 and the related consolidated statements of income, retained earnings, and cash flows for the years ended December 31, 20X3, 20X2, and 20X1 (none of which are presented herein); we expressed unqualified opinions on those consolidated financial statements. In our opinion, the information set forth in the selected financial data for each of the five years in the period ended December 31, 20X5, appearing on pages 18 through 22, is fairly stated in all material respects in relation to the consolidated financial statements from which it has been derived.

> **ENGAGEMENT STRATEGY:** The auditor should report only on the data derived from the audited financial statements. For example, if nonaccounting data are presented, such as number of employees, the auditor should specifically identify the data to which the report is applicable.

SECTION 558

REQUIRED SUPPLEMENTARY INFORMATION

Authoritative Pronouncements

SAS-120 — Required Supplementary Information

> **IMPORTANT NOTICE FOR 2011:** The Auditing Standards
> Board (ASB) is in the process of redrafting all of the auditing
> sections in *Codification of Statements on Auditing Standards*
> to converge U.S. GAAS with the International Standards on
> Auditing issued by the International Auditing and Assurance
> Standards Board. As part of this process, the newly redrafted
> standards will follow certain clarity drafting conventions
> adopted by the ASB. SAS-120 (which superseded the
> guidance in AU 558) represents the redrafted and clarified
> guidance for AU 558. Although the ASB expects that the
> redrafted standards will become effective on the same date,
> the effective date for the guidance in AU 558 has been accel-
> erated to address certain practice issues. SAS-120 is effective
> for audits of financial statements for periods beginning on or
> after December 15, 2010. Early application is permitted.

Overview

Although required supplementary information is not part of the basic financial statements, certain designated entities must disclose such information. The required supplementary information is considered to be an
essential part of the financial report for these designated entities. Although
this information does not have to be audited, certain prescribed procedures
established by AU 558 must be applied. The auditor's objective in
performing these procedures is to communicate through his or her report
whether any of the required supplementary information has not been presented and whether any material modifications have been identified that
should be made to the required supplementary information for it to conform with guidelines established by a designated accounting standard setter. AU 550 specifies the auditor's responsibilities for other information
that is not required supplementary information.

> **OBSERVATION:** The auditor also may be required to perform
> certain procedures on information as prescribed in an AICPA
> Audit Guide. For example, the Audit and Accounting Guide

titled *Common Interest Realty Associations* requires presentation of unaudited supplementary information about the funding of future major repairs and replacements of common property by these types of entities. It also sets forth procedures for the auditor to perform on this information.

Definitions

Term	Definition
Required supplementary information	Information that a designated accounting standard setter requires to accompany an entity's basic financial statements. This differs from other types of information outside the basic financial statements because a designated accounting standards setter considers the information an essential part of the financial reporting of certain entities and because authoritative guidelines for the measurement and presentation of the information have been established.
Designated accounting standard setter	A body designated by the AICPA council to establish GAAP pursuant to Rule 202, *Compliance with Standards*, and Rule 203, *Accounting Principles*. Designated bodies are the Federal Accounting Standards Advisory Board, Financial Accounting Standards Board, Governmental Accounting Standards Board, Public Company Accounting Oversight Board, and the International Accounting Standards Board.
Basic financial statements	Financial statements presented in accordance with an applicable financial reporting framework as established by a designated accounting standard setter, excluding required supplementary information.
Applicable financial reporting framework	The financial reporting framework used by management and those charged with governance in preparing the financial statements that is acceptable given the nature of the entity and the objective of the financial statements, or that is required by law or regulation.
Prescribed guidelines	The authoritative guidelines established by the designated accounting standard setter for the methods of measurement and presentation of the required supplementary information.

Requirements

The auditor is presumptively required to perform the following procedures in fulfilling responsibilities related to required supplementary information.

Procedures

1. Apply the following procedures to required supplementary information:

    a. Inquire of management about methods of preparing the information, including whether it has been prepared according to prescribed guidelines, whether any significant assumptions or interpretations underlie its measurement or presentation, and whether measurement or presentation methods have changed since the prior period and reasons for such changes.

    b. Compare the information for consistency with management's responses to the foregoing inquiries, the audited financial statements, and other knowledge obtained during the financial statement audit.

    c. Obtain written representations from management regarding the topics of management inquiry and acknowledging responsibility for the required supplementary information.

2. If unable to complete these procedures, consider whether management contributed to the inability to complete the procedures, and, if so, inform those charged with governance.

Reporting

3. Include an explanatory paragraph after the opinion paragraph in the auditor's report referring to the required supplementary information. If some or all of the required supplementary information is presented, the explanatory paragraph should include the following elements:

    a. A statement that [identify the applicable financial reporting framework] require that the [identify the required supplementary information] be presented to supplement the basic financial statements.

    b. A statement that such information, although not a part of the basic financial statements, is required by [identify designated accounting standard setter] who considers it to be an essential part of financial reporting and for placing the basic financial statements in an appropriate operational, economic, or historical context.

c. If the auditor is able to complete the prescribed procedures related to the required supplementary information: (1) a statement that the auditor has applied limited procedures, which consisted of inquiries of management and other limited procedures, as prescribed by auditing standards generally accepted in the United States of America regarding the methods of measurement and presentation of the required supplementary information; and (2) a statement that the limited procedures do not provide the auditor with evidence sufficient to express an opinion or any other form of assurance on the information.

d. If the auditor is unable to complete the prescribed procedures related to the required supplementary information: (1) a statement that the auditor was unable to apply to the information certain limited procedures prescribed by auditing standards generally accepted in the United States of America because [state the reasons]; and (2) a statement that the auditor does not express an opinion or any other form of assurance on the information.

e. If some of the required supplementary information is omitted: (1) a statement that management has omitted [description of the missing required supplementary information] that [identify the applicable financial reporting framework] require to be presented to supplement the basic financial statements; (2) a statement that such missing information, although not a part of the basic financial statements, is required by [identify designated accounting standard setter] who considers it to be an essential part of financial reporting and for placing the basic financial statements in an appropriate operational, economic, or historical context; and (3) a statement that the auditor's opinion on the basic financial statements is not affected by the missing information.

f. If the measurement or presentation of the required supplementary information departs materially from prescribed guidelines, a statement that the auditor's opinion on the basic financial statements is not affected but that material departures from prescribed guidelines exist [describe the material departures from the applicable financial reporting framework].

g. If the auditor has unresolved doubts about whether the required supplementary information conforms to prescribed guidelines, a statement that although the auditor's opinion on the basic financial statements is not affected, the results of the limited procedures have raised doubts regarding whether material modifications should be made to the information for it to conform with guidelines established by [identify designated accounting standard setter].

4. If all of the required supplementary information is omitted, the explanatory paragraph should just include the statements described in requirement 3e (above).

Analysis and Application of Procedures

Reporting

Required supplementary information is not part of the basic financial statements, so the auditor's opinion on the financial statements is not affected by the entity's presentation or lack of presentation of the required supplementary information. If the entity omits presentation of required supplementary information, the auditor does not have a responsibility to present it.

Practitioner's Aid

Exhibit AU 558-1 provides an example of an explanatory paragraph that can be used in the auditor's report when the required supplementary information is included, the auditor has applied the specified procedures, and no material departures from the prescribed guidelines have been identified.

EXHIBIT AU558-1 — EXPLANATORY PARAGRAPH WHEN REPORTING ON SUPPLEMENTARY INFORMATION

[Identify the applicable financial reporting framework (for example, accounting principles generally accepted in the United States of America)] require that the [*identify the required supplementary information*] on page XX be presented to supplement the basic financial statements. Such information, although not a part of the basic financial statements, is required by [*identify designated accounting standard setter*] who considers it to be an essential part of financial reporting for placing the basic financial statements in an appropriate operational, economic, or historical context. We have applied certain limited procedures to the required supplementary information in accordance with auditing standards generally accepted in the United States of America, which consisted of inquiries of management about

the methods of preparing the information and comparing the information for consistency with management's responses to our inquiries, the basic financial statements, and other knowledge we obtained during our audit of the basic financial statements. We do not express an opinion or provide any assurance on the information, because the limited procedures do not provide us with sufficient evidence to express an opinion or provide any assurance.

SECTION 560

SUBSEQUENT EVENTS

Authoritative Pronouncements

SAS-1 — Codification of Auditing Standards and Procedures (Section 560, Subsequent Events)

SAS-12 — Inquiry of a Client's Lawyer Concerning Litigation, Claims, and Assessments

SAS-98 — Omnibus Statement on Auditing Standards — 2002

SAS-113 — Omnibus Statement on Auditing Standards — 2006

> **IMPORTANT NOTICE FOR 2011:** The Auditing Standards Board (ASB) is in the process of redrafting all of the auditing sections in *Codification of Statements on Auditing Standards* to converge U.S. GAAS with the International Standards on Auditing issued by the International Auditing and Assurance Standards Board. As part of this process, the newly redrafted standards will follow certain clarity drafting conventions adopted by the ASB. These clarity drafting conventions include (1) establishing objectives for each standard; (2) including a definitions section, if appropriate; and (3) separating requirements from application guidance and other material. The ASB is planning to have all redrafted standards become effective on the same date, which is for audits of financial statements for periods ending on or after December 15, 2012. It is possible that the effective date might be delayed beyond that date. The ASB's clarity and convergence project will have a significant effect on the auditing standards applicable to audits of non-public companies, and the 2012 *GAAS Guide* will be appropriately modified to reflect these changes once the effective date of the standards is certain.

Overview

The auditor is responsible for collecting audit evidence pertaining to events that occur subsequent to the balance sheet date. Generally, the responsibility for identifying significant subsequent events continues through the date of the auditor's report, which is the date the auditor has gathered sufficient appropriate evidence to support the audit opinion. Subsequent events may affect the financial statements in two ways. First, the event may provide the basis for an adjusting entry at the date of the balance sheet. This occurs when the subsequent event affects the valuation of any account as of the balance sheet date. Second, the event may not affect the valuations at the balance sheet date, because the event is not associated with assets or liabilities that existed at the balance sheet date. For this reason, the subsequent event does not require an accrual adjustment, but it is likely to be disclosed in the financial statements.

> **PLANNING AID REMINDER:** It is sometimes difficult to classify a subsequent event, because usually there is an informational lag period between the date the auditor becomes aware of the event and the actual identification of the economic event that affects the valuation of an account. For example, during the subsequent-event period, a competitor might announce a new product that places a client's product at a significant disadvantage and probably requires an inventory write-down. Although the product announcement occurred after the balance sheet date, it is likely that the technological breakthrough occurred on or before the balance sheet date. Of course, it becomes speculative to try to pinpoint the economic event, because the client and the auditor probably have limited information. For this reason, SAS-1 states that subsequent events that affect the realization of receivables and inventories and the settlement of estimated liabilities generally require an adjustment to the financial statements.

> **PLANNING AID REMINDER:** SAS-98 makes it clear that the responsibilities described in this section apply only to subsequent events that may have existed as of the date of the balance sheet but before the financial statements are issued. They do not apply to events that occur after auditor's report date.

Promulgated Procedures Checklist

The auditor should use the following approach to identify and account for subsequent events that occur after the end of the client's fiscal year:

- Employ appropriate procedures to identify relevant subsequent events.

- Determine whether the subsequent event requires an audit adjustment.

- Determine whether the subsequent event requires disclosure in the financial statements.

Analysis and Application of Procedures

Employ appropriate procedures to identify relevant subsequent events

Audit procedures must be employed to obtain audit evidence associated with all subsequent events. These audit procedures may be classified as those associated with other phases of the audit engagement and those specifically designed to identify subsequent events. In many parts of the engagement, audit procedures call for the auditor to determine whether an account is presented in accordance with generally accepted accounting principles (GAAP) by reviewing subsequent events. For example, cash collected on account subsequent to the balance sheet date is associated with subsequent events, but it provides evidence to support the collectibility of accounts receivable as of the balance sheet date. However, SAS-1 identifies the following audit procedures that the auditor should perform in order to specifically identify possible subsequent events that might require an accrual adjustment or disclosure in the financial statements:

- Inquire of and discuss with members of management who have financial accounting responsibility whether:

  - Any material contingent liabilities or commitments existed at the date of the balance sheet or shortly thereafter.

  - Any significant change in owners' equity, long-term debt, or working capital has occurred since the balance sheet date.

  - Any material adjustments have been made during the subsequent period.

- Inquire of and discuss with members of management who have financial accounting responsibility the status of items that were accounted for in the financial statements on the basis of tentative or preliminary data.

- Read the available minutes of stockholders, directors, and other committee meetings during the subsequent period.

- Obtain from client's legal counsel a description and evaluation of any impending litigation, claims, and contingent liabilities.

- Obtain a letter of representation from management (usually the chief financial officer) dated as of the date of the auditor's report regarding any events occurring during the subsequent period that require adjustment to or disclosure in the financial statements.

- Follow any other procedures that are deemed appropriate depending on the results of the procedures described above.

Determine whether the subsequent event requires an audit adjustment

As noted earlier, SAS-1 describes two types of subsequent events. The first type relates to "events that provide additional evidence with respect to conditions that existed at the date of the balance sheet and affect the estimates inherent in the process of preparing financial statements." Evidence available to the auditor before the issuance of the financial statements should be used to evaluate estimates used by management. The auditor evaluates these estimates in light of subsequent events by making inquiries of management and having a current knowledge of the technological factors that affect the client's operations.

Determine whether the subsequent event requires disclosure
in the financial statements

The second type of subsequent event relates to "events that provide evidence with respect to conditions that did not exist at the date of the balance sheet being reported on but arose subsequent to that date." An example of this type of subsequent event would be fire or flood damages to property, plant, and equipment that occurred after the date of the balance sheet. The auditor may discover this type of subsequent event by reviewing the minutes of the board of directors' meetings after the balance sheet date, making inquiries of management, and obtaining written representations from management.

> **PLANNING AID REMINDER:** Examples of subsequent events that do not require an accrual adjustment are the issuance of additional capital stock or losses resulting from fire or flood after the balance sheet date. The second type of subsequent event is usually disclosed in a note to the financial statements. If the event is material, however, it may be more appropriate to show the effects of the subsequent event in the form of pro forma financial statements supplementary to the financial statements. The pro forma statement is presented as if the subsequent event had occurred on the last day of the period being audited.

Practitioner's Aids

Exhibit AU 560-1 illustrates an audit program for subsequent events.

EXHIBIT AU 560-1 — SUBSEQUENT EVENTS AUDIT PROGRAM

Use the following procedures as a guide to identify subsequent events that occur after the date of the financial statements but before the date of our audit report. This audit program is only a guide, and professional judgment should be exercised to determine how it should be modified by revising or adding procedures.

Initial and date each procedure as it is completed. If the procedure is not relevant to this particular engagement, place "N/A" (not applicable) in the space provided for an initial.

Client Name: _____

Date of Financial Statements: _____

Audit Report Date: _____

	Initials	*Date*	*Audit Documentation Reference*
1. Inquire of and discuss with appropriate management personnel whether any material contingent liabilities or commitments existed at the date of the balance sheet or shortly thereafter.	____	____	_____
2. Inquire of and discuss with appropriate management personnel whether any significant change in owners' equity, long-term debt, or working capital has occurred since the date of the balance sheet.	____	____	_____
3. Inquire of and discuss with appropriate management personnel whether any material adjustments have been made during the subsequent period.	____	____	_____
4. Inquire of and discuss with appropriate management personnel the status of items that were accounted for in the financial statements on the basis of tentative or preliminary data.	____	____	_____
5. Read the latest minutes of stockholders', directors', and other committee meetings that occurred during the subsequent period.	____	____	_____

	Initials	*Date*	*Audit Documentation Reference*

6. Obtain from the client's legal counsel a description and evaluation of any impending litigation, claims, and contingent liabilities. ___ ___ _____

7. Obtain a letter of representation from management regarding any events occurring during the subsequent period that require adjustment or disclosure. ___ ___ _____

8. Read the latest interim financial statements and compare them to (a) the year-end financial statements and (b) the interim financial information for the previous year. ___ ___ _____

9. Review journal entries made after the end of the year for unusual amounts, unusual activity, or other unusual characteristics. ___ ___ _____

10. Determine whether the client is considering changing any of its accounting policies or procedures. ___ ___ _____

11. Perform any other procedures deemed appropriate depending on the results of the procedures described above. ___ ___ _____

Reviewed by: _____

Date: _____

SECTION 561

SUBSEQUENT DISCOVERY OF FACTS EXISTING AT THE DATE OF THE AUDITOR'S REPORT

Authoritative Pronouncements

SAS-1 — Codification of Auditing Standards and Procedures (Section 561, Subsequent Discovery of Facts Existing at the Date of the Auditor's Report)

SAS-98 — Omnibus Statement on Auditing Standards — 2002

Auditing Interpretation No. 1 of AU 561 (February 1989) — Auditor's Association with Subsequently Discovered Information When the Auditor Has Resigned or Been Discharged

> **IMPORTANT NOTICE FOR 2011:** The Auditing Standards Board (ASB) is in the process of redrafting all of the auditing sections in *Codification of Statements on Auditing Standards* to converge U.S. GAAS with the International Standards on Auditing issued by the International Auditing and Assurance Standards Board. As part of this process, the newly redrafted standards will follow certain clarity drafting conventions adopted by the ASB. These clarity drafting conventions include (1) establishing objectives for each standard; (2) including a definitions section, if appropriate; and (3) separating requirements from application guidance and other material. The ASB is planning to have all redrafted standards become effective on the same date, which is for audits of financial statements for periods ending on or after December 15, 2012. It is possible that the effective date might be delayed beyond that date. The ASB's clarity and convergence project will have a significant effect on the auditing standards applicable to audits of non-public companies, and the 2012 *GAAS Guide* will be appropriately modified to reflect these changes once the effective date of the standards is certain.

Overview

Although the auditor is not required to continue auditing after the date of the report, in some instances he or she discovers facts after the report date that could impact the audited financial statements. The discovery of such facts may occur when the auditor performs interim audit work or other nonaudit service for the client.

> **OBSERVATION:** SAS-98 makes it clear that the responsibilities described in this section apply only to subsequent events that may have existed as of the date of the auditor's report and not the date the report was issued.

Promulgated Procedures Checklist

The auditor should perform the following procedures with respect to discovery of facts existing at the date of the auditor's report:

- Determine whether the discovered facts are relevant to the audited financial statements.

- If the discovered facts are considered relevant, take appropriate measures with respect to the audited financial statements.

- If the client does not cooperate with the auditor's conclusions and proposed remedies, notify the client's board of directors.

- If the client refuses to cooperate, communicate the problem to appropriate parties.

Analysis and Application of Procedures

Determine whether the discovered facts are relevant to the audited financial statements

If the auditor becomes aware (1) of material information that would have affected the report and (2) that persons are currently relying, or are likely to rely, on the financial statements covered by the report, the auditor should contact the client and discuss the matter with appropriate management personnel.

If the discovered facts are considered relevant, the auditor should take appropriate measures with respect to the audited financial statements

After appropriate discussion, if both the client and the auditor agree that the discovered facts are relevant to the audited financial statements, the auditor and client should take the following steps:

- The client should issue revised financial statements, and the auditor should issue a new report as soon as practical, describing the reasons for revision.

- If financial statements, accompanied by an auditor's report for a subsequent period, are to be issued imminently, the auditor may make the necessary disclosures and revisions therein.

- If doing so is appropriate, the client should be advised to discuss the new disclosures or revisions with the Securities and Exchange Commission (SEC), stock exchanges, and appropriate regulatory agencies where applicable.

- The auditor must satisfy himself or herself that the client has taken appropriate steps.

The auditor should document the following:

- When and by whom additional auditing procedures were performed as a result of subsequent discovery of facts that existed at the date of the report but that were not known to the auditor at that time

- When and by whom these additional procedures were reviewed

- The results obtained from performing any additional audit procedures

- The effect on the auditor's conclusions (including the continuing appropriateness of the original audit opinion issued) as a result of the subsequent discovery of facts that existed at the date of the audit report.

If the client does not cooperate with the auditor's conclusions and proposed remedies, the client's board of directors should be notified

If the client refuses to proceed as outlined above, the auditor should notify each member of the client's board of directors that (1) the client has refused to cooperate with the auditor in disclosing these subsequently discovered facts and (2) in the absence of disclosure by the client, to prevent further reliance on the report and the financial statements, the auditor will take the following additional steps:

- Notify any regulatory agencies involved, if applicable, that the report should no longer be relied on.

- Notify persons known to be relying, or likely to rely, on the financial statements that the auditor's report should no longer be relied on.

These notifications should contain the following:

- A description of the effects of the newly discovered information on the auditor's report and on the financial statements

- The most precise and factual information available about the financial statement misstatement

If the client refuses to cooperate, the auditor should communicate the problem to appropriate parties

In those circumstances where the client refuses to cooperate and, as a result, the auditor is unable to conduct an adequate investigation of the new information, the auditor's notifications need state only that new information has come to his or her attention and that if the new information is correct, the report should no longer be relied on or be associated with the financial statements.

> **ENGAGEMENT STRATEGY:** The auditor must use professional judgment in the circumstances described above. Consultation with legal counsel is usually advisable.

> **ENGAGEMENT STRATEGY:** Interpretation No. 1 of AU 561 states that the auditor's responsibility to investigate whether subsequently discovered information existed at the date of the auditor's report does not change even when the auditor has resigned or been discharged from the engagement.

Practitioner's Aids

EXHIBIT AU 561-1 — DISCOVERY OF FACTS AFTER THE DATE OF THE REPORT

Use the following procedures, which are adapted from guidance found in SAS-1, AU 561 (Subsequent Discovery of Facts Existing at the Date of the Auditor's Report), as a guide for evaluating the discovery of facts after the date of the report. The program is only a guide, and professional judgment should be exercised to determine how the guidance established in the auditing standard should be adapted to a particular engagement.

Initial and date each procedure as it is completed. If the procedure is not relevant to this engagement, place "N/A" (not applicable) in the space provided for an initial.

Client Name: _____

Date of Financial Statements: _____

	Initials	*Date*	*Audit Documentation Reference*

1. Determine whether the discovered facts are relevant to the financial statements by considering the following factors:

   • The report would have been affected if the CPA had known the information at the date of the audit report, _____ ____ _____

   • The matter would have been reflected in the financial statements, and _____ ____ _____

   • The CPA believes that there are third-party users relying on or likely to rely on the financial statements who would attach importance to the subsequently discovered information. _____ ____ _____

2. If the conditions described in 1 above exist, advise the client to inform third-party users currently relying or likely to rely on the financial statements, following the general guidance:

   • When the effects of the subsequently discovered information can be determined quickly, and the issuance of more current financial statements is not imminent, revised financial statements and a revised report should be issued. (Both the financial statements and the report should describe the reason for the revision.) _____ ____ _____

	Initials	Date	*Audit Documentation Reference*

- When the issuance of more recent financial statements is imminent, the disclosure of the revision can be made in the more recent financial statements; the earlier financial statements need not be reissued.

- When the effects of the subsequently discovered information cannot be determined without a prolonged investigation, third-party users who are currently relying or likely to rely on the financial statements and the associated report should be notified not to rely on them and should be informed that revised financial statements and a revised audit report will be issued when an investigation is completed.

3. If the client refuses to make appropriate disclosures to third-party users, inform each member of the board of directors of the refusal.

4. If the board of directors is notified but appropriate disclosures to third-party users still are not made, discuss the matter with legal counsel.

	Initials	*Date*	*Audit Documentation Reference*

5. If it appears there are or will be third-party users who will rely on the financial statements, consider the following:

- Notify the client that the CPA's report should no longer be associated with the client's financial statements.   ___ ___ _____

- Notify regulatory agencies having jurisdiction over the client that the CPA's report should no longer be associated with the client's financial statements.   ___ ___ _____

- To the extent practical, the CPA should notify each third-party user known to be relying on the financial statements that the auditor's report should no longer be relied upon.   ___ ___ _____

6. If the matters have been satisfactorily investigated and the subsequent information considered reliable, disclosures to regulatory authorities and third-party users should include the following:

- The nature of the subsequently acquired information and the effects on the financial statements.   ___ ___ _____

	Initials	Date	*Audit Documentation Reference*

- The effects of the subsequently acquired information on the CPA's report, if the information had been known to him or her at the date of the report and it had not been reflected in the financial statements. _____ ____ _____

7. If a satisfactory investigation is not conducted, make the following disclosure to regulatory authorities and third-party users:

- Describe the general nature of the problem (specific details are not required). _____ ____ _____

- State that the effects of the problem cannot be substantiated because the client did not cooperate in the investigation of the matter. _____ ____ _____

- State that if the information is correct, the CPA believes that his or her report should no longer be associated with the client's financial statements. No disclosure should be made unless the CPA believes that the financial statements are likely to be misleading and that his or her audit report should no longer be relied upon. _____ ____ _____

8. Other engagement procedures: _____
   _____

Reviewed by: _____

Date: _____
_____

AU 600

Other Types of Reports

Section 623: Special Reports 629

Section 625: Reports on the Application of Accounting
    Principles 655

Section 634: Letters for Underwriters and Certain
    Other Requesting Parties 663

SECTION 623

SPECIAL REPORTS

Authoritative Pronouncements

SAS-62 — Special Reports

SAS-77 — Amendments to Statements on Auditing Standards No. 22, "Planning and Supervision," No. 59, "The Auditor's Consideration of an Entity's Ability to Continue as a Going Concern," and SAS-62, "Special Reports"

Auditing Interpretation No. 9 (October 2000) — Auditors' Special Reports on Property and Liability Insurance Companies' Loss Reserves

Auditing Interpretation No. 10 (October 2000) — Reports on the Financial Statements Included in Internal Revenue Form 990 (Return of Organizations Exempt from Income Taxes)

Auditing Interpretation No. 11 (October 2000) — Reporting on Current-Value Financial Statements That Supplement Historical-Cost Financial Statements in a Presentation of Real Estate Entities

Auditing Interpretation No. 12 (January 2005) — Evaluation of the Appropriateness of Informative Disclosures in Insurance Enterprises' Financial Statements Prepared on a Statutory Basis

Auditing Interpretation No. 13 (February 1999) — Reporting on a Special-Purpose Financial Statement That Results in an Incomplete Presentation but Is Otherwise in Conformity with GAAP

Auditing Interpretation 14 (January 2005) — Evaluating the Adequacy of Disclosure and Presentation in Financial Statements Prepared in Conformity with an Other Comprehensive Basis of Accounting (OCBOA)

Auditing Interpretation 15 (January 2005) — Auditor Reports on Regulatory Accounting or Presentation When the Regulated Entity Distributes the Financial Statements to Parties Other Than the Regulatory Agency Either Voluntarily or Upon Specific Request

IMPORTANT NOTICE FOR 2011: The Auditing Standards Board (ASB) is in the process of redrafting all of the auditing sections in *Codification of Statements on Auditing Standards* to converge U.S. GAAS with the International Standards on Auditing issued by the International Auditing and Assurance

Standards Board. As part of this process, the newly redrafted standards will follow certain clarity drafting conventions adopted by the ASB. These clarity drafting conventions include: (1) establishing objectives for each standard; (2) including a definitions section, if appropriate; and (3) separating requirements from application guidance and other material. The ASB is planning to have all redrafted standards become effective on the same date, which is for audits of financial statements for periods ending on or after December 15, 2012. It is possible that the effective date might be delayed beyond that date. The ASB's clarity and convergence project will have a significant effect on the auditing standards applicable to audits of nonpublic companies, and the 2012 *GAAS Guide* will be appropriately modified to reflect these changes once the effective date of the standards is certain.

Overview

An auditor may be engaged to report on financial statements that are prepared on a comprehensive basis of accounting that is not GAAP or information presentations that do not constitute a set of financial statements. These reporting situations are discussed in this section.

Promulgated Procedures Checklist

The auditor may issue a special report in any one of the following five broad categories:

- Reporting on a comprehensive basis of accounting other than generally accepted accounting principles (GAAP)

- Reporting on specified elements, accounts, or items of a financial statement

- Reporting on compliance with contractual agreements or regulatory requirements related to audited financial statements

- Reporting on financial presentations to comply with contractual agreements or regulatory provisions

- Reporting on financial information presented in prescribed forms or schedules

Analysis and Application of Procedures

Reporting on a comprehensive basis of accounting other than GAAP

Financial statements may be issued by all types of entities or segments of entities, including commercial enterprises, not-for-profit organizations, individuals, estates, and governmental units. SAS-62 defines a "financial statement" as a "presentation of financial data, including accompanying notes, derived from accounting records that are intended to communicate an entity's economic resources or obligations at a point in time or the changes therein for a period of time in conformity with a comprehensive basis of accounting." For reporting purposes, SAS-62 considers a "financial statement" to consist of a statement of (1) financial position (balance sheet), (2) income or operations, (3) retained earnings, (4) cash flows, (5) changes in owners' equity, (6) assets and liabilities (excludes owners' equity accounts), (7) revenues and expenses, (8) summary of operations, (9) operations by product lines, and (10) cash receipts and disbursements. This broad definition does not restrict financial statements to those that are prepared in accordance with GAAP. Thus, an entity may prepare and issue a financial statement based on a comprehensive basis of accounting other than GAAP.

When financial statements based on an other comprehensive basis of accounting (OCBOA) are prepared, the accountant should determine whether the financial statements are properly labeled. Care must be taken in titling financial statements so that a reader of the statements will not infer that the financial statements are prepared in accordance with GAAP.

The earlier definition of "financial statement" referred to a presentation of financial data that intends to communicate an entity's economic resources or obligations in accordance with generally accepted accounting principles or a comprehensive basis of accounting other than generally accepted accounting principles. When GAAP-based financial statements are presented, such a statement is referred to as a balance sheet or a statement of financial position. When OCBOA-based financial statements are presented, it would be inappropriate to refer to the statement as a balance sheet or a statement of financial position. Instead, for example, if the financial statements are prepared on a modified cash basis, the title might be "Statement of Assets and Liabilities—Modified Cash Basis." If the financial statements are prepared on a regulatory accounting basis an appropriate name would be "Balance Sheet—Regulatory Accounting Basis."

The definitions of "financial statement" in Statement on Standards for Accounting and Review Services (SSARS) No. 1 (SSARS-1) (AR 100) (Compilation and Review of Financial Statements) and SAS-62 refer to presenting financial data related to changes in an entity's economic resources and obligations. When GAAP-based financial statements are presented, they are referred to as an income statement or a statement of operations. When OCBOA-based financial statements are presented, more appropriate names may be "Statement of Cash Receipts and Disbursements" (for a cash-based financial statement) and "Statement of Revenues and Expenses — Income Tax Basis" (for a tax-based financial statement).

A financial statement or presentation should be clearly and accurately titled. If the auditor concludes that a financial statement or presentation is not properly titled, an explanatory paragraph should be added to the auditor's special report, and the opinion on the statement or presentation should be qualified.

> **PLANNING AID REMINDER:** Under SAS-58 (AU 508) (Reports on Audited Financial Statements), if an auditor is requested to report on only one financial statement from a set of financial statements, there is no scope limitation of the audit. Under SAS-58 (AU 508), this type of engagement is classified as a limited reporting engagement.

Under the provisions of SAS-62, a comprehensive basis of accounting other than generally accepted accounting principles is restricted to the following.

- A basis of accounting that the reporting entity uses to comply with the requirements or financial reporting provisions of a governmental regulatory agency to whose jurisdiction the entity is subject

- A basis of accounting that the reporting entity uses or expects to use to file its income tax return for the period covered by the financial statements

- The cash receipts and disbursements basis of accounting, and modifications of the cash basis having substantial support, such as recording depreciation on fixed assets or accruing income taxes

- A definite set of criteria having substantial support that is applied to all material items appearing in financial statements, such as the price-level basis of accounting

> **PLANNING AID REMINDER:** Interpretation No. 11 of AU 623 states that an engagement to report on current-value financial statements that supplement historical-cost financial statements of a real estate entity may be accepted only if (1) the current-value financial statements are based on measurement and disclosure criteria that are reasonable and (2) the current-value financial statements are reliable (competent persons using the same criteria would arrive at similar financial statements that are not materially different from one another).

If an entity reports on a comprehensive basis of accounting not listed above, the auditor should determine whether the special-basis financial statements are presented in a manner that results in a material deviation from GAAP. If the entity is a business entity, the GAAP hierarchy is now codified in the accounting literature in accordance with ASC 105 (FAS-168) (see AU 411 for further discussion). If the entity is a governmental entity, the GAAP hierarchy is still codified in SAS-69 (AU 411) (The Meaning of "Present Fairly in Conformity with Generally Accepted Accounting Principles"). If the deviation(s) from GAAP is considered material, the auditor should observe the reporting standards established by SAS-58 (AU 508) when preparing his or her special report. That is, the auditor should express a qualified or adverse opinion on the financial statements.

Adequate disclosure

Generally accepted auditing standards are applicable to the audit of financial statements prepared in conformity with an other comprehensive basis of accounting. Thus, the auditor must consider the third reporting standard (adequate informative disclosures).

In determining whether financial statements prepared in conformity with an other comprehensive basis of accounting satisfy the adequate disclosure criterion, the auditor should consider the following concepts established in SAS-69 (AU 411):

- The accounting principles selected and applied should have general acceptance.

- The accounting principles should be appropriate in the circumstances.

- The financial statements, including the related notes, should be informative of matters that may affect their use, understanding, and interpretation.

- The information presented in the financial statements should be classified and summarized in a reasonable manner; that is, it should be neither too detailed nor too condensed.

- The financial statements should reflect the underlying events and transactions (in a manner that satisfies the purpose of the financial statements) within a range of acceptable limits; that is, limits that are reasonable and practicable to attain in financial statements.

The notes to the financial statements should include a summary of significant accounting policies to describe the basis of presentation and how the presentation differs from a presentation that conforms with GAAP.

> **ENGAGEMENT STRATEGY:** Interpretation No. 14 of AU 623 discusses the requirement established by AU 623 that OCBOA-based financial statements contain a summary of significant accounting policies that explains the basis of presentation and how that basis differs from generally accepted accounting principles. The Interpretation states that the disclosure may be brief, using language such as "The accompanying financial statements present financial results on the accrual basis of accounting used for federal income tax reporting." In addition, only the primary differences between GAAP and the tax basis need be included in the disclosure. Quantifying the differences is not necessary.

Finally, items that are presented as part of a financial statement prepared in conformity with an other comprehensive basis of accounting that are similar to items that would be presented as part of GAAP-based financial statements should include related disclosures that would be similar to disclosures that would appear in the GAAP-based financial statements. For example, if long-term debt is presented in financial statements prepared on a modified cash basis, information related to the terms, maturity, description, and restrictions of long-term debt must be disclosed. In addition, information on discontinued operations, extraordinary items, and accounting changes may be shown in the financial statement notes rather than on the face of the income statement. And disclosures that are not relevant to the basis of accounting are not required; for example, the disclosures related to estimates required by SOP 94-6 (Disclosure of Certain Significant Risks and Uncertainties) are not required in a cash basis presentation.

> **PLANNING AID REMINDER:** There is no comprehensive list of minimum disclosures for OCBOA-based financial statements. Professional judgment must be used to determine whether the basic concept of adequate disclosure has been achieved in the OCBOA-based financial statements.

> **PLANNING AID REMINDER:** Interpretation No. 12 of AU 623 states that the auditor should use the same analysis that is used in the evaluation of GAAP-based financial statements to determine whether financial statements based on accounting standards established by insurance regulators (statutory basis) satisfy the criterion of informative disclosure required by the third standard of reporting. Insurance companies should follow GAAP when preparing general-purpose financial statements and should follow appropriate accounting procedures established by each state's insurance department when preparing statutory financial statements. However, even when

preparing statutory financial statements, items included in an OCBOA set of financial statements that are the same as, or similar to, items included in a GAAP set of financial statements should have similar disclosures. This requirement holds even though the National Association of Insurance Commissioners' (NAIC) Accounting Practices and Procedures Manual states that "GAAP pronouncements do not become part of Statutory Accounting Principles until and unless adopted by the NAIC." GAAP pronouncements may not become part of Statutory Accounting Principles, but the disclosure provisions of these pronouncements remain binding on the external auditor in accounting for items that are the same (or similar) in an OCBOA presentation as in a GAAP presentation.

Reporting standards

The title of the special auditor's report should include the word "independent." In addition, the report should have a manual or printed signature and be dated no earlier than the date on which the auditor has obtained sufficient appropriate evidence to support the opinion.

SAS-62 requires that a four-paragraph format be used as the standard special report. The content of each paragraph is described in the following:

• Introductory paragraph

— State that the financial statements identified in the report were audited.

— State that the financial statements are the responsibility of company's management and that the auditor is responsible for expressing an opinion on the financial statements based on the audit.

• Scope paragraph

— State that the audit was conducted in accordance with U.S. generally accepted auditing standards (GAAS).

— State that GAAS require that the auditor plan and perform the audit to obtain reasonable assurance about whether the financial statements are free of material misstatement.

— State that an audit includes examining, on a test basis, evidence supporting the amounts and disclosures in the financial statements.

— State that an audit includes assessing the accounting principles used and significant estimates made by management.

— State that an audit includes evaluating the overall financial statement presentation.

— State that the auditor believes that his or her audit provides a reasonable basis for the opinion.

> **PUBLIC COMPANY IMPLICATION:** For public companies, an audit report on financial statements prepared using a comprehensive basis of accounting other than GAAP or on information presentations that do not constitute a set of financial statements must state that the audit was conducted in accordance with standards of the Public Company Accounting Oversight Board.

• Presentation basis paragraph

— State the basis of presentation and refer to the note to the financial statements that describes the basis.

— State that the basis of presentation is a comprehensive basis of accounting other than generally accepted accounting principles.

• Opinion paragraph

— Express an opinion on whether the financial statements are presented fairly, in all material respects, in conformity with the basis of accounting described.

Exhibit AU 623-1 is an example of a special auditor's report on financial statements prepared on the cash basis.

> **PLANNING AID REMINDER:** When financial statements that are prepared on a regulatory basis of accounting are to be generally distributed, the standard report form, as established by SAS-58 (AU 508), should be modified for departures from generally accepted accounting principles. The standard report may include an additional paragraph that expresses an opinion on whether the financial statements are presented in conformity with the regulatory basis of accounting.

When the auditor is reporting on financial statements that are prepared in conformity with accounting procedures established by a governmental regulatory agency, an additional paragraph should be included in the standard special auditor's report. The additional paragraph should state that the use of the report is for those within the entity or for filing with the regulatory agency. This additional paragraph should be included even though by law or regulation the report is part of the public record.

A regulated entity may distribute its financial statements, prepared using an OCBOA, to parties other than its regulatory agency either voluntarily or upon specific request. According to Interpretation 15 of AU 623, in this situation the auditor is precluded from using the report presented in Exhibit AU 623-1. Rather, the auditor must report using the guidance in AU 544 (Lack of Conformity with Generally Accepted Accounting Principles). The auditor's report is to be modified for the departure from GAAP and then in an additional paragraph he or she can opine on whether the financial statements are prepared in accordance with a regulatory basis of accounting. Exhibit AU 623-2 illustrates an auditor's report on an OCBOA-basis set of financial statements (prepared using a regulatory basis) when the regulated entity distributes the financial statements to parties other than its regulator, either voluntarily or upon receipt of a specific request.

Reporting on specified elements, accounts, or items of a financial statement

An auditor may be engaged to report on a specified element(s), account(s), or item(s) of a financial statement. Even though an engagement of this nature is limited in its scope, generally accepted auditing standards must be satisfied.

> **OBSERVATION:** The first reporting standard would not be applicable if the element, account, or item is presented on a basis other than GAAP. The other basis of accounting should not be confused with a comprehensive basis of accounting discussed earlier. For example, the other basis of accounting could be derived from a clause contained in a contract.

An engagement to express an opinion on an element, account, or item of a financial statement may be conducted as part of the audit of the financial statements or undertaken as a separate engagement. The basis for materiality in the limited-scope audit is the specific element, account, or item being reported on, and for this reason, generally a more detailed audit of the element, account, or item would be conducted.

> **PLANNING AID REMINDER:** Although the engagement may be limited to reporting on a specified element, account, or item of a financial statement, the scope of the audit includes all related matters and, if appropriate, other related accounts. For example, an engagement to report on accounts receivable requires that the credit sales system and the cash receipts system as part of the entity's internal control be considered.

ENGAGEMENT STRATEGY: SAS-62 states that "if a specified element, account, or item is, or is based on, an entity's net income or stockholders' equity or the equivalent thereof, the auditor should have audited the complete financial statements to express an opinion on the specified element, account, or item."

Reporting standards

When reporting on specified elements, accounts, or items, the title of the special auditor's report should include the word "independent." The following format should be used in the preparation of the standard special auditor's report on a specified element, account, or item of a financial statement:

- Introductory paragraph

  — State that the specified element, account, or item identified in the report was audited.

  — State, if applicable, that the audit was made in conjunction with the audit of the entity's financial statements. (Also disclose the date of the auditor's report and describe any departure from the standard auditor's report on the financial statement if the basis for the departure is considered relevant to the evaluation of the specified element, account, or item.)

  — State that the specified element, account, or item is the responsibility of the company's management and that the auditor is responsible for expressing an opinion on the specified element, account, or item based on the audit.

- Scope paragraph

  — State that the audit was conducted in accordance with GAAS.

  — State that GAAS require that the auditor plan and perform the audit to obtain reasonable assurance about whether the specified element, account, or item is free of material misstatement.

  — State that an audit includes examining, on a test basis, evidence supporting the amounts and disclosures in the presentation of the specified element, account, or item.

  — State that an audit includes assessing the accounting principles used and significant estimates made by management.

— State that an audit includes evaluating the overall presentation of the specified element, account, or item.

— State that the auditor believes that the audit provides a reasonable basis for his or her opinion.

- Presentation basis paragraph

— State the basis on which the specified element, account, or item is presented and, when applicable, any agreement specifying such basis if the presentation is not prepared in conformity with GAAP. (If the basis of presentation is another comprehensive basis of accounting, state so. Alternatively, the description contained in this paragraph may be incorporated into the introductory paragraph.)

- Opinion paragraph

— Express an opinion on whether the specified element, account, or item is fairly presented, in all material respects, in conformity with the basis of accounting described.

— If not presented fairly on the basis of accounting described or if the scope of the engagement has been limited, an explanatory paragraph preceding the opinion paragraph should state all substantive reasons for the above conclusions. The opinion paragraph should include modifying language and a reference to the explanatory paragraph(s).

When the auditor is reporting on a specified element, account, or item to satisfy a contract or agreement, and the information is not presented on a GAAP basis or an other comprehensive basis of accounting, an additional paragraph should be included in the standard special auditor's report. The additional paragraph should state that the distribution of the report is restricted solely to those that are parties to the contract or agreement. When the auditor is reporting on an element, account, or item that is presented on another comprehensive basis of accounting prescribed by a governmental regulatory agency, an additional paragraph should disclose that the distribution of the report is restricted solely to those within the entity and for filing with the regulatory agency. This additional paragraph should be included even though by law or regulation the report is part of the public record.

An additional paragraph may be added to the standard special auditor's report that describes the scope of the engagement in greater detail. SAS-62 permits an additional paragraph of this nature; however, the additional paragraph must be a separate paragraph and should not be merged into the standard scope paragraph described above.

Exhibit AU 623-3 is an example of a special auditor's report on accounts receivable.

SAS-62 states that a potential conflict exists when the auditor has expressed an adverse opinion or has disclaimed an opinion on the entity's basic financial statements, but has been requested to express an opinion on an element(s), account(s), or item(s) that is part of the basic financial statements. Under this circumstance, an opinion on the element, account, or item can be expressed only when the information being reported on does not constitute a major portion of the financial statement(s). To do otherwise would constitute a piecemeal opinion, which is prohibited by SAS-58 (AU 508). If the auditor decides to express an opinion on an element, account, or item, that report should be presented separately from the report on the entity's basic financial statements.

> **PLANNING AID REMINDER:** Interpretation No. 9 of AU 623 notes that the auditor should follow the guidance established by AU 623 (paragraphs 11 – 18) when he or she is requested to express an opinion on a company's loss and loss adjustment expense reserves and on the schedule of liabilities for losses and loss adjustment expenses that accompany the auditor's report on the financial statements filed by property and liability insurance company with state regulatory agencies.

Reporting on compliance with contractual agreements or regulatory requirements related to audited financial statements

Financial statement users, such as banks and regulatory agencies, may request that an entity's auditor specifically state whether the entity has observed a particular contract clause or administrative regulation. For example, a loan agreement may require that the entity's working capital not be less than a certain dollar amount. If the entity's financial statements are audited and the clause or regulation is subject to verification, the auditor may issue a negative assurance in an auditor's special report with respect to the contractual clause or regulation.

> **PLANNING AID REMINDER:** If compliance with laws and regulations consistent with *Government Auditing Standards* (the Yellow Book) is to be tested, the guidance established by SAS-116 (AU 801) (Compliance Audits) must be observed.

The negative assurance on matters contained in contractual agreements or regulatory requirements must have been related to the audit of the entity's basic financial statements. If an adverse opinion or disclaimer of opinion was expressed on the basic financial statements, a negative assurance on matters contained in contractual agreements or regulatory requirements should not be given.

> **PLANNING AID REMINDER:** If the matter for which the auditor is providing the assurance has not been subjected to auditing procedures as part of the audit of the entity's basic financial statements, guidance established in SSAE-3 (Compliance Attestation) should be followed.

Reporting standards

The negative assurance on the matter specified in the contractual agreement or regulatory requirement may be expressed in a separate report or added to the auditor's report on the basic financial statements.

Separate report

The title of the special auditor's report on matters contained in contractual agreements or regulatory requirements should include the word "independent." Also, the report should have a manual or printed signature and should be dated no earlier than the date on which the auditor has obtained sufficient appropriate audit evidence to support the opinion.

The separate report should be formatted in the manner described below.

* Introductory paragraph

  — State that the financial statements were audited in accordance with U.S. GAAS, include the date of the auditor's report on the audited financial statements, and, if applicable, disclose any departure from the standard auditor's report on the audited financial statements.

* Limited assurance paragraph

  — Identify the specific covenant or paragraphs of the agreement.

  — Provide a negative assurance on the aspects of the contractual agreement or regulatory requirements insofar as they relate to accounting matters.

— State that the negative assurance is being given in connection with the audit of the financial statements.

— State that the audit was not directed primarily toward obtaining knowledge regarding compliance with the contractual agreement or regulatory provision.

- Explanatory paragraph

  — Describe significant interpretations, if any, and their sources, that have been made by the entity's management relating to the contractual agreement or regulatory provision.

- Distribution paragraph

  — State that the distribution of the report is restricted to those within the entity and the parties to the contract or agreement or for filing with the regulatory agency.

Exhibit AU 623-4 is an example of a (separate) auditor's special report expressing a negative assurance on whether certain terms of a debt agreement have been observed.

Special report added to the standard audit report

The negative assurance on compliance with aspects of contractual agreements or regulatory requirements may be expressed in the auditor's report on the entity's basic financial statements. Under this reporting circumstance, three additional paragraphs, as described below, may need to be added to the standard (three-paragraph) auditor's report after the opinion paragraph.

- Fourth paragraph

  — Identify the specific covenant or paragraphs of the agreement.

  — Provide a negative assurance on the aspects of the contractual agreement or regulatory requirements insofar as they relate to accounting matters. Note that the negative assurance is being given in connection with the audit of the financial statements.

  — State that the audit was not directed primarily toward obtaining knowledge regarding compliance with the contractual agreement or regulatory provisions.

- Fifth paragraph

  — Describe significant interpretations, if any, and their sources, that the entity's management has made relating to the contractual agreement or regulatory provision.

- Sixth paragraph

  — State that the distribution of the report is restricted to those within the entity and the parties to the contract or agreement or for filing with the regulatory agency.

Reporting on financial presentations to comply with contractual agreements or regulatory provisions

An auditor may be requested to report on special-purpose financial statements that have been prepared to satisfy a contractual agreement or governmental regulatory requirements. SAS-62 identifies the following as types of special-purpose financial statement presentations:

> a. A special-purpose financial presentation prepared in compliance with a contractual agreement or regulatory provision that does not constitute a complete presentation of the entity's assets, liabilities, revenues and expenses, but is otherwise prepared in conformity with GAAP or an other comprehensive basis of accounting.

> b. A special-purpose financial presentation (may be a complete set of financial statements or a single financial statement) prepared on a basis of accounting prescribed in an agreement that does not result in a presentation in conformity with GAAP or an other comprehensive basis of accounting.

These special-purpose financial presentations are discussed below.

Incomplete presentations

Because of a contractual agreement or regulatory provision, an entity may be required to prepare a financial statement that is incomplete but nonetheless presents financial information that is prepared in accordance with GAAP or an other comprehensive basis of accounting. For example, an entity may be required by contract to present a statement of net assets sold as of a specific date. SAS-62 states that these presentations constitute a financial statement even though the presentations are incomplete, and accordingly, an auditor can express an opinion on incomplete financial presentations.

> **OBSERVATION:** Interpretation No. 13 of AU 623 states that an offering memorandum is not considered a "contractual agreement" as defined by SAS-62. However, an agreement between a client and a third party to prepare financial statements using a special-purpose presentation format is a "contractual agreement" as defined by SAS-62.

In the conduct of an engagement related to incomplete financial presentations, the basis for determining materiality should be the incomplete financial presentation taken as a whole. The presentation should omit only information that is not pertinent to satisfying the contractual agreement or regulatory provision. Information that is presented as part of the incomplete financial presentation and that is similar to information that would be presented as part of GAAP-based financial statements should include related disclosures that would be similar to disclosures that would appear in the GAAP-based financial statements. Finally, the incomplete financial presentation should be titled in a manner that would not suggest that the presentation is a complete financial statement.

Reporting standards

The title of the special auditor's report should include the word "independent," and the report should have a manual or printed signature. The report should be dated no earlier than the date on which the auditor has obtained sufficient appropriate audit evidence to support the opinion.

The format shown below should be used to prepare a special auditor's report on incomplete financial presentations.

*   Introductory paragraph

    — State that the financial statements identified in the report were audited.

    — State that the financial statements are the responsibility of the company's management and that the auditor is responsible for expressing an opinion on the financial statements based on the audit.

- Scope paragraph

  — State that the audit was conducted in accordance with U.S. GAAS.

  — State that GAAS require that the auditor plan and perform the audit to obtain reasonable assurance about whether the financial statements are free of material misstatement.

  — State that an audit includes examining, on a test basis, evidence supporting the amounts and disclosures in the financial statements.

  — State that an audit includes assessing the accounting principles used and significant estimates made by management.

  — State that an audit includes evaluating the overall financial statement presentation.

  — State that the auditor believes that the audit provides a reasonable basis for his or her opinion.

- Presentation basis paragraph

  — Explain what the presentation is intended to present and refer to the note to the special-purpose financial statements that describes the basis of presentation.

  — If the basis of presentation is in conformity with GAAP, state that the presentation is not intended to be a complete presentation of the entity's assets, liabilities, revenue, and expenses.

  — If the basis of presentation is an other comprehensive basis of accounting, state that the basis of presentation is a comprehensive basis of accounting other than GAAP and that it is not intended to be a complete presentation of the entity's assets, liabilities, revenues, and expenses on the basis described.

- Opinion paragraph

  — Express an opinion on whether the information is fairly presented, in all material respects.

  — State that the presentation is intended to present the information in conformity with U.S. GAAP or an other comprehensive basis of accounting.

- Distribution paragraph

  — State that the report is restricted to those within the entity, to the parties to the contract or agreement, for filing with a regulatory agency, or to those with whom the entity is negotiating directly. (A distribution paragraph is not necessary when the financial information must be filed with a regulatory agency and is to be included in a document that is distributed to the general public.)

Exhibit AU 623-5 is an example of a report on a statement of assets sold and liabilities transferred to comply with a contractual agreement.

Presentation not in accordance with GAAP or OCBOA

The terms of a contract might require an entity to prepare financial statements that are in accordance with neither GAAP nor another comprehensive basis of accounting. For example, an entity might be required to prepare financial statements that use unacceptable methods to value various accounts and transactions. The auditor might be requested to express an opinion on financial statements of this type, but it should be emphasized that this type of engagement is not the same as the engagement described earlier.

Reporting standards

The title of the special auditor's report should include the word "independent," and the report should have a manual or printed signature. The report should be dated no earlier than the date on which the auditor has obtained sufficient appropriate audit evidence to support the opinion.

The following format should be used to prepare a special auditor's report on financial statements prepared on a basis of accounting prescribed in an agreement that results in a presentation that is not in conformity with GAAP or OCBOA.

• Introductory paragraph

     — State that the special-purpose financial statements identified in the report were audited.

     — State that the financial statements are the responsibility of the company's management and that the auditor is responsible for expressing an opinion on the financial statements based on the audit.

• Scope paragraph

     — State that the audit was conducted in accordance with U.S. GAAS.

     — State that U.S. GAAS require that the auditor plan and perform the audit to obtain reasonable assurance about whether the financial statements are free of material misstatement.

— State that an audit includes examining, on a test basis, evidence supporting the amounts and disclosures in the financial statements.

— State that an audit includes assessing the accounting principles used and significant estimates made by management.

— State that an audit includes evaluating the overall financial statement presentation.

— State that the auditor believes that the audit provides a reasonable basis for his or her opinion.

• Presentation basis paragraph

— Explain what the presentation is intended to present, and refer to the note to the special-purpose financial statements that describes the basis of presentation.

— State that the presentation is not intended to be a presentation in conformity with GAAP.

• Explanatory paragraph

— Describe significant interpretations, if any — and their sources — that the entity's management have made relating to the contractual agreement.

• Opinion paragraph

— Express an opinion on whether the information is fairly presented, in all material respects, on the basis of accounting specified. If the information is not presented fairly on the basis of accounting described or if the scope of the engagement has been limited, an explanatory paragraph preceding the opinion paragraph should disclose all substantive reasons for the above conclusions. The opinion paragraph should include modifying language and a reference to the explanatory paragraph(s).

• Distribution paragraph

— State that the report is restricted to those within the entity, to the parties to the contract or agreement, for filing with a regulatory agency, or to those with whom the entity is negotiating directly.

Exhibit AU 623-6 is an example of a special auditor's report on financial statements prepared pursuant to a loan agreement that results in a presentation not in conformity with GAAP or an OCBOA.

Reporting on financial information presented in prescribed forms or schedules

An entity may be required to file financial information on a form supplied or approved by a governmental agency, institution, or other authority. In addition, an auditor may be engaged to express an opinion on the information in the form, and the wording of the auditor's report may also be part of the prescribed form. For example, a state agency may require certain not-for-profit entities to submit periodic financial reports on prescribed forms. Before signing the prescribed report, the auditor must be careful to protect him- or herself from making inappropriate statements in the report.

Under some circumstances, the auditor may be able to sign the prescribed report by modifying the report language in the form. If a significant amount of rewording is necessary, it might be more appropriate for the auditor to attach a separate auditor's report. The auditor can find guidance for writing a separate report by following the reporting formats on financial statements prepared in accordance with a comprehensive basis of accounting other than GAAP.

> **PLANNING AID REMINDER:** Interpretation No. 10 of AU 623 states that a special report situation may arise when a charitable organization presents its financial statements in a manner consistent with Internal Revenue Form 990 (Return of Organizations Exempt from Income Tax). These financial statements may be submitted to state and federal regulatory authorities. When the presentation materially departs from GAAP and the financial statements are intended solely for filing with a regulatory agency, a special report following the reporting format established for statements prepared on a comprehensive basis of accounting other than GAAP may be followed. When the presentation materially departs from GAAP and there is public distribution of the report, reporting requirements established by SAS-62 are not applicable. In this situation, the auditor must observe SAS-58 (AU 508) by issuing a qualified or adverse opinion on the financial statements.

Modifications to the standard auditor's special report

When an auditor concludes that an unqualified opinion is not applicable, the special auditor's report should be appropriately modified. If the deficiency is related to accounting principles used to prepare the financial presentation, the modification to the report should include an explanatory paragraph(s) that describes the deficiency, and the opinion paragraph should refer to the explanatory paragraph as the basis for the qualified or adverse opinion. On the other hand, if the deficiency is related to the scope of the audit engagement, an explanatory paragraph(s) should be added to the special auditor's report, and the opinion paragraph should refer to the explanatory paragraph as the basis for the qualified opinion or disclaimer of opinion. Under both circumstances (accounting deficiency and scope deficiency), the explanatory paragraph should precede the opinion paragraph.

In addition to modifications to the special auditor's report arising from accounting and scope deficiencies, the report should be modified under the following circumstances:

- There is a lack of consistent application of accounting principles.

- Substantial doubt exists about the entity's ability to continue as a going concern.

- Part of the audit was conducted by another auditor.

- The auditor expresses an opinion on the financial presentation that is different from the one expressed in a previous engagement on the same presentation.

- A matter is to be emphasized.

When an entity changes its basis of accounting from GAAP to a comprehensive basis of accounting other than GAAP, in the year of change the matter should not be treated as a consistency violation. Nonetheless, it may be appropriate to include an additional paragraph that discloses that a different basis of accounting was used to prepare financial statements in previous periods or that the entity has also prepared another report that uses generally accepted accounting principles as the basis of accounting.

In addition, when financial statements are prepared on a tax basis, a change in the tax laws would not constitute a violation of the consistency standard; however, it may be appropriate to disclose the matter in the financial statements.

Practitioner's Aids

The following exhibits are presented in this section:

- Exhibit AU 623-1 — Special Report on Cash-Based Financial Statements

- Exhibit AU 623-2 — Special Report on a Regulatory Basis of Accounting (Regulated Entity Releases the Report to Parties Other than the Regulator Either Voluntarily or Upon Specific Request)

- Exhibit AU 623-3 — Special Report on an Account in a Financial Statement

- Exhibit AU 623-4 — Special Report on Whether Certain Terms of a Debt Agreement Have Been Observed

- Exhibit AU 623-5 — Special Report on a Statement of Assets Sold and Liabilities Transferred

- Exhibit AU 623-6 — Special Report on Financial Statements Prepared Pursuant to a Loan Agreement

EXHIBIT AU 623-1 — SPECIAL REPORT ON CASH-BASED FINANCIAL STATEMENTS

We have audited the accompanying statements of assets and liabilities arising from cash transactions of X Company as of December 31, 20X5 and 20X4, and the related statements of revenues collected and expenses paid for the years then ended. These financial statements are the responsibility of the Company's management. Our responsibility is to express an opinion on these financial statements based on our audits.

We conducted our audits in accordance with auditing standards generally accepted in the United States of America. Those standards require that we plan and perform the audit to obtain reasonable assurance about whether the financial statements are free of material misstatement. An audit includes examining, on a test basis, evidence supporting the amounts and disclosures in the financial statements. An audit also includes assessing the accounting principles used and significant estimates made by management, as well as evaluating the overall financial statement presentation. We believe that our audits provide a reasonable basis for our opinion.

As described in Note X, these financial statements were prepared on the basis of cash receipts and disbursements, which is a comprehensive basis of accounting other than generally accepted accounting principles.

In our opinion, the financial statements referred to above present fairly, in all material respects, the assets and liabilities arising from cash transactions of X Company as of December 31, 20X5 and 20X4, and its revenues collected and expenses paid during the years then ended, on the basis of accounting described in Note X.

EXHIBIT AU 623-2 — SPECIAL REPORT ON A REGULATORY BASIS OF ACCOUNTING (REGULATED ENTITY RELEASES THE REPORT TO PARTIES OTHER THAN THE REGULATOR EITHER VOLUNTARILY OR UPON SPECIFIC REQUEST)

We have audited the accompanying statement of cash and unencumbered cash, cash receipts and disbursements, and disbursements —

budget and actual for each fund of [*city*], [*state*], as of and for the year ended June 30, 20X8. These financial statements are the responsibility of the City's management. Our responsibility is to express an opinion on these financial statements based on our audit.

We conducted our audit in accordance with auditing standards generally accepted in the United States of America. Those standards require that we plan and perform the audit to obtain reasonable assurance about whether the financial statements are free of material misstatement. An audit includes examining, on a test basis, evidence supporting the amounts and disclosures in the financial statements. An audit also includes assessing the accounting principles used and significant estimates made by management, as well as evaluating the overall financial statement presentation. We believe that our audit provides a reasonable basis for our opinion.

As described more fully in Note X, [*city*] has prepared these financial statements using accounting practices prescribed or permitted by [*name of regulatory agency*], whose practices differ from accounting principles generally accepted in the United States of America. The effects on the financial statements of the variances between these regulatory accounting practices and accounting principles generally accepted in the United States of America, although not reasonably determinable, are presumed to be material.

In our opinion, because of the effects of the matter discussed in the preceding paragraph, the financial statements referred to above do not present fairly, in conformity with accounting principles generally accepted in the United States of America, the financial position of each fund of [*city*] as of June 30, 20X8, or changes in financial position or cash flows for the year then ended.

In our opinion, the financial statements referred to above present fairly, in all material respects, the cash and unencumbered cash balances of each fund of [*city*] as of June 30, 20X8, and their respective cash receipts and disbursements, and budgetary results for the year then ended, on the basis of accounting described in Note X.

[*Signature of accounting firm*]

[*Date*]

EXHIBIT AU 623-3 — SPECIAL REPORT ON AN ACCOUNT IN A FINANCIAL STATEMENT

We have audited the accompanying schedule of accounts receivable of X Company as of December 31, 20X5. This schedule is the responsibility of the Company's management. Our responsibility is to express an opinion on this schedule based on our audit.

We conducted our audit in accordance with auditing standards generally accepted in the United States of America. Those standards require that we plan and perform the audit to obtain reasonable assurance about whether the schedule of accounts receivable is free of material misstatement. An audit includes examining, on a test basis, evidence supporting the amounts and disclosures in the schedule of accounts receivable. An audit also includes assessing the accounting principles used and significant estimates made by management, as well as evaluating the overall schedule presentation. We believe that our audit provides a reasonable basis for our opinion.

In our opinion, the schedule of accounts receivable referred to above presents fairly, in all material respects, the accounts receivable of X Company as of December 31, 20X5, in conformity with accounting principles generally accepted in the United States of America.

EXHIBIT AU 623-4 — SPECIAL REPORT ON WHETHER CERTAIN TERMS OF A DEBT AGREEMENT HAVE BEEN OBSERVED

We have audited, in accordance with auditing standards generally accepted in the United States of America, the balance sheet of X Company as of December 31, 20X5, and the related statements of income, retained earnings, and cash flows for the year then ended, and have issued our report thereon dated February 20, 20X6.

In connection with our audit, nothing came to our attention that caused us to believe that the Company failed to comply with the terms, covenants, provisions, or conditions of the restrictive terms of the loan agreement (dated March 4, 20X0), as explained in Section A of the agreement with First State Bank insofar as they relate to accounting matters. However, our audit was not directed primarily toward obtaining knowledge of such noncompliance.

This report is intended solely for the information and use of the boards of directors and managements of X Company and First State Bank and is not intended to be and should not be used by anyone other than these specified parties.

EXHIBIT AU 623-5 — SPECIAL REPORT ON A STATEMENT OF ASSETS SOLD AND LIABILITIES TRANSFERRED

We have audited the accompanying statement of net assets sold of X Company as of July 15, 20X5. This statement of net assets sold is the responsibility of X Company's management. Our responsibility is to express an opinion on the statement of net assets sold based on our audit.

We conducted our audit in accordance with auditing standards generally accepted in the United States of America. Those standards require that we plan and perform the audit to obtain reasonable assurance about whether the statement of net assets sold is free of material misstatement. An audit includes examining, on a test basis, evidence supporting the amounts and disclosures in the statement. An audit also includes assessing the accounting principles used and significant estimates made by management, as well as evaluating the overall presentation of the statement of net assets sold. We believe that our audit provides a reasonable basis for our opinion.

The accompanying statement was prepared to present the net assets of X Company sold to Z Company pursuant to the purchase agreement described in Note 1, and is not intended to be a complete presentation of X Company's assets and liabilities.

In our opinion, the accompanying statement of net assets sold presents fairly, in all material respects, the net assets of X Company as of July 15, 20X5, sold pursuant to the purchase agreement referred to in Note 1, in conformity with accounting principles generally accepted in the United States of America.

This report is intended solely for the information and use of the boards of directors and managements of X Company and Z Company and is not intended to be and should not be used by anyone other than these specified parties.

EXHIBIT AU 623-6 — SPECIAL REPORT ON FINANCIAL STATEMENTS PREPARED PURSUANT TO A LOAN AGREEMENT

We have audited the special-purpose statement of assets and liabilities of X Company as of December 31, 20X5 and 20X4, and the related special-purpose statements of revenues and expenses and cash flows for the years then ended. These financial statements are the responsibility of the Company's management. Our responsibility is to express an opinion on these financial statements based on our audits.

We conducted our audits in accordance with auditing standards generally accepted in the United States of America. Those standards require that we plan and perform the audit to obtain reasonable assurance about whether the financial statements are free of material misstatement. An audit includes examining, on a test basis, evidence supporting the amounts and disclosures in the financial statements. An audit also includes assessing the accounting principles used and significant estimates made by management, as well as evaluating the overall financial statement presentation. We believe that our audits provide a reasonable basis for our opinion.

The accompanying special-purpose financial statements were prepared for the purpose of complying with Section A of a loan agreement between the Company and the First State Bank as discussed in Note 1, and are not intended to be a presentation in conformity with accounting principles generally accepted in the United States of America.

In our opinion, the special-purpose financial statements referred to above present fairly, in all material respects, the assets and liabilities of X Company as of December 31, 20X5 and 20X4, and the revenues, expenses, and cash flows for the years then ended, on the basis of accounting described in Note 1.

This report is intended solely for the information and use of the boards of directors and managements of X Company and the First State Bank and is not and should not be used for anyone other than these specified parties.

SECTION 625

REPORTS ON THE APPLICATION OF ACCOUNTING PRINCIPLES

Authoritative Pronouncements

SAS-50 — Reports on the Application of Accounting Principles

SAS-97 — Amendment to Statement on Auditing Standards No. 50, Reports on the Application of Accounting Principles

Auditing Interpretation No. 1 (January 2005) — Requirement to Consult with the Continuing Accountant

> **IMPORTANT NOTICE FOR 2011:** The Auditing Standards Board (ASB) is in the process of redrafting all of the auditing sections in *Codification of Statements on Auditing Standards* to converge U.S. GAAS with the International Standards on Auditing issued by the International Auditing and Assurance Standards Board. As part of this process, the newly redrafted standards will follow certain clarity drafting conventions adopted by the ASB. These clarity drafting conventions include: (1) establishing objectives for each standard; (2) including a definitions section, if appropriate; and (3) separating requirements from application guidance and other material. The ASB is planning to have all redrafted standards become effective on the same date, which is for audits of financial statements for periods ending on or after December 15, 2012. It is possible that the effective date might be delayed beyond that date. The ASB's clarity and convergence project will have a significant effect on the auditing standards applicable to audits of nonpublic companies, and the 2012 *GAAS Guide* will be appropriately modified to reflect these changes once the effective date of the standards is certain.

Overview

Accountants are often requested to give an informal opinion on how a transaction should or could be accounted for or what type of opinion would be appropriate for a particular set of financial statements. Requests of this nature are frequently associated with prospective clients who are "shopping for an opinion." Unfortunately, such requests have resulted in a significant amount of adverse publicity for the accounting profession.

To provide guidance in this sensitive area, the Auditing Standards Board issued SAS-97, which is an amendment to SAS-50.

SAS-97 points out that an accountant may be asked by management or other interested parties (1) to explain how GAAP (or an other comprehensive basis of accounting) apply to new transactions experienced by a company or the development of new financial products or (2) to increase their knowledge of specific financial reporting issues. In this capacity the accountant may assume the role of the reporting accountant or the continuing accountant, which are defined by SAS-97 as follows:

> *Reporting accountant* — an accountant in public practice who prepares any written communication or provides oral advice on the application of accounting principles to specified transactions involving facts and circumstances of a specific entity, or the type of opinion that may be rendered on a specific entity's financial statements.

> *Continuing accountant* — an accountant who has been engaged to report on the financial statements of a specific entity.

Scope of Standards

The standards established by SAS-97 apply to the reporting accountant under the following circumstances:

- A written report is prepared on the application of GAAP to specified transactions (either those completed or those proposed) that involve facts and circumstances of a specific entity

- A written report is prepared on the type of opinion that may be expressed on a specific entity's financial statements

- Oral advice is offered by the reporting accountant that he or she intends to be used by a principal to the transaction as an important factor to be considered in reaching a decision on the application of GAAP to a specific transaction

- Oral advice is offered by the reporting accountant that he or she intends to be used by a principal to the transaction as an important factor to be considered in reaching a decision on the type of opinion that may be expressed on a specific entity's financial statements

> **OBSERVATION:** The scope of SAS-97 is intended to include oral advice so that the reporting accountant cannot circumvent professional standards simply by not preparing a written report.

> **PLANNING AID REMINDER:** SAS-50 allowed an accountant to prepare a written report on hypothetical transactions. SAS-97 prohibits such reports.

The standards established by SAS-97 do not apply to the following circumstances:

- A continuing accountant with respect to the specific entity whose financial statements that are being reported upon by the continuing accountant

- An accountant assisting in litigation involving accounting matters

- An accountant providing expert testimony concerning an accounting matter

- An accountant providing professional advice to another accountant in public practice

- An accountant preparing other communications such as position papers (newsletters, articles, tests, lectures, etc.) unless the guidance is rendered on a specific entity's financial statements

> **OBSERVATION:** The standards established by SAS-97 do not provide guidance for a continuing accountant (except as discussed later with respect to the communication between the reporting accountant and the continuing accountant), because the continuing accountant discusses the application of accounting principles to various transactions and the effect of the accounting for such transactions on the auditor's report as part of the normal audit process.

Promulgated Procedures Checklist

The reporting accountant should observe the following performance standards when reporting on engagement covered by SAS-97:

- Consider the circumstances of the request

- Observe specified generally accepted auditing standards

- Obtain sufficient information

- Communicate with the continuing accountant

- Observe reporting standards

Analysis and Application of Procedures

Consider the circumstances of the request

It should be recalled that the reporting accountant, as defined in SAS-90 (AU 380, AU 722), is not the accountant who is auditing the client's financial statements. For that reason the reporting accountant should be cautious in accepting an engagement (one that includes either a written report or oral advice) subject to the standards established by SAS-97 (AU 625). Specifically, the reporting accountant should "consider the circumstances under which the written report or oral advice is requested, the purpose of the request, and the intended use of the written report or oral advice."

> **OBSERVATION:** With the increased visibility of accountants in the press and the related close scrutiny of the profession as well as the possibility of litigation, accountants should be particularly careful in accepting engagements covered by SAS-97.

Observe specified generally accepted auditing standards

An engagement performed in accordance with the standards established by SAS-97 must satisfy the following generally accepted auditing standards:

- Due professional care is to be exercised in performing the engagement (see AU 230).

- The engagement is to be performed by a person or persons having adequate technical training and proficiency (see AU 210).

- The work is to be adequately planned and assistants, if any, are to be properly supervised (see AU 311).

Obtain sufficient information

SAS-97 requires that the reporting accountant "accumulate sufficient information to provide a reasonable basis for the professional judgment described in the report," and it specifically lists the following as procedures to be performed in this regard:

- Develop an understanding of the form and substance of the transaction(s).

- Review appropriate generally accepted accounting principles (see AU 411 [The Meaning of "Present Fairly in Conformity with Generally Accepted Accounting Principles"].).

- Consult with those having relevant expertise, if appropriate.

- Perform an investigation to identify credible precedents or analogies, if appropriate.

In addition to the above procedures, SAS-97 states that the reporting accountant should make inquiries of the continuing accountant concerning matters such as the following:

- The form and substance of the transaction

- How management has applied accounting principles to similar transactions

- Whether the method of accounting recommended by the continuing accountant is disputed by management

- Whether the continuing accountant has reached a different conclusion on the application of accounting principles or the type of opinion that may be rendered on the entity's financial statements

The reporting accountant should obtain permission from the entity's management to contact the continuing accountant and instruct management to authorize the continuing accountant to respond fully to the reporting accountant's request for information.

> **OBSERVATION:** The continuing accountant should respond to the reporting accountant's request for information in a manner similar to the guidance established by SAS-84 (AU 315) (Communications between Predecessor and Successor Auditors).

Auditing Interpretation No. 1 of AU 625 applies to situations where an accountant other than the entity's independent auditor is engaged on a continuing basis to help management apply GAAP. A non-public company may hire such an advisory accountant to perform bookkeeping services and to prepare the financial statements and notes, among other possible tasks. The advisory accountant is not engaged to provide a second opinion on the application of GAAP to specific transactions or to opine on the type of audit opinion that may be appropriate.

The advisory accountant is not required to consult with the continuing accountant if he or she (1) has full access to management, (2) has full knowledge of the form and substance of transactions where he or she is providing advice to management, and (3) is not being asked to provide a second opinion. The advisory accountant should document his or her conclusion, indicating that consultation with the continuing accountant was not necessary.

The advisory accountant should establish an understanding with management regarding the scope of the engagement. This understanding includes the recognition by management that they remain responsible for the proper treatment of events and transactions in the financial statements, and that management should consult with its continuing accountant on these issues. In addition, the entity's governance body (e.g., audit committee) and the continuing accountant should be informed of the retention of an advisory accountant. Finally, for those transactions where the advisory accountant is to provide advice to management, the advisory accountant must

- Obtain an understanding of the form and substance of the transaction

- Review the applicable GAAP

- If needed, consult with other professionals and experts

- If needed, perform research and other procedures to determine whether creditable precedents or analogies apply to the transaction(s) for which advice is to be rendered

> **OBSERVATION:** The difference between a "reporting accountant" and an "advisory accountant" pertains to the nature of the engagement and the term of the engagement. A reporting accountant is engaged to provide an opinion on the application of GAAP to a completed or anticipated transaction, or to issue an opinion on the type of audit report appropriate for the entity. The term of the engagement is typically onetime (or, at a minimum, sporadic). An advisory accountant is engaged to help management in executing accounting or reporting functions (e.g., the outsourcing of the controllership function), and the term of the service is typically permanent (or at least recurring).

Observe Reporting Standards

SAS-97 identifies the following as reporting standards that the reporting accountant should ordinarily observe when preparing a written report:

- Address the report to the requesting entity (e.g., management, board of directors, etc.)

- Brief description of the nature of the engagement and a statement that the engagement was performed in accordance with standards established by the AICPA

- Identification of the specific entity, a description of the transaction(s), a statement of the relevant facts, circumstances, and assumptions, and a statement about the source of the information

- A statement describing the appropriate accounting principle(s) (including the country of origin) to be applied or type of opinion that may be rendered on the entity's financial statements and, if appropriate, a description of the reasons for the reporting accountant's conclusion

- A statement that the responsibility for the proper accounting treatment rests with the preparers of the financial statements, who should consult with their continuing accountants

- A statement that any difference in the facts, circumstances, or assumptions presented might change the report

- A separate paragraph at the end of the report that includes the following elements:

  — A statement indicating that the report is intended solely for the information and use of the specified parties (nonetheless the report can be provided to the continuing accountant)

  — An identification of the specified parties to whom use is restricted

  — A statement indicating the report is not intended to be and should not be used by anyone other than the specified parties

    ENGAGEMENT STRATEGY: SAS-97 notes that the above reporting standards apply only to written reports but that "accountants may find this guidance useful in providing oral advice."

The accountant's report is divided into the following five sections: (1) introduction; (2) description of transaction(s); (3) appropriate accounting principles or opinion to be expressed; (4) concluding comments; and (5) restricted use. Generally the first, fourth, and fifth paragraphs follow, for the most part, a standard format. The second and third sections are unique to the specific accounting issue being raised.

Exhibit AU 625-1 is an example from SAS-97 of an accountant's report that covers the application of accounting principles.

Practitioner's Aids

Exhibit AU 625-1 is an example based on the reporting standards established by SAS-97 of an accountant's report on the application of accounting principles.

EXHIBIT AU 625-1 — ACCOUNTANT'S REPORT ON THE APPLICATION OF ACCOUNTING PRINCIPLES

[*Introduction*]

We have been engaged to report on the appropriate application of accounting principles generally accepted in [*country of origin of such principles*] to the specific transaction described below. This report is being issued to ABC Company for assistance in evaluating accounting principles for the described specific transaction. Our engagement has been conducted in accordance with standards established by the American Institute of Certified Public Accountants.

[*Description of Transaction*]

The facts, circumstances, and assumptions relevant to the specific transaction as provided to us by the management of ABC Company are as follows: [*describe the transaction*]
[*Appropriate Accounting Principles*]

[*Discuss generally accepted accounting principles*]

[*Concluding Comments*]

The ultimate responsibility for the decision on the appropriate application of accounting principles generally accepted in [*country of origin of such principles*] for an actual transaction rests with the preparers of financial statements, who should consult with their continuing accountants. Our judgment on the appropriate application of accounting principles generally accepted in [*country of origin of such principles*] for the described specific transaction is based solely on the facts provided to us as described above; should these facts and circumstances differ, our conclusion may change.

[*Restricted Use*]

This report is intended solely for the information and use of the board of directors and management of ABC Company and is not intended to be and should not be used by anyone other than these specified parties.

SECTION 634

LETTERS FOR UNDERWRITERS AND CERTAIN OTHER REQUESTING PARTIES

Authoritative Pronouncements

SAS-72—Letters for Underwriters and Certain Other Requesting Parties

SAS-76—Amendments to Statement on Auditing Standards No. 72, Letters for Underwriters and Certain Other Requesting Parties

SAS-86—Amendment to Statement on Auditing Standards No. 72, Letters for Underwriters and Certain Other Requesting Parties

Auditing Interpretation No. 1 (January 2001)—Letters to Directors Relating to Annual Reports on Form 10-K

Auditing Interpretation No. 3 (August 1998)—Commenting in a Comfort Letter on Quantitative Disclosures about Market Risk Made in Accordance with Item 305 of Regulation S-K

> **IMPORTANT NOTICE FOR 2011:** The Auditing Standards Board (ASB) is in the process of redrafting all of the auditing sections in *Codification of Statements on Auditing Standards* to converge U.S. GAAS with the International Standards on Auditing issued by the International Auditing and Assurance Standards Board. As part of this process, the newly redrafted standards will follow certain clarity drafting conventions adopted by the ASB. These clarity drafting conventions include: (1) establishing objectives for each standard; (2) including a definitions section, if appropriate; and (3) separating requirements from application guidance and other material. The ASB is planning to have all redrafted standards become effective on the same date, which is for audits of financial statements for periods ending on or after December 15, 2012. It is possible that the effective date might be delayed beyond that date. The ASB's clarity and convergence project will have a significant effect on the auditing standards applicable to audits of nonpublic companies, and the 2012 *GAAS Guide* will be appropriately modified to reflect these changes once the effective date of the standards is certain.

Overview

SAS-72 (Letters for Underwriters and Certain Other Requesting Parties), as amended by SAS-86 (AU 634) (Amendment to Statement on Auditing

Standards No. 72, Letters for Underwriters and Certain Other Requesting Parties), provides guidance to accountants in performing engagements to provide (1) letters to underwriters in conjunction with filings with the Securities and Exchange Commission (SEC) under the Securities Act of 1933 (the 1933 Act) and (2) letters to a requesting party in conjunction with other securities offerings.

SAS-72 supersedes SAS-49 (Letters for Underwriters). SAS-49 was issued in 1984, before the issuance of Statements on Standards for Attestation Engagements (Attestation Standards; Financial Forecasts and Projections; and Reporting on Pro Forma Financial Information). Therefore, the guidance and examples pertaining to letters (commonly referred to as "comfort letters") issued to underwriters and certain other parties (referred to hereafter as "requesting parties") had to be revised to reflect the issuance of these standards. Furthermore, since SAS-49 was issued, accountants have been requested to issue comfort letters to parties other than underwriters and in connection with securities offerings other than those registered under the Act. SAS-72 provides guidance on those parties to whom accountants may provide comfort letters.

> **PLANNING AID REMINDER:** Interpretation No. 1 of AU 634 (AU 9634.01 – .09) states that the auditor may perform some services requested by the board of directors relating to the annual report on Form 10-K.

Applicability of Statement on Auditing Standards No. 72

As part of the registration of securities under the 1933 Act, underwriters of the securities often ask an accountant to provide them with a comfort letter. The comfort letter is not a requirement of the 1933 Act and is not included in the registration statement. However, underwriters request it to assist them in discharging their duty of reasonable investigation and to help establish their affirmative defense under Section 11 of the 1933 Act (often referred to as "Section 11 investigation" or "due diligence"). Therefore, obtaining the accountant's comfort letter is one of many activities that underwriters undertake to respond to the liability imposed on them under Section 11 of the 1933 Act.

> **OBSERVATION:** SAS-72 states that the accountant may address the comfort letter to parties other than a named underwriter only when (1) the requesting party has a statutory due diligence defense under Section 11 of the 1933 Act and (2) legal counsel for the requesting party issues a written legal opinion to the accountant explicitly stating that such party has a statutory due diligence defense under Section 11 of the 1933 Act. If the

> requesting party cannot provide such a legal opinion letter from
> its counsel, the accountant should obtain a representation letter,
> as described below, from the requesting party.

SAS-72 states that the accountant may also provide comfort letters to other requesting parties, in addition to underwriters, in the following situations only if the representation letter described below is obtained:

- To a broker-dealer or other financial intermediary in connection with the following types of securities offerings:

    — For foreign offerings (e.g., Regulation S, Eurodollar, and other offshore offerings)

    — For transactions that are exempt from the registration requirements of Section 5 of the 1933 Act, including those pursuant to Regulation A, Regulation D, and Rule 144A

    — For offerings of securities issued or backed by governmental, municipal, banking, tax-exempt, or other entities that are exempt from registration under the 1933 Act

- To a buyer or a seller, or both, in connection with acquisition transactions involving an exchange of stock (e.g., Form S-4 or merger proxy situation)

A comfort letter (or alternative letter, described below) should be prepared only for parties referred to in paragraphs 3-5 of SAS-72. If another party requests a letter, the guidance in AU 634 does not apply.

SAS-76 (Amendments to Statement on Auditing Standards No. 72 on Letters for Underwriters) states that when a party specifically identified in paragraphs 3-5 of SAS-72 (other than an underwriter of a party with a due diligence defense based on Section 11 of the 1933 Act) requests a comfort letter *but does not provide the representations established by paragraphs 6 and 7 of SAS-72*, the accountant should not provide a comfort letter. However, the accountant may provide an alternative letter that does not include a negative assurance on the financial statements or specified elements, accounts, or items of those statements. In addition, the alternative letter should state the following:

- That the accountant had no responsibility for determining the procedures enumerated in the letter

- That the enumerated procedures do not constitute an audit of the financial statements

- That the enumerated procedures should not substitute for additional inquiries or procedures that the party may perform as part of considering the proposed offering

- That the letter is solely for the other party's information and should not be used for any other purpose

- That the accountant has no responsibility for updating the letter for events that may occur after the cutoff date

The guidance established by SAS-72 that applies to performing procedures related to a comfort letter also should apply to the procedures referred to in the alternative letter.

> **OBSERVATION:** Interpretation No. 3 of AU 634 states that the auditor should not offer positive or negative assurances on information related to Item 305 of Regulation S-K.

Required representation letter

The required representation letter from the requesting parties identified above should (1) be addressed to the accountant and signed by the requesting party and (2) include a statement that the review process to be applied by the requesting party is substantially consistent with the due diligence review process that would be performed pursuant to the 1933 Act. Exhibit AU 634-1 illustrates a representation letter as would be found in SAS-72.

If a nonunderwriter requests a comfort letter in connection with a securities offering registered pursuant to the 1933 Act, the second and third sentences of the representation letter should be revised as follows:

> This review process, applied to the information relating to the issuer, is substantially consistent with the due diligence review process that an underwriter would perform in connection with this placement of securities. We are knowledgeable with respect to the due diligence review process that an underwriter would perform in connection with a placement of securities registered pursuant to the Securities Act of 1933.

> **PLANNING AID REMINDER:** When the requesting party has provided the accountant with a representation letter regarding its due diligence review process as described above, the accountant should make reference to those representations in the comfort letter.

General guidance

Although SAS-72 provides guidance on comfort letters issued in various types of securities transactions, it generally addresses comfort letters issued in connection with securities offerings registered pursuant to the 1933 Act. Accordingly, guidance provided in SAS-72 with respect to comments made in comfort letters on compliance with SEC rules and regulations (e.g., Regulation S-X or S-K) generally applies when securities offerings are registered pursuant to the 1933 Act.

Scope of comfort procedures

The scope and conclusions in the comfort letter should be guided, wherever possible, by the pertinent sections of the underwriting agreement. Therefore, the accountant should obtain a draft copy of the underwriting agreement and review it at the earliest practicable date.

In requiring comfort letters from accountants, underwriters are seeking assistance in performing a reasonable investigation of data (unaudited financial information and other data) on the authority of an expert. Unfortunately, what constitutes a reasonable investigation of unaudited data sufficient to satisfy an underwriter's purpose has never been authoritatively established. Therefore, it is only the underwriter who can determine the amount of work sufficient to satisfy his or her due diligence requirement. Accordingly, accountants are willing to carry out procedures that will aid underwriters in discharging their responsibility for exercising due diligence, but cannot furnish any assurance on whether those procedures are sufficient for the underwriter's purpose.

To ensure that the accountant's professional responsibility is understood, the accountant should meet with the underwriter and the client and explain the typical procedures (as discussed later in this section) employed as a basis for the issuance of a comfort letter. SAS-72 states that the accountant should accompany any such discussion of procedures with a clear statement that the accountant cannot furnish any assurance regarding the sufficiency of the procedures and should include a statement to that effect in the comfort letter. Paragraph 4 of the sample comfort letter in this section illustrates this requirement.

Promulgated Procedures Checklist

The auditor should perform the following procedures with respect to letters for underwriters and certain other requesting parties:

- Prepare a draft comfort letter to the underwriter.

- Obtain a copy of the draft comfort letter from other accountants.

- Based on the circumstances of the engagement, prepare an appropriate comfort letter.

Analysis and Application of Procedures

Prepare a draft letter to the underwriter

After receiving a draft of the underwriting agreement or being informed of its contents, the accountant should furnish the underwriter with a draft of the proposed comfort letter that responds to the underwriting agreement. This practice offers the underwriter and the client the opportunity to review the draft letter and discuss with the accountant the procedures expected to be performed. The accountant should not make statements about performing, or imply that he or she will perform, the procedures he or she considers necessary in the circumstances, as this may lead to a misunderstanding about the accountant's responsibility for the sufficiency of the procedures for the underwriter's purposes.

To further emphasize the point that the underwriter and not the accountant is responsible for the sufficiency of the comfort procedures, SAS-72 indicates that the accountant may include a legend or a concluding paragraph on the draft letter to the underwriter to address its functions and limitations. SAS-72 contains the following example of such a paragraph:

> This draft is furnished solely for the purpose of indicating the form of letter that we would expect to be able to furnish [*name of underwriter*] in response to their request, the matters expected to be covered in the letter, and the nature of the procedures that we would expect to carry out with respect to such matters. On the basis of our discussions with [*name of underwriter*], it is our understanding that the procedures outlined in this draft letter are those they wish us to follow. Unless [*name of underwriter*] informs us otherwise, we shall assume that there are no additional procedures they wish us to follow. The text of the letter itself will depend, of course, on the results of the procedures, which we would not expect to complete until shortly before the letter is given and in no event before the cutoff date indicated therein.

In the absence of any discussions with the underwriter, the accountant should outline in the draft letter those procedures specified in the underwriting agreement that he or she is willing to perform. In this situation, the second sentence above should be revised as follows:

In the absence of any discussions with [*name of underwriter*], we have set out in this draft letter those procedures referred to in the draft underwriting agreement (of which we have been furnished a copy) that we are willing to follow.

Obtain a copy of the draft comfort letter from other accountants

SAS-72 indicates that comfort letters are sometimes requested from more than one accountant (e.g., in connection with registration statements to be used in the subsequent sale of shares issued in recently effected mergers or from predecessor auditors). The principal accountant should obtain a copy of the draft comfort letter written by the other accountant.

There also may be situations in which a registration statement includes the report of more than one accountant on financial statements included therein — for example, if a significant subsidiary or division is audited by other accountants. In that event, SAS-72 indicates that

- The principal accountant should read the comfort letter the other accountant has prepared. Such comfort letter should include statements similar to those contained in the principal accountant's comfort letter, including representations about the accountant's independence.

- The principal accountant should make the following comments in his or her comfort letter: (1) that the principal accountant has read the comfort letter prepared by the other accountant and (2) that procedures performed by the principal accountant relate only to the financial statements audited by the principal accountant and the consolidated financial statements.

Shelf registrations

A shelf registration statement enables an entity to register securities under the 1933 Act and then issue these securities over a period of time. At the effective date of the registration statement, an underwriter or lead underwriter may not have been named, although the accountant may have been asked to issue a comfort letter. SAS-72 indicates that since only the underwriter can determine the appropriate procedures to be performed with respect to the accountant's comfort letter, the accountant should not agree to issue a comfort letter to the client, to the counsel for the underwriter group (when a lead underwriter has not been named), or to an unspecified party such as "any or all underwriters to be selected." However, the accountant may issue a draft comfort letter to the client or the legal counsel representing the underwriter group, based on the actual procedures the accountant has performed. In this circumstance, the accountant should include a legend or a paragraph in the draft comfort letter addressing the letter's functions and limitations. The following is an example of such a paragraph as illustrated in SAS-72:

> This draft describes the procedures that we have performed and represents a letter we would be prepared to sign as of the effective date of the registration statement if the managing underwriter had been chosen at that date and had requested such a letter. On the basis of our discussions with [*name of client or legal counsel*], the procedures set forth are similar to those that experience indicates that underwriters often request in such circumstances. The text of the final letter will depend, of course, on whether the managing underwriter who is selected requests that other procedures be performed to meet his or her needs and whether the managing underwriter requests that any of the procedures be updated to the date of issuance of the signed letter.

Based on the circumstances of the engagement, prepare an appropriate comfort letter

The contents of comfort letters vary depending on the specific circumstances of the individual engagement. However, a comfort letter typically includes the following:

1. *Date* The comfort letter is usually dated on or shortly before the effective date of the registration statement.

2. *Addressee* The comfort letter is usually addressed to the parties to whom the accountant is giving assurance (e.g., the client and the underwriter).

3. *Introductory paragraph* This paragraph typically refers to the accountant's report on the audited financial statements and related schedules included or incorporated by reference in the registration statement.

4. *Independence* The comfort letter typically makes a brief statement regarding the accountant's independence.

5. *Compliance with SEC requirements* When the underwriting agreement requests the accountant to comment on compliance with SEC requirements, the accountant should add a paragraph in the comfort letter to that effect.

6. *Comments on information other than audited financial statements.*

7. *Comments on tables, statistics, and other financial data.*

8. *Concluding paragraph* To avoid misunderstanding by the requesting party, the comfort letter typically includes a paragraph about its purpose and intended use.

9. *Disclosure of subsequently discovered matters.*

Date

Ordinarily, the comfort letter is dated on or shortly before the effective date of the registration statement. Usually the underwriting agreement specifies the date to which the procedures described in the letter are to relate. This date, commonly referred to as the cutoff date, is customarily within five business days before the effective date of the registration statement.

> **PLANNING AID REMINDER:** SAS-72 indicates that the comfort letter should state that the procedures described therein do not cover the intervening period from the cutoff date to the date of the letter.

Underwriters also sometimes require that an additional comfort letter be issued and dated at or shortly before the closing date on which the entity or selling shareholders deliver the securities to the underwriter in exchange for the proceeds of the offering. SAS-72 does not prohibit the accountant from furnishing both of these letters. However, when both are required, the accountant should carry out the specified procedures as of the cutoff date of each letter.

Addressee

SAS-72 states that the accountant should not address or give the comfort letter to any parties other than the client, the named underwriter, the broker-dealer, the financial intermediary, or the buyer or seller, or both, in connection with acquisition transactions as discussed above.

Introductory paragraph

Although not required, it is customary, and desirable according to SAS-72, for the accountant to include an introductory paragraph in the comfort letter that describes which financial statements are included in the registration statement the accountant has audited. The following is an example of such a paragraph as illustrated in SAS-72:

> We have audited the [*identify the financial statements and financial statement schedules*] included [*incorporated by reference*] in

the registration statement (no. 33-00000) on Form X filed by the company under the Securities Act of 1933 (the Act); our reports with respect thereto are also included [*incorporated by reference*] in that registration statement. The registration statement, as amended as of [*date*], is herein referred to as the registration statement.

> **PLANNING AID REMINDER:** Occasionally, underwriters will request that the accountant's opinion on the financial statements contained in the registration statement be repeated in the comfort letter. There does not appear any valid reason to do so, and it should not be done; also, the accountant should not give negative assurance regarding his or her report. Furthermore, the accountant should not give negative assurance with respect to financial statements and schedules that have been audited and are reported on in the registration statement by other accountants.

Modified introductory paragraph

The introductory paragraph of the accountant's comfort letter should be modified when the accountant's report on audited financial statements and related schedules included in the registration statement contains the following material:

- An explanatory paragraph or emphasis-of-matter paragraph

- A qualified opinion on the financial statements

In these instances, the introductory paragraph should be modified to refer to and discuss such matters.

Reference to other reports in the introductory paragraph   The accountant may have previously reported on any of the following:

- Condensed financial statements derived from audited financial statements, in accordance with SAS-42 (AU 552) (Reporting on Condensed Financial Statements and Selected Financial Data)

- Selected financial data, in accordance with SAS-42 (AU 552)

- Interim financial information, in accordance with SAS-100 (AU 722) (Interim Financial Information)

- Pro forma financial information, in accordance with Statement on Standards for Attestation Engagements (Reporting on Pro Forma Financial Information [AT 401])

- A financial forecast, in accordance with SSAE-1 (AT 301)

- Management's discussion and analysis (MD&A)

In these situations, in the introductory paragraph of the comfort letter the accountant may refer to the previously issued reports. However, these reports should not be repeated in the comfort letter; nor should the accountant otherwise imply that he or she is reporting as of the date of the comfort letter or is assuming responsibility for the sufficiency of the procedures for the underwriter's purposes.

Independence

In conjunction with SEC filings, the underwriting agreement customarily requests that the accountant represent in the comfort letter that he or she is independent. A simple statement, such as the following, suffices:

> We are independent certified public accountants with respect to [*name of client*], within the meaning of the Act and the applicable published rules and regulations thereunder.

In a non-SEC filing, a statement such as the following suffices:

> We are independent certified public accountants with respect to [*name of client*], under Rule 101 of the AICPA Code of Professional Conduct and its interpretations and rulings.

SAS-72 indicates that the accountants for previously nonaffiliated companies recently acquired by the registrant would not be required to have been independent with respect to the company whose shares are being registered. In this situation, the statement regarding independence should be modified, as follows:

> As of [*date of the accountant's most recent report on the financial statements of the client*] and during the period covered by the financial statements on which we reported, we were independent certified public accountants with respect to [*name of client*] within the meaning of the Act and the applicable published rules and regulations thereunder.

Compliance with SEC requirements

Usually, the underwriting agreement requests that the accountant comment on whether the financial statements comply with SEC requirements. The accountant may do so in the comfort letter by adding a paragraph like the following:

> In our opinion [*include phrase* "except as disclosed in the reg-istration statement," *if applicable*], the [*identify the financial statements and financial statement schedules*] audited by us and included [*incorporated by reference*] in the registration statement comply as to form in all material respects with the applicable accounting requirements of the Act and the related published rules and regulations.

If there is a material departure from the pertinent published SEC require-ments, the accountant should disclose such departure in the comfort letter. Normally, representatives of the SEC will have agreed to such a departure. The following is an example of wording to be used in the comfort letter when the SEC has agreed to a departure from its published accounting requirements:

> In our opinion [*include phrase* "except as disclosed in the regis-tration statement," *if applicable*], the [*identify the financial state-ments and financial statement schedules*] audited by us and included [*incorporated by reference*] in the registration statement comply as to form in all material respects with the applicable accounting requirements of the Act and the related published rules and regulations; however, as agreed to by representatives of the SEC, separate financial statements and financial statement schedules of ABC Company (an equity investee) as required by rule 3-09 of Regulation S-X have been omitted.

> **PLANNING AID REMINDER:** SAS-100 states that if depar-tures from pertinent published SEC requirements either are not disclosed in the registration statement or have not been agreed to by representatives of the SEC, the accountant should care-fully consider whether to consent to the use of the accountant's report in the registration statement.

Commenting in comfort letter on information other than audited financial statements

The accountant's comfort letter often refers to information other than audited financial statements. The accountant's comments in the letter generally pertain to

- Unaudited condensed interim financial information
- Capsule financial information

- Pro forma financial information

- Financial forecasts

- Changes in capital stock, increases in long-term debt, and decreases in other specified financial statement items

As discussed above, the comfort letter should refer to the agreed-upon procedures, with the following exception: When the accountant has been asked to provide negative assurance on interim financial information or capsule financial information, the accountant does not need to specify the procedures involved in a SAS-100 (AU 722) review. The accountant should make no comments or suggestions that he or she has applied procedures that the accountant considered necessary for the underwriter's purposes. Terms or comments that are subjective and unclear (e.g., "general review," "limited review," "reconcile," "check," and "test") should not be used in describing the accountant's work, unless the procedures implied by these terms are described in the comfort letter.

Notwithstanding the above, SAS-72 states that the accountant should not comment in a comfort letter on certain unaudited financial information unless the accountant has obtained knowledge of the client's internal controls as they relate to the preparation of both annual and interim financial information. Such knowledge of internal controls is ordinarily acquired when the accountant audits the entity's financial statements. If the accountant has not acquired such knowledge, the accountant should perform the necessary procedures to obtain that knowledge in order to make the required comments in the comfort letter. This knowledge of internal controls is required when the accountant is requested to comment in a comfort letter on the following:

- Unaudited condensed interim financial information

- Capsule financial information

- A financial forecast when historical financial statements provide a basis for one or more significant assumptions for the forecast

- Changes in capital stock, increases in long-term debt, and decreases in selected financial statement items

> **ENGAGEMENT STRATEGY:** SAS-86 states that a auditor should not use the comment letter to comment on "compliance as to form of MD&A with rules and regulations adopted by the SEC." However, an auditor may accept an engagement to examine or review MD&A based on the guidance established by Statements on Standards for Attestation Engagements.

Unaudited condensed interim financial information The comfort letter should (1) identify the unaudited condensed interim financial information and

(2) state that the accountant has not audited such information in accordance with generally accepted auditing standards and, therefore, does not express an opinion on such information. (Paragraph 3 of the sample comfort letter at the end of this Section illustrates this requirement.)

The accountant's comments in the comfort letter regarding unaudited condensed interim financial information should provide negative assurance on whether:

1. Any material modifications should be made to such information for it to be in conformity with generally accepted accounting principles.

2. Such information complies as to form in all material respects with the applicable accounting requirements of the 1933 Act and the related rules and regulations. [Paragraph 5(a) of the sample comfort letter at the end of this Section illustrates this requirement.]

The accountant may provide such negative assurance in the comfort letter only when he or she has conducted a review of such information in accordance with SAS-100 (AU 722). In this case, the accountant may:

1. State in the comfort letter that he or she has performed the procedures identified in SAS-100 (AU 722). [Paragraph 4(a)(i) of the sample comfort letter at the end of this Section illustrates this requirement.]

2. If the accountant has issued a report on the review of the interim financial information, he or she may mention that fact in the comfort letter. In this case, the accountant should attach the review report to the comfort letter, unless the review report is already included or incorporated by reference in the registration statement.

If a review in accordance with SAS-100 (AU 722) has not been conducted, the accountant may not provide negative assurance in the comfort letter regarding the interim financial information. (The accountant is limited to reporting the procedures performed and results obtained.) (SAS-72, example O in the appendix, illustrates the wording in this case.)

Capsule financial information   A registration statement may contain capsule financial information (i.e., unaudited summarized interim information for periods subsequent to the date of the audited financial statements and for the corresponding period of the prior year or the date of the unaudited condensed interim financial information). The accountant may express a negative assurance on whether such capsule financial information conforms with generally accepted accounting principles and comment on whether the dollar amounts were determined on a basis substantially consistent with corresponding amounts in the audited financial statements only if both of the following conditions are met:

1. The capsule financial information meets the minimum reporting requirements established in paragraph 30 of APB-28 (Interim Financial Reporting).

2. The accountant has performed a SAS-100 (AU 722) review of the financial statements underlying the capsule financial information.

If the minimum reporting requirements in 1. above are not met, the accountant may provide only negative assurance on whether the dollar amounts were determined on a basis substantially consistent with corresponding amounts in the audited financial statements, as long as the accountant has performed a SAS-100 (AU 722) review.

> **ENGAGEMENT STRATEGY:** If the accountant determines that negative assurance cannot be given because the conditions discussed above are not met, he or she is limited to reporting in the comfort letter the procedures performed and the results obtained.

Pro forma financial information In a comfort letter, the accountant should not provide negative assurance on (1) pro forma financial information, (2) the application of pro forma adjustments to historical amounts, (3) the compilation of pro forma financial information, or (4) whether the pro forma financial information complies as to form in all material respects with the applicable accounting requirements of rule 11-02 of Regulation S-X unless one of the following conditions is met:

1. The accountant has performed an audit of the entity's annual financial statements (or a significant part of a business combination) and has obtained an appropriate level of knowledge of its accounting and financial reporting practices.

2. The accountant has performed a SAS-100 (AU 722) review of the entity's interim financial statements to which the pro forma adjustments were applied.

If the conditions indicated above are not met, the accountant's comments in the comfort letter are limited to the procedures performed and results obtained. (Example O in the appendix to SAS-72 illustrates the wording in this case.)

Financial forecasts SAS-72 states that to perform agreed-upon procedures and comment in the comfort letter on a financial forecast, the accountant should

1. Obtain knowledge of the entity's internal controls as they relate to the preparation of annual and interim financial statements, as discussed earlier.

2. Perform the procedures required for a compilation of a forecast, as prescribed in Appendix B of SSAE-1.

3. Follow the guidance in paragraphs 16 and 17 of SSAE-1 regarding reporting on the compilation of the financial forecast, and attach the report to the comfort letter.

> **OBSERVATION:** If the forecast is included in the registration statement, the forecast must be accompanied by an indication that the accountant has not examined the forecast and, therefore, does not express an opinion on it. If the accountant has issued a compilation report on the forecast in connection with the comfort letter, the accountant's report need not be included in the registration statement.

The accountant may not give negative assurance in the comfort letter on the procedures performed in connection with a financial forecast. Furthermore, the accountant may not give negative assurance on the forecast's compliance with rule 11-03 of Regulation S-X unless the accountant has performed an examination of the forecast in accordance with Financial Forecasts and Projections. (Examples E and O in the appendix to SAS-72 provide illustrations of the accountant's wording in a comfort letter in connection with financial forecasts.)

Subsequent changes   The underwriter usually will ask the accountant to comment in the comfort letter on changes in certain financial statement items during a period (commonly referred to as the change period) subsequent to that of the latest financial statements included, or incorporated by reference, in the registration statement. These comments usually relate to (1) changes in capital stock, (2) increases in long-term debt, (3) decreases in net current assets, (4) decreases in stockholders' equity, (5) decreases in net sales, and (6) decreases in total and per-share amounts of income before extraordinary items and of net income.

> **PLANNING AID REMINDER:** The accountant should base his or her comments solely on the limited procedures performed with respect to the period between the date of the latest financial statements made available and the cut-off date (i.e., the date to which the procedures described in the comfort letter are to relate). These procedures usually are limited to inquiries of company officials and the reading of minutes, which should be

made clear in the comfort letter. (Paragraph 6 of the sample comfort letter in Exhibit AU 634-2 illustrates this requirement.)

The accountant may, on the underwriter's request, provide negative assurance in the comfort letter on subsequent changes in specified financial statement items as of any date that is less than 135 days from the end of the most recent period for which the accountant has performed an audit or a SAS-100 (AU 722) review. (Paragraphs 5b and 6 of the sample comfort letter at the end of this Section illustrate appropriate wording for expressing such negative assurance when there have been no subsequent changes. Example M in the appendix to SAS-72 provides illustrations of appropriate wording when there have been subsequent changes.)

If the underwriter requests negative assurance with respect to subsequent changes as of any date that is 135 days or more after to the end of the most recent period for which the accountant has performed an audit or a SAS-100 (AU 722) review, the accountant may not provide such negative assurance. In this case, the accountant's comments in the comfort letter are limited to the procedures performed and results obtained. (Example O in the appendix to SAS-72 illustrates the wording in this case.)

> **PLANNING AID REMINDER:** In the comfort letter the accountant should use the terms "change," "increase," and "decrease" rather than "adverse change." The term "adverse change" implies that the accountant is making a judgment about the change, which might be misinterpreted by the underwriter.

Some subsequent changes may be disclosed in the registration statement and need not be repeated in the comfort letter. Under this circumstance, the accountant should use the phrase "except for changes, increases, or decreases that the registration statement discloses have occurred or may occur" in the comfort letter. [Paragraph 5b(i) of the sample comfort letter at the end of this Section illustrates wording that would be appropriate when the accountant is making such a statement.]

The change period, which ends on the cutoff date, ordinarily begins (1) immediately after the date of the latest balance sheet in the registration statement, for balance sheet items, and (2) immediately after the latest period for which such items are presented in the registration statement, for income statement items. If the underwriter requests the use of a different change period, the accountant may use the period requested. To avoid any misunderstanding about the change period and the date of the financial statements used in comparison, both dates should be identified in the comfort letter in both the draft and the final form of the letter.

When more than one accountant is involved in the audit of the financial statements of the entity, and the principal accountant has obtained a copy of the comfort letter of the other accountant that does not disclose matters that affect the negative assurance given, the principal accountant should make appropriate modifications to the comfort letter commenting on subsequent changes. The modifications consist of an addition to paragraph 4, a substitute for the applicable part of paragraph 5, and an addition to the last sentence of paragraph 6 of the sample comfort letter at the end of this section.

> 4c. We have read the letter dated [*date*] of [*the other accountants*] with regard to [*the related company*].
>
> 5. Nothing came to our attention as a result of the foregoing procedures (which, so far as [*the related company*] is concerned, consisted solely of reading the letter referred to in 4c), however, that caused us to believe that ...
>
> 6. On the basis of these inquiries and our reading of the minutes and the letter dated [*date*] of [*the other accountants*] with regard to [*the related company*], as described in 4, nothing came to our attention that caused us to believe that there was any such change, increase, or decrease, except in all instances for changes, increases, or decreases that the registration statement discloses have occurred or may occur.

Tables, statistics, and other financial information

The comfort letter may refer to tables, statistics, and other financial information in the registration statement only if the accountant has the expertise to make a competent statement on them. Therefore, comments in the comfort letter regarding such information should be limited to the following categories:

- Information that is expressed in dollars, or percentages derived from dollar amounts, and that has been obtained from accounting records that are subject to internal controls of the company's accounting system

- Information that has been derived directly from such accounting records by analysis or computation

- Quantitative information that has been obtained from an accounting record if the information is of a type that is subject to the same controls as the dollar amounts

The accountant should not comment in the comfort letter on tables, statistics, and other financial information relating to an unaudited period unless the accountant has obtained a knowledge of the client's internal control.

The registration statement may include certain financial information to comply with specific requirements of Regulation S-K, such as the following items:

- Item 301, "Selected Financial Data"

- Item 302, "Supplementary Financial Information"

- Item 402, "Executive Compensation"

- Item 503(d), "Ratio of Earnings to Fixed Charges"

The accountant is limited to providing negative assurance on conformity of the information presented in the registration statement with the disclosure requirements of Regulation S-K. The accountant may provide such negative assurance only if the following conditions are met:

1. The information presented is derived from the accounting records subject to the internal control policies and procedures of the entity's accounting system, or has been derived directly from such accounting records by analysis or computation.

2. The information presented can be evaluated against reasonable criteria that have been established by the SEC.

The accountant should describe in the comfort letter the procedures and related findings with respect to the other financial information. The accountant should use specific, unambiguous language — such as page numbers or paragraph numbers — in the comfort letter when referring to the other information being commented on. If applicable, the accountant should comment on the acceptability of the allocation methods the client used in computing such other financial information. The accountant should not use the phrase "presents fairly" when commenting on tables, statistics, and other financial information, since this phrase relates to presentations of financial statements. (Appropriate ways of expressing comments on tables, statistics, and other financial information addressing these points are illustrated in examples F, G, and H in the appendix to SAS-72.)

Concluding paragraph

The comfort letter ordinarily concludes with a paragraph describing the purpose and intended use of the letter, including a statement that it is strictly for the use of the addressees and the underwriter. (Paragraph 7 of the sample comfort letter in Exhibit AU 634-2 illustrates appropriate wording for a concluding paragraph.)

Disclosure of subsequently discovered matters

When the accountant discovers matters (e.g., decreases or changes in specified items not disclosed in the registration statement) that may require mention in the final comfort letter, the accountant should discuss them with the client so that appropriate consideration is given to whether disclosure should be made in the registration statement. The accountant should inform the client that if such disclosure is not made, such matters will be mentioned in the comfort letter. Also, the accountant should recommend that the client promptly inform the underwriter of the matters the accountant has discovered.

Exhibit AU 634-2 is a typical comfort letter, extracted from the appendix to SAS-72, which contains a variety of sample comfort letters.

Practitioner's Aids

Exhibit AU 634-1 is an example of a required representation letter as illustrated in SAS-72. Exhibit AU 634-2 is an example of a sample comfort letter as illustrated in the appendix to SAS-72.

EXHIBIT AU 634-1 — REPRESENTATION LETTER FROM REQUESTING PARTIES

Dear ABC Accountants:

[Name of financial intermediary], as principal or agent, in the placement of *[identify securities]* to be issued by *[name of issuer]*, will be reviewing certain information relating to *[issuer]* that will be included *[incorporated by reference]* in the document *[if appropriate, the document should be identified]*, which may be delivered to investors and utilized by them as a basis for their investment decision. This review process, applied to the information relating to the issuer, is [will be] substantially consistent with the due diligence review process that we would perform if this placement of securities *[or issuance of securities in an acquisition transaction]* were being registered pursuant to the Securities Act of 1933 (the Act). We are knowledgeable with respect to the due diligence review process that would be performed if this placement of securities were being registered pursuant to the Act. We hereby request that you deliver to us a "comfort" letter concerning the financial statements of the issuer and certain statistical and other data included in the offering document. We will contact you to identify the

procedures we wish you to follow and the form we wish the comfort letter to take.

Very truly yours,

[Name of financial intermediary]

EXHIBIT AU 634-2 — SAMPLE COMFORT LETTER

June 28, 20X6

[Addressee]

Dear Sirs:

We have audited the consolidated balance sheets of the Blank Company, Inc. (the company) and subsidiaries as of December 31, 20X5 and 20X4, and the consolidated statements of income, retained earnings (stockholders' equity), and cash flows for each of the three years in the period ended December 31, 20X5, and the related financial statement schedules all included in the registration statement (no. 33-00000) on Form S-1 filed by the company under the Securities Act of 1933 (the Act); our reports with respect thereto are also included in that registration statement.[1] The registration statement, as amended on June 28, 20X6, is herein referred to as the registration statement.[2] In connection with the registration statement:

1. We are independent certified public accountants with respect to the company within the meaning of the Act and the applicable published rules and regulations thereunder.

2. In our opinion [*include the phrase "except as disclosed in the registration statement," if applicable*], the consolidated financial statements and financial statement schedules audited by us and included in the registration statement comply as to form in all material respects with the applicable accounting requirements of the Act and the related published rules and regulations.

3. We have not audited any financial statements of the company as of any date or for any period subsequent to December 31, 20X5; although we have conducted an audit for the year ended December 31, 20X5, the purpose (and therefore the scope) of the

audit was to enable us to express our opinion on the consolidated financial statements as of December 31, 20X5, and for the year then ended, but not on the financial statements for any interim period within that year. Therefore, we are unable to and do not express any opinion on the unaudited condensed consolidated balance sheet as of March 31, 20X6, and the unaudited condensed consolidated statements of income, retained earnings (stockholders' equity), and cash flows for the three-month periods ended March 31, 20X6 and 20X5, included in the registration statement, or on the financial position, results of operations, or cash flows as of any date or for any period subsequent to December 31, 20X5.

4. For purposes of this letter we have read the 20X6 minutes of meetings of the stockholders, the board of directors, and [include other appropriate committees, if any] of the company and its subsidiaries as set forth in the minute books at June 23, 20X6, officials of the company having advised us that the minutes of all such meetings[3] through that date were set forth therein; we have carried out other procedures to June 23, 20X6, as follows (our work did not extend to the period from June 24, 20X6, to June 28, 20X6, inclusive):

   a. With respect to the three-month periods ended March 31, 20X6 and 20X5, we have:

      (i) Performed the procedures specified by the American Institute of Certified Public Accountants for a review of interim financial information as described in SAS No. 100, Interim Financial Information, on the unaudited condensed consolidated balance sheet as of March 31, 20X6, and unaudited condensed consolidated statements of income, retained earnings (stockholders' equity), and cash flows for the three-month periods ended March 31, 20X6 and 20X5, included in the registration statement.

      (ii) Inquired of certain officials of the company who have responsibility for financial and accounting matters whether the unaudited condensed consolidated financial statements referred to in a (i) comply as to form in all material respects with the applicable accounting requirements of the Act and the related published rules and regulations.

   b. With respect to the period from April 1, 20X6, to May 31, 20X6, we have:

    (i)   Read the unaudited consolidated financial statements[4,5] of the company and subsidiaries for April and May of both 20X5 and 20X6 furnished us by the company, officials of the company having advised that no such financial statements as of any date or for any period subsequent to May 31, 20X6, were available.

   (ii)   Inquired of certain officials of the company who have responsibility for financial and accounting matters whether the unaudited consolidated financial statements referred to in b (i) are stated on a basis substantially consistent with that of the audited consolidated financial statements included in the registration statement.

The foregoing procedures do not constitute an audit conducted in accordance with generally accepted auditing standards. Also, they would not necessarily reveal matters of significance with respect to the comments in the following paragraph. Accordingly, we make no representations regarding the sufficiency of the foregoing procedures for your purposes.

5.   Nothing came to our attention as a result of the foregoing procedures, however, that caused us to believe that:

  a.(i)   Any material modifications should be made to the unaudited condensed consolidated financial statements described in 4a(i), included in the registration statement, for them to be in conformity with generally accepted accounting principles.[6]

   (ii)   The unaudited condensed consolidated financial statements described in 4a(i) do not comply as to form in all material respects with the applicable accounting requirements of the Act and the related published rules and regulations.

  b.(i)   At May 31, 20X6, there was any change in the capital stock, increase in long-term debt, or decrease in consolidated net current assets or stockholder's equity of the consolidated companies as compared with amounts shown in the March 31, 20X6, unaudited condensed consolidated balance sheet included in the registration statement, or

   (ii)   for the period from April 1, 20X6, to May 31, 20X6, there were any decreases, as compared to the corresponding period in the preceding year, in consolidated net sales or in the total or per-share amounts of income before extraordinary items or of net income, except in all instances for changes, increases, or decreases that the registration statement discloses have occurred or may occur.

6. As mentioned in 4b, company officials have advised us that no consolidated financial statements as of any date or for any period subsequent to May 31, 20X6, are available; accordingly, the procedures carried out by us with respect to changes in financial statement items after May 31, 20X6, have, of necessity, been even more limited than those with respect to the periods referred to in 4. We have inquired of certain officials of the company who have responsibility for financial and accounting matters whether (a) at June 23, 20X6, there was any change in the capital stock, increase in long-term debt or any decreases in consolidated net current assets or stockholders' equity of the consolidated companies as compared with amounts shown on the March 31, 20X6, unaudited condensed consolidated balance sheet included in the registration statement or (b) for the period from April 1, 20X6, to June 23, 20X6, there were any decreases, as compared with the corresponding period in the preceding year, in consolidated net sales or in the total or per-share amounts of income before extraordinary items or of net income. On the basis of these inquiries and our reading of the minutes as described in 4, nothing came to our attention that caused us to believe that there was any such change, increase, or decrease, except in all instances for changes, increases, or decreases that the registration statement discloses have occurred or may occur.

7. This letter is solely for the information of the addressees and to assist the underwriters in conducting and documenting their investigation of the affairs of the company in connection with the offering of the securities covered by the registration statement, and it is not to be used, circulated, quoted, or otherwise referred to within or without the underwriting group for any purpose, including but not limited to the registration, purchase, or sale of securities, nor is it to be filed with or referred to in whole or in part in the registration statement or any other document, except that reference may be made to it in the underwriting agreement or in any list of closing documents pertaining to the offering of the securities covered by the registration statement.

¹ The example includes financial statements required by SEC regulations to be included in the filing. If additional financial information is covered by the comfort letter, appropriate modifications should be made.

² The example assumes that the accountants have not previously reported on the interim financial information. If the accountants have previously reported on the interim financial information, they may refer to that fact in the introductory paragraph of the comfort letter as follows:

> Also, we have reviewed the unaudited condensed consolidated financial statements as of March 31, 20X6 and 20X5, and for the three-month periods then ended, as indicated in our report dated May 15, 20X6, which is included (incorporated by reference) in the registration statement.

The report may be attached to the comfort letter (see paragraph 28 of SAS-72). The accountants may agree to comment in the comfort letter on whether the interim financial information complies as to form in all material respects with the applicable accounting requirements of the published rules and regulations of the SEC.

³ The accountants should discuss with the secretary those meetings for which minutes have not been approved. The letter should be modified to identify specifically the unapproved minutes of meetings that the accountants have discussed with the secretary.

⁴ If the interim financial information is incomplete, a sentence similar to the following should be added: ''The financial information for April and May is incomplete in that it omits the statements of cash flows and other disclosures.''

⁵ If there has been a change in accounting principle during the interim period, a reference to that change should be included therein.

⁶ SAS-100 (AU 722) does not require the accountants to modify the report on a review of interim financial information for a lack of consistency in the application of accounting principles provided that the interim financial information appropriately discloses such matters.

Note to Exhibit AU 634-2: This letter assumes the following circumstances: The prospectus (Part I of the registration statement) includes audited consolidated balance sheets as of December 31, 20X5 and 20X4, and audited consolidated statements of income, retained earnings (stockholders' equity), and cash flows for each of the three years in the period ended December 31, 20X5. Part I also includes an unaudited condensed consolidated balance sheet as of March 31, 20X6, and unaudited condensed consolidated statements of income, retained earnings (stockholders' equity), and cash flows for the three-month periods ended March 31, 20X6 and 20X5, reviewed in accordance with SAS-100 (AU 722) but not previously reported on by the accountants. Part II of the registration statement includes audited consolidated financial statement schedules for the three years ended December 31, 20X5. The cutoff date is June 23, 20X6, and the letter is dated June 28, 20X6. The effective date is June 28, 20X6. Each of the comments in the letter is in response to a requirement of the underwriting agreement. For purposes of this example, the income statement items of the current interim period are to be compared with those of the corresponding period of the preceding year.

> **PUBLIC COMPANY IMPLICATION:** Because comfort letters are associated with filings under the federal securities laws, references in Exhibit AU 634-2 to "independent certified public accountants" are to be changed to "independent registered public accounting firm"; references to "generally accepted auditing standards" are to be changed to "standards of the Public Company Accounting Oversight Board (United States)"; and references to "procedures of the American Institute of Certified Public Accountants" are to be changed to "standards of the Public Company Accounting Oversight Board."

AU 700

Special Topics

Section 711: Filings under Federal Securities Statutes 691

Section 722: Interim Financial Information 697

SECTION 711

FILINGS UNDER FEDERAL SECURITIES STATUTES

Authoritative Pronouncements

SAS-37 — Filings Under Federal Securities Statutes

Auditing Interpretation No. 1 (May 1983) — Subsequent Events Procedures for Shelf Registration Statements Updated After the Original Effective Date

Auditing Interpretation No. 2 (March 1995) — Consenting to Be Named as an Expert in an Offering Document in Connection with Securities Offerings Other Than Those Registered Under the Securities Act of 1933

Auditing Interpretation No. 3 (June 1992) — Consenting to the Use of an Audit Report in an Offering Document in Securities Offerings Other Than One Registered Under the Securities Act of 1993

> **IMPORTANT NOTICE FOR 2011:** The Auditing Standards Board (ASB) is in the process of redrafting all of the auditing sections in *Codification of Statements on Auditing Standards* to converge U.S. GAAS with the International Standards on Auditing issued by the International Auditing and Assurance Standards Board. As part of this process, the newly redrafted standards will follow certain clarity drafting conventions adopted by the ASB. These clarity drafting conventions include: (1) establishing objectives for each standard; (2) including a definitions section, if appropriate; and (3) separating requirements from application guidance and other material. The ASB is planning to have all redrafted standards become effective on the same date, which is for audits of financial statements for periods ending on or after December 15, 2012. It is possible that the effective date might be delayed beyond that date. The ASB's clarity and convergence project will have a significant effect on the auditing standards applicable to audits of nonpublic companies, and the 2012 *GAAS Guide* will be appropriately modified to reflect these changes once the effective date of the standards is certain.

Overview

SAS-37 provides guidance for the accountant whose report, based on a review of interim financial information, is presented or incorporated by reference in a filing under the Securities Act of 1933. SAS-37 also provides guidance for the auditor and accountant in the area of subsequent events that occur after filings with the Securities and Exchange Commission (SEC).

SAS-37 states that generally an accountant's responsibility for filings under federal securities statutes is no different from the accountant's responsibility in any other reporting engagement. However, the Securities Act of 1933 and its related rules and regulations contain specific duties and responsibilities for any expert whose report or valuation is used as part of a registration statement filed with the SEC. An accountant's report on a review of interim financial information is not a report under the existing rules of the SEC. If an accountant's report is based on a review of interim financial information, the SEC requires that any reference to such a report in any filing with the SEC contain a statement that the report is not a report on part of the registration statement under Sections 7 and 11 of the Securities Act of 1933. Thus, an accountant's report on a review of interim financial information is exempt under Sections 7 and 11 of the Securities Act of 1933. Section 11(a) is one of the most important sections of the Act, in specifying the duties and responsibilities of an auditor or an accountant:

> Section 11(a): If any part of a registration statement that becomes effective contains an untrue statement of a material fact or omits a material fact required in order to make the statement not misleading, any person acquiring such security may either at law or at equity sue:

1. Every person who signed the registration statement

2. Every person who was a director or partner

3. Every accountant, engineer, or appraiser, or any other expert professional

4. Every underwriter with respect to such securities

Although an accountant's report based on a review of interim financial information is exempt from Sections 7 and 11 of the Securities Act of 1933, an auditor's report on an examination of financial statements that is made in accordance with generally accepted auditing standards is not exempt.

A registration statement is effective on the twentieth day after filing, or after filing of the last amendment to the registration statement. The independent auditor's statutory duties and responsibilities for his or her reports, other than those based on an interim review of financial information, do not cease until the effective date of the registration statement. Thus, an auditor must perform certain audit procedures to include the period from the date of the financial statements covered by the report through the effective date of the registration statement. This is called the "subsequent-events period." To complete a review of subsequent events, the auditor must arrange for the client to keep him or her informed of the progress of the registration statement. In the subsequent-events period, the auditor should employ the same audit procedures used to identify subsequent events in regular audited statements.

Promulgated Procedures Checklist

The auditor should perform the following procedures related to filings under federal securities statutes:

- Perform standard subsequent review procedures.

- Perform subsequent review procedures specifically related to filings under federal securities statutes.

- Determine whether unaudited financial information incorporated through reference is appropriate.

- Review documents filed with the SEC.

Analysis and Application of Procedures

Perform standard subsequent review procedures

The auditor should perform the same procedures typically performed as part of the review for subsequent events related to the audit engagement. These procedures are discussed in AU 560.

Perform subsequent review procedures specifically related to filings under federal securities statutes

In addition to the usual audit procedures for the subsequent-events period, the auditor should perform the following procedures:

1. Read the entire prospectus and the pertinent parts of the registration statement thoroughly.

2. Make inquiries of responsible executives of the client regarding any financial and accounting matters of a material nature that may have occurred during the subsequent-events period.

3. Obtain client representation letters covering any subsequent events that have a material effect on the audited financial statements.

A predecessor auditor whose report for a prior period appears in a filing with the SEC is responsible for subsequent events from the date of the financial statements covered in the prior-period report to the effective date of the registration statement that materially relate to the prior-period financial statements. The predecessor auditor should perform the following procedures:

1. Read the pertinent portions of the prospectus and registration statement carefully.

2. Obtain a representation letter from the current auditor on whether anything of a material nature came to his or her attention during the examination, including subsequent events, for which the predecessor auditor is required to disclose or make an adjustment.

3. If adjustments or disclosures are discovered that affect the prior-period financial statements, the predecessor auditor needs to be satisfied about what procedures are necessary under the circumstances. Thus, the predecessor auditor may need to make inquiries and perform certain audit procedures in order to be satisfied.

If the client refuses to make adjustments or disclosures for subsequent events as deemed necessary by the auditor, the auditor should follow the procedures promulgated for Subsequent Discovery of Facts Existing at the Date of the Auditor's Report. These procedures are discussed in AU 561.

> **PLANNING AID REMINDER:** Interpretation No. 1 of AU 711 states that an auditor must perform subsequent-events procedures as described in SAS-37, paragraphs 10 and 11, with respect to filing a single shelf registration statement that permits companies to register a designated amount of securities for continuous or delayed offering when (1) a posteffective amendment to the shelf registration statement is filed pursuant to Item 512(a) of Regulation S-K or (2) a 1934 Act filing that includes or amends audited financial statements is incorporated by reference into the shelf registration statement.
>
> **OBSERVATION:** Interpretation No. 2 of AU 711 states that the auditor should not consent to be named, or referred to, as an expert with respect to a securities offering other than those registered under the Securities Act of 1933. Interpretation No. 3 of AU 711 states that an auditor may consent to the use of his or her audit report in an offering document other than the one registered under the Securities Act of 1933.

When subsequent events or subsequently discovered facts come to the auditor's attention, standards established by AU 560 (Subsequent Events) and AU 561 (Subsequent Discovery of Facts Existing at the Date of the Auditor's Report) should be observed.

Determine whether unaudited financial information incorporated through reference is appropriate

If unaudited financial statements or unaudited interim financial statements are presented or incorporated by reference in a filing with the SEC, and if the accountant subsequently determines that such statements are not in conformity with generally accepted accounting principles, the accountant must insist that the client make the appropriate disclosures or revisions. If the client refuses to make the appropriate changes, the accountant should consider withholding consent to the use of the report on the client's audited financial statements, if any, for filings with the SEC. The accountant should also seek the advice of legal counsel.

Review documents filed with the SEC

Usually, a prospectus contains an expert section that includes the names of the experts whose reports or valuations are included in the registration statement. An important procedure that the auditor or accountant should perform is to read all the pertinent sections of the prospectus, the registration statement, and any other documents filed with the SEC. No document filed with the SEC should imply that the independent auditor actually prepared the financial statements on which the report is based. Financial statements are prepared by, and are direct representations of, the management of an enterprise. The auditor or accountant should read the relevant sections of filings made to the SEC carefully to make sure that they contain no indication of responsibility for the financial statements greater than what was actually intended.

Practitioner's Aids

Exhibit AU 711-1, which is reproduced from SAS-37, illustrates acceptable wording to be included in a registration statement that describes the status of the accountant's review report that was part of the 10-Q filing and is then incorporated in the registration statement through reference.

EXHIBIT AU 711-1 — DESCRIPTION OF STATUS OF REVIEW REPORT INCORPORATED THROUGH REFERENCE IN A REGISTRATION STATEMENT

The consolidated balance sheets as of December 31, 20X5, and 20X4, and the consolidated statements of income, retained earnings, and cash flows for each of the three years in the period ended December 31, 20X5, incorporated by reference in this prospectus, have been included herein in reliance on the report of _____ independent public accountants, given on the authority of that firm as experts in auditing and accounting.

With respect to the unaudited interim financial information for the periods ended March 31, 20X6, and 20X5, incorporated by reference in this prospectus, the independent public accountants have reported that they have applied limited procedures in accordance with professional standards for a review of such information. However, their separate report included in the company's quarterly report on Form 10-Q for the quarter ended March 31, 20X6, and incorporated by reference herein, states that they did not audit and they do not express an opinion on that interim financial information. Accordingly, the degree of reliance on their report on such information should be restricted in light of the limited nature of the review procedures applied. The accountants are not subject to the liability provisions of Section 11 of the Securities Act of 1933 for their report on the unaudited interim financial information, because that report is not a "report" or a "part" of the registration statement prepared or certified by the accountants within the meaning of Sections 7 and 11 of the Act.

SECTION 722

INTERIM FINANCIAL INFORMATION

Authoritative Pronouncements

SAS-100 — Interim Financial Information

SAS-116 — Interim Financial Information

Overview

Interim financial information may be issued on a monthly or quarterly basis or at any other interval deemed appropriate by the client or a regulatory authority. SAS-100, as amended by SAS-116, notes that an interim period also includes data or information issued for a 12-month period ending on a date other than the client's normal year-end date.

> **IMPORTANT NOTICE FOR 2011:** The Auditing Standards Board (ASB) issued SAS-116 (Interim Financial Information), which amends SAS-110 to establish standards and provide guidance on the independent accountant's professional responsibilities when he or she is engaged to review interim financial information of a nonissuer. SAS-116 removes the guidance for reviews of the interim financial statements of issuers because such guidance appropriately resides in the auditing standards of the PCAOB. SAS-116 was issued in conjunction with the issuance of SSSARS-18 (Applicability of Statements on Standards for Accounting and Review Services). Together, SAS-116 and SSARS-18 require the accountant to follow the guidance in AU 722 when engaged by a nonissuer to review interim financial information.

Interim financial information may be presented alone or included in a note to the audited financial statements. SAS-116 applies when the accountant is engaged by a nonissuer to review interim financial information if

- The entity's latest financial statements have been audited by the accountant or a predecessor;

- The accountant has been engaged to audit the current-year financial statements or audited the entity's latest annual financial statements and expects to be engaged to audit the current-year financial statements; and

- The client prepares its interim financial information in accordance with the same financial reporting framework as that used to prepare the annual financial statements.

SAS-116 also applies to reviews of interim financial information that is condensed information if all of the following conditions are met:

- The condensed interim financial information purports to conform with an appropriate financial reporting framework, which includes appropriate form and content of interim financial statements;

- The condensed interim financial information includes a note that the financial information does not represent complete financial statements and should be read in conjunction with the entity's latest annual audited financial statements; and

- The condensed financial information accompanies the entity's latest audited annual financial statements or such audited annual financial statements are made readily available by the entity.

> **PLANNING AID REMINDER:** SAS-100, as amended by SAS-116, is applicable to interim financial information that is to be reviewed. Interim financial statements may be audited, in which case the auditor follows generally accepted auditing standards. The special accounting practices and modifications established by APB-28 (Interim Financial Reporting) and Financial Accounting Standards Board Interpretation No. 18 (FIN-18) (Accounting for Income Taxes in Interim Periods) should be followed in the preparation of the interim financial statements, with one exception: APB-28 states that the gross-profit method can be used to determine inventories at the interim date; however, if the interim financial statements are audited, the auditor would have to observe the inventory at or near the date of the interim statements.

> **PUBLIC COMPANY IMPLICATION:** The PCAOB's AS-7 (Engagement Quality Review) establishes standards for the performance of an engagement quality review. AS-7 applies to all firms registered with the PCAOB (prior to AS-7, only firms that were members of the AICPA's SECPS were required to perform a concurring review). In addition to applying to audits performed under PCAOB standards, AS-7 also applies to reviews. However, the procedures required to be performed by the engagement quality reviewer for a review of interim financial information would be more limited. For all such engagements, an engagement review would be required to be conducted before the report is issued. The engagement reviewer would be required to be a partner of the firm performing the engagement, another person in an equivalent position in the firm, or an individual outside the firm who is associated with a registered public accounting firm. The engagement reviewer would be required to have competence, independence, integrity, and objectivity. He or she would be required to have the

level of competence needed to have an overall responsibility for the engagement under review (although the quality reviewer is not actually serving as the engagement partner). To maintain objectivity, the engagement reviewer would not be permitted to make decisions for the engagement team or assume responsibilities of the team. In addition, a partner cannot serve as the engagement quality reviewer for a client if the partner had served as the engagement partner for either of the client's two previous audits; however, this prohibition does not apply to certain small auditing firms that are exempt from the audit partner rotation rules under SEC regulation. Certain review procedures are required on every audit engagement, and review procedures generally involve discussions with engagement personnel and review of documents. Review procedures must be performed with due professional care and professional skepticism. Required engagement quality review procedures are more limited when the service being reviewed is an interim review. In addition, the engagement quality reviewer would be required to review documentation in the areas that he or she reviewed. The engagement quality reviewer would be required to assess whether this documentation indicates that the engagement team responded appropriately to significant risks (audit engagements only) and whether the documentation supports conclusions reached by the engagement team (both for audit and review engagements). The engagement quality reviewer must adequately document his or her review procedures. The firm would not be permitted to issue its report (or communicate its conclusion to the client if no report was to be issued) until the engagement quality reviewer granted his or her concurring approval. The PCAOB has stated that compliance with ASB standards (e.g., SQCS-7) is not sufficient to comply with AS-7.

Responsibility and function of the accountant

The purpose of an audit is to determine whether the financial statements are presented fairly in accordance with generally accepted accounting principles. A review of interim financial information differs significantly from an audit of financial information, because a review does not include the collection of corroborative evidence through the performance of typical substantive audit tests. Basically, the review of interim financial information consists of the performance of certain inquiries and analytical procedures. For these reasons, a review provides limited assurance on the interim financial information.

SAS-100, as amended by SAS-116, states that the purpose of a review is to provide the accountant with a basis for reporting whether material modifications are necessary for the interim financial information to be in conformity with the applicable financial reporting framework. The accountant acquires the basis for reporting by applying the standards for a review of interim financial information in accordance with AU 722. The accountant issues a report containing an expression of limited assurance that, on the basis of the review, he or she is not aware of any material modification that should be made to the interim financial information for it to be in conformity with the applicable financial reporting framework.

Pre-engagement planning

Rule 201 of the Code of Professional Conduct states, in part, that a professional service engagement must be adequately planned and supervised. The Code defines professional services as one or more types of services performed in the practice of public accounting. Thus, Rule 201 is applicable to a review of interim financial information. In most instances, the auditor's review of interim financial information is a continuation of a professional relationship that has included the audit of the prior period's annual financial statements. For this reason, much of the pre-engagement planning is an extension of the audit engagement, which is discussed in AU 311.

Promulgated procedures checklist

The auditor should perform the following procedures when reporting on interim financial information:

- Establish an understanding with the client.
- Acquire knowledge of the entity's business and internal control.
- Perform analytical procedures and related inquiries.
- Perform inquiries and other review procedures.
- Consider making inquiries related to litigation, claims, and assessments.
- Consider making inquiries concerning the entity's ability to continue as a going concern.
- Consider performing extended interim review procedures.
- Obtain written representations from management.
- Evaluate the results of performing the review procedures.
- Consider communicating with management, audit committees, and others.
- Prepare appropriate documentation for the review engagement.

Analysis and Application of Procedures

Establish an understanding with the client

The accountant should establish an understanding with the client concerning the review of interim financial information in order that both parties clearly understand the purpose of the engagement. SAS-116 requires the accountant to document the understanding through a written communication with the client. SAS-100, as amended by SAS-116, points out that the understanding would generally encompass the following points:

- The objective of a review of interim financial information is to provide the accountant with a basis for communicating whether he or she is aware of any material modifications that should be made to the interim financial information for it to conform with the applicable financial reporting framework.

- A review includes obtaining sufficient knowledge of the entity's business and its internal control as it relates to the preparation of both annual and interim financial information to

  — Identify the types of potential misstatements in the interim financial information and consider the likelihood of their occurrence and

  — Select the inquiries and analytical procedures that will provide the accountant with a basis for communicating whether he or she is aware of any material modifications that should be made to the interim financial information for it to conform with the applicable financial reporting framework.

- Limitations of a review engagement, including acknowledgement that a review does not provide a basis for expressing an opinion on the interim financial information.

- Management is responsible for the entity's interim financial information.

- Management is responsible for establishing and maintaining effective internal control over financial reporting.

- Management is responsible for identifying and ensuring that the entity complies with the laws and regulations applicable to its activities.

- Management is responsible for making all financial records and related information available to the accountant.

- At the conclusion of the engagement, management will provide the accountant with a letter confirming certain representations made during the review.

- Management is responsible for adjusting the interim financial information to correct material misstatements. Although a review of interim financial information is not designed to obtain reasonable assurance that the interim financial information is free from material misstatement, management also is responsible for affirming in its representation letter to the accountant that the effects of any uncorrected misstatements aggregated by the accountant during the current engagement and pertaining to the current period(s) under review are immaterial, both individually and in the aggregate, to the financial information taken as a whole.

- The accountant is responsible for conducting the review in accordance with standards established by the AICPA. A review of interim financial information consists principally of performing analytical procedures and making inquiries of persons responsible for financial and accounting matters. It is substantially less in scope than an audit conducted in accordance with generally accepted auditing standards, the objective of which is the expression of an opinion regarding the financial statements taken as a whole. Accordingly, the accountant will not express an opinion on the interim financial information.

- A description of the expected form of the accountant's communication (whether as a written or oral report) upon completion of the engagement and a statement that if the entity states in any report, document, or written communication containing the interim financial information that the information has been reviewed by the accountant or makes other reference to the accountant's association, that the accountant's review report will be included in the document.

- A review is not designed to provide assurance on internal control or to identify control deficiencies. However, the accountant is responsible for communicating to management and those charged with governance any significant deficiencies or material weaknesses in internal control over financial reporting that come to his or her attention.

> **PLANNING AID REMINDER:** SAS-115 (Communication of Internal Control Related Matters Identified in an Audit), requires the auditor of financial statements to communicate in writing to management and those charged with governance significant deficiencies and material weaknesses that were identified. Although an audit of financial statements is not designed to perform procedures to detect control deficiencies,

SAS-115 requires the communications when the auditor identifies significant deficiencies and material weaknesses in internal control over financial reporting. The ASB adopted the PCAOB definitions of "control deficiency," "significant deficiency," and "material weakness."

PUBLIC COMPANY IMPLICATION: Although a review is not designed to provide assurance on internal control, the auditor's involvement in evaluating internal controls on an interim basis is likely to increase because of SEC and PCAOB requirements. First, management must disclose to the auditor (1) all changes during the quarter in internal control over financial reporting that materially affected, or are likely to materially affect, the entity's internal control, (2) all significant deficiencies and material weaknesses in the design and operation of internal control on a quarterly basis, and (3) any fraud, regardless of materiality, involving management or any other person who plays an important role in the entity's internal control over financial reporting. Second, because the auditor must issue its own opinion on the effectiveness of the entity's internal control over financial reporting as part of its annual audit report, it seems likely that internal control testing will occur throughout the year.

Acquire knowledge of the entity's business and internal control

In order to successfully execute a review of interim financial information, the accountant must have both an understanding of the client's business and its internal control used to prepare annual as well as interim financial information. This background (1) helps identify financial information that has the greatest potential for misstatement and (2) provides focus in determining which analytical procedures and inquiries should be made. SAS-100, as amended by SAS-116, states that procedures such as the following should be employed in order to acquire knowledge of the entity's business and internal control.

Review audit documentation of the previous year's audit, current year's interim review(s), and corresponding interim period(s) of the prior year and specifically:

- Consider corrected material misstatements.

- Consider nature of uncorrected misstatements.

- Identify risks as related to material misstatements due to fraud (including the risk of management overriding controls).

- Identify significant accounting and reporting matters, such as internal control significant deficiencies or material weaknesses that may still exist.

- Read the most recent annual and comparable prior interim period financial information.

- Consider the results of applying audit procedures to the current year's financial statements.

- Make inquiries of management concerning changes in its business activities.

- Make inquiries of management concerning changes in internal control (such as policies, procedures, and personnel) related to interim financial information that have occurred since the previous audit of annual financial information or prior review of interim financial information.

> **PUBLIC COMPANY IMPLICATION:** Management must disclose to the auditor all changes during the quarter in internal control over financial reporting that materially affected, or are likely to materially affect, the entity's internal control.

If the accountant has not previously reviewed a new client's interim financial information, he or she must nonetheless obtain an adequate understanding of the client's business and its internal control. Specifically, under this circumstance, the accountant should do the following:

- Make appropriate inquiries of the predecessor accountant.

- Obtain permission from the predecessor accountant in order to review his or her audit documentation for the previous annual audit and for any reviews made during the current year and consider the nature of the following:

  — Corrected material misstatements.

  — Nature of uncorrected misstatements.

  — Risks identified as related to material misstatements due to fraud (including the risk of management overriding controls).

  — Significant accounting and reporting matters, such as internal control weaknesses that may still exist.

> **OBSERVATION:** The accountant should also consider obtaining permission from the predecessor accountant in order to review his or her audit documentation for interim reviews made during the previous year.

When the predecessor accountant does not respond to the accountant's inquiries or allow access to audit documentation for previous engagements, the accountant must use alternative procedures in order to obtain an adequate understanding of the client's business and internal control.

Perform Analytical Procedures and Related Inquiries

Analytical procedures should be applied by the accountant in order to "identify and provide a basis for inquiry about the relationships and individual items that appear to be unusual and that may indicate a material misstatement." The specific analytical procedures and related inquiries employed should be based on the accountant's understanding of the client's business and internal control discussed in the previous section. SAS-100, as amended by SAS-116, identifies the following as analytical procedures that should be performed in a review of interim financial information:

- Compare the current interim information to the previous interim information.

- Compare the current interim information to the comparable period in the previous year.

- Compare the current year-to-date interim information to the comparable period in the previous year.

- Consider reasonable relationships between financial and nonfinancial information (the information may include material developed by client).

- Compare recorded amounts (including ratios derived from recorded amounts) to expectations developed by the accountant.

- Compare disaggregated revenue information with similar information for previous periods.

Perform Inquiries and Other Review Procedures

In addition to performing the analytical procedures described above to provide a basis for making inquiries of members of management, the following review procedures should be performed:

- Read minutes of meetings of stockholders, directors, and appropriate committees (for meetings where minutes are not available, make inquiries of appropriate personnel).

- Read reports prepared by other accountants who have reviewed subsidiaries, segments, etc. of the client (for reviews in which reports were not prepared, make inquiries of the other accountants).

Based on the performance of analytical procedures, the reading of minutes of meetings, the reading of reports prepared by other accountants, and other procedures that may have been performed, the following inquiries should be made of management:

- Has the interim financial information been prepared in accordance with the applicable financial reporting framework?

- What is the nature and purpose of unusual or complex situations that affect the interim financial information?

- What is the nature and purpose of significant transactions recognized during the last few days of the interim period?

- What is the status of unrecorded misstatements identified in the previous audit engagement or the previous interim review engagement?

- What is the explanation for a matter discovered during the current review engagement?

- Are there events that have occurred after the interim period that might affect interim financial information?

- Is there fraud or suspected fraud involving (1) management, (2) employees who have significant roles in internal control, or (3) others where the fraud could have a material implication for the interim financial information?

- Are there any allegations of fraud or suspected fraud made by various external parties or regulators?

- What is the nature and purpose of significant journal entries and other adjustments?

- Have there been communications from regulatory agencies concerning the financial information?

- What is the nature of significant deficiencies and material weaknesses in internal control that could have an effect on preparing both annual and interim financial information?

In addition to the above inquiries, SAS-100 requires that the following additional procedures be performed as part of the review of interim financial information:

- Determine that the interim financial information agrees (or reconciles) with the accounting records and make inquiries of management concerning the reliability of the accounting records.

- Based on the evidence gathered during the review engagement, read the interim financial information and consider whether the information appears to be reported in accordance with generally accepted accounting principles.

- Read the other information in documents containing the interim financial information to consider whether the information is materially inconsistent with the interim financial information.

Consider making inquiries related to litigation, claims, and assessments

Generally the accountant is not required to make inquiries of the client's lawyer concerning litigation, claims, and assessment in a review of interim financial information; however, SAS-100, as amended by SAS-116, states that if information comes to the accountant's attention that suggests that the interim financial information does not properly reflect such matters, appropriate inquiries should be directed to the client's lawyer.

Consider making inquiries concerning the entity's ability to continue as a going concern

Generally the accountant is not required to collect evidence that might identify conditions or events that raise substantial doubt about the client's ability to continue as a going concern, except under the following circumstances:

- During the course of the review engagement, information came to the attention of the accountant that raises such doubts.

- Such doubts existed at the date of the prior-period financial statements (either at the preceding year-end or at end of the preceding interim period), regardless of whether the auditor's consideration of management plans resulted in the auditor issuing an unmodified report.

- When either of these two circumstances exists, the accountant should do the following:

  — Inquire about management's plans for dealing with the possible negative impact of the conditions and events.

  — Determine whether the conditions are adequately disclosed in the interim financial information.

Consider performing extended interim review procedures

During the performance of the review of interim financial information, questions might arise as to whether the information conforms to the applicable financial reporting framework. Under this circumstance the accountant should perform extended review procedures in order to determine whether the interim financial information should be revised.

Obtain written representations from management

SAS-100, as amended by SAS-116, requires the accountant to obtain written representations from management for each interim financial information review engagement. The written representations should relate to the following:

- Representations concerning financial statements:

  — Management acknowledges responsibility for the fair presentation of the interim financial information in conformity with the applicable financial reporting framework.

  — Management believes that the interim financial information has been prepared in conformity with the applicable financial reporting framework.

- Representations concerning internal control:

  — Management acknowledges responsibility to establish and maintain controls that are sufficient to provide a reasonable basis for the preparation of reliable interim financial information in accordance with the applicable financial reporting framework.

  — Management has disclosed all significant deficiencies (including material weaknesses) in the design or operation of internal controls that could have an adverse affect on its ability to record, process, summarize, and report both annual and interim financial information.

  — Management is responsible for the design and implementation of programs and controls to prevent and detect fraud.

  — Management has communicated to the accountant knowledge of fraud or suspected fraud affecting the entity involving (1) management, (2) employees who have significant roles in internal control, or (3) others where the fraud could have a material effect on the interim financial information.

  — Management has communicated to the accountant knowledge of any allegations of fraud or suspected fraud affecting the entity received in communications from employees, former employees, analysts, regulators, short sellers, or others.

- Representations concerning completeness of information:

  — Management has made all financial records and related data available to the accountant.

  — Management represents that all minutes of meetings of stockholders, directors, and committees of directors or summaries of actions of recent meetings for which minutes have not been prepared have been made available to the accountant and that such minutes or summaries of actions are complete.

  — Management represents that all communications with regulatory authorities concerning noncompliance with or deficiencies in financial reporting practices have been made available to the accountant.

  — Management represents that there are no unrecorded transactions.

- Representations concerning recognition, measurement, and disclosure.

  — Management believes that the effects of any unrecorded financial misstatements in the financial statements determined by the accountant are immaterial.

  — Management has disclosed to the accountant plans that may have a material effect on the carrying value or classification of assets and liabilities.

  — Management has disclosed to the accountant related-party transactions, including related receivables and payables.

  — Management has disclosed to the accountant written or oral guarantees that create contingent liabilities.

  — Management has identified significant estimates and material concentrations that are required to be disclosed based on the guidance established by ASC 275 (AICPA's Statement of Position 94-6, Disclosure of Certain Significant Risks and Uncertainties).

  — Management has disclosed to the accountant violations or possible violations of laws or regulations that might have an effect on interim financial information.

  — Management has identified unasserted claims or assessments that are probable of assertion and that must be disclosed as required by ASC 450 (FAS-5, Accounting for Contingencies).

  — Management has identified other liabilities or gain or loss contingencies that must be disclosed as required by ASC 450 (FAS-5).

— Management represents satisfactory title to all owned assets, liens, or encumbrances on such assets and assets pledged as collateral.

— Management represents compliance with contractual agreements that may have implications for the interim financial information.

• Representations concerning subsequent events:

— Management has informed the accountant of subsequent events that might affect the interim financial information.

In addition to the specific representations required above by SAS-100, the accountant should consider the particular characteristics of the client to determine which additional representations should be made by management. For example, a client that operates in an industry addressed by an AICPA Accounting and Auditing Guide should consider whether other representations should be obtained from management.

An example of a representation letter for the review of interim financial information of a public company is presented in Exhibit AU 722-1.

Evaluate the results of performing the review procedures

The application of review procedures can identify likely misstatements, which are described by SAS-100, as amended by SAS-116, as "the accountant's best estimate of the total misstatement in the account balances or classes of transactions on which he or she has performed review procedures." These misstatements should be evaluated individually as well as in the aggregate to determine whether the interim information should be adjusted or otherwise modified. This evaluation is based on the accountant's professional judgment; however, SAS-100 states that factors such as the following should be considered:

• The amount and the reason for the misstatement

• The occurrence date of the misstatement (current period or the previous period)

• The basis for determining whether an item is material

• The possible effect of the misstatement on future interim or annual periods

For those uncorrected likely misstatements, the accountant should also consider the following:

• The appropriateness of offsetting a likely misstatement that is based on an estimate with a misstatement that is subject to measurement that is more precise

- The possible material effect on future financial information of current balance sheet misstatements that are considered immaterial

  OBSERVATION: When an accountant is not able to perform appropriate review procedures (including specific written representations from the client), a review report cannot be issued.

Consider communicating with management, audit committee, and others

SAS-100, as amended by SAS-116, requires the accountant to communicate with management and those charged with governance under the following circumstances:

- The interim financial information should be modified because of material misstatements.

- The entity issued the interim financial information before the review was completed.

If after being informed of these matters management does not respond appropriately, the accountant should inform those charged with governance. If those charged with governance do not subsequently respond appropriately, the accountant (perhaps in consultation with legal counsel) should consider whether to resign from the engagement.

  OBSERVATION: The accountant should also observe the guidance in AU 380 in determining additional matters that should be communicated to the client's audit committee.

  OBSERVATION: If matters concerning possible illegal acts or fraud arise, the accountant should follow the guidance established by SAS-54 (Illegal Acts by Clients) and SAS-99 (Consideration of Fraud in a Financial Statement Audit).

  OBSERVATION: If matters concerning internal control deficiencies over financial reporting come to the accountant's attention, the guidance established in SAS-115 (Communication of Internal Control Related Matters Identified in an Audit) should be considered. SAS-115 requires the auditor of financial statements to communicate in writing identified significant deficiencies and material weaknesses to management and those charged with governance.

When the accountant determines that a matter should be communicated to those charged with governance, he or she should communicate with those charged with governance or at least the chair of the audit committee (or similar subgroup with a different name) on a sufficiently timely basis to enable those charged with governance to take appropriate action.

Prepare appropriate documentation for the review engagement

The accountant should prepare appropriate documentation, such as review programs, various analyses, and memoranda to demonstrate what procedures were performed and to support the conclusions reached during the engagement. In addition, the review engagement documentation should include the following:

- Descriptions, client's responses, and conclusions related to any matters considered significant (such as possible departures from generally accepted accounting principles discovered during the engagement)

- Material that enables proper supervision and review of procedures

- Identification of members of the engagement review team

- Identification of evidence that enabled the accountant to determine that the interim financial information agrees (or reconciles) with the accounting records

Reporting Standards

The accountant is not required to issue a review report on a review of interim financial information. However, if the accountant is engaged to issue a written report or determines that a written report is applicable, his or her review report on interim financial information should be prepared according to the following guidelines:

- Include a title that uses the word "independent."

- State that the interim financial information has been reviewed.

- State that the interim financial information is the responsibly of management.

- State that the review was performed in accordance with standards established by the AICPA.

- Provide a general description of review procedures.

- State that the scope of a review engagement is substantially less than the scope of an audit in accordance with auditing standards generally accepted in the United States, the objective of which is to express an opinion on the information and no such opinion is expressed.

- State whether the accountant is aware of any material misstatements that should be made to the interim financial information for it to conform with the applicable financial reporting framework.

- Identify the country of origin of the accounting principles.

- Sign the review report.

- Date the review report.

> **OBSERVATION:** Each page of the interim financial information must be clearly marked as unaudited.

Exhibit AU 722-2 is an example of a standard review report.

Report Modifications

The following circumstances may preclude the issuance of a review report or require modification to the standard review report:

- Departures from generally accepted accounting principles

- Existence of substantial doubt related to going concern

- Emphasis of a matter

Departures from generally accepted accounting principles

If material deviations from the applicable financial reporting framework are discovered, the accountant should modify the review report on interim financial information by (1) including an explanatory paragraph (or paragraphs) that describes the deviation and, if possible, the effects of the deviation on the interim financial information and (2) modify the concluding paragraph by referring to the explanatory paragraph.

Exhibit AU 722-3 is an example of a review report on interim financial information that has a departure from GAAP.

When interim financial statements are presented, disclosures should be sufficient to constitute a fair presentation of financial position, results of operations, and cash flows. APB-28 (Interim Financial Reporting), however, establishes minimum disclosure requirements for interim financial information for publicly traded companies. If the accountant concludes that disclosures are not adequate, the review report should identify the inadequacy and, if practicable, include the required disclosure in the report.

Exhibit AU 722-4 is an example of a review report on interim financial information that includes an inadequate disclosure.

Existence of substantial doubt related to going concern

SAS-100, as amended by SAS-116, points out that the report on interim financial information does not have to be modified for the existence of substantial doubt related to the client's ability to continue as a going concern if all of the following conditions exist:

- The audit report for the previous year-end included an explanatory paragraph related to substantial doubt about the entity's ability to continue as a going concern

- The reason that was the basis for the substantial doubt question continues to exist at the current interim reporting date

- The condition is adequately disclosed in the current interim financial information

Although the foregoing conditions do not require a modification of the review report, an explanatory paragraph can be included in the report. An example of this type of report is presented in Exhibit AU 722-5.

Also, SAS-100, as amended by SAS-116, states that the report on interim financial information does not have to be modified if the auditor's report for the previous year did not include an explanatory paragraph due to the existence of substantial doubt regarding the entity's continuation as a going concern but that such a condition now exists as of the date of the interim financial report and the condition is adequately disclosed in the current financial information. Even though these conditions do not require a modification of the review report, an explanatory paragraph can be included in the report. An example of this type of report is presented in Exhibit AU 722-6.

Discovery of Facts Subsequent to the Date of the Review Report

Information might come to the attention of the accountant after the date of the review report that might have had an effect on the report if the information had been known to the accountant before the report was issued. SAS-100, as amended by SAS-116, does not provide specific guidance under this circumstance because of the potential diversity of the matters that might be discovered and the circumstances under which they might be discovered; however, SAS-100 does recommend that under these conditions the general guidance established by SAS-1 (AU 561) (Codification of Auditing Standards and Procedures — Subsequent Discovery of Facts Existing at the Date of the Auditor's Report) is helpful.

Client's Representation in Regulatory Filings, and Communications with Stockholders and Third Parties

In instances in which a client represents in a filing with a regulatory authority or communications with stockholders or third parties (that include the interim financial information) that the interim information has been reviewed by an accountant, the review report must be included as part of the filing or communication. If the client will not agree to the inclusion, SAS-100, as amended by SAS-116, requires that the accountant do the following:

- Inform the client that the accountant's name is not to be associated with or referred to in the document that contains the interim financial information.

- Consider recommending that the client consult legal counsel in order to determine how to address the issue.

- Consider taking other actions, including contacting legal counsel.

If a client represents in a filing with a regulatory authority or communications with stockholders or third parties (that include the interim financial information) that the interim information has been reviewed by an accountant and the accountant has not completed the review, the accountant should follow the guidance discussed in the previous section titled "Consider Communicating with Management, Audit Committee, and Others."

Interim Financial Information Included with Audited Financial Statements

Interim financial information may be included as supplementary information or as a note to the client's audited financial statements. Under both circumstances the interim information should be clearly marked as unaudited; however, the auditor's report need not indicate that the interim financial information has been reviewed. On the other hand, SAS-100, as amended by SAS-116, points out that the audit report should be modified in the following situations:

- When interim financial information does not appear to conform with the applicable financial reporting framework, the audit report should include an explanatory paragraph that describes the departure. (There is no need for this modification to the audit report if the departure from the applicable financial reporting framework has been included in the review report on the interim financial information and that report is included with the information.)

• When interim financial information is included in a note but has not been clearly marked as unaudited, the audit report should disclaim an opinion on the interim financial information.

> **OBSERVATION:** When the audit report is modified for the above reasons, that modification does not affect the opinion on the audited financial statements.

Practitioner's Aids

The following exhibits are presented in this section:

• Exhibit AU 722-1 — Client Representation Letter for a Review of Interim Financial Information

• Exhibit AU 722-2 — Standard Review Report on Interim Financial Information

• Exhibit AU 722-3 — Standard Review Report on Interim Financial Information That Contains a Departure from GAAP

• Exhibit AU 722-4 — Standard Review Report on Interim Financial Statements That Contain An Inadequate Disclosure

• Exhibit AU 722-5 — Review Report on Interim Financial Statements with An Explanatory Paragraph Related to a Going Concern Issue Referred to in the Previous Audit Report

• Exhibit AU 722-6 — Review Report on Interim Financial Statements with An Explanatory Paragraph Related to a Going Concern Issue Not Referred to in the Previous Audit

EXHIBIT AU 722-1 — CLIENT REPRESENTATION LETTER FOR A REVIEW OF INTERIM FINANCIAL INFORMATION

Bluefield Company
1400 Maple Street
Bluefield, NJ 08000

[*Date*]

Mr. Arthur Oldes
Arthur Oldes & Company
1040 Main Street
Bluefield, NJ 08000

Dear Mr. Oldes:

We are providing this letter in connection with your review of the [*identification of interim financial information*] of [*name of client*] as of [*dates*] and for the [*periods*] for the purpose of determining whether any material modifications should be made to the interim financial information, for it to conform with [*identify the applicable financial reporting framework, such as* accounting principles generally accepted in the United States of America]. We confirm that we are responsible for the fair presentation of the interim financial information in conformity with [*identify the applicable financial reporting framework*] and that we are responsible for establishing and maintaining controls that are sufficient to provide a reasonable basis for the preparation of reliable interim financial information in accordance with [*identify the applicable financial reporting framework*].

Certain representations in this letter are described as being limited to matters that are material. Items are considered material, regardless of size, if they involve an omission or misstatement of accounting information that, in the light of surrounding circumstances, makes it probable that the judgment of a reasonable person relying on the information would be changed or influenced by the omission or misstatement.

We confirm, to the best of our knowledge and belief, [as of [*date of accountant's report or completion of review*],] the following representations made to you during your review.

The interim financial information referred to above has been prepared and presented in conformity with [*identify the applicable financial reporting framework*].

We have made available to you:

All financial records and related data.

All minutes of the meetings of stockholders, directors, and committees of directors, or summaries of actions of recent meetings for which minutes have not yet been prepared. All significant board and committee actions are included in the summaries.

We believe that the effects of any uncorrected financial statement misstatements aggregated by you during the current review engagement and pertaining to the interim period(s) in the current year, as summarized in the accompanying schedule, are immaterial, both individually and in the aggregate to the interim financial information taken as a whole.

There are no significant deficiencies or material weaknesses in the design or operation of internal controls as it relates to the preparation of both annual and interim financial information.

We acknowledge our responsibility for the design and implementation of programs and controls to prevent and detect fraud.

We have no knowledge of any fraud or suspected fraud affecting the company involving:

Management;

Employees who have significant roles in internal control; or

Others where the fraud could have a material effect on the interim financial information.

We have no knowledge of any allegations of fraud or suspected fraud affecting the company received in communications from employees, former employees, analysts, regulators, short sellers, or others.

We have reviewed our representation letter to you dated [*date of representation letter relating to most recent audit*] with respect to the audited financial statements for the year ended [*prior year-end date*]. We believe that representations A, B, and C within that representation letter do not apply to the interim financial information referred to above. We now confirm those representations 1 through X, as they apply to the interim financial information referred to above, and incorporate them herein, with the following changes:

[*indicate changes*]

[*Add any representations related to new accounting or auditing standards that are being implemented for the first time.*]

To the best of our knowledge and belief, no events have occurred subsequent to the balance-sheet date and through the date of this letter that would require adjustment to or disclosure in the aforementioned interim financial information.

_____

[Name of chief executive officer and title]

_____

[Name of chief financial officer and title]

_____

[Name of chief accounting officer and title]

EXHIBIT AU 722-2 — STANDARD REVIEW REPORT ON INTERIM FINANCIAL INFORMATION

Independent Accountant's Report

Board of Directors
Bluefield Company
Bluefield, NJ 08000

We have reviewed the accompanying *[describe the interim financial information or statements reviewed]* of Bluefield Company as of June 30, 20X5, and for the three-month and six-month periods then ended. This interim financial information is the responsibility of the company's management.

We conducted our review in accordance with standards established by the American Institute of Certified Public Accountants. A review of interim financial information consists principally of applying analytical procedures and making inquiries of persons responsible for financial and accounting matters. It is substantially less in scope than an audit conducted in accordance with auditing standards generally accepted in the United States, the objective of which is the expression of an opinion regarding the financial information taken as a whole. Accordingly, we do not express such an opinion.

Based on our review, we are not aware of any material modifications that should be made to the accompanying interim financial information for it to be in conformity with accounting principles generally accepted in the United States of America.

[Signature of Accountant]

July 21, 20X5

*EXHIBIT AU 722-3—STANDARD REVIEW REPORT
ON INTERIM FINANCIAL INFORMATION THAT
CONTAINS A DEPARTURE FROM GAAP*

Independent Accountant's Report

Board of Directors
Bluefield Company
Bluefield, NJ 08000

We have reviewed the accompanying [*describe the interim financial information or statements reviewed*] of Bluefield Company as of June 30, 20X5, and for the three-month and six-month periods then ended. This interim financial information is the responsibility of the company's management.

We conducted our review in accordance with standards established by the American Institute of Certified Public Accountants. A review of interim financial information consists principally of applying analytical procedures and making inquiries of persons responsible for financial and accounting matters. It is substantially less in scope than an audit conducted in accordance with auditing standards generally accepted in the United States, the objective of which is the expression of an opinion regarding the financial information taken as a whole. Accordingly, we do not express such an opinion.

Based on information furnished to us by management, we believe that the company has excluded from debt in the accompanying balance sheet certain obligations related to defined benefits pension plans that we believe should be presented to conform with accounting principles generally accepted in the United State of America. This information indicates that if these obligations were presented at June 30, 20X5, long-term debt would increase by $_____, and net income and earnings per share would be increased (decreased) by $_____, $_____, $_____, and $_____, respectively for the three-month and six-month periods then ended.

Based on our review, with the exception of the matters described in the preceding paragraph(s), we are not aware of any material modifications that should be made to the accompanying interim financial information for it to be in conformity with accounting principles generally accepted in the United States of America.

[*Signature of Accountant*]

July 21, 20X5

EXHIBIT AU 722-4 — STANDARD REVIEW REPORT ON INTERIM FINANCIAL STATEMENTS THAT CONTAIN AN INADEQUATE DISCLOSURE

Independent Accountant's Report

Board of Directors
Bluefield Company
Bluefield, NJ 08000

We have reviewed the accompanying [*describe the interim financial statements reviewed*] of Bluefield Company as of June 30, 20X5, and for the three-month and six-month periods then ended. This interim financial information is the responsibility of the company's management.

We conducted our review in accordance with standards established by the American Institute of Certified Public Accountants. A review of interim financial information consists principally of applying analytical procedures and making inquiries of persons responsible for financial and accounting matters. It is substantially less in scope than an audit conducted in accordance with auditing standards generally accepted in the United States, the objective of which is the expression of an opinion regarding the financial information taken as a whole. Accordingly, we do not express such an opinion.

Management had informed us that the company is a defendant in litigation concerning personal injuries alleged to have occurred to a customer while on the company's premises. The amount of damages to be paid to the plaintiff, if any, cannot currently be determined. The interim financial information fails to disclose this matter, which we believe is required to be disclosed in conformity with accounting principles generally accepted in the United States.

Based on our review, with the exception of the matters described in the preceding paragraph, we are not aware of any material modifications that should be made to the accompanying interim financial information for it to be in conformity with accounting principles generally accepted in the United States of America.

[*Signature of Accountant*]

July 21, 20X5

EXHIBIT AU 722-5 — REVIEW REPORT ON INTERIM FINANCIAL STATEMENTS WITH AN EXPLANATORY PARAGRAPH RELATED TO A GOING CONCERN ISSUE REFERRED TO IN THE PREVIOUS AUDIT REPORT

Independent Accountant's Report

Board of Directors
Bluefield Company
Bluefield, NJ 08000

We have reviewed the accompanying interim financial information of Bluefield Company as of June 30, 20X5, and for the three-month and six-month periods then ended. This interim financial information is the responsibility of the company's management.

We conducted our review in accordance with standards established by the American Institute of Certified Public Accountants. A review of interim financial information consists principally of applying analytical procedures and making inquiries of persons responsible for financial and accounting matters. It is substantially less in scope than an audit conducted in accordance with auditing standards generally accepted in the United States, the objective of which is the expression of an opinion regarding the financial information taken as a whole. Accordingly, we do not express such an opinion.

Based on our review, we are not aware of any material modifications that should be made to the accompanying interim financial information for it to be in conformity with accounting principles generally accepted in the United States of America.

Note X of the Company's audited financial statements as of December 31, 20X4, and for the year then ended discloses that the Company [*describe the condition that raised substantial doubt*]. Our auditor's report on those financial statements includes an explanatory paragraph referring to the matters in Note X of those financial statements and indicating that these matters raised substantial doubt about the Company's ability to continue as a going concern. As indicated in Note 3 of the Company's unaudited interim financial information as of June 30, 20X6, and for the six months then ended, the Company was still [*describe the continuing condition that still exists*]. The accompanying interim financial information does not include any adjustments that might result from the outcome of this uncertainty.

[*Signature of Accountant*]

July 21, 20X5

EXHIBIT AU 722-6 — REVIEW REPORT ON INTERIM FINANCIAL STATEMENTS WITH AN EXPLANATORY PARAGRAPH RELATED TO A GOING CONCERN ISSUE NOT REFERRED TO IN THE PREVIOUS AUDIT REPORT

Independent Accountant's Report

Board of Directors
Bluefield Company
Bluefield, NJ 08000

We have reviewed the accompanying interim financial information of Bluefield Company as of June 30, 20X5, and for the three-month and six-month periods then ended. This interim financial information is the responsibility of the company's management.

We conducted our review in accordance with standards established by the American Institute of Certified Public Accountants. A review of interim financial information consists principally of applying analytical procedures and making inquiries of persons responsible for financial and accounting matters. It is substantially less in scope than an audit conducted in accordance with auditing standards generally accepted in the United States, the objective of which is the expression of an opinion regarding the financial information taken as a whole. Accordingly, we do not express such an opinion.

Based on our review, we are not aware of any material modifications that should be made to the accompanying interim financial information for it to be in conformity with accounting principles generally accepted in the United States of America.

As indicated in Note X, certain conditions indicate that the Company may be unable to continue as a going concern. The accompanying interim financial statements do not include any adjustments that might result from the outcome of this uncertainty.

[*Signature of Accountant*]

July 21, 20X5

AU 800

Compliance Auditing

Section 801: Compliance Auditing Considerations in Audits of
    Governmental Entities and Recipients of Governmental
    Financial Assistance 727

SECTION 801

COMPLIANCE AUDITING CONSIDERATIONS IN AUDITS OF GOVERNMENTAL ENTITIES AND RECIPIENTS OF GOVERNMENTAL FINANCIAL ASSISTANCE

Authoritative Pronouncements

SAS-117 — Compliance Audits

[This SAS supersedes SAS-74 (Compliance Auditing Considerations in Audits of Governmental Entities and Recipients of Governmental Financial Assistance).]

> **IMPORTANT NOTICE FOR 2011:** The Auditing Standards Board (ASB) is in the process of redrafting all of the auditing sections in *Codification of Statements on Auditing Standards* to converge U.S. GAAS with the International Standards on Auditing issued by the International Auditing and Assurance Standards Board. As part of this process, the newly redrafted standards will follow certain clarity drafting conventions adopted by the ASB. SAS-117 (which superseded SAS-74) represents the redrafted and clarified guidance for AU 801. Although the ASB expects that the redrafted standards will become effective on the same date, the effective date for the guidance in AU 801 has been accelerated to address certain practice issues. SAS-117 is effective for compliance audits for fiscal periods beginning on or after June 15, 2010. Early application is permitted.

Overview

The guidance in AU 801 applies when an auditor is engaged or required by law or regulation to perform a compliance audit in accordance with GAAS, the financial auditing standards under *Government Auditing Standards*, and a governmental audit requirement requiring an auditor to express an opinion on compliance. For example, AU 801 applies to an audit performed in accordance with the provisions of Office of Management and Budget (OMB) Circular A-133, *Audits of States, Local Governments and Non-Profit Organizations*.

AU 801 does not apply to an engagement that does not require that the audit be performed according to both GAAS and *Government Auditing Standards*. Under these circumstances, the engagement could be performed under AT 601 (Compliance Attestation), AT 101 (Attest Engagements), or AT 201 (Agreed-Upon Procedures Engagements), depending on the government requirements. AT 601 is also applicable when the governmental audit requirement requires an examination of an entity's compliance with specified requirements in accordance with the Statements on Standards for Attestation Engagements or an examination of an entity's internal control over compliance. If an entity is required to undergo a compliance audit and an examination of internal control over compliance, AU 801 applies to the compliance audit and AT 601 applies to the examination of internal control over compliance. Law or regulation does not always prescribe which standards the auditor should follow, so he or she will need to use professional judgment in this determination.

AU 801 assists the auditor in applying GAAS to a compliance audit, which is often performed in conjunction with a financial statement audit. Although AU Sections 100–700 and 900 address financial statement audits, only AU Sections 100–300 and 500 can generally be adapted to a compliance audit's objectives. When planning and performing a compliance audit, the auditor should obtain sufficient appropriate audit evidence to support his or her opinion. However, the auditor is not required to translate each financial statement audit procedure into a compliance audit procedure. AU 801 provides the auditor with more specific guidance on how to adapt and apply relevant AU Sections to a compliance audit.

Management is responsible for the entity's compliance with compliance requirements in a compliance audit. Management's responsibilities include (1) identifying the entity's government programs and understanding and complying with compliance requirements, (2) establishing and maintaining effective controls that provide reasonable assurance that the entity administers government programs in compliance with compliance requirements, (3) evaluating and monitoring the entity's compliance with compliance requirements, and (4) taking corrective action when instances of noncompliance are identified, including findings of the compliance audit.

In a compliance audit, the auditor's objective is to obtain sufficient appropriate audit evidence to form an opinion and report at the level specified in the governmental audit requirement on whether the entity complied in all material respects with the applicable compliance requirements. The auditor also has the objective of identifying any audit and reporting requirements specified in the governmental audit requirement that are supplementary to GAAS and *Governmental Auditing Standards* and perform procedures to address those requirements.

Definitions

Term	Definition
Audit findings	Matters the auditor is required to report on in accordance with the governmental audit requirement
Audit risk of noncompliance	Risk that the auditor expresses an inappropriate audit opinion on the entity's compliance when material noncompliance exists; function of the risks of material noncompliance and detection risk of noncompliance
Compliance audit	A program-specific or organization-wide audit of an entity's compliance with applicable compliance requirements
Compliance requirements	Laws, regulations, rules, and provisions of contracts or grant agreements applicable to government programs with which the entity is required to comply
Deficiency in internal control over compliance	A deficiency in internal control over compliance exists when the design or operation of a control over compliance does not allow management or employees to prevent, or detect and correct, noncompliance on a timely basis in the course of their normal activities
Detection risk of noncompliance	The risk that the procedures the auditor performs to reduce audit risk of noncompliance to an acceptably low level will not detect existing noncompliance that could be material, either individually or when aggregated with other instances of noncompliance
Government Auditing Standards	Standards and guidance issued by the Comptroller General of the United States, U.S. Government Accountability Office for financial audits, attestation engagements, and performance audits; also known as generally accepted government auditing standards (GAGAS) or the Yellow Book
Government program	The means by which governmental entities achieve their objectives
Grantor	A government agency that funds the government program
Known questioned costs	Questioned costs specifically identified by the auditor; a subset of likely questioned costs
Likely questioned costs	The auditor's best estimate of total questioned costs developed by extrapolating from audit evidence obtained, for example, by projecting known questioned costs identified in an audit sample to the entire population from which the sample was drawn

Term	Definition
Material noncompliance	If not otherwise identified in the governmental audit requirement, a failure to follow compliance requirements or a violation of prohibitions included in the applicable compliance requirements that results in noncompliance that is quantitatively or qualitatively material to the affected government program, either individually or when aggregated with other noncompliance
Material weakness in internal control over compliance	A deficiency or combination of deficiencies in internal control over compliance such that there is a reasonable possibility that material noncompliance with a compliance requirement will not be prevented, or detected and corrected, on a timely basis. A reasonable possibility exists when the event's likelihood is reasonably possible or probable.
Organization-wide audit	An audit of an entity's financial statements and its compliance with the applicable compliance requirements as they relate to one or more government programs that the entity administers
Pass-through entity	An entity that receives an award from a grantor or other entity and distributes all or part of it to another entity to administer a government program
Program-specific audit	An audit of an entity's compliance with applicable compliance requirements as they relate to one government program that the entity administers performed in conjunction with an audit of the entity's or program's financial statements
Questioned costs	Costs that are questioned by the auditor because (1) of a violation or possible violation of compliance requirements; (2) of lack of support by adequate documentation; or (3) the incurred costs appear unreasonable and do not reflect a prudent person's actions in the circumstances
Risk of material noncompliance	The risks that material noncompliance exists prior to the audit; consists of the inherent risk of noncompliance and the control risk of noncompliance
Significant deficiency in internal control over compliance	A deficiency or combination of deficiencies in internal control over compliance that is less severe than a material weakness in internal control over compliance yet important enough to merit attention by those charged with governance

Requirements

The auditor is presumptively required to perform the following procedures when performing a compliance audit.

Planning and Performing a Compliance Audit

1. Adapt and apply the relevant AU sections to the objectives of a compliance audit.

2. Establish and apply materiality levels for the compliance audit based on the governmental audit requirement.

3. Determine which of the entity's government programs and compliance requirements to test.

4. For each government program and compliance requirement tested, perform risk assessment procedures to understand the applicable compliance requirements and the entity's internal control over compliance with the applicable compliance requirements.

5. In performing risk assessment procedures, ask management if there are findings and recommendations in written communications from previous audit or attestation engagements or monitoring that directly relate to the compliance audit's objectives. Gain an understanding of management's response to any findings and recommendations that could have a material effect on the entity's compliance with applicable compliance requirements and use this information to assess risk and determine the nature, timing, and extent of the audit procedures for the compliance audit and the extent to which testing the implementation of any corrective actions is applicable to the audit objectives.

6. Assess the risks of material noncompliance due to fraud or error for each applicable compliance requirement and consider whether any of those risks are pervasive, affecting the entity's compliance with many compliance requirements.

7. Develop an overall response to any identified pervasive risks of material noncompliance.

8. Design and perform further audit procedures, including tests of details, in response to the assessed risks of material noncompliance to obtain sufficient appropriate audit evidence about the entity's compliance with each applicable compliance requirement. Risk assessment procedures, tests of controls, and analytical procedures by themselves are not sufficient to address these risks.

9. Tests of controls and their operating effectiveness over each applicable compliance requirement should be performed in response to the assessed risks of material noncompliance if (1) the auditor's risk assessment includes an expectation of the operating effectiveness of controls over compliance related to the applicable compliance requirements, (2) substantive procedures alone do not provide sufficient appropriate audit evidence, or (3) tests of controls over compliance are required by the governmental audit requirement.

10. Perform procedures to address any additional audit requirements specified in the governmental audit requirement supplementary to GAAS and *Government Auditing Standards.*

11. Request written representations from management tailored to the entity and the governmental audit requirement stating management's:

    a. Acknowledgement of responsibility for understanding and complying with the compliance requirements

    b. Acknowledgement of responsibility for establishing and maintaining controls providing reasonable assurance that the entity administers government programs in accordance with the compliance requirements

    c. Identification and disclosure to the auditor all of its government programs and related activities subject to the governmental audit requirement

    d. Making available to the auditor all contracts, grant agreements, amendments, and any other correspondence relevant to the programs and related activities subject to the governmental audit requirement

    e. Disclosure to the auditor of all known noncompliance with the applicable compliance requirements or stating that there was no such noncompliance

    f. Belief as to whether the entity has complied with the applicable compliance requirements excepting any noncompliance disclosed to the auditor

    g. Making available to the auditor all documentation related to compliance with the applicable compliance requirements

    h. Interpretation of any applicable compliance requirements subject to varying interpretations

    i. Disclosure to the auditor of any communications from grantors and pass-through entities about possible noncompliance with applicable compliance requirements, including communications to the date of the auditor's report

j. Disclosure to the auditor of findings received and related corrective actions taken up to the date of the auditor's report for previous audits, attestation engagements, and internal or external monitoring that directly relate to the compliance audit's objectives

k. Disclosure to the auditor of all known noncompliance with the applicable compliance requirements subsequent to the period covered by the auditor's report or stating that there is no known noncompliance

l. Responsibility for taking corrective action on audit findings of the compliance audit

12. Perform audit procedures up to the date of the auditor's report to obtain sufficient appropriate audit evidence that all subsequent events related to the entity's compliance during the period covered by the auditor's compliance report have been identified. Take into account the risk assessment in determining the nature and extent of the audit procedures, which should include but not be limited to inquiring of management about and considering any relevant internal auditors' reports, other auditors' reports, and reports from grantors and pass-through entities about the entity's noncompliance that were issued during the subsequent period, and information about the entity's noncompliance obtained through other professional engagements performed for the entity.

13. Form an opinion at the level specified by the governmental audit requirement on whether the entity complied in all material respects with the applicable compliance requirements and report appropriately. Evaluate likely questioned costs and other material noncompliance that may not result in questioned costs.

Reporting on a Compliance Audit

14. The auditor's report on compliance should include:

a. A title including the word "independent"

b. Identification of government programs covered by the compliance audit or reference to a schedule containing that information

c. Identification of applicable compliance requirements or reference to where they can be found

d. Identification of the period covered by the report

e. A statement that the entity's management is responsible for compliance with the applicable compliance requirements

f. A statement that the auditor is responsible for expressing an opinion on the entity's compliance with the applicable compliance requirements based on the compliance audit

g. A statement that the compliance audit was conducted in accordance with auditing standards generally accepted in the United States of America, standards applicable to financial audits contained in *Governmental Auditing Standards*, and the governmental audit requirement

h. A statement that the compliance audit included examining, on a test basis, evidence about the entity's compliance with those requirements and performing such other procedures as the auditor considered necessary in the circumstances

i. A statement that the auditor believes the compliance audit provides a reasonable basis for his or her opinion

j. A statement that the compliance audit is not a legal determination of the entity's compliance

k. The auditor's opinion on whether the entity complied with the applicable compliance requirements in all material respects at the level specified by the governmental audit requirement

l. If noncompliance is identified that results in an opinion modification or is required to be reported by the governmental audit requirement but does not result in an opinion modification, a description of the noncompliance or a reference to that description in an accompanying schedule

m. If the criteria used to evaluate compliance are established or determined by contractual agreement or regulatory provisions that are developed solely for the parties to the agreement or regulatory agency responsible for the provisions or are available only to the specified parties, a separate paragraph at the end of the report including (1) a statement that the report is intended solely for the information and use of the specified parties, (2) identification of the specified parties to whom use is restricted, and (3) a statement that the report should not be used by anyone other than the specified parties

n. The manual or printed signature of the auditor's firm

o. The date of the auditor's report

15. If the auditor's report on compliance is combined with a report on internal control over compliance required by the governmental audit requirement, the following items should be added to the report elements already listed:

    a. A statement that management is responsible for establishing and maintaining effective internal control over compliance

    b. A statement that the auditor considered the entity's internal control over compliance with the applicable compliance requirements in planning and performing the audit to determine the auditing procedures in order to express an opinion on compliance, but not an opinion on the effectiveness of internal control over compliance

    c. A statement that the auditor is not expressing an opinion on internal control over compliance

    d. A statement that the auditor's consideration of the entity's internal control over compliance was not designed to identify all internal control deficiencies that might be significant deficiencies or material weaknesses in internal control over compliance

    e. The definitions of "deficiency in internal control over compliance" and "material weakness in internal control over compliance"

    f. A description of any identified material weaknesses in internal control over compliance or reference to that description in an accompanying schedule

    g. If significant deficiencies in internal control over compliance were identified, the definition of "significant deficiency in internal control over compliance" and a description of the deficiencies or reference to that description in an accompanying schedule

    h. If no material weaknesses in internal control over compliance were identified, a statement to that effect

16. If the auditor chooses to issue a separate report on internal control over compliance required by the governmental audit requirement, the following items should be added to the report elements listed in requirement 15 (above):

    a. A title that includes the word "independent"

    b. A statement that the auditor audited the entity's compliance with applicable compliance requirements pertaining to [*identify the government program(s) and the period audited]* and a reference to the auditor's report on compliance

   c. A statement that the compliance audit was conducted in accordance with auditing standards generally accepted in the United States of America, standards applicable to financial audits contained in *Governmental Auditing Standards*, and the governmental audit requirement

   d. The manual or printed signature of the auditor's firm

   e. The date of the auditor's report

17. Noncompliance and other matters required to be reported by the governmental audit requirement should be reported in the manner specified by that requirement.

18. The auditor's opinion on compliance should be modified if (1) the compliance audit identifies noncompliance with the applicable compliance requirements that the auditor believes has a material effect on the entity's compliance or (2) there is a restriction on the scope of the compliance audit.

19. Communicate in writing to management and those charged with governance any identified significant deficiencies and material weaknesses in internal control over compliance, even if there is no governmental audit requirement to report on internal control over compliance.

20. Communicate to those charged with governance the auditor's responsibilities under GAAS, *Government Auditing Standards*, and the governmental audit requirement, an overview of the planned scope and timing of the compliance audit, and significant findings from the compliance audit.

Documentation

21. The auditor should document the following:

   a. Risk assessment procedures performed, including those performed to gain an understanding of internal control over compliance

   b. The auditor's responses to the assessed risks of material noncompliance, procedures performed, including any tests of controls over compliance, to test compliance with the applicable compliance requirements, and the results of those procedures

    c. Materiality levels and the basis on which they were determined

    d. How compliance with the specific governmental audit require-
ments supplementary to GAAS and *Government Auditing Standards* was achieved

Report Reissuance

22. If a report is reissued, it should include an explanatory paragraph stating the report is replacing a previously issued report, describing the reasons why the report is being reissued, and any changes from the previously issued report. If additional procedures are performed to obtain sufficient appropriate audit evidence for all of the government programs being reported on, the report date should be updated to the date the auditor obtained sufficient appropriate audit evidence about the events causing the auditor to perform the new procedures. If additional procedures are performed to obtain sufficient appropriate audit evidence for some of the government programs being reported on, the report should be dual dated with an updated report date being the date the auditor obtained sufficient appropriate audit evidence regarding the affected government programs and a reference to the affected government programs.

Analysis and Application of Procedures

Planning and Performing a Compliance Audit

Materiality

In a compliance audit, the auditor establishes materiality levels to:

- Determine the nature and extent of risk assessment procedures

- Identify and assess the risks of material noncompliance

- Determine the nature, timing, and extent of further audit procedures

- Evaluate whether the entity complied with the applicable compliance requirements

- Report noncompliance findings and other matters required to be reported by the governmental audit requirement

Materiality is generally considered in relation to the government program as a whole, although a different level of materiality may be specified by the governmental audit requirement for particular purposes. For example, OMB Circular A-133 requires reporting findings of noncompliance that are material in relation to one of fourteen types of compliance requirements identified in the OMB *Compliance Supplement.*

Identifying government programs and applicable compliance requirements

Some governmental audit requirements specifically identify the applicable compliance requirements, whereas others, such as the *Compliance Supplement* for OMB Circular A-133, provide a framework for the auditor to determine the applicable compliance requirements. When identifying and obtaining an understanding of applicable compliance requirements, the auditor may consult the *Compliance Supplement* used in OMB Circular A-133 audits, which contains compliance requirements that are typically applicable to federal government programs and suggested audit procedures for those requirements and also provides guidance for identifying compliance requirements for programs that are not included. The auditor may also consult the applicable program-specific audit guide issued by the grantor agency, which contains the compliance requirements pertaining to the government program and suggested audit procedures for those requirements.

If the *Compliance Supplement* or a program-specific audit guide is not applicable, the auditor may perform the following procedures to identify and obtain an understanding of the applicable compliance requirements:

- Read laws, regulations, rules, and provisions of contracts or grant agreements pertaining to the government program

- Inquire of management and other knowledgeable entity personnel

- Inquire of appropriate individuals outside the entity, such as the office of the federal, state, or local program official or auditor about the laws and regulations applicable to entities within their jurisdiction or a third-party specialist such as an attorney

- Read the minutes of meetings of the governing board of the entity being audited

- Read audit documentation about the applicable compliance requirements prepared during prior years' audits or other engagements

- Discuss the applicable compliance requirements with auditors who performed prior years' audits or other engagements

Risk assessment and audit procedures

The nature and extent of risk assessment procedures the auditor performs vary and are influenced by factors such as the following:

- The newness, complexity, and nature of the applicable compliance requirements

- The auditor's knowledge of the entity's internal control over compliance with the applicable compliance requirements obtained in previous audits or other professional engagements

- The services provided by the entity and how they are affected by external factors

- The level of oversight by the grantor or pass-through entity

- How management addresses findings

In assessing the risks of material noncompliance with the applicable compliance requirements, the auditor may consider the requirements' complexity and susceptibility to noncompliance, how long the entity has been subject to the requirements, how the entity has previously complied with the requirements, the potential effect on the entity of noncompliance, the degree of judgment involved in adhering to the requirements, and the auditor's assessment of the risks of material misstatement in the financial statement audit. Inherent and control risk of noncompliance may be evaluated individually or in combination.

> **OBSERVATION:** The risk of material noncompliance may be pervasive to the entity's noncompliance if an entity is experiencing financial difficulty and there is an increased risk that grant funds will be diverted for unauthorized purposes or an entity has a history of poor recordkeeping for its government programs.

In a compliance audit, audit procedures are designed to detect intentional and unintentional material noncompliance in order to obtain reasonable, but not absolute, assurance about the entity's compliance. Analytical procedures may contribute some substantive evidence, but they are generally less effective in a compliance audit than in a financial statement audit. Tests of details may be used to test for compliance in areas such as grant disbursements or expenditures, eligibility files, cost allocation plans, or periodic reports filed with grantor agencies.

Some governmental audit requirements such as OMB Circular A-133 require tests of the operating effectiveness of controls identified as likely to be effective even if the testing is inefficient. For compliance audits, audit evidence about the operating effectiveness of controls obtained in prior audits is not applicable.

Supplementary audit requirements

An example of supplementary audit requirements the auditor may need to adhere to are the requirements in OMB Circular A-133 to perform specified procedures to identify major programs and to follow up on prior audit findings and perform procedures to assess the reasonableness of the summary schedule of prior audit findings.

> **PLANNING AID REMINDER:** If a governmental agency's audit guidance for performing compliance audits has not been updated or it otherwise conflicts with current GAAS or *Government Auditing Standards*, comply with the most current applicable GAAS and *Government Auditing Standards*, not the outdated or conflicting guidance.

Written representations

Management may include qualifying language in the written representations indicating that the representations are made to the best of management's knowledge and belief. This qualifying language is not appropriate for the representations about management's responsibilities for understanding and complying with the compliance requirements, establishing and maintaining controls that provide reasonable assurance that the entity administers government programs in accordance with the compliance requirements, and taking corrective action on audit findings of the compliance audit.

Evaluating audit evidence and forming an opinion

In determining whether an entity has materially complied with the applicable compliance requirements, the auditor may consider factors such as:

- The frequency and nature of noncompliance with the applicable compliance requirements identified during the compliance audit

- The adequacy of the entity's system for monitoring compliance with the applicable compliance requirements and the possible effect of any noncompliance on the entity

- Whether any identified noncompliance with the applicable compliance requirements resulted in likely questioned costs that are material to the government program

The auditor should consider all noncompliance he or she identified in making this evaluation, regardless of whether the entity corrected the noncompliance after the auditor brought it to management's attention.

Reporting on a Compliance Audit

The auditor is not precluded from restricting the use of any report to intended users.

> **PLANNING AID REMINDER:** All combined reports on the entity's compliance and internal control over compliance should include the restricted-use paragraph.

> **OBSERVATION:** If a report is a matter of public record or available for public inspection, removing personally identifiable information in the report and findings of noncompliance will reduce the likelihood of sensitive information being disclosed.

Government Auditing Standards require that when the auditor communicates significant deficiencies or material weaknesses in internal control over compliance to management and those charged with governance, he or she obtain a response, preferably in writing, concerning their views on the findings, conclusions, and recommendations included in the auditor's report on internal control over compliance and any such written response be included in the auditor's report. If the written response is included in a document with the auditor's written communication to management and those charged with governance regarding identified significant deficiencies or material weaknesses in internal control over compliance, the auditor may add a paragraph to the communication disclaiming an opinion on such information.

> **PLANNING AID REMINDER:** Printed forms, schedules, and reports designed or adopted by government agencies sometimes contain prescribed wording. If the auditor has no basis to make a statement that is part of that prescribed wording, he or she should appropriately reword the document or attach an appropriately worded separate report.

Documentation

Specific documentation of how the auditor adapted and applied each of the applicable AU sections to the objectives of a compliance audit is not necessary; documentation of the audit strategy, audit plan, and the work performed is sufficient.

AU 900

Special Reports of the Committee on Auditing Procedure

Section 901: Public Warehouses — Controls and Auditing
Procedures for Goods Held 745

SECTION 901

PUBLIC WAREHOUSES — CONTROLS AND AUDITING PROCEDURES FOR GOODS HELD

Authoritative Pronouncements

SAS-1 — Codification of Auditing Standards and Procedures (Section 901, Public Warehouses — Controls and Auditing Procedures for Goods Held)

SAS-43 — Omnibus Statement on Auditing Standards

> **IMPORTANT NOTICE FOR 2011:** The Auditing Standards Board (ASB) is in the process of redrafting all of the auditing sections in *Codification of Statements on Auditing Standards* to converge U.S. GAAS with the International Standards on Auditing issued by the International Auditing and Assurance Standards Board. As part of this process, the newly redrafted standards will follow certain clarity drafting conventions adopted by the ASB. These clarity drafting conventions include: (1) establishing objectives for each standard; (2) including a definitions section, if appropriate; and (3) separating requirements from application guidance and other material. The ASB is planning to have all redrafted standards become effective on the same date, which is for audits of financial statements for periods ending on or after December 15, 2012. It is possible that the effective date might be delayed beyond that date. The ASB's clarity and convergence project will have a significant effect on the auditing standards applicable to audits of nonpublic companies, and the 2012 *GAAS Guide* will be appropriately modified to reflect these changes once the effective date of the standards is certain.

Overview

Generally, the direct confirmation of the inventory held by outside custodians provides sufficient evidence to validate the existence and ownership of the inventory. However, if the inventory held by outside custodians is significant in relation to current assets and total assets, the auditor must supplement the confirmation by performing the following procedures:

- Discuss with the client (owner of the goods) the client's control procedures in investigating the warehouseman, including tests of related audit evidence.

- Whenever practical and reasonable, observe the warehouseman's or client's count of goods.

- If warehouse receipts have been pledged as collateral, confirm details with the lenders to the extent the auditor deems necessary.

- Obtain an independent auditor's report on the warehouseman's control procedures relevant to custody of goods and, if applicable, pledge receipts; or apply alternative procedures at the warehouse to gain reasonable assurance that information received from the warehouseman is reliable (SAS-43).

Although these procedures are required by generally accepted auditing standards (GAAS), when the inventory of the auditor's client is held by a public warehouse, the public warehouse's auditor must also be concerned with the inventories owned by others but held by the public warehouse. In a special report issued by the Committee on Auditing Procedures (predecessor of the Auditing Standards Board) and incorporated as part of SAS-1 (Codification of Auditing Standards and Procedures), the following recommendations were made:

- Study and evaluate the system relating to the goods held for others.

- Test the system described above.

- Test the warehouse's accountability for recorded outstanding warehouse receipts.

- Observe physical counts whenever practical and reasonable.

- Confirm accountability with owners of the goods to the extent deemed necessary.

- Follow other audit procedures considered appropriate in the circumstances.

AT Section

Statements on Standards for Attestation Engagements

AT Section 20: Defining Professional Requirements in Statements
   on Standards for Attestation Engagements 749

AT Section 50: SSAE Hierarchy 751

AT Section 101: Attest Engagements 753

AT Section 201: Agreed-Upon Procedures Engagements 779

AT Section 301: Financial Forecasts and Projections 787

AT Section 401: Reporting on Pro Forma Financial
   Information 812

AT Section 501: Reporting on an Entity's Internal Control
   Over Financial Reporting 822

AT Section 601: Compliance Attestation 850

AT Section 701: Management's Discussion and Analysis 866

AT Section 801: Reporting on Controls at a Service
   Organization 897

AT SECTION 20

DEFINING PROFESSIONAL REQUIREMENTS IN STATEMENTS ON STANDARDS FOR ATTESTATION ENGAGEMENTS

Authoritative Pronouncements

SSAE-13 — Defining Professional Requirements in Statements on Standards for Attestation Engagements

Overview

SSAE-13 specifies the practitioner's performance responsibility under the Statements on Standards for Attestation Engagements. The standard provides guidance on when a practitioner *must* perform an attestation procedure, when the practitioner *should* perform an attestation procedure, and when a practitioner *may* perform an attestation procedure.

> **OBSERVATION:** SSAE-13 defines a practitioner's performance responsibilities with more specificity than has previously existed in the professional literature. Therefore, the authors expect that practitioners will be held to these performance standards by regulators and the judicial system. For these reasons, practitioners are well advised to pay particularly close attention to the inclusion of the words "must," "is required," "should, and "may" in existing and future professional standards.

A SSAE contains both professional requirements and related guidance in applying the standard. In fulfilling professional responsibilities, the practitioner has a responsibility to consider the entire text of a SSAE. There are two types of professional requirements imposed by a SSAE: (1) unconditional requirements and (2) presumptively mandatory requirements.

A practitioner must comply with an unconditional requirement, assuming that the circumstances that the requirement applies to exist. The existence of an unconditional requirement is indicated by the words "must" or "is required" in a SSAE.

In most cases, the practitioner is also required to comply with a presumptively mandatory requirement. In rare cases, a practitioner can depart from a presumptively mandatory requirement. But, in these rare cases, the practitioner must document (1) the reasons why the presumptively mandatory requirement was not followed and (2) how alternative procedures achieved the objectives that the presumptively mandatory requirement was designed to meet. The existence of a presumptively mandatory requirement is indicated by the word "should."

> **ENGAGEMENT STRATEGY:** The practitioner must achieve the objectives that a presumptively mandatory requirement is designed to achieve, either by performing the procedures specified in the SSAE or by employing alternative procedures that accomplish the same objective.

A SSAE may specify that a practitioner "should consider" a procedure. In this instance, there is a presumptive requirement that the practitioner will consider the procedure. However, although the practitioner essentially has to consider the procedure, the practitioner does not necessarily have to perform the procedure.

A SSAE also contains related guidance in applying the standard. This related guidance is also referred to as "explanatory material." Explanatory material in a SSAE is intended to be descriptive rather than imperative (i.e., it does not impose a performance obligation upon the practitioner). For example, explanatory material may (1) explain the objective of the professional requirements, (2) explain why particular attestation procedures are recommended or required, and (3) provide additional information that the practitioner may find helpful in applying his or her professional judgment. Explanatory material may discuss other procedures or actions that the practitioner might perform. These other procedures or actions are suggestive and do not impose a professional requirement on the practitioner. These suggested procedures and actions in a SSAE are denoted by the words "may," "might," or "could."

> **OBSERVATION:** SSAE-13 indicates that interpretive publications are not professional standards but, rather, provide guidance on the application of a SSAE to a particular circumstance. Interpretive guidance includes interpretations of the SSAEs, appendixes to SSAEs, and AICPA Statements of Position. The words "must" or "should" in an interpretive document do not represent unconditional requirements or presumptively mandatory requirements, respectively.

AT SECTION 50

SSAE HIERARCHY

Authoritative Pronouncements

SSAE-14—SSAE Hierarchy

Overview

A practitioner must follow the attestation standards in planning, conducting, and reporting on an attestation engagement. The attestation standards define the level of performance expected of the practitioner and are designed to ensure quality engagement performance. Attestation procedures are the specific steps performed by the practitioner in complying with the attestation standards.

There are 11 generally accepted attestation standards. These standards are listed and discussed in AT Section 101. The Auditing Standards Board, a senior technical body of the AICPA, issues Statements on Standards for Attestation Engagements (SSAEs). The SSAEs are essential in applying the 11 generally accepted attestation standards. Practitioners who perform an attestation engagement are required by Rule 202 of the AICPA's Code of Professional Conduct to comply with the generally accepted attestation standards and SSAEs.

Practitioners must apply professional judgment in applying the attestation standards. It should be rare for a practitioner to depart from presumptively mandatory requirements in performing an attestation engagement. If a practitioner departs from a presumptively mandatory requirement, he or she must document the reason for the departure and how the alternative procedures performed accomplished the objectives of the requirements that were not being followed.

In addition to the generally accepted attestation standards and SSAEs, there are other sources of guidance on performing attestation engagements. These other sources of guidance are attestation interpretations and other attestation publications.

Attestation interpretations are Interpretations of SSAEs, SSAE appendixes, attestation guidance in AICPA Audit and Accounting Guides, and AICPA attestation Statements of Position. The practitioner should consider these attestation interpretations in performing an engagement. If the practitioner chooses not to apply the guidance that is in an attestation interpretation, he or she should be prepared to explain how he or she met the SSAE requirement that was the subject of the attestation interpretation.

> **OBSERVATION:** An appendix to a SSAE that modifies another SSAE must be complied with in the same manner as the body of the SSAE.

Other attestation publications are a broad set of literature, including (1) other AICPA attestation publications, (2) attestation articles in professional journals and newsletters, (3) continuing education programs, (4) textbooks and guide books, and (5) state CPA society publications. Other attestation publications have no authoritative status, but the practitioner may consider and apply this guidance if it is relevant and appropriate to the engagement. In evaluating whether an attestation publication is appropriate, the practitioner should consider (1) the degree to which the publication is recognized as helpful in understanding and applying SSAEs and (2) the degree to which the issuer or author is recognized as an authority on attestation matters.

> **OBSERVATION:** An attestation publication that has been reviewed by the AICPA Audit and Attest Standards Staff is presumed to be appropriate.

AT SECTION 101

ATTEST ENGAGEMENTS

Authoritative Pronouncements

SSAE-10 — Attestation Standards: Revision and Recodification (Chapter 1)

> **OBSERVATION:** SSAE-10 supersedes SSAE-1 through SSAE-9.

SSAE-11 — Attest Documentation

SSAE-12 — Amendment to SSAE No. 10, Attestation Standards: Revision and Recodification

SSAE Interpretation No. 1 of AT 101 (January 2001) — Defense Industry Questionnaire on Business Ethics and Conduct

SSAE Interpretation No. 2 of AT 101 (January 2001) — Responding to Requests for Reports on Matters Relating to Solvency

SSAE Interpretation No. 3 of AT 101 (January 2001) — Applicability of Attestation Standards to Litigation Services

SSAE Interpretation No. 4 of AT 101 (January 2002) — Providing Access to or Photocopies of Working Papers to a Regulator

SSAE Interpretation No. 5 of AT 101 (September 2003) — Attest Engagements on Financial Information Included in XBRL Instance Documents

SSAE Interpretation No. 6 of AT 101 (January 2005) — Reporting on Attestation Engagements Performed in Accordance with Government Auditing Standards

SSAE Interpretation No. 7 of AT 101 (December 2008) — Reporting on the Design of Internal Control

Overview

Before standards for attest engagements (or attestation engagements) were promulgated, the professional standards did not specifically address certain types of auditing and accounting engagements. For example, there were no professional standards for engagements to report on (1) descriptions of computer software; (2) compliance with statutory, regulatory, and contractual requirements; (3) investment performance statistics; and (4) nonfinancial information supplementary to financial statements. These and other auditing and accounting engagements that are not addressed by other existing professional standards may be covered by the standards for attest engagements.

Statements on Standards for Attestation Engagements (SSAE) establish attestation standards that must be satisfied by an auditor when he or she is "engaged to issue or does issue an examination, a review, or an agreed-upon procedures report on subject matter, or an assertion about the subject matter (the assertion), that is the responsibility of another party" except in the following circumstances:

- Engagements performed in accordance with Statements on Auditing Standards (SASs)

- Engagements performed in accordance with Statements on Standards for Accounting and Review Services (SSARSs)

- Engagements performed in accordance with Statements on Standards for Consulting Services (SSCS)

- Engagements in which the auditor is the client's advocate (such as tax disputes with the Internal Revenue Service)

- Engagements to prepare tax returns or give tax advice

As suggested in the above definition, in an attest engagement subject to SSAE standards the auditor reports on subject matter or an assertion. SSAE-10 notes that the subject matter of an attest engagement can be varied and can provide an assurance on such data as the following:

- Historical or prospective performance or condition, such as historical financial information, prospective financial information, and backlog data.

- Physical characteristics, such as the number of square feet in a building.

- Historical events, such as the price of commodities on a specified date.

- Analytical material, such as break-even analysis.

- Systems and processes, such as internal controls.

- Compliance with established procedures, such as laws and regulations.

On the other hand, when the attest engagement deals with issuing a report on an "assertion about the subject matter," the auditor is concerned with whether the assertion is based on or in conformity with the criteria selected.

In an examination or a review attest engagement, the auditor should obtain a written assertion. The written assertion could be communicated to the auditor in a variety of ways, including as a representation letter addressed to the auditor or a declaration on a related schedule.

> **OBSERVATION:** When a written assertion is not obtained, a practitioner can report on the subject matter as explained later.

The responsible party in an attest engagement is "the person or persons, either as individuals or representatives of the entity, responsible for the subject matter." The practitioner cannot be the "responsible party" even when the practitioner has obtained information to help the responsible party to understand the nature of the written assertion. SSAE-10 points out that the responsible party must "accept responsibility for its assertion and the subject matter and must not base its assertion solely on the practitioner's procedures." In fact, the practitioner can accept an SSAE engagement only if one of the following conditions is satisfied:

> The party wishing to engage the practitioner is responsible for the subject matter, or has a reasonable basis for providing a written assertion about the subject matter if the nature of the subject matter is such that a responsible party does not otherwise exist.
>
> The party wishing to engage the practitioner is not responsible for the subject matter but is able to provide the practitioner, or have a third party who is responsible for the subject matter provide the practitioner, with evidence of the third party's responsibility for the subject matter.

> **PLANNING AID REMINDER:** Interpretation No. 3 of AT 101 states that attestation standards apply only to litigation service engagements in which a practitioner "is engaged to issue or does issue an examination, a review, or an agreed-upon procedures report on subject matter, or an assertion about the subject matter, that is the responsibility of another party."

> **PLANNING AID REMINDER:** Interpretation No. 1 of AT 101 states that SSAEs apply to an engagement in which a practitioner has been requested to express a written conclusion on a defense contractor's Statement of Responses to the Defense Industry Questionnaire on Business Ethics and Conduct and the additional attached questionnaire and responses.

> **OBSERVATION:** SSAE-12 points out that although a firm has deficiencies in its system of quality control or violates specific

policies or controls, it does not mean that a particular attest engagement was not performed in accordance with Statements on Standards for Attestation Engagements.

EXAMINATIONS AND REVIEWS

Due to the nature of attest engagements, SSAE standards require that the CPA establish an understanding of the engagement with the client. That understanding between the CPA and the client (preferably in writing) should include (1) the objectives of the engagement, (2) management's responsibilities with respect to the presentation, (3) the CPA's responsibilities, and (4) limitations of the attest engagement.

> **OBSERVATION:** The balance of this chapter discusses the general standards, fieldwork standards, and reporting standards in the context of an examination attest engagement and a review attest engagement. These standards also apply to agreed-upon procedures engagements, which is the subject matter of the following chapter.

Promulgated Procedures Checklist

The practitioner should perform the following procedures in an attest engagement:

- Preplan the attest engagement.
- Plan the attest engagement.
- Obtain sufficient evidence depending on the nature of the attest engagement.
- Prepare an appropriate report on the results of the attest engagement.
- Prepare appropriate workpapers.

Analysis and Application of Procedures

Preplan the attest engagement

Pre-engagement planning is an essential element of all professional engagements a CPA performs. The practitioner must determine whether the attest engagement will include an examination, a review, or the application of agreed-upon procedures. In addition, the practitioner must determine whether to accept or reject the attest engagement. The preengagement planning phase of an attest engagement is based on the first five general standards for attest engagements, which are discussed below.

General Standard No. 1 — Training and Proficiency

The first general attestation standard states that "the practitioner must have adequate technical training and proficiency to perform the attestation engagement." Adequate technical training is a combination of an appropriate educational background and practical experience. A CPA with adequate technical training should be competent enough to obtain and evaluate the necessary evidence to determine whether or not another party's written assertions are supportable. The CPA can develop proficiency only by applying knowledge he or she has gained in an actual attest engagement.

> **ENGAGEMENT STRATEGY:** Unlike the first standard of generally accepted auditing standards, the first general attestation standard does not refer to the practitioner's technical training and proficiency as an auditor. The scope of the attestation function described in the SSAE standards goes beyond the boundaries of financial reporting.

General Standard No. 2 — Knowledge of Subject Matter

The second general attestation standard states that "the practitioner must have adequate knowledge of the subject matter." Although it can be assumed that a CPA is familiar with financial reporting standards, it cannot be assumed that a CPA is familiar with the procedures and concepts of all attest engagements. Thus, before a CPA accepts an attest engagement, he or she should have an adequate understanding of the nature of the written assertion(s). Obviously, a CPA cannot express an opinion on the written assertions unless he or she has a certain level of expertise relating to the nature of the assertions.

The knowledge required to perform an attest engagement may be obtained through a variety of sources, including formal courses and professional experience. Under some circumstances, the CPA does not have to master a portion of the expertise but may obtain it through the use of specialists (SAS-73 [AU 336] [Using the Work of a Specialist]). When a CPA decides to use the work of a specialist, he or she must have a sufficient understanding of the subject matter to explain the objectives of the engagement to the specialist. The CPA must also be able to evaluate the work of the specialist to determine whether the objectives of the engagement have been achieved.

General Standard No. 3 — Suitable and Available Criteria

Not all engagements provide a basis for attestation. The third general standard requires that "the practitioner must have reason to believe that the subject matter is capable of evaluation against criteria that are suitable and available to users."

The fundamental element in the engagement is the existence of reasonable criteria that provide the basis for the written assertions. In an audit engagement, the reasonable criteria are generally accepted accounting principles (GAAP), which in turn provide a reasonable basis for the preparation of financial statements. Because of the diversity of attest engagements, there is no single set of reasonable criteria for all such engagements. However, SSAE standards note that criteria are considered to be suitable only if they have the following four characteristics:

1. Objective (free from bias)

2. Measurable (provide a reasonable basis for the consistent measurement of the subject matter)

3. Complete (no relevant factors that would alter a conclusion are omitted)

4. Relevant (related to the subject matter)

There is no single source of criteria for the various attest engagements, and the practitioner must use professional judgment to determine whether a specific set of criteria is suitable to a particular subject matter.

> **PLANNING AID REMINDER:** Criteria developed by an appropriate professional group that follows due process procedures are ordinarily considered suitable. For example, Interpretation No. 5 of AT 101 states that XBRL taxonomies and XBRL International Technical Specifications are suitable criteria for performing an attest engagement on XBRL Instance Documents. Another example of suitable criteria is the Auditing Standards Board's guidance in SOP 2003-02 (Attest Engagements on Greenhouse Gas Emissions Information) in performing attest engagements relating to the existence and ownership of greenhouse gas emissions credits. Conversely, in other cases a client (or other parties or groups that do not follow due process procedures and that do not represent a group of experts) may develop criteria to be used for the attest

engagement. In such cases, the practitioner must use the four characteristics listed above to determine the suitability of the criteria established for the attest engagement. An engagement should not be accepted "when the criteria are so subjective or vague that reasonably consistent measurements, qualitative or quantitative, of subject matter cannot ordinarily be obtained."

OBSERVATION: In some engagements the appropriateness of criteria may apply only to parties who have participated in the establishment of the criteria or that have a particular level or type of expertise. In these circumstances the practitioner should restrict the use of the engagement report.

PLANNING AID REMINDER: The suitability of criteria is determined without regard to the type of attest engagement. For example, if criteria are considered to be unsuitable for an examination attest engagement, they are also unsuitable for a review attest engagement.

Finally, SSAE standards require that criteria be available to users under at least one of the following circumstances:

- The criteria are publicly available.

- The criteria are clearly presented in the presentation of the subject matter or the assertion.

- The criteria are clearly presented in the practitioner's report.

- The criteria are commonly understood and are not unique to the attest engagement.

- The criteria are available only to the specified parties (and therefore the availability of auditor's report is restricted).

General Standard No. 4 — Independence

The fourth general attestation standard requires that "the practitioner must maintain independence in mental attitude in all matters relating to the engagement." Independence in fact is a mental state of mind wherein a CPA is impartial in determining the reliability of assertions made in the written communication. In reaching a conclusion, a CPA favors neither the asserter nor the user of the information. Independence in appearance means that the CPA should avoid situations or relationships that may suggest to an outside party that the CPA is not independent. The AICPA's Code of Professional Conduct, Rule 101 (Independence) is applicable to attest engagements.

> **PUBLIC COMPANY IMPLICATION:** The PCAOB also has jurisdiction over standard setting for attestation engagements performed for public companies. When assessing independence related to an attestation engagement for a public company, registered public accounting firms must ensure that they are in compliance with all of the SEC's rules, PCAOB's rules, and Rule 101 of the AICPA's Code of Professional Conduct.

General Standard No. 5 — Due Care

The fifth general attestation standard requires that "the practitioner must exercise due professional care in the planning and performance of the engagement and the preparation of the report." The CPA achieves due professional care by observing the two standards of fieldwork and the four reporting standards. For a CPA to agree to perform an attest engagement implies that the practitioner has a level of expertise that is possessed by other CPAs who perform similar services. Upon accepting the engagement, the CPA is expected to perform the engagement and exercise those skills to a degree expected by a reasonable person. However, this does not imply that the CPA's judgment is infallible or that he or she can be expected to fill the role of a guarantor of information contained in written reports. If the practitioner is not negligent in the execution of the engagement and conducts him- or herself in an honest manner, the due care standard generally will be satisfied.

Plan the attest engagement

Critical elements of every professional engagement include planning and supervision. The importance of these elements is recognized in the first standard of fieldwork, which states that an attest engagement should be adequately planned and that assistants, if any, should be properly supervised.

Fieldwork Standard No. 1 — Planning and Supervision

The first standard of fieldwork states that "the practitioner must adequately plan the work and must properly supervise any assistants." Planning allows the practitioner to develop a strategy for conducting an attest engagement. Adequate planning matches the objectives of the attest engagement with the specific procedures that must be performed to achieve the objectives. Each engagement plan is unique, because it is based on the specific characteristics of a particular engagement. SSAE standards identify the following as factors that should be considered by the practitioner in planning an attest engagement:

- The criteria that are the basis for the engagement

- Preliminary judgments about attestation risk and materiality related to the engagement.

- The likelihood of revision or adjustment of items within the assertion or the nature of the subject matter

- Possible conditions that may require that attestation procedures be modified or extended

- The nature of the attestation report that is expected to be issued by the auditor

In addition, an understanding with the client should be established and should include the following elements:

- The objectives of the attest engagement

- The responsibilities of management with respect to the attest engagement

- The responsibility of the practitioner with respect to the attest engagement

- The limitations of the attest engagement

If an appropriate understanding with the client cannot be reached, the practitioner should refuse the attest engagement.

> **PLANNING AID REMINDER:** The understanding with the client should be documented in the engagement files, preferably through a written communication with the client (an engagement letter).

Obtain sufficient evidence depending on the nature of the attest engagement

The second standard of fieldwork states that "the practitioner must obtain sufficient evidence to provide a reasonable basis for the conclusion that is expressed in the report."

Fieldwork Standard No. 2 — Sufficient Evidence

There are a variety of attest procedures that may be used to obtain evidential matter. The selection of specific procedures to be used in a specific attest engagement is based on professional judgment. In addition, SSAE standards provide the following guidelines:

- Evidence obtained from independent sources outside an entity provides greater assurance of an assertion's reliability than does evidence secured solely from within the entity.

- Information obtained through the practitioner's direct personal knowledge (such as through physical examination, observation, computation, operating tests, or inspection) is more persuasive than information not obtained through the practitioner's personal knowledge.

- Assertions developed under effective internal controls are more reliable than those developed under ineffective internal controls.

The above guidelines are concerned with the quality of the evidential matter that is obtained in an attest engagement, but the CPA must also be concerned with the quantity of the evidential matter. Here again, professional judgment must ultimately be used to identify what constitutes sufficient evidence in an attest engagement. In addition, SSAE standards provide that the practitioner should consider the following items in determining the sufficiency of evidential matter:

- Nature and materiality of the information in the presentation of the assertions taken as a whole

- Likelihood of misstatements

- Knowledge obtained during current and previous engagements

- The competence of the responsible party (often management) in the subject matter of the assertion

- Extent to which the information is affected by the asserter's judgment

- Inadequacies in the assertions' underlying data

The quality of evidence and the sufficiency of evidence must be determined in the context of the specific type of attest engagement. As described earlier, an attest engagement may be an examination engagement, a review engagement, or an agreed-upon procedures engagement.

Examination engagement   Attest procedures must be selected so that the quality and quantity of evidence obtained is sufficient to reduce the attestation risk (probability of not discovering materially misstated assertions) to a low level. Of course, the overall attestation risk cannot be quantified, but the CPA must exercise professional judgment in order to assess inherent risk and control risk and establish an appropriate level of detection risk. The practitioner has little influence, if any, on the levels of inherent risk and control risk in an attest engagement. However, the practitioner can influence the level of detection risk through the selection of attest procedures. The generalized relationships in Exhibit AT 101-1 can be used to establish an acceptable level of detection risk.

EXHIBIT AT 101-1—ACCEPTABLE LEVEL OF DETECTION RISK

Assessed Risk	*Effect on Detection Risk Level*
Inherent risk is assessed to be relatively high.	Detection risk should be established at a relatively low level.
Inherent risk is assessed to be relatively low.	Detection risk should be established at a relatively high level.
Control risk is assessed to be relatively high.	Detection risk should be established at a relatively low level.
Control risk is assessed to be relatively low.	Detection risk should be established at a relatively high level.

After considering inherent risk, control risk, and detection risk, the practitioner should attempt to achieve a low level of attestation risk. In an examination engagement, the practitioner can achieve a low level of attestation risk by relying on search and verification procedures, such as physical observation, confirmation, and inspection, in addition to inquiry and analytical procedures.

Review engagement   The level of assurance the practitioner provides in a review engagement is not as great as the level of assurance he or she provides in an examination engagement. In a review engagement, the practitioner expresses a limited assurance, whereas in an examination engagement, the practitioner expresses a positive assurance on the assertions. For this reason, the level of attestation risk that must be achieved in a review engagement is a moderate level, rather than a low level. On the basis of the interrelationship of inherent risk, control risk, and detection risk, the practitioner selects attest procedures that will result in an overall moderate level of attestation risk.

Generally, in a review engagement, the CPA limits attest procedures to inquiry and analytical procedures, in much the same manner as an accountant would in the conduct of a review of historical financial statements. This is not to suggest that other attest procedures, such as search and verification procedures, are not appropriate under some circumstances. For example, Exhibit AT 101-2 presents circumstances that may be encountered in a review engagement and the effects of the circumstances on attest procedures.

EXHIBIT AT 101-2 — CIRCUMSTANCES ENCOUNTERED IN REVIEW ENGAGEMENTS AND THEIR EFFECTS ON ATTEST PROCEDURES

Circumstance	Effects of Circumstance on Attest Procedures Used in a Review Engagement
Inquiry and analytical procedures cannot be performed.	Use other attest procedures to achieve a level of assurance that would have been achieved if the inquiry and analytical procedures had been performed.
Inquiry and analytical procedures are considered to be inefficient.	Use other attest procedures that are more efficient to achieve a level of assurance that would have been achieved if the less efficient inquiry and analytical procedures had been performed.
Inquiry and analytical procedures are employed, but results suggest that assertions might be incorrect or incomplete.	Use additional attest procedures to the extent deemed necessary to remove doubts about the accuracy or completeness of assertions.

ENGAGEMENT STRATEGY: Interpretation No. 4 of AT 101 notes that the guidance provided in Interpretation No. 1 of AU 339 for audit engagements also applies to attest engagements.

SSAE standards state that a practitioner should consider obtaining a representation letter from the responsible party in both an examination engagement and a review engagement. To some extent the content of the representation letter will be unique to the nature of the subject matter, but elements of the letter may include the following:

- Acknowledgment of responsibility for the subject matter and, when applicable, the assertion

- Acknowledgement of responsibility for selecting the criteria

- Acknowledgement of responsibility for the appropriateness of the criteria (when the responsible party is the client)

- The assertion about the subject matter

- Representation that all known matters contradicting the assertion have been made available to the practitioner

- Representation that communications from regulatory agencies related to the subject matter have been made available to the practitioner

- Statement that all relevant records have been made available to the practitioner

- Statement that material subsequent events related to the subject matter have been communicated to the practitioner

> **ENGAGEMENT STRATEGY:** In an attest engagement in which the client is the responsible party the client will ordinarily be capable of providing the practitioner with a written assertion about the subject matter. If the client does not provide a written assertion, the practitioner should (1) modify the engagement report because of the client-imposed scope limitation in an examination engagement, or (2) withdraw from a review engagement. However, when a party other than the client is the responsible party and that party does not provide a written assertion, SSAE standards point out that the practitioner "may be able to conclude that he or she has sufficient evidence to form a conclusion about the subject matter."

Prepare an appropriate report on the results of the attest engagement

Although the nature of attest engagements is varied, there are four reporting standards that must be observed in the preparation of the practitioner's report.

> **OBSERVATION:** The reporting standards do not apply unless the practitioner issues a report.

Reporting Standard No. 1 — Character of Engagement

The first reporting standard requires that "the practitioner must identify the subject matter of the assertion being reported on and state the character of the engagement in the report." The examination or review report should provide an assurance on the subject matter or the assertion, describe the nature and scope of the engagement, and identify the professional standards that apply to the engagement.

> **PLANNING AID REMINDER:** Interpretation No. 6 of AT 101 states that the practitioners performing attestation engagements under the Government Auditing Standards (i.e., the Yellow Book) are required to follow standards in the Yellow Book that go beyond the reporting standards in AT 101. For those engagements, Interpretation No. 6 of AT 101 states that the practitioner should modify the scope of the attestation report to indicate that the examination or review was "conducted in accordance with attestation standards established by the AICPA and the standards applicable to attestation engagements contained in accordance with Government Auditing Standards issued by the Comptroller General of the United States."

Reporting Standard No. 2 — Conclusions

SSAE standards require that the engagement report state the practitioner's conclusion "about the subject matter or the assertion in relation to the criteria against which the subject matter was evaluated."

The nature and scope of the attest engagement should enable the practitioner to draw a conclusion about whether there are material omissions or misstatements with respect to the subject matter or assertion. Professional judgment must be exercised to identify material misstatements. An item is considered material if a user of the information would be influenced by its omission or misstatement. Materiality is expressed in relative (percentage) terms rather than absolute (dollar) terms.

In an examination engagement, the practitioner's report should express a positive conclusion about whether the presentation of assertions is in accordance with the established or stated criteria. The practitioner may expand the report by adding paragraphs that emphasize certain matters relating to the attest engagement or the presentation of assertions. This type of report modification does not result in a qualified opinion, and the opinion paragraph of the report should not refer to the emphasized matters.

Circumstances that may lead to the expression of an opinion that is not unqualified are discussed later in this chapter under the section titled "Reporting Standard No. 3."

When a review engagement is completed, the practitioner's report expresses negative assurance on the subject matter or assertion. In addition to negative assurance, the report should state that the scope of a review is narrower than that of an examination, and it should disclaim a positive opinion on the presentation. The practitioner may expand the report by adding paragraphs that emphasize certain matters relating to the attest engagement. Other circumstances that may lead to the modification of a review report are discussed later in this section under the section titled "Reporting Standard No. 3."

Reporting Standard No. 3 — Significant Reservations

The third reporting standard is unique in that it explicitly requires that the attest report include all significant reservations the practitioner has with respect to the engagement, the subject matter and, if applicable, the assertions. When attestation standards have not been satisfied and the practitioner has significant reservations, an unqualified conclusion should not be expressed in the examination report or the review report. Significant reservations may be categorized as scope deficiencies and engagement reservations.

Scope deficiencies   The second standard of fieldwork requires that sufficient evidence be obtained to support the practitioner's report. When significant reservations exist because of the limited scope of the attest engagement, the practitioner should qualify or disclaim any assurance on the presentation of assertions or withdraw from the engagement.

Scope limitations may arise if all necessary or alternative procedures (examination and review engagements) cannot be performed because of the circumstances surrounding the engagement or because of restrictions imposed by the client. Generally, if the client imposes restrictions, the practitioner should withdraw from the engagement and issue no report or should disclaim any assurance on the presentation.

When the scope limitation is caused by the practitioner's inability to perform attest procedures or express a conclusion on the presentation of assertions, the significance of the restrictions determines whether a qualified conclusion, disclaimer of conclusion, or withdrawal from the engagement is appropriate. Specifically, the actions the practitioner should take depend on the following factors:

- Nature and magnitude of the scope restrictions

- Significance of restrictions to the presentation of assertions

- Nature of the service being performed (examination or review)

If the practitioner concludes that a qualified conclusion or disclaimer of conclusion should be expressed, the basis for the qualification or disclaimer must be described in the practitioner's report.

Engagement reservations   The practitioner may have reservations about the subject matter or the assertion concerning conformity of the subject matter with the criteria, which includes the adequacy of related disclosures. The nature of a reservation can relate to "the measurement, form, arrangement, content or underlying judgments and assumptions applicable to the subject matter or assertion and its appended notes." Professional judgment must be exercised to determine whether the reservation results in a qualified or adverse opinion in an examination engagement or a modified conclusion in a review engagement.

> **PLANNING AID REMINDER:** According to Interpretation No. 2 of AT 101, a CPA should provide no level of assurance, through an audit, a review, or an agreed-upon procedures engagement, that an entity (1) is not insolvent at the time debt is incurred or would not be rendered insolvent thereby, (2) does not have unusually small capital, or (3) has the ability to pay its debt as the debt matures. These and similar situations are referred to as matters relating to solvency.

> **ENGAGEMENT STRATEGY:** Although a CPA cannot provide assurance about matters relating to solvency, he or she can provide other services, such as the audit or review of the historical financial statements, the examination or review of pro forma financial information, or the examination or compilation of prospective financial information.

Reporting Standard No. 4 — Restricted Distribution

The fourth standard of reporting states that "the practitioner must state in the report that the report is intended solely for the information and use of the specified parties" under the following circumstances:

- When the criteria used to evaluate the subject matter are determined by the practitioner to be appropriate only for a limited number of parties who either participated in their establishment or can be presumed to have an adequate understanding of the criteria

- When the criteria used to evaluate the subject matter are available only to specified parties

- When reporting on subject matter and a written assertion has not been provided by the responsible party

- When the report is on an attestation engagement to apply agreed-upon procedures to the subject matter

When a restricted report is issued, that report should include the following points:

- A statement noting that the report is "intended solely for the information and use of the specified parties"

- Identification of the specified parties

- A statement that the report "is not intended to be and should not be used by anyone other than the specified parties"

Prepare appropriate workpapers

Attest documentation (attest files) should (1) facilitate the conduct and supervision of an engagement and (2) substantiate the attest report; however, the specific type and extent of documentation is to some degree dependent upon the characteristics of a particular attest engagement. Attest documentation should identify team members who performed specific tasks and those who reviewed the work. In addition, the documentation should allow those individuals responsible for the review and supervision of the engagement to "understand the nature, timing, extent, and result of attest procedures performed and the information obtained."

Retention of attest documentation

Attest documentation should be retained for the period of time that meets the objectives of the CPA firm (for example, the need for internal reviews) and satisfies the legal or regulatory requirements imposed by the state or regulatory authorities.

> **PUBLIC COMPANY IMPLICATION:** The PCAOB requires auditors to retain audit documentation for seven years from the audit report release date. The PCAOB will presumably develop retention requirements for documentation in support of attest engagements at some future point.

Confidentiality of attest documentation

A CPA firm should adopt reasonable administrative procedures to maintain the confidentiality (including unauthorized access) of its attest documentation in order to satisfy the Code of Professional Conduct (Rule 301) and any legal or regulatory requirements.

> **PLANNING AID REMINDER:** The documentation requirements described above are general and apply to all attest engagements. In addition, when the attest engagement involves the examination of prospective financial statements the attest documentation should "indicate that the process by which the entity develops its prospective financial statements was considered in determining the scope of the examination."

Reporting on the Design of Internal Control

SSAE-15 provides guidance for when an auditor is engaged to report on the effectiveness of internal control over financial reporting that is integrated with a financial statement audit. In a SSAE-15 engagement, the auditor tests both the design and operating effectiveness of internal control. A practitioner may be engaged to report only on the design of internal control. The practitioner can perform such an engagement using the guidance in AT 101 (in particular, see Interpretation No. 7 of AT 101).

One reason for requesting a practitioner to report on the design of internal control is that a client may be requested to prepare or file a pre-award survey (assertion) as part of applying for a governmental grant or contract. The assertion may be concerned with the effectiveness of the design of part or all of a client's internal control, and it may require the client's auditor to report on the assertion. Interpretation No. 7 of AT 101 states that the practitioner's consideration of a client's internal control as part of the audit of its financial statements is not a basis for reporting on the assertion included in the pre-award survey.

In order to report on the client's assertion concerning its internal control, the practitioner must perform an examination or an agreed-upon procedures (AUP) engagement based on the SSAE standards. And if the agreed-upon procedures engagement involves controls over compliance with specified requirements, the practitioner also should refer to the guidance in AT 601 (Compliance Attestation).

A practitioner also may be asked to report on whether controls that an entity plans to implement are suitably designed to provide reasonable assurance that control objectives, typically specified by a regulatory agency, will be met. A practitioner can report on the suitability of control design even though the controls have yet to be implemented, but he or she should modify both the scope and inherent limitations paragraphs of his or her report. The scope paragraph is modified to state that the controls identified in the report have not yet been implemented. The inherent limitations paragraph is modified to state that another limitation is that the identified controls may not be implemented when the entity's operations begin.

The practitioner cannot sign a form prescribed by a governmental agency that relates to the assertion the client made regarding its internal control unless the practitioner has performed an examination or AUP engagement. Additionally, the practitioner must read the prescribed form carefully to make sure it conforms to professional standards related to reporting on an entity's assertion about its internal control.

Additionally, a client may be requested by the governmental agency to file a pre-award survey (assertion) about its ability to establish an appropriately designed internal control, along with its practitioner's report on the assertion. Interpretation No. 7 of AT 101 states that a practitioner cannot report on an assertion concerning such an ability, because for such a statement "there are no suitable criteria for evaluating the entity's ability to establish suitably designed internal control." The governmental agency might be willing to accept a consulting (nonattest) engagement; however, in this case the practitioner's report may include the following:

- A statement that the practitioner is unable to perform an attest engagement on the entity's ability to establish suitably designed internal control, because there are no suitable criteria for evaluating the entity's ability to do so

- A description of the nature and scope of the practitioner's services

- The practitioner's findings

APPENDIX — ATTESTATION STANDARDS AND CONSULTING ENGAGEMENTS

An auditor may accept a consulting service engagement that includes an attest service as described in AT Section 101. The practitioner should perform the two separate phases of the single engagement by observing Statements on Standards for Consulting Services (SSCS) for the consulting phase of the engagement and Statements on Standards for Attestation Engagements (SSAE) for the attest phase. The practitioner should explain to the client the difference between the two services and should obtain the client's agreement that the attest service should be performed in accordance with professional standards. The agreement that an attest service is to be performed should be documented in the consulting engagement letter.

Practitioner's Aids

The following practitioner's aids are based on illustrations provided in SSAE-10:

- Exhibit AT 101-3 — Checklist for an examination report on a subject matter
- Exhibit AT 101-4 — Checklist for an examination report on an assertion
- Exhibit AT 101-5 — Checklist for a review report on a subject matter
- Exhibit AT 101-6 — Checklist for a review report on an assertion
- Exhibit AT 101-7 — Examination Report — Subject Matter
- Exhibit AT 101-8 — Examination Report — Assertion
- Exhibit AT 101-9 — Review Report — Subject Matter
- Exhibit AT 101-10 — Review Report — Assertion (Restricted Distribution)

EXHIBIT AT 101-3 — CHECKLIST FOR AN EXAMINATION REPORT ON A SUBJECT MATTER

An examination report on a subject matter should include the following:

- A title that includes the word "independent"
- An identification of the subject matter and the responsible party
- A statement that the subject matter is the responsibility of the responsible party
- A statement that the practitioner's responsibility is to express an opinion on the subject matter based on his or her examination
- A statement that the examination was conducted in accordance with attestation standards established by the American Institute of Certified Public Accountants and, accordingly, included procedures that the practitioner considered necessary in the circumstances
- A statement that the practitioner believes the examination provides a reasonable basis for his or her opinion
- The practitioner's opinion on whether the subject mater is based on (or in conformity with) the criteria in all material respects

- A statement restricting the use of the report to specified parties, if applicable

- The manual or printed signature of the practitioner's firm

- The date of the examination report

EXHIBIT AT 101-4 — CHECKLIST FOR AN EXAMINATION REPORT ON AN ASSERTION

An examination report on an assertion should include the following:

- A title that includes the word "independent"

- An identification of the assertion and the responsible party (If the assertion is not included in the practitioner's report, the first paragraph of the report should also contain a statement of the assertion.)

- A statement that the assertion is the responsibility of the responsible party

- A statement that the practitioner's responsibility is to express an opinion on the assertion based on his or her examination

- A statement that the examination was conducted in accordance with attestation standards established by the American Institute of Certified Public Accountants and, accordingly, included procedures that the practitioner considered necessary in the circumstances

- A statement that the practitioner believes the examination provides a reasonable basis for his or her opinion

- The practitioner's opinion on whether the assertion is presented (or fairly stated), in all material respects, based on the criteria

- A statement restricting the use of the report to specified parties, if applicable

- The manual or printed signature of the practitioner's firm

- The date of the examination report

EXHIBIT AT 101-5 — CHECKLIST FOR A REVIEW REPORT ON A SUBJECT MATTER

A review report on a subject matter should include the following:

- A title that includes the word "independent"

- An identification of the subject matter and the responsible party

- A statement that the subject matter is the responsibility of the responsible party

- A statement that the review was conducted in accordance with attestation standards established by the American Institute of Certified Public Accountants

- A statement that a review is substantially less in scope than an examination, the objective of which is an expression of an opinion on the subject matter, and accordingly, no such opinion is expressed in the review

- A statement about whether the practitioner is aware of any material modifications that should be made to the subject matter in order for it to be based on (or in conformity with), in all material respects, the criteria, other than those modifications, if any, indicated in his or her report

- A statement restricting the use of the report to specified parties, if applicable

- The manual or printed signature of the auditor's firm

- The date of the review report

EXHIBIT AT 101-6 — CHECKLIST FOR A REVIEW REPORT ON AN ASSERTION

A review report on an assertion should include the following:

- A title that includes the word "independent"

- An identification of the assertion and the responsible party (if the assertion is not included in the practitioner's report, the first paragraph of the report should also contain a statement of the assertion.)

- A statement that the assertion is the responsibility of the responsible party

- A statement that the review was conducted in accordance with attestation standards established by the American Institute of Certified Public Accountants

- A statement that a review is substantially less in scope than an examination, the objective of which is an expression of opinion on the subject matter, and accordingly, no such opinion is expressed in the review

- A statement about whether the practitioner is aware of any material modifications that should be made to the assertion in order for it to be presented (or fairly stated), in all material respects, based on (or in conformity with) the criteria, other than those modifications, if any, indicated in his or her report

- A statement restricting the use of the report to specified parties, if applicable

- The manual or printed signature of the practitioner's firm

- The date of the review report

EXHIBIT AT 101-7 — EXAMINATION REPORT — SUBJECT MATTER

Independent Accountant's Report

We have examined the [*identify the subject matter—for example*, the accompanying schedule of investment returns of XYZ Company for the year ended December 31, 20X5]. XYZ Company's management is responsible for the schedule of investment returns. Our responsibility is to express an opinion based on our examination.

Our examination was conducted in accordance with attestation standards established by the American Institute of Certified Public Accountant and, accordingly, included examining, on a test basis, evidence supporting [*identify the subject matter—for example*, XYZ Company's schedule of investment return] and performing such other procedures as we considered necessary in the circumstances. We believe that our examination provides a reasonable basis for our opinion.

[*Additional paragraph(s) may be added to emphasize certain matters relating to the attest engagement or the subject matter.*]

In our opinion, the schedule referred to above presents, in all material respects, [*identify the subject matter—for example*, the investment returns of XYZ Company for the year ended December 31, 20X5] based on [*identify criteria—for example*, the ABC criteria set for in Note 1].

[*Signature*]

[*Date*]

EXHIBIT AT 101-8—EXAMINATION REPORT—ASSERTION

Independent Accountant's Report

We have examined management's assertion that [*identify the assertion—for example*, the accompanying schedule of investment return of XYZ Company for the year ended December 31, 20X5 is presented in accordance with ABC criteria set for in Note 1]. XYZ Company's management is responsible for the assertion. Our responsibility is to express an opinion on the assertion based on our examination.

Our examination was conducted in accordance with attestation standards established by the American Institute of Certified Public Accountants and, accordingly, included examining, on a test basis, evidence supporting management's assertion and performing such other procedures as we considered necessary in the circumstances. We believe that our examination provides a reasonable basis for our opinion.

[*Additional paragraph(s) may be added to emphasize certain matters relating to the attest engagement or the assertion.*]

In our opinion, management's assertion referred to above is fairly stated, in all material respects, based on [*identify established or stated criteria—for example*, the ABC criteria set forth in Note 1].

[*Signature*]

[*Date*]

EXHIBIT AT 101-9 — REVIEW REPORT — SUBJECT MATTER

Independent Accountant's Report

We have reviewed the [*identify the subject matter — for example*, the accompanying schedule of investment returns of XYZ Company for the year ended December 31, 20X5]. XYZ Company's management is responsible for the schedule of investment returns.

Our review was conducted in accordance with attestation standards established by the American Institute of Certified Public Accountants. A review is substantially less in scope than an examination, the objective of which is the expression of an opinion on [*identify the subject matter — for example*, XYA Company's schedule of investment returns]. Accordingly, we do not express such an opinion.

[*Additional paragraph(s) may be added to emphasize certain matters relating to the attest engagement or the subject matter.*]

Based on our review, nothing came to our attention that caused us to believe that the [*identify the subject matter — for example*, schedule of investment returns of XYZ Company for the year ended December 31, 20X5] is not presented, in all material respects, in conformity with [*identify the criteria — for example*, the ABC criteria set forth in Note 1].

[*Signature*]

[*Date*]

EXHIBIT AT 101-10 — REVIEW REPORT — ASSERTION (RESTRICTED DISTRIBUTION)

Independent Accountant's Report

We have reviewed management's assertion that [*identify the assertion — for example*, the accompanying schedule of investment returns of XYZ Company for the year ended December 31, 20X5] is presented in accordance with the ABC criteria referred to in Note 1. XYZ Company's management is responsible for the assertion.

Our review was conducted in accordance with attestation standards established by the American Institute of Certified Public Accountants. A review is substantially less in scope than an examination, the objective of which is the expression of an opinion on management's assertion. Accordingly, we do not express such an opinion.

[*Additional paragraph(s) may be added to emphasize certain matters relating to the attest engagement or the assertion.*]

Based on our review, nothing came to our attention that caused us to believe that management's assertion referred to above is not fairly stated, in all material respects, based on [*identify the criteria—for example*, the ABC criteria referred to in the investment management agreement between XYZ Company and DEF Investment Managers, Ltd., dated November 15, 20X1].

This report is intended solely for the information and use of XYZ Company and [*identify other specified parties—for example*, DEF Investment Managers, Ltd.,] and is not intended to be and should not be used by anyone other than these specified parties.

[*Signature*]

[*Date*]

AT SECTION 201

AGREED-UPON PROCEDURES ENGAGEMENTS

Authoritative Pronouncements

SSAE-10 — Attestation Standards: Revision and Recodification (Chapter 2)

Overview

A practitioner should observe the Statements on Standards for Attestation Engagement (SSAE) standards when performing an agreed-upon procedures (AUP) engagement except in the following circumstances:

- Engagements in which an auditor reports on specified compliance requirements based solely on an audit of financial statements, as addressed in paragraphs 19 through 21 of SAS-62 (AU 623) (Special Reports)

- Engagements for which the objective is to report in accordance with SAS-74 (AU 801) (Compliance Auditing Considerations in Audits of Governmental Entities and Recipients of Governmental Financial Assistance), unless the terms of the engagement specify that the engagement be performed pursuant to the SSAEs

- Engagements covered by paragraph 58 of SAS-70 (AU 324) (Service Organizations, as amended), when the service auditor is requested to apply substantive procedures to user transactions or assets at the service organization and he or she makes specific reference in his or her service auditor's report to having carried out designated procedures (However, SSAE standards for agreed-upon procedures apply when the service auditor provides a separate report on the performance of agreed-upon procedures in an attestation engagement.)

- Engagements covered by SAS-72 (AU 634) (Letters for Underwriters and Certain Other Requesting Parties, as amended)

- Engagements that would not be considered as subject to SSAE standards as described in the chapter titled "Attest Engagements" (see AT 101)

In an AUP engagement the practitioner issues a report after performing specific procedures on the subject matter, the procedures having been agreed to by the practitioner and the specified party. In this engagement, the specified procedures can vary greatly, but the specified party is responsible for determining the sufficiency of the procedures. For this reason, the use of the practitioner's report must be restricted to the specified party or parties.

The general, fieldwork, and reporting standards for attestation engagements, as discussed in AT 101, must be observed in an AUP engagement.

Promulgated Procedures Checklist

The practitioner should perform the following procedures with respect to AUP engagements:

- Determine whether pre-engagement conditions exist.

- Perform appropriate engagement procedures.

- Prepare an appropriate report based on the scope of the engagement.

> **ENGAGEMENT STRATEGY:** General guidance for documenting an attest engagement is discussed in AT 101 (Attest Engagements).

Analysis and Application of Procedures

Determine whether pre-engagement conditions exist

Before the practitioner accepts an AUP engagement based on a written assertion, SSAE standards require that the following conditions be satisfied:

- The practitioner must be independent.

- There must be an agreement between the practitioner and the specified party on which procedures are to be performed.

- The specified party must take responsibility for the sufficiency of the agreed-upon procedures.

- The subject matter must be subject to reasonably consistent measurement.

- There must be an agreement between the practitioner and specified party on the criteria to be used for determining the findings.

- The application of the agreed-upon procedures is expected to result in reasonably consistent findings using the criteria agreed upon.

- There is an expectation that evidential matter exists that will provide a reasonable basis for expressing the practitioner's findings.

- There is an agreement between the practitioner and the specified party with respect to materiality, where applicable.

- The use of the practitioner's report is restricted.

   In addition to the above requirements, SSAE standards require that one of the following conditions exist:

- The party wishing to engage the practitioner is responsible for the subject matter, or has a reasonable basis for providing a written assertion about the subject matter when the nature of the subject matter is such that a responsible party does not otherwise exist.

- The party wishing to engage the practitioner is not responsible for the subject matter but is able to provide the practitioner, or have a third party who is responsible for the subject matter provide the practitioner, with evidence of the third party's responsibility for the subject matter.

   PLANNING AID REMINDER: When the AUP engagement relates to prospective financial information, a summary of significant assumptions must be included in the prospective financial statements.

Identification and sufficiency of procedures

Generally the practitioner should communicate directly with the specified party to determine which procedures are to be performed and to make it clear that the specified party is responsible for the sufficiency of the procedures. SSAE standards note that when the practitioner is unable to communicate directly with the specified party, procedures such as the following should be employed:

- Compare the procedures to be applied to written requirements established by the specified party.

- Discuss with a representative of the specified party the procedures to be employed.

- Review relevant contracts or correspondence from the specified party.

Understanding with the client

The terms of the AUP engagement should be understood by the practitioner and ideally should be expressed in an engagement letter. SSAE standards note that items that may be appropriate for the engagement letter include the following:

- Description of the engagement
- Identification of the subject matter (or the related assertion), the criteria used, and the responsible party
- An acknowledgment by the specified party with respect to the responsibility for the sufficiency of the agreed-upon procedures
- The practitioner's responsibilities
- Reference to attestation standards established by the AICPA
- Enumerating the agreed-upon procedures
- Description of disclaimers expected to be part of the practitioner's report
- The restricted nature of the practitioner's report
- Assistance expected to be provided to the practitioner
- The work of a specialist, if any
- Materiality thresholds

> **OBSERVATION:** In an AUP engagement the practitioner assumes the risk that (1) misapplication of the procedures might result in inappropriate findings being reported and (2) appropriate findings might not be reported or might be reported inaccurately.

Perform appropriate engagement procedures

Specified users, not the practitioner, are responsible for the nature, timing, and extent of agreed-upon procedures; however, the practitioner must have an adequate knowledge of the specific subject matter to which the agreed-upon procedures will be applied.

The specific procedures to be employed in an AUP engagement are dependent upon the nature of the engagement; however, in general the practitioner must "obtain evidential matter from applying the agreed-upon procedures to provide a reasonable basis for the findings or findings expressed in his or her report, but need not perform additional procedures outside the scope of the engagement to gather additional evidential matter." SSAE standards identify the following as appropriate procedures in an AUP engagement:

- Executing a sampling application after agreeing on relevant parameters

- Inspecting specified documents evidencing certain types of transactions or detailed attributes thereof

- Confirming specific information with third parties

- Comparing documents, schedules, or analyses with certain specified attributes

- Performing specific procedures on work performed by others (including the work of internal auditors)

- Performing mathematical computations

On the other hand, the following would be inappropriate procedures in an AUP engagement:

- Merely reading the work performed by others solely to describe their findings

- Evaluating the competency or objectivity of another party

- Obtaining an understanding about a particular subject

- Interpreting documents outside the scope of the practitioner's professional expertise

Use of a specialist

In some AUP engagements it is appropriate for a practitioner to use the work of a specialist; however, the practitioner and the specified party should explicitly agree to that use. The practitioner's report should explain the work performed by the specialist.

> **PLANNING AID REMINDER:** As one of the agreed-upon procedures, the practitioner may agree to apply procedures to the work product created by a specialist. This approach is not considered the "use of a specialist" in the context of an AUP engagement. SSAE standards note that the practitioner should not agree to simply read a specialist's report "solely to describe or repeat the findings, or take responsibility for all or a portion of any procedures performed by a specialist or the specialist's work product."

Use of an internal auditor or other personnel

The practitioner is responsible for performing the agreed-upon procedures, but he or she may use internal auditors or other personnel to accumulate data and perform other similar procedures. In addition, the practitioner may agree to perform procedures on information included in an internal practitioner's audit documentation; however, SSAE standards point out that the following would be inappropriate:

- Agree to simply read an internal auditor's report for the sole purpose of describing the findings in the engagement report

- Prepare an engagement report in a manner that suggests that the practitioner and the internal auditor share responsibility for the performance of the agreed-upon procedures

Prepare an appropriate report based on the scope of the engagement

Based on the performance of the agreed-upon procedures, the practitioner should formulate the findings that are to be expressed in his or her report. The findings should be expressed in a manner that is clear and unambiguous. The report may also include explanatory language such as an explanation of sampling risk and descriptions of controls.

> **PLANNING AID REMINDER:** SSAE standards prohibit the practitioner from expressing a negative assurance about the subject matter or the assertion.

Practitioner's Aids

The following practitioner's aids are based on illustrations provided in SSAE-10:

- Exhibit AT 201-1 — Checklist for an AUP report
- Exhibit AT 201-2 — AUP Engagement Report

EXHIBIT AT 201-1 — CHECKLIST FOR AN AUP REPORT

An AUP report should include the following:

- A title that includes the word "independent"
- An identification of the specified party

- An identification of the subject matter (or the written assertion) and the character of the engagement

- An identification of the responsible party and a statement that the subject matter is the responsibility of the responsible party

- A statement that the procedures were agreed to by the specified party

- A statement that the AUP engagement was conducted in accordance with attestation standards established by the American Institute of Certified Public Accountants

- A statement that the specified party is solely responsible for the sufficiency of the agreed-upon procedures; furthermore, the statement should disclaim any responsibility for the sufficiency of the procedures

- List the procedures performed and related findings

- Description of materiality thresholds, where applicable

- A statement that the practitioner was not engaged to and did not conduct an examination of the subject matter, the objective of which would be the expression of an opinion, a disclaimer of opinion on the subject matter, and a statement that if the practitioner had performed additional procedures, other matters might have come to his or her attention that would have been reported

- A statement restricting the use of the report to specified parties

- Reservations or restrictions related to procedures or findings, if applicable

- A description of the assistance provided by a specialist, if applicable

- The manual or printed signature of the practitioner's firm

- The date of the AUP report

PLANNING AID REMINDER: When the AUP engagement concerns prospective financial information, the guidance established in the chapter titled "Financial Forecasts and Projections" (AT 301) should be observed in preparing an agreed-upon procedures report for prospective financial information.

EXHIBIT AT 201-2 — AUP ENGAGEMENT REPORT

Independent Accountant's Report on Applying Agreed-Upon Procedures

To the Audit Committees and Managements of ABC Inc. and XYZ Fund:

We have performed the procedures enumerated below, which were agreed to by the audit committees and managements of ABC Inc. and XYZ Fund, solely to assist you in evaluating the accompanying Statement of Investment Performance Statistics of XYZ Fund (prepared in accordance with the criteria specified therein) for the year ended December 31, 20X1. XYZ Fund's management is responsible for the statement of investment performance statistics. This agreed-upon procedures engagement was conducted in accordance with attestation standards established by the American Institute of Certified Public Accountants. The sufficiency of these procedures is solely the responsibility of those parties specified in this report. Consequently, we make no representation regarding the sufficiency of the procedures described below either for the purpose for which this report has been requested or for any other purpose.

[Include paragraphs to enumerate procedures and findings.]

We were not engaged to and did not conduct an examination, the objective of which would be to express of an opinion on the accompanying Statement of Investment Performance Statistics of XYZ Fund. Accordingly, we do not express such an opinion. Had we performed additional procedures, other matters might have come to our attention that would have been reported to you.

This report is intended solely for the information and use of the audit committees and managements of ABC Inc. and XYZ Fund, and is not intended to be, and should not be, used by anyone other than these specified parties.

[Signature]

[Date]

AT SECTION 301

FINANCIAL FORECASTS AND PROJECTIONS

Authoritative Pronouncements

SSAE-10 — Attestation Standards: Revision and Recodification (Chapter 3)

Overview

A prospective financial statement is either a financial forecast or a financial projection that reflects an entity's expected statement of financial position, results of operations, statement of cash flows, and summaries of significant assumptions and accounting policies. A prospective financial statement is based on expected future economic conditions that represent the best knowledge and belief of the person or persons responsible for the underlying assumptions in the forecast or projection. A prospective financial statement is a financial forecast or projection that covers a period of time that is partially but not completely expired or a period of time wholly in the future. Financial statements that cover an expired period of time are not considered prospective financial statements.

> **ENGAGEMENT STRATEGY:** Pro forma financial statements attempt to reflect the effects of a possible transaction or event on historical financial statements. Pro forma financial statements are not considered to be prospective financial statements. Pro forma financial information is discussed in the chapter titled "Reporting on Pro Forma Financial Information" (AT 401).

The person or persons who establish the underlying assumptions for the prospective financial statements are referred to in the attestation standards as the "responsible party" or "responsible parties." As a rule, the responsible party for a prospective financial statement is the management of an enterprise, but it may be a prospective buyer or some other outsider. A practitioner who is engaged to report on prospective financial statements may assist the responsible party in identifying assumptions and gathering information for the forecast or projection. However, all of the underlying assumptions and the preparation and presentation of the prospective financial statements are the responsibility of the responsible party. Thus, the term *preparation of prospective financial statements* should not be used in the practitioner's report or in any other correspondence relating to the engagement.

Under the attestation standards, a practitioner who is engaged to report on prospective financial statements must determine whether such statements are intended for general use or for limited use. Prospective financial statements that are issued for general use are those that are intended to be used by parties that are not negotiating directly with the responsible party. Since the parties not negotiating directly are generally unable to make direct inquiries about the prospective financial statements, the most useful presentation for them is one that reflects the responsible party's best knowledge and belief of the expected results. Thus, only a financial forecast is appropriate for general use.

Prospective financial statements that are issued for limited use are those that are intended to be used only by the responsible party and those parties negotiating directly with the responsible party. Since the parties are negotiating directly and are able to make direct inquiries of the responsible party, either a financial forecast or a financial projection is appropriate for limited use.

A financial forecast reflects an entity's expected statement of financial position, results of operations, and statement of cash flows, based on the responsible party's assumptions of the conditions that are expected to exist during the forecast period and the course of action that is expected to be taken if the expected conditions materialize. A financial projection reflects an entity's expected statement of financial position, results of operations, and statement of cash flows, based on the responsible party's assumptions of the conditions that will exist during the projection period if one or more hypothetical assumptions occur and the course of action that will be taken if the hypothetical assumptions materialize. Thus, a financial forecast is based on expected future economic conditions and the course of action to be taken if the expected conditions materialize, whereas a financial projection is based on expected future economic conditions that will exist if one or more hypothetical assumptions occur and the course of action that will be taken if the hypothetical assumptions materialize.

A prospective financial statement may be prepared as a single set of estimates or as a range of estimates. To facilitate comparisons, prospective financial statements should be presented in the same format as that used for historical financial statements. The attestation standards require the following minimum presentation standards for prospective financial statements:

1. Sales or gross revenues

2. Gross profit or cost of sales

3. Unusual or infrequently occurring items

4. Provision for income taxes

5. Discontinued operations or extraordinary items

6. Income from continuing operations

7. Net income

8. Basic and diluted earnings per share

9. Significant changes in financial position

10. Description of what the responsible party intends the prospective financial statements to present, a statement that assumptions are based on information about circumstances and conditions existing at the time the prospective information was prepared, and a caveat that the prospective results might not be achieved

11. Summary of significant assumptions

12. Summary of significant accounting policies

Types of Engagements

A practitioner can accept the following engagements for prospective financial statements:

• Examination engagement

• Compilation engagement

• Agreed-upon procedures engagement

> **OBSERVATION:** SSAE standards require that a practitioner perform one of the three types of engagements for prospective financial statements when the practitioner "(a) submits, to his or her client or others, prospective financial statements that he or she has assembled, or assisted in assembling, that are or reasonably might be expected to be used by another (third) party or (b) reports on prospective financial statements that are, or reasonably might be expected, to be used by another (third) party."

EXAMINATION ENGAGEMENT

The purpose of an examination of prospective financial statements is to express an opinion on whether the statements are presented in conformity with American Institute of Certified Public Accountants (AICPA) guidelines and to determine whether the responsible party's assumptions provide a reasonable basis for the preparation of the prospective financial statements.

> **PLANNING AID REMINDER:** For financial projections, the practitioner must determine whether the given hypothetical assumptions provide a reasonable basis for the responsible party's presentation.

Materiality is a highly subjective factor that the practitioner must consider in the examination of prospective financial statements in the same manner as he or she would do in the evaluation of historical financial statements. Because of the higher degree of uncertainty associated with prospective financial statements, prospective financial information cannot be expected to be as precise as historical financial information. Thus, the range or reasonableness for evaluating prospective financial information is broader than the range an auditor would use to evaluate historical financial information.

> **PLANNING AID REMINDER:** An examination of prospective financial statements must observe the general, fieldwork, and reporting standards for an attestation engagement as described in the chapter titled "Attest Engagements" (AT 101).

Promulgated Procedures Checklist

The practitioner should perform the following procedures in an examination engagement for prospective financial statements:

- Establish an understanding with the responsible party

- Plan the examination engagement

- Obtain sufficient evidence to provide a reasonable basis for the report

- Obtain sufficient evidence concerning the reasonableness of assumptions

- Obtain sufficient evidence concerning the preparation and presentation of the prospective financial statements

- Prepare an appropriate report on the prospective financial statements

> **PLANNING AID REMINDER:** General guidance for documenting an attest engagement is discussed in AT 101 (Attest Engagements).

Analysis and Application of Procedures

Establish an understanding with the responsible party

The practitioner should establish an understanding with the responsible party that includes (1) the objective of the engagement, (2) the responsibilities of the responsible party, (3) the practitioner's responsibilities, and (4) limitations of the examination engagement. This understanding should be documented in the attest files, preferably through written communication with the responsible party.

> **PLANNING AID REMINDER:** When the client and the responsible party are not the same, the understanding must encompass the client as well as the responsible party.

Plan the examination engagement

SSAE standards identify the following as some of the factors that are important in the proper planning of an examination engagement:

- Accounting principles to be used and the type of presentation

- The level of attestation risk related to the engagement

- Initial assessment of materiality

- Elements of the prospective financial statements that are likely to require revision

- Conditions that could change the nature, timing, or extent of examination procedures

- Understanding of the entity's business environment

- The responsible party's experience in preparing prospective financial statements

- The period of time covered by the prospective financial statements

- The process used to develop the prospective financial statements

- Understanding key factors (such as costs of production; competitiveness of markets; pace of technology within the industry; and past patterns of revenues, costs, and management policies) that will affect the prospective financial statements

Obtain sufficient evidence to provide a reasonable basis for the report

In an examination of prospective financial statements the accountant must collect sufficient evidential matter "to restrict attestation risk to a level that is, in his or her professional judgment, appropriate for the level of assurance that may be imparted by his or her examination report." The Statements on Standards for Attestation Engagements (SSAE) standards describe the purpose of an examination of prospective financial statements as follows:

> The practitioner provides assurance only about whether the prospective financial statements are presented in conformity with AICPA presentation guidelines and whether the assumptions provide a reasonable basis for management's forecast, or a reasonable basis for management's projection given the hypothetical assumptions.

There is no single list of engagement procedures that must be executed by the auditor in an examination of prospective financial statements; however, the SSAE standards point out that the following factors should be considered in determining the extent of examination procedures:

- The nature and materiality of the item under examination in relationship to the prospective financial statements taken as a whole

- The likelihood of misstatement

- Existing evidence obtained during the current engagement as well as previous engagements

- The competency of the responsible party in the preparation of prospective financial statements

- The degree to which the prospective financial statements are affected by judgments made by the responsible party

- The adequacy of the data that supports the prospective financial statements

Obtain sufficient evidence concerning the reasonableness of assumptions

Evidence must be collected to determine if assumptions used in the preparation of the prospective financial statements are reasonable.

Financial forecasts

The SSAE standards state that in a financial forecast engagement the practitioner can be satisfied with respect to the reasonableness of assumptions made by the responsible party if the examination procedures lead to the following conclusions:

- The responsible party has explicitly identified all factors expected to materially affect the operations of the entity during the prospective period and has developed appropriate assumptions with respect to such factors.

- The assumptions are suitably supported.

Financial projections

The SSAE standards state that in a financial projection engagement (given the hypothetical assumptions) the practitioner can be satisfied with respect to the reasonableness of assumptions made by the responsible party if the examination procedures lead to the following conclusions:

- The responsible party has explicitly identified all factors that would materially affect the operations of the entity during the prospective period if the hypothetical assumptions were to materialize and developed appropriate assumptions with respect to such factors.

- The other assumptions are suitably supported given the hypothetical assumptions.

> **ENGAGEMENT STRATEGY:** In determining whether assumptions are suitably supported in a financial forecast the auditor must be able to conclude that "the preponderance of information supports each significant assumption." For a financial projection, the practitioner must be satisfied that the assumptions provide a reasonable basis for the projection, given the hypothetical assumptions. In a financial projection engagement the practitioner does not have to obtain support for the hypothetical assumptions.

The determination of whether there is a preponderance of information is highly subjective and does not suggest that a particular outcome is the only outcome that will actually occur. The practitioner's conclusion must be concerned with whether assumptions provide a reasonable basis for the preparation of the prospective financial statements. The following should be considered when determining whether there is suitable support for assumptions:

- Have sufficient pertinent sources of information about the assumptions been considered? Examples of external sources the accountant might consider are government publications, industry publications, economic forecasts, existing or proposed legislation, and reports of changing technology. Examples of internal sources are budgets, labor agreements, patents, royalty agreements and records, sales backlog records, debt agreements, and actions of the board of directors involving entity plans.

- Are the assumptions consistent with the sources from which they are derived?

- Are the assumptions consistent with each other?

- Are the historical financial information and other data used in developing the assumptions sufficiently reliable for that purpose? Reliability can be assessed by inquiry and analytical and other procedures, some of which may have been completed in past examinations or reviews of the historical financial statements. If historical financial statements have been prepared for an expired part of the prospective period, the practitioner should consider the historical data in relation to the prospective results for the same period, where applicable. If the prospective financial statements incorporate such historical financial results and that period is significant to the presentation, the practitioner should make a review of the historical information in conformity with the applicable standards.

- Are the historical financial information and other data used in developing the assumptions comparable over the periods specified? Were the effects of any lack of comparability considered in developing the assumptions?

- Are the logical arguments or theory, considered with the data supporting the assumptions, reasonable?

Obtain sufficient evidence concerning the preparation and presentation of the prospective financial statements

With respect to the evaluation of the preparation and presentation of prospective financial statements, the practitioner should collect evidence to satisfy him- or herself that

- Suitably supported assumptions are reflected in the statements.

- Computations to convert the assumptions to dollar values are mathematically correct.

- Assumptions are internally consistent.

- Generally accepted accounting principles used in the preparation of the prospective financial statements are the same principles (1) used in the latest historical financial statements and (2) expected to be used in the historical financial statements that will cover the same reporting period as the prospective financial statements (for financial projections the accounting principles should be consistent with the purpose of the presentation).

- Prospective financial statements are presented in accordance with AICPA guidelines.

- Assumptions have been adequately disclosed based on AICPA presentation guidelines.

Written representations should be obtained from the responsible party with respect to the prospective financial statements.

Prepare an appropriate report on the prospective financial statements

SSAE standards require that an examination report on prospective financial statements include the following:

- A title that includes the word "independent"

- An identification of the prospective financial statements presented

- An identification of the responsible party and a statement that the prospective financial statements are the responsibility of the responsible party

- A statement that the practitioner's responsibility is to express an opinion on the prospective financial statements

- A statement that the examination of the prospective financial statements was made in accordance with AICPA standards, and included such procedures as considered necessary by the practitioner

- A statement that the practitioner believes that the examination provides a reasonable basis for the opinion expressed

- The practitioner's opinion that the prospective financial statements are presented in conformity with AICPA presentation guidelines and that the underlying assumptions provide a reasonable basis for the forecast or a reasonable basis for the projection, given the hypothetical assumptions

- A caveat that the prospective results might not be achieved

- A statement that the practitioner assumes no responsibility to update the report for events and circumstances occurring after the date of the report

- Identification of the purpose of the prospective financial statements (for a projection only)

- Statement that restricts the distribution of the report (for a projection only)

- The manual or printed signature of the practitioner's firm

- The date of the examination report

Exhibit AT 301-1 is an example taken from SSAE-10 of a standard report on an examination of a forecast.

EXHIBIT AT 301-1 — STANDARD REPORT ON AN EXAMINATION OF A FORECAST

Independent Accountant's Report

We have examined the accompanying forecasted balance sheet, statements of income, retained earnings, and cash flows of XYZ Company as of December 31, 20X5, and for the year then ending. XYZ Company's management is responsible for the forecast. Our responsibility is to express an opinion on the forecast based on our examination.

Our examination was conducted in accordance with attestation standards established by the American Institute of Certified Public Accountants and, accordingly, included such procedures as we considered necessary to evaluate both the assumptions used by management and the preparation and presentation of the forecast. We believe that our examination provides a reasonable basis for our opinion.

In our opinion, the accompanying forecast is presented in conformity with guidelines for presentation of a forecast established by the American Institute of Certified Public Accountants, and the underlying assumptions provide a reasonable basis for management's forecast. However, there will usually be differences between the forecasted and actual results, because events and circumstances frequently do not occur as expected, and those differences may be material. We have no responsibility to update this report for events and circumstance occurring after the date of this report.

[*Signature*]

[*Date*]

Exhibit AT 301-2 is an example taken from SSAE-10 of a standard report on an examination of a projection.

EXHIBIT AT 301-2—STANDARD REPORT ON AN EXAMINATION OF A PROJECTION

Independent Accountant's Report

We have examined the accompanying projected balance sheet, statements of income, retained earnings, and cash flows of XYZ Company as of December 31, 20X5, and for the year then ending. XYZ Company's management is responsible for the projection, which was prepared for [*state special purpose, for example*, "the purpose of negotiating a loan to expand XYA Company's plant"]. Our responsibility is to express an opinion on the projection based on our examination.

Our examination was conducted in accordance with attestation standards established by the American Institute of Certified Public Accountants and, accordingly, included such procedures as we considered necessary to evaluate both the assumptions used by management and the preparation and presentation of the projection. We believe that our examination provides a reasonable basis for our opinion.

In our opinion, the accompanying projection is presented in conformity with guidelines for presentation of a projection established by the American Institute of Certified Public Accountants, and the underlying assumptions provide a reasonable basis for management's projection [*describe the hypothetical assumption, for example*, "assuming the granting of the requested loan for the purpose of expanding XYZ Company's plant as described in the summary of significant assumptions."] However, even if [*describe hypothetical assumption, for example*, "the loan is granted and the plant is expanded"], there will usually be differences between the projected and actual results, because events and circumstances frequently do not occur as expected, and those differences may be material. We have no responsibility to update this report for events and circumstance occurring after the date of this report.

The accompanying projection and this report are intended solely for the information and use of [*identify specified parties, for example*, "XYZ Company and DEF National Bank"] and is not intended to be and should not be used by anyone other than these specified parties.

[*Signature*]

[*Date*]

Modifications of the examination report

A practitioner may encounter a variety of circumstances that might require that the standard report on prospective financial statements be modified. The following summarizes these modifications.

Departure from presentation guidelines

A practitioner may conclude that AICPA presentation guidelines have not been followed in the preparation or presentation of the prospective financial statements. When the deviations are considered to be material, either a qualified opinion or an adverse opinion should be expressed. If the practitioner decides to modify the opinion, an explanatory paragraph(s) should be included in the report in which the deviations are described. When a qualified opinion is expressed, the opinion paragraph should refer to the explanatory paragraph and use the qualifying language "except for." When an adverse opinion is expressed, the practitioner should refer to the deviations described in the explanatory paragraph and state that the prospective financial statements are not presented in accordance with AICPA presentation guidelines.

If the presentation deficiency results from the entity's nondisclosure of significant assumptions, the practitioner should express an adverse opinion and describe the omitted assumptions.

Lack of reasonable basis

A practitioner should express an adverse opinion on the prospective financial statements when a significant assumption does (or assumptions do) not provide a reasonable basis for a forecast (or, given the hypothetical assumptions, a significant assumption does [or assumptions do] not provide a reasonable basis for a projection).

Scope limitation

A disclaimer of opinion should be expressed when procedures that the accountant considers necessary cannot be performed. The report should describe the nature of the scope limitation in an explanatory paragraph.

Use of another practitioner

When another practitioner is involved in the engagement and reports on his or her portion of the examination, the principal practitioner must decide whether or not to make reference to the work of the other practitioner.

Emphasis of a matter

A practitioner may emphasize a specific item or event in his or her report and still express an unqualified opinion on the prospective financial statements. The item or event that is emphasized should be described in a separate paragraph of the practitioner's report, but the opinion paragraph should make no reference to the item or event emphasized.

Comparative information

Historical financial statements or summarizations of such statements may be included in the document that contains the prospective financial statements or that summarizes the prospective financial information. The practitioner's report on the prospective financial statements should include a reference to the historical financial statements, as follows:

> The historical financial statements for the year ended December 31, 20X5, and our report thereon are set forth on pages XX through XX of this document.

Larger engagement

The examination of prospective financial statements may be only a part of a larger engagement. For example, a feasibility study may include the examination of prospective financial statements. When a practitioner reports on the expanded engagement, the report should be tailored to fit the complete nature of the engagement.

COMPILATION ENGAGEMENT

A compilation of prospective financial statements does not provide a basis for the practitioner to express an opinion on the financial statements. When a compilation report is issued, the practitioner gives no assurance that AICPA presentation guidelines have been followed or that assumptions used in the preparation of the statements are reasonable. The practitioner should not compile prospective financial statements that exclude a summary of significant assumptions. In addition, a compilation engagement is inappropriate when a financial projection does not identify the hypothetical assumptions that are used or fails to describe the limitation of the usefulness of the presentation.

A compilation of prospective financial statements must satisfy the following standards:

- The engagement must be performed by a person having adequate technical training and proficiency to compile prospective financial statements.

- Due professional care should be exercised in the performance of the engagement and the preparation of the report.

- The work should be adequately planned and assistants, if any, should be properly supervised.

- Appropriate compilation procedures should be performed as a basis for reporting on the compiled prospective financial statements.

> **PLANNING AID REMINDER:** SSAE standards note that a compilation may include the "assembling, to the extent necessary, the prospective financial statements based on the responsible party's assumptions."

Promulgated Procedures Checklist

The practitioner should perform the following procedures in a compilation engagement for prospective financial statements:

- Establish an understanding with the responsible party

- Make inquiries about accounting principles

- Make inquiries about key factors and assumptions

- Identify significant assumptions

- Consider the internal consistency of assumptions

- Test the mathematical accuracy of computations

- Read the prospective financial statements

- Inquire about historical transactions

- Obtain written representations from the responsible party

- Consider extended engagement procedures

- Prepare an appropriate report on the prospective financial statements

> **ENGAGEMENT STRATEGY:** General guidance for documenting an attest engagement is discussed in AT 101.

Analysis and Application of Procedures

Establish an understanding with the responsible party

The practitioner should establish an understanding with the responsible party that includes (1) the objective of the engagement, (2) the responsibilities of the responsible party, (3) the practitioner's responsibilities, and (4) limitations of the compilation engagement. This understanding should be documented in the attest files, preferably through written communication with the responsible party.

Make inquiries about accounting principles

SSAE standards require the practitioner to make the following inquiries about the accounting principles used in the preparation of the prospective financial statements:

- For existing entities, compare the accounting principles used to those used in the preparation of previous historical financial statements and inquire whether such principles are the same as those expected to be used in the historical financial statements covering the prospective period.

- For entities to be formed or for entities formed that have not commenced operations, compare specialized industry accounting principles used, if any, to those typically used in the industry. Inquire whether the accounting principles used for the prospective financial statements are those that are expected to be used when, or if, the entity commences operations.

Make inquiries about key factors and assumptions

The practitioner should make inquiries of the responsible party concerning key factors and assumptions used to prepare the prospective financial statements. Key factors include such items as the entity's sales, production, service, and financing activities.

Identify significant assumptions

SSAE standards require that the practitioner "list, or obtain a list of, the responsible party's significant assumptions providing the basis for the prospective financial statements. Consider whether there are any obvious omissions in light of the key factors on which the prospective results of the entity appear to depend."

Consider the internal consistency of assumptions

The practitioner should read the assumptions established by the responsible party and consider whether they are internally consistent.

Test the mathematical accuracy of computations

Part of the compilation procedures should include testing the mathematical accuracy of translating assumptions into prospective financial statements.

Read the prospective financial statements

SSAE standards require that the practitioner read the prospective financial statements, including the summary of significant assumptions, and consider whether

- The statements, including the disclosures of assumptions and accounting policies, appear to be presented in conformity with the AICPA presentation guidelines for prospective financial statements.

- The statements, including the summary of significant assumptions, appear to be appropriate in relation to the auditor's knowledge of the entity, the industry in which the entity operates, and (1) for a financial forecast, the expected conditions and course of action in the prospective period and (2) for a financial projection, the purpose of the presentation.

Inquire about historical transactions

In some instances a significant part of the period covered by the prospective financial statements will have expired. Under this circumstance the practitioner should make inquires about the results of operations or significant portions of the operations (such as sales volume) and significant cash flows. The practitioner should consider the effects of these historical transactions on the prospective financial statements. When historical financial statements have been prepared for an expired portion of the period, the practitioner should read those financial statements and consider the results in relation to the prospective financial statements.

Obtain written representations from the responsible party

The practitioner should obtain written representations about the prospective financial statements, including assumptions upon which they are made. For a financial forecast, SSAE standards require that the written representations include the following statements:

- The financial forecast presents, to the best of the responsible party's knowledge and belief, the expected financial position, results of operations, and cash flows.

- The financial forecast reflects the responsible party's judgment, based on present circumstances, of the expected conditions and its expected course of action.

- The financial forecast is presented in conformity with guidelines for presentation of a forecast established by the AICPA.

- The assumptions on which the forecast is based are reasonable.

- To the best of the responsible party's knowledge and belief, the item or items subject to the assumptions are expected to actually fall within the range and that the range was not selected in a biased or misleading manner (applies only when the financial forecast contains a range).

For a financial projection SSAE standards require that the written representations include the following:

- State that the financial projection presents, to the best of the responsible party's knowledge and belief, the expected financial position, results of operations, and cash flows for the projection period given the hypothetical assumptions.

- State that the financial projection reflects the responsible party's judgment, based on present circumstances, of expected conditions and its expected course of action given the occurrence of the hypothetical events.

- Identify the hypothetical assumptions and describe the limitations on the usefulness of the presentations.

- State that the assumptions are appropriate.

- Indicate whether the hypothetical assumptions are improbable.

- State that to the best of the responsible party's knowledge and belief, given the hypothetical assumptions, the item or items subject to the assumptions are expected to actually fall within the range and that the range was not selected in a biased or misleading manner (applies only when the financial projection contains a range).

- State that the financial projection is presented to conform with the guidelines for presentation of a projection established by the AICPA.

Consider extended engagement procedures

If, after completing the compilation procedures, the auditor concludes that certain information is incomplete or inappropriate, the client should be requested to make proper revisions. If the financial information is not properly revised, generally the auditor should withdraw from the engagement.

> **PLANNING AID REMINDER:** The omission of disclosures (except for those related to significant assumptions) does not require that the practitioner withdraw from the engagement.

Prepare an appropriate report on the prospective financial statements

SSAE standards require that a compilation report on prospective financial statements include the following:

- An identification of the prospective financial statements presented

- A statement that the practitioner has compiled the prospective financial statements in accordance with attestation standards established by the AICPA

- A statement that that a compilation is limited in scope and does not enable the practitioner to express an opinion or any other form of assurance on the statement or assumptions

- A caveat that the prospective results might not be achieved

- A statement that the practitioner assumes no responsibility to update the report for events and circumstances occurring after the date of the report

- The manual or printed signature of the practitioner's firm

- The date of the compilation report

Exhibit AT 301-3 is an example taken from SSAE-10 of a standard report on a compilation of a financial statement forecast.

EXHIBIT AT 301-3 — STANDARD REPORT ON A COMPILATION OF A FINANCIAL STATEMENT FORECAST

We have compiled the accompanying forecasted balance sheet, statements of income, retained earnings, and cash flows of XYZ Company as of December 31, 20X5, and for the year then ending, in accordance with attestation standards established by the American Institute of Certified Public Accountants.

A compilation is limited to presenting in the form of a forecast information that is the representation of management and does not include evaluation of the support for the assumptions underlying the forecast. We have not examined the forecast and, accordingly, do not express an opinion or any other form of assurance on the accompanying statements or assumptions. Furthermore, there will usually be differences between the forecasted and actual results, because events and circumstances frequently do not occur as expected, and those differences may be material. We have no responsibility to update this report for events and circumstances occurring after the date of this report.

[*Signature*]

[*Date*]

Exhibit AT 301-4 is an example taken from SSAE-10 of a standard report on a compilation of projected financial statements.

EXHIBIT AT 301-4 — STANDARD REPORT ON A COMPILATION OF PROJECTED FINANCIAL STATEMENTS

We have compiled the accompanying projected balance sheet, statements of income, retained earnings, and cash flows of XYZ Company as of December 31, 20X5, and for the year then ending, in accordance with attestation standards established by the American Institute of Certified Public Accountants. The accompanying projection was prepared for [*state special purpose, for example*, "the purpose of negotiating a loan to expand XYZ Company's plant"].

A compilation is limited to presenting in the form of a projection information that is the representation of management and does not include evaluation of the support for the assumptions underlying the projection. We have not examined the projections, and accordingly, do not express an opinion or any other form of assurance on the accompanying statements or assumptions. Furthermore, even if [*describe hypothetical assumption, for example*, "the loan is granted and the plan is expanded"], there will usually be differences between the projected and actual results, because events and circumstances frequently do not occur as expected, and those differences may be material. We have no responsibility to update this report for events and circumstances occurring after the date of this report.

The accompanying projection and this report are intended solely for the information and use of [*identify specified parties, for example,* "XYZ Company and DEF Bank"] and is not intended to be and should not be used by anyone other than these specified parties.

[*Signature*]

[*Date*]

Modifications of the examination report

The compilation report should be modified when prospective financial statements are presented on a comprehensive basis of accounting other than generally accepted accounting principles (GAAP) and the basis of accounting is not disclosed in the prospective financial statements.

> **PLANNING AID REMINDER:** A practitioner may compile prospective financial statements that have presentation deficiencies or omit disclosures (except those related to the disclosure of significant assumptions) provided that (1) the deficiencies or omissions are presented in the practitioner's report and (2) to the practitioner's knowledge the responsible party did not create the presentation deficiencies or omissions with the intent to deceive those who are expected to use the prospective financial statements.

AGREED-UPON PROCEDURES ENGAGEMENT

When a practitioner accepts an agreed-upon procedures (AUP) engagement related to prospective financial statements the general, fieldwork, and reporting standards discussed in the chapter titled "Attest Engagements" (AT 101) and the guidance discussed in the chapter titled "Agreed-Upon Procedures Engagements" (AT 201) must be observed. In addition, SSAE standards state that an AUP engagement on prospective financial statements can be accepted only if all of the following conditions are satisfied:

• The practitioner is independent.

• The practitioner and the specified party agree to the procedures to be performed.

• The specified party accepts responsibility for the sufficiency of the agreed-upon procedures.

• A summary of significant assumptions is included in the prospective financial statements.

- The prospective financial statements "are subject to reasonably consistent evaluation against criteria that are suitable and available to the specified parties."

- The practitioner and the specified party agree to the criteria to be used in determining the findings.

- The procedures agreed to are expected to create reasonably consistent findings based on the criteria used.

- Evidential matter related to the engagement is expected to exist in order to provide a reasonable basis for expressing the findings in the accountant's report.

- The practitioner and the specified party agree to materiality limits (where applicable).

- The report is to be restricted to use only by the specified party.

Promulgated Procedures Checklist

The practitioner should perform the following procedures with respect to AUP engagements:

- Determine whether pre-engagement conditions exist.

- Perform appropriate engagement procedures.

- Prepare an appropriate report based on the scope of the engagement.

> **ENGAGEMENT STRATEGY:** General guidance for documenting an attest engagement is discussed in AT 101 (Attest Engagements).

Analysis and Application of Procedures

Determine whether pre-engagement conditions exist

This procedure is discussed in the chapter titled "Attest Engagements" (AT 101).

Perform appropriate engagement procedures

This procedure is discussed in the chapter titled "Attest Engagements" (AT 101).

Prepare an appropriate report based on the scope of the engagement

SSAE standards require that an AUP report on prospective financial statements include the following:

- A title that includes the word "independent"

- An identification of the specified party

- Reference to the prospective financial statements and the character of the engagement

- A statement that the procedures performed were agreed to by the specified party

- An identification of the responsible party

- A statement that the prospective financial statements are the responsibility of the responsible party

- A statement that the engagement was conducted in accordance with attestation standards established by the American Institute of Certified Public Accountants

- A statement that the sufficiency of the procedures is the sole responsibility of the specified parties

- Disclaim responsibility for the sufficiency of the procedures

- List the agreed-upon procedures and related findings

- Describe the agreed-upon materiality limits (where applicable)

- A statement that the practitioner was not engaged to examine the prospective financial statements

- Disclaim an opinion on the prospective financial statements

- A statement restricting the use of the auditor's report

- If applicable, reservations or restrictions concerning procedures or findings

- A caveat that the prospective results might not be achieved

- A statement that the practitioner is not responsible to update the report for events or circumstances that have occurred after the date of the report

- If applicable, a description of the nature of work performed by a specialist

- The manual or printed signature of the practitioner's firm

- The date of the report

Exhibit AT 301-5 is an example taken from SSAE-10 of a report on an AUP engagement for prospective financial statements.

EXHIBIT AT 301-5 — REPORT ON AN AUP ENGAGEMENT FOR PROSPECTIVE FINANCIAL STATEMENTS

At your request, we have performed certain agreed-upon procedures, as enumerated below, with respect to the forecasted balance sheet and the related forecasted statements of income, retained earnings, and cash flows of DEF Company, a subsidiary of ABC Company, as of December 31, 20X5, and for the year then ending. These procedures, which were agreed to by the Boards of Directors of XYZ Corporation and ABC Company, were performed solely to assist you in evaluating the forecast in connection with the proposed sale of DEF Company to XYZ Corporation. DEF Company's management is responsible for the forecast.

This agreed-upon procedures engagement was conducted in accordance with attestation standards established by the American Institute of Certified Public Accountants. The sufficiency of these procedures is solely the responsibility of the specified parties. Consequently, we make no representation regarding the sufficiency of the procedures described below either for the purpose for which this report has been requested or for any other purpose.

[Include paragraphs to enumerate procedures and findings.]

We were not engaged to and did not conduct an examination, the objective of which would be the expression of an opinion on the accompanying prospective financial statements. Accordingly, we do not express an opinion on whether the prospective financial statements are presented in conformity with AICPA presentation guidelines or on whether the underlying assumptions provide a reasonable basis for the presentation. Had we performed additional procedures, other matters might have come to our attention that would have been reported to you. Furthermore, there will usually be differences between the forecasted and actual results, because events and circumstances frequently do not occur as expected, and those differences may be material. We have no responsibility to update this report for events and circumstances occurring after the date of this report.

This report is intended solely for the information and use of the Boards of Directors of ABC Company and XYZ Corporation and is not intended to be and should not be used by anyone other than these specified parties.

[*Signature*]

[*Date*]

PARTIAL PRESENTATIONS

When prospective financial statements exclude one or more of the minimum presentation guidelines established by the AICPA (as discussed earlier in this chapter), the information is considered a "partial presentation." Due to the limited nature of a partial presentation, the practitioner's report should be restricted to the specified party who will be negotiating directly with the responsible party.

SSAE standards do not establish specific engagement procedures that should be used in a partial presentation engagement, because of the limited content of the presentation. However, the standards do point out that the auditor "may find it necessary for the scope of the examination or compilation of some partial presentations to be similar to that for the examination or compilation of a presentation of prospective financial statements."

> **PLANNING AID REMINDER:** The practitioner should carefully consider the interrelationship of elements, accounts, and items in complete financial statements to determine whether all key factors have been considered and all significant assumptions have been disclosed by the responsible party in the partial presentation.

OTHER INFORMATION

In some instances the practitioner may compile, review, or audit historical financial statements that are included in the practitioner-submitted document that also includes prospective financial statements. Under this circumstance the prospective financial statements must be examined, compiled, or subjected to agreed-upon procedures, except when all of the following conditions exist:

- The prospective financial statements are identified as a "budget."

- The budgetary period covered by the prospective financial statements does not extend beyond the end of the current fiscal year.

- The budget is presented with interim historical financial statements for the current year.

> **PLANNING AID REMINDER:** When the budgetary exception applies as described above, the practitioner should report on the "budget" and (1) state that the auditor did not examine or compile the budget and (2) disclaim an opinion or any assurance on the budget. The budget may exclude the summary of significant assumptions and accounting polices if the practitioner believes the omission was not made to mislead those reasonably expected to use the budget: however, the omission must be referred to in the practitioner's report.

When the prospective financial statements are included in a client-prepared document that includes compiled, reviewed, or audited financial statements, the practitioner should not agree to the use of his or her name except under one of the following circumstances:

- The practitioner has examined, compiled or applied agreed-upon procedures to the prospective financial statements and the related report is included in the document.

- The prospective financial statements are accompanied by an indication by either the responsible party or the practitioner that the practitioner has performed no service with respect to the prospective financial statements and takes no responsibility for them.

- The prospective financial statements have been examined, compiled or subjected to agreed-upon procedures by another practitioner and that practitioner's report is included in the document.

> **PLANNING AID REMINDER:** When the practitioner has not examined, reviewed, or applied agreed-upon procedures to the prospective financial statements, the standards discussed in SAS-8 (AU 550) (Other Information in Documents Containing Audited Financial Statements) must be followed.

AT SECTION 401

REPORTING ON PRO FORMA FINANCIAL INFORMATION

Authoritative Pronouncements

SSAE-10 — Attestation Standards: Revision and Recodification (Chapter 4)

Overview

Pro forma financial information reflects the effects of applying significant assumptions, such as a proposed transaction, to an enterprise's historical financial statements or information. The more common uses of pro forma financial information include showing the effects of transactions such as a business combination, change in capitalization, change in form of business organization, proposed sale or purchase, or the disposition of a significant segment of a business. When pro forma financial information is presented, the following should be observed:

- Pro forma financial information should be labeled to distinguish it from historical financial information.

- The transactions or events that are being integrated into the historical financial information should be clearly described.

- The historical financial information that is the basis for the pro forma financial information should be clearly identified.

- The assumptions used by management in constructing the pro forma financial information should be clearly identified.

- Any significant uncertainties related to management's assumptions should be clearly identified.

- A clear indication must be made that the pro forma financial information should be read in conjunction with the related historical financial information.

- It must be clearly indicated that the pro forma financial information is not necessarily indicative of what would have occurred had the transaction taken place at an earlier date.

> **OBSERVATION:** Reporting on pro forma financial information does not apply to post-balance-sheet events or transactions that are included in historical financial statements for the purposes of a more meaningful presentation (for example, revision

of earnings per share for a stock split or the revision of debt maturities).

PLANNING AID REMINDER: The general and fieldwork standards described in the chapter titled "Attestation Engagements" should be observed in an engagement to report on pro forma financial information.

A practitioner may accept an engagement to examine or review pro forma financial information if all of the following conditions exist:

- The document that includes the pro forma financial information also includes (or incorporates by reference) the most recent historical financial statements [if pro forma financial information is presented for an interim period, the document must also include (or incorporate by reference) the historical interim financial information that covers the same period as the pro form presentation].

- The historical financial statements that are the basis for the pro forma financial information must have been audited or reviewed.

- The auditor must have an adequate level of knowledge of the accounting and financial reporting practices of the reporting entity.

PLANNING AID REMINDER: A practitioner has an appropriate level of knowledge of the reporting entity when he or she has audited or reviewed the entity's historical financial statements. In a proposed business combination the practitioner must have an appropriate level of knowledge of the two entities involved in the transaction. SSAE standards note that "if another practitioner has performed such an audit or review, the need by a practitioner reporting on the pro forma financial information for an understanding of the entity's accounting and financial reporting is not diminished, and that practitioner should consider whether, under the particular circumstances, he or she can acquire sufficient knowledge of these matters to perform the procedures necessary to report on the pro forma financial information."

PLANNING AID REMINDER: The type of pro forma financial information engagement that a practitioner can accept depends on the type of service performed on the related historical financial statements. That is, an audit of the pro forma financial information can be performed only when the historical financial statements have been audited. Only a review of the pro forma financial information can be performed when the historical financial statements have only been reviewed. The rationale for these guidelines is that the level of assurance that can be made for pro forma financial information can be no higher than the level of assurance the practitioner made with respect to the historical financial statements.

The objectives, as stated in the Statements on Standards for Attestation Engagements (SSAE) standards, of an examination (reasonable assurance) and a review (negative assurance) of pro forma financial information are presented in Exhibit AT 401-1.

EXHIBIT AT 401-1 — OBJECTIVES OF EXAMINATIONS AND REVIEWS OF PRO FORMA FINANCIAL INFORMATION

	Examination Engagement	Review Engagement
Management's assumptions	They provide a reasonable basis for presenting the significant effects directly attributable to the underlying transaction (or event)	No information came to the practitioner's attention during the engagement to suggest they do not provide a reasonable basis for presenting the significant effects directly attributable to the underlying transaction (or event)
Related pro forma adjustments	They give appropriate effect to those assumptions	No information came to the practitioner's attention during the engagement to suggest they do not give appropriate effect to those assumptions
The pro forma column	It reflects the proper application of those adjustments to the historical financial statements	No information came to the practitioner's attention during the engagement to suggest it does not reflect the proper application of those adjustments to the historical financial statements

Promulgated Procedures Checklist

As noted earlier, the starting point for a pro forma engagement is the historical financial statements, which have been audited or reviewed by the practitioner. In addition to those procedures, the practitioner should perform the following procedures in an examination or review of pro forma financial information:

- Obtain an understanding of the underlying transaction (or event)

- Obtain a level of knowledge of each constituent part of the combined entity in a business combination

- Discuss the assumptions made by management

- Evaluate the completeness of the pro forma adjustments

- Obtain sufficient evidence to support the pro forma adjustments

- Evaluate the presentation and consistency of assumptions

- Test the mathematical accuracy of the pro forma adjustments

- Obtain written representation from management

- Read the pro forma financial information

- Prepare an appropriate report on the pro forma financial information

> **PLANNING AID REMINDER:** General guidance for documenting an attest engagement is discussed in AT 101 (Attest Engagements).

Analysis and Application of Procedures

Obtain an understanding of the underlying transaction (or event)

The practitioner must understand the nature of the transaction that is the basis for converting the historical financial statements into pro forma financial information. Obtaining this understanding could include the reading of contracts and agreements between the parties involved in the transaction and by making inquiries of appropriate management personnel.

Obtain a level of knowledge of each constituent part of the combined entity in a business combination

As noted earlier in this section, the performance of a pro forma financial information engagement is based on the assumption that the practitioner has an adequate understanding of the parties involved in a business combination or a proposed combination. Generally, this knowledge already exists because the practitioner would have audited or reviewed the financial statements of the parties involved in the combination. However, if the practitioner has not audited or reviewed one of the parties to the combination, the SSAE standards note that an adequate level of knowledge may be obtained by "communicating with other practitioners who have audited or reviewed the historical financial information on which the pro forma financial statements is based."

Discuss the assumptions made by management

The auditor should discuss the significant assumptions made by management to integrate the transaction into the historical financial statements in order to create the pro forma financial information.

Evaluate the completeness of the pro forma adjustments

Once the assumptions made by management are understood, the practitioner should determine whether all significant pro forma adjustments directly related to the transaction have been made to the historical financial statements.

Obtain sufficient evidence to support the pro forma adjustments

Professional judgment must be used to determine what constitutes sufficient evidential matter for each pro forma adjustment. For example, the practitioner may obtain appraisal reports to support the assignment of fair values in a purchase transaction or review debt agreements.

> **ENGAGEMENT STRATEGY:** Generally, a greater level of evidential matter is required in an examination than in a review engagement.

Evaluate the presentation and consistency of assumptions

Generally a variety of assumptions are necessary in order to provide a basis for the creation of pro forma financial information. SSAE standards require that the practitioner "evaluate whether management's assumptions that underlie the pro forma adjustments are presented in a sufficiently clear and comprehensive manner." In addition, the practitioner should determine whether the pro forma adjustments are internally consistent and properly reflect the data used to create them.

Test the mathematical accuracy of the pro forma adjustments

The practitioner should test the mathematical accuracy of the pro forma adjustments and the conversion of the historical column to the pro forma column.

Obtain written representation from management

As part of the pro forma financial information engagement, the following written representations should be obtained from management:

- Management takes responsibility for the assumptions.

- Assumptions provide a reasonable basis for presenting the effects of the transaction or event.

- The pro forma adjustments are based on these assumptions.

- The pro forma financial information reflects the pro forma adjustments.

- Significant effects related to the transaction or event are appropriately disclosed in the pro forma financial information.

Read the pro forma financial information

Based on the practitioner's knowledge of the entities involved in the transaction and the understanding of the transaction itself, the pro forma financial information should be read to determine if:

- They properly describe the transaction or event, pro forma adjustments, significant assumptions, and significant uncertainties.

- They properly identify the sources of the historical financial information that serves as the basis for the pro forma financial information.

Prepare an appropriate report on the pro forma financial information

The reporting guidelines in Exhibit AT 401-2 should be followed in the preparation of an examination/review of pro forma financial information.

EXHIBIT AT 401-2—REPORTING GUIDELINES FOR PREPARATION/REVIEW OF PRO FORMA FINANCIAL INFORMATION

Guidelines for an Examination	Guidelines for a Review
Title that includes the word "independent"	Title that includes the word "independent"
Identification of the pro forma financial information	Identification of the pro forma financial information
Reference to the historical financial statements that are the basis for the preparation of the pro forma financial information and state that they were audited (if the report was modified, the modification should be described)	Reference to the historical financial statements that are the basis for the preparation of the pro forma financial information and state that they were audited or reviewed (if the report was modified, the modification should be described)
Identification of the responsible party and state that the responsible party is responsible for the presentation	Identification of the responsible party and state that the responsible party is responsible for the presentation
Statement that the practitioner's responsibility is to express an opinion on the information based on the results of the engagement	
Statement that the examination was made in accordance with AICPA standards, and included such procedures as considered necessary by the practitioner	Statement that the review was made in accordance with AICPA standards
Statement that the practitioner believes that the examination provides a reasonable basis for the opinion expressed	Statement that a review is substantially less in scope than an examination, the objective of which is an expression of opinion on the pro forma financial information, and accordingly, no such opinion is expressed

Guidelines for an Examination	Guidelines for a Review
Separate paragraph that explains the objective and limitations of pro forma financial information	Separate paragraph that explains the objective and limitations of pro forma financial information
Opinion as to whether management's assumptions provide a reasonable basis for presenting the significant effects of the transaction, whether the pro forma adjustments are appropriate, and whether the pro forma column properly reflects the adjustments.	Conclusion as to whether any information came to the practitioner's attentions to cause him or her to believe that management's assumptions do not provide a reasonable basis for presenting the significant effects of the transaction, whether the pro forma adjustments are appropriate and whether the pro forma column properly reflects the adjustments
Manual or printed signature of the practitioner's firm	Manual or printed signature of the practitioner's firm
Date of the examination report	Date of the review report

> **OBSERVATION:** The practitioner may decide that the use of the report may be restricted, in which case an appropriate paragraph would be added to the examination/review report.

Exhibit AT 401-3 is an example taken from SSAE-10 of an examination report on pro forma financial information.

EXHIBIT AT 401-3 — EXAMINATION REPORT ON PRO FORMA FINANCIAL INFORMATION

Independent Accountant's Report

We have examined the pro forma adjustments reflecting the transaction (or event) described in Note 1 and the application of those adjustments to the historical amounts in the accompanying pro forma condensed balance sheet of X Company as of December 31, 20X5, and the pro forma condensed statement of income for the year then ended. The historical condensed financial statements are derived from the historical financial statements of X company, which were audited by us, and of Y Company, which were audited by other accountants, appearing elsewhere herein (or incorporated by reference). Such pro forma adjustments are based on management's assumptions described in Note 2. X Company's management is responsible for the pro forma financial information. Our responsibility is to express an opinion on the pro forma financial information based on our examination.

Our examination was conducted in accordance with attestation standards established by the American Institute of Certified Public Accountants and, accordingly, included such procedures as we considered necessary in the circumstances. We believe that our examination provides a reasonable basis for our opinion.

The objective of this pro forma financial information is to show what the significant effects on the historical financial information might have been had the transaction (or event) occurred at an earlier date. However, the pro forma condensed financial statements are not necessarily indicative of the results of operations or related effects on financial position that would have been attained had the above-mentioned transaction (or event) actually occurred earlier.

In our opinion, management's assumptions provide a reasonable basis for presenting the significant effects directly attributable to the above-mentioned transaction (or event) described in Note 1, the related pro forma adjustments give appropriate effect to those assumptions, and the pro forma column reflects the proper application of those adjustments to the historical financial statement amounts in the pro forma condensed balance sheet as of December 31, 20X5, and the pro forma condensed statement of income for the year then ended.

[*Signature*]

[*Date*]

Exhibit AT 401-4 is an example taken from SSAE-10 of a review report on pro forma financial information.

EXHIBIT AT 401-4 — REVIEW REPORT ON PRO FORMA FINANCIAL INFORMATION

Independent Accountant's Report

We have reviewed the pro forma adjustments reflecting the transaction (or event) described in Note 1 and the application of those adjustments to the historical amounts in the accompanying pro forma condensed balance sheet of X Company as of March 31, 20X6, and the pro forma condensed statement of income for the three months then ended. These historical condensed financial statements are derived from the historical unaudited financial statements of X Company, which were reviewed by us, and of Y Company, which were reviewed by other accountants, appearing elsewhere herein (or incorporated by reference). Such pro forma adjustments are based on management's assumptions as described in Note 2. X Company's management is responsible for the pro forma financial information.

Our review was conducted in accordance with attestation standards established by the American Institute of Certified Public Accountants. A review is substantially less in scope than an examination, the objective of which is the expression of an opinion on management's assumptions, the pro forma adjustments and the application of those adjustments to historical financial information. Accordingly, we do not express such an opinion.

The objective of this pro forma financial information is to show what the significant effects on the historical financial information might have been had the transaction (or event) occurred at an earlier date. However, the pro forma condensed financial statements are not necessarily indicative of the results of operations or related effects on financial position that would have been attained had the above-mentioned transaction (or event) actually occurred earlier.

Based on our review, nothing came to our attention that causes us to believe that management's assumptions do not provide a reasonable basis for presenting the significant effects directly attributable to the above-mentioned transaction (or event) described in Note 1, that the related pro forma adjustments do not give appropriate effect to those assumptions, or that the pro forma column does not reflect the proper application of those adjustments to the historical financial statement amounts in the pro forma condensed balance sheet as of March 31, 20X6, and the pro forma condensed statement of income for the three months then ended.

[*Signature*]

[*Date*]

AT SECTION 501

REPORTING ON AN ENTITY'S INTERNAL CONTROL OVER FINANCIAL REPORTING

Authoritative Pronouncements

SSAE-15 — An Examination of an Entity's Internal Control over Financial Reporting That Is Integrated with an Audit of Its Financial Statements

Overview

The basic concepts of internal control and the auditor's consideration of internal control in a financial statement audit are discussed in AU 314. Internal control over financial reporting is a process — designed and overseen by those charged with governance, management, and others — designed to provide reasonable assurance that the financial statements are prepared in accordance with the applicable financial reporting framework. Effective internal control provides reasonable assurance over the reliability of financial reporting.

Guidance for reporting on internal control is established by the Statements on Standards for Attestation Engagements (SSAE) and is discussed in this section. An auditor may accept an engagement to report on a client's internal control only if the following conditions are satisfied:

- Management accepts responsibility for the effectiveness of internal control over financial reporting.

- Management evaluates the effectiveness of internal control over financial reporting using a suitable and available control framework.

- Management supports its assessment of the effectiveness of internal control over financial reporting with sufficient appropriate evidence.

- Management provides a report on the effectiveness of internal control over financial reporting that accompanies the auditor's report.

> **PUBLIC COMPANY IMPLICATION:** As a result of the issuance of AS-5 by the PCAOB, the guidance in AT 501 only applies to reporting on an entity's internal control over financial reporting for nonpublic companies. SSAE-15 largely converges the standards for reporting on internal control over financial reporting for nonpublic companies with the guidance on

reporting on internal control over financial reporting for public companies as contained in AS-5.

> **OBSERVATION:** SSAE-15 refers to the auditor rather than the practitioner (as is typical within the attestation standards) because it only applies when an engagement to examine the design and operating effectiveness of internal control over financial reporting is integrated with an audit of the financial statements.

In addition, the guidance in SSAE-15 does *not* apply in the following circumstances:

- An engagement to examine the design of internal control (such an engagement can be performed under the standards in AT 101 (Attest Engagements))

- An engagement to examine controls over the effectiveness and efficiency of operations (such an engagement can be performed under the standards in AT 101 (Attest Engagements))

- An engagement to examine controls over compliance with laws and regulations (such an engagement can be performed under the standards in AT 601 (Compliance Attestation))

- An engagement to examine controls over the processing of transactions by a service organization (such an engagement can be performed under the standards in AU 324 (Service Organizations))

- An engagement to perform agreed-upon procedures on controls (such an engagement can be performed under the standards in AT 201 (Agreed-Upon Procedures Engagements))

- In addition, an auditor is precluded from accepting an engagement to review ICFR or a written assertion thereon.

Under SSAE-15, the auditor can be retained to report either directly on the entity's internal control over financial reporting (ICFR) or on management's assertion relating to ICFR. ICFR is typically examined as of the end of the entity's fiscal year; however, management may retain the auditor to examine ICFR as of a date other than year-end. In addition, the auditor can be retained to examine ICFR during a period of time.

> **OBSERVATION:** Unlike AS-5, which requires the same auditor to perform the financial statement and ICFR audits, SSAE-15 does not explicitly require the same firm to provide both

services. Nevertheless, SSAE-15 encourages entities to use the same auditor to provide both services, and it states that certain regulators require the same auditor to provide both services.

An auditor engaged to opine on ICFR should comply with the general, fieldwork, and reporting standards (AT Section 101), and the specific performance and reporting standards in SSAE-15. In addition, if management refuses to furnish a written assertion on its assessment as to the effectiveness of ICFR, the auditor should withdraw from the engagement. If the auditor cannot withdraw from the engagement because of law or regulation, he or she should disclaim an opinion.

EXAMINATION ENGAGEMENT

The purpose of an examination engagement that reports on an entity's internal control over financial reporting is to express an opinion on (1) the effectiveness of the entity's internal control, in all material respects, based on the applicable control framework or (2) whether the responsible party's written assertion about the effectiveness of internal control is fairly stated, in all material respects, based on the applicable control framework. The auditor should use the same framework as management to evaluate ICFR, which typically is the framework developed by the Committee of Sponsoring Organizations (COSO) of the Treadway Commission, *Internal Control—Integrated Framework*. In order to express an opinion concerning the effectiveness of its internal control, the practitioner must collect sufficient appropriate evidence that supports the opinion.

> **PLANNING AID REMINDER:** The opinion expressed is based on management's assertion or the internal controls taken as a whole, and it is not directed to a specific control policy or procedure or to the separate components of internal control.

Promulgated Procedures Checklist

The auditor should perform the following procedures when reporting on an entity's ICFR:

- Consider management's responsibility for supporting its ICFR assertion.
- Plan the engagement.
- Perform a risk assessment.
- Analyze fraud risk.

- Determine materiality.

- Consider using the work of others.

- Use a top-down approach.

- Identify significant accounts and disclosures.

- Understand likely sources of misstatement.

- Test design effectiveness.

- Test operating effectiveness.

- Match evidence to risk.

- Determine nature, timing, and extent of testing.

- Consider use of service organizations.

- Integrate with financial statement audit.

- Evaluate identified deficiencies.

- Obtain written representations.

- Fulfill communication responsibilities.

- Prepare an appropriate report on the entity's (client's) ICFR.

- Consider subsequent events

> **PLANNING AID REMINDER:** General guidance for documenting an attest engagement is discussed in AT 101 (Attest Engagements).

Analysis and Application of Procedures

Consider management's responsibility for supporting its ICFR assertion

Management is responsible for documenting its controls and related control objectives, and the documentation serves as a basis for management's internal control assertion. The extent of the documentation needed depends on the size and complexity of the entity. Examples of documentation include (1) policy and accounting manuals, (2) narrative memoranda, (3) flowcharts, (4) decision tables, (5) procedural write-ups, and (5) questionnaires.

Management's monitoring activities also provide evidence as to the design and operating effectiveness of internal control. Monitoring includes periodically testing and assessing controls, and identifying and reporting deficiencies to appropriate individuals in the entity. Monitoring can be performed through ongoing activities or separate evaluations.

The selection of methods used to document internal control is a managerial decision based on the size and complexity of the entity's operations, and it may include documentation methods such as policy manuals, memoranda, flowcharts, questionnaires, and accounting manuals. These methods should document the relationship between internal controls and the control objectives.

> **ENGAGEMENT STRATEGY:** Although management is responsible for the documentation of its internal control, the auditor may be engaged to help management identify the methods they are using to document the controls.
>
> **PUBLIC COMPANY IMPLICATION:** The extent to which the auditor can be used to help management document internal controls for a public company is more limited than for private companies. Documentation assistance must be preapproved by the audit committee only after the audit committee carefully considers whether the auditor's involvement in documenting controls would impair the auditor's independence, either in fact or in appearance.

Plan the engagement

Proper planning of the engagement requires that the auditor consider a number of factors that may be relevant to forming an opinion related to the client's internal control. SSAE standards list the following as some of the factors that may be relevant in planning the engagement:

- Knowledge of the entity's internal control based on previous engagements.

- Matters affecting the entity's industry (e.g., financial reporting practices, economic conditions, and laws and regulations).

- Matters affecting the entity's business (e.g., organization, operating characteristics, and capital structure).

- The effect of recent changes to the entity, its operations, or its internal control.

- The auditor's preliminary judgments about materiality and risk.

- Internal control deficiencies previously communicated to management or those charged with governance.

- Legal or regulatory matters affecting the entity.

- The type and extent of available evidence related to assessing ICFR.

- Preliminary judgments about the effectiveness of ICFR.

- Public information about the entity related to the risk of material financial statement misstatements and about the effectiveness of ICFR.

- Knowledge about entity risks obtained as part of the client acceptance and retention process.

- The relative complexity of the entity.

The auditor should realize that the nature of an entity's controls should vary based on its size and complexity, and the documentation of controls are typically more extensive for a larger, more complex entity than for a smaller, less complex one. The auditor should adjust (scale) the audit approach accordingly. Factors to consider in assessing the complexity of an entity include (1) the number of business lines, (2) the complexity of business processes and financial reporting systems, (3) the relative degree of centralization of the accounting function, (4) involvement by senior management in the day-to-day activities of the business, and (5) the number of levels of management. One additional factor that the practitioner should consider when planning the engagement is the extent to which the internal control is documented.

In addition, the planning of the engagement is affected by whether the client has multiple locations. The amount of audit work performed at a location or business unit should reflect the risk of a material misstatement to the financial statements resulting from the activities of the location or business unit. The auditor does not have to examine those locations that either alone or in combination with others do not present a reasonable possibility of material misstatement to the financial statements. For other low-risk locations or business units, the auditor should assess whether he or she can rely on (1) entity-level controls and (2) work performed by others (e.g., internal audit).

Perform a risk assessment

SSAE-15 states that the auditor's risk assessment procedures underlie the entire process of auditing ICFR. The auditor should focus more of his or her effort on areas of higher risk. In addition, there should be a direct relation between the risk that a material weakness could exist in a particular area and the amount of audit attention devoted to the area. The auditor does not have to test those controls that even if deficient would not expose the entity to a reasonable possibility of material misstatement to the financial statements. Finally, the auditor should recognize that internal control is less likely to prevent, or detect and correct, a material misstatement due to fraud than misstatements due to error.

Analyze fraud risk

The auditor is specifically required to analyze fraud risk in an audit of ICFR. The auditor should address whether controls adequately address the risk of material misstatement due to fraud and to management override of controls. Controls that might be responsive to fraud risks include

- Controls over significant unusual transactions, particularly those that occur late in the period or via unusual journal entries

- Controls over journal entries and adjustments made as part of the period-end financial reporting process

- Controls over related-party transactions

- Controls related to significant management estimates

- Controls that reduce managerial incentives or pressures to falsify reported financial results

If the auditor concludes that an entity's antifraud programs and controls are deficient, he or she should consider this fact when planning the financial statement audit. Deficiencies in antifraud programs and controls should lead the auditor to modify the nature, timing, and extent of audit procedures in the financial statement audit.

Determine materiality

Materiality should be the same for the audit of ICFR as for the financial statement audit.

Consider using the work of others

In an audit of ICFR, the auditor may use work performed by, or receive direct assistance from, internal auditors, entity personnel other than internal audit, and outside parties working under the direction of management and those charged with governance. In determining how extensively the auditor can rely on the work of others, he or she is to assess the competence and objectivity of other parties that the auditor is considering relying upon. There is a direct relation between reliance and competence and objectivity. Given a higher assessed level of competence and objectivity, the auditor can place greater reliance on work performed by others. In addition, the less audit risk in an area, the more reliance that can be placed on the work of others.

Use a top-down approach

In planning an audit of ICFR, the auditor is to use a top-down approach, beginning with controls at the financial statement level and then working down to controls related to significant accounts and disclosures and related assertions. The auditor should analyze the financial statements to determine which accounts, transaction classes, and disclosures present a reasonable possibility of a material misstatement. In addition, the auditor should consider entity-level controls. Entity-level controls include (1) controls related to the control environment, (2) controls related to management override, (3) the entity's risk assessment process, (4) centralized processing and controls, (5) controls that monitor the results of operations, (6) controls to monitor other controls (e.g., internal audit, those charged with governance), and (7) controls over the period-end financial reporting process. Effective entity-level controls reduce the amount of audit effort needed in testing controls at the account and transaction level (i.e., referred to as control activities in COSO's internal control framework). After assessing entity-level controls, the auditor should identify significant accounts and disclosures and their relevant assertions, and controls that address risk at the assertion level. The auditor should focus his or her efforts in those areas that pose a reasonable possibility of a material misstatement to the financial statements.

In evaluating entity-level controls, the control environment is the first among equals or, as expressed by COSO, the foundation upon which all the other elements of internal control rest. In evaluating the control environment, the auditor should assess whether management's philosophy and operating style promote effective internal control. In addition, the auditor should assess whether there is evidence of sound integrity and ethical values, especially on the part of senior management. Finally, the auditor should evaluate whether those charged with governance understand and exercise oversight responsibility related to financial reporting and internal control. (The auditor should also refer to AU Section 314 for further guidance in evaluating the control environment.)

Another entity-level control that is particularly important to accurate financial reporting is the client's period-end financial reporting process, which includes

- Procedures for entering transaction totals in the general ledger

- Procedures for selecting and applying accounting principles

- Procedures to initiate, authorize, record, and process journal entries in the general ledger

- Procedures used to record recurring and nonrecurring financial statement adjustments

- Procedures for preparing the financial statements and related disclosures

In assessing a client's period-end financial reporting process, the auditor should evaluate

- How the entity produces its financial statements (e.g., inputs, procedures performed, and outputs)

- The extent of information technology involvement in the period-end financial reporting process

- The participation from management in the process

- The locations involved in the period-end financial reporting process

- The types of adjusting and consolidating entries

- The oversight of the process by management and those charged with governance

Identify significant accounts and disclosures

To perform an effective audit of ICFR the auditor should identify the client's significant accounts and disclosures and their relevant assertions. To do this, the auditor evaluates quantitative and qualitative risk factors related to financial statement line items and disclosures. Risk factors related to accounts, classes of transactions, and disclosures include

- Size and composition

- Susceptibility to misstatement due to error or fraud

- Nature of the account, transaction class, or disclosure

- Volume of activity and the complexity of transactions

- Accounting and reporting complexities

- Possibility of significant contingent liabilities

- Existence of related-party transactions

- Changes from the prior period

The accounts, transaction classes, and disclosures, and their relevant assertions identified in an ICFR audit also pertain to a financial statement audit. In identifying significant accounts and disclosures, the auditor's objective is to identify likely sources of potential material misstatement.

Understand likely sources of misstatement

Given the importance and need for judgment in understanding likely sources of misstatement, the auditor should either perform the work in this area or supervise the work of others in this area. Procedures that the auditor should perform to understand likely sources of misstatement include

- Understanding the flow of transactions related to relevant assertions (e.g., initiation, authorization, processing, and recording)

- Identifying the points within the process where misstatements could occur

- Identifying controls that address the risks of misstatement

- Identifying controls to prevent, or timely detect and correct, the unauthorized acquisition, use, or disposition of the entity's assets

- Understanding how IT affects the flow of transactions

Performing a walk-through is often the best way to understand the likely sources of misstatement. A walk-through involves following a transaction from initiation through the entity's processes until it is reflected in the financial records. In addition, a walk-through includes questioning entity personnel about their understanding of procedures and controls, especially at those points where important processing procedures occur.

Test design effectiveness

Controls are designed effectively if they meet the entity's control objectives — assuming the controls are implemented as designed — and would prevent, or detect and timely correct, misstatements that could lead to a material misstatement in the financial statements. In testing design effectiveness, the auditor evaluates whether there are any deficiencies in the design of controls. A deficiency in control design exists if (1) a necessary control is missing or (2) the applicable control objective would not be met even if the control operated as designed.

Design effectiveness can be tested using inquiry, observation, and inspection of relevant documentation. Walk-throughs that incorporate the foregoing procedures are often sufficient for evaluating design effectiveness.

Test operating effectiveness

In testing operating effectiveness, the auditor evaluates whether there are any deficiencies in the operation of controls. A deficiency in control operation exists if (1) a properly designed control does not operate as designed or (2) the person performing the control lacks the needed competence or authority.

In testing the operating effectiveness of ICFR, the tests should be designed to determine (1) how the control was applied, (2) whether the control was applied consistently, and (3) who applied the control. The auditor can make these determinations by applying a variety of examination procedures, including inquiry, inspection of documents, observation of activities, and reapplication or reperformance of internal control procedures.

The extent to which examination procedures should be performed is a matter of professional judgment. Generally, the nature, timing, and extent of tests of operating effectiveness are based on the preliminary assessment of risk and the client's entity-level controls. Specific factors that a practitioner may consider in determining what constitutes sufficient evidential matter include the following:

- The nature of the control

- The significance of the control in achieving the objectives of the control criteria

- The nature and extent of tests of operating effectiveness that the client performs

> **ENGAGEMENT STRATEGY:** The absence of misstatements in an account balance, transaction class, or disclosure related to a control does not necessarily mean that the control is effective. A control should be tested directly in order to conclude that it is effective.

> **PLANNING AID REMINDER:** The auditor's objective is to provide an opinion on the entity's internal control overall, not an opinion on the effectiveness of each individual control. Thus, an auditor can vary the evidence obtained about the effectiveness of individual controls based on the risks associated with the individual control.

For many clients, automated controls are increasingly important. A benchmarking strategy may be effective for testing automated controls. A benchmarking strategy is appropriate if general computer controls are effective and if the general computer controls are retested every year. General computer controls are controls over program changes, access to programs and databases, and computer operations. In using a benchmarking strategy, the auditor needs to verify that the automated application control has not changed since the baseline was established. The auditor can examine compilation dates for computer programs. In the case of purchased software, changes to the underlying code may not be possible and the auditor may instead verify that configuration settings have not been changed. If these procedures are followed, the auditor can conclude that the automated application control continues to be effective without retesting the operation of the automated application control.

A client may perform various tests of the operational effectiveness of its internal control. The auditor must decide to what extent, if at all, he or she should rely on the work performed by client personnel when drawing a conclusion about the client's internal control. If the auditor plans to rely to some degree on the work performed by client personnel, he or she should test some of the work performed. Obviously, an auditor would place more reliance on work he or she performs him- or herself than on tests performed by the client. Auditors must make fundamental judgments about the testing process; for example, it would be inappropriate for a client to decide what constitutes sufficient evidence or a material weakness.

The auditor must decide what period of time the test procedures should be applied to. To some extent, the nature of a control determines the period over which it should be tested. For example, some procedures are performed only periodically (e.g., controls over the preparation of interim financial statements and the physical inventory count) and others are continuous (e.g., controls over payroll transactions).

Match evidence to risk

The audit evidence needed depends on the risk associated with the control (more risk, more evidence needed; less risk, less evidence). The risk associated with a control includes the risk that the control is not effective and, if the control is not effective, the risk that a material weakness exists. Factors affecting the risk associated with a control include

- Nature and materiality of the misstatements that the control addresses

- Inherent risk associated with the account and assertions

- Changes in the volume or nature of transactions

- The account's history of errors

- Effectiveness of entity-level controls

- Nature of the control

- Frequency of the control's operation (e.g., daily, weekly, monthly, etc.)

- Extent to which the control relies on the effectiveness of other controls

- Competence of the personnel performing the control or monitoring performance

- Whether the control is manual or automated

- Complexity of the control, and extent of judgment needed to apply the control

When the auditor detects deviations in the operation of a control, he or she should consider the effect of these deviations on the auditor's assessment of risk as well as on the auditor's evaluation of the operating effectiveness of the control. An individual control can have some deviations and still be viewed as effective.

Determine nature, timing, and extent of testing

The auditor should vary the nature, timing, and extent of his or her testing in response to the risk associated with a control. The nature of testing relates to the type of auditing procedures performed. Not all auditing procedures are equally effective. Generally, the quality of audit evidence obtained follows this descending order: (1) reperformance, including recalculation, (2) inspection of relevant documentation, (3) observation, and (4) inquiry. Exclusive reliance on inquiry, given that inquiry generally provides the weakest form of evidence, is insufficient for testing a control.

> **ENGAGEMENT STRATEGY:** The nature of evidence gathered depends on the extent of the client's documentation of control procedures. Some controls (e.g., tone at the top, management's philosophy and operating style) do not provide documentary evidence, and the lack of documentary evidence may be more pronounced in smaller entities. In cases where documentary evidence is lacking, the auditor may have to rely on inquiry, observation of activities, and review of less formal documentation. Where inquiry is an important procedure, the auditor may want to consider asking similar questions of multiple individuals, including client personnel in operating positions.

Testing controls over a longer period of time provides more evidence than testing controls over a shorter period of time. And testing controls closer to year-end provides more evidence than testing controls earlier in the year, although controls have to be tested over a period that is long enough to assess their operating effectiveness. In addition, the more extensively (i.e., sample size) a control is tested, the more evidence the testing provides. Moreover, the auditor should consider the results from the prior year's testing of ICFR in planning the current year's examination of ICFR. Audit procedures to test controls should be varied from year to year — that is, an element of unpredictability should be built in to the auditor's tests.

A client may remediate control deficiencies during the year. If sufficient time remains in the year to test the operating effectiveness of the remediated control, the auditor can test it because the opinion on the effectiveness of ICFR is as of year-end. The auditor does not have to test the superseded control for the ICFR audit; however, he or she does need to consider the effect of deficiencies in the superseded control in planning the financial statement audit.

An auditor may test the operating effectiveness of a control as of an interim date and desire to roll forward his or her conclusion to the period-end date. The auditor needs more evidence as to the continuing effectiveness of the control if (1) the risks associated with the control are greater, (2) the evidence obtained about the control's operating effectiveness at the interim date was limited, (3) there is a longer period of time between the interim date and the year end date, and (4) changes have occurred in internal control since the interim date.

Consider use of service organizations

A service organization's services may be part of an entity's information and communication component of internal control. The auditor should obtain (1) an understanding of the controls at the service organization, (2) an understanding of controls at the user organization over the activities of the service organization, and (3) evidence that the relevant controls are operating effectively. To assess whether controls at the service organization are operating effectively, the auditor should perform one or more of the following procedures:

- Obtain a service auditor's report on controls placed in operation and tests of operating effectiveness of these controls (i.e., a SAS-70 Type II report)

- Obtain a service auditor's report on the application of agreed-upon procedures

- Test the user organization's controls over the activities of the service organization

- Perform tests of controls at the service organization (directly by the auditor)

The auditor should also refer to the guidance in AU Section 324 if a service organization is part of the client's internal control system.

> **ENGAGEMENT STRATEGY:** If an auditor intends to rely on a SAS-70 Type II report, he or she needs to assess (1) the time period covered by the service auditor's report in relation to the date that the auditor is reporting on ICFR, (2) the scope of the controls tested at the service organization (i.e., were the controls at the service organization that are applicable to the auditor's ICFR examination tested), (3) the nature of the tests of controls at the service organization, and (4) the nature of the Type II opinion. Depending on the results of the assessment, the auditor may need to perform additional procedures relating to controls at the service organization. Additionally, the auditor should make inquiries as to the reputation, competence, and independence of the auditor who issued the Type II report.

> **OBSERVATION:** The auditor is not to refer to the Type II audit report in his or her ICFR report.

Integrate with financial statement audit

The auditor's conclusions about ICFR should affect the financial statement audit. Specifically, the nature, timing, and extent of audit procedures in the financial statement audit should reflect conclusions about the effectiveness of the client's ICFR. In addition, the auditor's findings during the financial statement audit should affect the audit of ICFR. For example, areas where misstatements are identified may suggest that internal control in that area is not effective.

> **PLANNING AID REMINDER:** Although the ICFR audit should affect (be integrated with) the financial statement audit and vice versa, the auditor typically needs to test more controls in order to issue an ICFR opinion than would be tested when only expressing an opinion on the financial statements.

> **PLANNING AID REMINDER:** Regardless of the assessed level of risk, the auditor should perform substantive procedures for all relevant assertions for each material account balance, transaction class, and disclosure. Therefore, even if inherent risk is low and internal control is effective, the auditor must still perform some substantive procedures for material account balances, transaction classes, and disclosures.

Evaluate identified deficiencies

In evaluating the internal control deficiencies identified during the ICFR audit, the auditor evaluates whether any single deficiency or deficiencies considered together constitute either a significant deficiency or a material weakness. A significant deficiency is a deficiency or combination of deficiencies that is less severe than a material weakness but important enough to warrant consideration by those charged with governance. Therefore, a significant deficiency does not change the nature of an unmodified report on ICFR and is not included in the auditor's report, but it is communicated to those charged with governance. A material weakness is a deficiency or combination of deficiencies such that there is a reasonable possibility that a material misstatement in the financial statements will not be prevented, or detected and corrected, on a timely basis. The term "reasonable possibility" as used here means that a material misstatement in the financial statements is either "reasonably possible" or "probable" as those terms are defined in ASC 450 (FAS-5, Accounting for Contingencies). If there is even one material weakness, the auditor cannot conclude that ICFR is effective (i.e., the auditor must issue an adverse opinion on the effectiveness of ICFR).

The severity of an identified deficiency depends on the magnitude of the potential misstatement as a result of the deficiency and the likelihood that a misstatement will occur as a result of the deficiency. Factors that affect the magnitude of a potential misstatement are (1) the financial statement amounts or transaction totals affected by the deficiency and (2) the volume of activity in the account or transaction class affected by the deficiency. In evaluating deficiencies, the auditor should recognize that the likelihood of a small misstatement is greater than the likelihood of a large misstatement. Factors that affect the likelihood of a misstatement are

- Nature of accounts, transactions, disclosures, and assertions
- Susceptibility of related asset or liability to loss or fraud
- Subjectivity, complexity, and judgment involved with the account
- Relation of the control to other controls

- Interaction among the deficiencies

- Possible future consequences of the deficiency

> **PLANNING AID REMINDER:** The severity of a deficiency does not depend on whether a misstatement has already occurred.

Multiple deficiencies that affect the same account, disclosure, assertion, or internal control component increase the likelihood that a material weakness exists. In some cases, clients have a second control that compensates for a deficiency in the tested control. A compensating control can limit the severity of an identified deficiency (in the tested control) and thereby prevent the deficiency from rising to the level of a significant deficiency or material weakness. However, a compensating control does not eliminate the underlying deficiency. In order for a compensating control to mitigate a control deficiency it must operate at a level of precision sufficient to prevent, or detect and timely correct, a material misstatement in the financial statements. The auditor should test the operating effectiveness of any compensating control that he or she plans to rely on.

There are certain indicators that suggest that a material weakness may exist:

- Identification of fraud committed by senior management, regardless of materiality

- Restatements of previously issued financial statements to correct a material misstatement due to error or fraud

- Identification of a material misstatement by the auditor in the financial statements being audited that was not detected by management (i.e., the auditor is not part of the client's internal control system)

- Ineffective oversight of financial reporting and internal control by those charged with governance

> **PLANNING AID REMINDER:** If the auditor concludes that a deficiency or combination of deficiencies is not a material weakness, he or she should assess whether a prudent official would reach the same judgment given the same information as that known to the auditor.

Obtain written representations

The auditor should obtain written representations from management in an ICFR audit, including

- A statement that responsibility for establishing and maintaining internal control is that of management

- A statement that management has performed an evaluation of the effectiveness of internal control based on control criteria (control criteria should be specified)

- A statement that management did not rely on the auditor's procedures in making its assertion

- Management's assertion about the effectiveness of internal control based on the control criteria as of a specified date

- A statement that management has communicated to the auditor all deficiencies in the design or operation of internal control, separately identifying deficiencies it believes to be significant deficiencies and material weaknesses

- A statement that management has described any material fraud and any other fraud that involves management or other employees who have a significant role in the entity's internal control, even though the fraud is not material

- A statement that significant deficiencies or material weaknesses communicated to management and those charged with governance in the prior year have been corrected, or where such corrections have not occurred that, specifically, identifies them

- A statement that subsequent to the date of the report there were no events, changes in internal control, or occurrences of other factors that might significantly affect internal control, including the remediation of significant deficiencies and material weaknesses

A failure to obtain written representations from management represents a scope limitation. The auditor should consider the effect of management's refusal to provide such representations on his or her ability to rely on other representations, including representations related to the financial statement audit.

Fulfill communication responsibilities

The auditor is to communicate in writing to management and those charged with governance all significant deficiencies and material weaknesses identified during the integrated audit. If any of these significant deficiencies or material weaknesses were previously communicated, the auditor can simply refer to the communication by date. And if the auditor concludes that audit committee oversight of financial reporting and internal control is ineffective, he or she is to communicate this in writing to the board of directors or other, similar governing body. These required communications should occur by the report release date. The report release date is the date the auditor allows the entity to use his or her report.

> **PLANNING AID REMINDER:** Communication of significant deficiencies and material weaknesses can occur later than the report release date for a governmental entity. The required communications must be made within 60 days of the report release date. This exception only exists if the required communications will be publicly available prior to management's report on internal control, the entity's financial statements, and the auditor's report thereon.

The client may be able to remediate internal control deficiencies during the year if it receives timely communication. Therefore, the auditor can orally communicate to management significant internal control matters. However, oral communication does not eliminate the auditor's responsibility to communicate significant deficiencies and material weaknesses in writing, even if the matters are remediated during the year. In addition, all internal control deficiencies (beyond significant deficiencies and material weaknesses) are to be communicated to management in writing within 60 days of the report release date, and those charged with governance are to be notified when this communication takes place.

> **PLANNING AID REMINDER:** The auditor is precluded from issuing a report containing "negative assurance" about internal control. For example, the auditor should not issue a report indicating that no deficiencies were identified.

Prepare an appropriate report on the entity's (client's) ICFR

The auditor's opinion on the effectiveness of ICFR should reflect evidence obtained from all sources, specifically from the auditor's testing of internal control and from testing performed during the financial statement audit. In addition, the auditor should consider reports issued during the year by any internal audit group that may exist. The auditor should ensure that management has issued its own report on the effectiveness of ICFR and that management's report contains the following elements:

- A statement that management is responsible for internal control

- A description of what was examined, typically controls over the preparation of financial statements in accordance with GAAP

- A description of the framework used to evaluate controls, typically COSO's *Internal Control — Integrated Framework* (1992)

- Management's assertion about the effectiveness of ICFR

- A description of any material weaknesses

- The date as of which management's assertion is made

> **OBSERVATION:** If management refuses to include its own report on ICFR, the auditor should withdraw from the engagement. If precluded from withdrawing by law or regulation, the auditor should disclaim an opinion on ICFR.

The reporting guidelines in Exhibit AT 501-1 should be followed in the preparation of report on internal control.

EXHIBIT AT 501-1 — REPORTING GUIDELINES FOR PREPARATION OF AN EXAMINATION REPORT ON AN ENTITY'S INTERNAL CONTROL

Required Elements of the Audit Report on the Effectiveness of ICFR

- Title that includes the word "independent"

- Statement that management is responsible for maintaining effective internal control and for evaluating the effectiveness of ICFR

- An identification of management's assessment of ICFR (refer to management's report)

- Statement that the auditor is responsible for issuing an opinion on ICFR or on management's assertion regarding internal control (i.e., the auditor can either report directly on internal control or on management's assertion regarding internal control)

- Statement that the engagement was performed in accordance with AICPA attestation standards

- Statement that the AICPA attestation standards require the auditor to gather reasonable assurance as to whether internal control was maintained in all material respects

- A description of the attestation procedures performed (e.g., understanding control, assessing risk, testing and evaluating design and operating effectiveness, and other procedures as deemed necessary)

- A statement that the auditor believes that he or she has a reasonable basis for the opinion

- A definition of internal control (the auditor is to use the same definition as that used by management)

- Separate paragraph describing the inherent limitations of internal control, along with a warning that the effectiveness of the internal control may be inadequate for future periods

- An opinion on whether the entity has maintained, in all material respects, effective internal control as of a specified date based on the control criteria (or the auditor's opinion on management's internal control assertion)

- Manual or printed signature of the firm

- Date of the report

The auditor can issue a combined report on ICFR and the financial statements or separate reports on each. If separate reports are issued, the auditor should add a paragraph to the report on the financial statements stating that he or she audited ICFR and the type of report issued, and a paragraph to the ICFR report stating that he or she audited the financial statements and indicating the type of report issued. Because the financial statement and ICFR audits are integrated they should be dated the same.

Exhibit AT 501-2 is an example taken from SSAE-15 of an examination on the effectiveness of an entity's internal control over financial reporting.

EXHIBIT AT 501-2 — EXAMINATION ON THE EFFECTIVENESS OF AN ENTITY'S INTERNAL CONTROL OVER FINANCIAL REPORTING

Independent Auditor's Report

We have examined W Company's internal control over financial reporting as of December 31, 20XX, based on [*identify criteria*]. W Company's management is responsible for maintaining effective internal control over financial reporting, and for its assertion of the effectiveness of internal control over financial reporting, included in the accompanying [*title of management's report*]. Our responsibility is to express an opinion on W Company's internal control over financial reporting based on our examination.

We conducted our examination in accordance with attestation standards established by the American Institute of Certified Public Accountants. Those standards require that we plan and perform the examination to obtain reasonable assurance about whether effective internal control over financial reporting was maintained in all material respects. Our examination included obtaining an understanding of internal control over financial reporting, assessing the risk that a material weakness exists, and testing and evaluating the design and operating effectiveness of internal control based on the assessed risk. Our examination also included performing such other procedures as we considered necessary in the circumstances. We believe that our examination provides a reasonable basis for our opinion.

An entity's internal control over financial reporting is a process effected by those charged with governance, management, and other personnel, designed to provide reasonable assurance regarding the preparation of reliable financial statements in accordance with [*applicable financial reporting framework, such as accounting principles generally accepted in the United States of America*]. An entity's internal control over financial reporting includes those policies and procedures that (1) pertain to the maintenance of records that in reasonable detail accurately and fairly reflect the transactions and dispositions of the assets of the entity; (2) provide reasonable assurance that transactions are recorded as necessary to permit preparation of financial statements in accordance with [*applicable financial reporting framework, such as accounting principles generally accepted in the United States of America*] and that receipts and expenditures of the entity are being made only in accordance with authorizations of management and those charged with governance; and (3) provide reasonable assurance regarding prevention, or timely detection and correction of unauthorized acquisition, use, or disposition of the entity's assets that could have a material effect on the financial statements.

Because of its inherent limitations, internal control over financial reporting may not prevent, or detect and correct misstatements. Also, projections of any evaluation of effectiveness to future periods are subject to the risk that controls may become inadequate because of changes in conditions, or that the degree of compliance with the policies or procedures may deteriorate.

In our opinion, W Company maintained, in all material respects, effective internal control over financial reporting as of December 31, 20XX, based on [*identify criteria*].

We also have audited, in accordance with auditing standards generally accepted in the United States of America, the [*identify financial statements*] of W Company and our report dated [*date of report, which should be the same as the date of the report on the examination of internal control*] expressed [*include nature of opinion*].

[*Signature*]

[*Date*]

Exhibit AT 501-3 is an example taken from SSAE-15 of an examination on management's written assertion on the effectiveness of an entity's internal control over financial reporting.

EXHIBIT AT 501-3 — EXAMINATION ON MANAGEMENT'S WRITTEN ASSERTION ON THE EFFECTIVENESS OF AN ENTITY'S INTERNAL CONTROL OVER FINANCIAL REPORTING

Independent Auditor's Report

We have examined management's assertion, included in the accompanying [*title of management's report*], that W Company maintained effective internal control over financial reporting as of December 31, 20XX, based on [*identify criteria*]. W Company's management is responsible for maintaining effective internal control over financial reporting, and for its assertion of the effectiveness of internal control over financial reporting, included in the accompanying [*title of management's report*]. Our responsibility is to express an opinion on management's assertion based on our examination.

We conducted our examination in accordance with attestation standards established by the American Institute of Certified Public Accountants. Those standards require that we plan and perform the examination to obtain reasonable assurance about whether effective internal control over financial reporting was maintained in all material respects. Our examination included obtaining an understanding of internal control over financial reporting, assessing the risk that a material weakness exists, and testing and evaluating the design and operating effectiveness of internal control based on the assessed risk. Our examination also included performing such other procedures as we considered necessary in the circumstances. We believe that our examination provides a reasonable basis for our opinion.

An entity's internal control over financial reporting is a process effected by those charged with governance, management, and other personnel designed to provide reasonable assurance regarding the preparation of reliable financial statements in accordance with [applicable financial reporting framework, such as accounting principles generally accepted in the United States of America]. An entity's internal control over financial reporting includes policies and procedures that (1) pertain to the maintenance of records that in reasonable detail accurately and fairly reflect the transactions and dispositions of the assets of the entity; (2) provide reasonable assurance that transactions are recorded as necessary to permit preparation of financial statements in accordance with [applicable financial reporting framework, such as accounting principles generally accepted in the United States of America], and that receipts and expenditures of the entity are being made only in accordance with authorizations of management and those charged with governance; and (3) provide reasonable assurance regarding prevention, or timely detection and correction, of unauthorized acquisition, use, or disposition of the entity's assets that could have a material effect on the financial statements.

Because of its inherent limitations, internal control over financial reporting may not prevent, or detect and correct misstatements. Also, projections of any evaluation of effectiveness to future periods are subject to the risk that controls may become inadequate because of changes in conditions, or that the degree of compliance with the policies or procedures may deteriorate.

In our opinion, management's assertion that W Company maintained effective internal control over financial reporting as of December 31, 20XX, is fairly stated, in all material respects, based on [identify criteria].

We have also audited, in accordance with auditing standards generally accepted in the United States of America the [identify financial *statements*] of W Company, and our report dated [*date of report, which should be the same as the date of the report on the examination of internal control*] expressed [*include nature of opinion*].

[*Signature*]

[*Date*]

Report modifications

SSAE standards state that the auditor should modify the standard report (on either a direct opinion on internal control or on a written assertion on internal control) if any of the following circumstances exist:

- Material weakness
- Management's report is incomplete or not properly presented
- Scope limitation
- Reliance in part on the report of another auditor
- Other information is included in management's report

Material weakness

If one or more material weaknesses exist, the auditor is to issue an adverse opinion on internal control (unless a scope limitation exists). In the report, the auditor is to define a material weakness and identify the material weakness included in management's assertion.

If management fails to describe the material weakness in its report, the auditor should state that a material weakness has been omitted from management's report and he or she should describe the material weakness in the audit report. The auditor's discussion should include the actual and potential effects of the material weakness on the financial statements. In addition, the auditor should communicate in writing to those charged with governance that a material weakness was excluded from management's report. Finally, the auditor should disclose whether the material weakness affected the financial statement audit report.

> **PLANNING AID REMINDER:** When a material weakness exists, SSAE-15 states that the auditor should report directly on the effectiveness of internal control rather than on the written assertion.

Management's report is incomplete or not properly presented

If a required element of management's report is missing or inadequate, the auditor should ask management to correct its report. If management refuses to make the needed correction, the auditor should modify his or her report by including an explanatory paragraph describing the deficiency in management's report.

Scope limitation

When significant examination procedures deemed necessary to achieve the standard of sufficient appropriate evidence cannot be performed, the auditor should disclaim an opinion or withdraw from the engagement. If the auditor disclaims an opinion, his or her report should state that an opinion is not being expressed and explain the reasons for the disclaimer. The auditor should neither include in the report a description of any procedures performed nor describe the characteristics of internal control.

If the auditor disclaims an opinion, he or she should describe all material weaknesses that he or she is aware of. The auditor also should communicate in writing to management and those charged with governance that an opinion on internal control cannot be expressed because of a scope limitation.

Reliance in part on the report of another auditor

If internal control components of the entity are examined by another auditor, an auditor may still report on the entity's internal control over financial reporting. Under this circumstance, the auditor must decide whether or not to serve as the principal auditor and, if he or she serves as principal auditor, whether to refer to the work of the other auditor in the examination report. Specific guidance for making these determinations is discussed in AU 543 (Part of Audit Performed by Other Independent Auditors). Although the guidance is discussed in the context of an audit of financial statements, SSAE standards state that the general guidance is also applicable to the examination of management's assertion about its internal control.

Other information is included in management's report

Management's report may contain additional information beyond that which the auditor is engaged to report on. For example, management may make a statement discussing the trade-off between the costs of remediating internal control deficiencies and the benefits to be achieved from the remediation, or management may discuss corrective actions taken to address identified deficiencies. The auditor is to disclaim an opinion on additional information included in management's report by adding an additional last paragraph to the auditor's standard ICFR report.

> **PLANNING AID REMINDER:** The last paragraph may be worded as follows, "We do not express an opinion or any other form of assurance on [*describe additional information, such as management's cost-benefit statement*]."

If the auditor believes that the additional information contained in management's report contains a material misstatement of fact, he or she should discuss the matter with the client. If the auditor concludes that a material misstatement of fact remains after discussing the matter with the client, he or she may want to consult with his or her legal counsel. At a minimum, the auditor should communicate in writing to management and those charged with governance his or her belief that a material misstatement of fact exists in management's report.

Consider subsequent events

After the date of management's assertion about its internal control but before the date of the examination report, there may have been changes in policies, procedures, or other factors that may have a significant effect on the entity's internal control. SSAE standards state that to determine whether such changes have occurred, the auditor should determine whether the following reports were issued subsequent to the date of the examination report, and, if so, he or she should read them:

- Other reports issued by independent practitioner(s) that identify deficiencies

- Relevant reports issued by internal auditors

- Reports on the client's internal control issued by regulatory agencies

- Information generated through other professional engagements that relates to the effectiveness of the client's internal control

If the subsequent event indicates that a material weakness existed at the date being reported on, the auditor should issue an adverse opinion and refer to the material weakness. In this case the auditor must report directly on internal control because an adverse opinion is being issued (i.e., the auditor cannot report on management's assertion regarding internal control). If the subsequent event indicates that a material weakness came into existence after the date being reported on, the auditor should describe the event in an explanatory paragraph or refer to the related discussion in management's report.

AT SECTION 601

COMPLIANCE ATTESTATION

Authoritative Pronouncements

SSAE-10 — Attestation Standards: Revision and Recodification (Chapter 6)

Overview

The Statements on Standards for Attestation Engagements (SSAE) standards provide guidance for an engagement in which the practitioner either (1) reports on the client's compliance with requirements of specified laws, regulations, rules, contracts, or grants (referred to as compliance with specified requirements) or (2) reports on the effectiveness of the client's internal control over compliance with specified requirements.

> **PLANNING AID REMINDER:** When a practitioner is engaged to report on compliance with specified requirements, the general, fieldwork, and reporting standards discussed in AT 101 should be observed, along with the standards established in this chapter.

Although the standards discussed in this chapter are concerned with engagements related to compliance with specified requirements, the guidance does not apply to the following engagements:

- Audits of financial statements that are subject to generally accepted auditing standards (GAAS)

- Certain audit reports on specified compliance requirements based solely on the audit of financial statements [see paragraphs 19 through 21 of SAS-62 (AU 623) (Special Reports)]

- Reports on engagements that are subject to the standards established by SAS-74 (AU 801) (Compliance Auditing Considerations in Audits of Governmental Entities and Recipients of Governmental Financial Assistance), unless the terms of the engagement specifically require the type of attest report discussed in this chapter

- Engagements subject to SAS-72 (AU 634) (Letters for Underwriters and Certain Other Requesting Parties)

- Report engagements related to a broker or dealer's internal control as required by Rule 17a-5 of the Securities Exchange Act of 1934

A compliance attestation engagement can take either the form of an agreed-upon procedures engagement or an examination.

AGREED-UPON PROCEDURES ENGAGEMENT

SSAE standards state that the purpose of an agreed-upon procedures (AUP) compliance attestation engagement is "to present specific findings to assist users in evaluating an entity's compliance with specified requirements or the effectiveness of an entity's internal control over compliance based on procedures agreed upon by the users of the report." A practitioner may accept an AUP compliance attestation engagement if both of the following conditions are satisfied:

- The responsible party accepts responsibility for compliance with the specified requirements and the effectiveness of the internal control over compliance.

- The responsible party evaluates compliance with the specified requirements or the effectiveness of the internal control over compliance.

Engagement Procedures

An AUP engagement must satisfy the standards established in this chapter as well as the guidance discussed in the chapter titled "Agreed-Upon Procedures Engagements" (AT 201).

As part of the AUP engagement, SSAE standards require that the practitioner obtain an understanding of the specified compliance requirements by considering the following:

- Laws, regulations, rules, contracts, and grants that relate to the compliance requirements

- Experienced gained from previous engagement and regulatory reports

- Inquiries made of appropriate management personnel

- Inquiries made of external parties such as specialists and regulators

Reporting Guidance

The practitioner's AUP report should include the following items:

- A title that includes the word "independent"
- An identification of the specified party

- An identification of the subject matter (or the written assertion), the period or point in time covered by the engagement, and the character of the engagement

- An identification of the responsible party and a statement that the subject matter is the responsibility of the responsible party

- A statement that the procedures were agreed to by the specified party and were performed to assist the specified party in evaluating compliance with the specified requirements or the effectiveness of internal control over compliance

- A statement that the AUP engagement was conducted in accordance with attestation standards established by the American Institute of Certified Public Accountants

- A statement that the specified party is solely responsible for the sufficiency of the agreed-upon procedures and disclaim any responsibility for the sufficiency of the procedures

- List of the procedures performed and related findings

- Description of materiality thresholds, where applicable

- A statement that the practitioner was not engaged to and did not conduct an examination of the compliance with specified requirements (or the effectiveness of internal control over compliance), a disclaimer of opinion, and a statement that if the practitioner had performed additional procedures, other matters might have come to his or her attention that would have been reported

- A statement restricting the use of the report to specified parties

- Reservations or restrictions related to procedures or findings, if applicable

- A description of the assistance provided by a specialist, if applicable

- The manual or printed signature of the practitioner's firm

- The date of the AUP report

Exhibit AT 601-1 is an example taken from SSAE-10 of an AUP engagement on an entity's compliance with specified requirements.

EXHIBIT AT 601-1—AUP REPORT ON AN ENTITY'S COMPLIANCE WITH SPECIFIED REQUIREMENTS

Independent Accountant's Report on Applying Agreed-Upon Procedures

We have performed the procedures enumerated below, which were agreed to by the [*identify specify parties*], solely to assist the specified parties in evaluating [*name of entity*]'s compliance with [*list specified requirements*] during the [*period*] ended [*date*]. Management is responsible for [*name of entity*]'s compliance with those requirements.

This agreed-upon procedures engagement was conducted in accordance with attestation standards established by the American Institute of Certified Public Accountants. The sufficiency of these procedures is solely the responsibility of those parties specified in this report. Consequently, we make no representation regarding the sufficiency of the procedures described below either for the purpose for which this report has been requested or for any other purpose. [*Include paragraphs to enumerate procedures and findings.*]

We were not engaged to and did not conduct an examination, the objective of which would be the expression of an opinion on compliance. Accordingly, we do not express such an opinion. Had we performed additional procedures, other matters might have come to our attention that would have been reported to you.

This report is intended solely for the information and use of [*list or refer to specified parties*] and is not intended to be and should not be used by anyone other than these specified parties.

[*Signature*]

[*Date*]

EXAMINATION ENGAGEMENT

SSAE standards state that the purpose of an examination engagement is "to express an opinion on an entity's compliance (or assertion related thereto), based on the specified criteria." A practitioner may accept an examination compliance attestation engagement if all of the following conditions are satisfied:

- The responsible party accepts responsibility for compliance with the specified requirements and the effectiveness of the internal control over compliance.

- The responsible party evaluates compliance with the specified requirements.

- Sufficient evidential matter exists or could be developed to support the responsible party's evaluation.

Promulgated Procedures Checklist

The practitioner should perform the following procedures in an examination engagement:

- Obtain an understanding of compliance requirements.
- Plan the examination engagement.
- Consider relevant internal control components.
- Obtain sufficient evidential matter.
- Consider subsequent events.
- Obtain written representations from the client.
- Prepare an appropriate compliance report.

> **ENGAGEMENT STRATEGY:** General guidance for documenting an attest engagement is discussed in AT 101.

Analysis and Application of Procedures

Obtain an understanding of compliance requirements

Since the scope of compliance attestation is broad and the standards can be applied to a variety of circumstances, it is difficult to generalize about the practitioner's knowledge of compliance requirements. Basically, the practitioner must develop an understanding of the specified compliance requirements. SSAE standards identify the following as sources of information that can provide the practitioner with an adequate understanding:

- Specific laws, regulations, rules, contracts, and grants on which the specified requirements are based

- Experience developed from previous similar examination engagements

- Information contained in relevant regulatory reports

- Conversations with management personnel concerning the specified requirements

- Conversations with external parties, including regulatory authorities and specialists in the area

Plan the examination engagement

One of the fundamental components of a compliance attestation engagement is the assessment of attestation risk, defined as follows:

> The risk that the practitioner may unknowingly fail to modify appropriately his or her opinion on management's assertion.

When the practitioner offers an opinion on an entity's compliance with specified requirements, there is always a chance that the opinion will be incorrect. Simply stated, it is impossible for the practitioner to reduce the attestation risk to zero because, for example, sampling methods must be used, judgments must be made, and management personnel can collude to deceive the practitioner.

To assess attestation risk, the practitioner must consider (1) inherent risk, (2) control risk, and (3) detection risk.

"Inherent risk" relates to the fundamental characteristics of the entity. These characteristics provide the background or context in which a particular activity is performed. Not surprisingly, the practitioner uses a significant degree of professional judgment in assessing inherent risk.

Although there is no comprehensive list of factors that contribute to inherent risk, the SSAE standards state that the practitioner should consider the same risk factors that would be considered in an audit of the financial statements, including the fraud risk factors identified in SAS-99 (AU 316). In addition, SSAE standards list the following as other factors that should be considered in assessing inherent risk:

- Level of complexity of specified compliance requirements

- Period of time that the entity has been subject to the specified compliance requirements

- Practitioner's prior experience with the entity's compliance with the specified requirements

- Possible ramifications of lack of compliance with the specified requirements

"Control risk" refers to the probability that material deviations from specified compliance requirements exist. Thus, the design of the client's internal control with respect to specified requirements will have an impact on the level of control risk. Control risk, like inherent risk, cannot be changed by the practitioner. In general, the stronger the internal control for specified requirements, the more likely it is that material compliance deviations will be prevented or detected by the system on a timely basis. Thus, the practitioner must carefully assess control risk at a level that accurately reflects the internal control policies and procedures that have been adopted by the client. (Of course, the practitioner can make recommendations for improving the system, which may affect future engagements.)

As referred to earlier, the practitioner's assessment of the internal control over compliance with specified requirements is based on obtaining an understanding of relevant internal control policies and procedures.

"Detection risk" is the risk that a practitioner's procedures will lead to the conclusion that material deviations from specified requirements do not exist when in fact such deviations do exist. During the planning phase of the engagement, the practitioner should consider inherent risk, control risk, and detection risk and select an examination strategy that will result in a low level of attestation risk once the engagement is complete. There is an inverse relationship between the practitioner's assessment of inherent risk and control risk and the level of detection risk. If the inherent risk and control risk are higher, the practitioner should establish a lower level of detection risk. The level of detection risk established has a direct effect on the design of the nature, timing, and extent of compliance tests performed.

From a broad perspective, the concept of materiality in a compliance attestation engagement is similar to its role in an audit of financial statements. Immaterial deviations [from generally accepted accounting principles (GAAP) or from established or agreed-upon criteria] will generally exist in both types of engagements, but it is unreasonable to direct the focus of the engagements to immaterial items.

Although the concept of materiality applies to both types of engagements, it is probably more difficult to apply the concept in a compliance attestation engagement. First, because the engagement can be directed to a variety of specified requirements, it is very difficult to generalize about the examination approach. Second, the specified requirements may or may not be quantifiable in monetary terms. Third, there has been little research, if any, into what the focal point should be for determining materiality in a compliance attestation engagement. SSAE standards provide little guidance for determining materiality, except to state that the following may affect the determination of materiality:

- The nature of management's assertion and the compliance requirements, which may or may not be quantifiable in monetary terms

- The nature and frequency of noncompliance identified with appropriate consideration of sampling risk

- Qualitative considerations, including the needs and expectations of the report's users

> **PLANNING AID REMINDER:** Some compliance attestation engagements require the practitioner to prepare a supplemental report identifying all or certain deviations discovered. Any threshold guidance established for reporting items in the supplemental report should not have an effect on the auditor's determination of a materiality threshold for the primary examination report.

In many engagements, the operations of the entity will encompass two or more locations. As part of the planning of the compliance attestation engagement, the practitioner should decide whether the internal control policies and procedures at all of the locations or some of the locations should be considered. SSAE standards point out that the practitioner should consider factors such as the following when determining the scope of the engagement with respect to the component units:

- The degree to which the specified requirements apply to each component

- The assessment of materiality in the context of each component's operations

- The degree to which records are processed at each component

- The effectiveness of control environment policies and procedures over each component's operations

- The similarities of operations among components

- The nature and extent of operations at each component

Consider relevant internal control components

The practitioner should obtain an understanding of the relevant internal control policies and procedures related to the entity's ability to comply with the specified requirements. This understanding enables the practitioner to plan the engagement properly and determine the planned assessed level of control risk. In gaining this understanding, the practitioner should have developed insight into the strengths and weaknesses of the internal control by identifying the processing steps and procedures that are (1) most likely to result in the occurrence of material noncompliance and (2) most likely to reduce the likelihood that material noncompliance will occur.

> **PLANNING AID REMINDER:** The consideration of the internal control in a compliance attestation engagement is very similar to the consideration of the internal control in an audit of financial statements. In an audit of financial statements, the auditor (1) obtains an understanding of the entity and its environment, including internal control, (2) determines the planned assessed level of the risk of material misstatement, (3) generally performs tests of controls, and (4) designs substantive procedures based on the assessed level of the risk of material misstatement. In a compliance attestation engagement, the practitioner (1) obtains an understanding of internal control, (2) determines the planned assessed level of control risk, (3) generally performs tests of controls, and (4) designs compliance tests based on the assessed level of control risk. Thus, the only difference is that in a compliance attestation engagement the auditor performs tests of compliance rather than substantive procedures as the final step.

The understanding of internal control may be obtained by performing such procedures as (1) making inquiries of appropriate client personnel, (2) inspecting relevant documents and records, (3) observing the entity's relevant activities and operations, and (4) if applicable, reviewing workpapers from the previous engagement(s). The understanding of internal control includes an analytical phase and a corroborative phase. In the analytical phase, the practitioner's responsibility is to gain an understanding of relevant internal controls. In the corroborative phase (tests of controls), the practitioner must determine the effectiveness of the design of internal controls and the operations of the relevant internal controls.

The evidential matter obtained through these and other examination procedures should provide the practitioner with a basis for the design of tests of compliance. SSAE standards specifically note that the nature and extent of tests of compliance procedures can be affected by a variety of factors, including the following:

- The newness and complexity of the specified requirements
- The practitioner's experience with the client's relevant internal control based on previous engagements
- The nature of the specified compliance requirements
- The characteristics of the client and its industry
- The assessment as to what constitutes material noncompliance

> **PLANNING AID REMINDER:** During the engagement, the practitioner may discover noncompliance that is considered "significant" but not material. Under this circumstance, guidance established by SAS-115 (AU 325) (Communication of Internal Control Related Matters Noted in an Audit) should be considered.

> **PLANNING AID REMINDER:** If the practitioner decides that the work of a specialist is required in a compliance attestation engagement, the guidance established by SAS-73 (AU 336) (Using the Work of a Specialist) should be observed. If the practitioner decides to consider a client's internal audit function, the guidance established by SAS-65 (AU 322) (The Auditor's Consideration of the Internal Audit Function in an Audit of Financial Statements) should be observed.

Obtain sufficient evidential matter

Based on the assessed level of control risk, which is the final phase in the development of an understanding of the client's internal control, the practitioner must perform tests of compliance. The extent to which these tests should be performed is a matter of professional judgment and in general a practitioner should follow the guidance established in SAS-39 (AU 350) (Audit Sampling).

> **PLANNING AID REMINDER:** If the client is subject to regulatory requirements, the engagement approach should include "reviewing reports of significant examinations and related communications between regulatory agencies and the entity and, when appropriate, making inquiries of the regulatory agencies, including inquiries about examinations in progress."

Consider subsequent events

SSAE standards identify two types of subsequent events that the practitioner should consider in the compliance attestation engagement. The first type of subsequent event provides additional information about the entity's compliance during the period covered by engagement. In a manner similar to the approach used in an audit of financial statements, the practitioner should perform, between the end of the period covered by the engagement and the date of the report, specific subsequent-event procedures to evaluate the appropriateness of management's assertions. While there is no comprehensive list of subsequent audit procedures, SSAE standards list the following as examples:

• Review relevant internal audit reports that have been issued during the subsequent period.

• Determine whether relevant reports by other practitioners have been issued during the subsequent period.

• Consider whether relevant subsequent events have been discovered due to the conduct of other professional engagements for the client.

• Consider reports on the entity's noncompliance issued by regulatory agencies during the subsequent period.

The second type of subsequent events relates to noncompliance events that actually occur between the end of the period covered by the engagement and the date of the report. Although the scope of the engagement focuses on the period covered by the engagement, the practitioner must nonetheless take into consideration subsequent noncompliance events. SSAE standards state that if the noncompliance is significant, the noncompliance event should be described in the practitioner's report.

Obtain written representations from the client

The practitioner should obtain written representations from management concerning an examination to express an opinion on compliance with specified requirements. SSAE standards state that appropriate management personnel should make the following representations:

• State that the responsible party is responsible for complying with the specified requirements.

- State that the responsible party is responsible for establishing and maintaining effective internal control with respect to compliance with specified requirements.

- State that the responsible party has evaluated the entity's compliance with specified requirements or controls over compliance with the specified requirements.

- State the responsible party's assertion about compliance with the specified requirements or about the effectiveness of internal controls, based on the stated or established criteria.

- State that the responsible party has informed the practitioner of all known noncompliance.

- State that the responsible party has made available to the practitioner all documentation relevant to the engagement.

- State the responsible party's interpretation of any specified requirements that have alternative interpretations.

- State that the responsible party has communicated to the practitioner all communications from regulatory agencies, internal auditors, and other auditors concerning possible noncompliance, including communications received up to the date of the practitioner's report.

- State that the responsible party has informed the practitioner of any noncompliance that occurred from the date covered by the engagement through the date of the practitioner's report.

Prepare an appropriate compliance report

Once the practitioner has obtained sufficient evidence, the practitioner states an opinion on the entity's compliance with the specified internal controls.

In a compliance attestation engagement to report on specified controls, the practitioner may report in either of the following ways:

- Report directly on the entity's compliance with the specified controls.

- Report on the responsible party's written assertion concerning compliance with the specified controls.

The reporting guidelines in Exhibit AT 601-2 should be followed in the preparation of a compliance report.

EXHIBIT AT 601-2 — REPORTING GUIDELINES FOR
PREPARATION OF A COMPLIANCE EXAMINATION
REPORT

Guidance for Reporting Directly on the Specified Controls	**Guidance for Reporting on the Responsible Party's Written Assertion Concerning the Specified Controls**
Title that includes the word "independent"	Title that includes the word "independent"
Identification of specified compliance requirements, including the period covered, and the responsible party	Identification of the responsible party's assertion, including the period covered, and the responsible party
Statement that management is responsible for compliance with the specified requirements	Statement that management is responsible for compliance with the specified requirements
Statement that the practitioner's responsibility is to express an opinion on the compliance with specified requirements	Statement that the practitioner's responsibility is to express an opinion on the responsible party's assertion on compliance with specified requirements
Statement that the examination was performed in accordance with attestation standards established by the AICPA, a brief description of the nature of the examination, and a statement that the practitioner believes that the examination provided a reasonable basis for the opinion expressed	Statement that the examination was performed in accordance with attestation standards established by the AICPA, a brief description of the nature of the examination, and a statement that the practitioner believes that the examination provided a reasonable basis for the opinion expressed
Statement that the practitioner's examination did not make a legal determination with respect to compliance with specified requirements	Statement that the practitioner's examination did not make a legal determination with respect to compliance with specified requirements
An opinion on the compliance with specified requirements	An opinion on whether the responsible party's assertions about compliance is fairly stated in all material respects based on the specified criteria

Guidance for Reporting Directly on the Specified Controls	Guidance for Reporting on the Responsible Party's Written Assertion Concerning the Specified Controls
Statement restricting the use of the report, when appropriate	Statement restricting the use of the report, when appropriate
Manual or printed signature of the practitioner's firm	Manual or printed signature of the practitioner's firm
Date of the examination report	Date of the examination report

PLANNING AID REMINDER: SSAE standards (fourth reporting standard) require that the auditor restrict the use of the report when the criteria used in the examination are (1) determined by the auditor to be appropriate only for a limited number of parties who either participated in their establishment or can be presumed to have an adequate understanding of the criteria or (2) available only to specified parties.

Exhibit AT 601-3 is an example taken from SSAE-10 of an examination on the compliance with specified requirements.

EXHIBIT AT 601-3 — EXAMINATION ON THE COMPLIANCE WITH SPECIFIED REQUIREMENTS

Independent Accountant's Report

We have examined [*name of entity*] compliance with [*list specified compliance requirements*] during the [*period*] ended [*date*]. Management is responsible for [*name of entity*]'s compliance with those requirements. Our responsibility is to express an opinion on [*name of entity*]'s compliance based on our examination.

Our examination was conducted in accordance with attestation standards established by the American Institute of Certified Public Accountants and, accordingly, included examining, on a test basis, evidence about [*name of entity*]'s compliance with those requirements and performing such other procedures as we considered necessary in the circumstances. We believe that our examination provides a reasonable basis for our opinion. Our examination does not provide a legal determination of [*name of entity*]'s compliance with specified requirements.

In our opinion, [*name of entity*] complies, in all material respects, with the aforementioned requirements for the year ended December 31, 20X5.

[*Signature*]

[*Date*]

Exhibit AT 601-4 is an example taken from SSAE-10 of an examination on management's assertion concerning compliance with specified requirements.

EXHIBIT AT 601-4— EXAMINATION ON MANAGEMENT'S ASSERTION CONCERNING COMPLIANCE WITH SPECIFIED REQUIREMENTS

Independent Accountant's Report

We have examined management's assertion, included in the accompanying [*title of management report*], that [*name of entity*] complied with [*list specified compliance requirements*] during the [*period*] ended [*date*]. Management is responsible for [*name of entity*]'s compliance with those requirements. Our responsibility is to express an opinion on management's assertion about [*name of entity*]'s compliance based on our examination.

Our examination was conducted in accordance with attestation standards established by the American Institute of Certified Public Accountants and, accordingly, included examining, on a test basis, evidence about [*name of entity*]'s compliance with those requirements and performing such other procedures as we considered necessary in the circumstances. We believe that our examination provides a reasonable basis for our opinion. Our examination does not provide a legal determination of [*name of entity*]'s compliance with specified requirements.

In our opinion, management's assertion that [*name of entity*] complied with the aforementioned requirements during the [*period*] ended [*date*] is fairly stated, in all material respects.

[*Signature*]

[*Date*]

In some instances it is necessary to interpret the specified requirements established by laws, regulations, rules, contracts, or grants. If the practitioner's examination report is based on significant interpretations, the auditor may add an additional paragraph to the report explaining the nature of the interpretation and its source.

SSAE standards note that it may be necessary to modify the examination report for the following reasons:

- Material noncompliance with specified requirements exists. (During the examination, the practitioner may discover a noncompliance that he or she believes has a material effect on the entity's compliance with the specified requirements. Under this circumstance the practitioner should report directly on the entity's specified compliance requirements and not on the responsible party's assertion.)

- Scope of the engagement has been restricted. (When there is a restriction in the scope of the engagement, the practitioner should report in a manner described in the chapter titled "Attest Engagements" [AT 101].)

- Reference is made to the work of another practitioner. (When the work of another practitioner is used as the basis for reporting on the client's compliance with specified requirements, the practitioner should report in a manner described in the chapter titled "Reporting on an Entity's Internal Control Over Financial Reporting" [AT 501].)

AT SECTION 701

MANAGEMENT'S DISCUSSION AND ANALYSIS

Authoritative Pronouncements

SSAE-10 — Attestation Standards: Revision and Recodification (Chapter 7)

Overview

A practitioner may be engaged to examine or review management's discussion and analysis (MD&A) (a written assertion) that is presented to conform to the rules and regulations adopted by the Securities and Exchange Commission (SEC). This service is considered an attestation engagement subject to the standards established in the Statements on Standards for Attestation Engagements (SSAE) standards. Under these standards the practitioner may perform either an examination or review of MD&A. Examinations and reviews should satisfy the general, fieldwork, and reporting standard discussed in the chapter titled "Attest Engagements" (AT 101), as well as the guidance discussed in this chapter.

> **OBSERVATION:** A practitioner may perform an agreed-upon procedures engagement on MD&A if the standards established in the chapter titled "Agreed-Upon Procedures Engagements" (AT 201) are observed.

> **OBSERVATION:** Because only public companies are required to prepare an MD&A, presumably most attestation engagements on MD&A have been performed for public companies. The PCAOB has the statutory authority to set auditing and attestation standards for public companies. It is reasonable to assume that the standards for issuing an attestation report on MD&A for a public company might be modified by the PCAOB in the future.

EXAMINATION ENGAGEMENT

SSAE standards state that the objective of an examination of MD&A information is for the practitioner to express an opinion on the information taken as a whole by reporting on the following:

- Whether the presentation includes, in all material respects, the required elements of the rules and regulations adopted by the SEC

- Whether the historical financial amounts have been accurately derived, in all material respects, from the entity's financial statements

- Whether the underlying information, determinations, estimates, and assumptions of the entity provide a reasonable basis for the disclosures contained therein

A practitioner may examine a MD&A presentation in order to express an opinion on the presentation if (1) the practitioner has audited at least the latest financial statements to which the MD&A information pertains and (2) either the practitioner or a predecessor practitioner has audited the prior years' financial statements to which the MD&A information pertains.

When a predecessor practitioner has audited one or more of the financial statements for the period covered by the MD&A information, the successor practitioner must determine whether it is possible to "acquire sufficient knowledge of the business and of the entity's accounting and financial reporting practices for such period" so that the following can be satisfied:

- The types of potential material misstatements in MD&A can be identified and the likelihood of their occurrence can be determined.

- Procedures can be performed that will provide the practitioner with a basis for expressing an opinion on whether the MD&A presentation includes, in all material respects, the required elements of the rules and regulations adopted by the SEC.

- Procedures can be performed that will provide the practitioner with a basis for expressing an opinion on the MD&A presentation with respect to whether the historical financial amounts have been accurately derived, in all material respects, from the entity's financial statements for such a period.

- Procedures can be performed that will provide the practitioner with a basis for expressing an opinion on whether the underlying information, determinations, estimates, and assumptions of the entity provide a reasonable basis for the disclosures contained therein.

The practitioner examining the MD&A information may decide to review the workpapers (for the financial statement audit and the examination or review of MD&A information) of the predecessor practitioner; however, the review of the predecessor practitioner's workpapers alone does not provide a basis sufficient to express an opinion on the MD&A information that applies to the periods for which the predecessor practitioner was involved. The results of the review of the predecessor auditor's workpapers should be used to determine the nature, extent, and timing of the examination engagement procedures (which are discussed below) with respect to the MD&A information covered by the work of the predecessor practitioner. In addition, the auditor should "make inquiries of the predecessor practitioner and management as to audit adjustments proposed by the predecessor practitioner that were not recorded in the financial statements."

> **PLANNING AID REMINDER:** The practitioner should follow the standards established by SAS-84 (AU 315) (Communications Between Predecessor and Successor Auditors) to determine whether to accept an audit engagement with respect to the financial statements. When the requested engagement also encompasses the examination of MD&A information, the successor auditor should expand the inquiries directed to the predecessor auditor so that they include questions concerning the previous MD&A engagement. If the successor auditor is requested to examine the MD&A information after being engaged to audit the client's financial statements, the successor auditor should review the predecessor auditor's workpapers related to the previous MD&A engagement.

Promulgated Procedures Checklist

The practitioner should plan and execute the MD&A engagement in order to determine, with reasonable assurance, whether any material misstatements in the MD&A information exist. SSAE standards require that, in order to achieve this objective, the practitioner perform the following procedures during the engagement:

- Plan the engagement.

- Obtain an understanding of MD&A requirements.

- Obtain an understanding of the client's methods used to prepare MD&A information.

- Consider relevant portions of the entity's internal control applicable to the preparation of MD&A.

- Obtain sufficient evidence, including testing for completeness.

- Consider the effect of events subsequent to the balance-sheet date.

- Obtain written representations from management.

- Prepare an appropriate examination report.

PLANNING AID REMINDER: General guidance for documenting an attest engagement is discussed in AT 101.

Analysis and Application of Procedures

Plan the engagement

In an examination engagement, the practitioner must collect evidence sufficient to limit attestation risk to an "appropriate low level." The components of attestation risk in an examination are similar to those that are related to an audit of financial statements, and they are described by the SSAE standards as follows:

> *Inherent risk* — The susceptibility of an assertion within MD&A to a material misstatement, assuming that there are no related controls (inherent risk varies depending on the nature of each assertion included in the MD&A information)

> *Control risk* — The risk that a material misstatement that could occur in an assertion within MD&A and not be prevented or detected on a timely basis by the entity's controls (some control risk will always exist because of the inherent limitations of any internal control)

> *Detection risk* — The risk that the practitioner will not detect a material misstatement that exists in an assertion within MD&A (the establishment of an acceptable level of detection risk is related to the auditor's assessment of inherent risk and control risk)

The foregoing risk factors should be integrated into the planning phase of the engagement by taking into consideration the following factors:

• The anticipated level of attestation risk related to assertions embodied in the MD&A presentation

• Preliminary judgments about materiality levels for attest purposes

• The items within the MD&A presentation that are likely to require revision or adjustment

• Conditions that may require extension or modification of attest procedures

The focus of the examination of MD&A information is the assertions (explicit or implicit) that are included in the client's MD&A presentation. There are four broad assertions:

1. *Occurrence assertion:* The occurrence assertion is concerned with whether transactions included in the MD&A information actually occurred during the period covered by the presentation.

2. *Consistency assertion:* The consistency assertion focuses on whether the information in the MD&A presentation is consistent with information included in the financial statements and related financial records. The assertion is also concerned with whether nonfinancial data have been "accurately derived from related records."

3. *Completeness assertion:* The completeness assertion is concerned with whether descriptions of transactions and events included in MD&A information are sufficient to adequately reflect the entity's financial condition, changes in financial condition, results of operations, and material commitments for capital resources. This assertion also requires that relevant "known events, transactions, conditions, trends, demands, commitments, or uncertainties" that will or may affect these transactions and events be properly presented in the MD&A information.

4. *Presentation and disclosure assertion:* The presentation and disclosure assertion focuses on the proper classification, description, and disclosure of information included in the MD&A presentation.

> **ENGAGEMENT STRATEGY:** The assertions listed above are similar to the assertions that the auditor is concerned with when the client's financial statements are audited, and they are discussed in AU 326 in this book. However, the examination of assertions related to a MD&A engagement is limited to the assertions described in the SSAE standards (not the assertions described in SAS-106 [AU 326] [Audit Evidence]). For example, if a client asserts that revenues increased due to a strengthening of the dollar relative to other foreign currencies, the auditor should determine the completeness of that assertion, but he or she would not be concerned with the completeness of the assertion related to total revenues, which would have been evaluated as part of the audit of the entity's financial statements.

The practitioner must use professional judgment to determine the specific planning strategy to be used in a particular MD&A engagement;

however, SSAE standards note that planning should consider factors such as the following:

- Industry characteristics (such as economic conditions, accounting principles, and legal considerations)

- An understanding of the client's internal control (and recent changes thereto) with respect to the preparation of MD&A information that may have been obtained during the audit of the entity's financial statements

- Specific characteristics of the entity (such as business form, capital structure, and distribution systems)

- The type of relevant information provided to external parties (such as press releases and presentations to financial analysts)

- The approach the client used to analyze operating activities (such as budgeted versus actual result comparisons) and the types of reports presented to its board of directors to keep the board members informed of day-to-day operations as well as long-range planning strategies

- Management's familiarity with MD&A rules and regulations

- The purpose of the MD&A information, if the entity is nonpublic

- Initial judgments about materiality, inherent risk, and factors related to MD&A internal controls

- Fraud risk factors and other relevant conditions identified as part of the audit of the entity's latest financial statements

- The client's documentation to support MD&A information

- The possible need for a specialist due to the complexity of the material included in the MD&A information (when a specialist is required, the guidance established by SAS-73 [AU 336] [Using the Work of a Specialist] may be followed)

- The existence of an internal audit function (when an internal audit function exists, the guidance established by SAS-65 [AU 322] [The Auditor's Consideration of the Internal Audit Function in an Audit of Financial Statements] may be followed)

- The intended use of the MD&A (if issued by a nonpublic entity)

In addition, the practitioner should take into consideration the results of auditing the client's financial statements. For example, the planning of the

MD&A engagement may be affected by such matters as the type of audit adjustments proposed and the types of misstatements identified. If the practitioner's report on the client's financial statements is other than unqualified, that fact may have an impact on the planning of the MD&A engagement.

> **ENGAGEMENT STRATEGY:** When the auditor has not previously examined MD&A information for the client, the auditor should obtain an understanding of the internal controls relative to the preparation of the MD&A information for the previous year(s).

Public companies often consist of various subsidiaries, branches, and other operating entities. SSAE standards note that the practitioner should consider factors such as the following in order to determine the procedures to be applied to a particular operating component:

- The significance of each component to the MD&A information taken as a whole

- The degree to which centralized records are maintained

- The effectiveness of controls over the various operating components

- The activities conducted at an operating component location

- The similarity of activities and related internal controls at each operating component

Obtain an understanding of MD&A requirements

The auditor must develop an understanding of the MD&A rules and regulations adopted by the SEC. These rules and regulations are established in the following SEC publications and related Interpretations:

- Item 303 of Regulation S-K and related Financial Reporting Releases

- Item 303 of Regulation S-B (for small-business issues)

- Item 9 of Form 20-F (for foreign companies)

> **PLANNING AID REMINDER:** The SEC rules and regulations listed above establish "reasonable criteria" as required by General Standard No. 3.

Obtain an understanding of the client's methods used to prepare MD&A information

For developing the MD&A information, the client should have established procedures (similar in concept to its established procedures for the preparation of its financial statements) that conform to the rules and regulations established by the SEC. The practitioner should obtain from the client a description (oral or written) of the procedures the client used to prepare the MD&A information. The description should include such matters as the following:

• The sources of the information

• The manner in which the information is obtained

• The factors that management considered relevant in determining the materiality of information

• The identification of any changes in procedures from the prior year

Consider the relevant portions of the entity's internal control applicable to the preparation of MD&A

The practitioner must consider the client's internal controls that relate to its preparation of MD&A information in much the same manner as the auditor evaluates internal controls in the audit of an entity's financial statements. In order to satisfy the SSAE standards, the practitioner should follow the steps listed below when considering internal controls in an examination of MD&A information:

Step 1: Obtain an understanding of the client's internal controls.

Step 2: Assess the control risk.

Step 3: Perform tests of controls (when control risk is assessed at a level less than the maximum level).

Step 4: Determine the nature, timing, and extent of substantive procedures.

Step 5: Document the assessment of control risk.

Step 1

In all examination engagements, the practitioner must adequately understand those controls relevant to the client's preparation of MD&A

information. Relevant controls are concerned with the recording, processing, summarizing, and reporting of financial and nonfinancial data consistent with the assertions embodied in the MD&A presentation. Thus, the practitioner needs to understand internal controls that increase the likelihood that the MD&A information will be prepared in accordance with rules and regulations established by the SEC.

The practitioner generally obtains an understanding of the entity's internal controls that relate to the MD&A presentation by employing the following procedures:

- Making appropriate inquiries of client personnel

- Inspecting relevant entity documents

- Observing relevant control activities

Step 2

Once the practitioner has obtained an understanding of the client's internal control, it is possible to assess the level of control risk for a particular engagement. The practitioner should have documented the system and, based on that documentation, identified potential misstatements (including material omissions of MD&A information). The assessment of the level of control risk provides the practitioner with a general strategy for planning the remaining internal control evaluation. If the practitioner believes the internal control is well designed, the level of control risk will be assessed at a relatively low level for a given assertion. On the other hand, if the internal control appears to be poorly designed, the level of control risk will be assessed at a maximum level.

Step 3

In order to assess control risk at a relatively low level, the practitioner must perform tests of controls. Tests of controls are used to determine the effectiveness of (1) the design of internal controls and (2) operations of internal controls that relate to the preparation of the MD&A information in accordance with the rules and regulations established by the SEC. For example, if the MD&A information includes statistics, such as the average net sales per square foot of retail space, the auditor must test the internal controls related to how this information is accumulated and reported.

Step 4

Based on his or her assessment of inherent risk and assessment of control risk resulting from the understanding of the entity's internal control and perhaps tests of control (if control risk is assessed at a level less than the maximum), the practitioner determines an acceptable level of detection risk. Detection risk is the risk that the practitioner will not detect a material misstatement in an assertion that is included or that should be included in the MD&A presentation. The establishment of a level of acceptable detection risk is used as a basis for determining the nature, timing, and extent of substantive procedures.

Step 5

The assessment of control risk for a particular assertion (or group of assertions related to a component of the MD&A presentation) must be documented. The assessment must be related to the results of obtaining an understanding of the client's relevant internal controls and, perhaps, to the performance of tests of controls. SSAE standards note that "the form and extent of this documentation is influenced by the size and complexity of the entity, as well as the nature of the entity's control applicable to the preparation of MD&A."

Obtain sufficient evidence (including testing completeness)

In order to obtain sufficient evidence to allow the practitioner to offer a reasonable assurance on the client's presentation of MD&A information, SSAE standards require the practitioner to perform the following procedures:

- Read the MD&A and compare the content with the audited financial statements for consistency; compare financial amounts to the audited financial statements and related accounting records and analyses; and recompute the increases, decreases, and percentages disclosed.

- Compare nonfinancial amounts to the audited financial statements, if applicable, or to other records (see the discussion below for nonfinancial data).

- Consider whether the explanations in MD&A are consistent with the information obtained during the audit; through inquiry (including inquiry of officers and other executives having responsibility for operational areas) and inspection of client records, investigate further those explanations that cannot be substantiated by information in the audit work-papers.

- Examine internally generated documents (for example, variance analyses and business plans or programs) and externally generated documents (for example, correspondence, contracts, or loan agreements) in support of the existence, occurrence, or expected occurrence of events, transactions, conditions, trends, demands, commitments, or uncertainties disclosed in the MD&A.

- Obtain available prospective financial information (for example, budgets; sales forecasts; forecasts of labor, overhead, and materials cost; capital expenditure requests; and financial forecasts and projections) and compare such information to forward-looking MD&A disclosures. Ask management about the procedures used to prepare the prospective financial information. Evaluate whether the underlying information, determinations, estimates, and assumptions of the entity provide a reasonable basis for the MD&A disclosures of events, transactions, conditions, trends, demands, commitments, or uncertainties.

- Consider obtaining available prospective financial information relating to prior periods and comparing actual results with forecasted and projected amounts.

- Ask officers and other executives who have responsibility for operational areas (such as sales, marketing, and production) and financial and accounting matters about their plans and expectations for the future that could affect the entity's liquidity and capital resources.

- Consider obtaining external information concerning industry trends, inflation, and changing prices and comparing the related MD&A disclosures with such information.

- Compare the information in MD&A with the rules and regulations adopted by the SEC, and consider whether the presentation includes the required elements of such rules and regulations.

- Read the minutes of meetings to date of the board of directors and other significant committees to identify matters that may affect MD&A; consider whether such matters are appropriately addressed in MD&A.

- Ask officers about the entity's prior experience with the SEC and the extent of comments received upon review of documents by the SEC; read correspondence between the entity and the SEC with respect to such review, if any.

- Obtain public communications (for example, press releases and quarterly reports) and the related supporting documentation dealing with historical and future results; consider whether MD&A is consistent with such communications.

- Consider obtaining other types of publicly available information (for example, analyst reports and news articles); compare the MD&A presentation with such information.

Nonfinancial data

MD&A information may include a variety of nonfinancial data, such as number of customers, backorders, and capacity utilization rates. SSAE standards note that the practitioner must determine whether the definitions used by management for such nonfinancial data are reasonable for the particular disclosure in the MD&A and whether there are reasonable criteria for the measurement. If nonfinancial data have such characteristics, the practitioner should apply appropriate examination procedures, taking into consideration the materiality of the data in relationship to the MD&A information taken as a whole and the assessed level of control risk.

Testing completeness

The information (especially explanations) included in MD&A does not arise simply from the client's observance of SEC rules and regulations. As part of the test of completeness, the auditor should consider whether the MD&A discloses matters that could significantly impact future financial condition and results of operations of the entity by considering information that he or she obtained through the following:

- As the result of the audit of the entity's financial statements
- Through inquiries of the client's personnel with respect to current events, conditions, economic changes, commitments, and uncertainties that are unique to the client or to the industry in which it operates
- By the application of other engagement procedures

> **PLANNING AID REMINDER:** SSAE standards note that if the MD&A engagement is characterized by a high level of inherent risk, it may be appropriate for the practitioner to expand the engagement by performing extended procedures, including additional inquiries of client personnel and examining additional documentation.

Consider the effect of events subsequent to the balance sheet date

The practitioner should consider events that may have an effect on the MD&A presentation but occur after the period covered by the MD&A information and prior to the issuance of the examination report. Relevant events would be those that have a material impact on the client's financial condition (including liquidity and capital resources), changes in financial condition, results of operations, and material commitments for capital resources. Attestation standards require that the MD&A presentation disclose subsequent events or matters such as the following:

- Items that are expected to have a material effect on (1) net sales or revenues and (2) income from continuing operations

- Items that are expected to have a material effect on the entity's liquidity

- Items that are expected to have a material effect on the entity's capital resources

- Items that are expected to have an impact on the entity in a manner that would make reported financial results a poor predictor of future operating results or financial condition

The identification of subsequent events may require that the MD&A presentation be adjusted or that additional disclosures be included in the material.

> **PLANNING AID REMINDER:** SSAE standards note that when MD&A information is included in a 1933 Securities Act document (or incorporated through reference), examination procedures must be extended to the filing date or "as close to it as is reasonable and practicable in the circumstances." This time extension also applies when the examination report is included in a 1933 Securities Act document.

Generally the practitioner's fieldwork extends beyond the date of the auditor's report on the client's financial statements. For this reason SSAE standards (as part of the consideration of the possible occurrence of subsequent events) requires that the auditor perform the following procedures:

- Read available minutes of meetings of stockholders, the board of directors, and other appropriate committees; for meetings whose minutes are not available, inquire about matters dealt with at the meetings.

- Read the latest available interim financial statements for periods subsequent to the date of the auditor's report and compare them with the financial statements for the periods covered by the MD&A. Discuss with officers and other executives who have responsibility for operational, financial, and accounting matters (limited where appropriate to major locations) such matters as the following:

  — Whether the interim financial statements have been prepared on the same basis as the audited financial statements

— Whether any significant changes took place in the entity's operations, liquidity, or capital resource in the subsequent period

— The current status of items in the financial statements for which the MD&A has been prepared that were accounted for on the basis of tentative, preliminary, or inconclusive data

— Whether any unusual adjustments were made during the period from the balance sheet date to the date of inquiry

- Make inquiries of members of senior management about the current status of matters concerning litigation, claims, and assessments identified during the audit of the financial statements and about any new matters or unfavorable developments. Consider obtaining updated legal letters from legal counsel.

- Consider whether any changes have occurred in economic conditions or in the industry that could have a significant effect on the entity.

- Obtain written representations from appropriate officials about whether any events occurred subsequent to the latest balance sheet date that would require disclosure in the MD&A.

- Make additional inquiries or perform other procedures considered necessary and appropriate to address questions that arise in carrying out the foregoing procedures, inquiries, and discussions.

Obtain written representations from management

Attest standards require that an auditor obtain written representations from the client in an MD&A examination (and a review) engagement. The purpose of written representations is to confirm oral representations made by management during the engagement and to reduce the likelihood of misunderstandings between the client and the auditor. The written representations may be documented in a client representation letter. Although no comprehensive list of items exists that must be included in a client representation letter (or other form of written communication), SSAE standards identify the following as items that management should include:

- Acknowledgment that management is responsible for the preparation of the MD&A information and that it has prepared the information in accordance with the rules and regulations established by the SEC

- A statement that the historical financial amounts have been accurately derived from the client's financial statements and are reflected in the MD&A presentation

- An affirmation of the belief that the underlying information, determinations, estimates, and assumptions provide a reasonable basis for the MD&A presentation

- A statement that all significant documentation that relates to the compliance with the SEC rules and regulations has been made available

- Confirmation that complete minutes of all meetings of stockholders, the board of directors, and committees of directors have been made available

- A statement about whether the client (if it is a public entity) has received relevant communications from the SEC

- A statement about whether events subsequent to the latest balance sheet date that would require disclosure in the MD&A have occurred

- A statement about whether forward-looking information is included in MD&A information and, if it is included, whether the following is also true:

  — The forward-looking information is based on the client's best estimate of expected events and operations and is consistent with budgets, forecasts, or operating plans prepared for such periods.

  — The same accounting principles used in the preparation of the financial statements were used to prepare the MD&A presentation.

  — The latest versions of budgets, forecasts, or operating plans have been provided, and the practitioner has been informed of any anticipated changes or modifications to such information that could affect the disclosures contained in the MD&A presentation.

- A statement that, if voluntary information is included and subject to SEC rules and regulations, such voluntary information has been prepared in accordance with SEC rules and regulations

- A statement that, if pro forma information is included in the MD&A information, the following is also true:

  — The client is responsible for establishing the assumptions upon which the pro forma adjustments are based.

  — The client believes that the assumptions used provide a reasonable basis for the pro forma adjustments, and the pro forma column accurately reflects the application of the adjustments to the historical financial statements.

— The pro forma information appropriately discloses the significant effects directly attributable to the transaction or event that is the basis for the pro forma adjustments.

> **PLANNING AID REMINDER:** The guidance established in SAS-85 (AU 333) (Management Representations) should be followed to determine the date of the representations and who should sign them. When a client refuses to provide the practitioner with appropriate written representations, the practitioner should not issue an unqualified opinion on the MD&A information but, rather, should decide whether a qualified opinion, a disclaimer of opinion, or withdrawal from the engagement is appropriate. (If the engagement is a review, the practitioner should generally withdraw from the engagement.) The fact that a client will not provide an appropriate written representation suggests that the practitioner should not rely on other representations the client has made.

> **PLANNING AID REMINDER:** When a client provides written representation concerning a matter but does not allow the practitioner to apply appropriate examination procedures to the matter, the auditor should express a qualified opinion or a disclaimer of an opinion in an examination engagement, and in a review engagement he or she should withdraw.

Prepare an appropriate examination report

Based on the results of applying examination procedures, the practitioner should form an opinion on the MD&A presentation. The report must be accompanied by the financial statements covered by the MD&A information, the auditor's report(s) on those financial statements, and the MD&A presentation itself.

> **PLANNING AID REMINDER:** When the client is a nonpublic company, one of the following conditions should be met: (1) a written statement should be included in the MD&A information stating that the information has been prepared in accordance with the rules and regulations established by the SEC, (2) a separate written assertion from management should accompany the MD&A presentation, or (3) a separate written assertion from management should be included in the representation letter.

The examination report should include the following items:

- A title that includes the word "independent"

- An identification of the MD&A presentation, including the period that is covered

- A statement that management is responsible for the preparation of the MD&A pursuant to the rules and regulations adopted by the SEC, and a statement that the practitioner's responsibility is to express an opinion on the presentation based on his or her examination

- A reference to the auditor's report on the related financial statements and, if the report was other than a standard report, the substantive reasons why

- A statement that the examination was made in accordance with attestation standards established by the American Institute of Certified Public Accountants (AICPA), and a description of the scope of an examination of MD&A

- A statement that the practitioner believes the examination provides a reasonable basis for the opinion given

- A paragraph stating the following:

  — That the preparation of MD&A requires management to interpret the criteria, make determinations as to the relevancy of information to be included, and make estimates and assumptions that affect reported information

  — That actual results in the future may differ materially from management's present assessment of information regarding the estimated future impact of transactions and events that have occurred or are expected to occur, expected sources of liquidity and capital resources, operating trends, commitments, and uncertainties

- If the entity is a nonpublic entity, a statement that, although the entity is not subject to the rules and regulations of the SEC, the MD&A presentation is intended to be a presentation in accordance with the rules and regulations adopted by the SEC

- The practitioner's opinion on the following:

  — Whether the presentation includes, in all material respects, the required elements of the rules and regulations adopted by the SEC

— Whether the historical financial amounts have been accurately derived, in all material respects, from the entity's financial statements

— Whether the underlying information, determinations, estimates, and assumptions of the entity provide a reasonable basis for the disclosures contained therein

- The manual or printed signature of the practitioner's firm
- The date of the examination report

Exhibit AT 701-1 is an example taken from SSAE-10 of an examination report on an entity's MD&A presentation.

EXHIBIT AT 701-1 — EXAMINATION REPORT ON AN ENTITY'S MD&A PRESENTATION

We have examined XYZ Company's Management's Discussion and Analysis taken as a whole, included [*incorporated by reference*] in the Company's [*insert description of registration statement or document*]. Management is responsible for the preparation of the Company's Management's Discussion and Analysis, pursuant to the rules and regulations adopted by the Securities and Exchange Commission. Our responsibility is to express an opinion on the presentation based on our examination. We have audited, in accordance with standards of the Public Company Accounting Oversight Board (United States), the financial statements of XYZ Company as of December 31, 20X5 and 20X4, and for each of the years in the three-year period ending December 31, 20X5. In our report dated [*month*] XX, 20X6, we expressed an unqualified opinion on those financial statements.

Our examination of Management's Discussion and Analysis was made in accordance with attestation standards established by the American Institute of Certified Public Accountants and, accordingly, included examining, on a test basis, evidence supporting the historical amounts and disclosures in the presentation. An examination also includes assessing the significant determinations made by management as to the relevancy of information to be included and the estimates and assumptions that affect reported information. We believe that our examination provides a reasonable basis for our opinion.

The preparation of Management's Discussion and Analysis requires management to interpret the criteria, make determinations as to the relevancy of information to be included, and make estimates and assumptions that affect reported information. Management's Discussion and Analysis includes information regarding the estimated future impact of transactions and events that have occurred or are expected to occur, expected sources of liquidity and capital resources, operating trends, commitments, and uncertainties. Actual results in the future may differ materially from management's present assessment of this information because events and circumstances frequently do not occur as expected.

In our opinion, the Company's presentation of Management's Discussion and Analysis includes, in all material respects, the required elements of the rules and regulations adopted by the Securities and Exchange Commission; the historical financial amounts included therein have been accurately derived, in all material respects, from the Company's financial statements; and the underlying information, determinations, estimates, and assumptions of the Company provide a reasonable basis for the disclosures contained therein.

[*Signature*]

[*Date*]

OBSERVATION: Only public companies are required to file an MD&A with the Securities and Exchange Commission. Such audits are performed in accordance with standards of the Public Company Accounting Oversight Board (United States). If a nonpublic company voluntarily includes an MD&A and retains an accounting firm to issue an attestation report, the audit must be performed in accordance with generally accepted auditing standards.

The standard examination report on MD&A presentations may be modified for the following reasons:

- A material element as required by SEC rules and regulations is omitted from the presentation (a qualified or adverse opinion should be expressed).

- Historical financial amounts have not been accurately derived (in all material respects) from the client financial statements (a qualified or adverse opinion should be expressed).

- Underlying information, determinations, estimates, and assumptions used by the client do not provide the practitioner a reasonable basis on which to prepare the MD&A presentation (a qualified or adverse opinion should be expressed).

- The practitioner is unable to perform procedures deemed appropriate for the MD&A engagement (a qualified opinion or a disclaimer of opinion should be expressed, or the practitioner should withdraw from the engagement).

- The practitioner decided to refer to the work of another practitioner.

- The practitioner has been engaged to examine the client MD&A presentation after it has been filed with the SEC.

- The practitioner has decided to emphasize a matter.

REVIEW ENGAGEMENT

SSAE standards state that the objective of a review of MD&A information is for the practitioner to report on whether any information came to his or her attention to cause him or her to believe that

- The MD&A presentation does not include, in all material respects, the required elements of the rules and regulations adopted by the SEC.

- The historical financial amounts included therein have not been accurately derived, in all material respects, from the entity's financial statements.

- The underlying information, determinations, estimates, and assumptions of the entity do not provide a reasonable basis for the disclosures contained therein.

A practitioner may review a MD&A presentation if (1) the practitioner has audited at least the latest financial statements to which the MD&A information pertains and (2) either the practitioner or a predecessor practitioner has audited the prior years' financial statements to which the MD&A information pertains.

When a predecessor practitioner has audited one or more of the financial statements for the period covered by the MD&A information, the successor practitioner must determine whether it is possible to "acquire sufficient knowledge of the business and of the entity's accounting and financial reporting practices for such period" so that the following can be satisfied:

- The types of potential material misstatements in MD&A can be identified and the likelihood of their occurrence can be determined.

- Procedures can be performed that will provide the practitioner with a basis for determining whether any information obtained in the engagement suggests that

  — The MD&A information excludes material information required by SEC rules and regulations.

  — The historical financial amounts included in the MD&A information have not been accurately derived from the historical financial statements.

  — The underlying information, determinations, estimates, and assumptions of the entity do not provide a reasonable basis for the disclosures included in the MD&A presentation.

Promulgated Procedures Checklist

The practitioner should plan and execute the MD&A engagement in order to provide limited assurance that the material misstatements in the MD&A information will be identified. According to SSAE standards, to achieve this objective the practitioner should perform the following:

- Plan the engagement.

- Obtain an understanding of MD&A requirements.

- Obtain an understanding of the client's methods used to prepare MD&A information.

- Consider relevant portions of the entity's internal control applicable to the preparation of MD&A.

- Apply analytical procedures and make inquires of management and other appropriate personnel.

- Consider the effect of events subsequent to the balance sheet date.

- Obtain written representations from management.

- Prepare an appropriate review report.

> **PLANNING AID REMINDER:** General guidance for documenting an attest engagement is discussed in AT 101 (Attest Engagements).

Analysis and Application of Procedures

Plan the engagement

The practitioner must use professional judgment in determining the specific planning strategy to be used in a particular MD&A engagement; however, SSAE standards note that in planning the review engagement, the practitioner should consider factors such as the following:

- Industry characteristics (such as economic conditions, accounting principles, and legal considerations)

- Specific characteristics of the entity (such as business form, capital structure, and distribution systems)

- Relevant information provided to external parties (such as press releases and presentations to financial analysts)

- Management's familiarity with MD&A rules and regulations

- The purpose of the MD&A information, if the entity is nonpublic

- Matters identified during the audit or review of the client's financial statements that may provide insight into the preparation and reporting of MD&A information

- Matters identified during the examination or review concerning the prior years' MD&A presentations

- Initial judgments about materiality levels

- Items that are either relatively complex or subjective that provide a basis for assertions in the MD&A information

- The existence of an internal audit function and the degree to which the function was involved in the verification of MD&A information

Consider relevant portions of the entity's internal control applicable to the preparation of MD&A

SSAE standards state that as a basis for performing appropriate analytical procedures and inquiries of client personnel, the practitioner must develop an adequate understanding of the client's internal controls related to its preparation and presentation of MD&A information. Although the standards do not provide specific guidance on how this is to be accomplished, the practitioner's knowledge of internal controls must be sufficient to accomplish the following:

- Identification of types of potential misstatements in MD&A, including types of material omissions, and consideration of the likelihood of their occurrence

- Selection of the inquiries and analytical procedures that will provide a basis for reporting whether any information causes the practitioner to believe the following:

  — That the MD&A presentation does not include, in all material respects, the required elements of the rules and regulations adopted by the SEC, or that the historical financial amounts included therein have not been accurately derived, in all material respects, from the entity's financial statements

  — That the underlying information, determinations, estimates, and assumptions of the entity do not provide a reasonable basis for the disclosures contained therein

Apply analytical procedures and make inquiries of management and other appropriate personnel

The practitioner should apply a variety of analytical procedures and make specific inquiries of client personnel. The results of these procedures should be evaluated in the context of the practitioner's understanding of other relevant information that he or she knows. Although there is no specific list of analytical procedures and inquiries that should be performed in a review engagement, SSAE standards point out that the auditor should generally employ the following procedures:

- Compare information in the MD&A presentation with the audited financial statement and related accounting records and analyses.

- Recompute increases, decreases, and percentage changes relative to financial amounts included in or derived from the financial statements.

- Compare nonfinancial amounts in the MD&A presentation with audited amounts in the financial statements, if appropriate, or in other records.

- Inquire about the types of records that support the nonfinancial amounts, and determine the existence of the records.

- Determine whether the nonfinancial information is relevant to users and is clearly defined in the MD&A information, and inquire about whether the definition of nonfinancial information was consistently applied.

- Consider whether explanations included in the MD&A presentation are consistent with information obtained as part of the audit of the client's financial statements, and direct any related inquiries to appropriate personnel.

- Compare prospective financial information (such as budgets) to forward-looking information included in the MD&A presentation.

- Make inquiries of relevant personnel concerning procedures used to develop prospective financial information and forward-looking information.

- Consider whether information obtained suggests that underlying information, determinations, estimates, and assumptions of the entity do not provide a reasonable basis for the disclosures of trends, demands, commitments, events, or uncertainties.

- Make inquiries of appropriate operational personnel (such as production and marketing) and financial personnel as to plans that could have an effect on the client's liquidity and capital resources.

- Determine whether the MD&A presentation includes disclosures required by the SEC.

- Consider whether the MD&A presentation properly reflects any relevant matters discussed in the minutes of meetings of the board of directors and other significant committees.

- Make inquiries about the experience the client has had with the SEC relative to MD&A presentations made in previous years, and read any correspondence between the client and the SEC relative to these matters.

- Make inquiries concerning the nature of public communications that include historical and future results. Determine whether those communications are consistent with the MD&A presentation.

Although a review engagement is characterized by the use of analytical procedures and inquiries of management personnel, the practitioner should use whatever procedures he or she deems appropriate (including corroborative procedures) if it appears that the MD&A presentation is "incomplete or contains inaccuracies or is otherwise unsatisfactory."

ENGAGEMENT STRATEGY: The practitioner might find the general guidance for the application of analytical procedures

in SAS-56 (AU 329) (Analytical Procedures) helpful in applying the procedures to a review of MD&A information.

Obtain an understanding of MD&A requirements

In order to develop an understanding of MD&A requirements established
by the SEC for a review engagement, the practitioner should follow the
guidance discussed earlier for an examination engagement.

Obtain an understanding of the client's methods used to prepare MD&A information

In a review engagement, in order to develop an understanding of the
client's methods used to create MD&A information, the auditor should
follow the guidance discussed earlier for an examination engagement.

Consider the effect of events subsequent to the balance-sheet date

In order to consider the effect of an event occurring subsequent to the
balance sheet date in a review engagement, the practitioner should follow
the guidance discussed earlier for the occurrence of this situation in an
examination engagement.

Obtain written representations from management

In a review engagement, the practitioner should obtain written representations similar to those obtained in an examination engagement, as discussed
earlier. However, when the client refuses to provide the practitioner with
appropriate written representations in a review engagement, the practitioner should withdraw from the engagement.

Prepare an appropriate review report

Based on the results of applying review procedures, the practitioner should
consider which report would be appropriate to issue on the MD&A
presentation. However, the report must be accompanied by the financial
statements covered by the MD&A information, the auditor's report(s) on
those financial statements, and the MD&A presentation.

> **PLANNING AID REMINDER:** When the client is a public
> company and the MD&A presentation covers an interim

period, the presentation should be accompanied by (1) the related interim financial statements and the review report applicable to the MD&A presentation and (2) the most recent comparative financial statements and the related MD&A presentation. (The information may be included by reference to filings with the SEC.)

PLANNING AID REMINDER: When the client is a nonpublic company, there should be a statement that the MD&A information has been prepared in accordance with rules and regulations established by the SEC. The statement may be included in the MD&A presentation itself or presented as a separate statement that accompanies the MD&A presentation. If the presentation for a nonpublic company relates to an interim period, the MD&A presentation should be accompanied by (1) the entity's most recent annual MD&A presentation and the related examination or review report and (2) the related interim financial statements and the most recent annual financial statements.

The review report should include the following items:

- A title that includes the word "independent"

- An identification of the MD&A presentation, including the period covered

- A statement that management is responsible for preparing the MD&A pursuant to the rules and regulations adopted by the SEC

- A reference to the auditor's report on the related financial statements and, if the report was other than a standard report, the substantive reasons for it

- A statement that the review was made in accordance with attestation standards established by the AICPA

- A description of the procedures for a review of MD&A

- A statement that a review of MD&A is substantially less in scope than an examination, the objective of which is an expression of opinion regarding the MD&A presentation and that, accordingly, no such opinion is expressed

- A paragraph stating the following:

  — That the preparation of MD&A requires management to interpret the criteria, make determinations as to the relevancy of information to be included, and make estimates and assumptions that affect reported information

— That future results may differ materially from management's present assessment of information regarding the estimated future impact of transactions and events that have occurred or are expected to occur, expected sources of liquidity and capital resources, operating trends, commitments, and uncertainties

- If the entity is a nonpublic entity, a statement that, although the entity is not subject to the rules and regulations of the SEC, the MD&A presentation is intended to be a presentation in accordance with the rules and regulations adopted by the SEC

- A statement about whether any information came to the practitioner's attention that caused him or her to believe any of the following:

  — That the presentation does not include, in all material respects, the required elements of the rules and regulations adopted by the SEC

  — That the historical financial amounts have not been accurately derived, in all material respects, from the entity's financial statements

  — That the underlying information, determinations, estimates, and assumptions of the entity do not provide a reasonable basis for the disclosures contained therein

- If the entity is a public entity or nonpublic entity that is making an offering of securities to the public, a statement restricting the use of the report to specified parties

- The manual or printed signature of the practitioner's firm

- The date of the review report

Exhibit AT 701-2 is an example taken from SSAE-10 of a report for a review engagement on an entity's MD&A presentation.

EXHIBIT AT 701-2 — REVIEW REPORT ON AN ENTITY'S MD&A PRESENTATION

We have reviewed XYZ Company's Management's Discussion and Analysis taken as a whole, included [*incorporated by reference*] in the Company's [*insert description of registration statement or document*]. Management is responsible for the preparation of the Company's Management's Discussion and Analysis pursuant to the rules and regulations adopted by the Securities and Exchange

Commission. We have audited, in accordance with the standards of the Public Company Accounting Oversight Board (United States), the financial Statements of XYZ Company as of December 31, 20X5 and 20X4, and for each year in the three-year period ended December 31, 20X5, and in our report date [*month*] XX, 20X6, we expressed an unqualified opinion on those financial statements.

We conducted our review of Management's Discussion and Analysis in accordance with attestation standards established by the American Institute of Certified Public Accounts. A review of Management's Discussion and Analysis consists principally of applying analytical procedures and making inquiries of persons responsible for financial, accounting, and operating matters. It is substantially less in scope than an examination, the objective of which is the expression of an opinion on the presentation. Accordingly, we do not express such an opinion.

The preparation of Management's Discussion and Analysis requires management to interpret the criteria, make determinations as to the relevancy of information to be included, and make estimates and assumptions that affect reported information. Management's Discussion and Analysis includes information regarding the estimated future impact of transactions and events that have occurred or are expected to occur, expected sources of liquidity and capital resources, operating trends, commitments, and uncertainties. Actual results in the future may differ materially from management's present assessment of this information because events and circumstances frequently do not occur as expected.

Based on our review, nothing came to our attention that caused us to believe that the Company's presentation of Management's Discussion and Analysis does not include, in all material respects, the required elements of the rules and regulations adopted by the Securities and Exchange Commission, that the historical financial amounts included therein have not been accurately derived, in all material respects, from the Company's financial statements, or that the underlying information, determinations, estimates and assumptions of the Company do not provide a reasonable basis for the disclosures contained therein.

The report is intended solely for the information and use of [*list or refer to specified parties*] and is not intended to be and should not be used by anyone other than the specified parties.

[*Signature*]

[*Date*]

> **OBSERVATION:** Only public companies are required to file an MD&A with the Securities and Exchange Commission. Such audits are performed "in accordance with standards of the Public Company Accounting Oversight Board (United States)." If a nonpublic company voluntarily includes an MD&A and retains an accounting firm to issue an attestation report, the audit must be performed in accordance with generally accepted auditing standards.

The standard review report on MD&A presentations may be modified for the following reasons:

- A material element as required by SEC rules and regulations is omitted from the presentation (modify the review report by describing the omission).

- Historical financial amounts have not been accurately derived (modify the review report by describing the misstated information).

- Underlying information, determinations, estimates, and assumptions used by the client do not provide a reasonable basis upon which to prepare the MD&A presentation (modify the review report by describing the deficiency).

- The practitioner decides to emphasize a matter with respect to the MD&A presentation (a standard review report is issued with an explanatory paragraph describing the nature of the matter emphasized).

The practitioner's review report may also be modified when another practitioner has examined or reviewed (and issued a separate report on) MD&A information for a component that represents a significant part of the overall financial statements. Under this circumstance the principal practitioner's report should refer to the work of the other practitioner as a basis for offering the limited assurance on the MD&A presentation. When the other practitioner has not issued a separate report on the (component) MD&A presentation, there should be no reference to the work of the other practitioner in the review report on the MD&A presentation. (This does not mean that the principal practitioner cannot refer in the review report to the fact that a component's financial statements were audited by another auditor.)

> **PLANNING AID REMINDER:** When the practitioner is unable to perform appropriate review procedures or the client is unwilling to provide appropriate written representations, the practitioner should not issue a review report on the MD&A presentation.

OTHER ISSUES

Combined Reporting

A practitioner may be engaged to report on the results of (1) an examination on an MD&A presentation related to the latest annual financial statements and (2) a review of an MD&A presentation on interim financial information for a period that is subsequent to the date of the annual financial statements. When the two engagements are "completed at the same time," the practitioner can issue a single report that incorporates both a separate examination format and a separate review format (except that the explanatory paragraph in the review report is omitted).

> **ENGAGEMENT STRATEGY:** In some instances the client may prepare a combined MD&A presentation for an annual period and an interim period. SSAE standards note that if the discussion of liquidity and capital resources applies only as of the most recent interim period (not as of the date of the annual financial statements), the auditor is "limited to performing the highest level of service that is provided with respect to the historical financial statements of any of the periods covered by the MD&A presentation." Thus, if annual financial statements are audited and the interim financial statements are reviewed, the combined MD&A presentation can be reviewed but cannot be examined.

Engagement of the Auditor Subsequent to Filing of MD&A Presentation

Public companies are required to report significant subsequent events on Form 8-K, on Form 10-Q, or in a registration statement. They are not required to modify previously filed MD&A presentations for the occurrence of subsequent events. If the practitioner is engaged to examine or review an MD&A presentation after the document has been filed, the auditor should consider whether subsequent events have been reported in Form 8-K or Form 10-Q or in a registration statement, rather than whether the MD&A presentation has been modified to reflect the subsequent event. However, under this circumstance the following sentence should be added to the opinion paragraph in an examination engagement and to the concluding paragraph in a review engagement:

The accompanying Management's Discussion and Analysis does not consider events that have occurred subsequent to [*month*] XX, 20X6, the date as of which it was filed with the Securities and Exchange Commission.

> **PLANNING AID REMINDER:** If the client has not notified the SEC of a material subsequent event, the practitioner should express a qualified or adverse opinion on the MD&A presentation in a examination engagement (or in a review engagement appropriately modifying the review report), assuming that the auditor concludes that it is appropriate to issue a report on the MD&A information. This circumstance may occur when the SEC filing has not yet been completed but management intends to make the appropriate filing on a timely basis. However, if the subsequent event is not disclosed in a proper manner, the practitioner must decide whether to withdraw from both the MD&A engagement and the audit engagement.

Communicating with the Client's Audit Committee

Under the following circumstances (assuming the client refuses to correct the deficiency), the practitioner should communicate the deficiency to the entity's audit committee (or others with equivalent authority):

- Material inconsistencies exist between the MD&A presentation and other information included in the document containing the MD&A material.

- Material inconsistencies exist between the MD&A presentation and the historical financial statements.

- Material omissions are made in the MD&A presentation.

- Material misstatements of facts are made in the MD&A presentation.

> **FRAUD POINTER:** If the practitioner has evidence as a result of performing the attestation or review engagement that fraud might have occurred — even if the fraud is inconsequential — it should be communicated to an appropriate level of management.

AT SECTION 801

REPORTING ON CONTROLS AT A SERVICE ORGANIZATION

Authoritative Pronouncements

SSAE 16 — Reporting on Controls at a Service Organization

> **IMPORTANT NOTICE FOR 2011:** The Auditing Standards Board (ASB) issued Statement on Standards for Attestation Engagements (SSAE) No. 16, *Reporting at a Service Organization*, in April 2010. The purpose of SSAE No. 16 is to move the guidance for service auditors contained in AU 324 from auditing standards to the attest standards. The guidance for user auditors will continue to reside in the audit standards. As of April 2010, the ASB had completed a revision to AU 324 that is part of the ASB's process of redrafting all of the auditing sections in *Codification of Statements on Auditing Standards* to converge U.S. GAAS with the International Standards on Auditing issued by the International Auditing and Assurance Standards Board. The redrafted AU 324 conforms the guidance for user auditors contained in AU 324 to the clarity drafting conventions adopted by the ASB. Although the guidance in SSAE No. 16 is effective for service auditors' reports for periods ending on or after June 15, 2011 (with early application permitted), the redrafted AU 324 guidance for user auditors will become effective with all other redrafted standards. The ASB is planning to have all redrafted standards become effective on the same date, which is for audits of financial statements for periods ending on or after December 15, 2012. It is possible that the effective date might be delayed beyond that date. The ASB's clarity and convergence project will have a significant effect on the auditing standards applicable to audits of nonpublic companies, and the 2012 *GAAS Guide* will be appropriately modified to reflect these changes once the effective date of the standards is certain.

Overview

AT 801 addresses examination engagements performed by a service auditor to report on controls at service organizations that provide services to user entities when those controls are likely to be part of the user entities' information and communication systems relevant to financial reporting. While this is the central focus, AT 801 may also be applied to engagements to report on other service organization controls such as those affecting user entities' regulatory compliance, production, or quality control or those at a shared service center providing services to a group of related entities. Guidance for auditors of entities that use service centers to provide services is contained in audit standards (AU 324).

The objectives of the service auditor in these engagements are (1) to obtain reasonable assurance about whether in all material respects and based on suitable criteria the description of management's service organization system is fairly presented and controls are suitably designed (and operated effectively when included in the scope of the engagement) to achieve the control objectives stated in management's description and (2) to report in accordance with the findings.

ROLE OF THE SERVICE AUDITOR

When a service auditor reports on the processing of transactions by a service organization, the general standards — and the relevant standards of fieldwork and reporting — should be observed. Although the service auditor must be independent with respect to the service organization, it is not necessary to be independent from every user organization.

The service organization should determine what type of engagement the service auditor should perform; however, in an ideal situation, the user organization would discuss the matter with the service organization and its auditors to ensure that all parties will be satisfied with the service auditor's report.

Definitions

Term	Definition
Carve-out method	Method of dealing with services provided by a subservice organization in which the service organization's description of its system identifies the nature of the services provided by the subservice organization. The service organization's system description and the scope of the service auditor's engagement exclude the subservice organization's relevant control objectives and related controls and include the service organization's controls for monitoring control effectiveness at the subservice organization.

Term	Definition
Complementary user entity controls	Controls the service organization assumes will be implemented by user entities. If these controls are necessary to achieve the control objectives stated in the description of the service organization's system, they should be identified as such in the description.
Control objectives	The aim or purpose of specified controls at the service organization that ordinarily address the risks the controls are intended to mitigate. In the context of internal control over financial reporting, control objectives generally relate to assertions addressing the risk that specific controls will not provide reasonable assurance that a misstatement or omission is prevented or detected and corrected on a timely basis.
Controls at a service organization	Policies and procedures at a service organization that are likely relevant to user entities' internal control over financial reporting. These policies and procedures are designed, implemented, and maintained to provide reasonable assurance about achievement of control objectives relevant to the services covered by the service auditor's report. (This does not include controls unrelated to achievement of control objectives stated in the service organization's system description, such as controls related to preparation of the service organization's financial statements.)
Controls at a subservice organization	Subservice organization policies and procedures designed, implemented, and maintained for the same reasons as controls at a service organization.
Criteria	Standards or benchmarks used to measure and present the subject matter and against which the service auditor evaluates the subject matter. Management is responsible for selecting criteria. Suitable criteria (see AT 101) are required for reasonably consistent evaluation or measurement of a subject matter. Criteria need to be available to the intended users to enable their understanding of how the subject matter has been evaluated or measured.
Inclusive method	Method of dealing with services provided by a subservice organization in which the service organization's system description identifies the nature of the services provided by the subservice organization as well as the subservice organization's relevant control objectives and related controls included in the scope of the service auditor's engagement. (This method is generally feasible if the service and subservice organizations are related or if their contract provides for issuance of such a report.)

Term	Definition
Internal audit function	Service organization internal auditors and others such as a compliance or risk department who perform activities that are similar to those of internal auditors.
Report on a description of a service organization's system and the suitability of the design of controls (Type 1 report)	A report comprising (1) a description of the service organization's system, prepared by management of the service organization; (2) a written assertion by the service organization's management about whether in all material respects, based on suitable criteria and as of a specified date, the description of the service organization's system fairly presents such system's design and implementation, and the controls related to the description's control objectives were suitably designed to achieve those objectives; and (3) a service auditor's report expressing an opinion on these written assertions.
Report on a description of a service organization's system and the suitability of the design and operating effectiveness of controls (Type 2 report)	A report comprising (1) a description of the service organization's system, prepared by management of the service organization; (2) a written assertion by the service organization's management about whether in all material respects, based on suitable criteria and throughout the specified period, the description of the service organization's system fairly presents the system's design and implementation and that the controls related to the description's control objectives were suitably designed and operated effectively to achieve those objectives; and (3) a service auditor's report expressing an opinion on these written assertions and including a description of the service auditor's tests of controls and their results.
Service auditor	A practitioner who reports on controls at a service organization.
Service organization	An organization or segment of an organization providing services to user entities that are part of the user entities' information and communication systems relevant to financial reporting.
Service organization's system	The policies and procedures designed, implemented, and maintained to provide user entities with the services covered by the service auditor's report. A management-prepared description of the service organization's system identifies the services covered, the period related to the description, control objectives specified by management or an outside party, any outside party specifying the control objectives, and the related controls.
Subservice organization	A service organization used by another service organization to perform services provided to user entities that are part of the user entities' information and communication systems relevant to financial reporting.

Term	Definition
Test of controls	A procedure designed to evaluate the operating effectiveness of controls in preventing or detecting and correcting internal control deficiencies that could result in nonachievement of the control objectives stated in the service organization's system description.
User auditor	An auditor who audits and reports on user entity financial statements.
User entity	An entity that uses a service organization.

Requirements

The service auditor is presumptively required to apply the following procedures for reporting on controls at a service organization.

Identification of Management

1. Determine who within management or the governance structure is the appropriate person to interact with, including consideration of which person(s) have the appropriate responsibilities for and knowledge of the matters related to controls at the service organization.

Acceptance and Continuance

2. Unless otherwise required by law or regulation, only continue or accept a service auditor's engagement if:

   a. The service auditors possess the capabilities and competence to perform the engagement.

   b. Preliminary knowledge of the engagement circumstances indicates the criteria will be suitable and available to intended users, there will be access to sufficient, appropriate evidence, and the service organization's system description and scope of the engagement will not be limited to the extent they are not useful to user entities and their auditors.

   c. Management of the service organization, in agreeing to the engagement terms, acknowledges and accepts responsibility for:

      i. Preparing and presenting the service organization's system description and an accompanying written assertion that will be provided to user entities;

ii.   Having a basis for their assertion;

iii. Selecting and stating in the assertion criteria used;

iv.   Specifying and stating the control objectives in the description and identifying any other party specifying control objectives;

v.   Identifying the risks that threaten achievement of the control objectives and designing, implementing, and documenting controls at the service organization to address those risks to control objectives; and

vi.   Providing the service auditor with all information relevant to the service organization's system description and accompanying assertion and any additional relevant information requested, unrestricted access to service organization personnel to obtain evidence for the engagement, and written representations at the engagement's conclusion.

3. If management refuses to provide a written assertion, withdraw from the engagement due to a scope limitation. If withdrawal is prevented by law or regulation, disclaim an opinion.

4. If management requests a change in the engagement scope before engagement completion, the service auditor should be satisfied there is reasonable justification for the change before agreeing.

5. If management will not provide a written assertion, the service auditor may not perform a service auditor's engagement under AT 101 (Attest Engagements).

Assess Criteria Suitability

6. Assess whether management used suitable criteria in preparing and presenting the service organization's system description and evaluating whether controls were suitably designed (and operating effectively if a Type 2 report) to achieve the description's stated control objectives.

7. Minimum suitable criteria for evaluating fair presentation of the service organization's system description include whether the description presents how:

i.   The system was designed and implemented to process relevant transactions, including the classes of transactions processed;

ii.   The procedures by which transactions are initiated, authorized, recorded, processed, corrected, and reported for user entities and the related accounting records prepared to support those processes;

iii. Significant events and conditions are captured;

iv.   The process used to prepare reports for user entities;

    v. Specified control objectives and controls designed to achieve those objectives;

   vi. Other aspects of the service organization's internal control system relevant to achieving the description's stated control objectives; and

  vii. That it does not omit or distort information relevant to the description and acknowledges the description may not include all system aspects important to every user entity and auditor.

8. Minimum suitable criteria for evaluating if controls are suitably designed to achieve stated control objectives include whether risks threatening achievement of the description's stated control objectives have been identified and if identified controls would, if operating as described, provide reasonable assurance that those risks would not prevent achievement of the control objectives.

9. Minimum suitable criteria for evaluating whether controls operate effectively to provide reasonable assurance that the stated control objectives would be achieved include whether the controls were consistently applied as designed and whether manual controls were applied by individuals with sufficient competence and authority.

Materiality

10. Evaluate materiality when planning and performing the engagement regarding fair presentation of the service organization's system description and suitability of the design (and operating effectiveness if a Type 2 report) of controls to achieve the description's stated control objectives.

Obtain an Understanding of the Service Organization's System

11. Obtain an understanding of the service organization's system and controls included in the scope of the engagement. Obtain information for use in identifying risks that the service organization's system description is not fairly presented or the description's stated control objectives were not achieved due to intentional acts by service organization personnel,

Obtain Evidence Regarding Description

12. Obtain and read the service organization's system description and evaluate whether aspects of the description included in the scope of the engagement are presented fairly, including whether the descrip-

tion's stated control objectives are reasonable, controls identified in the description were implemented, and any complementary user controls and services provided by a subservice organization are adequately described (including which method, inclusive or carve-out, is used).

13. Determine whether the service organization's system description has been implemented through inquiries of management and other service organization personnel and other procedures.

Obtain Evidence Regarding Design Effectiveness

14. Determine which service organization controls are necessary to achieve the description's stated control objectives and assess whether they were suitably designed to achieve those objectives by identifying risks threatening achievement of the objectives and evaluating the linkage of controls identified in the description with those risks.

Obtain Evidence Regarding Control Operating Effectiveness

15. For a Type 2 engagement, test controls necessary to achieve the description's stated control objectives and assess their operating effectiveness throughout the period. Evidence obtained in prior engagements does not provide a basis for a reduction in testing even if supplemented with evidence obtained during the current period.

16. Inquire about changes in the service organization's controls implemented during the period covered by the service auditor's report. Changes significant to user entities and their auditors should be in the service organization's system description or, if not in the description, should be described in the service auditor's report. If superseded controls are relevant to achievement of the description's stated control objectives, determine if it is possible to test the controls before and after the change and, if not, the effect on the service auditor's report.

17. When designing and performing tests of controls, perform other procedures in combination with inquiry to obtain evidence about how, by whom or what means, and with what consistency the control was applied; determine if any controls to be tested depend on other controls and if it is necessary to obtain evidence about those controls' operating effectiveness; and determine an effective method for selecting the items to be tested to meet the procedure's objectives.

18. Determine the extent of tests of controls and if sampling is appropriate by considering the population characteristics, including the nature, frequency, and expected deviation rate of the controls to be tested.

19. Investigate the nature and cause of any deviations identified, including considering whether the deviations may be the result of intentional acts by service organization personnel. Determine whether identified deviations are within the expected deviation rate and the control operated effectively, additional testing of the control or compensating controls is necessary to reach a conclusion about operating effectiveness, or the testing performed provides an appropriate basis for concluding the control did not operate effectively.

20. If a discovered deviation is considered an anomaly and no compensating controls have been identified, perform additional procedures to obtain a high degree of certainty the deviation is not representative of the population.

Using the Work of Others

21. Obtain an understanding of the aspects of the internal audit function relevant to the engagement.

22. If intending to use work of the internal audit function, evaluate their objectivity, technical competence, and due professional care and the effect of any constraints or restrictions placed on the internal audit function by management or those charged with governance. This might include evaluating the specialist's capabilities, competence, and objectivity and inquiring about interests and relationships that could threaten that objectivity. It might also include obtaining an understanding of the specialist's field of expertise to enable a determination of the nature, scope, and objectives of the specialist's work and an evaluation of the adequacy of that work for the service auditor's purposes.

23. In judging the effect of the internal audit function's work on the service auditor's procedures, evaluate the significance of that work to the service auditor's conclusions and the degree of subjectivity involved in evaluating the evidence gathered in support of those conclusions.

24. Perform procedures to evaluate the adequacy of work performed by the internal audit function if the service auditor uses that work or receives direct assistance from the internal audit function. Consider the adequacy of the scope of the work and whether the evaluation of the internal audit function remains appropriate. Evaluate whether:

    i.   Work is performed by people with appropriate skill and expertise;

    ii. Work is properly supervised, reviewed, and documented;

    iii. Sufficient, appropriate evidence is obtained to be able to draw reasonable conclusions;

    iv. Conclusions reached are appropriate in the circumstances;

    v. Any prepared reports are consistent with results; and

    vi. Any exceptions or unusual matters disclosed by the internal audit function are properly resolved.

25. If work of the internal audit function has been used in performing tests of controls in a Type 2 report, the description of those tests and results should include a description of the internal auditor's work and the service auditor's procedures with respect to that work.

26. Establish a written understanding with the specialist regarding the nature, scope, and objectives of the specialist's work, the service auditor's and specialist's respective roles, and the nature, timing, and extent of communication between the parties, including the form of any report to be provided.

27. The service auditor's opinion should not refer to work of the internal audit function or a specialist that was used. The service auditor's sole responsibility for the opinion expressed is not reduced by using the work of others.

Written Representations

28. Ask management to provide written representations based on its knowledge and belief:

    a. That reaffirm the assertion accompanying the service organization's system description

    b. About whether all records, documentation, unusual matters they are aware of, and other information relevant to the engagement have been made available to the service auditor

    c. That they have disclosed to the service auditor any of the following about which they are aware:

        i. Instances of noncompliance with laws and regulations or uncorrected errors that may affect user entities;

        ii. Knowledge of any actual, suspected, or alleged intentional acts by the service organization's management or employees, such as overrides of controls or misappropriation of user entity assets, that could adversely affect the fair presentation of the service organization's system description or the completeness or achievement of the description's stated control objectives;

      iii. Design deficiencies in controls, including those for which management believes the cost of corrective action exceeds the benefits; instances where controls have not operated as described; and

      iv. Subsequent events regarding the services covered by the engagement that could have a significant effect on user entities.

29. If the service organization's system description uses the inclusive method and a subservice organization is used, obtain the written representations described above from management of the subservice organization.

30. Written representations should be in the form of a representation letter addressed to the service auditor with the same date as the service auditor's report.

31. If management does not provide one or more of the requested written representations: discuss the matter with management, consider the assessment of management's integrity and determine effects on the engagement, and take appropriate actions, including determining the possible effect on the opinion in the service auditor's report.

Other Information

32. Read other information included in a document containing the service organization's system description and the service auditor's report to identify any material inconsistencies with the description. If the service auditor becomes aware of a material inconsistency or an apparent misstatement of fact in the other information, discuss the matter with management. If management refuses to correct this inconsistency or misstatement, take further appropriate action.

Subsequent Events

33. Inquire whether management is aware of any events subsequent to the period covered by the service organization's system description up to the date of the service auditor's report that could have a significant effect on controls at the service organization or on the service auditor's report. If so, and the event is not disclosed in the description, disclose it in the service auditor's report.

34. There is no obligation after the date of the service auditor's report to perform any procedures regarding the service organization's system description or the suitability of the design or operating effectiveness of controls.

Documentation

35. Prepare documentation sufficient to enable an experienced auditor with no previous connection to the audit to understand (1) the nature, timing, and extent of the audit procedures performed to comply with AT 801 and applicable legal and regulatory requirements; (2) the results of procedures performed and the evidence obtained; and (3) conclusions reached on significant matters arising during the engagement and significant professional judgments made in reaching those conclusions.

36. Document the nature, timing, and extent of audit procedures performed by recording (1) the identifying characteristics of specific items or matters tested; (2) who performed procedures and the date the procedures were completed; and (3) who reviewed the work performed and the date and extent of the review.

37. If the service auditor uses the work of internal audit, document the conclusions reached regarding the evaluation of the adequacy of the work of the internal audit function and procedures performed by the service auditor on that work.

38. Document discussions of significant matters with service organization personnel and others. Include when and with whom the discussions occurred.

39. If information was identified that is inconsistent with the service auditor's final conclusion regarding a significant finding, document how the inconsistency was addressed.

40. Complete the assembly of the final engagement file on a timely basis after the date of the service auditor's report no later than 60 days following the service auditor's report release date.

41. Do not discard any documentation after assembly of the final engagement file has been completed before the end of its retention period.

42. If documentation needs to be modified or added to after assembly of the final engagement file is complete, document the specific reasons for making the changes, when and by whom the changes were made and reviewed, and any effect they have on the service auditor's conclusions.

Preparing the Service Auditor's Report

43. Include the following elements in the service auditor's report:

   a. A title clearly indicating the report is an independent service auditor's report.

   b. An addressee.

   c. Identification of:

i. The service organization's system description prepared by the service organization's management and management's assertion about the matters identified in the definitions of Type 1 and Type 2 reports;

ii. An identification of any parts of the service organization's system description not covered by the service auditor's report;

iii. If stated control objectives can only be achieved if complementary user entity controls are suitably designed and operating effectively, the service auditor's report should include a statement that the service auditor has not evaluated such suitability of the design or operating effectiveness of the user controls; and

iv. If services of a subservice organization were used, an identification of those services and whether the inclusive or carve-out method was used. Depending on if the inclusive or carve-out method was used, respectively, there should be a statement that the service organization's system description includes or excludes the control objectives and related controls at the subservice organization and that the service auditor's procedures included or excluded procedures at or related to the subservice organization.

44. Identification of the criteria.

45. A statement of the inherent limitations of the potential effectiveness of controls at the service organization and the risk of projecting any evaluation of the service organization's system description or any conclusions about the effectiveness of controls in achieving the related control objectives stated in the description to the future.

46. A description of the service organization's and service auditor's responsibilities, including a statement that management of the service organization is responsible for:

a. Preparing and presenting the service organization's system description and the accompanying assertion;

b. Providing the services covered by the service organization's system description;

c. Specifying and stating the description's control objectives;

d. Identifying the risks that threaten the achievement of the control objectives;

e. Selecting the criteria;

f. Designing, implementing, and maintaining controls to achieve the related control objectives stated in the description; and

g. Selecting the criteria.

47. A statement that the service auditor's responsibility is to express an opinion on the fairness of the presentation of management's description of the service organization's system and on the suitability of the design and (operating effectiveness if a Type 2 report) of the controls to achieve the objectives stated in the description.

48. A statement that the engagement was performed in accordance with Statements on Standards for Attestation Engagements.

49. A statement that the basis for the auditor's opinion is the performance of audit procedures to obtain reasonable assurance and a statement, in a Type 1 report, that procedures regarding the operating effectiveness of controls have not been performed and no opinion is expressed on such effectiveness.

50. The service auditor's opinion on whether, in all material respects, based on the criteria specified in management's assertion that as of the specified date for a Type 1 report or throughout the specified period for a Type 2 report:

a. The service organization's system description fairly presents the system that was designed and implemented;

b. The controls related to the description's stated control objectives were suitably designed to provide reasonable assurance that those objectives would be achieved if the controls operated effectively, and

c. For a Type 2 report, that those controls were tested and operated effectively.

51. A paragraph at the end of the report containing the following elements:

a. A statement restricting the use of the service auditor's report (and description of tests of controls and their results in the case of a Type 2 report) to customers as of the end of the period (Type 1 report), customers during some or all of the period covered by the report (Type 2 report), user auditors, and service organization management; and

b. A statement that the report is not intended to be and should not be used by anyone other than these specified parties.

52. The date of the service auditor's report.

53. The service auditor's name and the city where the office with responsibility for the engagement is maintained.

54. If application of complementary user entity controls is necessary to achieve the description's stated control objectives, add a phrase to the opinion paragraph of the report to indicate this.

55. For the opinion on the suitable design of controls, add the phrase "and customers applied the complementary user entity controls contemplated in the design of XYZ Service Organization's controls as of [*date*] (for a Type 1 report) or throughout the period [*date*] to [*date*] (for a Type 2 report.)"

56. For the opinion on the operating effectiveness of controls in a Type 2 report, add the phrase "if customers applied the complementary user entity controls contemplated in the design of XYZ Service Organization's controls throughout the period [*date*] to [*date*]."

57. In a Type 2 report, include a separate section after the opinion or an attachment describing the tests of controls and results indicating which controls were tested, the period covered by testing, whether items tested were a sample or the entire population, and the nature of testing in sufficient detail to enable user auditors to determine the effect of such tests on their risk assessments. If deviations have been identified, they should be reported along with the extent of testing performed leading to identification of the deviations, the nature of the deviations, and the deviations noted.

58. Modify the opinion and include a clear description of all reasons for the modification if the service auditor concludes that management's description of the service organization system is not fairly presented in all material respects; controls are not suitably designed to provide reasonable assurance that the description's stated control objectives would be achieved if the controls operated as described; that, in the case of a Type 2 report, those controls did not operate effectively; or the service auditor is unable to obtain sufficient, appropriate audit evidence.

59. Modify the report if information comes to the service auditor's attention, irrespective of specified control objectives, causing the conclusion that design deficiencies exist that could adversely affect the ability of the service organization to initiate, authorize, record, process, or report financial data to user organizations without error, and that user organizations would not generally be expected to have controls in place to mitigate such design deficiencies.

Other Communication Responsibilities

60. If the service auditor becomes aware of incidents of noncompliance with laws and regulations, fraud, or uncorrected errors attributable to the service organization that may affect user entities, determine the effect of such incidents on the service organization's system description, the achievement of the control objectives, and the service auditor's report. Determine whether this information has been communicated appropriately to affected user entities and, if it has not been communicated and management is unwilling to do so, take appropriate action, which could include withdrawing from the engagement and communicating the reasons for withdrawal to those charged with governance depending on the significance of the matter.

Analysis and Application of Procedures

Acceptance and Continuance

The auditor must determine whether he or she has the capabilities and competence to perform the engagement, including having knowledge of the industry, an understanding of the information technology and systems, experience evaluating risks as they relate to suitable design of controls, and experience in the design and execution of tests of controls and the evaluation of the results.

> **PLANNING AID REMINDER:** The service auditor does not need to be independent of each user entity to perform a service auditor's engagement.

If management requests a change in the scope of an engagement before its completion, the auditor must be satisfied there is reasonable justification for the change. Reasons that do not justify a change in scope include excluding certain service organization controls from the engagement or changing from a Type 2 to a Type 1 report because of the likelihood the opinion would be modified without such changes.

Assess Criteria Suitability

The auditor must determine that the subject matter of the engagement is capable of evaluation against criteria that are suitable and available to users. Management is responsible for selecting the criteria and for determining whether they are appropriate.

Materiality

In an engagement to report on controls at a service organization, the concept of materiality relates to information being reported on, not the financial statements of user entities. An item or aggregation of items is material in the context of a service auditor's engagement when a reasonable person, such as a member of a user entity's management or user auditor, would be influenced by the item's misstatement or omission. Materiality related to the fair presentation of the service organization's system description and design of controls primarily considers qualitative factors such as whether the description includes significant aspects of processing significant transactions or omits or distorts relevant information, or whether the controls, as designed, have the ability to provide reasonable assurance that the description's stated control objectives would be achieved. Materiality related to the operating effectiveness of controls considers quantitative and qualitative factors, such as tolerable and observed deviation rates and the nature and cause of any observed deviations.

Obtain an Understanding of the Service Organization's System

Obtaining an understanding of the service organization's system and related controls assists the service auditor in:

- Identifying the system's boundaries and how the system interfaces with other systems

- Assessing the fair presentation of the service organization's system description

- Determining which controls are necessary to achieve the description's stated control objectives, and whether controls were suitably designed (and operating effectively in the case of a Type 2 report) to achieve those objectives

There are many procedures the auditor may perform to obtain this understanding, including inquiring of management and other service organization personnel, observing operations, inspecting documents and records of transaction processing, inspecting agreements between the service organization and user entities to identify common terms, and reperforming application of controls.

There are also procedures the auditor may perform to obtain information for use in identifying risks that the service organization's system description is not fairly presented or the description's stated control objectives were not achieved due to intentional acts by service organization personnel. These procedures include discussing among audit team members factors at the service organization that could affect these risks, inquiring of management and others within the organization to obtain their views about these risks and how they are addressed, considering if factors exist at the organization that increase these risks, and considering other information coming to the auditor's attention helpful in identifying these risks.

Intentional acts could include management override of controls, misappropriation of user entity assets by service organization personnel, or creation of false or misleading documents or records of user organization transactions processed by the service organization by service organization personnel.

> **PLANNING AID REMINDER:** Factors that could increase the risk of management override include unrealistic processing schedules, significant increases in processing volumes exceeding normal processing capacity, and an environment in which established procedures and controls are not consistently followed. Factors that could increase the risk of misappropriation of assets include inadequate supervision or monitoring, processing or maintaining records of large amounts of cash or investments, inadequate segregation of duties or independent checks, and inadequate physical or electronic safeguards over cash or investments.

Obtain Evidence

In evaluating the fair presentation of the service organization's system description, the auditor may perform procedures such as:

- Considering the user entities' nature and how they are affected by the service organization's services

- Reading standard contracts with user entities to understand the service organization's contractual obligations

- Observing procedures performed by service organization personnel

- Reviewing the service organization's policy and procedure manuals and other system documentation

- Performing walk-throughs of transactions through the service organization's system

Procedures the auditor may perform to determine whether the system described has been implemented include inquiry of management and other service organization personnel, observation, inspection of records and other documentation, and reperformance of transaction processing and control application. If the inclusive method is used, the description should adequately differentiate between service and subservice organization controls. If the carve-out method is used, the description should identify the functions performed, but it does not need to describe detailed processing or controls at the subservice organization.

When obtaining evidence regarding the design of controls, the auditor should take compensating controls into account. If the auditor evaluates certain activities as ineffective in achieving a particular control objective, compensating controls may exist that still allow the auditor to conclude that controls related to the description's stated control objective are suitably designed to achieve that objective.

In obtaining evidence about the operating effectiveness of controls, evidence about the suitability of control design and implementation may provide evidence of operating effectiveness if there is some automation that provides for consistent operation of the control as it was designed and implemented. Some control procedures do not leave evidence of their operation, so the auditor may need to test operating effectiveness of such procedures throughout the reporting period to obtain sufficient evidence. To determine the effect of changes in service organization controls that were implemented during the period covered by the service auditor's report, the auditor should gather information about the nature and extent of the changes, how they affect processing at the service organization, and how they might affect assertions in financial statements of user entities.

Type 2 reports ordinarily cover a minimum period of six months. Reports covering a shorter time period may describe the reasons in the service organization's system description and service auditor's report. Reasons for a shorter reporting period include:

- The service auditor was engaged close to the report issuance date so controls cannot be tested for operating effectiveness for a six month period

- The service organization, system, or application has been operating for less than six months

- Significant changes have been made to controls and it is not practicable to issue a report covering the system before and after the changes or to wait six months before issuing a report

Written Representations

Written representations described in the requirements section are separate from management's written assertion that accompanies the service organization's system description provided to user entities. In some circumstances, these written representations may be obtained from parties in addition to service organization management, such as those charged with governance.

Preparing the Service Auditor's Report

Type 1 and Type 2 reports should be addressed to the service organization. An example of a Type 1 report (Exhibit AT 801-1) and a Type 2 report (Exhibit AT 801-2) are presented at the end of this section.

> **PUBLIC COMPANY IMPLICATION:** Under the PCAOB's AS-5, only a Type 2 report is acceptable, because the auditor must be comfortable that internal controls at the service organization are properly designed and operating effectively.

In a Type 2 report's description of tests of controls, the inclusion of any information about causative factors for identified deviations can be useful to readers of the report.

There are many modifications that can be made to service auditor's reports. The auditor may issue a qualified opinion because the service organization's system description is not fairly presented in all material respects, controls are not suitably designed (or do not operate effectively for a Type 2 report) to provide reasonable assurance of the achievement of the description's stated control objectives, or the auditor is unable to obtain sufficient appropriate evidence. In any of these circumstances, an explanatory paragraph should be inserted before a modified opinion paragraph and all other report paragraphs remain unchanged. The opinion paragraph is modified as follows, "In our opinion, except for the matter described in the preceding paragraph, and based on the criteria described in management's assertion on page [*aa*], in all material respects ... "

The auditor may also issue a report that includes a disclaimer of opinion on other information included in management's description of the service organization's system that is not covered by the service auditor's report. In this situation, the service auditor's report would be modified only by including an illustrative explanatory paragraph following the opinion paragraph.

Other Communication Responsibilities

When an auditor becomes aware of noncompliance with laws and regulations, fraud, or uncorrected errors at the service organization, there are several actions that may be taken:

• Obtain legal advice about the consequences of different courses of action

- Communicate with those charged with governance at the service organization

- Modify the service auditor's opinion or add an emphasis of a matter paragraph

- Communicate with third parties such as a regulator when required

- Withdraw from the engagement

Practitioner's Aids

Exhibit AT 801-1 is an example of a Type 1 report and Exhibit AT 801-2 is an example of a Type 2 report.

EXHIBIT AT 801-1 — TYPE 1 REPORT

We have examined X Service Organization's description on pages [*bb – cc*] of the [*type or name of*] system made available to customers of the system for processing their transactions as of [*date*], and the suitability of the design of controls to achieve the related control objectives stated in the description.

Service Organization's Responsibilities

On page XX of the description, X Service Organization has provided an assertion about the fairness of the presentation of the description and suitability of the design of the controls to achieve the related control objectives stated in the description. X Service Organization is responsible for preparing the description and for the assertion, including the completeness, accuracy, and method of presentation of the description and the assertion, providing the services covered by the description, specifying the control objectives and stating them in the description, identifying the risks that threaten the achievement of the control objectives, selecting the criteria, and designing, implementing, and documenting controls to achieve the related control objectives stated in the description.

Service Auditor's Responsibilities

Our responsibility is to express an opinion on the fairness of the presentation of the description and on the suitability of the design of controls to achieve the related control objectives stated in the description, based on our examination. We conducted our examination in accordance with attestation standards established by the

American Institute of Certified Public Accountants. Those standards require that we plan and perform our examination to obtain reasonable assurance, in all material respects, about whether the description is fairly presented and the controls were suitably designed to achieve the related control objectives stated in the description as of [*date*].

An examination of a description of a service organization's system and the suitability of the design of controls to achieve the related control objectives stated in the description involves performing procedures to obtain evidence about the fairness of the presentation of the description of the system and the suitability of the design of the controls to achieve the related control objectives stated in the description. Our procedures included assessing the risks that the description is not fairly presented and that the controls were not suitably designed to achieve the related control objectives stated in the description. An examination engagement of this type also includes evaluating the overall presentation of the description and the suitability of the control objectives stated therein, and the suitability of the criteria specified by the service organization and described at page [*aa*].

We did not perform any procedures regarding the operating effectiveness of the controls stated in the description and, accordingly, do not express an opinion thereon.

We believe that the evidence we obtained is sufficient and appropriate to provide a reasonable basis for our opinion.

Inherent Limitations

Because of their nature, controls at a service organization may not prevent or detect and correct all errors or omissions in processing or reporting transactions. The projection to the future of any evaluation of the fairness of the presentation of the description, or any conclusions about the suitability of the design of the controls to achieve the related control objectives is subject to the risk that the controls at a service organization may become ineffective or fail.

Opinion

In our opinion, in all material respects, based on the criteria described in X Service Organization's assertion

a.   The description fairly presents the [*type or name of*] system that was designed and implemented as of [*date*], and
b.   The controls related to the control objectives stated in the description of X Service Organization's system were suitably

designed to provide reasonable assurance that the control objectives would be achieved if the controls operated effectively as of [*date*].

Restricted Use

This report is intended solely for the information and use of management of X Service Organization, user entities of X Service Organization's [*type or name of*] system as of [*date*], and the independent auditors of such user entities, who have a sufficient understanding to consider it, along with other information including information about controls implemented by the user entities themselves, when obtaining an understanding of user entities information and communication systems relevant to financial reporting. This report is not intended to be and should not be used by anyone other than these specified parties.

[Service auditor's signature]

[Date of the service auditor's report]

[Service auditor's city and state]

EXHIBIT AT 801-2 — TYPE 2 REPORT

We have examined X Service Organization's description of its [*type or name of*] system for processing user entities' transaction throughout the period [*date*] to [*date*] and the suitability of the design and operating effectiveness of controls to achieve the related control objectives stated in the description.

Service Organization's Responsibilities

On page XX of the description, X Service Organization has provided an assertion about the fairness of the presentation of the description and suitability of the design of the controls to achieve the related control objectives stated in the description. X Service Organization is responsible for preparing the description and for the assertion, including the completeness, accuracy, and method of presentation of the description and the assertion, providing the services covered by the description, specifying the control objectives and stating them in the description, identifying the risks that threaten the achievement of the control objectives, selecting the criteria, and designing, implementing, and documenting controls to achieve the related control objectives stated in the description.

Service Auditor's Responsibilities

Our responsibility is to express an opinion on the fairness of the presentation of the description and on the suitability of the design and operating effectiveness of the controls to achieve the related control objectives stated in the description, based on our examination. We conducted our examination in accordance with attestation standards established by the American Institute of Certified Public Accountants. Those standards require that we plan and perform our examination to obtain reasonable assurance about whether, in all material respects, the description is fairly presented and the controls were suitably designed and operating effectively to achieve the related control objectives stated in the description throughout the period [*date*] to [*date*].

An examination of a description of a service organization's system and the suitability of the design and operating effectiveness of the service organization's controls to achieve the related control objectives stated in the description involves performing procedures to obtain evidence about the fairness of the presentation of the description and the suitability of the design and operating effectiveness of those controls to achieve the related control objectives stated in the description. Our procedures included assessing the risks that the description is not fairly presented and that the controls were not suitably designed or operating effectively to achieve the related control objectives stated in the description. Our procedures included testing the operating effectiveness of those controls that we consider necessary to provide reasonable assurance that the related control objectives stated in the description were achieved. An examination engagement of this type also includes evaluating the overall presentation of the description and the suitability of the control objectives stated therein, and the suitability of the criteria specified by the service organization and described at page [*aa*]. We believe that the evidence we obtained is sufficient and appropriate to provide a reasonable basis for our opinion.

Inherent Limitations

Because of their nature, controls at a service organization may not prevent or detect and correct all errors or omissions in processing or reporting transactions. Also, the projection to the future of any evaluation of the fairness of the presentation of the description, or conclusions about the suitability of the design or operating effectiveness of the controls to achieve the related control objectives is subject to the risk that controls at a service organization may become inadequate or fail.

Opinion

In our opinion, in all material respects, based on the criteria described in X Service Organization's assertion on page [*aa*],

a. The description fairly presents the [*type or name of*] system that was designed and implemented throughout the period [*date*] to [*date*].

b. The controls related to the control objectives stated in the description were suitably designed to provide reasonable assurance that the control objectives would be achieved if the controls operated effectively throughout the period [*date*] to [*date*].

c. The controls we tested, which were those necessary to provide reasonable assurance that the control objectives stated in the description were achieved, operated effectively throughout the period [*date*] to [*date*].

Description of Tests of Controls

The specific controls tested and the nature, timing, and results of those tests are listed on pages [*yy – zz*].

Restricted Use

This report, including the description of tests of controls and results thereof on pages [*yy – zz*] is intended solely for the information and use of X Service Organization, user entities of X Service Organization's [*type or name of*] system during some or all of the period [*date*] to [*date*], and the independent auditors of such entities, who have a sufficient understanding to consider it, along with other information including information about controls implemented by user entities themselves, when assessing the risks of material misstatements of user entities' financial statements. This report is not intended to be and should not be used by anyone other than these specified parties.

[Service auditor's signature]

[Date of the service auditor's report]

[Service auditor's city and state]

AR Section

Statements on Standards for Accounting and Review Services

AR Section 60: Framework for Performing and Reporting on
    Compilation and Review Engagements 925

AR Section 80: Compilation of Financial Statements 932

AR Section 90: Review of Financial Statements.................. 953

AR Section 110: Compilation of Specified Elements, Accounts,
    or Items of a Financial Statement 1017

AR Section 120: Compilation of Pro Forma Financial
    Information 1019

AR Section 200: Reporting on Comparative Financial
    Statements 1021

AR Section 300: Compilation Reports on Financial Statements
    in Certain Prescribed Forms 1037

AR Section 400: Communications between Predecessor and
    Successor Accountants 1041

AR Section 600: Reporting on Personal Financial Statements
    Included in Written Personal Financial Plans 1066

AR SECTION 60

FRAMEWORK FOR PERFORMING AND REPORTING ON COMPILATION AND REVIEW ENGAGEMENTS

Authoritative Pronouncements

SSARS-19 — Compilation and Review Engagements

Overview

In SSARS-19 the Accounting and Review Services Committee establishes a framework for performing and reporting on compilation engagements. The framework includes defining (1) key terms, (2) the objective of compilation and review engagements, (3) the requirements applicable to these types of engagements, (4) the sources and levels of authority of standards and guidance for performing compilation and review engagements, (5) the elements of compilation and review engagements, and (6) materiality within the context of compilation and review engagements.

Definitions

Term	Definition
Applicable financial reporting framework	The financial reporting framework adopted by management and, when appropriate, those charged with governance
Assurance engagement	An engagement in which an accountant issues a report designed to enhance third-party and management confidence about the outcome of an evaluation or measurement of financial statements against an applicable financial reporting framework
Attest engagement	An engagement requiring independence
Financial reporting framework	A set of criteria used to determine measurement, recognition, presentation, and disclosure of all material items appearing in the financial statements
Financial statements	A structured representation of historical financial information, including related notes. The term ordinarily refers to a complete set of financial statements as determined by the applicable financial reporting framework, but it can also refer to a single financial statement or financial statements without notes.
Management	The person(s) with executive responsibility for the entity's operations

Term	Definition
Nonissuer	A company not required to file reports with the Securities and Exchange Commission
Other comprehensive basis of accounting (OCBOA)	A definite set of criteria other than accounting principles generally accepted in the United States of America or International Financial Reporting Standards (IFRS) that has substantial support underlying the preparation of financial statements. Examples include the following:
	— A basis of accounting that insurance companies use in accordance with state insurance commission rules
	— A basis of accounting a reporting entity uses or expects to use to file its income tax return
	— The cash basis of accounting and modifications of the cash basis that have substantial support, for example, recording depreciation on fixed assets
Review evidence	Information used by an accountant to provide a reasonable basis for obtaining limited assurance
Submission of financial statements	Presenting financial statements to management that an accountant has prepared
Third party	All persons, including those charged with governance, except for members of management
Those charged with governance	The person(s) responsible for overseeing the entity's strategic direction and obligations related to the entity's accountability

Objectives

The objective of a compilation is to help management present financial information in the form of financial statements without obtaining or providing any assurance regarding the financial statements' need for material modifications in order to conform to the applicable financial reporting framework. A compilation engagement differs significantly from a review or financial statement audit because it is an attest engagement, but it is not an assurance engagement.

> **OBSERVATION:** For the purposes of SSARSs, when discussing compilation engagements, the term "financial statements" includes other specified financial statement elements, accounts, or items and pro-forma financial information when applicable.

The objective of a review is to obtain limited assurance through accumulation of review evidence that there are no material modifications that should be made to the financial statements in order for the statements to be in conformity with the applicable financial reporting framework. A review engagement is both an attest engagement and an assurance engagement, and it differs significantly from a financial statement audit because the accountant does not obtain assurance that he or she will become aware of all significant matters that would be disclosed in an audit.

Requirements

Accountants performing compilations or reviews are responsible for considering the entire text of a SSARS in their work on an engagement and in understanding and applying the professional requirements of relevant SSARSs. There are two categories of professional requirements used in SSARSs, and they impose different responsibilities on the accountant. Unconditional requirements are indicated by the words "must" or "is required" and require an accountant to comply with the requirement in all cases in which the circumstances the requirement applies to exist. Presumptively mandatory requirements are indicated by the word "should," and they also require an accountant to comply with the requirement if the circumstances the requirement applies to exist. However, the accountant may depart from presumptively mandatory requirements in rare circumstances if he or she documents the justification for the departure and how the alternative procedures performed sufficiently achieve the objectives of the requirement. If a SSARS states that an accountant "should consider" a procedure or action, he or she is presumptively required to consider, not carry out, the procedure or action.

Explanatory material consists of text within a SSARS that may provide further explanation and guidance on the professional requirements or identify and describe other procedures or actions relating to the accountant's activities. Explanatory material is indicated by the words "may," "might," and "could" and does not impose a professional requirement to perform suggested procedures or actions, rather it indicates material requiring the accountant's attention and understanding. Whether the accountant performs procedures or actions described in explanatory material depends on his or her professional judgment given the engagement circumstances.

Compilation and Review Standards and Guidance

Different sources of guidance are available to accountants performing compilations and reviews. Compilation and review engagements of nonissuers must be performed in accordance with SSARSs, except for certain reviews of interim financial information. SSARSs require the accountant to exercise professional judgment in their application.

Interpretative publications are not standards for accounting and review services, but are recommendations on the application of SSARS in certain circumstances. Interpretative publications can consist of SSARSs' compilation and review interpretations, SSARSs' appendices, AICPA Audit and Accounting Guide compilation and review guidance, and AICPA Statements of Position. The accountant should be aware of and consider any applicable interpretative publications and, although the guidance does not have to be applied, the accountant should be prepared to explain how he or she complied with SSARSs provisions addressed by the guidance.

Other compilation and review publications are available that do not have authoritative status but may help accountants understand and apply SSARS. Such publications include AICPA accounting and review publications; the AICPA's annual *Compilation and Review Alert;* compilation and review articles in professional journals and the AICPA's *The CPA Letter;* continuing professional education programs and other instructional materials, books, programs, and checklists; and compilation and review publications published by state CPA societies, other organizations, and individuals. If an accountant chooses to apply the guidance in an other compilation and review publication, he or she should be satisfied that it is relevant and appropriate to the circumstances. AICPA publications reviewed by the AICPA Audit and Attest Standards staff are presumed to be appropriate.

In addition to the SSARS, accountants who are members of the AICPA must also comply with other standards in performing compilation and review engagements. The AICPA's Code of Professional Conduct requires that accountants maintain objectivity and integrity and comply with all other applicable provisions when performing a compilation or review engagement. AICPA members are also governed by Statements on Quality Control Standards, which establish standards and provide guidance on a firm's system of quality control. The firm should have quality control policies and procedures in place to provide reasonable assurance that personnel comply with SSARS in compilation and review engagements. The nature and extent of those policies and procedures will depend on the firm's size, degree of operating autonomy, the nature of its practice, its organization, and appropriate cost-benefit considerations.

> **OBSERVATION:** Deficiencies or instances of noncompliance with a firm's quality control policies do not necessarily indicate that a particular compilation or review engagement was not performed in accordance with SSARSs.

Compilation or Review Engagement Elements

There are five elements of a compilation or review engagement:

1. A three-party relationship involving management, an accountant, and intended users

2. An applicable financial reporting framework

3. Financial statements or financial information

4. Sufficient appropriate review evidence (in a review)

5. A written communication or report

Three-Party Relationship

Management, or the responsible party, is one party to the relationship. Management takes responsibility for the preparation and fair presentation of the financial statements in accordance with the applicable financial reporting framework and for designing, implementing, and maintaining internal control. If management is unwilling to accept these responsibilities, the accountant cannot issue an unmodified compilation or review report. During a compilation or review engagement, the accountant may make suggestions about the form and content of the financial statements or prepare them, in whole or in part, based on information from management.

An accountant in the practice of public accounting as defined by the AICPA code is a second party to the relationship. If an accountant is not in the practice of public accounting, it is inappropriate that he or she issue a written communication or report under SSARSs. In some cases, the accountant may be requested to perform additional services along with the compilation or review, which is acceptable as long as he or she adheres to professional standards in performing those services.

The third parties to the relationship are the intended users of the financial statements or financial information, which in some cases may be management.

Applicable Financial Reporting Framework

Management and, when applicable, those charged with governance are responsible for choosing an entity's applicable financial reporting framework and its accounting policies when there are acceptable alternatives within the framework. Examples of financial reporting frameworks include accounting principles generally accepted in the United States of America issued by the Financial Accounting Standards Board, the Governmental Accounting Standards Board, or the Federal Accounting Standards Advisory Board; IFRSs issued by the International Accounting Standards Board; and OCBOA.

Financial Statements or Financial Information

A compilation or review engagement may be for a complete set of financial statements or an individual financial statement that may be for a period of one year or more or less than one year, depending on management's needs.

Evidence

In a review engagement, the accountant should perform procedures sufficient to obtain limited assurance that no material modifications should be made to the financial statements in order for the statements to conform with the applicable financial reporting framework. Review evidence from analytical procedures and inquiries typically provide the accountant with a reasonable basis for obtaining limited assurance.

> **PLANNING AID REMINDER:** The accountant has no responsibility to obtain any evidence about the completeness or accuracy of the financial statements in a compilation engagement.

Written Communication or Report

When performing a compilation, a written communication or report is required unless the accountant withdraws from the engagement. An accountant who is not independent may still issue a compilation report as long as he or she complies with compilation standards. When performing a review, a written review report is required unless the accountant withdraws from the engagement.

Materiality

The accountant's determination of materiality is a matter of professional judgment, and is to reflect his or her views of the needs of financial statement users. Materiality is generally discussed in the applicable financial reporting framework. However, if materiality is not discussed, the following provides the accountant with a framework for evaluating materiality:

- Misstatements, including omissions, are considered to be material if individually or in the aggregate they could reasonably be expected to influence the economic decisions of users taken on the basis of the financial statements

- Judgments about materiality are affected by circumstances as well as a misstatement's size and nature

- Judgments about whether matters are material to financial statement users are made considering the common financial information needs of the users as a group

AR SECTION 80

COMPILATION OF FINANCIAL STATEMENTS

Authoritative Pronouncements

SSARS 19—Compilation and Review Engagements

Overview

Statements on Standards for Accounting and Review Services (SSARS) cover two different levels of service that an accountant can provide for unaudited financial statements of nonpublic entities. The first level of service is referred to as a compilation. The accountant's report on a compilation includes a statement that an audit or a review was not performed and no opinion or other assurance is expressed on the accompanying financial statements. The second level of service is called a review. The accountant's report on a review includes a statement of limited assurance that the financial statements are in accordance with generally accepted accounting principles (GAAP) or an other comprehensive basis of accounting.

The objective of the compilation service is to present in the form of financial statements information that is the representation of management. In a compilation service, the accountant does not express any assurance on the financial statements. The accountant is required to comply with the provisions of SSARS-19 when he or she is engaged to report on compiled financial statements or submitting financial statements to a client.

Establishing an Understanding

The accountant should establish an understanding with management and, when applicable, with those charged with governance regarding the services to be performed for compilation engagements, and this understanding should be documented with a written engagement letter with management. The understanding should include the engagement objectives, management's and accountant's responsibilities, and engagement limitations, incorporating the following matters:

- A compilation's objective is to assist management in presenting financial information in the form of financial statements.

- The accountant uses information from management without obtaining any assurance that there are no material modifications that should be made to the financial statements.

- Management is responsible for preparing and presenting the financial statements in accordance with the applicable financial reporting framework.

- Management is responsible for designing, implementing, and maintaining internal control relevant to the preparation and fair presentation of the financial statements.

- Management is responsible for preventing and detecting fraud.

- Management is responsible for identifying and ensuring the entity's compliance with applicable laws and regulations.

- Management is responsible for making all financial records and related information available to the accountant.

- The accountant is responsible for conducting the engagement in accordance with SSARSs issued by the AICPA.

- A compilation differs significantly from a review or audit of financial statements; therefore, the accountant will not express an opinion or provide any assurance about the financial statements.

- The engagement cannot be relied upon to disclose errors, fraud, or illegal acts.

- The accountant will inform management of any material errors and any evidence or information coming to his or her attention during the compilation that fraud or an illegal act may have occurred.

- If applicable, the effect of any independence impairments on the expected form of the accountant's compilation report.

Exhibit AR 80-1 provides an example engagement letter for financial statement compilations.

Other matters may also be included in the understanding with management and, when applicable, those charged with governance, including the following:

- Fees and billings

- Any arrangements or limitation of the accountant's or client's liability, such as indemnifying the accountant for liability based on knowing misrepresentations from management where permitted

- Conditions under which access to compilation documents may be granted to others

- Additional services to be provided relating to regulatory requirements

If compiled financial statements are not expected to be used by a third party and a compilation report will not be issued, this should be addressed in the engagement letter.

> **OBSERVATION:** If the accountant is performing a compilation for restricted use, add the following paragraph to the engagement letter: "The financial statements will not be accompanied by a report and are for management's use only and are not to be used by a third party."

There are additional matters to be addressed in the engagement letter for a restricted-use compilation such as the following: there may be material departures from the applicable financial reporting framework and any effects of those departures may not be disclosed; substantially all disclosures and the statement of cash flows as required by the applicable financial reporting framework may not be included; and reference to any supplementary information.

At the outset of an engagement the accountant might know that a departure, or departures, from GAAP exists. In this event, it might be appropriate to include in the engagement letter information to the effect that a modified report will be issued reflecting the departure(s) from GAAP instead of the standard compilation or review report. This procedure should eliminate misunderstanding about what type of report the client will receive when the engagement is completed.

Compilation Performance Requirements

An accountant adheres to several requirements in performing a compilation engagement. He or she should have an understanding of the client's industry and its accounting principles and practices. This requirement does not prevent the accountant from accepting an engagement for an industry in which he or she has no previous experience, but it does mean that he or she is responsible for obtaining the required level of knowledge.

Developing an understanding of the client

The accountant should obtain an understanding of the client's business, including knowledge of the client's organization, operating characteristics, and the nature of its assets, liabilities, revenues, and expenses. The accountant should also obtain an understanding of the accounting principles and practices used by the client, remaining alert to any unusual accounting policies and procedures that come to his or her attention. This understanding may include changes in accounting principles and practices and differences in the client as compared to normal industry practices.

Consider whether the client needs other accounting services

On the basis of the accountant's general knowledge of the client's business, he or she should consider the need to perform other accounting services. (Such services may be limited to consulting on a specific accounting matter or involve adjusting all or many of the significant accounts in the general ledger.) The need for such services may result from the accountant discovering, for example, that

- The accounting records are inadequate.

- The accounting or bookkeeping personnel do not possess sufficient abilities or experience.

- The accounting basis used to maintain the books is incorrect.

- The information to be disclosed in the financial statements is not available.

Read the financial statements

After the accountant has obtained the required knowledge of the client and the industry the client operates in, has completed any other accounting services deemed necessary, and prepared the financial statements, he or she should read the financial statements.

Reading the financial statements is one of the more important procedures in a compilation engagement. The accountant must apply all the knowledge and understanding previously obtained and use his or her professional expertise effectively. Questions the accountant must answer include the following:

- Do the financial statements appear to be in the proper form and complete?

- Do the financial statements appear to be free from obvious material errors?

- Are all necessary disclosures made in reasonable detail?

Any information that the accountant is aware of, from any source, should be considered for possible indications that the financial statements may be inaccurate, incomplete, or otherwise unsatisfactory.

Financial statements that may be inaccurate or incomplete

Although doing so is not required, the accountant may have made inquiries or performed other procedures regarding information provided by the entity. If these inquiries or procedures make the accountant aware that information supplied by the entity is incorrect, incomplete, unsatisfactory, or that fraud or an illegal act may have occurred, he or she should request that management consider the effect of these matters on the financial statements and communicate their conclusions to him or her. The accountant should consider the effects of management's conclusions, obtaining additional information if he or she believes the financial statements may be materially misstated. If management refuses to provide additional or revised information, the accountant should withdraw from the engagement and consider the need for consulting legal counsel.

Consider obtaining a client representation letter

Compilation standards do not require that client representations be obtained. However, because of the very limited procedures required for a compilation and the possibility of misunderstandings regarding accounting information, having obtained a client representation letter may be useful, especially when the client does not understand that the financial statements are its responsibility.

Documentation of the compilation engagement

Documentation should be prepared for each engagement in sufficient detail to provide a clear understanding of the work performed. The form, content, and extent of documentation varies depending on the engagement circumstances and the accountant's professional judgment. Documentation should include (1) the engagement letter documenting the understanding with the client, (2) any findings or issues the accountant finds significant in his or her professional judgment, and (3) written or oral communications to management regarding fraud or illegal acts that come to the accountant's attention.

Financial Statement Reporting

When they are reasonably expected to be used by a third party, financial statements should be accompanied by a written report in order to prevent misinterpretation of the degree of responsibility the accountant is assuming regarding them. The following are the basic elements of the accountant's report:

- *Title* The title should clearly indicate it is the accountant's compilation report and, if applicable, may indicate that the accountant is independent.

- *Addressee* The report should be addressed appropriately.

- *Introductory paragraph* This paragraph should identify the entity whose financial statements have been compiled and the financial statements that have been compiled, state that the financial statements have been compiled, specify the date or period covered by the financial statements, and include a statement that the accountant has not audited or reviewed the financial statements and does not express an opinion or provide any assurance about whether the financial statements are in accordance with the applicable financial reporting framework.

- *Management's responsibility for the financial statements and for internal control over financial reporting* A statement that management is responsible for preparing and fairly presenting the financial statements in accordance with the applicable financial reporting framework and for designing, implementing, and maintaining internal control relevant to the preparation and fair presentation of the financial statements.

- *Accountant's responsibility* A statement that the accountant is responsible for conducting the compilation in accordance with SSARS issued by the AICPA and that a compilation's objective is to assist management in presenting financial information in the form of financial statements without providing assurance that there are no material modifications that should be made to the statements.

- *Accountant's signature* The accounting firm or accountant's manual or printed signature.

- *Date of the report* The compilation report date should be the date the compilation is completed.

Exhibit AR 80-2 provides an example of a standard accountant's compilation report.

The accountant should not describe any procedures performed as part of the compilation engagement in the report. Each page of the compiled financial statements should contain a reference such as "See accountant's compilation report." Financial statements prepared in accordance with an OCBOA are not considered appropriate in form unless they include a description of the OCBOA, including a summary of significant accounting policies and a description of the primary differences from GAAP, and informative disclosures similar to those required by GAAP if the financial statements contain items similar to those in financial statements prepared in accordance with GAAP.

> **OBSERVATION:** SSARS-13 (Compilation of Specified Elements, Accounts, or Items of a Financial Statement) and SSARS-14 (Compilation of Pro Forma Financial Information) enable an accountant to compile elements, accounts, or items of a financial statement and pro-forma financial information. These SSARS expand the applicability of SSARS (which were formerly only applicable to financial statements) to allow an accountant to compile and report on such items in accordance with SSARS. Examples of specified elements, accounts, or items of a financial statement that an accountant can now compile under the standards include schedules of rentals, royalties, profit participation, and provision of income taxes. Pro-forma financial information shows what the significant effects on historical financial statements might have been had a consummated or proposed transaction (or event) occurred at an earlier date. The new standards establish specific responsibilities for accountants engaged to compile specified elements, accounts, or items of a financial statement and pro-forma financial information. SSARS-13 is summarized in AR 110 and SSARS-14 is summarized in AR 120.

All types of financial statements may be compiled or reviewed and may be for any type of nonissuer business organization, including an estate, a trust, or an individual. The financial statements may reflect the operations of not-for-profit organizations, governments, governmental agencies, or other nonpublic entities that prepare their financial statements using a comprehensive basis of accounting other than GAAP. Whenever the term "GAAP" is used in connection with a compilation or review, its meaning also includes "an other comprehensive basis of accounting." As mentioned previously, compilation and review standards are not applicable to forecasts, projections, or similar financial presentations, or to financial information included in tax returns.

Financial Statements that Omit Substantially All Disclosures

If financial statements omit substantially all disclosures required by the applicable financial reporting framework, the accountant may still compile the statements if the omission is not due to the intent to mislead financial statement users. When reporting on such financial statements, the paragraph on the accountant's responsibility should be followed by a paragraph containing statements that management has omitted substantially all disclosures required by the applicable financial reporting framework; if those disclosures were included, they might influence the users' conclusions about the entity's financial position, results of operations, and cash flows; and the financial statements are not intended for those who are uninformed about such matters. An example of such a paragraph is as follows:

> Management has elected to omit substantially all of the disclosures required by accounting principles generally accepted in the United States of America. If the omitted disclosures were included in the financial statements, they might influence the user's conclusions about the company's financial position, results of operations, and cash flows. Accordingly, the financial statements are not designed for those who are not informed about such matters.

> **PLANNING AID REMINDER:** If the entity only includes disclosures about a few matters, those disclosures should be labeled "Selected Information — Substantially All Disclosures Required by [*identify the applicable financial reporting framework (for example, "Accounting Principles Generally Accepted in the United States of America"*)] Are Not Included."

A similar situation arises when the statement of cash flows is omitted from a presentation that includes a balance sheet and an income statement. Under GAAP, a statement of cash flows is a required statement, and reference to such omission must be made in the accountant's compilation report. The following is the recommended fourth paragraph that should be added to the accountant's compilation report when a statement of cash flows or disclosures are omitted:

> Management has elected to omit substantially all the disclosures (and the statement of cash flows) required by generally accepted accounting principles. If the omitted disclosures were included in the financial statements, they might influence the user's conclusions about the Company's financial position, results of operations, and cash flows. Accordingly, these financial statements are not designed for those who are not informed about such matters.

If only the statement of cash flows is omitted, the fourth paragraph should read as follows:

A statement of cash flows for the year ended December 31, 20X1, has not been presented. Generally accepted accounting principles require that such a statement be presented when financial statements purport to present financial position and results of operations.

Accountant Is Not Independent

If the accountant is not independent, the compilation report should be modified to include a final paragraph stating the accountant's lack of independence. This disclosure could be phrased as follows: "I am (We are) not independent with respect to ABC Company." Exhibit AR 80-3 provides an example of such a report. The accountant may disclose a description about the reasons for his or her lack of independence, but if these reasons are disclosed, then all reasons should be included in the description. The following are example descriptions of reasons for a lack of independence:

- A member of the engagement team had a direct financial interest in the company.

- An immediate family member of a member of the engagement team was employed by the company.

- Certain accounting services performed impaired independence.

Financial Statements Not Expected to Be Used by a Third Party

The accountant does not need to issue a compilation report if the financial statements are not expected to be used by a third party. A reference should be included on each page of the financial statements restricting their use, such as "Restricted for Management's Use Only." If the accountant becomes aware that the financial statements have been distributed to third parties, discuss the situation with the client and consider requesting that the client have the statements returned. If the client does not comply with a request to have the statements returned, the accountant should notify known third parties that the financial statements are not intended for third-party use and preferably consult his or her attorney.

Emphasis of a Matter

The accountant may use his or her discretion to add an emphasis-of-matter paragraph regarding a matter disclosed in the financial statements. This information should be presented in a separate paragraph in the report and may include matters such as uncertainties, that the entity is part of a larger entity, that the entity had significant transactions with related parties, unusually important subsequent events, or accounting matters not involving a change in accounting principle that affect the comparability of the financial statements with those of the prior period.

Emphasis-of-a-matter paragraphs should never be used as a substitute for management's disclosures. For this reason, an accountant should not include an emphasis paragraph in a compilation report on financial statements that omit substantially all disclosures unless the matter is disclosed in the financial statements.

Departures from the Applicable Financial Reporting Framework

The accountant may become aware of material departures from the applicable financial reporting framework and, if the financial statements are not revised, should consider the effects on the report. The omission of substantially all disclosures and/or the statement of cash flows, although such omissions constitute a departure from GAAP, is permitted in a compilation because of the special disclosure provisions. If the accountant concludes that modification of the standard report is adequate to disclose the departure, a separate paragraph should be included in the report disclosing the departure and its effects on the financial statements if the effects have been determined by management or are known based on the accountant's procedures. An example of this type of report is provided in Exhibit AR 80-4.

If management has not determined the effects, the accountant is not required to determine the effects so long as the report states that such a determination has not been made. If the accountant believes modification of the report is not adequate to indicate the financial statement deficiencies, he or she should withdraw from the engagement and not perform any further services regarding those financial statements.

Restricted Use Reports

A general use report is not restricted to specified parties and is normally used in financial statement reports prepared in conformity with an applicable financial reporting framework. However, the accountant is not precluded from restricting the use of any report. A restricted use report is intended only for one or more specified third parties. A report's use should be restricted when it is based on measurement or disclosure criteria contained in contractual agreements or regulatory provisions that are not in conformity with an applicable financial reporting framework.

If a single combined report is used covering subject matter requiring a restriction on use and subject matter not requiring a restriction on use, the report's use should be restricted to the specified parties. A separate restricted use report may be included in a document also containing a general use report when required by law or regulation. In this situation, both reports maintain their intended use.

If the accountant is asked to add additional parties as specified parties to a restricted use report after completion of the engagement, he or she may do so but should obtain affirmative acknowledgement from the other parties, preferably in writing, regarding their understanding of the nature of the engagement, the measurement or disclosure criteria used, and the related report.

A restricted use report should contain a separate paragraph at the end of the report including:

- A statement that the report is intended solely for the information and use of specified parties.

- Identification of the specified parties included in the restricted use (the parties may be listed in the report or the report may refer to a listing elsewhere in the document).

- A statement that the report is not intended to be and should not be used by anyone other than the specified parties.

Entity's Ability to Continue as a Going Concern

The accountant may become aware during a compilation engagement that there is uncertainty about the entity's ability to continue as a going concern for a reasonable period of time, not exceeding one year beyond the date of the compiled financial statements. In these situations, the accountant should request that management consider possible effects of the going concern uncertainty on the financial statements, including the need for disclosure and consider the reasonableness of management's conclusions and the adequacy of any related disclosures.

If the accountant concludes that management's conclusions are not reasonable or that disclosure is inadequate, he or she should follow the guidance regarding departures from an applicable financial reporting framework and, depending on what the accountant considers necessary, should either modify the report or withdraw from the engagement. The accountant may emphasize an uncertainty about the entity's ability to continue as a going concern in the report as long as the uncertainty is disclosed in the financial statements.

Subsequent Events

Whether during performance of compilation procedures or subsequent to the date of the compilation report but prior to the report's release, the accountant may become aware that a subsequent event with a material effect on the compiled financial statements has occurred. In this situation, the accountant should request that management consider the possible effects on the financial statements and any applicable related disclosures. If the accountant determines the subsequent event is not adequately accounted for in the financial statements or disclosed in the notes, the guidance regarding departures from an applicable financial reporting framework should be followed and, depending on what the accountant considers necessary, he or she should either modify the report or withdraw from the engagement. A subsequent event may have such a material effect on the entity that the accountant may choose to include an emphasis of matter paragraph to direct the reader's attention to the event and its effects if the matter is disclosed in the financial statements.

Subsequent Discovery of Facts Existing at the Date of the Report

The accountant may become aware of facts existing at the date of the report subsequent to that date that, had the accountant been aware of those facts, may have caused him or her to believe the information supplied by the entity was incorrect, incomplete, or otherwise unsatisfactory. In these circumstances, consulting with legal counsel is advised because of the legal implications involved.

The accountant has no obligation to perform other compilation procedures with respect to the financial statements after the date of the compilation report unless new information comes to the accountant's attention. However, when information comes to the accountant's attention that would have been investigated had it been known during the course of the compilation, the accountant should try to determine whether the information is reliable and whether the facts existed at the date of the report. The accountant should discuss the matter with management and, as necessary, those charged with governance. The accountant should obtain additional or revised information if (1) the matter's nature and effect would have affected the accountant's report or the financial statements if the information had been known at the report date and included in the financial statements and (2) the accountant believes there are users or likely users of the financial statements that would find the information important.

If the accountant concludes that action should be taken to prevent further use of the report or financial statements, he or she should advise the client to appropriately disclose the newly discovered facts and their impact on the financial statements to current and likely financial statement users. If the effect of the subsequently discovered information can be readily determined, disclosure should consist of issuing revised financial information and a new report as soon as practicable, disclosing the reasons for the revision in a note to the financial statements and referring to them in the report when applicable. If issuance of subsequent financial statements is imminent, appropriate disclosure can be made in those statements rather than reissuing the earlier statements. If the effect of the subsequently discovered information on the financial statements cannot promptly be determined, appropriate disclosure consists of the client informing current or likely financial statement users that the statements should not be used and that revised financial statements and a new accountant's report will be issued as soon as practicable.

The accountant should take whatever steps he or she feels are necessary to ensure the specified disclosures have been made. If the client refuses to make the specified disclosures, the accountant should notify persons at the highest level of the entity of such refusal and that, without those disclosures, the accountant will have to take steps to prevent further use of the financial statements and accountant's report. Unless otherwise recommended by the accountant's attorney, the accountant should take the following steps in these circumstances:

1. Notify the client that the accountant's report must no longer be associated with the financial statements.

2. Notify regulatory agencies with jurisdiction over the client that the accountant's report should no longer be used.

3. Notify each person known to the accountant to be using the financial statements that the financial statements and accountant's report should no longer be used.

Any disclosure made by the accountant to those other than the client should include a description of the nature of the subsequently acquired information and its effect on the financial statements. Also, the information disclosed should be as precise and factual as possible without going beyond what is reasonably necessary to describe the nature and effects of the information and without commenting on anyone's conduct or motives.

Supplementary Information

The accountant should clearly indicate the degree of responsibility taken with respect to information presented for supplementary analysis purposes with the basic financial statements. If the accountant compiled both the financial statements and the supplementary information, the report should refer to the supplementary information or the accountant should issue a separate report on the supplementary information.

When the engagement does not include compiling supplementary information, there should be no chance that readers of the financial statements will misunderstand the responsibility of the accountant. Misunderstanding may be avoided by (1) the client clearly stating (in a preamble to the supplementary information) that the accountant has not compiled the supplementary information or (2) the accountant adding a separate paragraph stating that the supplementary information has not been compiled.

Communications with Management and Others

When information comes to the accountant's attention that fraud or an illegal act may have occurred, it should be brought to management's attention unless the matter deals with a clearly inconsequential illegal act. If the fraud or illegal act involves senior management, the accountant should report the matter to someone at a higher level in the entity, such as the owner-manager or those charged with governance. Communication may be written or oral, but if the communication is oral, it should be documented. If the matter involves an owner of the entity, the accountant should consider withdrawing from the engagement.

The accountant is typically precluded by ethical and legal confidentiality obligations from disclosing information that fraud or an illegal act may have occurred to parties other than the client's management or those charged with governance. There are exceptions that may impose a duty to disclose such information, such as complying with legal and regulatory requirements, communicating with a successor accountant, or responding to a subpoena.

Change in Engagement Type

During, but before the completion of, an engagement, a client may ask to change the level of service the accountant is performing. If the request for change in services is from a lower level to a higher level — for example, from a review to an audit or from a compilation to a review — no problem arises. A problem does arise, however, when the change is to a lower level of service than that which was being provided. This request may be due to a change in the entity's circumstances affecting its requirements for an audit or review or a misunderstanding about the nature of services to be provided. Either of these reasons is typically considered a reasonable basis for requesting a change in the engagement. The request may also be due to a scope restriction, imposed by the client or by circumstance.

In considering whether a request to change to a compilation engagement is reasonable, the accountant should consider the client's reasons for the request, especially the implications of a scope restriction, the additional effort required to complete the audit or review engagement, and the estimated additional cost to complete the audit or review.

> **PLANNING AID REMINDER:** There are situations that ordinarily preclude the accountant from issuing a compilation report. One such situation is when the accountant has been prohibited from corresponding with the entity's legal counsel in an audit.

If in the accountant's judgment a change to a lower level of service is acceptable, the accountant should perform the service in accordance with the standards applicable to the changed engagement. The accountant should make no mention in the report of the original engagement, any procedures accomplished for the original engagement, or any scope limitation that resulted in the changed service.

Practitioner's Aids

EXHIBIT AR 80-1 — COMPILATION ENGAGEMENT LETTER

Exhibit AR 80-1 is an example of a standard engagement letter for a compilation.

[*Appropriate Salutation*]

This letter is to confirm our understanding of the terms and objectives of our engagement and the nature and limitations of the services we will provide.

We will perform the following services:

We will compile, from information you provide, the annual [*and interim, if applicable*] financial statements of ABC Company as of December 31, 20X1, and issue an accountant's report thereon in accordance with Statements on Standards for Accounting and Review Services (SSARSs) issued by the American Institute of Certified Public Accountants (AICPA).

The objective of a compilation is to assist you in presenting financial information in the form of financial statements. We will utilize information that is your representation without undertaking to obtain or provide any assurance that there are no material modifications that should be made to the financial statements in order for the statements to be in conformity with [*the applicable financial reporting framework (for example,* accounting principles generally accepted in the United States of America*)*].

You are responsible for

a. The preparation and fair presentation of the financial statements in accordance with [*the applicable financial reporting framework (for example,* accounting principles generally accepted in the United States of America*)*].

b. Designing, implementing, and maintaining internal control relevant to the preparation and fair presentation of the financial statements.

c. Preventing and detecting fraud.

d. Identifying and ensuring that the entity complies with the laws and regulations applicable to its activities.

e. Making all financial records and related information available to us.

We are responsible for conducting the engagement in accordance with SSARSs issued by the AICPA.

A compilation differs significantly from a review or an audit of financial statements. A compilation does not contemplate performing inquiry, analytical procedures, or other procedures performed in a review. Additionally, a compilation does not contemplate obtaining an understanding of the entity's internal control; assessing fraud risk; testing accounting records by obtaining sufficient appropriate evidence through inspection, observation, confirmation, or the examination of source documents (for example, cancelled checks or bank images); or other procedures ordinarily performed in an audit. Accordingly, we will not express an opinion or provide any assurance regarding the financial statements being compiled.

Our engagement cannot be relied upon to disclose errors, fraud, or illegal acts. However, we will inform the appropriate level of management of any material errors, and of any evidence or information that comes to our attention during the performance of our compilation procedures that fraud may have occurred. In addition, we will report to you any evidence or information that comes to our attention during the performance of our compilation procedures regarding illegal acts that may have occurred, unless they are clearly inconsequential.

[*If, during the period covered by the engagement letter, the accountant's independence is or will be impaired, insert the following:*

We are not independent with respect to ABC Company. We will disclose that we are not independent in our compilation report.]

If, for any reason, we are unable to complete the compilation of your financial statements, we will not issue a report on such statements as a result of this engagement.

Our fees for these services are $XXX (and include any other information regarding billings).

We will be pleased to discuss this letter with you at any time. If the foregoing is in accordance with your understanding, please sign the copy of this letter in the space provided and return it to us.

Sincerely yours,

[*Signature of Accountant*]

Acknowledged:

ABC Company

[*Signature of President*]

[*Date*]

EXHIBIT AR 80-2 — STANDARD ACCOUNTANT'S COMPILATION REPORT

Exhibit AR 80-2 is an example of a standard compilation report on financial statements prepared in accordance with accounting principles generally accepted in the United States of America.

Accountant's Compilation Report

[*Appropriate Salutation*]

I (we) have compiled the accompanying balance sheet of ABC Company as of December 31, 20X1, and the related statements of income, retained earnings, and cash flows for the year then ended. I (we) have not audited or reviewed the accompanying financial statements and, accordingly, do not express an opinion or provide any assurance about whether the financial statements are in accordance with accounting principles generally accepted in the United States of America.

Management (owners) is (are) responsible for the preparation and fair presentation of the financial statements in accordance with accounting principles generally accepted in the United States of America and for designing, implementing, and maintaining internal control relevant to the preparation and fair presentation of the financial statements.

My (our) responsibility is to conduct the compilation in accordance with Statements on Standards for Accounting and Review Services issued by the American Institute of Certified Public Accountants. The objective of a compilation is to assist management in presenting financial information in the form of financial statements without undertaking to obtain or provide any assurance that there are no material modifications that should be made to the financial statements.

[*Signature of accounting firm or accountant, as appropriate*]

[*Date*]

EXHIBIT AR 80-3 — COMPILATION REPORT WHEN INDEPENDENCE IS IMPAIRED

Exhibit AR 80-3 is an example of a compilation report on financial statements prepared in accordance with accounting principles generally accepted in the United States of America when the accountant's independence has been impaired and the accountant decides not to disclose the reason for the independence impairment.

Accountant's Compilation Report

[*Appropriate Salutation*]

I (we) have compiled the accompanying balance sheet of ABC Company as of December 31, 20X1, and the related statements of income, retained earnings, and cash flows for the year then ended. I (we) have not audited or reviewed the accompanying financial statements and, accordingly, do not express an opinion or provide any assurance about whether the financial statements are in accordance with accounting principles generally accepted in the United States of America.

Management (owners) is (are) responsible for the preparation and fair presentation of the financial statements in accordance with accounting principles generally accepted in the United States of America and for designing, implementing, and maintaining internal control relevant to the preparation and fair presentation of the financial statements.

My (our) responsibility is to conduct the compilation in accordance with Statements on Standards for Accounting and Review Services issued by the American Institute of Certified Public Accountants. The objective of a compilation is to assist management in presenting financial information in the form of financial statements without undertaking to obtain or provide any assurance that there are no material modifications that should be made to the financial statements.

I am (we are) not independent with respect to ABC Company.

[*Signature of accounting firm or accountant, as appropriate*]

[*Date*]

EXHIBIT AR 80-4 – COMPILATION REPORT DISCLOSING A GAAP DEPARTURE

Exhibit AR 80-4 is an example of a compilation report on financial statements disclosing a departure from accounting principles generally accepted in the United States of America.

Accountant's Compilation Report

[*Appropriate Salutation*]

I (we) have compiled the accompanying balance sheet of ABC Company as of December 31, 20X1, and the related statements of income, retained earnings, and cash flows for the year then ended. I (we) have not audited or reviewed the accompanying financial statements and, accordingly, do not express an opinion or provide any assurance about whether the financial statements are in accordance with accounting principles generally accepted in the United States of America.

Management (owners) is (are) responsible for the preparation and fair presentation of the financial statements in accordance with accounting principles generally accepted in the United States of America and for designing, implementing, and maintaining internal control relevant to the preparation and fair presentation of the financial statements.

My (our) responsibility is to conduct the compilation in accordance with Statements on Standards for Accounting and Review Services issued by the American Institute of Certified Public Accountants. The objective of a compilation is to assist management in presenting financial information in the form of financial statements without undertaking to obtain or provide any assurance that there are no material modifications that should be made to the financial statements. During our compilation, I (we) did become aware of a departure (certain departures) from accounting principles generally accepted in the United States of America that is (are) described in the following paragraph.

As disclosed in Note X to the financial statements, accounting principles generally accepted in the United States of America require that land be stated at cost. Management has informed me (us) that the company has stated its land at appraised value and that, if accounting principles generally accepted in the United States of America had been followed, the land account and stockholders' equity would have been decreased by $500,000.

[*Signature of accounting firm or accountant, as appropriate*]

[*Date*]

EXHIBIT AR 80-5 — COMPILATION PROGRAM

Use the following procedures as a guide for performing a compilation engagement. The compilation program is only a guide, and professional judgment should be exercised to determine how the procedures should be modified by revising or adding procedures to the compilation program.

Initial and date each procedure as it is completed. If the procedure is not relevant to this particular compilation engagement, place "N/A" (not applicable) in the space provided for an initial and cross-reference the omitted procedure to another workpaper that explains why the procedure was omitted.

Client Name: _____

Date of Financial Statements: _____

	Initials	Date	Workpaper Reference
1. Acquire an adequate understanding of the accounting principles and practices of the client's industry.	____	___	_____
2. Develop a general understanding of the nature of the client's business transactions.	____	___	_____
3. Develop a general understanding of the stated qualifications of the client's accounting personnel.	____	___	_____
4. Develop a general understanding of the accounting basis used to prepare the client's financial statements.	____	___	_____
5. Develop a general understanding of the form and content of the client's financial statements.	____	___	_____
6. Consider whether other professional services are needed in order to complete the compilation engagement.	____	___	_____
7. Read the financial statements.	____	___	_____
8. On the basis of information collected by using other compilation procedures and/or information that otherwise has come to our attention, consider whether additional or revised information must be obtained.	____	___	_____

9. Other compilation procedures used: ————————————————

————————————————————————————————————

————————————————————————————————————

Reviewed By: _____

Date: _____

————————————————————————————————————

AR SECTION 90

REVIEW OF FINANCIAL STATEMENTS

Authoritative Pronouncements

SSARS-19 — Compilation and Review Engagements

Overview

Accountants are required to comply with the provisions of AR 90 when engaged to review financial statements. The exception to this requirement is when the accountant is reviewing interim financial information and the entity's latest annual financial statements have been audited by the accountant or a predecessor; the accountant has been engaged to audit the entity's current-year financial statements or he or she audited the prior financial statements and expects to be engaged to audit the current-year financial statements; and the entity prepares its interim financial information in accordance with the same financial reporting framework used to prepare its annual financial statements. When these conditions exist, the accountant is to follow the guidance in SAS-116 (as codified in AU 722), not the guidance in AR 90, when performing the review engagement.

> **PLANNING AID REMINDER:** An accountant cannot perform a review engagement if his or her independence is impaired for any reason.

The objective of a review engagement is to express limited assurance that there are no material modifications that should be made to the financial statements in order for them to be in conformity with GAAP. A review is a level of service higher than a compilation because it results in an expression of limited assurance. The limited assurance is contained in a report by the accountant stating that he or she is not aware of any material modifications that should be made to the financial statements in order for them to be in conformity with GAAP. The accountant must perform sufficient inquiry and analytical procedures to give a reasonable basis for that conclusion, and the accountant must obtain representations from management for all financial statements and periods covered by his or her review report. These inquiries and analytical procedures are the major difference between a review and a compilation.

A review is a level of service lower than an audit of financial statements. It does not provide a basis for expressing an opinion under GAAS, because it does not require many of the significant procedures required in an audit.

A review does not contemplate obtaining an understanding of the entity's internal control, assessing fraud risks, tests of accounting records by obtaining sufficient appropriate evidence, or other procedures ordinarily performed in an audit. Therefore a review provides only limited assurance that there are no material modifications that should be made to the financial statements for them to conform with GAAP.

A review engagement may involve reporting on all the basic financial statements or on only one financial statement, such as a balance sheet or a statement of income. A review may not include reporting on financial statements that omit substantially all disclosures required by GAAP, unless such omissions are completely disclosed in the accountant's report. This obviously is not a practical alternative.

Establishing an Understanding

The accountant should establish an understanding with management and, when applicable, with those charged with governance regarding the services to be performed for review engagements and document this understanding with a written engagement letter with management. The understanding should include the engagement objectives, management and accountant's responsibilities, and engagement limitations, incorporating the following matters:

- A review's objective is to obtain limited assurance that there are no material modifications that should be made to the financial statements.

- Management is responsible for preparing and presenting the financial statements in accordance with the applicable financial reporting framework.

- Management is responsible for designing, implementing, and maintaining internal control relevant to the preparation and fair presentation of the financial statements.

- Management is responsible for preventing and detecting fraud.

- Management is responsible for identifying and ensuring the entity's compliance with applicable laws and regulations.

- Management is responsible for making all financial records and related information available to the accountant.

- Management will provide the accountant with a letter confirming certain representations made during the review at the engagement's conclusion.

- The accountant is responsible for conducting the engagement in accordance with SSARSs issued by the AICPA.

- A review primarily involves applying analytical procedures to management's financial data and making inquiries of company management.

- A review is substantially less in scope than an audit of financial statements; therefore, the accountant will not express an opinion regarding the financial statements as a whole.

- The engagement cannot be relied upon to disclose errors, fraud, or illegal acts.

- The accountant will inform management of any material errors and any evidence or information coming to the accountant's attention during the review that fraud or an illegal act may have occurred. Illegal acts that are clearly inconsequential need not be reported and an understanding may be established with the entity in advance regarding the nature of any such matters to be communicated.

Exhibit AR 90-1 provides an example engagement letter for financial statement reviews.

Other matters may also be included in the understanding with management and, when applicable, those charged with governance. These matters include:

- Fees and billings

- Conditions under which access to review documents may be granted to others

- Additional services to be provided relating to regulatory requirements

- Any arrangements or limitation of the accountant's or client's liability, such as indemnifying the accountant for liability based on knowing misrepresentations from management where permitted

> **PLANNING AID REMINDER:** Liability limitation agreements such as those described above may be restricted or prohibited by regulators.

Additional matters should be addressed in the engagement letter if circumstances apply, including that there may be material departures from the applicable financial reporting framework and that any effects of those departures may not be disclosed as well as reference to any supplementary information.

Review Performance Requirements

In a review engagement, the accountant is required to perform procedures to accumulate review evidence that provides a reasonable basis for obtaining limited assurance that no material modifications should be made to the financial statements in order for them to be in conformity with the applicable financial reporting framework. These procedures should take into account the accountant's understanding of the client's industry and knowledge of the client. Analytical procedures and inquiry ordinarily provide the accountant with the evidence necessary to obtain limited assurance; however, if the accountant needs additional evidence to obtain limited assurance that the financial statements are not materially misstated, he or she should perform additional procedures.

Knowledge of the industry

The accountant should have an understanding of the client's industry and the accounting principles and practices used in the industry. This requirement does not prevent the accountant from accepting an engagement for an industry in which he or she has no previous experience, but it does mean that he or she is responsible for obtaining the required level of knowledge. CPAs may obtain that knowledge through, for example, the study of AICPA industry guides, industry publications, and financial statements of entities in the industry.

Knowledge of the client

The accountant's knowledge of the client should be sufficient to assist in determining the specific nature, timing, and extent of review procedures to be performed. The accountant should obtain an understanding of the client's business, including knowledge of the client's organization; operating characteristics; the nature of its assets, liabilities, revenues, and expenses; and material transactions with related parties. The accountant should also obtain an understanding of the accounting principles and practices used by the client in measuring, recognizing, recording, and disclosing all significant accounts and disclosures in the financial statements, remaining alert to any unusual accounting policies and procedures that come to his or her attention.

The required level of understanding of a client's business may be obtained by:

- Previous or current experience in providing the client services such as audits, tax return preparation, compiling of financial statements, and consultation on various financial matters

- Inquiry of client personnel

- Previous or current experience with other entities in the same industry as the client

Designing and Performing Review Procedures

Review procedures should be focused on areas where the accountant believes there are increased risks of misstatements. However, during the performance of review procedures, the accountant's understanding of areas of increased risk may be modified. Exhibit AR 90-4 provides an example of a review program and Exhibit AR 90-5 provides a checklist that can serve as a guide in performing review procedures.

Analytical Procedures

Effective analysis of the results of analytical procedures generally requires an understanding of financial and nonfinancial relationships, knowledge of the client and its industry, and an understanding of the purposes and limitations of analytical procedures. Analytical procedures to be performed for the purpose of a review should be designed to detect relationships and individual items that appear to be unusual and that may indicate a material misstatement. Analytical procedures may be performed at the financial statement or detailed account level and the nature, timing, and extent of the procedures used are a matter of professional judgment. Analytical procedures involve comparing expectations developed by the accountant to recorded amounts or ratios developed from those recorded amounts. An accountant cannot perform effective analytical procedures without first developing expectations related to the results of the procedures. The accountant develops expectations using his or her knowledge of the client and its industry to identify plausible relationships that are reasonably expected to exist. Sources of information used to develop these expectations include:

- Financial information for comparable prior periods, considering known changes

- Anticipated results; for example, budgets, forecasts, or extrapolations from interim or annual data

- Relationships among financial information elements within the period

- Information regarding the industry in which the client operates

- Relationships of financial information with relevant nonfinancial information (e.g., airline revenue to seat miles flown)

The accountant should investigate the results of analytical procedures that are inconsistent with other relevant information or that differ significantly from expected values by inquiring of management and performing other necessary procedures. Although it is not required, the accountant may need to corroborate management's responses to inquiries with other evidence when management is unable to provide an explanation or the explanation along with other evidence obtained is not considered adequate.

Examples of financial statements that would be expected to conform to a predictable relationship are

- Sales and accounts receivable

- Sales and cost of sales

- Interest expense and debt

- Sales and commissions and freight out

- Depreciation and property (also maintenance and repairs)

Moreover, the accountant should consider adjustments made to the financial statements in previous periods, because they might affect his or her judgment on the results of other analytical procedures. In addition, the accountant should consider whether similar adjustments should be made during the current period.

The following approach is appropriate for performing analytical procedures:

1. Identify immaterial account balances or classes of transactions. Apply no analytical procedures to them.

2. Identify account balances or classes of transactions to which other accounting services (bookkeeping or payroll services, for example) have been applied. The accountant should consider the evidence that he or she already has and whether any material errors are likely to remain. If the accountant believes he or she already has sufficient evidence for those account balances or classes of transactions to reduce the risk of material misstatement to a moderate level, he or she should not apply analytical procedures to them.

3. For the remaining account balances and classes of transactions, the accountant should develop expectations (for example, using historical trends adjusted for known changes) for them and document those expectations when those expectations are not otherwise readily determinable from the documentation of the work performed. Exhibit AR 90-8 illustrates how an accountant might document expectations in a review engagement.

4. The accountant should consider how close the existing account balance or class of transactions comes to the expectation developed in item 3. If the differences are small, no additional evidence is needed.

5. If the differences are large, material errors could exist. The accountant should inquire about valid business reasons for the difference. If the results of inquiry are plausible and agree with other evidence, it might be that no additional evidence is needed.

6. If additional evidence is needed, the accountant should apply additional procedures or obtain other suitable evidence. The accountant should document any additional procedures performed in response to significant differences between the expectations and recorded amounts.

Exhibit AR 90-7 lists potential analytical procedures that may be used in a review engagement.

Inquiries and Other Review Procedures

The accountant should consider performing the following:

- Make inquiries of management with responsibility for financial and accounting matters about the following (the accountant may also direct inquiries to those charged with governance and others within the entity, if appropriate):

  — Whether the financial statements have been prepared in conformity with the applicable financial reporting framework

  — The entity's accounting principles and practices and the methods followed in applying them and the entity's procedures for recording, classifying, and summarizing transactions and disclosing information in the financial statements

  — Unusual or complex situations that may have an effect on the financial statements

  — Significant transactions occurring or recognized near the end of the reporting period

— The status of uncorrected misstatements identified during the previous engagement

— Questions that have arisen during the application of review procedures

— Events subsequent to the date of the financial statements that could have a material effect on the financial statements

— Knowledge of any fraud or suspected fraud affecting the entity involving management or others where the fraud could have a material effect on the financial statements

— Significant journal entries and other adjustments

— Communications from regulatory agencies

• Inquire about actions taken at stockholder meetings, board of director and committee meetings, or comparable meetings that may affect the financial statements

• Read the financial statements to consider whether they appear to conform with the applicable financial reporting framework

• Obtain reports from any other accountants engaged to audit or review the financial statements of significant components of the reporting entity, its subsidiaries, and other investees

In addition, the CPA might have identified other questions during the review engagement. The accountant must use professional judgment to determine the extent of inquiries required, and the inquiries must be sufficiently comprehensive to cover all significant amounts and matters. When determining the extent and type of inquiries, the accountant should consider the following items:

• Nature and significance of an item

• Probability of misstatement

• Extent to which management's judgment enters into the determination of a particular item

• Knowledge obtained during a previous or the current engagement

• Qualifications of accounting personnel

• Deficiencies in financial data or the accounting system

Although the accountant is not required to corroborate management's responses with other evidence, he or she should consider the reasonableness and consistency of management's responses given the results of other review procedures and his or her knowledge of the client and its industry. Exhibit AR 90-6 provides a checklist of possible inquiries.

Incorrect, Incomplete, or Otherwise Unsatisfactory Information

The performance of a review does not provide assurance that the accountant will become aware of all significant matters, nor does it provide assurance that inaccuracies or the omission of necessary disclosures will come to his or her attention. However, if the accountant becomes aware during the performance of review procedures that information is incorrect, incomplete or otherwise unsatisfactory, he or she should request management consider the effects of these matters and communicate its findings to him or her. The accountant should then consider management's findings and any effect they may have on the review report.

If the accountant believes the financial statements may be materially misstated, he or she should perform any additional procedures necessary to obtain limited assurance that material modifications to the financial statements are not needed for the statements to be in conformity with the applicable financial reporting framework. Such other procedures may include:

- Further inquiry of responsible persons

- Other accounting services

- Consultation with the client on matters such as the proper accounting principles to be applied in recording transactions or the proper treatment of transactions for tax purposes

When the CPA concludes that additional review procedures should be performed, the circumstances surrounding the questionable information should dictate the degree of corroborative evidence that should be collected. In general, the decision to collect additional evidence does not mean that the level of assurance for a particular item has increased from that of a review engagement (limited assurance) to that of an audit engagement (reasonable assurance). For example, if the CPA is concerned with the nature of a large nontrade note receivable that is presented as a current asset, it does not mean that the CPA must confirm the receivable with the outside party. An appropriate explanation by the client may satisfy the CPA that the note is properly classified in the balance sheet. On the other hand, because of the circumstances of the particular engagement, the CPA may employ extended review procedures that would normally be considered more rigorous than those related to a typical audit engagement.

If the accountant determines that the financial statements are materially misstated, the guidance regarding departures from an applicable financial reporting framework should be followed and, depending on what the accountant considers necessary, he or she should either modify the report or withdraw from the engagement.

Management Representations

The accountant is required to obtain written representations from management for all financial statements and periods covered by the accountant's review report. The specific representations obtained will depend on the engagement circumstances and the nature and basis of presentation of the financial statements. The accountant should request that management provide a written representation related to matters specific to the entity's business or industry as well as to the following matters:

- Management's acknowledgement of its responsibility for preparing and fairly presenting the financial statements

- Management's belief that the financial statements are fairly presented

- Management's acknowledgement of its responsibility for designing, implementing, and maintaining internal control relevant to the preparation and fair presentation of the financial statements

- Management's acknowledgement of its responsibility to prevent and detect fraud

- Knowledge of any fraud or suspected fraud affecting the entity involving management or others where the fraud could have a material effect on the financial statements

- Management's full and truthful response to all inquiries

- Completeness of information

- Information concerning subsequent events

> **FRAUD POINTER:** Given the importance of communications from employees and outside parties in detecting fraud (i.e., tips), the accountant should have management include in its representation letter that no such tips from employees or outside parties have been received.

Exhibit AR 90-2 provides an example management representation letter for financial statement reviews.

In certain situations, the accountant should consider obtaining an updating representation letter from management. One such situation is when a predecessor auditor is requested to reissue a report on the financial statements of a prior period that are to be presented on a comparative basis with reviewed financial statements of a subsequent period. In this case, the updating representation letter should state whether any information has come to management's attention that would cause management to believe any of its previous representations should be modified and whether any events have occurred subsequent to the balance sheet date of the latest financial statements that would require adjustment to or disclosure in those financial statements.

Management's representations should be made as of the date of the accountant's review report. The accountant does not need to possess the management representation letter as of the date of the accountant's review report as long as management has acknowledged they will sign the letter without modification and it is received before release of the report. The representation letter should be addressed to the accountant and signed by members of management the accountant believes are responsible for and knowledgeable about the matters covered in the representation letter, which typically includes the chief executive officer, chief financial officer, or others with equivalent positions in the entity.

> **OBSERVATION:** The accountant must obtain a representation letter for each review engagement that results in the issuance of a review report. For example, if the accountant reviews and reports on quarterly interim financial statements, he or she must obtain a representation letter for each of the four separate and distinct review engagements.

Review Engagement Documentation

Documentation should be prepared for each engagement in sufficient detail to provide a clear understanding of the work, including the nature, timing, extent, and results of review procedures performed; the review evidence obtained and its source; and the conclusions reached. Documentation provides support for the assertion in the review report that the review was performed in accordance with SSARS and for the conclusion that the accountant is not aware of any material modifications that should be made to the financial statements in order for them to be in conformity with the applicable financial reporting framework.

The form, content, and extent of documentation varies depending on the engagement circumstances and the accountant's professional judgment. Documentation should include the following:

- The engagement letter documenting the understanding with the client

- Analytical procedures performed, including the expectations and the factors considered in developing expectations, results of comparing expectations to ratios or recorded amounts, and management's responses to inquiries about relationships that are inconsistent or that differ significantly from expectations

- Any additional review procedures performed in response to significant unexpected differences found in analytical procedures and the results of those additional procedures

- Significant matters covered in the accountant's inquiry procedures and the responses

- Any findings or issues the accountant finds significant in his or her professional judgment

- Significant unusual matters considered during performance of review procedures and the results of this consideration

- Written or oral communications to management regarding fraud or illegal acts that come to the accountant's attention

- The representation letter

In addition to review documentation, the accountant may provide support through written documentation in other engagement or quality control files or through oral explanations. However, oral explanations alone do not provide sufficient support for the accountant's work or conclusions.

Financial Statement Reporting

Reviewed financial statements should be accompanied by a written report in order to prevent misinterpretation of the degree of responsibility the accountant is assuming regarding the financial statements. The following are the basic elements of the accountant's report:

- *Title* The title should clearly indicate it is the accountant's review report and include the word "independent"

- *Addressee* The report should be addressed appropriately

- *Introductory paragraph* This paragraph should identify the entity whose financial statements have been reviewed and the financial statements that have been reviewed; state that the financial statements have been reviewed; specify the date or period covered by the financial statements; include a statement that a review primarily involves management inquiries and applying analytical procedures to management's financial data; and include a statement that a review is substantially less in scope than an audit and, therefore, the accountant does not express an opinion about the financial statements as a whole

- *Management's responsibility for the financial statements and for internal control over financial reporting* A statement that management is responsible for preparing and fairly presenting the financial statements in accordance with the applicable financial reporting framework and for designing, implementing, and maintaining internal control relevant to the preparation and fair presentation of the financial statements

- *Accountant's responsibility* A statement that the accountant is responsible for conducting the review in accordance with SSARS issued by the AICPA, that those standards require the accountant to perform procedures to obtain limited assurance that there are no material modifications that should be made to the statements, and that the accountant believes the results of those procedures provide a reasonable basis for the report

- *Results of engagement* A statement by the accountant that he or she is unaware of any material modifications needed to the financial statements for them to be in accordance with the applicable financial reporting framework (i.e., negative assurance), other than those modifications that the accountant indicates in the report

- *Accountant's signature* The accounting firm's or accountant's manual or printed signature

- *Date of the report* The review report date should not be earlier than the date the accountant has obtained sufficient review evidence to provide a reasonable basis for the conclusion that limited assurance has been obtained that no material modifications should be made to the financial statements in order for them to be in conformity with the applicable financial reporting framework

Any additional procedures that may have been performed should not be described in the accountant's review report, and no reference should be made to the consistent application of GAAP.

Exhibit AR 90-3 provides an example of a standard accountant's review report.

Each page of the reviewed financial statements should contain a reference such as "See Independent Accountant's Review Report." The accountant may issue a review report on one financial statement and not on other related financial statements if the scope of his or her inquiry and analytical procedures has not been restricted. Financial statements prepared in accordance with an OCBOA are not considered appropriate in form unless they include a description of the OCBOA, including a summary of significant accounting policies and a description of the primary differences from GAAP, and informative disclosures similar to those required by GAAP if the financial statements contain items similar to those in financial statements prepared in accordance with GAAP.

A review is incomplete and does not provide a sufficient basis for issuing a review report if the accountant is unable to perform the necessary inquiries and analytical procedures or the client does not provide the accountant with a representation letter. In these circumstances, the accountant should consider whether it is appropriate to issue a compilation report on the financial statements. If the limitation is due to a scope restriction, the accountant should consider whether that restriction is imposed by the client or by circumstance. If the limitation is due to lack of a representation letter, the accountant is ordinarily precluded from issuing a compilation report.

Emphasis of a Matter

The accountant may use his or her discretion to add an emphasis-of-matter paragraph regarding a matter disclosed in the financial statements. This information should be presented in a separate paragraph in the report.

> **OBSERVATION:** Emphasized matters may include uncertainties, that the entity is part of a larger entity, that the entity had significant transactions with related parties, unusually important subsequent events, or accounting matters not involving a change in accounting principle that affect the comparability of the financial statements across periods.

Departures from the Applicable Financial Reporting Framework

The accountant may become aware of material departures from the applicable financial reporting framework (including inadequate disclosure) and, if the financial statements are not revised, should consider the effects on the report. If the accountant concludes that modification of the standard report is adequate to disclose the departure, a separate paragraph should be included in the report disclosing the departure and its effects on the financial statements if the effects have been determined by management or are known based on the accountant's procedures. If management has not determined the effects, the accountant is not required to determine them so long as the report states that such a determination has not been made.

If the accountant believes modification of the report is not adequate to indicate the financial statement deficiencies, he or she should withdraw from the engagement and not perform any further services regarding those financial statements.

> **PLANNING AID REMINDER:** The accountant may wish to consult with legal counsel when withdrawing from an engagement.

If the accountant decides that a modification to the review report is sufficient to disclose the departure from GAAP, the third and fourth paragraphs of the report should read as follows:

> Based on our review, with the exception of the matter described in the following paragraph, we are not aware of any material modifications that should be made to the accompanying financial statements in order for them to be in conformity with generally accepted accounting principles.
>
> As disclosed in Note X to the financial statements, generally accepted accounting principles require that inventory cost consist of material, labor, and overhead. Management has informed us that the inventory of finished goods in the accompanying financial statements is stated at material and direct labor cost only. The effects of this departure from generally accepted accounting principles on financial position, results of operations, and cash flows have not been determined by management.

Restricted Use Reports

A general use report is not restricted to specified parties and is normally used in financial statement reports prepared in conformity with an applicable financial reporting framework. However, the accountant is not precluded from restricting the use of any report. A restricted use report is intended only for one or more specified third parties. A report's use should be restricted when it is based on measurement or disclosure criteria contained in contractual agreements or regulatory provisions that are not in conformity with an applicable financial reporting framework.

If a single combined report is used covering subject matter requiring a restriction on use and subject matter not requiring a restriction on use, the report's use should be restricted to the specified parties. A separate restricted use report may be included in a document also containing a general use report when required by law or regulation. In this situation, both reports maintain their intended use.

The accountant should consider informing the client that restricted use reports are not intended for distribution to nonspecified parties regardless of whether a separate general use report is contained in the same document. However, the accountant is not responsible for controlling the report's distribution. Therefore, a restricted use report should alert readers to its intended use by indicating that it is not intended to and should not be used by anyone other than the specified parties.

A restricted use report should contain a separate paragraph at the end of the report including the following:

• A statement that the report is intended solely for the information and use of specified parties

• Identification of the specified parties included in the restricted use (these parties may be listed in the review report or the report may refer to a listing elsewhere in the document)

• A statement that the report is not intended to be and should not be used by anyone other than the specified parties

Entity's Ability to Continue as a Going Concern

The accountant may become aware during a review engagement that there is uncertainty about the entity's ability to continue as a going concern for a reasonable period of time, not exceeding one year beyond the date of the reviewed financial statements. In these situations, the accountant should request that management consider possible effects of the going concern uncertainty on the financial statements, including the need for disclosure and consider the reasonableness of management's conclusions and the adequacy of any related disclosures.

If the accountant concludes that management's conclusions are not reasonable or that disclosure is inadequate, he or she should follow the guidance regarding departures from an applicable financial reporting framework and, depending on what the accountant considers necessary, either modify the report or withdraw from the engagement. The accountant may emphasize an uncertainty about the entity's ability to continue as a going concern in the report as long as the uncertainty is disclosed in the financial statements.

Exhibit AR 90-9 contains guidance that might be helpful when evaluating an entity's ability to continue as a going concern.

Subsequent Events

Whether during performance of review procedures or subsequent to the date of the review report but prior to the report's release, the accountant may become aware that a subsequent event with a material effect on the reviewed financial statements has occurred. In this situation, the accountant should request that management consider the possible effects on the financial statements and any applicable related disclosures. If the accountant determines the subsequent event is not adequately accounted for in the financial statements or disclosed in the notes, the guidance regarding departures from an applicable financial reporting framework should be followed and, depending on what the accountant considers necessary, he or she should either modify the report or withdraw for the engagement.

> **OBSERVATION:** Two types of subsequent events require consideration by management. The first type consists of events that provide additional evidence with respect to conditions that existed at the date of the financial statements. The financial statements should be adjusted for any changes in estimates resulting from the use of such evidence. The second type consists of events that provide evidence with respect to conditions that did not exist at the date of the balance sheet being reported on but that arose subsequent to that date. These events should not result in adjustments of the financial statements but rather be reflected via a note to the financial statements.

Subsequent Discovery of Facts Existing at the Date of the Report

The accountant may become aware of facts existing at the date of the report subsequent to that date that, had he or she been aware of them, may have caused him or her to believe the information supplied by the entity was incorrect, incomplete, or otherwise unsatisfactory. In these circumstances, consulting with legal counsel is advised because of the legal implications involved.

The accountant has no obligation to perform other review procedures with respect to the financial statements after the date of the review report unless new information comes to the accountant's attention. However, when information comes to the accountant's attention that would have been investigated had it been known during the course of the review, the accountant should try to determine whether the information is reliable and whether the facts existed at the date of the report. The accountant should discuss the matter with management and, as necessary, those charged with governance. The accountant should perform the additional procedures necessary to obtain limited assurance that no material modifications should be made to the financial statements in order for the statements to be in conformity with the applicable financial reporting framework if (1) the matter's nature and effect would have affected the accountant's report or the financial statements if the information had been known at the report date and included in the financial statements and (2) the accountant believes there are users or likely users of the financial statements that would find the information important. Consideration should be given to the time elapsed since the financial statements were issued.

If the accountant concludes that action should be taken to prevent further use of the report or financial statements, he or she should advise the client to appropriately disclose the newly discovered facts and their impact on the financial statements to current and likely financial statement users. If the effect of the subsequently discovered information can be readily determined, disclosure should consist of issuing revised financial information and a new report as soon as practicable, disclosing the reasons for the revision in a note to the financial statements, and referring to them in the report when applicable. If issuance of subsequent financial statements is imminent, appropriate disclosure can be made in those statements rather than reissuing the earlier statements because disclosure would not be delayed. If the effect of the subsequently discovered information on the financial statements cannot promptly be determined, appropriate disclosure consists of the client informing current or likely financial statement users that the statements should not be used and that revised financial statements and a new accountant's report will be issued as soon as practicable.

The accountant should take whatever steps he or she feels are necessary to ensure the specified disclosures have been made. If the client refuses to make the specified disclosures, the accountant should notify persons at the highest level of the entity of such refusal and that without those disclosures the accountant will have to take steps to prevent further use of the financial statements and his or her report. The accountant's knowledge that people exist who are using the financial statements and accountant's report and would attach importance to the information as well as the accountant's ability to communicate with these people will affect the steps he or she is able to take. Unless otherwise recommended by the accountant's attorney, the accountant should take the following steps in these circumstances as applicable:

1. Notify the client that the accountant's report must no longer be associated with the financial statements

2. Notify regulatory agencies with jurisdiction over the client that the accountant's report should no longer be used

3. Notify each person known to the accountant to be using the financial statements that the financial statements and accountant's report should no longer be used

Any disclosure made by the accountant to those other than the client should include a description of the nature of the subsequently acquired information and its effect on the financial statements. Also, the information disclosed should be as precise and factual as possible without going beyond what is reasonably necessary to describe the nature and effects of the information and without commenting on anyone's conduct or motives. If the client has not cooperated with the accountant, he or she may disclose this lack of cooperation in attempting to substantiate information coming to his or her attention and that, if the information is true, the accountant believes the review report must no longer be used or associated with the financial statements.

Supplementary Information

The accountant should clearly indicate the degree of responsibility taken with respect to information presented for supplementary analysis purposes with the basic financial statements. This indication should state that other data accompanying the financial statements are presented only for additional analysis and either have been subjected to the procedures applied in reviewing the financial statements and the accountant did not become aware of any material modifications that should be made to the data, or that the data have not been subjected to the procedures applied in reviewing the financial statements but were compiled from management's information without audit or review and the accountant does not express an opinion or provide any assurance on the data.

Communications with Management and Others

When information comes to the accountant's attention that fraud or an illegal act may have occurred, it should be brought to management's attention unless the matter deals with a clearly inconsequential illegal act. If the fraud or illegal act involves senior management, the accountant should report the matter to someone at a higher level in the entity, such as the owner-manager or those charged with governance. Communication may be written or oral, but if the communication is oral, it should be documented. If the matter involves an owner of the entity, the accountant should consider withdrawing from the engagement. The accountant should also consider consulting with his or her legal counsel whenever information comes to his or her attention that fraud or an illegal act may have occurred.

The accountant is typically precluded by ethical and legal confidentiality obligations from disclosing information that fraud or an illegal act may have occurred to parties other than the client's management or those charged with governance. There are exceptions that may impose a duty to disclose such information, such as complying with legal and regulatory requirements, communicating with a successor accountant, or responding to a subpoena.

Change in Engagement Type

An accountant may be requested to change from an audit to a review engagement before completion of the audit. This request may be due to a change in the entity's circumstances affecting its requirements for an audit or a misunderstanding about the nature of services to be provided. Either of these reasons is typically considered a reasonable basis for requesting a change in the engagement.

In considering whether a request to change to a review engagement is reasonable, the accountant should consider the client's reasons for the request, especially the implications of a scope restriction whether imposed by client or circumstance, evaluating the possibility that information affected by the scope restriction could be incorrect, incomplete, or otherwise unsatisfactory. Also, if audit procedures are substantially complete or the cost to complete the additional procedures is insignificant, the accountant should consider the reasonableness of accepting a change in the engagement.

A review report may not be issued if the review procedures deemed necessary by the accountant have not been completed to his or her satisfaction. In such situations, there is no adequate basis for expressing the limited assurance contemplated by a review. Moreover, the circumstances may be such that the accountant may not issue a compilation report. Information the accountant obtains during the performance of an incomplete review cannot be ignored if the engagement is reduced to a compilation.

When determining whether to issue a compilation report where a review is incomplete, the accountant should consider the same points that would be considered for an engagement that is changed from a higher service level to a lower service level.

Review standards require that an accountant perform whatever additional procedures he or she deems necessary under the circumstances. Additional procedures may include corresponding with the client's legal counsel or confirming balances and transactions. If the client will not agree to such correspondence or will not sign a representation letter, there is a scope limitation, which is usually considered to be of such significance that the accountant should not issue a review report.

Practitioner's Aids

EXHIBIT AR 90-1 — REVIEW ENGAGEMENT LETTER

Exhibit AR 90-1 is an example of a standard engagement letter for a review.

[Appropriate Salutation]

This letter is to confirm our understanding of the terms and objectives of our engagement and the nature and limitations of the services we will provide.

We will perform the following services:

We will review the financial statements of ABC Company as of December 31, 20X8, and issue an accountant's report thereon in accordance with Statements on Standards for Accounting and Review Services (SSARSs) issued by the American Institute of Certified Public Accountants (AICPA).

The objective of a review is to obtain limited assurance that there are no material modifications that should be made to the financial statements in order for the statements to be in conformity with *[the applicable financial reporting framework (for example,* accounting principles generally accepted in the United States of America*)]*.

You are responsible for

a. The preparation and fair presentation of the financial statements in accordance with *[the applicable financial reporting framework (for example,* accounting principles generally accepted in the United States of America*)]*.

b. Designing, implementing, and maintaining internal control relevant to the preparation and fair presentation of the financial statements.

c. Preventing and detecting fraud.

d. Identifying and ensuring that the entity complies with the laws and regulations applicable to its activities.

e. Making all financial records and related information available to us.

f. Providing us, at the conclusion of the engagement, with a letter that confirms certain representations made during the review.

We are responsible for conducting the engagement in accordance with SSARS issued by the AICPA.

A review includes primarily applying analytical procedures to your financial data and making inquiries of company management. A review is substantially less in scope than an audit, the objective of which is the expression of an opinion regarding the financial statements as a whole. A review does not contemplate obtaining an understanding of the entity's internal control; assessing fraud risk; testing accounting records by obtaining sufficient appropriate audit evidence through inspection, observation, confirmation, or the examination of source documents (for example, cancelled checks or bank images); or other procedures ordinarily performed in an audit. Accordingly, we will not express an opinion regarding the financial statements as a whole.

Our engagement cannot be relied upon to disclose errors, fraud, or illegal acts. However, we will inform the appropriate level of management of any material errors and any evidence or information that comes to our attention during the performance of our review procedures that fraud may have occurred. In addition, we will report to you any evidence or information that comes to our attention during the performance of our review procedures regarding illegal acts that may have occurred, unless they are clearly inconsequential.

If, for any reason, we are unable to complete the review of your financial statements, we will not issue a report on such statements as a result of this engagement.

Our fees for these services [...].

We will be pleased to discuss this letter with you at any time. If the foregoing is in accordance with your understanding, please sign the copy of this letter in the space provided and return it to us.

Sincerely yours,

[*Signature of Accountant*]

Acknowledged:

ABC Company

[*Signature of President*]

[*Date*]

EXHIBIT AR 90-2 — MANAGEMENT REPRESENTATION LETTER

Exhibit AR 90-2 is an example management representation letter for financial statement reviews.

[*Date (The date of the representation letter should not be earlier than the date of the accountant's review report)*]

To [*the Accountant*]

We are providing this letter in connection with your review of the [*identification of financial statements*] of [*name of entity*] as of [*dates (for example,* December 31, 20X1 and December 31, 20X2*)*] and for the [*periods of review (for example,* for the years then ended*)*] for the purpose of obtaining limited assurance that there are no material modifications that should be made to the financial statements in order for the statements to be in conformity with [*the applicable financial reporting framework (for example,* accounting principles generally accepted in the United States of America*)*]. We confirm that we are responsible for the fair presentation of the financial statements in accordance with [*the applicable financial reporting framework*] and the selection and application of the accounting policies.

Certain representations in this letter are described as being limited to matters that are material. Items are considered material, regardless of size, if they involve an omission or misstatement of accounting information that, in the light of surrounding circumstances, makes it probable that the judgment of a reasonable person using the information would be changed or influenced by the omission or misstatement.

We confirm, to the best of our knowledge and belief (as of [*the date of the accountant's review report*]), the following representations made to you during your review:

1. The financial statements referred to previously are fairly presented in accordance with [*the applicable financial reporting framework (for example,* accounting principles generally accepted in the United States of America*)*].

2. We have made the following available to you

    a. Financial records and related data.

    b. Minutes of the meetings of stockholders, directors, and committees of directors, or summaries of actions of recent meetings for which minutes have not yet been prepared.

3. No material transactions exist that have not been properly recorded in the accounting records underlying the financial statements.

4. We acknowledge our responsibility for the preparation and fair presentation of the financial statements in accordance with [*the applicable financial reporting framework (for example,* accounting principles generally accepted in the United States of America*)*].

5. We acknowledge our responsibility for designing, implementing, and maintaining internal control relevant to the preparation and fair presentation of the financial statements.

6. We acknowledge our responsibility to prevent and detect fraud.

7. We have no knowledge of any fraud or suspected fraud affecting the entity involving management or others where the fraud could have a material effect on the financial statements, including any communications received from employees, former employees, or others.

8. We have no plans or intentions that may materially affect the carrying amounts or classification of assets and liabilities.

9. No material losses exist (such as from obsolete inventory or purchase or sales commitments) that have not been properly accrued or disclosed in the financial statements.

10. None of the following exist:

    a. Violations or possible violations of laws or regulations, whose effects should be considered for disclosure in the financial statements or as a basis for recording a loss contingency

    b. Unasserted claims or assessments that our lawyer has advised us are probable of assertion that must be disclosed in accordance with Financial Accounting Standards Board (FASB) *Accounting Standards Codification* (ASC) 450, *Contingencies.*

    c. Other material liabilities or gain or loss contingencies that are required to be accrued or disclosed by FASB ASC 450.

11. The company has satisfactory title to all owned assets, and no liens or encumbrances on such assets exist, nor has any asset been pledged as collateral, except as disclosed to you and reported in the financial statements.

12. We have complied with all aspects of contractual agreements that would have a material effect on the financial statements in the event of noncompliance.

13. The following have been properly recorded or disclosed in the financial statements:

    a. Related-party transactions, including sales, purchases, loans, transfers, leasing arrangements, and guarantees, and amounts receivable from or payable to related parties.

    b. Guarantees, whether written or oral, under which the company is contingently liable.

    c. Significant estimates and material concentrations known to management that are required to be disclosed in accordance with the FASB ASC 275, *Risks and Uncertainties.*
    [*Add additional representations that are unique to the entity's business or industry.*]

14. We are in agreement with the adjusting journal entries you have recommended, and they have been posted to the company's accounts (if applicable).

15. To the best of our knowledge and belief, no events have occurred subsequent to the balance-sheet date and through the date of this letter that would require adjustment to or disclosure in the aforementioned financial statements.

16. We have responded fully and truthfully to all inquiries made to us by you during your review.

[*Name of Owner or Chief Executive Officer and Title*]

[*Name of Chief Financial Officer and Title, when applicable*]

> **OBSERVATION:** The accountant may decide based on engagement circumstances or the client's industry that other matters should be specifically included in the letter or that some of the representations included in the illustrative letter above are not necessary. SSARS-19 includes examples of representations that may be tailored to an entity's business or industry.

EXHIBIT AR 90-3 — STANDARD ACCOUNTANT'S REVIEW REPORT

Exhibit AR 90-3 is an example of a standard review report on financial statements prepared in accordance with accounting principles generally accepted in the United States of America.

Independent Accountant's Review Report

[Appropriate Salutation]

I (we) have reviewed the accompanying balance sheet of ABC Company as of December 31, 20X8, and the related statements of income, retained earnings, and cash flows for the year then ended. A review includes primarily applying analytical procedures to management's (owners') financial data and making inquiries of company management (owners). A review is substantially less in scope than an audit, the objective of which is to express an opinion regarding the financial statements as a whole. Accordingly, I (we) do not express such an opinion.

Management (owners) is (are) responsible for the preparation and fair presentation of the financial statements in accordance with accounting principles generally accepted in the United States of America and for designing, implementing, and maintaining internal control relevant to the preparation and fair presentation of the financial statements.

My (our) responsibility is to conduct the review in accordance with Statements on Standards for Accounting and Review Services issued by the American Institute of Certified Public Accountants. These standards require me (us) to perform procedures to obtain limited assurance that there are no material modifications that should be made to the financial statements. I (We) believe that the results of my (our) procedures provide a reasonable basis for our report.

Based on my (our) review, I am (we are) not aware of any material modifications that should be made to the accompanying financial statements in order for them to be in conformity with accounting principles generally accepted in the United States of America.

[Signature of accounting firm or accountant, as appropriate]

[Date]

EXHIBIT AR 90-4 — REVIEW PROGRAM

Use the following procedures as a guide for performing a continuing review engagement. The review program is only a guide, and professional judgment should be exercised to determine how the procedures should be modified by revising procedures listed or adding procedures to the review program.

Initial and date each procedure as it is completed. If the procedure is not relevant to this particular review engagement, place "N/A" (not applicable) in the space provided for an initial.

Client Name: _____

Date of Financial Statements: _____

Date of Review Report: _____

	Initials	Date	Workpaper Reference
1. Acquire an adequate understanding of accounting principles and practices of the client's industry and methods of applying them.	_____	___	_____
2. Develop an understanding of the client's organization.	_____	___	_____
3. Develop an understanding of the client's operating characteristics.	_____	___	_____
4. Develop an understanding of the nature of the client's assets, liabilities, revenues, and expenses.	_____	___	_____
5. Make inquiries concerning the client's accounting principles, practices, and methods.	_____	___	_____
6. Make inquiries concerning the client's procedures for recording, classifying, and summarizing transactions and accumulating information for disclosure in the financial statements.	_____	___	_____

	Initials	Date	Workpaper Reference
7. Make inquiries concerning actions taken at meetings of stockholders, board of directors, or other meetings that may affect the financial statements.	____	___	_____
8. Make inquiries concerning the consistent application of GAAP.	____	___	_____
9. Make inquiries concerning changes in the client's business activities or accounting principles and the implication for financial statements.	____	___	_____
10. Make inquiries concerning occurrence of subsequent events that may have a material effect on the financial statements.	____	___	_____
11. Make inquiries regarding the extent of unusual or complex situations that might exist and that have a material effect on the financial statements.	____	___	_____
12. Make inquiries about whether significant transactions occurred or were recognized in the last several days of the reporting period.	____	___	_____
13. Inquire about the status of uncorrected misstatements identified in prior engagements.	____	___	_____
14. Inquire regarding whether management has any knowledge of fraud or suspected fraud affecting the entity that might involve management or others that could materially misstate the financial statements.	____	___	_____
15. Make inquiries concerning the types of significant journal entries or other adjustments that exist.	____	___	_____
16. Inquire regarding whether the client has received communications from regulatory agencies.	____	___	_____
17. Apply analytical procedures to identify relationships and individual items that appear to be unusual.	____	___	_____

	Initials	*Date*	*Workpaper Reference*
18. Consider whether other professional services are needed before starting the review engagement.	____	____	_____
19. If appropriate, obtain reports from other accountants.	____	____	_____
20. Consider whether other review procedures should be performed on the basis of the results of performing the minimum review procedures.	____	____	_____
21. Read the financial statements to consider if they conform with GAAP.	____	____	_____
22. Obtain a client representation letter.	____	____	_____
23. Other review procedures: _____			

Reviewed By: _____

Date: _____

EXHIBIT AR 90-5 — REVIEW QUESTIONNAIRE CHECKLIST

Use the following checklist as a guide for performing review procedures. The checklist is only a guide, and professional judgment should be exercised to determine how the checklist should be modified by revising questions listed or adding questions to the checklist where appropriate.

Initial and date each question as it is considered. If the question is not relevant to this particular review engagement, place "N/A" (not applicable) in the space provided for an initial. If the answer to the question is "no" or if additional explanation is needed with respect to a question, provide a proper cross-reference to another workpaper.

Client Name: _____

Date of Financial Statements: _____

	Initials	Date	Workpaper Reference

1. Have we acquired an adequate understanding of specialized accounting principles and practices of the client's industry by

   • Reviewing relevant AICPA Accounting/Audit Guides? ____ ____ _____

   • Reviewing financial statements of other entities in the same industry? ____ ____ _____

   • Consulting with other individuals familiar with accounting practices in the specialized industry? ____ ____ _____

   • Reading periodicals, textbooks, and other publications? ____ ____ _____

   • Performing other procedures? ____ ____ _____

2. Have we developed an understanding of the client's organization, including

   • The form of business organization? ____ ____ _____

   • The history of the client? ____ ____ _____

   • The principals involved in the organizational chart or similar analysis? ____ ____ _____

   • Other relevant matters? ____ ____ _____

3. Have we developed an understanding of the client's operating characteristics, including

   • An understanding of the client's products and services? ____ ____ _____

   • Identification of operating locations? ____ ____ _____

   • An understanding of production methods? ____ ____ _____

   • Other operating characteristics? ____ ____ _____

4. Have we developed an understanding of the nature of the client's assets, liabilities, revenues, and expenses by

   • Reviewing the client's chart of accounts? ____ ____ _____

	Initials	Date	Workpaper Reference
• Reviewing the previous year's financial statements?	_____	___	_____
• Considering the relationships between specific accounts and the nature of the client's business?	_____	___	_____
• Performing other procedures?	_____	___	_____

5. Have we made inquiries concerning accounting principles, practices, and methods?   _____   ___   _____

6. Have we made inquiries concerning the accounting procedures used by the client, including

   • Recording transactions?   _____   ___   _____
   • Classifying transactions?   _____   ___   _____
   • Summarizing transactions?   _____   ___   _____
   • Accumulating information for making disclosures in the financial statements?   _____   ___   _____
   • Other accounting procedures?   _____   ___   _____

7. Have we made inquiries concerning the effect on the financial statements due to actions taken at meetings of

   • Stockholders?   _____   ___   _____
   • The board of directors?   _____   ___   _____
   • Other committees?   _____   ___   _____

8. If there were changes in the application of accounting principles

   • Did the change in accounting principle include the adoption of another acceptable accounting principle?   _____   ___   _____
   • Was the change properly justified?   _____   ___   _____
   • Were the effects of the change presented in the financial statements, including adequate disclosure, in a   _____   ___   _____

	Initials	Date	Workpaper Reference

manner consistent with FAS-154 (ASC 250)?

- Were there other matters that we took into consideration? ___ ___ _____

9. Have we made inquiries concerning changes in the client's business activities that may require the adoption of different accounting principles, and have we considered the implication of this change for the financial statements? ___ ___ _____

10. Have we made inquiries concerning the occurrence of events subsequent to the date of the financial statements that may require

- Adjustments to the financial statements? ___ ___ _____

- Disclosures in the financial statements? ___ ___ _____

11. Have we made inquiries regarding the extent of unusual or complex situations that might exist and that have a material effect on the financial statements? ___ ___ _____

12. Have we made inquiries about whether significant transactions occurred or were recognized in the last several days of the reporting period? ___ ___ _____

13. Have we inquired about the status of uncorrected misstatements identified in prior engagements? ___ ___ _____

14. Have we inquired regarding whether management has any knowledge of fraud or suspected fraud affecting the entity that might involve management or others that could ___ ___ _____

	Initials	*Date*	*Workpaper Reference*

materially misstate the financial statements?

15. Have we made inquiries concerning the types of significant journal entries or other adjustments that exist?

16. Have we inquired regarding whether the client has received communications from regulatory agencies?

17. Have we performed analytical procedures, including

   • Comparing current financial statements with comparable prior period(s)?

   • Comparing current financial statements with anticipated results?

   • Studying financial statement elements and expected relationships?

   • Other analytical procedures?

   • Documenting our expectations?

18. Have we considered whether other professional services are needed in order to complete the review engagement, including

   • Preparing a working trial balance?

   • Preparing adjusting journal entries?

   • Consulting matters fundamental to the preparation of acceptable financial statements?

   • Preparing tax returns?

   • Providing bookkeeping or data processing services that do not include the generation of financial statements?

	Initials	Date	Workpaper Reference

- Considering other services that may be necessary before a review can be performed?

19. Have we obtained reports from other CPA(s) who reported on the financial statements of components of the client-reporting entity? _____ ____ _____

20. Have we read the financial statements to determine whether they appear to be in accordance with GAAP based on the information that has come to our attention? _____ ____ _____

21. Have we obtained a client representation letter? _____ ____ _____

22. Have we used other procedures to resolve questions during the review arrangement? _____ ____

Reviewed By: _____

EXHIBIT AR 90-6 — INQUIRY CHECKLIST FOR A REVIEW ENGAGEMENT

Use this checklist to document inquiries made concerning accounting procedures used by the client. The checklist is only a guide, and professional judgment should be exercised to determine how the checklist should be modified by revising questions listed or adding questions where appropriate.

If a question is not relevant to this particular review engagement, place "N/A" (not applicable) in the space provided for a comment. If an additional explanation is needed in response to the question, provide a proper cross-reference to another workpaper. Note the source of the information in the space provided after each question.

Client Name: _____

Date of Financial Statements: _____

Sources of Information: _____

_____

_____

_____

Date: _____

_____

	Yes	No	*Date of Inquiry*	*Comment*

GENERAL

1. What are the procedures for recording, classifying, and summarizing transactions in the financial statements, including relevant disclosures? ___ ___ _____ _____

2. Do general ledger control accounts agree with subsidiary ledger accounts? ___ ___ _____ _____

3. Have the financial statements been prepared in accordance with generally accepted accounting principles consistently applied? ___ ___ _____ _____

CASH

1. Have bank balances been reconciled with book balances? ___ ___ _____ _____

   Source:

2. Have old or unusual reconciling items between bank balances and book balances been reviewed and adjustments made where necessary? ___ ___ _____ _____

   Source:

3. Has a proper cutoff of cash transactions been made? ___ ___ _____ _____

   Source:

4. ___ ___ _____ _____

	Yes	No	*Date of* *Inquiry*	*Comment*

Are there any restrictions on the avail-ability of cash balances?

Source:

5. Have cash funds been counted and re-conciled with control accounts?

| | — | — | —— | —— |

Source:

6. Have cash overdrafts been classified as current liabilities?

| | — | — | —— | —— |

Source:

7. Have amounts that represent tempo-rary investments been identified and reclassified?

| | — | — | —— | —— |

Source:

INVESTMENTS IN MARKETABLE EQUITY SECURITIES

1. Have investments in marketable equi-ty securities been classified into trad-ing securities and available-for-sale securities?

| | — | — | —— | —— |

Source:

2. Have trading securities and available-for-sale securities been carried at mar-ket value on the balance sheet?

| | — | — | —— | —— |

Source:

3. Has management determined market value based on prices in active mar-kets and, if not, how has market value been obtained?

| | — | — | —— | —— |

Source:

4.

| | — | — | —— | —— |

	Yes	No	Date of Inquiry	Comment

Have available-for-sale securities been classified into a current and non-current portfolio?

Source:

5. Have unrealized changes in the market value of trading securities since the prior year's financial statements been recorded in the income statement?

Source:

6. Has the cumulative difference between the market value of available-for-sale securities and their book value been recorded as a component of stockholders' equity? Have changes in this account been recognized as a component of Other Comprehensive Income during the year?

Source:

7. Have marketable equity securities been evaluated to determine reductions that are other than temporary?

Source:

8. Have gains or losses from the sale of marketable equity securities been reported on the income statement?

Source:

9. Have dividends received on marketable equity securities been reported on the income statement?

Source:

	Yes	No	Date of Inquiry	Comment

10. Has an analysis been made to accrue dividends declared but not paid at the end of the period?

   Source:

11. Have reclassifications between trading securities and available-for-sale securities been accounted for in accordance with FAS-115 (ASC 320) (Accounting for Certain Investments in Debt and Equity Securities) and related FASB Staff Guidance?

   Source:

INVESTMENTS IN DEBT
SECURITIES

1. Have investments in marketable debt securities been classified into trading securities, available-for-sale securities, and hold-to-maturity securities?

   Source:

2. Have trading securities and available-for-sale securities been carried at market value on the balance sheet?

   Source:

3. Has management determined market value based on prices in active markets and, if not, how has market value been determined?

   Source:

4. Have hold-to-maturity securities been carried at amortized cost, where amortized cost is determined using the effective interest method (unless the

| | *Date of* | |
Yes	No	*Inquiry*	*Comment*

results from using the straight-line method of amortizing premium or discount are immaterially different)?

Source:

5. Have available-for-sale securities and hold-to-maturity securities been classified into a current and noncurrent portfolio?

Source:

6. Have unrealized changes in the market value of trading securities since the prior year's financial statements been recorded in the income statement?

Source:

7. Has the cumulative difference between the market value of available-for-sale securities and their book value been recorded as a component of stockholders' equity? Have changes in this account been recognized as a component of Other Comprehensive Income during the year?

Source:

8. Have marketable debt securities been evaluated to determine reductions that are other than temporary?

Source:

9. Have gains or losses from the sale of marketable debt securities been reported on the income statement?

Source:

10.

	Yes	No	Date of Inquiry	Comment

Has interest income been recognized on the income statement, including an analysis of accrued interest income at the end of the period?

Source:

RECEIVABLES

1. Has a reasonable allowance been made for doubtful accounts?

    Source:

2. Have receivables considered uncollectible been written off?

    Source:

3. If appropriate, has interest been reflected?

    Source:

4. Has a proper cutoff of sales transactions been made?

    Source:

5. Are there any receivables from employees and related parties?

    Source:

6. Are any receivables pledged, discounted, or factored?

    Source:

7. Have receivables been properly classified between current and noncurrent?

	Yes	No	Date of Inquiry	Comment

Source:

8. Have noncurrent receivables been evaluated to determine whether they carry a reasonable interest rate? __ __ ____ _____

Source:

INVENTORIES

1. Have inventories been physically counted? (If not, how have inventory quantities been determined?) __ __ ____ _____

Source:

2. Have general ledger control accounts been adjusted to agree with physical inventories? __ __ ____ _____

Source:

3. If physical inventories are taken at a date other than the balance sheet date, have appropriate procedures been used to record changes in inventory between the date of the count and the balance sheet date? __ __ ____ _____

Source:

4. Were consignments in or out considered in taking physical inventories? __ __ ____ _____

Source:

5. Has inventory been valued using an inventory method consistent with that of the previous period? __ __ ____ _____

Source:

6. Does inventory cost include material, labor, and overhead where applicable? __ __ ____ _____

	Yes	No	Date of Inquiry	Comment

Source:

7. Have write-downs for obsolescence or cost in excess of net realizable value been made? — — ____ _____

Source:

8. Have proper cutoffs of purchases, goods in transit, and returned goods been made? — — ____ _____

Source:

9. Are there any inventory encumbrances? — — ____ _____

Source:

10. Have there been any exchanges during the period that involve similar items? — — ____ _____

Source:

PROPERTY, PLANT, AND EQUIPMENT

1. Have gains or losses on disposal of property or equipment been properly reflected? — — ____ _____

Source:

2. Have the criteria for capitalizing property, plant, and equipment been established, and have they been applied during the fiscal period? — — ____ _____

Source:

3. Does the repairs and maintenance account only include expenses? — — ____ _____

Source:

4. — — ____ _____

	Yes	No	Date of Inquiry	Comment

Are property, plant, and equipment stated at cost?

Source:

5. Have depreciation methods been applied in a consistent manner? ___ ___ _____ _____

Source:

6. Are there any unrecorded additions, retirements, abandonments, sales, or trade-ins? ___ ___ _____ _____

Source:

7. Does the client have material lease agreements, and have they been properly reflected in the financial statements? ___ ___ _____ _____

Source:

8. Is any property, plant, or equipment mortgaged or otherwise encumbered? ___ ___ _____ _____

Source:

9. Have there been any exchanges during the period that involved similar items? ___ ___ _____ _____

Source:

10. Has the client evaluated its fixed assets for possible evidence of impairment and, if impaired, has the appropriate write-off been recognized on the income statement? ___ ___ _____ _____

Source:

PREPAID EXPENSES

	Yes	No	Date of Inquiry	Comment

1. Have the items included in prepaid expenses been evaluated to determine whether they are appropriately classified as prepayments?   ___ ___ ___ ___

    Source:

2. Has a rational and systematic method been used to amortize prepaid expenses, and has the method been used in a manner consistent with the previous period?   ___ ___ ___ ___

    Source:

INTANGIBLE ASSETS

1. Have the items included in intangible assets been evaluated to determine whether they are appropriately classified as intangible assets?   ___ ___ ___ ___

    Source:

2. Have intangible assets with indefinite useful lives been evaluated for possible impairment and, if impaired, has the appropriate write-off been recognized on the income statement?   ___ ___ ___ ___

    Source:

3. Has the straight-line method been used to amortize the cost of intangible assets with determinative useful lives and has the amortization method been used in a manner consistent with the previous period?   ___ ___ ___ ___

    Source:

	Yes	No	*Date of Inquiry*	*Comment*

OTHER ASSETS

1. Have the items included in other assets been evaluated to determine whether they are appropriately classified?

    Source:

2. Has each item classified as other assets been accounted for in accordance with GAAP?

    Source:

3. Have any of the other assets been mortgaged or otherwise encumbered?

    Source:

ACCOUNTS AND NOTES PAYABLE AND ACCRUED LIABILITIES

1. Have all significant payables been reflected in the financial statements?

    Source:

2. Have all short-term liabilities been properly classified?

    Source:

3. Have all significant accruals, such as payroll, interest, and provisions for pension and profit-sharing plans, been properly reflected in the financial statements?

    Source:

		Date of	
Yes	*No*	*Inquiry*	*Comment*

4. Have any of the liabilities been collateralized?

   Source:

5. Are there any payables to employees and related parties?

   Source:

LONG-TERM LIABILITIES

1. Have the terms and other provisions of long-term liability agreements been properly reflected in the financial statements?

   Source:

2. Have liabilities been evaluated to determine whether they are properly classified as noncurrent?

   Source:

3. Has interest expense been properly reflected in the financial statements?

   Source:

4. Has there been compliance with restrictive covenants of loan agreements?

   Source:

5. Have any of the long-term liabilities been collateralized or subordinated?

   Source:

6. Has pension liability been determined in accordance with FAS-87 (ASC 715) (including, if applicable, the computation of a minimum liability)?

   Source:

	Yes	*No*	*Date of Inquiry*	*Comment*

INCOME AND OTHER TAXES

1. Has provision been made for current- and prior-year federal income taxes payable?

   Source:

2. Have any assessments or reassessments been received, and are tax examinations in process?

   Source:

3. Have differences between accounting methods used in the financial statements and those used in the tax return been properly reflected in the financial statements?

   Source:

4. Has the income statement been prepared to reflect intraperiod income tax allocation?

   Source:

5. Has provision been made for state and local income, franchise, sales, and other taxes payable?

   Source:

OTHER LIABILITIES, CONTINGENCIES, AND COMMITMENTS

1. Have the items included in other liabilities been evaluated to determine whether they are properly classified?

	Yes	No	*Date of Inquiry*	*Comment*

Source:

2. Have the items included in other liabilities been evaluated to determine whether they are current or noncurrent?

Source:

3. Are there any contingent liabilities such as discounted notes, drafts, endorsements, warranties, litigation, unsettled asserted claims, and unasserted potential claims?

Source:

4. Are there any material contractual obligations for construction or purchase of real property and equipment and any commitments or options to purchase or sell company securities?

Source:

EQUITY

1. Have changes in equity accounts for the period been properly accounted for and presented in the financial statements?

Source:

2. Have all classes of authorized capital stock been identified and properly reflected in the financial statements?

Source:

3. Has the par or stated value of the various classes of stock been identified and properly reflected in the financial statements?

	Yes	No	*Date of Inquiry*	*Comment*

Source:

4. Has there been a reconciliation between the number of outstanding shares of capital stock and subsidiary records?

Source:

5. Have capital stock preferences, if any, been properly disclosed?

Source:

6. Have stock options been granted?

Source:

7. Has the client made any acquisitions of its own capital stock?

Source:

8. Has a determination been made as to whether there are any restrictions on retained earnings or other capital accounts?

Source:

REVENUES AND EXPENSES

1. Has the propriety and reasonableness of revenue recognition methods been considered?

2. Has there been a proper cutoff for the recognition of revenues from the sale of major products and services?

Source:

3. Has there been a proper cutoff for the measurement of expenses and pur-

	Yes	No	Date of Inquiry	Comment

chases of inventory made during the period?

Source:

4. Are revenues and expenses properly classified in the financial statements? ___ ___ _____ _____

Source:

5. Has an evaluation been made to determine whether the financial statements properly include discontinued operations or items that may be considered extraordinary? ___ ___ _____ _____

Source:

OTHER

1. Have there been any material transactions between the client and related parties? ___ ___ _____ _____

Source:

2. Have there been evaluations to determine whether there are any material uncertainties? ___ ___ _____ _____

Source:

3. Has the status of material uncertainties previously disclosed been evaluated? ___ ___ _____ _____

Source:

4. Are there any subsequent events that have a material effect on the financial statements? ___ ___ _____ _____

Source:

	Yes	No	*Date of Inquiry*	*Comment*

CONSOLIDATION

1. Have all subsidiaries been evaluated to determine whether they should be included in the consolidated financial statements?

    Source:

2. Have all divisions and branches been included in the client's financial statements?

    Source:

3. Have all intercompany and intracompany accounts and transactions been eliminated?

    Source:

4. For intercorporate investments not consolidated, has there been an evaluation as to whether the equity method or the cost method should be used to account for the investment?

    Source:

5. Has there been any change in the accounting for an intercorporate investment?

    Source:

STATEMENT OF CASH FLOWS

1. Has a statement of cash flows been prepared?

	Yes	No	Date of Inquiry	Comment

Source:

2. Has there been an evaluation to determine whether the focus of the statement should be cash, or cash and cash equivalents?   __ __ _____ _____

Source:

3. If the direct method of determining cash flows from operations is not used, has a supplemental reconciliation been included in the financial statement disclosures?   __ __ _____ _____

Source:

EXHIBIT AR 90-7 — ANALYTICAL PROCEDURES FOR A REVIEW ENGAGEMENT

Use this form to document the performance of analytical procedures for a review engagement. The form is only a guide, and professional judgment should be exercised to determine how the form should be modified by omitting or adding analytical procedures.

Client Name: _____

Date of Financial Statements: _____

COMPARISON OF CURRENT FINANCIAL STATEMENTS WITH COMPARABLE PRIOR-PERIOD FINANCIAL STATEMENTS

The following ratios were computed:

_____ Using financial data that reflect review adjustments proposed to date.

_____ Using financial data that do not reflect review adjustments.

Formula

LIQUIDITY RATIOS

1. Current ratio

$$\frac{\text{Current Assets}}{\text{Current Liabilities}}$$

2. Acid-test ratio

$$\frac{\text{Quick Assets}}{\text{Current Liabilities}}$$

3. Days' sales in accounts receivable

$$\frac{\text{Average Accounts Receivable} \times 365 \text{ Days}}{\text{Net Credit Sales}}$$

4. Current liabilities to total assets

$$\frac{\text{Current Liabilities}}{\text{Total Assets}}$$

ACTIVITY RATIOS

1. Inventory turnover

$$\frac{\text{Cost of Goods Sold}}{\text{Average Inventory}}$$

2. Receivable turnover

$$\frac{\text{Net Credit Sales}}{\text{Average Accounts Receivable}}$$

3. Asset turnover

$$\frac{\text{Net Sales}}{\text{Average Total Assets}}$$

4. Gross profit percentage

$$\frac{\text{Gross Profit}}{\text{Net Sales}}$$

PROFITABILITY RATIOS

1. Bad debt to sales

$$\frac{\text{Bad Debt Expense}}{\text{Net Sales}}$$

2. Rate of return on total assets used

$$\frac{\text{Net Income}}{\text{Total Assets}}$$

3. Rate of return on equity (investment)

$$\frac{\text{Net Income}}{\text{Total Equity}}$$

4. Net margin

$$\frac{\text{Net Income}}{\text{Net Sales}}$$

COVERAGE RATIOS

1. Debt to total assets

$$\frac{\text{Total Debt}}{\text{Total Assets}}$$

2. Interest expense to sales

$$\frac{\text{Interest Expense}}{\text{Net Sales}}$$

	Formula
3. Number of times interest earned	Income before Interest and Taxes / Interest Expense

OTHER RATIOS

1. Effective tax rate	Income Taxes / Income before Taxes
2. Bad debt rate	Allowance for Bad Debts / Accounts Receivable
3. Depreciation rate	Depreciation Expense / Depreciable Property
4. Accounts payable to purchases	Accounts Payable / Purchases
5. Dividend rate	Dividends / Common Stock (Market Value)
6. Interest rate	Interest Expense / Average Interest-Bearing Debt
7. Payroll rate	Payroll Expense / Net Sales
8. Dividend return	Dividend Income / Average Equity Investments
9. Interest income return	Interest Income / Average Debt Investments

OTHER

COMPARISON OF CURRENT FINANCIAL STATEMENTS WITH ANTICIPATED RESULTS

PLANNING AID REMINDER: SSARS-19 requires a practitioner performing a review engagement to independently develop expectations of ratios and account balances (including changes in them) before analyzing the client's data. SSARS require that the accountant document those expectations when they are not otherwise readily determinable from the documentation of the work performed. Exhibit AR 90-7 contains an example of documentation.

Acct # Account Name	20XX		
	Actual	Budgeted	Difference
Cash in bank — name			
Petty cash			
Cash in bank — payroll			
Investment marketable equity securities (current)			
Accounts receivable			
Allowance for doubtful accounts			
Other receivables (current)			
Accrued interest receivable			
Notes receivable (current)			
Discount on notes receivable			
Dividends receivable			
Inventory (year-end balance)			
Prepaid insurance			
Prepaid rent			
Prepaid advertising			
Land			
Buildings			
Accumulated depreciation — buildings			
Delivery equipment			
Accumulated depreciation — delivery equipment			
Fixtures			
Accumulated depreciation — fixtures			
Office equipment			
Accumulated depreciation — office equipment			
Property — capital leases			
Investment — marketable equity securities (noncurrent)			
Other receivables (noncurrent)			
Land held for investment			
Accounts payable			
Accrued liabilities			
Payroll taxes and other withholdings			
Interest payable			
Notes payable			
Discounts/premiums — notes payable			

| | 20XX | | |
Acct # Account Name	Actual	Budgeted	Difference
Obligations — capital leases (current)			
Dividends payable			
Income taxes payable			
Notes payable (noncurrent)			
Bonds payable			
Discounts/premiums — bonds payable			
Obligation — capital leases (noncurrent)			
Common stock			
Paid-in capital in excess of par			
Treasury stock			
Accumulated other comprehensive income			
Unappropriated retained earnings			
Appropriated retained earnings			
Sales			
Sales returns and allowances			
Sales discounts			
Cost of goods sold			
Purchases			
Freight-in			
Bad debt expense			
Utilities expense			
Travel expense			
Advertising expense			
Delivery expense			
Miscellaneous expense			
Insurance expense			
Rent expense			
Professional fees expense			
Salaries and wages expense			
Payroll taxes expense			
Depreciation expense — buildings			
Depreciation expense — delivery equipment			
Depreciation expense — fixtures			
Depreciation expense — office equipment			
Depreciation expense — capital leases			
Repairs and maintenance expense			

	20XX		
Acct # Account Name	*Actual*	*Budgeted*	*Difference*

Miscellaneous income
Dividend income
Interest income
Interest expense
Loss/gain on sale of assets
Loss on exchange of assets
Loss due to permanent decline in
    value of security investments
Loss/gain on sale of investments
Income tax expense
Totals

Prepared By: _____

Reviewed By: _____

STUDY OF FINANCIAL STATEMENT ELEMENTS AND UNEXPECTED RELATIONSHIPS

Unexpected Relationships	*Summary of Analysis*

OTHER ANALYTICAL PROCEDURES

Summary of findings: _____

_____

_____

_____

_____

_____

_____

_____

_____

_____

_____

Prepared By: _____

Date: _____

Reviewed By: _____

Date: _____

EXHIBIT AR 90-8 — DOCUMENTING EXPECTATIONS WHEN PERFORMING ANALYTICAL PROCEDURES IN A REVIEW ENGAGEMENT

In review engagements, the accountant must perform inquiry and analytical procedures to provide the basis for the review report. When performing analytical procedures, the accountant first forms an expectation of the recorded amounts or ratios in such a way that a material difference between the expectation and the recorded amount or ratio is indicative of a possible material misstatement requiring further explanation. An accountant cannot perform effective analytical procedures without first developing expectations as to the results of those analytical procedures.

Based on the accountant's understanding of the client and its industry, the accountant develops expectations by identifying plausible relationships (such as number of stores and sales) that are reasonably expected to exist. Several data sources might be used by the accountant to form the expectation. AR 90 requires the accountant to document expectations and factors considered in the development of those expectations where significant expectations are not otherwise readily determinable from the documentation of the work performed.

The following is an example of how an accountant might document expectations.

Documenting an Expectation Related to an Increase in Revenue

An accountant is engaged to conduct a review of financial statements of a company that manufactures medical products for use in cancer treatments. Because of increased cancer detection rates due to advanced medical technologies, the accountant reasonably expects product sales to have increased during the fiscal period due to greater demand for cancer treatment products. Using his or her knowledge of the client, the accountant expects a 10 percent to 15 percent increase in sales. Additionally, the accountant concludes that receivables should increase, and that loans payable and interest expense would also increase due to additional borrowing of funds to handle production demands.

Example Documentation

Lifeway Medical Supply Corporation
Analytical Procedures
For the Year Ended December 31, 20X9

Expectations

The following are factors that should affect the relationship between current and prior-year revenue account amounts:

- Increase in cancer treatment spending due to earlier cancer detection and treatment improvements in the medical field, resulting in increased product sales. Expected increase is between 10 percent and 15 percent. A similar expectation exists for an increase in accounts receivable.

- To fund expenses related to additional production demands, the client borrowed additional funds from its lenders. Thus, loans payable and interest expense is expected to increase between 10 percent and 15 percent.

- No significant increases are expected in either days sales in inventory or inventory turnover. Although there will be some inventory buildup, it is not expected to correspond with an increase in sales because the cancer treatment products are expected to be sold near the date of completion. Increases in days sales in inventory or inventory turnover are not expected to change by more than 5 percent.

Balance sheets are available for the current year and the two years prior to the current year and income statements accounts are available for the current and prior year.

Trend Analysis

	December 31, 20X9	December 31, 20X8	Change	Percentage Change
Sales	$5,000,000	$4,350,000	$650,000	14.94%
Cost of Sales	$3,560,000	$3,132,000	$428,000	13.67%
Gross margin	$1,440,000	$1,218,000		
Gross margin as a percentage of sales	28.80%	28.00%		
Selling expenses	$460,000	$368,000	$92,000	25.00%
Interest expense	$96,000	$84,000	$12,000	14.29%

Balance Sheet Ratio Analysis

	December 31, 20X9	December 31, 20X8	December 31, 20X7
Accounts Rec., net	$2,200,000	$1,686,000	$1,406,000
Inventory	$2,000,000	$1,664,000	$1,388,000
Notes Payable	$996,000	$874,000	$836,000

Change in Receivables

Accounts receivable increased 30.5 percent from the prior year, which is in excess of the expected increase of between 10 percent and 15 percent. As a result, additional inquiries about the increase in accounts receivable will be made of the client and the associated reasons will be documented.

Days in Receivables

Days sales in receivables = Accounts receivables, net at end of period / (Net sales/365)

Days in Receivables for 20X9:
$2,200,000 / ($5,000,000/365) = 160.6 days

Days in Receivables for 20X8:
$1,686,000 / ($4,350,000/365) = 141.5 days

The increase in 19 days sales in receivables (160.6 – 141.5 days) represents a 13.5 percent increase. Inquiries about the increase in days sales in receivables will be made as part of the additional inquiries about the increase in accounts receivable.

Change in Inventory

Inventory increased 20.2 percent from the prior year, which is in excess of the expected increase of between 10 percent and 15 percent that would be associated with the increase in sales by the same percentage amounts. As a result, additional inquiries about the increase in inventory will be made of the client and the associated reasons will be documented.

Days sales in inventory

Days sales in inventory = Inventory at end of period / (Total cost of goods sold / 365)

Days sales in inventory for 2009:
$2,000,000 / ($3,560,000 / 365) = 205.1 days

Days sales in inventory for 2008:
$1,664,000 / ($3,132,000 / 365) = 193.9 days

The increase of 11.2 days sales in inventory (205.1 – 193.9 days) represents a 5.8 percent increase. Because this increase is greater than expected, further inquiries will be made of the client and reasons for the difference will be documented.

Inventory Turnover

Inventory turnover = Cost of goods sold / Average inventory

Inventory turnover for 20X9:
    $3,560,000 / (($2,000,000 + $1,664,000) / 2) = 1.94 times

Inventory turnover for 20X8:
    $3,132,000 / (($1,664,000 + $1,388,000) / 2) = 2.05 times

The inventory turnover decrease of 5.4% is beyond the expected change of no more than 5%. Because this change is greater than expected, further inquiries will be made of the client and reasons for the difference will be documented.

The increase in notes payable is also reasonable (13.9%) when considered in light of the corresponding increase in interest expense and the expectation associated with the notes payable account. However, because the increase in selling expenses is 25 percent, additional inquiries about that increase will be made of the client and the associated reasons will be documented.

EXHIBIT AR 90-9 — CONSIDERING GOING CONCERN

An entity's continuance as a going concern is assumed in financial reporting in the absence of significant information to the contrary. Often information that indicates uncertainty about an entity's ability to continue as a going concern relates to its ability to continue to meet its obligations as they become due without substantial disposition of assets outside the ordinary course of business, restructuring debt, externally forced revisions of its operations, or similar actions.

Conditions Often Leading to Substantial Doubt

Certain conditions, when considered together, may lead to there being substantial doubt about an entity's ability to continue as a going concern for a reasonable period of time, typically not to exceed one year beyond the date of the financial statements. Conditions or events that may indicate a substantial doubt about the entity's ability to continue as a going concern include the following:

- Negative trends that might include, for example, recurring operating losses, working capital deficiencies, negative cash flows from operating activities, adverse key financial ratios.

- Other indications of possible financial difficulties that might include, for example, default on loan or similar agreements, arrearages in dividends, denial of usual trade credit from suppliers, restructuring of debt, noncompliance with statutory capital requirements, need to seek new sources or methods of financing or to dispose of substantial assets.

- Internal matters that might include, for example, work stoppages or other labor difficulties, substantial dependence on the success of a particular project, uneconomic long-term commitments, need to significantly revise operations.

- External matters that have occurred might include, for example, legal proceedings, legislation, or similar matters that might jeopardize an entity's ability to operate; loss of a key franchise, license, or patent; loss of a principal customer or supplier; uninsured or underinsured catastrophe such as a drought, earthquake, or flood.

Management's Plans to Address Conditions

Management should have plans to address these identified adverse conditions and events. Examples of management's plans might include the following:

- Plans to dispose of assets: Considerations should be made about

  — Whether there are any restrictions on the disposal of assets

  — The marketability of assets to be sold

  — Potential direct or indirect effects of the disposal of assets

- Plans to borrow money or restructure debt: Considerations should be made about

  — Availability of debt financing

  — Existing or committed arrangements to restructure debt

  — Possible effects of management's borrowing plans on existing restrictions on additional borrowing

- Plans to reduce or delay expenditures: Considerations should be made about

  — Feasibility of plans to reduce overhead or administrative expenditures

  — Impact of reduced or delayed expenditures

- Plans to increase ownership equity: Considerations should be made about

  — Feasibility of plans to increase ownership equity, including existing or committed arrangements to raise additional capital

  — Existing or committed arrangements to reduce current dividend requirements

Financial Statement Disclosure

When management concludes that there is substantial doubt about the entity's ability to continue as a going concern, management should consider disclosing the following:

- Pertinent conditions and events giving rise to the assessment of the uncertainty about the entity's ability to continue as a going concern for a reasonable period of time.

- The possible effects of such conditions and events and any mitigating factors.

- Possible discontinuance of operations.

- Management's plans

- Information about the recoverability or classification of recorded asset amounts or the amounts or classification of liabilities.

Management should consider the need for disclosure of the principal conditions and events that initially caused management to believe there was an uncertainty. The consideration of disclosure may include the possible effects of such conditions and events, and any mitigating factors, including management's plans.

AR SECTION 110
COMPILATION OF SPECIFIED ELEMENTS, ACCOUNTS, OR ITEMS OF A FINANCIAL STATEMENT

Authoritative Pronouncements

SSARS-13 — Compilation of Specified Elements, Accounts, or Items of a Financial Statement

Overview

The Accounting and Review Services Committee issued SSARS-13 in 2005 to provide new guidance that expands SSARS to apply when an accountant is engaged to compile or issues a compilation report on one or more specified elements, accounts, or items of a financial statement.

Defining elements, accounts, or items

SSARS-13 notes that elements, accounts, or items of a financial statement constitute accounting information that is part of, but less than, a financial statement. Such information also encompasses accounting information contained in the client's accounts that supports the elements, accounts, or items presented in the financial statements. Although accounting information is generally expressed in monetary amounts (or percentages derived from monetary amounts), it may also include quantitative information derived from accounting records that is not expressed in monetary terms.

Specified elements may be taken directly from the financial statements (or notes). They may also represent any component or combination of components derived from the financial statements. Specified elements may be individual financial statement line items or a combination of several line items. They may also be general ledger accounts that make up all or part of a financial statement line item. The following are examples of specified element presentations:

- Total sales from the income statement

- Summary of all amounts included in property, plant, and equipment at a specified date

- Schedule of accounts receivable at a specified date

- Schedule of balances in cash accounts at a specified date

- Schedule of construction costs incurred

Although AR Section 110 provides guidance for compiling specified elements, accounts, or items of financial statement, nothing precludes the accountant from preparing or assisting in the preparation of one of more specified elements, accounts, or items of a financial statement, and submitting the presentation to the client without the issuance of a compilation report.

A compilation of a specified element is limited to presenting financial information that is the representation of management (or the owners) without undertaking to express any assurance on the information.

Performance requirements

When an accountant is engaged to compile or issues a compilation report on one or more specified elements, accounts, or items of a financial statement, he or she must establish an understanding with the entity, preferably in writing, regarding the services to be performed. If the accountant becomes aware of fraud or an illegal act that may have occurred, he or she must adhere to the communication requirements contained in AR Section 80.

The accountant must also adhere to the compilation performance requirements contained in AR Section 80. Before issuance of a compilation report on one or more specified elements, accounts, or items of a financial statement, the accountant should read the compiled information to consider whether it appears to be appropriate in form and free of obvious material errors, including arithmetical or clerical mistakes and mistakes in the application of accounting principles.

Reporting requirements

When an accountant is engaged to compile or issues a compilation report on one or more specified elements, accounts, or items of a financial statement, AR 110 specifies explicit report elements.

Any other procedures that the accountant might have performed before or during the compilation engagement should not be described in the report. In addition, each page of the compiled specified elements, accounts, or items of a financial statement should include a reference such as "See Accountant's Compilation Report."

AR SECTION 120

COMPILATION OF PRO FORMA FINANCIAL INFORMATION

Authoritative Pronouncements

SSARS-14—Compilation of Pro Forma Financial Information

Overview

The Accounting and Review Services Committee issued SSARS-14 in 2005 to provide new guidance that expands SSARS to apply when an accountant is engaged to compile pro forma financial information. By definition a presentation of pro forma financial information is not a financial statement presentation and thus did not previously come under the scope of SSARS. However, SSARS-14 expands SSARS-1 to apply when an accountant is engaged to compile or issues a compilation report on pro forma financial information.

Defining pro forma financial information

The objective of pro forma financial information is to show what the significant effects on historical financial information might have been had a consummated or proposed transaction (or event) occurred at an earlier date. Pro forma financial information is commonly used to show the effects of transactions such as the following:

- Business combination

- Change in capitalization

- Disposition of a significant portion of the business

- Change in the form of business organization or status as an autonomous entity

- Proposed sale of securities and the application of the proceeds

Pro forma financial information is generally achieved by applying pro-forma adjustments to historical financial statements. Pro forma adjustments should be based on management's assumptions and give effect to all significant effects directly attributable to the transaction (or event).

Accountant responsibility for pro forma financial information

Although AR Section 120 provides guidance for compiling pro forma financial information, nothing precludes an accountant from preparing or assisting in the preparation of pro forma financial information and submitting the presentation to the client without the issuance of a compilation report. However, an accountant who prepares or assists a client in preparing a presentation of pro forma financial information should consider how the presentation will be used. The accountant should consider the potential for being associated with the presentation and the likelihood that the user may inappropriately infer through that association an unintended level of assurance. If the accountant believes that he or she will be associated with the information, he or she should consider issuing a compilation report so that users will not infer a level of assurance that does not exist.

An engagement to compile pro forma financial information may be undertaken as a separate engagement or in conjunction with a compilation of financial statements. When an accountant is engaged to compile pro forma financial information, he or she should establish an understanding with the entity, preferably in writing, regarding the services to be performed. The understanding should include a description of the nature and limitations of the services to be performed and a description of the report.

When an accountant is engaged to compile pro forma financial information, he or she must adhere to the performance requirements contained in SSARS-1 for compilations. Before issuing the compilation report, the accountant should read the compiled pro forma financial information, including the summary of significant assumptions and consider whether it appears to be appropriate in form and free of obvious material errors.

SSARS-14 specifies the basic elements of a compilation report on pro forma financial information. Each page of the compiled pro forma financial information should include a reference, such as "See Accountant's Compilation Report."

AR SECTION 200

REPORTING ON COMPARATIVE FINANCIAL STATEMENTS

Authoritative Pronouncements

SSARS-2 — Reporting on Comparative Financial Statements

SSARS-11 — Standards for Accounting and Review Services (May 2004)

SSARS-12 — Omnibus Statement on Standards for Accounting and Review Services — 2005

SSARS-15 — Elimination of Certain References to Statements on Auditing Standards and Incorporation of Appropriate Guidance into Statements on Standards for Accounting and Review Services

SSARS-17 — Omnibus Statement on Standards for Accounting and Review Services — 2008

SSARS Interpretation 1 — Reporting on Financial Statements That Previously Did Not Omit Substantially All Disclosures (November 2002)

Overview

"Comparative financial statements" are defined as "financial statements of two or more periods presented in columnar form." The periods may be other than annual, such as the three months (quarter) ended March 31, 20X6 (current period), compared to the three months ended March 31, 20X5 (prior period). The statements may cover more than two periods; for example, statements for the five years ended May 31, 20X7. However, each type of financial statement (for example, balance sheet, statement of income) for all periods presented must be on the same page in columnar form. The columns may be in vertical or horizontal format.

When financial statements of more than one period are presented in columnar form, the accountant must report on all periods presented. A *reissued* report is one that has been issued subsequent to the date of the original report but with its original date. A reissued report should be dual-dated if it is revised for specific events. An *updated* report is issued by a continuing accountant and bears the same date as the current report. It may or may not contain the same conclusions reached in the original report, and it should consider information that the accountant becomes aware of during the current engagement.

Financial statements that have been compiled, reviewed, or audited and that are accompanied by appropriate reports may *not* be presented in columnar form with financial statements that are *not* compiled, reviewed, or audited. In such cases, the accountant should advise the client that the report and the accountant's name should not be used in connection with such comparative financial statements. In other words, the accountant may *not* report on client-prepared comparative financial statements containing statements that *were not* compiled, reviewed, or audited and statements that *were* compiled, reviewed, or audited. However, the client-prepared statements may be presented on a separate page of a document that includes, on another separate page of the same document, the accountant's compiled, reviewed, or audited financial statements. In this event, each page of the client-prepared statements must bear a comment that the accountant has not compiled, reviewed, or audited the statements and assumes no responsibility for them.

Substantially all disclosures may be omitted in compiled financial statements; however, it is inappropriate for an accountant to issue reviewed or audited financial statements that omit substantially all disclosures. Thus, only when all periods are compiled and all periods omit substantially all disclosures can an accountant report on comparative financial statements that omit substantially all disclosures.

Promulgated Procedures Checklist

The structure of the CPA's report on comparative financial statements depends upon the various reporting circumstances that can be encountered in an engagement. The following are common reporting circumstances:

- All periods covered by the financial statements are compiled or reviewed.

- The current period's financial statements are reviewed, while the prior period financial statements are compiled.

- The current period's financial statements are compiled, while the prior period financial statements are reviewed.

- The current or prior period's financial statements are audited, while the other period's financial statements are compiled or reviewed.

- There has been a change in the report on the prior period's financial statements.

- Other accountants have compiled or reviewed the financial statements of the prior period or periods.

- An exception exists on the highest level of service rendered.

- The status of the client (public versus nonpublic) has changed.

Analysis and Application of Procedures

All periods covered by the financial statements are compiled or reviewed

When periods presented in comparative financial statements are either all compiled or all reviewed, the continuing accountant should update the report on the prior period, or periods, and issue it as part of the report on the current period. An example of a report on all periods compiled is presented in Exhibit AR 200-1. An example of a report on all periods reviewed is presented in Exhibit AR 200-2.

The current period's financial statements are reviewed, while the prior period financial statements are compiled

When the accountant performs a level of service in the current period that is higher than that performed in the prior period, he or she should update the report on the prior period, or periods, and issue it as the last paragraph of the report on the current period. An example of the standard report in this situation is presented in Exhibit AR 200-3.

The current period's financial statements are compiled, while the prior period financial statements are reviewed

When the accountant performs a level of service in the current period that is lower than that of the prior period, he or she may report on such comparative financial statements by (1) issuing two separate reports, (2) issuing a compilation report on the current period and adding a last paragraph for the prior period, or (3) issuing a combined compilation and review report.

If the accountant elects to issue two separate reports, the current period will be covered in a compilation report. The prior period will be covered in a review report bearing its original date.

If the accountant elects to issue a compilation report with a last paragraph referring to the prior period, certain information must be included. The last paragraph should contain a description of the degree of responsibility the accountant is assuming for the prior period, the date of the accountant's original report, and a statement that the accountant has not performed any procedures in connection with the prior period's review after the date of the prior-period review report. An example of such an additional last paragraph is presented in Exhibit AR 200-4.

The combined report should include the current-period compilation report and the reissued review report for the prior period. The combined report should be dated as of the completion of the current-period compilation engagement. The report should also mention that the accountant has not performed any procedures in connection with the prior-period review report after the date of that report.

The current or prior period's financial statements are audited, while the other period's financial statements are compiled or reviewed

SAS-26 (AU 504) (Association with Financial Statements) provides the reporting standards that should be followed when current-period financial statements are audited and included with prior-period compiled or reviewed financial statements. When the financial statements are those of a nonissuer, the accountant's opinion on the current-year audited financial statements should be expanded to include a final separate paragraph describing the compilation or review of the prior-period financial statements. When prior-period financial statements were compiled, the separate paragraph may be worded as follows:

> The 20X8 financial statements were compiled by us, and our report thereon, dated January 31, 20X9, stated that we did not audit or review those financial statements and, accordingly, express no opinion or other form of assurance on them.

When prior-period financial statements were reviewed, the separate paragraph may be worded as follows:

> The 20X8 financial statements were reviewed by us, and our report thereon, dated January 31, 20X9, stated that we were not aware of any material modifications that should be made to those statements for them to be in conformity with generally accepted accounting principles. However, a review is substantially less in scope than an audit and does not provide a basis for the expression of an opinion on the financial statements taken as a whole.

When the prior-period financial statements have been audited, the accountant should issue a compilation report or review report on the current-period financial statements and should either (1) reissue the audit report for the prior period or (2) add a separate paragraph to the current-period compilation or review report describing the responsibility assumed for the prior-period financial statements. The description paragraph should include the date of the prior-period audit report, a statement that the financial statements were previously examined, the type of opinion expressed and whether the opinion was other than unqualified, the substantive reasons for the qualification, and, finally, a statement that no auditing procedures have been performed since the date of the prior-period audit report. An example of this type of paragraph is as follows:

> The financial statements for the year ended December 31, 20X8, were audited by us (other accountants) and we (they) expressed an unqualified opinion on them in our (their) report dated March 1, 20X9, but we (they) have not performed any auditing procedures since that date.

There has been a change in the report on the prior period's financial statements

Before or during the current-period engagement, a continuing accountant may become aware of information that affects the prior-period report; for example, a modification in the prior-period report to disclose a departure from generally accepted accounting principles (GAAP) may no longer be applicable, or a modification to disclose a departure from GAAP may become necessary. In this event, the accountant's report on the prior-period statements should be expanded to include an additional separate paragraph. This separate paragraph should contain (1) the date of the original report; (2) the reasons for the change in the original report; and (3) if applicable, a statement to the effect that the prior-period financial statements have been changed. Exhibit AR 200-5 provides an example of such an explanatory paragraph.

If the revised report is reissued (issued separately from the report on the current financial statements), it should be dual-dated. The second date should be the date when substantially all the information that resulted in the revision of the report was obtained. This date may be the same date as that used for the current year's report.

Other accountants have compiled or reviewed the financial statements of the prior period or periods

Predecessor accountant reissues unchanged report

The successor accountant should consider the provisions of SSARS-4 (Communication Between Predecessor and Successor Accountants) when communicating with the predecessor accountant (auditor) and when determining the types of communications that are appropriate under the circumstances. SSARS-4 indicates that the successor accountant should obtain the permission of the client before communicating with the predecessor accountant.

A predecessor accountant is not required to reissue a compilation or review report. However, the predecessor accountant may reissue the report on prior-period financial statements, at the client's request, if the accountant makes satisfactory arrangements with the former client and complies with the following provisions before reissuing the report:

1. Evaluates whether the prior-period report is still appropriate by considering (1) the form and style of the report presentation; (2) the effects of any subsequent events; and (3) as a result of changes, whether a modification is required or should be deleted

2. Reads the current-period financial statements and the accompanying accountant's report

3. Compares the prior-period financial statements to previously issued financial statements and the financial statements of the current period

4. Obtains a letter from the current accountant stating that he or she is (is not) aware of any matter that might have a material effect on the prior-period financial statements

If, as a result of the above procedures, the predecessor accountant becomes aware of information that may affect the prior-period report on the financial statements, he or she should perform (1) procedures similar to those that would have been performed if the accountant had been aware of such information during the prior engagement and (2) any other procedures considered necessary under the circumstances. Because of the seriousness of the situation, the procedures may include discussion with the successor accountant and review of pertinent portions of the current-period workpapers. If the predecessor accountant cannot complete the necessary procedures, he or she should not reissue the report on the prior-period financial statements. Under these circumstances, the predecessor accountant may consider the need to consult with legal counsel regarding appropriate action.

> **ENGAGEMENT STRATEGY:** The situation may be such that the predecessor accountant should consider the guidance SAS-1 (AU 561) provides to an auditor when a subsequent discovery of facts existing at the date of the accountant's prior report.

After performing the required procedures, if the predecessor accountant is not aware of any information that would require restatement or revision of the prior-period report, the predecessor accountant should reissue the report on the former client's request. The reissued report should be dated as it was originally. No reference should be made to any subsequent procedures performed, including the representation letter from the successor accountant and the report that the successor accountant will issue on the current period.

Predecessor accountant issues changed report

After following the prescribed procedures, the predecessor accountant may determine that a prior-period report cannot be reissued exactly as it was issued originally. In this event, the prior-period report and/or financial statements should be appropriately revised, and the report should contain a separate explanatory paragraph. The separate explanatory paragraph should disclose (1) the date of the original report and the date of the revised report, if different; (2) all of the substantive reasons for the change to the original report; and (3) if applicable, a statement to the effect that the financial statements of the prior period have been changed.

AR Section 200 previously required that either the predecessor or the successor accountant report on changed prior-period financial statements, as restated. The successor accountant was precluded from reporting on the restatement adjustment only.

The issuance of SSARS-12 revised AR Section 200 to allow the successor accountant to report on the restatement adjustment while stating that a predecessor accountant reported on the financial statements of the prior period before restatement. SSARS-12 amends AR 200 to include example reporting in these circumstances.

Predecessor accountant's report not reissued

A predecessor accountant may decide not to reissue the original prior-period report and not to issue any changed report on the prior period. In this event, the successor accountant should either (1) refer to the report of the predecessor accountant in the current report or (2) compile, review, or audit the prior-period financial statements.

SSARS-11 addressed a technical correction to SSARS-2. SSARS provide guidance to be followed when the financial statements of a prior period have been compiled or reviewed by a predecessor accountant whose report is not presented and the successor accountant has not compiled or reviewed those financial statements. SSARS-11 revised SSARS-2, footnote 9, to conform with the guidance found in SAS-58 (AU 508), footnote 29, which states that a successor auditor may name the predecessor auditor if the predecessor auditor's practice was acquired by or merged with that of the successor auditor.

If the predecessor accountant's report is not to be reissued and the successor accountant is not engaged to compile, review, or audit the prior-period financial statements, the successor accountant should expand the report on the current period to include a separate paragraph containing the following information:

1. Without naming the prior-period accountants, a statement that the prior-period financial statements were compiled, reviewed, or audited by other accountants (auditors)

2. The date of the prior-period report

3. A description of the form of disclaimer, limited assurance, or other opinion given in the prior-period report

4. Quotation or description of any modification in the prior-period report and of any matter emphasized in the report

An example of a separate paragraph for a compilation appears in Exhibit AR 200-6. An example of a separate paragraph for a review appears in Exhibit AR 200-7.

The successor accountant may compile, review, or audit prior-period financial statements even though they have already been compiled, reviewed, or audited by the predecessor accountant. This is particularly true when the client wants to upgrade the services of the prior period. Under these circumstances, the successor accountant (auditor) should consider the guidance provided by SSARS-4. The client must give both the predecessor accountant and the successor accountant permission to communicate with each other. The predecessor accountant may provide information that may affect the successor accountant's decision to accept the engagement. In addition to making specific inquiries of the predecessor accountant, the successor accountant may have an opportunity to review the predecessor accountant's workpapers for the prior period.

Considerations when the predecessor accountant has ceased operations

When the accountant presents a compilation or review report with a compilation, review, or audit report of a prior period, and the prior-period report was prepared by a predecessor accountant that has ceased operations, the successor auditor should follow SSARS-11 (Standards for Accounting and Review Services). SSARS-11 revises SSARS-2 to state that the successor practitioner may name the predecessor practitioner if the predecessor practitioner's practice was acquired by or merged with the successor practitioner's practice.

> **OBSERVATION:** In some cases when the predecessor accountant has ceased operations, the successor accountant might believe that the prior-period financial statements should be revised. In this case, the successor auditor might consider the Notice to Practitioners titled "Audit, Review, and Compliance Considerations When a Predecessor Accountant has Ceased Operations" (a nonauthoritative practice aid) issued by the AICPA in February 1991. The Notice to Practitioners recommends that when the accountant believes that prior-period financial statements should be revised but the predecessor accountant has ceased operations, the successor accountant should suggest that the client notify "the party responsible for winding up the affairs of the predecessor firm" of the matter. If the client refuses to make the communication or if the reaction of the client's predecessor accountant is unsatisfactory, the successor accountant should discuss the matter with legal counsel.

An exception exists on the highest level of service rendered

SSARS-1 requires that the accountant report on the highest level of service rendered. For example, when a compilation is performed followed by a review of the same set of financial statements, the review report should be issued. An exception occurs, however, when the prior-period financial statements *do not* omit substantially all disclosures required by GAAP and the current-period financial statements *do* omit these disclosures. In this instance, the current period must be a compilation engagement, because when financial statements omit substantially all the disclosures required by GAAP, the accountant can only issue a compilation report. It is inappropriate for an accountant to issue a review report or an audit report on financial statements that omit substantially all disclosures. Thus, only when *all* periods are *compiled* and *all* periods omit substantially all disclosures can an accountant report on comparative financial statements that omit substantially all disclosures.

However, a situation may arise where the accountant has issued compiled financial statements that omit substantially all disclosures for the current period but issued a review report in the prior period and the client now requests *comparative* compiled financial statements that omit substantially all disclosures. In order for the financial statements to be comparative, the client must ask the accountant to compile the prior-period statements and omit substantially all disclosures. Although SSARS-1 requires that the accountant issue a report on the highest level of service for the prior period, SSARS-2 provides for an exception. Under SSARS-2, the accountant can reissue a prior-period report on the basis of a lower level of service if the following steps are taken:

1. The accountant must fully comply with all the standards applicable to reporting on compiled financial statements that omit substantially all disclosures.

2. A separate paragraph must be included in the accountant's report that discloses (1) the type of previous services rendered by the accountant in the prior period and (2) the date of the accountant's previous report.

Exhibit AR 200-8 presents an example of the required separate paragraph that is added to the end of the compilation report on the comparative financial statements that omit substantially all disclosures.

> **OBSERVATION:** An accountant might be asked to issue a compilation report on financial statements that omit substantially all disclosures for financial statements that had previously been audited. Or the accountant might be asked to issue a compilation report on financial statements that omit substantially all disclosures for financial statements that had previously been reviewed or compiled and did not omit substantially all disclosures. Or the accountant might be asked to issue a compilation report on financial statements that omit substantially all disclosures for financial statements that had previously been audited. Or the accountant might be asked to issue a compilation report on financial statements that omit substantially all disclosures for financial statements that had previously been reviewed or compiled and did not omit substantially all disclosures. Or the accountant might be asked to issue a compilation report on financial statements that omit substantially all disclosures for financial statements that were previously audited, reviewed, or compiled (with disclosures included) to accompany current-year compiled financial statements (that omit substantially all required disclosures) so that comparative financial statements can be issued and reported upon. Interpretation No. 1 of AR 200 addresses the accountant's reporting obligation if the previous audit report was qualified, adverse, or a disclaimer of opinion, and if the previous review or compilation report was modified. In such instances, the accountant must add a separate paragraph to his or her report that discloses (1) the type of service rendered by the accountant in a prior period, (2) the date of the accountant's previous report, and (3a) the fact

that a qualified report, adverse report, or disclaimer of opinion was issued and the reasons for the opinion issued or (3b) the fact that a modified compilation or review report was issued (or a compilation or review report was issued with an emphasis of matter) and the reasons for the modification or emphasis of matter.

The status of the client (issuer versus nonissuer) has changed

A company is an issuer or a nonissuer entity according to its status for the current period. If a company is classified as a nonissuer for the current period, an accountant can issue a compilation report or review report. If a company is classified as an issuer for the current period, however, the accountant usually cannot issue a compilation report or review report and must follow standards for public companies (standards of the Public Company Accounting Oversight Board).

A situation may arise where a company is an issuer entity for the current period and was a nonissuer entity in the prior period. The standards applicable to this situation are those applicable to the current period. Since the company is a public company in the current period, generally accepted auditing standards apply and compilation or review standards do not apply. Thus, a compilation report or review report issued for the prior period cannot be reissued or referred to in the audit report for the current period.

If a company is a nonissuer in the current period and its financial statements are compiled or reviewed, and if the company was a public company in the prior period and its financial statements were audited, the rules for "Current Period Compiled or Reviewed and Prior Period Audited" are used. In this event, the accountant should issue a compilation report or review report on the current period and either (1) reissue the audit report for the prior period or (2) add a separate paragraph to the current-period compilation report or review report describing the responsibility assumed by the accountant for the prior-period financial statements. The description paragraph should include the date of the prior-period report; a statement that the financial statements were previously examined; the type of opinion expressed, and if the opinion was other than unqualified, the substantive reasons for the qualification; and, finally, a statement that no auditing procedures have been performed since the date of the prior-period audit report. Exhibit AR 200-9 presents an example of a report where the current period has been compiled and the prior period has been audited.

If a company is a nonissuer in the current period and its financial statements are compiled or reviewed and an unaudited disclaimer of opinion was issued in the prior period, the unaudited disclaimer of opinion may not be reissued or referred to in the report on the financial statements for the current period. Under these circumstances, the accountant should comply with the compilation or review standards or perform an audit on the prior period and report accordingly.

Practitioner's Aids

The following practitioner's aids are presented in this section:

- Exhibit AR 200-1 — Report on Comparative Financial Statements Where All Periods Have Been Compiled

- Exhibit AR 200-2 — Report on Comparative Financial Statements Where All Periods Have Been Reviewed

- Exhibit AR 200-3 — Report on Comparative Financial Statements Where the Current Period Is Reviewed and the Prior Period Is Compiled

- Exhibit AR 200-4 — Additional Paragraph to a Compilation Report on the Current Period That Refers to the Prior Period That Had Been Reviewed

- Exhibit AR 200-5 — Explanatory Paragraph Added to a Current Report That Refers to a Change in a Previous Report Issued by the Accountant

- Exhibit AR 200-6 — Separate Paragraph Added to the Current Report That Refers to the Predecessor Accountant's Compilation Report

- Exhibit AR 200-7 — Separate Paragraph Added to the Current Report That Refers to the Predecessor Accountant's Review Report

- Exhibit AR 200-8 — Compilation Report on Comparative Financial Statements That Omit Substantially All Disclosures but Where the Prior Year Had Originally Been Reviewed by the Accountant

- Exhibit AR 200-9 — Report on Comparative Financial Statements Where the Current Year Is Compiled and the Prior Year Is Audited

EXHIBIT AR 200-1 — REPORT ON COMPARATIVE FINANCIAL STATEMENTS WHERE ALL PERIODS HAVE BEEN COMPILED

We have compiled the accompanying balance sheets of ABC Company as of March 31, 20X9 and 20X8, and the related statements of income, retained earnings, and cash flows for the years then ended, in accordance with Statements on Standards for Accounting and Review Services issued by the American Institute of Certified Public Accountants.

A compilation is limited to presenting in the form of financial statements information that is the representation of management. We have not audited or reviewed the accompanying financial statements and, accordingly, do not express an opinion or any other form of assurance on them.

EXHIBIT AR 200-2 — REPORT ON COMPARATIVE FINANCIAL STATEMENTS WHERE ALL PERIODS HAVE BEEN REVIEWED

We have reviewed the accompanying balance sheets of ABC Company as of December 31, 20X9 and 20X8, and the related statements of income, retained earnings, and cash flows for the years then ended, in accordance with Statements on Standards for Accounting and Review Services issued by the American Institute of Certified Public Accountants. All information included in these financial statements is the representation of the management of ABC Company.

A review consists principally of inquiries of company personnel and analytical procedures applied to financial data. It is substantially less in scope than an examination in accordance with generally accepted auditing standards, the objective of which is the expression of an opinion regarding the financial statements taken as a whole. Accordingly, we do not express such an opinion.

Based on our reviews, we are not aware of any material modifications that should be made to the accompanying financial statements in order for them to be in conformity with generally accepted accounting principles.

EXHIBIT AR 200-3 — REPORT ON COMPARATIVE FINANCIAL STATEMENTS WHERE THE CURRENT PERIOD IS REVIEWED AND THE PRIOR PERIOD IS COMPILED

We have reviewed the accompanying balance sheet of ABC Company as of December 31, 20X9, and the related statements of income, retained earnings, and cash flows for the year then ended in accordance with Statements on Standards for Accounting and Review Services issued by the American Institute of Certified Public

Accountants. All information included in these financial statements is the representation of the management of ABC Company.

A review consists principally of inquiries of company personnel and analytical procedures applied to financial data. It is substantially less in scope than an examination in accordance with generally accepted auditing standards, the objective of which is the expression of an opinion regarding the financial statements taken as a whole. Accordingly, we do not express such an opinion.

Based on our review, we are not aware of any material modifications that should be made to the 20X9 financial statements in order for them to be in conformity with generally accepted accounting principles.

The accompanying 20X8 financial statements of ABC Company were compiled by us. A compilation is limited to presenting in the form of financial statements information that is the representation of management. We have not audited or reviewed the 20X8 financial statements and, accordingly, do not express an opinion or any other form of assurance on them.

EXHIBIT AR 200-4—ADDITIONAL PARAGRAPH TO A COMPILATION REPORT ON THE CURRENT PERIOD THAT REFERS TO THE PRIOR PERIOD THAT HAD BEEN REVIEWED

The accompanying 20X8 financial statements of ABC, Inc., were previously reviewed by me, and my report dated March 1, 20X9, stated that I was not aware of any material modifications that should be made to those statements in order for them to be in conformity with generally accepted accounting principles. I have not performed any procedures in connection with that review engagement after the date of my report on the 20X8 financial statements.

EXHIBIT AR 200-5—EXPLANATORY PARAGRAPH ADDED TO A CURRENT REPORT THAT REFERS TO A CHANGE IN A PREVIOUS REPORT ISSUED BY THE ACCOUNTANT

In my previous review report, dated March 1, 20X9, on the 20X8 financial statements, I referred to a departure from generally accepted accounting principles because the Company carried its land at appraised values. However, as disclosed in note X, the Company has restated its 20X8 financial statements to reflect its land at cost in accordance with generally accepted accounting principles.

EXHIBIT AR 200-6 — SEPARATE PARAGRAPH ADDED TO THE CURRENT REPORT THAT REFERS TO THE PREDECESSOR ACCOUNTANT'S COMPILATION REPORT

The 20X8 financial statements of ABC Company were compiled by other accountants whose report, dated February 1, 20X9, stated that they did not express an opinion or any other form of assurance on those statements.

EXHIBIT AR 200-7 — SEPARATE PARAGRAPH ADDED TO THE CURRENT REPORT THAT REFERS TO THE PREDECESSOR ACCOUNTANT'S REVIEW REPORT

The 20X8 financial statements of ABC Company were reviewed by other accountants whose report, dated March 1, 20X9, stated that they were not aware of any material modifications that should be made to those statements in order for them to be in conformity with generally accepted accounting principles.

EXHIBIT AR 200-8 — COMPILATION REPORT ON COMPARATIVE FINANCIAL STATEMENTS THAT OMIT SUBSTANTIALLY ALL DISCLOSURES BUT WHERE THE PRIOR YEAR HAD ORIGINALLY BEEN REVIEWED BY THE ACCOUNTANT

We have compiled the accompanying balance sheets of ABC Company as of December 31, 20X9 and 20X8, and the related statements of income, retained earnings, and cash flows for the years then ended, in accordance with Statements on Standards for Accounting and Review Services issued by the American Institute of Certified Public Accountants.

A compilation is limited to presenting in the form of financial statements information that is the representation of management. We have not audited or reviewed the accompanying financial statements and, accordingly, do not express an opinion or any other form of assurance on them.

Management has elected to omit substantially all the disclosures required by generally accepted accounting principles. If the omitted disclosures were included in the financial statements, they might influence the user's conclusions about the company's financial position, results of operations, and cash flows. Accordingly, these financial statements are not designed for those who are not informed about such matters.

The accompanying 20X8 financial statements were compiled by us from financial information that did not omit substantially all of the disclosures required by generally accepted accounting principles and that we previously reviewed, as indicated in our report dated March 1, 20X9.

EXHIBIT AR 200-9 — REPORT ON COMPARATIVE FINANCIAL STATEMENTS WHERE THE CURRENT YEAR IS COMPILED AND THE PRIOR YEAR IS AUDITED

We have compiled the accompanying balance sheet of ABC Company as of December 31, 20X9, and the related statements of income, retained earnings, and cash flows for the year then ended, in accordance with Statements on Standards for Accounting and Review Services issued by the American Institute of Certified Public Accountants.

A compilation is limited to presenting in the form of financial statements information that is the representation of management. We have not audited or reviewed the accompanying 20X9 financial statements and, accordingly, do not express an opinion or any other form of assurance on them.

The financial statements for the year ended December 31, 20X8, were audited by us (other accountants) and we (they) expressed an unqualified opinion on them in our (their) report dated March 1, 20X9, but we (they) have not performed any auditing procedures since that date.

AR SECTION 300

COMPILATION REPORTS ON FINANCIAL STATEMENTS IN CERTAIN PRESCRIBED FORMS

Authoritative Pronouncements

SSARS-3 — Compilation Reports on Financial Statements in Certain Prescribed Forms

SSARS Interpretation 1 — Omission of Disclosures in Financial Statements Included in Certain Prescribed Forms (May 1982)

SSARS-15 — Elimination of Certain References to Statements on Auditing Standards and Incorporation of Appropriate Guidance into Statements on Standards for Accounting and Review Services

SSARS-17 — Omnibus Statement on Standards for Accounting and Review Services — 2008

Overview

In December 1981, the American Institute of Certified Public Accountants (AICPA) Accounting and Review Services Committee issued SSARS-3 (Compilation Reports on Financial Statements Included in Certain Prescribed Forms). The purpose of SSARS-3 is to provide an alternative report format when the prescribed form or related instructions call for departures from generally accepted accounting principles (GAAP) (or from a comprehensive basis of accounting other than GAAP). Thus, when a prescribed form is designed with material departures from GAAP, the accountant may issue (1) the standard compilation report with a description of the departures from GAAP or (2) the report described in SSARS-3, which makes no reference to the specific departures from GAAP.

Promulgated Procedures Checklist

The CPA should perform the following procedures in determining whether to report on financial statements formatted in certain prescribed forms:

- Determine whether the prescribed form is appropriate.
- Prepare an appropriate compilation report.

Analysis and Application of Procedures

Determine whether the prescribed form is appropriate

A "prescribed form" is any "standard form designed or adopted by the body to which it is to be submitted." A form designed or adopted by the client is not considered to be a prescribed form. Prescribed forms include financial statement formats used by industry trade associations, banks, and regulatory authorities.

> **OBSERVATION:** The Robert Morris Associates (association of bank lending officers) and the AICPA have developed a Business Credit Information Package (BCIP) to be used by nonpublic businesses requesting loans from financial institutions. The BCIP includes, among other documents, a prescribed form for the preparation of financial statements that does not require all GAAP disclosures. This form of financial statement presentation falls within the requirements established by SSARS-3.

Prepare an appropriate compilation report

SSARS-3 adopts the basic philosophy that a body that prescribes a form for financial statements has defined the requirements it considers sufficient to meet its informational needs. Thus, except for when an audit report or a review report has been requested, the accountant's compilation report need not refer to departures from generally accepted accounting principles (including disclosure). Exhibit AR 300-1 is an example of a compilation report on financial statements included in a prescribed form that specifies measurement principles that do not conform to GAAP.

The SSARS Interpretation (May 1982) titled "Omission of Disclosures in Financial Statements Included in Certain Prescribed Forms" states that in a compilation report on financial statements included in a prescribed form, an accountant may refer to the review report previously issued on the financial statements if the difference between the previously reviewed financial statements and the financial statements included in the prescribed form is limited to the omission of disclosures not required by the form.

The following sentence might be added to the third paragraph presented in Exhibit AR 300-1:

> These financial statements were compiled by us from financial statements for the same period that we previously reviewed, as indicated in our report dated February 12, 20X9.

During the performance of the compilation, the accountant may discover departures from generally accepted accounting principles not sanctioned by the prescribed form or related instructions. Also, the accountant may discover departures from the prescribed format or instructions. In either case, such a departure requires that the accountant modify the compilation report by including a separate paragraph that describes the departure.

Practitioner's Aids

EXHIBIT AR 300-1 — COMPILATION REPORT ON FINANCIAL STATEMENTS INCLUDED IN A PRESCRIBED FORM

We have compiled the accompanying balance sheet of X Company as of December 31, 20X8, and the related statements of income, retained earnings, and cash flows for the year then ended included in the accompanying prescribed form in accordance with Statements on Standards for Accounting and Review Services issued by the American Institute of Certified Public Accountants.

Our compilation was limited to the presentation of information that is the representation of management in the form prescribed by the West Virginia Fine Arts Commission. We have not audited or reviewed the financial statements referred to above and, accordingly, do not express an opinion or any other form of assurance on them.

These financial statements (including related disclosures) are presented in accordance with the requirements of the West Virginia Fine Arts Commission, which differ from generally accepted accounting principles. Accordingly, these financial statements are not designed for those who are not informed about such differences.

AR SECTION 400

COMMUNICATIONS BETWEEN PREDECESSOR AND SUCCESSOR ACCOUNTANTS

Authoritative Pronouncements

SSARS-4 — Communications between Predecessor and Successor Accountants

SSARS-9 — Omnibus Statement on Standards for Accounting and Review Services — 2002

SSARS-15 — Elimination of Certain References to Statements on Auditing Standards and Incorporation of Appropriate Guidance into Statements on Standards for Accounting and Review Services

SSARS-17 — Omnibus Statement on Standards for Accounting and Review Services — 2008

SSARS Interpretation 1 — Reports on the Application of Accounting Principles (November 2002)

Overview

SSARS-4, as amended by SSARS-9, provides the following definitions:

> *Successor accountant:* An accountant who has been invited to make a proposal for an engagement to compile or review financial statements and is considering accepting the engagement or an accountant who has accepted such an engagement.

> *Predecessor accountant:* An accountant who (a) has reported on the most recent compiled or reviewed financial statements or was engaged to perform but did not complete a compilation or review of the financial statements, and (b) has resigned, declined to stand for reappointment, or been notified that his or her services have been, or may be, terminated.

The successor accountant may (but is not required to) communicate with the predecessor accountant, with the prospective client's permission, in order to determine whether a compilation or review engagement should be accepted. SSARS-9 notes that the inquiries "should be specific and reasonable regarding matters that will assist the successor accountant in determining whether to accept the engagement" and may include areas of inquiry such as the following:

- Management (owner's) integrity

- Disagreements concerning accounting principles, the performance of engagement procedures, or "similarly significant matters"

- Management cooperation with requests for additional or revised information

- Fraud or illegal acts

- The reason for the change of accountants

The predecessor accountant should respond promptly and fully to inquiries posed by the successor accountant except in cases of unusual circumstances such as litigation. When the response is limited, the predecessor accountant should inform the successor accountant about the situation.

The successor accountant may also request, with the client's permission, a review of the predecessor accountant's working papers. SSARS-9 notes that the predecessor accountant should determine which working papers should be made available to and copied by the successor accountant. SSARS-4 notes that the predecessor accountant may decide to request a written communication from the successor accountant before allowing access to working papers. Exhibit AR 400-1 reproduces an example letter that appears in SSARS-9 whereby the predecessor accountant requests a written communication from the successor accountant regarding the use of the predecessor accountant's working papers.

> **OBSERVATION:** If the successor accountant discovers during the engagement that the financial statements compiled or reviewed by the predecessor accountant may have to be revised, the successor accountant should request the client to inform the predecessor accountant of this possibility. SSARS-9 states that if the client refuses to inform the predecessor accountant of the matter or is not satisfied with the predecessor accountant's response to the notification, the successor accountant should consider the impact (including withdrawal from the engagement or consultation with legal counsel) of such developments on the current engagement.

Promulgated Procedures Checklist

The successor accountant should perform the following procedures with respect to communications between the predecessor accountant and the successor accountant:

- Consider whether circumstances make it advisable to make inquiries of the predecessor accountant.

- Determine whether the predecessor accountant should be advised that prior-period financial statements must be revised.

Analysis and Application of Procedures

Consider whether circumstances make it advisable to make inquiries of the predecessor accountant

Although the successor accountant is not required to make inquiries of the predecessor accountant, circumstances surrounding the engagement might suggest that such inquiries ought to be made. SSARS-4 does not attempt to provide general or specific guidelines for defining which circumstances may suggest a need to communicate with the predecessor accountant, but it lists four examples that may lead the successor accountant to contact the predecessor accountant: (1) frequent changes of accountants, (2) limited information about the client and its principals, (3) existing information that raises questions about the client and its principals, or (4) the change of accountants at a date significantly after the end of the accounting period for which the service is to be provided.

Before the oral or written inquiries are made, the successor accountant must obtain the consent of the client, so that the predecessor accountant is not put in the position of violating Rule 301 (Confidential Client Information) of the AICPA's Code of Professional Conduct. If the client refuses to authorize the successor accountant to communicate with the predecessor accountant, the successor accountant should evaluate the basis for such refusal in deciding whether to accept the engagement. The predecessor accountant is expected to respond promptly and fully to the successor accountant's inquiries — except under unusual circumstances, such as impending litigation with respect to services performed by the predecessor accountant. If the predecessor accountant refuses to respond to the inquiries, he or she should explain to the successor accountant that responses are limited by circumstances.

The following items are identified as typical inquiries that the successor accountant might make:

- Information about the management's or owners' integrity

- Disagreements about accounting matters or the performance of procedures

- The degree of cooperation of management or the owners in providing additional or revised information

- The predecessor's knowledge of fraud or illegal acts perpetrated by the client

- The predecessor accountant's explanation of why there was a change of accountants

Other inquiries

SSARS-4 notes that a successor accountant may wish to make inquiries of the predecessor accountant as a typical part of the acceptance of any engagement, even if circumstances do not suggest that there may be problems with the client's management or its owners. For example, the successor accountant may simply wish to inquire about the adequacy of underlying financial data or about recurring problem areas of the engagement. Again, the predecessor accountant is expected to respond to reasonable requests from the successor accountant. However, the predecessor accountant still must obtain the client's permission to release information to the successor accountant.

The fact that the predecessor accountant has responded to inquiries or has made workpapers available to the successor accountant does not provide a basis for referring to the work of the predecessor accountant in the successor accountant's report. However, the predecessor accountant's report may be used when comparative financial statements are presented. The reporting formats for comparative financial statements when predecessor and successor accountants are involved are discussed in AR 200.

Determine whether the predecessor accountant should be advised that prior-period financial statements must be revised

During the engagement, the accountant may become aware of information that requires the revision of financial statements that the predecessor accountant reported on. Under this circumstance, SSARS-7 requires that the successor accountant request that the client communicate the information to the predecessor accountant.

> **PLANNING AID REMINDER:** Accountants may be asked by entities that are not their clients to give advice on how a transaction should or could be accounted for and what type of opinion or assurance would be appropriate for a particular set of financial statements. In some instances, these requests are made by prospective clients who are shopping for an

opinion. To provide guidance in this area, the Auditing Standards Board issued SAS-50 (AU 625) (Reports on the Application of Accounting Principles). SSARS Interpretation No. 1 of AR 400 states that standards established by SAS-50 (AU 625) are applicable to requests related to compilations and reviews as well as audit engagements.

EXHIBIT AR 400-1 — PREDECESSOR ACCOUNTANT'S LETTER REQUESTING A WRITTEN COMMUNICATION FROM THE SUCCESSOR ACCOUNTANT CONCERNING ACCESS TO WORKING PAPERS

[*Date*]

[*Successor Accountant*]

[*Address*]

We have previously [reviewed *or* compiled], in accordance with Statements on Standards for Accounting and Review Services, the December 31, 20X5, financial statements of Bluefield Company. In connection with your [review *or* compilation] of Bluefield Company's 20X6 financial statements, you have requested access to our working papers prepared in connection with that engagement. Bluefield Company has authorized our firm to allow you to review those working papers.

Our [review *or* compilation] and the working papers prepared in connection therewith of Bluefield Company's financial statements were not planned or conducted in contemplation of your [review *or* compilation]. Therefore, items of possible interest to you might not have been specifically addressed. Our use of professional judgment for the purpose of this engagement means that matters may have existed that would have been assessed differently by you. We make no representation about the sufficiency or appropriateness of the information in our working papers for your purposes.

We understand that the purpose of your review is to obtain information about Bluefield Company and our 20X5 results to assist you in your 20X6 engagement of Bluefield Company. For that purpose only, we will provide you access to our working papers that relate to that objective.

Upon request, we will provide copies of those working papers that provide factual information about Bluefield Company. You agree to subject any such copies or information otherwise derived from our working papers to your normal policy for retention of working papers and protection of confidential client information. Furthermore, in the event of a third-party request for access to your working papers prepared in connection with your [review *or* compilation] of Bluefield Company, you agree to obtain our permission before voluntarily allowing any such access to our working papers or information otherwise derived from our working papers, and to obtain on our behalf any releases that you obtain from such third party. You agree to advise us promptly and provide us a copy of any subpoena, summons, or other court order for access to your working papers that include copies of our working papers or information otherwise derived therefore.

Please confirm your agreement with the foregoing by signing and dating a copy of this letter and returning it to us.

Very truly yours,

[*Predecessor Accountant*]

By: _____

Accepted:

[*Successor Accountant*]

By: _____

Date: _____

Note: SSARS-9 points out that to encourage the predecessor accountant to provide access to working papers, it may be desirable to add the following paragraph to the letter illustrated above:

Because your review of our working papers is undertaken solely for the purpose described above and may not entail a review of all our working papers, you agree that (1) the information obtained from the review will not be used by you for any other purposes, (2) you will not comment, orally or in writing, to anyone as a result of that review about whether our engagement was performed in accordance with Statements on Standards for Accounting and Review Services, and (3) you will not provide expert testimony or litigation services or otherwise accept an engagement to comment on issues relating to the quality of our engagement.

AR SECTION 600

REPORTING ON PERSONAL FINANCIAL STATEMENTS INCLUDED IN WRITTEN PERSONAL FINANCIAL PLANS

Authoritative Pronouncements

SSARS-6 — Reporting on Personal Financial Statements Included in Written Personal Financial Plans

SSARS Interpretation 1 — Submitting a Personal Financial Plan to a Client's Advisers (May 1991)

Overview

SSARS-1 states that an accountant associated with unaudited financial statements of a nonissuer must either compile or review the financial statements. SSARS-6 (Reporting on Personal Financial Statements Included in Written Personal Financial Plans) provides an exception to this general requirement.

Promulgated Procedures Checklist

The accountant should perform the following procedures when reporting on personal financial statements included in written personal financial plans:

• Determine whether the standards established by SSARS-1 have to be observed.

• Prepare the appropriate report on the financial statements.

Analysis and Application of Procedures

Determine whether the standards established by SSARS-1 have to be observed

When an accountant prepares a written personal financial plan that includes unaudited personal financial statements, the requirements established by SSARS-1 (as amended) do not have to be observed if the following conditions exist:

- An understanding with the client is reached (preferably in writing) that the financial statements (1) will be used only by the client or the client's advisers to develop personal financial goals and objectives and (2) will not be used to obtain credit or for any purpose other than the establishment of goals and objectives related to the financial plan.

- During the engagement, nothing came to the accountant's attention that would suggest that the personal financial statements would be (1) used to obtain credit or (2) used for any purpose other than the establishment of financial goals and objectives for the client.

> **PLANNING AID REMINDER:** SSARS Interpretation No. 1 of AR 600 states that actual implementation of the personal financial plan by the client or the client's advisers (investment adviser, attorney, insurance broker, etc.) is part of "developing a client's personal financial goals and objectives."

Prepare the appropriate report on the financial statements

If the accountant concludes that the exemption criteria described above have been satisfied, a written report should be prepared. The accountant's report should include the following comments:

- That the unaudited financial statements were prepared to facilitate the development of the client's personal financial plan

- That the unaudited financial statements may be incomplete or may contain other departures from generally accepted accounting principles and should not be used to obtain credit or for any purpose other than the establishment of the personal financial plan

- That the unaudited financial statements have not been audited, reviewed, or compiled by the accountant

An example of an accountant's report on personal financial statements included in a written personal financial plan is presented in Exhibit AR 600-1.

Each personal financial statement should contain a reference to the accountant's report (such as "See accountant's report").

PLANNING AID REMINDER: Although SSARS-6 provides an exemption to the requirements established by SSARS-1, the accountant is not precluded from observing the standards established by SSARS-1. It should also be noted that when an accountant decides to audit, review, or compile personal financial statements, SOP 82-1 (ASC 274) (Accounting and Financial Reporting for Personal Financial Statements) requires that the personal financial statements present assets at their estimated current values and liabilities at their estimated current amounts at the date of the financial statements when presented in accordance with generally accepted accounting principles (GAAP). However, if the personal financial statements are presented at historical cost, instead of at current value, the presentation constitutes an other comprehensive basis of accounting.

Practitioner's Aids

EXHIBIT AR 600-1 — ALTERNATIVE ACCOUNTANT'S REPORT ON PERSONAL FINANCIAL STATEMENTS INCLUDED IN WRITTEN PERSONAL FINANCIAL PLANS

The accompanying Statement of Financial Condition of [*name of client*], as of December 31, 20X8, was prepared solely to help you develop your personal financial plan. Accordingly, it may be incomplete or contain other departures from generally accepted accounting principles and should not be used to obtain credit or for any purposes other than developing your financial plan. We have not audited, reviewed, or compiled the statement.

APPENDIX A

The Sarbanes-Oxley Act of 2002

Introduction

The United States Congress passed, and President Bush signed into law, the Sarbanes-Oxley Act (SOX) in the summer of 2002. This legislation is viewed as the most far-reaching legislation affecting the accounting profession since the issuance of the securities laws of the 1930s that created the Securities and Exchange Commission (SEC). Provided here is an overview of the key components of SOX and related rules implemented by the SEC.

The Sarbanes-Oxley Act applies to SEC registrants and their auditors. Although SOX does not apply to private companies, not-for-profit organizations, or governmental entities, state boards of accountancy might incorporate portions of the act into state accountancy rules and regulations that apply to all audits. Other regulators are considering whether provisions similar to those in SOX should be mandated for other types of entities.

The Sarbanes-Oxley Act comprises 11 sections:

1. The Public Company Accounting Oversight Board (PCAOB)
2. Auditor independence
3. Corporate responsibility
4. Enhanced financial disclosures
5. Analyst conflicts of interest
6. Commission resources and authority
7. Studies and reports
8. Corporate and criminal fraud accountability
9. White-collar crime penalty enhancements
10. Corporate tax returns
11. Corporate fraud and accountability

SOX is a direct result of alleged financial reporting fraud at a number of major corporations, which increasingly became a matter of concern in the fall of 2001 with the first disclosure of problems at Enron. Those problems, combined with other alleged frauds at Global Crossing, Qwest, Adelphia Communications, Tyco, and WorldCom increased public scrutiny of the financial reporting and related audit process. The resulting public outrage at these allegations of financial reporting fraud was reflected by the overwhelming votes in favor of SOX in both houses of Congress. SOX passed the Senate 99-0, and only three votes were cast against it in the House of Representatives.

Public Company Accounting Oversight Board

Among the more important provisions of SOX is the creation of the Public Company Accounting Oversight Board (PCAOB). The PCAOB's mission is to "Oversee the audits of public companies, to protect the interests of investors, and to further the public interest in the preparation of informative, accurate, and independent audit reports." The PCAOB is responsible for overseeing all aspects of the public accounting profession related to audits of SEC registrants (public companies). Much of the AICPA's former self-regulatory efforts over public company audits were obviated by the creation of the PCAOB.

All accounting firms that audit public company financial statements must register to practice with the PCAOB. In addition, the PCAOB has the authority to establish or adopt auditing, quality control, ethics, and independence standards for auditors of public companies. As part of its enforcement authority, the PCAOB conducts inspections of registered public accounting firms to assess compliance with SOX, SEC, and PCAOB rules, and other professional standards. Finally, the PCAOB investigates allegations of substandard performance by auditors of public companies and has the power to discipline offending accounting firms and individual auditors of public companies.

The PCAOB has five full-time members, only two of whom can be licensed CPAs. The SEC appoints board members after consulting with the Chairman of the Board of Governors of the Federal Reserve System and the U.S. Secretary of the Treasury. The term of service is five years, and board members are limited to two terms.

The PCAOB's current members are Daniel Goelzer (Acting Chairman), Bill Gradison, Charles Niemeier, and Steve Harris. There is one open position. Goelzer and Niemeier are CPAs and have experience in public accounting, although they more recently practiced as securities lawyers. Both men have prior experience with the SEC. Gradison has served as a member of the U.S. House of Representatives, as a mayor of Cincinnati, and as president of a health-care industry association. Harris previously served as the Staff Director and Chief Counsel to the U.S. Senate Banking, Housing, and Urban Affairs Committee under Senator Sarbanes, and he was one of the primary drafters of the Sarbanes-Oxley Act.

The accounting and auditing practice experience of the PCAOB's board members appears to be limited. Thus, it is likely that the board will rely heavily on its professional staff, particularly in setting auditing standards for audits of public companies. The PCAOB's Chief Auditor is Martin Baumann, who was previously the Director of the Office of Research and Analysis at the PCAOB and who prior to joining the PCAOB had a more than 30-year career with PricewaterhouseCoopers. Other professionals in the Office of the Chief Auditor include individuals with significant experience in the public accounting profession.

The PCAOB assesses and collects a registration fee and an annual fee from each registered public accounting firm. These fees are to be sufficient to recover the costs of both processing registrations and the required annual report that each registered accounting firm is to file with the PCAOB. Public companies are also assessed an annual accounting support fee.

Although the PCAOB is charged with promulgating auditing standards, SOX specifically requires that these standards include the following provisions:

- Registered public accounting firms must maintain workpapers in sufficient detail to support their conclusions in the audit report. The workpapers must be retained for at least seven years.

- The issuance of an audit report must be approved by a concurring or second partner. Each audit report must describe the scope of the auditor's internal control testing. The auditor must include, either in the audit report or in a separate report, the following items: (1) the auditor's findings from the internal control testing, (2) an overall evaluation of the entity's internal control structure and procedures, and (3) a description of any material weaknesses in internal controls.

- Quality control standards related to required internal firm consultations on accounting and auditing questions must be adhered to.

The PCAOB adopted the AICPA's Statements on Auditing Standards (SAS) that existed as of April 16, 2003 as its "Interim Auditing Standards." Since April 2003, the PCAOB has issued seven Auditing and Related Professional Practice Standards (one of which has been superseded) and numerous rules.

The PCAOB inspects public accounting firms that regularly audit more than 100 public companies on an annual basis. Other public accounting firms that audit at least one public company are inspected no less often than once every three years. Inspections involve reviews of audit engagements and of the firm's quality control system. The PCAOB can report violations of (1) the Sarbanes-Oxley Act, (2) PCAOB and SEC rules, (3) the firm's own quality control standards, and (4) professional standards to the SEC and each appropriate state regulatory authority.

Registered public accounting firms and their employees are required to cooperate with PCAOB investigations. Firms that fail to cooperate in

PCAOB investigations can be suspended or disbarred from being able to audit public companies, as can individual CPAs. Although the PCAOB does not have subpoena power (the PCAOB is specifically designated as a nongovernmental entity), there are procedures for the PCAOB to obtain needed information for an investigation using an SEC-issued subpoena. Documents and information gathered by the PCAOB in the course of an investigation are not subject to civil discovery. PCAOB sanctions include the suspension or disbarment of firms or individual CPAs from auditing public companies, as well as monetary penalties as high as $750,000 for individuals and $15 million for firms.

SOX amends the Securities Acts of 1933 and 1934 to define as "generally accepted accounting principles" those principles promulgated by a standards-setting body when the standards-setting body meets a number of requirements set out in SOX. The FASB's current structure meets the requirements set out in SOX. Thus, the PCAOB does not establish accounting standards.

The PCAOB's funding and the funding of the accounting standards-setting body (currently the FASB) are recoverable from annual accounting support fees. These annual accounting support fees are assessed against and are recoverable from public companies, where the amount of the fee due from each issuer is a function of the issuer's relative market capitalization.

Auditor Independence

SOX specifically prohibits accounting firms from performing any of the following services for a public company audit client:

- Bookkeeping services

- Financial information systems design and implementation

- Appraisal or valuation services, fairness opinions, or contribution-in-kind reports

- Actuarial services

- Internal audit outsourcing services

- Management or human resources functions

- Broker or dealer, investment adviser, or investment banking services

- Legal services and expert services unrelated to the audit

Many of these nonaudit services were already prohibited by SEC rules. However, the provision of any other nonaudit services for an audit client, including tax work, is now allowed only if approved in advance by the audit committee. In addition, the audit committee must preapprove all audit, review, or attest engagements required under the securities laws, as well as other audit services (e.g., comfort letters for underwriters, statutory audits, etc.).

Reporting to the Audit Committee

SOX requires the auditor to provide a timely report to the audit committee containing the following information: (1) a discussion of critical accounting policies and practices; (2) alternative accounting treatments discussed with management, the ramifications of these alternatives, and the auditor's preferred treatment; and (3) other material communications between the auditor and management (e.g., the management letter, schedule of unadjusted audit differences, engagement letter, independence letter). These required communications are in addition to, and do not supplant, the existing required communications from the auditor to the audit committee in already existing auditing professional standards (see, in particular, SAS-89 (AU 333, AU 380), SAS-99 (AU 230, AU 312, AU 316, AU 333), SAS-114 (AU 380), SAS-115 (AU 325), and SAS-116 (AU 722)). Although SAS-114, SAS-115, and SAS-116 have not been adopted by the PCAOB, it is likely that auditors will make similar communications to the audit committees of public companies. SAS-115 requires auditors to communicate certain internal control related matters to the audit committee. Required communications to the audit committee relating to internal control are specified in AS-5. In addition, as the 2011 edition of CCH's *GAAS Guide* went to press, the PCAOB had outstanding an exposure draft of a standard on auditor communications to audit committees.

Mandatory Audit Partner Rotation

SOX requires that the lead audit partner and concurring partner on an audit of a public company be rotated every five years, and these individuals must remain off the engagement for at least five years. The SEC's interpretation of SOX extended this rotation requirement to other audit partners. Other audit partners must rotate after seven years and they must remain off the engagement for at least two years. The SEC defines other audit partners as (1) partners with decision-making responsibility on significant accounting, auditing, and reporting matters, (2) partners who maintain regular contact with management and the audit committee, and (3) lead partners on subsidiaries whose assets or revenues constitute 20% or more of the consolidated totals.

Audit Firm Personnel Movement to the Client

A registered public accounting firm is not independent of a public company if an individual who has direct responsibility for, or oversight of, those who prepare the company's financial statements and related information was employed by the registered public accounting firm and worked on the audit engagement within one year prior to the beginning of the current year's audit. Individuals who have responsibility for, or oversight of, the company's financial reporting process would include, at a minimum, the company's CEO, president, chief operating officer, CFO, controller, chief accounting officer, general counsel, treasurer, director of internal audit, director of financial reporting, or a member of the board of directors.

Required Disclosures of Services and Fees

Public companies must disclose in their annual proxy statement the services performed and the fees received by their registered public accounting firm during the previous year. These fees must be categorized into one of four categories: (1) audit fees, (2) audit-related fees, (3) tax fees, and (4) all other fees. Audit fees include fees for the annual audit and reviews of interim financial information, comfort letters, statutory audits, attest services, and consents and assistance related to documents filed with the SEC. Audit-related fees include fees for employee benefit plan audits, due diligence services related to mergers and acquisitions, accounting consultations and audits in connection with acquisitions, and attest services not required by statute or regulation. Tax fees and all other fees are self-explanatory.

Corporate Responsibility

SOX imposes increased responsibilities on audit committees and senior management for accurate financial reporting. In addition, SOX imposes penalties on senior management if financial statements have to be restated due to noncompliance with GAAP and related SEC regulations. SOX also proscribes any attempt by management or others acting at the direction of management to exert pressure on the auditor relating to the conduct of the audit.

Audit Committee Responsibilities

SOX specifies that the audit committee is directly responsible for the appointment, compensation, and oversight of the external auditor. SOX also requires that all members of the audit committee be independent. Audit committees are to establish procedures for handling complaints related to accounting, internal controls, and auditing matters, including complaints that are submitted anonymously. Audit committees are to be given the authority to retain independent counsel and other advisers, if they deem this to be necessary. Finally, each public company must provide the funding that the audit committee believes is necessary to compensate the registered public accounting firm. National securities exchanges (e.g., NYSE) and national securities associations (e.g., NASDAQ) are prohibited from listing securities issued by a company that is not in compliance with SOX's audit committee rules.

CEO and CFO Certifications

SOX requires the CEO and CFO of each public company to certify in each annual and quarterly report filed with the SEC the following conditions:

- That the CEO and CFO have reviewed the report

- To the best of the officers' knowledge, the report does not contain any material omissions or misstatements

- That the financial statements and other financial information included in the report fairly present the entity's financial condition and results of operations (compliance with GAAP if the financial statements are not fairly stated is not a defense under the terms of SOX)

- That the signing officers are responsible for the entity's internal control system, that the internal control system is appropriately designed, that the effectiveness of the internal control system has been evaluated within 90 days of the report, and that the officers' conclusions about the effectiveness of internal controls are included within the report

- That the signing officers have disclosed to their auditors and the audit committee significant deficiencies in the design or operation of the entity's internal control as well as any fraud (even if immaterial) involving management or employees with a significant role in the entity's internal control structure

- Whether there have been any significant changes in internal control subsequent to the date of its evaluation

Penalties in Cases of Restatements

SOX also requires the CEO and CFO of any issuer restating its financial statements because of material noncompliance with SEC financial reporting requirements to forfeit any bonus or incentive-based or equity-based compensation received within one year of the filing date of the financial statements that are subsequently restated. Profits realized from the sale of securities during this 12-month period also must be forfeited.

Improper Influence on the Conduct of an Audit

SOX makes it unlawful for any officer or director or any other person operating under an officer or director's direction, to coerce, manipulate, mislead, or fraudulently influence the external auditor in the audit of financial statements if that person knows or should have known that such action, if successful, could result in making the financial statements materially misleading. An attempt to coerce or manipulate the auditor implies compelling the auditor to act in a certain way through pressure, threats, trickery, intimidation, or some other form of purposeful action.

The SEC defines an "officer" as the CEO, president, vice presidents, secretary, treasurer, principal financial officer (often the CFO), controller, and principal accounting officer (CAO). In addition, the SEC defines "direction" as a broader concept than purely supervision. Examples of persons who might be under the direction of an officer or director but not under their supervision include customers, vendors, creditors, attorneys, securities professionals, and even other partners or employees of the accounting firm. According to the SEC, improper influence can happen (1) before the audit (e.g., during negotiations for the retention of the auditor), (2) during the audit, and (3) after the audit (e.g., when the auditor is considering whether to consent to the use of, reissuance of, or the withdrawal of a prior audit report). The SEC states that improper influence on the conduct of an audit is an illegal act, and Section 10A of the 1934 Exchange Act requires the auditor to file a report with the SEC when the auditor becomes aware of the client's participation in an illegal act.

The SEC provides numerous examples of behavior that is or might indicate improper influence on the conduct of an audit, including

- Offering or paying bribes or other financial incentives (e.g., offers of future employment or offers of contracts for nonaudit services)

- Providing an auditor with an inaccurate or misleading legal analysis

- Canceling or threatening to cancel existing nonaudit or audit engagements if the auditor objects to the company's accounting

- Seeking to have a partner removed from the engagement because a partner objects to the company's accounting

- Blackmail

- Physical threats

- Knowingly providing the auditor inadequate or misleading information that is key to the audit

- Pressuring the auditor to transfer managers or principals from the audit engagement

- And when predicated by an intent to defraud: (1) verbal abuse, (2) creating undue time pressure, (3) not providing information to the auditors on a timely basis, and (4) not being available to discuss matters with the auditor on a timely basis

Enhanced Financial Disclosures

The SOX section on financial disclosures requires certain behavior by management, prohibits certain activities, and significantly enhances financial statement disclosures.

Audit Adjustments

SOX requires public companies to reflect in the financial statements all material adjustments to the financial statements identified by the external auditor. Thus, there should be no waived or passed adjustments that have a material effect on the financial statements.

Disclosure of Off-Balance-Sheet Transactions

Companies must disclose all material off-balance-sheet transactions, arrangements, and obligations. The SEC now requires companies to explain their off-balance sheet arrangements in a new, and separately captioned, section of the MD&A section of the Form 10-K. Also, most companies are now required to include a table that presents an overview of certain known contractual obligations.

Pro Forma Financial Information

SOX specifically prohibits misleading pro forma financial information. Pro forma financial information also must be reconciled with what would be required under GAAP.

Loans to and Stock Transactions by Executives

SOX generally prohibits personal loans to executives. In addition, stock transactions by directors, officers, and principal stockholders must be disclosed by the close of the second business day after the date of the stock transaction.

Internal Control Reports

SOX requires internal control reports in each annual report. Management must state that it is responsible for internal control over financial reporting and it must provide an assessment of the effectiveness of that internal control. Management must identify the framework it used in evaluating its internal controls over financial reporting (in all likelihood, the COSO framework, *Internal Control—Integrated Framework,* will be used in the United States).

Internal controls over financial reporting are designed to provide reasonable assurance that financial statements are prepared in accordance with GAAP. As such, internal controls are designed to

- Ensure the maintenance of records that in reasonable detail accurately and fairly reflect the transactions and dispositions of the company

- Provide reasonable assurance that transactions are recorded as necessary to permit preparation of financial statements in accordance with GAAP, and that receipts and expenditures are being made only in accordance with authorizations of management and the directors

- Provide reasonable assurance regarding prevention or timely detection of unauthorized acquisition, use, or disposition of the company's assets

Management's assessment of internal control over financial reporting must include an assessment of both the system's design and operating effectiveness. Controls that must be evaluated include those relating to

- Initiating, recording, processing, and reconciling account balances, classes of transactions, and disclosures
- Initiation and processing of nonroutine and nonsystematic transactions
- The selection and application of appropriate accounting policies
- The prevention, identification, and detection of fraud

Finally, the company's external auditor must issue its own opinion on the effectiveness of the company's internal control over financial reporting.

Code of Ethics

Public companies are required to state whether or not they have a code of ethics that applies to the company's principal executive officer, principal financial officer, principal accounting officer or controller and, if not, why not. The code of ethics must address requirements related to

- Honest and ethical conduct
- Full, fair, accurate, timely, and understandable disclosure in SEC filings and other public communications
- Compliance with applicable governmental laws, rules, and regulations
- Prompt internal reporting to an appropriate person of violations of the code
- Accountability for adherence to the code

The company must disclose its code of ethics, if one exists. The company can disclose its code of ethics as an exhibit to its annual report, on its Web site, or by providing without charge a copy of the code of ethics to any person upon request. Finally, any changes or waivers (including an implicit waiver) to the code of ethics for senior officers must be disclosed in a Form 8-K filing to the SEC.

Audit Committee Financial Expert

Public companies must disclose whether or not the audit committee contains at least one financial expert and, if not, why not. The company must disclose the name of the audit committee financial expert and state whether the expert is independent of management. An audit committee financial expert should possess

- An understanding of GAAP and financial statements

- An ability to assess the general application of GAAP to accounting for estimates, accruals, and reserves

- Experience in preparing, auditing, analyzing, or evaluating financial statements (or actively supervising individuals who perform these tasks) of comparable breadth and complexity to those of the company

- An understanding of internal control over financial reporting

- An understanding of audit committee functions

It is important to note that because a large proportion of board members have current or prior experience as a CEO, a principal executive officer with significant operations involvement but little financial or accounting involvement, would not meet the SEC's definition as exercising active supervision and therefore would not qualify as an audit committee financial expert.

Rapid Disclosure of Material Events

A company is required to disclose in plain English on a rapid and current basis (generally within four business days of the event's occurrence) any material change in the company's financial condition and results of operations. Items that are required to be disclosed on Form 8-K include

- Entering into a material definitive agreement not in the ordinary course of business (e.g., business combination agreements)

- Terminating a material definitive agreement not in the ordinary course of business

- New obligations under the terms of a material direct financial obligation (e.g., a short-term debt obligation arising in other than the ordinary course of business, a long-term debt obligation, and a lease, whether capital or operating), or if the company becomes directly or contingently liable for a material obligation arising from an off-balance sheet arrangement

- An event that accelerates (e.g., default) or increases a direct financial obligation or an obligation under an off-balance sheet arrangement

- Expected costs associated with an exit or disposal plan if the exit or disposal plan meets the FAS-146 (ASC 420) (Accounting for Costs Associated with Exit or Disposal Activities) criteria

- Material asset impairment charges required to be recognized under GAAP

- A notice of delisting or a failure to continue to meet listing requirements received from a national securities exchange (e.g., NYSE) or association (e.g., NASDAQ)

- The sale of equity securities in a transaction that is not registered under the Securities Acts

- Material modifications to the rights held by any holders of a company's securities

- A determination by the company that its previously issued financial statements should no longer be relied upon because of an error in the financial statements, including situations where the company's auditor indicates that previously issued audit reports should no longer be relied upon

- If a director resigns from the board or chooses not to stand for reelection due to a disagreement with management, or if a director is removed from the board for cause

Analyst Conflicts of Interest

The Sarbanes-Oxley Act seeks to increase the objectivity and independence of securities analysts. SOX specifically requires that

- Analysts' research reports no longer be subject to clearance or approval by investment bankers

- Investment bankers be prohibited from providing input into the performance evaluations of research analysts

- Investment bankers be prohibited from threatening retaliation or retaliating against research analysts for reports that might adversely affect investment-banking relationships with existing or prospective clients

- Structural and institutional safeguards be established to protect research analysts from review, pressure, or oversight by investment bankers.

SOX also requires the disclosure of analyst conflicts of interest in both public appearances and published research reports. When discussing a particular company in a public appearance or research report, the analyst must disclose how much of the company's debt or equity securities the analyst's firm or the analyst personally owns. The analyst must disclose whether he or she personally or his or her firm has received any compensation from the company that is the subject of the research report. If the analyst is recommending a company's securities, he or she must disclose whether the company is a current client of his or her employer or if it has been a client during the past year. The analyst must also disclose whether his or her compensation is tied to investment banking revenues.

SEC Resources and Authority

SOX provides substantial incremental funding for the SEC. The SEC used a portion of this funding to hire a significant number of additional qualified professionals to oversee auditors and the public accounting profession.

The Sarbanes-Oxley Act also clarifies the ability of the SEC to censure individuals and to bar, either temporarily or permanently, individuals from practicing before the SEC. These remedies are available to the SEC if an individual

- Lacks the qualifications needed to represent others

- Lacks character or integrity

- Has engaged in unethical or improper professional conduct

- Has willfully violated, or helped others to willfully violate (i.e., aided and abetted) the securities laws

SOX defines "improper professional conduct" to include an intentional or knowing violation of applicable professional standards, including a violation attributable to reckless conduct. Improper professional conduct also includes two types of negligent conduct:

1. A single instance of highly unreasonable conduct, leading to a violation of professional standards, when the firm or the practitioner should have known that heightened scrutiny was warranted

2. Repeated instances of unreasonable conduct leading to a violation of professional standards, which suggests that the individual may lack the competence to practice before the SEC

Studies and Reports

SOX required either the SEC or the Government Accountability Office (GAO) (formerly known as the General Accounting Office) to conduct five types of studies. These studies involve examination of issues related to (1) the consolidation of the public accounting profession, (2) the role of credit rating agencies in the securities markets, (3) violations of securities laws, (4) SEC enforcement actions and restatements of financial statements, and (5) the role and functioning of investment banks in the securities markets.

The GAO studied the effects on the securities markets of the consolidation of the public accounting profession that began in the late 1980s, and it issued its report on July 30, 2003. The study included (1) factors leading to the consolidation of the profession, (2) the impact of this consolidation on capital formation and the securities markets, and (3) solutions to any problems identified, including ways to increase competition and increase the number of accounting firms able to audit large national and multinational companies. The study considered whether the consolidation of the public accounting profession has affected business organizations with regard to higher costs, lower quality, less choice, and lack of auditor independence.

The GAO found that the Big 4 firms have the potential for significant market power, although there is no evidence to date that competition has been impaired. The GAO failed to find any link between consolidation in the public accounting profession and either audit quality or audit independence. The GAO identified significant barriers to smaller accounting firms joining the ranks of the Big 4 and concluded that market forces are unlikely to expand the ranks of the four largest firms. The GAO updated this study in a report released in January of 2008. Although the GAO found that concentration continued in the audit market for large public companies, it made no recommendation for change.

The SEC studied the role of credit rating agencies in the securities markets and issued its report in January 2003. The study examined threats to the ability of credit rating agencies to accurately assess the risks of issuers. The study also examined barriers to the entry of new credit rating agencies and ways to remove those barriers.

As a result of this study, the U.S. Congress passed, and President Bush signed (September 29, 2006), the Credit Rating Agency Reform Act of 2006. The act amends the 1934 Securities Exchange Act and is designed to both improve the quality of credit ratings and to protect investors by increasing accountability, transparency, and competition in the credit rating industry. The Act creates a voluntary registration and regulatory program, overseen by the SEC, for credit rating agencies that want to be designated as a "nationally recognized statistical rating organization (NRSRO)."

The SEC has issued a rule to implement the Credit Rating Agency Reform Act. Under the SEC's rule, a credit rating agency seeking designation as a NRSRO must meet the following requirements: (1) be in business as a credit rating agency for at least the last three years and (2) issue credit ratings certified by qualified institutional buyers to one or more of the following groups: financial institutions, brokers, or dealers; insurance companies; corporate issuers; asset-backed securities issuers; and issuers of government or municipal securities. In order to qualify as a credit rating agency, the agency must (1) be engaged in the business of issuing credit ratings through a readily accessible means, for free or for a reasonable fee, (2) employ a quantitative or qualitative (or both) methodology in determining ratings, and (3) receive fees from either issuers, investors, or market participants.

The SEC studied violations of securities laws between 1998 and 2001 and issued its report in January 2003. The study investigated how many public accountants, public accounting firms, investment bankers, investment advisers, brokers, dealers, attorneys, and other securities professionals were found to have aided and abetted in the violation of securities laws but who were not sanctioned or disciplined as a primary violator in either an administrative action or civil proceeding. The SEC also determined how many such individuals were found to have been primary violators of the securities laws. Finally, the SEC categorized the specific violations of securities laws, including sanctions imposed on the violators.

The SEC found that 1,596 securities professionals violated federal securities laws (or aided and abetted others in their violations of such laws) between 1998 and 2001. Public accountants and public accounting firms were not among the most frequent violators of federal securities laws. The sections of federal securities law most frequently violated were Section 10(b) of the 1934 Exchange Act and Section 17(a) of the 1933 Securities Act (which both relate to the antifraud provisions of the related securities acts).

The SEC conducted a study of its enforcement releases and financial statement restatements during the five-year period prior to the passage of SOX and issued its report in January 2003. The focus of the study was to identify the financial reporting areas most susceptible to fraud, inappropriate manipulation, or inappropriate earnings management. The SEC studied enforcement actions issued during the five-year period between July 31, 1997 and July 31, 2002 that were based on improper financial reporting, fraud, audit failure, or auditor independence violations. The most frequent area involving an enforcement action was improper revenue recognition. A significant number of enforcement actions also involved improper expense recognition, including improper capitalization or deferral of expenses, improper use of reserves, and other understatements of expenses. In approximately 75% of the cases the enforcement action was brought against one or more members of senior management. Eighteen enforcement actions were brought against auditing firms and 89 actions were brought against individual auditors. Enforcement actions against auditors typically resulted from lack of audit evidence, lack of skepticism, and lack of independence.

The GAO conducted a study to determine whether investment banks helped companies manipulate their earnings and obfuscate their true financial condition. SOX specifically required the GAO to address the role investment banks played in designing derivative transactions and special-purpose entities for the Enron Corporation and in swapping of fiber-optic capacity by Global Crossing. The GAO issued its report on March 17, 2003. The GAO found that certain investment banks facilitated complex financial transactions with Enron despite allegedly knowing that the intent of these transactions was to obfuscate Enron's true financial condition. The GAO also found that control groups within financial institutions and bank regulators have increased their review and scrutiny of structured finance transactions in the wake of the problems at Enron and Global Crossing.

Corporate and Criminal Fraud Accountability

SOX imposes severe criminal penalties for prohibited forms of document destruction and for violations of the securities laws. Prison sentences of up to 20 years can be imposed for the destruction, alteration, or falsification of records in federal investigations and bankruptcy. Auditors must retain for seven years their workpapers and other relevant documents related to audit conclusions. Failure to comply with these SEC rules and regulations can result in prison terms of up to 10 years. An individual who knowingly attempts to execute or executes a scheme or artifice to defraud any person relative to the securities laws faces prison sentences of up to 25 years.

SOX changed the bankruptcy laws to specify that debts incurred as a result of violations of the securities laws are not dischargeable in bankruptcy. The length of time to file a civil suit under the securities laws was extended to two years after discovering the violation or five years after the violation occurred.

SOX provides whistleblowers with certain protections against retaliation by the public company or its agents. Parties can be imprisoned for up to 10 years for knowingly retaliating against an individual for providing truthful information to a law enforcement officer regarding the commission of a federal offense.

White-Collar Crime Penalty Enhancements

SOX amends the U.S. Code by increasing the criminal penalties for both mail and wire fraud from five years to 20 years. In addition, SOX imposes criminal penalties on CEOs and CFOs when they certify financial reports that do not comport with the requirements of the act. The penalties are a fine of as much as $1 million and imprisonment for as many as 10 years for improper certifications, and a fine of as much as $5 million and imprisonment for as many as 20 years for willfully improper certifications.

Corporate Tax Returns

The Sarbanes-Oxley Act contains a sense of the Senate, which is not a legal requirement, that CEOs should sign the corporate tax return.

Corporate Fraud and Accountability

SOX imposes fines and potential prison terms of up to 20 years for tampering with a record, document, or other object or otherwise impeding an official proceeding. In addition, criminal penalties available under the Securities and Exchange Act of 1934 have been increased.

In some cases, public companies attempt to make large payments to officers, directors, and others when the company is under investigation for possible violations of securities laws. SOX empowers the SEC to petition a federal district court to restrain a public company from making extraordinary payments to officers, directors, and others during the course of an investigation. The proposed payments would be placed in escrow for 45 days, and one extension of the 45-day period may be obtained. If the company is charged with a securities law violation, the contemplated extraordinary payments would continue to be held in escrow until the case is resolved.

SOX makes it easier for the SEC to suspend or permanently prohibit an individual from serving as an officer or director of a public company if the individual has violated Section 10(b) of the 1934 Securities and Exchange Act or Section 17(a) of the 1933 Securities Act. Previously, the SEC had to bring an action in federal court to bar an individual from serving as an officer or director of a public company.

Emerging Trends

In the eight years that SOX has been in effect, trends that are a result of the act have emerged:

- Audit committees are more engaged in financial reporting oversight than ever before, they are meeting more often and they are increasingly taking control of the relation with the external auditor. However, there are still too many cases where the audit committee, although legally charged with overseeing the external audit process, defers to management.

- Audit fees have increased, in some cases by a substantial percentage. However, in more recent years, likely due to the recession, there has been substantial downward pressure on audit fees.

- The PCAOB is having a pervasive impact on the practice of public accounting.

- Accounting standards issued by the FASB are likely to be more principles-based, and the FASB and the International Accounting Standards Board are increasingly working together to issue converged accounting standards that have broad applicability around the globe.

- Aspects of SOX are likely to affect private companies, not-for-profit organizations, and governmental entities, and the auditors who serve these companies, particularly in states with more aggressive regulation and in certain regulated industries.

- Some formerly public companies have gone private, at least in part due to the significant compliance burden imposed by SOX.

- Private companies that hope to go public or be acquired by a public company are taking steps to comply with most of SOX's provisions.

Further consequences from Sarbanes-Oxley will only become apparent with the passage of time.

Recent Developments

The Sarbanes-Oxley Act of 2002 has been criticized heavily by certain groups. Many of these criticisms were tied to the cost and complexity of issuing a management report on the effectiveness of internal control over financial reporting (Section 404a) and the related auditor issuance of an opinion on management's assessment process, as well as the auditor's own opinion on the effectiveness of the company's internal control over financial reporting (Section 404b). As a result of these criticisms, the SEC undertook a number of initiatives.

The SEC extended the effective date of Section 404 for smaller public companies (i.e., nonaccelerated filers) for a number of years. However, for fiscal years ending after December 15, 2007, companies with a market capitalization below $75 million will have to include in their Form 10-K a management report on the effectiveness of internal control over financial reporting. Unlike larger public companies, due to continuing deferrals of the requirements of Section 404b the external auditor is not yet required to issue an opinion on the effectiveness of internal control. The SEC issued a rule in the final quarter of 2009 indicating that these deferrals of the requirements in Section 404b will end. In fiscal years ending after June 15, 2010, the external auditor will issue a separate opinion on the effectiveness of internal control over financial reporting. However, there are a number of bills pending in the U.S. Congress that would permanently exempt smaller companies (i.e., non-accelerated filers) from having an external auditor report on the effectiveness of the company's internal control over financial reporting. As the 2011 edition of CCH's *GAAS Guide* went to press, this issue remained unresolved.

The SEC also asked the Committee of Sponsoring Organizations of the Treadway Commission (COSO) to develop implementation guidance for applying its internal control framework for smaller public companies. In 2006 COSO issued *Internal Control over Financial Reporting — Guidance for Smaller Public Companies*, which provides implementation guidance for applying COSO's internal control framework in a manner that seeks to maintain the effectiveness of internal control reporting while reducing its cost and complexity. COSO has released *Guidance on Monitoring Internal*

Control Systems, which is designed to help management better utilize the results of monitoring to support their conclusions about the effectiveness of internal control over financial reporting.

In early 2006 a small accounting firm and a private special-interest group filed suit in federal court challenging the constitutionality of the PCAOB. The U.S. District Court hearing the case found for the PCAOB, as did a three-judge panel of the Court of Appeals for the D.C. Circuit. In May 2009 the U.S. Supreme Court announced that it would hear the case in its 2009–2010 year. The Supreme Court heard arguments on the case in December 2009 and a decision by the Court was issued in June 2010. The Supreme Court held that the Sarbanes-Oxley Act's provisions making PCAOB Board members removable by the Securities and Exchange Commission (SEC) only for good cause were inconsistent with the Constitution's separation of powers. Because the Court severed these provisions from the Act, however, no legislation was necessary to bring the Board's structure within constitutional requirements. The consequence of the Court's decision is that PCAOB Board members will be removable by the SEC at will, rather than only for good cause.

Finally, the SEC has issued a document that provides guidance to management in performing its evaluation of the effectiveness of internal control over financial reporting. In addition, the PCAOB has released a standard on auditor reporting on internal control (AS-5) that replaces the Board's previous standard, AS-2. Both documents share a number of similarities, including (1) emphasizing that evaluating internal control should follow a top-down risk-based process, (2) greater reliance on ongoing monitoring as support for management's evaluation and greater reliance on the work of others to support the auditor's opinion, and (3) numerous changes to afford management and the auditor more flexibility in evaluating the design and operating effectiveness of internal control, which are designed to reduce the cost and burden of internal control reporting.

Accounting Resources on the Web

Presented here are World Wide Web URLs of interest to practitioners. Because of the constantly changing nature of the Internet, addresses change and new resources become available every day. To find additional resources, use search engines such as Google (http://www.google.com), the Open Directory Project (http://www.dmoz.org), and Yahoo! (http://www.yahoo.com).

"Agreed-Upon Procedures and Results Assessment of Federal Audit Clearinghouse Database Fiscal Year 1998 Audit Reports"
www.oig.doc.gov/oig/reports/2000/ESA-Census-ATL-12556-07-2000.pdf

"Choosing an External Auditor"
www.auditforum.org/mid%2øamerica/midam_exauditor.htm

Accountants World   http://www.accountantsworld.com/

Accounting Research Manager
http://www.accountingresearchmanager.com/

Accounting Resources on the Internet   http://accounting.rutgers.edu/

Action Without Borders–Idealist.org
http://www.idealist.org/if/i/en/npofaq

AICPA http://www.aicpa.org

AICPA Library Service
http://www.olemiss.edu/depts/general_library/aicpa

American Accounting Association   http://www.aaahq.org

American Legal Publishing Corp.
http://amlegal.com/library

Association of Certified Fraud Examiners (ACFE)
http://www.acfe.org/

Association of College and University Auditors (ACUA)
http://www.acua.org

Association of Government Accountants (AGA)
http://www.agacgfm.org/homepage.aspx

Association of Local Government Auditors (ALGA)
http://www.GovernmentAuditors.org/

Association of School Business Officials   http://www.asbointl.org/

Automated Clearing House   http://www.fms.treas.gov/ach/

BoardSource   http://www.boardsource.org/

Bureau of Labor Statistics   http://www.bls.gov/

Cash Management Improvement Act   http://www.fms.treas.gov/cmia/

Catalog of Federal Domestic Assistance (CFDA)   http://www.cfda.gov/

CCH INCORPORATED   http://CCHGroup.com/

Code of Federal Regulations   http://www.gpoaccess.gov/cfr/

Compliance Assistance Employment Law Guide
http://www.dol.gov/compliance/guide/dbra.htm

Compliance Supplement
http://www.whitehouse.gov/omb/circulars/a133_compliance/04/04toc.html

COSO (Committee of Sponsoring Organizations of the Treadway Commission)   http://www.coso.org/

Council of State Governments (CSG)   http://www.csg.org/csg/default

Council on Foundations   http://www.cof.org/

Data Collection Form
http://harvester.census.gov/fac/collect/formoptions.html

Department of Education OIG's Non-Federal Audit Team
www2.ed.gov/about/offices/list/oig/nonfed/nfteam.html

Electronic Privacy Information Center   http://www.epic.org/

Evangelical Council for Financial Accountability (ECFA)
http://www.ecfa.org/

FASB   http://www.fasb.org/

Federal Agencies Web Locator   http://www.lib.lsu.edu/gov/

Federal Audit Clearinghouse   http://harvester.census.gov/sac/

Federal Financial Accounting Standards Board (FASAB)
http://www.fasab.gov/

Federal Inspectors General (IGnet)   http://www.ignet.gov/

Federal Register   http://www.gpoaccess.gov/fr/index.html

FEDSTATS   http://www.fedstats.gov/

Forensic Accounting Information
http://www.forensic-accounting-information.com/

GASB   http://www.gasb.org/

Government Accountability Office   http://www.gao.gov/

General Services Administration   http://www.gsa.gov/

Government Accounting Standards
http://www.gao.gov/govaud/ybk01.htm

Government Finance Officers Association (GFOA)
http://www.gfoa.org/

Government Printing Office   http://www.gpo.gov/

GSA Forms   http://www.gsa.gov/forms

Health and Human Resources (HHS)   http://www.hhs.gov/

IGnet Federal Inspectors General
http://www.ignet.gov/

Infomine government publications
http://infomine.ucr.edu/cgi-bin/search?category=govpub

Information about Tax-Exempt Organizations
http://www.irs.ustreas.gov/charities/eo/index.html

Institute of Internal Auditors, The (IIA)   http://www.theiia.org/

Institute of Management Accountants (IMA)   http://www.imanet.org/

Intergovernmental Audit Forums   http://www.auditforum.org/

Internal Audit and Fraud Investigation Articles
http://www.mrsciacfe.cjb.net/

International Accounting Standards Board   http://www.iasb.org

International City/County Managers Association
http://www.icma.org/

International Federation of Accountants   http://ifac.org

International Financial Reporting Standards   http://www.ifrs.com

International Organization of Securities Commission
http://www.iosco.org/about/

IRS Digital Daily   http://www.irs.gov/

IT Audit (The IIA)   http://www.itaudit.org/

Legal Information Institute (Cornell Law School)
http://www.law.cornell.edu/statutes.html

Legal Services Corporation (LSC)   http://www.lsc.gov/

LSU Libraries Government Documents
http://www.lib.lsu.edu/govdocs/index.html

National Archives and Records Administration Code of Federal Regulations   http://www.gpoaccess.gov/cfr/index.html

National Association of College and University Business Officers (NACUBO)   http://www.nacubo.org/

National Association of Local Government Auditors (NALGA)
http://www.nalga.org/

National Association of State Auditors, Comptrollers, and Treasurers (NASACT)   http://www.nasact.org/

National Association of State Boards of Accountancy (NASBA)
http://www.nasba.org/

National Association of State Budget Officers   http://www.nasbo.org/

National Conference of State Legislatures (NCSL)
http://www.ncsl.org/

National Labor Relations Board   http://www.nlrb.gov/

North American Industry Classification System (NAICS)
http://www.census.gov/epcd/www/naics.html

Occupational Employment Statistics   http://stats.bls.gov/oes/home.htm

Office of Federal Contract Compliance Programs (OFCCP)
http://www.dol.gov/ofccp/regs/compliance/ca_irca.htm

Office of Management and Budget   http://www.whitehouse.gov/omb

PCIE Single Audit Guidance
http://www.ignet.gov/pande/audit/psingle.html

Police List of Resources: Electronic Crime
http://police.sas.ab.ca/prl/elect.html

Privacy Foundation   http://www.privacyfoundation.org/

Prompt Payment Act Interest Rate
http://www.treasurydirect.gov/govt/rates/tcir/tcir_opdprmt2.htm

ProSystem fx   http://CCHGroup.com/ProSystem/default.htm

Public Company Accounting Oversight Board
http://www.pcaobus.org

SAB-99   http://www.sec.gov/interps/account/sab99.htm

SAB-101   http://www.sec.gov/interps/account/sab101.htm

Sarbanes-Oxley Act of 2002
http://www.gpo.gov/fdsys/pkg/PLAW-107publ204/content-detail.html

SEC Edgar Database   http://www.sec.gov/edgar.shtml

SEC Staff Accounting Bulletins
http://www.sec.gov/interps/account.shtml

Securities and Exchange Commission   http://www.sec.gov/

Software and Information Industry Association (SIIA)
http://www.siia.net/

State and local links
http://www.Statelocal.gov

Sterling Codifiers, Inc.
http://Sterlingcodifiers.com/codebook/index.php?book_id=408

The Library of Congress   http://www.loc.gov/

Thomas: Legislative Information   http://thomas.loc.gov/

Treasury — Financial Management Service   http://www.fms.treas.gov/

Uniform CPA Examination   http://www.cpa-exam.org/

U.S. Conference of Mayors   http://www.usmayors.org/

U.S. Department of Agriculture   http://www.usda.gov/

U.S. Department of Commerce   http://www.commerce.gov/

U.S. Department of Defense   http://www.defense.gov

U.S. Department of Education   http://www.ed.gov/

U.S. Department of Energy   http://www.energy.gov/

U.S. Department of Health and Human Services   http://www.dhhs.gov/

U.S. Department of Housing and Urban Development
http://www.hud.gov/

U.S. Department of Labor Wage and Hour Division
http://www.dol.gov/whd/index.htm

U.S. Department of Labor   http://www.dol.gov/

U.S. Department of State   http://www.state.gov/

U.S. Department of the Interior   http://www.doi.gov/

U.S. Department of the Treasury's Listing of Approved Sureties
http://www.fms.treas.gov/c570/c570.html

U.S. Department of Transportation   http://www.dot.gov/

U.S. Dept. of Treasury Financial Management Service
http://www.fms.treas.gov/

U.S. Environmental Protection Agency http://www.epa.gov/

U.S. GAO Bid Protest Decisions
http://www.gao.gov/decisions/bidpro/bidpro.htm

U.S. General Services Administration http://www.gsa.gov/

U.S. government forms http://www.gsa.gov/forms

U.S. House of Representatives Current Floor Proceedings
http://clerk.house.gov/

U.S. House of Representatives http://www.house.gov/

U.S. HUD Office of Inspector General
http://www.hud.gov/offices/oig/

U.S. HUD Office of Labor Relations
http://www.hud.gov/offices/olr/index.cfm

U.S. Senate http://www.senate.gov/

U.S. Small Business Administration http://www.sba.gov/

U.S. State & Local Gateway http://www.statelocal.gov/

U.S. Treasury http://www.treas.gov/

University of Michigan Documents Center
http://www.lib.umich.edu/govdocs/

Yellow Book http://www.gao.gov/govaud/ybk01.htm

Cross-Reference

STATEMENTS ON AUDITING STANDARDS (SASs) AND SAS INTERPRETATIONS

ORIGINAL PRONOUNCEMENT	GAAS GUIDE REFERENCE
SAS-1 — Codification of Auditing Standards and Procedures	
Responsibilities and Functions of the Independent Auditor	AU 110
• No Interpretations	
Generally Accepted Auditing Standards	Superseded by SAS-95.
Nature of the General Standards	AU 201
• No Interpretations	
Training and Proficiency of the Independent Auditor	AU 210
• No Interpretations	
Independence	AU 220
• No Interpretations	
Due Care in the Performance of Work	Amended by SAS-104.
• No Interpretations	
Inventories	AU 331
• No Interpretations	
Adherence to Generally Accepted Accounting Principles	AU 410
• Auditing Interpretation No. 3 of AU 410 (February 1997) — The Impact of the Auditor's Report of a FASB Statement Prior to the Statement's Effective Date	
Consistency of Application of Generally Accepted Accounting Principles	AU 420
• Auditing Interpretation No. 2 of AU 420 (February 1974) — The Effect of APB Opinion 28 on Consistency	

ORIGINAL PRONOUNCEMENT   GAAS GUIDE REFERENCE

- Auditing Interpretation No. 3 of AU 420 (April 1989) — Impact of the Auditor's Report of LIFO to LIFO Change in Comparative Financial Statements

- Auditing Interpretation No. 8 of AU 420 (June 1993) — The Effect of Accounting Changes by an Investee on Consistency

- Auditing Interpretation No. 10 of AU 420 (December 1980) — Change in Presentation of Accumulated Benefit Information in the Financial Statements of a Defined Benefit Pension Plan

- Auditing Interpretation No. 12 of AU 420 (April 2002) — The Effect on the Auditor's Report of an Entity's Adoption of a New Accounting Standard That Does Not Require the Entity to Disclose the Effect of the Change in the Year of Adoption

Dating of the Independent Auditor's Report   AU 530

- No Interpretations

Part of Audit Performed by Other Independent Auditors   AU 543

- Auditing Interpretation No. 1 of AU 543 (November 1996) — Specific Procedures Performed by the Other Auditor at the Principal Auditor's Request

- Auditing Interpretation No. 2 of AU 543 (April 1979) — Inquiries of the Principal Auditor by the Other Auditor

- Auditing Interpretation No. 3 of AU 543 (April 1979) — Form of Inquiries of the Principal Auditor Made by the Other Auditor

- Auditing Interpretation No. 4 of AU 543 (April 1979) — Form of Principal Auditor's Response to Inquiries from Other Auditors

- Auditing Interpretation No. 5 of AU 543 (April 1979) — Procedures of the Principal Auditor

- Auditing Interpretation No. 6 of AU 543 (December 1981) — Application of Additional Procedures Concerning the Audit Performed by the Other Auditor

ORIGINAL PRONOUNCEMENT	GAAS GUIDE REFERENCE
Lack of Conformity with Generally Accepted Accounting Principles	AU 544
• No Interpretations	
Subsequent Events	AU 560
• No Interpretations	
Subsequent Discovery of Facts Existing at the Date of the Auditor's Report	AU 561
• Auditing Interpretation No. 1 of AU 561 (February 1989) — Auditor's Association with Subsequently Discovered Information When the Auditor Has Resigned or Been Discharged	
Public Warehouses — Controls and Auditing Procedures for Goods Held	AU 901
• No Interpretations	
SAS-2 — Reports on Audited Financial Statements	Superseded by SAS-58.
SAS-3 — The Effects of EDP on the Auditor's Study and Evaluation of Internal Control	Superseded by SAS-48.
SAS-4 — Quality Control Considerations for a Firm of Independent Auditors	Superseded by SAS-25.
SAS-5 — The Meaning of "Present Fairly in Conformity with Generally Accepted Accounting Principles" in the Independent Auditor's Report	Superseded by SAS-69.
SAS-6 — Related Party Transactions	Superseded by SAS-45.
SAS-7 — Communications Between Predecessor and Successor Auditors	Superseded by SAS-84.
SAS-8 — Other Information in Documents Containing Audited Financial Statements	Superseded by SAS-118.
SAS-9 — The Effect of an Internal Audit Function on the Scope of the Independent Auditor's Examination	Superseded by SAS-65.
SAS-10 — Limited Review of Interim Financial Information	Superseded by SAS-24.
SAS-11 — Using the Work of a Specialist	Superseded by SAS-73.
SAS-12 — Inquiry of a Client's Lawyer Concerning Litigation, Claims, and Assessments	AU 337 and AU 560
• Auditing Interpretation No. 1 of AU 337 (March 1977) —Specifying Relevant Date in an Audit Inquiry Letter	

ORIGINAL PRONOUNCEMENT   GAAS GUIDE REFERENCE

- Auditing Interpretation No. 2 of AU 337 (March 1977) — Relationship Between Date of Lawyer's Response and Auditor's Report

- Auditing Interpretation No. 3 of AU 337 (March 1977) — Form of Audit Inquiry Letter When Client Represents That No Unasserted Claims and Assessments Exist

- Auditing Interpretation No. 4 of AU 337 (March 1977) — Documents Subject to Lawyer-Client Privilege

- Auditing Interpretation No. 5 of AU 337 (June 1983)—Alternative Wording of the Illustrative Audit Inquiry Letter to a Client Lawyer

- Auditing Interpretation No. 6 of AU 337 (June 1983) — Client Has Not Consulted a Lawyer

- Auditing Interpretation No. 7 of AU 337 (February 1997) — Assessment of a Lawyer's Evaluation of the Outcome of Litigation

- Auditing Interpretation No. 8 of AU 337 (June 1983) — Use of the Client's Inside Counsel in the Evaluation of Litigation, Claims, and Assessments

- Auditing Interpretation No. 9 of AU 337 (February 1990) — Use of Explanatory Language about the Attorney–Client Privilege or the Attorney Work-Product Privilege

- Auditing Interpretation No. 10 of AU 337 (January 1997) — Use of Explanatory Language Concerning Unasserted Possible Claims or Assessments in Lawyer's Response to Audit Inquiry Letters

SAS-13 — Reports on a Limited Review of Interim Financial Information   Superseded by SAS-24.

SAS-14 — Special Reports   Superseded by SAS-62.

SAS-15 — Reports on Comparative Financial Statements   Superseded by SAS-58.

SAS-16 — The Independent Auditor's Responsibility for the Detection of Errors or Irregularities   Superseded by SAS-53.

ORIGINAL PRONOUNCEMENT	GAAS GUIDE REFERENCE
SAS-17 — Illegal Acts by Clients	Superseded by SAS-54.
SAS-18 — Unaudited Replacement Cost Information	Withdrawn
SAS-19 — Client Representations	Superseded by SAS-85.
SAS-20 — Required Communication of Material Weaknesses in Internal Accounting Control	Superseded by SAS-60.
SAS-21 — Segment Information	Rescinded [See Interpretation (August 1998) in AU 326.]
SAS-22 — Planning and Supervision	Superseded by SAS-108.
SAS-23 — Analytical Review Procedures	Superseded by SAS-56.
SAS-24 — Review of Interim Financial Information	Superseded by SAS-36.
SAS-25 — The Relationship of Generally Accepted Auditing Standards to Quality Control Standards	AU 161
• No Interpretations	
SAS-26 — Association with Financial Statements	AU 504
• Auditing Interpretation No. 1 of AU 504 (November 2002) — Annual Report Disclosure of Unaudited Fourth Quarter Interim Data	
• Auditing Interpretation No. 4 of AU 504 (November 1979) — Auditor's Identification with Condensed Financial Data	
• Auditing Interpretation No. 5 of AU 504 (November 1979) — Applicability of Guidance on Reporting When Not Independent	
SAS-27 — Supplementary Information Required by the Financial Accounting Standards Board	Superseded by SAS-52.
SAS-28 — Supplementary Information on the Effects of Changing Prices	Superseded by SAS-52.
SAS-29 — Reporting on Information Accompanying the Basic Financial Statements in Auditor-Submitted Documents	Superseded by SAS-119.
SAS-30 — Reporting on Internal Control	Superseded by SSAE-2.
SAS-31 — Evidential Matter	Superseded by SAS-106.

ORIGINAL PRONOUNCEMENT	GAAS GUIDE REFERENCE
SAS-32 — Adequacy of Disclosures in Financial Statements	AU 431
• No Interpretations	
SAS-33 — Supplementary Oil and Gas Reserve Information	Superseded by SAS-45.
SAS-34 — The Auditor's Considerations When a Question Arises about an Entity's Continued Existence	Superseded by SAS-59.
SAS-35 — Special Reports — Applying Agreed-Upon Procedures to Specified Elements, Accounts, or Items of a Financial Statement	Superseded by SAS-75.
SAS-36 — Review of or Performing Procedures on Interim Financial Information	Superseded by SAS-71.
SAS-37 — Filings under Federal Securities Statutes	AU 711
• Auditing Interpretation No. 1 of AU 711 (May 1983) — Subsequent Events Procedures for Shelf Registration Statements Updated after the Original Effective Date	
• Auditing Interpretation No. 2 of AU 711 (March 1995) — Consenting to Be Named as an Expert in an Offering Document in Connection with Securities Offerings Other Than Those Registered Under the Securities Act of 1933	
• Auditing Interpretation No. 3 of AU 711 (June 1992) — Consenting to the Use of an Audit Report in an Offering Document in Securities Offerings Other Than One Registered Under the Securities Act of 1993	
SAS-38 — Letters for Underwriters	Superseded by SAS-49.
SAS-39 — Audit Sampling	AU 350; amended by SAS-111
• Auditing Interpretation No. 1 of AU 350 (January 1985) — Applicability	
SAS-40 — Supplementary Mineral Reserve Information	Superseded by SAS-52.
SAS-41 — Working Papers	Superseded by SAS-96.
SAS-42 — Reporting on Condensed Financial Statements and Selected Financial Data	AU 552
• No Interpretations	
SAS-43 — Omnibus Statement on Auditing Standards	AU 331, AU 350, AU 420, and AU 901

ORIGINAL PRONOUNCEMENT	GAAS GUIDE REFERENCE

SAS-44 — Special-Purpose Reports on Internal Accounting Control at Service Organizations

Superseded by SAS-70.

SAS-45 — Omnibus Statement on Auditing Standards — 1983

AU 334 and AU 350

- Auditing Interpretation No. 4 of AU 334 (April 1979) — Exchange of Information Between the Principal and Other Auditor on Related Parties

- Auditing Interpretation No. 5 of AU 334 (April 1979) — Examination of Identified Related Party Transactions with a Component

- Auditing Interpretation No. 6 of AU 334 (May 1986) — The Nature and Extent of Auditing Procedures for Examining Related Party Transactions

- Auditing Interpretation No. 7 of AU 334 (May 2000) — Management's and Auditor's Responsibilities With Regard to Related Party Disclosures Prefaced by Terminology Such As "Management Believes That"

SAS-46 — Consideration of Omitted Procedures after the Report Date

AU 390

- No Interpretations

SAS-47 — Audit Risk and Materiality in Conducting an Audit

Superseded by SAS-107.

SAS-48 —The Effects of Computer Processing on the Examination of Financial Statements

Superseded by SAS-106 and SAS-107.

SAS-49 — Letters for Underwriters

Superseded by SAS-72.

SAS-50 — Reports on the Application of Accounting Principles

Amended by SAS-97.

- Auditing Interpretation No. 1 of AU 625 (January 2005) — Requirement to Consult with the Continuing Accountant

SAS-51 — Reporting on Financial Statements Prepared for Use in Other Countries

AU 534

- Auditing Interpretation No. 1 of AU 534 (May 1996) — Financial Statement for General Use Only Outside of the U.S. in Accordance with International Accounting Standards and International Standards on Auditing

ORIGINAL PRONOUNCEMENT	GAAS GUIDE REFERENCE

- Auditing Interpretation No. 2 of AU 534 (May 2008) — Financial Statements Prepared in Conformity with International Financial Reporting Standards as Issued by the International Accounting Standards Board

- Auditing Interpretation No. 3 of AU 534 (May 2008) — Financial Statements Audited in Accordance with International Standards on Auditing

SAS-52 — Omnibus Statement on Auditing Standards — 1987 (Required Supplementary Information)   AU 551 and AU 558

- Auditing Interpretation No. 1 of AU 558 (February 1989) — Supplementary Oil and Gas Information

SAS-53 — The Auditor's Responsibility to Detect and Report Errors and Irregularities   Superseded by SAS-82.

SAS-54 — Illegal Acts by Clients   AU 317

- Auditing Interpretation No. 1 of AU 317 (October 1978) — Consideration of the Internal Control Structure in a Financial Statement Audit and the Foreign Corrupt Practices Act

- Auditing Interpretation No. 2 of AU 317 (October 1978) — Material Weakness in Internal Control and the Foreign Corrupt Practices Act

SAS-55 — Consideration of Internal Control in a Financial Statement Audit   Superseded by SAS-109 and SAS-110.

SAS-56 — Analytical Procedures   AU 329

- No Interpretations

SAS-57 — Auditing Accounting Estimates   AU 342

- Auditing Interpretation No. 1 of AU 342 (October 2000) — Performance and Reporting Guidance Related to Fair Value Disclosures

SAS-58 — Reports on Audited Financial Statements   AU 508

- Auditing Interpretation No. 1 of AU 508 (October 2000) — Report of an Outside Inventory-Taking Firm as an Alternative Procedure for Observing Inventories

ORIGINAL PRONOUNCEMENT   GAAS GUIDE REFERENCE

- Auditing Interpretation No. 8 of AU 508 (October 2000) — Reporting on Financial Statements Prepared on a Liquidation Basis of Accounting

- Auditing Interpretation No. 12 of AU 508 (January 1989) — Reference in Auditor's Standard Report to Management's Report

- Auditing Interpretation No. 14 of AU 508 (May 2008) — Reporting on Audits Conducted in Accordance with Auditing Standards Generally Accepted in the United States of America and in Accordance with International Standards on Auditing

- Auditing Interpretation No. 15 of AU 508 (November 2002) — Reporting as Successor Auditor When Prior-Period Audited Financial Statements Were Audited by a Predecessor Auditor Who Has Ceased Operations

- Auditing Interpretation No. 16 of AU 508 (June 2003) — Effect on Auditor's Report of Omission of Schedule of Investments by Investment Partnerships That Are Exempt from Securities and Exchange Commission Registration under the Investment Company Act of 1940

- Auditing Interpretation No. 17 of AU 508 (June 2004) — Clarification in the Audit Report of the Extent of Testing of Internal Control over Financial Reporting in Accordance with Generally Accepted Auditing Standards

- Auditing Interpretation No. 18 of AU 508 (June 2004) — Reference to PCAOB Standards in an Audit Report on a Nonissuer

- Auditing Interpretation No. 19 of AU 508 (May 2008) — Financial Statements Prepared in Conformity with International Financial Reporting Standards as Issued by the International Accounting Standards Board

SAS-59 — The Auditor's Consideration of an Entity's Ability to Continue as a Going Concern   AU 341

- Auditing Interpretation No. 1 of AU 341 (August 1995) — Elimination of a Going Concern Explanatory Paragraph from a Reissued Report

ORIGINAL PRONOUNCEMENT	GAAS GUIDE REFERENCE
SAS-60 — Communication of Internal Control Related Matters Noted in an Audit	Superseded by SAS-112.
SAS-61 — Communication with Audit Committees	Superseded by SAS-114.
SAS-62 — Special Reports	AU 410, AU 544, and AU 623

- Auditing Interpretation No. 9 of AU 623 (October 2000) — Auditors' Special Reports on Property and Liability Insurance Companies' Loss Reserves

- Auditing Interpretation No. 10 of AU 623 (October 2000) — Reports on the Financial Statements Included in Internal Revenue Form 990 (Return of Organizations Exempt from Income Tax)

- Auditing Interpretation No. 11 of AU 623 (October 2000) — Reporting on Current-Value Financial Statements That Supplement Historical-Cost Financial Statements in a Presentation of Real Estate Entities

- Auditing Interpretation No. 12 of AU 623 (January 2005) — Evaluation of the Appropriateness of Informative Disclosures in Insurance Enterprises' Financial Statements Prepared on a Statutory Basis

- Auditing Interpretation No. 13 of AU 623 (February 1999) — Reporting on a Special-Purpose Financial Statement That Results in an Incomplete Presentation but Is Otherwise in Conformity with GAAP

- Auditing Interpretation No. 14 of AU 623 (January 2005)—Evaluating the Adequacy of Disclosure and Presentation in Financial Statements Prepared in Conformity with an Other Comprehensive Basis of Accounting (OCBOA)

- Auditing Interpretation No. 15 of AU 623 (January 2005) — Auditor Reports on Regulatory Accounting or Presentation When the Regulated Entity Distributes the Financial Statements to Parties Other Than the Regulatory Agency Either Voluntarily or Upon Specific Request

SAS-63 — Compliance Auditing Applicable to Governmental Entities and Other Recipients of Governmental Financial Assistance Superseded by SAS-68.

ORIGINAL PRONOUNCEMENT	GAAS GUIDE REFERENCE

SAS-64 — Omnibus Statement on Auditing Standards —1990

AU 341, AU 508, and AU 543

SAS-65 — The Auditor's Consider of the Internal Audit Function in an Audit of Financial Statements

AU 322

- No Interpretations

SAS-66 — Communication of Matters About Interim Financial Information Filed or to Be Filed with Specified Regulatory Agencies — An Amendment to SAS No. 36, Review of Interim Financial Information

Superseded by SAS-71.

SAS-67 — The Confirmation Process

AU 330 and AU 331

- Auditing Interpretation No. 1 of AU 330 (November 2008) — Use of Electronic Confirmations

SAS-68 — Compliance Auditing Applicable to Governmental Entities and Other Recipients of Governmental Financial Assistance

Superseded by SAS-74.

SAS-69 — The Meaning of "Present Fairly in Conformity with Generally Accepted Accounting Principles"

AU 411

- Auditing Interpretation No. 3 of AU 411 (October 2000) — The Auditor's Consideration of Management's Adoption of Accounting Principles for New Transactions or Events

SAS-70 — Service Organizations

AU 324

- Auditing Interpretation No. 1 of AU 324 (April 1995) — Describing Tests of Operating Effectiveness and the Results of Such Tests

- Auditing Interpretation No. 2 of AU 324 (April 1995) — Service Organizations That Use the Services of Other Service Organizations (Subservice Organizations)

- Auditing Interpretation No. 4 of AU 324 (February 2002) — Responsibilities of Service Organizations and Service Auditors with Respect to Forward-Looking Information in a Service Organization's Description of Controls

- Auditing Interpretation No. 5 of AU 324 (February 2002) — Statements about the Risk of Projecting Evaluations of the Effectiveness of Controls to Future Periods

ORIGINAL PRONOUNCEMENT	GAAS GUIDE REFERENCE
SAS-71 — Interim Financial Information	Superseded by SAS-100.
SAS-72 — Letters for Underwriters and Certain Other Requesting Parties	AU 634

- Auditing Interpretation No. 1 of AU 634 (January 2001) — Letters to Directors Relating to Annual Reports on Form 10-K

- Auditing Interpretation No. 3 of AU 634 (August 1998) — Commenting in a Comfort Letter on Quantitative Disclosures about Market Risk Made in Accordance with Item 305 of Regulations S-K

SAS-73 — Using the Work of a Specialist   AU 336

- Auditing Interpretation No. 1 of AU 336 (December 2001) — The Use of Legal Interpretations as Evidential Matter to Support Management's Assertion That a Transfer of Financial Assets Has Met the Isolation Criterion in Paragraph 9(a) of Financial Accounting Standards Board Statement No. 140

SAS-74 — Compliance Auditing Considerations in Audits of Governmental Entities and Recipients of Governmental Financial Assistance   Superseded by SAS-117.

SAS-75 — Engagements to Apply Agreed-Upon Procedures to Specified Elements, Accounts, or Items of a Financial Statement   Withdrawn

SAS-76 — Amendments to Statement on Auditing Standards No. 72, Letters for Underwriters and Certain Other Requesting Parties   AU 634

SAS-77 — Amendments to Statements on Auditing Standards No. 22, "Planning and Supervision," No. 59, "The Auditor's Consideration of an Entity's Ability to Continue as a Going Concern," and No. 62, "Special Reports"   AU 341, AU 544, and AU 623

SAS-78 — Consideration of Internal Control in a Financial Statement Audit: An Amendment to SAS-55   Superseded by SAS-109.

SAS-79 — Amendments to Statement on Auditing Standards No. 58, "Reports on Audited Financial Statements"   AU 508

- No Interpretations

ORIGINAL PRONOUNCEMENT	GAAS GUIDE REFERENCE

SAS-80 — Amendment to Statement on Auditing Standards No. 31, Evidential Matter

Superseded by SAS-106.

SAS-81 — Auditing Investments

Superseded by SAS-92.

SAS-82 — Consideration of Fraud in a Financial Statement Audit

Superseded by SAS-99.

SAS-83 — Establishing an Understanding with the Client

Superseded by SAS-108.

SAS-84 — Communications Between Predecessor and Successor Auditors

AU 315

- No Interpretations

SAS-85 — Management Representations

AU 333 and AU 508

- Auditing Interpretation No. 1 of AU 333 (March 1979) — Management Representations on Violations and Possible Violations of Laws and Regulations

SAS-86 — Amendment to Statement on Auditing Standards No. 72, Letters for Underwriters and Certain Other Requesting Parties

AU 634

- No Interpretations

SAS-87 — Restricting the Use of an Auditor's Report

AU 532

- No Interpretations

SAS-88 — Service Organizations and Reporting on Consistency

AU 324 and AU 420

- No Interpretations

SAS-89 — Audit Adjustments

AU 333 and AU 380

- No Interpretations

SAS-90 — Audit Committee Communications

Superseded by SAS-100 and SAS-114.

SAS-91 — Federal GAAP Hierarchy

AU 411

- No Interpretations

SAS-92 — Auditing Derivative Instruments, Hedging Activities, and Investments in Securities

AU 332

- Auditing Interpretation No. 1 (July 2005) — Auditing Investments in Securities Where a Readily Determinable Fair Value Does Not Exist

ORIGINAL PRONOUNCEMENT	GAAS GUIDE REFERENCE
SAS-93 — Omnibus Statement on Auditing Standards — 2000	AU 315, AU 411, AU 508, and AU 622
• No Interpretations	
SAS-94 — The Effect of Information Technology on the Auditor's Consideration of Internal Control in a Financial Statement Audit	Superseded by SAS-109.
SAS-95 — Generally Accepted Auditing Standards	AU 150; amended by SAS-105
• No Interpretations	
SAS-96 — Audit Documentation	Superseded by SAS-103.
SAS-97 — Amendment to Statement on Auditing Standards No. 50, Reports on the Application of Accounting Principles	AU 625
• No Interpretations	
SAS-98 — Omnibus Statement on Auditing Standards — 2002	
• No Interpretations	AU 150, AU 161, AU 312, AU 324, AU 508, AU 530, AU 550, AU 551, AU 558, AU 560, and AU 561
SAS-99 — Consideration of Fraud in a Financial Statement Audit	AU 230, AU 312, AU 316, and AU 333
• No Interpretations	
SAS-100 — Interim Financial Information	AU 722, amended by SAS-116
• No Interpretations	
SAS-101 — Auditing Fair Value Measurements and Disclosures	AU 328
• Auditing Interpretation No. 1 (July 2005) — Auditing Interests in Trusts Held by a Third-Party Trustee and Reported at Fair Value	
SAS-102 — Defining Professional Requirements in Statements on Auditing Standards	AU 120
• No Interpretations	
SAS-103 — Audit Documentation	AU 339, as redrafted
• No Interpretations	
SAS-104 — Amendment to SAS No. 1, Codification of Auditing Standards and Procedures "Due Professional Care in the Performance of Work"	AU 230
• No Interpretations	

ORIGINAL PRONOUNCEMENT	GAAS GUIDE REFERENCE
SAS-105 — Amendment to SAS No. 95, Generally Accepted Auditing Standards	AU 150
• No Interpretations	
SAS-106 — Audit Evidence	AU 326
• No Interpretations	
SAS-107 — Audit Risk and Materiality in Conducting an Audit	AU 312
• No Interpretations	
SAS-108 — Planning and Supervision	AU 311
• No Interpretations	
SAS-109 — Understanding the Entity and Its Environment and Assessing the Risks of Material Misstatement	AU 314
• No Interpretations	
SAS-110 — Performing Audit Procedures in Response to Assessed Risks and Evaluating the Audit Evidence Obtained	AU 318
• No Interpretations	
SAS-111 — Amendment to SAS No. 39, Audit Sampling	AU 350
• No Interpretations	
SAS-112 — Communication of Internal Control Related Matters Identified in an Audit	Superseded by SAS-115.
SAS-113 — Omnibus Statement on Auditing Standards — 2006	AU 150, AU 316, AU 328, AU 333, AU 341, AU 342, and AU 560
• No Interpretations	
SAS-114 — The Auditor's Communication with Those Charged with Governance	AU 311, AU 341, and AU 380, as redrafted
• No Interpretations	
SAS-115 — Communicating Internal Control Related Matters Identified in an Audit	AR 325
• Auditing Interpretation No. 1 (March 2010) — Communication of Deficiencies in Internal Control over Compliance in an Office of Management and Budget Circular A-133 Audit	
• Auditing Interpretation No. 2 (November 2009) — Communication of Significant Deficiencies and Material Weaknesses Prior to the Completion of the Compliance Audit for Participants in Office of Management and Budget Single Audit Pilot Project	

ORIGINAL PRONOUNCEMENT   GAAS GUIDE REFERENCE

- Auditing Interpretation No. 3 (November 2009) — Communication of Significant Deficiencies and Material Weaknesses Prior to the Completion of the Compliance Audit for Auditors That are Not Participants in Office of Management and Budget Single Audit Pilot Project

- Auditing Interpretation No. 4 (November 2009) — Appropriateness of Identifying No Significant Deficiencies or No Material Weaknesses in an Interim Communication

SAS-116 — Interim Financial Information   AU 722

- No Interpretations

SAS-117 — Compliance Audits   AU 801

- No Interpretations

SAS-118 — Other Information In Documents Containing Audited Financial Statements   AU 550

- No Interpretations

SAS-119 — Supplementary Information in Relation to the Financial Statements as a Whole   AU 551

- No Interpretations

SAS-120 — Required Supplementary Information   AU 558

- No Interpretations

STATEMENTS ON QUALITY CONTROL STANDARDS (SQCSs)

ORIGINAL PRONOUNCEMENT   GAAS GUIDE REFERENCE

SQCS-7—A Firm's System of Quality Control   AU 161

- No Interpretations

STATEMENTS ON STANDARDS FOR ACCOUNTING AND REVIEW SERVICES (SSARS) AND SSARS INTERPRETATIONS

ORIGINAL PRONOUNCEMENT   GAAS GUIDE REFERENCE

SSARS-1 — Compilation and Review of Financial Statements   Superseded by SSARS-19.

SSARS-2 — Reporting on Comparative Financial Statements   AR 200

- SSARS Interpretation No. 1 of AR 200 (November 2002) — Reporting on Financial Statements That Previously Did Not Omit Substantially All Disclosures

ORIGINAL PRONOUNCEMENT	GAAS GUIDE REFERENCE
SSARS-3 — Compilation Reports on Financial Statements Included in Certain Prescribed Forms	AR 300
• SSARS Interpretation No. 1 of AR 300 (May 1982) — Omission of Disclosures in Financial Statements Included in Certain Prescribed Forms	
SSARS-4 — Communication Between Predecessor and Successor Accountants	AR 400
• SSARS Interpretation No. 1 of AR 400 (November 2002) — Reports on the Application of Accounting Principles	
SSARS-6 — Reporting on Personal Financial Statements Included in Written Personal Financial Plans	AR 600
• SSARS Interpretation No. 1 of AR 600 (May 1991) — Submitting a Personal Financial Plan to a Client's Advisers	
SSARS-7 — Omnibus Statement on Standards for Accounting and Review Services — 1992	AR 400
• No Interpretations	
SSARS-8 — Amendments to Statement on Standards for Accounting and Review Services No. 1, Compilation and Review of Financial Statements	Superseded by SSARS-19.
SSARS-9 — Omnibus Statement on Standards for Accounting and Review Services — 2002	AR 400
• No Interpretations	
SSARS-10 — Performance of Review Engagements	Superseded by SSARS-19.
SSARS-11 — Standards for Accounting and Review Services	AR 200
• SSAE Interpretation No. 26 of AR 100 (May 2004) — Communicating Possible Fraud and Illegal Acts to Management and Others	
SSARS-12 — Omnibus Statement on Standards for Accounting and Review Services — 2005	AR 200
• No Interpretations	
SSARS-13 — Compilation of Specified Elements, Accounts, or Items of a Financial Statement	AR 110
• No Interpretations	

ORIGINAL PRONOUNCEMENT	GAAS GUIDE REFERENCE
SSARS-14 — Compilation of Pro Forma Financial Information	AR 120
• No Interpretations	
SSARS-15 — Elimination of Certain References to Statements on Auditing Standards and Incorporation of Appropriate Guidance into Statements on Standards for Accounting and Review Services	AR 200, AR 300, and AR 400
• No Interpretations	
SSARS-16 — Defining Professional Requirements in Statements on Standards for Accounting and Review Services	Superseded by SSARS-19.
SSARS-17 — Omnibus Statement on Standards for Accounting and Review Services — 2008	AR 200, AR 300, and AR 400
• No Interpretations	
SSARS-18 — Applicability of Statements on Standards for Accounting and Review Services	Superseded by SSARS-19.
SSARS-19 — Compilation and Review Engagements	AR 60, AR 80, and AR 90
• No Interpretations	

STATEMENTS ON STANDARDS FOR ATTESTATION ENGAGEMENTS (SSAEs) AND SSAE INTERPRETATIONS

ORIGINAL PRONOUNCEMENT	GAAS GUIDE REFERENCE
SSAE-10 — Attestation Standards: Revision and Recodification: Chapter 1 — Attest Engagements	AT 101; amended by SSAE-14
• SSAE Interpretation No. 1 of AT 101 (January 2001) — Defense Industry Questionnaire on Business Ethics and Conduct	
• SSAE Interpretation No. 2 of AT 101 (January 2001) — Responding to Requests for Reports on Matters Relating to Solvency	
• SSAE Interpretation No. 3 of AT 101 (January 2001) — Applicability of Attestation Standards to Litigation Services	
• SSAE Interpretation No. 4 of AT 101 (January 2002) — Providing Access to or Photocopies of Working Papers to a Regulator	

ORIGINAL PRONOUNCEMENT	GAAS GUIDE REFERENCE

- SSAE Interpretation No. 5 of AT 101 (September 2003) — Attest Engagements on Financial Information Included in XBRL Instance Documents

- SSAE Interpretation No. 6 of AT 101 (January 2005) — Reporting on Attestation Engagements Performed in Accordance with Government Auditing Standards

- SSAE Interpretation No. 7 of AT 101 (December 2008) — Reporting on the Design of Internal Control

SSAE-10 — Attestation Standards: Revision and Recodification: Chapter 2 — Agreed-Upon Procedures Engagements   AT 201

- No Interpretations

SSAE-10 — Attestation Standards: Revision and Recodification: Chapter 3 — Financial Forecasts and Projections   AT 301

- **No Interpretations**

SSAE-10 — Attestation Standards: Revision and Recodification: Chapter 4 — Reporting on Pro Forma Financial Information   AT 401

- No Interpretations

SSAE-10 — Attestation Standards: Revision and Recodification: Chapter 5 — Reporting on An Entity's Internal Control Over Financial Reporting   Superseded by SSAE-15.

SSAE-10 — Attestation Standards: Revision and Recodification: Chapter 6 — Compliance Attestation   AT 601

- No Interpretations

SSAE-10 — Attestation Standards: Revision and Recodification: Chapter 7 — Management's Discussion and Analysis   AT 701

OBSERVATION: SSAE-10 revises and recodifies SSAE-1 through SSAE-9.

ORIGINAL PRONOUNCEMENT	GAAS GUIDE REFERENCE
SSAE-11 — Attest Documentation	AT 101

- No Interpretations

SSAE-12 — Amendment to SSAE No. 10, Attestation Standards: Revision and Recodification   AT 101

- No Interpretations

ORIGINAL PRONOUNCEMENT	GAAS GUIDE REFERENCE
SSAE-13 — Defining Professional Requirements in Statements on Standards for Attestation Engagements	AT 20
• No Interpretations	
SSAE-14 — SSAE Hierarchy	AT 50
• No Interpretations	
SSAE-15 — An Examination of an Entity's Internal Control over Financial Reporting That Is Integrated with an Audit of Its Financial Statements	AT 501
• No Interpretations	
SSAE-16 — Reporting on Controls at a Service Organization	AT 801
• No Interpretations	

Index

A

Accountants
    advisory, 659–660
    compilation of financial
        statements. *See* Compilation of
        financial statements
    continuing, 655, 658–659
    reporting. *See* Reporting
        accountant
    responsibility in interim financial
        information, 699–700
    review of financial statements. *See*
        Review of financial statements
Account balances
    assertions, 69, 259
    audit responses to assessed risks,
        197–199
    audit risk, 77–79, 84–87
    beginning balances, evidence to
        support, 148–149
    detection risk, 82–83
Accounting
    auditing practice, defined,
        15–16
    changes. *See* Accounting changes
    contingencies, for. *See* FAS-5
    estimates. *See* Accounting
        estimates
    GAAP. *See* Generally accepted
        accounting principles
    hierarchy. *See* Accounting
        hierarchy
    PCAOB. *See* Public Company
        Accounting Oversight Board
    understanding entity policies,
        116–117
Accounting and review services
    (AR 50), 925
Accounting and Review Services
    Committee (ARSC). *See specific*
    SSARS
Accounting changes. *See also* FAS-154
    inappropriate treatment of change
        in accounting principle, 538

justification for change in
    accounting principles, 539
reporting change to unacceptable
    accounting principle, 537–538
Accounting estimates, 407–429
    advice and support for client,
        418–419
    alternative approaches, 424
    assumptions, 420–421, 423
    auditing. *See* AU 342; SAS-57
    auditor evaluation of estimates,
        428–429
    balance sheet, 414–415
    basis for, 427
    biases, 169
    client's involvement, 417–418
    communication of, 424–428
    defined, 407
    disclosures, 425–428
    evidence related to soft accounting
        information, 422–424
    fair value, 277–278, 412–415
    final estimates, 421–423
    financial statement estimates,
        428–429
    GAAP applications, 506
    high risks, identifying, 416–417
    hindsight, use of, 423
    limitations of, 427
    management's good faith effort,
        422
    management's internal control,
        408–409
    misstatements, 86
    model, 419–420, 423, 427
    overview, 407–409
    procedures checklist, 409
    ranges of estimates, 423–424
    reasonableness, 409–412
    recognition criteria, 427–428
    reliability of, 422
    revenue recognition, 184
    role of estimates, 419
    soft accounting information,
        416–428

Accounting hierarchy
federal governmental entities, 492,
497–498
GAAP, 491, 497–498
nongovernmental entities,
494–496
SSARS, 925
state and local governmental
entities, 492, 496–497
Accounting Research Bulletin
(ARB-45, Long-Term Construction-
Type Contracts), 175
Accounting Trends and Techniques,
493
Accounts receivable
confirmations, 315–316, 321–323
defined, 315
Accuracy assertion, 259
Activity ratios, 297
Adjustments
audit adjustments (SAS-89), 342,
1056–1057
dating of auditor's report, 562
due to fraud, 123, 205–206
due to subsequent events, 615
restatement. *See* Restatement
adjustments
Adverse auditor's report, 533,
554–555
Advisory accountant, 659–660
Advisory Committee on the Auditing
Profession, 157, 525
Agreed-upon procedures engagements,
779–786. *See also* AT 201
authoritative pronouncements, 779
compliance attestation, 851–853
engagement report, 786
internal auditor, use of, 784
overview, 779–780
pre-engagement conditions,
780–781
procedures analysis and
application, 780–784
procedures checklist, 780
prospective financial statement,
806–810
report checklist, 784–785
report on scope, 784

specialist, use of, 783
understanding with the client,
781–782
Agreements
absence of, 178
debt agreements. *See* Debt
agreements
side agreements, 176
AICPA. *See* American Institute of
Certified Public Accountants
American Institute of Certified Public
Accountants (AICPA)
*Accounting Trends and
Techniques,* 493
Antifraud Programs and Controls
Task Force, 100, 162
Audit and Accounting Guides,
11–12
Audit Guide. *See* Audit Guide
Code of Professional Conduct. *See*
Code of Professional Conduct
fieldwork standards, 9
Financial Report Survey, 493
general auditing standards, 8–9
"Management Override of Internal
Controls: The Achilles' Heel of
Fraud Prevention," 100, 162
Practice Alert 01-1 (Common Peer
Review Recommendations), 16
Practice Alert 03-1 (Audit
Confirmations), 184, 307, 308,
312, 316, 358
Practice Alert 98-2 (professional
skepticism), 36–39
standards of reporting, 9–10
Statements of Position, 11, 12. *See
also specific SOP*
Statements on Auditing Standards,
5–7, 10. *See also specific SAS*
TIS 8200.05, 102
TIS 8200.06, 200
TIS 8200.07, 206
TIS 8200.09, 81
TIS 8200.11, 102
TIS 8200.12, 115–116
TIS 8200.13, 131
TIS 8200.15, 247–248
web site, 16

Analyst conflicts of interest,
1060 – 1061
Analytical procedures, 281 – 305. *See
also* AU 329; SAS-56
audit evidence, 266 – 267
Audit Guide, 283 – 288
auditor expectations, 283
authoritative pronouncements, 281
control environment, 107
documentation, 294 – 296
in engagement planning, 289 – 290
evaluation of results, 288
expectations, 290
final review, 303 – 305
financial information review, 291
financial statement comparisons,
297 – 301
fraud information gathered,
163 – 164
for fraud risks, 170 – 171
identification of differences, 286
interim financial information, 705
investigation of differences,
286 – 288
MD&A, 888 – 890
nature of account or assertion,
283 – 284
overview, 281 – 282
performance, documentation,
296 – 302
preliminary review, 302 – 303
procedures analysis and
application, 289 – 294
procedures checklist, 288 – 289
process of, 283 – 288
ratio analysis, 284, 285
reasonableness tests, 284, 285
regression analysis, 284, 285 – 286
reliability of data, 284
revenue recognition, 182
review of financial statements,
957 – 959, 1004 – 1014
substantive procedures, 291 – 294
trend analysis, 284 – 285
Antifraud programs and controls,
119 – 120. *See also* Fraud
Antifraud Programs and Controls Task
Force, 100, 162

APB-18 (The Equity Method of
Accounting for Investments in
Common Stock), 334
APB-20 (Accounting Changes). *See*
FAS-154
APB-28 (Interim Financial Reporting),
677, 698, 713
AR 50 (Standards for Accounting and
Review Services), 925
AR 60 (Framework for Performing and
Reporting on Compilation and
Review Engagements), 925 – 931
authoritative pronouncements, 925
definitions, 925 – 926
elements of engagement, 929 – 930
evidence, 930
explanatory material in SSARS,
927
financial reporting framework, 930
financial statements, 930
materiality, 931
objectives, 926 – 927
overview, 925
SSARS compliance, 927
standards and guidance,
928 – 929
three-party relationship, 929
written communication or report,
930
AR 80 (Compilation of financial
statements), 932 – 952
accounting services needed by
client, 935
authoritative pronouncements, 932
change in engagement type,
945 – 946
client representation letter, 936
communications with management
and others, 945
departures from reporting
framework, 941, 950 – 951
disclosures omitted from financial
statements, 938 – 940
documentation of engagement, 936
elements of accountant's report,
937
emphasis-of-matter paragraph in
report, 940 – 941

AR 80 (Compilation of financial
   statements) *(cont.)*
   engagement letter, 946–948
   establishing an understanding,
      932–934
   going concern uncertainty, 942
   inaccurate or incomplete financial
      statements, 936
   independence of accountant, lack
      of, 940, 949–950
   management and governance,
      establishing understanding with,
      932–934
   overview, 932
   performance requirements,
      934–936
   procedures checklist, 951–952
   reading financial statements, 935
   report, 936–942
   restricted use reports, 941–942
   sample reports, 948–951
   standard report (example),
      948–949
   subsequent discovery of facts,
      943–944
   subsequent events, 943
   supplementary information,
      944–945
   third party use of financial
      statements, 940
   understanding client, 934–935
AR 90 (Review of Financial
   Statements), 953–1016
   analytical procedures, 957–959,
      1004–1014
   authoritative pronouncements, 953
   change in engagement type,
      972–973
   client, knowledge of, 956–957
   communications with management
      and others, 971–972
   departures from reporting
      framework, 966–967
   documentation, 963–964
   elements of report, 964–965
   emphasis-of-matter paragraph in
      report, 966
   engagement letter, 973–975

   establishing understanding with
      management and governance,
      954–956
   expectations, documenting,
      1010–1014
   fraud detection, 962
   going concern uncertainty,
      968–969, 1014–1016
   incorrect, incomplete, or
      unsatisfactory information,
      961–962
   industry, knowledge of, 956
   inquiries, 959–961
   inquiry checklist, 986–1004
   management representations,
      962–963, 975–977
   overview, 953–954
   performance requirements, 956–957
   procedures, designing and
      performing, 957–963
   procedures checklist, 979–981
   report, 964–968, 978
   restricted use reports, 967–968
   review program, 979–981
   review questionnaire checklist,
      981–986
   standard report (example), 978
   subsequent discovery of facts,
      969–971
   subsequent events, 969
   supplementary information, 971
AR 110 (Compilation of Specified
   Elements, Accounts, or Items of a
   Financial Statement), 1017–1018
   compilation of financial
      statements, 938
AR 120 (Compilation of Pro Forma
   Financial Information), 1019–1020
   compilation of financial
      statements, 938
AR 200 (Reporting on Comparative
   Financial Statements), 1021–1036
   all periods have been compiled,
      1032–1033
   all periods have been compiled or
      reviewed, 1023
   all periods have been reviewed,
      1033

authoritative pronouncements, 1021

change in previous report, 1025, 1034–1035

current or prior period is audited and other period is compiled or reviewed, 1024–1025

current period is reviewed and prior period is compiled, 1023, 1033–1034

current period refers to prior period, 1034

current year is compiled and prior year is audited, 1031–1032, 1036

highest level of service rendered, exception, 1029–1031

omission of all disclosures, 1029–1031, 1035–1036

overview, 1021–1022

predecessor accountant's reports, 1024–1028, 1035–1036

procedures analysis and application, 1023–1032

procedures checklist, 1022–1023

status of client as issuer has changed, 1031–1032

AR 300 (Compilation Reports on Financial Statements in Certain Prescribed Forms), 1037–1039

AR 400 (Communications Between Predecessor and Successor Accountants), 1041–1045

authoritative pronouncements, 1040

overview, 1040–1041

procedures analysis and application, 1042–1044

procedures checklist, 1041–1042

request for access to working papers, 1044–1045

AR 600 (Reporting on Personal Financial Statements Included in Written Personal Financial Plans), 1046–1048

ARB-45 (Long-Term Construction-Type Contracts), 175

ARSC (Accounting and Review Services Committee). *See specific SSARS*

AS-1 (References in Auditors' Reports to the Standards of the Public Company Accounting Oversight Board), 524–525

AS-3 (Audit Documentation), 380–381, 386, 581

AS-5 (An Examination of an Entity's Internal Control over Financial Reporting that is Integrated with an Audit of Its Financial Statements), 822, 823, 1053

AS-6 (Evaluating Consistency of Financial Statements and Conforming Amendments), 501–502

AS-7 (Engagement Quality Review), 18–19

ASB (Auditing Standards Board) redrafting of standards, 23

Assertions

account balances, 69, 259

accuracy, 259

attest engagements, 754–755

audit responses to assessed risks, 197–200

classes of transactions, 69, 259

completeness. *See* Completeness assertions

consistency, 870

control risk, 81–82

cutoff, 259

derivatives and securities, 339–341

examination report, 773, 776

existence. *See* Existence assertions

ICFR, 825–826

inventory, 214–215

occurrence. *See* Occurrence assertion

presentation and disclosure. *See* Presentation and disclosure assertion

review report, 774–775, 777–778

rights and obligations, 259

transaction classes, 69, 259

Assertions *(cont.)*
   valuation and allocation, 259
Assessment
   default to maximum, 82
   inquiries. *See* AU 337; SAS-12
   risk. *See* Risk assessment
Assets
   accounting estimates, 428–429
   accounting for transfers
    (FAS-140), 367
   goodwill and intangibles
    (FAS-142), 274
   impairment or disposal (FAS-144),
    417, 424
   misappropriation of, 157–158
   special reports, 652–653
   transfer of financial assets
    (FAS-140), 367–368
Assistants
   disagreements, 57
   questions during audit, 57
   responsibilities of audit, 56–57
   review of work of, 57–58
Association with financial statements
   (AU 504, SAS-26), 515–521
   association, defined, 515
   auditor is not independent, 518
   authoritative pronouncements, 515
   comparative financial statements,
    519–520, 521
   compilation description, 521
   comprehensive basis other than
    GAAP, 518
   disclaimer of opinion, 520–521
   modified disclaimer, 520
   overview, 515–516
   public entity unaudited financial
    statements, 517–519
   reporting analysis and application,
    517–520
   reporting checklist, 516–517
   review description, 521
Assumptions
   accounting estimates, 420–421,
    423
   fair value, 277
   pro forma financial information,
    816–817

Assurance
   in auditor's reports, 529
   limited assurance paragraph, 641
   negative. *See* Negative assurances
   reasonable assurance, 35–36
AT 20 (Defining Professional
   Requirements in Statements on
   Standards for Attestation
   Engagements), 749–750
AT 50 (SSAE Hierarchy), 751–752
AT 101 (Attest Engagements),
   753–778
   authoritative pronouncements, 753
   examination report, assertion, 773,
    776
   examination report, subject matter,
    772–773, 775–776
   examinations and reviews, 756
   internal control, design of,
    770–771
   overview, 753–756
   procedures analysis and
    application, 756–770
   procedures checklist, 756
   review report, assertion, 774–775,
    777–778
   review report, subject matter, 774,
    777
AT 201 (Agreed-Upon Procedures
   Engagements), 779–786
   authoritative pronouncements, 779
   engagement report, 786
   overview, 779–780
   procedures analysis and
    application, 780–784
   procedures checklist, 780
   report checklist, 784–785
AT 301 (Financial Forecasts and
   Projections), 787–811
   agreed-upon procedures
    engagement, 806–810
   authoritative pronouncements, 787
   compilation engagements,
    799–800
   examination engagement,
    789–799
   historical financial statements, 810
   overview, 787–789

partial presentations, 810
procedures analysis and
application, 801 – 806
procedures checklist, 800
AT 401 (Reporting on Pro Forma
Financial Information), 812 – 821
authoritative pronouncements, 812
comfort letters, 672
overview, 812 – 814
procedures analysis and
application, 815 – 821
procedures checklist, 815
AT 501 (Reporting on an Entity's
Internal Control Over Financial
Reporting), 822 – 849
authoritative pronouncements, 822
overview, 822 – 824
procedures analysis and
application, 825 – 849
procedures checklist, 824 – 825
AT 601 (Compliance Attestation),
850 – 865
agreed-upon procedures
engagements, 851 – 853
authoritative pronouncements, 850
examination engagement,
854 – 865
overview, 850 – 851
procedures analysis and
application, 854 – 865
procedures checklist, 854
AT 701 (Management's Discussion and
Analysis), 866 – 896
auditor engagement subsequent to
filing, 895 – 896
authoritative pronouncements, 866
combined reporting, 895
communication with audit
committee, 896
examination engagement,
866 – 885
overview, 866 – 868
procedures analysis and
application, 869 – 886,
887 – 894
procedures checklist, 868 – 869,
886
review engagements, 885 – 894

AT 801 (Reporting on Controls at a
Service Organization), 897 – 921
authoritative pronouncements, 897
overview, 897 – 898
procedures analysis and
application, 912 – 917
Type 1 report (example), 917 – 919
Type 2 report (example), 919 – 921
Attest engagement, 753 – 778. *See also*
AT 101
authoritative pronouncements, 753
character of engagement, 766
conclusions, 766 – 767
documentation, 769 – 770
due care, 760
engagement reservations, 768
evidence, 761 – 765
examination engagement, 762 – 763
examination report, assertion, 773,
776
examination report, subject matter,
772 – 773, 775 – 776
examinations and reviews, 756
greenhouse gas emissions (SOP
2003-02), 758
independence, 759 – 760
internal control design, reporting
on, 770 – 771
knowledge of subject matter,
757 – 758
overview, 753 – 756
planning and supervision, 760 – 761
pre-engagement planning,
756 – 760
procedures analysis and
application, 756 – 770
procedures checklist, 756
prospective financial statement,
788 – 789
reporting standards, 765 – 769
reservations, 767, 768
restricted distribution, 768 – 769
review engagements, 763 – 765
review report, assertion, 774 – 775,
777 – 778
review report, subject matter, 774,
777
scope deficiencies, 767 – 768

Attest engagement *(cont.)*
    standards. *See* Standards for
      Attestation Engagements (SSAE)
    suitable and available criteria,
      758–759
    training and proficiency of
      practitioner, 757
    workpapers, 769
Attribute sampling, 432
AU 110 (Responsibilities and
  Functions of the Independent
  Auditor), 3–4
AU 120 (Defining Professional
  Requirements in Statements on
  Auditing Standards), 5–7
AU 150 (Generally Accepted Auditing
  Standards), 8–13
AU 161 (The Relationship of Generally
  Accepted Auditing Standards to
  Quality Control Standards), 14–19
AU 201 (General Standards), 23
AU 210 (Training and Proficiency of
  the Independent Auditor), 24–26
AU 220 (Independence), 27–32
AU 230 (Due Care in the Performance
  of Work), 33–39
AU 311 (Planning and Supervision),
  43–67
    assistant responsibilities, 56–57
    audit engagement planning
      checklist, 60–66
    audit engagement supervision
      checklist, 66–67
    auditor independence, 50–51
    audit plan, 54–55
    authoritative pronouncements, 43
    communication with predecessor
      auditor, 46
    documentation of understanding,
      49–50
    engagement letter, 49, 58–60
    engagement strategy, 51–54
    inventories, 324
    IT specialists, 55–56
    management communications, 56
    overview, 43–45
    procedures analysis and
      application, 46–58

    procedures checklist, 45–46
    reports and communications,
      53–54
    risk assessment and response,
      proposed standards, 44–45
    specialized skills, 55–56
    understanding with the client,
      46–49
AU 312 (Audit Risk and Materiality in
  Conducting an Audit), 68–95
    account balance level, 77–79
    aggregating and netting
      misstatements, 93–94
    assertions, 69
    assessing materiality, 91–93
    authoritative pronouncements, 68
    class-of-transactions level, 77–79
    communication of misstatements to
      management, 88–89
    control risk, 80–82
    derivatives and securities,
      336–337
    detection risk, 82–84
    documentation of audit results,
      89–90
    financial statement level, 71–74
    fraud, detection of, 69–70
    GAAP precedent over industry
      practice, 88
    inherent risk, 80
    intentional misstatements, 87–88,
      94–95
    "materiality" bulletin, 91
    misstatements, 69–71
    overview, 68–71
    during planning phase, 71–84
    procedures analysis and
      application, 71–90
    procedures checklist, 71
    qualitative considerations, 76–77,
      90–91
    quantitative materiality
      considerations, 74–76
    substantive procedures, 84–87
AU 314 (Understanding the Entity and
  Its Environment and Assessing the
  Risk of Material Misstatement),
  96–143

authoritative pronouncements, 96
control environment, 99 – 103, 132
entity risk factor examples, 133
external factors, 136
factors of risk of material
  misstatement, 141 – 142
information system objectives, 134
information technology, 104 – 105
internal control over financial
  reporting, 135
material misstatement risks and
  auditor's responses, 143
overview, 96 – 99
procedures analysis and
  application, 106 – 131
procedures checklist, 106
reporting standards, 137 – 138
small and midsized entities,
  139 – 140
AU 315 (Communications Between
  Predecessor and Successor Auditors),
  144 – 154
  access to audit files, 147 – 148
  authoritative pronouncements, 144
  client consent and acknowledgment
    letter, 152
  consistency standard, 148 – 149
  discovery of misstatements, 150
  before engagement acceptance,
    145 – 146
  evidence to support beginning
    account balances, 148 – 149
  letter of understanding, 150 – 152
  overview, 144 – 145
  planning and supervision, 46
  procedures analysis and
    application, 145 – 150
  procedures checklist, 145
  prospective client evaluation form,
    153 – 154
  reasonable requests, 147 – 148
  reaudits, 149 – 150
AU 316 (Consideration of Fraud in a
  Financial Statement Audit), 155 – 186
  analytical procedures, 163 – 164,
    170 – 171, 182
  assessing fraud risks throughout the
    engagement, 170

authoritative pronouncements, 155
brainstorming sessions, 109,
  159 – 160
communication of fraud to
  management, 173 – 174
communication with governance,
  480
documenting, 174
evaluate audit evidence, 170
fraudulent financial reporting,
  156 – 157
information gathering, 160 – 165
inquiries, 161 – 163
journal entries, 205 – 206
misappropriation of assets,
  157 – 158
misstatement related to fraud,
  165 – 166, 172 – 173
overview, 155 – 158
potential for material misstatement,
  159
procedures analysis and
  application, 159 – 174
procedures checklist, 158
professional skepticism, 158, 160
related programs and controls, 166
response to results of assessment,
  166
risk assessment at completion of
  fieldwork, 171 – 172
risk identification, 160 – 161,
  165 – 166
AU 317 (Illegal Acts by Clients),
  187 – 193
  authoritative pronouncements, 187
  overview, 187 – 189
  procedures analysis and
    application, 190 – 193
  procedures checklist,
    189 – 190
AU 318 (Performing Audit Procedures
  in Response to Assessed Risks and
  Evaluating the Audit Evidence
  Obtained), 194 – 217
  assessed risks, 194 – 210
  audit evidence, 210 – 212
  authoritative pronouncements, 194
  documentation, 212

AU 318 (Performing Audit Procedures in Response to Assessed Risks and Evaluating the Audit Evidence Obtained) *(cont.)*
  financial statement level response, 196
  inventory assertions, 214–215
  overview, 194–196
  proposed PCAOB standards, 195–196
  relevant assertion level response, 197–200
  substantive procedures, 205–210, 214–217
  tests of controls, 200–205, 213
AU 322 (The Auditor's Consideration of the Internal Audit Function in an Audit of Financial Statements), 218–224
  authoritative pronouncements, 218
  overview, 218–219
  procedures analysis and application, 219–224
  procedures checklist, 219
AU 324 (Service Organizations), 225–244
  authoritative pronouncements, 225
  controls report, 241–244
  overview, 226–228
  procedures checklist, 228
  service auditor procedures, 233–241
  user auditor procedures, 228–232
AU 325 (Communication of Internal Control Related Matters Noted in an Audit), 245–256
  authoritative pronouncements, 245
  material weaknesses, 246, 247–249, 253–256
  overview, 246–247
  possible deficiencies, 248, 252–253
  procedures analysis and application, 247–252
  procedures checklist, 247
  written communication about significant deficiencies and material weaknesses, 253–256

AU 326 (Audit Evidence), 257–268
  authoritative pronouncements, 257
  overview, 257–258
  procedures analysis and application, 258–268
  procedures checklist, 258
AU 328 (Auditing Fair Value Measurements and Disclosures), 269–280
  audit committee communications, 280
  authoritative pronouncements, 269
  estimates, 277–278
  GAAP conformity, 274–275
  overview, 269–271
  procedures analysis and application, 273–280
  procedures checklist, 272
  testing, 275–277
AU 329 (Analytical Procedures), 281–305
  analytical review, 302–303
  Audit Guide, 283–288
  authoritative pronouncements, 281
  final review, 303–305
  financial statement comparisons, 297–301
  fraud information gathered, 163–164
  overview, 281–282
  performance, documentation, 296–302
  procedures analysis and application, 289–294
  procedures checklist, 288–289
  process of, 283–288
  substantive procedures, 291–294
AU 330 (The Confirmation Process), 306–323
  accounts receivable, 315–316, 321–323
  authoritative pronouncements, 306
  designing requests, 307–312
  examples, 317–323
  lease obligation, 319
  mortgage obligation, 320
  negative confirmation, 318
  overview, 306–307

positive confirmation, 318
procedures analysis and
application, 307–316
procedures checklist, 307
AU 331 (Inventories), 324–331
authoritative pronouncements, 324
confirmations, 330–331
observation procedures, 327–329
overview, 324
procedures analysis and
application, 325–327
procedures checklist, 324–325
successor auditor procedures, 149
AU 332 (Auditing Derivative
Instruments, Hedging Activities, and
Investments in Securities),
332–341
assertions, 338–341
authoritative pronouncements, 332
overview, 332–333
procedures analysis and
application, 335–338
procedures checklist, 334–335
securities, 334
services affecting substantive
procedures, 338
substantive procedures, 338–341
AU 333 (Management
Representations), 342–352
authoritative pronouncements, 342
letter example, 349–352
overview, 342–343
procedures analysis and
application, 344–349
procedures checklist, 343–344
AU 334 (Related Parties), 353–360
authoritative pronouncements, 353
overview, 353–354
procedures analysis and
application, 354–360
procedures checklist, 354
AU 336 (Using the Work of a
Specialist), 361–368
authoritative pronouncements, 361
overview, 361–363
procedures analysis and
application, 364–368
procedures checklist, 363

AU 337 (Inquiry of a Client's Lawyer
Concerning Litigation, Claims, and
Assessments), 369–378
audit inquiry letter to legal counsel,
375–378
authoritative pronouncements, 369
letter of audit inquiry,
372–374
litigation, claims, and assessment
to be accrued or disclosed,
371–372
overview, 370
procedures analysis and
application, 371–375
procedures checklist, 370–371
AU 339 (Audit Documentation),
379–394
access to, 392–394
authoritative pronouncements, 379
checklist of SAS requirements,
388–392
fieldwork standards, 381–387
overview, 379–381
regulatory agency access to
documentation, 392–394
AU 341 (The Auditor's Consideration
of an Entity's Ability to Continue as
a Going Concern), 395–406
authoritative pronouncements, 395
evaluating entity's ability to
continue, 404–406
management's plans, 398–399
overview, 396
procedures analysis and
application, 396–404
procedures checklist, 396
substantial-doubt conditions, 397
AU 342 (Auditing Accounting
Estimates), 407–429
auditor evaluation of estimates,
428–429
authoritative pronouncements, 407
overview, 407–409
procedures analysis and
application, 409–415
procedures checklist, 409
soft accounting information,
416–428

AU 350 (Audit Sampling), 430–471
  authoritative pronouncements, 430
  nonstatistical sampling for tests of
    detail, 457–471
  overview, 430–435
  procedures analysis and
    application, 436–448, 449–457,
    458–469
  procedures checklist, 435–436,
    448, 457
  size of sample, 469–471
  tests of controls, 435–448
  tests of details, 448–471
AU 380 (The Auditor's
  Communication with Those Charged
  with Governance), 472–482
  accounting principles, 494
  adequacy of communication,
    479–480
  auditor's responsibilities under
    GAAS, 476
  authoritative pronouncements, 472
  form of communication, 478–479
  matters to be communicated,
    475–478
  overview, 472–473
  procedures analysis and
    application, 473–480
  procedures checklist, 473
  recipients of communication,
    473–475
  scope and timing of audit, 477
  significant finding from the audit,
    477–478
  significant findings, topic and nature
    of communications, 481–482
  timing, 479
AU 390 (Consideration of Omitted
  Procedures After the Report Date)
  assessment of significance of
    omitted procedures, 484–485
  audit documentation, 381
  authoritative pronouncements, 483
  overview, 483
  procedures analysis and
    application, 484–485
  procedures checklist, 484
  proper course of actions, 485

AU 410 (Adherence to Generally
  Accepted Accounting Principles),
  489–490
AU 411 (The Meaning of "Present
  Fairly in Conformity with Generally
  Accepted Accounting Principles"),
  491–498
  authoritative pronouncements, 491
  federal GAAP hierarchy, 497–498
  nongovernmental entity accounting
    hierarchy, 494–496
  overview, 491–494
  state and local government
    accounting hierarchy, 496–497
AU 420 (Consistency of Application of
  Generally Accepted Accounting
  Principles), 499–507
  authoritative pronouncements, 499
  overview, 500–502
  reporting analysis and application,
    503–507
  reporting checklist, 502–503
AU 431 (Adequacy of Disclosures in
  Financial Statements)
  authoritative pronouncements, 508
  engagement program, 509–511
  overview, 508–509
AU 435 (Segment Information), 512
AU 504 (Association with Financial
  Statements), 515–521
  authoritative pronouncements, 515
  compilation description, 521
  disclaimer of opinion, 520–521
  overview, 515–516
  redrafting of standards by ASB,
    515–521
  reporting analysis and application,
    517–520
  reporting checklist, 516–517
  review description, 521
AU 508 (Reports on Audited Financial
  Statements)
  auditor's report when predecessor
    auditor's report no presented, 559
  auditor's report when standards are
    followed, 559–560
  authoritative pronouncements,
    522–523, 522–560

balance sheet, reports on, 557
comparative financial statements, on, 557 – 558
dating the auditor's report, 564
disclaimer report, 556 – 557
overview, 523 – 532
qualified auditor's report, 553 – 554, 555 – 556
reporting standards analysis and application, 533 – 552
reporting standards checklist, 532 – 533
AU 530 (Dating of the Independent Auditor's Report)
authoritative pronouncements, 561
dual-dating, 348, 563
events requiring adjustment, 562
overview, 561 – 564
reissuance of the audit report, 563 – 564
single-dating method, 563
AU 532 (Restricting the use of an Auditor's Report), 565 – 570
authoritative pronouncements, 565
financial statements before loan agreements, 569 – 570
overview, 565 – 566
reporting standards analysis and application, 567 – 568
reporting standards checklist, 566 – 567
special-purpose financial statements, 569
AU 534 (Reporting on Financial Statements Prepared for use in Other Countries)
authoritative pronouncements, 571
dual statements, 575 – 576
foreign and U.S. distribution, 576
foreign auditing standards, 573
general standards and fieldwork standards, 572 – 573
overview, 571 – 572
procedures analysis and application, 572 – 576
procedures checklist, 572
U.S.-style standard auditor's report, 572 – 573, 577

AU 543 (Part of Audit Performed by Other Independent Auditors)
authoritative pronouncements, 578
basic audit procedures, 579 – 580
inquiry of other auditor to principal auditor, 583 – 584
overview, 578
principal auditor's response to other auditor, 584 – 585
procedures analysis and application, 579 – 582
procedures checklist, 579
reaudits, 150
reference to work of others in the audit report, 583
reputation of predecessor auditor, 148 – 149
AU 544 (Lack of Conformity with Generally Accepted Accounting Principles), 586 – 587
AU 550 (Other Information in Documents Containing Audited Financial Statements), 588 – 593
authoritative pronouncements, 588
definitions, 589
overview, 588 – 589
procedures analysis and application, 591 – 593
required procedures, 589 – 591
AU 551 (Reporting on Information Accompanying the Basic Financial Statements in Auditor-Submitted Documents), 594 – 551
authoritative pronouncements, 594
definitions, 595
explanatory paragraph used to report on supplementary information, 600 – 601
overview, 594 – 595
procedures analysis and application, 599 – 600
reporting procedures, 597 – 599
reporting supplementary information separately, 601
required procedures, 595 – 599

AU 552 (Reporting on Condensed
Financial Statements and Selected
Financial Data)
  authoritative pronouncements, 602
  overview, 602–603
  procedures analysis and
    application, 603–605
AU 558 (Required Supplementary
Information), 606–611
  authoritative pronouncements, 606
  definitions, 607
  overview, 606–607
  reporting, 608–610
  required procedures, 608
AU 560 (Subsequent Events),
612–617
  audit program, 615–617
  authoritative pronouncements, 612
  overview, 612–613
  procedures analysis and
    application, 613–615
  procedures checklist, 613
AU 561 (Subsequent Discovery of
Facts Existing at the Date of the
Auditor's Report)
  audit documentation, 381
  authoritative pronouncements, 618
  discovery of misstatements, 150
  overview, 618–619
  procedures analysis and
    application, 619–621
  procedures checklist, 619,
    621–625
  restatement adjustments, 551
AU 623 (Special Reports)
  account in a financial statement,
    651–652
  authoritative pronouncements, 629
  cash-based financial statements,
    649–650
  debt agreements, 652
  financial statements prepared
    pursuant to loan agreement,
    653–654
  overview, 629–630
  procedures analysis and
    application, 630–649
  procedures checklist, 630

  regulatory basis of accounting,
    650–651
  statement of assets sold, 652–653
  statement of liabilities transferred,
    652–653
AU 625 (Reports on the Application of
Accounting Principles)
  authoritative pronouncements, 655
  example, 661–662
  overview, 655
  procedures analysis and
    application, 657–660
  procedures checklist, 657
  reporting standards, 660–661
  scope of standards, 656–657
AU 634 (Letters for Underwriters and
Certain Other Requesting Parties)
  authoritative pronouncements, 663
  comfort letter, 683–688
  overview, 663–667
  procedures analysis and
    application, 667–682
  procedures checklist, 667
  representation letter, 682–683
AU 711 (Filings Under Federal
Securities Statutes)
  authoritative pronouncements, 691
  dating the auditor's report, 564
  overview, 691–693
  procedures analysis and
    application, 693–695
  procedures checklist, 693
  status of review report, 695–696
AU 722 (Interim Financial
Information)
  analytical procedures and related
    inquiries, 705
  in audited financial statements,
    715–716
  authoritative pronouncements, 697
  client representation letter,
    716–719
  client's representation, 715
  discovery of facts subsequent to
    date of review report, 714
  going concern issues, 722–724
  inquiries and other review
    procedures, 705–712

overview, 697–700
procedures analysis and
    application, 701–705
procedures checklist, 700
reporting standards, 712–713
report modifications, 713–714
standard review report, 719–722
AU 801 (Compliance Auditing
  Consideration in Audits of
  Governmental Entities and
  Recipients of Governmental
  Financial Assistance), 727–741
    authoritative pronouncements, 727
    definitions, 729–730
    overview, 727–728
    planning and performing audit,
        731–733
    procedures analysis and
        application, 737–741
    procedures checklist, 727
    required procedures, 731–737
AU 901 (Public Warehouses —
  Controls and Auditing Procedures for
  Goods Held), 745–746
Audit adjustments, SAS-89, 342,
    1056–1057
Audit and Accounting Guides, 11–12
Audit committees
    fair value communications, 280
    financial expert, SOX
        requirements, 1059
    illegal acts, communication of,
        192–193
    internal control matters, reporting,
        1053
    MD&A, 896
    public company requirements, 474
    reporting accountant, defined, 657
    SOX requirements, 50, 1053, 1054
Audit Confirmations (AICPA Practice
    Alert 03-1), 184, 307, 308, 312, 316,
    358
Audit documentation, 379–394. *See
    also* AS-3; AU 339; SAS-103
    access to, 386–387, 392–394
    assembly, retention, and protection
        of, 385–386
    auditor's understanding, 130–131

audit results, 89–90
audit sampling, 447, 457
authoritative pronouncements, 379
checklist of SAS requirements,
    388–392
confidentiality, 386
dating of auditor's report, 384–385
departure from GAAS, 384
fieldwork standards, 381–387
going concern, audit results,
    403–404
items tested, 383
nature and extent of
    documentation, 382–383
overview, 379–381
protection of, 385–386
purpose, 379
regulatory agency access to,
    386–387, 392–394
required documentation, 386
retention of, 385–386
SAS-96, 68, 729
significant findings, 383–384
Audit engagement, purpose of, 3
Audit evidence. *See* Evidence
Audit Guide
    accounting estimates, 184
    analytical procedures, 182–183,
        283–288
    audit procedures, 179–186
    audit risk level, 180
    audit sampling, 461
    consideration of fraud in financial
        statements, 182
    evidence, evaluation by auditor,
        186
    evidence, integrity of, 178
    incomplete earnings process, 179
    indicators of improper revenue
        recognition, 178–179
    internal control over revenue
        recognition, 181
    inventory, observance of, 184–185
    knowledge of business, 180–181
    lack of delivery, 179
    related party transactions, 182
    revenue recognition, 175–186
    transactions, 183

Auditing Interpretations
  accounting estimates, 407, 412
  Assessment of a Lawyer's
    Evaluation of the Outcome of
    Litigation (February 1997), 369
  association with financial
    statements, 515, 516, 518
  audit documentation, 379,
    386–387
  audit evidence, 257, 260, 262, 267
  auditor's reports, 522, 525,
    527–529, 536, 540–541, 550
  audit sampling, 430, 431
  comfort letters, 665
  communications, 43
  continuing accountant, 655, 659
  fair value measurements, 269, 272
  foreign auditing standards, 571, 576
  GAAP, adherence to, 489–490
  GAAP, consistent application of,
    499, 501, 504
  GAAP, presenting fairly in
    conformity with, 491, 493–494
  going concern, 395
  illegal acts by clients, 187, 188, 189
  inquiry of client's lawyer, 369, 372,
    373–374, 376–377
  investments in securities, 332, 334
  legal consultation, 349
  letters to directors, 663, 664
  management representations, 342,
    349
  part of audit performed by other
    independent auditors, 578, 580,
    582, 585
  planning and supervision, 53
  purpose, 11
  related party transactions,
    353–356, 358
  securities filings, 691, 694
  segment information, 512
  service organizations, 225,
    240–241, 244
  specialists, use of, 361, 368
  special reports, 629, 632–634,
    636, 640, 643, 648
  subsequent discovery of facts,
    618, 621

Auditing Standards Board (ASB)
  redrafting of standards, 23
Auditors
  controls, evaluation of, 127
  independence and unaudited
    financial statement, 518, 521
  internal, in agreed-upon procedures
    engagements, 784
  mandatory audit partner rotation,
    1053
  part of audit performed by other
    independent auditors. See AU 543
  predecessors. See Predecessor
    auditors
  presumptively mandatory
    requirements, 6, 10
  professional requirements, 5–7
  reports. See Auditor's reports
  responsibilities and functions, 3–4
  service. See Service auditors
  successors. See Successor auditors
  training and proficiency (AU 210;
    SAS-1), 24–26
  unconditional requirements, 6
  user. See User auditor
Auditor's reports
  adverse report, 554–555
  assurances, 528–529
  audit evidence, 539–541
  auditing standards disclosure, 528
  audit standards, 559–560
  balance sheet only, 557
  change to unacceptable accounting
    principle, 537–538
  combined statement of income and
    comprehensive income, 531
  comparative financial statements,
    547–552, 557–558
  components, 523–524
  comprehensive income,
    529–532
  dating, 561–564. See also AU 530
  departure from accounting
    principles, 535–536
  departure from GAAP,
    533–534
  disclaimers, 556–557
  disclosures, adequacy, 536–537

emphasis of a matter, 544–545
format standards, 523–524
going concern uncertainties, 542–543
inappropriate treatment of change in accounting principle, 538
independence, 545–546
introductory paragraph, 525
justification for change in accounting principles, 539
limited engagement, 542
loss contingencies, 543–544
negative assurances, 546
opinion paragraph, 526
part of audit performed by other independent auditors, 579–582
piecemeal opinion, 546
predecessor auditor, by, 548–550, 559
qualified report, 553–554, 555–556
reporting standards checklist, 532–533
restricted use. See AU 532; SAS-87
scope limitations, 541, 555–556
scope paragraph, 525
separate statement of comprehensive income, 530–531
special reports, 642, 648–649
standard report, example, 526–527
statement of change in equity, 531–532
successor auditor, by, 550–552
Audit procedures
audit evidence, 263–267
control activities, 124
control environment, 118–119
extent of further procedures, 199–200
illegal acts, indirect effect of, 188–189
information and communication systems, 122
material misstatement risk, 197–198
monitoring, 125–126
in response to assessed risks. See AU 318; SAS-110
risk assessment, 121
timing, 198–199

Audit risk. See also AU 312; SAS-107
acceptable level of, 72
conditions, 72
defined, 69
derivatives and securities, 336–337
nonquantitative terms, 72
quantitative terms, 72
sampling risk, 82, 432–435, 445–446, 452–454
Audit sampling, 430–471. See also AU 350; SAS-39
allowable risk of assessing control risk too low, 442
attribute sampling, 432
audit documentation, 383–384
audit risk, 432–435
authoritative pronouncements, 430
block sampling, 440
detection risk, 82
deviation, 437, 443, 445, 446–447
documentation, 447, 457
expected misstatement, 454–455
haphazard sampling, 440
inventories, 326
judgment factors, 441, 451
nonsampling plans, 431
nonstatistical sampling plans, 431–432, 444. See also Nonstatistical sampling plans
objective, 449
overview, 430–435
population, 437–438, 443, 449–450, 452, 455–456, 459
procedures analysis and application, 436–448, 449–457, 458–469
procedures checklist, 435–436, 448, 457
projected misstatement, 456
random-number sampling, 439
risk level, 452–454
sample selection, 438–439, 455
sampling risk, 82, 432–435, 445–446, 456
sampling unit, 438, 449
sequential sampling, 439–440
size of population, 460–461
size of sample, 440–442, 444, 448, 450, 458–459, 463–465

Audit sampling (cont.)
  statistical sampling plans,
    431–432, 435–448
  systematic sampling, 439–440
  testing period, 438
  test objectives, 436–437
  tests of controls, 433–435,
    435–448
  tests of details, 448–471
  tolerable misstatement, 454
  tolerable rate, 442
  variable sampling, 432, 448–457
"Audits of States, Local Governments
  and Non-Profit Organizations," 566
Audit team
  control environment discussions,
    109–110
  discussions of fraud, 57
Authorizations, 104

B

Balance sheet
  accounting estimates, 414–415
  auditor's report, 557
Beginning balances, evidence to
  support, 148–149
Block sampling, 440
Brainstorming sessions, 109–110
  fraud detection, 159–160
Business combinations, 816
Business risk, 113–114, 122

C

CAATs (computer-assisted audit
  techniques), 264
Capsule financial information,
  676–677
Cash-based financial statements,
  special reports, 649–650
Cash flow
  accounting estimates, 428
  change in statement format, 504
  CON-7, 269
  statement. See Statement of Cash
    Flows

CEO and CFO certifications,
  1054–1055
Certification of statements on auditing,
  3, 5
Certified Public Accountant
  examination, 25
Channel stuffing, 176–177
Circular A-123, 566
Claims, inquiries. See AU 337; SAS-12
Classes of transactions
  assertions, 69, 259
  audit responses to assessed risks,
    197–199
  audit risk, 77–79, 84–87
  detection risk, 82–83
Classification assertion, 259
Clients
  compilation and review
    engagements, representation
    letter, 716–719
  consent and acknowledgment
    letter, 152
  prospective client evaluation form,
    153–154
  understanding. See Understanding
Code of ethics
  quality control, 17
  SOX requirements, 1058
Code of Professional Conduct
  compilation and review
    engagements, 928
  confidentiality of attest
    documentation, 770
  GAAS compliance, 8–9
  independence, 28–29
  quality control standards, 17
  Rule 201, pre-engagement
    planning, 700
  Rule 202, GAAS and SSAEs, 526,
    751
  Rule 203, auditor's opinions, 526,
    535–536
  Rule 301, disclosing confidential
    information, 146
Codification of Auditing Standards and
  Procedures. See SAS-1
Collusion, internal control limitations,
  103

Combined reporting, MD&A, 895
Combining information, 596–597
Comfort letters
    alternative letter, 665
    to broker-dealers, 664–665
    buyers or sellers of stock, 665
    capsule financial information,
        676–677
    concluding paragraph, 681
    contents, 670
    draft letter, 667–670
    financial forecasts, 677–678
    information other than audited
        financial statements, 674–675
    pro forma financial information,
        677
    registration of securities, 664, 666
    sample, 683–688
    scope of procedures, 666–667
    subsequent events, 678–681, 682
    tables, statistics, and other
        information, 680–681
    unaudited condensed interim
        financial information, 675–676
    underwriters, for, 663, 683–688
Committee of Sponsoring
    Organizations of the Treadway
    Commission (COSO)
        "Fraudulent Financial Reporting:
            1998-2007, An Analysis of U.S.
            Public Companies," 157, 165,
            279, 398, 404
        internal control, 824
        internal control, defined, 97, 98
        risk assessment by the entity, 100
Common Interest Realty Associations,
    607
Communication
    accounting estimates, 424–428
    audit committees, with. *See* Audit
        committees
    compilation and review
        engagements, 930
    compilation of financial
        statements, 945
    fraud, team member
        communications, 57

of fraud to management, 173–74
information systems. *See*
    Information and communication
    systems
interim financial information,
    711–712
internal control matters, 839–840
with management in audit
    planning, 56
material weaknesses, 250
of misstatements to management,
    88–89
planning and supervision, 53–54
predecessor and successor auditors.
    See AR 400; AU 315; SAS-84;
    SSARS-4
review of financial statements,
    971–972
significant deficiencies, 250
soft accounting information, nature
    of, 424–428
subsequent discovery of facts,
    620–621
Communication with those charged
    with governance, 472–482
    adequacy of communication,
        479–480
    auditor's responsibilities under
        GAAS, 476
    authoritative pronouncements, 472
    form and timing of, 478–480
    form of communication, 478–479
    matters to be communicated,
        475–478
    overview, 472–473
    procedures analysis and
        application, 473–480
    procedures checklist, 473
    recipients of communication,
        473–475
    scope and timing of audit, 477
    significant finding from the audit,
        477–478
    significant findings, topic and
        nature of communications,
        481–482
    timing, 479

Comparative financial statements
  association with financial
    statements, 519–520, 521
  auditor's reports, 547–552,
    558–559
  defined, 1021
  predecessor auditor reporting,
    548–550
  reporting. *See* Reporting on
    comparative financial statements
  updated opinion, 547–548
Compensating control, defined, 249
Compilation engagements, 925–931.
  See also Compilation of financial
  statements
  authoritative pronouncements, 925
  definitions, 925–926
  elements of, 929–930
  evidence, 930
  explanatory material in SSARS,
    927
  financial reporting framework, 930
  financial statements, 930
  materiality, 931
  objectives, 926–927
  overview, 925
  prescribed forms (SSARS-3),
    1037–1039
  pro forma financial information
    (AR 120), 1019–1020
  prospective financial statement,
    799–806
  reporting on comparative financial
    statements, 521
  SSARS compliance, 927
  standards and guidance, 928–929
  three-party relationship, 929
  written communication or report,
    930
Compilation of financial statements,
  932–952. *See also* Compilation
  engagements
  accounting services needed by
    client, 935
  authoritative pronouncements, 932
  change in engagement type,
    945–946
  client representation letter, 936

  communications with management
    and others, 945
  departures from reporting
    framework, 941, 950–951
  disclosures omitted from financial
    statements, 938–940
  documentation of engagement, 936
  elements of accountant's report,
    937
  emphasis-of-matter paragraph in
    report, 940–941
  engagement letter, 946–948
  establishing an understanding,
    932–934
  going concern uncertainty, 942
  inaccurate or incomplete financial
    statements, 936
  independence of accountant, lack
    of, 940, 949–950
  management and governance,
    establishing understanding with,
    932–934
  overview, 932
  performance requirements,
    934–936
  procedures checklist, 951–952
  reading financial statements, 935
  reports, 936–942, 948–951
  restricted use reports, 941–942
  sample reports, 948–951
  standard report (example),
    948–949
  subsequent discovery of facts,
    943–944
  subsequent events, 943
  supplementary information,
    944–945
  third party use of financial
    statements, 940
  understanding client, 934–935
Compilation reports on financial
  statements in certain prescribed
  forms (AR 300, SSARS-3),
  1037–1039
Completeness assertions
  audit evidence, 259
  derivatives and securities, for,
    339–340

management representations,
345–346
MD&A, 870
Compliance attestation, 850–865. *See
also* AT 601
agreed-upon procedures
engagements, 851–853
authoritative pronouncements, 850
evidence, 859
examination engagement,
854–865
internal control components,
858–859
overview, 850–851
procedures analysis and
application, 854–865
procedures checklist, 854
reporting, 861–865
special reports (SSAE-3), 640
subsequent events, 860
written representations, 860–861
Compliance audits, 727–741
applicable compliance
requirements, 738
authoritative pronouncements, 727
definitions, 729–730
documentation, 736–737, 741
evidence, 733, 740–741
management representations,
732–733, 740
materiality, 737–738
overview, 727–728
planning and performing audit,
731–733
procedures analysis and
application, 737–741
reissuance of report, 737
report, 733–737, 741
required procedures, 731–737
risk assessment, 739–740
supplementary requirements, 740
Compliance Supplement, 738
Comprehensive income
audit reports (FAS-130), 528
combined statement of income, 531
components, 529–530
defined, 529
reporting (FAS-130), 529–530

separate statement of, 530–531
statement of change in equity,
531–532
Computer-assisted audit techniques
(CAATs), 264
CON-2 (Qualitative Characteristics of
Accounting Information)
materiality, defined, 68–69
materiality characteristics, 91
CON-7 (Using Cash Flow Information
and Present Value in Accounting
Measurements), 269
Condensed financial statements
comfort letters, 675–676
reporting, 602–605
Confidentiality
audit documentation, 386
Rule 301, disclosing confidential
information, 146
Confirmation, 306–323. *See also* AU
330; SAS-67
accounts receivable, 315–316,
321–323
audit documentation, 389
audit evidence, 266
audit objectives, 312–313
designing requests, 307–312
electronic confirmations, 312–313
examples, 317–323
information being confirmed,
310–311
inventory, 330–331
lease obligation, 319
mortgage obligation, 320
negative confirmation, 308–310,
318
overview, 306–307
positive confirmation, 308–310, 318
prior auditor experience, 310
procedures analysis and
application, 307–316
procedures checklist, 307
request form, 308–310
respondent characteristics,
311–312
revenue recognition, 183–184
third parties, from, 313–315
unconfirmed balances, 314–315

Conflict of interest, SOX requirements, 1060 – 1061

Consideration of Fraud in a Financial Statement Audit. *See* SAS-99

Consistency assertion, 870

Consistency standard, 148 – 149

Consolidated information, 596 – 597

Construction-type contracts (ARB-45, SOP 81-1), 175

Contingencies
  accounting for. *See* FAS-5
  loss contingencies, 543 – 544
  reporting of, 543 – 544

Continuance of engagement, planning and supervision, 50 – 51

Continuing accountant
  defined, 655
  inquiries from reporting accountant, 658 – 659

Continuing professional education (CPE), 25

Contracts, financial presentations, 643 – 646

Control
  internal control. *See* Internal control
  override by management, 167 – 169, 206, 208

Control activities
  audit procedures, 123
  defined, 97 – 98
  environment, 101
  examples, 101, 135
  small and midsized entities, 140

Control environment
  auditor objectives of internal control, 102 – 103
  audit procedures, 118 – 119
  control activities, 101
  defined, 97
  elements, 99
  examples, 132
  information and communication systems, 101
  internal control limitations, 103
  monitoring, 101 – 102
  risk assessment, 100
  small and midsized entities, 139

Control risk
  assessment of, 80 – 82
  calculation formula, 82 – 83
  compliance attestation, 856
  defined, 80, 336 – 337, 462
  derivatives and securities, 336 – 337
  in examination engagement, 869

COSO. *See* Committee of Sponsoring Organizations of the Treadway Commission (COSO)

Coverage ratios, 298

Credit Rating Agency Reform Act, 1062 – 1063

Criteria, suitable and available, 758 – 759

Cutoff assertion, 259

Cutoff tests, 183

D

Dates
  auditor's reports, 528, 561 – 564
  of comfort letters, 670 – 671
  dual-dating. *See* Dual-dated reports
  single-dating method, 563

Debt agreements
  financial statements prepared pursuant to, 653 – 654
  mortgage confirmations, 320
  product financing arrangements (FAS-49), 175
  restricted audit report, 569 – 570
  short-term obligations to be refinanced (FAS-6), 343
  SOX requirements, 1057
  special reports, 652, 653 – 654

Decision tree for tests of controls, 213

Default to maximum assessment, 82

Defense industry, attest engagements, 753, 755

Deficiency
  defined, 48
  internal control, 837 – 838
  material weakness. *See* Material weakness
  significant. *See* Significant deficiency

Defining Professional Requirements in Statements on Auditing Standards (AU 120; SAS-102), 5–7
Defining Professional Requirements on Statements on Standards for Accounting and Review Services (SSARS-16), 926
Derivative instruments, 332–341
  accounting for (FAS-133), 274, 332
  auditing. *See* AU 332; SAS-92
  characteristics, 332–333
  classifications, 333
Detection risk
  account balance or class of transaction level, 82–83
  calculation formula, 82–83
  compliance attestation, 856
  defined, 82
  in examination engagement, 763, 869
Deviation conditions in audit sampling, 437, 443, 445, 446–447
Disclaimers
  auditor is not independent, 545–546
  auditor's reports, 556–557
  modified, 520
  unaudited financial statements, 520
Disclosures
  accounting estimates, 425–428
  adequacy, in financial statements (AU 431, SAS-32), 508–511, 536–537
  adequacy of, 210, 633–634
  assertions. *See* Presentation and disclosure assertion
  audit responses to assessed risks, 197–199
  of confidential information, 146
  fair value, 278–279
  fees for services, 1054
  financial statements, adequacy, 185
  going concern, 400–401
  inadequate interim financial statements, 721–722
  management representations, 345
  omissions in financial statements, 938–940

reasonably adequate, 536–537
related party, 359–360
SOX requirements, 1056–1060
subsequent events, 615
Discovery of facts after date of report. *See* Subsequent discovery of facts
Distribution paragraph
  in attest engagements, 768–769
  incomplete financial presentations, 645
  separate report, 642
  special auditor's report, 647
Documentation
  analytical procedures, 294–296
  attest engagement, 769–770
  audit. *See* Audit documentation
  compilation of financial statements engagement, 936
  compliance audits, 736–737, 741
  consideration of fraud, 174
  engagement understandings, 46–48, 49–50
  responses to assessed risks, 212
  review of financial statements, 963–964, 1010–1014
Dual-dated reports
  auditor's reports, 348
  independent auditor's reports, 563
  reissued reports, 548
Dual financial statements, 575–576
Dual-purpose tests, 202
Due care in performance of work
  in attest engagements, 760
  authoritative pronouncements, 33
  overview, 33–36
  professional skepticism, 34–35, 36–39
  reasonable assurance, 35–36
Due diligence, 664

E

EITF 2000-21 (Accounting for Revenue Arrangements with Multiple Deliverables), 175

Elimination of Certain References on
Auditing Standards and
Incorporation of Appropriate
Guidance into Statements on
Standards for Accounting and
Review Services. *See* SSARS-15
Emerging Issue Task Force. *See
specific EITF*
Emphasis of a matter
auditor's reports, 544 – 545
in compilation reports, 940 – 941
review of financial statements
report, 966
Engagement letter
compilation of financial
statements, 946 – 948
planning and supervision,
49 – 50, 58 – 60
review of financial statements,
973 – 975
sample, 58 – 60
Engagements
acceptance and continuance
standards, 17
agreed-upon procedures
engagements. *See* Agreed-upon
procedures engagements
attest. *See* Attest engagement
compilation. *See* Compilation
engagements
continuance, 50 – 51
examination. *See* Examination
engagement
performance standards, 18
planning and supervision, 46 – 48,
50 – 54
reports and communications,
53 – 54
review. *See* Review engagements
strategy, 51 – 54
understandings, 46 – 48
Entity
business risks, 113 – 114
control environment,
110 – 115
financial performance, 114 – 115
industry and regulatory factors,
112, 136

internal control applications, small
to midsized, 139 – 140
nature of, 112 – 113
objectives, 113 – 114
reporting standards, 137 – 138
strategies, 113 – 114
Equity method of accounting for
investments in common stock (APB-
18), 334
Errors. *See also* Misstatement
corrections, GAAP applications,
505
defined, 69
Estimates. *See* Accounting estimates
Ethics
quality control, 17
SOX requirements, 1058
Evidence
assertions, 258 – 260
in attest engagements, 761 – 765
in auditor's reports, 539 – 541
audit procedures, in response to
assessed risks. *See* AU 318;
SAS-110
audit procedures, types and
performance, 263 – 267
beginning balances, 148 – 149
compilation engagements, 930
compliance attestation, 859
compliance audits, 733, 740 – 741
evaluation by auditor, 186
evaluation for possible fraud, 170
evaluation of, 268
evaluation of sufficiency and
appropriateness, 210 – 212
generally. *See* AU 326; SAS-106
going concern, 400 – 404
information technology of client,
267
internal control, match to risk,
833 – 834
MD&A, 875 – 877
pro forma adjustments, 816
for prospective financial
statements, 792 – 794
revenue recognition, integrity of
evidence, 178
review engagements, 930

risk assessment, 262–263
specialist effects, 365
substantive procedures, 262–263
sufficient appropriate, 260–262
tests of controls, 262–263
Examination
assertion reports, 773, 776
subject matter reports, 772–773,
775–776
Examination engagement
compliance attestation, 854–865
evidence, in attest engagement,
762–763
internal control, 824
MD&A, 866–885
prospective financial statement,
789–799
Existence assertions
audit evidence, 259
for derivatives and securities, 334
derivatives and securities, for, 339
Expectations in analytical procedures,
290
review of financial statements,
1010–1014
Expenses, accounting estimates, 429
Explanatory material
emphasis of a matter, 544–545
overview, 7
Explanatory paragraph
interim financial information,
722–724
scope limitations, 540
separate report, 641
special auditor's reports, 647
supplementary information,
reporting on, 600–601, 608–611
updated opinion different from
previous opinion, 548

F

Fair value
accounting estimates, 412–415
audit committee communications,
280
auditing. *See* AU 328; SAS-101
authoritative pronouncements, 269

defined, 269
determination, 269, 273
disclosures, 278–279
estimates, 277–278
GAAP conformity, 274–275
management representations,
279–280
overview, 269–271
procedures analysis and
application, 273–280
procedures checklist, 272
public company implications,
333–334, 366
results of audit procedures, 279–280
specialist, use of, 275
subsequent events, 278
testing measurements and
disclosures, 275–277
understanding client's process,
273–274
FAS-5 (Accounting for Contingencies)
accounting estimates, 425,
427–428
fraudulent financial reporting, 156
illegal acts, 191
litigation, claims, and assessment
inquiries, 370, 371
loss contingencies, reporting, 543
management representations, 345
reasonable possibility, 837
reporting of, 543
training and proficiency of
independent auditor, 25
FAS-6 (Classification of Short-Term
Obligations Expected to Be
Refinanced), 343
FAS-13 (capitalizing leases), 157
FAS-14 (Financial Reporting for
Segments of a Business Enterprise),
512
FAS-45 (Accounting for Franchise Fee
Revenue), 176
FAS-48 (Revenue Recognition When
Right of Return Exists), 176
FAS-49 (Accounting for Product
Financing Arrangements), 175
FAS-52 (Foreign Currency
Translation), 530

FAS-57 (Related Party Disclosures)
applicable parties, 354 – 355
conditions for, 354 – 356
in financial statements, 359 – 360
guidelines, 354
transaction examples, 355
FAS-66 (Accounting for Sales of Real
Estate), 175
FAS-87 (Employers' Accounting for
Pensions)
accounting estimates, 416
comprehensive income, 529
qualifications of specialists, 364
FAS-95 (Statement of Cash Flows),
504
FAS-107 (Disclosures about Fair Value
of Financial Instruments), 413
FAS-109 (Accounting for Income
Taxes), 362
FAS-115 (Accounting for Certain
Investments in Debt and Equity
Securities)
accounting estimates, 424
commercial enterprises, 334
comprehensive income, 530
FAS-123R (Share-Based Payment), 424
FAS-124 (Accounting for Certain
Investments Held by Not-for-Profit
Organizations), 334
FAS-130 (Reporting Comprehensive
Income)
audit reports, 527
comprehensive income, defined,
529
FAS-131 (Disclosures about Segments
of an Enterprise and Related
Information), 512
FAS-133 (Accounting for Derivative
Instruments and Hedging Activities),
274, 332
FAS-136 (Transfers of Assets to a Not-
for-Profit Organization or Charitable
Trust that Raises or Holds
Contributions for Others), 272
FAS-140 (Accounting for Transfers and
Servicing of Financial Assets and
Extinguishments of Liabilities),
367 – 368

FAS-142 (Goodwill and Other
Intangible Assets), 274
FAS-144 (Accounting for the
Impairment or Disposal of Long-
Lived Assets), 417, 424
FAS-146 (Accounting for Costs
Associated with Exit or Disposal
Activities), 1060
FAS-154 (Accounting Changes and
Error Corrections — A Replacement
of APB Opinion No. 20 and FASB
Statement No. 3)
accounting changes defined, 500
accounting estimates, 506
FIFO to LIFO change, 504
reports on audited financial
statements, 538
FAS-157 (Fair Value Measurements),
270, 332
accounting estimates, 412
FAS-168 (The FASB Accounting
Standards Codification and the
Hierarchy of Generally Accepted
Accounting Principles), 492,
494 – 495
FASB (Financial Accounting Standards
Board), 535
Fees for services, 1054
Fieldwork standards
accounting estimates, 407 – 429
analytical procedures, 281 – 305
audit documentation, 381 – 387
audit risk and materiality, 68 – 95
derivative instruments, hedging
activities, and securities
investments, 332 – 341
documentation, 379 – 394
evaluating fraud risk, 171 – 172
evidence, 257 – 268
fair value measurements and
disclosures, 269 – 280
fraud, consideration of, 155 – 186
GAAS, 9
going concern considerations,
395 – 406
governance, communications with,
472 – 482
illegal acts by clients, 187 – 193

inquiries of client's lawyer, 369–378

internal audit function, 218–224

internal controls, 245–256

inventories, 324–331

management representations, 342–352

omitted procedures, consideration of after report date, 483–485

planning and supervision, 43–67

predecessor and successor auditors, communications, 144–154

related party transactions, 353–360

service organizations, 225–244

specialists, use of, 361–368

understanding entity and its environment, risk assessment, 96–143

Filings under federal securities statutes. See AU 711; SAS-37

FIN-18 (Accounting for Income Taxes in Interim Periods), 698

Financial Accounting Standards Board (FASB), 535

Financial forecasts, 787–811. See also AT 301

agreed-upon procedures engagement, 806–810

authoritative pronouncements, 787

comfort letters, 677–678

compilation engagements, 799–800

compilation report, 804–805

evidence, 793

examination engagement, 789–799

generally. See AT 301

historical financial statements, 810–811

overview, 787–789

partial presentations, 810

reporting, 796–797

Financial performance of the entity, 114–115

Financial projections. See also AT 301

compilation report, 805–806

evidence, 793–794

overview, 787–789

reporting, 797–799

Financial reporting

compilation and review engagements, 930

fraudulent, 156–157

internal control, 117–118, 135

small and midsized entities, 139–140

Financial Report Survey, 493

Financial statements

accounting estimates, 428–429

adequacy of, 210

association with. See AU 504; SAS-26

audit, with internal control, 836–837

audit risk and materiality, 71–74

cash-based, 649–650

comparative. See Comparative financial statements

compilation of. See Compilation of financial statements

condensed, 602–605

consistency, 501–502

defined, 630

disclosures, adequacy of (AU 431, SAS-32), 508–511

documents containing, other information, 588–593

dual statements, 575–576

management representations, 344

misstatements in, 69–71

personal, 1046–1048

prescribed forms (AR 300, SSARS-3), 1037–1039

prospective. See Prospective financial statement

related party transactions, 359–360

reports on auditing (SAS-58), 389

responses to assessed risks, 196

restated, 551

review of. See Review of financial statements

revised, 551

Financial statements *(cont.)*
  special-purpose. *See* Special-
    purpose financial statements
  unaudited. *See* Unaudited financial
    statements
A Firm's System of Quality Control
  (SQCS-7), 14–16
Forecasts. *See* Financial forecasts
Foreign
  financial statements. *See* AU 534;
    SAS-51
  Form 20-F, 872
Foreign currency (FAS-52), 529
Form 8-K, 895, 1058, 1059
Form 10-K, 663, 664
Form 10-Q, 695, 895
Form 20-F, 872
Form 990 (Return of Organizations
  Exempt from Income Tax)
  prescribed forms of financial
    information, 648
  Reports on the Financial
    Statements Included in Internal
    Revenue Form 990 (Return of
    Organizations Exempt from
    Income Taxes) (October 2000),
    629, 648
Form S-4, 665
Franchise fee revenue, accounting for
  (FAS-45), 176
Fraud. *See also* Illegal acts; SAS-99
  accounting estimates, 408, 411
  accounting principles, 494
  account level risk assessment, 84
  analytical procedures, 107,
    170–171
  antifraud program evaluation,
    119–120
  Antifraud Programs and Controls
    Task Force, 100, 162
  audit approach and identified risks,
    166–167
  audit evidence, 211, 262, 265, 268
  auditor's response to intentional
    misstatements, 87–88
  audit sampling, 437
  biases in accounting estimates, 169
  brainstorming sessions, 159–160
  business basis for significant
    unusual transactions, 169–170
  characteristics of, 35–36
  communications before
    engagement acceptance, 146
  communication to management,
    173–174
  conditions of fraud, 164
  confirmations, 311–312, 316
  control environment, 100
  defined, 155
  detection of, 69–70
  documentation, 174
  documents containing audited
    financial statements, 592–593
  fair value, 279
  financial reporting, 156–157
  in financial statement audit. *See*
    AU 316; SAS-99
  "Fraudulent Financial Reporting:
    1998-2007, An Analysis of U.S.
    Public Companies," 157, 165,
    279, 398, 404
  going concern, 398, 404
  identification of risks, 160–161,
    165–166
  illegal acts, 191, 192
  information gathering, 160–165
  inquiries, 161–163
  inquiry of a client's lawyer, 372
  internal audit function, 221–222
  internal control, 100, 103, 118, 828
  inventories, 325
  isolated occurrence, 212
  journal entries and adjustments,
    123, 205–206
  management override of controls,
    167–169, 206, 208
  "Management Override of Internal
    Controls: The Achilles' Heel of
    Fraud Prevention," 100, 162
  management representations, 343,
    346, 347
  material misstatement, 165–166,
    172–173, 590
  MD&A, 896
  misappropriation of assets,
    157–158

nature, timing, and extent of procedures, 167
predictability of audit procedures, 167
prevention, 119–120
professional skepticism, 34–35, 110
related parties, 356
responding to misstatements, 172–173
response to results of assessment, 166
revenue in certain industries, 175–186
review of financial statements, 962
risk assessment in context of related programs and controls, 166
risk assessment throughout the engagement, 170
risk factors, 164
sampling risk, 433
SOX requirements, 1064–1065, 1065
specialists, 363
team member communications, 57
timing of substantive procedures, 208–209

G

GAAP. *See* Generally accepted accounting principles
GAAS. *See* Generally accepted auditing standards
Gains and losses, accounting estimates, 429
GAO (Government Accountability Office), 1062–1064
GASB-31 (Accounting and Financial Reporting for Certain Investments and for External Investment Pools), 334
General Accounting Office, 1062–1064
Generally accepted accounting principles (GAAP)
  accounting estimates, 506
  accounting hierarchy, 491, 497–498

adherence to (AU 410), 489–490
changes to acceptable accounting principle, 505
change with material effect in the future, 507
compilation of financial statements, 932, 938, 939, 941, 950–951
consistency of application. *See* AU 420
defined, 491
departure from, auditor's reports, 533–534, 553–554
error corrections, 505
fair value measurements, 271, 274–275
foreign auditing standards, 573–575
industry practice conflicts, 88
interim financial information, 713, 720–721
investments, 334
lack of conformity (AU 544), 586–587
present fairly in conformity with, 491–498
reporting entity, 506–507
reporting on comprehensive basis of accounting other than GAAP, 630–636
review of financial statements, 953–954, 967
special-purpose financial statements, 645–646
subsequent events, 614
substantially different transactions or events, 507
Generally accepted auditing standards (GAAS). *See also* SAS-95; SAS-98
  auditor's communication with those charged with governance, 476
  authoritative pronouncements, 8
  documentation of departure from, 384
  fieldwork standards, 9
  general standards, 8–9
  interpretative publications, 11–12

Generally accepted auditing standards
(GAAS). *(cont.)*
    overview, 8 – 13. *See also* SAS-95
    presumptively mandatory
        requirements, 10, 13
    quality control standards (AU 161;
        SAS-25), 14 – 19
    report on the application of
        accounting principles, 658
    standards of reporting, 9 – 10
    statements on auditing standards, 10
General standards. *See also* SAS-1
    authoritative pronouncements, 23
    due care in performance of work, 33
    GAAS, 8 – 9
    independence, 27 – 32
    nature of, 23
    overview, 23
    training and proficiency of
        independent auditor, 24 – 26
Going concern, 395 – 406. *See also* AU
    341; SAS-59; SAS-77
    audit documentation, 389
    auditor's report uncertainties,
        542 – 543
    audit results, documenting,
        403 – 404
    authoritative pronouncements, 395
    compilation of financial statements
        and, 942
    disclosures, 400 – 401, 1016
    evaluating entity's ability to
        continue, 404 – 406
    interim financial information, 707,
        714, 722 – 724
    management's plans to address,
        398 – 399, 1015 – 1016
    overview, 396
    procedures analysis and
        application, 396 – 404
    procedures checklist, 396
    relevant information during
        engagement, 396 – 398
    report modifications, 401 – 403
    review of financial statements,
        uncertainty, 968 – 969,
        1014 – 1016
    substantial-doubt conditions, 397

Governance
    auditor's communication with. *See*
        SAS-114
    communication with. *See*
        Communication with those
        charged with governance
    compilation of financial statements
        and, 932 – 934, 945
    financial expertise of, 120
    independence of, 120
    internal control, communication of,
        250
    review of financial statements,
        954 – 956
Government
    auditing standards, 334
    "Audits of States, Local
        Governments and Non-Profit
        Organizations," 566
    compliance audits. *See* Compliance
        audits
    federal, GAAP hierarchy, 492,
        497 – 498
    GASB, 535
    GASB-31, 334
    Government Accountability Office
        (GAO), 1062 – 1064
    Government Auditing Standards
        (the Yellow Book), 640, 729
    state and local, accounting
        hierarchy, 492, 496 – 497
Government Auditing Standards
    (Yellow Book), 640, 729, 741
Greenhouse gas emissions
    (SOP 2003-02), 758

H

Haphazard sampling, 440
Hedging
    accounting for (FAS-133), 274,
        332 – 333
    auditing, 332 – 341. *See also* AU
        332; SAS-92
Hierarchy
    accounting. *See* Accounting
        hierarchy
    SSAE, 751 – 752

Human resources, quality control
  standards, 17–18

I

Illegal acts. *See also* Fraud
  by clients. *See* AU 317; SAS-54
  defined, 187
  direct effects on financial
    statements, 188
  indirect effects on financial
    statements, 188–189
  procedures analysis and
    application, 190–193
  procedures checklist, 189–190
  reporting, 193
Income, comprehensive. *See*
  Comprehensive income
Income taxes
  accounting for (FAS-109), 362
  in interim periods (FIN-18), 698
Incomplete presentations, 643–644
Incorrect acceptance, 459–465
Independence. *See also* SAS-1
  in attest engagements, 759–760
  auditor is not independent,
    545–546
  authoritative pronouncements, 27
  comfort letters, 673
  compilation of financial
    statements, lack of independence
    of accountant, 940, 949–950
  defined, 29
  general standards, 27–32
  governance, 120
  overview, 27–32
  planning and supervision, 50–51
  Rule 101, 29–30
  SOX requirements, 1052–1054
  unaudited financial statement and,
    518, 521
Industry
  entity and its environment, 112
  GAAP vs. industry practice, 88
  review of financial statements and,
    956
Information and communication
  systems

audit procedures, 122
control environment, 101
defined, 97
IT. *See* Information technology
  (IT)
objectives, 134
small and midsized entities, 140
Information technology (IT)
  audit evidence and, 264, 267
  authorizations, 104
  internal control and, 104–105
  internal control risks, 105
  planning of audit engagement,
    55–56
  recording, 104
  reporting, 104
Inherent risk
  assessment of, 80–81
  calculation formula, 82–83
  compliance attestation,
    855–856
  defined, 80, 336, 462
  derivatives and securities, 336
  in examination engagement, 869
  nonstatistical sampling, 462
Inquiries
  audit evidence, 264–265
  auditor's response to inquiry by
    other auditor, 584–585
  client's lawyer. *See* AU 337;
    SAS-12
  confirmation, 266
  interim financial information,
    705–712
  oral representations, 374
  from other auditor to principal
    auditor, 579
  reporting accountant to continuing
    accountant, 658–659
  review of financial statements,
    959–961, 986–1004
Inspection
  audit evidence, records or
    documents, 264
  control environment, 108
  tangible assets, 264
Insurance, auditing loss reserves (SOP
  92-4), 362

Intentional misstatements
    auditor's response to, 87 – 88
    immaterial misstatements, 94 – 95
Interim financial information. *See also*
  AU 722; SAS-100
    analytical procedures and related
      inquiries, 705
    APB-28, 677, 698, 713
    in audited financial statements,
      715 – 716
    authoritative pronouncements, 697
    client representation letter,
      716 – 719
    client's representation, 715
    comfort letters, 675 – 676
    discovery of facts subsequent to
      date of review report, 714
    going concern issues, 714,
      722 – 724
    inadequate disclosure, 721 – 722
    income taxes (FIN-18), 698
    independence standards, 30
    inquiries and other review
      procedures, 705 – 712
    overview, 697 – 700
    PCAOB auditing standards, 4
    procedures analysis and
      application, 701 – 705
    procedures checklist, 700
    reporting standards, 712 – 713
    report modifications, 713 – 714
    review procedures, 705 – 712
    standard review report,
      719 – 722
    understanding with the client,
      701 – 703
Internal audit function
    authoritative pronouncements, 218
    competence, 220 – 221
    evaluation of work, 224
    in financial statement audit. *See*
      AU 322; SAS-65
    material misstatement risk
      assessment, 221 – 222
    objectivity, 220 – 221
    overview, 218 – 219
    procedures checklist, 219

    reliance on, 222 – 224
    understanding of internal control,
      221
Internal control
    accounting estimates, 408 – 409
    auditor objectives, 102 – 103
    auditor's evaluation, 127
    communications. *See* AU 325;
      SAS-112
    compliance attestation, 858 – 859
    components, 97 – 98
    defined, 97
    extent of understanding needed,
      118
    financial reporting, 117 – 118, 135
    financial reporting, small and
      midsized entities, 139 – 140
    interim financial information,
      703 – 705
    internal audit function, 221
    limitations, 103
    MD&A, 873 – 875, 887 – 888
    public company reporting, 48, 98,
      116, 231
    reporting. *See* AT 501
    service organization, 230 – 231
    small and midsized entities,
      139 – 140
    SOX requirements, 1057 – 1058
    understanding of, 115 – 126
Internal Revenue Service, 629, 648,
  Form 990 (Return of Organizations
  Exempt from Income Tax)
International Standards on Auditing
    financial statements, 571. *See also*
      AU 534; SAS-51
    reporting standards, 526, 528
Internet resources, 1069 – 1075
Interpretive publications. *See*
  Publications, interpretive
Introductory paragraph
    auditor's reports, 525
    in comfort letters, 671 – 675
    incomplete financial presentations,
      644
    separate report, 641
    special auditor's reports, 646

specified elements, accounts, or
items, 638
standard special report, 635
Inventory, 324–331. *See also* AU 331
authoritative pronouncements, 324
confirmations, 330–331
FIFO to LIFO change, 504
held by outside custodian,
326–327
material weaknesses, 256
observance of, 184–185, 327–329
overview, 324
perpetual records, 325–326
physical counts, 325
previous count substantiation, 326
procedures analysis and
application, 325–327
procedures checklist, 324–325
public warehouses, 745–746
reaudits, 150
statistical sampling, 326
substantive procedures,
214–215
Investment accounting (GASB-31), 334
Investment company audits, 536–537
Investment pool auditing standards, 334
IT. *See* Information technology

J

Journal entries, examination for fraud,
123, 205–206
Judgmental matters, 128–129

K

Known misstatements, 70

L

Lack of conformity with generally
accepted accounting principles,
586–587
Lawyer inquiries. *See* AU 337; SAS-12
Leases
capitalization (FAS-13), 157
confirmation, 319

Letters
client consent and
acknowledgment, 152
compilation and review
engagements, client
representation letter, 975–977
compilation of financial
statements, client representation
letter, 936
engagement. *See* Engagement letter
inquiries. *See* Inquiries
from management. *See*
Management representations
management representations,
review engagement, 975–977
predecessor to successor auditors,
letters of understanding, 150–152
regulatory agency request for
access to documentation,
392–394
representation letter. *See*
Representation letter
underwriters, for. *See* Underwriter
letters
updating representation letter, 348
Liability
accounting estimates, 429
extinguishments (FAS-140),
367–368
special reports, 652–653
Likelihood of material misstatement, 126
Likely misstatements
defined, 70
substantive procedures, 84
Limited assurance paragraph, 641
Liquidity ratios, 297
Litigation
attest engagements, 753, 755
inquiries. *See* AU 337; SAS-12
interim financial information, 707
Loans. *See* Debt agreements
Loss contingencies
defined, 543
probable, 543
reasonably possible, 543
remote, 543
reporting of, 543–544
Losses, accounting estimates, 429

M

Management
  accounting estimates, 408–409, 422
  communication of fraud, 173–174
  communication of misstatements, 88–89
  communications of internal control, 250
  compilation of financial statements and, 932–934, 945
  control environment inquiries, 107–108
  controls over nonroutine transactions and judgmental matters, 128–129
  derivatives and securities, intent of, 337–338
  fair value representations, 279–280
  financial performance measures, 114–115
  going concern issues, plans, 398–399, 1015–1016
  implication of fraud, 70
  information sources of, 126
  "Management Override of Internal Controls: The Achilles' Heel of Fraud Prevention," 100, 162
  MD&A. *See* Management's discussion and analysis
  override of controls, 167–169, 206
  planning of audit engagement, 56
  representations. *See* Management representations
  review of financial statements, 954–956, 971–972
  tone at the top, 120
Management representations. *See also* AU 333; SAS-85
  authoritative pronouncements, 342
  compliance audits, 732–733, 740
  inconsistencies, 347
  interim financial information, 708–710
  letter example, 349–352
  MD&A, 879–881, 890
  minimum requirements, 346–347
  from other parties, 347–348
  overview, 342–343
  procedures analysis and application, 344–349
  procedures checklist, 343–344
  pro forma financial information, 817
  refusal to provide written representations, 348–349
  revenue recognition, 185
  review of financial statements, 962–963, 975–977
  supplementary information, 596–597
  updating representation letter, 348
  written representations, 344–346
Management's discussion and analysis (MD&A), 866–896
  analytical procedures, 888–890
  auditor engagement subsequent to filing, 895–896
  authoritative pronouncements, 866
  combined reporting, 895
  comfort letters, 672, 675
  communication with audit committee, 896
  evidence, 875–877
  examination engagement, 866–885
  examination report, 881–885
  internal control, 873–875, 887–888
  management representations, 879–881, 890
  nonfinancial data, 877
  overview, 866–868
  procedures analysis and application, 869–886, 887–894
  procedures checklist, 868–869, 886
  review engagements, 885–894
  review report, 885–894
  subsequent events, 877–879, 890, 895–896
  testing completeness, 877
Managing earnings, 93
Materiality. *See also* SAB-99; SAS-107

aggregate, 92
compilation engagements, 931
compliance attestation, 856–857
compliance audits, 737–738
defined, 68–69, 91
derivatives and securities,
  336–337
factor, 92
internal control, 828
in prospective financial statements,
  790
qualitative, 76–77, 90–91
quantitative, 74–76
rapid disclosure, SOX
  requirements, 1059–1060
review engagements, 931
supplementary information,
  596–597, 599
unconfirmed balances, 314–315
Material misstatement. *See also* AU
  314
  auditor's response, 143
  audit responses to assessed risks,
    197–200
  documents containing audited
    financial statements, 589,
    590–591, 592–593
  financial reporting factors,
    141–142
  financing factors, 141
  internal audit function and risk
    assessment, 221–222
  operating factors, 141
  risk assessment, 79, 126–129. *See
    also* AU 314; SAS-109
Material weakness
  areas of controls, 249
  communication of, 250
  defined, 48, 246
  examples, 253–256
  identification, 247–249
  internal control, 846
  small business enterprise,
    examples, 254–256
  written communication, 253–256
MD&A. *See* Management's discussion
  and analysis

Merger proxy, 665
Midsized entities. *See* Small and
  midsized entities
Misappropriation of assets, 157–158
Misstatement
  aggregating and netting, 93–94
  audit sampling, expected
    misstatement, 460
  communication of misstatements to
    management, 88–89
  discovery by successor auditors,
    150
  in financial statements, 69–71
  intentional, 87–88, 94–95
  known, 70
  likelihood of, 126
  likely, 70, 84–87
  material. *See* Material
    misstatement
  nonstatistical sampling, 460,
    466–469
  offsetting, 84–85
  potential for, due to fraud, 159
  responding to misstatements
    related to fraud, 172–173
  risk assessment, 126–129
  sampling, expected misstatement,
    454–455
  sampling, projected misstatement
    in, 456
  as significant deficiency, 249
  tolerable. *See* Tolerable
    misstatement
  understanding sources of, 831
Modifications to reports
  going concern, 401–403
  interim financial information,
    713–714
  standard auditor's special reports,
    648–649
Monitoring
  audit procedures, 125–126
  control environment, 101–102
  defined, 98
  quality control standards, 18
  small and midsized entities, 140
Mortgage confirmations, 320

N

NASDAQ, 474

Nationally recognized statistical rating organization (NRSRO), 1062–1063

Nature of entity and reporting standards, 137–138

Nature of the entity, 112–113

Negative assurances
  in auditor's reports, 546
  capsule financial information, 676–677
  special reports, 642

Negative confirmations, 308–310, 318

New York Stock Exchange (NYSE)
  audit committee requirements, 474
  internal audit function, 219

Nonaudit services for public companies, 546

Nonaudit services of public companies, 54

Nonfinancial data in MD&A, 877

Nongovernmental entity accounting hierarchy, 493, 494–496

Nonroutine transactions, 128–129

Nonsampling plans, 431

Nonsampling risk, 82

Nonstatistical sampling plans
  evaluation of results, 466–469
  inherent risk, 462
  misstatements, 466–469
  overview, 431–432
  risk of incorrect acceptance, 459–465, 462–463
  sample selection, 465–466
  sampling for tests of detail, 457–471
  sampling risk, 445–446, 467
  size of population, 460–461
  size of sample, 444, 463–465, 469–471
  tests of controls, 435–448
  tests of details, 457–471
  tolerable misstatement, 463
  variable sampling in tests of details, 448–457

Not-for-profit organizations
  accounting standards (FAS-124), 334

"Audits of States, Local Governments and Non-Profit Organizations," 566
  transfers of assets (FAS-136), 272

NRSRO (nationally recognized statistical rating organization), 1062–1063

NYSE (New York Stock Exchange), 219, 474

O

Observation
  audit evidence, 264
  control environment, 108

OCBOA (Other comprehensive basis of accounting), 645–646

Occurrence assertion
  audit evidence, 258, 259
  derivatives and securities, for, 338–339
  MD&A, 870

Off-balance-sheet transactions, 1057

Office of Management and Budget (OMB)
  "Audits of States, Local Governments and Non-Profit Organizations," 566
  Circular A-123, 566

OMB Circular A-133, 738, 740

Omitted procedures, consideration of after report date. *See* SAS-46

Omnibus Statement on Standards for Accounting and Review Services–2008. *See* SSARS-17

Opinion paragraph
  incomplete financial presentations, 645
  special auditor's reports, 647
  specified elements, accounts, or items, 639
  standard special report, 636

Opinions
  adverse opinion, 533, 554–555
  in auditor's reports, 526
  comparative financial statements, different opinions, 558–559

condensed financial statements, on, 603 – 605

departure from GAAP, 533 – 534

paragraphs. *See* Opinion paragraph

piecemeal opinion, 546

on selected financial data, 604 – 605

updated, different from previous opinion, 547 – 548

Other comprehensive basis of accounting (OCBOA), 645 – 646

P

Part of audit performed by other independent auditors. *See* AU 543

PCAOB. *See* Public Company Accounting Oversight Board

Pensions, accounting for. *See* FAS-87

Performing Audit Procedures in Response to Assessed Risks and Evaluating the Audit Evidence Obtained. *See* AU 318; SAS-110

Personal financial statements

accounting for (SOP 82-1), 1048

reporting (AR 600, SSARS-6), 1046 – 1048

submitting to advisers, 1046, 1047

Personnel management, assignment based on fraud risk, 166 – 167

Piecemeal opinion, 546

Planning and supervision, 43 – 67

analytical procedures, 289 – 290

assistant responsibilities, 56 – 57

attest engagements, 760 – 761

audit engagement planning checklist, 60 – 66

audit engagement supervision checklist, 66 – 67

auditor independence, 50 – 51

audit plan, 54 – 55

audit sampling, 458 – 459

authoritative pronouncements, 43

communication with predecessor auditor, 46

compliance audits, 731 – 733, 737 – 741

documentation of understanding, 49 – 50

engagement letter, 49 – 50, 58 – 60

engagement strategy, 51 – 54

examination engagement, 791

IT specialists, 55 – 56

management communications, 56

overview, 43 – 45

pre-engagement, 700, 756 – 760

procedures analysis and application, 46 – 58

procedures checklist, 45 – 46

reports and communications, 53 – 54

risk assessment and response, proposed standards, 44 – 45

soft accounting information audits, 416 – 422

specialized skills, 55 – 56

understanding with the client, 46 – 49

Positive confirmations, 308 – 310, 318

PPPO report

audit procedures, 234

defined, 233

example, 241 – 242

preparation, 233 – 240

purpose, 234

Type 1 SAS-70 report, 234

PPPO/TOE report

audit procedures, 234

defined, 233

example, 242 – 244

preparation, 233 – 240

purpose, 234

Type 2 SAS-70 report, 234

Practicable, defined, 509, 534

Practice Alert 01-1 (Common Peer Review Recommendations), 16

Practice Alert 03-1 (Audit Confirmations), 184, 307, 308, 312, 316, 358

Practice Alert 98-2 (professional skepticism), 36 – 39

Predecessor auditors

communications before engagement acceptance, 46

communications with successor auditors. *See* AR 400; AU 315; SAS-84; SAS-109; SSARS-4

Predecessor auditors *(cont.)*
    comparative financial statements,
        1024–1028
    defined, 1040
    letter of understanding, 150–152
    reporting by, 548–550, 559
Pre-engagement planning
    attest engagements, 756–760
    interim financial information, 700
Prescribed form of financial
    information, 647–648
Presentation and disclosure assertion
    audit evidence, 259
    derivatives and securities, for, 341
    fieldwork standards, 69
    MD&A, 870
Presentation basis paragraph
    incomplete financial presentations,
        645
    special auditor's reports, 646–647
    specified elements, accounts, or
        items, 638
    standard special report, 636
Present fairly in conformity with
    generally accepted accounting
    principles, 491–498. *See also* AU
    411; SAS-69
    authoritative pronouncements, 491
    federal GAAP hierarchy, 497–498
    new transactions or events,
        493–494
    nongovernmental entity accounting
        hierarchy, 494–496
    overview, 492–494
    state and local government
        accounting hierarchy,
        496–497
Presumptively mandatory
    requirements, 6, 10, 13
Professional judgment in nonstatistical
    sampling, 468–469
Professional requirements, AU 120,
    5–7. *See also* SAS-102
Professional skepticism
    of audit evidence, 261
    during audit team discussions, 110
    for confirmations, 311–312

    defined, 158, 160
    due care in performance of work,
        34–35, 36–39
    during engagements, 158, 160
Professional standards (AU 20,
    SSAE-13), 749–750
Proficiency in attest engagements, 757
Profitability ratios, 297
Pro forma financial information. *See
    also* AT, 401
    authoritative pronouncements, 812
    comfort letters, 677
    compilation of (AR 120,
        SSARS-14), 1019–1020
    defined, 1019–1020
    examination and review objectives,
        814
    examination report, 819–820
    overview, 812–814
    procedures analysis and
        application, 815–821
    procedures checklist, 815
    reporting guidelines, 818–819
    review report, 820–821
    SOX requirements, 1057
    SSARS-14, 926, 1019–1020
Projections. *See* Financial projections
Property, plant, and equipment, 256
Prospective financial statement,
    787–811
    agreed-upon procedures
        engagement, 806–810
    authoritative pronouncements, 787
    compilation engagements,
        799–806
    evidence, 792–795
    examination engagement,
        789–799
    historical financial statements,
        810–811
    overview, 787–789
    partial presentations, 810
    reporting, 795–799
Publications, interpretive
    AICPA Audit and Accounting
        Guides, 11–12
    purpose, 7, 11

Public Company Accounting Oversight
Board (PCAOB)
  AS-3, 380–381, 386, 581
  AS-5, 822, 823, 1053
  AS-6, 501–502
  AS-7, 18–19
  attest documentation, 769
  auditing standards, 4
  auditor's reports, 524–525
  fraud detection, 156, 157
  independence standards, 28–29,
    31–32
  professional standards, 5, 8
  proposed risk assessment
    standards, 195–196
  risk, 44–45, 70–71, 98–99, 282
  risk assessment and response,
    proposed standards, 155–156
  Rule 3526, 475–476
  SOX requirements, 12, 1050–1052
  Staff Audit Practice Alert No. 2,
    270, 333–334, 366
  Staff Audit Practice Alert No. 3,
    111–112
  Staff Audit Practice Alert No. 4,
    270–271
Public company implications
  attest engagements, 760
  audit committees, auditor
    communication with, 474
  audit documentation, 380–381,
    386, 769
  auditing standards, 12
  auditor's communication with
    those charged with governance,
    475–476
  auditor's reports, 549–550
  audit reports, 524–525, 528–529
  audit sampling, 437
  comfort letters, 688
  communication with audit
    committees, 474
  fair value measurements, 270–271
  "Fraudulent Financial Reporting:
    1998-2007, An Analysis of U.S.
    Public Companies," 157, 165,
    279, 398, 404
  GAAP conformity, 493, 502
  independence standards, 28–29,
    31–32
  interim financial information, 703,
    704
  internal audit function, 219
  internal control assessment, 589
  internal control effectiveness, 249
  internal control over financial
    reporting, 822–823, 826
  internal control report, 48, 98, 116,
    231
  management representations, 347
  materiality considerations, 76–77
  material weaknesses, 251
  nonaudit services, 54, 546
  part of audit performed by other
    independent auditors, 581
  PPPO and PPPO/TOE reports, 234
  professional standards, 6
  related parties, 357
  revenue recognition, 177–178
  risk assessment of internal control,
    100
  SAS-1, auditor responsibilities, 3, 4
  SAS-102, professional
    requirements, 7
  special reports, 635
  understanding with the client, 50
Public warehouses, 745–746
Purchases, material weaknesses,
  255–256

Q

Qualified auditor's reports, 553–554,
  555–556
Qualitative characteristics of
  accounting information. *See* CON-2
Qualitative materiality, 76–77,
  90–91
Quality control standards
  authoritative pronouncements, 14
  checklist, 16
  documentation of operation,
    18–19
  engagement acceptance and
    continuance, 17
  engagement performance, 18

Quality control standards *(cont.)*
    Engagement Quality Review,
        755–756
    ethical requirements, 17
    firm's system of quality control
        (SQCS-7), 14–16
    GAAS and, 14
    human resources, 17–18
    leadership responsibilities, 17
    monitoring, 18
    overview, 14–16
Quantitative materiality, 74–76

R

Random-number sampling, 439
Ratios
    activity, 297
    analysis, 284, 285
    coverage, 298
    liquidity, 297
    profitability, 297
Reasonable assurance, 35–36
Reasonable detail, 94–95
Reasonableness test, 284, 285
    accounting estimates, 409–412
Reaudits, 149–150
Recalculation procedure for audit
    evidence, 266
Reclassification, statement of cash
    flows, 504
Registrations
    comfort letters, 664, 666
    Regulation S-K, 681
    shelf, 669–670, 691, 694
    status of review report, 695–696
Regression analysis, 284, 285–286
Regulation S-B, 872
Regulation S-K
    comfort letters, 663, 665
    interim financial information, 694
    MD&A, 872
    registration statements, 681
Regulation S-X, 678
Regulatory agency
    access to audit documentation,
        386–387, 392–394

compliance reporting, 640–642
interim financial information, 715
reporting on financial
    presentations, 643–646
special reports, 650–651
Reissuance of reports
    audit reports, 563–564
    compliance audits, 737
    defined, 1021
    predecessor auditor reporting,
        548–550
Related-party transactions, 353–360.
    See also AU 334; SAS-45
    audit procedures, 356–358
    authoritative pronouncements, 353
    conditions for, 354–356
    disclosures. *See* FAS-57
    overview, 353–354
    procedures analysis and
        application, 354–360
    procedures checklist, 354
    revenue recognition, 177, 182
Relationships of specialists, 365
Reperformance of procedure for audit
    evidence, 266
Reporting
    application of accounting
        principles. *See* SAS-50
    on auditing financial statements.
        See SAS-58
    change in reporting entity,
        506–507
    compilation and review
        engagements, 930
    compilation of financial
        statements, accountant's report,
        936–942, 948–951
    compliance attestation,
        861–865
    compliance audits, 733–736, 741
    dual-dated reports, 348, 548, 563
    entity standards, 137–138
    financial statements prepared
        for use in other countries.
        See SAS-51
    fraudulent financial reporting,
        156–157

illegal acts, effect of, 193
information accompanying
    financial statements. *See* AU 551;
    SAS-29
information technology, 104
internal control. *See* Reporting on
    an entity's internal control over
    financial reporting
planning and supervision, 53–54
pro forma financial information.
    See AT 401
reissued. *See* Reissuance of reports
review of financial statements,
    964–968, 978
single (current) year, 503
specialists and, 366–367
special reports. *See* AU 623;
    SAS-62
standards generally, 9–10
subsequent year, 503–504
supplementary information,
    597–599, 601, 608–610
timing of, 53–54
Reporting accountant
    advisory accountant vs., 659–660
    circumstances of audit request, 657
    defined, 655, 657
    fieldwork standards, 656
    inquiries from continuing
        accountant, 658–659
    procedures checklist, 657
    sufficient information, 658–659
Reporting on an entity's internal
    control over financial reporting,
    822–849
    authoritative pronouncements, 822
    communication, 839–840
    deficiencies, 837–838
    evaluation of elements, 117–118
    evidence, match to risk, 833–834
    examination engagement, 824
    examples of control activities, 135
    financial statement audit, 836–837
    fraud risk, 828
    ICFR assertion, 825–826
    ICFR reporting, 840–846
    identify accounts and disclosures,
        830–831

management report includes other
    information, 847–848
management report incomplete or
    improper, 847
materiality, 828
material weakness, 846
misstatement, understanding
    sources of, 831
nature, timing, extent of testing,
    834–835
overview, 822–824
planning, 826–827
procedures analysis and
    application, 825–849
procedures checklist, 824–825
reliance on report of another
    auditor, 847
report modifications, 846
risk assessment, 827–828
scope limitation, 847
service organizations, use of,
    835–836
small and midsized entities,
    139–140
subsequent events, 848–849
test design effectiveness, 831–832
test operating effectiveness,
    832–833
top-down approach, 829–830
using the work of others, 828–829
written representations, 838–839
Reporting on comparative financial
    statements (AR 200, SSARS-2),
    1021–1036
    all periods have been compiled,
        1032–1033
    all periods have been reviewed,
        1033
    authoritative pronouncements, 1021
    change in previous report, 1025,
        1034–1035
    current period is compiled and prior
        period is reviewed, 1023–1024
    current period is reviewed and prior
        period is compiled, 1023–1025,
        1033–1034
    current period refers to prior
        period, 1024–1025, 1034

Reporting on comparative financial statements *(cont.)*
  current year is compiled and prior year is audited, 1031 – 1032, 1036
  highest level of service rendered, exception, 1029 – 1031
  omission of all disclosures, 1029 – 1031, 1035 – 1036
  overview, 1021 – 1022
  predecessor accountant has ceased operations, 1028 – 1029
  predecessor accountant's reports, 1024 – 1028, 1035 – 1036
  procedures analysis and application, 1023 – 1032
  procedures checklist, 1022 – 1023
  reissuance of unchanged report, 1025 – 1027
Representation letter
  from requesting parties, 666, 682 – 683
  review of interim financial information, 716 – 719
  updating, 348
Representations
  inquiry of client's lawyer, oral representations, 374
  letters. *See* Representation letter
  management. *See* Management representations
Required supplementary information (AU 558), 606 – 611
Resources on the web, 1069 – 1075
Responsible party
  attest engagement, 755
  prospective financial statement, 787, 791, 802 – 803
Restatement adjustments
  reporting standards, 549 – 551
  retroactive restatement of subsequent events, 503
  SOX penalties, 1055
  unaudited financial statements, 551 – 552
Restricted use reports
  auditor's reports. *See* AU 532; SAS-87

  compilation of financial statements, 941 – 942
  review of financial statements, 967 – 968
Retroactive restatement, 503
Revenue recognition, 175 – 186
  audit procedures, 179 – 186
  in certain industries, 175 – 186
  channel stuffing, 176 – 177
  comprehensive income. *See* Comprehensive income
  evidence, integrity of, 178
  indicators of improper recognition, 178 – 179
  nature of business, 177 – 178
  pronouncements, 175 – 176
  related party transactions, 177, 182
  SAB-101, 176, 177 – 178
  SAB-104, 176, 177 – 178
  side agreements, 176
  significant unusual transactions, 177
  of software (SOP 97-2), 176
Revenues, accounting estimates, 429
Review engagements, 925 – 931. *See also* Review of financial statements
  assertion reports, 774 – 775, 777 – 778
  authoritative pronouncements, 925
  definitions, 925 – 926
  elements of, 929 – 930
  evidence, 930
  evidence, in attest engagement, 763 – 765
  explanatory material in SSARS, 927
  financial reporting framework, 930
  financial statements, 930
  interim financial information, 705 – 712
  materiality, 931
  MD&A, 885 – 894
  objectives, 926 – 927
  overview, 925
  performance of (SSARS-10), 926
  reporting on comparative financial statements, 521

SSARS compliance, 927
standards. *See* SSARS-11
standards and guidance, 928–929
subject matter reports, 774, 777
three-party relationship, 929
written communication or report,
930
Review of financial statements,
953–1016. *See also* Review
engagements
analytical procedures, 957–959,
1004–1014
authoritative pronouncements, 953
change in engagement type,
972–973
client, knowledge of, 956–957
communications with management
and others, 971–972
departures from reporting
framework, 966–967
documentation, 963–964
elements of report, 964–965
emphasis-of-matter paragraph in
report, 966
engagement letter, 973–975
establishing understanding with
management and governance,
954–956
expectations, documenting,
1010–1014
fraud detection, 962
going concern uncertainty,
968–969, 1014–1016
incorrect, incomplete, or
unsatisfactory information,
961–962
industry, knowledge of, 956
inquiries, 959–961
inquiry checklist, 986–1004
management representations,
962–963, 975–977
overview, 953–954
performance requirements,
956–957
procedures, designing and
performing, 957–963
procedures checklist, 979–981

questionnaire checklist, 981–986
report, 964–968, 978
restricted use reports, 967–968
review program, 979–981
standard report (example), 978
subsequent discovery of facts,
969–971
subsequent events, 969
supplementary information, 971
Revision and recodification. *See*
SSAE-10; SSAE-12
Rights and obligations assertion
audit evidence, 259
derivatives and securities, for, 340
Risk
assessment. *See* Risk assessment
audit risk. *See* AU 312
control. *See* Control risk
detection. *See* Detection risk
disclosures. *See* SOP 94-6
incorrect acceptance, 459–465
inherent. *See* Inherent risk
judgmental matters, 128–129
nature of, 128
nonroutine transactions, 128–129
nonsampling, 82
sampling, 82
significance, 127
Risk assessment
analytical procedures, 107
audit evidence, 262–263
auditor's response, 212
audit team discussions, 109–110
compliance audits, 739–740
control environment, 106–110
control risk, 80–82
defined, 97
financial statement level, 71–74
information sources, 109
inherent risk, 80–81
inspection, 108
internal control, 100, 827–828
internal control risk factors, 133
management inquiries, 107–108
material misstatement, 81,
126–129
observation, 108

Risk assessment *(cont.)*
  procedures, 71–90
  proposed PCAOB standards,
    155–156
  proposed standards, 44–45
  small and midsized entities,
    139–140
  substantive procedures, 84–87
  throughout the engagement, 129
Robert Morris Associates, 1038
Rule 201, pre-engagement planning,
  700
Rule 202, GAAS and SSAEs, 526, 751
Rule 203, auditor's opinions, 526,
  535–536
Rule 301, disclosing confidential
  information, 146, 770
Rules of Conduct, general standards,
  28–30

S

SAB-99 (Materiality)
  aggregating and netting
    misstatements, 93–94
  assessing materiality, 91–93
  intentional immaterial
    misstatements, 94–95
  qualitative considerations, 76–77
SAB-101 (Revenue Recognition in
  Financial Statements), 176, 177–178
SAB-104 (Revenue Recognition), 176,
  177–178
Sales
  incomplete earnings process, 179
  lack of delivery, 179
  material weaknesses, 255
  real estate (FAS-66), 175
Sampling. *See* Audit sampling
Sarbanes-Oxley Act of 2002 (SOX),
  1049–1067
  analyst conflicts of interest,
    1060–1061
  audit committees, 50
  auditing standards, 12
  auditor independence, 1052–1054
  auditor responsibilities, 4
  audit sampling, 437

background, 1049–1050
corporate fraud and accountability,
  1065
corporate responsibility, 1054–1055
corporate tax returns, 1064
disclosure requirements, 1056–1060
due care in the performance of
  work, 34
fraud accountability, 1064–1065
implications. *See* Public company
  implications
improper influence on the conduct
  of audit, 1055–1056
independence, 28, 32
internal control report, 48, 98, 116,
  231
nonaudit services for public
  companies, 546
PCAOB, 1050–1052. *See also*
  Public Company Accounting
  Oversight Board
PCAOB standards, 12
recent developments, 1066–1067
restatement penalties, 1055
SEC resources and authority, 1061
studies and reports, 1062–1064
trends, 1065–1067
white-collar crime penalties, 1064
SAS-1 (Codification of Auditing
  Standards and Procedures), 324–331
  adherence to GAAP, 489
  audit documentation, 388
  dating of the independent auditor's
    report, 561
  discovery of misstatements, 150
  due care in performance of work,
    33, 34, 36
  error corrections, 505
  fair value, 278
  functions of auditor, 3
  GAAP, defined, 491
  GAAP application, 499
  general standards, 23
  independence, 27–32
  interim financial information, 714
  inventories, 324, 326. *See also* AU,
    331
  inventory and related procedures, 149

lack of conformity with generally accepted accounting principles, 586–587

part of audit performed by other independent auditors, 578

professional skepticism, 34

public warehouses, 745–746

reaudits, 149

redrafting of standards by ASB, 23

reputation of predecessor auditor, 148–149

responsibilities of auditor, 3

SAS-104 amendment, 33

subsequent discovery of facts, 618

subsequent events, 278, 612

training and proficiency of independent auditor, 24–26

SAS-8 (Other Information in Documents Containing Audited Financial Statements). *See also* AU 550

prospective financial statement, 811

selected financial data, 604

SAS-12 (Inquiry of a Client's Lawyer Concerning Litigation, Claims, and Assessments), 369–378

audit documentation, 388

audit inquiry letter to legal counsel, 375–378

authoritative pronouncements, 369

letter of audit inquiry, 372–374

litigation, claims, and assessment to be accrued or disclosed, 371–372

management representations, 349

overview, 370

procedures analysis and application, 371–375

procedures checklist, 370–371

redrafting of standards by ASB, 369

subsequent events, 612

training and proficiency of independent auditor, 25

SAS-21 (Segment Information), 512

SAS-22 (Planning and Supervision), 395

SAS-25 (The Relationship of Generally Accepted Auditing Standards to Quality Control Standards), 14

SAS-26 (Association with Financial Statements), 515–521

authoritative pronouncements, 515

compilation description, 521

disclaimer of opinion, 520–521

overview, 515–516

reporting analysis and application, 517–520

reporting checklist, 516–517

review description, 521

SAS-29 (Reporting on Information Accompanying the Basic Financial Statements in Auditor-Submitted Documents)

dating of the independent auditor's report, 561

independence rules, 30

SAS-32 (Adequacy of Disclosure in Financial Statements)

engagement program, 509–511

overview, 508–509

practical, defined, 536

SAS-37 (Filings under Federal Securities Statutes)

authoritative pronouncements, 691

overview, 691–693

procedures analysis and application, 693–695

procedures checklist, 693

selected financial data, 604

status of review report, 695–696

SAS-39 (Audit Sampling), 430–471

authoritative pronouncements, 430

compliance attestation, 859

nonstatistical sampling for tests of detail, 457–471

overview, 430–435

PPPO/TOE report, 234

procedures analysis and application, 436–448, 449–457, 458–469

procedures checklist, 435–436, 448, 457

redrafting of standards by ASB, 430

SAS-111 amendment, 430

size of sample, 469–471

tests of controls, 435–448

tests of details, 448–471

SAS-42 (Reporting on Condensed
Financial Statements and Selected
Financial Data)
 authoritative pronouncements, 602
 comfort letters, 672
 independence rules, 30
 overview, 602–603
 procedures analysis and
  application, 603–605
 procedures checklist, 602
 redrafting of standards by ASB, 602
SAS-43 (Omnibus Statement on
Auditing Standards)
 audit sampling, 430
 GAAP application, 499
 inventories. *See* AU 331
 public warehouses, 745–746
 statement of cash flows format
  changes, 504
SAS-45 (Related Parties), 353–360
 authoritative pronouncements, 353
 overview, 353–354
 procedures analysis and
  application, 354–360
 procedures checklist, 354
 revenue recognition, 182
 specialists, 365
 transaction examples, 355
SAS-46 (Consideration of Omitted
Procedures after the Report Date)
 assessment of significance of
  omitted procedures, 484–485
 audit documentation, 388
 overview, 483
 procedures analysis and
  application, 484–485
 procedures checklist, 484
 proper course of actions, 485
 redrafting of standards by ASB, 483
SAS-49 (Letters for Underwriters), 663
SAS-50 (Reports on the Application of
Accounting Principles)
 amendment SAS-97, 655. *See also*
  SAS-97
 authoritative pronouncements, 655
 communications between
  predecessor and successor
  accountants, 1044

 example, 661–662
 hypothetical transaction reports,
  656
 overview, 655
 procedures analysis and
  application, 657–660
 procedures checklist, 657
 reporting standards, 660–661
 scope of standards, 656–657
SAS-51 (Reporting on Financial
Statements Prepared for Use in Other
Countries)
 audit documentation, 388
 authoritative pronouncements, 571
 dual statements, 575–576
 foreign and U.S. distribution, 576
 foreign auditing standards, 573
 general standards and fieldwork
  standards, 572–573
 independence rules, 30
 overview, 571–572
 procedures analysis and
  application, 572–576
 procedures checklist, 572
 U.S.-style standard auditor's report,
  573–575, 577
SAS-54 (Illegal Acts by Clients)
 audit documentation, 389
 authoritative pronouncements, 187
 illegal acts, defined, 187
 intentional misstatements, 87–88
 overview, 187–189
 procedures analysis and
  application, 190–193
 procedures checklist, 189–190
 redrafting of standards by ASB,
  187
SAS-56 (Analytical Procedures),
281–305
 analytical review, 302–303
 audit documentation, 389
 authoritative pronouncements, 281
 control environment, 107
 fair value estimates, 277–278
 final review, 303–305
 financial statement comparisons,
  297–301
 for fraud risks, 170–171

MD&A, 889–890
overview, 281–282
performance, documentation, 296–302
procedures analysis and application, 289–294
procedures checklist, 288–289
process of, 283–288
redrafting of standards by ASB, 281
revenue recognition, 182–183
substantive procedures, 291–294
SAS-57 (Auditing Accounting Estimates), 407–429
  auditor evaluation of estimates, 428–429
  authoritative pronouncements, 407
  overview, 407–409
  procedures analysis and application, 409–415
  procedures checklist, 409
  revenue recognition, 184
  soft accounting information, 416–428
  specialists, 365
SAS-58 (Reports on Auditing Financial Statements), 522–560
  accounting change, 539
  adverse auditor's report, 554–555
  audit documentation, 389
  audit evidence, 540
  auditor's report when predecessor auditor's report no presented, 559
  auditor's report when standards are followed, 559–560
  authoritative pronouncements, 522
  balance sheet, reports on, 557
  comparative financial statements, 547, 558–559
  components, 523–524
  disclaimer report, 556–557
  emphasized matters, 544–545
  foreign and U.S. financial statements, 576
  justification for change in accounting principles, 539
  lack of conformity with generally accepted accounting principles, 587

limited reporting engagement, 631
loss contingencies, 544
overview, 523–532
qualified auditor's report, 553–554, 555–556
reporting standards analysis and application, 533–552
reporting standards checklist, 532–533
SAS-98 amendment, 547
special reports, 632, 636, 639, 648
statement of cash flows, 536
SAS-59 (The Auditor's Consideration of an Entity's Ability to Continue as a Going Concern)
  audit documentation, 389
  authoritative pronouncements, 395
  evaluating entity's ability to continue, 404–406
  management's plans, 398–399
  overview, 396
  procedures analysis and application, 396–404
  procedures checklist, 396
  redrafting of standards by ASB, 395
  SAS-77 amendment, 395. *See also* SAS-77
  substantial-doubt conditions, 397
SAS-62 (Special Reports)
  account in a financial statement, 651–652
  adherence to GAAP, 489
  agreed-upon procedures engagements, 779
  association with financial statements, 516
  authoritative pronouncements, 629
  cash-based financial statements, 649–650
  compliance attestation, 850
  comprehensive basis other than GAAP, 630–636
  debt agreements, 652
  financial statement, defined, 630
  financial statements prepared on comprehensive basis other than GAAP, 518

SAS-62 (Special Reports) *(cont.)*
  financial statements prepared
    pursuant to loan agreement,
    653–654
  independence rules, 30
  lack of conformity with generally
    accepted accounting principles,
    586–587
  management representations, 346
  overview, 629–630
  procedures analysis and
    application, 630–650
  procedures checklist, 630
  regulatory basis of accounting,
    650–651
  report as byproduct of audit, 567
  SAS-77 amendment, 395. *See also*
    SAS-77
  special-purpose financial
    statements, 567, 643
  statement of assets sold, 652–653
  statement of liabilities transferred,
    652–653
  work of specialists, 362
SAS-64 (Omnibus Statement on
  Auditing Standards — 1990)
  going concern considerations, 395,
    401
  part of audit performed by other
    independent auditors, 578
  reports on audited financial
    statements, 522
SAS-65 (The Auditor's Consideration
  of the Internal Audit Function in an
  Audit of Financial Statements),
  218–224
  authoritative pronouncements, 218
  competence, 220–221
  compliance attestation, 859
  confirmations, 312
  MD&A, 871
  objectivity, 220–221
  overview, 218–219
  procedures analysis and
    application, 219–224
  procedures checklist, 219
  reaudits, 150

SAS-67 (The Confirmation Process)
  accounts receivable, 315–316,
    321–323
  audit documentation, 389
  audit objectives, 312–313
  authoritative pronouncements, 306
  designing requests, 307–312
  inventories, 324
  lease obligation, 319
  mortgage obligation, 320
  negative confirmation, 318
  overview, 306–307
  positive confirmation, 318
  procedures analysis and
    application, 307–316
  procedures checklist, 307
  redrafting of standards by ASB, 306
  revenue recognition, 183
SAS-69 (The Meaning of "Present
  Fairly in Conformity with Generally
  Accepted Accounting Principles")
  auditor assurances, 529
  authoritative pronouncements, 491
  federal GAAP hierarchy, 497–498
  lack of conformity with generally
    accepted accounting principles,
    586
  nongovernmental entity accounting
    hierarchy, 494–496
  overview, 492–494
  special reports, 633
  state and local government
    accounting hierarchy, 496–497
SAS-70 (Service Organizations)
  agreed-upon procedures
    engagements, 779
  derivatives and securities, 337
  description of controls, 237–239
  fair value measurements, 273
  independence rules, 30
  overview, 226–228
  PPPO report, 233–240
  PPPO/TOE report, 233–240
  restricted use auditor's report, 566
  Type 1 SAS-70 report, 234
  Type 2 SAS-70 report, 234, 835,
    836

SAS-72 (Letters for Underwriters and
Certain Other Requesting Parties)
  agreed-upon procedures
    engagements, 779
  authoritative pronouncements, 663
  comfort letter, 683 – 688
  compliance attestation, 850
  overview, 663 – 667
  procedures analysis and
    application, 667 – 682
  procedures checklist, 667
  representation letter, 682 – 683
  restricted use auditor's report, 566
  SAS-76 amendment, 663
  SAS-86 amendment, 663, 675
SAS-73 (Using the Work of a
Specialist), 361 – 368
  accounting estimates, 422
  in attest engagements, 757
  authoritative pronouncements, 361
  compliance attestation, 859
  fair value determination, 275
  information technology skills, 105
  MD&A, 871
  overview, 361 – 363
  procedures analysis and
    application, 364 – 368
  procedures checklist, 363
  reaudits, 150
  redrafting of standards by ASB,
    361
  training and proficiency of
    independent auditor, 25
SAS-74 (Compliance Auditing
Consideration in Audits of
Governmental Entities and
Recipients of Governmental
Financial Assistance). *See also*
SAS-117
  agreed-upon procedures
    engagements, 779
  audit documentation, 389
  compliance attestation, 850
  special reports, 640
  understanding with the client, 50
SAS-76 (Amendments to Statement on
Auditing Standards No. 72, Letters
for Underwriters and Certain Other
Requesting Parties), 663, 665

SAS-77 (Amendments to Statements on
Auditing Standards No. 22,
"Planning and Supervision," No. 59
"The Auditor's Consideration of an
Entity's Ability to Continue as a
Going Concern," and SAS-62,
"Special Reports")
  going concern considerations, 395,
    401
  lack of conformity with generally
    accepted accounting principles,
    586
  SAS-62 amendment, 629
SAS-78 (Consideration of Internal
Control in a Financial Statement
Audit: An Amendment to SAS-55),
225
SAS-79 (Amendments to Statement on
Auditing Standards No. 58, "Reports
on Audited Financial Statements"),
522, 544
SAS-84 (Communications Between
Predecessor and Successor Auditors),
144 – 154
  access to audit files, 147 – 148
  communication of fraud to
    management, 174
  discovery of misstatements, 150
  before engagement acceptance,
    145 – 146
  inquiries from reporting accountant
    to continuing accountant, 659
  letter of understanding from
    predecessor to successor auditor,
    150 – 152
  MD&A, 868
  overview, 144 – 145
  planning and supervision, 46
  reasonable requests, 147 – 148
  reaudits, 149 – 150
  redrafting of standards by ASB,
    144
  reputation of predecessor auditor,
    148 – 149
SAS-85 (Management Representations)
  audit documentation, 379, 390
  authoritative pronouncements, 342
  letter example, 349 – 352
  MD&A, 881

SAS-85 (Management Representations)
(*cont.*)
  overview, 342–343
  procedures analysis and
    application, 344–349
  procedures checklist, 343–344
  redrafting of standards by ASB,
    342–343
  reports on audited financial
    statements, 522
  written representations, 162
SAS-86 (Amendment to Statement on
  Auditing Standards No. 72, Letters
  for Underwriters and Certain Other
  Requesting Parties), 663, 675
SAS-87 (Restricting the Use of an
  Auditor's Report)
  basis of reporting criteria,
    566–567
  financial statements before loan
    agreements, 567
  overview, 565–566
  report as byproduct of audit, 568
  reporting standards, 567–568
  special-purpose financial
    statements, 569
SAS-88 (Service Organizations and
  Reporting on Consistency),
  225–244
  change in reporting entity, 506–507
  GAAP application, 499
  internal control, 225, 230
  redrafting of standards by ASB, 225
SAS-89 (Audit Adjustments), 342
  revenue recognition, 185
  SOX requirements, 1056–1057
SAS-90 (Audit Committee
  Communications), 657
SAS-91 (Federal GAAP Hierarchy), 491
SAS-92 (Auditing Derivative
  Instruments, Hedging Activities, and
  Investments in Securities), 332–341
  assertions, 339–341
  authoritative pronouncements, 332
  fair value measurements, 270
  overview, 332–333
  procedures analysis and
    application, 335–338

  procedures checklist, 334–335
  securities, 334
  services affecting substantive
    procedures, 338
  substantive procedures, 338–341
SAS-93 (Omnibus Statement on
  Auditing Standards — 2000)
  GAAP, 491
  overview, 144–145
  redrafting of standards by ASB,
    144
  reports on audited financial
    statements, 522
SAS-95 (Generally Accepted Auditing
  Standards)
  audit documentation, 389
  interpretive publications, 7
  overview, 8–13
  redrafting of standards to follow
    clarity drafting conventions, 8
  SAS-105 amendment, 8
SAS-96 (Audit Documentation), 68, 729
SAS-97 (Amendment to Statement on
  Auditing Standards No. 50, Reports
  on the Application of Accounting
  Principles)
  authoritative pronouncements, 655
  example, 661–662
  overview, 655
  procedures analysis and
    application, 657–660
  procedures checklist, 657
  reporting standards, 660–661
  scope of standards, 656–657
SAS-98 (Omnibus Statement on
  Auditing Standards — 2002)
  comparative financial statements,
    547
  dating of independent auditor's
    reports, 561, 562
  GAAS, 8
  inquiries on subsequent events, 239
  overview, 15, 68
  reports on audited financial
    statements, 522
  service organizations, 225
  subsequent discovery of facts, 618
  subsequent events, 612, 613

SAS-99 (Consideration of Fraud in a
Financial Statement Audit)
accounting estimates, 411
account level risk assessment, 84
analytical procedures, 163 – 164,
171, 288
antifraud programs and controls,
119 – 120
audit documentation, 389 – 390
Audit Guide procedures, 182
auditor's response to intentional
misstatements, 87 – 88
audit sampling, 437
brainstorming sessions, 109,
159 – 160
characteristics of fraud, 35 – 36
communication of fraud to
management, 173 – 174
communications before
engagement acceptance, 146
compliance attestation, 855
control environment evaluation, 118
documentation of consideration of
fraud, 174
due care in performance of work,
33
evaluate audit evidence, 170
fair value, 273 – 274
fraud, defined, 155
fraud opportunities, 408
fraud risk factors, 164
fraudulent financial reporting,
156 – 157
GAAP conformity, 494
illegal acts, 188
information gathering, 73, 162
information to identify risks of
material misstatement, 160 – 161
interim financial information, 711
internal audit function, 221 – 222
internal control limitations, 103
inventories, 325
journal entries and adjustments,
123, 205 – 206
management representations, 342,
346
material misstatement, 97, 165 – 166
overview, 68, 155 – 158

potential for material misstatement,
159
professional skepticism, 34 – 35,
158
reasonable assurance, 36
redrafting of standards by ASB, 155
response to results of assessment,
166
revenue recognition, 184
risk assessment procedures, 106
sampling risk, 433
specialists, 363
team member communications, 57
unusual transactions, 171
SAS-100 (Interim Financial
Information)
analytical procedures and related
inquiries, 705
in audited financial statements,
715 – 716
authoritative pronouncements, 697
client representation letter,
716 – 719
client's representation, 715
comfort letters, 672, 674 – 677, 679
discovery of facts subsequent to
date of review report, 714
going concern issues, 722 – 724
independence rules, 30
inquiries and other review
procedures, 705 – 712
overview, 697 – 700
procedures analysis and
application, 701 – 705
procedures checklist, 700
reporting standards, 712 – 713
report modifications, 713 – 714
standard review report, 719 – 722
understanding with the client, 50,
701 – 703
SAS-101 (Auditing Fair Value
Measurements and Disclosures),
269 – 280
audit committee communications,
280
authoritative pronouncements, 269
GAAP conformity, 274 – 275
independent estimates, 277 – 278

SAS-101 (Auditing Fair Value
Measurements and Disclosures)
(cont.)
overview, 269–271
procedures analysis and
application, 273–280
procedures checklist, 272
testing, 275–277
understanding client's process,
273–274
SAS-102 (Defining Professional
Requirements in Statements on
Auditing Standards)
application of requirements, 10, 13
auditor responsibilities, 5–7
departure from GAAS,
documentation of, 384
redrafting of standards to follow
clarity drafting conventions, 5
terminology, degree of
responsibility, 13
SAS-103 (Audit Documentation)
audit sampling, 447, 457
authoritative pronouncements, 379
checklist of SAS requirements,
388–392
dating of independent auditor's
reports, 561
fieldwork standards, 381–387
going concern, 395
overview, 379–381
redrafting of standards by ASB,
379–381
regulatory agency access to
documentation, 386–387,
392–394
SAS-104 (Amendment to Statement on
Auditing Standards No. 1,
Codification of Auditing Standards
and Procedures), 33
SAS-105 (Amendment to Statement on
Auditing Standards No. 95,
Generally Accepted Auditing
Standards), 8
SAS-106 (Audit Evidence)
assertions, 69
audit sampling, 462
authoritative pronouncements, 257

confirmation, 307
MD&A, 870
overview, 257–258
procedures analysis and
application, 258–268
procedures checklist, 258
qualifications of specialists, 364
redrafting of standards by ASB,
257
SAS-107 (Audit Risk and Materiality in
Conducting an Audit), 68–95
acceptable level of audit risk, 72
accounting estimates, 86
account level audit procedures,
77–79
assessment factors, 72–73
audit documentation, 390
audit risk level, 87
audit sampling, 462
control risk, defined, 80, 462
control risk assertion, 81–82
default to maximum assessment, 82
derivatives and securities,
336–337
detection risk, defined, 82
documentation of audit results,
89–90
fair value, 279
inherent risk, defined, 80–81, 462
known misstatements, 70
likely misstatements, 70
locations or components, at, 74
management representations, 346
materiality level, 75–76
overview, 68–70
preliminary analysis, 75
qualitative considerations, 76
redrafting of standards by ASB, 68
reduced materiality level, 79
risk assessment procedures, 72–74
substantive procedures, 84–87
SAS-108 (Planning and Supervision)
audit documentation, 390
overview, 43
redrafting of standards by ASB, 43
specialist, 362
understanding with the client,
48–49, 50

SAS-109 (Understanding the Entity and
  Its Environment and Assessing the
  Risks of Material Misstatement)
    audit documentation, 390 – 391
    authoritative pronouncements, 96
    control environment, 99 – 103, 132
    control risk assessment, 230 – 231
    derivatives and securities, 337
    entity risk factor examples, 133
    external factors, 136
    factors of risk of material
      misstatement, 141 – 142
    fair value, 273
    fraud due to risk of material
      misstatement, 160 – 161
    fraud risk assessment in context of
      related programs and controls, 166
    governmental entities, 729
    information system objectives, 134
    information technology, 104 – 105
    internal control over financial
      reporting, 135
    material misstatement risks and
      auditor's responses, 143
    overview, 96 – 99
    PPPO/TOE reports, 234
    procedures analysis and
      application, 106 – 131
    procedures checklist, 106
    redrafting of standards by ASB, 96
    reporting standards, 137 – 138
    revenue recognition, internal
      control over, 181
    small and midsized entities,
      139 – 140
    user auditor, 227 – 228
SAS-110 (Performing Audit Procedures
  in Response to Assessed Risks and
  Evaluating the Audit Evidence
  Obtained)
    assessed risks, 194 – 210
    audit documentation, 391
    audit evidence, 210 – 212
    authoritative pronouncements, 194
    documentation, 212
    financial statement level response,
      196
    inventory assertions, 214 – 215

overview, 194 – 196
    redrafting of standards by ASB,
      194
    relevant assertion level response,
      197 – 200
    substantive procedures, 205 – 210,
      214 – 217
    tests of controls, 200 – 205, 213
    user auditor, 227 – 228
SAS-111 (Amendment to Statement on
  Auditing Standards No. 39, Audit
  Sampling), 430
SAS-112 (Communication of Internal
  Control Related Matters Identified in
  an Audit)
    report as byproduct of audit, 568
    reporting to the audit committee,
      1053
SAS-113 (Omnibus Statement on
  Auditing Standards – 2006), 8
    accounting estimates, 407
    consideration of fraud in a financial
      statement audit, 155
    fair value measurements, 269
    going concern considerations, 395
    management representations, 342
    subsequent events, 612
SAS-114 (The Auditor's
  Communication with Those Charged
  with Governance), 472 – 482
    accounting principles, 167
    audit documentation, 391
    authoritative pronouncements, 472
    fair value measurements, 280
    going concern considerations, 395
    matters to be communicated,
      475 – 478
    overview, 472 – 473
    procedures analysis and
      application, 473 – 480
    procedures checklist, 473
    redrafting of standards by ASB,
      472
    reporting to audit committee, 1053
    restricted auditor's report, 568
    significant findings, topic and
      nature of communications,
      481 – 482

SAS-115 (Communication of Internal
  Control Related Matters Identified in
  an Audit)
  audit documentation, 392
  authoritative pronouncements, 245
  communication of internal control,
    250–251
  communications of fraud to
    management, 173
  compensating control, defined, 249
  compliance attestation, 859
  deficiencies, 248
  deficiencies and material
    weaknesses, 48
  examples of possible deficiencies,
    252–253
  governmental entities, 729
  material weakness, 246, 247–249,
    253–256
  overview, 246–247
  procedures analysis and
    application, 247–252
  procedures checklist, 247
  redrafting of standards by ASB, 245
  significant deficiencies, 246,
    247–249, 253–256
  small business material
    weaknesses, examples, 254–256
  written reports, 250–252
SAS-116 (Interim Financial
  Information), 391–392
SAS-117 (Compliance Audits),
  727–741
  authoritative pronouncements, 727
  definitions, 729–730
  overview, 727–728
  planning and performing audit,
    731–733, 737–741
  procedures analysis and
    application, 737–741
  procedures checklist, 727
  required procedures, 731–737
SAS-118 (Other Information in
  Documents Containing Audited
  Financial Statements), 588–593
  accounting estimates, 415
  authoritative pronouncements, 588
  definitions, 589

material inconsistencies, 590, 592
misstatements of fact, 590–591,
  592–593
overview, 588–589
procedures analysis and
  application, 591–593
reading other information, 590,
  591–592
required procedures, 589–591
SAS-119 (Supplementary Information
  in Relation to the Financial
  Statements as a Whole), 594
SAS-120 (Required Supplementary
  Information), 606
Scanning of audit evidence, 267
Scope limitations
  in attest engagements, 767–768
  internal control, 847
  limited reporting engagement, 542,
    631
  qualified auditor's reports, 555–556
  reporting of, 541
Scope of engagement
  agreed-upon procedures
    engagements, 784
  auditor's reports, scope paragraph,
    525
  audit risk and, 79
  considerations, 52–53
Scope paragraph
  incomplete financial presentations,
    644
  special auditor's reports, 646
  specified elements, accounts, or
    items, 638
  standard special report, 635
SEC. *See* Securities and Exchange
  Commission
Section 11 investigation, 664
Securities
  accounting for. *See* FAS-115
  analysts, SOX conflict of interest
    requirements, 1060–1061
  auditing of. *See* AU 332; SAS-92
  auditing standards, 334
  filings under federal securities
    statutes. *See* SAS-37
  registration of, 664, 666

Securities Act of 1933
  accountant's reports, 691
  comfort letters, 664
  dating auditor's reports, 564
  MD&A information, 878
  Section 7, 691–692
  Section 11, 691–692
  Section 11 investigation, 664
  selected financial data, 604
  shelf registrations, 669–670, 691, 694
Securities and Exchange Commission (SEC)
  comparative financial statements, 519
  compliance, comments in comfort letters, 673–674
  direction, defined, 1055
  fraud detection, 157
  "Fraud Related SEC Enforcement Actions Against Auditors: 1987-1997," 36
  improper influence on the conduct of audit, 1056
  officer, defined, 1055
  resources and authority under SOX, 1061
  Staff Accounting Bulletins. *See specific SAB*
Securities Exchange Act of 1934
  compliance attestation, 850
  Credit Rating Agency Reform Act, 1062–1063
Segment information, 512
Segregation of duties, 103
Selected financial data, reporting of. *See* AU 552; SAS-42
Sequential sampling, 439–440
Service auditors
  acceptance of, 901–902, 912
  assessing criteria suitability, 902–903, 912
  communications, 912, 916–917
  continuance of, 901–902, 912
  controls placed in operation, 231
  defined, 227, 900
  documentation, 908

  evidence of service organization's system and controls, obtaining, 903–905, 914–915
  identification of management, 901
  internal control information, 230–231
  management representations, 905–906, 915–916
  material inconsistencies with description, 907
  materiality, 903, 913
  overview, 897–898
  preparation of report, 908–911, 916
  professional reputation, 231–232
  reporting procedures, 901–912, 912–917
  role of, 232–233, 898
  service audit report, 233–239
  subsequent events, 239, 907
  tests of operating effectiveness, 231
  Type 1 report (example), 917–919
  Type 2 report (example), 919–921
  understanding of service organization's system, 903, 913–914
  use of service auditor's work, 232
  work of others, using, 905–906
  written representations, 239–241
Service organizations, 897–921
  defined, 227
  definitions, 898–901
  derivatives and securities, for, 338
  generally. *See* AU 324; SAS-70
  internal control, 835–836
  procedures analysis and application, 912–917
  reporting on consistency. *See* SAS-88
  reporting procedures of service auditors, 901–917
  role of service auditor, 898
  subservice organizations, 225, 240
  Type 1 report (example), 917–919
  Type 2 report (example), 919–921
  understanding of, by service auditor, 903, 913–914

Share-Based Payment (FAS-123R), 424
Shelf registration, 669–670, 691, 694
Side agreements, 176
Significance
    assertions, 258–260
    deficiencies. *See* Significant
        deficiency
    defined, 126
    material misstatement, 126
    risks requiring audit attention, 127
Significant deficiency
    areas of controls, 249
    communication of, 250–251
    defined, 246
    examples, 253–256
    identification, 247–249
    internal control, 837–838
    written communication, 253–256
Single-dated reports, 563
Skepticism. *See* Professional
    skepticism
Small and midsized entities
    material weaknesses, examples,
        254–256
    risk assessment, 139–140
Soft accounting information, auditing,
    416–428
Software revenue recognition
    (SOP 97-2), 176
SOP 81-1 (Accounting for Performance
    of Construction-Type and Certain
    Production-Type Contracts), 175
SOP 82-1 (Accounting and Financial
    Reporting for Personal Financial
    Statements), 1048
SOP 92-4 (Auditing Insurance Entities'
    Loss Reserves), 362
SOP 94-6 (Disclosure of Certain
    Significant Risks and Uncertainties)
    accounting estimates, 425
    engagement program, 509–511
    fair value, 279
    financial statement disclosures,
        509–511
    loss contingencies, 543
    management representations, 185,
        345
    special reports, 634

SOP 97-2 (Software Revenue
    Recognition), 176
SOP 2003-02 (Attest Engagement on
    Greenhouse Gas Emissions
    Information), 758
SOX. *See* Sarbanes-Oxley Act of 2002
Specialists. *See also* AU 336; SAS-73
    in agreed-upon procedures
        engagements, 783
    audit evidence, effects on, 365
    audit report, effects on, 366–367
    extent of work, 365–366
    fair value, 275
    IT. *See* Information technology
    planning of audit engagement,
        55–56
    qualifications, 364–365
    relationships, 365
    transfer of financial assets,
        367–368
Special-purpose financial statements
    contractual agreements or
        regulatory provisions, 643, 927
    incomplete presentations,
        643–644
    presentation not in accordance with
        GAAP or OCBOA, 645–646
    reporting standards, 644–645
    restricting use of reports, 567, 569
Special reports. *See* AU 623; SAS-62;
    SAS-77
Specified elements, accounts, or items
    compilation (AR 110),
        1017–1018
    compilation (SSARS-13),
        1017–1018
    opinion paragraph, 639
    presentation basis paragraph, 638
SQCS-7 (A Firm's System of Quality
    Control), 14–16, 18–19, 1092
SSAE. *See generally* Standards for
    Attestation Engagements; *below are
    specific SSAEs by number*
SSAE-1 (comfort letters), 672, 678
SSAE-3 (Compliance Attestation),
    special reports, 640
SSAE-10 (Attestation Standards:
    Revision and Recodification)

agreed-upon procedures
engagements, 779. *See also* AT
201
attest engagements, 753. *See also*
AT 101
compliance attestation, 850,
852–853, 863–865
MD&A, 866, 883–884, 892–893
pro forma financial information,
812, 819–821. *See also* AT 401
responsible party, 755
subject matter, 754
SSAE-11 (Attest Documentation), 753
SSAE-12 (Amendment to SSAE No.
10, Attestation Standards: Revision
and Recodification), 753, 755–756
SSAE-13 (Defining Professional
Requirements in Statements on
Standards for Attestation
Engagements), 749–750
SSAE-14 (SSAE Hierarchy), 751–752
SSAE-15 (An Examination of an
Entity's Internal Control Over
Financial Reporting That Is
Integrated With an Audit of Its
Financial Statements)
attestation engagements, 770–771
reporting internal control over
financial reporting, 822–824,
842, 844, 846
SSAE-16 (Reporting on Controls at a
Service Organization), 897–921
redrafting of standards by ASB, 897
SSAE Interpretations, 753, 755, 758,
764, 766, 768
SSARS. *See generally* Statements on
Standards for Accounting and
Review Services; *below are specific
SSARS by number*
SSARS-1 (Compilation and Review of
Financial Statements)
financial statement, defined, 631
personal financial statements,
1046–1048
SSARS-2 (Reporting on Comparative
Financial Statements), 1021–1036
all periods have been compiled,
1032–1033

all periods have been reviewed,
1033
authoritative pronouncements,
1021
change in previous report, 1025,
1034–1035
current period is compiled and
prior period is reviewed,
1023–1024
current period is reviewed and prior
period is compiled, 1023–1025,
1033–1034
current period refers to prior
period, 1024–1025, 1034
current year is compiled and prior
year is audited, 1031–1032, 1036
highest level of service rendered,
exception, 1029–1031
omission of all disclosures,
1029–1031, 1035–1036
overview, 1021–1022
predecessor accountant has ceased
operations, 1028–1029
predecessor accountant's reports,
1024–1028, 1035–1036
procedures analysis and
application, 1023–1032
procedures checklist, 1022–1023
reissuance of unchanged report,
1025–1027
status of client as issuer has
changed, 1031–1032
SSARS-3 (Compilation Reports on
Financial Statements in Certain
Prescribed Forms), 1037–1039
SSARS-4 (Communication Between
Predecessor and Successor
Accountants)
authoritative pronouncements,
1040
overview, 1040–1041
procedures analysis and
application, 1042–1044
procedures checklist, 1041–1042
reissuance of unchanged report,
1025–1027
request for access to working
papers, 1044–1045

SSARS-6 (Reporting on Personal
Financial Statements Included in
Written Personal Financial Plans),
1046–1048
SSARS-7 (Omnibus Statement on
Standards for Accounting and
Review Services — 1992), 926, 1043
SSARS-9 (Omnibus Statement on
Standards for Accounting and Review
Services — 2002), 1040–1041
SSARS-10 (Performance of Review
Engagements), 926
SSARS-11 (Standards for Accounting
and Review Services)
    reporting on comparative financial
    statements, 1021
    review engagement, 926
    SSARS hierarchy, 925
SSARS-12 (Omnibus Statement on
Standards for Accounting and
Review Services — 2005), 1021
SSARS-13 (Compilation of Specified
Elements, Accounts, or Items of a
Financial Statement), 1017–1018
    compilation of financial
    statements, 938
SSARS-14 (Compilation of Pro Forma
Financial Information), 1019–1020
    compilation of financial
    statements, 938
SSARS-15 (Elimination of Certain
References to Statements on
Auditing Standards and
Incorporation of Appropriate
Guidance into Statements on
Standards for Accounting and
Review Services)
    communications between
    predecessor and successor
    accountants, 1040
    compilation reports on financial
    statements in certain prescribed
    forms, 1037
    reporting on comparative financial
    statements, 1021
SSARS-16 (Defining Professional
Requirements in Statements on
Standards for Accounting and
Review, Services), 926

SSARS-17 (Omnibus Statement on
Standards for Accounting and
Review Services – 2008)
    communications between
    predecessor and successor
    accountants, 1040
    compilation reports on financial
    statements in certain prescribed
    forms, 1037
    reporting on comparative financial
    statements, 1021
SSARS-18 (Applicability of Statements
on Standards for Accounting and
Review Services), 926
SSARS-19 (Compilation and Review
Engagements), 925–931. See also
Compilation of financial statements;
Review of financial statements
    authoritative pronouncements, 925,
    932
    definitions, 925–926
    elements of engagement, 929–930
    evidence, 930
    explanatory material in SSARS,
    927
    financial reporting framework, 930
    financial statements, 930
    materiality, 931
    objectives, 926–927
    overview, 925
    review of financial statements, 953
    SSARS compliance, 927
    standards and guidance, 928–929
    three-party relationship, 929
    written communication or report,
    930
SSARS Interpretations
    comparative financial statements,
    1021, 1030
    compilation and review
    engagements, 926, 927
    compilation reports on financial
    statements in certain prescribed
    forms, 1037, 1038
    personal financial plans, 1047
    personal financial statements, 1046
    predecessor and successor
    accountant communications,
    1040, 1044

SSCS (Statements on Standards for Consulting Services), attest engagement, 771

Staff Audit Practice Alert No. 2 (Matters Related to Auditing Fair Value Measurements of Financial Instruments and the Use of Specialists), 270, 333–334, 366, 413

Staff Audit Practice Alert No. 3 (Audit Considerations in the Current Economic Environment), 111–112

Standards for Accounting and Review Services (AR 50), 925

Standards for Attestation Engagements (SSAE). *See also "SSAE" by number*
hierarchy, 751–752
independence rules, 30
interpretations. *See specific SSAE Interpretation*

Standards of fieldwork. *See* Fieldwork standards

Standards of reporting, GAAS, 9–10

Statement of Cash Flows
adequacy of disclosures, 536
FAS-95, 504
qualified auditor's reports, 555

Statements of Position (SOP), purpose of, 11, 12. *See also specific SOP*

Statements on Auditing Standards. *See also specific SAS*
GAAS Guide sections, cross-reference table, 1077–1092
Meaning of "Present Fairly in Conformity with Generally Accepted Accounting Principles," for Nongovernmental Entities (proposed), 493
overview, 10
professional requirements, 5–7. *See also* SAS-102

Statements on Quality Control Standards (SQCS-7), 14–16, 18–19, 1092

Statements on Standards for Accounting and Review Services (SSARS). *See also specific SSARS*
GAAS Guide sections, cross-reference table, 1092–1094

independence rules, 31

Statements on Standards for Attestation Engagements (SSAE). *See also specific AT*
GAAS Guide sections, cross-reference table, 1094–1096
purpose of, 754, 784

Statements on Standards for Consulting Services (SSCS), attest engagement, 771

Statistical sampling plans
overview, 431–432
sampling risk, 446
size of sample, 444
tests of controls, 435–448

Statistics, in comfort letters, 680–681

Stock
equity method of accounting (APB-18), 334
share-based payment (FAS-123R), 424
SOX requirements, 1057
stockholder communications of interim financial information, 715

Strategy for audit engagement, 51–54

Studies and reports by GAO, 1062–1064

Subject matter
examination report, 772–773, 775–776
review report, 774, 777

Subsequent discovery of facts, 618–625
audit documentation, 381
authoritative pronouncements, 618
compilation of financial statements, 943–944
discovery of misstatements, 150
interim financial information, 714
overview, 618–619
procedures analysis and application, 619–621
procedures checklist, 619, 621–625
restatement adjustments, 551
review of financial statements, 969–971

Subsequent events, 612–617
    adjustments, 615
    audit program, 615–617
    authoritative pronouncements, 612
    comfort letters, 678–681, 682
    compilation of financial
        statements, 943
    compliance attestation, 860
    disclosures, 615
    discovery of facts. *See* Subsequent
        discovery of facts
    error corrections, 505
    fair value, 278
    FIFO to LIFO change, 504
    interim financial information, 714
    internal control, 848–849
    management representations, 345
    MD&A, 877–879, 890, 895–896
    overview, 612–613
    procedures analysis and
        application, 613–615
    procedures checklist, 613
    reporting, 503–504
    retroactive restatement, 503
    review engagement, 693
    review of financial statements, 969
    service auditor, discovery by, 239
    subsequent-events period, 693
Substantial-doubt question, 397,
    401–402
Substantive procedures
    analytical procedures, 291–294
    audit evidence, 262–263
    derivatives and securities, 337,
        338–341
    for detection risk, 129
    extent of, 209
    inventory assertions, 214–215
    nature of, 207–208
    presentation and disclosure
        evaluation, 210
    in response to assessed risks,
        205–210
    for risk assessment, 84–87
    roll forward from interim to period
        end, 216–217
    sampling risk, 433–435
    timing, 208–209

Successor auditors
    communications with predecessor
        auditors. *See* AR 400; AU 315;
        SAS-84; SAS-109; SSARS-4
    defined, 1040
    discovery of misstatements, 150
    letter of understanding, 150–152
    reporting by, 550–552
Supervision. *See* Planning and
    supervision
Supplementary information, 594–551
    authoritative pronouncements, 594,
        606
    definitions, 595, 607
    explanatory paragraph used to
        report on supplementary
        information, 600–601, 608–611
    overview, 594–595, 606–607
    procedures analysis and
        application, 599–600
    procedures checklist, 607
    reporting, 597–599, 601, 608–610
    required procedures, 595–599, 608
Systematic sampling, 439–440

T

Tables, in comfort letters, 680–681
Tests
    accounting estimates
        reasonableness test, 409–412
    of controls. *See* Tests of controls
    cutoff tests, 183
    design effectiveness, 831–832
    nature, timing, extent of, 834–835
    nonstatistical sampling tests of
        details, 469–471
    operating effectiveness, 231,
        832–833
    reasonableness test, 284, 285
    sampling tests of details, 448–471
Tests of controls
    audit evidence, 262–263
    audit sampling, 433–435,
        435–448
    decision tree, 213
    dual-purpose tests, 202
    extent of, 204–205

nature of, 201–202
in response to assessed risks,
200–205
sampling risk, 433–435
timing, 202–204
Third parties
compilation and review
engagements, 929
confirmations from, 313–315
financial statements, use of, 940
inventory confirmations, 330–331
inventory storage, 326–327
TIS. *See* American Institute of Certified
Public Accountants (AICPA)
Tolerable misstatement
audit sampling, 454, 463
determination, 77–79
nonstatistical sampling, 460
Tolerable rate of control risk, 442
Tone at the top, 16
Training, in attest engagements, 757
Transactions
classes of. *See* Classes of
transactions
hypothetical, 656
new, 493–494
nonroutine, 128
off-balance-sheet, 1057
vouch transactions, 183
Transfers of assets, impact of
specialists (FAS-140), 367–368
Trend analysis, 284–285
Type 1 report, service auditor's,
917–919
Type 1 SAS-70 report, 234
Type 2 report, service auditor's,
919–921
Type 2 SAS-70 report, 234

U

Unaudited financial statements
accounting basis other than GAAP,
520–521
auditor independence, 518, 521
disclaimers, 520–521
of public entity, 517–519
restatement adjustments, 551–552

Uncertainty. *See* Going concern
Unconditional requirements, 6
Understanding. *See also* AU, 312
in agreed-upon procedures
engagements, 781–782
compilation of financial
statements, 934–935
compilation of financial statements
engagement, 932–934
documentation of, 49–50, 130–131
of environment. *See* AU 314;
SAS-109
interim financial information,
701–703
of internal control, 115–126
letter of understanding from
predecessor to successor auditor,
150–152
planning and supervision, 46–49
review of financial statements,
954–956
Underwriter letters
agreed-upon procedures
engagements, 779
authoritative pronouncements, 663
comfort letter, 683–688
compliance attestation, 850
overview, 663–667
procedures analysis and
application, 667–682
procedures checklist, 667
representation letter, 682–683
restricted use auditor's reports, 566
SAS-49 (Letters for Underwriters),
663
SAS-76 amendment, 663
SAS-86 amendment, 663, 675
Unusual transactions
fraud, 171
revenue recognition, 177
Updated report, defined, 1021
User auditor
defined, 227
procedures analysis and
application, 228–232
procedures checklist, 228
role of, 227–228
User organization, defined, 227

Users of reports. *See* Distribution
  paragraph

V

Valuation and allocation assertion
  audit evidence, 259
  derivatives and securities, for,
  340–341
Variable sampling, 432, 448–457
Vouch transactions, 183

W

Warehouses, 745–746
Web resources, 1069–1075
Web site, AICPA, 16

White-collar crime penalties, 1064
Working papers. *See* Audit
  documentation
Written representations
  compliance attestation, 860–861
  interim financial information,
  708–710
  internal control, 838–839
  from service organizations,
  239–241

Y

Yellow Book (Government Auditing
  Standards)
  compliance audits, 729, 741
  special reports, 640

About the CD-ROM

System Requirements

- IBM PC or compatible computer with CD-ROM drive

- Microsoft Word 7.0 for Windows or compatible word processor

- 2.6 MB available on hard drive

The CD-ROM provided with CCH's *GAAS Guide* contains electronic versions of the more than 100 exhibits presented in the book.

Subject to the conditions in the license agreement and the limited warranty, which are reproduced at the end of the book, you may duplicate the files on this disk, modify them as necessary, and create your own customized versions. Installing the disk contents and/or using the disk in any way indicates that you accept the terms of the license agreement.

If you experience any difficulties installing or using the files included on this disk and cannot resolve the problems using the information presented in this section, call 800 835 0105 or visit our Web site: http://support.cch.com.

Accounting Research Manager™

Accounting Research Manager is the most comprehensive, up-to-date, and objective online database of financial reporting literature. It includes all authoritative and proposed accounting, auditing, and SEC literature, plus independent, expert-written interpretive guidance. And, in addition to our standard accounting and SEC libraries, you can enjoy the full spectrum of financial reporting with our Audit library.

The Audit library covers auditing standards, attestation engagement standards, accounting and review services standards, audit risk alerts, and other vital auditing-related guidance. You'll also have online access to our best-selling *GAAS Practice Manual, Knowledge-Based Audit*™ *Procedures, Compilations & Reviews, CPA's Guide to Effective Engagement Letters, CPA's Guide to Management Letter Comments*, and be kept-up-to-date on the latest authoritative literature via the *GAAS Update Service*.

With **Accounting Research Manager**, you maximize the efficiency of your research time, while enhancing your results. Learn more about our content, our experts and how you can request a FREE trial by visiting us at **http://www.accountingresearchmanager.com**.

CD-ROM Contents

File	File Name	File Type
Exhibit AU 230-1 — Professional Skepticism	AU230-01	RTF
Exhibit AU 311-1 — Engagement Letter	AU311-01	RTF
Exhibit AU 311-2 — Audit Engagement Planning Checklist	AU311-02	RTF
Exhibit AU 311-3 — Audit Engagement Supervision Checklist	AU311-03	RTF
Exhibit AU 314-01 — Examples of Elements of The Control Environment	AU314-01	PPT
Exhibit AU 314-02 — Examples of Factors Affecting Entity Risks	AU314-02	PPT
Exhibit AU 314-03 — Objectives of Information Systems	AU314-03	PPT
Exhibit AU 314-04 — Examples of Control Activities Germane to Internal Control over Financial Reporting	AU314-04	PPT
Exhibit AU 314-05 — Examples of Industry, Regulatory, and Other External Factors	AU314-05	PPT
Exhibit AU 314-06 — Nature of the Entity and Relevant Standards of Financial Reporting	AU314-06	RTF
Exhibit AU 314-07 — Application of Internal Control Concepts to Small and Midsized Entities	AU314-07	RTF
Exhibit AU 314-08 — Factors That Might Indicate a Heightened Risk of Material Misstatement	AU314-08	RTF
Exhibit AU 314-09 — Relationship of Assessed Risks of Material Misstatement and Auditor's Responses	AU314-09	RTF
Exhibit AU 315-1 — Letter of Understanding from Predecessor to Successor Auditor	AU315-01	RTF
Exhibit AU 315-2 — Client Consent and Acknowledgment Letter	AU315-02	RTF
Exhibit AU 315-3 — Prospective Client Evaluation Form	AU315-03	RTF

File	File Name	File Type
Exhibit AU 316-1 — Guidance for Auditing Revenue in Certain Industries	AU316-01	RTF
Exhibit AU 318-01 — Decision Tree for Designing and Performing Current Year Tests of Controls	AU318-01	RTF
Exhibit AU 318-02 — Examples of Substantive Procedures Relevant to Inventory Assertions	AU318-02	RTF
Exhibit AU 318-03 — Examples of Roll Forward of Substantive Procedures from Interim to Period End	AU318-03	RTF
Exhibit AU 324-1 — Report on Controls Placed at a Service Organization (PPPO)	AU324-01	RTF
Exhibit AU 324-2 — Report on Controls Placed in Operation at a Service Organization and Tests of Operating Effectiveness (PPPO/TOE)	AU324-02	RTF
Exhibit AU 325-1 — Examples of Possible Deficienies	AU325-01	RTF
Exhibit AU 325-2 — Example of a Written Communication about Significant Deficiencies and Material Weaknesses	AU325-02	RTF
Exhibit AU 325-3 — Examples of Possible Material Weaknesses: Small Business Enterprise	AU325-03	RTF
Exhibit AU 329-1 — Documentation of the Effect of Analytical Procedures on the Planning of Substantive Audit Procedures	AU329-01	RTF
Exhibit AU 329-2 — Performance of Analytical Procedures	AU329-02	RTF
Exhibit AU 329-03 — Example of Preliminary Analytical Review	AU329-03	RTF
Exhibit AU 329-04 — Example of Final Analytical Review	AU329-04	RTF
Exhibit AU 330-1 — Positive Confirmation	AU330-01	RTF
Exhibit AU 330-2 — Negative Confirmation	AU330-02	RTF

File	File Name	File Type
Exhibit AU 330-3 — Obligation under Long-Term Leases	AU330-03	RTF
Exhibit AU 330-4 — Mortgage Obligation	AU330-04	RTF
Exhibit AU 330-5 — Audit Program — Confirmation of Accounts Receivable	AU330-05	RTF
Exhibit AU 330-6 — Summary of Accounts Receivable Confirmation Statistics	AU330-06	RTF
Exhibit AU 331-1 — Audit Program: Inventory Observation Procedures	AU331-01	RTF
Exhibit AU 331-2 — Confirmation Request for Inventory Held by Another Party	AU331-02	RTF
Exhibit AU 332-1 — Services that Affect Substantive Procedures	AU332-01	RTF
Exhibit AU 332-2 — Illustrative Substantive Procedures for Derivatives and Securities	AU332-02	RTF
Exhibit AU 333-1 — Management Representation Letter	AU333-01	RTF
Exhibit AU 337-1 — Illustrative Audit Inquiry Letter to Legal Counsel	AU337-01	RTF
Exhibit AU 337-2 — Illustrative Audit Inquiry Letter to Legal Counsel Whereby Management Has Requested That the Lawyer Prepare the List of Pending or Threatened Litigation, Claims, and Assessments	AU337-02	RTF
Exhibit AU 339-1 — SASs that Identify Specific Audit Documentation	AU339-01	RTF
Exhibit AU 339-2 — Letter for Regulatory Agency That Requests Access to Audit Documentation	AU339-02	RTF
Exhibit AU 341-1 — Conditions and Events That May Raise a Substantial-Doubt Question	AU341-01	RTF
Exhibit AU 341-2 — Plans and Factors Relevant to the Evaluation of Management's Plans	AU341-02	RTF

File	File Name	File Type
Exhibit AU 341-3 — Evaluating an Entity's Ability to Continue as a Going Concern	AU341-03	RTF
Exhibit AU 342-1 — Nonauthoritative Guidance for Auditing Soft Accounting Information	AU342-01	RTF
Exhibit AU 342-02 — Common Financial Statement Estimates Requiring Auditor Evaluation	AU342-02	RTF
Exhibit AU 350-1 — Audit Judgment Factors Used in Nonstatistical and Statistical Sampling to Determine Sample Size for Tests of Controls	AU350-01	RTF
Exhibit AU 350-2 — Audit Judgment Factors Used to Determine Sample Size for Substantive Procedures	AU350-02	RTF
Exhibit AU 350-3 — Illustrative Sample Sizes	AU350-03	RTF
Exhibit AU 350-4 — Selecting the Sample	AU350-04	RTF
Exhibit AU 350-5 — Misstatements and Professional Judgment	AU350-05	RTF
Exhibit AU 350-6 — Required Sample Size for Nonstatistical Tests of Details	AU350-06	RTF
Exhibit AU 380-1 — Topic and Nature of Communications about Significant Findings	AU380-01	RTF
Exhibit AU 390-1 — Omission of Engagement Procedures Discovered after the Report Date	AU390-01	RTF
Exhibit AU 411-1 — Sources of GAAP for Non-Governmental Entities	AU411-01	RTF
Exhibit AU 411-2 — State and Local Government Accounting Hierarchy	AU411-02	RTF
Exhibit AU 411-3 — Federal GAAP Hierarchy	AU411-03	RTF
Exhibit AU 431-1 — Engagement Program for SOP 94-6	AU431-01	RTF
Exhibit AU 504-1 — Disclaimer of Opinion on Unaudited Financial Statements	AU504-01	RTF

File	File Name	File Type
Exhibit AU 504-2 — Disclaimer of Opinion on Unaudited Financial Statements That Are Prepared on a Comprehensive Basis of Accounting Other Than Generally Accepted Accounting Principles	AU504-02	RTF
Exhibit AU 504-3 — Disclaimer of Opinion on Unaudited Financial Statements Because the Accountant Is Not Independent	AU504-03	RTF
Exhibit AU 504-4 — Description of a Compilation in a Separate Paragraph When Reporting on Audited and Unaudited Financial Statements in Comparative Form	AU504-04	RTF
Exhibit AU 504-5 — Description of a Review in a Separate Paragraph When Reporting on Audited and Unaudited Financial Statements in Comparative Form	AU504-05	RTF
Exhibit AU 508-1 — Standard Auditor's Report	AU508-01	RTF
Exhibit AU 508-2 — Qualified Auditor's Report	AU508-02	RTF
Exhibit AU 508-3 — Adverse Auditor's Report	AU508-03	RTF
Exhibit AU 508-4 — Qualified Auditor's Report Because Statement of Cash Flow Is Omitted	AU508-04	RTF
Exhibit AU 508-5 — Qualified Auditor's Report Because of a Scope Limitation	AU508-05	RTF
Exhibit AU 508-6 — Disclaimer Report	AU508-06	RTF
Exhibit AU 508-7 — Auditor's Report Only on the Balance Sheet	AU508-07	RTF
Exhibit AU 508-8 — Accounting and Reporting Standards for Loss Contingencies	AU508-08	RTF
Exhibit AU 508-9 — Auditor's Report on Comparative Financial Statements	AU508-09	RTF

File	File Name	File Type
Exhibit AU 508-10 — Auditor's Report on Comparative Financial Statements with Different Opinions	AU508-10	RTF
Exhibit AU 508-11 — Auditor's Report When a Predecessor Auditor's Report Is Not Presented	AU508-11	RTF
Exhibit AU 508-12 — Auditor's Report When the Standards of Both the Auditing Standards Board and the Public Company Accounting Oversight Board Are Followed in Performing the Audit	AU508-12	RTF
Exhibit AU 532-1 — Restricted Audit Report on Special-Purpose Financial Statement Presentation	AU532-01	RTF
Exhibit AU 532-2 — Restricted Audit Report on Financial Statements Prepared Pursuant to a Loan Agreement	AU532-02	RTF
Exhibit AU 534-1 — U.S.-Style Standard Auditor's Report	AU534-01	RTF
Exhibit AU 543-1 — Reference to the Work of Another Auditor in the Audit Report	AU543-01	RTF
Exhibit AU 543-2 — Example of Inquiry by the Other Auditor Directed to the Principal Auditor	AU543-02	RTF
Exhibit AU 543-3 — Example of Principal Auditor's Response to Inquiry Made by Other Auditor	AU543-03	RTF
Exhibit AU 551-1 — Explanatory Paragraph Used When Reporting on Supplementary Information	AU551-01	RTF
Exhibit AU 551-2 — Reporting on Supplementary Information Separately from the Financial Statements As a Whole	AU551-02	RTF
Exhibit AU 558-1 — Explanatory Paragraph When Reporting on Supplementary Information	AU558-01	RTF
Exhibit AU 560-1 — Subsequent Events Audit Program	AU560-01	RTF

File	File Name	File Type
Exhibit AU 561-1 — Discovery of Facts after the Date of the Report	AU561-01	RTF
Exhibit AU 623-1 — Special Report on Cash-Based Financial Statements	AU623-01	RTF
Exhibit AU 623-2 — Special Report on a Regulatory Basis of Accounting (Regulated Entity Releases the Report to Parties Other than the Regulator Either Voluntarily or Upon Specific Request)	AU623-02	RTF
Exhibit AU 623-3 — Special Report on an Account in a Financial Statement	AU623-03	RTF
Exhibit AU 623-4 — Special Report on Whether Certain Terms of a Debt Agreement Have Been Observed	AU623-04	RTF
Exhibit AU 623-5 — Special Report on a Statement of Assets Sold and Liabilities Transferred	AU623-05	RTF
Exhibit AU 623-6 — Special Report on Financial Statements Prepared Pursuant to a Loan Agreement	AU623-06	RTF
Exhibit AU 625-1 — Accountant's Report on the Application of Accounting Principles	AU625-01	RTF
Exhibit AU 634-1 — Representation Letter from Requesting Parties	AU634-01	RTF
Exhibit AU 634-2 — Sample Comfort Letter	AU634-02	RTF
Exhibit AU 711-1 — Description of Status of Review Report Incorporated through Reference in a Registration Statement	AU711-01	RTF
Exhibit AU 722-1 — Client Representation Letter for a Review of Interim Financial Information	AU722-01	RTF
Exhibit AU 722-2 — Standard Review Report on Interim Financial Information	AU722-02	RTF
Exhibit AU 722-3 — Standard Review Report on Interim Financial Information That Contains a Departure from GAAP	AU722-03	RTF

File	File Name	File Type
Exhibit AU 722-4 — Standard Review Report on Interim Financial Statements That Contain an Inadequate Disclosure	AU722-04	RTF
Exhibit AU 722-5 — Review Report on Interim Financial Statements with an Explanatory Paragraph Related to a Going Concern Issue Referred to in the Previous Audit Report	AU722-05	RTF
Exhibit AU 722-6 — Review Report on Interim Financial Statements with an Explanatory Paragraph Related to a Going Concern Issue Not Referred to in the Previous Audit Report	AU722-06	RTF
Exhibit AT 101-01 — Acceptable Level of Detection Risk	AT101-01	RTF
Exhibit AT 101-02 — Circumstances Encountered in Review Engagements and their Effects on Attest Procedures	AT101-02	RTF
Exhibit AT 101-03 — Checklist for an Examination Report on a Subject Matter	AT101-03	RTF
Exhibit AT 101-04 — Checklist for an Examination Report on an Assertion	AT101-04	RTF
Exhibit AT 101-05 — Checklist for a Review Report on a Subject Matter	AT101-05	RTF
Exhibit AT 101-06 — Checklist for a Review Report on an Assertion	AT101-06	RTF
Exhibit AT 101-07 — Examination Report — Subject Matter	AT101-07	RTF
Exhibit AT 101-08 — Examination Report — Assertion	AT101-08	RTF
Exhibit AT 101-09 — Review Report — Subject Matter	AT101-09	RTF
Exhibit AT 101-10 — Review Report — Assertion (Restricted Distribution)	AT101-10	RTF
Exhibit AT 201-01 — Checklist for an AUP Report	AT201-01	RTF
Exhibit AT 201-02 — AUP Engagement Report	AT201-02	RTF

File	File Name	File Type
Exhibit AT 301-01 — Standard Report on an Examination of a Forecast	AT301-01	RTF
Exhibit AT 301-02 — Standard Report on an Examination of a Projection	AT301-02	RTF
Exhibit AT 301-03 — Standard Report on a Compilation of a Financial Statement Forecast	AT301-03	RTF
Exhibit AT 301-04 — Standard Report on a Compilation of Projected Financial Statements	AT301-04	RTF
Exhibit AT 301-05 — Report on an AUP Engagement for Prospective Financial Statements	AT301-05	RTF
Exhibit AT 401-01 — Objectives of Examinations and Reviews of Pro Forma Financial Information	AT401-01	RTF
Exhibit AT 401-02 — Reporting Guidelines for Preparation/Review of Pro Forma Financial Information	AT401-02	RTF
Exhibit AT 401-03 — Examination Report on Pro Forma Financial Information	AT401-03	RTF
Exhibit AT 401-04 — Review Report on Pro Forma Financial Information	AT401-04	RTF
Exhibit AT 501-01 — Reporting Guidelines for Preparation of an Examination Report on an Entity's Internal Control	AT501-01	RTF
Exhibit AT 501-02 — Examination on the Effectiveness of an Entity's Internal Control over Financial Reporting	AT501-02	RTF
Exhibit AT 501-03 — Examination on the Written Assertion on the Effectiveness of an Entity's Internal Control over Financial Reporting	AT501-03	RTF
Exhibit AT 601-01 — AUP Report on an Entity's Compliance with Specified Requirements	AT601-01	RTF

File	File Name	File Type
Exhibit AT 601-02 — Reporting Guidelines for Preparation of a Compliance Examination Report	AT601-02	RTF
Exhibit AT 601-03 — Examination on the Compliance with Specified Requirements	AT601-03	RTF
Exhibit AT 601-04 — Examination on Management's Assertion Concerning Compliance with Specified Requirements	AT601-04	RTF
Exhibit AT 701-01 — Examination Report on an Entity's MD&A Presentation	AT701-01	RTF
Exhibit AT 701-02 — Review Report on and Entity's MD&A Presentation	AT701-02	RTF
Exhibit AT801-01 — Type 1 Report	AT801-01	RTF
Exhibit AT801-02 — Type 2 Report	AT801-02	RTF
Exhibit AR80-01 — Compilation Engagement Letter	AR080-01	RTF
Exhibit AR80-02 — Standard Accountant's Compilation Report	AR080-02	RTF
Exhibit AR80-03 — Compilation Report When Independence Is Impaired	AR080-03	RTF
Exhibit AR80-04 — Compilation Report Disclosing A Gaap Departure	AR080-04	RTF
Exhibit AR80-05 — Compilation Program	AR080-05	RTF
Exhibit AR90-01 — Review Engagement Letter	AR090-01	RTF
Exhibit AR90-02 — Management Representation Letter	AR090-02	RTF
Exhibit AR90-03 — Standard Accountant's Review Report	AR090-03	RTF
Exhibit AR90-04 — Review Program	AR090-04	RTF
Exhibit AR90-05 — Review Questionnaire Checklist	AR090-05	RTF
Exhibit AR90-06 — Inquiry Checklist for a Review Engagement	AR090-06	RTF
Exhibit AR90-07 — Analytical Procedures for a Review Engagement	AR090-07	RTF

File	File Name	File Type
Exhibit AR90-08 — Documenting Expectations When Performing Analytical Procedures in a Review Engagement	AR090-08	RTF
Exhibit AR90-09 — Considering Going Concern	AR090-09	RTF
Exhibit AR 200-1 — Report on Comparative Financial Statements Where All Periods Have Been Compiled	AR200-01	RTF
Exhibit AR 200-2 — Report on Comparative Financial Statements Where All Periods Have Been Reviewed	AR200-02	RTF
Exhibit AR 200-3 — Report on Comparative Financial Statements Where the Current Period Is Reviewed and the Prior Period Is Compiled	AR200-03	RTF
Exhibit AR 200-4 — Additional Paragraph to a Compilation Report on the Current Period that Refers to the Prior Period That Had Been Reviewed	AR200-04	RTF
Exhibit AR 200-5 — Explanatory Paragraph Added to a Current Report that Refers to a Change in a Previous Report Issued by the Accountant	AR200-05	RTF
Exhibit AR 200-6 — Separate Paragraph Added to the Current Report that Refers to the Predecessor Accountant's Compilation Report	AR200-06	RTF
Exhibit AR 200-7 — Separate Paragraph Added to the Current Report that Refers to the Predecessor Accountant's Review Report	AR200-07	RTF
Exhibit AR 200-8 — Compilation Report on Comparative Financial Statements that Omit Substantially All Disclosures but Where the Prior Year Had Originally Been Reviewed by the Accountant	AR200-08	RTF

File	**File Name**	**File Type**
Exhibit AR 200-9 — Report on Comparative Financial Statements Where the Current Year Is Compiled and the Prior Year Is Audited	AR200-09	RTF
Exhibit AR 300-1 — Compilation Report on Financial Statements Included in a Prescribed Form	AR300-01	RTF
Exhibit AR 400-01 — Predecessor Accountant's Letter Requesting a Written Communication from the Successor Accountant Concerning Access to Working Papers	AR400-01	RTF
Exhibit AR 600-1 — Alternative Accountant's Report on Personal Financial Statements Included in Written Personal Financial Plans	AR600-01	RTF